Pearson Arab World Editions – Business & Economics

The Arab world's location between three continents ensures its place at the centre of an increasingly integrated global economy, as distinctive as any business culture. We think learning should be as dynamic, relevant and engaging as the business environment. Our new Arab World Editions for Business & Economics provide this uniquely Arab perspective for students in and of the Arab world.

Each Arab World Edition integrates cases, companies, research, people and discussions representing the diverse economic, political, and cultural situations across the nations that span the Arab world, whilst retaining the quality, research, and relevant global perspectives of the world's leading business thinkers.

We hope that you find this edition a valuable contribution to your teaching or business studies. We aim to set a new benchmark for contextualised learning with our adapted and new titles, and hope that they will prove a valuable contribution in the success of students and teachers along each step of their business programme.

Supplementary support includes PowerPoint slides, instructor manuals, test bank generators and MyLab online tutorial and homework systems.

Titles span a range of subjects and disciplines, including:

- Management – Robbins & Coulter
- Strategic Management: Concepts and Cases – David
- Economics – Hubbard & O'Brien
- Statistics for Business – Benghezal
- Principles of Managerial Finance – Gitman
- Marketing Management – Kotler & Keller
- Organizational Behavior – Robbins & Judge
- Human Resource Management – Dessler
- Introductory Mathematical Analysis for Business, Economics and Life and Social Sciences – Haeussler

To find out more, go to www.pearson.com/middleeast/awe

PEARSON

economics

Arab World Edition

R. Glenn Hubbard
Columbia University

Anthony Patrick O'Brien
Lehigh University

Ashraf Galal Eid
King Fahd University of Petroleum
and Minerals

Amany El Anshasy
United Arab Emirates University

Acquisitions Editor: Rasheed Roussan
Senior Development Editor: Sophie Bulbrook
Project Editor: Kate Sherington
Editorial Assistant: Fay Gibbons
Copy-editor: Valerie Bingham
Proofreader: Jim Caunter
Design Manager: Sarah Fach
Permissions Editor: Samsita Sinha
Picture Researcher: Zohir Naciri
Indexer: Indexing Specialists (UK) Ltd
Marketing Manager: Sue Mainey
Production Controller: Christopher Crow
Cover Designer: Sarah Fach
Typesetter: Integra
Typeface: 10.5/12, Minion

Printed in Malaysia (CTP-VVP)

Pearson Education Limited
Edinburgh Gate
Harlow
Essex CM20 2JE
England

and Associated Companies throughout the world

First published 2011

20 19
IMP 10

ISBN: 978-1-4082-5530-8

For my precious parents, my beloved wife Halah, my brother Mohamed, and my dearest daughter Hala
—*Ashraf Galal Eid*

For Yusef and Yusr
—*Amany El Anshasy*

About the Authors

R. Glenn Hubbard is the dean and Russell L. Carson Professor of Finance and Economics in the Graduate School of Business at Columbia University and professor of economics in Columbia's Faculty of Arts and Sciences. He is also a research associate of the National Bureau of Economic Research and a director of Automatic Data Processing, Black Rock Closed-End Funds, Duke Realty, Information Services Group, KKR Financial Corporation, MetLife, and Ripplewood Holdings. He received his Ph.D. in economics from Harvard University in 1983. From 2001 to 2003, he served as chairman of the White House Council of Economic Advisers and chairman of the OECD Economy Policy Committee, and from 1991 to 1993, he was deputy assistant secretary of the U.S. Treasury Department. He currently serves as co-chair of the nonpartisan committee on Capital Markets Regulation. Hubbard's fields of specialization are public economics, financial markets and institutions, corporate finance, macroeconomics, industrial organization, and public policy. He is the author of more than 100 articles in leading journals, including *American Economic Review, Brookings Papers on Economic Activity, Journal of Finance, Journal of Financial Economics, Journal of Money, Credit, and Banking, Journal of Political Economy, Journal of Public Economics, Quarterly Journal of Economics, RAND Journal of Economics*, and *Review of Economics and Statistics*. His research has been supported by grants from the National Science Foundation, the National Bureau of Economic Research, and numerous private foundations.

Anthony Patrick O'Brien is a professor of economics at Lehigh University. He received his Ph.D. from the University of California, Berkeley, in 1987. He has taught principles of economics for more than 15 years, in both large sections and small honors classes. He received the Lehigh University Award for Distinguished Teaching. He was formerly the director of the Diamond Center for Economic Education and was named a Dana Foundation Faculty Fellow and Lehigh Class of 1961 Professor of Economics. He has been a visiting professor at the University of California, Santa Barbara, and the Graduate School of Industrial Administration at Carnegie Mellon University. O'Brien's research has dealt with such issues as the evolution of the U.S. automobile industry, the sources of U.S. economic competitiveness, the development of U.S. trade policy, the causes of the Great Depression, and the causes of black–white income differences. His research has been published in leading journals, including *American Economic Review, Quarterly Journal of Economics, Journal of Money, Credit, and Banking, Industrial Relations, Journal of Economic History*, and *Explorations in Economic History*. His research has been supported by grants from government agencies and private foundations. In addition to teaching and writing, O'Brien also serves on the editorial board of the *Journal of Socio-Economics*.

Ashraf Galal Eid is an assistant professor of Economics in the Finance and Economics Department, College of Industrial Management, at King Fahd University of Petroleum and Minerals, Saudi Arabia. He also holds the position of Associate Professor of Public Economics in the Public Finance Department, Faculty of Commerce, at Alexandria University, Egypt. He received his Ph.D. degree in applied economics from Western Michigan University in 2004 and a Masters degree from the same university. He conducted his post-doctoral studies at Michigan State University. He gained his teaching experience in Saudi Arabia, Egypt, Lebanon, and the U.S., teaching several economics courses, such as Principles of Economics, Public Finance, Money and Banking, Intermediate Macroeconomics, and Managerial Economics, to undergraduate, MBA, and EMBA students. In 2004, he received the Outstanding Graduate Teaching Award from the Graduate College, Western Michigan University, and in the academic year 2006-2007, he was awarded the Fulbright Research Grant. His main fields of interest for research are the economics of R&D and technology changes, macroeconomics, and public finance. His research papers appear in international journals such as *Education Economics, Atlantic Economic Journal, Journal of Applied Business and Economics, and Journal of Energy & Environment*. He has also presented his research papers at international conferences for the Midwest Economic Association, the International Council for Small Business, the International Association for Management of Technology, and the Economic and Business Historical Society, among others. He is a member of the American Economic Association, the International Association for Management of Technology, and the Economic Science Association.

Amany A. El Anshasy is an assistant professor of economics in the Faculty of Business and Economics, United Arab Emirates University, UAE. She also holds the position of Assistant Professor of Public Finance in the Faculty of Commerce, Alexandria University, Egypt. She received her Ph.D. degree in economics in 2006 from George Washington University in the U.S. She also holds a Master of Philosophy degree in economics from the same university. In 1993, she received an MA degree in Development Economics from the International Institute of Social Studies (Erasmus University Rotterdam) in The Hague, Netherlands. She has taught many economics and public finance courses, including courses in taxation, public economics, principles of microeconomics, principles of macroeconomics, theory of macroeconomics, project economics, energy and environmental economics. Her current research interests are related to the political economy of the Middle East; growth, governance and democratic institutions; the interplay between natural resources and institutions; and the effects of oil price volatility on oil-exporters' economies.

Brief contents

Contents

PART 4: Special Topics: the Need for the Government and International Trade

CHAPTER 13: Externalities, Environmental Policy, and Public Goods   416

PART 6: Markets for Factors of
Production and Short-Run Fluctuations

CHAPTER 18: The Markets for Labor
and Other Factors of Production **580**

CHAPTER 19: Output and Expenditure in the Short Run   616

CHAPTER 19 Appendix: The Algebra of Macroeconomic Equilibrium   655

CHAPTER 20: Aggregate Demand and Aggregate Supply Analysis   658

CHAPTER 20 Appendix: Macroeconomic Schools of Thought   691

PART 7: Monetary Policy, Fiscal Policy, and the International Economy

CHAPTER 23 Appendix: A Closer Look at the Multiplier **795**

CHAPTER 24: Inflation, Unemployment, and Central Bank Policy **802**

CHAPTER 25: Macroeconomics in an Open Economy **832**

FLEXIBILITY CHART

The following chart helps you organize your syllabus based on your teaching preferences and objectives:

Core	Policy	Optional
CHAPTER 1: Economics: Foundations and Models *Discusses the role of models in economic analysis.*	**CHAPTER 4:** Economic Efficiency, Government Price Setting, and Taxes	**CHAPTER 1 Appendix:** Using Graphs and Formulas
CHAPTER 2: Trade-offs, Comparative Advantage, and the Market System *Includes coverage of the role of the entrepreneur, property rights, and the legal system in a market system.*	**CHAPTER 13:** Externalities, Environmental Policy, and Public Goods	**CHAPTER 4 Appendix:** Quantitative Demand and Supply Analysis *Provides a quantitative analysis of rent control.*
CHAPTER 3: Where Prices Come From: The Interaction of Demand and Supply	**CHAPTER 22:** Monetary Policy *Uses the aggregate demand and aggregate supply model to show the effects of monetary policy on real GDP and the price level.*	**CHAPTER 14: Appendix: Multinational Firms** *Covers the benefits and challenges of operating overseas businesses.*
CHAPTER 5: Elasticity: The Responsiveness of Demand and Supply	**CHAPTER 23:** Fiscal Policy *Uses the aggregate demand and aggregate supply model to show how taxes and government spending affect the economy. Includes significant coverage of the supply-side effects of fiscal policy.*	**CHAPTER 6:** Consumer Choice and Behavioral Economics *Covers utility theory and unique coverage of social influences on behavior and network externalities.*
CHAPTER 7: Technology, Production, and Costs		**CHAPTER 7 Appendix:** Using Isoquants and Isocosts to Understand Production and Costs *Provides a formal analysis of how firms choose the combination of inputs to produce a given level of output.*
CHAPTER 8: Firms in Perfectly Competitive Markets		**CHAPTER 12:** Pricing Strategy *A unique chapter that covers price discrimination, cost-plus pricing, and two-part tariffs.*
CHAPTER 9: Monopolistic Competition: The Competitive Model in a More Realistic Setting		**CHAPTER 19:** Output and Expenditure in the Short Run *Uses the Keynesian 45°-line aggregate expenditure model to introduce students to the short-run relationship between spending and production. The discussion of monetary and fiscal policy in later chapters uses only the aggregate demand and aggregate supply model, which allows instructors to omit Chapter 19.*
CHAPTER 10: Oligopoly: Firms in Less Competitive Markets *Includes full coverage of game theory and unique coverage of Porter's Five Forces model of competition.*		**CHAPTER 19 Appendix:** The Algebra of Macroeconomic Equilibrium *Uses equations to represent the aggregate expenditure model described in the chapter.*
CHAPTER 11: Monopoly and Antitrust Policy		**CHAPTER 20 Appendix:** Macroeconomic Schools of Thought *Covers the monetarist model, the new classical model, and the real business cycle model.*
CHAPTER 14: Comparative Advantage and the Gains from International Trade		**CHAPTER 24:** Inflation, Unemployment, and Central Bank Policy *Discusses the short-run and long-run Phillips curves. Also covers the roles of expectations formation and central bank credibility in monetary policy.*
CHAPTER 15: GDP: Measuring Total Production and Income *Covers how total production is measured and the difference between real and nominal variables.*		
CHAPTER 16: Unemployment and Inflation *Covers the three types of unemployment, how inflation is measured, and the difference between real and nominal interest rates.*		
CHAPTER 17: Economic Growth, the Financial System, and Business Cycles *Provides an overview of key macroeconomic issues by discussing the business cycle in the context of long-run growth. Discusses the roles of entrepreneurship, financial institutions, and policy in economic growth.*		

Core	Policy	Optional

CHAPTER 18: The Markets for Labor and Other Factors of Production *Covers all factors of production in one chapter and includes coverage of discrimination, unions, compensating differentials, and personnel economics.*

CHAPTER 20: Aggregate Demand and Aggregate Supply Analysis *Carefully develops the AD-AS model and then makes the model dynamic to better account for actual movements in real GDP and the price level.*

CHAPTER 21: Money, Banks, and the Federal Reserve System *Explores the role of money in the economy, the money supply process and the role of Central Banks*

CHAPTER 25: Macroeconomics in an Open Economy *Explains the linkages among countries at the macroeconomic level and how policymakers in all countries take these linkages into account when conducting monetary and fiscal policy.*

FEATURES MATRIX

	Chapter Title	Chapter Opener	Making the Connection	An Inside Look
1	Economics: Foundations and Models	The Rising Economic Powers in the East: The Arab World and The Global Economy	Will Women Have Fewer or More Babies if the Government Pays Them To? • Should the Host Governments Protect the Migrant Workers?	Gulf Companies Learn the Price of GlobalizationSource: *Financial Times*
2	Trade-Offs, Comparative Advantage, And The Market System	Managers Making Choices at BMW: The Cases of BMW-Egypt	Trade-Offs: The Pattern of Charitable Giving in the Arab World • A Story of the Market System in Action: How Do You Make an iPod? • Property Rights in Cyberspace: You Tube and MySpace	The Impact of the Egyptian Revolution on Local Car Feeding Industry Source: *Al Ahram Wekly*
3	Where Prices Come From: The Interaction of Demand and Supply	Apple and the Demand for iPods	Why Supermarkets Need to Understand Substitutes and Complements • Google Responds to a Growing Arab World Demand for Internet Navigation by launching "Ahlan Online" • Apple Forecasts the Demand for iPods and other Consumer Electronics • The Falling Price of LCD Televisions • Global Fashion Trends Reveals a Growing Demand for Arabian Styles	'Perfect' Oil Price Hides Divisions within OPEC Source: *Financial Times*
4	Economic Efficiency, Government Price Setting, and Taxes	Why Does the Dubai Government Control Apartment Rents?	The Consumer Surplus from Satellite Television • Price Floors in Labor Markets: The Debate over Minimum Wage Policy • Does Holiday Gift Giving Have a Deadweight Loss? • Is The Burden of the Social Insurance Tax in Egypt Really Shared Equally between Workers and Firms?	Is Rent Control Really Effective? Source: *Gulf News*
5	Elasticity: The Responsiveness of Demand and Supply	Do People Care about the Prices of Books?	The Price Elasticity of Demand for Breakfast Cereal • Determining the Price Elasticity of Demand for DVDs by Market Experiment • Short-run Price Elasticity, Long-run Price Elasticity, and Income Elasticity in the Crude Oil Market • What Are Oil Prices So Unstable?	Etisalat Offer a Price Cut for iPhones and Roaming Services Sources:1. *Arabian Business;* 2. *Arabian Business.*
6	Consumer Choice and Behavioral Economics	Did Amr Diab Make You Switch to Drinking Pepsi-Cola?	Why Do Firms Pay Mohamed Aboutrika to Endorse Their Products? • How can we explain the long lines at Al-Baik Restaurant? • Why Do Hilton Hotels and other Firms Hide Their Prices? • Why Don't Students Study More?	Was Nokia Right to Choose Mohamed Hamaki to Endorse Its New Music Service? Source: AMEinfo.com
7	Technology, Production, and Costs	Sony Uses a Cost Curve to Determine the Price of Radios	Improving Inventory Control at Wal-Mart and Bread Quality at Carrefour • Fixed Costs in the Publishing Industry • Adam Smith's Famous Account of the Division of Labor in a Pin Factory • Economies and Diseconomies of Scale in the Car Industry	Lower Manufacturing Costs Push Down the Price of Flat-Panel TVs Source: *Wall Stree Journal*

	Chapter Title	Chapter Opener	Making the Connection	An Inside Look
8	Firms in Perfectly Competitive Markets	Perfect Competition in the Retail Market for Mobile Phones	The Medical Screening Industry: When to Make Money and When to Lose • Easy Entry Makes the Long Run Pretty Short in the Apple iPhone Apps Store • "Lose Money But Do Not Lose the Market Share"	An industry based on a thousand-year old tradition faces collapseSource: AL-SHORFA.COM
9	Monopolistic Competition: The Competitive Model in a More Realistic Setting	Costa Coffee Expansion in the Middle East: Growth through Product Differentiation	The Rise and Fall of Apple's Macintosh Computer • A Regional Brand on a Global Mission: Aramex to Join the "Big Four:" UPS, DHL, FedEx, and TNT • Can Dunkin' Donuts' Marketing Strategy Help it Compete with Starbucks? • Is Being the First Firm in the Market a Key to Success?	The Growing Competition among Coffeehouses in the Arab World Source: Arroya.com
10	Oligopoly: Firms in Less Competitive Markets	Competing With Carrefour	The Price War Is Escalating between Qatar's Two Telecom Operators • Is There a Dominant Strategy for Bidding on Souq.com? • Du's Decision Not to Indulge in a Price War with Etisalat, UAE's Former Telecom Monopoly • How Jordan's Fastlink (now Zain) Coped with the Threat of New Competition from Mobilcom in early 2000	Can LuLu Hypermarket Compete with Carrefour in the Middle East? Source: *Gulf News*
11	Monopoly and Antitrust Policy	Fixed-Line Telecom Services: A Long-Time Monopoly in the Middle East	Is Xbox 360 a Close Substitute for PlayStation 3? • The End of the Arab World's Mobile Telecom Monopolies • Are Diamond Profits Forever? The De Beers Diamond Monopoly • Is Egypt's Steel Industry a Monopoly? The Case of Ezz-Dekhela	Kuwait—Telecoms, Mobile, Broadband and Forecasts Source: Budde.com
12	Pricing Strategy	Getting into Dream Park: One Price Does Not Fit All	How Colleges Use Yield Management • Price Discrimination at Foreign Restaurants in the Gulf Countries • Cost-Plus Pricing in the Publishing Industry	Electricity Bills: One Price Does Not Fit All Users Sources: 1. *Daily News Egypt*; 2.*Jordan Times*
13	Externalities, Environmental Policy, and Public Goods	Economic Policy and the Environment	The Importance of Adopting Industrial Energy-efficiency Strategies in the Arab World • Masdar: Building a Leading-Edge Clean Energy Technology in Abu Dhabi • Can Tradable Permits Reduce Global Warming? • Should the Government Run the Health Care System? • How Middle East Chefs and Chain Suppliers Are Dealing with Decreasing Seafood Stocks	Oil-producing Nations Take a Different View on Carbon Taxes Source: *Financial Times*

	Chapter Title	Chapter Opener	Making the Connection	An Inside Look
14	Comparative Advantage and the Gains from International Trade	Trade Policy: Who Wins and Who Loses?	Would the Greater Arab Free Trade Area Agreement (GAFTA) help Arabs Boost Exports? • The GCC Common Market: Are There Potential Gains? Who Wins and Who Loses? • Why the Egyptian Economy Is Compared with the South Korean Economy • Qualified Industrial Zones and the Middle East Free Trade Area • The WTO Strategy for the Arab Region	The GCC-Singapore Free Trade Agreement Source: *Gulf News*
15	Measuring Total Production and Income	Emirates Airlines Feel the Impact of the Global Recession and the Fluctuations in GDP	Corruption and the Underground Economy: How Severe Is Corruption in the Arab World? • The Global Financial Crisis and Arab Economies' Nominal and Real GDP	The Government Spending Component of GDP Can Make up for the Decline in Other Components to Help Avoid a Recession Source: IMF
16	Unemployment and Inflation	Unemployment and Inflation: Two Persistent Problems in yhe Arab World	How Should We Classify Unemployment in the Arab Countries? • Why a Lower Inflation Rate Is Like a Tax Cut for Orascom Telecom Bondholders	Food Prices, Housing Prices, and the "Youthquack": Major Problems Facing the Arab World Sources: 1. *Arab Times*; 2.The Majlis
17	Economic Growth, the Financial System, and Business Cycles	Economic Growth in the Arab World: What Is Missing?	The Connection between Economic Prosperity and Health • What Explains Rapid Economic Growth in Botswana?	Economic Growth and Inflation Rate: Are They Positively Related? Source: suite101.com
18	The Markets for Labor and Other Factors of Production	Why Is Real Madrid Paying Cristiano Ronaldo $17 Million per Year?	Will Your Future Income Depend on Which Courses You Take in College? • Restricting Immigration and the Supply of Labor in the Arab Gulf • Technology and the Earnings of "Superstars"	Would Flexible Employment Enhance Labor Market Efficiency and Increase Labor Force Participation in the GCC E17countries? Source: AMEinfo.com
19	Output and Expenditure in the Short Run	The Fluctuating Demand in the Arab World: The Effects of the Recent Global Financial Crisis	The Construction Boom in the Gulf (2005–2008) Induces Steel Production Capacity Growth • Business Attempts to Control Inventories, Then…and Now • The Multiplier in Reverse: The Great Depression of the 1930s	Jordan Expected Thousands of Workers Home from the Gulf: Is it Good News for the Jordanian Economy? Source: *Global Post*

	Chapter Title	Chapter Opener	Making the Connection	An Inside Look
20	Aggregate Demand and Aggregate Supply Analysis	The Fortunes of Aramex Follow the Business Cycle	In a Global Economy, How Can You Tell the Imports from the Domestic Goods? • Saudi's Slow Economic Recovery • Can FedEx and the US Economy Withstand High Oil Prices?	How FedEx Middle East Weathered the Recent Global Recession Source: Arabian supply chain.com
21	Money, Banks, and the Central Bank	A New Sudanese Pound Is Worth a Thousand Old Pounds	Money without a Government? The Strange Case of the Iraqi Dinar • Do We Still Need the Fils, Piaster, or Penny? • Is Money the Same as Income or Wealth? • The German Hyperinflation of the Early 1920s	Lowering the Discount Rate Failed to Encourage Bank Lending in Kuwait Source: *Arab Times*
22	Monetary Policy	Monetary Policy, Drake and Scull, and the Housing Market in Dubai	Why Does *Khaleej Times* Care about Monetary Policy? • With Monetary Policy, It's the Interest Rates—Not the Money—That Counts • How Does the Central Bank Measure Inflation?	Dubai Housing Market Slowdown Affects the Rate of Inflation in the UAE Source: AMEinfo.com
23	Fiscal Policy	Arab Governments to the Rescue	Is Losing Your Job Good for Your Health? • Did Fiscal Policy Fail during the Great Depression? • Should Arab NonOil-Based Economies Adopt the "Flat Tax"?	How Severe is the Lebanese Public Debt? Source: *Daily Star*
24	Inflation, Unemployment, and Central Bank Policy	How Do Central Banks React to Economic Downturns?	Do Workers Understand Inflation? • Does the Natural Rate of Unemployment Ever Change?	The Monetary Policy of the Central Bank of Jordan Source: *Jordanian Times*
25	Macroeconomics in an Open Economy	Chinese Products Threaten Local Industries in Both Developed and Developing Countries	Exchange Rates in the Financial Pages • What Explains the Fall and Rise and Fall of the Dollar? • Why Is the United States Called the "World's Largest Debtor"?	Can the US Current Account Deficit Be Sustained? Source: *Economist*

Preface

When George Lucas was asked why he made *Star Wars*, he replied, "It's the kind of movie I like to see, but no one seemed to be making them. So, I decided to make one." We realized that no one seemed to be writing the kind of textbook we wanted to use in our classes. So, after years of supplementing texts with fresh, lively, real-world examples from newspapers, magazines, and professional journals, we decided to write an economics text that not only delivers complete economics coverage with many real-world business examples, but also presents the unique socio-economic characteristics of the Arab world. Our goal is to introduce to instructors and students of economics the necessary link between economic theories and real life examples of the Arab and Middle East region and keep our classes "widget free."

THE ARAB WORLD EDITION

The Arab World Edition meets the aspirations of both instructors and students in the region. This unique edition explains the theoretical ideas and applies them to real life examples and case studies from the Arab region, without ignoring the international aspects. Therefore, this edition directly addresses the Arab countries' characteristics, problems, and economic policies. Arab students will find this textbook readable, simple, and full of case studies and policy analysis that stem from their region. The book also serves as a time saver for economics instructors as they will find all the needed Arab news, case studies, economic policies, and data within each chapter. We believe that students find the study of economics more interesting and easier to master when they see economic analysis applied to the real-world issues that concern them. Given how much has happened recently in the world economy in general, and the Arab economies specifically, we believe we needed the Arab World Edition to provide students with a better understanding of recent economic events and the policy responses to them. The impact of the recent global financial crisis on inflation and economic growth in the Arab countries, the expected effect of minimum wage laws in Saudi Arabia and Bahrain, the opening of car-assembly factories in Egypt, and the public debt problem in Lebanon are examples of case studies and news analyses we are discussing throughout the book.

Here are some key empirical studies and changes in the Arab World Edition:

- Chapter 1, "Economics:Foundations and Models" shows how changes and fluctuations in the global economy today became more relevant for the Arab world, particularly businesses in the Gulf, as a direct result of the Arab economies greater integration in the world economy.

- Chapter 2, "Trade-offs, Comparative Advantage, and the Market System" discusses the impact of the 25th of January Egyptian revolution on the local car-feeding industry and how some managers managed to keep their factories running while others decided to shut down their factories.

- Chapter 4, "Economic Efficiency, Government Price Setting, and Taxes" discusses the effectiveness of rent control policy in the city of Dubai and whether landlords are sticking with the rent cap.

- Chapter 9, "Monopolistic Competition: The Competitive Model in a More Realistic Setting" discusses how world leading coffeehouses such as Costa and Starbucks, among many others, are competing hard in the Arab world by differentiating their products and creating a unique "café experience" to attract the growing young Arab population.

- Chapter 10, "Oligopoly: Firms in Less Competitive Markets" explains how hypermarkets such as Carrefour and LuLu are striving to win the race for market share in the Arab world.

- Chapter 11, "Monopoly and Antitrust Policy" shows how the telephone fixed-line industry is still monopolized by national companies in the Arab world such as Saudi Telecom, Etisalat UAE, Qtel Qatar, Ogero Telecom Lebanon, Orange- Jordan Telecom, and Telecom Egypt while the wireless telecommunication industry moves away from monopolization.

- Chapter 12, "Pricing Strategy" explains the price discrimination policy applied in the electricity sector in Jordan and Egypt.

- Chapter 13, "Externalities, Environmental Policy, and Public Goods" discusses how MASDAR city in Abu Dhabi will soon become a cutting-edge clean energy provider with its state-of-the-art green technology and post-graduate research institute, the Masdar Institute of Science and Technology.

- Chapter 14, "Comparative Advantage and the Gains from International Trade" introduces a new section on the importance of trade to the Arab economy.

- Chapter 16, "Unemployment and Inflation" explains the demographics of unemployment in the Arab world with a focus on youth unemployment.

- Chapter 17, "Economic Growth, the Financial System, and Business Cycles" explores the relationship between economic growth and inflation in the Gulf Cooperation Council (GCC) countries, Syria, Lebanon, Jordan, and Egypt.

- Chapter 21, "Money, Banks, and the Central Bank" shows how, in just 20 years, the new Sudanese pound is worth one thousand old pounds.

- Chapter 22, "Monetary Policy" discusses the impact of the drying-up of lending amid the financial crisis of 2008 and the Dubai housing market slowdown on the rate of inflation in the UAE.

- Chapter 23, "Fiscal Policy" includes a new section on budget deficits, surpluses, and government debt in oil-based and non-oil-based Arab economies.

- The majority of *Making the Connections* are updated using Arab world case studies. For example:

  Chapter 5 covers the short run price elasticity, long run price elasticity, and income elasticity in the crude oil market.

  Chapter 8 covers the impact of the recent financial crisis on the apparel industry in Egypt.

  Chapter 9 covers the successful story of Aramex in Jordan.

  Chapter 10 covers the price war between Qatar's two telecom operators.

  Chapter 14 covers the GCC common market and the qualified industrial zones in the Middle East.

  Chapter 18 covers the supply of labor in the Arab Gulf.

  Chapter 20 covers the economic recovery in Saudi Arabia in 2010.

  Chapter 23 covers the discussion on whether Arab non-oil-based economies should adopt the "flat tax".

- The majority of figures and tables have been updated using the latest data available from the Arab world.

- The majority of chapter openers are updated with new information and data about the Arab world.

Note: US$ have been used throughout the text as the standard currency, so that readers from different parts of the Arab world, using different currencies in their own lives, have a common benchmark, or frame of reference.

The Foundation:
Contextual Learning and Modern Organization

We believe a course is a success if students can apply what they have learned in both personal and business settings and if they have developed the analytical skills to understand what they read in the media. That's why we explain economic concepts by using many real-world business examples and applications in the chapter openers, graphs, *Making the Connection* feature, *An Inside Look* feature, and end-of-chapter problems. This approach helps both business majors and liberal arts majors become educated consumers, voters, and citizens. In addition to our widget-free approach, we also have a modern organization and place interesting policy topics early in the book to pique student interest.

Here are several chapters that illustrate our approach in both microeconomics and macroeconomics.

Microeconomics

We are convinced that students learn to apply economic principles best if they are taught in a familiar context. Whether they open an art studio, do social work, trade on Wall Street, or work for the government, students would benefit from understanding the economic forces behind their work. And though business students will have many opportunities to see economic principles in action in various courses, liberal arts students may not. We therefore use many diverse real-world business and policy examples to illustrate economic concepts and to develop educated consumers, voters, and citizens.

Here are several chapters that illustrate our approach:

- **A STRONG SET OF INTRODUCTORY CHAPTERS.** The introductory chapters provide students with a solid foundation in the basics. We emphasize the key ideas of marginal analysis and economic efficiency. In Chapter 4, "Economic Efficiency, Government Price Setting, and Taxes," we use the concepts of consumer surplus and producer surplus to measure the economic effects of price ceilings and price floors as they relate to the familiar examples of rental properties and the minimum wage. (We revisit consumer surplus and producer surplus in Chapter 14, "Comparative Advantage and the Gains from International Trade," where we discuss outsourcing and analyze government policies that affect trade; in Chapter 11, "Monopoly and Antitrust Policy," where we examine the effect of market power on economic efficiency; and in Chapter 12, "Pricing Strategy," where we examine the effect of firm pricing policy on economic efficiency.)

- **EARLY COVERAGE OF POLICY ISSUES.** To expose students to policy issues early in the course, we discuss outsourcing in Chapter 1, "Economics: Foundations and Models," rent control and the minimum wage in Chapter 4, "Economic Efficiency, Government Price Setting, and Taxes," air pollution, global warming, and whether the government should run the health care system in Chapter 13, "Externalities, Environmental Policy, and Public Goods," and government policy toward illegal drugs in Chapter 5, "Elasticity: The Responsiveness of Demand and Supply."

- **COMPLETE COVERAGE OF MONOPOLISTIC COMPETITION.** We devote a full chapter to monopolistic competition (Chapter 9, "Monopolistic Competition: The Competitive Model in a More Realistic Setting") prior to covering oligopoly and monopoly in Chapter 10, "Oligopoly: Firms in Less Competitive Markets," and Chapter 11, "Monopoly and Antitrust Policy." Although many instructors cover monopolistic competition very briefly or dispense with it entirely, we think it is an overlooked tool for reinforcing the basic message of how markets work in a context that is much more familiar to students than the agricultural examples that dominate other discussions of perfect competition. We use the monopolistic competition model to introduce the downward-sloping demand curve material usually introduced in the monopoly chapter. This helps students grasp the important point that nearly all firms—not just monopolies—face downward-sloping demand curves. Covering monopolistic competition directly after perfect competition also allows for the early discussion of topics such as brand management and the sources of competitive success. Nevertheless, we wrote the chapter so that instructors who prefer to cover monopoly (Chapter 11, "Monopoly and Antitrust Policy") directly after perfect competition (Chapter 8, "Firms in Perfectly Competitive Markets") can do so without loss of continuity.

- **EXTENSIVE, REALISTIC GAME THEORY COVERAGE.** In Chapter 10, "Oligopoly: Firms in Less Competitive Markets," we use game theory to analyze competition among oligopolists. Game theory helps students understand how companies with market power make strategic decisions in many competitive situations. We use familiar companies such as Carrefour, Coca-Cola, PepsiCo, and Dell in our game theory applications.

- **UNIQUE COVERAGE OF PRICING STRATEGY.** In Chapter 12, "Pricing Strategy," we explore how firms use pricing strategies to increase profits. Students encounter pricing strategies everywhere—when they buy a movie ticket, book a flight for spring break or mid-year vacation, or research book prices online. We use these relevant, familiar examples to illustrate how companies use strategies such as price discrimination, cost-plus pricing, and two-part tariffs.

Macroeconomics

Students come to study macroeconomics with a strong interest in understanding events and developments in the economy. We try to capture that interest and develop students' economic intuition and understanding in this text. We present macroeconomics in a way that is modern and based in the real world of business and economic policy. And we believe we achieve this presentation without making the analysis more difficult. We avoid the recent trend of using simplified versions of intermediate models, which are often more detailed and more complex than what students need to understand the basic macroeconomic issues. Instead, we use a more realistic version of the familiar aggregate demand and aggregate supply model to analyze short-run fluctuations and monetary and fiscal policy. We also avoid the "dueling schools of thought" approach often used to teach macroeconomics at the principles level. We emphasize the many areas of macroeconomics where most economists agree. And we present throughout real business and policy situations to develop students' intuition.

Here are a few highlights of our approach to macroeconomics:

- **A BROAD DISCUSSION OF MACRO STATISTICS.** Many students pay at least some attention to the financial news and know that the release of statistics by government agencies can cause movements in stock and bond prices. A background in macroeconomic statistics helps clarify some of the policy issues encountered in later chapters. In Chapter 15, "GDP: Measuring Total Production and Income," and Chapter 16, "Unemployment and Inflation," we provide students with an understanding of the uses and potential shortcomings of the key macroeconomic statistics, without getting bogged down in the minutiae of how the statistics are constructed. Chapter 22, "Monetary Policy," discusses why central banks prefer to measure inflation using the personal consumption expenditures price index rather than the consumer price index.

- **EARLY COVERAGE OF LONG-RUN TOPICS.** We place key macroeconomic issues in their long-run context in Chapter 17, "Economic Growth, the Financial System, and Business Cycles" where we put the business cycle in the context of underlying long-run growth and discuss what actually happens during the phases of the business cycle. We believe this material is important if students are to have the understanding of business cycles they will need to interpret economic events, yet this material is often discussed only briefly or omitted entirely in other books. We know that many instructors prefer to have a short-run orientation to their macro courses, with a strong emphasis on policy. Accordingly, we have structured Chapter 17 so that its discussion of long-run growth would be sufficient for instructors who want to move quickly to short-run analysis.

- **A DYNAMIC MODEL OF AGGREGATE DEMAND AND AGGREGATE SUPPLY.** We take a fresh approach to the standard aggregate demand and aggregate supply model. We realize there is no good, simple alternative to using the *AD-AS* model when explaining movements in the price level and in real GDP. But we know that more instructors are dissatisfied with the *AD-AS* model than with any other aspect of the macro principles course. The key problem, of course, is that *AD-AS* is a static model that attempts to account for dynamic changes in real GDP and the price level. Our approach retains the basics of the *AD-AS* model but makes it more accurate and useful by making it more dynamic. We emphasize two points: First, changes in the position of the short-run (upward-sloping) aggregate supply curve depend mainly on the state of expectations of the inflation rate. Second, the existence of growth in the economy means that the long-run (vertical) aggregate supply curve shifts to the right every year. This "dynamic" *AD-AS* model provides students with a more accurate understanding of the causes and consequences of fluctuations in real GDP and the price level.

  We introduce the *AD-AS* model in Chapter 20, "Aggregate Demand and Aggregate Supply Analysis," and use it to discuss monetary policy in Chapter 22, "Monetary Policy," and fiscal policy in Chapter 23, "Fiscal Policy." Instructors may safely omit the sections on the dynamic *AD-AS* model without any loss in continuity to the discussion of macroeconomic theory and policy. Chapter 22, "Monetary Policy," includes a graph, Figure 22-6, "Monetary Policy," that shows expansionary and contractionary policy using only the basic *AD-AS* model, which makes it possible to skip the dynamic *AD-AS* discussion of monetary policy. Chapter 23, "Fiscal Policy," also includes a graph, Figure 23-4, "Fiscal Policy," that shows expansionary and contractionary policy using only the basic *AD-AS* model, which makes it possible to skip the dynamic *AD-AS* discussion of fiscal policy. Chapter 24, "Inflation, Unemployment, and Central Bank Policy," uses only the basic *AD-AS* model in discussing the Phillips curve.

- **EXTENSIVE COVERAGE OF MONETARY POLICY.** Because of the central role monetary policy plays in the economy and in students' curiosity about business and financial news, we devote two chapters—Chapters 22, "Monetary Policy," and 24, "Inflation, Unemployment, and Central Bank Policy"—to the topic. We emphasize the issues involved in the Central Bank's choice of monetary policy targets, and we include coverage of the Taylor rule. The Arab World Edition includes coverage of the Central Banks' policies in the Arab countries aimed at dealing with the 2008 global financial crisis.

- **COVERAGE OF BOTH THE DEMAND-SIDE AND SUPPLY-SIDE EFFECTS OF FISCAL POLICY.** Our discussion of fiscal policy in Chapter 23, "Fiscal Policy," carefully distinguishes between automatic stabilizers and discretionary fiscal policy. We also provide significant coverage of the supply-side effects of fiscal policy.

- **A SELF-CONTAINED BUT THOROUGH DISCUSSION OF THE KEYNESIAN IN-COME-EXPENDITURE APPROACH.** The Keynesian income-expenditure approach (the "45°-line diagram," or "Keynesian cross") is useful for introducing students to the short-run relationship between spending and production. Many instructors, however, prefer to omit this material. Therefore, we use the 45°-line diagram only in Chapter 19, "Output and Expenditure in the Short Run." The discussion of monetary and fiscal policy in later chapters uses only the *AD-AS* model, making it possible to omit Chapter 19.

- **COVERAGE OF INTERNATIONAL ASPECTS.** We include two chapters devoted to discuss how Arab countries are integrated in the world economy: Chapter 14, "Comparative Advantage and the Gains from International Trade," and Chapter 25, "Macroeconomics in an Open Economy." Having a good understanding of the international trading and financial systems is essential to understanding the macroeconomy and to satisfying students' curiosity about the economic world around them. In addition to the material in our two international chapters, we weave international comparisons into the narratives of several chapters, including our discussion of labor market institutions in Chapter 24, "Inflation, Unemployment, and Central Bank Policy," and potential GDP in Chapter17, "Economic Growth, the Financial System, and Business Cycles."

- **FLEXIBLE CHAPTER ORGANIZATION.** Because we realize that there are a variety of approaches to teaching principles of macroeconomics, we have structured our chapters for maximum flexibility. For example, our discussion of the Keynesian 45°-line diagram is confined to Chapter 19 so that instructors who do not use this approach can proceed directly to aggregate demand and aggregate supply analysis in Chapter 20, "Aggregate Demand and Aggregate Supply Analysis." While we devote two chapters to monetary policy, the first of these—Chapter 22, "Monetary Policy"—is a self-contained discussion, so instructors may safely omit the material in Chapter 24, "Inflation, Unemployment, and Central Bank Policy," if they choose to. Finally, instructors may choose to omit the two international chapters (Chapter 14, "Comparative Advantage and the Gains from International Trade," and Chapter 25, "Macroeconomics in an Open Economy,"), or cover just one of these two chapters. Please refer to the flexibility chart on **pages xxii and xxiii** to help select the chapters and order best suited to your classroom needs.

Special Features:
A Real-World, Hands-on Approach to Learning Economics

Business Cases and *Inside Look* News Articles

Each chapter-opening case provides a real-world context for learning, sparks students' interest in economics, and helps to unify the chapter. Companies are integrated in the narrative, graphs, and pedagogical features of the chapter. Here are a few examples of international and regional companies we explore in this Arab World Edition:

- Managers making choices at BMW: The cases of BMW-Egypt and BMW-US (**Chapter 2**, "Trade-offs, Comparative Advantage, and the Market System")

- Can Apple's iPod continue to dominate the market? (**Chapter 3**, "Where Prices Come From: The Interaction of Demand and Supply")

- Did Amr Diab make you switch to drinking Pepsi-Cola? (**Chapter 6**, "Consumer Choice and Behavioral Economics")

- Competing with Carrefour (**Chapter 10**, "Oligopoly: Firms in Less Competitive Markets")

- Costa Coffee expansion in the Arab world (**Chapter 9**, "Monopolistic Competition: The Competitive Model in a More Realistic Setting")

- Getting into Dream Park: One price does not fit all (**Chapter 12**, "Pricing Strategy")

- Emirates Airlines feel the impact of the global recession and the fluctuations in GDP (**Chapter 15**, "GDP: Measuring Total Production and Income")

- The fortunes of Aramex follow the business cycle. (**Chapter 20**, "Aggregate Demand and Aggregate Supply")

An Inside Look is a two-page feature that shows students how to apply the concepts from the chapter to the analysis of a news article. Select articles deal with policy issues and are titled *An Inside Look at Policy*. Articles are from international and regional sources such as *Financial Times*, *Economist*, *Al-Ahram Weekly*, *Gulf News*, *Arab Times*, and *Arabian Business*. The feature presents an excerpt from an article, analysis of the article, graph(s), and critical thinking questions.

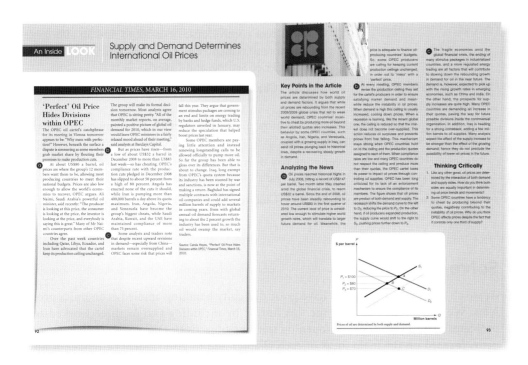

Here are some examples of the articles featured in *An Inside Look*:

- "'Perfect' Oil Price Hides Divisions within OPEC," *Financial Times*, (**Chapter 3**, "Where Prices Come From: The Interaction of Demand and Supply")
- "Etisalat Launches Special Roaming Rates In Egypt And Ksa," *Arabian Business*, (**Chapter 5**, "Elasticity: The Responsiveness of Demand and Supply")
- "Oil Producing Nations Take a Different View on Carbon Taxes," Financial Times, (Chapter 13, "Externalities, Environmental Policy, and Public Goods")
- "First GCC Trade Accord Signed With Singapore," *Gulf News*, (**Chapter 14**, "Comparative Advantage and the Gains from International Trade")
- "GCC Inflation Down; Rising Food Prices Need 'Attention': CBK Gov. Kuwait Inflation at 13-Month High," Arab Times, (**Chapter 16**, "Unemployment and inflation")
- "How Severe is the Lebanese Public Debt?," *The Daily Star*, (**Chapter 23**, "Fiscal Policy")

Economics in Your Life

After the chapter-opening real-world business case, we have added a personal dimension to the chapter opener with a feature titled *Economics in Your Life*, which asks students to consider how economics affects their own lives. The feature piques the interest of students and emphasizes the connection between the material they are learning and their own experiences.

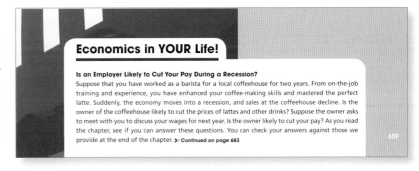

Economics in YOUR Life!

Is an Employer Likely to Cut Your Pay During a Recession?

Suppose that you have worked as a barista for a local coffeehouse for two years. From on-the-job training and experience, you have enhanced your coffee-making skills and mastered the perfect latte. Suddenly, the economy moves into a recession, and sales at the coffeehouse decline. Is the owner of the coffeehouse likely to cut the prices of lattes and other drinks? Suppose the owner asks to meet with you to discuss your wages for next year. Is the owner likely to cut your pay? As you read the chapter, see if you can answer these questions. You can check your answers against those we provide at the end of the chapter. Continued on page 683

659

> **CHAPTER 20**   Aggregate Demand and Aggregate Supply Analysis   **683**

Economics in YOUR Life!

» Continued from page 659

At the beginning of this chapter, we asked you to consider whether during a recession your employer is likely to reduce your pay and cut the prices of the products he or she sells. In this chapter, the dynamic aggregate demand and aggregate supply model showed that even during a recession, the price level rarely falls. A typical firm is therefore unlikely to cut its prices during a recession. So, the owner of the coffeehouse you work in will probably not cut the price of lattes unless sales have declined drastically. We also saw that most firms are more reluctant to cut wages than to increase them because wage cuts can have a negative effect on worker morale and productivity. Given that you are a highly skilled barista, your employer is particularly unlikely to cut your wages for fear that you might quit and work for a competitor.

At the end of the chapter, we use the chapter concepts to answer the questions asked at the beginning of the chapter.

Here are examples of the topics we cover in the new "Economics in Your Life" feature:

- Will you buy an iPod or a Zune? (**Chapter 3**, "Where Prices Come From: The Interaction of Demand and Supply")

- Does rent control make it easier to find an affordable apartment? (**Chapter 4**, "Economic Efficiency, Government Price Setting, and Taxes")

- What's the best country to work in? (**Chapter 15**, "GDP: Measuring Total Production and Income")

- If you spend more, will the economy grow more? (**Chapter 17**, "Economic Growth, the Financial System, and Business Cycles")

- Is an employer likely to cut your pay during a recession? (**Chapter 20**, "Aggregate Demand and Aggregate Supply Analysis")

- How big a raise should you ask for? (**Chapter 24**, "Inflation, Unemployment, and the Central Bank Policy")

Solved Problems

As we all know, many students have great difficulty handling applied economics problems. We help students overcome this hurdle by including two or three worked-out problems tied to select chapter-opening learning objectives. Our goals are to keep students focused on the main ideas of each chapter and to give students a model of how to solve an economic problem by breaking it down step by step. There are additional exercises in the end-of-chapter *Problems and Applications* section tied to every *Solved Problem*.

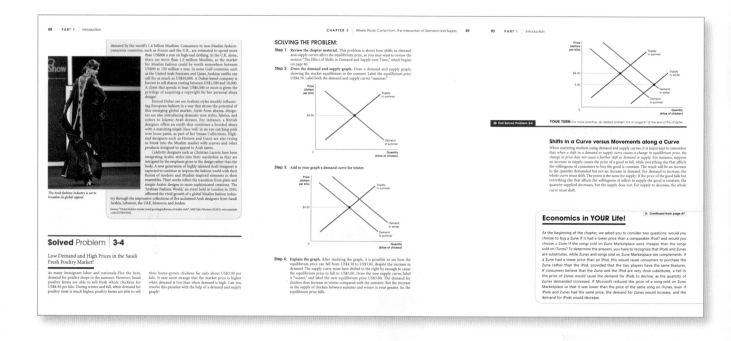

Additional *Solved Problems* appear in the following areas:

- The Instructor's Manual
- PowerPoint® slides
- The *Test Item Files* includes problems tied to the *Solved Problems* in the main book.

Making the Connection

Each chapter includes a number of *Making the Connection* features that present real-world reinforcement of key concepts and help students learn how to interpret what they read on the Web or in newspapers. Most *Making the Connection* features use relevant, stimulating, and provocative news stories focused on businesses and policy issues. The majority of the *Making the Connection* features are updated using real-life examples from the Arab world. Some *Making the Connection* features have a supporting end-of-chapter problem to allow students to test their understanding of the topic discussed. Here are some of the new *Making the Connection* features:

- Trade-Offs: The Pattern of Charitable Giving in the Arab World (**Chapter 2**, "Trade-offs, Comparative Advantage, and the Market System")
- Google Responds to a Growing Arab World Demand on Internet Navigation by launching "Ahlan Online" (**Chapter 3**, "Where Prices Come From: The Interaction of Demand and Supply")
- The Importance of Adopting Industrial Energy-Efficiency Strategies in the Arab World (**Chapter 13**, "Externalities, Environmental Policy, and Public Goods")
- The WTO Strategy for the Arab Region (**Chapter 14**, "Comparative Advantage and the Gains from International Trade")
- Why the Egyptian Economy is compared to the South Korean Economy (**Chapter 14**, "Comparative Advantage and the Gains from International Trade")
- Why Do Firms Pay Mohamed Aboutrika to Endorse Their Products? (**Chapter 6**, "Consumer Choice and Behavioral Economics")
- The Rise and Fall of Apple's Macintosh Computer (**Chapter 9**, "Monopolistic Competition: The Competitive Model in a More Realistic Setting")
- The End of the Arab World's Mobile Telecom Monopolies (**Chapter 11**, "Monopoly and Antitrust Policy")
- Price Discrimination at Foreign Restaurants in the Gulf Countries (**Chapter 12**, "Pricing Strategy")
- In a Global Economy, How Can You Tell the Imports from the Domestic Goods? (**Chapter 20**), "Aggregate Demand and Aggregate Supply Analysis")
- Saudi's Slow Economic Recovery (**Chapter 20**, "Aggregate Demand and Aggregate Supply Analysis")
- Do We Still Need the Fils, Piaster, or penny? (**Chapter 21**, "Money, Banks, and the Federal Reserve System")
- Why Does Khaleej Times Care about Monetary Policy? (**Chapter 22**, "Monetary Policy")
- Is Losing Your Job Good for Your Health? (**Chapter 23**, "Fiscal Policy")

CHAPTER 3 | Where Prices Come From: The Interaction of Demand and Supply 73

Making the Connection

Google Responds to a Growing Arab World Demand for Internet Navigation by launching Ahlan Online

Internet users in the Arab world have gone up 228 percent from just 16.5 million in 2004 to 56 million in 2010. Egypt witnessed the largest increase (20 percent) followed by Morocco (18 percent) and Saudi Arabia (17 percent). Meanwhile, the UAE has the regions' highest Internet penetration rate with 60 percent of the population online. It is also estimated that the number of personal computers in the Arab world more than doubled in 5 years. Between 2004 and 2009 this number surged from 11 million to 26 million personal computers. Recent statistics shows that 30 percent of the new users online are under the age of 18. The research additionally indicated that top online activities in the region consist of an entertainment and/ or communication element.

Understanding these demographical dynamics, Google responded to the rising demand for basic guidance on net navigation, search tips and more by launching Ahlan Online; catering specifically to new, first-time Arab Internet users. Ahlan Online is an Arabic website that provides Middle Eastern and North African (MENA) users with the necessary skills they need to navigate the Internet using Google tools. The site is designed to provide educational tips and guidance on basic online usage such as Google search, Gmail, Google Talk (chat), and Privacy settings (web safety). It will thus assist new users to rapidly learn the basic Google tools and practices of the Internet. Ahlan Online will continue to be enhanced based on users' feedback and needs, in addition to increasingly providing interactive guidance for a greater number of Google products and applications.

The initial phase for the user-friendly website is designed to focus on the current needs of the region and will cover six topics: browser, search, mail, chat, sharing and collaboration, and privacy. The site is compromised of Arabic language educational videos and simple tutorials; it will allow users to learn the ways of Internet through an interactive lesson in Arabic as well as gain tips on how to navigate across a multitude of Google products especially relevant for new users.

Sources: "Middle East Internet Users Increase to 56 million", Menareport.com, April 21, 2010; and www.google.com/ahlan.

YOUR TURN: For more practice, do problem 1.8 on page 95 at the end of this chapter.

Graphs and Summary Tables

Graphs are an indispensable part of the principles of economics course but are a major stumbling block for many students. Every chapter except Chapter 1 includes end-of-chapter problems that require students to draw, read, and interpret graphs. We use four devices to help students read and interpret graphs:

1. Detailed captions
2. Boxed notes
3. Color-coded curves
4. Summary tables with graphs

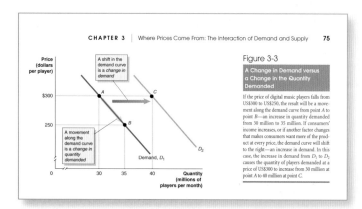

Figure 3-3

A Change in Demand versus a Change in the Quantity Demanded

If the price of digital music players falls from US$300 to US$250, the result will be a movement along the demand curve from point A to point B—an increase in quantity demanded from 30 million to 35 million. If consumers' income increases, or if another factor changes that makes consumers want more of the product at every price, the demand curve will shift to the right—an increase in demand. In this case, the increase in demand from D_1 to D_2 causes the quantity of players demanded at a price of US$300 to increase from 30 million at point A to 40 million at point C.

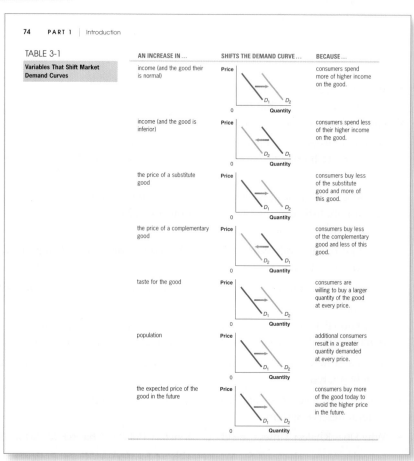

TABLE 3-1

Variables That Shift Market Demand Curves

AN INCREASE IN...	SHIFTS THE DEMAND CURVE...	BECAUSE...
income (and the good their is normal)		consumers spend more of higher income on the good.
income (and the good is inferior)		consumers spend less of their higher income on the good.
the price of a substitute good		consumers buy less of the substitute good and more of this good.
the price of a complementary good		consumers buy less of the complementary good and less of this good.
taste for the good		consumers are willing to buy a larger quantity of the good at every price.
population		additional consumers result in a greater quantity demanded at every price.
the expected price of the good in the future		consumers buy more of the good today to avoid the higher price in the future.

New Review Questions and Problems and Applications—Grouped by Learning Objective to Improve Assessment

All the end-of-chapter material—*Summary, Review Questions,* and *Problems and Applications*—is grouped under learning objectives. We reorganized chapter *Summaries* and placed them together in one section, which is separated from the *Review Questions* and *Problems and Applications* section. The goals of this new organization are to make it easier for instructors to assign problems based on learning objectives, both in the book and in MyEconLab, and to help students efficiently track and review chapter summaries. If students have difficulty with a particular learning objective, an instructor can easily identify which end-of-chapter questions and problems support that objective and assign them as homework or discuss them in class. Every exercise in a chapter's *Problems and Applications* section is available in MyEconLab. Using MyEconLab, students can complete these and many other exercises online, get tutorial help, and receive instant feedback and assistance on those exercises they answer incorrectly. Also, student learning will be enhanced by having the summary material grouped by learning objective, which will allow students to focus on the parts of the chapter they found most challenging. Each major section of the chapter, paired with a learning objective, has at least two review questions and three problems.

We also include one or more end-of-chapter problems that test the students' understanding of the content presented in the *Solved Problem* and *Making the Connection* special features in the chapter. Instructors can cover the feature in class and assign the corresponding problem for homework. The Test Item File also includes test questions that pertain to these special features.

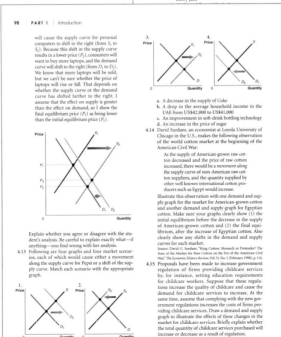

Integrated Supplements

Resources for the Instructor

Instructor's Manual

The *Instructor's Manual* includes chapter-by-chapter summaries, learning objectives, extended examples and class exercises, teaching outlines incorporating key terms and definitions, teaching tips, topics for class discussion, new *Solved Problems*, and solutions to all review questions and problems in the book. The *Instructor's Manual* is available for download from the Instructor's Resource Center.

Test Item File

The Test Item File includes 2,000 multiple-choice questions, true/false, short-answer, and graphing questions. There are questions to support each key feature in the book. Test questions are annotated with the following information:

- **Difficulty:** 1 for straight recall, 2 for some analysis, 3 for complex analysis
- **Type:** multiple-choice, true/false, short-answer, essay
- **Topic:** the term or concept the question supports
- **Skill:** fact, definition, analytical, conceptual
- Learning objective
- **AACSB** (see description that follows)
- Page number
- **Special feature in the main book:** chapter-opening business example, Economics in Your Life, Solved Problem, Making the Connection, and An Inside Look.

The Association to Advance Collegiate Schools of Business (AACSB)

The Test Item File connects select questions to the general knowledge and skill guidelines found in the AACSB Assurance of Learning Standards.

What is the AACSB?

AACSB is a not-for-profit corporation of educational institutions, corporations, and other organizations devoted to the promotion and improvement of higher education in business administration and accounting. A collegiate institution offering degrees in business administration or accounting may volunteer for AACSB accreditation review. The AACSB makes initial accreditation decisions and conducts periodic reviews to promote continuous quality improvement in management education. Pearson Education is a proud member of the AACSB and is pleased to provide advice to help you apply AACSB Assurance of Learning Standards.

What are AACSB Assurance of Learning Standards?

One of the criteria for AACSB accreditation is the quality of the curricula. Although no specific courses are required, the AACSB expects a curriculum to include learning experiences in such areas as:

- Communication
- Ethical Reasoning
- Analytic Skills

- Use of Information Technology
- Multicultural and Diversity
- Reflective Thinking

These six categories are AACSB Assurance of Learning Standards. Questions that test skills relevant to these standards are tagged with the appropriate standard. For example, a question testing the moral questions associated with externalities would receive the Ethical Reasoning tag.

How Can Instructors Use the AACSB Tags?

Tagged questions help you measure whether students are grasping the course content that aligns with the AACSB guidelines noted above. This in turn may suggest enrichment activities or other educational experiences to help students achieve these skills.

TestGen

The computerized TestGen package allows instructors to customize, save, and generate classroom tests. The test program permits instructors to edit, add, or delete questions from the Test Item File; edit existing graphics and create new graphics; analyze test results; and organize a database of tests and student results. This software allows for extensive flexibility and ease of use. It provides many options for organizing and displaying tests, along with search and sort features. The software and the Test Item File can be downloaded from the Instructor's Resource Center (accessed via www.pearsoned.co.uk/awe/hubbard).

PowerPoint® Lecture Presentation

A comprehensive set of PowerPoint® slides that can be used by instructors for class presentations or by students for lecture preview or review. The presentation includes all the graphs, tables, and equations in the textbook.

Instructors may download these PowerPoint® presentations from the Instructor's Resource Center (accessed via www.pearsoned.co.uk/awe/hubbard).

myeconlab

Get Ahead of the Curve

For the Instructor

MyEconLab is an online course management, testing, and tutorial resource. Instructors can choose how much, or how little, time to spend setting up and using MyEconLab.

Each chapter contains two Sample Tests, Study Plan Exercises, and Tutorial Resources. Student use of these materials requires no initial set-up by their instructor. The online Gradebook records each student's performance and time spent on the Tests and Study Plan and generates reports by student or by chapter.

Instructors can assign Tests, Quizzes, and Homework in MyEconLab using four resources:

- Pre-loaded Sample Test questions
- Problems similar to the end-of-chapter problems
- Test Item File questions
- Self-authored questions using Econ Exercise Builder

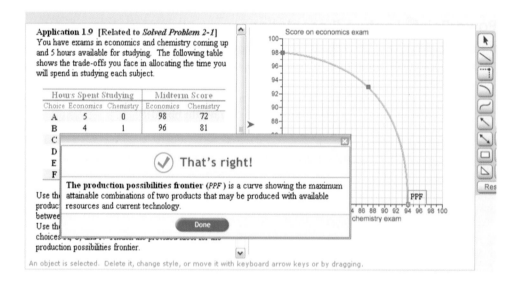

Exercises use multiple-choice, graph drawing, and free-response items, many of which are generated algorithmically so that each time a student works them, a different variation is presented.

MyEconLab grades every problem, even those with graphs. When working homework exercises, students receive immediate feedback with links to additional learning tools.

For the Student

MyEconLab puts students in control of their learning through a collection of testing, practice, and study tools tied to the online, interactive version of the textbook and other medial resources.

Within MyEconLab's structured environment, students practice what they learn, test their understanding, and pursue a personalized Study Plan generated from their performance on Sample Tests and tests created by their instructors. At the core of MyEconLab are the following features:

- Sample Tests, two per chapter
- Personal Study Plan
- Tutorial Instruction
- Graphing Tool

Sample Tests

Two Sample Tests for each chapter are pre-loaded in MyEconLab, enabling students to practice what they have learned, test their understanding, and identify areas in which they need to do further work. Students can study on their own, or they can complete assignments created by their instructor.

Personal Study Plan

Based on a student's performance on tests, MyEconLab generates a personal Study Plan that shows where he or she needs further study. The Study Plan consists of a series of additional practice exercises with detailed feedback and guided solutions and keyed to other tutorial resources.

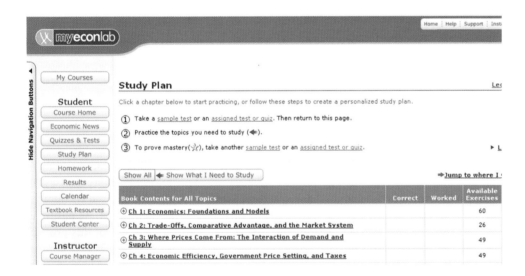

Tutorial Instruction

Launched from many of the exercises in the Study Plan, MyEconLab provides tutorial instruction in the form of step-by-step solutions and other media-based explanations.

Graphing Tool

A graphing tool is integrated into the Tests and Study Plan exercises to enable students to make and manipulate graphs. This feature helps students understand how concepts, numbers, and graphs connect.

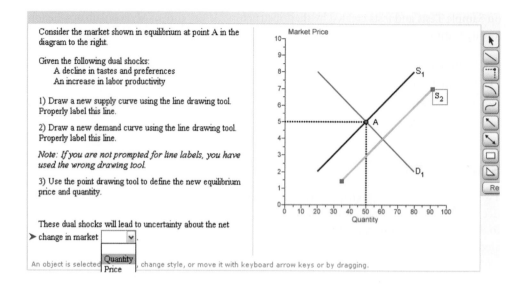

Additional MyEconLab Tools

MyEconLab also includes the following additional features:

1. **Economics in the News**—Links to regional articles from the Financial Times

2. **eText**—While working in the Study Plan or completing homework assignments, part of the tutorial resources available is a link directly to the relevant page of the text so the student can review the appropriate material to help them complete the exercise

3. **Glossary Flashcards**—every key term is available as a flashcard, allowing students to quiz themselves on vocabulary from one or more chapters at a time

4. **Ask the Author**—e-mail economic related questions to the author

A Word of Thanks

We would like to express our deep appreciation to the Pearson team, as we benefited greatly from their dedication and professionalism. Sophie Bulbrook, the Senior Development Editor and Editorial Team Leader of Arab World Editions, worked really hard for more than a year to ensure that this book was as good as it could be. Sophie's support, advice, and encouragement were crucial to us, especially during the writing stage of the manuscript. Acquisitions Editor Rasheed Roussan is the person who first started the arrangements of this project. Rasheed was always a great help to us with his kind words and advice. He was very keen to dedicate much of his time to make this project a success. We were also pleased to work with Kate Sherington, Project Editor, and Fay Gibbons, Editorial Assistant. Their editorial comments were very helpful. We would also like to extend our thanks to all reviewers of the Arab World Edition for their time and effort, and for their valuable remarks.

A good part of the burden of a project of this magnitude is borne by our families. We appreciate the patience, support, and encouragement of our spouses and children.

Ashraf Galal Eid
Amany El Anshasy

Acknowledgments

We would like to thank the following reviewers for their thoughtful comments and suggestions for this new *Arab World Edition*:

Dr. Khalid M. Kisswani, Gulf University for Science & Technology, Kuwait

Wasseem Mina, United Arab Emirates University, UAE

Usamah Husni Ramadan, American University of Beirut, Lebanon

Amer Al-Roubaie, Ph.D. Ahlia University, Bahrain

Professor Hussein Al-Talafha, Yarmouk University, Jordan

Dr. Abdullah A. Alshebel, King Saud University, Saudi Arabia

Dr. George Fahmy Rezk, Arab Academy for Science & Technology, Egypt

Zahera Tayseer Mohammad, College of Business Administration (CBA), Saudi Arabia

This text would also not have been possible without the many contributions of reviewers, consultant board members, and accuracy checkers in previous editions of *Economics*. We'd like to thank them all for their valuable insight and suggestions, which have informed our work on this adaptation.

PART 1

Introduction

Chapter 1

Economics: Foundations and Models

The Rising Economic Powers in the East: The Arab World and the Global Economy

You probably see the words "Made in China" every time you go shopping, for a variety of goods, including running shoes, clothing, towels, and sheets. Even sophisticated and high-technology products, such as cars and electronics, are now designed and manufactured in China. The rise of China and other economies, such as India, in the past few years, coupled with significant signs of weakened U.S. and European economies, has created an increasing perception that the economic power is shifting eastward. Yet, the experience of the current global slowdown has highlighted the degree to which emerging markets still depend on demand in the world's biggest consumer market in the U.S. and other developed nations.

To what extent would Arab states benefit from these rising powers? The geographical location of the Arab nations, as the passage between the East and the West, gives the region a great advantage and raises its potential to benefit from the expected future growth in the developing world in the East. For example, all of the Gulf Cooperation Council (GCC) states, which comprises Bahrain, Kuwait, Oman, Qatar, Saudi Arabia, and the United Arab Emirates (UAE), have strong historical trade links with key Asian and African emerging markets. In addition, they are working on establishing strong investment profiles in these key developing economies. Qatar, in 2009, for example, opened an investment office in China to take advantage of the lucrative investment opportunities in the fast-growing economy. Qatar Investment Authority, Qatar's sovereign investment fund, has offices in India as well and is negotiating large stakes in Indian companies. In 2008, the China Dubai Capital investment fund was established to target and pursue investment opportunities in China. It was created by the international investment arm of Dubai Holding (Dubai International Capital LLC), and the leading China private equity firm, First Eastern Investment Group. The competition is now intensifying between the GCC states and other countries seeking to build similar strong trade and investment links in the emerging markets of the East.

Some forecasts show that the GCC's share of the world economy is expected to grow steadily between now and 2020. Given sufficient foreign investment flows to the region and a growth in government revenues from sources other than oil, this growth could be sustained even if oil prices remained low. In fact, there is an argument that much higher oil prices—of US$100 – 200 billion—could reduce the incentives for economic reform.

In addition, the newly rising powers of the East may play a greater role in international institutions, pushing for better representation on the UN Security Council and at the International Monetary Fund (IMF). This new trend towards the representation of a larger group of governments is highly welcomed in the Gulf nations, whose economic power was acknowledged with the participation of Saudi Arabia as part of the G20. Ultimately, the GCC states will soon make an increased contribution to international institutions and the world trade. **AN INSIDE LOOK** on **page 18** discusses the price the Gulf economy has to pay for greater integration in the global economy.

Sources: The Economist Intelligence Unit Report, "The GCC in 2020: Outlook for the Gulf and the Global Economy," *The Economist*, March 2009; "Qatar Holding to Open Office in China," Reuters, November 2, 2009; and "Dubai International Capital and First Eastern Launch China Dubai Capital," www.cpifinancial.net, April 14, 2008.

Economics in YOUR Life!

Are You Likely to Find a Job in the GCC Area upon Your Graduation?

According to the *Statistical Bulletin of the GCC General Secretariat*, 435,000 graduates are currently unemployed in the GCC countries.[1] In the next 10 years, 100,000 Emiratis will be seeking employment, including 70,000 in Abu Dhabi, according to estimates from the Abu Dhabi Tawteen Council. Jobseekers in Oman increased to 88,000 by the end of 2008, from 24,000 by the end of 2007. Suppose that you are a GCC national who is planning on working as an economist, a software engineer, a lawyer, a business consultant, a financial analyst, or in another industry that is expected to grow in the next decade: would you expect to find a job upon your graduation, or do you believe that unemployment will grow despite the need for more workers to sustain the expected growth in the GCC economies? As you read the chapter, see if you can answer this question. You can check your answer against the one we provide at the end of the chapter. **> Continued on page 16**

In this book, we use economics to answer questions such as the following:

- How are the prices of goods and services determined?

- How does pollution affect the economy, and how should government policy deal with these effects?

- Why do firms engage in international trade, and how do government policies affect international trade?

- Why does government control the prices of some goods and services, and what are the effects of those controls?

Economists do not always agree on the answers to every question. In fact, as we will see, economists engage in lively debate on some issues. In addition, new problems and issues are constantly arising. So, economists are always at work developing new methods to analyze and answer these questions.

Scarcity The situation in which unlimited wants exceed the limited resources available to fulfill those wants.

All the questions we discuss in this book illustrate a basic fact of life: people must make choices as they try to attain their goals. We must make choices because we live in a world of **scarcity**, which means that although our wants are unlimited, the resources available to fulfill those wants are limited. You might like to have a 60-inch plasma television in every room of your home, but unless you are a close relative of Bill Gates, you probably lack the money to purchase them. Every day, you must make choices about how to spend your limited income on the many goods and services available. The finite amount of time available to you also limits your ability to attain your goals. If you spend an hour studying for your economics midterm, you have one less hour available to study for your history midterm. Firms and the government are in the same situation as you: they have limited resources available as they attempt to attain their goals. **Economics** is the study of the choices consumers, business managers, and government officials make to attain their goals, given their scarce resources.

Economics The study of the choices people make to attain their goals, given their scarce resources.

We begin this chapter by discussing three important economic ideas that we will return to many times in the book: *People are rational. People respond to incentives. Optimal decisions are made at the margin.* Then we consider the three fundamental questions that any economy must answer: *What* goods and services will be produced? *How* will the goods and services be produced? *Who* will receive the goods and services? Next we consider the role of *economic models* in helping analyze the many issues presented throughout this book. **Economic models** are simplified versions of reality used to analyze real-world economic situations. Later in this chapter, we explore why economists use models and how they construct them. Finally, we discuss the difference between microeconomics and macroeconomics, and we preview some important economic terms.

Economic model A simplified version of reality used to analyze real-world economic situations.

1.1 | Explain these three key economic ideas: *People are rational. People respond to incentives. Optimal decisions are made at the margin.*

Three Key Economic Ideas

Market A group of buyers and sellers of a good or service and the institution or arrangement by which they come together to trade.

As you try to achieve your goals, whether they are buying a new computer or finding a part-time job, you will interact with other people in *markets*. A **market** is a group of buyers and sellers of a good or service and the institution or arrangement by which they come together to trade. Most of economics involves analyzing what happens in markets.

Throughout this book, as we study how people make choices and interact in markets, we will return to three important ideas:

1 People are rational.

2 People respond to economic incentives.

3 Optimal decisions are made at the margin.

People Are Rational

Economists generally assume that people are rational. This assumption does *not* mean that economists believe everyone knows everything or always makes the 'best' decision. It means that economists assume that consumers and firms use all available information as they act to achieve their goals. Rational individuals weigh the benefits and costs of each action, and they choose an action only if the benefits outweigh the costs. For example, if Microsoft charges a price of US$239 for a copy of Windows, economists assume that the managers at Microsoft have estimated that a price of US$239 will earn Microsoft the most profit. The managers may be wrong; perhaps a price of US$265 would be more profitable, but economists assume that the managers at Microsoft have acted rationally on the basis of the information available to them in choosing the price. Of course, not everyone behaves rationally all the time. Still, the assumption of rational behavior is very useful in explaining most of the choices that people make.

People Respond to Economic Incentives

Human beings act from a variety of motives, including religious belief, envy, and compassion. Economists emphasize that consumers and firms consistently respond to *economic* incentives. This fact may seem obvious, but it is often overlooked. For example, it is not clearly understood why banks are not taking steps to improve security in the face of an increase in robberies. A significant improvement in banks' security may require, for example, doubling or tripling the number of armed guards outside their doors and installing bullet-resistant glass or plastic in front of tellers' windows. Some of you will be surprised to know that very few banks may adopt these measures. But think about it carefully. The economic incentive to banks is clear: given the very small probability that a bank robbery will happen in a specific branch in a year-period, it becomes far less costly to put up with bank robberies than to take additional security measures. The fact that banks respond to economic incentives as they do to the threat of robberies should not be surprising to economists.

In each chapter, the *Making the Connection* feature discusses a news story or another application related to the chapter material. Read the following *Making the Connection* for a discussion of whether people respond to economic incentives even when making the decision to have children.

Making the Connection | **Will Women Have Fewer or More Babies if the Government Pays Them To?**

The populations of the United States, Japan, and most European countries are aging as birthrates decline and the average person lives longer. The governments of these countries have programs to pay money to retired workers, such as the Social Security system. Most of the money for these programs comes from taxes paid by people currently working. As the population ages, there are fewer workers paying taxes relative to the number of retired people receiving government payments. The result is a funding crisis that countries can solve only by either reducing government payments to retired workers or by raising the taxes paid by current workers.

(continued)

The Arab world is facing the opposite problem. The population has grown at an average rate of 2.6 per cent per year compared with a 1.5 per cent growth rate in the rest of the world. For the population of a country to be stable, the average woman must have 2.1 children. By 2000, the average total fertility rate in the region was 4.1, which exceeded the world's average of 2.7. This rate is projected to fall to 3.1 between 2015 and 2020. An important policy question is: would women respond to an economic incentive by reducing the number of children if the government paid those who have fewer children; or would they have more children if the government pays a grant for each newborn child?

Population policy has changed in many Arab countries since 2001. The majority of the Arab governments began acknowledging the negative effect of rapid population growth on their resources. In 1976, the only Arab countries that considered their population growth rate to be too high and intervened to lower it were Egypt, Morocco, and Tunisia. Thirty years later, the only country that succeeded in sharply cutting its average birthrate was Tunisia.

The government of Tunisia adopted an aggressive policy to reduce the rate of birth. The policy was devised to deter families from having more children and encourage having a smaller number of children. Government financial aid was restricted to three children. The policy, including other measures such as raising the age of marriage and legalizing abortion, worked. In Egypt, on the other hand, fearing social unrest, especially among religious segments of society, the government opted to have a large-scale family advising program, instead of using deterrents or incentives. The policy seems to have had a very small impact on Egyptian birthrates to date.

In some European countries birthrates have fallen so low that the total population will soon begin to decline. One example is the small European country of Estonia. The Estonian government used economic incentives in an attempt to increase the birthrate. Beginning in 2004, the government began paying working women who take time off after having a baby their entire salary for up to 15 months. Women who did not work received US$200 per month, which is a substantial amount, given that the average income in Estonia is US$650 per month. In fact, the birthrate in Estonia increased from 1.3 children per woman in the late 1990s to 1.7 children per woman in 2008.

Estonia is not alone; more than 45 other countries in Europe and Asia have taken steps to try to raise their birthrates. People may respond to economic incentives even when making the very personal decision of how many children to have.

Sources: UN-ESCWA, "Population and Development: The Demographic Profile of the Arab Countries," United Nations, 2003; and Marcus Walker, "In Estonia, Paying Women to Have Babies Is Paying Off", *Wall Street Journal*, October 20, 2006, p. A1.

YOUR TURN: Test your understanding by doing related problem 1.5 on page 21 at the end of this chapter.

Optimal Decisions Are Made at the Margin

Some decisions are 'all or nothing': An entrepreneur decides whether to open a new restaurant. He or she either starts the new restaurant or doesn't. You decide whether to enter graduate school or to take a job instead. You either enter graduate school or you don't. But most decisions in life are not all or nothing. Instead, most decisions involve doing a little more or a little less. If you are trying to decrease your spending and increase your saving, the decision is not really a choice between saving every dollar you earn or spending it all. Rather, many small choices are involved, such as whether to buy a caffè mocha at Starbucks every day or to cut back to three times per week.

Economists use the word *marginal* to mean an extra or additional benefit or cost of a decision. Should you watch another hour of TV or spend that hour studying? The *marginal benefit* (or, in symbols, *MB*) of watching more TV is the additional enjoyment you receive. The *marginal cost* (or *MC*) is the lower grade you receive from having studied a little less. Should Apple Computer produce an additional 300,000 iPods? Firms receive *revenue* from selling goods. Apple's marginal benefit is the additional revenue it receives from selling 300,000 more iPods. Apple's marginal cost is the additional cost—for wages, parts, and so forth—of producing 300,000 more iPods. *Economists reason that the optimal decision is to continue any activity up to the point where the marginal benefit equals the marginal cost—in symbols, where* MB = MC. Often we apply this rule without consciously thinking about it. Usually you will know whether the additional enjoyment from watching a television program is worth the additional cost involved in not spending that hour studying, without giving it a lot of thought. In business situations, however, firms often have to make careful calculations to determine, for example, whether the additional revenue received from increasing production is greater or less than the additional cost of the production. Economists refer to analysis that involves comparing marginal benefits and marginal costs as **marginal analysis**.

In each chapter of this book, you will see the special feature *Solved Problem*. This feature will increase your understanding of the material by leading you through the steps of solving an applied economic problem. After reading the problem, you can test your understanding by working the related problems that appear at the end of the chapter.

Marginal analysis Analysis that involves comparing marginal benefits and marginal costs.

Solved Problem | 1-1

Apple Computer Makes a Decision at the Margin

Suppose Apple is currently selling 3,000,000 iPods per year. Managers at Apple are considering whether to raise production to 3,300,000 iPods per year. One manager argues, "Increasing production from 3,000,000 to 3,300,000 is a good idea because we will make a total profit of US$100 million if we produce 3,300,000." Do you agree with her reasoning? What, if any, additional information do you need to decide whether Apple should produce the additional 300,000 iPods?

SOLVING THE PROBLEM:

Step 1: **Review the chapter material.** The problem is about making decisions, so you may want to review the section "Optimal Decisions Are Made at the Margin," which begins on page 6. Remember to think "marginal" whenever you see the word "additional" in economics.

Step 2: **Explain whether you agree with the manager's reasoning.** We have seen that any activity should be continued to the point where the marginal benefit is equal to the marginal cost. In this case, that involves continuing to produce iPods up to the point where the additional revenue Apple receives from selling more iPods is equal to the marginal cost of producing them. The Apple manager has not done a marginal analysis, so you should not agree with her reasoning. Her statement about the *total* profit of producing 3,300,000 iPods is not relevant to the decision of whether to produce the last 300,000 iPods.

Step 3: **Explain what additional information you need.** You will need additional information to make a correct decision. You will need to know the additional revenue Apple would earn from selling 300,000 more iPods and the additional cost of producing them.

YOUR TURN: For more practice, do related problems 1.3, and 1.4 on page 21 at the end of this chapter.

⟫ End Solved Problem 1-1

1.2 | Discuss how an economy answers these questions: *What* goods and services will be produced? *How* will the goods and services be produced? *Who* will receive the goods and services?

The Economic Problem That Every Society Must Solve

Trade-off The idea that because of scarcity, producing more of one good or service means producing less of another good or service.

Opportunity cost The highest-valued alternative that must be given up to engage in an activity.

We have already noted the important fact that we live in a world of scarcity. As a result, any society faces the economic problem that it has only a limited amount of economic resources—such as workers, machines, and raw materials—and so can produce only a limited amount of goods and services. Therefore, society faces **trade-offs**: producing more of one good or service means producing less of another good or service. In fact, the best way to measure the cost of producing a good or service is the value of what has to be given up to produce it. The **opportunity cost** of any activity—such as producing a good or service—is the highest-valued alternative that must be given up to engage in that activity. The concept of opportunity cost is very important in economics and applies to individuals as much as it does to firms or to society as a whole. Consider the example of someone who could receive a salary of US$80,000 per year working as a manager at a firm but opens her own firm instead. In that case, the opportunity cost of her managerial services to her own firm is US$80,000, even if she does not explicitly pay herself a salary.

Trade-offs force society to make choices, particularly when answering the following three fundamental questions:

1 *What* goods and services will be produced?

2 *How* will the goods and services be produced?

3 *Who* will receive the goods and services produced?

Throughout this book, we will return to these questions many times. For now, we briefly introduce each question.

What Goods and Services Will Be Produced?

How will society decide whether to produce more economics textbooks or more HD-DVD players? More schools or more football stadiums? Of course, 'society' does not make decisions; only individuals make decisions. The answer to the question of what will be produced is determined by the choices made by consumers, firms, and the government. Every day, you help decide which goods and services will be produced when you choose to buy an iPod rather than an HD-DVD player or a caffè mocha rather than a chai tea. Similarly, Apple must choose whether to devote its scarce resources to making more iPods or more MacBook laptop computers. The government must choose whether to spend more of its limited budget on building healthcare facilities or on national security and the armed forces. In each case, consumers, firms, and the government face the problem of scarcity by trading off one good or service for another. And each choice made comes with an opportunity cost measured by the value of the best alternative given up.

How Will the Goods and Services Be Produced?

Firms choose how to produce the goods and services they sell. In many cases, firms face a trade-off between using more workers or using more machines. For example, a local service station has to choose whether to provide car repair services using more diagnostic computers and fewer auto mechanics or more auto mechanics and fewer diagnostic computers. Similarly, movie studios have to choose whether to produce animated films using highly skilled animators to draw them by hand or fewer animators and more computers.

Who Will Receive the Goods and Services Produced?

In the Arab world, who receives the goods and services produced depends largely on how income is distributed. Individuals with the highest income have the ability to buy the most goods and services. Often, people are willing to give up some of their income—and, therefore, some of their ability to purchase goods and services—by donating to charities to increase the incomes of poorer people. An important policy question, however, is whether the government should intervene to make the distribution of income more equal. Such intervention already occurs in many Arab countries, because people with higher incomes pay a larger fraction of their incomes in taxes and because the government makes payments to people with low incomes. There is disagreement over whether the current attempts to redistribute income are sufficient or whether there should be more or less redistribution.

Centrally Planned Economies versus Market Economies

Societies organize their economies in two main ways to answer the three questions of what, how, and who. A society can have a **centrally planned economy** in which the government decides how economic resources will be allocated. Or a society can have a **market economy** in which the decisions of households and firms interacting in markets allocate economic resources.

From 1917 to 1991, the most important centrally planned economy in the world was that of the Soviet Union, which was established when Vladimir Lenin and his Communist Party staged a revolution and took over the Russian Empire. In the Soviet Union, the government decided what goods to produce, how to produce them, and who would receive them. Government employees managed factories and stores. The objective of these managers was to follow the government's orders rather than to satisfy the wants of consumers. Centrally planned economies like the Soviet Union have not been successful in producing low-cost, high-quality goods and services. As a result, the standard of living of the average person in a centrally planned economy tends to be quite low. All centrally planned economies have also been political dictatorships. Dissatisfaction with low living standards and political repression finally led to the collapse of the Soviet Union in 1991. Today, only a few small countries, such as Cuba and North Korea, still have completely centrally planned economies.

All the high-income democracies, such as the United States, Canada, Japan, and the countries of Western Europe, are market economies. Most Arab countries nowadays are moving towards becoming market economies, but are still struggling with heavy government intervention. Market economies rely primarily on privately owned firms to produce goods and services and to decide how to produce them. Markets, rather than the government, determine who receives the goods and services produced. In a market economy, firms must produce goods and services that meet the wants of consumers, or the firms will go out of business. In that sense, it is ultimately consumers who decide what goods and services will be produced. Because firms in a market economy compete to offer the highest-quality products at the lowest price, they are under pressure to use the lowest-cost methods of production. For example, in the past 10 years, some U.S. firms, particularly in the electronics and furniture industries, have been under pressure to reduce their costs to meet competition from Chinese firms.

In a market economy, the income of an individual is determined by the payments he receives for what he has to sell. If he is a civil engineer and firms are willing to pay a salary of US$85,000 per year for engineers with his training and skills, that is the amount of income he will have to purchase goods and services. If the engineer also owns a house that he rents out, his income will be even higher. One of the attractive features of markets is that they reward hard work. Generally, the more extensive the training a person has received and the longer the hours the person works, the higher the person's income will be. Of course, luck—both good and bad—also plays a role

Centrally planned economy An economy in which the government decides how economic resources will be allocated.

Market economy An economy in which the decisions of households and firms interacting in markets allocate economic resources.

here, as elsewhere in life. We can conclude that market economies answer the question "Who receives the goods and services produced?" with the answer "Those who are most willing and able to buy them."

The Modern 'Mixed' Economy and the Arab Economies

Starting in the early 1960s and continuing throughout the 1970s, governments played a large role in most Arab economies. The role of the government ranged from building strong armies, building infrastructure, and providing public education to establishing industries and controlling most markets. The objective of most Arab governments then was to provide strong economic and social support to the newly independent Arab economies. Some government intervention was also meant to reduce unemployment and poverty through expanding public-sector employment and establishing a large Social Security system. As a result, government intervention in the economy dramatically increased in countries such as Egypt and Syria. By the middle of the 1980s, many Arab economies started realizing, after years of adopting a model that is closer to a centrally planned economy than to a market economy, that the proceeds of development and growth of more than two decades were not so high. In fact, some Arab countries ended up accumulating huge piles of debts. In more recent years, international organizations such as the IMF and the World Bank played a significant role in advising most Arab countries, and shaping their policies to limit government intervention and to downsize the public sector, allowing greater market freedom.

Therefore, most Arab economies are today believed to be *mixed economies*. A **mixed economy** is primarily a market economy with most economic decisions resulting from the interaction of buyers and sellers in markets, but in a mixed economy the government plays a significant role in the allocation of resources. In fact, most economies today are effectively mixed economies. Some economists argue that the extent of government intervention in countries such as the U.S., Canada, Japan, and those of Western Europe including the U.K., makes it no longer accurate to refer to their economies as pure market economies. As we will see in later chapters, economists continue to debate the role government should play in a market economy.

Similarly, one of the most important developments in the international economy in recent years has been the movement of China from being a centrally planned economy to being a more mixed economy. The Chinese economy had suffered decades of economic stagnation following the takeover of the government by Mao Zedong and the Communist Party in 1949. Although China remains a political dictatorship, production of most goods and services is now determined in the market rather than by the government. The result has been rapid economic growth that in the near future may lead to total production of goods and services in China surpassing total production in the United States.

Efficiency and Equity

Market economies tend to be more efficient than centrally planned economies. There are two types of efficiency: *productive efficiency* and *allocative efficiency*. **Productive efficiency** occurs when a good or service is produced at the lowest possible cost. **Allocative efficiency** occurs when production is in accordance with consumer preferences. Markets tend to be efficient because they promote competition and facilitate voluntary exchange. **Voluntary exchange** refers to the situation in which both the buyer and seller of a product are made better off by the transaction. We know that the buyer and seller are both made better off because, otherwise, the buyer would not have agreed to buy the product or the seller would not have agreed to sell it. Productive efficiency is achieved when competition among firms in markets forces the firms to produce goods and services at the lowest cost. Allocative efficiency is achieved when the combination of competition among firms and voluntary exchange between firms and consumers results in firms producing the mix of goods and services that consumers prefer most. Competition will force firms

Mixed economy An economy in which most economic decisions result from the interaction of buyers and sellers in markets but in which the government plays a significant role in the allocation of resources.

Productive efficiency The situation in which a good or service is produced at the lowest possible cost.

Allocative efficiency A state of the economy in which production is in accordance with consumer preferences; in particular, every good or service is produced up to the point where the last unit provides a marginal benefit to society equal to the marginal cost of producing it.

Voluntary exchange The situation that occurs in markets when both the buyer and seller of a product are made better off by the transaction.

to continue producing and selling goods and services as long as the additional benefit to consumers is greater than the additional cost of production. In this way, the mix of goods and services produced will be in accordance with consumer preferences.

Although markets promote efficiency, they don't guarantee it. Inefficiency can arise from various sources. To begin with, it may take some time to achieve an efficient outcome. When DVD players were introduced, for example, firms did not instantly achieve productive efficiency. It took several years for firms to discover the lowest-cost method of producing this good. As we will discuss in Chapter 4, governments sometimes reduce efficiency by interfering with voluntary exchange in markets. For example, many governments limit the imports of some goods from foreign countries. This limitation reduces efficiency by keeping goods from being produced at the lowest cost. The production of some goods damages the environment. In this case, government intervention can increase efficiency because, without such intervention, firms may ignore the costs of environmental damage and thereby fail to produce the goods at the lowest possible cost.

Just because an economic outcome is efficient does not necessarily mean that society finds it desirable. Many people prefer economic outcomes that they consider fair or equitable, even if those outcomes are less efficient. **Equity** is harder to define than efficiency, but it usually involves a fair distribution of economic benefits. For some people, equity involves a more equal distribution of economic benefits than would result from an emphasis on efficiency alone. For example, some people support taxing people with higher incomes to provide the funds for programs that aid the poor. Although governments may increase equity by reducing the incomes of high-income people and increasing the incomes of the poor, efficiency may be reduced. People have less incentive to open new businesses, to supply labor, and to save if the government takes a significant amount of the income they earn from working or saving. The result is that fewer goods and services are produced, and less saving takes place. As this example illustrates, *there is often a trade-off between efficiency and equity*. In this case, the total amount of goods and services produced falls, although the distribution of the income to buy those goods and services is made more equal. Government policymakers often confront this trade-off.

Equity The fair distribution of economic benefits.

1.3 | Understand the role of models in economic analysis.

Economic Models

Economists rely on economic theories, or *models* (the words *theory* and *model* are used interchangeably), to analyze real-world issues, such as the economic effects of outsourcing. As mentioned earlier, economic models are simplified versions of reality. Economists are certainly not alone in relying on models: an engineer may use a computer model of a bridge to help test whether it will withstand high winds, or a biologist may make a physical model of a nucleic acid to better understand its properties. One purpose of economic models is to make economic ideas sufficiently explicit and concrete so that individuals, firms, or the government can use them to make decisions. For example, we will see in Chapter 3 that the model of demand and supply is a simplified version of how the prices of products are determined by the interactions among buyers and sellers in markets.

Economists use economic models to answer questions. For example, they may use a model of economic growth to analyze the question of how trading and investment treaties with emerging markets in the East would affect the prospects of economic growth in a particular group of countries, such as the Arab world countries. Sometimes economists use an existing model to analyze an issue, but in other cases, they must develop a new model. To develop a model, economists generally follow these steps:

1 Decide on the assumptions to be used in developing the model.

2 Formulate a testable hypothesis.

3 Use economic data to test the hypothesis.

4 Revise the model if it fails to explain well the economic data.

5 Retain the revised model to help answer similar economic questions in the future.

The Role of Assumptions in Economic Models

Any model is based on making assumptions because models have to be simplified to be useful. We cannot analyze an economic issue unless we reduce its complexity. For example, economic models make *behavioral assumptions* about the motives of consumers and firms. Economists assume that consumers will buy the goods and services that will maximize their well-being or their satisfaction. Similarly, economists assume that firms act to maximize their profits. These assumptions are simplifications because they do not describe the motives of every consumer and every firm. How can we know if the assumptions in a model are too simplified or too limiting? We discover this when we form hypotheses based on these assumptions and test these hypotheses using real-world information.

Forming and Testing Hypotheses in Economic Models

Economic variable Something measurable that can have different values, such as the wages of software programmers.

A *hypothesis* in an economic model is a statement that may be either correct or incorrect about an *economic variable*. An **economic variable** is something measurable that can have different values, such as the wages. An example of a hypothesis in an economic model is the statement that relying on foreign labor in many Arab counties increases unemployment among nationals. An economic hypothesis is usually about a *causal relationship*; in this case, the hypothesis states that employing foreign labor causes, or leads to, fewer jobs being available for nationals, raising calls for labor nationalization.

Before accepting a hypothesis, we must test it. To test a hypothesis, we must analyze statistics on the relevant economic variables. In our example, we must gather statistics on employment in the relevant Arab countries and perhaps on other variables as well. Testing a hypothesis can be tricky. For example, showing that the employment among nationals fell at a time when foreign labor was increasing would not be enough to demonstrate that foreign labor *caused* a rise in the rate of unemployment among nationals. Just because two things are *correlated*—that is, they happen at the same time—does not mean that one caused the other. For example, suppose that the number of trained national workers greatly increased at the same time that foreign labor was increasing. In that case, unless foreign labor replaced national labor, the fall in employment among nationals may have been caused by the increased number of national workers looking for certain jobs rather than by the effects of larger foreign labour. Over a period of time, many economic variables change, which complicates testing hypotheses. In fact, when economists disagree about a hypothesis, it is often because of disagreements over interpreting the statistical analysis used to test the hypothesis.

Note that hypotheses must be statements that could, in principle, turn out to be incorrect. Statements such as "labor nationalization is good" or "labor nationalization is bad" are value judgments rather than hypotheses because it is not possible to disprove them.

Economists accept and use an economic model if it leads to hypotheses that are confirmed by statistical analysis. In many cases, the acceptance is tentative, however, pending the gathering of new data or further statistical analysis. In fact, economists often refer to a hypothesis having been "not rejected," rather than having been "accepted," by statistical analysis. But what if statistical analysis clearly rejects a hypothesis? For example, what if a model leads to a hypothesis that the nationalization of the labor force in the Arab Gulf states lowers the rates of unemployment, but this hypothesis is rejected by the data? In that case, the model must be reconsidered. It may be that an assumption used in the model was too simplified or too limiting. For example, perhaps the model used to determine the effect of foreign labor on the rates of unemployment assumed that national labor receive the same wages as foriegn labor. In fact, national labor is usually paid higher salaries than foriegn labor; this difference may explain why our hypothesis was rejected by the economic statistics.

The process of developing models, testing hypotheses, and revising models occurs not just in economics but also in disciplines such as physics, chemistry, and biology. This process is often referred to as the *scientific method*. Economics is a *social science* because it applies the scientific method to the study of the interactions among individuals.

Normative and Positive Analysis

Throughout this book, as we build economic models and use them to answer questions, we need to bear in mind the distinction between *positive analysis* and *normative analysis*. **Positive analysis** is concerned with *what is*, and **normative analysis** is concerned with *what ought to be*. Economics is about positive analysis, which measures the costs and benefits of different courses of action.

We can use the Jordanian government's minimum wage law to compare positive and normative analysis. In 2008, under this law, it was illegal for an employer to hire a worker at a wage less than 110 Jordanian dinar per month (about US$ 150).[2] Without the minimum wage law, some firms and some workers would voluntarily agree to a lower wage. Because of the minimum wage law, some workers have difficulty finding jobs, and some firms end up paying more for labor than they otherwise would have. A positive analysis of the minimum wage law uses an economic model to estimate how many workers have lost their jobs because of the law, its impact on the costs and profits of businesses, and the gains to workers receiving the minimum wage. After economists complete this positive analysis, the decision as to whether the minimum wage law is a good idea or a bad idea is a normative one and depends on how people evaluate the trade-off involved. Supporters of the law believe that the losses to employers and to workers who are unemployed as a result of the law are more than offset by the gains to workers who receive higher wages than they would without the law. Opponents of the law believe the losses are greater than the gains. The assessment by any individual would depend, in part, on that person's values and political views. The positive analysis provided by an economist would play a role in the decision but can't by itself decide the issue one way or the other.

Positive analysis Analysis concerned with what is.

Normative analysis Analysis concerned with what ought to be.

Economics as a Social Science

Because economics is based on studying the actions of individuals, it is a social science. Economics is therefore similar to other social science disciplines, such as psychology, political science, and sociology. As a social science, economics considers human behavior—particularly decision-making behavior—in every context, not just in the context of business. Economists have studied such issues as how families decide the number of children to have, why people have difficulty losing weight or attaining other desirable goals, and why people often ignore relevant information when making decisions. Economics also has much to contribute to questions of government policy. As we will see throughout this book, economists have played an important role in formulating government policies in areas such as the environment, health care, and poverty.

Making the Connection | ## Should the Host Governments Protect the Migrant Workers?

Each year millions of unskilled workers from India, Pakistan, Bangladesh, Indonesia, and elsewhere leave their homes and families in search of jobs and a better future. Their search often leads them to the oil-rich Gulf Corporation Council (GCC) countries of Saudi Arabia, the UAE, Kuwait, Qatar, Bahrain, and Oman. These migrant workers come from regions with high levels of unemployment, low wages, and poor living conditions. They come in search of jobs, hoping for a better future for themselves and their families. Through hard work, they expect to be able to support their families back home and accumulate sufficient savings to return home one day to buy a house or set up a business.

The host countries are in need of laborers to fill thousands of jobs created annually as a consequence of the investment of oil revenues in construction, agriculture, manufacturing, and services. While many of these countries have their own pool of able local laborers, they often find it difficult to fulfill these vacancies. The lack of a minimum wage level and other labor laws make salaries and employment conditions unattractive to the local population. In addition, the stigma attached to certain employment, especially manual work, causes local laborers to shy away from available vacancies. As a result, thousands of jobs are regularly filled by 'guest' workers from Southeast Asian countries.

Should host governments protect migrant workers?

Most workers who take these jobs are recruited in their home country by local employment agencies. They are promised high salaries, accommodation, insurance benefits, and long-term employment contracts. Once they arrive in the host country, their dream of better jobs and a higher standard of living is quickly shattered. Many find themselves housed in cramped labor camps, working long hours for wages that are barely enough to cover food and other basic necessities. For the first few years of their contract deductions are made from their meagre wages to cover the cost of their air travel to the host country, visa fees, insurance, and other outlays made by their employer. As security against the migrants absconding, their passports are confiscated and held until completion of their contracts. Local laws prohibit them from changing employment until fulfillment of their contractual obligation. Any violation is grounds for dismissal and a placement of a lifetime ban on their return to the host country. Organized demands for better wages or working conditions are also causes for discharge, deportation, and banishment.

Many international human rights organizations have criticized the GCC countries for their labor laws and their treatment of guest workers. The GCC governments, however, believe that the present conditions actually *help* workers by providing employment to otherwise unemployed people. They accuse the international organizations of interference in local laws and the free flow of labor.

YOUR TURN: Test your understanding by doing related problem 3.7 on page 22 at the end of this chapter.

1.4 LEARNING OBJECTIVE

1.4 | Distinguish between microeconomics and macroeconomics.

Microeconomics and Macroeconomics

Microeconomics The study of how households and firms make choices, how they interact in markets, and how the government attempts to influence their choices.

Economic models can be used to analyze decision making in many areas. We group some of these areas together as *microeconomics* and others as *macroeconomics*. **Microeconomics** is the study of how households and firms make choices, how they interact in markets, and how the government attempts to influence their choices. Microeconomic issues include explaining how consumers react to changes in product prices and how firms decide what prices to charge. Microeconomics also involves policy issues, such as analyzing the most efficient way to reduce teenage smoking, analyzing the costs and benefits of approving the sale of a new prescription drug, and analyzing the most efficient way to reduce air pollution.

Macroeconomics The study of the economy as a whole, including topics such as inflation, unemployment, and economic growth.

Macroeconomics is the study of the economy as a whole, including topics such as inflation, unemployment, and economic growth. Macroeconomic issues include explaining why economies experience periods of recession and increasing unemployment and why over the long run, some economies have grown much faster than others. Macroeconomics also involves policy issues, such as whether government intervention can reduce the severity of recessions.

The division between microeconomics and macroeconomics is not hard and fast. Many economic situations have *both* a microeconomic and a macroeconomic aspect. For example, the level of total investment by firms in new machinery and equipment helps to determine how rapidly the economy grows—which is a macroeconomic issue. But to understand how much new machinery and equipment firms decide to purchase, we have to analyze the incentives individual firms face—which is a microeconomic issue.

1.5 | Become familiar with important economic terms.

A Preview of Important Economic Terms

In the following chapters, you will encounter certain important terms again and again. Becoming familiar with these terms is a necessary step in learning economics. Here we provide a brief introduction to some of these terms. We will discuss them all in greater depth in later chapters:

- **Entrepreneur.** An entrepreneur is someone who operates a business. In a market system, entrepreneurs decide what goods and services to produce and how to produce them. An entrepreneur starting a new business puts his or her own funds at risk. If an entrepreneur is wrong about what consumers want or about the best way to produce goods and services, the entrepreneur's funds can be lost. This is not an unusual occurrence: it is common for about half of new businesses close within four years. Without entrepreneurs willing to assume the risk of starting and operating businesses, economic progress would be impossible in a market system.

- **Innovation.** There is a distinction between an *invention* and *innovation.* An invention is the development of a new good or a new process for making a good. An innovation is the practical application of an invention. (*Innovation* may also be used more broadly to refer to any significant improvement in a good or in the means of producing a good.) Much time often passes between the appearance of a new idea and its development for widespread use. For example, the first digital electronic computer—the ENIAC—was developed in 1945, but the first IBM personal computer was not introduced until 1981, and widespread use of computers did not have a significant effect on the productivity of businesses until 1990s.

- **Technology.** A firm's technology is the processes it uses to produce goods and services. In the economic sense, a firm's technology depends on many factors, such as the skill of its managers, the training of its workers, and the speed and efficiency of its machinery and equipment.

- **Firm, company, or business.** A firm is an organization that produces a good or service. Most firms produce goods or services to earn profits, but there are also non-profit firms, such as universities and some hospitals. Economists use the terms *firm, company,* and *business* interchangeably.

- **Goods.** Goods are tangible merchandise, such as books, computers, or DVD players.

- **Services.** Services are activities done for others, such as providing haircuts or investment advice.

- **Revenue.** A firm's revenue is the total amount received for selling a good or service. It is calculated by multiplying the price per unit by the number of units sold.

- **Profit.** A firm's profit is the difference between its revenue and its costs. Economists distinguish between *accounting profit* and *economic profit.* In calculating accounting profit, we exclude the cost of some economic resources that the firm does not pay for explicitly. In calculating economic profit, we include the opportunity cost of all resources used by the firm. When we refer to *profit* in this book, we mean economic profit. It is important not to confuse *profit* with *revenue*.

- *Household.* A household consists of all persons occupying a home. Households are suppliers of factors of production—particularly labor—used by firms to make goods and services. Households also demand goods and services produced by firms and governments.

- *Factors of production or economic resources.* Firms use factors of production to produce goods and services. The main factors of production are labor, capital, human capital, natural resources—including land—and entrepreneurial ability. Households earn income by supplying the factors of production to firms.

- *Capital.* The word *capital* can refer to *financial capital* or to *physical capital.* Financial capital includes stocks and bonds issued by firms, bank accounts, and holdings of money. In economics, though, *capital* refers to physical capital, which includes manufactured goods that are used to produce other goods and services. Examples of physical capital are computers, factory buildings, machine tools, warehouses, and trucks. The total amount of physical capital available in a country is referred to as the country's *capital stock*.

- *Human capital.* Human capital refers to the accumulated training and skills that workers possess. For example, college-educated workers generally have more skills and are more productive than workers who have only high school degrees.

Economics in YOUR Life!

>> Continued from page 3

At the beginning of the chapter, we posed the question: "Is it likely that you will find a job after your graduation in the GCC economy?" If the GCC continues its rapid growth and establishes itself as a growing knowledge-based economy, the rate of unemployment should naturally decline over the next two decades. But guaranteeing a job opportunity for every graduate depends on whether the educational system in the GCC will address the challenge of matching higher-education programs to the needs of economic, social, and cultural development. That requires creating an educational infrastructure capable of attracting global talents in teaching and research. Tying education to labor market needs in the region will ensure providing a sustainable supply of workers trained in local knowledge relevant to the nations' long-term ambitions. Failing to do so would simply mean that the labor market in the Gulf will continue its dependence on foreign labor and that the rate of unemployment among nationals will be on the rise despite the growing economy. In addition, the extent to which the diversification efforts of the GCC economies succeed will determine the scope of new opportunities to exploit the human resource development. So, finding a job in the GCC countries in the future hinges on whether your educational training matches available jobs' technical requirements. That in turn depends on the success of education and labor market policies.

Conclusion

The best way to think of economics is as a group of useful ideas about how individuals make choices. Economists have put these ideas into practice by developing economic models. Consumers, business managers, and government officials use these models every day to help make choices. In this book, we explore many key economic models and give examples of how to apply them in the real world.

Most students taking an introductory economics course do not major in economics or become professional economists. Whatever your major may be, the economic principles you will learn in this book will improve your ability to make choices in many aspects of your life. These principles will also improve your understanding of how decisions are made in business and government.

Reading the newspaper and other periodicals is an important part of understanding the current business climate and learning how to apply economic concepts to a variety of real-world events. At the end of each chapter, you will see a two-page feature entitled *An Inside Look*. This feature consists of an excerpt of an article that either relates to the company introduced at the start of the chapter, or to the concepts discussed throughout the chapter. A summary and analysis and supporting graphs highlight the economic key points of the article. Read *An Inside Look* on the next page to learn how more integration in the global economy has exposed the Gulf's private sector to global shocks Test your understanding by answering the *Thinking Critically* questions.

FINANCIAL TIMES APRIL 15, 2009

Gulf Companies Learn the Price of Globalization

The private sectors of the six oil-exporting countries of the Gulf Cooperation Council are, by varying degrees, experiencing their worst crisis since the oil price crash of 1998–99. Historically, corporate profitability was hit by cuts in public expenditure as Gulf governments recoiled from plummeting oil revenues. This time, the accumulation of sovereign wealth funds is enabling governments to raise expenditure despite falling oil receipts. But as the GCC has opened to the outside world over the past decade, the private sector's exposure to economic contagion has grown.

In the old days, fluctuations in oil prices were the main driver of corporate profits in the GCC for two main reasons. First, government expenditure, which is the primary economic stimulant in Gulf countries given their expansive public sectors, tended to track changes in oil receipts. Second, Gulf economies were largely insulated from global capital flows given their then limited opportunities for foreign investment and the lower reliance of companies and banks on external debt financing.

An example of this causality is the last period of substantial oil price decline, when global oil prices slid to an average of US$13 a barrel in 1998. The resulting cuts in government expenditure across the Gulf had an adverse effect on domestic demand as public consumption and investment fell. Local companies, reliant on government contracts, saw their businesses contract. Even though global growth slowed in 1998, the GCC countries did not experience significant capital outflows. Local equity and real estate markets were largely barred to non-residents and many economic sectors were off-limits to foreign investors.

Yet today, the chain of causality between oil prices, government expenditure, and private-sector profitability is less clear cut. The main reasons for this are that the accumulation of sovereign wealth funds has enabled most Gulf governments to break the link between oil revenues and public expenditure, at least over the short- to medium-term. Second, private sectors in the Gulf have closer ties to the outside world. In contrast to the late 1990s, most GCC governments are defying the collapse in their revenues and are raising, rather than cutting, expenditure in nominal dollar terms. These increases are stimulating flagging private sectors.

Furthermore, companies and banks across the Gulf are today more directly exposed to global financial and market turmoil than in past crises because of closer economic links to the outside world. Foreigners can now purchase equities on all GCC stock markets. Five out of six GCC states now allow foreign ownership of property in designated areas. Banks have become more vulnerable to swings in external sentiment, particularly during last year's speculation over Gulf currency revaluation. Some GCC banks and financial institutions have been exposed to exotic financial instruments. Foreign direct investment is much freer these days. GCC companies and banks have also made significant investments outside the Gulf over the past 10 years, thereby increasing their exposure to global economic trends. They also have higher external debt burdens than previously from tapping international capital markets to fund expansion.

Of course, oil prices still matter because they continue indirectly to influence the confidence of consumers and investors in the long-term economic health of the Gulf States. Yet for those parts of the private sector that are not directly dependent on national oil companies, this crisis can be distinguished from previous ones by the greater role played by globalization rather than falling oil prices.

Source: "Gulf Companies Learn the Price of Globalization," The Financial Times, April 15, 2009.

Key Points in the Article

The article discusses the recent integration of the Gulf countries into the global economy. While global integration, as we read in the chapter opener, will increase the potential for their future high growth, it comes at a cost. The article argues that, in the past, episodes of lower oil prices and the slowdown in growth in the non-oil private sector were mainly due to a contraction in government spending as a result of lower oil receipts. On the contrary, in the recent 2008/2009 crisis, globalization played a major role in the slowdown in the Gulf economies. Despite the increase in government spending, the private sector became much exposed to economic crises in the global economy as a result of more capital flows, larger foreign direct investment, and the bank's greater integration in the global financial system.

Analyzing the News

a We have seen in this chapter that economists use models to analyze economic issues such as the effects of expanding trade and foriegn direct investment flows on countries' economic performance. In the past, the GCC economies were tied to the international economy through oil exports that accounted for most of government revenues. When oil prices surge, government revenues also soar, leading to a fast growth in public spending, and vice versa. The expansion of government services, economic infrastructure, and government contracts used to boost private-sector non-oil activities. On the other hand, falling oil prices result in lower levels of government spending and slower private-sector growth.

b In recent years, the oil surpluses have been invested in the financial markets of the U.S., Europe, and the emerging markets. The return from investing the oil receipts allowed the GCC governments to support a falling demand at times of low oil prices, preventing a decline in non-oil activities. Therefore, unlike the experience from the past few decades, government spending became a stabilizing element in the economy.

c In the past decade, the GCC states have started transforming their economies to become fully integrated in the global economy. The Gulf became the newly growing financial hub in the region, and direct foreign investment became the catalyst for economic growth. While this has been a source of potential growth, it also became the main source of economic fluctuations. These countries pay a price for global integration in terms of greater exposure to external shocks and global crises. So, in the latest global financial crises, the slowdown in major countries in Europe and the U.S. was the main reason behind the slowdown in economic activity in the Gulf.

Thinking Critically

1. Why does greater exposure to global crises play a fundamental role in destabilizing the GCC, economies?
2. What are the potential benefits of being integrated in the global economy?

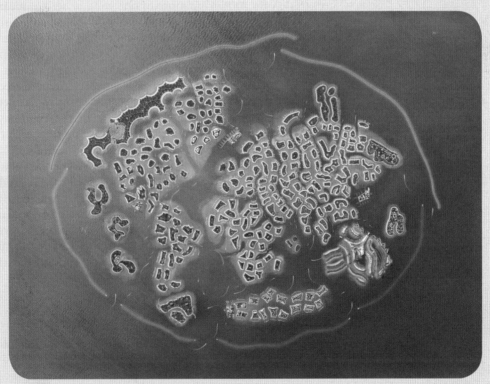

The GCC countries are becoming more integrated in the global economy.

Key Terms

Summary

1.1 LEARNING OBJECTIVE

Explain these three key economic ideas: *People are rational. People respond to incentives. Optimal decisions are made at the margin,* **pages 4–7.**

Three Key Economic Ideas

Economics is the study of the choices consumers, business managers, and government officials make to attain their goals, given their scarce resources. We must make choices because of **scarcity**, which means that although our wants are unlimited, the resources available to fulfill those wants are limited. Economists assume that people are rational in the sense that consumers and firms use all available information as they take actions intended to achieve their goals. Rational individuals weigh the benefits and costs of each action and choose an action only if the benefits outweigh the costs. Although people act from a variety of motives, ample evidence indicates that they respond to economic incentives. Economists use the word **marginal** to mean extra or additional. The optimal decision is to continue any activity up to the point where the marginal benefit equals the marginal cost.

1.2 LEARNING OBJECTIVE

Discuss how an economy answers these questions: *What* goods and services will be produced? *How* will the goods and services be produced? *Who* will receive the goods and services? **pages 8–11.**

The Economic Problem That Every Society Must Solve

Society faces **trade-offs**: producing more of one good or service means producing less of another good or service. The **opportunity cost** of any activity—such as producing a good or service—is the highest-valued alternative that must be given up to engage in that activity. The choices of consumers, firms, and governments determine what goods and services will be produced. Firms choose how to produce the goods and services they sell. In the Arab world, who receives the goods and services produced depends largely on how income is distributed in the marketplace. In a **entrally planned economy**, most economic decisions are made by the government. In a **market economy**, most economic decisions are made by consumers and firms. Most economies, including those of the Arab world, are **mixed economies** in which most economic decisions are made by consumers and firms but in which the government also plays a significant role. There are two types of efficiency: productive efficiency and allocative efficiency. **Productive efficiency** occurs when a good or service is produced at the lowest possible cost. **Allocative efficiency** occurs when production is in accordance with consumer preferences. **Voluntary exchange** is the situation that occurs in markets when both the buyer and seller of a product are made better off by the transaction. **Equity** is more difficult to define than efficiency, but it usually involves a fair distribution of economic benefits. Government policymakers often face a trade-off between equity and efficiency.

1.3 LEARNING OBJECTIVE

Understand the role of models in economic analysis, **pages 11–14.**

Economic Models

Economists rely on economic models when they apply economic ideas to real-world problems. **Economic models** are simplified versions of reality used to analyze real-world economic situations. Economists accept and use an economic model if it leads to hypotheses that are confirmed by statistical analysis. In many cases, the acceptance is tentative, however, pending the gathering of new data or further statistical analysis. Economics is a **social science** because it applies the scientific method to the study of the interactions among individuals. Economics is concerned with positive analysis rather than normative analysis. **Positive analysis** is concerned with what is. **Normative**

analysis is concerned with what ought to be. Because economics is based on studying the actions of individuals, it is a social science. As a social science, economics considers human behavior in every context of decision making, not just in business.

Microeconomics and Macroeconomics

Microeconomics is the study of how households and firms make choices, how they interact in markets, and how the government attempts to influence their choices. **Macroeconomics** is the study of the economy as a whole, including topics such as inflation, unemployment, and economic growth.

1.4 LEARNING OBJECTIVE

Distinguish between microeconomics and macroeconomics, **pages 14–15.**

A Preview of Important Economic Terms

Becoming familiar with important terms is a necessary step in learning economics. These important economic terms include *capital, entrepreneur, factors of production, firm, goods, household, human capital, innovation, profit, revenue,* and *technology.*

1.5 LEARNING OBJECTIVE

Become familiar with important economic terms, **pages 15–16.**

Review, Problems and Applications

myeconlab Visit www.pearsoned.co.uk/awe/hubbard to complete these exercises online and get instant feedback.
Get Ahead of the Curve

1.1 LEARNING OBJECTIVE   Explain these three key economic ideas: *People are rational. People respond to incentives. Optimal decisions are made at the margin,* **pages 4–7.**

Review Questions

1.1 Briefly discuss each of the following economic ideas: People are rational. People respond to incentives. Optimal decisions are made at the margin.

1.2 What is scarcity? Why is scarcity central to the study of economics?

Problems and Applications

1.3 **(Related to *Solved Problem 1-1* on page 7)** Suppose Dell is currently selling 250,000 Pentium 4 laptops per month. A manager at Dell argues, "The last 10,000 laptops we produced increased our revenue by US$8.5 million and our costs by US$8.9 million. However, because we are making a substantial total profit of US$25 million from producing 250,000 laptops, I think we are producing the optimal number of laptops." Briefly explain whether you agree with the manager's reasoning.

1.4 **(Related to *Solved Problem 1-1* on page 7)** Two students are discussing Solved Problem 1-1:

Ahmed: "I think the key additional information you need to know in deciding whether to produce 300,000 more iPods is the amount of profit you currently are making while producing 3,000,000. Then you can compare the profit earned from selling 3,300,000 iPods with the profit earned from selling 3,000,000. This information is more important than the additional revenue and additional cost of the last 300,000 iPods produced."

Ali: "Actually, Ahmed, knowing how much profits change when you sell 300,000 more iPods is exactly the same as knowing the additional revenue and the additional cost."

Briefly evaluate their arguments.

1.5 **(Related to the *Making the Connection* on page 5)** Estonia has attempted to increase the country's birthrate by making payments to women who have babies. Can you suggest how to change the program and adapt it to an Arab country, such as the UAE, that seeks to increase its population? Make sure you change the program in ways that might make it more likely that UAE women will have more children, rather than simply changing the timing of when they have children as in Estonia. What information would we need in the future (after the implementation of the program) to know whether UAE women are responding to the government's incentives by having more children or simply by having them earlier?

Discuss how an economy answers these questions: *What* goods and services will be produced? *How* will the goods and services be produced? *Who* will receive the goods and services? **pages 8–11.**

Review Questions

2.1 What are the three economic questions that every society must answer? Briefly discuss the differences in how centrally planned, market, and mixed economies answer these questions.

2.2 What is the difference between productive efficiency and allocative efficiency?

2.3 What is the difference between efficiency and equity? Why do government policymakers often face a trade-off between efficiency and equity?

Problems and Applications

2.4 Does the Lebanese-Mexican businessman Carlos Slim, the richest person in the world, face scarcity? Does everyone? Are there any exceptions?

2.5 Would you expect new and better machinery and equipment to be adopted more rapidly in a market economy or in a centrally planned economy? Briefly explain.

2.6 Centrally planned economies have been less efficient than market economies.
  a. Has this happened by chance, or is there some underlying reason?
  b. If market economies are more economically efficient than centrally planned economies, would there ever be a reason to prefer having a centrally planned economy rather than a market economy?

2.7 Thomas Sowell, an economist at the Hoover Institution at Stanford University in the U.S., has written, "All economic systems not only provide people with goods and services, but also restrict or prevent them from getting as much of these goods and services as they wish." Why is it necessary for all economic systems to do this? How does a market system prevent people from getting as many goods and services as they wish?

Source: Thomas Sowell, *Applied Economics: Thinking Beyond Stage One*, New York: Basic Books, 2004, p. 16.

2.8 Suppose that your local police department recovers 100 tickets to the Football league finals from blackmarket ticket dealers. The police department decides to distribute these to residents and announces that tickets will be given away at 10 a.m. Monday at a public park.
  a. What groups of people will be most likely to try to get the tickets? Think of specific examples and then generalize.
  b. What is the opportunity cost of distributing the tickets this way?
  c. Productive efficiency occurs when a good or service (such as the distribution of tickets) is produced at the lowest possible cost. Is this an efficient way to distribute the tickets? If possible, think of a more efficient method of distributing the tickets.
  d. Is this an equitable way to distribute the tickets? Explain.

Understand the role of *models* in economic analysis, **pages 11–14.**

Review Questions

3.1 Why do economists use models? How are economic data used to test models?

3.2 Describe the five steps by which economists arrive at a useful economic model.

3.3 What is the difference between normative analysis and positive analysis? Is economics concerned mainly with normative analysis or mainly with positive analysis? Briefly explain.

Problems and Applications

3.4 Do you agree or disagree with the following assertion: "The problem with economics is that it assumes consumers and firms always make the correct decision. But we know everyone's human, and we all make mistakes."

3.5 Suppose an economist develops an economic model and finds that "it works great in theory, but it fails in practice." What should the economist do next?

3.6 Dr Khaled's theory is that the price of mushrooms is determined by the activity of subatomic particles that exist in another universe parallel to ours. When the subatomic particle emissions are high, the price of mushrooms is high. When subatomic particle emissions are low, the price of mushrooms also is low. How would you go about testing Dr Khaled's theory? Discuss whether this theory is useful.

3.7 **(Related to the *Making the Connection* on page 13)** The *Making the Connection* explores the debate over the immigration of skilled workers. What is the impact of labor law on local workers employment, wages, and working conditions? How will changes to the minimum wage and other labor laws affect the flow of migrant workers to the host country? Think about some local labor laws in your own home country. Do they encourage local employment? Do they help attract workers to your country?

3.8 Explain which of the following statements represent positive analysis and which represent normative analysis.

   a. A 50-cent-per-pack tax on cigarettes will reduce smoking by teenagers by 12 percent.

   b. The government should spend more on cancer research.

   c. Rising paper prices will increase textbook prices.

   d. The price of coffee at Starbucks is too high.

1.4 LEARNING OBJECTIVE   Distinguish between *microeconomics* and *macroeconomics*, **pages 14–15.**

Review Questions

4.1 Briefly discuss the difference between microeconomics and macroeconomics.

Problems and Applications

4.2 Briefly explain whether each of the following is primarily a microeconomic issue or a macroeconomic issue.

   a. The effect of higher cigarette taxes on the quantity of cigarettes sold.

   b. The effect of higher income taxes on the total amount of consumer spending.

   c. The reasons for the economies of East Asian countries growing faster than the economies of sub-Saharan African countries.

   d. The reasons for low rates of profit in the airline industry.

4.3 Briefly explain whether you agree with the following assertion: "Microeconomics is concerned with things that happen in one particular place, such as the unemployment rate in one city. In contrast, macroeconomics is concerned with things that affect the country as a whole, such as how the rate of teenage smoking would be affected by an increase in the tax on cigarettes."

Appendix

Using Graphs and Formulas

Review the use of graphs and formulas.

Graphs are used to illustrate key economics ideas. Graphs appear not just in economics textbooks but also on websites and in newspaper and magazine articles that discuss events in business and economics. Why the heavy use of graphs? Because they serve two useful purposes: (1) They simplify economic ideas, and (2) they make the ideas more concrete so they can be applied to real-world problems. Economic and business issues can be complicated, but a graph can help cut through complications and highlight the key relationships needed to understand the issue. In that sense, a graph can be like a street map.

For example, suppose you take a bus to Dubai to see Burj Khalifa. After arriving at the bus terminal, you will probably use a map similar to the one shown below to find your way.

Maps are very familiar to just about everyone, so we don't usually think of them as being simplified versions of reality, but they are. This map does not show much more than the streets in this part of Dubai and some of the most important buildings. The names, addresses, and telephone numbers of the people who live and work in the area aren't given. Almost none of the stores and buildings those people work and live in are shown either. The map doesn't tell which streets allow curbside parking and which don't. In fact, the map tells almost nothing about the messy reality of life in this section of Dubai, except how the streets are laid out, which is the essential information you need to get from the bus terminal to Burj Khalifa.

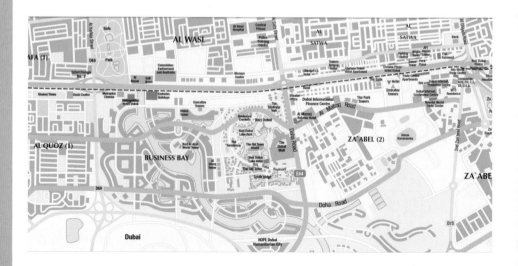

Think about someone who says, "I know how to get around in the city, but I just can't figure out how to read a map." It certainly is possible to find your destination in a city without a map, but it's a lot easier with one. The same is true of using graphs in economics. It is possible to arrive at a solution to a real-world problem in economics and business without using graphs, but it is usually a lot easier if you do use them.

Often, the difficulty students have with graphs and formulas is a lack of familiarity. With practice, all the graphs and formulas in this text will become familiar to you. Once you are familiar with them, you will be able to use them to analyze problems that would otherwise seem very difficult. What follows is a brief review of how graphs and formulas are used.

Graphs of One Variable

Figure 1A-1 displays values for *Arab countries' shares* in the total Arab labor force, using two common types of graphs. Labor force shares show a country's population aged 15 and older who meet the International Labor Organization (ILO) definition of the economically active as a percentage of Arab countries' *total* labor force. In this case, the information is for countries: the 'Big four'—Egypt, Algeria, Sudan, and Morocco—as well as Saudi Arabia, Iraq, Syria, Yemen, Tunisia, and the rest of the 22 Arab states combined. Panel (a) displays the information on labor force shares as a *bar graph*, where the labor force share of each country is represented by the height of its bar. Panel (b) displays the same information as a *pie chart*, with the labor force share of each country represented by the size of its slice of the pie.

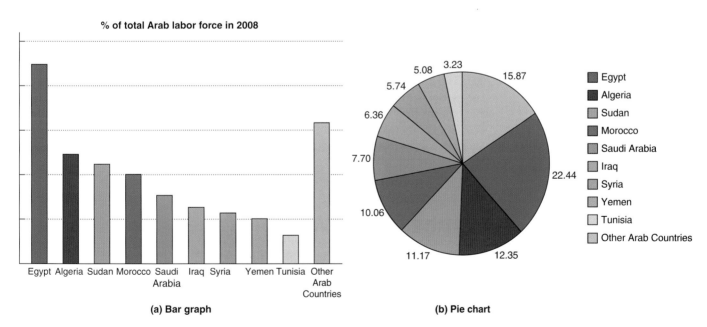

(a) Bar graph   **(b) Pie chart**

Figure 1A-1 | Bar Graphs and Pie Charts

Values for an economic variable are often displayed as a bar graph or as a pie chart. In this case, panel (a) shows labor force share data for the Arab world countries as a bar graph, where the labor force share of each country is represented by the height of its bar. Panel (b) displays the same information as a pie chart, with the labor force share of each country represented by the size of its slice of the pie.
Source: World Bank, World Development Indicators (2009).

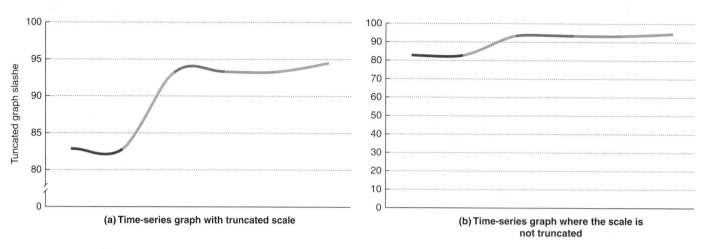

(a) Time-series graph with truncated scale

(b) Time-series graph where the scale is not truncated

Figure 1A-2 | Time-Series Graphs

Both panels present time-series graphs of Kuwait's adult literacy rate during each year from 2002 to 2007. Panel (a) has a truncated scale on the vertical axis, and panel (b) does not. As a result, the fluctuations in Kuwait's adult literacy rate appear smaller in panel (b) than in panel (a).
Source: United Nations Development Program: Human Development Report (2009).

Information on economic variables is also often displayed in *time-series graphs*. Time-series graphs are displayed on a coordinate grid. In a coordinate grid, we can measure the value of one variable along the vertical axis (or *y*-axis), and the value of another variable along the horizontal axis (or *x*-axis). The point where the vertical axis intersects the horizontal axis is called the *origin*. At the origin, the value of both variables is zero. The points on a coordinate grid represent values of the two variables. Kuwait had the highest literacy rate in the Arab world in 2007. So, in Figure 1A-2 we measure Kuwait's adult literacy rate as a percentage of the population aged 15 and above on the vertical axis, and we measure time on the horizontal axis. In time-series graphs, the height of the line at each date shows the value of the variable measured on the vertical axis. Both panels of Figure 1A-2 show Kuwait's adult literacy rate during each year from 2002 to 2007. The difference between panel (a) and panel (b) illustrates the importance of the scale used in a time-series graph. In panel (a), the scale on the vertical axis is truncated, which means that it does not start with zero. In panel (b), the scale is not truncated. In panel (b), the increase in Kuwait's adult literacy rate since 2002 appears smaller than in panel (a). (Technically, the horizontal axis is also truncated because we start with the year 2002, not the year 0.)

Graphs of Two Variables

We often use graphs to show the relationship between two variables. For example, suppose you are interested in the relationship between the price of a pepperoni pizza and the quantity of pizzas sold per week in Beirut, Lebanon. A graph showing the relationship between the price of a good and the quantity of the good demanded at each price is called a *demand curve*. (As we will discuss later, in drawing a demand curve for a good, we have to hold constant any variables other than price that might affect the willingness of consumers to buy the good.) Figure 1A-3 shows the data you have collected on price and quantities.

The Figure shows a two-dimensional grid on which we measure the price of pizza along the *y*-axis and the quantity of pizza sold per week along the *x*-axis. Each point on the grid represents one of the price and quantity combinations listed in the table. We can connect the points to form the demand curve for pizza in Beirut. Notice that the scales on both axes in the graph are truncated. In this case, truncating the axes allows the graph

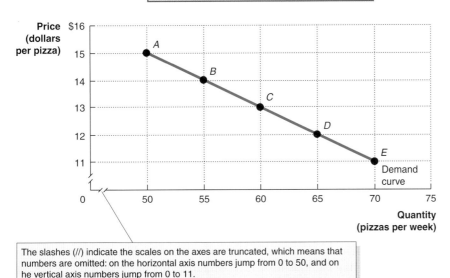

Price (dollars per pizza)	Quantity (pizzas per week)	Points
15	50	A
14	55	B
13	60	C
12	65	D
11	70	E

The slashes (//) indicate the scales on the axes are truncated, which means that numbers are omitted: on the horizontal axis numbers jump from 0 to 50, and on he vertical axis numbers jump from 0 to 11.

Figure 1A-3

Plotting Price and Quantity Points in a Graph

The figure shows a two-dimensional grid on which we measure the price of pizza along the vertical axis (or *y*-axis) and the quantity of pizza sold per week along the horizontal axis (or *x*-axis). Each point on the grid represents one of the price and quantity combinations listed in the table. By connecting the points with a line, we can better illustrate the relationship between the two variables.

to illustrate more clearly the relationship between price and quantity by excluding low prices and quantities.

Slopes of Lines

Once you have plotted the data in Figure 1A-3, you may be interested in how much the quantity of pizza sold increases as the price decreases. The *slope* of a line tells us how much the variable we are measuring on the *y*-axis changes as the variable we are measuring on the *x*-axis changes. We can use the Greek letter delta (Δ) to stand for the change in a variable.

The slope is sometimes referred to as the rise over the run. So, we have several ways of expressing slope:

$$\text{Slope} = \frac{\text{Change in value on the vertical axis}}{\text{Change in value on the horizontal axis}} = \frac{\Delta y}{\Delta x} = \frac{\text{Rise}}{\text{Run}}$$

Figure 1A-4 reproduces the graph from Figure 1A-3. Because the slope of a straight line is the same at any point, we can use any two points in the figure to calculate the slope of the line.

For example, when the price of pizza decreases from US$14 to US$12, the quantity of pizza sold increases from 55 per week to 65 per week. Therefore, the slope is:

$$\text{Slope} = \frac{\Delta \text{Price of pizza}}{\Delta \text{Quantity of pizza}} = \frac{(\$12 - \$14)}{(65 - 55)} = \frac{-2}{10} = -0.2$$

The slope of this line gives us some insight into how responsive consumers in Beirut are to changes in the price of pizza. The larger the value of the slope (ignoring the negative sign), the steeper the line will be, which indicates that not many additional pizzas are sold when the price falls. The smaller the value of the slope, the flatter the line will be, which indicates a greater increase in pizzas sold when the price falls.

Figure 1A-4

We can calculate the slope of a line as the change in the value of the variable on the *y*-axis divided by the change in the value of the variable on the *x*-axis. Because the slope of a straight line is constant, we can use any two points in the figure to calculate the slope of the line. For example, when the price of pizza decreases from US$14 to US$12, the quantity of pizza demanded increases from 55 per week to 65 per week. So, the slope of this line equals, 2 divided by 10, or –0.2.

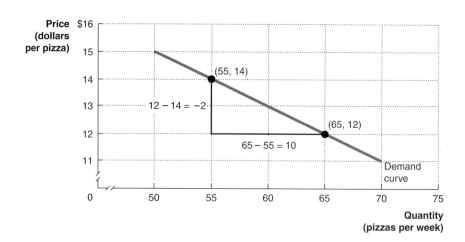

Taking into Account More Than Two Variables on a Graph

The demand curve graph in Figure 1A-4 shows the relationship between the price of pizza and the quantity of pizza sold, but we know that the quantity of any good sold depends on more than just the price of the good. For example, the quantity of pizza sold in a given week in Beirut can be affected by such other variables as the price of burgers, whether an advertising campaign by local pizza parlors has begun that week, and so on. Allowing the values of any other variables to change will cause the position of the demand curve in the graph to change.

Suppose, for example, that the demand curve in Figure 1A-4 was drawn holding the price of burgers constant at US$1.50. If the price of burgers rises to US$2.00, then some consumers will switch from buying burgers to buying pizza, and more pizzas will be sold at every price. The result on the graph will be to shift the line representing the demand curve to the right. Similarly, if the price of burgers falls from US$1.50 to US$1.00, some consumers will switch from buying pizza to buying burgers, and fewer pizzas will be sold at every price. The result on the graph will be to shift the line representing the demand curve to the left.

The table in Figure 1A-5 shows the effect of a change in the price of burgers on the quantity of pizza demanded. For example, suppose at first we are on the line labeled *Demand curve*$_1$. If the price of pizza is US$14 (point *A*), an increase in the price of burgers from US$1.50 to US$2.00 increases the quantity of pizzas demanded from 55 to 60 per week (point *B*) and shifts us to *Demand curve*$_2$. Or, if we start on *Demand curve*$_1$ and the price of pizza is US$12 (point *C*), a decrease in the price of burgers from US$1.50 to US$1.00 decreases the quantity of pizzas demanded from 65 to 60 per week (point *D*) and shifts us to *Demand curve*$_3$. By shifting the demand curve, we have taken into account the effect of changes in the value of a third variable—the price of burgers. We will use this technique of shifting curves to allow for the effects of additional variables many times in this book.

Positive and Negative Relationships

We can use graphs to show the relationships between any two variables. Sometimes the relationship between the variables is *negative*, meaning that as one variable increases in value, the other variable decreases in value. This was the case with the price of pizza and the quantity of pizzas demanded. The relationship between two variables can also be *positive*, meaning that the values of both variables increase or decrease together. For example, when the level of total income—or *disposable personal income*—received by households in Jordan increases, the level of total *consumption spending*, which is spending by households on goods and services, also increases. Figure 1A-6 shows the values for Jordan's income and consumption spending for the years 1990–2008 (the values are

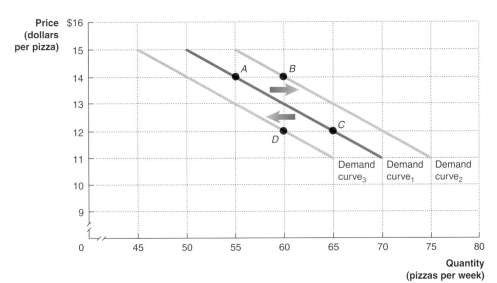

	Quantity (pizzas per week)		
Price (dollars per pizza)	When the Price of Hamburgers = $1.00	When the Price of Hamburgers = $1.50	When the Price of Hamburgers = $2.00
$15	45	50	55
14	50	55	60
13	55	60	65
12	60	65	70
11	65	70	75

Figure 1A-5

Showing Three Variables on a Graph

The demand curve for pizza shows the relationship between the price of pizzas and the quantity of pizzas demanded, *holding constant other factors that might affect the willingness of consumers to buy pizza.* If the price of pizza is US$14 (point *A*), an increase in the price of burgers from US$1.50 to US$2.00 increases the quantity of pizzas demanded from 55 to 60 per week (point *B*) and shifts us to Demand curve₂. Or, if we start on *Demand curve₁* and the price of pizza is US$12 (point *C*), a decrease in the price of burgers from US$1.50 to US$1.00 decreases the quantity of pizza demanded from 65 to 60 per week (point *D*) and shifts us to *Demand curve₃*.

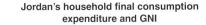
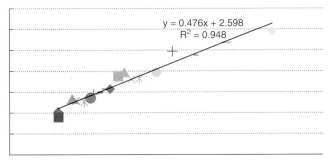

Jordan's household final consumption expenditure and GNI

$y = 0.476x + 2.598$
$R^2 = 0.948$

Figure 1A-6

Graphing the Positive Relationship between Income and Consumption

In a positive relationship between two economic variables, as one variable increases, the other variable also increases. This figure shows the positive relationship between Gross National Income of Jordan and consumption spending. As income in Jordan has increased, so has consumption spending.
Source: World Bank, World Development Indicators, 2009.

in billions of dollars). The graph plots national income measured along the horizontal axis and consumption spending measured along the vertical axis. Notice that not all points fall exactly on the line. This is often the case with real-world data. To examine the relationship between two variables, economists often use the straight line that best fits the data.

Determining Cause and Effect

When we graph the relationship between two variables, we often want to draw conclusions about whether changes in one variable are causing changes in the other variable. Doing so, however, can lead to incorrect conclusions. For example, suppose you graph the number of homes in a neighborhood that have a fire burning in the fireplace and the number of leaves on trees in the neighborhood. You would get a relationship like that shown in panel (a) of Figure 1A-7 The more fires burning in the neighborhood,

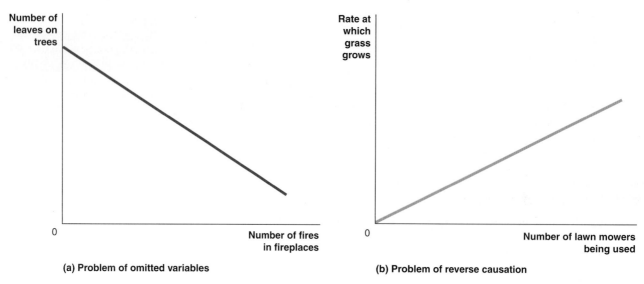

Figure A1-7 | Determining Cause and Effect

Using graphs to draw conclusions about cause and effect can be hazardous. In panel (a), we see that there are fewer leaves on the trees in a neighborhood when many homes have fires burning in their fireplaces. We cannot draw the conclusion that the fires cause the leaves to fall because we have an *omitted variable*—the season of the year. In panel (b), we see that more lawn mowers are used in a neighborhood during times when the grass grows rapidly and fewer lawn mowers are used when the grass grows slowly. Concluding that using lawn mowers *causes* the grass to grow faster would be making the error of *reverse causality*.

the fewer leaves the trees have. Can we draw the conclusion from this graph that using a fireplace causes trees to lose their leaves? We know, of course, that such a conclusion would be incorrect. In spring and summer, there are relatively few fireplaces being used, and the trees are full of leaves. In the fall, as trees begin to lose their leaves, fireplaces are used more frequently. And in winter, many fireplaces are being used and many trees have lost all their leaves. The reason that the graph in Figure 1A-7 is misleading about cause and effect is that there is obviously an *omitted variable* in the analysis—the season of the year. An omitted variable is one that affects other variables, and its omission can lead to false conclusions about cause and effect.

Although in our example the omitted variable is obvious, there are many debates about cause and effect where the existence of an omitted variable has not been clear. For instance, it has been known for many years that people who smoke cigarettes suffer from higher rates of lung cancer than do nonsmokers. For some time, tobacco companies and some scientists argued that there was an omitted variable—perhaps psychological temperament—that made some people more likely to smoke and more likely to develop lung cancer. If this omitted variable existed, then the finding that smokers were more likely to develop lung cancer would not have been evidence that smoking *caused* lung cancer. In this case, however, nearly all scientists eventually concluded that the omitted variable did not exist and that, in fact, smoking does cause lung cancer.

A related problem in determining cause and effect is known as *reverse causality*. The error of reverse causality occurs when we conclude that changes in variable *X* cause changes in variable *Y* when, in fact, it is actually changes in variable *Y* that cause changes in variable *X*. For example, panel (b) of Figure 1A-7 plots the number of lawn mowers being used in a neighborhood against the rate at which grass on lawns in the neighborhood is growing. We could conclude from this graph that using lawn mowers *causes* the grass to grow faster. We know, however, that in reality, the causality is in the other direction: rapidly growing grass during the spring and summer causes the increased use of lawn mowers. Slowly growing grass in the fall or winter or during periods of low rainfall causes decreased use of lawn mowers.

Once again, in our example, the potential error of reverse causality is obvious. In many economic debates, however, cause and effect can be more difficult to determine. For example, changes in the money supply, or the total amount of money in the economy, tend to occur at the same time as changes in the total amount of income people in the economy earn. A famous debate in economics was about whether the changes in the money supply caused the changes in total income or whether the changes in total income caused the changes in the money supply. Each side in the debate accused the other side of committing the error of reverse causality.

Are Graphs of Economic Relationships Always Straight Lines?

The graphs of relationships between two economic variables that we have drawn so far have been straight lines. The relationship between two variables is *linear* when it can be represented by a straight line. Few economic relationships are actually linear. For example, if we carefully plot data on the price of a product and the quantity demanded at each price, holding constant other variables that affect the quantity demanded, we will usually find a curved—or *nonlinear*—relationship rather than a linear relationship. In practice, however, it is often useful to approximate a nonlinear relationship with a linear relationship. If the relationship is reasonably close to being linear, the analysis is not significantly affected. In addition, it is easier to calculate the slope of a straight line, and it also is easier to calculate the area under a straight line. So, in this textbook, we often assume that the relationship between two economic variables is linear even when we know that this assumption is not precisely correct.

Slopes of Nonlinear Curves

In some situations, we need to take into account the nonlinear nature of an economic relationship. For example, panel (a) of Figure 1A-8 shows the hypothetical relationship between Apple's total cost of producing iPods and the quantity of iPods produced. The relationship is curved, rather than linear. In this case, the cost of production is increasing at an increasing rate, which often happens in manufacturing. Put a different way, as we move up the curve, its slope becomes larger. (Remember that with a straight line, the slope is always constant.) To see this effect, first remember that we calculate the slope of a curve by dividing the change in the variable on the y-axis by the change in the variable on the x-axis. As we move from point A to point B, the quantity produced increases by 1 million iPods, while the total cost of production increases by US\$50 million. Farther up the curve, as we move from point C to point D, the change in quantity is the same—1 million iPods—but the change in the total cost of production is now much larger: US\$250 million. Because the change in the y variable has increased, while the change in the x variable has remained the same, we know that the slope has increased.

To measure the slope of a nonlinear curve at a particular point, we must measure the slope of the *tangent line* to the curve at that point. A tangent line will only touch the curve at that point. We can measure the slope of the tangent line just as we would the slope of any straight line. In panel (b), the tangent line at point B has a slope equal to:

$$\frac{\Delta \text{Cost}}{\Delta \text{Quantity}} = \frac{75}{1} = 75$$

The tangent line at point C has a slope equal to:

$$\frac{\Delta \text{Cost}}{\Delta \text{Quantity}} = \frac{150}{1} = 150$$

Once again, we see that the slope of the curve is larger at point C than at point B.

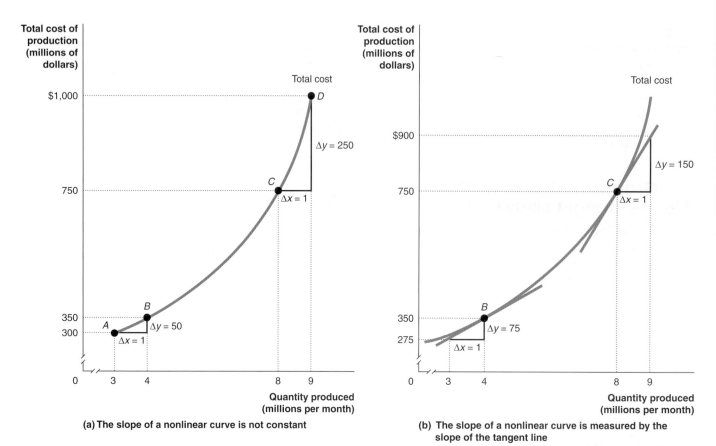

Figure 1A-8 | The Slope of a Nonlinear Curve

The relationship between the quantity of iPods produced and the total cost of production is curved, rather than liner. In panel (a), in moving from point A to point B, the quantity produced increases by 1 million iPods, while the total cost of production increases by US$50 million. Farther up the curve, as we move from point C to point D, the change in quantity is the same—1 million iPods—but the change in the total cost of production is now much larger: US$250 million.

Because the change in the y variable has increased, while the change in the x variable has remained the same, we know that the slope has increased. In panel (b), we measure the slope of the curve at a particular point by the slope of the tangent line. The slope of the tangent line at point B is 75, and the slope of the tangent line at point C is 150.

Formulas

We have just seen that graphs are an important economic tool. In this section, we will review several useful formulas and show how to use them to summarize data and to calculate important relationships.

Formula for a Percentage Change

One important formula is the percentage change. The *percentage change* is the change in some economic variable, usually from one period to the next, expressed as a percentage. An important macroeconomic measure is the real gross domestic product (GDP). *GDP* is the value of all the final goods and services produced in a country during a year. "Real GDP is corrected for the effects of inflation. When economists say that the Saudi economy grew 3.8 percent during 2010, they mean that GDP was 3.8 percent higher in 2010 than it was in 2009. The formula for making this calculation is:

$$\left(\frac{GDP_{2010} - GDP_{2009}}{GDP_{2009}} \right) \times 100$$

or, more generally, for any two periods:

$$\text{Percentage change} = \frac{\text{Value in the second period} - \text{Value in the first period}}{\text{Value in the first period}} \times 100$$

In this case, if, for example, GDP was US$599,700 billion in 2009 and US$622,500 billion in 2010. So, the growth rate of the Saudi economy during 2010 was:

$$\left(\frac{\$622,500 - \$599,700}{\$599,700} \right) \times 100 = 3.8$$

Notice that it didn't matter that in using the formula, we ignored the fact that GDP is measured in billions of dollars. In fact, when calculating percentage changes, *the units don't matter*. The percentage increase from US$599,700 billion to US$622,500 billion is exactly the same as the percentage increase from US$599,700 to US$622,500.

Formulas for the Areas of a Rectangle and a Triangle

Areas that form rectangles and triangles on graphs can have important economic meaning. For example, Figure 1A-9 shows the demand curve for Pepsi. Suppose that the price is currently US$2.00 and that 125,000 bottles of Pepsi are sold at that price. A firm's *total revenue* is equal to the amount it receives from selling its product, or the quantity sold multiplied by the price. In this case, total revenue will equal 125,000 bottles times US$2.00 per bottle, or US$250,000.

The formula for the area of a rectangle is:

$$\text{Area of a rectangle} = \text{Base} \times \text{Height}$$

In Figure A1-9, the green-shaded rectangle also represents the firm's total revenue because its area is given by the base of 125,000 bottles multiplied by the price of US$2.00 per bottle.

We will see in later chapters that areas that are triangles can also have economic significance. The formula for the area of a triangle is:

$$\text{Area of a triangle} = \frac{1}{2} \times \text{Base} \times \text{Height}$$

The blue-shaded area in Figure A1-10 is a triangle. The base equals 150,000 − 125,000, or 25,000. Its height equals US$2.00 − US$1.50, or US$0.50. Therefore, its area equals 1/2 × 25,000 × US$0.50, or US$6,250. Notice that the blue area is a triangle only if the demand curve is a straight line, or linear. Not all demand curves are linear. However, the formula for the area of a triangle will usually still give a good approximation, even if the demand curve is not linear.

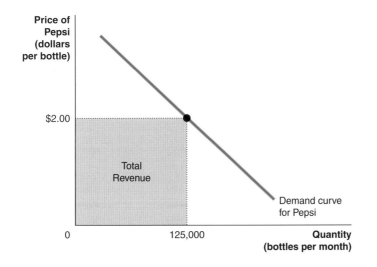

Figure 1A-9

Showing a Firm's Total Revenue on a Graph

The area of a rectangle is equal to its base multiplied by its height. Total revenue is equal to quantity multiplied by price. Here, total revenue is equal to the quantity of 125,000 bottles times the price of US$2.00 per bottle, or US$250,000. The area of the green-shaded rectangle shows the firm's total revenue.

Figure 1A-10

The Area of a Triangle

The area of a triangle is equal to 1/2 multiplied by its base multiplied by its height. The area of the blue-shaded triangle has a base equal to 150,000, 125,000, or 25,000, and a height equal to US$2.00, US$1.50, or US$0.50. Therefore, its area equals 1/2 × 25,000 × US$0.50, or US$6,250.

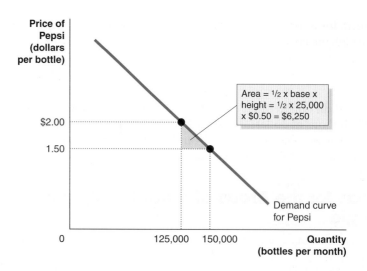

Summary of Using Formulas

You will encounter several other formulas in this book. Whenever you must use a formula, you should follow these steps:

1 Make sure you understand the economic concept that the formula represents.

2 Make sure you are using the correct formula for the problem you are solving.

3 Make sure that the number you calculate using the formula is economically reasonable. For example, if you are using a formula to calculate a firm's revenue and your answer is a negative number, you know you made a mistake somewhere.

Problems and Applications

 Visit www.pearsoned.co.uk/awe/hubbard to complete these exercises online and get instant feedback.

Get Ahead of the Curve

LEARNING OBJECTIVE   Review the use of graphs and formulas, **pages 24–34.**

1A.1 The following table gives the relationship between the price of custard pies and the number of pies Yusef buys per week.

PRICE	QUANTITY OF PIES	WEEK
$3.00	6	July 2
2.00	7	July 9
5.00	4	July 16
6.00	3	July 23
1.00	8	July 30
4.00	5	August 6

a. Is the relationship between the price of pies and the number of pies Yusef buys a positive relationship or a negative relationship?

b. Plot the data from the table on a graph similar to Figure A1-3. Draw a straight line that best fits the points.

c. Calculate the slope of the line.

1A.2 The following table gives information on the quantity of glasses of lemonade demanded on sunny and overcast days. Plot the data from the table on a graph similar to Figure 1A-5. Draw two straight lines representing the two demand curves—one for sunny days and one for overcast days.

PRICE (DOLLARS PER GLASS)	QUANTITY (GLASSES OF LEMONADE PER DAY)	WEATHER
$0.80	30	Sunny
0.80	10	Overcast
0.70	40	Sunny
0.70	20	Overcast
0.60	50	Sunny
0.60	30	Overcast
0.50	60	Sunny
0.50	40	Overcast

1A.3 Using the information in Figure 1A-2, calculate the percentage change in literacy rates in Kuwait from one year to the next. Between which years did rates rise fastest?

1A.4 Imagine that GDP in 2000 was US$5,292 million and that GDP in 2001 was US$5,189 million. What was the percentage change in real GDP from 2000 to 2001? What do economists call the percentage change in real GDP from one year to the next?

1A.5 Assume that the demand curve for Pepsi passes through the following two points:

PRICE PER BOTTLE OF PEPSI	NUMBER OF BOTTLES OF PEPSI SOLD
$2.50	100,000
1.25	200,000

a. Draw a graph with a linear demand curve that passes through these two points.

b. Show on the graph the areas representing total revenue at each price. Give the value for total revenue at each price.

1A.6 What is the area of the blue triangle shown in the following figure?

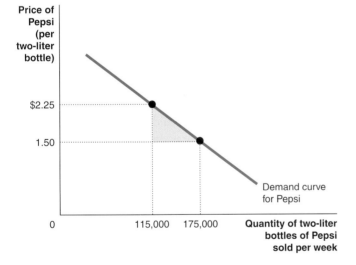

1A.7 Calculate the slope of the total cost curve at point *A* and at point *B* in the following figure.

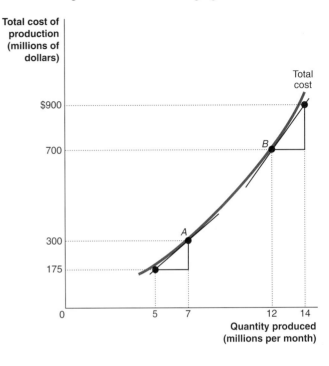

≫ End Appendix Learning Objective

Trade-offs, Comparative Advantage, and the Market System

Managers Making Choices at BMW: The Cases of BMW-Egypt and BMW-US

When you think of cars that combine fine engineering, high performance, and cutting-edge styling, you are likely to think of BMW. The Bayerische Motoren Werke, or Bavarian Motor Works, was founded in Germany in 1916. Today, BMW employs more than 100,000 workers in 23 factories in 15 countries to produce eight car models. In 2007, it had worldwide sales of nearly 1.5 million cars.

To compete in the automobile market, the managers of BMW must make many strategic decisions, such as whether to introduce a new car model. In 2006, for example, BMW announced that it would introduce a hydrogen-powered version of the 7-Series sedan and was also working on fuel-cell powered cars. Another strategic decision BMW's managers face is where to focus their advertising. In the late 1990s, for example, some of BMW's managers opposed advertising in China because they were skeptical about the country's sales potential. Other managers, however, argued that rising incomes were rapidly increasing the size of the Chinese market. BMW decided to advertise in China, and it has become

the company's fourth-largest market, with sales increasing by 38 percent in 2009 alone.

Over the years, BMW's managers have also faced the strategic decision of whether to concentrate production in factories in Germany or to build new factories in its overseas markets. Keeping production in Germany makes it easier for BMW's managers to supervise production and to employ German workers, who generally have high levels of technical training. Building factories in other countries, however, has two benefits. First, the lower wages paid to workers in other countries reduce the cost of manufacturing vehicles. Second, BMW can reduce political friction by producing vehicles in the same country in which it sells them. In 2003, BMW opened a plant at Shenyang, in northeast China, to build its 3-Series and 5-Series cars. Previously, in 1994, BMW opened a U.S. factory in Spartanburg, South Carolina, which currently produces the Z4 roadster and X5 sports utility vehicle (SUV) for sale both in the United States and worldwide. In addition, in 2004, BMW opened a US$60 million assembly factory in 6th of October City, Egypt. As indicated by the just-auto editorial team, the new factory is said to be one of the most modern car plants in the region. Under the company's Completely Knocked Down (CKD) strategy, specific parts and components are put together as kits

in precisely defined levels of assembly and shipped to Egypt. In compliance with local law, a high percentage of locally manufactured components is added and then finally assembled into a complete car. The factory comprises 'state of the art' body and paint shops and a final assembly line.

"With our partner we have established the right basis for our ambitious targets and durable success in Egypt. With the new factory and new dealerships we aim from the first full year of operation to achieve a higher production and sales volume than we ever had in the past, on the Egyptian market," said Leuder Payan, the senior vice-president of the BMW group. The factory sells locally assembled 3 and 5 series models in Egypt, and also exports to the Arab and European Union for Eastern and Southern Africa (COMESA) markets. Moreover, owing to the high customs duties on imported luxury cars in Egypt (135 percent on cars with an engine size greater than 1.6 liters), BMW managers decided, in 2008, to open new assembly lines that produce premium models such as 7 series and X3.

Managers also face smaller-scale—or tactical—business decisions. For instance, for many years, BMW used two workers to attach the gearbox to the engine in each car. In 2002, an alternative method of attaching the gearbox using a robot, rather than workers, was developed.

In choosing which method to use, managers at BMW faced a trade-off because the robot method had a higher cost, but installed the gearbox in exactly the correct position, which reduces engine noise when the car is driven. Ultimately, the managers decided to adopt the robot method. A similar tactical business decision must be made in scheduling production at BMW's 6th of October assembly factory, in Egypt. For example, managers must decide every month the quantity of each model that should be assembled.

AN INSIDE LOOK on **page 58** discusses how domestic car feeding factories' managers in Egypt responded to the low demand for cars after the January 25th (2011) revolution.

Sources: Just-auto.com editorial team, "Egypt: BMW Opens New Assembly Plant," www.just-auto.com, May 14, 2004; and Alex Dziadosz, "As Luxury Car Sales Slip Abroad, New BMW Lines Roll into Egypt", dailynewsegypt.com, Nov. 19, 2008.

LEARNING Objectives

After studying this chapter, you should be able to:

2.1 Use a **production possibilities frontier** to analyze opportunity costs and trade-offs, page 38.

2.2 Understand **comparative advantage** and explain how it is the basis for **trade**, page 44.

2.3 Explain the basic idea of how a **market system** works, page 49.

Economics in YOUR Life!

The Trade-offs When You Buy a Car

When you buy a car, you probably consider factors such as safety and gas mileage. To increase gas mileage, automobile manufacturers make cars small and light. Large cars absorb more of the impact of an accident than do small cars. As a result, people are usually safer driving large cars than small cars. What can we conclude from these facts about the relationship between safety and gas mileage? Under what circumstances would it be possible for car manufacturers to make cars safer and more fuel efficient? As you read the chapter, see if you can answer these questions. You can check your answer against those provided at the end of the chapter. ▶ Continued on page 57

Scarcity The situation in which unlimited wants exceed the limited resources available to fulfill those wants.

Ⅰn a market system, managers at most firms must make decisions like those made by BMW's managers. The decisions managers face reflect a key fact of economic life: *Scarcity requires trade-offs*. **Scarcity** exists because we have unlimited wants but only limited resources available to fulfill those wants. Goods and services are scarce. So, too, are the economic resources, or *factors of production*—workers, capital, natural resources, and entre- preneurial ability—used to make goods and services. Your time is scarce, which means you face trade-offs: If you spend an hour studying for an economics exam, you have one less hour to spend studying for a psychology exam or going to the movies. If your university decides to use some of its scarce budget funds to buy new computers for the computer labs, those funds will not be available to buy new books for the library or to resurface the student parking lot. If BMW decides to devote some of the scarce workers and machinery in its 6th of October assembly plant to producing more 3 series, those resources will not be available to produce more X3 SUVs.

Many of the decisions of households and firms are made in markets. One key activity that takes place in markets is trade. Trade involves the decisions of millions of households and firms spread around the world. By engaging in trade, people can raise their standard of living. In this chapter, we provide an overview of how the market system coordinates the independent decisions of these millions of households and firms. We begin our analysis of the economic consequences of scarcity and the working of the market system by introducing an important economic model: the *production possibilities frontier*.

2.1 LEARNING OBJECTIVE

2.1 | Use a production possibilities frontier to analyze opportunity costs and trade-offs.

Production Possibilities Frontiers and Opportunity Costs

As we saw in the opening to this chapter, BMW operates an automobile factory in 6th of October City of Egypt, where it assembles 3 series and 5 series, among other models. Because the firm's resources—workers, machinery, materials, and entre- preneurial skills—are limited, BMW faces a trade-off: resources devoted to producing 3 series are not available for producing 5 series and vice versa. Chapter 1 explained that economic models can be useful in analyzing many questions. We can use a simple model called the *production possibilities frontier* to analyze the trade-offs BMW faces in its 6th of October City plant. A **production possibilities frontier** (*PPF*) is a curve showing the maximum attainable combinations of two products that may be pro- duced with available resources and current technology. In BMW's case, the two prod- ucts are 3 series and 5 series, and the resources are BMW's workers, materials, robots, and other machinery.

Production possibilities frontier (*PPF*) A curve showing the maximum attainable combinations of two products that may be produced with available resources and current technology.

Graphing the Production Possibilities Frontier

Figure 2-1 uses a production possibilities frontier to illustrate the trade-offs that BMW faces. The numbers from the table are plotted in the graph. The line in the graph is BMW's production possibilities frontier. If BMW uses all its resources to produce 3 series, it can produce 800 per day—point *A* at one end of the production possibili- ties frontier. If BMW uses all its resources to produce 5 series, it can produce 800 per day—point *E* at the other end of the production possibilities frontier. If BMW devotes resources to producing both vehicles, it could be at a point like *B*, where it produces 600 cars of 3 series and 200 cars of 5 series.

BMW's Production Choices at its 6ᵗʰ of October City Plant		
Choice	Quantity of 3 Series Produced	Quantity of 5 Series Produced
A	800	0
B	600	200
C	400	400
D	200	600
E	0	800

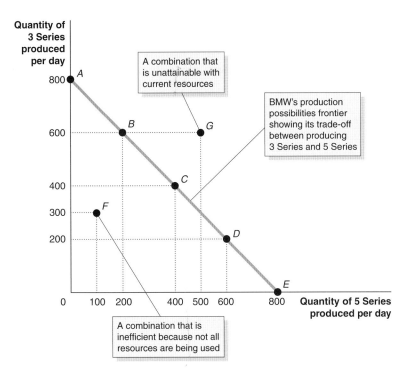

Figure 2-1

BMW's Production Possibilities Frontier

BMW faces a trade-off: to build one more 3 series car, it must build one less 5 series. The production possibilities frontier illustrates the trade-off BMW faces. Combinations on the production possibilities frontier—like points *A*, *B*, *C*, *D*, and *E*—are *technically efficient* because the maximum output is being obtained from the available resources. Combinations inside the frontier—like point *F*—are *inefficient* because some resources are not being used. Combinations outside the frontier—like point *G*—are *unattainable* with current resources.

All the combinations either on the frontier—like *A*, *B*, *C*, *D*, and *E*—or inside the frontier—like point *F*—are *attainable* with the resources available. Combinations on the frontier are *efficient* because all available resources are being fully utilized, and the fewest possible resources are being used to produce a given amount of output. Combinations inside the frontier—like point *F*—are *inefficient* because maximum output is not being obtained from the available resources—perhaps because the assembly line is not operating at capacity. BMW might like to be beyond the frontier—at a point like *G*, where it would be producing 600 cars of 3 series and 500 cars of 5 series—but points beyond the production possibilities frontier are *unattainable*, given the firm's current resources. To produce the combination at *G*, BMW would need more machines or more workers.

Notice that if BMW is producing efficiently and is on the production possibilities frontier, the only way to produce more of one vehicle is to produce less of the other vehicle. Recall from Chapter 1 that the **opportunity cost** of any activity is the highest-valued alternative that must be given up to engage in that activity. For BMW, the opportunity cost of producing one more of 5 series is the number of 3 series the company will not be able to produce because it has shifted those resources to producing 5 series. For example, in moving from point *B* to point *C*, the opportunity cost of producing 200 more 5 series cars per day is the 200 fewer 3 series cars that can be produced.

What point on the production possibilities frontier is best? We can't tell without further information. If consumer demand for 5 series is greater than demand for 3 series, the company is likely to choose a point closer to *E*. If demand for 3 series is greater than demand for 5 series, the company is likely to choose a point closer to *A*.

Opportunity cost The highest-valued alternative that must be given up to engage in an activity.

Solved Problem | 2-1

Drawing a Production Possibilities Frontier for a Sweet Shop in Lebanon

A sweet shop in Lebanon specializes in cakes and baklawa. The best worker at the sweet shop, Zeyad, has 5 hours per day to devote to baking.

a. Use the information given to complete the following table:

	HOURS SPENT MAKING		QUANTITY MADE	
CHOICE	CAKES	TRAYS OF BAKLAWA	CAKES	TRAYS OF BAKLAWA
A	5	0		
B	4	1		
C	3	2		
D	2	3		
E	1	4		
F	0	5		

b. Use the data in the table to draw a production possibilities frontier graph illustrating Zeyad's trade-offs between making cakes and making baklawa. Label the vertical axis "Quantity of cakes made." Label the horizontal axis "Quantity of baklawa made." Make sure to label the values where Zeyad's production possibilities frontier intersects the vertical and horizontal axes.

c. Label the points representing choice D and choice E. If Zeyad is at choice D, what is his opportunity cost of making more baklawa?

SOLVING THE PROBLEM:

Step 1: **Review the chapter material.** This problem is about using production possibilities frontiers to analyze trade-offs, so you may want to review the section "Graphing the Production Possibilities Frontier," which begins on page 38.

Step 2: **Answer question (a) by filling in the table.** If Zeyad can produce 1 cake in 1 hour, then with choice A, he will make 5 cakes and 0 trays of baklawa. Because he can produce 2 baklawa trays in 1 hour, with choice B, he will make 4 cakes and 2 baklawa trays. Using similar reasoning, you can fill in the remaining cells in the table as follows:

	HOURS SPENT MAKING		QUANTITY MADE	
CHOICE	CAKES	TRAYS OF BAKLAWA	CAKES	TRAYS OF BAKLAWA
A	5	0	5	0
B	4	1	4	2
C	3	2	3	4
D	2	3	2	6
E	1	4	1	8
F	0	5	0	10

Step 3: **Answer question (b) by drawing the production possibilities frontier graph.** Using the data in the table in Step 2, you should draw a graph that looks like this:

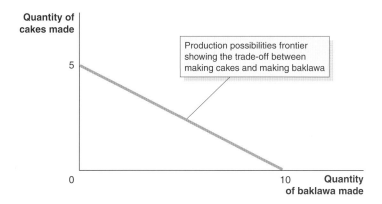

If Zeyad devotes all 5 hours to making cakes, he will make 5 cakes. Therefore, his production possibilities frontier will intersect the vertical axis at 5 cakes made. If Zeyad devotes all 5 hours to making baklawa, he will make 10 baklawa trays. Therefore, his production possibilities frontier will intersect the horizontal axis at 10 baklawa trays made.

Step 4: **Answer question (c) by showing choices *D* and *E* on your graph.** The points for choices *D* and *E* can be plotted using the information from the table:

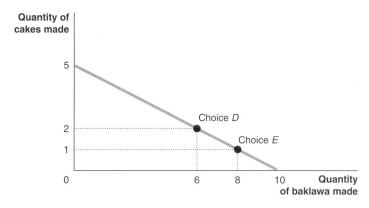

Moving from choice *D* to choice *E* increases Zeyad's production of baklawa trays by 2 but lowers his production of cakes by 1. Therefore, his opportunity cost of making 2 more baklawa trays is making 1 less cake.

YOUR TURN: For more practice, do related problem 1.9 on page 61 at the end of this chapter.

>> End Solved Problem 2-1

Making the Connection	**Trade-Offs: The Pattern of Charitable Giving in the Arab World**

Charitable giving is a fundamental feature of the Arab culture, which is characterized by generosity, caring, and social bonding, and also because Arabs are keen to follow the teachings of Islam and Christianity regarding religious giving. Until recently, people in the Arab world gave charitable donations on a person–to-person basis rather than to organized charitable agencies that aim to provide support to developmental programs, such as education, health care, and infrastructure. There are three main reasons behind this. First, some Arab families

(Continued)

underestimated the long-term benefits of developmental programs and preferred to see the immediate effect of their donation, so they directly targeted poor families, giving them financial and in-kind support (such as food and clothes). Second, the lack of transparency and the existence of some degree of corruption meant that people preferred to be in direct contact with the recipients of charitable giving. Third, Muslims were skeptical about whether their Zakah payment, which is one of the pillars of Islam, could be used to support developmental programs.

Person-to-person giving, however, results in a very low portion of the donations being directed to developmental programs. For example, the Center for Development Services (CDS), Egypt, carried out a national study on philanthropy (charitable donations) in Egypt, in 2004. One of the main findings of the study was that only 0.6 percent of the total donations and volunteering activities made by Egyptains in the study sample related to human development, such as helping people to start projects and depend on themselves. The trade-off is clear in this example: as more donations are devoted to achieving short-term goals (relieving poverty through giving direct financial or in-kind support to the poor), less will be available to for other uses, such as financing long-term developmental programs.

A noticeable change in the pattern of charitable giving emerged in the past decade when people started to support private charititable agencies that target human development. For instance, Ruwwad, a Jordanian charitable organization created in 2004, ventured into the underprivileged Jabal al-Nathif neighborhood in Amman, mainly focusing on improving the quality of life of poor people. Ruwwad is investing in human development programs such as building schools, clinics, and libraries, and providing scholarships for poor students to attend Jordanian universities. But since the idea of receiving such help was new to the poor, especially elderly people, it took them two years to realize that Ruwwad was there only to help them, and that there were no political motives behind the organization's generosity.

More funds for the Children's Cancer Hospital Egypt meant less funds for other charities.

As the number of such charitable agencies started to increase, Ruwaad had to compete for people's donations. The agency that succeeds in attracting the biggest portion of people's donations is usually the one that performs successful campaigns through TV satellite channels and the Internet. A well-known example in Egypt is the Children's Cancer Hospital Egypt (CCHE), which depends completely on charitable giving and was successful in its advertisment campaign to win sufficient financial support not only from Egyptians but also from citizens of other Arab countries. This success was criticized and attacked by many other hospitals that are also in need of financial support, particularly those that offer similar services, such as the National Cancer Institute (NCI), which suffered a significant shortage in charitable giving as a result. Again, the trade-off is obvious: since donations are limited, the more charitable giving is directed to the CCHE, the less will be available to the NCI.

Sources: Marwa El Daly, Areeg El Badrawi, and Radwa Al Gaaly, "Philanthropy for Social Development," Center for Development Services, Cairo, 2005, pp. 86–87; Roula Khalaf, "Jordan Sees Benefit of Private Sector Aid," *Financial Times*, November 25, 2009.

YOUR TURN: Test your understanding by doing related problem 1.10 on page 62 at the end of this chapter.

Increasing Marginal Opportunity Costs

We can use the production possibilities frontier to explore issues related to the economy as a whole. For example, suppose we divide all the goods and services produced in the economy into just two types: military goods and civilian goods. In Figure 2-2,

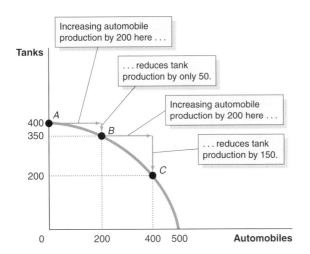

Figure 2-2

Increasing Marginal Opportunity Cost

As the economy moves down the production possibilities frontier, it experiences *increasing marginal opportunity costs* because increasing automobile production by a given quantity requires larger and larger decreases in tank production. For example, to increase automobile production from 0 to 200—moving from point *A* to point *B*—the economy has to give up only 50 tanks. But to increase automobile production by another 200 vehicles—moving from point *B* to point *C*—the economy has to give up 150 tanks.

we let tanks represent military goods and automobiles represent civilian goods. If all the country's resources are devoted to producing military goods, 400 tanks can be produced in one year. If all resources are devoted to producing civilian goods, 500 automobiles can be produced in one year. Devoting resources to producing both goods results in the economy being at other points along the production possibilities frontier.

Notice that this production possibilities frontier is bowed outward rather than being a straight line. Because the curve is bowed out, the opportunity cost of automobiles in terms of tanks depends on where the economy currently is on the production possibilities frontier. For example, to increase automobile production from 0 to 200—moving from point *A* to point *B*—the economy has to give up only 50 tanks. But to increase automobile production by another 200 vehicles—moving from point *B* to point *C*—the economy has to give up 150 tanks.

As the economy moves down the production possibilities frontier, it experiences *increasing marginal opportunity costs* because increasing automobile production by a given quantity requires larger and larger decreases in tank production. Increasing marginal opportunity costs occurs because some workers, machines, and other resources are better suited to one use than to another. At point *A*, some resources that are well suited to producing automobiles are forced to produce tanks. Shifting these resources into producing automobiles by moving from point *A* to point *B* allows a substantial increase in automobile production, without much loss of tank production. But as the economy moves down the production possibilities frontier, more and more resources that are better suited to tank production are switched into automobile production. As a result, the increases in automobile production become increasingly smaller, while the decreases in tank production become increasingly larger. We would expect in most situations that production possibilities frontiers will be bowed outward rather than linear, as in the BMW example discussed earlier.

The idea of increasing marginal opportunity costs illustrates an important economic concept: *The more resources already devoted to any activity, the smaller the payoff to devoting additional resources to that activity.* For example, the more hours you have already spent studying economics, the smaller the increase in your test grade from each additional hour you spend—and the greater the opportunity cost of using the hour in that way. The more funds a firm has devoted to research and development during a given year, the smaller the amount of useful knowledge it receives from each additional dollar—and the greater the opportunity cost of using the funds in that way. The more funds the government spends cleaning up the environment during a given year, the smaller the reduction in pollution from each additional dollar—and, once again, the greater the opportunity cost of using the funds in that way.

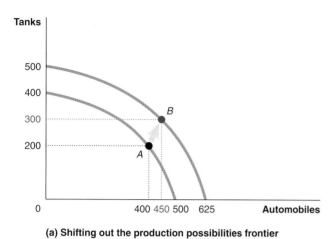

(a) Shifting out the production possibilities frontier

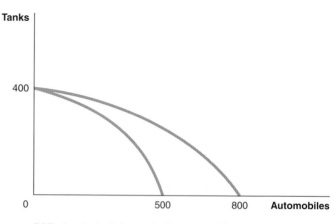

(b) Technological change in the automobile industry

Figure 2-3 | Economic Growth

Panel (a) shows that as more economic resources become available and technological change occurs, the economy can move from point A to point B, producing more tanks and more automobiles. Panel (b) shows the results of technological advance in the automobile industry that increases the quantity of vehicles workers can produce per year while leaving the maximum quantity of tanks that can be produced unchanged. Shifts in the production possibilities frontier represent *economic growth*.

Economic Growth

At any given time, the total resources available to any economy are fixed. Therefore, if Egypt produces more automobiles, it must produce fewer of something else—tanks, in this example. Over time, though, the resources available to an economy may increase. For example, both the labor force and the capital stock—the amount of physical capital available in the country—may increase. The increase in the available labor force and the capital stock shifts the production possibilities frontier outward for the Egyptian economy and makes it possible to produce both more automobiles and more tanks. Panel (a) of Figure 2-3 shows that the economy can move from point A to point B, producing more tanks and more automobiles.

Similarly, technological advance makes it possible to produce more goods with the same amount of workers and machinery, which also shifts the production possibilities frontier outward. Technological advance need not affect all sectors equally. Panel (b) of Figure 2-3 shows the results of technological advance in the automobile industry that increases the quantity of automobile workers can produce per year while leaving unchanged the quantity of tanks that can be produced.

Shifts in the production possibilities frontier represent **economic growth** because they allow the economy to increase the production of goods and services, which ultimately raises the standard of living.

Economic growth The ability of an economy to produce increasing quantities of goods and services.

2.2 LEARNING OBJECTIVE

2.2 | Understand comparative advantage and explain how it is the basis for trade.

Comparative Advantage and Trade

We can use the ideas of production possibilities frontiers and opportunity costs to understand the basic economic activity of *trade*. Markets are fundamentally about **trade**, which is the act of buying and selling. Sometimes we trade directly, as when children trade a falafel sandwich for a lollipop. But often we trade indirectly: we sell our labor services as, say, an accountant, a salesperson, or a nurse for money, and then we use the money to buy goods and services. Although in these cases, trade takes place indirectly, ultimately the accountant, salesperson, or nurse is trading his or her services for food, clothing, and other goods and services. One of the great benefits to trade is that it makes it possible for people to become better off by increasing both their production and their consumption.

Trade The act of buying or selling.

Specialization and Gains from Trade

Consider the following situation: You and your neighbor both have fruit trees on your property. Initially, suppose you have only apple trees and your neighbor has only cherry trees. In this situation, if you both like apples and cherries, there is an obvious opportunity for both of you to gain from trade: you trade some of your apples for some of your neighbor's cherries, making you both better off. But what if there are apple and cherry trees growing on both of your properties? In that case, there can still be gains from trade. For example, your neighbor might be very good at picking apples, and you might be very good at picking cherries. It would make sense for your neighbor to concentrate on picking apples and for you to concentrate on picking cherries. You can then trade some of the cherries you pick for some of the apples your neighbor picks. But what if your neighbor is actually better at picking both apples and cherries than you are?

We can use production possibilities frontiers (*PPFs*) to show how your neighbor can benefit from trading with you even though she is better than you are at picking both apples and cherries. (For simplicity, and because it will not have any effect on the conclusions we draw, we will assume that the *PPFs* in this example are straight lines.) The table in Figure 2-4 shows how many apples and how many cherries you and your neighbor can pick in one week. The graph in the figure uses the data from the table to construct *PPFs*. Panel (a) shows your *PPF*. If you devote all your time to picking apples, you can pick 20 kilos of apples per week. If you devote all your time to picking cherries, you can pick 20 kilos per week. Panel (b) shows that if your neighbor devotes all her time to picking apples, she can pick 30 kilos. If she devotes all her time to picking cherries, she can pick 60 kilos.

The production possibilities frontiers in Figure 2-4 show how many apples and cherries you and your neighbor can consume, *without trade*. Suppose that when you don't trade with your neighbor, you pick and consume 8 kilos of apples and

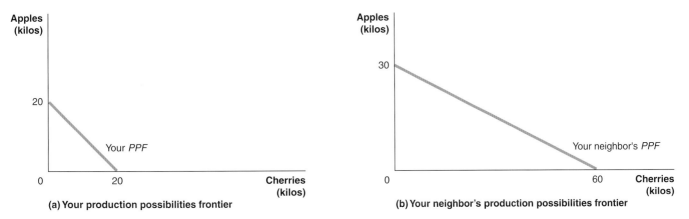

	You		Your Neighbor	
	Apples	Cherries	Apples	Cherries
Devote all time to picking apples	20 kilos	0 kilos	30 kilos	0 kilos
Devote all time to picking cherries	0 kilos	20 kilos	0 kilos	60 kilos

(a) Your production possibilities frontier

(b) Your neighbor's production possibilities frontier

Figure 2-4 | Production Possibilities for You and Your Neighbor, without Trade

The table in this figure shows how many kilos of apples and how many kilos of cherries you and your neighbor can each pick in one week. The graphs in the figure use the data from the table to construct production possibilities frontiers (*PPFs*) for you and your neighbor. Panel (a) shows your *PPF*. If you devote all your time to picking apples and none of your time to picking cherries, you can pick 20 kilos. If you devote all your time to picking cherries, you can pick 20 kilos. Panel (b) shows that if your neighbor devotes all her time to picking apples, she can pick 30 kilos. If she devotes all her time to picking cherries, she can pick 60 kilos.

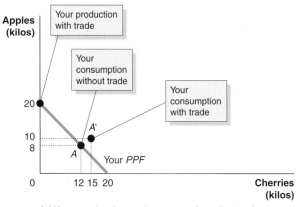

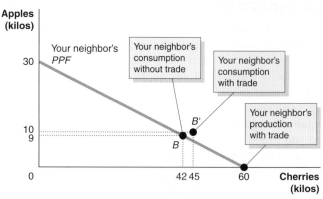

Figure 2-5 | Gains from Trade

When you don't trade with your neighbor, you pick and consume 8 kilos of apples and 12 kilos of cherries per week—point *A* in panel (a). When your neighbor doesn't trade with you, she picks and consumes 9 kilos of apples and 42 kilos of cherries per week—point *B* in panel (b). If you specialize in picking apples, you can pick 20 kilos. If your neighbor specializes in picking cherries, she can pick

60 kilos. If you trade 10 kilos of your apples for 15 kilos of your neighbor's cherries, you will be able to consume 10 kilos of apples and 15 kilos of cherries—point *A'* in panel (a). Your neighbor can now consume 10 kilos of apples and 45 kilos of cherries—point *B'* in panel (b). You and your neighbor are both better off as a result of trade.

---

12 kilos of cherries per week. This combination of apples and cherries is represented by point *A* in panel (a) of Figure 2-5. When your neighbor doesn't trade with you, she picks and consumes 9 kilos of apples and 42 kilos of cherries per week. This combination of apples and cherries is represented by point *B* in panel (b) of Figure 2-5.

After years of picking and consuming your own apples and cherries, suppose your neighbor comes to you one day with the following proposal: She offers to trade you 15 kilos of her cherries for 10 kilos of your apples next week. Should you accept this offer? You should accept because you will end up with more apples and more cherries to consume. To take advantage of her proposal, you should specialize in picking only apples rather than splitting your time between picking apples and picking cherries. We know this will allow you to pick 20 kilos of apples. You can trade 10 kilos of apples to your neighbor for 15 kilos of her cherries. The result is that you will be able to consume 10 kilos of apples and 15 kilos of cherries (point *A'* in panel (a) of Figure 2-5). You are clearly better off as a result of trading with your neighbor: You now can consume 2 more kilos of apples and 3 more kilos of cherries than you were consuming without trading. You have moved beyond your *PPF*!

Your neighbor has also benefited from the trade. By specializing in picking only cherries, she can pick 60 kilos. She trades 15 kilos of cherries to you for 10 kilos of apples. The result is that she can consume 10 kilos of apples and 45 kilos of cherries (point *B'* in panel (b) of Figure 2-5). This is 1 more kilo of apples and 3 more kilos of cherries than she was consuming before trading with you. She also has moved beyond her *PPF*. Table 2-1 summarizes the changes in production and consumption that result from your trade with your neighbor. (In this example, we chose one specific rate of trading cherries for apples—15 kilos of cherries for 10 kilos of apples. There are, however, many other rates of trading cherries for apples that would also make you and your neighbor better off.)

Absolute Advantage versus Comparative Advantage

Absolute advantage The ability of an individual, a firm, or a country to produce more of a good or service than competitors, using the same amount of resources.

Perhaps the most remarkable aspect of the previous example is that your neighbor benefits from trading with you even though she is better than you at picking both apples and cherries. **Absolute advantage** is the ability of an individual, a firm, or a country

	YOU		YOUR NEIGHBOR	
	APPLES (IN KILOS)	CHERRIES (IN KILOS)	APPLES (IN KILOS)	CHERRIES (IN KILOS)
Production *and* consumption *without* trade	8	12	9	42
Production *with* trade	20	0	0	60
Consumption *with* trade	10	15	10	45
Gains from trade (increased consumption)	2	3	1	3

TABLE 2-1

A Summary of the Gains from Trade

to produce more of a good or service than competitors, using the same amount of resources. Your neighbor has an absolute advantage over you in producing both apples and cherries because she can pick more of each fruit than you can in the same amount of time. Although it seems that your neighbor should pick her own apples *and* her own cherries, we have just seen that she is better off specializing in cherry picking and leaving the apple picking to you.

We can consider further why both you and your neighbor benefit from specializing in picking only one fruit. First, think about the opportunity cost to each of you of picking the two fruits. We saw from the *PPF* in Figure 2-4 that if you devoted all your time to picking apples, you would be able to pick 20 kilos of apples per week. As you move down your *PPF* and shift time away from picking apples to picking cherries, you have to give up 1 kilo of apples for each kilo of cherries you pick (the slope of your *PPF* is −1). (For a review of calculating slopes, see the appendix to Chapter 1) Therefore, your opportunity cost of picking 1 kilo of cherries is 1 kilo of apples. By the same reasoning, your opportunity cost of picking 1 kilo of apples is 1 kilo of cherries. Your neighbor's *PPF* has a different slope, so she faces a different trade-off: as she shifts time from picking apples to picking cherries, she has to give up 0.5 kilo of apples for every 1 kilo of cherries she picks (the slope of your neighbor's *PPF* is −0.5). As she shifts time from picking cherries to picking apples, she gives up 2 kilos of cherries for every 1 kilo of apples she picks. Therefore, her opportunity cost of picking 1 kilo of apples is 2 kilos of cherries, and her opportunity cost of picking 1 kilo of cherries is 0.5 kilo of apples.

Table 2-2 summarizes the opportunity costs for you and your neighbor of picking apples and cherries. Note that even though your neighbor can pick more apples in a week than you can, the *opportunity cost* of picking apples is higher for her than for you because when she picks apples, she gives up more cherries than you do. So, even though she has an absolute advantage over you in picking apples, it is more costly for her to pick apples than it is for you. The table also shows that her opportunity cost of picking cherries is lower than your opportunity cost of picking cherries. **Comparative advantage** is the ability of an individual, a firm, or a country to produce a good or service at a lower opportunity cost than competitors. In apple picking, your neighbor has an *absolute advantage* over you, but you have a *comparative advantage* over her. Your neighbor has both an absolute and a comparative advantage over you in picking cherries. As we have seen, you are better off specializing in picking apples, and your neighbor is better off specializing in picking cherries.

Comparative advantage The ability of an individual, a firm, or a country to produce a good or service at a lower opportunity cost than competitors.

TABLE 2-2

Opportunity Costs of Picking Apples And Cherries

	OPPORTUNITY COST OF PICKING 1 KILO OF APPLES	OPPORTUNITY COST OF PICKING 1 KILO OF CHERRIES
YOU	1 kilo of cherries	1 kilo of apples
YOUR NEIGHBOR	2 kilos of cherries	0.5 kilo of apples

Comparative Advantage and the Gains from Trade

We have just derived an important economic principle: *The basis for trade is comparative advantage, not absolute advantage.* The fastest apple pickers do not necessarily do much apple picking. If the fastest apple pickers have a comparative advantage in some other activity—picking cherries, playing in the football league, or being industrial engineers—they are better off specializing in that other activity. Individuals, firms, and countries are better off if they specialize in producing goods and services for which they have a comparative advantage and obtain the other goods and services they need by trading. We will return to the important concept of comparative advantage in Chapter 14, which is devoted to the subject of international trade.

Solved Problem | **2-2**

Comparative Advantage and the Gains from Trade

Suppose that Kuwait and the United Arab Emirates both produce Arabic coffee and tea. These are the combinations of the two goods that each country can produce in one day:

KUWAIT		UAE	
ARABIC COFFEE (IN TONS)	TEA (IN TONS)	ARABIC COFFEE (IN TONS)	TEA (IN TONS)
0	60	0	50
10	45	10	40
20	30	20	30
30	15	30	20
40	0	40	10
		50	0

a. Who has a comparative advantage in producing tea? Who has a comparative advantage in producing Arabic coffee?

b. Suppose that Kuwait is currently producing 30 tons of Arabic coffee and 15 tons of tea and the UAE is currently producing 10 tons of Arabic coffee and 40 tons of tea. Demonstrate that Kuwait and the UAE can both be better off if they specialize in producing only one good and engage in trade.

c. Illustrate your answer to question (b) by drawing a *PPF* for the UAE and a *PPF* for Kuwait. Show on your *PPF*s the combinations of Arabic coffee and tea produced and consumed in each country before and after trade.

SOLVING THE PROBLEM:

Step 1: **Review the chapter material.** This problem concerns comparative advantage, so you may want to review the section "Absolute Advantage versus Comparative Advantage," which begins on page 46.

Step 2: **Answer question (a) by calculating who has a comparative advantage in each activity.** Remember that a country has a comparative advantage in producing a good if it can produce the good at the lowest opportunity cost. When Kuwait produces 1 more ton of Arabic coffee, it produces 1.5 fewer tons of tea. On the one hand, when the UAE produces 1 more ton of Arabic coffee, it produces 1 less ton of tea. Therefore, UAE'S opportunity cost of producing Arabic coffee—1 ton of tea—is lower than Kuwait's—1.5 tons of tea. On the other hand, when Kuwait produces 1 more ton of tea, it produces 0.67 ton less of Arabic coffee. When the UAE produces 1 more ton of tea, it produces 1 less ton of Arabic coffee. Therefore, Kuwait's opportunity cost of producing tea—0.67 ton of Arabic coffee—is lower than that of the UAE—1 ton of

Arabic coffee. We can conclude that the UAE has a comparative advantage in the production of Arabic coffee and Kuwait has a comparative advantage in the production of tea.

Step 3: **Answer question (b) by showing that specialization makes Kuwait and the United Arab Emirates better off.** We know that Kuwait should specialize where it has a comparative advantage and the UAE should specialize where it has a comparative advantage. If both countries specialize, Kuwait will produce 60 tons of tea and 0 tons of Arabic coffee, and the UAE will produce 0 tons of tea and 50 tons of Arabic coffee. After both countries specialize, the UAE could then trade 30 tons of Arabic coffee to Kuwait in exchange for 40 tons of tea. (Other mutually beneficial trades are possible as well.) We can summarize the results in a table:

	BEFORE TRADE		AFTER TRADE	
	ARABIC COFFEE (IN TONS)	TEA (IN TONS)	ARABIC COFFEE (IN TONS)	TEA (IN TONS)
KUWAIT	30	15	30	20
UNITED ARAB EMIRATES	10	40	20	40

The UAE is better off after trade because it can consume the same amount of tea and 10 more tons of Arabic coffee. Kuwait is better off after trade because it can consume the same amount of Arabic coffee and 5 more tons of tea.

Step 4: **Answer question (c) by drawing the *PPF*s.**

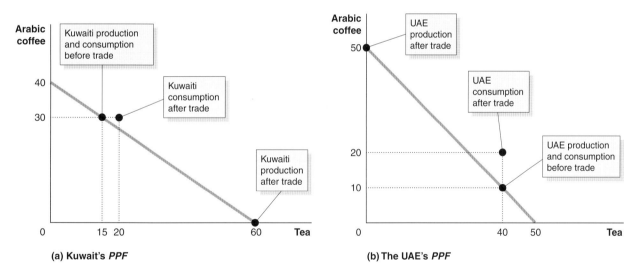

(a) Kuwait's *PPF*

(b) The UAE's *PPF*

YOUR TURN: For more practice, do related problems 2.5 and 2.6 on page 63 at the end of this chapter.

>> **End Solved Problem 2-2**

2.3 | Explain the basic idea of how a market system works.

The Market System

We have seen that households, firms, and the government face trade-offs and incur opportunity costs because of the scarcity of resources. We have also seen that trade allows people to specialize according to their comparative advantage. By engaging in trade, people can raise their standard of living. Of course, trade in the modern world is much more complex than the examples we have considered so far. Trade today involves the decisions of millions of people spread around the world. But how does an economy make trade possible, and how are the decisions of these millions of people coordinated? In the Arab world and most other countries, trade is carried out in markets. Markets also determine the answers to the three fundamental questions discussed in Chapter 1: *What* goods and services will be produced? *How* will the goods and services be produced? and *Who* will receive the goods and services?

Market A group of buyers and sellers of a good or service and the institution or arrangement by which they come together to trade.

Recall that the definition of **market** is a group of buyers and sellers of a good or service and the institution or arrangement by which they come together to trade. Markets take many forms: they can be physical places, like a local pizza parlor or the Saudi Stock Exchange (Tadawul), or virtual places, like eBay.com and eWaseet.com. In a market, the buyers are demanders of goods or services, and the sellers are suppliers of goods or services. Households and firms interact in two types of markets: *product markets* and *factor markets*. **Product markets** are markets for goods—such as computers—and services—such as medical treatment. In product markets, households are demanders, and firms are suppliers. **Factor markets** are markets for the *factors of production*. **Factors of production** are the inputs used to make goods and services. Factors of production are divided into four broad categories:

Product markets Markets for goods—such as computers—and services—such as medical treatment.

Factor markets Markets for the factors of production, such as labor, capital, natural resources, and entrepreneurial ability.

Factors of production Labor, capital, natural resources, and other inputs used to produce goods and services.

- *Labor* includes all types of work, from the part-time labor of teenagers working at small stores to the work of top managers in large corporations.

- *Capital* refers to physical capital, such as computers and machine tools, that is used to produce other goods.

- *Natural resources* include land, water, oil, iron ore, and other raw materials (or 'gifts of nature') that are used in producing goods.

- An *entrepreneur* is someone who operates a business. *Entrepreneurial ability* is the ability to bring together the other factors of production to successfully produce and sell goods and services.

The Circular Flow of Income

Two key groups participate in markets:

- A *household* consists of all the individuals in a home. Households are suppliers of factors of production—particularly labor—used by firms to make goods and services. Households use the income they receive from selling the factors of production to purchase the goods and services supplied by firms. We are used to thinking of households as suppliers of labor because most people earn most of their income by going to work, which means they are selling their labor services to firms in the labor market. But households own the other factors of production, as well, either directly or indirectly, by owning the firms that have these resources. All firms are owned by households. Small firms, like a neighborhood restaurant, might be owned by one person. Large firms, like Microsoft or BMW, are owned by millions of households who own shares of stock in them. When firms pay profits to the people who own them, the firms are paying for using the capital and natural resources that are supplied to them by those owners. So, we can generalize by saying that in factor markets, households are suppliers, and firms are demanders.

- *Firms* are suppliers of goods and services. Firms use the funds they receive from selling goods and services to buy the factors of production needed to make the goods and services.

Circular-flow diagram A model that illustrates how participants in markets are linked.

We can use a simple economic model called the **circular-flow diagram** to see how participants in markets are linked. Figure 2-6 shows that in factor markets, households supply labor and other factors of production in exchange for wages and other payments from firms. In product markets, households use the payments they earn in factor markets to purchase the goods and services supplied by firms. Firms produce these goods and services using the factors of production supplied by households. In the figure,

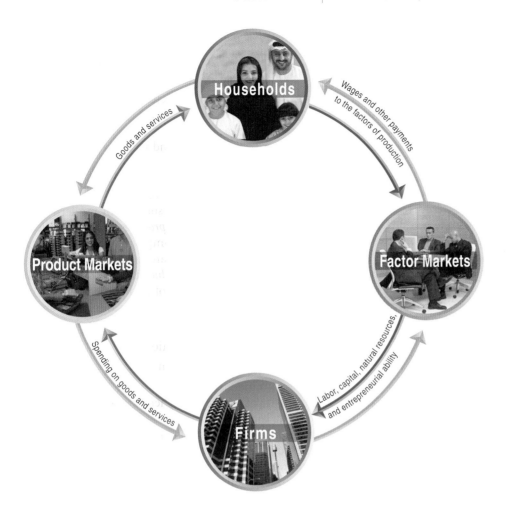

Figure 2-6

The Circular-Flow Diagram

Households and firms are linked together in a circular flow of production, income, and spending. The blue arrows show the flow of the factors of production. In factor markets, households supply labor, entrepreneurial ability, and other factors of production to firms. Firms use these factors of production to make goods and services that they supply to households in product markets. The red arrows show the flow of goods and services from firms to households. The green arrows show the flow of funds. In factor markets, households receive wages and other payments from firms in exchange for supplying the factors of production. Households use these wages and other payments to purchase goods and services from firms in product markets. Firms sell goods and services to households in product markets, and they use the funds to purchase the factors of production from households in factor markets.

the blue arrows show the flow of factors of production from households through factor markets to firms. The red arrows show the flow of goods and services from firms through product markets to households. The green arrows show the flow of funds from firms through factor markets to households and the flow of spending from households through product markets to firms.

Like all economic models, the circular-flow diagram is a simplified version of reality. For example, Figure 2-6 leaves out the important role of government in buying goods from firms and in making payments, such as Social Security or unemployment insurance payments, to households (these payments are mainly directed to old age, disabled, and unemployed people). The figure also leaves out the roles played by banks, the stock and bond markets, and other parts of the financial system in aiding the flow of funds from lenders to borrowers. Finally, the figure does not show that some goods and services purchased by domestic households are produced in foreign countries and some goods and services produced by domestic firms are sold to foreign households. The government, the financial system, and the international sector are explored further in later chapters. Despite these simplifications, the circular-flow diagram in Figure 2-6 is useful for seeing how product markets, factor markets, and their participants are linked together. One of the great mysteries of the market system is that it manages to successfully coordinate the independent activities of so many households and firms.

The Gains from Free Markets

A **free market** exists when the government places few restrictions on how a good or a service can be produced or sold or on how a factor of production can be employed. Governments in all modern economies intervene more than is

Free market A market with few government restrictions on how a good or service can be produced or sold or on how a factor of production can be employed.

consistent with a fully free market. In that sense, we can think of the free market as being a benchmark against which we can judge actual economies. There are relatively few government restrictions on economic activity in the United States, Canada, the countries of Western Europe, Hong Kong, Singapore, and Estonia. So these countries come close to the free market benchmark. In countries such as Cuba, North Korea, and some of the Arab countries such as Syria, Libya, and Egypt (in the 1960s), the free market system has been rejected in favor of centrally planned economies with extensive government control over product and factor markets. Countries that come closest to the free-market benchmark have been more successful than countries with centrally planned economies in providing their people with rising living standards.

The Scottish philosopher Adam Smith is considered the father of modern economics because his book *An Inquiry into the Nature and Causes of the Wealth of Nations*, published in 1776, was an early and very influential argument for the free market system. Smith was writing at a time when extensive government restrictions on markets were still very common. In many parts of Europe, the *guild system* still prevailed. Under this system, governments would give guilds, or organizations of producers, the authority to control the production of a good. For example, the shoemakers' guild controlled who was allowed to produce shoes, how many shoes they could produce, and what price they could charge. In France, the clothmakers' guild even dictated the number of threads in the weave of cloth. The guild system was also found in the Arab world in the seventeenth century, the time of the Ottoman Empire. For example, studies on the economic history of the Middle East found that there were around 300 guilds in Cairo, Egypt, that contain almost all workers working in profitable occupations except the high bureaucracy, the army, and the *ulama* (Muslim scholars). The role of the government was clear in the Egyptian guilds as each guild was headed by a special officer, or *shaykh*, who was appointed by the government. The officer was often ignorant of the guild traditions and his main job was to provide protection to the guild members, collect taxes, and maintain government policy inside the guild[1].

Smith argued that such restrictions reduced the income, or wealth, of a country and its people by restricting the quantity of goods produced. Some people at the time supported the restrictions of the guild system because it was in their financial interest to do so. If you were a member of a guild, the restrictions served to reduce the competition you faced. But other people sincerely believed that the alternative to the guild system was economic chaos. Smith argued that these people were wrong and that a country could enjoy a smoothly functioning economic system if firms were freed from guild restrictions.

The Market Mechanism

In Smith's day, defenders of the guild system worried that if, for instance, the shoemakers' guild did not control shoe production, either too many or too few shoes would be produced. Smith argued that prices would do a better job of coordinating the activities of buyers and sellers than the guilds could. A key to understanding Smith's argument is the assumption that *individuals usually act in a rational, self-interested way*. In particular, individuals take those actions most likely to make themselves better off financially. This assumption of rational, self-interested behavior underlies nearly all economic analysis. In fact, economics can be distinguished from other fields that study human behavior—such as sociology and psychology—by its emphasis on the assumption of self-interested behavior. Adam Smith understood—as economists today understand—that people's motives can be complex. But in analyzing people in the act of buying and selling, the motivation of financial reward usually provides the best explanation for the actions people take.

For example, suppose that a significant number of consumers switch from buying regular gasoline-powered cars to buying gasoline/electric-powered hybrid cars, such as the Toyota Prius, as in fact happened in the United States during the 2000s. Firms will find that they can charge relatively higher prices for hybrid cars than they can for regular cars. The self-interest of these firms will lead them to respond to consumers' wishes by producing more hybrids and fewer regular cars. Or suppose that consumers decide that they want to eat less bread, pasta, and other foods high in carbohydrates, as many did following the increase in popularity of the Atkins and South Beach diets (these diets depend mainly on eating protein, mostly from meat, and food that is low in carbohydrates). Then the prices firms can charge for bread and pasta will fall. The self-interest of firms will lead them to produce less bread and pasta, which in fact is what happened.

In the case where consumers want more of a product, and in the case where they want less of a product, the market system responds without a guild or the government giving orders about how much to produce or what price to charge. In a famous phrase, Smith said that firms would be led by the "invisible hand" of the market to provide consumers with what they wanted. Firms would respond to changes in prices by making decisions that ended up satisfying the wants of consumers.

Making the Connection | A Story of the Market System in Action: How Do You Make an iPod?

The iPod is a product of Apple, which has its headquarters in Cupertino, in the U.S. State of California. It seems reasonable to assume that iPods are also manufactured in California. In fact, Apple produces none of the components of the iPod, nor does it assemble the components into a finished product. Far from being produced entirely by one company in one place, the iPod requires the coordinated activities of thousands of workers and dozens of firms, spread around the world.

Several Asian firms, including Asustek, Inventec Appliances, and Foxconn, assemble the iPod, which is then shipped to Apple for sale in the United States and all over the world. But the firms doing final assembly don't make any of the components. For example, the iPod's hard drive is manufactured by the Japanese firm, Toshiba, although Toshiba actually assembles the hard drive in factories in China and the Philippines. Apple purchases the controller chip that manages the iPod's functions from PortalPlayer, which is based in Santa Clara, California. But PortalPlayer actually has the chip manufactured for it by Taiwan Semiconductor Manufacturing Corporation, and the chip's processor core was designed by ARM, a British company. Taiwan Semiconductor Manufacturing Corporation's factories are for the most part not in Taiwan, but in mainland China and Eastern Europe.

The market coordinates the activities of the many people spread around the world who contribute to the making of an iPod

All told, the iPod contains 451 parts, designed and manufactured by firms around the world. Many of these firms are not even aware of which other firms are also producing components for the iPod. Few of the managers of these firms have met managers of the other firms or shared knowledge of how their particular components are produced. In fact, no one person from Steve Jobs, the head of Apple, on down possesses the knowledge of how to produce all of the components that are assembled into an iPod. Instead, the invisible hand of the market has led these firms to contribute their knowledge to the process that

(Continued)

ultimately results in an iPod available for sale in a store in Dubai. Apple has so efficiently organized the process of producing the iPod that you can order a custom iPod with a personal engraving and have it delivered from an assembly plant in China to your doorstep in the UAE in as little as three days.

Hal Varian, an economist at the University of California, Berkeley, has summarized the iPod story: "Those clever folks at Apple figured out how to combine 451 mostly generic parts into a valuable product. They may not make the iPod, but they created it."

Sources: Hal Varian, "An iPod Has Global Value: Ask the (Many) Countries That Make It," *New York Times*, June 28, 2007; Greg Linden, Kenneth L. Kraemer, Jaon Dedrick, "Who Captures Value in a Global Innovation System? The Case of Apple's iPod," Personal Computing Industry Center, June 2007.

YOUR TURN: Test your understanding by doing related problem 3.8 on page 64 at the end of this chapter.

The Role of the Entrepreneur

Entrepreneur Someone who operates a business, bringing together the factors of production—labor, capital, and natural resources—to produce goods and services.

Entrepreneurs are central to the working of the market system. An **entrepreneur** is someone who operates a business. Entrepreneurs must first determine what goods and services they believe consumers want, and then they must decide how to produce those goods and services most profitably. Entrepreneurs bring together the factors of production—labor, capital, and natural resources—to produce goods and services. They put their own funds at risk when they start businesses. If they are wrong about what consumers want or about the best way to produce goods and services, they can lose those funds. In fact, it is not unusual for entrepreneurs who eventually achieve great success to fail at first. For instance, early in their careers, both Henry Ford and Sakichi Toyoda, who eventually founded the Toyota Motor Corporation, started companies that quickly failed.

The Legal Basis of a Successful Market System

In a free market, government does not restrict how firms produce and sell goods and services or how they employ factors of production, but the absence of government intervention is not enough for a market system to work well. Government has to provide secure rights to private property for a market system to work at all. In addition, government can aid the working of the market by enforcing contracts between private individuals through an independent court system. Many economists would also say the government has a role in facilitating the development of an efficient financial system as well as systems of education, transportation, and communication. The protection of private property and the existence of an independent court system to impartially enforce the law provide a *legal environment* that will allow a market system to succeed.

Protection of Private Property For a market system to work well, individuals must be willing to take risks. Someone with US$250,000 can be cautious and keep it safely in a bank—or even in cash, if the person doesn't trust the banking system. But the market system won't work unless a significant number of people are willing to risk their funds by investing them in businesses. Investing in businesses is risky in any country. Many businesses fail every year in the Arab world as well as in developed countries. But if someone starts a new business or invests in an existing business in the Arab world, he or she doesn't have to worry that the government, the military, or criminal gangs might decide to seize the business or demand payments for not destroying the business. Unfortunately, in many poor countries, owners of businesses are not well protected from having their businesses seized by the government or from having their profits taken by criminals. Where these problems exist, opening a business can be extremely risky. Cash can be concealed easily, but a business is difficult to conceal and difficult to move.

Property rights are the rights individuals or firms have to the exclusive use of their property, including the right to buy or sell it. Property can be tangible, physical property, such as a store or factory. Property can also be intangible, such as the right to an idea.

In any modern economy, *intellectual property rights* are very important. Intellectual property includes books, films, software, and ideas for new products or new ways of producing products. To protect intellectual property, governments grant a *patent* that gives an inventor—which is often a firm—the exclusive right to produce and sell a new product for a period of 20 years from the date the product was invented. For instance, because Microsoft has a patent on the Windows operating system, other firms cannot sell their own versions of Windows. Governments grant patents to encourage firms to spend money on the research and development necessary to create new products. If other companies could freely copy Windows, Microsoft would not have spent the funds necessary to develop it. Just as a new product or a new method of making a product receives patent protection, books, films, and software receive *copyright* protection.

Property rights The rights individuals or firms have to the exclusive use of their property including the right to buy or sell it.

Making the Connection | Property Rights in Cyberspace: YouTube and MySpace

The development of the Internet has led to new problems in protecting intellectual property rights. People can copy and e-mail songs, newspaper and magazine articles, and even entire motion pictures and television programs or post them on websites. Controlling unauthorized copying is more difficult today than it was when 'copying' meant making a physical copy of a book, CD, or DVD. The popularity of YouTube and MySpace highlights the problem of unauthorized copying of videos and music. YouTube, founded in 2005, quickly became an enormous success because it provided an easy way to upload videos, which could then be viewed by anyone with an Internet connection. By 2009, thousands of new videos were being uploaded each day, and the site was receiving more than 70 million visitors per month. YouTube earned substantial profits from selling online advertising. Unfortunately, many of the videos on the site contained copyrighted material.

At first, YouTube's policy was to remove any video containing unauthorized material if the holder of the copyright complained. Then YouTube began to negotiate with the copyright holders to pay a fee in return for allowing the copyrighted material to remain on the site. For music videos, YouTube was usually able to obtain the needed permission directly from the recording company. Things were more complicated when videos on YouTube used copyrighted songs as background music. In those cases, YouTube needed to obtain permissions from the songwriters as well as the record company, which could be a time-consuming process. Obtaining permission to use videos that contained material from television shows or movies was even more complicated because sometimes dozens of people— including the actors, directors, and composers of music—held rights to the television show or movie. YouTube's vice president for business development was quoted as saying, "It's almost like technology has pushed far beyond the business practices and the law, and now everything needs to kind of catch up." In November 2006, YouTube agreed to be purchased by Google for US$1.65 billion, which made the young entrepreneurs who started the company very wealthy. The willingness of YouTube's owners to sell their company to Google was motivated at least

Recording artists like Nancy Ajram may worry that the copyrights for their songs are not being protected on the Internet.

(Continued)

partly by the expectation that Google had the resources to help them resolve their copyright problems.

MySpace had similar problems because many web pages on the site contained copyrighted music or videos. Universal Music sued MySpace after music from rapper Jay-Z's latest album started appearing on the site even before the album was released. In its lawsuit, Universal claimed that the illegal use of its copyrighted music had "created hundreds of millions of dollars of value for the owners of MySpace." Music, television, and movie companies believe that the failure to give the full protection of property rights to the online use of their material reduces their ability to sell CDs and DVDs.

The problem of software piracy is also severe in many developing countries because of weak software copyright laws. The Business Software Alliance, an industry lobby group, conducted a survey in 2007 on software piracy rates worldwide and found that the U.S. has the world's lowest piracy rate, at 21 percent, while Vietnam, the Ukraine, China, and Zimbabwe are found to have the highest software piracy as more than 90 per cent of their software was illegal. In the Arab world, the UAE has the lowest piracy rate (35 percent), followed by Saudi Arabia (51 percent) and Qatar (54 percent), compared with an average 58 percent for the Middle East and Africa. This is because of strict intellectual property laws adopted in the 1990s in the Emirates.

Sources: Kevin J. Delaney, Ethan Smith, and Brooks Barnes, "YouTube Finds Signing Rights Deals Complex, Frustrating," *Wall Street Journal*, November 3, 2006, p. B1; Ethan Smith and Julia Angwin, "Universal Music Sues MySpace Claiming Copyright Infringement," *Wall Street Journal*, November 18, 2006, p. A3; Maija Pesola, "Software Sector Fears US$200bn Piracy Losses," *Financial Times*, May 18, 2005.

YOUR TURN: Test your understanding by doing related problem 3.14 on page 64 at the end of this chapter.

Enforcement of Contracts and Property Rights Much business activity involves someone agreeing to carry out some action in the future. For example, you may borrow US$20,000 to buy a car and promise the bank—by signing a loan contract—that you will pay back the money over the next five years. Or Microsoft may sign a licensing agreement with a small technology company, agreeing to use that company's technology for a period of several years in return for a fee. Usually these agreements take the form of legal contracts. For a market system to work, businesses and individuals have to rely on these contracts being carried out. If one party to a legal contract does not fulfill its obligations—perhaps the small company had promised Microsoft exclusive use of its technology but then began licensing it to other companies—the other party could go to court to have the agreement enforced.

But going to court to enforce a contract or private property rights will be successful only if the court system is independent and judges are able to make impartial decisions on the basis of the law. In the Arab world, the court systems have enough independence from other parts of the government and enough protection from intimidation by outside forces—such as criminal gangs—that they are able to make their decisions based on the law.

If property rights are not well enforced, fewer goods and services will be produced. This reduces economic efficiency, leaving the economy inside its production possibilities frontier.

>> Continued from page 37

Economics in YOUR Life!

At the beginning of the chapter, we asked you to think about two questions: when buying a new car, what is the relationship between safety and gas mileage? and under what circumstances would it be possible for car manufacturers to make cars safer and more fuel efficient? To answer the first question, you have to recognize that there is a trade-off between safety and gas mileage. With the technology available at any particular time, an automobile manufacturer can increase gas mileage by making a car smaller and lighter. But driving a lighter car increases your chances of being injured if you have an accident. The trade-off between safety and gas mileage would look much like the relationship in Figure 2-1 on page 39. To get more of both safety and gas mileage, automobile makers would have to discover new technologies that allow them to make the car lighter and safer at the same time. Such new technologies would make points like G in Figure 2-1 attainable.

Conclusion

We have seen that by trading in markets, people are able to specialize and pursue their comparative advantage. Trading on the basis of comparative advantage makes all participants in trade better off. The key role of markets is to facilitate trade. In fact, the market system is a very effective means of coordinating the decisions of millions of consumers, workers, and firms. At the center of the market system is the consumer. To be successful, firms must respond to the desires of consumers. These desires are communicated to firms through prices. To explore how markets work, we must study the behavior of consumers and firms. We continue this exploration of markets in Chapter 3, when we develop the model of demand and supply.

Before moving on to Chapter 3, read *An Inside Look* on the next page to learn how the managers of domestic car feeding factories in Egypt responded to the low demand for cars after the revolution of January 25, 2011.

The Impact of the Egyptian Revolution on Local Car Feeding Industry

AL AHRAM WEEKLY, MARCH 11, 2011

Egypt's Car Feeding Industries Feel the Brunt of the Post-Revolution Slowdown

(a) Since their clients, car manufacturers, have ceased production due to low demand, 120 car feeding factories were forced to shut down end of February and will remain closed until further notice. According to Nabih El-Semari, head of the feeder industries division at the Federation of Egyptian Industries, many of the other feeder industries have managed to stay open because they work at very low capacity utilization.

There are roughly 480 feeding factories in the country, 60 percent of which are car feeders, El-Semari said, adding that factory owners are dealing with the losses in different ways. "Some owners had to lay off employees, others cut down their salaries," he said.

Mohamed Abdu, business unit manager at Mobica, the furniture manufacturer and a feeding company for car manufacturers in Egypt employing about 600 workers, says that his company decided to keep all of its employees despite the absence of any work during February. "We have started to work at 20 percent of normal capacity starting March when some of our clients, like General Motors Egypt, decided to resume production," he said.

Abdu says that Mobica, which manufactures car furniture for passenger cars and pick-up trucks through five factories, was expected to increase production by 15 percent in 2011 before the revolution started. "We produced 68,000 full car furniture in 2010," he stated. "We would be lucky to produce half that amount by the end of the year."

"I expect a 50 percent decrease in production at all feeding factories until the end of 2011," El-Semari said. He added that the division is trying to ease the burden on the factories by requesting assistance from the various concerned ministries such as the ministries of trade and Industry and finance. "We recommended a 50 percent reduction on sales taxes as a start," he pointed out.

"Moreover, the real state taxes on these factories should be cancelled, permanently, because it has always been an added burden on the administrative expenses which results in a more expensive product and favors the competitors," El-Semari stressed.

El-Semari also disclosed that other recommendations have been sent to the former prime minister Ahmed Shafik, but he resigned before taking any action. "I also suggested a temporary halt to all international agreements, especially cutting down customs duties on imported cars, to give local manufacturers a chance to stand on their feet," he said.

(b) El-Semari believes that the revolution is not the sole reason for the pitiful condition of the feeding industry. "The problems facing car feeding companies as a result of the political unrest have been maximized through poor planning by the Industrial Development Authority (IDA)," he explained.

There are now 13 factories for car manufacturing and assembling in Egypt, more than any other country, El-Semari said. "The big number of factories, allowed by IDA, makes feeding factories produce in small quantities for each car manufacturer, which results in a higher production cost and a lower profit margin," he added.

Nonetheless, El-Semari says he welcomes the opening of one more factory as an exception. "Toyota was planning to open a factory this year, and it would be of great benefit to the industry," he said, explaining that being the top seller in the world means more business for feeding companies because they can work with any of Toyota's factories worldwide in large-quantity deals.

Source: Ahmed Kotb, "Egypt's Car Feeding Industries Feel the Brunt of the Post-Revolution Slowdown," *Al Ahram Weekly*, March 11, 2011.

Key Points in the Article

This article discusses the extent to which the local car feeding industry was affected by the January 25th revolution in Egypt (2011). The direct impact of the low local production of cars, due to the revolution, is that some managers of car feeding industries had to make the tough decision to shut down their factories, while others kept the factories running at much lower capacity. The expected opening of a Toyota assembly line in 2011 is welcomed by managers of car feeding industries since Toyota cars are highly demanded in Egypt.

Analyzing the News

(a) Demand for car feeding industry products is mainly derived from demand for cars. On February 1, 2011, many car manufacturers, such as General Motors (GM), Nissan, Daimler, and BMW, decided to close their assembly plants temporarily in Egypt to ensure the safety of their employees as the political unrest continued to rise. Even after some of these car manufacturers (such as Nissan) reopened their plants a couple of weeks later, the production of cars in Egypt was expected to decrease sharply because of the low local demand for cars. As a result, 120 car feeding factories had to shut down while other car feeding factories remained in business with an expected production level of 50 percent of their capacity. This simply meant that the production possibility frontier for the car feeding industry shifted leftward, owing to the shutting down of many factories. In addition, it was clear that the remaining factories that stayed in the market were not producing at full capacity. Assuming that domestic car feeding factories produce only two main types of

products: car furniture and windshields, Figure 1 shows the reduction in car feeding industry products represented by a leftward shift of the car feeding industry production possibility frontier from PPF_{2010} to PPF_{2011}. It is also expected that, during 2011, the industry will produce at a point inside the production possibility frontier (PPF_{2011}), point "b", compared with point "a", which is the point of production in 2010 (assuming that the industry was producing at full capacity).

(b) Car feeding factories suffer from high cost of production as large number of factories sell their products to limited number of car assembly plants. This means that many car feeding factories are likely to produce small quantities and might not be able to utilize their full capacity (we discuss in Chapter 7 how a large production enables factories to decrease the unit cost of production). The expected opening of a Toyota car assembly plant in 2011 is going to help car feeding factories to utilize their capacity since there is high demand for Toyota cars by consumers not only in Egypt but also in many Arab countries. This means that a large quantity of car feeding products will be demanded by the new Toyota plant. Thus, many car feeding factories would like to switch their production toward the new Toyota plant to benefit from the large scale of production. To show the impact of opening a

new Toyota car assembly plant on car feeding factories in Egypt, let us assume that, in 2011, Mobica factory managers decided to produce car furniture for two main car manufacturers: Daimler and Toyota. As shown in Figure 2, because of the low demand in 2011, Mobica is producing below capacity at point "c". As demand for cars starts to pick up in 2012, as expected, and to benefit from the large demand by the new Toyota plant, Mobica managers are expected to allocate more resources to the production of car furniture to Toyota. In this case, Mobica managers will not face a trade-off between producing car furniture for Daimler and Toyota but, rather, they will use their idle resources and manage to move from producing at a point inside Mobica's production possibility frontier, point "c", to a point on the PPF, point "d".

Thinking Critically

1. After the January 25th revolution in Egypt, 120 car feeding factories' managers decided to shut down until the market conditions improve. What would be the costs to those factories of shutting down for a period of months? If shutting down the factories is costly, why did the managers of those car feeding factories take this decision?

2. Under which circumstances would Mobica factory managers face a trade-off between Daimler cars furniture and Toyota cars furniture?

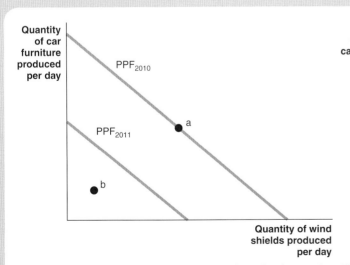

Figure 1. The reduction in car feeding industry products after the Egyptian revolution in 2011.

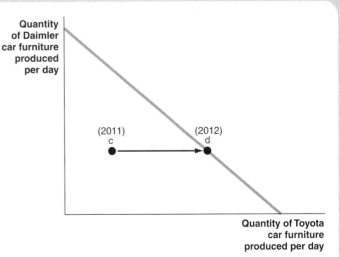

Figure 2. The impact of opening the new Toyota plant on the Mobica factory.

Key Terms

Summary

2.1 LEARNING OBJECTIVE

Use a production possibilities frontier to analyze opportunity costs and trade-offs, **pages 38–44.**

Production Possibilities Frontiers and Opportunity Costs

The **production possibilities frontier (*PPF*)** is a curve that shows the maximum attainable combinations of two products that may be produced with available resources. The *PPF* is used to illustrate the trade-offs that arise from **scarcity**. Points on the frontier are technically efficient. Points inside the frontier are inefficient, and points outside the frontier are unattainable. The **opportunity cost** of any activity is the highest valued alternative that must be given up to engage in that activity. Because of increasing marginal opportunity costs, production possibilities frontiers are usually bowed out rather than straight lines. This illustrates the important economic concept that the more resources that are already devoted to any activity, the smaller the payoff to devoting additional resources to that activity is likely to be. **Economic growth** is illustrated by shifting a production possibilities frontier outward.

2.2 LEARNING OBJECTIVE

Understand comparative advantage and explain how it is the basis for trade, **pages 44–49.**

Comparative Advantage and Trade

Fundamentally, markets are about **trade**, which is the act of buying or selling. People trade on the basis of comparative advantage. An individual, a firm, or a country has a **comparative advantage** in producing a good or service if it can produce the good or service at the lowest opportunity cost. People are usually better off specializing in the activity for which they have a comparative advantage and trading for the other goods and services they need. It is important not to confuse comparative advantage with absolute advantage. An individual, a firm, or a country has an **absolute advantage** in producing a good or service if it can produce more of that good or service from the same amount of resources. It is possible to have an absolute advantage in producing a good or service without having a comparative advantage.

2.3 LEARNING OBJECTIVE

Explain the basic idea of how a market system works, **pages 49–56.**

The Market System

A **market** is a group of buyers and sellers of a good or service and the institution or arrangement by which they come together to trade. **Product markets** are markets for goods and services, such as computers and medical treatment. **Factor markets** are markets for the **factors of production**, such as labor, capital, natural resources, and entrepreneurial ability. A **circular-flow diagram** shows how participants in product markets and factor markets are linked. Adam Smith argued in his 1776 book *The Wealth of Nations* that in a **free market** where the government does not control the production of goods and services, changes in prices lead firms to produce the goods and services most desired by consumers. If consumers demand more of a good, its price will rise. Firms respond to rising prices by increasing production. If consumers demand less of a good, its price will fall. Firms respond to falling prices by producing less of a good. An **entrepreneur** is someone who operates a business. In a market system, entrepreneurs are responsible for organizing the production of goods and services. A market system will work well only if there is protection for **property rights**, which are the rights of individuals and firms to use their property.

Review, Problems and Applications

2.1 LEARNING OBJECTIVE   Use a production possibilities frontier to analyze opportunity costs and trade-offs, **pages 38-44.**

Review Questions

1.1 What do economists mean by scarcity? Can you think of anything that is not scarce according to the economic definition?

1.2 What is a production possibilities frontier? How can we show economic efficiency on a production possibilities frontier? How can we show inefficiency? What causes a production possibilities frontier to shift outward?

1.3 What does increasing marginal opportunity costs mean? What are the implications of this idea for the shape of the production possibilities frontier?

Problems and Applications

1.4 Draw a production possibilities frontier that shows the trade-off between the production of cotton and the production of soybeans.
 a. Show the effect that a prolonged drought would have on the initial production possibilities frontier.
 b. Suppose genetic modification makes soybeans resistant to insects, allowing yields to double. Show the effect of this technological change on the initial production possibilities frontier.

1.5 **(Related to the *Chapter Opener* on page 36)** One of the trade-offs BMW faces is between safety and gas mileage. For example, adding steel to a car makes it safer but also heavier, which results in lower gas mileage. Draw a hypothetical production possibilities frontier that BMW engineers face that shows this trade-off.

1.6 Suppose you win free tickets to a movie plus all you can eat at the snack bar for free. Would there be a cost to you to attend this movie? Explain.

1.7 Suppose we can divide all the goods produced by an economy into two types: consumption goods and capital goods. Capital goods, such as machinery, equipment, and computers, are goods used to produce other goods.
 a. Use a production possibilities frontier graph to illustrate the trade-off to an economy between producing consumption goods and producing capital goods. Is it likely that the production possibilities frontier in this situation would be a straight line (as in Figure 2-1 on page 39) or bowed out (as in Figure 2-2 on page 43)? Briefly explain.
 b. Suppose a technological advance occurs that affects the production of capital goods but not consumption goods. Show the effect on the production possibilities frontier.
 c. Suppose that country A and country B currently have identical production possibilities frontiers but

that country A devotes only 5 percent of its resources to producing capital goods over each of the next 10 years, whereas country B devotes 30 percent. Which country is likely to experience more rapid economic growth in the future? Illustrate using a production possibilities frontier graph. Your graph should include production possibilities frontiers for country A today and in 10 years and production possibilities frontiers for country B today and in 10 years.

1.8 Use the production possibilities frontier for a country to answer the following questions.

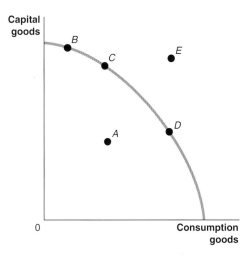

 a. Which point(s) are unattainable? Briefly explain why.
 b. Which point(s) are efficient? Briefly explain why.
 c. Which point(s) are inefficient? Briefly explain why.
 d. At which point is the country's future growth rate likely to be the highest? Briefly explain why.

1.9 **(Related to *Solved Problem 2-1* on page 40)** You have exams in economics and accounting coming up and five hours available for studying. The following table shows the trade-offs you face in allocating the time you will spend in studying each subject.

CHOICE	HOURS SPENT STUDYING		MIDTERM SCORE	
	ECONOMICS	ACCOUNTING	ECONOMICS	ACCOUNTING
A	5	0	95	70
B	4	1	93	78
C	3	2	90	84
D	2	3	86	88
E	1	4	81	90
F	0	5	75	91

a. Use the data in the table to draw a production possibilities frontier graph. Label the vertical axis "Score on economics exam" and label the horizontal axis "Score on accounting exam." Make sure to label the values where your production possibilities frontier intersects the vertical and horizontal axes.

b. Label the points representing choice *C* and choice *D*. If you are at choice *C*, what is your opportunity cost of increasing your accounting score?

c. Under what circumstances would *A* be a sensible choice?

1.10 (Related to the *Making the Connection* on page 41) Suppose the president is attempting to decide whether the government should spend more on research to find a cure for heart disease. He asks you, one of his economic advisors, to prepare a report discussing the relevant factors he should consider. Discuss the main issues you would deal with in your report.

1.11 Lawrence Summers served as the U.S. Secretary of the Treasury in the Clinton administration and later as the president of Harvard University. He has been quoted as giving the following moral defense of the economic approach:

> There is nothing morally unattractive about saying: We need to analyze which way of spending money on health care will produce more benefit and which less, and using our money as efficiently as we can. I don't think there is anything immoral about seeking to achieve environmental benefits at the lowest possible costs.

Would it be more moral to reduce pollution without worrying about the cost or by taking the cost into account? Briefly explain.

Source: David Wessel, "Precepts from Professor Summers," *Wall Street Journal*, October 17, 2002.

1.12 In *The Wonderful Wizard of Oz* and his other books about the Land of Oz, L. Frank Baum observed that

if people's wants were modest enough, most goods would not be scarce. According to Baum, this was the case in Oz:

> There were no poor people in the Land of Oz, because there was no such thing as money.... Each person was given freely by his neighbors whatever he required for his use, which is as much as anyone may reasonably desire. Some tilled the lands and raised great crops of grain, which was divided equally among the whole population, so that all had enough. There were many tailors and dressmakers and shoemakers and the like, who made things that any who desired them might wear. Likewise there were jewelers who made ornaments for the person, which pleased and beautified the people, and these ornaments also were free to those who asked for them. Each man and woman, no matter what he or she produced for the good of the community, was supplied by the neighbors with food and clothing and a house and furniture and ornaments and games. If by chance the supply ever ran short, more was taken from the great storehouses of the Ruler, which were afterward filled up again when there was more of any article than people needed...
>
> You will know, by what I have told you here, that the Land of Oz was a remarkable country. I do not suppose such an arrangement would be practical with us.

Do you agree with Baum that the economic system in Oz wouldn't work in the contemporary Arab world? Briefly explain why or why not.

Source: L. Frank Baum, *The Emerald City of Oz*, pp. 30–31. First edition published in 1910.

2.2 LEARNING OBJECTIVE   Understand comparative advantage and explain how it is the basis for trade,

pages 44–49.

Review Questions

2.1 What is absolute advantage? What is comparative advantage? Is it possible for a country to have a comparative advantage in producing a good without also having an absolute advantage? Briefly explain.

2.2 What is the basis for trade? What advantages are there to specialization?

Problems and Applications

2.3 Look again at the information in Figure 2-4 on page 45. Choose a rate of trading cherries for apples

different than the rate used in the text (15 kilos of cherries for 10 kilos of apples) that will allow you and your neighbor to benefit from trading apples and cherries. Prepare a table like Table 2-1 on page 39 to illustrate your answer.

2.4 Using the same amount of resources, Jordan and Egypt can both produce shirts and boots, as shown in the following production possibilities frontiers.

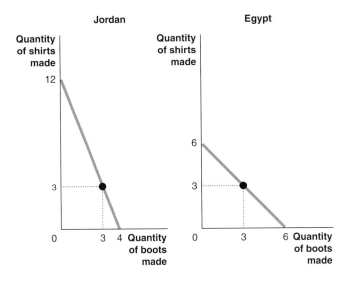

a. Who has a comparative advantage in producing boots? Who has a comparative advantage in producing shirts? Explain your reasoning.
b. Does either country have an absolute advantage in producing both goods? Explain.
c. Suppose that both countries are currently producing three pairs of boots and three shirts. Show that both can be better off if they specialize in producing one good and then engage in trade.

2.5 (Related to *Solved Problem 2-2* on page 48) Suppose Saudi Arabia and Oman both produce oil and olive oil. The following table shows combinations of both goods that each country can produce in a day, measured in thousands of barrels.

OMAN		SAUDI ARABIA	
OIL	OLIVE OIL	OIL	OLIVE OIL
0	8	0	4
2	6	1	3
4	4	2	2
6	2	3	1
8	0	4	0

a. Who has the comparative advantage in producing oil? Explain.
b. Can these two countries gain from trading oil and olive oil? Explain.

2.6 (Related to *Solved Problem 2-2* on page 48) Suppose that Bahrain and Qatar both produce fish and dates. The following table shows combinations of the goods that each country can produce in a day.

BAHRAIN		QATAR	
DATES (KILOS)	FISH (KILOS)	DATES (KILOS)	FISH (KILOS)
0	8	0	15
1	6	1	12
2	4	2	9
3	2	3	6
4	0	4	3
		5	0

a. Who has a comparative advantage in producing dates? Who has a comparative advantage in producing fish?
b. Suppose that Bahrain is currently producing 1 kilo of dates and 6 kilos of fish, and Qatar is currently producing 3 kilos of dates and 6 kilos of fish. Demonstrate that Bahrain and Qatar can both be better off if they specialize in producing only one good and then engage in trade.

2.7 In the 1950s, the economist Bela Balassa compared 28 manufacturing industries in the United States and Britain. In every one of the 28 industries, Balassa found that the U.S. had an absolute advantage. In these circumstances, would there have been any gain to the U.S. from importing any of these products from Britain? Explain.

2.8 In colonial America, the population was spread thinly over a large area, and transportation costs were very high because it was difficult to ship products by road for more than short distances. As a result, most of the free population lived on small farms where they not only grew their own food but also usually made their own clothes and very rarely bought or sold anything for money. Explain why the incomes of these farmers were likely to rise as transportation costs fell. Use the concept of comparative advantage in your answer.

2.9 Some have argued that a country should only import those products that could not be produced there. Do you believe that this would be a good policy? Explain.

2.3 LEARNING OBJECTIVE   Explain the basic idea of how a market system works, **pages 49–56.**

Review Questions

3.1 What is the circular-flow diagram, and what does it demonstrate?
3.2 What are the two main categories of participants in markets? Which participants are of greatest importance in determining what goods and services are produced?
3.3 What is a free market? In what ways does a free market economy differ from a centrally planned economy?

3.4 What is an entrepreneur? Why do entrepreneurs play a key role in a market system?
3.5 Under what circumstances are firms likely to produce more of a good or service? Under what circumstances are firms likely to produce less of a good or service?
3.6 What are private property rights? What role do they play in the working of a market system? Why are independent courts important for a well-functioning economy?

Problems and Applications

3.7 Identify whether each of the following transactions will take place in the factor market or in the product market and whether households or firms are supplying the good or service or demanding the good or service:

    a. Khaled buys a BMW X5 SUV.

    b. BMW increases employment at its 6th of October City plant.

    c. Khaled works 20 hours per week at McDonald's.

    d. Khaled sells land he owns to McDonald's so it can build a new restaurant.

3.8 **(Related to the *Making the Connection* on page 53)** In *The Wealth of Nations*, Adam Smith wrote the following (Book I, Chapter II): "It is not from the benevolence of the butcher, the brewer, or the baker, that we expect our dinner, but from their regard to their own interest." Briefly discuss what he meant by this.

3.9 In a commencement address to economics graduates at the University of Texas, Robert McTeer, Jr., who was then the president of the Federal Reserve Bank of Dallas, argued, "For my money, Adam Smith's invisible hand is the most important thing you've learned by studying economics." What's so important about the idea of the invisible hand?

Source: Robert D. McTeer, Jr., "The Dismal Science? Hardly!" *Wall Street Journal*, June 4, 2003.

3.10 Evaluate the following argument: "Adam Smith's analysis is based on a fundamental flaw: He assumes that people are motivated by self-interest. But this isn't true. I'm not selfish, and most people I know aren't selfish."

3.11 Writing in the *New York Times*, Michael Lewis argued that "a market economy is premised on a system of incentives designed to encourage an ignoble human trait: self-interest." Do you agree that self-interest is an "ignoble human trait"? What incentives does a market system provide to encourage self-interest?

Source: Michael Lewis, "In Defense of the Boom," *New York Times*, October 27, 2002.

3.12 An editorial in *BusinessWeek* magazine offered this opinion: "Economies should be judged on a simple measure: their ability to generate a rising standard of living for all members of society, including people at the bottom." Briefly discuss whether you agree.

Source: "Poverty: The Bigger Picture," *BusinessWeek*, October 7, 2002.

3.13 An estimated 400 million to 600 million people worldwide are squatters who live on land to which they have no legal title, usually on the outskirts of cities in developing countries. Economist Hernando de Soto persuaded Peru's government to undertake a program to make it cheap and easy for such squatters to obtain a title to the land they had been occupying. How would this creation of property rights be likely to affect the economic opportunities available to squatters?

Source: Alan B. Krueger, "A Study Looks at Squatters and Land Title in Peru," *New York Times*, January 9, 2003.

3.14 **(Related to the *Making the Connection* on page 55)** A columnist for the *Wall Street Journal* argued that most copyright holders are not damaged by having their material shown on YouTube:

> It's [laughable] to suggest that content owners are hurt by videos of teenagers lip-synching to hip-hop songs, that the market for sports DVDs is destroyed by fans being allowed to relive a team's great moment, or that artists reusing footage of famous televised events destroys interest in documentaries.

Do you agree with the argument that the copyright owners of the material mentioned should not be paid a fee if their material is on YouTube? Are there other types of material not mentioned by this columnist with which the copyright holders might suffer significant financial damages by having their material available on YouTube?

Source: Jason Fry, "The Revolution May Be Briefly Televised," *Wall Street Journal*, November 13, 2006.

Where Prices Come From: The Interaction of Demand and Supply

Apple and the Demand for iPods

During the last three months of 2008, Apple sold US$1.82 billion worth of iPods. iPods seemed to be everywhere, but during 2008 it became clear that the market for digital music players was becoming much more competitive.

Steve Jobs and Steve Wozniak started Apple in 1976. Working out of Jobs's parents' garage, the two friends created the Apple I computer. By 1980, although Jobs was still only in his mid-twenties, Apple had become the first firm in history to join the Fortune 500 list of largest U.S. firms in less than five years. Apple's success in the computer business has been up and down, but when the company introduced the iPod digital music player in 2001, it had a runaway success on its hands. The most obvious reasons for the iPod's success are its ease of use and sleek design. But also important has been iTunes,

Apple's online music store. Apple decided to offer individual songs, as well as whole albums, for download at a price of just US$0.99 per song. After paying a royalty to the record company, Apple makes very little profit from the songs it sells on iTunes. Apple was willing to accept a small profit on the sale of each song to make the purchase of the iPod more attractive to consumers.

At a price of several hundred dollars, the iPod might be relatively expensive, but purchasing the music is very inexpensive. In addition, the songs on iTunes are playable only on iPods, and iPods can only play songs downloaded from iTunes (although with enough technical skill, it's possible to get around both restrictions). So, owners of other digital music players do not have easy access to iTunes, and iPod owners have little incentive to download music from other online sites. In addition, because Apple makes the iPod and owns iTunes, the two systems work smoothly

together, which is not the case for many of Apple's competitors. Microsoft's Vice-President Bryan Lee says, "That's something that Apple has played up very well. One brand, one device, one service."

By early 2008, more than 150 million iPods had been sold and more than 4 billion songs had been downloaded from iTunes. Clearly, the strategy of selling an expensive digital music player and selling the music cheaply has been very successful for Apple. But how long will the iPod's dominance last? By 2008, competitors were flooding into the market. New digital music players, such as Microsoft's Zune, Toshiba's Gigabeat, and iRiver's H10, among many others, were rapidly gaining customers. In addition, firms were introducing new 'music phones' that combined the features of a cellphone with the features of a digital music player. Although this wave of competition might be bad news for Apple, it could be good news for consumers by increasing the choices available and lowering prices. **AN INSIDE LOOK** on **page 92** discusses how international oil prices follow the changes in both international oil supply and world demand conditions.

Sources: Nick Wingfield and Robert Guth, "iPod, TheyPod: Rivals Imitate Apple's Success," *Wall Street Journal,* September 18, 2006, p. B1; and Nick Wingfield, "iPod Demand Lifts Apple's Results," *Wall Street Journal,* January 18, 2007, p. A2.

LEARNING Objectives

After studying this chapter, you should be able to:

3.1 Discuss the variables that influence **demand** page 68.

3.2 Discuss the variables that influence **supply** page 76.

3.3 Use a graph to illustrate **market equilibrium** page 80.

3.4 Use **demand and supply graphs** to predict changes in prices and quantities, page 84.

Economics in YOUR Life!

Will you buy an iPod or a Zune?

Suppose you are about to buy a new digital music player and that you are choosing between Apple's iPod and Microsoft's Zune. As the industry leader, the iPod has many advantages over a new entrant like Zune. One strategy Microsoft can use to overcome those advantages is to compete based on price. Would you choose a Zune if it had a lower price than a comparable iPod? Would you choose a Zune if the songs sold on Zune Marketplace were cheaper than the songs sold on iTunes? As you read the chapter, see if you can answer these questions. You can check your answers against those we provide at the end of the chapter. **>> Continued on page 90**

I n Chapter 1 we explored how economists use models to predict human behavior. In Chapter 2, we used the model of production possibilities frontiers to analyze scarcity and trade-offs. In this chapter and the next, we explore the model of demand and supply, which is the most powerful tool in economics, and use it to explain how prices are determined.

Recall from Chapter 1 that economic models rely on assumptions and that these assumptions are simplifications of reality. In some cases, the assumptions of the model may not seem to describe exactly the economic situation being analyzed. For example, the model of demand and supply assumes that we are analyzing a *perfectly competitive market*. In a **perfectly competitive market**, there are many buyers and sellers, all the products sold are identical, and there are no barriers to new firms entering the market. These assumptions are very restrictive and apply exactly to only a few markets, such as the markets for wheat and other agricultural products. Experience has shown, however, that the model of demand and supply can be very useful in analyzing markets where competition among sellers is intense, even if there are relatively few sellers and the products being sold are not identical. In fact, in recent studies the model of demand and supply has been successful in analyzing markets with as few as four buyers and four sellers. In the end, the usefulness of a model depends on how well it can predict outcomes in a market. As we will see in this chapter, the model of demand and supply is often very useful in predicting changes in quantities and prices in many markets.

We begin considering the model of demand and supply by discussing consumers and the demand side of the market, then we turn to firms and the supply side. As you will see, we will apply this model throughout this book to understand business, the economy, and economic policy.

Perfectly competitive market A market that meets the conditions of (1) many buyers and sellers, (2) all firms selling identical products, and (3) no barriers to new firms entering the market.

3.1 | Discuss the variables that influence demand.

The Demand Side of the Market

Chapter 2 explained that in a market system, consumers ultimately determine which goods and services will be produced. The most successful businesses are the ones that respond best to consumer demand. But what determines consumer demand for a product? Certainly, many factors influence the willingness of consumers to buy a particular product. For example, consumers who are considering buying a digital music player, such as Apple's iPod or Microsoft's Zune, will make their decisions based on, among other factors, the income they have available to spend and the effectiveness of the advertising campaigns of the companies that sell digital music players. The main factor in consumer decisions, though, will be the price of the digital music player. So, it makes sense to begin with price when analyzing the decisions of consumers to buy a product. It is important to note that when we discuss demand, we are considering not what a consumer *wants* to buy but what the consumer is both willing and *able* to buy.

Demand Schedules and Demand Curves

Tables that show the relationship between the price of a product and the quantity of the product demanded are called **demand schedules**. The table in Figure 3-1 shows the number of players consumers would be willing to buy over the course of a month at five different prices. The amount of a good or a service that a consumer is willing and able to purchase at a given price is referred to as the **quantity demanded**. The graph in Figure 3-1 plots the numbers from the table as a **demand curve**, a curve that shows the relationship between the price of a product and the quantity of the product demanded. (Note that for convenience, we made the demand curve in Figure 3-1 a straight line, or linear. There is no reason that all demand curves need to be straight lines.) The demand curve in Figure 3-1

Demand schedule A table showing the relationship between the price of a product and the quantity of the product demanded.

Quantity demanded The amount of a good or service that a consumer is willing and able to purchase at a given price.

Demand curve A curve that shows the relationship between the price of a product and the quantity of the product demanded.

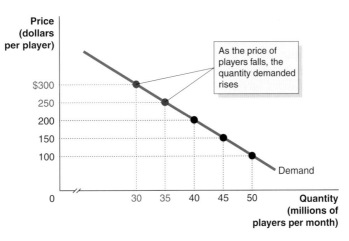

Demand Schedule	
Price (dollars per player)	Quantity (millions of players per month)
$300	30
250	35
200	40
150	45
100	50

Figure 3-1

A Demand Schedule and Demand Curve

As the price changes, consumers change the quantity of digital music players they are willing to buy. We can show this as a *demand schedule* in a table or as a *demand curve* on a graph. The table and graph both show that as the price of players falls, the quantity demanded rises. When the price of a player is US$300, consumers buy 30 million. When the price drops to US$250, consumers buy 35 million. Therefore, the demand curve for digital music players is downward sloping.

shows the **market demand**, or the demand by all the consumers of a given good or service. The market for a product, such as restaurant meals, that is purchased locally would include all the consumers in a city or a relatively small area. The market for a product that is sold internationally, such as digital music players, would include all the consumers in the world.

The demand curve in Figure 3-1 slopes downward because consumers will buy more players as the price falls. When the price of players is US$300, consumers buy 30 million players per month. If the price of players falls to US$250, consumers buy 35 million players. Buyers demand a larger quantity of a product as the price falls because the product becomes less expensive relative to other products and because they can afford to buy more at a lower price.

> **Market demand** The demand by all the consumers of a given good or service.

The Law of Demand

The inverse relationship between the price of a product and the quantity of the product demanded is known as the **law of demand**: holding everything else constant, when the price of a product falls, the quantity demanded of the product will increase, and when the price of a product rises, the quantity demanded of the product will decrease. The law of demand holds for any market demand curve. Economists have never found an exception to it. In fact, Nobel Prize–winning economist George Stigler once remarked that the surest way for an economist to become famous would be to discover a market demand curve that sloped upward rather than downward.

> **Law of demand** The rule that, holding everything else constant, when the price of a product falls, the quantity demanded of the product will increase, and when the price of a product rises, the quantity demanded of the product will decrease.

What Explains the Law of Demand?

It makes sense that consumers will buy more of a good when the price falls and less of a good when the price rises, but let's look more closely at why this is true. When the price of digital music players falls, consumers buy a larger quantity because of the *substitution effect* and the *income effect*.

Substitution Effect The **substitution effect** refers to the change in the quantity demanded of a good that results from a change in price, making the good more or less expensive *relative* to other goods that are *substitutes*. When the price of digital music players falls, consumers will substitute buying music players for buying other goods, such as radios or compact stereos.

> **Substitution effect** The change in the quantity demanded of a good that results from a change in price, making the good more or less expensive relative to other goods that are substitutes.

The Income Effect The **income effect** of a price change refers to the change in the quantity demanded of a good that results from the effect of a change in the good's price on consumers' purchasing power. Purchasing power is the quantity of goods a consumer can buy with a fixed amount of income. When the price of a good falls, the increased purchasing power of consumers' incomes will usually lead them to purchase a larger quantity of the good. When the price of a good rises, the decreased purchasing power of consumers' incomes will usually lead them to purchase a smaller quantity of the good.

> **Income effect** The change in the quantity demanded of a good that results from the effect of a change in the good's price on consumers' purchasing power.

Note that although we can analyze them separately, the substitution effect and the income effect happen simultaneously whenever a price changes. Thus, a fall in the price of digital music players leads consumers to buy more players, both because the players are now cheaper relative to substitute products and because the purchasing power of the consumers' incomes has increased.

Holding Everything Else Constant: The *Ceteris Paribus* Condition

Notice that the definition of the law of demand contains the phrase *holding everything else constant*. In constructing the market demand curve for digital music players, we focused only on the effect that changes in the price of players would have on the quantity of players consumers would be willing and able to buy. We were holding constant other variables that might affect the willingness of consumers to buy players. Economists refer to the necessity of holding all variables other than price constant in constructing a demand curve as the **ceteris paribus** condition; *ceteris paribus* is Latin for all else equal.

What would happen if we allowed a change in a variable—other than price—that might affect the willingness of consumers to buy music players? Consumers would then change the quantity they demand at each price. We can illustrate this effect by shifting the market demand curve. A shift of a demand curve is *an increase or a decrease in demand.* A movement along a demand curve is *an increase or a decrease in the quantity demanded.* As Figure 3-2 shows, we shift the demand curve to the right if consumers decide to buy more of the good at each price, and we shift the demand curve to the left if consumers decide to buy less at each price.

Variables That Shift Market Demand

Many variables other than price can influence market demand. These five are the most important:

- Income
- Prices of related goods
- Tastes
- Population and demographics
- Expected future prices.

We next discuss how changes in each of these variables affect the market demand curve for digital music players.

Ceteris paribus (all else equal)
The requirement that when analyzing the relationship between two variables—such as price and quantity demanded—other variables must be held constant.

Figure 3-2

Shifting the Demand Curve

When consumers increase the quantity of a product they wish to buy at a given price, the market demand curve shifts to the right, from D_1 to D_2. When consumers decrease the quantity of a product they wish to buy at any given price, the demand curve shifts to the left, from D_1 to D_3.

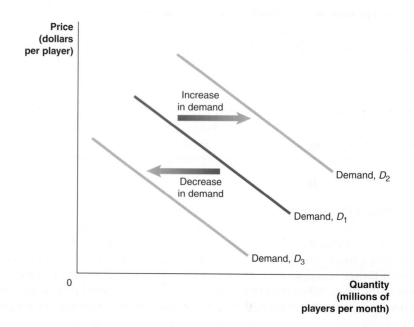

Income The income that consumers have available to spend affects their willingness and ability to buy a good. Suppose that the market demand curve in Figure 3-1 represents the willingness of consumers to buy digital music players when average household income is US$43,000. If household income rises to US$45,000, the demand for players will increase, which we show by shifting the demand curve to the right. A good is a **normal good** when demand increases following a rise in income and decreases following a fall in income. Most goods are normal goods, but the demand for some goods falls when income rises and rises when income falls. For instance, as your income rises, you might buy less canned tuna fish or fewer hot dogs and buy more shrimp or prime rib. A good is an **inferior good** when demand decreases following a rise in income and increases following a fall in income. So, for you hot dogs and tuna fish would be examples of inferior goods—not because they are of low quality but because you buy less of them as your income increases.

Normal good A good for which the demand increases as income rises and decreases as income falls.

Inferior good A good for which the demand increases as income falls and decreases as income rises.

Prices of Related Goods The prices of other goods can also affect consumers' demand for a product. Suppose that the market demand curve in Figure 3-1 represents the willingness and ability of consumers to buy digital music players during a year when the average price of compact stereos, such as the Bose Wave music system, is US$500. If the average price of these stereo systems falls to US$400, how will the market demand for digital music players change? Fewer players will be demanded at every price. We show this by shifting the demand curve for players to the left.

Goods and services that can be used for the same purpose—such as digital music players and compact stereos—are **substitutes**. When two goods are substitutes, the more you buy of one, the less you will buy of the other. A decrease in the price of a substitute causes the demand curve for a good to shift to the left. An increase in the price of a substitute causes the demand curve for a good to shift to the right.

Substitutes Goods and services that can be used for the same purpose.

Many consumers play songs downloaded from a website, such as iTunes or Zune Marketplace, on their digital music players. Suppose the market demand curve in Figure 3-1 represents the willingness of consumers to buy players at a time when the average price to download a song is US$0.99. If the price to download a song falls to US$0.49, consumers will buy more song downloads *and* more digital music players: the demand curve for music players will shift to the right.

Making the Connection | Why Supermarkets Need to Understand Substitutes and Complements

Supermarkets sell what sometimes seems like a bewildering variety of goods. The first row of the following table shows the varieties of eight products stocked by five supermarkets.

	COFFEE	FROZEN PIZZA	HOT DOGS	ICE CREAM	POTATO CHIPS	REGULAR CEREAL	SPAGHETTI SAUCE	YOGURT
Varieties in five supermarkets	391	337	128	421	285	242	194	288
Varieties introduced in a 2-year period	113	109	47	129	93	114	70	107
Varieties removed in a 2-year period	135	86	32	118	77	75	36	51

Source: Juin-Kuan Chong, Teck-Hua Ho, and Christopher S. Tang, "A Modeling Framework for Category Assortment Planning," *Manufacturing & Service Operations Management*, 2001, Vol. 3, No. 3, pp. 191–210.

(Continued)

Supermarkets are also constantly adding new varieties of goods to their shelves and removing old varieties. The second row of the table shows that these five supermarkets added 113 new varieties of coffee over a two-year period, while the third row shows that they eliminated 135 existing varieties. How do supermarkets decide which varieties to add and which to remove?

Christopher Tang is a professor at the Anderson Graduate School of Management at the University of California, Los Angeles (UCLA) in the U.S. In an interview with the *Baltimore Sun*, Tang argues that supermarkets should not necessarily remove the slowest-selling goods from their shelves but should consider the relationships among the goods. In particular, they should consider whether the goods being removed are substitutes or complements with the remaining goods. A lobster bisque soup, for example, could be a relatively slow seller but might be a complement to other soups because it can be used with them to make a sauce. In that case, removing the lobster bisque would hurt sales of some of the remaining soups. Tang suggests the supermarket would be better off removing a slow-selling soup that is a substitute for another soup. For example, the supermarket might want to remove one of two brands of cream of chicken soup.

Source: Lobster bisque example from Lorraine Mirabella, "Shelf Science in Supermarkets," *Baltimore Sun*, March 17, 2002, p. 16.

YOUR TURN: For more practice, do problem 1.5 on page 95 at the end of this chapter.

Complements Goods and services that are used together.

Products that are used together—such as digital music players and song downloads—are **complements**. When two goods are complements, the more consumers buy of one, the more they will buy of the other. A decrease in the price of a complement causes the demand curve for a good to shift to the right. An increase in the price of a complement causes the demand curve for a good to shift to the left.

Tastes Consumers can be influenced by an advertising campaign for a product. If Apple, Microsoft, Toshiba, and other makers of digital music players begin to heavily advertise on television and online, consumers are more likely to buy players at every price, and the demand curve will shift to the right. An economist would say that the advertising campaign has affected consumers' *taste* for digital music players. Taste is a catchall category that refers to the many subjective elements that can enter into a consumer's decision to buy a product. A consumer's taste for a product can change for many reasons. Sometimes trends play a substantial role. For example, the popularity of low-carbohydrate diets caused a decline in demand for some goods, such as bread and donuts, and an increase in demand for beef. In general, when consumers' taste for a product increases, the demand curve will shift to the right, and when consumers' taste for a product decreases, the demand curve for the product will shift to the left.

Demographics The characteristics of a population with respect to age, race, and gender.

Population and Demographics Population and demographic factors can affect the demand for a product. As the population in the Arab world increases, so will the number of consumers, and the demand for most products will increase. The **demographics** of a population refers to its characteristics, with respect to age, race, and gender. As the demographics of a country or region change, the demand for particular goods will increase or decrease because different categories of people tend to have different preferences for those goods. For instance, 65 percent of the Arab world is 30 years of age or younger, increasing the demand for education and jobs and other products heavily used by younger people.

Making the Connection

Google Responds to a Growing Arab World Demand for Internet Navigation by launching Ahlan Online

Internet users in the Arab world have gone up 228 percent from just 16.5 million in 2004 to 56 million in 2010. Egypt witnessed the largest increase (20 percent) followed by Morocco (18 percent) and Saudi Arabia (17 percent). Meanwhile, the UAE has the regions' highest Internet penetration rate with 60 percent of the population online. It is also estimated that the number of personal computers in the Arab world more than doubled in 5 years. Between 2004 and 2009 this number surged from 11 million to 26 million personal computers. Recent statistics shows that 30 percent of the new users online are under the age of 18. The research additionally indicated that top online activities in the region consist of an entertainment and/ or communication element.

Understanding these demographical dynamics, Google responded to the rising demand for basic guidance on net navigation, search tips and more by launching Ahlan Online; catering specifically to new, first-time Arab Internet users. Ahlan Online is an Arabic website that provides Middle Eastern and North African (MENA) users with the necessary skills they need to navigate the Internet using Google tools. The site is designed to provide educational tips and guidance on basic online usage such as Google search, Gmail, Google Talk (chat), and Privacy settings (web safety). It will thus assist new users to rapidly learn the basic Google tools and practices of the Internet. Ahlan Online will continue to be enhanced based on users' feedback and needs, in addition to increasingly providing interactive guidance for a greater number of Google products and applications.

The initial phase for the user-friendly website is designed to focus on the current needs of the region and will cover six topics: browser, search, mail, chat, sharing and collaboration, and privacy. The site is compromised of Arabic language educational videos and simple tutorials; it will allow users to learn the ways of Internet through an interactive lesson in Arabic as well as gain tips on how to navigate across a multitude of Google products especially relevant for new users.

Sources: "Middle East Internet Users Increase to 56 million", Menareport.com, April 21, 2010; and www.google.com/ahlan.

YOUR TURN: For more practice, do problem 1.8 on page 95 at the end of this chapter.

Expected Future Prices Consumers choose not only which products to buy but also when to buy them. If enough consumers become convinced that digital music players will be selling for lower prices three months from now, the demand for players will decrease now, as some consumers postpone their purchases to wait for the expected price decrease. Alternatively, if enough consumers become convinced that the price of players will be higher three months from now, the demand for players will increase now, as some consumers try to beat the expected price increase.

Table 3-1 on page 74 summarizes the most important variables that cause market demand curves to shift. You should note that the table shows the shift in the demand curve that results from an *increase* in each of the variables. A *decrease* in these variables would cause the demand curve to shift in the opposite direction.

TABLE 3-1

Variables That Shift Market Demand Curves

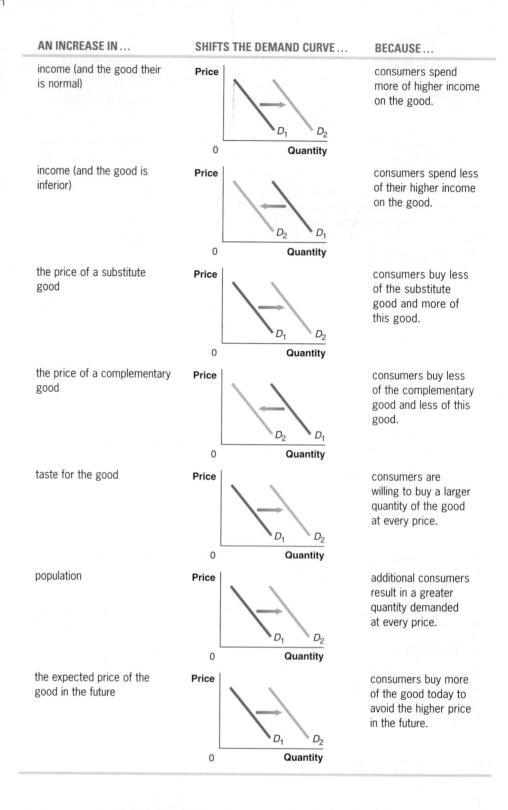

AN INCREASE IN...	SHIFTS THE DEMAND CURVE...	BECAUSE...
income (and the good their is normal)		consumers spend more of higher income on the good.
income (and the good is inferior)		consumers spend less of their higher income on the good.
the price of a substitute good		consumers buy less of the substitute good and more of this good.
the price of a complementary good		consumers buy less of the complementary good and less of this good.
taste for the good		consumers are willing to buy a larger quantity of the good at every price.
population		additional consumers result in a greater quantity demanded at every price.
the expected price of the good in the future		consumers buy more of the good today to avoid the higher price in the future.

A Change in Demand versus a Change in Quantity Demanded

It is important to understand the difference between a *change in demand* and a *change in quantity demanded*. A change in demand refers to a shift of the demand curve. A shift occurs if there is a change in one of the variables, *other than the price of the product*, that affects the willingness of consumers to buy the product. A change in quantity demanded refers to a movement along the demand curve as a result of a change in the product's

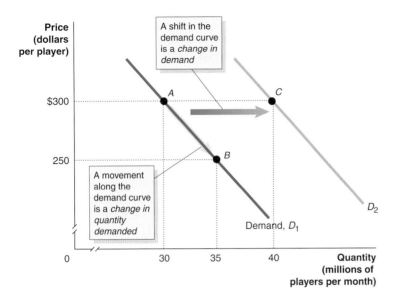

Price (dollars per player)

A shift in the demand curve is a *change in demand*

A movement along the demand curve is a *change in quantity demanded*

Demand, D_1

D_2

Quantity (millions of players per month)

Figure 3-3

A Change in Demand versus a Change in the Quantity Demanded

If the price of digital music players falls from US$300 to US$250, the result will be a movement along the demand curve from point *A* to point *B*—an increase in quantity demanded from 30 million to 35 million. If consumers' income increases, or if another factor changes that makes consumers want more of the product at every price, the demand curve will shift to the right—an increase in demand. In this case, the increase in demand from D_1 to D_2 causes the quantity of players demanded at a price of US$300 to increase from 30 million at point *A* to 40 million at point *C*.

price. Figure 3-3 illustrates this important distinction. If the price of digital music players falls from US$300 to US$250, the result will be a movement along the demand curve from point *A* to point *B*—an increase in quantity demanded from 30 million to 35 million. If consumers' incomes increase, or if another factor changes that makes consumers want more of the product at every price, the demand curve will shift to the right—an increase in demand. In this case, the increase in demand from D_1 to D_2 causes the quantity of digital music players demanded at a price of US$300 to increase from 30 million at point *A* to 40 million at point *C*.

Making the Connection | Apple Forecasts the Demand for iPods and other Consumer Electronics

One of the most important decisions that the managers of any large firm have to make is which new products to develop. A firm must devote people, time, and money to designing the product, negotiating with suppliers, formulating a marketing campaign, and many other tasks. But any firm has only limited resources and so faces a trade-off: resources used to develop one product will not be available to develop another product. Ultimately, the products a firm chooses to develop will be those which it believes will be the most profitable. So, to decide which products to develop, firms need to forecast the demand for those products.

David Sobotta, who worked at Apple for 20 years, eventually becoming its national sales manager, has described the strategy Apple has used to decide which consumer electronics products will have the greatest demand. Sobotta describes discussions at Apple during 2002 about whether to develop a tablet personal computer. A tablet PC is a laptop with a special screen that allows the computer to be controlled with a stylus or pen and that has the capability of converting handwritten input into text. The previous year, Bill Gates, chairman of Microsoft, had predicted that "within five years…[tablet PCs] will be the most popular form of PC sold in America." Representatives of the federal government's National Institutes of Health also urged Apple to develop a tablet PC, arguing that it would be particularly useful to doctors, nurses, and hospitals. Apple's managers then decided not to develop a tablet PC, however, because they believed the technology was too

(Continued)

Will Apple's iPhone match the success of its iPod?

complex for the average computer user and did not believe that the demand from doctors and nurses would be very large. Despite Bill Gates's prediction, in 2006, tablets made up only 1 percent of the computer market. Apple decided to pursue the project later on.

According to Sobotta, "Apple executives had a theory that the route to success will not be through selling thousands of relatively expensive things, but millions of very inexpensive things like iPods." In fact, although many business analysts were skeptical that the iPod would succeed, demand grew faster than even Apple's most optimistic forecasts. By the beginning of 2007, 100 million iPods had been sold. So, it was not very surprising when in early 2007, Apple Chief Executive Officer Steve Jobs announced that the company would be combining the iPod with a cellphone to create the iPhone. With more than 900 million cellphones sold each year, Apple expects the demand for the iPhone to be very large. As Sobotta noted, "And there's an 'Apple gap': mobile phone users often find their interfaces confusing.... Apple's unique ability to simplify while innovating looks like a good fit there."

Upon the release of the new gadget, Apple forecasted that it would sell 10 million iPhones during the product's first year on the market, with much larger sales expected in future years. Again, time proved that Apple's forecast of a large demand for the iPhone turned out to be correct. In April 2010, Steve Jobs announced that the company was able to sell over 50 million iPhones as of that date.

Sources: David Sobotta, "Technology: What Jobs Told Me on the iPhone," *The Guardian* (London), January 4, 2007, p. 1; Connie Guglielmo, "Apple First-Quarter Profit Rises on iPod, Mac Sales," Bloomberg.com, January 17, 2007; and www.apple.com, April 20, 2010.

YOUR TURN: For more practice, do problem 1.10 on page 96 at the end of this chapter.

3.2 LEARNING OBJECTIVE

3.2 | Discuss the variables that influence supply.

The Supply Side of the Market

Just as many variables influence the willingness and ability of consumers to buy a particular good or service, many variables also influence the willingness and ability of firms to sell a good or service. The most important of these variables is price. The amount of a good or service that a firm is willing and able to supply at a given price is the **quantity supplied**. Holding other variables constant, when the price of a good rises, producing the good is more profitable, and the quantity supplied will increase. When the price of a good falls, the good is less profitable, and the quantity supplied will decrease. In addition, as we saw in Chapter 2, devoting more and more resources to the production of a good results in increasing marginal costs. So, if, for example, Apple, Microsoft, and Toshiba increase production of digital music players during a given time period, they are likely to find that the cost of producing the additional players increases as they run existing factories for longer hours and pay higher prices for components and higher wages for workers. With higher marginal costs, firms will supply a larger quantity only if the price is higher.

Quantity supplied The amount of a good or service that a firm is willing and able to supply at a given price.

Supply Schedules and Supply Curves

A **supply schedule** is a table that shows the relationship between the price of a product and the quantity of the product supplied. The table in Figure 3-4 is a supply schedule showing the quantity of digital music players that firms would be willing to supply per month at different prices. The graph in Figure 3-4 plots the numbers from the supply

Supply schedule A table that shows the relationship between the price of a product and the quantity of the product supplied.

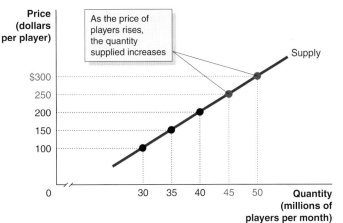

Supply Schedule	
Price (dollars per player)	Quantity (millions of players per month)
$300	50
250	45
200	40
150	35
100	30

As the price of players rises, the quantity supplied increases

Figure 3-4

Supply Schedule and Supply Curve

As the price changes, Apple, Microsoft, Toshiba, and the other firms producing digital music players change the quantity they are willing to supply. We can show this as a *supply schedule* in a table or as a *supply curve* on a graph. The supply schedule and supply curve both show that as the price of players rises, firms will increase the quantity they supply. At a price of US$250, firms will supply 45 million players. At a price of US$300 per player, firms will supply 50 million players.

schedule as a *supply curve*. A **supply curve** shows the relationship between the price of a product and the quantity of the product supplied. The supply schedule and supply curve both show that as the price of players rises, firms will increase the quantity they supply. At a price of US$250 per player, firms will supply 45 million players per year. At the higher price of US$300, they will supply 50 million. (Once again, we are assuming for convenience that the supply curve is a straight line, even though not all supply curves are actually straight lines.)

Supply curve A curve that shows the relationship between the price of a product and the quantity of the product supplied.

The Law of Supply

The *market supply curve* in Figure 3-4 is upward sloping. We expect most supply curves to be upward sloping according to the **law of supply**, which states that, holding everything else constant, increases in price cause increases in the quantity supplied, and decreases in price cause decreases in the quantity supplied. Notice that the definition of the law of supply—like the definition of the law of demand—contains the phrase *holding everything else constant*. If only the price of the product changes, there is a movement along the supply curve, which is *an increase or a decrease in the quantity supplied*. As Figure 3-5 shows, if any other variable that affects the willingness of firms to supply a good changes, the supply curve will shift, which is *an increase or decrease in supply*. When

Law of supply The rule that, holding everything else constant, increases in price cause increases in the quantity supplied, and decreases in price cause decreases in the quantity supplied.

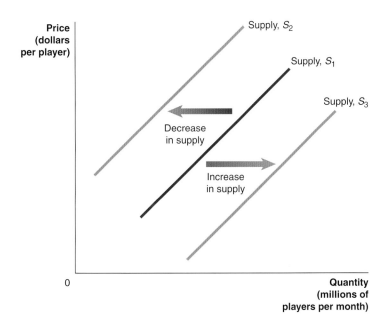

Figure 3-5

Shifting the Supply Curve

When firms increase the quantity of a product they wish to sell at a given price, the supply curve shifts to the right. The shift from S_1 to S_3 represents an *increase in supply*. When firms decrease the quantity of a product they wish to sell at a given price, the supply curve shifts to the left. The shift from S_1 to S_2 represents a *decrease in supply*.

firms increase the quantity of a product they wish to sell at a given price, the supply curve shifts to the right. The shift from S_1 to S_3 represents *an increase in supply*. When firms decrease the quantity of a product they wish to sell at a given price, the supply curve shifts to the left. The shift from S_1 to S_2 represents *a decrease in supply*.

Variables That Shift Supply

The following are the most important variables that shift supply:

- Prices of inputs
- Technological change
- Prices of substitutes in production
- Number of firms in the market
- Expected future prices.

We next discuss how each of these variables affects the supply of digital music players.

Prices of Inputs The factor most likely to cause the supply curve for a product to shift is a change in the price of an *input*. An input is anything used in the production of a good or service. For instance, if the price of a component of digital music players, such as the microprocessor, rises, the cost of producing music players will increase, and players will be less profitable at every price. The supply of players will decline, and the market supply curve for players will shift to the left. Similarly, if the price of an input declines, the supply of players will increase, and the supply curve will shift to the right.

Technological change A positive or negative change in the ability of a firm to produce a given level of output with a given quantity of inputs.

Technological Change A second factor that causes a change in supply is *technological change*. **Technological change** is a positive or negative change in the ability of a firm to produce a given level of output with a given quantity of inputs. Positive technological change occurs whenever a firm is able to produce more output using the same amount of inputs. This shift will happen when the *productivity* of workers or machines increases. If a firm can produce more output with the same amount of inputs, its costs will be lower, and the good will be more profitable to produce at any given price. As a result, when positive technological change occurs, the firm will increase the quantity supplied at every price, and its supply curve will shift to the right. Normally, we expect technological change to have a positive impact on a firm's willingness to supply a product. Negative technological change is relatively rare, although it could result from a natural disaster or a war that reduces the ability of a firm to supply as much output with a given amount of inputs. Negative technological change will raise a firm's costs, and the good will be less profitable to produce. Therefore, negative technological change causes a firm's supply curve to shift to the left.

Prices of Substitutes in Production Firms often choose which good or service they will produce. Alternative products that a firm could produce are called *substitutes in production*. To this point, we have considered the market for all types of digital music players. But suppose we now consider separate markets for music players with screens capable of showing videos and for smaller players, without screens, that play only music. If the price of video music players increases, video music players will become more profitable, and Apple, Microsoft, and the other companies making music players will shift some of their productive capacity away from smaller players and toward video players. The companies will offer fewer smaller players for sale at every price, so the supply curve for smaller players will shift to the left.

Number of Firms in the Market A change in the number of firms in the market will change supply. When new firms *enter* a market, the supply curve shifts to the right, and when existing firms leave, or *exit*, a market, the supply curve for digital music players shifts to the left. For instance, when Microsoft introduced the Zune, the market supply curve for digital music players shifted to the right.

Expected Future Prices If a firm expects that the price of its product will be higher in the future than it is today, it has an incentive to decrease supply now and increase it in the future. For instance, if Apple believes that prices for digital music players are temporarily low—perhaps because of a price war among firms making players—it may store some of its production today to sell tomorrow, when it expects prices will be higher.

Table 3-2 summarizes the most important variables that cause market supply curves to shift. You should note that the table shows the shift in the supply curve that results from an *increase* in each of the variables. A *decrease* in these variables would cause the supply curve to shift in the opposite direction.

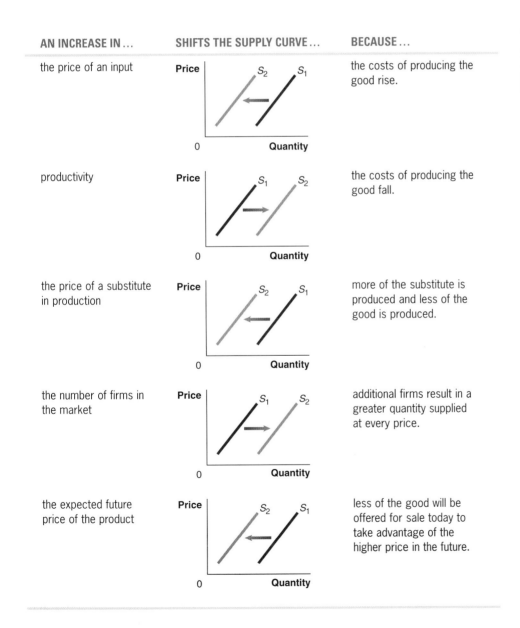

AN INCREASE IN...	SHIFTS THE SUPPLY CURVE...	BECAUSE...
the price of an input		the costs of producing the good rise.
productivity		the costs of producing the good fall.
the price of a substitute in production		more of the substitute is produced and less of the good is produced.
the number of firms in the market		additional firms result in a greater quantity supplied at every price.
the expected future price of the product		less of the good will be offered for sale today to take advantage of the higher price in the future.

TABLE 3-2

Variables That Shift Market Supply Curve

Figure 3-6

A Change in Supply versus a Change in the Quantity Supplied

If the price of digital music players rises from US$200 to US$250, the result will be a movement up the supply curve from point *A* to point *B*—an increase in quantity supplied by Apple, Microsoft, and Toshiba and the other firms from 40 million to 45 million. If the price of an input decreases or another factor changes that makes sellers supply more of the product at every price, the supply curve will shift to the right—an increase in supply. In this case, the increase in supply from s_1 to s_2 causes the quantity of digital music players supplied at a price of US$250 to increase from 45 million at point *b* to 55 million at point *C*.

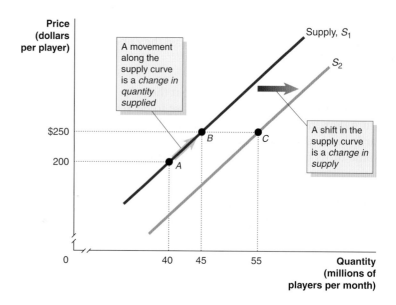

A Change in Supply versus a Change in Quantity Supplied

We noted earlier the important difference between a change in demand and a change in quantity demanded. There is a similar difference between a *change in supply* and a *change in quantity supplied*. A change in supply refers to a shift of the supply curve. The supply curve will shift when there is a change in one of the variables, *other than the price of the product*, that affects the willingness of suppliers to sell the product. A change in quantity supplied refers to a movement along the supply curve as a result of a change in the product's price. Figure 3-6 illustrates this important distinction. If the price of music players rises from US$200 to US$250, the result will be a movement up the supply curve from point *A* to point *B*—an increase in quantity supplied from 40 million to 45 million. If the price of an input decreases or another factor makes sellers supply more of the product at every price change, the supply curve will shift to the right—an increase in supply. In this case, the increase in supply from S_1 to S_2 causes the quantity of digital music players supplied at a price of US$250 to increase from 45 million at point *B* to 55 million at point *C*.

3.3 LEARNING OBJECTIVE   3.3 | Use a graph to illustrate market equilibrium.

Market Equilibrium: Putting Demand and Supply Together

The purpose of markets is to bring buyers and sellers together. As we saw in Chapter 2, instead of being chaotic and disorderly, the interaction of buyers and sellers in markets ultimately results in firms being led to produce those goods and services consumers desire most. To understand how this process happens, we first need to see how markets work to reconcile the plans of buyers and sellers.

In Figure 3-7, we bring together the market demand curve for digital music players and the market supply curve. Notice that the demand curve crosses the supply curve at only one point. This point represents a price of US$200 and a quantity of 40 million players. Only at this point is the quantity of players consumers are willing to buy equal to the quantity of players firms are willing to sell. This is the point of **market equilibrium**. Only at market equilibrium will the quantity demanded equal the quantity supplied. In this case, the *equilibrium price* is US$200, and the *equilibrium quantity* is 40 million. As we noted at the beginning of the chapter, markets that

Market equilibrium A situation in which quantity demanded equals quantity supplied.

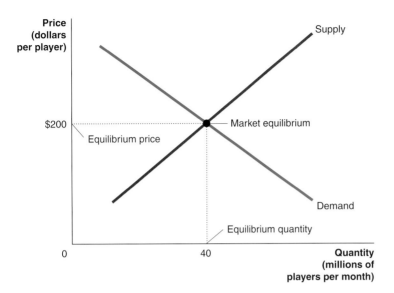

Figure 3-7

Market Equilibrium

Where the demand curve crosses the supply curve determines market equilibrium. In this case, the demand curve for digital music players crosses the supply curve at a price of US$200 and a quantity of 40 million. Only at this point is the quantity of players consumers are willing to buy equal to the quantity of players Apple, Microsoft, Toshiba, and the other firms are willing to sell: The quantity demanded is equal to the quantity supplied.

have many buyers and many sellers are competitive markets, and equilibrium in these markets is a **competitive market equilibrium**. In the market for digital music players, there are many buyers but fewer than 20 firms. Whether 20 firms is enough for our model of demand and supply to apply to this market is a matter of judgment. In this chapter, we are assuming that the market for digital music players has enough sellers to be competitive.

Competitive market equilibrium A market equilibrium with many buyers and many sellers.

How Markets Eliminate Surpluses and Shortages

A market that is not in equilibrium moves toward equilibrium. Once a market is in equilibrium, it remains in equilibrium. To see why, consider what happens if a market is not in equilibrium. For instance, suppose that the price in the market for digital music players was US$250, rather than the equilibrium price of US$200. As Figure 3-8 shows, at a price of US$250, the quantity of players supplied would be 45 million, and the quantity of players demanded would be 35 million. When the quantity supplied is greater than the quantity demanded, there is a **surplus** in the market. In this case, the surplus is equal to 10 million players (45 million − 35 million = 10 million). When

Surplus A situation in which the quantity supplied is greater than the quantity demanded.

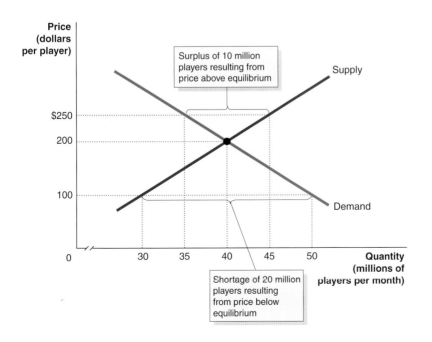

Figure 3-8

The Effect of Surpluses and Shortages on the Market Price

When the market price is above equilibrium, there will be a *surplus*. In the figure, a price of US$250 for digital music players results in 45 million being supplied but only 35 million being demanded, or a surplus of 10 million. As Apple, Microsoft, Toshiba, and the other firms cut the price to dispose of the surplus, the price will fall to the equilibrium of US$200. When the market price is below equilibrium, there will be a *shortage*. A price of US$100 results in 50 million players being demanded but only 30 million being supplied, or a shortage of 20 million. As consumers who are unable to buy a player offer to pay higher prices, the price will rise to the equilibrium of US$200.

there is a surplus, firms have unsold goods piling up, which gives them an incentive to increase their sales by cutting the price. Cutting the price will simultaneously increase the quantity demanded and decrease the quantity supplied. This adjustment will reduce the surplus, but as long as the price is above US$200, there will be a surplus, and downward pressure on the price will continue. Only when the price has fallen to US$200 will the market be in equilibrium.

Shortage A situation in which the quantity demanded is greater than the quantity supplied.

If, however, the price were US$100, the quantity supplied would be 30 million, and the quantity demanded would be 50 million, as shown in Figure 3-8. When the quantity demanded is greater than the quantity supplied, there is a **shortage** in the market. In this case, the shortage is equal to 20 million digital music players (50 million − 30 million = 20 million). When a shortage occurs, some consumers will be unable to buy a digital music player at the current price. In this situation, firms will realize that they can raise the price without losing sales. A higher price will simultaneously increase the quantity supplied and decrease the quantity demanded. This adjustment will reduce the shortage, but as long as the price is below US$200, there will be a shortage, and upward pressure on the price will continue. Only when the price has risen to US$200 will the market be in equilibrium.

At a competitive market equilibrium, all consumers willing to pay the market price will be able to buy as much of the product as they want, and all firms willing to accept the market price will be able to sell as much of the product as they want. As a result, there will be no reason for the price to change unless either the demand curve or the supply curve shifts.

Demand and Supply Both Count

Always keep in mind that it is the interaction of demand and supply that determines the equilibrium price. Neither consumers nor firms can dictate what the equilibrium price will be. No firm can sell anything at any price unless it can find a willing buyer, and no consumer can buy anything at any price without finding a willing seller.

Solved Problem | 3-3

Demand and Supply Both Count:
A Tale of Two Metals

If you were to visit a Damas store in Dubai, you may notice that the setting of a diamond ring can be made of platinum or gold. If you were thinking of buying one, you may wonder which ring is likely to be worth more: a ring made of platinum or one made of gold? As you may already know, a platinum setting will cost you more. Both gold and platinum have superior qualities and beauty that put them top of the list of the metals used in the jewelry industry. But, gold traditionally constitutes most of jewelry trading, especially in India and the Arab world. The demand for gold rings would seem to be much greater than the demand for platinum rings. Yet, when you look at the spot market prices (as of April 30, 2010) you find that an ounce of platinum is worth US$1,737, while an ounce of gold is sold for only US$1,177.

Use a demand and supply graph to explain how platinum has a higher market price than gold, even though the

worldwide demand for gold (around 3,385 tons) is greater than the demand for platinum (around 220 tons).

Demand for gold is greater than that of platinum, but platinum still has a higher market price because the supply of gold is greater.

SOLVING THE PROBLEM:

Step 1: **Review the chapter material.** This problem is about prices being determined at market equilibrium, so you may want to review the section "Market Equilibrium: Putting Demand and Supply Together," which begins on page 80.

Step 2: **Draw demand curves that illustrate the greater demand for gold.** Begin by drawing two demand curves. Label one "Demand for gold" and the other "Demand for platinum." Make sure that the gold demand curve is much farther to the right than the platinum demand curve.

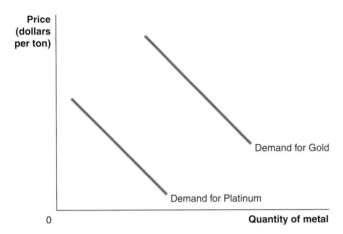

Step 3: **Draw supply curves that illustrate the equilibrium price of platinum being higher than the equilibrium price of gold.** Based on the demand curves you have just drawn, think about how it might be possible for the market price of gold to be lower than the market price of platinum. The only way this can be true is if the supply of gold is much greater than the supply of platinum. Draw on your graph a supply curve for gold and a supply curve for platinum that will result in an equilibrium price of platinum of US$1,737 and an equilibrium price of gold of US$1,177. You have now solved the problem.

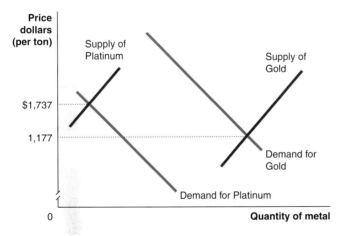

EXTRA CREDIT: The explanation for this puzzle is that both demand and supply count when determining market price. The demand for gold is much greater than the demand for platinum, but platinum is very rare and its supply is very small. Geologists believe that all the platinum ever mined would fill a room measuring less than 25 feet on each side. The 'above-the-ground' platinum supplies would last about a year. This compares with an above-the-ground supply of about 25 years for gold. Note that the supply curves for platinum and gold slope up even though only a fixed quantity of each is available in nature. The upward slope of the supply curves occurs because the higher the price, the larger the quantity mined (newly extracted) of both metals and the quantity that will be offered for sale by people who currently own them.

>> **End Solved Problem 3-3**

YOUR TURN: For more practice, do related problem 3.4 on page 96 at the end of this chapter.

3.4 LEARNING OBJECTIVE

3.4 | Use demand and supply graphs to predict changes in prices and quantities.

The Effect of Demand and Supply Shifts on Equilibrium

We have seen that the interaction of demand and supply in markets determines the quantity of a good that is produced and the price at which it sells. We have also seen that several variables cause demand curves to shift, and other variables cause supply curves to shift. As a result, demand and supply curves in most markets are constantly shifting, and the prices and quantities that represent equilibrium are constantly changing. In this section, we see how shifts in demand and supply curves affect equilibrium price and quantity.

The Effect of Shifts in Supply on Equilibrium

When Microsoft decided to start selling the Zune music player, the market supply curve for music players shifted to the right. Figure 3-9 shows the supply curve shifting from S_1 to S_2. When the supply curve shifts to the right, there will be a surplus at the original equilibrium price, P_1. The surplus is eliminated as the equilibrium price falls to P_2, and the equilibrium quantity rises from Q_1 to Q_2. If existing firms exit the market, the supply curve will shift to the left, causing the equilibrium price to rise and the equilibrium quantity to fall.

Figure 3-9

The Effect of an Increase in Supply on Equilibrium

If a firm enters a market, as Microsoft entered the market for digital music players when it launched the Zune, the equilibrium price will fall, and the equilibrium quantity will rise.

1. As Microsoft enters the market for digital music players, a larger quantity of players will be supplied at every price, so the market supply curve shifts to the right, from S_1 to S_2, which causes a surplus of players at the original price, P_1.
2. The equilibrium price falls from P_1 to P_2.
3. The equilibrium quantity rises from Q_1 to Q_2.

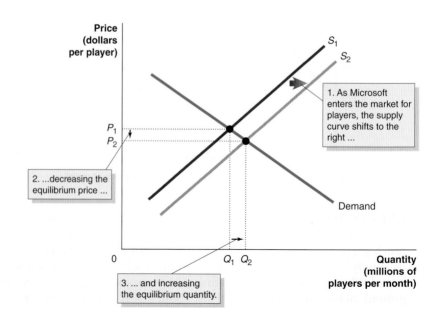

Making the Connection

The Falling Price of LCD Televisions

Research on flat-screen televisions using liquid crystal displays (LCDs) began in the 1960s. However, it was surprisingly difficult to use this research to produce a television priced low enough for many consumers to purchase. One researcher noted, "In the 1960s, we used to say 'In ten years, we're going to have the TV on the wall.' We said the same thing in the seventies and then in the eighties." A key technical problem in manufacturing LCD televisions was making glass sheets large enough, thin enough, and clean enough to be used as LCD screens. Finally, in 1999, Corning, Inc. developed a process to manufacture glass that was less than 1 millimeter thick and very clean because it was produced without being touched by machinery.

Corning's breakthrough led to what the *Wall Street Journal* described as a "race to build new, better factories." The firms producing the flat screens are all located in Taiwan, South Korea, and Japan. The leading firms are Korea's Samsung Electronics and LG Phillips LCD, Taiwan's AU Optronics, and Japan's Sharp Corporation. In 2004, AU Optronics opened a new factory with 2.4 million square feet of clean room in which the LCD screens are manufactured. This factory is nearly five times as large as the largest factory in which Intel makes computer chips. In all, 10 new factories manufacturing LCD screens came into operation between late 2004 and late 2005. The figure shows that this increase in supply drove the price of a typical large LCD television from US$4,000 in the fall of 2004 to US$1,600 at the end of 2006, increasing the quantity demanded worldwide from 8 million to 46 million.

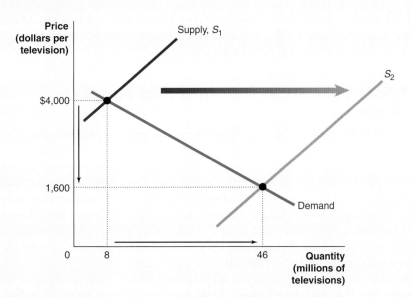

Sources: David Richards, "Sony and Panasonic Flat Screen Kings," Smarthouse.com, February 13, 2007; Evan Ramstad, "Big Display: Once a Footnote, Flat Screens Grow into Huge Industry," *Wall Street Journal*, August 30, 2004, p. A1; and Michael Schuman, "Flat Chance: Prices on Cool TVs Are Dropping as New Factories Come on Line," *Time*, October 18, 2004, pp. 64–66.

YOUR TURN: For more practice, do problem 4.6 on page 97 at the end of this chapter.

Figure 3-10

The Effect of an Increase in Demand on Equilibrium

Increases in income and population will cause the equilibrium price and quantity to rise:

1. As population and income grow, the quantity demanded increases at every price, and the market demand curve shifts to the right, from D_1 to D_2, which causes a shortage of digital music players at the original price, P_1.
2. The equilibrium price rises from P_1 to P_2.
3. The equilibrium quantity rises from Q_1 to Q_2.

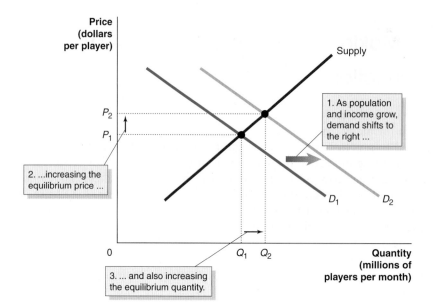

The Effect of Shifts in Demand on Equilibrium

When population growth and income growth occur, the market demand for music players shifts to the right. Figure 3-10 shows the effect of a demand curve shifting to the right, from D_1 to D_2. This shift causes a shortage at the original equilibrium price, P_1. To eliminate the shortage, the equilibrium price rises to P_2, and the equilibrium quantity rises from Q_1 to Q_2. By contrast, if the price of a complementary good, such as downloads from music websites, were to rise, the demand for music players would decrease. This change would cause the demand curve for players to shift to the left, and the equilibrium price and quantity would both decrease.

The Effect of Shifts in Demand and Supply over Time

Whenever only demand or only supply shifts, we can easily predict the effect on equilibrium price and quantity. But what happens if *both* curves shift? For instance, in many markets, the demand curve shifts to the right over time, as population and income grow. The supply curve also often shifts to the right as new firms enter the market and positive technological change occurs. Whether the equilibrium price in a market rises or falls over time depends on whether demand shifts to the right more than does supply. Panel (a) of Figure 3-11 shows that when demand shifts to the right more than supply, the equilibrium price rises. But, as panel (b) shows, when supply shifts to the right more than demand, the equilibrium price falls.

Table 3-3 on page 87 summarizes all possible combinations of shifts in demand and supply over time and the effects of the shifts on equilibrium price (*P*) and quantity (*Q*). For example, the entry in red in the table shows that if the demand curve shifts to the right and the supply curve also shifts to the right, then the equilibrium quantity will increase, while the equilibrium price may increase, decrease, or remain unchanged. To make sure you understand each entry in the table, draw demand and supply graphs to check whether you can reproduce the predicted changes in equilibrium price and quantity. If the entry in the table says the predicted change in equilibrium price or quantity can be either an increase or a decrease, draw two graphs similar to panels (a) and (b) of Figure 3-11, one showing the equilibrium price or quantity increasing and the other showing it decreasing. Note also that in the ambiguous cases where either price or quantity might increase or decrease, it is also possible that price or quantity might remain unchanged. Be sure you understand why this is true.

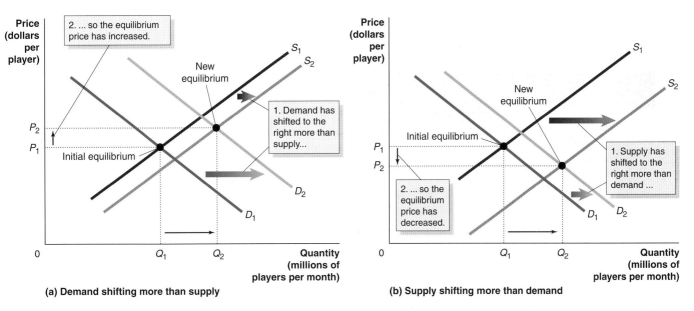

Figure 3-11 | Shifts in Demand and Supply over Time

Whether the price of a product rises or falls over time depends on whether demand shifts to the right more than supply.

In panel (a), demand shifts to the right more than supply, and the equilibrium price rises.
1. Demand shifts to the right more than supply.
2. Equilibrium price rises from P_1 to P_2.

In panel (b), supply shifts to the right more than demand, and the equilibrium price falls.
1. Supply shifts to the right more than demand.
2. Equilibrium price falls from P_1 to P_2

	SUPPLY CURVE UNCHANGED	SUPPLY CURVE SHIFTS TO THE RIGHT	SUPPLY CURVE SHIFTS TO THE LEFT	**TABLE 3-3**
DEMAND CURVE UNCHANGED	Q unchanged P unchanged	Q increases P decreases	Q decreases P increases	**How Shifts in Demand and Supply Affect Equilibrium Price (P) and Quantity (Q)**
DEMAND CURVE SHIFTS TO THE RIGHT	Q increases P increases	Q increases P increases or decreases	Q increases or decreases P increases	
DEMAND CURVE SHIFTS TO THE LEFT	Q decreases P decreases	Q increases or decreases P decreases	Q decreases P decreases or decreases	

Making the Connection

Global Fashion Trends Reveals a Growing Demand for Arabian Styles

After a growing acceptance and support from top global fashion icons, according to the French Fashion University Esmod Dubai, a leading fashion institute in the Arab world, the Arab fashion industry is set to broaden its global appeal. The international Muslim fashion industry has a potential market estimated at more than US$96 billion, based on estimates of international

(Continued)

demand by the world's 1.6 billion Muslims. Consumers in non-Muslim fashion-conscious countries, such as France and the U.K., are estimated to spend more than US$600 a year on high-end clothing. In the U.K. alone, there are more than 1.5 million Muslims, so the market for Muslim fashion could be worth somewhere between US$90 to 150 million a year. In some Gulf countries, such as the United Arab Emirates and Qatar, Arabian outfits can sell for as much as US$10,000. A Dubai-based company is known to sell abayas costing between US$1,500 and 10,000. A client that spends at least US$6,500 or more is given the privilege of acquiring a copyright for her personal abaya design!

Esmod Dubai can see Arabian styles steadily influencing European fashion in a way that shows the potential of this emerging global market. Aside from abayas, designers are also introducing dramatic new styles, fabrics, and colors to Islamic-Arab dresses. For instance, a British designer offers an outfit that combines a hooded abaya with a matching niqab (face veil) in an eye-catching pink over loose pants, as part of her Imaan Collections. High-end designers such as Hermes and Gucci are also trying to break into the Muslim market with scarves and other products designed to appeal to Arab tastes.

Celebrity designers such as Christian Lacroix have been integrating Arabic styles into their wardrobes as they are intrigued by the emphasis given to the design rather than the body. A new generation of highly talented Arab designers is expected to continue to impress the fashion world with their fusion of modern and Muslim-inspired elements in their ensembles. Their works reflect the transition from plain and simple Arabic designs to more sophisticated creations. The 'Arabian Fashion World,' an event held in London in 2010, affirmed the vivid growth of a global Muslim fashion industry through the impressive collections of five acclaimed Arab designers from Saudi Arabia, Lebanon, the UAE, Morocco, and Jordan.

The Arab fashion industry is set to broaden its global appeal

Source: "Global fashion trends reveal growing influence of Arabic style", *AME Info*, February 28 2010, www.ameinfo.com/225284.html.

Solved Problem | 3-4

Low Demand and High Prices in the Saudi Fresh Poultry Market?

As many immigrant labor and nationals Flee the heat, demand for poultry drops in the summer. However, Saudi poultry farms are able to sell fresh whole chickens for US$4.50 per kilo. During winter and fall, when demand for poultry meat is much higher, poultry farms are able to sell their home-grown chickens for only about US$3.00 per kilo. It may seem strange that the market price is higher when demand is low than when demand is high. Can you resolve this paradox with the help of a demand and supply graph?

SOLVING THE PROBLEM:

Step 1: **Review the chapter material.** This problem is about how shifts in demand and supply curves affect the equilibrium price, so you may want to review the section "The Effect of Shifts in Demand and Supply over Time," which begins on page 86.

Step 2: **Draw the demand and supply graph.** Draw a demand and supply graph, showing the market equilibrium in the summer. Label the equilibrium price US$4.50. Label both the demand and supply curves "summer."

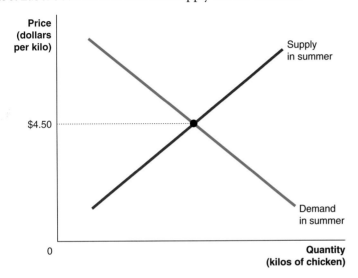

Step 3: **Add to your graph a demand curve for winter.**

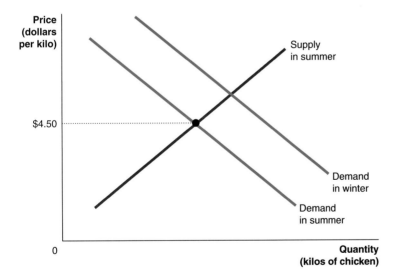

Step 4: **Explain the graph.** After studying the graph, it is possible to see how the equilibrium price can fall from US$4.50 to US$3.00, despite the increase in demand: The supply curve must have shifted to the right by enough to cause the equilibrium price to fall to US$3.00. Draw the new supply curve, label it "winter," and label the new equilibrium price US$3.00. The demand for chicken does increase in winter compared with the summer. But the increase in the supply of chicken between summer and winter is even greater. So, the equilibrium price falls.

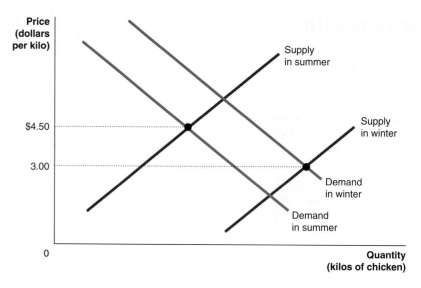

>> End Solved Problem 3-4

YOUR TURN: For more practice, do related problem 4.4 on page 97 at the end of this chapter.

Shifts in a Curve versus Movements along a Curve

When analyzing markets using demand and supply curves, it is important to remember that *when a shift in a demand or supply curve causes a change in equilibrium price, the change in price does not cause a further shift in demand or supply.* For instance, suppose an increase in supply causes the price of a good to fall, while everything else that affects the willingness of consumers to buy the good is constant. The result will be an increase in the quantity demanded but not an increase in demand. For demand to increase, the whole curve must shift. The point is the same for supply: If the price of the good falls but everything else that affects the willingness of sellers to supply the good is constant, the quantity supplied decreases, but the supply does not. For supply to decrease, the whole curve must shift.

Economics in YOUR Life!

>> Continued from page 67

At the beginning of the chapter, we asked you to consider two questions: would you choose to buy a Zune if it had a lower price than a comparable iPod? and would you choose a Zune if the songs sold on Zune Marketplace were cheaper than the songs sold on iTunes? To determine the answers, you have to recognize that iPods and Zunes are substitutes, while Zunes and songs sold on Zune Marketplace are complements. If a Zune had a lower price than an iPod, this would cause consumers to purchase the Zune rather than the iPod, provided that the two players have the same features. If consumers believe that the Zune and the iPod are very close substitutes, a fall in the price of Zunes would cause the demand for iPods to decline, as the quantity of Zunes demanded increased. If Microsoft reduced the price of a song sold on Zune Marketplace so that it was lower than the price of the same song on iTunes, even if iPods and Zunes had the same price, the demand for Zunes would increase, and the demand for iPods would decrease.

Conclusion

The interaction of demand and supply determines market equilibrium. The model of demand and supply provides us with a powerful tool for predicting how changes in the actions of consumers and firms will cause changes in equilibrium prices and quantities. As we have seen in this chapter, the model can often be used to analyze markets that do not meet all the requirements for being perfectly competitive. As long as there is intense competition among sellers, the model of demand and supply can often successfully predict changes in prices and quantities. We will use the model in the next chapter to analyze economic efficiency and the results of government-imposed price floors and price ceilings. Before moving on, read *An Inside Look* on the next page to learn how international oil prices are determined by the interaction of both the supply and the demand sides of the market.

Supply and Demand Determines International Oil Prices

FINANCIAL TIMES, MARCH 16, 2010

'Perfect' Oil Price Hides Divisions within OPEC

The OPEC oil cartel's catchphrase for its meeting in Vienna tomorrow appears to be: "Why mess with perfection?" However, beneath the surface a dispute is simmering as some members grab market share by flouting their promises to make production cuts.

At about US$80 a barrel, oil prices are where the group's 12 members want them to be, allowing most producing countries to meet their national budgets. Prices are also low enough to allow the world's economies to recover, OPEC argues. Ali Naimi, Saudi Arabia's powerful oil minister, said recently: "The producer is looking at this price, the consumer is looking at the price, the investor is looking at the price, and everybody is saying this is great." Many of Mr Naimi's counterparts from other OPEC countries agree.

Over the past week countries including Qatar, Libya, Ecuador, and Iran have advocated that the cartel keep its production ceiling unchanged.

The group will make its formal decision tomorrow. Most analysts agree that OPEC is sitting pretty. "All of the monthly market reports, on average, painted a positive picture of global oil demand for 2010, which in our view would leave OPEC ministers in a fairly relaxed mood ahead of their meeting," said analysts at Barclays Capital.

But as prices have risen—from a low of about US$32 a barrel in December 2008 to more than US$83 last week—so has cheating. OPEC's compliance rate with the production cuts pledged in December 2008 has slipped to about 50 percent from a high of 80 percent. Angola has enacted none of the cuts it should, while Iran is pumping more than 400,000 barrels a day above its quota maximum. Iran, Angola, Nigeria, and Venezuela have become the group's biggest cheats, while Saudi Arabia, Kuwait, and the UAE have maintained compliance of more than 75 percent.

Some analysts and traders note that despite recent upward revisions in demand—especially from China—markets remain oversupplied and OPEC faces some risk that prices will fall this year. They argue that government stimulus packages are coming to an end and limits on energy trading by banks and hedge funds, which U.S. regulators unveiled in January, may reduce the speculation that helped boost prices last year.

Some OPEC members are paying little attention and instead renewing longstanding calls to be allowed officially to pump more oil. So far the group has been able to gloss over its differences. But that is about to change. Iraq, long exempt from OPEC's quota system because its industry has been stunted by war and sanctions, is now at the point of making a return. Baghdad has signed multiple contracts with international oil companies and could add several million barrels of supply to markets in coming years. Even with global annual oil demand forecasts returning to about the 2 percent growth the industry has been used to, so much oil would swamp the market, say traders.

Source: Carola Hoyos, "'Perfect' Oil Price Hides Divisions within OPEC," *Financial Times*, March 16, 2010.

Key Points in the Article

The article discusses how world oil prices are determined by both supply and demand factors. It argues that while oil prices are rebounding from the recent 2008/2009 global crisis that led to weak world demand, OPEC countries' incentive to cheat by producing more oil beyond their allotted quotas also increases. This behavior by some OPEC countries, such as Angola, Iran, Nigeria, and Venezuela, coupled with a growing supply in Iraq, can send oil prices plunging back to historical lows, despite a recovering steady growth in demand.

Analyzing the News

(a) Oil prices reached historical highs in July 2008, hitting a record of US$147 per barrel. Two month latter they crashed amid the global financial crisis, to reach US$32 a barrel. Since the end of 2008, oil prices have been steadily rebounding to hover around US$83 in the first quarter of 2010. The current level of price is considered low enough to stimulate higher world growth rates, which will translate to larger future demand for oil. Meanwhile, the price is adequate to finance oil-producing countries' budgets. So, some OPEC producers are calling for keeping current production ceilings unchanged, in order not to 'mess' with a 'perfect' price.

(b) At every meeting, OPEC members revise the production ceiling they set for the cartel's producers in order to ensure satisfying market demand and meanwhile reduce the instability in oil prices. When demand is high this ceiling is usually increased, cooling down prices. When a recession is looming, like the recent global one, the ceiling is reduced so that the market does not become over-supplied. This action reduces oil surpluses and prevents prices from free falling. This mechanism stays strong when OPEC countries hold on to the ceiling and the production quotas assigned to each of them. When compliance rates are low and many OPEC countries do not respect the ceiling and produce more than their quotas, the OPEC cartel loses its power to impact oil prices through controlling oil supplies. OPEC has been long criticized for its lack of an enforcement mechanism to ensure the compliance of its members. The figure shows that oil prices are product of both demand and supply. The recession shifts the demand curve to the left to D_2, reducing the price to P_2. On the other hand, if oil producers expanded production, the supply curve would shift to the right to S_2, pushing prices further down to P_3.

(c) The fragile economies amid the global financial crisis, the ending of many stimulus packages in industrialized countries, and a more regulated energy trading are all factors that will contribute to slowing down the rebounding growth in demand for oil in the near future. The demand is, however, expected to pick up with the rising growth rates in emerging economies, such as China and India. On the other hand, the prospects for supply increases are quite high. Many OPEC countries are demanding an increase in their quotas, paving the way for future possible divisions inside the controversial organization. In addition, Iraq is heading for a strong comeback, adding a few million barrels to oil supplies. Many analysts expect the effect of the supply increase to be stronger than the effect of the growing demand; hence they do not preclude the possibility of lower oil prices in the future.

Thinking Critically

1. Like any other good, oil prices are determined by the interaction of both demand and supply sides. How do you think both sides are equally important in determining oil price trends and movements?
2. Some OPEC countries have a tendency to cheat by producing beyond their quotas, negatively contributing to the instability of oil prices. Why do you think OPEC affects prices despite the fact that it controls only one third of supply?

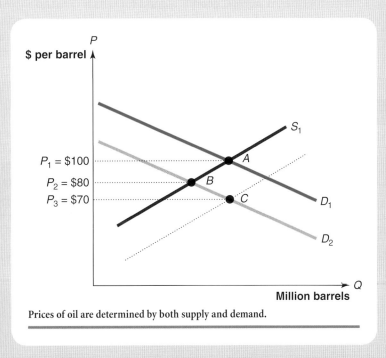

Prices of oil are determined by both supply and demand.

Key Terms

Ceteris paribus
  (all else equal), p. 70

Competitive market
  equilibrium, p. 81

Complements, p. 71

Demand curve, p. 68

Demand schedule, p. 68

Demographics, p. 72

Income effect, p. 69

Inferior good, p. 71

Law of demand, p. 69

Law of supply, p. 77

Market demand, p. 69

Market equilibrium, p. 80

Normal good, p. 71

Perfectly competitive
  market, p. 68

Quantity demanded, p. 68

Quantity supplied, p. 76

Shortage, p. 82

Substitutes, p. 71

Substitution effect, p. 69

Supply curve, p. 77

Supply schedule, p. 76

Surplus, p. 81

Technological change, p. 78

Summary

3.1 LEARNING OBJECTIVE

Discuss the variables that influence demand, **pages 68–76.**

The Demand Side of the Market

The model of demand and supply is the most powerful in economics. The model applies exactly only to **perfectly competitive markets**, where there are many buyers and sellers, all the products sold are identical, and there are no barriers to new sellers entering the market. But the model can also be useful in analyzing markets that don't meet all of these requirements. The **quantity demanded** is the amount of a good or service that a consumer is willing and able to purchase at a given price. A **demand schedule** is a table that shows the relationship between the price of a product and the quantity of the product demanded. A **demand curve** is a graph that shows the relationship between the price of a good and the quantity of the good consumers are willing and able to buy over a period of time. **Market demand** is the demand by all consumers of a given good or service. The **law of demand** states that **ceteris paribus**—holding everything else constant—the quantity of a product demanded increases when the price falls and decreases when the price rises. Demand curves slope downward because of the **substitution effect**, which is the change in quantity demanded that results from a price change making one good more or less expensive relative to another good, and the **income effect**, which is the change in quantity demanded of a good that results from the effect of a change in the good's price on consumer purchasing power. Changes in income, the prices of related goods, tastes, population and demographics, and expected future prices all cause the demand curve to shift. **Substitutes** are goods that can be used for the same purpose. **Complements** are goods that are used together. A **normal good** is a good for which demand increases as income increases. An **inferior good** is a good for which demand decreases as income increases. **Demographics** are the characteristics of a population with respect to age, race, and gender. A change in demand refers to a shift of the demand curve. A change in quantity demanded refers to a movement along the demand curve as a result of a change in the product's price.

3.2 LEARNING OBJECTIVE

Discuss the variables that influence supply, **pages 76–80.**

The Supply Side of the Market

The **quantity supplied** is the amount of a good that a firm is willing and able to supply at a given price. A **supply schedule** is a table that shows the relationship between the price of a product and the quantity of the product supplied. A **supply curve** shows on a graph the relationship between the price of a product and the quantity of the product supplied. When the price of a product rises, producing the product is more profitable, and a greater amount will be supplied. The **law of supply** states that, holding everything else constant, the quantity of a product supplied increases when the price rises and decreases when the price falls. Changes in the prices of inputs, technology, the prices of substitutes in production, expected future prices, and the number of firms in a market all cause the supply curve to shift. **Technological change** is a positive or negative change in the ability of a firm to produce a given level of output with a given quantity of inputs. A change in supply refers to a shift of the supply curve. A change in quantity supplied refers to a movement along the supply curve as a result of a change in the product's price.

Market Equilibrium: Putting Demand and Supply Together

Market equilibrium occurs where the demand curve intersects the supply curve. A **competitive market equilibrium** has a market equilibrium with many buyers and many sellers. Only at this point is the quantity demanded equal to the quantity supplied. Prices above equilibrium result in **surpluses**, with the quantity supplied being greater than the quantity demanded. Surpluses cause the market price to fall. Prices below equilibrium result in **shortages**, with the quantity demanded being greater than the quantity supplied. Shortages cause the market price to rise

3.3 LEARNING OBJECTIVE

Use a graph to illustrate market equilibrium, **pages 80–84.**

The Effect of Demand and Supply Shifts on Equilibrium

In most markets, demand and supply curves shift frequently, causing changes in equilibrium prices and quantities. Over time, if demand increases more than supply, equilibrium price will rise. If supply increases more than demand, equilibrium price will fall.

3.4 LEARNING OBJECTIVE

Use demand and supply graphs to predict changes in prices and quantities, **pages 84–90.**

Review, Problems and Applications

myeconlab Visit www.pearsoned.co.uk/awe/hubbard to complete these exercises online and get instant feedback.
Get Ahead of the Curve

3.1 LEARNING OBJECTIVE   Discuss the variables that influence demand, **pages 68–76.**

Review Questions

1.1 What is a demand schedule? What is a demand curve?
1.2 What do economists mean when they use the Latin expression *ceteris paribus*?
1.3 What is the difference between a change in demand and a change in quantity demanded?
1.4 What is the law of demand? What are the main variables that will cause the demand curve to shift? Give an example of each.

Problems and Applications

1.5 (Related to the *Making the Connection* on page 71) For each of the following pairs of products, state which are complements, which are substitutes, and which are unrelated.
    a. Pepsi and Coke
    b. Al-islami hot dogs and Faragulla hot dog buns
    c. Halwani's chocolate halawa and Vitrac's strawberry jam
    d. iPods and financial calculators
1.6 (Related to the *Chapter Opener* on page 66) Suppose Apple discovers that it is selling relatively few downloads of television programs on iTunes. Are downloads of television programs substitutes or complements for downloads of music? For downloads of movies? How might the answers to these questions affect Apple's decision about whether to continue offering downloads of television programs on iTunes?
1.7 State whether each of the following events will result in a movement along the demand curve for

McDonald's Big Mac hamburgers or whether it will cause the curve to shift. If the demand curve shifts, indicate whether it will shift to the left or to the right and draw a graph to illustrate the shift.
    a. The price of Burger King's Whopper hamburger declines.
    b. McDonald's distributes coupons for US$1.00 off on a purchase of a Big Mac.
    c. Because of a shortage of potatoes, the price of French fries increases.
    d. Kentucky Fried Chicken raises the price of a bucket of fried chicken.
1.8 (Related to the *Making the Connection* on page 73) Name three products whose demand is likely to increase rapidly if the following demographic groups increase at a faster rate than the population as a whole:
    a. Teenagers
    b. Children under five
    c. People over age 65
1.9 Suppose the data in the following table present the price of a base model Ford Explorer sport utility vehicle (SUV) and the quantity of Explorers sold. Do these data indicate that the demand curve for Explorers is upward sloping? Explain.

YEAR	PRICE (US$)	QUANTITY
2006	27,865	325,265
2007	28,325	330,648
2008	28,765	352,666

1.10 (Related to the *Making the Connection* on page 75) In early 2007, Apple forecast that it would sell 10 million iPhones during the product's first year on the market. What factors could affect the accuracy of this forecast? Is the forecast likely to be more or less accurate than Apple's forecast of how many iPods they would sell during the same time period? Briefly explain.

3.2 LEARNING OBJECTIVE   Discuss the variables that influence supply, **pages 76–80.**

Review Questions

2.1 What is a supply schedule? What is a supply curve?

2.2 What is the law of supply? What are the main variables that will cause a supply curve to shift? Give an example of each.

Problems and Applications

2.3 Briefly explain whether each of the following statements describes a change in supply or a change in the quantity supplied.

   a. To take advantage of high prices for oil during winter, oil producers decide to increase output.

   b. The success of Apple's iPod leads more firms to begin producing digital music players.

2.4 Will each firm in a given industry always supply the same quantity as every other firm at each price? What factors might cause the quantity of digital music players supplied by each firm at each price to be different?

2.5 If the price of a good increases, is the increase in the quantity of the good supplied likely to be smaller or larger, the longer the time period being considered? Briefly explain.

3.3 LEARNING OBJECTIVE   Use a graph to illustrate market equilibrium, **pages 80–84.**

Review Questions

3.1 What do economists mean by market equilibrium?

3.2 What happens in a market if the current price is above the equilibrium price? What happens if the current price is below the equilibrium price?

Problems and Applications

3.3 Briefly explain whether you agree with the following statement: "When there is a shortage of a good, consumers eventually give up trying to buy it, so the demand for the good declines, and the price falls until the market is finally in equilibrium."

3.4 **(Related to *Solved Problem 3-3* on page 82)** In *The Wealth of Nations*, Adam Smith discussed what has come to be known as the "diamond and water paradox":

Nothing is more useful than water: but it will purchase scarce anything; scarce anything can be had in exchange for it. A diamond, on the contrary, has scarce any value in use; but a very great quantity of other goods may frequently be had in exchange for it.

Graph the market for diamonds and the market for water. Show how it is possible for the price of water to be much lower than the price of diamonds, even though the demand for water is much greater than the demand for diamonds.

3.5 Briefly explain under what conditions zero would be the equilibrium quantity.

3.6 If a market is in equilibrium, is it necessarily true that all buyers and all sellers are satisfied with the market price? Briefly explain.

3.4 LEARNING OBJECTIVE   Use demand and supply graphs to predict changes in prices and quantities, **pages 84–90.**

Review Questions

4.1 Draw a demand and supply curve to show the effect on the equilibrium price in a market in the following two situations:

   a. The demand curve shifts to the right.

   b. The supply curve shifts to the left.

4.2 If, over time, the demand curve for a product shifts to the right more than the supply curve does, what will happen to the equilibrium price? What will happen to the equilibrium price if the supply curve shifts to the right more than the demand curve? For each case, draw a demand and supply graph to illustrate your answer.

Problems and Applications

4.3 As oil prices rose during 2006, the demand for alternative fuels increased. Ethanol, one alternative fuel, is made from corn. This was also accompanied by a general increase in the price of corn and food products that are made of corn, such as tortilla.

    a. Draw a demand and supply graph for the corn market and use it to show the effect on this market of an increase in the demand for ethanol. Be sure to indicate the equilibrium price and quantity before and after the increase in the demand for ethanol.

    b. Draw a demand and supply graph for the tortilla market and use it to show the effect on this market of an increase in the price of corn. Once again, be sure to indicate the equilibrium price and quantity before and after the increase in the demand for ethanol.

    Source: Mark Gongloff, "Tortilla Soup," *Wall Street Journal*, January 25, 2007.

4.4 **(Related to *Solved Problem 3-4* on page 88)** The demand for watermelons is highest during summer and lowest during winter. Yet watermelon prices are normally lower in summer than in winter. Use a demand and supply graph to demonstrate how this is possible. Be sure to carefully label the curves in your graph and to clearly indicate the equilibrium summer price and the equilibrium winter price.

4.5 As occupancy rates at luxury hotels have grown, prices have risen; that comes despite an increase in the number of rooms. Use a demand and supply graph to explain how these three things could be true: an increase in the equilibrium quantity of hotel rooms occupied, an increase in the equilibrium price of hotel rooms, and an increase in the number of hotel rooms available.

4.6 **(Related to the *Making the Connection* on page 85)** The average price of a high-definition plasma or LCD television fell between 2001 and 2006, from more than US$8,000 to about US$1,500. During that period, Sharp, Matsushita Electric Industrial, and Samsung all began producing plasma or LCD televisions. Use a demand and supply graph to explain what happened to the quantity of plasma and LCD televisions sold during this period.

4.7 The demand for full-size pickup trucks declined as a result of rising gas prices and a decline in housing construction (construction firms are an important part of the market for pickup trucks). At the same time, Toyota began production of trucks.

    a. Draw a demand and supply graph illustrating these developments in the market for full-size pickup trucks. Be sure to indicate changes in the equilibrium price and equilibrium quantity.

    b. Briefly discuss whether this problem provides enough information to determine whether the equilibrium quantity of trucks increased or decreased.

4.8 Beginning in the late 1990s, many consumers were having their vision problems corrected with laser surgery. An article in the *Wall Street Journal* noted two developments in the market for laser eye surgery. The first involved increasing concerns related to side effects from the surgery, including blurred vision and, occasionally, blindness. The second development was that the companies renting eye-surgery machinery to doctors had reduced their charges. One large company had cut its charge from US$250 per patient to US$100. Use a demand and supply graph to illustrate the effects of these two developments on the market for laser eye surgery.

Source: Laura Johannes and James Bandler, "Slowing Economy, Safety Concerns Zap Growth in Laser Eye Surgery," *Wall Street Journal*, January 8, 2001, p. B1.

4.9 Historically, the production of many perishable foods, such as dairy products, was highly seasonal. Thus, as the supply of those products fluctuated, prices tended to fluctuate tremendously—typically by 25 to 50 percent or more—over the course of the year. One impact of mechanical refrigeration, which was commercialized on a large scale in the last decade of the nineteenth century, was that suppliers could store perishables from one season to the next. Economists have estimated that as a result of refrigerated storage, wholesale prices rose by roughly 10 percent during peak supply periods, while they fell by almost the same amount during the off season. Use a demand and supply graph for each season to illustrate how refrigeration affected the market for perishable food.

Source: Lee A. Craig, Barry Goodwin, and Thomas Grennes, "The Effect of Mechanical Refrigeration on Nutrition in the US," *Social Science History*, Vol. 28, No. 2 (Summer 2004), pp. 327–328.

4.10 Briefly explain whether each of the following statements is true or false.

    a. If the demand and supply for a product both increase, the equilibrium quantity of the product must also increase.

    b. If the demand and supply for a product both increase, the equilibrium price of the product must also increase.

    c. If the demand for a product decreases and the supply of the product increases, the equilibrium price of the product may increase or decrease, depending on whether supply or demand has shifted more.

4.11 A student writes the following: "Increased production leads to a lower price, which in turn increases demand." Do you agree with his reasoning? Briefly explain.

4.12 A student was asked to draw a demand and supply graph to illustrate the effect on the laptop computer market of a fall in the price of computer hard drives, *ceteris paribus*. She drew the graph on the next page and explained it as follows:

    Hard drives are an input to laptop computers, so a fall in the price of hard drives will cause the supply curve for personal computers to shift to the right (from S_1 to S_2). Because this shift in the supply curve results in a lower price (P_2), consumers will want to buy more laptops, and the demand curve will shift to the right (from D_1 to D_2). We know that more laptops will be sold, but we can't be sure whether the price of laptops will rise or fall. That depends on whether the supply curve or the demand curve has shifted farther to the right. I assume that the effect on supply is greater than the effect on demand, so I show the final equilibrium price (P_3) as being lower than the initial equilibrium price (P_1).

Explain whether you agree or disagree with the student's analysis. Be careful to explain exactly what—if anything—you find wrong with her analysis.

4.13 Following are four graphs and four market scenarios, each of which would cause either a movement along the supply curve for Pepsi or a shift of the supply curve. Match each scenario with the appropriate graph.

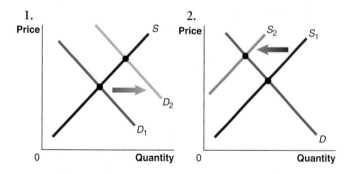

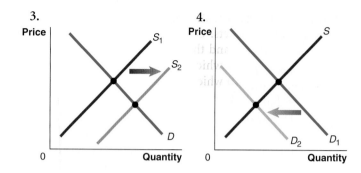

a. A decrease in the supply of Coke
b. A drop in the average household income in the UAE from US$42,000 to US$41,000
c. An improvement in soft-drink bottling technology
d. An increase in the price of sugar

4.14 David Surdam, an economist at Loyola University of Chicago in the U.S., makes the following observation of the world cotton market at the beginning of the American Civil War:

> As the supply of American-grown raw cotton decreased and the price of raw cotton increased, there would be a *movement along* the supply curve of non-American raw cotton suppliers, and the quantity supplied by other well known international cotton producers such as Egypt would increase.

Illustrate this observation with one demand and supply graph for the market for American-grown cotton and another demand and supply graph for Egyptian cotton. Make sure your graphs clearly show (1) the initial equilibrium before the decrease in the supply of American-grown cotton and (2) the final equilibrium, after the increase of Egyptian cotton. Also clearly show any shifts in the demand and supply curves for each market.

Source: David G. Surdam, "King Cotton: Monarch or Pretender? The State of the Market for Raw Cotton on the Eve of the American Civil War," *The Economic History Review*, Vol. 51, No. 1 (February 1998), p. 116.

4.15 Proposals have been made to increase government regulation of firms providing childcare services by, for instance, setting education requirements for childcare workers. Suppose that these regulations increase the quality of childcare and cause the demand for childcare services to increase. At the same time, assume that complying with the new government regulations increases the costs of firms providing childcare services. Draw a demand and supply graph to illustrate the effects of these changes in the market for childcare services. Briefly explain whether the total quantity of childcare services purchased will increase or decrease as a result of regulation.

4.16 On the right are the supply and demand functions for two markets. One of the markets is for BMW automobiles, and the other is for a cancer-fighting drug, without which lung cancer patients will die. Briefly explain which diagram most likely represents which market

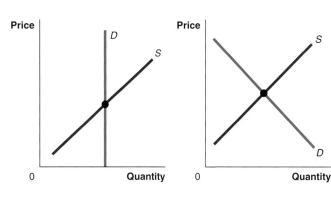

Economic Efficiency, Government Price Setting, and Taxes

Why Does the Dubai Government Control Apartment Rents?

Despite the drop in apartment rents in Dubai in 2009, owing to the global financial crisis, rent prices rose sharply in the first decade of this century as demand for renting houses increased rapidly. This was mainly because of the high growth rate in Dubai's 1.4 million population (2007 estimates). Dubai's population growth rate was about 8 percent a year until 2008. After a remarkable 40 percent increase in rent prices in 2005, the Dubai government decided to be the first emirate in the United Arab Emirates to introduce a rent cap when, in November 2005, Sheikh Mohammed Bin Rashid Al Maktoum, vice president and prime minister of the UAE, and ruler of Dubai, issued a decree capping the increase at a maximum of 15 percent of the annual rent. This rent-control policy showed a significant sign of success when, in 2007, rents rose by only 16 percent. On May 2, 2009, the rent cap was reduced as Sheikh Mohammed issued a decree stating that the rent increase should not exceed 7 percent of the annual rent of the property, with effect from January 1, 2010.

The rent-control policy aims at supressing the high inflation rate that prevailed in Dubai before the global financial crisis of 2008. Rent is an important part of the consumer basket, especially for expatriates, providing residents with affordable houses and helping them to predict their annual increase in rent so that they will be able to take more precise decision regarding their future career in Dubai. Expatriates welcomed the new decree not only as it would help many people to save money, but also as it would enabled them to return their families to Dubai. The sharp increase in rent in 2005 had pushed many expatriates to send their families back to their home countries because they were not able to afford the rent of more than one-bedroom apartment, and caused many others to search for roommates. (It should be said here that the Dubai rent-control policy is not 100 percent binding as it allows the landlord to increase rent beyond the 7 percent limit if both the landlord and the tenant agree upon the increase.)

As we will see in this chapter, however, rent control can also cause significant problems for tenants. **AN INSIDE LOOK AT POLICY** on **page 124** explores the debate over rent control laws in the UAE.

Sources: Ashfaq Ahmed, "Seven Per Cent Rent Cap in Dubai," *Gulf News*, May 3, 2009; and Simeon Kerr, "Dubai Property Boom on Slide but No Price Fall Yet," *Financial Times*, September 27, 2007.

Economics in YOUR Life!

Does Rent Control Make It Easier to Find an Affordable Apartment?

Suppose you have job offers in two cities. One factor in deciding which job to accept is whether you can find an affordable apartment. If one city has rent control, are you more likely to find an affordable apartment in that city, or would you be better off looking for an apartment in a city without rent control? As you read the chapter, see if you can answer this question. You can check your answer against the one we provide at the end of the chapter. >> Continued on page 122

W e saw in Chapter 3 that, in a competitive market, the price adjusts to ensure that the quantity demanded equals the quantity supplied. Stated another way, in equilibrium, every consumer willing to pay the market price is able to buy as much of the product as the consumer wants, and every firm willing to accept the market price can sell as much as it wants. Even so, consumers would naturally prefer to pay a lower price, and sellers would prefer to receive a higher price. Normally, consumers and firms have no choice but to accept the equilibrium price if they wish to participate in the market. Occasionally, however, consumers succeed in having the government imposes a **price ceiling**, which is a legally determined maximum price that sellers may charge. Rent control is an example of a price ceiling. Workers also sometimes succeed in having the government impose a **price floor**, which is a legally determined minimum wage that workers may receive.

Another way in which the government intervenes in markets is by imposing taxes. The government relies on the revenue raised from taxes to finance its operations. As we will see, though, imposing taxes alters the equilibrium in a market.

Unfortunately, whenever the government imposes a price ceiling, a price floor, or a tax, there are predictable negative economic consequences. It is important for government policy-makers and voters to understand these negative consequences when evaluating the effects of these policies. Economists have developed the concepts of *consumer surplus, producer surplus*, and *economic surplus*, which we discuss in the next section. In the sections that follow, we use these concepts to analyze the economic effects of price ceilings, price floors, and taxes. (As we will see in later chapters, these concepts are also useful in many other contexts.)

Price ceiling A legally determined maximum price that sellers may charge.

Price floor A legally determined minimum price that sellers may receive.

4.1 | Distinguish between the concepts of consumer surplus and producer surplus.

Consumer Surplus and Producer Surplus

Consumer surplus measures the dollar benefit consumers receive from buying goods or services in a particular market. Producer surplus measures the dollar benefit firms receive from selling goods or services in a particular market. Economic surplus in a market is the sum of consumer surplus plus producer surplus. As we will see, *when the government imposes a price ceiling or a price floor, the amount of economic surplus in a market is reduced*—in other words, price ceilings and price floors reduce the total benefit to consumers and firms from buying and selling in a market. To understand why this is true, we need to understand how consumer surplus and producer surplus are determined.

Consumer Surplus

Consumer surplus measures the difference between the highest price a consumer is willing to pay and the price the consumer actually pays. For example, suppose you are in Carrefour and you see a DVD of *Spider-Man 3* on the rack. No price is indicated on the package, so you bring it over to the register to check the price. As you walk to the register, you think to yourself that US$20 is the highest price you would be willing to pay. At the register, you find out that the price is actually US$12, so you buy the DVD. Your consumer surplus in this example is US$8: the difference between the US$20 you were willing to pay and the US$12 you actually paid.

We can use the demand curve to measure the total consumer surplus in a market. Demand curves show the willingness of consumers to purchase a product at different prices. Consumers are willing to purchase a product up to the point where the marginal benefit of consuming a product is equal to its price. The **marginal benefit** is the additional benefit to a consumer from consuming one more unit of a good or service. As a simple example, suppose there are only four consumers in the market for tea: Hala, Aliaa, Zeyad, and Housam. Because these four consumers have different tastes for tea and different incomes, the marginal benefit each of them receives from consuming a

Consumer surplus The difference between the highest price a consumer is willing to pay and the price the consumer actually pays.

Marginal benefit The additional benefit to a consumer from consuming one more unit of a good or service.

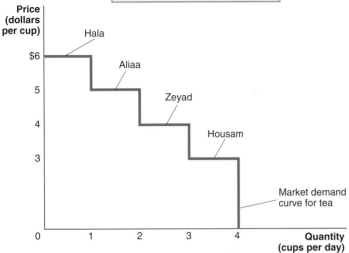

Consumer	Highest Price Willing to Pay
Hala	$6
Aliaa	5
Zeyad	4
Housam	3

Figure 4-1

Deriving the Demand Curve for Tea

With four consumers in the market for tea, the demand curve is determined by the highest price each consumer is willing to pay. For prices above US$6, no tea is sold because US$6 is the highest price any consumer is willing to pay. For prices of US$3 and below, all four consumers are willing to buy a cup of tea.

cup of tea will be different. Therefore, the highest price each is willing to pay for a cup of tea is also different. In Figure 4-1, the information from the table is used to construct a demand curve for tea. For prices above US$6 per cup, no tea is sold because US$6 is the highest price any of the consumers is willing to pay. At a price of US$5, both Hala and Aliaa are willing to buy, so two cups are sold. At prices of US$3 and below, all four consumers are willing to buy, and four cups are sold.

Suppose the market price of tea is US$3.50 per cup. As Figure 4-2 shows, the demand curve allows us to calculate the total consumer surplus in this market. In

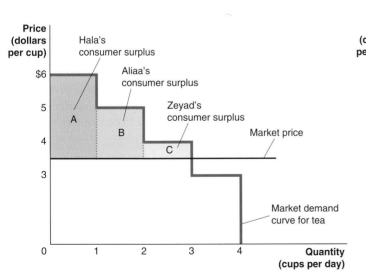

(a) Consumer surplus with a market price of $3.50

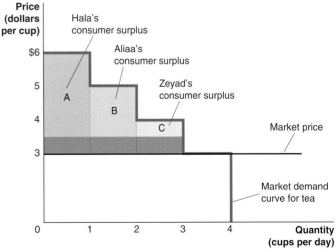

(b) Consumer surplus with a market price of $3.00

Figure 4-2 | Measuring Consumer Surplus

Panel (a) shows the consumer surplus for Hala, Aliaa, and Zeyad when the price of tea is US$3.50 per cup. Hala's consumer surplus is equal to the area of rectangle *A* and is the difference between the highest price she would pay—US$6—and the market price of US$3.50. Aliaa's consumer surplus is equal to the area of rectangle *B*, and Zeyad's

consumer surplus is equal to the area of rectangle *C*. Total consumer surplus in this market is equal to the sum of the areas of rectangles *A*, *B*, and *C*, or the total area below the demand curve and above the market price. In panel (b), consumer surplus increases by the shaded area as the market price declines from US$3.50 to US$3.00.

Figure 4-3

Total Consumer Surplus in the Market for Tea

The demand curve tells us that most buyers of tea would have been willing to pay more than the market price of US$2.00. For each buyer, consumer surplus is equal to the difference between the highest price he or she is willing to pay and the market price actually paid. Therefore, the total amount of consumer surplus in the market for tea is equal to the area below the demand curve and above the market price. Consumer surplus represents the benefit to consumers in excess of the price they paid to purchase the product.

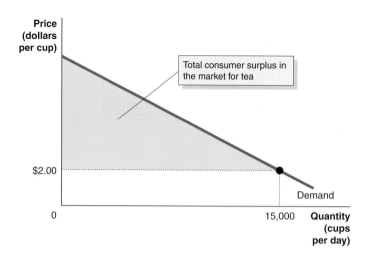

panel (a), we can see that the highest price Hala is willing to pay is US$6, but because she pays only US$3.50, her consumer surplus is US$2.50 (shown by the area of rectangle *A*). Similarly, Aliaa's consumer surplus is US$1.50 (rectangle *B*), and Zeyad's consumer surplus is US$0.50 (rectangle *C*). Housam is unwilling to buy a cup of tea at a price of US$3.50, so he doesn't participate in this market and receives no consumer surplus. In this simple example, the total consumer surplus is equal to US$2.50 + US$1.50 + US$0.50 = US$4.50 (or the sum of the areas of rectangles *A, B,* and *C*). Panel (b) shows that a lower price will increase consumer surplus. If the price of tea drops from US$3.50 per cup to US$3.00, Hala, Aliaa, and Zeyad each receive US$0.50 more in consumer surplus (shown by the shaded areas), so total consumer surplus in the market rises to US$6.00. Housam now buys a cup of tea but doesn't receive any consumer surplus because the price is equal to the highest price he is willing to pay. In fact, Housam is indifferent as to buying the cup or not—his well-being is the same either way.

The market demand curves shown in Figures 4-1 and 4-2 do not look like the smooth curves we saw in Chapter 3. This is because this example uses a small number of consumers, each consuming a single cup of tea. With many consumers, the market demand curve for tea will have the normal smooth shape shown in Figure 4-3. In this figure, the quantity demanded at a price of US$2.00 is 15,000 cups per day. We can calculate total consumer surplus in Figure 4-3 the same way we did in Figures 4-1 and 4-2: by adding up the consumer surplus received on each unit purchased. Once again, we can draw an important conclusion: *The total amount of consumer surplus in a market is equal to the area below the demand curve and above the market price.* Consumer surplus is shown as the blue area in Figure 4-3 and represents the benefit to consumers in excess of the price they paid to purchase the product—in this case, tea.

Making the Connection | The Consumer Surplus from Satellite Television

Consumer surplus allows us to measure the benefit consumers receive in excess of the price they paid to purchase a product. Recently, Austan Goolsbee and Amil Petrin, economists at the Graduate School of Business at the University of Chicago in the U.S., estimated the consumer surplus that households receive from subscribing to satellite television. To do this, they estimated the demand curve for satellite television and then computed the shaded area shown in the graph.

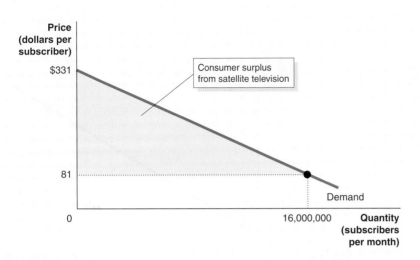

In 2001, the year for which the study was conducted, 16 million consumers in the U.S. paid to subscribe to DIRECTV or DISH Network, the two main providers of satellite television in the U.S. The demand curve shows that many consumers would have been willing to pay more than US$81 rather than do without satellite television. Goolsbee and Petrin calculated that the consumer surplus for households subscribing to satellite television averaged US$127 per month, which is the difference between the price they would have paid and the US$81 they did pay. The shaded area on the graph represents the total consumer surplus in the market for satellite television. Goolsbee and Petrin estimate that the value of this area is US$2 billion. This is one year's benefit to the consumers who subscribe to satellite television.

Source: Austan Goolsbee and Amil Petrin, "The Consumer Gains from Direct Broadcast Satellites and the Competition with Cable TV," *Econometrica*, Vol. 72, No. 2, March 2004, pp. 351–381.

YOUR TURN: Test your understanding by doing related problem 1.8 on page 127 at the end of this chapter.

Producer Surplus

Just as demand curves show the willingness of consumers to buy a product at different prices, supply curves show the willingness of firms to supply a product at different prices. The willingness to supply a product depends on the cost of producing it. Firms will supply an additional unit of a product only if they receive a price equal to the additional cost of producing that unit. **Marginal cost** is the additional cost to a firm of producing one more unit of a good or service. Consider the marginal cost to the firm Ahmed Tea of producing one more cup: in this case, the marginal cost includes the ingredients for making the tea and the wages paid to the worker preparing the tea. Often, the marginal cost of producing a good increases as more of the good is produced during a given period of time. This is the key reason—as we saw in Chapter 3—that supply curves are upward sloping.

Panel (a) of Figure 4-4 shows Ahmed Tea's producer surplus. For simplicity, we show Ahmed producing only a small quantity of tea. The figure shows that Ahmed's marginal cost of producing the first cup of tea is US$1.00. Its marginal cost of producing the second cup is US$1.25, and so on. The marginal cost of each cup of tea is the lowest price Ahmed is willing to accept to supply that cup. The supply curve, then, is also a marginal cost curve. Suppose the market price of tea is US$1.75 per cup. On the first cup of tea, the price is US$0.75 higher than the lowest price Ahmed is willing to accept. **Producer surplus** is the difference between the lowest price a firm would be willing to accept and the price it actually receives. Therefore, Ahmed's producer surplus on

Marginal cost The additional cost to a firm of producing one more unit of a good or service.

Producer surplus The difference between the lowest price a firm would be willing to accept and the price it actually receives.

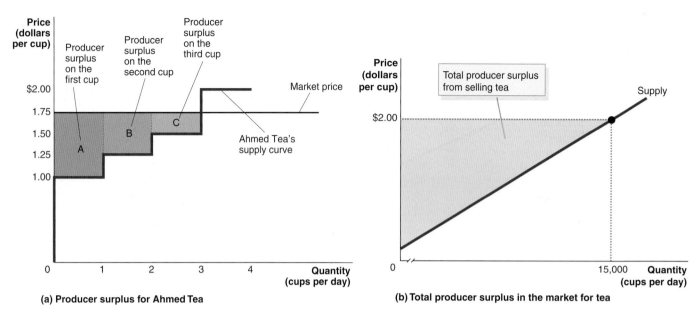

Figure 4-4 | Calculating Producer Surplus

Panel (a) shows Ahmed Tea's producer surplus. Producer surplus is the difference between the lowest price a firm would be willing to accept and the price it actually receives. The lowest price Ahmed Tea is willing to accept to supply a cup of tea is equal to its marginal cost of producing that cup. When the market price of tea is US$1.75, Ahmed receives a producer surplus of US$0.75 on the first cup (the area of rectangle A), US$0.50 on the second cup (rectangle B), and US$0.25 on the third cup (rectangle C). In panel (b), the total amount of producer surplus tea sellers receive from selling tea can be calculated by adding up for the entire market the producer surplus received on each cup sold. In the figure, total producer surplus is equal to the area above the supply curve and below the market price, shown in red.

the first cup is US$0.75 (shown by the area of rectangle A). Its producer surplus on the second cup is US$0.50 (rectangle B). Its producer surplus on the third cup is US$0.25 (rectangle C). Ahmed will not be willing to supply the fourth cup because the marginal cost of producing it is less than the market price. Ahmed Tea's total producer surplus is equal to US$0.75 + US$0.50 + US$0.25 = US$1.50 (or the sum of rectangles A, B, and C). A higher price will increase producer surplus. For example, if the market price of tea rises from US$1.75 to US$2.00, Ahmed Tea's producer surplus will increase from US$1.50 to US$2.25. (Make sure you understand how the new level of producer surplus was calculated.)

The supply curve shown in panel (a) of Figure 4-4 does not look like the smooth curves we saw in Chapter 3 because this example uses a single firm producing only a small quantity of tea. With many firms, the market supply curve for tea will have the normal smooth shape shown in panel (b) of Figure 4-4. In panel (b), the quantity supplied at a price of US$2.00 is 15,000 cups per day. We can calculate total producer surplus in panel (b) in the same way we did for panel (a): by adding up the producer surplus received on each cup sold. Therefore, *the total amount of producer surplus in a market is equal to the area above the market supply curve and below the market price*. The total producer surplus tea sellers receive from selling tea is shown as the red area in panel (b) of Figure 4-4.

What Consumer Surplus and Producer Surplus Measure

We have seen that consumer surplus measures the benefit to consumers from participating in a market, and producer surplus measures the benefit to producers from participating in a market. It is important, however, to be clear what we mean by this. In a sense, consumer surplus measures the *net* benefit to consumers from participating in a market rather than the *total* benefit. That is, if the price of a product were zero, the consumer surplus in a market would be all of the area under the demand curve. When the price is not zero, consumer surplus is the area below the demand curve and above the market price. So, consumer surplus in a market is equal to the total benefit received by consumers minus the total amount they must pay to buy the good.

Similarly, producer surplus measures the *net* benefit received by producers from participating in a market. If producers could supply a good at zero cost, the producer surplus in a market would be all of the area below the market price. When cost is not zero, producer surplus is the area below the market price and above the supply curve. So, producer surplus in a market is equal to the total amount firms receive from consumers minus the cost of producing the good.

4.2 | Understand the concept of economic efficiency.

The Efficiency of Competitive Markets

In Chapter 3, we defined a *competitive market* as a market with many buyers and many sellers. An important advantage of the market system is that it results in efficient economic outcomes. But what do we mean by *economic efficiency*? The concepts we have developed so far in this chapter give us two ways to think about the economic efficiency of competitive markets. We can think in terms of marginal benefit and marginal cost. We can also think in terms of consumer surplus and producer surplus. As we will see, these two approaches lead to the same outcome, but using both can increase our understanding of economic efficiency.

Marginal Benefit Equals Marginal Cost in Competitive Equilibrium

Figure 4-5 again shows the market for tea. Recall from our discussion that the demand curve shows the marginal benefit received by consumers, and the supply curve shows the marginal cost of production. To achieve economic efficiency in this market, the marginal benefit from the last unit sold should equal the marginal cost of production. The figure shows that this equality occurs at competitive equilibrium where 15,000 cups per day are produced, and marginal benefit and marginal cost are both equal to US$2.00. Why is this outcome economically efficient? Because every cup of tea has been produced where the marginal benefit to buyers is greater than or equal to the marginal cost to producers.

Another way to see why the level of output at competitive equilibrium is efficient is to consider what would be true if output were at a different level. For instance, suppose that output of tea were 14,000 cups per day. Figure 4-5 shows that at this level of output, the marginal benefit from the last cup sold is US$2.20, whereas the marginal cost is only

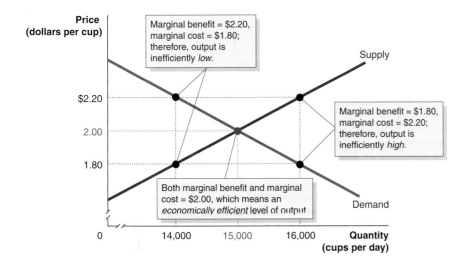

Figure 4-5

Marginal Benefit Equals Marginal Cost Only at Competitive Equilibrium

In a competitive market, equilibrium occurs at a quantity of 15,000 cups and price of US$2.00 per cup, where marginal benefit equals marginal cost. This is the economically efficient level of output because every cup has been produced where the marginal benefit to buyers is greater than or equal to the marginal cost to producers.

US$1.80. This level of output is not efficient because 1,000 more cups could be produced for which the additional benefit to consumers would be greater than the additional cost of production. Consumers would willingly purchase those cups, and tea sellers would willingly supply them, making both consumers and sellers better off. Similarly, if the output of tea were 16,000 cups per day, the marginal cost of the 16,000th cup is US$2.20, whereas the marginal benefit is only US$1.80. Tea sellers would only be willing to supply this cup at a price of US$2.20, which is US$0.40 higher than consumers would be willing to pay. In fact, consumers would not be willing to pay the price tea sellers would need to receive for any cup beyond the 15,000th.

To summarize, we can say this: *Equilibrium in a competitive market results in the economically efficient level of output, where marginal benefit equals marginal cost.*

Economic Surplus

Economic surplus in a market is the sum of consumer surplus and producer surplus. In a competitive market, with many buyers and sellers and no government restrictions, economic surplus is at a maximum when the market is in equilibrium. To see this, let's look again at the market for tea shown in Figure 4-6. The consumer surplus in this market is the blue area below the demand curve and above the line indicating the equilibrium price of US$2.00. The producer surplus is the red area above the supply curve and below the price line.

Deadweight Loss

To show that economic surplus is maximized at equilibrium, consider the situation in which the price of tea is *above* the equilibrium price, as shown in Figure 4-7. At a price of US$2.20 per cup, the number of cups consumers are willing to buy per day drops from 15,000 to 14,000. At competitive equilibrium, consumer surplus is equal to the sum of areas *A*, *B*, and *C*. At a price of US$2.20, fewer cups are sold at a higher price, so consumer surplus declines to just the area of *A*. At competitive equilibrium, producer surplus is equal to the sum of areas *D* and *E*. At the higher price of US$2.20, producer surplus changes to be equal to the sum of areas *B* and *D*. The sum of consumer and producer surplus—economic surplus—has been reduced to the sum of areas *A*, *B*, and *D*. Notice that this is less than the original economic surplus by an amount equal to areas *C* and *E*. Economic surplus has declined because at a price of US$2.20, all the cups between the 14,000th and the 15,000th, which would have been produced in competitive equilibrium, are not being produced. These 'missing' cups are not providing any consumer or producer surplus, so economic surplus has declined. The reduction in economic surplus resulting from a market not being in competitive equilibrium is called the **deadweight loss**. In the figure, it is equal to the sum of areas *C* and *E*.

Economic surplus The sum of consumer surplus and producer surplus.

Deadweight loss The reduction in economic surplus resulting from a market not being in competitive equilibrium.

Figure 4-6

Economic Surplus Equals the Sum of Consumer Surplus and Producer Surplus

The economic surplus in a market is the sum of the blue area representing consumer surplus and the red area representing producer surplus.

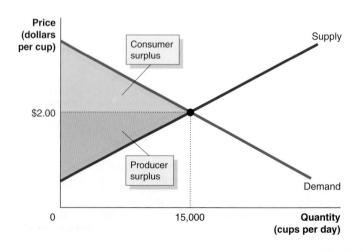

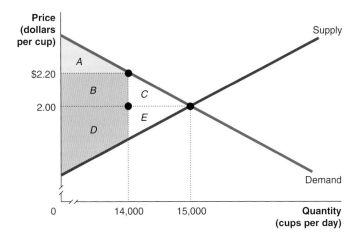

	At Competitive Equilibrium	At a Price of $2.20
Consumer Surplus	A + B + C	A
Producer Surplus	D + E	B + D
Deadweight Loss	None	C + E

Figure 4-7

When a Market Is Not in Equilibrium, There Is a Deadweight Loss

Economic surplus is maximized when a market is in competitive equilibrium. When a market is not in equilibrium, there is a deadweight loss. When the price of tea is US$2.20, instead of US$2.00, consumer surplus declines from an amount equal to the sum of areas *A*, *B*, and *C* to just area *A*. Producer surplus increases from the sum of areas *D* and *E* to the sum of areas *B* and *D*. At competitive equilibrium, there is no deadweight loss. At a price of US$2.20, there is a deadweight loss equal to the sum of areas *C* and *E*.

Economic Surplus and Economic Efficiency

Consumer surplus measures the benefit to consumers from buying a particular product, such as tea. Producer surplus measures the benefit to firms from selling a particular product. Therefore, economic surplus—which is the sum of the benefit to firms plus the benefit to consumers—is the best measure we have of the benefit to society from the production of a particular good or service. This gives us a second way of characterizing the economic efficiency of a competitive market: *Equilibrium in a competitive market results in the greatest amount of economic surplus, or total net benefit to society, from the production of a good or service.* Anything that causes the market for a good or service not to be in competitive equilibrium reduces the total benefit to society from the production of that good or service.

Now we can give a more general definition of *economic efficiency* in terms of our two approaches: **Economic efficiency** is a market outcome in which the marginal benefit to consumers of the last unit produced is equal to its marginal cost of production and in which the sum of consumer surplus and producer surplus is at a maximum.

Economic efficiency A market outcome in which the marginal benefit to consumers of the last unit produced is equal to its marginal cost of production and in which the sum of consumer surplus and producer surplus is at a maximum.

4.3 | Explain the economic effect of government-imposed price ceilings and price floors.

4.3 LEARNING OBJECTIVE

Government Intervention in the Market: Price Floors and Price Ceilings

Notice that we have *not* concluded that every *individual* is better off if a market is at competitive equilibrium. We have only concluded that economic surplus, or the *total* net benefit to society, is greatest at competitive equilibrium. Any individual producer would rather charge a higher price, and any individual consumer would rather pay a lower price, but usually producers can sell and consumers can buy only at the competitive equilibrium price.

Producers or consumers who are dissatisfied with the competitive equilibrium price can lobby the government to legally require that a different price be charged. When the government does intervene, it can either attempt to aid sellers by requiring that a price be above equilibrium—a price floor—or aid buyers by requiring that a price be below equilibrium—a price ceiling. To affect the market outcome, a price floor must be set above the equilibrium price and a price ceiling must be set below the equilibrium price. Otherwise, the price ceiling or price floor will not be *binding* on buyers and sellers. The preceding section demonstrates that moving away from competitive equilibrium will reduce economic efficiency. We can use the concepts of consumer surplus, producer surplus, and deadweight loss to see more clearly the economic inefficiency of binding price floors and price ceilings.

Price Floors: Government Policy in Agricultural Markets

The Great Depression of the 1930s was the greatest economic disaster in industrial countries' history, affecting every sector of their economies. Many farmers were unable to sell their products or could sell them only at very low prices. For example, U.S. farmers were able to convince the federal government to intervene to raise prices by setting price floors for many agricultural products. U.S. government intervention in agriculture—often referred to as the 'farm program'—has continued ever since. Some governments in the Arab world also set price floors for agricultural products. A famous example is the price floor set by the Egyptian government on cotton. Until the mid-1990s, the Egyptian government used to set a specific price for cotton. In 1993, a liberalization program started in Egypt, which changed the cotton price strategy by setting a guaranteed price floor that allowed cotton farmers to sell at any higher price. To see how a price floor in an agricultural market works, suppose that the equilibrium price in the wheat market is US$3.00 per kilo but the government decides to set a price floor of US$3.50 per kilo. As Figure 4-8 shows, the price of wheat rises from US$3.00 to US$3.50, and the quantity of wheat sold falls from 2.0 billion kilos per year to 1.8 billion. Initially, suppose that production of wheat also falls to 1.8 billion kilos.

Just as we saw in the earlier example of the market for tea (refer to Figure 4-7), the producer surplus received by wheat farmers increases by an amount equal to the area of the red rectangle *A* and falls by an amount equal to the area of the yellow triangle *C*. The area of the red rectangle *A* represents a transfer from consumer surplus to producer surplus. The total fall in consumer surplus is equal to the area of the red rectangle *A* plus the area of the yellow triangle *B*. Wheat farmers benefit from

Figure 4-8

The Economic Effect of a Price Floor in the Wheat Market

If wheat farmers convince the government to impose a price floor of US$3.50 per kilo, the amount of wheat sold will fall from 2.0 billion kilos per year to 1.8 billion. If we assume that farmers produce 1.8 billion kilos, producer surplus then increases by the red rectangle *A*—which is transferred from consumer surplus—and falls by the yellow triangle *C*. Consumer surplus declines by the red rectangle *A* plus the yellow triangle *B*. There is a deadweight loss equal to the yellow triangles *B* and *C*, representing the decline in economic efficiency due to the price floor. In reality, a price floor of US$3.50 per kilo will cause farmers to expand their production from 2.0 billion to 2.2 billion kilos, resulting in a surplus of wheat.

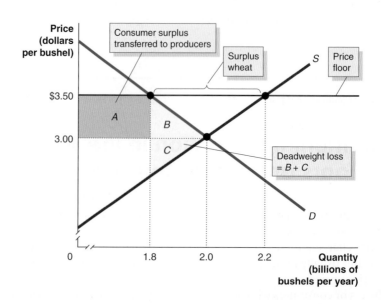

this program, but consumers lose. There is also a deadweight loss equal to the areas of the yellow triangles *B* and *C*, which represents the decline in economic efficiency due to the price floor. There is a deadweight loss because the price floor has reduced the amount of economic surplus in the market for wheat. Or, looked at another way, the price floor has caused the marginal benefit of the last kilo of wheat to be greater than the marginal cost of producing it. We can conclude that a price floor reduces economic efficiency.

We assumed initially that farmers reduce their production of wheat to the amount consumers are willing to buy. In fact, as Figure 4-8 shows, a price floor will cause the quantity of wheat that farmers want to supply to increase from 2.0 billion to 2.2 billion kilos. Because the higher price also reduces the amount of wheat consumers wish to buy, the result is a surplus of 0.4 billion kilos of wheat (the 2.2 billion kilos supplied minus the 1.8 billion demanded).

Making the Connection | Price Floors in Labor Markets: The Debate over Minimum Wage Policy

The minimum wage may be the most controversial 'price floor.' Supporters see the minimum wage as a way of raising the incomes of low-skilled workers. Opponents argue that it results in fewer jobs and imposes large costs on small businesses.

Recently, there has been an increasing demand by people, human rights organizations, and labor unions in the Arab world to increase the minimum wage so that poor, low-skilled workers can cope with the high cost of living. Yet, Arab governments hesitate to take this step, fearing that if businesses are forced to pay higher wages, higher unemployment will result. The current minimum wage varies significantly between Arab countries, ranging from a monthly rate of US$800 in Saudi Arabia and US$200 in Lebanon, to US$6 in Egypt (many Arab countries are considering an increase in their minimum wage after the political unrest that some of them faced in 2011.)

It is illegal for an employer to pay less than the minimum wage. For most workers, the minimum wage is irrelevant because it is well below the wage that employers are voluntarily prepared to pay them. But for low-skilled workers—such as janitors —the minimum wage is above the wage they would otherwise receive. The following figure shows the effect of the minimum wage on employment in the market for low-skilled labor.

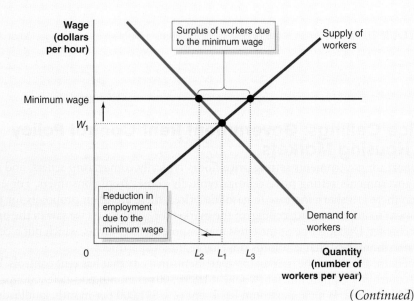

(Continued)

Without a minimum wage, the equilibrium wage would be W_1, and the number of workers hired would be L_1. With a minimum wage set above the equilibrium wage, the quantity of workers demanded by employers declines from L_1 to L_2, and the quantity of labor supplied increases to L_3, leading to a surplus of workers unable to find jobs equal to $L_3 - L_2$. The quantity of labor supplied increases because the higher wage attracts more people to work. For instance, some teenagers may decide that working after school is worthwhile at the minimum wage of US\$200 per month in Lebanon but would not be worthwhile at a lower wage.

This analysis is very similar to our analysis of the wheat market in Figure 4-8. Just as a price floor in the wheat market leads to less wheat consumed, a price floor in the labor market should lead to fewer workers hired. Views differ sharply among economists, however, concerning how large a reduction in employment the minimum wage causes. For instance, David Card of the University of California, Berkeley, and Alan Krueger of Princeton University conducted a study of fast-food restaurants in the U.S. states of New Jersey and Pennsylvania that indicates that the effect of minimum wage increases on employment is very small. Card and Krueger's study has been very controversial, however. Other economists have examined similar data and have come to the different conclusion that the minimum wage leads to a significant decrease in employment.

Whatever the extent of employment losses from the minimum wage, because it is a price floor, it will cause a deadweight loss, just as a price floor in the wheat market does. Therefore, many economists favor alternative policies for attaining the goal of raising the incomes of low-skilled workers. One policy many economists support is the *earned income tax credit*. The earned income tax credit reduces the amount of tax that low-income wage earners would otherwise pay to the government. Workers with very low incomes who do not owe any tax receive a payment from the government. Compared with the minimum wage, the earned income tax credit can increase the incomes of low-skilled workers without reducing employment. The earned income tax credit also places a lesser burden on the small businesses that employ many low-skilled workers, and it might cause a smaller loss of economic efficiency. Unfortunately, due to the lack of resources of many Arab governments, the earned income tax credit is not applied in the Arab world.

Sources: David Card and Alan B. Krueger, *Myth and Measurement: The New Economics of the Minimum Wage*, Princeton, NJ: Princeton University Press, 1995; David Neumark and William Wascher, "Minimum Wages and Employment: A Case Study of the Fast-Food Industry in New Jersey and Pennsylvania: Comment," *American Economic Review*, Vol. 90, No. 5, December 2000, pp. 1362–1396; and David Card and Alan B. Krueger, "Minimum Wages and Employment: A Case Study of the Fast-Food Industry in New Jersey and Pennsylvania: Reply," *American Economic Review*, Vol. 90, No. 5, December 2000, pp. 1397–1420.

YOUR TURN: Test your understanding by doing related problem 3.11 on page 130 at the end of this chapter.

Price Ceilings: Government Rent Control Policy in Housing Markets

Support for governments setting price floors typically comes from sellers, and support for governments setting price ceilings typically comes from consumers. For example, when there is a sharp increase in gasoline prices, there are often proposals for the government to impose a price ceiling on the market for gasoline. As we saw in the opener to this chapter, Dubai is one of the cities that imposes rent controls, which put a ceiling on the maximum rent that landlords can charge for an apartment.

Figure 4-9 shows the market for apartments in a city that has rent controls. Without rent control, the equilibrium rent would be US\$1,500 per month, and 2,000,000 apartments would be rented. With a maximum legal rent of US\$1,000 per month, landlords reduce the quantity of apartments supplied to 1,900,000. The fall in the quantity of apartments

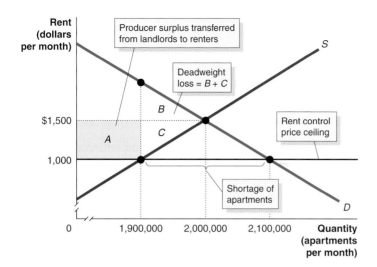

Figure 4-9

The Economic Effect of a Rent Ceiling

Without rent control, the equilibrium rent is US$1,500 per month. At that price, 2,000,000 apartments would be rented. If the government imposes a rent ceiling of US$1,000, the quantity of apartments supplied falls to 1,900,000, and the quantity of apartments demanded increases to 2,100,000, resulting in a shortage of 200,000 apartments. Producer surplus equal to the area of the blue rectangle *A* is transferred from landlords to renters, and there is a deadweight loss equal to the areas of yellow triangles *B* and *C*.

supplied is the result of some apartments being converted to offices or sold off as condominiums, some small apartment buildings being converted to single-family homes, and, over time, some apartment buildings being abandoned. In some cities that apply rent control policy such as New York City, rent control has resulted in whole city blocks being abandoned by landlords who were unable to cover their costs with the rents they were allowed to charge. In London, when rent controls were applied to rooms and apartments located in a landlord's own home, the quantity of these apartments supplied dropped by 75 percent.

In Figure 4-9, with the rent ceiling of US$1,000, the quantity of apartments demanded rises to 2,100,000. There is a shortage of 200,000 apartments. Consumer surplus increases by rectangle *A* and falls by triangle *B*. Rectangle *A* would have been part of producer surplus if rent control were not in place. With rent control, it is part of consumer surplus. Rent control causes the producer surplus received by landlords to fall by rectangle *A* plus triangle *C*. Triangles *B* and *C* represent the deadweight loss. There is a deadweight loss because rent control has reduced the amount of economic surplus in the market for apartments. Rent control has caused the marginal benefit of the last apartment rented to be greater than the marginal cost of supplying it. We can conclude that a price ceiling, such as rent control, reduces economic efficiency. The appendix to this chapter shows how we can make quantitative estimates of the deadweight loss, and it shows the changes in consumer surplus and producer surplus that result from rent control.

Renters as a group benefit from rent controls—total consumer surplus is larger—but landlords lose. Because of the deadweight loss, the total loss to landlords is greater than the gain to renters. Notice also that although renters as a group benefit, the number of renters is reduced, so some renters are made worse off by rent controls because they are unable to find an apartment at the legal rent.

Black Markets

To this point, our analysis of rent controls is incomplete. In practice, renters may be worse off and landlords may be better off than Figure 4-9 makes it seem. We have assumed that renters and landlords actually abide by the price ceiling, but sometimes they don't. Because rent control leads to a shortage of apartments, renters who would otherwise not be able to find apartments have an incentive to offer landlords rents above the legal maximum. When governments try to control prices by setting price ceilings or price floors, buyers and sellers often find a way around the controls. The result is a **black market** where buying and selling take place at prices that violate government price regulations.

In a housing market with rent controls, the total amount of consumer surplus received by renters may be reduced and the total amount of producer surplus received by landlords may be increased if apartments are being rented at prices above the legal price ceiling.

Black market A market in which buying and selling take place at prices that violate government price regulations.

Solved Problem | 4-3

What's the Economic Effect of a 'Black Market' for Apartments?

In many cities with rent controls, the actual rents paid can be much higher than the legal maximum. Because rent controls cause a shortage of apartments, desperate tenants are often willing to pay landlords rents that are higher than the law allows, perhaps by writing a check for the legally allowed rent and paying an additional amount in cash. Look again at Figure 4-9 on page 113. Suppose that competition among tenants results in the black market rent rising to US$2,000 per month. At this rent, tenants demand 1,900,000 apartments. Use a graph showing the market for apartments to compare this situation with the one shown in Figure 4-9. Be sure to note any differences in consumer surplus, producer surplus, and deadweight loss.

SOLVING THE PROBLEM:

Step 1: **Review the chapter material.** This problem is about price controls in the market for apartments, so you may want to review the section "Price Ceilings: Government Rent Control Policy in Housing Markets," which begins on page 112.

Step 2: **Draw a graph similar to Figure 4-9, with the addition of the black market price.**

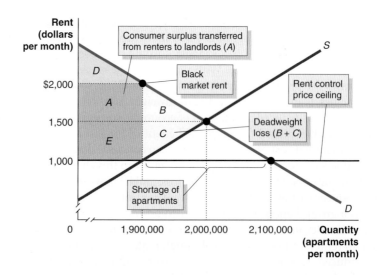

Step 3: **Analyze the changes from Figure 4-9.** Because the black market rent is now US$2,000—even higher than the original competitive equilibrium rent of US$1,500—compared with Figure 4-9, consumer surplus declines by an amount equal to the red rectangle *A* plus the red rectangle *E*. The remaining consumer surplus is the blue triangle *D*. Note that the rectangle *A*, which would have been part of consumer surplus without rent control, represents a transfer from renters to landlords. Compared with the situation shown in Figure 4-9, producer surplus has increased by an amount equal to rectangles *A* and *E*, and consumer surplus has declined by the same amount. Deadweight loss is equal to triangles *B* and *C*, the same as in Figure 4-9.

EXTRA CREDIT: This analysis leads to a surprising result: With an active black market in apartments, rent control may leave renters as a group worse off—with less consumer surplus—than if there were no rent control. There is one more possibility to consider, however. If enough landlords become convinced that they can get away with charging rents above the legal ceiling, the quantity of apartments supplied will increase. Eventually, the market could even end up at the competitive equilibrium, with an equilibrium rent of US$1,500 and equilibrium quantity of 2,000,000 apartments. In that case the rent control price ceiling becomes nonbinding, not because it was set below the equilibrium price but because it was not legally enforced.

YOUR TURN: For more practice, do related problems 3.13 on page 130 and 3.21 on page 131 at the end of this chapter.

>> **End Solved Problem 4-3**

Rent controls can also lead to an increase in racial and other types of discrimination. With rent controls, more renters are looking for apartments than there are apartments to rent. Landlords can afford to indulge their prejudices by refusing to rent to people they don't like. In cities without rent controls, landlords face more competition, which makes it more difficult to turn down tenants on the basis of irrelevant characteristics, such as race.

Making the Connection

Does Holiday Gift Giving Have a Deadweight Loss

The deadweight loss that results from rent control occurs, in part, because consumers rent fewer apartments than they would in a competitive equilibrium. Their choices are *constrained* by government. When you receive a gift, you are also constrained because the person who gave the gift has already chosen the product. In many cases, you would have chosen a different gift for yourself. Economist Joel Waldfogel of the University of Pennsylvania points out that gift giving results in a deadweight loss. The amount of the deadweight loss is equal to the difference between the gift's price and the dollar value the recipient places on the gift. Waldfogel surveyed his students, asking them to list every gift they had received for Christmas, to estimate the retail price of each gift, and to state how much they would have been willing to pay for each gift. Waldfogel's students estimated that their families and friends had paid US$438 on average for the students' gifts. The students themselves, however, would have been willing to pay only US$313 to buy the presents. If the deadweight losses experienced by Waldfogel's students were extrapolated to the whole population, the deadweight loss of Christmas gift giving could be as much as US$13 billion.

Gift giving may lead to deadweight loss.

If the gifts had been cash, the people receiving the gifts would not have been constrained by the gift givers' choices, and there would have been no deadweight loss. If your sister had given you cash instead of that sweater you didn't like, you could have bought whatever you wanted. Why then do people continue giving presents rather than cash? One answer is that most people receive more satisfaction from giving or receiving a present than from giving or receiving cash. If we take this satisfaction into account, the deadweight loss from gift

(Continued)

giving will be lower than in Waldfogel's calculations. In fact, a later study by economists John List of the University of Maryland and Jason Shogren of the University of Wyoming showed that as much as half the value of a gift to a recipient was its sentimental value. As Professor Shogren concluded, "People get a whole heck of a lot of value out of doing something for others and other people doing something for them. Aunt Helga gave you that ugly scarf, but hey, it's Aunt Helga."

Sources: Mark Whitehouse, "How Christmas Brings Out the Grinch in Economists," *Wall Street Journal*, December 23, 2006, p. A1; Joel Waldfogel, "The Deadweight Loss of Christmas," *American Economic Review*, Vol. 83, No. 4, December 1993, pp. 328–336; and John A. List and Jason F. Shogren, "The Deadweight Loss of Christmas: Comment," *American Economic Review*, Vol. 88, No, 5, 1998, pp. 1350–1355.

YOUR TURN: Test your understanding by doing related problem 3.14 on page 130 at the end of this chapter.

The Results of Government Price Controls: Winners, Losers, and Inefficiency

When the government imposes price floors or price ceilings, three important results occur:

- Some people win.
- Some people lose.
- There is a loss of economic efficiency.

The winners with rent control are the people who are paying less for rent because they live in rent-controlled apartments. Landlords may also gain if they break the law by charging rents above the legal maximum for their rent-controlled apartments, provided that those illegal rents are higher than the competitive equilibrium rents would be. The losers from rent control are the landlords of rent-controlled apartments who abide by the law and renters who are unable to find apartments to rent at the controlled price. Rent control reduces economic efficiency because fewer apartments are rented than would be rented in a competitive market (refer again to Figure 4-9). The resulting deadweight loss measures the decrease in economic efficiency.

Positive and Normative Analysis of Price Ceilings and Price Floors

Are rent controls, government price guarantee programs, and other price ceilings and price floors bad? As we saw in Chapter 1, questions of this type have no right or wrong answers. Economists are generally skeptical of government attempts to interfere with competitive market equilibrium. Economists know the role competitive markets have played in raising the average person's standard of living. They also know that too much government intervention has the potential to reduce the ability of the market system to produce similar increases in living standards in the future.

But recall from Chapter 1 the difference between positive and normative analysis. Positive analysis is concerned with *what is*, and normative analysis is concerned with *what should be*. Our analysis of rent control and of the federal farm programs in this chapter is positive analysis. We discussed the economic results of these programs. Whether these programs are desirable or undesirable is a normative question. Whether the gains to the winners more than make up for the losses to the losers and for the decline in economic efficiency is a matter of judgment and not strictly an economic question. Price ceilings and price floors continue to exist partly because people who understand their downside still believe they are good policies and therefore support them. The policies also persist because many people who support them do not understand the economic analysis in this chapter and so do not understand the drawbacks to these policies.

4.4 | Analyze the economic impact of taxes.

The Economic Impact of Taxes

When the government taxes a good to raise revenue, however, it affects the market equilibrium for that good. Just as with a price ceiling or price floor, one result of a tax is a decline in economic efficiency. Analyzing taxes is an important part of the field of economics known as *public finance*. In this section, we will use the model of demand and supply and the concepts of consumer surplus, producer surplus, and deadweight loss to analyze the economic impact of taxes.

The Effect of Taxes on Economic Efficiency

Whenever a government taxes a good or service, less of that good or service will be produced and consumed. For example, a tax on cigarettes will raise the cost of smoking and reduce the amount of smoking that takes place. We can use a demand and supply graph to illustrate this point. Figure 4-10 shows the market for cigarettes.

Without the tax, the equilibrium price of cigarettes would be US$4.00 per pack, and 4 billion packs of cigarettes would be sold per year (point *A*). If the government requires sellers of cigarettes to pay a US$1.00-per-pack tax, then their cost of selling cigarettes will increase by US$1.00 per pack. This causes the supply curve for cigarettes to shift up by US$1.00 because sellers will now require a price that is US$1.00 greater to supply the same quantity of cigarettes. In Figure 4-10, for example, without the tax, sellers would be

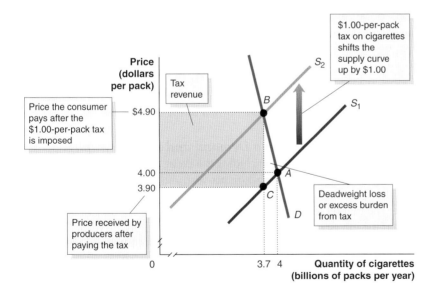

Figure 4-10 | The Effect of a Tax on the Market for Cigarettes

Without the tax, market equilibrium occurs at point *A*. The equilibrium price of cigarettes is US$4.00 per pack, and 4 billion packs of cigarettes are sold per year. A US$1.00-per-pack tax on cigarettes will cause the supply curve for cigarettes to shift up by US$1.00, from S_1 to S_2. The new equilibrium occurs at point *B*. The price of cigarettes will increase by US$0.90, to US$4.90 per pack, and the quantity sold will fall to 3.7 billion packs. The tax on cigarettes has increased the price paid by consumers from US$4.00 to US$4.90 per pack. Producers receive a price of US$4.90 per pack (point *B*), but after paying the US$1.00 tax, they are left with US$3.90 (point *C*). The government will receive tax revenue equal to the green shaded box. Some consumer surplus and some producer surplus will become tax revenue for the government and some will become deadweight loss, shown by the yellow-shaded area.

willing to supply a quantity of 3.7 billion packs of cigarettes at a price of US$3.90 per pack (point *C*). With the tax, they will supply only 3.7 billion packs of cigarettes if the price is US$4.90 per pack (point *B*). The shift in the supply curve will result in a new equilibrium price of US$4.90 and a new equilibrium quantity of 3.7 billion packs (point *B*).

The government will collect tax revenue equal to the tax per pack multiplied by the number of packs sold, or US$3.7 billion. The area shaded in green in Figure 4-10 represents the government's tax revenue. Consumers will pay a higher price of US$4.90 per pack. Although sellers appear to be receiving a higher price per pack, after they have paid the tax, the price they receive falls from US$4.00 per pack to US$3.90 per pack. There is a loss of consumer surplus because consumers are paying a higher price. The price producers receive falls, so there is also a loss of producer surplus. Therefore, the tax on cigarettes has reduced *both* consumer surplus and producer surplus. Some of the reduction in consumer and producer surplus becomes tax revenue for the government. The rest of the reduction in consumer and producer surplus is equal to the deadweight loss from the tax, shown by the yellow-shaded triangle in the figure.

We can conclude that the true burden of a tax is not just the amount paid to government by consumers and producers but also includes the deadweight loss. The deadweight loss from a tax is referred to as the *excess burden* of the tax. *A tax is efficient if it imposes a small excess burden relative to the tax revenue it raises.* One contribution economists make to government tax policy is to provide advice to policymakers on which taxes are most efficient.

Tax Incidence: Who Actually Pays a Tax?

The answer to the question "Who pays a tax?" seems obvious: whoever is legally required to send a tax payment to the government pays the tax. But there can be an important difference between who is legally required to pay the tax and who actually *bears the burden* of the tax. The actual division of the burden of a tax is referred to as **tax incidence**. Many Arab governments currently levy excise taxes (a specific tax imposed on manufactured goods) on cigarettes for health purposes and also to raise revenue, such as in Lebanon, Jordan, Egypt, Morocco, and Tunisia. In contrast, very few Arab countries impose an excise tax on gasoline (since most of them subsidize gasoline for economic and social purposes). Lebanon is one of the few Arab countries that imposes an excise tax on gasoline, of US$8.33 (12,500 Lebanese lira) per 20 liters. An excise tax on gasoline is also applied at Federal government and local government levels in the U.S. Sellers of cigarettes and gas station owners collect excise tax and forward the tax receipts to the government, but who actually bears the burden of the tax?

Tax incidence The actual division of the burden of a tax between buyers and sellers in a market.

Determining Tax Incidence on a Demand and Supply Graph Suppose that the retail price of gasoline in Lebanon—including the excise tax—is US$1.08 per liter, that 140 billion liters of gasoline are sold in Lebanon per year, and that excise tax is 10 cents per liter. Figure 4-11 allows us to analyze the incidence of the tax.

Consider the market for gasoline if there were no excise tax on gasoline. This equilibrium occurs at the intersection of the demand curve and supply curve, S_1. The equilibrium price is US$1.00 per liter, and the equilibrium quantity is 144 billion liters. If the government imposes a 10-cents-per-liter tax, the supply curve for gasoline will shift up by 10 cents per liter. At the new equilibrium, where the demand curve intersects the supply curve, S_2, the price has risen by 8 cents per liter, from US$1.00 to US$1.08. Notice that only in the extremely unlikely case that demand is a vertical line will the market price rise by the full amount of the tax. Consumers are paying 8 cents more per liter. Sellers of gasoline receive a new higher price of US$1.08 per liter, but after paying the 10-cents-per-liter tax, they are left with US$0.98 per liter, or 2 cents less than they had been receiving in the old equilibrium.

Although the sellers of gasoline are responsible for collecting the tax and forwarding it to the government, they do not bear most of the burden of the tax. In this case, consumers pay 8 cents of the tax because the market price has risen by 8 cents, and sellers pay 2 cents of the tax because after sending the tax to the government, they receive 2 cents less per liter of gasoline sold. Expressed in percentage terms, consumers pay 80 percent of the tax, and sellers pay 20 percent of the tax.

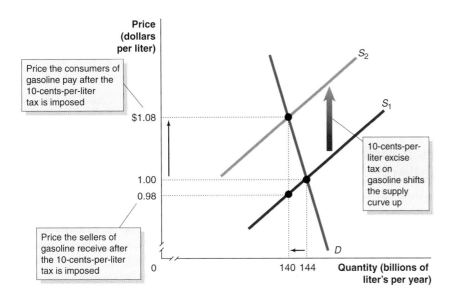

Figure 4-11

The Incidence of a Tax on Gasoline

With no tax on gasoline, the price would be US$1.00 per liter, and 144 billion liters of gasoline would be sold each year. A 10-cents-per-liter excise tax shifts up the supply curve from S_1 to S_2, raises the price consumers pay from US$1.00 to US$1.08, and lowers the price producers receive from US$1.00 to US$0.98. Therefore, consumers pay 8 cents of the 10-cents-per-liter tax on gasoline, and producers pay 2 cents.

Solved Problem | **4-4**

When Do Consumers Pay All of a Sales Tax Increase?

Briefly explain whether you agree with the following statement: "If the Lebanese government raises the excise tax on gasoline by US$0.25, then the price of gasoline will rise by US$0.25. Consumers can't get by without gasoline, so they have to pay the whole amount of any increase in the sales tax." Illustrate your answer with a graph.

SOLVING THE PROBLEM:

Step 1: **Review the chapter material.** This problem is about tax incidence, so you may want to review the section "Tax Incidence: Who Actually Pays a Tax?" which begins on page 118.

Step 2: **Draw a graph like Figure 4-11 to illustrate the circumstances when consumers will pay all of an increase in a sales tax.**

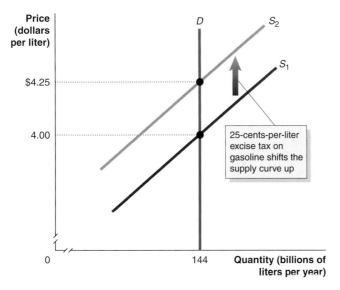

Step 3: **Use the graph to evaluate the statement.** The graph shows that consumers will pay all of an increase in a sales tax only if the demand curve is a vertical

line. It is very unlikely that the demand for gasoline looks like this because we expect that for every good, an increase in price will cause a decrease in the quantity demanded. Because the demand curve for gasoline is not a vertical line, the statement is incorrect.

>> End Solved Problem 4-4

YOUR TURN: For more practice, do related problem 4.5 on page 132 at the end of the chapter.

Does It Matter Whether the Tax Is on Buyers or Sellers?

We have already seen the important distinction between the true burden of a tax and whether buyers or sellers are legally required to pay a tax. We can reinforce this point by noting explicitly that the incidence of a tax does *not* depend on whether a tax is collected from the buyers of a good or from the sellers. Figure 4-12 illustrates this point by showing the effect on equilibrium in the market for gasoline if a 10-cents-per-liter tax is imposed on buyers rather than on sellers. That is, we are now assuming that instead of sellers having to collect the 10-cents-per-liter tax at the pump, buyers are responsible for keeping track of how many liters of gasoline they purchase and sending the tax to the government. (Of course, it would be very difficult for buyers to keep track of their purchases or for the government to check whether they were paying all of the tax they owed. That is why the government collects the tax on gasoline from sellers.)

Figure 4-12 is similar to Figure 4-11 except that it shows the gasoline tax being imposed on buyers rather than sellers. In Figure 4-12, the supply curve does not shift because nothing has happened to change the willingness of sellers to change the quantity of gasoline they supply. The demand curve has shifted, however, because consumers now have to pay a 10-cent tax on every liter of gasoline they buy. Therefore, at every quantity, they are willing to pay a price 10 cents less than they would have without the tax. We indicate this in the figure by shifting the demand curve down by 10 cents, from D_1 to D_2. Once the tax has been imposed and the demand curve has shifted down, the new equilibrium quantity of gasoline is 140 billion liters, which is exactly the same as in Figure 4-11.

The new equilibrium price after the tax is imposed appears to be different in Figure 4-12 than in Figure 4-11, but if we include the tax, buyers will pay and sellers will receive the same price in both figures. To see this, notice that in Figure 4-11, buyers paid sellers a price of US$1.08 per liter. In Figure 4-12, they pay sellers only US$0.98, but they must also pay the government a tax of 10 cents per liter. So, the total price buyers pay remains US$1.08 per liter. In Figure 4-11, sellers receive US$1.08 per liter from buyers, but after they pay the tax of 10 cents per liter, they are left with US$0.98, which is the same amount they receive in Figure 4-12.

Figure 4-12

The Incidence of a Tax on Gasoline Paid by Buyers

With no tax on gasoline, the demand curve is D_1. If a 10-cents-per-liter tax is imposed that consumers are responsible for paying, the demand curve shifts down by the amount of the tax, from D_1 to D_2. In the new equilibrium, consumers pay a price of US$1.08 per liter, including the tax. Producers receive US$0.98 per liter. This is the same result we saw when producers were responsible for paying the tax.

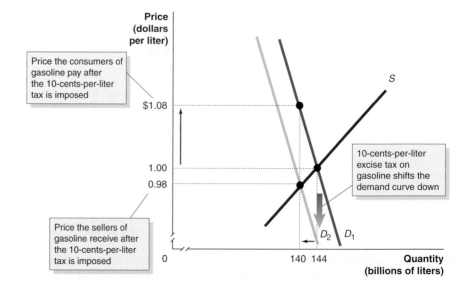

Price the consumers of gasoline pay after the 10-cents-per-liter tax is imposed

10-cents-per-liter excise tax on gasoline shifts the demand curve down

Price the sellers of gasoline receive after the 10-cents-per-liter tax is imposed

Making the Connection | Is The Burden of the Social Insurance Tax in Egypt Really Shared Equally between Workers and Firms?

Everyone who receives a paycheck has several different taxes withheld from it by their employers, who forward these taxes directly to the government. In fact, many people are shocked after getting their first job, when they discover the gap between their gross pay and their net pay after taxes have been deducted. In many countries, the largest tax many people of low or moderate income pay is the social security (insurance) tax. The tax revenue is earmarked to provide income and health care to the elderly and disabled. The social security tax is usually divided (equally or unequally) between employers and workers. For example, the Congress of the United States passed the Federal Insurance Contributions Act (FICA) that requires employers and workers to share equally the burden of the tax. Currently, the FICA is 15.3 percent of wages, with 7.65 percent paid by workers by being withheld from their paychecks and the other 7.65 percent paid by employers. In Egypt, the social insurance tax is 40 percent on basic salaries and is divided unequally between employers and workers as employers are required to pay 26 percent while 14 percent is paid by workers by being taken from their monthly salaries.

But does requiring workers and employers to each pay half the tax mean that the burden of the tax is also shared equally? And do employers in Egypt really bear about two-thirds of the social security tax burden? Our discussion in this chapter shows us that the answer is no. In the labor market, employers are buyers, and workers are sellers. As we saw in the example of government taxes on gasoline, whether the tax is collected from buyers or from sellers does not affect the incidence of the tax. Most economists believe, in fact, that the burden of the social security tax falls almost entirely on workers. The following figure, which shows the market for labor, illustrates why.

How much social insurance tax do you think these Egyptian employees pay?

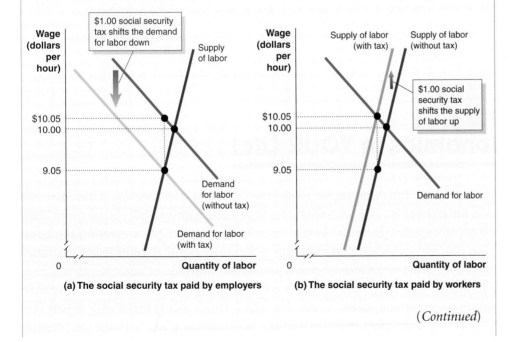

(a) The social security tax paid by employers

(b) The social security tax paid by workers

(Continued)

In the market for labor, the demand curve reflects the quantity of labor demanded by employers at various wages, and the supply curve reflects the quantity of labor supplied by workers at various wages. The intersection of the demand curve and the supply curve determines the equilibrium wage. In both panels, the equilibrium wage without a social security tax is US$10 per hour. For simplicity, let's assume that the social security tax equals US$1 per hour of work. In panel (a), we assume that employers must pay the tax. The tax causes the demand for labor curve to shift down by US$1 at every quantity of labor because firms now must pay a US$1 tax for every hour of labor they hire. We have drawn the supply curve for labor as being very steep because most economists believe the quantity of labor supplied by workers does not change much as the wage rate changes. Workers pay US$0.95 of the tax because their wages fall from US$10 before the tax to US$9.05 after the tax. Firms pay only US$0.05 of the tax because the amount they pay for an hour of labor increases from US$10 before the tax to US$10.05 after the tax. In panel (a), after the tax is imposed, the equilibrium wage declines from US$10 per hour to US$9.05 per hour. Firms are now paying a total of US$10.05 for every hour of work they hire: US$9.05 in wages to workers and US$1 in tax to the government. In other words, workers have paid US$0.95 of the US$1 tax, and firms have paid only US$0.05.

Panel (b) shows that this result is exactly the same if the tax is imposed on workers rather than on firms. In this case, the tax causes the supply curve for labor to shift up by US$1 at every quantity of labor because workers must now pay a tax of US$1 for every hour they work. After the tax is imposed, the equilibrium wage increases to US$10.05 per hour. But workers receive only US$9.05 after they have paid the US$1.00 tax. Once again, workers have paid US$0.95 of the US$1 tax, and firms have paid only US$0.05.

Although the figure presents a simplified analysis, it reflects the conclusion of most economists who have studied the incidence of the social security tax: even though parliaments in different countries require the distribution of the tax in some way (equal shares between employers and workers in the U.S., or two-thirds of the tax to be paid by employers and one-third to be paid by workers in Egypt, for example), in fact, the burden of the tax falls almost entirely on workers. This conclusion would not be changed even if parliament revised the law to require either employers or workers to pay all of the tax. The forces of demand and supply working in the labor market, and not the parliament, determine the incidence of the tax.

YOUR TURN: Test your understanding by doing related problem 4.6 on page 132 at the end of this chapter.

>> Continued from page 101

Economics in YOUR Life!

At the beginning of the chapter, we posed the following question: if you have two job offers in different cities, one with rent control and one without, will you be more likely to find an affordable apartment in the city with rent control? In answering the question, this chapter has shown that although rent control can keep rents lower than they might otherwise be, it can also lead to a permanent shortage of apartments. You may have to search for a long time to find a suitable apartment, and landlords may even ask you to give them payments 'under the table,' which would make your actual rent higher than the controlled rent. Finding an apartment in a city without rent control should be much easier, although the rent may be higher.

Conclusion

The model of demand and supply introduced in Chapter 3 showed that markets free from government intervention eliminate surpluses and shortages and do a good job of responding to the wants of consumers. We have seen in this chapter that both consumers and firms sometimes try to use the government to change market outcomes in their favor. The concepts of consumer and producer surplus and deadweight loss allow us to measure the benefits consumers and producers receive from competitive market equilibrium. They also allow us to measure the effects of government price floors and price ceilings and the economic impact of taxes.

Read *An Inside Look at Policy* on the next page for a discussion of the debate over rent control in the UAE.

GULF NEWS, MAY 31, 2008

UAE Landlords Find Ways to Beat the Rent Cap

Each emirate has enforced its own rules when it comes to rent, such as introducing a rent cap or prohibiting landlords from raising the rent during the first two years of a tenancy contract. Dubai/Abu Dhabi/Fujairah: The rule of thumb is that everybody should follow the rules.

One should especially follow the rules that were made to help balance the relationship between landlords and tenants. Each emirate has enforced its own rules when it comes to rent, such as introducing a rent cap or prohibiting landlords from raising the rent during the first two years of a tenancy contract.

In a recent *Gulf News* poll, 79 percent said the rent caps do not work across the emirates, while the remaining 21 percent said that they do.

City Talk took to the streets and asked residents whether the rent cap has worked for them and if they faced any problem with rent increases.

Tarek Khalifa, a business consultant from Egypt, 25, said: "I am here in the UAE on a project and so I am fortunate enough not to be looking for a flat because. from what I hear from my friends, rent has doubled and tripled in the last two years. My friends are suffering, either to find a flat that's affordable, or to keep up with expenses involved in their current flat."

G. Greta, an Indian secretary, said: "The landlord of the building where I have lived in for almost 11 years has increased the rent by 45 percent, even though the rent cap is only 5 percent. The increase does not cover maintenance, not to mention the monthly tips that we are obliged to give to our building watchman, which results in a burden on our savings."

Rabee Kafina, an engineer from Palestine, 27, said: "I am living in Sharjah and for the first two years the rent did not change. But now the rent has gone up all of a sudden by 45 percent, and that is not fair."

Umali James, a salesman from Malawi, 29, said: "The rent cap is good news but the landlords do not abide by it, and that is very upsetting. My rent is always going up. Most recently, the rent was doubled and the real-estate agents said it was because the building was going to be renovated, but it never happened."

Mylene D. Cedillo, a Filipina office assistant, 29, said: "Introducing a rent cap was definitely a positive move by the local authorities, and it was needed to stop greedy landlords, but in reality things have not changed for many.

"This year our landlord doubled our rent and even though we knew it was against the law we did not want to take up the matter with relevant authorities. If the law was changed, forcing landlords to seek approval from the municipality for any increase, that will take the pressure off tenants and ensure the law was correctly implemented."

Saeed Abrar Hussain, a Pakistani accountant, 25, said: "The rent cap is not effective. I cannot afford the rent anymore because it increases every year by 10 percent. The government should take active steps to make sure the rent cap is maintained properly."

Ali Abdul Hussain, a car rental agent from Iraq, 43, said: "The rent cap has not achieved anything for many people and landlords are getting away with unreasonable hikes. All residents in the building I live in have been told the rent will increase by a large margin. Many people don't know where to go or how the rent cap works and landlords are exploiting this."

…Sanjeev Menon, a media incharge from India, 42, said: "Our landlord increased the rent by 50 percent and asked us to vacate the property next year, so, for us, the rent cap did not work. I did not challenge the rent increase because I was not sure if it will be worth it."

Source: Mariam M. Al Serkal, Dina El Shammaa, and Fuad Ali, Staff Reporters, "UAE Landlords Find Ways to Beat the Rent Control," *Gulf News*, May 31, 2008.

Key Points in the Article

The article discusses the effectiveness of the rent-control law in the UAE. As we discussed in the chapter opener, Dubai was the first city in the Emirates to introduce a rent cap on the percentage by which landlords can increase annual rent to tenants. The purpose of rent-control laws is to ensure that low-income people can find affordable housing, and also to suppress the inflation rate. As the article explains, rent controls impose substantial costs on landlords that push them to look for any loopholes in the law that will enable them to circumvent it. And if landlords succeed in bypassing the rent-control law, it will become ineffective.

Analyzing the News

a The rent cap law in the UAE does not distinguish between low-income and high-income tenants, so some rent-controlled apartments are rented to people with high incomes. In other words, the law is not designed to help low-income tenants as it is a universal law that is applied on all types of apartments. The law is clearly a way to control the high inflation rate in the UAE. However, a rent-control law may actually increase the rent that some tenants pay. The figure in Solved Problem 4-3 on page 114 shows that the rent-control laws create a shortage of apartments, and that the resulting black market rent is often higher than the rent without rent-control laws.

b Strict rent-control laws reduce the price at which a landlord can sell a rent-controlled apartment compound (this applies to the 21 percent of voters in the *Gulf News* poll who said that the rent-control policy does work, as indicated in the previous article). Clearly, this hurts the landlord, but it can also harm tenants. The lower selling price for rent-controlled apartment compounds makes building those compounds less profitable. If developers can't make a profit building rent-controlled apartment compounds, then they won't build them. Over time, the number of compounds would decrease as old compounds become run down and developers lack the incentive to build new ones. The supply of rent-con-trolled apartments would decrease, making the apartment shortage worse. The figure below shows the effect of the decrease in rent-controlled apartment compounds as a shift of the supply curve to the left, from S_1 to S_2. This shift causes the shortage of apartments to increase from $(Q_1 - Q_2)$ to $(Q_1 - Q_3)$. In addition, the black market rent also increases from Black market$_1$ to Black market$_2$.

c On the other hand, rent-control laws might not be binding and might have loopholes. In this case, landlords will find several ways to get their desired rent. For example, as pointed out in the article, landlords can either charge a new, highly priced, expense item to tenants, such as maintenance expenses, or terminate, stop renewing, the contract with the existing tenant in order to lease the apartment at a higher rent to a new tenant, as long as this doesn't contradict with the rent-cap law (this case complies with the opinion of the 79 percent of voters in the Gulf News poll, who said that the rent-cap policy doesn't work). This will mainly happen when the demand for apartments is significantly higher than the supply of apartments, which is the case of many cities in the UAE, especially Dubai and Abu Dhabi. And if this scenario prevails, then the supply curve of apartments will not shift backward and will stay at S_1.

Thinking Critically About Policy

1. Despite the costs that are associated with rent-control laws, rent-control laws are very popular with tenants and politicians. Why would some tenants support rent-control laws? Do all tenants in the market gain from rent-control laws?

2. Economists are critical of rent-control laws for several reasons. One reason is that the laws create a deadweight loss. The magnitude of this deadweight loss depends on the slopes of the demand and supply curves. Look at the figure for Solved Problem 4-3 on page 114. The deadweight loss equals $B + C$, which is the yellow area. What causes the deadweight loss? What would the supply curve have to look like for the deadweight loss to equal zero?

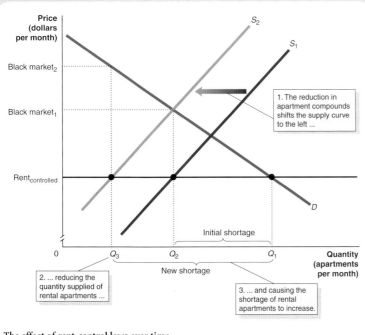

The effect of rent-control laws over time.

125

Key Terms

Summary

4.1 LEARNING OBJECTIVE

Distinguish between the concepts of consumer surplus and producer surplus, **pages 102–107.**

Consumer Surplus and Producer Surplus

Although most prices are determined by demand and supply in markets, the government sometimes imposes *price ceilings* and *price floors*. A **price ceiling** is a legally determined maximum price that sellers may charge. A **price floor** is a legally determined minimum price that sellers may receive. Economists analyze the effects of price ceilings and price floors using *consumer surplus* and *producer surplus*. **Marginal benefit** is the additional benefit to a consumer from consuming one more unit of a good or service. The demand curve is also a marginal benefit curve. **Consumer surplus** is the difference between the highest price a consumer is willing to pay for a product and the price the consumer actually pays. The total amount of consumer surplus in a market is equal to the area below the demand curve and above the market price. **Marginal cost** is the additional cost to a firm of producing one more unit of a good or service. The supply curve is also a marginal cost curve. **Producer surplus** is the difference between the lowest price a firm is willing to accept and the price it actually receives. The total amount of producer surplus in a market is equal to the area above the supply curve and below the market price.

4.2 LEARNING OBJECTIVE

Understand the concept of economic efficiency, **pages 107–109.**

The Efficiency of Competitive Markets

Equilibrium in a competitive market is **economically efficient**. **Economic surplus** is the sum of consumer surplus and producer surplus. Economic efficiency is a market outcome in which the marginal benefit to consumers from the last unit produced is equal to the marginal cost of production and where the sum of consumer surplus and producer surplus is at a maximum. When the market price is above or below the equilibrium price, there is a reduction in economic surplus. The reduction in economic surplus resulting from a market not being in competitive equilibrium is called the **deadweight loss**.

4.3 LEARNING OBJECTIVE

Explain the economic effect of government-imposed price ceilings and price floors, **pages 109–117.**

Government Intervention in the Market: Price Floors and Price Ceilings

Producers or consumers who are dissatisfied with the market outcome can attempt to convince the government to impose price floors or price ceilings. Price floors usually increase producer surplus, decrease consumer surplus, and cause a deadweight loss. Price ceilings usually increase consumer surplus, reduce producer surplus, and cause a deadweight loss. The results of the government imposing price ceilings and price floors are that some people win, some people lose, and a loss of economic efficiency occurs. Price ceilings and price floors can lead to a **black market**, where buying and selling takes place at prices that violate government price regulations. Positive analysis is concerned with what is, and normative analysis is concerned with what should be. Positive analysis shows that price ceilings and price floors cause deadweight losses. Whether these policies are desirable or undesirable, though, is a normative question.

4.4 LEARNING OBJECTIVE

Analyze the economic impact of taxes, **pages 117–123.**

The Economic Impact of Taxes

Most taxes result in a loss of consumer surplus, a loss of producer surplus, and a deadweight loss. The true burden of a tax is not just the amount paid to government by consumers and producers but also includes the deadweight loss. The deadweight loss from a tax is the excess burden of the tax. **Tax incidence** is the actual division of the burden of a tax. In most cases, consumers and firms share the burden of a tax levied on a good or service.

Review, Problems and Applications

myeconlab Visit www.pearsoned.co.uk/awe/hubbard to complete these exercises online and get instant feedback.

Get Ahead of the Curve

4.1 LEARNING OBJECTIVE   Distinguish between the concepts of consumer surplus and producer surplus, pages 102–107.

Review Questions

1.1 What is marginal benefit? Why is the demand curve referred to as a marginal benefit curve?

1.2 What is marginal cost? Why is the supply curve referred to as a marginal cost curve?

1.3 What is consumer surplus? How does consumer surplus change as the equilibrium price of a good rises or falls?

1.4 What is producer surplus? How does producer surplus change as the equilibrium price of a good rises or falls?

Problems and Applications

1.5 Suppose that a frost in Lebanon reduces the size of the orange crop, which causes the supply curve for oranges to shift to the left. Briefly explain whether each of the following will increase or decrease. Use demand and supply to illustrate your answers.
   a. Consumer surplus
   b. Producer surplus

1.6 A student makes the following argument: "When a market is in equilibrium, there is no consumer surplus. We know this because in equilibrium, the market price is equal to the price consumers are willing to pay for the good." Briefly explain whether you agree with the student's argument.

1.7 The following graph illustrates the market for a breast cancer–fighting drug, without which breast cancer patients cannot survive. What is the consumer surplus in this market? How does it differ from the consumer surplus in the markets you have studied up to this point?

1.8 (Related to the *Making the Connection* on page 104) The Making the Connection states that the value of the area representing consumer surplus from satellite television is US$2 billion. Use the information from the graph in the *Making the Connection* to show how this value was calculated. (For a review of how to calculate the area of a triangle, see the appendix to Chapter 1.)

1.9 The graph in the below shows the market for tickets to a concert that will be held in a local arena that seats 15,000 people. What is the producer surplus in this market? How does it differ from the producer surplus in the markets you have studied up to this point?

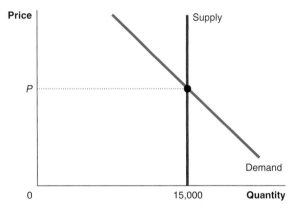

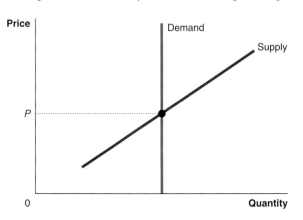

4.2 LEARNING OBJECTIVE   Understand the concept of economic efficiency, **pages 107–109.**

Review Questions

2.1 Define economic surplus and deadweight loss?

2.2 What is economic efficiency? Why do economists define efficiency in this way?

Problems and Applications

2.3 Suppose you were assigned the task of coming up with a single number that would allow someone to compare the economic activity in one country to that in another country. How might such a number be related to economic efficiency and consumer and producer surplus?

2.4 Briefly explain whether you agree with the following statement: "If at the current quantity marginal benefit is greater than marginal cost, there will be a deadweight loss in the market. However, there is no deadweight loss when marginal cost is greater than marginal benefit."

2.5 Briefly explain whether you agree with the following statement: "If consumer surplus in a market increases, producer surplus must decrease."

2.6 Does an increase in economic surplus in a market always mean that economic efficiency in the market has increased? Briefly explain.

2.7 Using the graph below, explain why economic surplus would be smaller if Q_1 or Q_3 were the quantity produced than if Q_2 is the quantity produced.

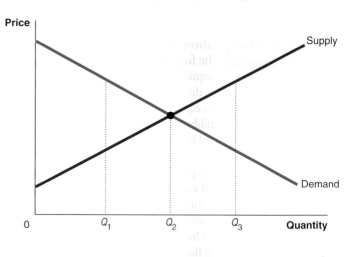

4.3 LEARNING OBJECTIVE   Explain the economic effect of government-imposed price ceilings and price floors, **pages 109–117.**

Review Questions

3.1 Why do some consumers tend to favor price controls while others tend to oppose them?

3.2 Do producers tend to favor price floors or price ceilings? Why?

3.3 What is a black market? Under what circumstances do black markets arise?

3.4 Can economic analysis provide a final answer to the question of whether the government should intervene in markets by imposing price ceilings and price floors? Why or why not?

Problems and Applications

3.5 The graph in the next column shows the market for apples. Assume the government has imposed a price floor of US$10 per crate.

a. How many crates of apples will be sold after the price floor has been imposed?

b. Will there be a shortage or a surplus? If there is a shortage or a surplus, how large will it be?

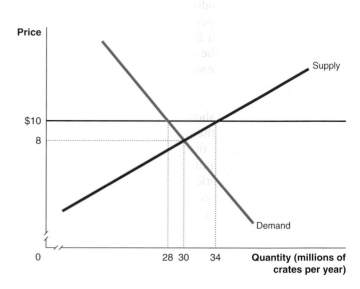

c. Will apple producers benefit from the price floor? If so, explain how they will benefit.

PRICE (PER CRATE) IN US$	QUANTITY DEMANDED (MILLIONS OF CRATES PER YEAR)	QUANTITY SUPPLIED (MILLIONS OF CRATES PER YEAR)
10	120	20
15	110	60
20	100	100
25	90	140
30	80	180
35	70	220

3.6 Use the information on the orange market in the table to answer the following questions.

a. What are the equilibrium price and quantity? How much revenue do orange producers receive when the market is in equilibrium? Draw a graph showing the market equilibrium and the area representing the revenue received by orange producers.

b. Suppose the government decides to impose a price floor of US$30 per crate. Now how many crates of oranges will consumers purchase? How much revenue will orange producers receive? Assume that the government does not purchase any surplus oranges. On your graph from question (a), show the price floor, the change in the quantity of oranges purchased, and the revenue received by orange producers after the price floor is imposed.

c. Suppose the government imposes a price floor of US$30 per crate and purchases any surplus oranges from producers. Now how much revenue will orange producers receive? How much will the government spend purchasing surplus oranges? On your graph from question (a), show the area representing the amount the government spends to purchase the surplus oranges.

3.7 Suppose that the government sets a price floor for milk that is above the competitive equilibrium price.

a. Draw a graph showing this situation. Be sure your graph shows the competitive equilibrium price, the price floor, the quantity that would be sold in competitive equilibrium, and the quantity that is sold with the price floor.

b. Compare the economic surplus in this market when there is a price floor and when there is no price floor.

3.8 During 2007, the Venezuelan government allowed consumers to buy only a limited quantity of sugar. The government also imposed a ceiling on the price of sugar. As a result, both the quantity of sugar consumed and the market price of sugar were below the competitive equilibrium price and quantity. Draw a graph to illustrate this situation. On your graph, be sure to indicate the areas representing consumer surplus, producer surplus, and deadweight loss.

3.9 Refer again to question 3.8. An article in the *New York Times* contained the following (Hugo Chávez is the president of Venezuela):

José Vielma Mora, the chief of Seniat, the government's tax agency, oversaw a raid this month on a warehouse here where officials seized about 165 tons of sugar. Mr. Vielma said the raid exposed hoarding by vendors who were unwilling to sell the sugar at official prices. He and other officials in Mr. Chávez's government have repeatedly blamed the shortages on producers, intermediaries and grocers.

Do you agree that the shortages in the Venezuelan sugar market are the fault of "producers, intermediaries and grocers"? Briefly explain.

Source: Simon Romero, "Chavez Threatens to Jail Price Control Violators," *New York Times*, February 17, 2007.

3.10 To drive a taxi legally in Amman, you must have a license issued by the city government. Suppose that city officials have issued only 12,187 licenses. Let's assume this puts an absolute limit on the number of taxi rides that can be supplied in Amman on any day because no one breaks the law by driving a taxi without a license. Let's also assume that each taxi can provide 6 trips per day. In that case, the supply of taxi rides is fixed at 73,122 (or 6 rides per taxi X 12,187 taxis). We show this in the following graph, with a vertical line at this quantity. *Assume that there are no government controls on the prices that drivers can charge for rides.* Use the graph to answer the following questions.

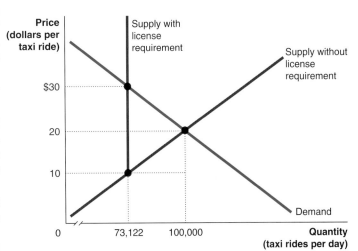

a. What would the equilibrium price and quantity be in this market if there were no license requirement?

b. What are the price and quantity with the license requirement?

c. Indicate on the graph the areas representing consumer surplus and producer surplus if there were no license requirement.

d. Indicate on the graph the areas representing consumer surplus, producer surplus, and deadweight loss with the license requirement.

3.11 (Related to the *Making the Connection* on page 111) Some U.S. economists studying the effects of the minimum wage law have found that it tends to reduce the employment of black teenagers relative to white teenagers. Does the graph in the *Making the Connection* on page 111 help you understand why black teenagers may have been disproportionately affected by the minimum wage? Briefly explain.

3.12 (Related to the *Chapter Opener* on page 100) Suppose the competitive equilibrium rent for a standard two-bedroom apartment in Dubai is US$600. Now suppose the city council passes a rent-control law imposing a price ceiling of US$500. Use a demand and supply graph to illustrate the impact of the rent-control law. Suppose that shortly after the law is passed, a large employer in the area announces that it will close a plant in Dubai and lay off 5,000 workers. Show on your graph how this will affect the market for rental property in Dubai.

3.13 (Related to *Solved Problem 4-3* on page 114) Use the information on the market for apartments in Abu Dhabi City in the table below to answer the following questions.

RENT IN US$	QUANTITY DEMANDED	QUANTITY SUPPLIED
500	375,000	225,000
600	350,000	250,000
700	325,000	275,000
800	300,000	300,000
900	275,000	325,000
1,000	250,000	350,000

a. In the absence of rent control, what is the equilibrium rent and what is the equilibrium quantity of apartments rented? Draw a demand and supply graph of the market for apartments to illustrate your answer. In equilibrium, will there be any renters who are unable to find an apartment to rent or any landlords who are unable to find a renter for an apartment?

b. Suppose the government sets a ceiling on rents of US$600 per month. What is the quantity of apartments demanded, and what is the quantity of apartments supplied?

c. Assume that all landlords abide by the law. Use a demand and supply graph to illustrate the impact of this price ceiling on the market for apartments. Be sure to indicate on your graph each of the following: (i) the area representing consumer surplus after the price ceiling has been imposed, (ii) the area representing producer surplus after the price ceiling has been imposed, and (iii) the area representing the deadweight loss after the ceiling has been imposed.

d. Assume that the quantity of apartments supplied is the same as you determined in (b). But now assume that landlords ignore the law and rent this quantity of apartments for the highest rent they can get. Briefly explain what this rent will be.

3.14 (Related to the *Making the Connection* on page 115) Joel Waldfogel argues that there may be a deadweight loss to holiday gift giving. An article in the *Wall Street Journal* suggests that retail stores might be better off if the tradition of holiday gift giving ended: "In theory, smoother sales throughout the year would be better for retailers, enabling them to avoid the extra costs of planning and stocking up for the holidays." Owners of many stores disagree, however. The owner of a store in New York City was quoted in the article as arguing: "Christmas is the lifeblood of the retail business. It's a time of year when people don't have a choice. They *have* to spend." Do you believe the efficiency of the economy would be improved if the tradition of holiday gift giving ended? Briefly explain your reasoning.
Source: Mark Whitehouse, "How Christmas Brings Out the Grinch in Economists," *Wall Street Journal*, December 23, 2006, p. A1.

3.15 Briefly explain whether you agree or disagree with the following statement: "If there is a shortage of a good, it must be scarce, but there is not a shortage of every scarce good."

3.16 A student makes the following argument:

> A price floor reduces the amount of a product that consumers buy because it keeps the price above the competitive market equilibrium. A price ceiling, on the other hand, increases the amount of a product that consumers buy because it keeps the price below the competitive market equilibrium.

Do you agree with the student's reasoning? Use a demand and supply graph to illustrate your answer.

3.17 An advocate of medical care system reform makes the following argument:

> The 15,000 kidneys that are transplanted in the United States each year are received free from organ donors. Despite this, because of hospital and doctor's fees, the average price of a kidney transplant is US$250,000. As a result, only rich people or people with very good health insurance can afford these transplants. The government should put a ceiling of US$100,000 on the price of kidney transplants. That way, middle-income people will be able to afford them, the demand for kidney transplants will increase, and more kidney transplants will take place.

Do you agree with the advocate's reasoning? Use a demand and supply graph to illustrate your answer.

3.18 (Related to the *Chapter Opener* on page 100) The cities of Dammam and Dhahran in Saudi Arabia are 10 km apart. Dhahran City enacts a rent-control law that puts a ceiling on rents well below their competitive market value. Predict the impact of this law on the competitive equilibrium rent in Dammam, which does not have a rent-control law. Illustrate your answer with a demand and supply graph.

3.19 (Related to the *Chapter Opener* on page 100) Suppose that the competitive equilibrium rent in the city of Dubai is currently US$1,000 per month. The government decides to enact rent control and to establish a price ceiling for apartments of US$750 per month. Briefly explain whether rent control is likely to make each of the following people better or worse off.
a. Someone currently renting an apartment in Dubai
b. Someone who will be moving to Dubai next year and who intends to rent an apartment
c. A landlord who intends to abide by the rent-control law
d. A landlord who intends to ignore the law and illegally charge the highest rent possible for his apartments

3.20 (Related to the *Chapter Opener* on page 100) The following is from an article in the *New York Times*:

> Imagine finding the perfect apartment, only to learn that the landlord is denying you the place because you are on a blacklist of supposedly high-risk renters. Nothing is wrong with your credit rating, but your name showed up on the list because a private screening service found it in housing court records about a dispute you had with a previous landlord—a dispute that was resolved in your favor.

Is it more likely that a 'blacklist' of 'high-risk' tenants will exist in a city with rent control or one without rent control? Briefly explain.
Source: Motoko Rich, "A Blacklist of Renters," *New York Times*, April 8, 2004.

3.21 (Related to *Solved Problem 4-3* on page 114) Suppose that initially the U.S. gasoline market is in equilibrium, at a price of US$3.00 per gallon and a quantity of 45 million gallons per month. Then, due to sustainable harsh weather conditions that resulted in a closure of many seaports in the United States, imports of oil into the U.S. are disrupted, shifting the supply curve for gasoline from S_1 to S_2. The price of gasoline begins to rise, and consumers protest. The U.S. federal government responds by setting a price ceiling of US$3.00 per liter. Use the graph to answer the following questions.

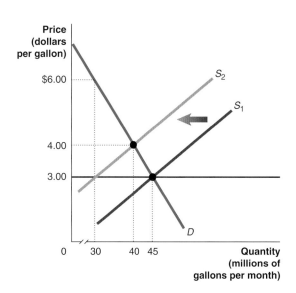

a. If there were no price ceiling, what would be the equilibrium price of gasoline, the quantity of gasoline demanded, and the quantity of gasoline supplied? Now assume that the price ceiling is imposed and that there is no black market in gasoline. What are the price of gasoline, the quantity of gasoline demanded, and the quantity of gasoline supplied? How large is the shortage of gasoline?
b. Assume that the price ceiling is imposed and there is no black market in gasoline. Show on the graph the areas representing consumer surplus, producer surplus, and deadweight loss.
c. Now assume that there is a black market and the price of gasoline rises to the maximum that consumers are willing to pay for the amount supplied by producers at US$3.00 per gallon. Show on the graph the areas representing producer surplus, consumer surplus, and deadweight loss.
d. Are consumers made better off with the price ceiling than without it? Briefly explain.

3.22 In the Arab world, Amazon.com and many other retailers sell books, DVDs, and music CDs for less than the price marked on the package. In Japan, retailers are not allowed to discount prices in this way. Who benefits and who loses from this Japanese law?

3.23 An editorial in *The Economist* discusses the fact that in most countries it is illegal for individuals to buy or sell body parts, such as kidneys.
a. Draw a demand and supply graph for the market for kidneys. Show on your graph the legal maximum price of zero and indicate the quantity of kidneys supplied at this price. (Hint: Because we know that some kidneys are donated, the quantity supplied will not be zero.)

b. The editorial argues that buying and selling kidneys should be legalized:

> With proper regulation, a kidney market would be a big improvement over the current sorry state of affairs. Sellers could be checked for disease and drug use, and cared for after operations…. Buyers would get better kidneys, faster. Both sellers and buyers would do better than in the illegal market, where much of the money goes to middlemen.

Do you agree with this argument? Should the government treat kidneys like other goods and allow the market to determine the price?

Source: "Psst, Wanna Buy a Kidney?" *The Economist*, November 18, 2006, p. 15.

4.4 LEARNING OBJECTIVE   Analyze the economic impact of taxes, **pages 117–123.**

Review Questions

4.1 What is meant by tax incidence?

4.2 Does it matter whether buyers or sellers are legally responsible for paying a tax? Briefly explain.

Problems and Applications

4.3 Suppose the current equilibrium price of cheese pizzas is US$10, and 10 million pizzas are sold per month. After the Egyptian government imposes a US$0.50 per pizza tax, the equilibrium price of pizzas rises to US$10.40, and the equilibrium quantity falls to 9 million. Illustrate this situation with a demand and supply graph. Be sure your graph shows the equilibrium price before and after the tax, the equilibrium quantity before and after the tax, and the areas representing consumer surplus after the tax, producer surplus after the tax, tax revenue collected by the government, and deadweight loss.

4.4 Use the graph of the market for cigarettes in the next column to answer the following questions.

a. According to the graph, how much is the government tax on cigarettes?

b. What price do producers receive after paying the tax?

c. How much tax revenue does the government collect?

4.5 (Related to *Solved Problem 4-4* on page 119) Suppose the Egyptian government decides to levy a sales tax on pizza of US$1.00 per pie. Briefly explain whether you agree with the following statement by a representative of the pizza industry:

> The pizza industry is very competitive. As a result, pizza sellers will have to pay the whole tax because they are unable to pass any of it on to consumers in the form of higher prices. Therefore, a sales tax of US$1.00 per pie will result in pizza sellers receiving US$1.00 less on each pie sold, after paying the tax.

Illustrate your answer with a graph.

4.6 (Related to the *Making the Connection* on page 121) If the price consumers pay and the price sellers receive are not affected by whether consumers or sellers collect a tax on a good or service, why does the government usually require sellers and not consumers to collect a tax?

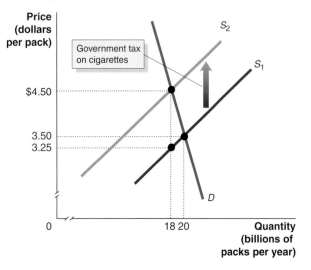

Appendix

Quantitative Demand and Supply Analysis

Graphs help us understand economic change *qualitatively*. For instance, a demand and supply graph can tell us that if household incomes rise, the demand curve for a normal good will shift to the right, and its price will rise. Often, though, economists, business managers, and policymakers want to know more than the qualitative direction of change; they want a *quantitative estimate* of the size of the change.

In Chapter 4, we carried out a qualitative analysis of rent controls. We saw that imposing rent controls involves a trade-off: Renters as a group gain, but landlords lose, and the market for apartments becomes less efficient, as shown by the deadweight loss. To better evaluate rent controls, we need to know more than just that these gains and losses exist; we need to know how large they are. A quantitative analysis of rent controls will tell us how large the gains and losses are.

LEARNING OBJECTIVE

Use **quantitative** demand and supply **analysis**.

Demand and Supply Equations

The first step in a quantitative analysis is to supplement our use of demand and supply curves with demand and supply *equations*. We noted briefly in Chapter 3 that economists often statistically estimate equations for demand curves. Supply curves can also be statistically estimated. For example, suppose that economists have estimated that the demand for apartments in Dubai is:

$$Q^D = 3,000,000 - 1,000P$$

and the supply of apartments is:

$$Q^S = -450,000 + 1,300P$$

We have used Q^D for the quantity of apartments demanded per month, Q^S for the quantity of apartments supplied per month, and P for the apartment rent in dollars per month. In reality, both the quantity of apartments demanded and the quantity of apartments supplied will depend on more than just the rental price of apartments in Dubai. For instance, the demand for apartments in Dubai will also depend on the average incomes of families in the Dubai area and on the rents of apartments in surrounding cities. For simplicity, we will ignore these other factors.

With no government intervention, we know that at competitive market equilibrium, the quantity demanded must equal the quantity supplied, or:

$$Q^D = Q^S$$

We can use this equation, which is called an *equilibrium condition*, to solve for the equilibrium monthly apartment rent by setting the demand equation equal to the supply equation:

$$3,000,000 - 1,000P = -450,000 + 1,300P$$

$$3,450,000 = 2,300P$$

$$P = \frac{3,450,000}{2,300} = US\$1,500$$

Figure 4A-1

Graphing Supply and Demand Equations

After statistically estimating supply and demand equations, we can use the equations to draw supply and demand curves. In this case, the equilibrium rent for apartments is US$1,500 per month, and the equilibrium quantity of apartments rented is 1,500,000. The supply equation tells us that at a rent of US$346, the quantity of apartments supplied will be zero. The demand equation tells us that at a rent of US$3,000, the quantity of apartments demanded will be zero. The areas representing consumer surplus and producer surplus are also indicated on the graph.

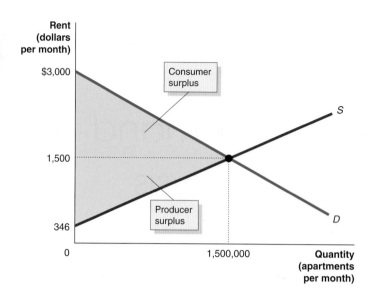

We can then substitute this price back into either the supply equation or the demand equation to find the equilibrium quantity of apartments rented:

$$Q^D = 3,000,000 - 1,000P = 3,000,000 - 1,000(1,500) = 1,500,000$$

$$Q^S = -450,000 + 1,300P = -450,000 + 1,300(1,500) = 1,500,000$$

Figure 4A-1 illustrates the information from these equations in a graph. The figure shows the values for rent when the quantity supplied is zero and when the quantity demanded is zero. These values can be calculated from the demand equation and the supply equation by setting Q^D and Q^S equal to zero and solving for price:

$$Q^D = 0 = 3,000,000 - 1,000P$$

$$P = \frac{3,000,000}{1,000} = US\$3,000$$

and:

$$Q^S = 0 = -450,000 + 1,300P$$

$$P = \frac{-450,000}{-1,300} = US\$346.15$$

Calculating Consumer Surplus and Producer Surplus

Figure 4A-1 shows consumer surplus and producer surplus in this market. Recall that the sum of consumer surplus and producer surplus equals the net benefit that renters and landlords receive from participating in the market for apartments. We can use the values from the demand and supply equations to calculate the value of consumer surplus and producer surplus. Remember that consumer surplus is the area below the demand curve and above the line representing market price. Notice that this area forms a right triangle because the demand curve is a straight line—it is *linear*. As we noted in the appendix to Chapter 1, the area of a triangle is equal to ½ multiplied by the base of the triangle multiplied by the height of the triangle. In this case, the area is:

$$\frac{1}{2} \times (1,500,000) \times (3,000 - 1,500) = US\$1,125,000,000$$

So, this calculation tells us that the consumer surplus in the market for rental apartments in Dubai would be about US$1.125 billion.

We can calculate producer surplus in a similar way. Remember that producer surplus is the area above the supply curve and below the line representing market price. Because our supply curve is also a straight line, producer surplus on the figure is equal to the area of the right triangle:

$$\frac{1}{2} \times 1{,}500{,}000 \times (1{,}500 - 346) = \text{US\$}865{,}500{,}000$$

This calculation tells us that the producer surplus in the market for rental apartments in Dubai is about US$865 million.

We can use this same type of analysis to measure the impact of rent control on consumer surplus, producer surplus, and economic efficiency. For instance, suppose the city imposes a rent ceiling of US$1,000 per month. Figure 4A-2 can help guide us as we measure the impact.

First, we can calculate the quantity of apartments that will actually be rented by substituting the rent ceiling of US$1,000 into the supply equation:

$$Q^S = 450{,}000 + (1{,}300 \times 1{,}000) = 850{,}000$$

We also need to know the price on the demand curve when the quantity of apartments is 850,000. We can do this by substituting 850,000 for quantity in the demand equation and solving for price:

$$850{,}000 = 3{,}000{,}000 - 1{,}000P$$

$$P = \frac{-2{,}150{,}000}{-1{,}000} = \text{US\$}2{,}150$$

Compared with its value in competitive equilibrium, consumer surplus has been reduced by a value equal to the area of the yellow triangle B but increased by a value equal to the area of the blue rectangle A. The area of the yellow triangle B is:

$$\frac{1}{2} \times (1{,}500{,}000 - 850{,}000) \times (2{,}150 - 1{,}500) = \text{US\$}211{,}250{,}000$$

and the area of the blue rectangle A is base multiplied by height, or:

$$(\text{US\$}1{,}500 - \text{US\$}1{,}000) \times (850{,}000) = \text{US\$}425{,}000{,}000$$

The value of consumer surplus in competitive equilibrium was US$1,125,000,000. As a result of the rent ceiling, it will be increased to:

$$(\text{US\$}1{,}125{,}000{,}000 + \text{US\$}425{,}000{,}000) - \text{US\$}211{,}250{,}000 = \text{US\$}1{,}338{,}750{,}000$$

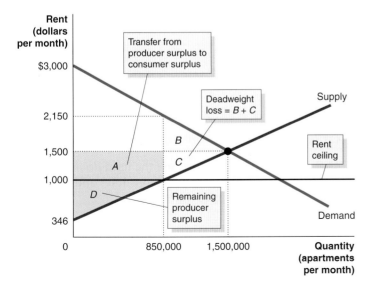

Figure 4A-2

Calculating the Economic Effect of Rent Controls

Once we have estimated equations for the demand and supply of rental housing, a diagram can guide our numeric estimates of the economic effects of rent control. Consumer surplus falls by an amount equal to the area of the yellow triangle B and increases by an amount equal to the area of the blue rectangle A. The difference between the values of these two areas is US$213,750,000. Producer surplus falls by an amount equal to the area of the blue rectangle A plus the area of the yellow triangle C. The value of these two areas is US$587,500,000. The remaining producer surplus is equal to the area of triangle D, or US$278,000,000. Deadweight loss is equal to the area of triangle B plus the area of triangle C, or US$373,750,000.

Compared with its value in competitive equilibrium, producer surplus has been reduced by a value equal to the area of the yellow triangle *C* plus a value equal to the area of the blue rectangle. The area of the yellow triangle *C* is:

$$\tfrac{1}{2} \times 1,500,000 - 850,00) \times (1,500 - 1,000) = \text{US\$162,500,000}$$

We have already calculated the area of the blue rectangle *A* as US\$425,000,000. The value of producer surplus in competitive equilibrium was US\$865,500,000. As a result of the rent ceiling, it will be reduced to:

$$\text{US\$865,500,000} - \text{US\$162,500,000} - \text{US\$425,000,000} = \text{US\$278,000,000}$$

The loss of economic efficiency, as measured by the deadweight loss, is equal to the value represented by the areas of the yellow triangles *B* and *C*, or:

$$\text{US\$211,250,000} + \text{US\$162,500,000} = \text{US\$373,750,000}$$

The following table summarizes the results of the analysis (the values are in millions of US dollars).

CONSUMER SURPLUS		PRODUCER SURPLUS		DEADWEIGHT LOSS	
COMPETITIVE EQUILIBRIUM	RENT CONTROL	COMPETITIVE EQUILIBRIUM	RENT CONTROL	COMPETITIVE EQUILIBRIUM	RENT CONTROL
$1,125	$1,338.75	$865.50	$278	$0	$373.75

Qualitatively, we know that imposing rent controls will make consumers better off, make landlords worse off, and decrease economic efficiency. The advantage of the analysis we have just gone through is that it puts dollar values on the qualitative results. We can now see how much consumers have gained, how much landlords have lost, and how great the decline in economic efficiency has been. Sometimes the quantitative results can be surprising. Notice, for instance, that after the imposition of rent control, the deadweight loss is actually greater than the remaining producer surplus.

Economists often study issues where the qualitative results of actions are apparent, even to non-economists. You don't have to be an economist to understand who wins and loses from rent control or that if a company cuts the price of its product, its sales will increase. Business managers, policymakers, and the general public do, however, need economists to measure quantitatively the effects of different actions—including policies such as rent control—so that they can better assess the results of these actions.

Review, Problems and Applications

 Visit www.pearsoned.co.uk/awe/hubbard to complete these exercises online and get instant feedback.
Get Ahead of the Curve

LEARNING OBJECTIVE　Use Quantitative Demand and Supply Analysis, **page 133–136.**

Review Questions

4A.1 In a linear demand equation, what economic information is conveyed by the intercept on the price axis?

4A.2 Suppose you were assigned the task of choosing a price that maximized economic surplus in a market. What price would you choose? Why?

4A.3 Consumer surplus is used as a measure of a consumer's net benefit from purchasing a good or service. Explain why consumer surplus is a measure of net benefit.

4A.4 Why would economists use the term *deadweight loss* to describe the impact on consumer and producer surplus from a price control?

Problems and Applications

4A.5 Suppose that you have been hired to analyze the impact on employment from the imposition of a minimum wage in the labor market. Further suppose that you estimate the supply and demand functions for labor, where L stands for the quantity of labor (measured in thousands of workers) and W stands for the wage rate (measured in dollars per hour):

Demand: $L^D = 100 - 4W$

Supply: $L^S = 6W$

First, calculate the free-market equilibrium wage and quantity of labor. Now suppose the proposed minimum wage is US$12. How large will the surplus of labor in this market be?

4A.6 The following graphs illustrate the markets for two different types of labor. Suppose an identical minimum wage is imposed in both markets. In which market will the minimum wage have the largest impact on employment? Why?

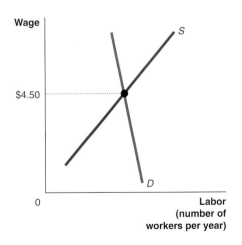

4A.7 Suppose that you are the vice president of operations of a manufacturing firm that sells an industrial lubricant in a competitive market. Further suppose that your economist gives you the following supply and demand functions:

Demand: $Q^D = 45 - 2P$

Supply: $Q^S = -15 + P$

What is the consumer surplus in this market? What is the producer surplus?

4A.8 The following graph shows a market in which a price floor of US$3.00 per unit has been imposed. Calculate the values of each of the following.
  a. The deadweight loss
  b. The transfer of producer surplus to consumers or the transfer of consumer surplus to producers
  c. Producer surplus after the price floor is imposed
  d. Consumer surplus after the price floor is imposed

4A.9 Construct a graph like the one in this appendix on page 135, but assume that the rent ceiling is US$1,200 rather than US$1,000.

>> **End Appendix Learning Objective**

Chapter 5

Elasticity: The Responsiveness of Demand and Supply

Do People Care about the Prices of Books?

Some observers have been predicting for years that the printed book will be replaced with the electronic book. The printed book is still holding its own, however. In 2006, U.S. consumers spent almost US$54 billion to buy 3.2 billion copies of new printed books. By contrast, although thousands of books were available in electronic format, total sales amounted to only a few million dollars. On the other hand, the printed-books industry in the Arab world is not faced with this 'e-books' competition as very few titles are available electronically. The UNESCO and country official documentation statistics show that the number of printed books' titles in the largest publishing Arab country, Egypt, increased in the IT revolution era from 1,410 in 1999 to an average of 7,000 title annually in the past 5 years.

While the printed book lives on, book publishers face a problem unique to the industry: unlike most retailers, bookstores have the right to return unsold books. For example, when a local supermarket orders shampoo, apple juice, or dog food, it knows that if it has overestimated consumer demand, it will be stuck with the unsold items. By contrast, to give bookstores an incentive to order more books, publishers have given the stores the right to return unsold

copies. On average, bookstores return 35 percent of books to publishers.

The high return rate of books means that publishers have to be very careful when deciding how many copies of a book to print and ship to bookstores. In 2007, Scholastic, the largest publisher of children's books in the world, published the final installment of the hugely popular Harry Potter series. Barnes & Noble bookstores (USA) and Jarir bookstores (Saudi Arabia) have special membership programs that give their customers a discount (10 to 20 percent) on most books. But on *Harry Potter and the Deathly Hallows*, Barnes & Noble offered a 40 percent discount. The company was willing to accept a small profit on each book in hopes of selling a very large quantity. Scholastic could not simply print all the books ordered by bookstores like Barnes & Noble because it feared that the bookstores might overestimate the quantity of books actually demanded by consumers. Executives at Scholastic knew that the number of copies of the book demanded by consumers would depend in part on the price of the book. In the same trend, Jarir Bookstores recently offered a store voucher of 50 Saudi riyals (SR) for every customer who spends SR200 (around US$50) on books in English. Again, this is an incentive to readers to buy more English books at the expense of lower profit for Jarir Bookstores. But how responsive are consumers

to changes in book prices and other bookstores' incentives? Will a lower price significantly increase sales? Publishers debate this point.

For example, Stephen Rubin, president and publisher of Doubleday, has made the following argument about book prices: "I am just convinced that there is no difference between US$22 and US$23. Let's face it. If you want a book in translation from a Czech writer, you are going to buy the book—price is not a factor if it is a book that you really want." On the other hand, Barnes & Noble's program of discounting books for members will be effective only if consumers are sufficiently responsive to lower prices for books. As Bill Armstrong, an industry analyst, put it: "[Barnes & Noble's discount program] will only be a success if these lower prices produce greater unit volume enough to offset the lower price per book." **AN INSIDE LOOK** on **page 164** discusses the effectiveness of Etisalat telecommunication company discounted service policy for call roaming and price cut of iPhones.

Sources: Henry Sanderson, "Barnes & Noble Disappoints Investors with Outlook," *Wall Street Journal*, March 5, 2007; data on book sales from U.S. Census Bureau, *The 2007 Statistical Abstract* Najib Harabi. "Knowledge Intensive Industries: Four Case Studies of Creative Industries in Arab Countries," World Bank Project; *Learning Event on Developing Knowledge Economy Strategies to Improve Competitiveness in the MENA Region*, May 17–21, 2009, Alexandria, Egypt; and "The Book industry in Egypt," Frankfurt Book Fair website, www.buchmesse.de/imperia/celum/documents/summary_book_industry_egypt_6992.pdf.

LEARNING Objectives

After studying this chapter, you should be able to:

5.1 Define the **price elasticity of demand** and understand how to measure it, page 140.

5.2 Understand the **determinants of** the **price elasticity** of **demand**, page 146.

5.3 Understand the relationship between the **price elasticity of demand** and **total revenue**, page 148.

5.4 Define the **cross-price elasticity of demand** and the **income elasticity** of demand, and understand their determinants and how they are measured, page 152.

5.5 Use **price elasticity** and **income elasticity** to analyze economic issues, page 155.

5.6 Define the **price elasticity of supply** and understand its main determinants and how it is measured, page 157.

Economics in YOUR Life!

How Much Do Book Prices Matter to You?

We have just seen that there is a debate in the publishing industry about how responsive consumers are to changes in book prices. Barnes & Noble was willing to reduce the price of *Harry Potter and the Deathly Hallows* and Jarir Bookstores offered store vouchers to buyers of books in English as they believed that doing so would significantly increase sales. Some book executives, like Stephen Rubin of Doubleday, seem to think that prices do not matter. What factors would make you more or less sensitive to price when purchasing a book? Are Barnes & Noble's and Jarir Bookstore's strategies likely to succeed? As you read the chapter, see if can answer these questions. You can check your answers against those we provide at the end of the chapter. >> Continued on page 162

Elasticity A measure of how much one economic variable responds to changes in another economic variable.

W̲hether you are managing a publishing company, bookstore, or coffee shop, you need to know how an increase or decrease in the price of your products will affect the quantity consumers are willing to buy. We saw in Chapter 3 that cutting the price of a good increases the quantity demanded and that raising the price reduces the quantity demanded. But the critical question is this: *How much* will the quantity demanded change as a result of a price increase or decrease? Economists use the concept of **elasticity** to measure how one economic variable—such as the quantity demanded—responds to changes in another economic variable—such as the price. For example, the responsiveness of the quantity demanded of a good to changes in its price is called the *price elasticity of demand*. Knowing the price elasticity of demand allows you to compute the effect of a price change on the quantity demanded.

We also saw in Chapter 3 that the quantity of a good that consumers demand depends not just on the price of the good but also on consumer income and on the prices of related goods. As a manager, you would also be interested in measuring the responsiveness of demand to these other factors. As we will see, we can use the concept of elasticity here as well. We also are interested in the responsiveness of the quantity supplied of a good to changes in its price, which is called the *price elasticity of supply*.

Elasticity is an important concept not just for business managers but for policymakers as well. If the government wants to discourage teenage smoking, it can raise the price of cigarettes by increasing the tax on them. If we know the price elasticity of demand for cigarettes, we can calculate how many fewer cigarettes will be demanded at a higher price. In this chapter, we will also see how policymakers use the concept of elasticity.

5.1 | Define the price elasticity of demand and understand how to measure it.

The Price Elasticity of Demand and Its Measurement

We know from the law of demand that when the price of a product falls, the quantity demanded of the product increases. But the law of demand tells firms only that the demand curves for their products slope downward. More useful is a measure of the responsiveness of the quantity demanded to a change in price. This measure is called the **price elasticity of demand**.

Measuring the Price Elasticity of Demand

Price elasticity of demand The responsiveness of the quantity demanded to a change in price, measured by dividing the percentage change in the quantity demanded of a product by the percentage change in the product's price.

We might measure the price elasticity of demand by using the slope of the demand curve because the slope of the demand curve tells us how much quantity changes as price changes. Using the slope of the demand curve to measure price elasticity has a drawback, however: The measurement of slope is sensitive to the units chosen for quantity and price. For example, suppose a US$1 decrease in the price of *Harry Potter and the Deathly Hallows* leads to an increase in the quantity demanded from 10.1 million books to 10.2 million books. The change in quantity is 0.1 million books, and the change in price is −US$1, so the slope is 0.1/−1 = −0.1. But if we measure price in cents, rather than dollars, the slope is 0.1/−100 = −0.001. If we measure price in dollars and books in thousands, instead of millions, the slope is 100/−1 = −100. Clearly, the value we compute for the slope can change dramatically, depending on the units we use for quantity and price.

To avoid this confusion over units, economists use *percentage changes* when measuring the price elasticity of demand. Percentage changes are not dependent on units. (For a review of calculating percentage changes, see the appendix to Chapter 1.) No matter what units we use to measure the quantity of wheat, 10 percent more wheat is 10 percent more wheat. Therefore, the price elasticity of demand is measured by dividing the percentage change in the quantity demanded by the percentage change in the price. Or:

$$\text{Price elasticity of demand} = \frac{\text{Percentage change in quantity demanded}}{\text{Percentage change in price}}$$

It's important to remember that *the price elasticity of demand is not the same as the slope of the demand curve.*

   If we calculate the price elasticity of demand for a price cut, the percentage change in price will be negative, and the percentage change in quantity demanded will be positive. Similarly, if we calculate the price elasticity of demand for a price increase, the percentage change in price will be positive, and the percentage change in quantity will be negative. Therefore, the price elasticity of demand is always negative. In comparing elasticities, though, we are usually interested in their relative size. So, we often drop the minus sign and compare their *absolute values*. In other words, although −3 is actually a smaller number than −2, a price elasticity of −3 is larger than a price elasticity of −2.

Elastic Demand and Inelastic Demand

If the quantity demanded is responsive to changes in price, the percentage change in quantity demanded will be *greater* than the percentage change in price, and the price elasticity of demand will be greater than 1 in absolute value. In this case, demand is **elastic**. For example, if a 10 percent fall in the price of bagels results in a 20 percent increase in the quantity of bagels demanded, then:

$$\text{Price elasticity of demand} = \frac{20\%}{-10\%} = -2$$

and we can conclude that the price of bagels is **elastic**.

   When the quantity demanded is not very responsive to price, however, the percentage change in quantity demanded will be *less* than the percentage change in price, and the price elasticity of demand will be less than 1 in absolute value. In this case, demand is **inelastic**. For example, if a 10 percent fall in the price of wheat results in a 5 percent increase in the quantity of wheat demanded, then:

$$\text{Price elasticity of demand} = \frac{5\%}{-10\%} = -0.5$$

and we can conclude that the demand for wheat is **inelastic**.

   In the special case in which the percentage change in the quantity demanded is equal to the percentage change in price, the price elasticity of demand equals −1 (or 1 in absolute value). In this case, demand is **unit-elastic**.

Elastic demand Demand is elastic when the percentage change in quantity demanded is greater than the percentage change in price, so the price elasticity is greater than 1 in absolute value.

Inelastic demand Demand is inelastic when the percentage change in quantity demanded is less than the percentage change in price, so the price elasticity is less than 1 in absolute value.

Unit-elastic demand Demand is unit-elastic when the percentage change in quantity demanded is equal to the percentage change in price, so the price elasticity is equal to 1 in absolute value.

An Example of Computing Price Elasticities

Suppose you own a small bookstore and you are trying to decide whether to cut the price you are charging for a Naguib Mahfouz novel. You are currently at point *A* in Figure 5-1: selling 16 copies of the novel per day at a price of US\$30 per copy. How many more copies you will sell by cutting the price to US\$20 depends on the price elasticity of demand for this novel. Let's consider two possibilities: If D_1 is the demand curve for this novel in your store, your sales will increase to 28 copies per day, point *B*. But if D_2 is your demand curve, your sales will increase only to 20 copies per day, point *C*. We might expect—correctly, as we will see—that between these points, demand curve D_1 is *elastic*, and demand curve D_2 is *inelastic*.

   To confirm that D_1 is elastic between these points and that D_2 is inelastic, we need to calculate the price elasticity of demand for each curve. In calculating price elasticity between two points on a demand curve, though, we run into a problem because we get a different value for price increases than for price decreases. For example, suppose we calculate the price elasticity for D_2 as the price is cut from US\$30 to US\$20. This reduction is a 33 percent price cut that increases the quantity demanded from 16 books to

Figure 5-1

Elastic and Inelastic Demand Curves

Along D_1, cutting the price from US$30 to US$20 increases the number of copies sold from 16 per day to 28 per day, so demand is elastic between point A and point B. Along D_2, cutting the price from US$30 to US$20 increases the number of copies sold from 16 per day to only 20 per day, so demand is inelastic between point A and point C.

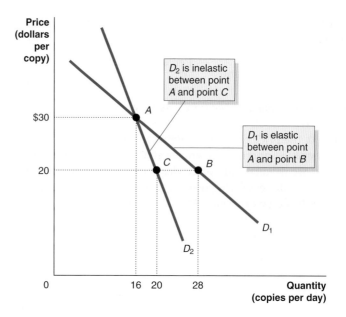

20 books, or by 25 percent. Therefore, the price elasticity of demand between points A and C is 25/−33 = −0.8. Now let's calculate the price elasticity for D_2 as the price is *increased* from US$20 to US$30. This is a 50 percent price increase that decreases the quantity demanded from 20 books to 16 books, or by 20 percent. So, now our measure of the price elasticity of demand between points A and C is −20/50 = −0.4. It can be confusing to have different values for the price elasticity of demand between the same two points on the same demand curve.

The Midpoint Formula

We can use the *midpoint formula* to ensure that we have only one value of the price elasticity of demand between the same two points on a demand curve. The midpoint formula uses the *average* of the initial and final quantities and the initial and final prices. If Q_1 and P_1 are the initial quantity and price and Q_2 and P_2 are the final quantity and price, the midpoint formula is:

$$\text{Price elasticity of demand} = \frac{(Q_2 - Q_1)}{\left(\dfrac{Q_1 + Q_2}{2}\right)} \div \frac{(P_2 - P_1)}{\left(\dfrac{P_1 + P_2}{2}\right)}$$

The midpoint formula may seem challenging at first, but the numerator is just the change in quantity divided by the average of the initial and final quantities, and the denominator is just the change in price divided by the average of the initial and final prices.

Let's apply the formula to calculating the price elasticity of D_2 in Figure 5-1. Between point A and point C on D_2, the change in quantity is 4, and the average of the two quantities is 18. Therefore, there is a 22.2 percent change in quantity. The change in price is −US$10, and the average of the two prices is US$25. Therefore, there is a −40 percent change in price. So, the price elasticity of demand is 22.2/−40.0 = −0.6. Notice these three results from calculating the price elasticity of demand using the midpoint formula: First, as we suspected from examining Figure 5-1, demand curve D_2 is inelastic between points A and C. Second, our value for the price elasticity calculated using the midpoint formula is between the two values we calculated earlier. Third, the midpoint formula will give us the same value whether we are moving from the higher price to the lower price or from the lower price to the higher price.

We can also use the midpoint formula to calculate the elasticity of demand between point A and point B on D_1. In this case, there is a 54.5 percent change in quantity and a −40 percent change in price. So, the elasticity of demand is 54.5/−40.0 = −1.4. Once again, as we suspected, demand curve D_1 is price elastic between points A and B.

Solved Problem | 5-1

Calculating the Price Elasticity of Demand

W. W. Norton & Co., book publishers, have suggested a retail price of US$35 for *The Arabian Nights: Sindbad and Other Popular Stories.* Suppose you own a small bookstore, and you believe that if you keep the price of the book at US$35, you will be able to sell 40 copies per day. You are considering cutting the price to US$25. The graph below shows two possible increases in the quantity sold as a result of your price cut. Use the information in the graph to calculate the price elasticity between these two prices on each of the demand curves. Use the midpoint formula in your calculations. State whether each demand curve is elastic or inelastic between these two prices.

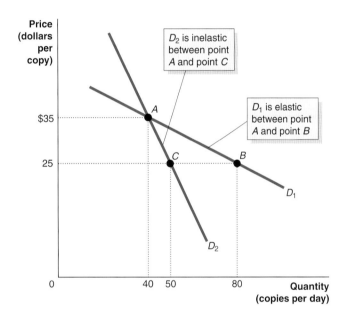

SOLVING THE PROBLEM:

Step 1: **Review the chapter material.** This problem requires calculating the price elasticity of demand, so you may want to review the material in the section "The Midpoint Formula," which begins on page 142.

Step 2: **As the first step in using the midpoint formula, calculate the average quantity and the average price for demand curve D_1.**

$$\text{Average quantity} = \frac{40 + 80}{2} = 60$$

$$\text{Average price} = \frac{\$35 + \$25}{2} = \$30$$

Step 3: **Now calculate the percentage change in the quantity demanded and the percentage change in price for demand curve D_1.**

$$\text{Percentage change in quantity demanded} = \frac{80 - 40}{60} \times 100 = 66.7\%$$

$$\text{Percentage change in price} = \frac{\$25 - \$35}{\$30} \times 100 = -33.3\%$$

Step 4: **Divide the percentage change in the quantity demanded by the percentage change in price to arrive at the price elasticity for demand curve D_1.**

$$\text{Price elasticity of demand} = \frac{66.7\%}{-33.3\%} = -2$$

Because the elasticity is greater than 1 in absolute value, D_1 is price *elastic* between these two prices.

Step 5: **Calculate the price elasticity of demand curve D_2 between these two prices.**

$$\text{Percentage change in quantity demanded} = \frac{50 - 40}{45} \times 100 = 22.2\%$$

$$\text{Percentage change in price} = \frac{\$25 - \$35}{\$30} \times 100 = -33.3\%$$

$$\text{Price elasticity of demand} = \frac{22.2\%}{-33.3\%} = -0.7$$

Because the elasticity is less than 1 in absolute value, D_2 is price *inelastic* between these two prices.

>> **End Solved Problem 5-1**

YOUR TURN: For more practice, do related problem 1.6 on page 167 at the end of this chapter.

When Demand Curves Intersect, the Flatter Curve Is More Elastic

Remember that elasticity is not the same thing as slope. While slope is calculated using changes in quantity and price, elasticity is calculated using percentage changes. But it *is* true that if two demand curves intersect, the one with the smaller slope (in absolute value)—the flatter demand curve—is more elastic, and the one with the larger slope (in absolute value)—the steeper demand curve—is less elastic. In Figure 5-1, demand curve D_1 is more elastic than demand curve D_2.

Polar Cases of Perfectly Elastic and Perfectly Inelastic Demand

Perfectly inelastic demand The case where the quantity demanded is completely unresponsive to price, and the price elasticity of demand equals zero.

Although they do not occur frequently, you should be aware of the extreme, or polar, cases of price elasticity. If a demand curve is a vertical line, it is **perfectly inelastic**. In this case, the quantity demanded is completely unresponsive to price, and the price elasticity of demand equals zero. However much price may increase or decrease, the quantity remains the same. For only a very few products will the quantity demanded be completely unresponsive to the price, making the demand curve a vertical line. The drug insulin is an example. Diabetics must take a certain amount of insulin each day. If the price of insulin declines, it will not affect the required dose and thus will not increase the quantity demanded. Similarly, a price increase will not affect the required dose or decrease the quantity demanded. (Of course, some diabetics will not be able to afford insulin at a higher price. If so, even in this case, the demand curve may not be completely vertical and, therefore, not perfectly inelastic.)

Perfectly elastic demand The case where the quantity demanded is infinitely responsive to price, and the price elasticity of demand equals infinity.

If a demand curve is a horizontal line, it is **perfectly elastic**. In this case, the quantity demanded would be infinitely responsive to price, and the price elasticity of demand equals infinity. If a demand curve is perfectly elastic, an increase in price causes the quantity demanded to fall to zero. Once again, perfectly elastic demand curves are rare, and it is important not to confuse *elastic* with *perfectly elastic*. Table 5-1 summarizes the different price elasticities of demand.

IF DEMAND IS...	THEN THE ABSOLUTE VALUE OF PRICE ELASTICITY IS	
elastic	greater than 1	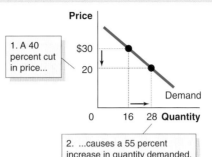
inelastic	less than 1	
unit-elastic	equal to 1	
perfectly elastic	equal to infinity	
perfectly inelastic	equal to 0	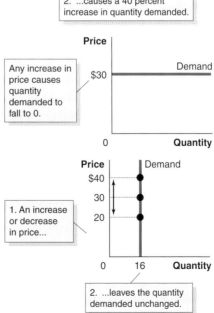

TABLE 5-1

Summary of the Price Elasticities of Demand

(Note that the percentage increases shown in the boxes in the graphs were calculated using the midpoint formula on page 142.)

5.2 | Understand the determinants of the price elasticity of demand.

The Determinants of the Price Elasticity of Demand

We have seen that the demand for some products may be elastic, while the demand for other products may be inelastic. In this section, we examine why price elasticities differ among products. The key determinants of the price elasticity of demand are as follows:

- Availability of close substitutes
- Passage of time
- Necessities versus luxuries
- Definition of the market
- Share of the good in the consumer's budget.

Availability of Close Substitutes

The availability of substitutes is the most important determinant of price elasticity of demand because how consumers react to a change in the price of a product depends on what alternatives they have. When the price of gasoline rises, consumers have few alternatives, so the quantity demanded falls only a little. But if Domino's raises the price of pizza, consumers have many alternatives, so the quantity demanded is likely to fall quite a lot. In fact, a key constraint on a firm's pricing policies is how many close substitutes exist for its product. In general, *if a product has more substitutes available, it will have more elastic demand. If a product has fewer substitutes available, it will have less elastic demand.*

Passage of Time

It usually takes consumers some time to adjust their buying habits when prices change. If the price of chicken falls, for example, it takes a while before consumers decide to change from eating chicken for dinner once per week to eating it twice per week. If the price of gasoline increases, it also takes a while for consumers to decide to shift toward buying more fuel-efficient cars to reduce the quantity of gasoline they buy. *The more time that passes, the more elastic the demand for a product becomes.*

Luxuries versus Necessities

Goods that are luxuries usually have more elastic demand curves than goods that are necessities. For example, the demand for milk is inelastic because milk is a necessity, and the quantity that people buy is not very dependent on its price. Tickets to a concert are a luxury, so the demand for concert tickets is much more elastic than the demand for milk. *The demand curve for a luxury is more elastic than the demand curve for a necessity.*

Definition of the Market

In a narrowly defined market, consumers have more substitutes available. If the price of Kellogg's Corn Flakes rises, many consumers will start buying another brand of corn flakes. If the prices of all brands of corn flakes rise, the responsiveness of consumers will be lower. If the prices of all breakfast cereals rise, the responsiveness of consumers will be even lower. *The more narrowly we define a market, the more elastic demand will be.*

Making the Connection | The Price Elasticity of Demand for Breakfast Cereal

MIT economist Jerry Hausman has estimated the price elasticity of demand for breakfast cereal. He divided breakfast cereals into three categories: children's cereals, such as Trix and Froot Loops; adult cereals, such as Special K and Grape-Nuts; and family cereals, such as Corn Flakes and Raisin Bran. Some of the results of his estimates are given in the following table.

CEREAL	PRICE ELASTICITY OF DEMAND
Post Raisin Bran	−2.5
All family breakfast cereals	−1.8
All types of breakfast cereals	−0.9

Source: Jerry A. Hausman, "The Price Elasticity of Demand for Breakfast Cereal," in Timothy F. Bresnahan and Robert J. Gordon, eds., *The Economics of New Goods*, Chicago: University of Chicago Press, 1997. Used with permission of The University of Chicago Press.

What happens when the price of Raisin Bran cereal increases?

Just as we would expect, the price elasticity for a particular brand of raisin bran was larger in absolute value than the elasticity for all family cereals, and the elasticity for all family cereals was larger than the elasticity for all types of breakfast cereals. If Post increases the price of its Raisin Bran by 10 percent, sales will decline by 25 percent, as many consumers switch to another brand of raisin bran. If the prices of all family breakfast cereals rise by 10 percent, sales will decline by 18 percent, as consumers switch to child or adult cereals. In both of these cases, demand is elastic. But if the prices of all types of breakfast cereals rise by 10 percent, sales will decline by only 9 percent. Demand for all breakfast cereals is inelastic.

Source: Jerry A. Hausman, "Valuation of New Goods under Perfect and Imperfect Competition," in Timothy F. Bresnahan and Robert J. Gordon, eds., *The Economics of New Goods*, Chicago: University of Chicago Press, 1997. Used with permission of The University of Chicago Press.

YOUR TURN: Test your understanding by doing related problem 2.4 on page 169 at the end of this chapter.

Share of a Good in a Consumer's Budget

Goods that take only a small fraction of a consumer's budget tend to have less elastic demand than goods that take a large fraction. For example, most people buy salt infrequently and in relatively small quantities. The share of the average consumer's budget that is spent on salt is very low. As a result, even a doubling of the price of salt is likely to result in only a small decline in the quantity of salt demanded. 'Big-ticket items,' such as houses, cars, and furniture, take up a larger share in the average consumer's budget. Increases in the prices of these goods are likely to result in significant declines in quantity demanded. In general, *the demand for a good will be more elastic the larger the share of the good in the average consumer's budget.*

Is the Demand for Books Perfectly Inelastic?

At the beginning of the chapter we quoted Stephen Rubin, publisher of Doubleday, as saying, "I am just convinced that there is no difference between US$22 and US$23.... Price is not a factor if it is a book that you really want." Taken literally, Rubin seems to be arguing that the demand for books is perfectly inelastic because only when demand is perfectly inelastic is price "not a factor." It's unlikely that this is what he means because if demand were really perfectly inelastic, he could charge US$200 or US$2,000 instead of charging US$23 and still sell the same number of books. It is more likely he is arguing that demand is inelastic, so that even though he will sell fewer books at a price of US$23 than at a price of US$22, the decline in sales will be small.

Notice also that the book he mentions is a "translation from a Czech writer." Specialized books of this type will have relatively few substitutes (although a consumer can buy a used copy or borrow a copy from the library). A cut in price is unlikely to attract many new customers, and an increase in price is unlikely to cause many existing customers to not buy. This lack of substitutes is the main factor that makes demand inelastic. The situation may be different for novels written by popular Arab novelists, such as Naguib Mahfouz, Ghada Samman, or Ihsan Abdel Quddous. Many consumers in the Arab world see books written by these authors as close substitutes. Someone looking for a 'good read' on an airplane trip or at the beach may switch from Naguib Mahfouz to Ghada Samman if the price of the Naguib Mahfouz book is significantly higher.

5.3 | Understand the relationship between the price elasticity of demand and total revenue.

The Relationship between Price Elasticity of Demand and Total Revenue

Total revenue The total amount of funds received by a seller of a good or service, calculated by multiplying price per unit by the number of units sold.

A firm is interested in price elasticity because it allows the firm to calculate how changes in price will affect its **total revenue**, which is the total amount of funds it receives from selling a good or service. Total revenue is calculated by multiplying price per unit by the number of units sold. When demand is inelastic, price and total revenue move in the same direction: an increase in price raises total revenue, and a decrease in price reduces total revenue. When demand is elastic, price and total revenue move inversely: an increase in price reduces total revenue, and a decrease in price raises total revenue.

To understand the relationship between price elasticity and total revenue, consider Figure 5-2. Panel (a) shows a demand curve for one of Naguib Mahfouz's novels (as in Figure 5-1 on page 142). This demand curve is inelastic between point A and point B. The total revenue received by a bookseller at point A equals the price of US$30 multiplied by the 16 copies sold, or US$480. This amount equals the areas of the rectangles C and D in the figure because together the rectangles have a height of US$30 and a base of 16 copies. Because this demand curve is inelastic between point A and point B (it was demand curve D_2 in Figure 5-1), cutting the price to US$20 (point B) reduces total revenue. The new total revenue is shown by the areas of rectangles D and E, and it is equal to US$20 multiplied by 20 copies, or US$400. Total revenue falls because the increase in the quantity demanded is not large enough to make up for the decrease in price. As a result, the US$80 increase in revenue gained as a result of the price cut—dark-green rectangle E—is less than the US$160 in revenue lost—light-green rectangle C.

Panel (b) of Figure 5-2 shows a demand curve that is elastic between point A and point B (it was demand curve D_1 in Figure 5-1). In this case, cutting the price increases total revenue. At point A, the areas of rectangles C and D are still equal to US$480, but at point B, the areas of rectangles D and E are equal to US$20 multiplied by 28 copies, or US$560. Here, total revenue rises because the increase in the quantity demanded is large enough to offset the lower price. As a result, the US$240 increase in revenue gained as a result of the price cut—dark-green rectangle E—is greater than the US$160 in revenue lost—light-green rectangle C.

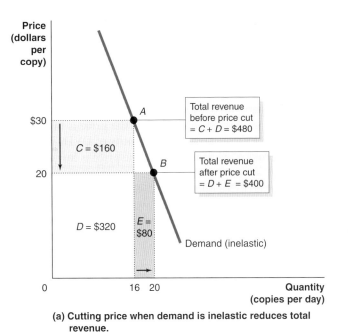

(a) Cutting price when demand is inelastic reduces total revenue.

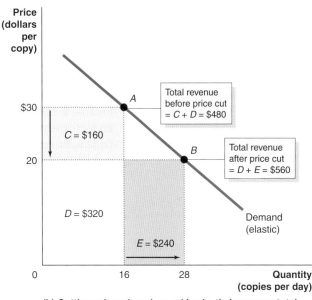

(b) Cutting price when demand is elastic increases total revenue.

Figure 5-2 | The Relationship between Price Elasticity and Total Revenue

When demand is inelastic, a cut in price will decrease total revenue. In panel (a), at point A, the price is US$30, 16 copies are sold, and total revenue received by the bookseller equals US$30 × 16 copies, or US$480. At point B, cutting price to US$20 increases the quantity demanded to 20 copies, but the fall in price more than offsets the increase in quantity. As a result, revenue falls to US$20 × 20 copies, or US$400.

When demand is elastic, a cut in price will increase total revenue. In panel (b), at point A, the area of rectangles C and D is still equal to US$480. But at point B, the area of rectangles D and E is equal to US$20 × 28 copies, or US$560. In this case, the increase in the quantity demanded is large enough to offset the fall in price, so total revenue increases.

The third, less common, possibility is that demand is unit elastic. In that case, a change in price is exactly offset by a proportional change in quantity demanded, leaving revenue unaffected. Therefore, when demand is unit-2 elastic, neither a decrease in price nor an increase in price affects revenue. Table 5-2 summarizes the relationship between price elasticity and revenue.

IF DEMAND IS...	THEN...	BECAUSE...
elastic	an increase in price reduces revenue	the decrease in quantity demanded is proportionally *greater* than the increase in price.
elastic	a decrease in price increases revenue	the increase in quantity demanded is proportionally *greater* than the decrease in price.
inelastic	an increase in price increases revenue	the decrease in quantity demanded is proportionally *smaller* than the increase in price.
inelastic	a decrease in price reduces revenue	the increase in quantity demanded is proportionally *smaller* than the decrease in price.
unit-elastic	an increase in price does not affect revenue	the decrease in quantity demanded is proportionally *the same as* the increase in price.
unit-elastic	a decrease in price does not affect revenue	the increase in quantity demanded is proportionally *the same as* the decrease in price.

TABLE 5-2

The Relationship between Price Elasticity and Revenue

Elasticity and Revenue with a Linear Demand Curve

Along most demand curves, elasticity is not constant at every point. For example, a straight-line, or linear, demand curve for DVDs is shown in panel (a) of Figure 5-3. The numbers from the table are plotted in the graphs. The demand curve shows that when the price falls by US$1, consumers always respond by buying 2 more DVDs per month. When the price is high and the quantity demanded is low, demand is elastic. This is true because a US$1 fall in price is a smaller percentage change when the price is high, and an increase of 2 DVDs is a larger percentage change when the quantity of DVDs is small. By similar reasoning, we can see why demand is inelastic when the price is low and the quantity demanded is high.

Panel (a) in Figure 5-3 shows that when price is between US$8 and US$4 and quantity is between 0 and 6, demand is elastic. Panel (b) shows that over this same range, total revenue will increase as price falls. For example, in panel (a), as price falls from US$7 to

Price	Quantity Demanded	Total Revenue
$8	0	$0
7	2	14
6	4	24
5	6	30
4	8	32
3	10	30
2	12	24
1	14	14
0	16	0

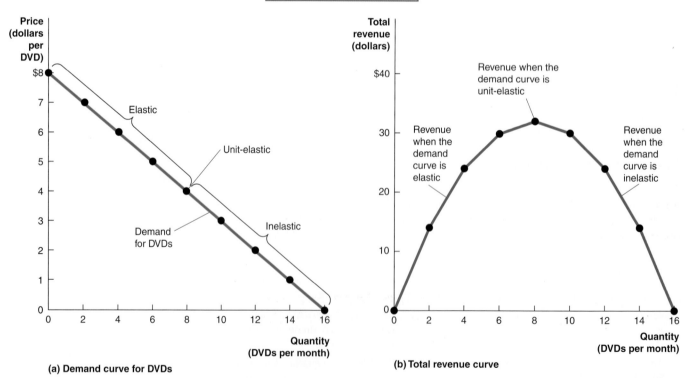

(a) Demand curve for DVDs

(b) Total revenue curve

Figure 5-3 | Elasticity Is Not Constant Along a Linear Demand Curve

The data from the table are plotted in the graphs. Panel (a) shows that as we move down the demand curve for DVDs, the price elasticity of demand declines. In other words, at higher prices, demand is elastic, and at lower prices, demand is inelastic. Panel (b)
shows that as the quantity of DVDs sold increases from zero, revenue will increase until it reaches a maximum of US$32 when 8 DVDs are sold. As sales increase beyond 8 DVDs, revenue falls because demand is inelastic on this portion of the demand curve.

US$6, quantity demand increases from 2 to 4, and in panel (b), total revenue increases from US$14 to US$24. Similarly, when price is between US$4 and zero and quantity is between 8 and 16, demand is inelastic. Over this same range, total revenue will decrease as price falls. For example, as price falls from US$3 to US$2 and quantity increases from 10 to 12, total revenue decreases from US$30 to US$24.

Solved Problem | **5-3**

Price and Revenue Don't Always Move in the Same Direction

Briefly explain whether you agree or disagree with the following statement: "The only way to increase the revenue from selling a product is to increase the product's price."

SOLVING THE PROBLEM:

Step 1: **Review the chapter material.** This problem deals with the effect of a price change on a firm's revenue, so you may want to review the section "The Relationship between Price Elasticity and Total Revenue," which begins on page 148.

Step 2: **Analyze the statement.** We have seen that a price increase will increase revenue only if demand is inelastic. In Figure 5-3, for example, increasing the rental price of DVDs from US$1 to US$2 *increases* revenue from US$14 to US$24 because demand is inelastic along this portion of the demand curve. But increasing the price from US$5 to US$6 *decreases* revenue from US$30 to US$24 because demand is elastic along this portion of the demand curve. If the price is currently US$5, increasing revenue would require a price *cut*, not a price increase. As this example shows, the statement is incorrect and you should disagree with it.

YOUR TURN: For more practice, do related problem 3.6 on page 169 at the end of this chapter.

>> **End Solved Problem 5-3**

Estimating Price Elasticity of Demand

To estimate the price elasticity of demand, economists need to know the demand curve for a product. To calculate the price elasticity of demand for new products, firms often rely on market experiments. With market experiments, firms try different prices and observe the change in quantity demanded that results.

| Making the Connection | **Determining the Price Elasticity of Demand for DVDs by Market Experiment** |

DVDs were a relatively new product in 2001. The movie studios producing them were unsure of the price elasticity of the demand curves they were facing, so they experimented with different prices to help determine the price elasticity. Following are four films and the prices for DVDs and VHS tapes that the studios suggested stores such as Blockbuster charge for them:

(Continued)

FILM	DVD PRICE	VHS PRICE
Rugrats in Paris	$22.46	$22.99
The Mummy Returns	26.98	22.98
Miss Congeniality	16.69	22.98
The Perfect Storm	24.98	22.99

VHS tapes had been on the market for many years, and the studios had determined their pricing strategies, given their estimates of the price elasticity of demand. As a result, the prices of VHS tapes were usually very similar; for these four films, the prices were almost identical. The prices of DVDs were much less standardized because the studios were unsure of their price elasticities. Tom Adams, the head of Adams Market Research, a company that does research on the home video market, summed up the situation: "The studios have different views of the market, so they are setting different suggested retail prices, and the stores are discounting those prices to different degrees."

After several years of market experiments, the movie studios had more accurate estimates of the price elasticity of DVDs, and the prices of most DVDs became similar. For instance, in 2007, nearly all newly released DVDs had a list price of about US$29, which was often discounted to about US$17 when they were sold online or in discount department stores, such as Wal-Mart. When HD-DVDs were introduced, the studios apparently felt confident that they understood their price elasticity, because in 2007 most had list prices of US$39.95, discounted to US$27.95 in many online stores.

When DVDs were first introduced, the movie studios were uncertain about their price elasticity of demand.

Sources: Geraldine Fabrikant, "Sale of DVDs Are Challenging Movie Rental Business," *New York Times*, April 16, 2001; prices from Amazon.com.

YOUR TURN: Test your understanding by doing related problem 3.12 on page 170 at the end of this chapter.

5.4 | Define the cross-price elasticity of demand and the income elasticity of demand, and understand their determinants and how they are measured.

Other Demand Elasticities

Elasticity is an important concept in economics because it allows us to quantify the responsiveness of one economic variable to changes in another economic variable. In addition to price elasticity, two other demand elasticities are important: *cross-price elasticity of demand* and *income elasticity of demand*.

Cross-Price Elasticity of Demand

Suppose you work at Apple and you need to predict the effect of an increase in the price of Microsoft's Zune on the quantity of iPods demanded, holding other factors constant. You can do this by calculating the **cross-price elasticity of demand**, which is the percentage change in the quantity of iPods demanded divided by the percentage change in the price of Zunes—or, in general:

Cross-price elasticity of demand The percentage change in quantity demanded of one good divided by the percentage change in the price of another good.

$$\text{Cross-price elasticity of demand} = \frac{\text{Percentage change in quanity demanded of one good}}{\text{Percentage change in price of another good}}$$

TABLE 5-3

Summary of Cross-Price Elasticity of Demand

IF THE PRODUCTS ARE...	THEN THE CROSS-PRICE ELASTICITY OF DEMAND WILL BE...	EXAMPLE
substitutes	positive	Two brands of digital music players
complements	negative	Digital music players and song downloads from online music stores
unrelated	zero	Digital music players and peanut butter

The cross-price elasticity of demand is positive or negative, depending on whether the two products are substitutes or complements. Recall that substitutes are products that can be used for the same purpose, such as two brands of digital music players. Complements are products that are used together, such as digital music players and song downloads from online music sites. An increase in the price of a substitute will lead to an increase in quantity demanded, so the cross-price elasticity of demand will be positive. An increase in the price of a complement will lead to a decrease in the quantity demanded, so the cross-price elasticity of demand will be negative. Of course, if the two products are unrelated—such as digital music players and peanut butter—the cross-price elasticity of demand will be zero. Table 5-3 summarizes the key points concerning the cross-price elasticity of demand.

Cross-price elasticity of demand is important to firm managers because it allows them to measure whether products sold by other firms are close substitutes for their products. For example, Amazon.com and Barnesandnoble.com are the leading online booksellers and Alkitab.com is a leading seller of Arabic books in the U.S. We might predict that if Amazon raises the price of Naguib Mahfouz's novel, many consumers will buy it from Barnesandnoble.com or Alkitab.com instead. But Jeff Bezos, Amazon's chief executive officer, has argued that because of Amazon's reputation for good customer service and because more customers are familiar with the site, ordering a book from Barnesandnoble.com or Alkitab.com is not a good substitute for ordering a book from Amazon. In effect, Bezos is arguing that the cross-price elasticity between Amazon's books and Barnesandnoble.com's books is low. Economists Judith Chevalier of Yale University and Austan Goolsbee of the University of Chicago used data on prices and quantities of books sold on these websites to estimate the cross-price elasticity. They found that the cross-price elasticity of demand between books at Amazon and books at Barnesandnoble.com was 3.5. This estimate means that if Amazon raises its prices by 10 percent, the quantity of books demanded on Barnesandnoble.com will increase by 35 percent. This result indicates that, contrary to Jeff Bezos's argument, consumers do consider books sold on the two websites to be close substitutes.

Income Elasticity of Demand

The **income elasticity of demand** measures the responsiveness of quantity demanded to changes in income. It is calculated as follows:

$$\text{Income elasticity of demand} = \frac{\text{Percentage change in quantity demanded}}{\text{Percentage change in income}}$$

Income elasticity of demand A measure of the responsiveness of quantity demanded to changes in income, measured by the percentage change in quantity demanded divided by the percentage change in income.

As we saw in Chapter 3, if the quantity demanded of a good increases as income increases, then the good is a *normal good*. Normal goods are often further subdivided into *luxury goods* and *necessity goods*. A good is a luxury if the quantity demanded is very responsive to changes in income, so that a 10 percent increase in income results in more than a 10 percent increase in quantity demanded. Expensive jewelry and vacation homes are examples of luxuries. A good is a necessity if the quantity demanded is not very responsive to changes in income, so that a 10 percent increase in income results in less than a 10 percent increase in quantity demanded. Food and clothing are examples

TABLE 5-4

Summary of Income Elasticity of Demand

IF THE INCOME ELASTICITY OF DEMAND IS...	THEN THE GOOD IS...	EXAMPLE
positive but less than 1	normal and a necessity	Milk
positive and greater than 1	normal and a luxury	Caviar
negative	inferior	High-fat meat/dry beans

of necessities. A good is *inferior* if the quantity demanded falls when income increases. Ground beef with a high fat content is an example of an inferior good. We should note that normal goods, inferior goods, necessities, and luxuries are just labels economists use for goods with different income elasticities; they are not intended to be value judgments about the worth of these goods.

Because most goods are normal goods, during periods of economic expansion, when consumer income is rising, most firms can expect—holding other factors constant—that the quantity demanded of their products will increase. Sellers of luxuries can expect particularly large increases. In the Gulf countries, starting from the mid-1970s, rapid increases in income resulted in large increases in demand for luxuries, such as meals in expensive restaurants, luxury apartments, and high-performance automobiles. During recessions, falling consumer income can cause firms to experience increases in demand for inferior goods. For example, the demand for bus or train trips increases as consumers cut back on air travel, and supermarkets find that the demand for processed meat, such as beefburgers, increases relative to the demand for steak. Table 5-4 summarizes the key points about the income elasticity of demand.

Making the Connection | Short-run Price Elasticity, Long-run Price Elasticity, and Income Elasticity in the Crude Oil Market

In the summer of 2008, oil prices reached an unprecedented level of US$147 per barrel. This high price triggered many researchers to study the main factors that caused this phenomenon. James D. Hamilton, professor of economics at University of California, San Diego, reviewed a number of theories that investigated the main factors behind the high price of oil during 2008. His study reached the following conclusion: "Unquestionably the three key features in any account are the low-price elasticity of demand, the strong growth in demand from China, the Middle East, and other newly industrialized economies, and the failure of global production to increase. These facts explain the initial strong pressure on prices that may have triggered commodity speculation in the first place. Speculation could have edged producers like Saudi Arabia into the discovery that small production declines could increase current revenues and may be in their long-run interests as well."

All studies that Hamilton surveyed show that the price elasticity of demand is significantly low in the short run and is estimated to be in the range of −0.05 to −0.34, while in the long run it is found to be three to four times the short-run one in most of the studies (remember that, as we discussed earlier in Learning Objective 5.2, *the more time that passes, the more elastic the demand for a product becomes*). The connection between price elasticity of demand and total revenue (Learning Objective 5.3) is clear in Hamilton's conclusion when he infers that a small reduction in the production of oil in Saudi Arabia could increase oil revenues. This could be explained as follows: the higher price of oil, as a result of a decline in the production of oil, accompanied by a low-price elasticity of demand, leads to an increase in Saudi Arabia's oil revenues. In addition, income elasticity

(Continued)

of demand on crude oil is found to be positive and in some studies greater than 1. This means that crude oil is a normal good since the demand on crude oil increases when the country's income increases (we discussed the concept of normal goods in Learning Objective 5.4). This will lead to a further increase in oil revenues for oil exporting countries. The following table summarizes the short-run price elasticity of demand, long-run price elasticity of demand, and income elasticity of demand in the studies surveyed by Hamilton.

ESTIMATES OF DEMAND ELASTICITIES

STUDY	PRODUCT	METHOD	SHORT-RUN PRICE ELASTICITY	LONG-RUN ELASTICITY	LONG-RUN INCOME ELASTICITY
Dahl and Sterner (1991)	Gasoline	Literature survey	–0.26	0.86	1.21
Espey (1998)	Gasoline	Literature survey	–0.26	–0.58	0.88
Graham and Glaister (2004)	Gasoline	Literature survey	–0.25	–0.77	0.93
Brons et al. (2008)	Gasoline	Literature survey	–0.34	–0.84	–
Dahl (1993)	Oil (developing countries)	Literature survey	–0.07	–0.3	1.32
Cooper (2003)	Oil (average of 23 countries)	Annual time-series regression	–0.05	0.21	–

Source: James D. Hamilton, "Understanding Crude Oil Prices," *The Energy Journal*, International Association for Energy Economics, Vol. 30(2), pp. 179–206. This table is copyrighted and reprinted by permission from the International Association for Energy Economics. The table first appeared in *The Energy Journal*.

5.5 | Use price elasticity of demand and the relationship between price elasticity of demand and total revenue to analyze economic issues.

Using Elasticity to Analyze Microsoft Windows' Price Cut in the Gulf Region

The concept of price elasticity can help us understand many economic issues. For example, in early 2008, Microsoft announced a price cut on boxed copies of its operating system Windows Vista Home Basic, Vista Home Premium, and Vista Ultimate in the Gulf region. The price cut was significant and ranges from 20 percent to 47 percent, depending on the version of the operating system. The retail price for Vista Home Basic went down from US$204 to US$109, while the decline in the price of the other two versions was less sharp as it went down from US$244 to US$150 for Home Premium, and from US$407 to US$326 for Vista Ultimate. Brad Brooks, the corporate vice president for Windows Consumer Product Marketing, defended the price cut policy as follows: "Today, the vast majority of Windows licenses are sold with PCs; retail stand-alone sales, in contrast, have been primarily from customers who value being early adopters and those building their own machines. We've observed market behaviour, however, that suggests an opportunity to expand Windows stand-alone sales to other segments of the consumer market." How can we interpret Brooks' explanation in terms of price elasticity of demand? The answer is simple: those "other segments" of consumers that Microsoft wants to approach have high elasticity of demand on stand-alone versions of Windows. So, if the price of these stand-alone Windows versions is high, their demand will drop sharply. In order for Microsoft to target those consumers and expand its customers, it has to offer them an attractive lower price that pushs them to increase the quantity demanded of stand-alone Windows versions signifcantly, by more than the percentage of reduction in the price, and thus realize an increase in total revenue. On the other hand, customers who rush to buy new versions of Windows as soon as they are released in the market—technology lovers—have low price elasticity of demand on Windows. So even though the price of a new Windows version is high, they will buy it to enjoy being the first users of the most updated version of Windows.[1]

Solved Problem | 5-5

Using Price Elasticity to Analyze Policy toward Illegal Drugs

An ongoing policy debate in some countries in the Western world concerns whether to legalize the use of drugs such as marijuana and cocaine. Some researchers estimate that legalizing cocaine would cause its price to fall by as much as 95 percent. Proponents of legalization argue that legalizing drug use would lower crime rates by eliminating the main reason for the murderous gang wars that plague many big cities and by reducing the incentive for drug addicts to commit robberies and burglaries. Opponents of legalization argue that lower drug prices would lead more people to use drugs.

a. Suppose the price elasticity of demand for cocaine is −2. If legalization causes the price of cocaine to fall by 95 percent, what will be the percentage increase in the quantity of cocaine demanded?

b. If the price elasticity is −0.02, what will be the percentage increase in the quantity demanded?

c. Discuss how the size of the price elasticity of demand for cocaine is relevant to the debate over its legalization.

SOLVING THE PROBLEM:

Step 1: **Review the chapter material.** This problem deals with applications of the price elasticity of demand formula, so you may want to review the section "Measuring the Price Elasticity of Demand," which begins on page 140.

Step 2: **Answer question (a) using the formula for the price elasticity of demand.**

$$\text{Price elasticity of demand} = \frac{\text{Percentage change in quantity demanded}}{\text{Percentage change in price}}$$

We can plug into this formula the values we are given for the price elasticity and the percentage change in price:

$$-2 = \frac{\text{Percentage change in quantity demanded}}{-95\%}$$

Or, rearranging:

$$\text{Percentage change in quantity demanded} = -2 \times -95\% = 190\%$$

Step 3: **Use the same method to answer question (b).** We only need to substitute −0.02 for −2 as the price elasticity of demand:

$$\text{Percentage change in quantity demanded} = -0.02 \times -95\% = 1.9\%$$

Step 4: **Answer question (c) by discussing how the size of the price elasticity of demand for cocaine helps us to understand the effects of legalization.** Clearly, the higher the absolute value of the price elasticity of demand for cocaine, the greater the increase in cocaine use that would result from legalization. If the price elasticity is as high as in question (a), legalization will lead to a large increase in use. If, however, the price elasticity is as low as in question (b), legalization will lead to only a small increase in use.

EXTRA CREDIT: One estimate puts the price elasticity at −0.28, which suggests that even a large fall in the price of cocaine might lead to only a moderate increase in cocaine use. However, even a moderate increase in cocaine use would have costs. Some studies have shown that cocaine users are more likely to commit crimes, to abuse their children, to have higher medical expenses, and to be less productive workers. Moreover, many people object to the use of cocaine and other narcotics on moral grounds and would oppose legalization even if it led to no increase in use. Ultimately, whether the use of cocaine and other drugs should be legalized is a normative issue. Economics can contribute to the discussion but cannot decide the issue.

Source for estimate of price elasticity of cocaine: Henry Saffer and Frank Chaloupka, "The Demand for Illicit Drugs," *Economic Inquiry,* Vol. 37, No. 3, July 1999, pp. 401–411.

YOUR TURN: For more practice, do related problems 5.2 and 5.3 on page 171 at the end of this chapter.

>> **End Solved Problem 5-5**

5.6 | Define the price elasticity of supply and understand its main determinants and how it is measured.

5.6 LEARNING OBJECTIVE

The Price Elasticity of Supply and Its Measurement

We can use the concept of elasticity to measure the responsiveness of firms to a change in price just as we used it to measure the responsiveness of consumers. We know from the law of supply that when the price of a product increases, the quantity supplied increases. To measure how much quantity supplied increases when price increases, we use the *price elasticity of supply*.

Measuring the Price Elasticity of Supply

Just as with the price elasticity of demand, we calculate the **price elasticity of supply** using percentage changes:

$$\text{Price elasticity of supply} = \frac{\text{Percentage change in quantity supplied}}{\text{Percentage change in price}}$$

Notice that because supply curves are upward sloping, the price elasticity of supply will be a positive number. We categorize the price elasticity of supply the same way we categorized the price elasticity of demand: if the price elasticity of supply is less than 1, then supply is *inelastic.* For example, the price elasticity of supply of gasoline from U.S. oil refineries is about 0.20, and so it is inelastic. A 10 percent increase in the price of gasoline will result in only a 2 percent increase in the quantity supplied. If the price elasticity of supply is greater than 1, then supply is *elastic.* If the price elasticity of supply is equal to 1, then supply is *unit elastic.* As with other elasticity calculations, when we calculate the price elasticity of supply, we hold the values of other factors constant.

Price elasticity of supply The responsiveness of the quantity supplied to a change in price, measured by dividing the percentage change in the quantity supplied of a product by the percentage change in the product's price.

Determinants of the Price Elasticity of Supply

Whether supply is elastic or inelastic depends on the ability and willingness of firms to alter the quantity they produce as price increases. Often, firms have difficulty increasing the quantity of the product they supply during any short period of time. For example, a pizza parlor cannot produce more pizzas on any one night than is possible using the ingredients on hand. Within a day or two it can buy more ingredients, and within a few months it can hire more cooks and install additional ovens. As a result, the supply curve for pizza and most other products will be inelastic if we measure it over a short period of time, but increasingly elastic the longer the period of time over which we measure it. Products that require resources that are themselves in fixed supply are an exception to this rule. For example, a Lebanese fruit preserves manufacturer may rely on a particular variety of grape to produce grape jam. If all the land on which that grape can be grown is already planted in vineyards, then the supply of that grape jam will be inelastic even over a long period.

Making the Connection | Why Are Oil Prices So Unstable?

Bringing oil to market is a long process. Oil companies hire geologists to locate fields for exploratory oil well drilling. If an exploratory well indicates that significant amounts of oil are present, the company begins full-scale development of the field. The process from exploration to pumping significant amounts of oil can take years. Because it takes so long to bring additional quantities of oil to market, the price elasticity of supply for oil is very low. Substitutes are limited for oil-based products—such as gasoline—so the price elasticity of demand for oil is also low.

As the following graph shows, the combination of inelastic supply and inelastic demand results in shifts in supply causing large changes in price. In the graph, a reduction in supply that shifts the market supply curve from S_1 to S_2 causes the equilibrium quantity of oil to fall only by 5 percent, from 80 million barrels per day to 76 million, but the equilibrium price rises by 22 percent, from US$40 per barrel to US$50 per barrel.

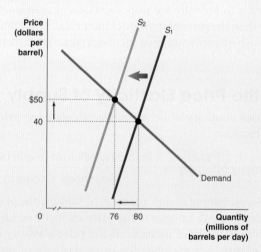

The world oil market is heavily influenced by the Organization of Petroleum Exporting Countries (OPEC). OPEC has 11 members, including Saudi Arabia, Kuwait, the United Arab Emirates, Qatar, and other Arab countries, as well as Iran, Venezuela, Nigeria, and Indonesia. Together these countries own 75 percent of the world's proven oil reserves with Saudi Arabia said to possess 25 percent of the world's proven oil reserves, and is also ranked as the largest exporter of oil. Periodically, OPEC has attempted to force up the price of oil by reducing the quantity of oil its members supply. As we will discuss further in Chapter 10, since the 1970s, the attempts by OPEC to reduce the quantity of oil on world markets have been successful only sporadically: periods during which OPEC members

(Continued)

cooperate and reduce supply alternate with periods in which the members fail to cooperate and supply increases. As a result, the supply curve for oil shifts fairly frequently. Combined with the low price elasticities of oil supply and demand, these shifts in supply have caused the price of oil to fluctuate significantly over the past 30 years, from as low as US$11 per barrel to more than US$75 per barrel.

Over longer periods of time, higher oil prices also lead to greater increases in the quantity supplied; in other words, the price elasticity of supply for oil increases. This increase happens because higher prices increase the economic incentive to explore for oil and to recover oil from more costly sources, such as under the oceans, in the Arctic, or at greater depths in the earth. When supply is more elastic, a given shift in supply results in a smaller increase in price. This effect is illustrated in the following graph. Compared with the preceding graph, the same decrease in supply increases the equilibrium price to US$45 per barrel rather than US$50 per barrel (and also causes a smaller decrease in the equilibrium quantity).

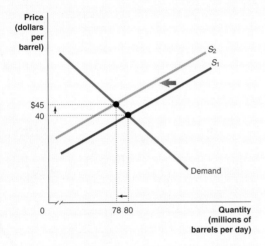

YOUR TURN: Test your understanding by doing related problem 6.3 on page 172 at the end of this chapter.

Polar Cases of Perfectly Elastic and Perfectly Inelastic Supply

Although it occurs infrequently, it is possible for supply to fall into one of the polar cases of price elasticity. If a supply curve is a vertical line, it is *perfectly inelastic*. In this case, the quantity supplied is completely unresponsive to price, and the price elasticity of supply equals zero. However much price may increase or decrease, the quantity remains the same. Over a brief period of time, the supply of some goods and services may be perfectly inelastic. For example, a parking lot may have only a fixed number of parking spaces. If demand increases, the price to park in the lot may rise, but no more spaces will become available. Of course, if demand increases permanently, over a longer period of time, the owner of the lot may buy more land to add additional spaces.

If a supply curve is a horizontal line, it is *perfectly elastic*. In this case, the quantity supplied is infinitely responsive to price, and the price elasticity of supply equals infinity. If a supply curve is perfectly elastic, a very small increase in price causes a very large increase in quantity supplied. Just as with demand curves, it is important not to confuse a supply curve being elastic with its being perfectly elastic and not to confuse a supply curve being inelastic with its being perfectly inelastic. Table 5-5 summarizes the different price elasticities of supply.

TABLE 5-5

Summary of the Price Elasticities of Supply

(Note that the percentage increases shown in the boxes in the graphs were calculated using the midpoint formula on page 142.)

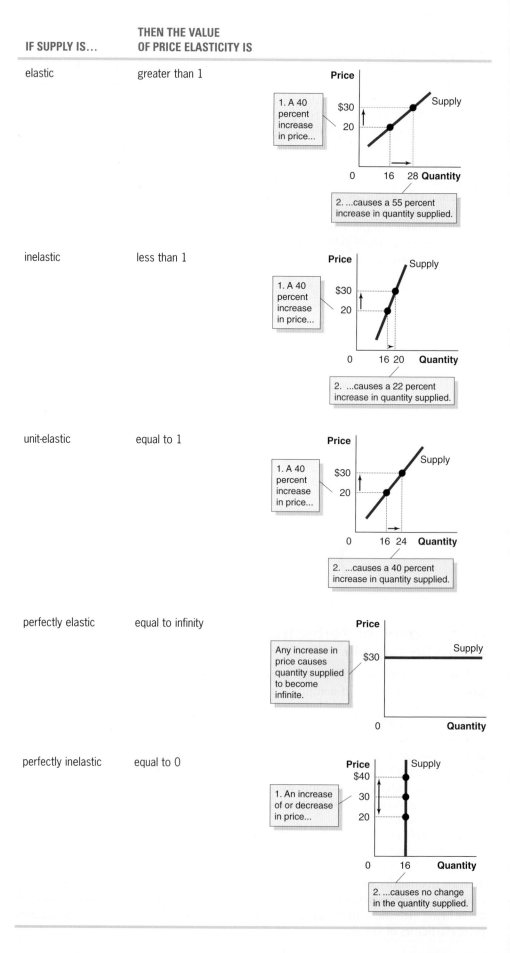

IF SUPPLY IS...	THEN THE VALUE OF PRICE ELASTICITY IS
elastic	greater than 1
inelastic	less than 1
unit-elastic	equal to 1
perfectly elastic	equal to infinity
perfectly inelastic	equal to 0

Using Price Elasticity of Supply to Predict Changes in Price

Figure 5-4 illustrates the important point that, when demand increases, the amount that price increases depends on the price elasticity of supply. The figure shows the demand and supply for parking spaces at a beach resort. In panel (a), on a typical summer weekend, equilibrium occurs at point *A*, where Demand (typical) intersects a supply curve that is inelastic. The increase in demand for parking spaces during *Eid al-Fitr* or Christmas holidays shifts the demand curve to the right, moving the equilibrium to point *B*. Because the supply curve is inelastic, the increase in demand results in a large increase in price—from US$2.00 per hour to US$4.00—but only a small increase in the quantity of spaces supplied—from 1,200 to 1,400.

In panel (b), supply is elastic, perhaps because the resort has vacant land that can be used for parking during periods of high demand. As a result, the shift in equilibrium from point *A* to point *B* results in a smaller increase in price and a larger increase in the quantity supplied. An increase in price from US$2.00 per hour to US$2.50 is sufficient to increase the quantity of parking supplied from 1,200 to 2,100. Knowing the price elasticity of supply makes it possible to predict more accurately how much price will change following an increase or a decrease in demand.

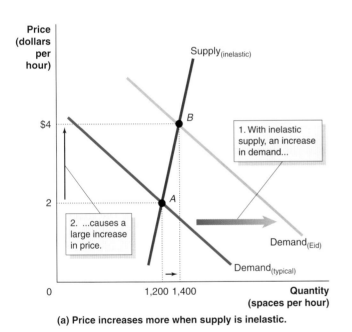

(a) Price increases more when supply is inelastic.

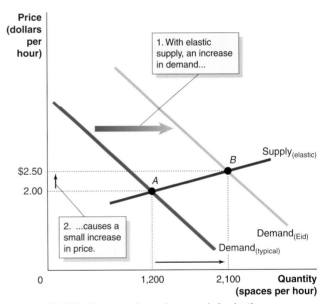

(b) Price increases less when supply is elastic.

Figure 5-4 | Changes in Price Depend on the Price Elasticity of Supply

In panel (a), Demand (typical) represents the typical demand for parking spaces on a summer weekend at a beach resort. Demand (Eid) represents demand during Eid al-Fitr holiday. Because supply is inelastic, the shift in equilibrium from point *A* to point *B* results in a large increase in price—from US$2.00 per hour to US$4.00—but only a small increase in the quantity of spaces supplied—from

1,200 to 1,400. In panel (b), supply is elastic. As a result, the shift in equilibrium from point *A* to point *B* results in a smaller increase in price and a larger increase in the quantity supplied. An increase in price from US$2.00 per hour to US$2.50 is sufficient to increase the quantity of parking supplied from 1,200 to 2,100.

Economics in YOUR Life!

>> Continued from page 139

At the beginning of the chapter, we asked you to think about two questions: what factors would make you more or less sensitive to price when purchasing a book? and are Barnes & Noble and Jarir bookstores' strategies of heavily discounting copies of *Harry Potter and the Deathly Hallows* and offering store vouchers to buyers of books in English in the hope of selling a very large quantity likely to succeed? If you have never read any Harry Potter books nor any books in English, you are probably neither a fan of the Harry Potter series nor someone who likes to read in the English language. This means that you are unlikely to purchase any of these books at any price. If you read all the earlier books in the Harry Potter series as soon as they came out and love to read in English, you are very likely to consider purchasing these books even at a high price. However, if you usually wait to purchase inexpensive paperback editions of books you like to read, you are more likely to purchase the hardcover book if Barnes & Noble or Jarir discount it. The answer to the second question depends on the prevalence of this last type of consumer. The more price-conscious consumers there are in the market, the more responsive to price will be the quantity demanded for the hardcover version, and the more likely it is for Barnes & Noble's and Jarir's revenues to increase in response to the drop in price.

Conclusion

In this chapter, we have explored the important concept of elasticity. Table 5-6 summarizes the various elasticities we discussed in this chapter. Computing elasticities is important in economics because it allows us to measure how one variable changes in response to changes in another variable. For example, by calculating the price elasticity of demand for its product, a firm can make a quantitative estimate of the effect of a price change on the revenue it receives. Similarly, by calculating the price elasticity of demand for cigarettes, the government can better estimate the effect of an increase in cigarette taxes on smoking.

Before going further in analyzing how firms decide on the prices to charge and the quantities to produce, we need to look at how firms are organized. We do this in the next chapter. Read *An Inside Look* on page 164 to use the concept of elasticity to analyze Etisalat telecommunication company's discounted service policy for call roaming and price cut of iPhones.

PRICE ELASTICITY OF DEMAND

Formula: $\dfrac{\text{Percentage change in quantity demanded}}{\text{Percentage change in price}}$

Midpoint Formula: $\dfrac{(Q_2 - Q_1)}{\left(\dfrac{Q_1 + Q_2}{2}\right)} \div \dfrac{(P_2 - P_1)}{\left(\dfrac{P_1 + P_2}{2}\right)}$

TABLE 5-6

Summary of Elasticities

	ABSOLUTE VALUE OF PRICE ELASTICITY	EFFECT ON TOTAL REVENUE OF AN INCREASE IN PRICE
Elastic	Greater than 1	Total revenue falls
Inelastic	Less than 1	Total revenue rises
Unit-elastic	Equal to 1	Total revenue unchanged

CROSS-PRICE ELASTICITY OF DEMAND

Formula: $\dfrac{\text{Percentage change in quantity demanded of one good}}{\text{Percentage change in price of another good}}$

TYPES OF PRODUCTS	VALUE OF CROSS-PRICE ELASTICITY
Substitutes	Positive
Complements	Negative
Unrelated	Zero

INCOME ELASTICITY OF DEMAND

Formula: $\dfrac{\text{Percentage change in quantity demanded}}{\text{Percentage change in income}}$

TYPES OF PRODUCTS	VALUE OF INCOME ELASTICITY
Normal and a necessity	Positive but less than 1
Normal and a luxury	Positive and greater than 1
Inferior	Negative

PRICE ELASTICITY OF SUPPLY

Formula: $\dfrac{\text{Percentage change in quantity supplied}}{\text{Percentage change in price}}$

	VALUE OF PRICE ELASTICITY
Elastic	Greater than 1
Inelastic	Less than 1
Unit-elastic	Equal to 1

Etisalat Offer a Price Cut for iPhones and Roaming Services

ARTICLE 1: ARABIAN BUSINESS, MAY 15, 2009

Exclusive: Etisalat Sees Surge in iPhone Sales After Price Cut

Sales of the iPhone were "modest" in the UAE compared with Saudi Arabia after the February launch, but demand will rise following recent price cuts, Etisalat's chairman told *Arabian Business* on Friday.

In an interview at the World Economic Forum in Jordan, Mohammed Omran also revealed that disagreement with its local partner may have cost Etisalat Iran's third mobile licence.

On May 5, the company slashed the price of its iPhone 3G packages in the UAE, which it says will save customers up to 22 percent from their initial asking prices.

The decision came after the company asked the UAE Telecom Regulatory Authority (TRA) to authorize a price cut. "We introduced the iPhone in Saudi Arabia cheaper than in the UAE and we have seen good market growth there, while in the UAE it was modest," Omran said. "When we equate the UAE with Saudi Arabia in terms of offering, we will be able to add more customers."

Etisalat owns a 26.25 percent stake in Saudi operator Mobily. Etisalat has signaled its interest to enter the Moroccan, Syrian, and Lebanese markets. Its Indian operations will "probably" launch in October, Omran said.

Source: Soren Billing, "Exclusive: Etisalat Sees Surge in iPhone Sales after Price Cut," arabian-business.com, May 15, 2009.

ARTICLE 2: ARABIAN BUSINESS, JULY 13, 2008

Etisalat Launches Special Roaming Rates in Egypt and KSA

Etisalat has launched a new roaming alliance initiative that offers special rates for customers roaming in two of its group networks—Egypt (Etisalat Misr) and Saudi Arabia (Mobily). Wasel prepaid and postpaid customers of Etisalat, who roam in Saudi Arabia through Mobily and in Egypt through Etisalat Misr, would be charged a flat rate at 1.40 United Arab Emirates dirham (AED) per minute for local calls, AED4.65 per minute for calls back to UAE, and AED1.10 for each SMS.

The alliance is part of the company's vision to leverage collaborations across its group to deliver a unique value proposition to its customer base of 64 million and to enhance the appeal of mobile services to roaming customers.

"Etisalat's global reach across the 16 markets we operate in gives us a unique opportunity to leverage our group synergies for the benefit of our customers. This launch is just the first phase of our Roaming Alliance Offer and we would like to extend this eventually to all our customers across the various markets we operate in, in addition to exploring roaming partnerships with other operators," said Essa Al Haddad, chief marketing officer, Etisalat.

To avail themselves of the offer, customers need to manually switch to the Mobily network (Mobily or Etihad Etisalat or 420-03) in KSA and Etisalat Misr (Etisalat or EGY-03 or 602-03) in Egypt. Outbound roaming customers can check roaming rates by dialing "*177#" on their mobile phone.

"This is part of our commitment to our customers to deliver outstanding customer value from our perspective as a truly global brand considering our growing reach and expansion across international markets," Essa Al Haddad added.

Source: Vineetha Menon, "Etisalat Launches Special Roaming Rates in Egypt and KSA," arabian-business.com, July 13, 2008.

Key Points in the Articles

Many telecommunication companies have attractive programs that provide their customers with price discounts. From a company's point of view, whether a discount program is a good idea depends on how customers respond—that is, it depends on the price elasticity of demand. In the two articles, Etisalat reduced the price of iPhones in the UAE and also offered its customers in Egypt and Saudi Arabia a discounted tariff for their roaming calls. If the lower prices cause enough additional iPhone sales and roaming calls to be made, then total revenue will rise. This is why companies offer discount programs: they believe the programs raise total profits. However, not all discount programs increase total profits as this depends on by how much sales increase after the discounted price.

Analyzing the News

(a) The discounted price of iPhones in the UAE succeeded in increasing the sales of iPhones, which means that the demand on iPhones is elastic. But will an iPhone price cut increase the revenue of Etisalat? Figure 1 shows the effect of a decrease in price on the quantity of iPhones sold, and Figure 2 shows the effect on total revenue. A decrease in price will increase total revenue only if the firm is operating on the elastic region of the demand curve, which is the case of Etisalat as the reduction in iPhone price resulted in a sharp increase in the quantity sold. That is exactly what Figure 2 shows.

(b) Etisalat managers know that the demand on roaming calls is highly elastic since travelers usually have several alternatives for contacting their relatives and friends in the country they are visiting, such as: buying a prepaid line from the hosting country, using the fixed line in a hotel or a public phone, sending emails, or chatting over Skype or Yahoo messenger. As we learned in Learning Objective 5.2, the more the availability of close substitutes, the higher the price elasticity of demand will be. Thus, Etisalat found that the only way to increase consumption of roaming calls was to reduce the price per minute, which will not work unless Etisalat is operating on the elastic part of the demand curve, as mentioned in point (a).

Thinking Critically

1. The purpose of discounted services and programs is to increase sales and profits. However, a firm's competitors often have discount programs as well. Suppose Etisalat and Zain both institute discounted calling services at the same time. Will revenue at Etisalat necessarily increase, even if Etisalat is currently on the elastic region of the demand curve?

2. The Internet has made it easy for travelers to communicate with their relatives and friends. What effect has the Internet had on the demand curve for roaming calls?

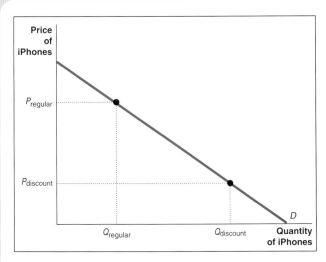

Figure 1. The discount program increases sales.

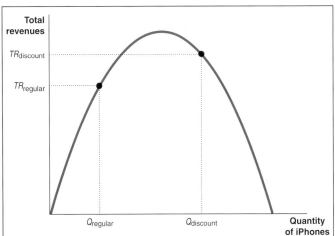

Figure 2. The discount program may not increase total revenues.

Key Terms

Summary

5.1 LEARNING OBJECTIVE

Define the price elasticity of demand and understand how to measure it, **pages 140–145.**

The Price Elasticity of Demand and Its Measurement

Elasticity measures how much one economic variable responds to changes in another economic variable. The **price elasticity of demand** measures how responsive quantity demanded is to changes in price. The price elasticity of demand is equal to the percentage change in quantity demanded divided by the percentage change in price. If the quantity demanded changes more than proportionally when price changes, the price elasticity of demand is greater than 1 in absolute value, and demand is **elastic**. If the quantity demanded changes less than proportionally when price changes, the price elasticity of demand is less than 1 in absolute value, and demand is **inelastic**. If the quantity demanded changes proportionally when price changes, the price elasticity of demand is equal to 1 in absolute value, and demand is **unit-elastic**. **Perfectly inelastic demand curves** are vertical lines, and **perfectly elastic** demand curves are horizontal lines. Relatively few products have perfectly elastic or perfectly inelastic demand curves.

5.2 LEARNING OBJECTIVE

Understand the determinants of the price elasticity of demand, **pages 146–148.**

The Determinants of the Price Elasticity of Demand

The main determinants of the price elasticity of demand for a product are the availability of close substitutes, the passage of time, whether the good is a necessity or a luxury, how narrowly the market for the good is defined, and the share of the good in the consumer's budget.

5.3 LEARNING OBJECTIVE

Understand the relationship between the price elasticity of demand and total revenue, **pages 148–152.**

The Relationship between Price Elasticity of Demand and Total Revenue

Total revenue is the total amount of funds received by a seller of a good or service. When demand is inelastic, a decrease in price reduces total revenue, and an increase in price increases total revenue. When demand is elastic, a decrease in price increases total revenue, and an increase in price decreases total revenue. When demand is unit elastic, an increase or a decrease in price leaves total revenue unchanged.

5.4 LEARNING OBJECTIVE

Define the cross-price elasticity of demand and the income elasticity of demand, and understand their determinants and how they are measured, **pages 152–155.**

Other Demand Elasticities

Other important demand elasticities are the **cross-price elasticity of demand**, which is equal to the percentage change in quantity demanded of one good divided by the percentage change in the price of another good, and the **income elasticity of demand**, which is equal to the percentage change in the quantity demanded divided by the percentage change in income.

5.5 LEARNING OBJECTIVE

Use price elasticity of demand and the relationship between price elasticity of demand and total revenue to analyze economic issues, **pages 155–157.**

Using Elasticity to Analyze Microsoft Windows Price Cut in the Gulf Region

Price elasticity and the relationship between price elasticity of demand and total revenue can be used to analyze many economic issues. One example is Microsoft Windows' price cut in the Gulf region in 2008. Because Microsoft decided to target new segments of consumers for its stand-alone Windows Vista operating system, more than a year after releasing it to the Gulf market—to those consumers with high price elasticity of demand—it had to offer them an attractive lower price to increase Windows sales significantly. The price cut was sharp and ranged from 20 to 47 percent. This price cut should induce the quantity demanded for stand-alone Windows versions to increase by more than the percentage of reduction in the price to insure an increase in Microsoft's total revenue. Microsoft had already taken advantage of consumers with low price elasticity of demand on newly released Windows versions by selling them Windows Vista at high price level at the time of its first release.

The Price Elasticity of Supply and Its Measurement

The **price elasticity of supply** is equal to the percentage change in quantity supplied divided by the percentage change in price. The supply curves for most goods are inelastic over a short period of time, but they become increasingly elastic over longer periods of time. Perfectly inelastic demand curves are vertical lines, and perfectly elastic supply curves are horizontal lines. Relatively few products have perfectly elastic or perfectly inelastic supply curves.

5.6 LEARNING OBJECTIVE

Define the price elasticity of supply and understand its main determinants and how it is measured, **pages 157–163.**

Review, Problems and Applications

5.1 LEARNING OBJECTIVE   Define the price elasticity of demand and understand how to measure it,

pages 140–145.

Review Questions

1.1 Write the formula for the price elasticity of demand. Why isn't elasticity just measured by the slope of the demand curve?

1.2 If a 10 percent increase in the price of Cap'n Crunch cereal causes a 25 percent reduction in the number of boxes of cereal demanded, what is the price elasticity of demand for Cap'n Crunch cereal? Is demand for Cap'n Crunch elastic or inelastic?

1.3 What is the midpoint method for calculating price elasticity of demand? How else can you calculate the price elasticity of demand? What is the advantage of the midpoint method?

1.4 Draw a graph of a perfectly inelastic demand curve. Think of a product that would have a perfectly inelastic demand curve. Explain why demand for this product would be perfectly inelastic.

Problems and Applications

1.5 Suppose the following table gives data on the price of wheat and the number of kilos of wheat sold in 2008 and 2009.

YEAR	PRICE (DOLLARS PER KILO) IN US$	QUANTITY (KILOS)
2008	3.00	8 million
2009	2.00	12 million

a. Calculate the change in the quantity of wheat demanded divided by the change in the price of wheat. Measure the quantity of wheat in kilos.

b. Calculate the change in the quantity of wheat demanded divided by the change in the price of wheat, but this time measure the quantity of wheat in millions of kilos. Compare your answer with the one you computed in (a).

c. Finally, assuming that the demand curve for wheat did not shift between 2008 and 2009, use the information in the table to calculate the price elasticity of demand for wheat. Use the midpoint formula in your calculation. Compare the value for the price elasticity of demand to the values you calculated in a and b.

1.6 (Related to *Solved Problem 5-1* on page 143) You own a hot dog stand that you set up outside the student union every day at lunch time. Currently, you are selling hot dogs for a price of US$3, and you sell 30 hot dogs a day. You are considering cutting the price to US$2. The following graph shows two possible increases in the quantity sold as a result of your price cut. Use the information in the graph to calculate the price elasticity between these two prices on each of the demand curves. Use the midpoint formula to calculate the price elasticities.

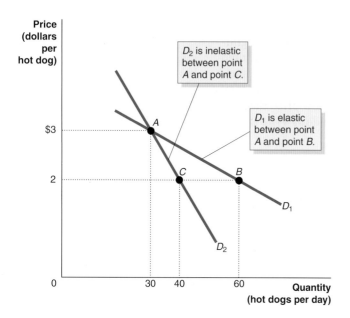

1.7 In fall 2006, Pace University in New York raised its annual tuition from US$24,751 to US$29,454. Freshman enrollment declined from 1,469 in fall 2005 to 1,131 in fall 2006. Assuming that the demand curve for places in the freshmen class at Pace did not shift between 2005 and 2006, use this information to calculate the price elasticity of demand. Use the midpoint formula in your calculation. Is the demand for places in Pace's freshmen class elastic or inelastic? Did the total amount of tuition Pace received from its freshman class rise or fall in 2006 compared with 2005?
Source: Karen W. Arenson, "At Universities, Plum Post at Top Is Now Shaky," *New York Times*, January 9, 2007.

1.8 Consider the following excerpt from a newspaper story on increases in college tuition:

> Facing stiff competition, Hendrix College, a small liberal arts institution in Conway, Ark., decided two years ago to bolster its academic offerings, promising students at least three hands-on experiences outside the classroom, including research, internships and service projects. It also raised tuition and fees 29 percent, to US$21,636.... As a result, 409 students enrolled in the

freshman class this year, a 37 percent increase. "What worked was the buzz," said J. Timothy Cloyd, the Hendrix president. "Students saw that they were going to get an experience that had value, and the price positioning conveyed to them the value of the experience."

Does this excerpt provide enough information to calculate the price elasticity of demand for places in Hendrix College's freshman class? Briefly explain.
Source: Jonathan D. Glater and Alan Finder, "In New Twist on Tuition Game, Popularity Rises with the Price," *New York Times*, December 12, 2006.

1.9 In summer 2007, Sony decided to cut the price of its PlayStation 3 video game console from US$600 to US$500. One industry analyst forecast that the price cut would increase sales from 80,000 units per month to 120,000 units per month. Assuming the analyst's forecast is correct, use the midpoint formula to calculate the price elasticity of demand for PlayStation 3.
Source: "Sony Cuts Price on PlayStation 3 by US$100," *New York Times*, July 9, 2007.

1.10 In 1916, the Ford Motor Company sold 500,000 Model T Fords at a price of US$440 each. Henry Ford believed that he could increase sales of the Model T by 1,000 cars for every dollar he cut the price. Use this information to calculate the price elasticity of demand for Model T Fords. Use the midpoint formula in your calculation.

1.11 The publisher of a magazine gives his staff the following information:

Current price	US$2.00 per issue
Current sales	150,000 copies per month
Current total costs	US$450,000 per month

He tells the staff, "Our costs are currently US$150,000 more than our revenues each month. I propose to eliminate this problem by raising the price of the magazine to US$3.00 per issue. This will result in our revenue being exactly equal to our cost." Do you agree with the publisher's analysis? Explain. (*Hint:* Remember that a firm's revenue is equal to the price of the product multiplied by the quantity sold.)

5.2 LEARNING OBJECTIVE   Understand the determinants of the price elasticity of demand, **pages 146–148.**

Review Questions

2.1 Is the demand for most agricultural products elastic or inelastic? Why?

2.2 What are the key determinants of the price elasticity of demand for a product? Which determinant is the most important?

Problems and Applications

2.3 Briefly explain whether the demand for each of the following products is likely to be elastic or inelastic.
   a. Milk
   b. Frozen cheese pizza
   c. Cola
   d. Prescription medicine

2.4 (Related to the *Making the Connection* on page 147) A study of the price elasticities of products sold in supermarkets contained the following data:

PRODUCT	PRICE ELASTICITY OF DEMAND
Soft drinks	−3.18
Canned soup	−1.62
Cheese	−0.72
Toothpaste	−0.45

a. For which products is the demand inelastic? Discuss reasons why the demand for each product is either elastic or inelastic.

b. Use the information in the table to predict the change in the quantity demanded for each product following a 10 percent price increase.

Source: Stephen J. Hoch, Byung-do Kim, Alan L. Montgomery, and Peter E. Rossi, "Determinants of Store-Level Price Elasticity," *Journal of Marketing Research*, Vol. 32, February 1995, pp. 17–29.

5.3 LEARNING OBJECTIVE   Understand the relationship between the price elasticity of demand and total revenue, **pages 148–152.**

Review Questions

3.1 If the demand for orange juice is inelastic, will an increase in the price of orange juice increase or decrease the revenue received by orange juice sellers?

3.2 The price of organic apples falls and apple growers find that their revenue increases. Is the demand for organic apples elastic or inelastic?

Problems and Applications

3.3 A newspaper story on the effect of higher milk prices on the market for ice cream contained the following: "As a result [of the increase in milk prices], retail prices for ice cream are up 4 percent from last year.... And ice cream consumption is down 3 percent." Given this information, compute the price elasticity of demand for ice cream. Will the revenue received by ice cream suppliers have increased or decreased following the price increase? Briefly explain.

Source: John Curran, "Ice Cream, They Scream: Milk Fat Costs Drive Up Ice Cream Prices," Associated Press, July 23, 2001.

3.4 Use the following graph for Hala's Frozen Yogurt Stand to answer the questions that follow.

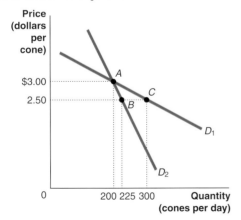

a. Use the midpoint formula to calculate the price elasticity of demand for D_1 between point A and point C and the price elasticity of demand for D_2 between point A and point B. Which demand curve is more elastic, D_1 or D_2? Briefly explain.

b. Suppose Hala is initially selling 200 cones per day at a price of US$3.00 per cone. If she cuts her price

to US$2.50 per cone and her demand curve is D_1, what will be the change in her revenue? What will be the change in her revenue if her demand curve is D_2?

3.5 An article in the *Wall Street Journal* noted the following:

Instead of relying on a full-coach, round-trip unrestricted fare of about US$2,000 between Cleveland and Los Angeles... Continental [Airlines] since June has offered a US$716 unrestricted fare in that market.... Through October, the test resulted in about the same revenue that Continental thinks it would have collected with its higher fare.

What is the value of the price elasticity of demand on this airline route? Is Continental likely to be better off charging the low fare or the high fare? Briefly explain.

Source: Scott McCartney, "Airlines Try Cutting Business Fares, Find They Don't Lose Revenue," *Wall Street Journal*, Nov. 22, 2002.

3.6 (Related to *Solved Problem 5-3* on page 151) Briefly explain whether you agree or disagree with Manager 2's reasoning:

Manager 1: "The only way we can increase the revenue we receive from selling our frozen pizzas is by cutting the price."

Manager 2: "Cutting the price of a product never increases the amount of revenue you receive. If we want to increase revenue, we have to increase price."

3.7 (Related to the *Chapter Opener* on page 138) Consider the following description of a pricing decision by academic book publishers:

A publisher may have issued a monograph several years ago, when both costs and book prices were lower, and priced it at US$14.95. The book is still selling reasonably well and would continue to do so at US$19.95. Why not, then, raise the price? The only danger is miscalculation: By raising the price you may reduce sales to the point where you make less money overall, even while making more per copy.

Assume that the situation described in the last sentence happens. What does this tell us about the price elasticity of demand for that book? Briefly explain.

Source: Beth Luey, *Handbook for Academic Authors*, 4th ed., Cambridge, UK: Cambridge University Press, 2002, p. 250.

3.8 Each summer, Lebanon, hosts Baalbeck International Festival, an outdoor music event held in the Roman ruins of the Baalbek Temples. Suppose that the organizers had been charging US$7 per day to park in the parking areas, and one year they raised the fee to US$10 per day. Although fewer people now used the parking areas, the increased rate (from US$7 to US$10) increased the revenues for the annual festival. Using the information in the following table, calculate the price elasticity of demand for parking spaces near the Baalbek Temples during the Baalbeck International Festival. Use the midpoint price elasticity of demand formula. Assume that nothing happened to shift the demand curve for parking places. Be sure to state whether demand is elastic or inelastic.

BAALBEK PARKING RATE REVENUE		
YEAR	RATE	REVENUE
2010	$10	$83,760
2009	7	77,791

3.9 Declining circulation hasn't stopped papers from raising subscription prices. In most cases, these increases, while boosting revenue per copy, almost always result in a decline in readership.
a. What is a newspaper's 'circulation'?
b. To what is 'revenue per copy' equal?
c. Why would a newspaper's management increase its subscription price if the result was a decline in the quantity of newspapers sold?

3.10 (Related to the *Chapter Opener* on page 138) Look again at the quote from Stephen Rubin of Doubleday at the beginning of this chapter. Suppose

that Everyman publishers is selling *The Cairo Trilogy* by Naguib Mahfouz at a price of US$28.95.
a. Assume that the demand for this book is perfectly inelastic. Draw a demand curve showing the effect on the quantity demanded of raising the price from US$28.95 to US$39.95. Assume that sales are 500,000 at a price of US$28.95. What is the change in revenue as a result of the price change?
b. Now assume that the price elasticity of demand is -2. Draw another demand curve showing the effect of raising the price from US$28.95 to US$39.95. Be sure to show the quantity demanded at each price. Now what is the change in revenue as a result of the price change?

3.11 Suppose that the authorities increased the toll on two bridges from US$0.50 to US$1.00. Use the information in the table to answer the questions. (Assume that nothing other than the toll change occurred during the months that would affect consumer demand.)

NUMBER OF VEHICLES CROSSING THE BRIDGE			
MONTH	TOLL	BRIDGE 1	BRIDGE 2
November	$0.50	519,337	728,022
December	1.00	433,691	656,257

a. Calculate the price elasticity of demand for each bridge, using the midpoint formula.
b. How much total revenue did the commission collect from these bridges in November? How much did it collect in December? Relate your answer to your answer in part (a).

3.12 (Related to the *Making the Connection* on page 151) Suppose you check out the prices of two products on Amazon.com: Conventional DVD players and HD (or Blu-Ray) DVD players. For which type of players would you expect manufacturers to be offering similar players at about the same prices and for which type of players would you expect prices to be more spread out? Briefly explain.

5.4 LEARNING OBJECTIVE　Define the cross-price elasticity of demand and the income elasticity of demand,
and understand their determinants and how they are measured, **pages 152–155.**

Review Questions

4.1 Define the cross-price elasticity of demand. What does it mean if the cross-price elasticity of demand is negative? What does it mean if the cross-price elasticity of demand is positive?

4.2 Define the income elasticity of demand. Use income elasticity to distinguish a normal good from an inferior good. Is it possible to tell from the income elasticity of demand whether a product is a luxury good or a necessity good?

Problems and Applications

4.3 In spring 2002, lettuce prices doubled, from about US$1.50 per head to about US$3.00. The reaction of one consumer was quoted in a newspaper article: "I will not buy [lettuce] when it's US$3 a head," she said, adding that other green vegetables can fill in for lettuce. "If bread were US$5 a loaf we'd still have to buy it. But lettuce is not that important in our family."

a. For this consumer's household, which product has the higher price elasticity of demand: bread or lettuce? Briefly explain.

b. Is the cross-price elasticity of demand between lettuce and other green vegetables positive or negative for this consumer? Briefly explain.

Source: Justin Bachman, "Sorry, Romaine Only," Associated Press, March 29, 2002.

4.4 In the following graph, the demand for hot dog buns has shifted outward because the price of hot dogs has fallen from US$2.20 to US$1.80 per package. Calculate the cross-price elasticity of demand between hot dogs and hot dog buns.

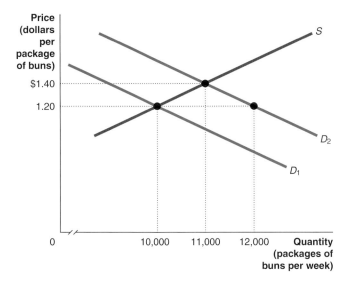

4.5 Are the cross-price elasticities of demand between the following pairs of products likely to be positive or negative? Briefly explain.
a. Pepsi and Coca-Cola
b. French fries and ketchup
c. Steak and chicken
d. HD-DVD players and HD-DVDs

4.6 After World War II, the Japanese government intervened in the economy to provide aid to certain industries that it believed would be most important in the recovery from war. One of the requirements for receiving government aid was that an industry had to be producing a good with a high income elasticity of demand. Why do you think the Japanese government made this a requirement?

4.7 Rank the following four goods from lowest income elasticity of demand to highest income elasticity of demand. Briefly explain your ranking.
a. Bread
b. Pepsi
c. Mercedes-Benz automobiles
d. Personal computers

5.5 LEARNING OBJECTIVE   Use price elasticity of demand and the relationship between price elasticity of demand and total revenue to analyze economic issues, **pages 155–157.**

Review Questions

5.1 Technology lovers have low price elasticity of demand on newly released software while elderly people have been found to have high price elasticity of demand on new technology. How can these facts explain Microsoft price strategy in the Gulf region?

Problems and Applications

5.2 **(Related to *Solved Problem 5-5* on page 156)** According to a study by the U.S. Centers for Disease Control and Prevention, the price elasticity of demand for cigarettes is –0.25. Americans purchase about 480 billion cigarettes each year.
a. If the U.S. federal tax on cigarettes were increased enough to raise the price of cigarettes by 50 percent, what would be the effect on the quantity of cigarettes demanded?
b. Is raising the tax on cigarettes a more effective way to reduce smoking if the demand for cigarettes is elastic or if it is inelastic? Briefly explain.

Source: "Response to Increases in Cigarette Prices by Race/Ethnicity, Income, and Age Groups—United States, 1976–1993," *Morbidity and Mortality Weekly Report*, July 31, 1998.

5.3 **(Related to *Solved Problem 5-5* on page 156)** The price elasticity of demand for cocaine has been estimated at –0.28. Suppose that a successful war on illegal drugs reduces the supply of cocaine in the United States enough to result in a 20 percent increase in its price. What will be the percentage reduction in the quantity of cocaine demanded?

Source: Henry Saffer and Frank Chaloupka, "The Demand for Illicit Drugs," *Economic Inquiry*, Vol. 37, No. 3, July 1999, pp. 401–411.

5.4 The price elasticity of demand for most agricultural products is quite low. What effect is this likely to have on how much the prices of these products change from year to year? Illustrate your answer with a demand and supply graph.

5.5 Suppose that the head of the Cotton Growers Association in Egypt makes the following statement:

> The government will continue to implement a price floor in the market for cotton. But the government will not be able to buy any surplus cotton produced at the price floor or to pay us any other subsidy. Because the demand for cotton is elastic, I believe this program will make us worse off, and I say we should oppose it.

Explain whether you agree or disagree with this reasoning.

5.6 Review the concept of economic efficiency from Chapter 4 before answering the following question: Will there be a greater loss of economic efficiency from a price ceiling when demand is elastic or inelastic? Illustrate your answer with a demand and supply graph.

5.6 LEARNING OBJECTIVE   Define the price elasticity of supply and understand its main determinants and how it is measured, **pages 157–163.**

Review Questions

6.1 Write the formula for the price elasticity of supply. If an increase of 10 percent in the price of frozen pizzas results in a 9 percent increase in the quantity of frozen pizzas supplied, what is the price elasticity of supply for frozen pizzas? Is the supply of pizzas elastic or inelastic?

6.2 What is the main determinant of the price elasticity of supply?

6.3 **(Related to the *Making the Connection* on page 158)** Suppose the demand for oil declines. Will the equilibrium price of oil decline more if the supply of oil is elastic or if it is inelastic? Illustrate your answer with a demand and supply graph.

6.4 Use the midpoint formula for calculating elasticity to calculate the price elasticity of supply between point *A* and point *B* for each panel of Figure 5-4 on page 161.

6.5 Briefly explain whether you agree with the following statement: "The longer the period of time following an increase in the demand for apples, the greater the increase in the equilibrium quantity of apples and the smaller the increase in the equilibrium price."

6.6 On most days, the price of a rose is US$1, and 8,000 roses are purchased. On Mother's Day, the price of a rose jumps to US$2, and 30,000 roses are purchased.

  a. Draw a demand and supply diagram that shows why the price jumps.

  b. Based on this information, what do we know about the price elasticity of demand for roses? What do we know about the price elasticity of supply for roses? Calculate values for the price elasticity of demand and the price elasticity of supply or explain why you can't calculate these values.

PART 2

Microeconomic Foundation: Consumers and Firms

Chapter 6: Consumer Choice and Behavioral Economics

Chapter 7: Technology, Production, and Costs

Consumer Choice and Behavioral Economics

Did Amr Diab Make You Switch to Pepsi-Cola?

In 2005, PepsiCo hired superstar Amr Diab to appear in television commercials as part of an innovative marketing campaign for Pepsi-Cola. PepsiCo had released a television commercial featuring singing superstar Enrique Iglesias as an emperor, being entertained in a coliseum by international popstars-turned-gladiators Britney Spears, Beyoncé, and Pink. In a special version of the advertisement for Middle East customers, Iglesias was replaced by Amr Diab as emperor. Why would the Pepsi-Cola Company hire Amr Diab? According to Tarek Kabil, president of PepsiCo for Egypt and North Africa, "Most Egyptians find it amusing to see their stars alongside international ones." But not only Egyptians like to see their stars

in commercials with international ones. Many people in the Arab world like advertisements to be oriented towards them, either through the combination of famous Arabs with international celebrities (Haifaa Wahby was also hired by Pepsi to make an advertisement with the famous French football player Tierry Henry) or by asking international superstars to speak the Arab language, as in the case of the football player Lionel Messi, who speaks in Arabic in an advertisement to market KFC products.

In Ramadan of 2011, Pepsi hired the young Egyptian star, Donia Samir Ghanim, to advertise its products. The advertisement became popular and was appreciated by many people, especially young adults, not only because it looked great, but also because it involved an ethical motivation to give to the poor.

Celebrities appear constantly in television, magazine, and online advertising. What do firms hope to

gain from celebrity endorsements? The obvious answer is that firms expect celebrity advertising will increase sales of their products. But why should consumers buy more of a product just because a celebrity endorses it? In this chapter, we will examine how consumers make decisions about which products to buy. Firms must understand consumer behavior to determine whether strategies such as using celebrities in their advertising are likely to be effective.

In the same trend, by the 1910s, the Coca-Cola company had moved from using unnamed young women drinking Coke in its advertising to using movie stars. The attempt to associate Coke with celebrities in the minds of consumers continued through the following decades. From the 1950s on, Coke's television commercials often featured popular singers of the time, and still do today, featuring singers such as Nancy Ajram.

Firms' attempts to distinguish their products in the minds of consumers from the products of rival firms will be an important theme in several of the following chapters. Advertising is one way in which firms try to distinguish their products. AN INSIDE LOOK on page 198 discusses why Nokia chose Mohamed Hamaki to endorse its "Comes with Music" service in the Middle East and Africa.

Source: Rehab El-Bakry, "A Star Is Branded," American Chamber of Commerce in Egypt *Business Monthly*, September 2005.

LEARNING Objectives

After studying this chapter, you should be able to:

6.1 Use the concept of **utility** to explain the **law of demand**, page 176.

6.2 Explain how **social influences** can affect **consumption choices**, page 184.

6.3 Describe the **behavioral economics** approach to understanding decision making, page 186.

APPENDIX Use **indifference curves** and **budget lines** to understand consumer behavior, page 205.

Economics in YOUR Life!

Do You Make Consistent Decisions?

Economists generally assume that people make decisions in a rational, consistent way. But are people actually as consistent as economists assume? Consider the following situation: You bought a concert ticket for US$75 to see Amr Diab live, which is the most you were willing to pay. While you are in line to enter the concert hall, someone offers you US$90 for the ticket. Would you sell the ticket? Would an economist think it is rational to sell the ticket? As you read the chapter, see if you can answer these questions. You can check your answers against those we provide at the end of the chapter. >> Continued on page 197

W̲e begin this chapter by exploring how consumers make decisions. In Chapter 1, we saw that economists usually assume that people act in a rational, self-interested way. In explaining consumer behavior, this means economists believe consumers make choices that will leave them as satisfied as possible, given their *tastes*, their *incomes*, and the *prices* of the goods and services available to them. We will see how the downward-sloping demand curves we encountered in Chapters 3 and 4 result from the economic model of consumer behavior. We will also see that in certain situations, knowing the best decision to make can be difficult. In these cases, economic reasoning provides a powerful tool for consumers to improve their decision making. Finally, we will see that *experimental economics* has shown that factors such as social pressure and notions of fairness can affect consumer behavior. We will look at how businesses take these factors into account when setting prices. In the appendix to this chapter, we extend the analysis by using indifference curves and budget lines to understand consumer behavior.

6.1 | Define utility and explain how consumers choose goods and services to maximize their utility.

Utility and Consumer Decision Making

We saw in Chapter 3 that the model of demand and supply is a powerful tool for analyzing how prices and quantities are determined. We also saw that, according to the *law of demand* whenever the price of a good falls, the quantity demanded increases. In this section, we will show how the economic model of consumer behavior leads to the law of demand.

The Economic Model of Consumer Behavior in a Nutshell

Imagine walking through a shopping mall, trying to decide how to spend your clothing budget. If you had an unlimited budget, your decision would be easy: just buy as much of everything as you want. Given that you have a limited budget, what do you do? Economists assume that consumers act so as to make themselves as well off as possible. Therefore, you should choose the one combination of clothes that makes you as well off as possible from among those combinations that you can afford. Stated more generally, the economic model of consumer behavior predicts that consumers will choose to buy the combination of goods and services that makes them as well off as possible from among all the combinations that their budgets allow them to buy.

This prediction may seem obvious and not particularly useful. But as we explore the implication of this prediction, we will see that it leads to conclusions that are both useful and not obvious.

Utility

Ultimately, how well off you are from consuming a particular combination of goods and services depends on your tastes, or preferences. There is an old saying—"There's no accounting for tastes"—and economists don't try to. If you buy Coca-Cola instead of Pepsi, even though Pepsi has a lower price, you must receive more enjoyment or satisfaction from drinking Coca-Cola. Economists refer to the enjoyment or satisfaction people receive from consuming goods and services as **utility**. So we can say that the goal of a consumer is to spend available income so as to maximize utility. But utility is a difficult concept to measure because there is no way of knowing exactly how much enjoyment or satisfaction someone receives from consuming a product. Similarly, it is not possible to compare utility across consumers. There is no way of knowing for sure whether one consumer Hala, receives more or less satisfaction than her friend Farida from drinking a bottle of Coca-Cola.

Utility The enjoyment or satisfaction people receive from consuming goods and services.

Two hundred years ago, economists hoped to measure utility in units called 'utils.' The util would be an objective measure in the same way that temperature is: if it is 35 degrees in Amman and 35 degrees in Dubai, it is just as warm in both cities. These economists wanted to say that if Farida's utility from eating a beefburger is 10 utils and Hala's utility is 5 utils, then Farida receives exactly twice the satisfaction from eating a beefburger that Hala does. In fact, it is *not* possible to measure utility across people. It turns out that none of the important conclusions of the economic model of consumer behavior depend on utility being directly measurable (a point we demonstrate in the appendix to this chapter). Nevertheless, the economic model of consumer behavior is easier to understand if we assume that utility is something directly measurable, like temperature.

The Principle of Diminishing Marginal Utility

To make the model of consumer behavior more concrete, let's see how a consumer makes decisions in a case involving just two products: cheese pizza and Coke. To begin, consider how the utility you receive from consuming a good changes with the amount of the good you consume. For example, suppose that you have just arrived at a party to watch the final game of the African Cup of Nations where the hosts are serving cheese pizza, and you are very hungry. In this situation, you are likely to receive quite a lot of enjoyment, or utility, from consuming the first slice of pizza. Suppose this satisfaction is measurable and is equal to 20 units of utility, or utils. After eating the first slice, you decide to have a second slice. Because you are no longer as hungry, the satisfaction you receive from eating the second slice of pizza is less than the satisfaction you received from eating the first slice. Consuming the second slice increases your utility by only an *additional* 16 utils, which raises your *total* utility from eating the two slices to 36 utils. If you continue eating slices, each additional slice gives you less and less additional satisfaction.

The table in Figure 6-1 shows the relationship between the number of slices of pizza you consume while watching the final game and the amount of utility you receive. The second column in the table shows the total utility you receive from eating a particular number of slices. The third column shows the additional utility, or **marginal utility** (*MU*), you receive from consuming one additional slice. (Remember that in economics, 'marginal' means additional.) For example, as you increase your consumption from 2 slices to 3 slices, your total utility increases from 36 to 46, so your marginal utility from consuming the third slice is 10 utils. As the table shows, by the time you eat the fifth slice of pizza that evening, your marginal utility is very low: only 2 utils. If you were to eat a sixth slice, you would become slightly nauseated, and your marginal utility would actually be a *negative* 3 utils.

Figure 6-1 also plots the numbers from the table as graphs. Panel (a) shows how your total utility rises as you eat the first five slices of pizza and then falls as you eat the sixth slice. Panel (b) shows how your marginal utility declines with each additional slice you eat and finally becomes negative when you eat the sixth slice. The height of the marginal utility line at any quantity of pizza in panel (b) represents the change in utility as a result of consuming that additional slice. For example, the change in utility as a result of consuming 4 slices instead of 3 is 6 utils, so the height of the marginal utility line in panel (b) is 6 utils.

The relationship illustrated in Figure 6-1 between consuming additional units of a product during a period of time and the marginal utility received from consuming each additional unit is referred to as the **law of diminishing marginal utility**. For nearly every good or service, the more you consume during a period of time, the less you increase your total satisfaction from each additional unit you consume.

Marginal utility (*MU*) The change in total utility a person receives from consuming one additional unit of a good or service.

Law of diminishing marginal utility The principle that consumers experience diminishing additional satisfaction as they consume more of a good or service during a given period of time.

The Rule of Equal Marginal Utility per Dollar Spent

The key challenge for consumers is to decide how to allocate their limited incomes among all the products they wish to buy. Every consumer has to make trade-offs: if you have US$100 to spend on entertainment for the month, then the more DVDs you buy,

Figure 6-1

Total and Marginal Utility from Eating Pizza

The table shows that for the first 5 slices of pizza, the more you eat, the more your total satisfaction or utility increases. If you eat a sixth slice, you start to feel ill from eating too much pizza, and your total utility falls. Each additional slice increases your utility by less than the previous slice, so your marginal utility from each slice is less than the one before. Panel (a) shows your total utility rising as you eat the first 5 slices and falling with the sixth slice. Panel (b) shows your marginal utility falling with each additional slice you eat and becoming negative with the sixth slice. The height of the marginal utility line at any quantity of pizza in panel (b) represents the change in utility as a result of consuming that additional slice. For example, the change in utility as a result of consuming 4 slices instead of 3 is 6 utils, so the height of the marginal utility line in panel (b) for the fourth slice is 6 utils

Number of Slices	Total Utility from Eating Pizza	Marginal Utility from the Last Slice Eaten
0	0	--
1	20	20
2	36	16
3	46	10
4	52	6
5	54	2
6	51	-3

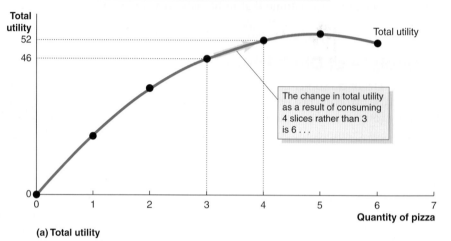

(a) Total utility

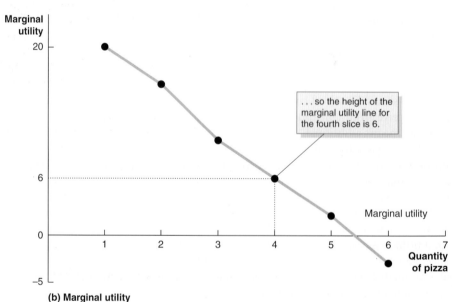

(b) Marginal utility

Budget constraint The limited amount of income available to consumers to spend on goods and services.

the fewer movies you can see in the theater. Economists refer to the limited amount of income you have available to spend on goods and services as your **budget constraint**. The principle of diminishing marginal utility helps us understand how consumers can best spend their limited incomes on the products available to them.

Suppose you attend the African Cup of Nations party at a restaurant, and you have US$10 to spend on refreshments. Pizza is selling for US$2 per slice, and Coke is selling

TABLE 6-1 | Total Utility and Marginal Utility from Eating Pizza and Drinking Coke

NUMBER OF SLICES OF PIZZA	TOTAL UTILITY FROM EATING PIZZA	MARGINAL UTILITY FROM THE LAST SLICE	NUMBER OF CUPS OF COKE	TOTAL UTILITY FROM DRINKING COKE	MARGINAL UTILITY FROM THE LAST CUP
0	0	—	0	0	—
1	20	20	1	20	20
2	36	16	2	35	15
3	46	10	3	45	10
4	52	6	4	50	5
5	54	2	5	53	3
6	51	−3	6	52	−1

for US$1 per cup. Table 6-1 shows the relationship between the amount of pizza you eat, the amount of Coke you drink, and the amount of satisfaction, or utility, you receive. The values for pizza are repeated from the table in Figure 6-1. The values for Coke also follow the principle of diminishing marginal utility.

How many slices of pizza and how many cups of Coke do you buy if you want to maximize your utility? If you did not have a budget constraint, you would buy 5 slices of pizza and 5 cups of Coke because that would give you total utility of 107 (54 + 53), which is the maximum utility you can achieve. Eating another slice of pizza or drinking another cup of Coke during the evening would lower your utility. Unfortunately, you do have a budget constraint: you have only US$10 to spend. To buy 5 slices of pizza (at US$2 per slice) and 5 cups of Coke (at US$1 per cup), you would need US$15.

To select the best way to spend your US$10, remember this key economic principle: *Optimal decisions are made at the margin.* That is, most of the time, economic decision makers—consumers, firms, and the government—are faced with decisions about whether to do a little more of one thing or a little more of an alternative. In this case, you are choosing to consume a little more pizza or a little more Coke. BMW-Egypt chooses to manufacture more 3 series or more SUVs in its 6th of October City factory. Parliament and the Health Department choose to spend more for research on heart disease or more for research on breast cancer. Every economic decision maker faces a budget constraint, and every economic decision maker faces trade-offs.

The key to making the best consumption decision is to maximize utility by following the *rule of equal marginal utility per dollar spent.* As you decide how to spend your income, you should buy pizza and Coke up to the point where the last slice of pizza purchased and the last cup of Coke purchased give you equal increases in utility *per dollar.* By doing this, you will have maximized your total utility.

It is important to remember that to follow this rule, you must equalize your marginal utility per dollar spent, *not* your marginal utility from each good. Buying tickets for your favorite football team or for the opera or buying a BMW may give you a lot more satisfaction than drinking a cup of Coke, but the football tickets may well give you less satisfaction *per dollar* spent. To decide how many slices of pizza and how many cups of Coke to buy, you must convert the values for marginal utility in Table 6-1 into marginal utility per dollar. You can do this by dividing marginal utility by the price of each good, as shown in Table 6-2.

In column (3), we calculate marginal utility per dollar spent on pizza. Because the price of pizza is US$2 per slice, the marginal utility per dollar from eating one slice of pizza equals 20 divided by US$2, or 10 utils per dollar. Similarly, we show in column (6) that because the price of Coke is US$1 per cup, the marginal utility per dollar from

TABLE 6-2 | Converting Marginal Utility to Marginal Utility per Dollar

(1) SLICES OF PIZZA	(2) MARGINAL UTILITY (MU_{Pizza})	(3) MARGINAL UTILITY PER DOLLAR $\left(\dfrac{MU_{Pizza}}{P_{Pizza}}\right)$	(4) CUPS OF COKE	(5) MARGINAL UTILITY (MU_{Coke})	(6) MARGINAL UTILITY PER DOLLAR $\left(\dfrac{MU_{Coke}}{P_{Coke}}\right)$
1	20	10	1	20	20
2	16	8	2	15	15
3	10	5	3	10	10
4	6	3	4	5	5
5	2	1	5	3	3
6	–3	–1.5	6	–1	–1

drinking 1 cup of Coke equals 20 divided by US$1, or 20 utils per dollar. To maximize the total utility you receive, you must make sure that the utility per dollar of pizza for the last slice of pizza is equal to the utility per dollar of Coke for the last cup of Coke. Table 6-2 shows that there are three combinations of slices of pizza and cups of Coke where marginal utility per dollar is equalized. Table 6-3 lists the combinations, the total amount of money needed to buy each combination, and the total utility received from consuming each combination.

If you buy 4 slices of pizza, the last slice gives you 3 utils per dollar. If you buy 5 cups of Coke, the last cup also gives you 3 utils per dollar, so you have equalized your marginal utility per dollar. Unfortunately, as the third column in the table shows, to buy 4 slices and 5 cups, you would need US$13, and you have only US$10. You could also equalize your marginal utility per dollar by buying 1 slice and 3 cups, but that would cost just US$5, leaving you with US$5 to spend. Only when you buy 3 slices and 4 cups have you equalized your marginal utility per dollar and spent neither more nor less than the US$10 available.

We can summarize the two conditions for maximizing utility:

1 $\dfrac{MU_{Pizza}}{P_{Pizza}} = \dfrac{MU_{Coke}}{P_{Coke}}$

2 Spending on pizza + Spending on Coke = Amount available to be spent

The first condition shows that the marginal utility per dollar spent must be the same for both goods. The second condition is the budget constraint, which states that total spending on both goods must equal the amount available to be spent. Of course, these conditions for maximizing utility apply not just to pizza and Coke but to any two pairs of goods.

TABLE 6-3 | Equalizing Marginal Utility per Dollar Spent

COMBINATIONS OF PIZZA AND COKE WITH EQUAL MARGINAL UTILITIES PER DOLLAR	MARGINAL UTILITY PER DOLLAR (MARGINAL UTILITY/PRICE)	TOTAL SPENDING	TOTAL UTILITY
1 slice of pizza and 3 cups of Coke	10	$2 + $3 = $5	20 + 45 = 65
3 slices of pizza and 4 cups of Coke	5	$6 + $4 = $10	46 + 50 = 96
4 slices of pizza and 5 cups of Coke	3	$8 + $5 = $13	52 + 53 = 105

Solved Problem | 6-1

Finding the Optimal Level of Consumption

The following table shows Aliaa's utility from consuming ice cream cones and cans of ice tea.

NUMBER OF ICE CREAM CONES	TOTAL UTILITY FROM ICE CREAM CONES	MARGINAL UTILITY FROM LAST CONE	NUMBER OF CANS OF ICE TEA	TOTAL UTILITY FROM CANS OF ICE TEA	MARGINAL UTILITY FROM LAST CAN
0	0	—	0	0	—
1	30	30	1	40	40
2	55	25	2	75	35
3	75	20	3	101	26
4	90	15	4	119	18
5	100	10	5	134	15
6	105	5	6	141	7

a. Khaled inspects this table and concludes, "Aliaa's optimal choice would be to consume 4 ice cream cones and 5 cans of ice tea because with that combination, her marginal utility from ice cream cones is equal to her marginal utility from ice tea." Do you agree with Khaled's reasoning? Briefly explain.

b. Suppose that Aliaa has an unlimited budget to spend on ice cream cones and cans of ice tea. Under these circumstances, how many ice cream cones and how many cans of ice tea will she consume?

c. Suppose that Aliaa has US$7 per week to spend on ice cream cones and ice tea. The price of an ice cream cone is US$2, and the price of a can of ice tea is US$1. If Aliaa wants to maximize her utility, how many ice cream cones and how many cans of ice tea should she buy?

SOLVING THE PROBLEM:

Step 1: **Review the chapter material.** This problem involves finding the optimal consumption of two goods, so you may want to review the section "The Rule of Equal Marginal Utility per Dollar Spent," which begins on page 177.

Step 2: **Answer question (a) by analyzing Khaled's reasoning.** Khaled's reasoning is incorrect. To maximize utility, Aliaa needs to equalize marginal utility per dollar for the two goods.

Step 3: **Answer question (b) by determining how Aliaa would maximize utility with an unlimited budget.** With an unlimited budget, consumers maximize utility by continuing to buy each good as long as their utility is increasing. In this case, Aliaa will maximize utility by buying 6 ice cream cones and 6 cans of ice tea.

Step 4: **Answer question (c) by determining Aliaa's optimal combination of ice cream cones and cans of ice tea.** will maximize her utility if she spends her US$7 per week so that the marginal utility of ice cream cones divided by the price of ice cream cones is equal to the marginal utility of ice tea divided by the price of ice tea. We can use the following table to solve this part of the problem:

QUANTITY	ICE CREAM CONES		CANS OF ICE TEA	
	MU	$\frac{MU}{P}$	MU	$\frac{MU}{P}$
1	30	15	40	40
2	25	12.5	35	35
3	20	10	26	26
4	15	7.5	18	18
5	10	5	15	15
6	5	2.5	7	7

Aliaa will maximize her utility by buying 1 ice cream cone and 5 cans of ice tea. At this combination, the marginal utility of each good divided by its price equals 15. She has also spent all of her US$7.

YOUR TURN: For more practice, do related problems 1.7 and 1.8 on pages 201–202 at the end of this chapter.

» End Solved Problem 6-1

What if the Rule of Equal Marginal Utility per Dollar Does Not Hold?

The idea of getting the maximum utility by equalizing the ratio of marginal utility to price for the goods you are buying can be difficult to grasp, so it is worth thinking about in another way. Suppose that instead of buying 3 slices of pizza and 4 cups of Coke, you buy 4 slices and 2 cups. Four slices and 2 cups cost US$10, so you would meet your budget constraint by spending all the money available to you, but would you have gotten the maximum amount of utility? No, you wouldn't have. From the information in Table 6-1, we can list the additional utility per dollar you are getting from the last slice and the last cup and the total utility from consuming 4 slices and 2 cups:

Marginal utility per dollar for the fourth slice of pizza = 3 utils per dollar

Marginal utility per dollar for the second cup of Coke = 15 utils per dollar

Total utility from 4 slices of pizza and 2 cups of Coke = 87 utils

Obviously, the marginal utilities per dollar are not equal. The last cup of Coke gave you considerably more satisfaction per dollar than did the last slice of pizza. You could raise your total utility by buying less pizza and more Coke. Buying 1 less slice of pizza frees up US$2 that will allow you to buy 2 more cups of Coke. Eating 1 less slice of pizza reduces your utility by 6 utils, but drinking 2 additional cups of Coke raises your utility by 15 utils (make sure you see this), for a net increase of 9. You end up equalizing your marginal utility per dollar (5 utils per dollar for both the last slice and the last cup) and raising your total utility from 87 utils to 96 utils.

The Income Effect and Substitution Effect of a Price Change

We can use the rule of equal marginal utility per dollar to analyze how consumers adjust their buying decisions when a price changes. Suppose you are back at the restaurant for the African Cup of Nations party, but this time the price of pizza is US$1.50 per slice, rather than US$2. You still have US$10 to spend on pizza and Coke.

When the price of pizza was US$2 per slice and the price of Coke was US$1 per cup, your optimal choice was to consume 3 slices of pizza and 4 cups of Coke. The fall in the price of pizza to US$1.50 per slice has two effects on the quantity of pizza you consume: the *income effect* and the *substitution effect*. First, consider the income effect. When the price of a good falls, you have more purchasing power. In our example, 3 slices of pizza and 4 cups of Coke now cost a total of only US$8.50 instead of US$10.00. An increase in purchasing power is essentially the same thing as an increase in income. The change in the quantity of pizza you will demand because of this increase in purchasing power—holding all other factors constant—is the **income effect** of the price change. Recall from Chapter 3 that if a product is a *normal good*, a consumer increases the quantity demanded as the consumer's income rises, but if a product is an *inferior good*, a consumer decreases the quantity demanded as the consumer's income rises. So, if we assume that for you pizza is a normal good, the income effect of a fall in price causes you to consume more pizza. If pizza had been an inferior good for you, the income effect of a fall in the price would have caused you to consume less pizza.

Income effect The change in the quantity demanded of a good that results from the effect of a change in price on consumer purchasing power, holding all other factors constant.

TABLE 6-4

Income Effect and Substitution Effect of a Price Change

		INCOME EFFECT		SUBSTITUTION EFFECT
PRICE DECREASE	Increases the consumer's purchasing power, which…	…if a normal good, causes the quantity demanded to increase.	…if an inferior good, causes the quantity demanded to decrease.	Lowers the opportunity cost of consuming the good, which causes the quantity of the good demanded to increase.
PRICE INCREASE	Decreases the consumer's purchasing power, which…	…if a normal good, causes the quantity demanded to decrease.	…if an inferior good, causes the quantity demanded to increase.	Raises the opportunity cost of consuming the good, which causes the quantity of the good demanded to decrease.

The second effect of the price change is the substitution effect. When the price of pizza falls, pizza becomes cheaper *relative* to Coke, and the marginal utility per dollar for each slice of pizza you consume increases. If we hold constant the effect of the price change on your purchasing power and just focus on the effect of the price being lower relative to the price of the other good, we have isolated the **substitution effect** of the price change. The lower price of pizza relative to the price of Coke has lowered the *opportunity cost* to you of consuming pizza because now you have to give up less Coke to consume the same quantity of pizza. Therefore, the substitution effect from the fall in the price of pizza relative to the price of Coke will cause you to eat more pizza and drink less Coke. In this case, both the income effect and the substitution effect of the fall in price cause you to eat more pizza. If the price of pizza had risen, both the income effect and the substitution effect would have caused you to eat less pizza. Table 6-4 summarizes the effect of a price change on the quantity demanded.

We can use Table 6-5 to determine the effect of the fall in the price of pizza on your optimal consumption. Table 6-5 has the same information as Table 6-2, with one change: The marginal utility per dollar from eating pizza has been changed to reflect the new lower price of US$1.50 per slice. Examining the table, we can see that the fall in the price of pizza will result in your eating 1 more slice of pizza, so your optimal consumption now becomes 4 slices of pizza and 4 cups of Coke. You will be spending all of your US$10, and the last dollar you spend on pizza will provide you with about the same marginal utility per dollar as the last dollar you spend on Coke. You will not be receiving exactly the same marginal utility per dollar spent on the two products. As Table 6-5

Substitution effect The change in the quantity demanded of a good that results from a change in price making the good more or less expensive relative to other goods, holding constant the effect of the price change on consumer purchasing power.

TABLE 6-5 | Adjusting Optimal Consumption to a Lower Price of Pizza

NUMBER OF SLICES OF PIZZA	MARGINAL UTILITY FROM LAST SLICE (MU_{Pizza})	MARGINAL UTILITY PER DOLLAR $\left[\dfrac{MU_{Pizza}}{P_{Pizza}}\right]$	NUMBER OF CUPS OF COKE	MARGINAL UTILITY FROM LAST CUP (MU_{COKE})	MARGINAL UTILITY PER DOLLAR $\left(\dfrac{MU_{Coke}}{P_{Coke}}\right)$
1	20	13.33	1	20	20
2	16	10.67	2	15	15
3	10	6.67	3	10	10
4	6	4	4	5	5
5	2	1.33	5	3	3
6	−3	—	6	−1	—

shows, the last slice of pizza gives you 4 utils per dollar, and the last cup of Coke gives you 5 utils per dollar. But this is as close as you can come to equalizing marginal utility per dollar for the two products, unless you can buy a fraction of a slice of pizza or a fraction of a cup of Coke.

6.2 | Use the concept of utility to explain the law of demand.

Where Demand Curves Come From

We saw in Chapter 3 that, according to the *law of demand*, whenever the price of a product falls, the quantity demanded increases. Now that we have covered the concepts of total utility, marginal utility, and the budget constraint, we can look more closely at why the law of demand holds.

In our example of optimal consumption of pizza and Coke at the African Cup of Nations party, we found the following:

Price of pizza = US$2 per slice ⇒ Quantity of pizza demanded = 3 slices

Price of pizza = US$1.50 per slice ⇒ Quantity of pizza demanded = 4 slices

In panel (a) of Figure 6-2, we plot the two points showing the optimal number of pizza slices you choose to consume at each price. In panel (b) of Figure 6-2, we draw a line connecting the two points. This downward-sloping line represents your demand curve for pizza. We could find more points on the line by changing the price of pizza and using the information in Table 6-2 to find the new optimal number of slices of pizza you would demand at each price.

To this point in this chapter, we have been looking at an individual demand curve. As we saw in Chapter 3, however, economists are typically interested in market demand curves. We can construct the market demand curve from the individual demand curves for all the consumers in the market. To keep things simple, let's assume that there are only three consumers in the market for pizza: you, Ayman, and Ahmed. The table in Figure 6-3 shows the individual demand schedules for the three consumers. Because

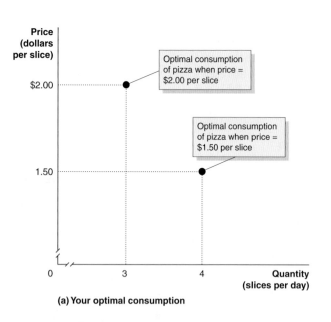
(a) Your optimal consumption

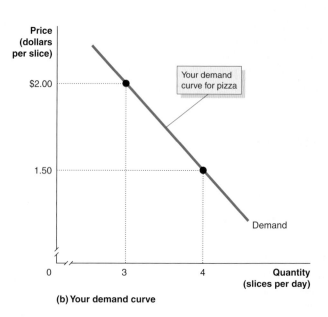
(b) Your demand curve

Figure 6-2 | Deriving the Demand Curve for Pizza

A consumer responds optimally to a fall in the price of a product by consuming more of that product. In panel (a), the price of pizza falls from US$2 per slice to US$1.50, and the optimal quantity of slices consumed rises from 3 to 4. When we graph this result in panel (b), we have the consumer's demand curve.

	Quantity (slices per day)			
Price (dollars per slice)	You	Ayman	Ahmed	Market
$2.50	2	4	1	7
2.00	3	5	3	11
1.50	4	6	5	15
1.00	5	7	7	19
0.50	6	8	9	23

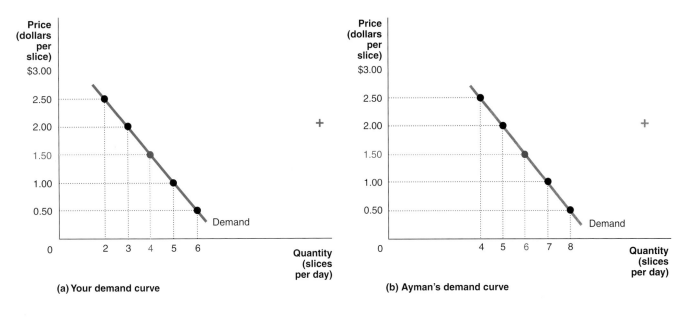

(a) Your demand curve (b) Ayman's demand curve

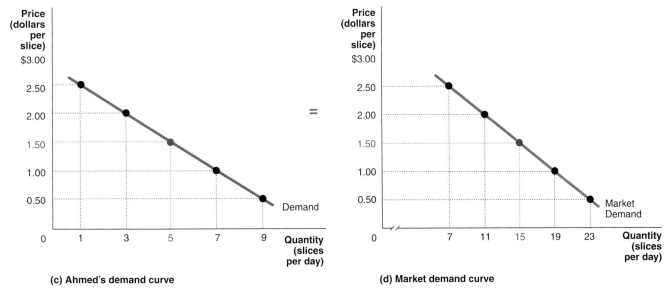

(c) Ahmed's demand curve (d) Market demand curve

Figure 6-3 | Deriving the Market Demand Curve from Individual Demand Curves

The table shows that the total quantity demanded in a market is the sum of the quantities demanded by each buyer. We can find the market demand curve by adding horizontally the individual demand curves in parts (a), (b), and (c). For instance, at a price of $1.50, your quantity demanded is 4 slices, Ayman's quantity demanded is 6 slices, and Ahmed's quantity demanded is 5 slices. Therefore, part (d) shows a price of $1.50, and a quantity demanded of 15 is a point on the market demand curve.

consumers differ in their incomes and their preferences for products, we would not expect every consumer to demand the same quantity of a given product at each price. The final column gives the market demand, which is simply the sum of the quantities demanded by each of the three consumers at each price. For example, at a price of US$1.50 per slice, your quantity demanded is 4 slices, Ayman's quantity demanded is 6 slices, and Ahmed's quantity demanded is 5 slices. So, at a price of US$1.50, a quantity of 15 slices is demanded in the market. The graphs in the figure show that we can obtain the market demand curve by adding horizontally the individual demand curves.

Remember that according to the law of demand, market demand curves always slope downward. We now know that this is true because the income and substitution effects of a fall in price cause consumers to increase the quantity of the good they demand. There is a complicating factor, however. As we discussed earlier, only for normal goods will the income effect result in consumers increasing the quantity of the good they demand when the price falls. If the good is an inferior good, then the income effect leads consumers to *decrease* the quantity of the good they demand. The substitution effect, on the other hand, results in consumers increasing the quantity they demand of both normal and inferior goods when the price falls. So, when the price of an inferior good falls, the income and substitution effects work in opposite directions: the income effect causes consumers to decrease the quantity of the good they demand, whereas the substitution effect causes consumers to increase the quantity of the good they demand. Is it possible, then, that consumers might actually buy less of a good when the price falls? If this happened, the demand curve would be upward sloping.

For a market demand curve to be upward sloping, the good would have to be an inferior good, and the income effect would have to be larger than the substitution effect. Goods that have both of these characteristics are called *Giffen goods*. Although we can conceive of there being Giffen goods, none has ever been discovered because for all actual goods, the substitution effect is larger than the income effect. Therefore, even for an inferior good, a fall in price leads to an increase in quantity demanded, and a rise in price leads to a decrease in the quantity demanded.

6.3 LEARNING OBJECTIVE

6.3 | Explain how social influences can affect consumption choices.

Social Influences on Decision Making

Sociologists and anthropologists have argued that social factors such as culture, customs, and religion are very important in explaining the choices consumers make. Economists have traditionally seen such factors as being relatively unimportant, if they take them into consideration at all. Recently, however, some economists have begun to study how social factors influence consumer choice.

For example, people seem to receive more utility from consuming goods they believe are popular. As the economists Gary Becker, a university professor at the University of Chicago and a Nobel Prize laureate, and Kevin Murphy, a Distinguished Service Professor of Economics at the University of Chicago, put it:

> The utility from drugs, crime, going bowling, owning a Rolex watch, voting Democratic, dressing informally at work, or keeping a neat lawn depends on whether friends and neighbors take drugs, commit crimes, go bowling, own Rolex watches, vote Democratic, dress informally, or keep their lawns neat.

This reasoning can help to explain why one restaurant is packed, while another restaurant that serves essentially the same food and has a similar décor has many fewer customers. Consumers decide which restaurant to go to partly on the basis of food and décor but also on the basis of the restaurant's popularity. People receive utility from being seen eating at a popular restaurant because they believe it makes them appear knowledgeable and fashionable. For example, many people in the Arab world now like to take a part of their work or study to one of the famous American, Canadian, or European coffee shops such as Costa Coffee, Starbucks, and Brioche, so that they can work or study while eating. The popularity of these coffee shops comes partially from the 'imitation in consumption'. In other words, whenever consumption takes place publicly, many consumers base their purchasing decisions on what other consumers are buying. Examples of public consumption include eating in restaurants, attending sporting events, wearing clothes or jewelry, and driving cars. In all these cases, the decision to buy a product depends partly on the characteristics of the product and partly on how many other people are buying the product.

The Effects of Celebrity Endorsements

In many cases, it is not just the number of people who use a product that makes it desirable but the types of people who use it. If consumers believe that movie stars or professional athletes use a product, demand for the product will often increase. This may be partly because consumers believe public figures are particularly knowledgeable about products: "Ahmed Helmy, the famous Egyptian celebrity, knows more about cars than I do, so I'll buy the same car he is driving." But many consumers also feel more fashionable and closer to famous people if they use the same products these people do. These considerations help to explain why companies are willing to pay millions of dollars to have celebrities endorse their products. As we saw at the beginning of this chapter, Coke has been using celebrities in its advertising for decades.

Making the Connection | **Why Do Firms Pay Mohamed Aboutrika to Endorse Their Products?**

Mohamed Aboutrika is one of the best Arab football players in recent years. Aboutrika, known in Egypt as "the Magico" or "the Prince of Hearts," started to gain his popularity when, in 2004, he joined the Egyptian football team Al-Ahly, "the African Club of the [20th] Century." He was described by Gabriele Marcotti, a UK-based Italian sports journalist, as "the best footballer on Earth not plying his trade in Europe or South America." Aboutrika played a vital role in helping Egypt to become African champions twice and in helping Al-Ahly to win three African Champions League crowns. As well as being a great footballing talent, Aboutrika is seen as a role model by many Arabs because of his respectful personality and his humanitarian activities.

Even though Aboutrika is a great footballer, should consumers care what products he uses or what humanitarian activities he is involved in? A number of companies, and not-for-profit institutions, apparently believe that consumers, and charity-givers, do care. For example, Vodafone telecommunications company, Best Cheese Company, and Children's Cancer Hospital Egypt (not-for-profit institution) hired him to market their products and attract more consumers and charity-givers.

There may be little doubt that consumers care what products Aboutrika uses, but *why* do they care? It might be that they believe Aboutrika has better information than they do about the products he endorses. A young man who loves football might believe that if Aboutrika markets Teama cheese, maybe this kind of cheese is better than any other kind. But it seems more likely that people buy products associated with Aboutrika or other celebrities because using these products makes them feel closer to the celebrity endorser or because it makes them appear to be fashionable.

Consumers and charity-givers care what products and humanitarian activities celebrities like Mohamed Aboutrika endorse.

YOUR TURN: Test your understanding by doing related problem 3.9 on page 203 at the end of this chapter.

Network Externalities

Network externality The situation where the usefulness of a product increases with the number of consumers who use it.

Technology can play a role in explaining why consumers buy products that many other consumers are already buying. There is a **network externality** in the consumption of a product if the usefulness of the product increases with the number of consumers who use it. For example, if you owned the only cellphone in the world, it would not be very useful. The usefulness of cellphones increases with the number of people who own them. Similarly, your willingness to buy an iPod depends in part on the number of other people who own iPods. The more people who own iPods, the more music that will be available to download and the more useful an iPod is to you.

Some economists have suggested the possibility that network externalities may have a significant downside because they might result in consumers buying products that contain inferior technologies. This outcome could occur because network externalities can create significant *switching costs* to changing products: when a product becomes established, consumers may find it too costly to switch to a new product that contains a better technology. The selection of products may be *path dependent*. This means that because of switching costs, the technology that was first available may have advantages over better technologies that were developed later. In other words, the path along which the economy has developed in the past is important.

One example of path dependency and the use of an inferior technology is the QWERTY order of the letters along the top row of most computer keyboards. This order became widely used when manual typewriters were developed in the late nineteenth century. The metal keys on manual typewriters would stick together if a user typed too fast, and the QWERTY keyboard was designed to slow down typists and minimize the problem of the keys sticking together. With computers, the problem that QWERTY was developed to solve no longer exists, so keyboards could be changed easily to have letters in a more efficient layout. But because the overwhelming majority of people have learned to use keyboards with the QWERTY layout, there might be significant costs to them if they had to switch, even if a new layout ultimately made them faster typists.

Other products that supposedly embodied inferior technologies are VHS video recorders—supposedly inferior to Sony Betamax recorders—and the Windows computer operating system—supposedly inferior to the Macintosh operating system. Some economists have argued that because of path dependence and switching costs, network externalities can result in *market failures*. A market failure is a situation in which the market fails to produce the efficient level of output. If network externalities result in market failure, government intervention in these markets might improve economic efficiency. Many economists are skeptical, however, that network externalities really do lead to consumers being locked into products with inferior technologies. In particular, economists Stan Leibowitz of the University of Texas, Dallas, and Stephen Margolis of North Carolina State University have argued that in practice, the gains from using a superior technology are larger than the losses due to switching costs. After carefully studying the cases of the QWERTY keyboard, VHS video recorders, and the Windows computer operating system, they have concluded that there is no good evidence that the alternative technologies were actually superior. The implications of network externalities for economic efficiency remain controversial among economists.

Does Fairness Matter?

If people were only interested in making themselves as well off as possible in a material sense, they would not be concerned with fairness. There is a great deal of evidence, however, that people like to be treated fairly and that they usually attempt to treat others fairly, even if doing so makes them worse off financially. Tipping servers in restaurants is an example. Diners in restaurants typically add 15 percent to their food bills as tips to their servers. Tips are not *required*, but most people see it as very unfair not to tip, unless the service has been exceptionally bad. You could argue that people leave tips not to be fair but because they are afraid that if they don't leave a tip, the next time they visit the restaurant they will receive poor service. Studies have shown, however, that most people leave tips at restaurants even while on vacation or in other circumstances where they are unlikely to visit the restaurant again.

There are many other examples where people willingly part with money when they are not required to do so and when they receive nothing material in return. The most obvious example is making donations to charity. Apparently, donating money to charity or leaving tips in restaurants that they will never visit again gives people more utility than they would receive from keeping the money and spending it on themselves.

A Test of Fairness in the Economic Laboratory: The Ultimatum Game Experiment Economists have used experiments to increase their understanding of the role that fairness plays in consumer decision making. Experimental economics has been widely used during the past two decades, and a number of experimental economics laboratories exist in the United States and Europe. Economists Maurice Allais (France), Reinhard Selten (Germany), and Vernon Smith (U.S.) were awarded the Nobel Prize in Economics in part because of their contributions to experimental economics. Experiments make it possible to focus on a single aspect of consumer behavior. The *ultimatum game*, first popularized by Werner Güth of the Max Planck Institute of Economics, is an experiment that tests whether fairness is important in consumer decision making. Various economists have conducted the ultimatum game experiment under slightly different conditions, but with generally the same result. In this game, a group of volunteers—often college students—are divided into pairs. One member of each pair is the 'allocator,' and the other member of the pair is the 'recipient.'

Each pair is given an amount of money, say US$20. The allocator decides how much of the US$20 each member of the pair will get. There are no restrictions on how the allocator divides up the money. He or she could keep it all, give it all to the recipient, or anything in between. The recipient must then decide whether to accept the allocation or reject it. If the recipient decides to accept the allocation, each member of the pair gets to keep his or her share. If the recipient decides to reject the allocation, both members of the pair receive nothing.

If neither the allocator nor the recipient cared about fairness, optimal play in the ultimatum game is straightforward: the allocator should propose a division of the money in which the allocator receives US$19.99 and the recipient receives US$0.01. The allocator has maximized his or her gain. The recipient should accept the division because the alternative is to reject the division and receive nothing at all: even a penny is better than nothing.

In fact, when the ultimatum game experiment is carried out, both allocators and recipients act as if fairness is important. Allocators usually offer recipients at least a 40 percent share of the money, and recipients almost always reject offers of less than a 10 percent share. Why do allocators offer recipients more than a negligible amount? It might be that allocators do not care about fairness but fear that recipients do care and will reject offers they consider unfair. This possibility was tested in an experiment known as the *dictator game* carried out by Daniel Kahneman (a psychologist who shared the Nobel Prize in Economics), Jack Knetsch, and Richard Thaler, using students at Cornell University in the US. In this experiment, the allocators were given only two possible divisions of US$20: either US$18 for themselves and US$2 for the recipient or an even division of US$10 for themselves and US$10 for the recipient. One important difference from the ultimatum game was that *the recipient was not allowed to reject the division*. Of the 161 allocators, 122 chose the even division of the US$20. Because there was no possibility of the US$18/US$2 split being rejected, the allocators must have chosen the even split because they valued acting fairly.

Why would recipients in the ultimatum game ever reject any division of the money in which they receive even a very small amount, given that even a small amount of money is better than nothing? Apparently, most people value fairness enough that they will refuse to participate in transactions they consider unfair, even if they are worse off financially as a result.

Business Implications of Fairness If consumers value fairness, how does that affect firms? One consequence is that firms will sometimes not raise prices of goods and services, even when there is a large increase in demand, because they are afraid their customers will consider the price increases unfair and may buy elsewhere.

For example, some popular Arab singers, such as Mohamed Mounir of Egypt, insist that the ticket price of their concerts is set at a relatively low price. This usually results in a shortage in the supply of seats for people who want to attend the concert. For example, many more fans of Mohamed Mounir wanted to buy tickets at a low price for a concert he was performing at the Egyptian Opera House than could be accommodated there. Figure 6-4 illustrates this situation.

Notice that the supply curve in Figure 6-4 is a vertical line, which indicates that the capacity of the Opera House is fixed at 1,644 seats. At a price of US$15 per ticket, there was a shortage of more than 400 tickets. Why didn't the theater raise ticket prices to US$25, where the quantity supplied would equal the quantity demanded?

Let's look at another example in which it seems that businesses could increase their profits by raising prices. At popular restaurants, there are often long lines of people waiting to be served. Some of the people will wait hours to be served, and some won't be served at all before the restaurant closes. Why doesn't the restaurant raise prices high enough to eliminate the lines?

In each of the previous two cases, it appears that a firm could increase its profits by raising prices. The seller would be selling the same quantity—of seats in a theater or meals in a restaurant—at a higher price, so profits should increase. Economists have provided two explanations of why firms sometimes do not raise prices in these situations. Gary Becker, winner of the Nobel Prize in Economics, has suggested that the products involved—theatrical plays, football games, rock concerts, or restaurant meals—are all products that buyers consume together with other buyers. In those situations, the

Figure 6-4

The Market for Tickets for a Mohamed Mounir concert

The Opera House could have raised prices for the Mohamed Mounir musical concert to US$25 per ticket and still sold all of the 1,644 tickets available. Instead, the theater kept the price of tickets at US$15, even though the result was a shortage of more than 400 seats. Is it possible that this strategy maximized profits?

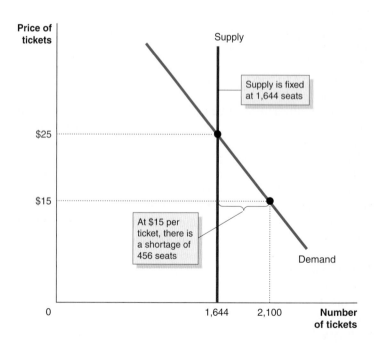

amount consumers wish to buy may be related to how much of the product other people are consuming. People like to consume, and be seen consuming, a popular product. In this case, a popular restaurant that increased its prices enough to eliminate lines might find that it had also eliminated its popularity.

Daniel Kahneman (U.S.), Jack Knetsch (Canada), and Richard Thaler (U.S.) have offered another explanation for why firms don't always raise prices when doing so would seem to increase their profits. In surveys of consumers, these researchers found that most people considered it fair for firms to raise their prices following an increase in costs but unfair to raise prices following an increase in demand. For example, Kahneman, Knetsch, and Thaler conducted a survey in which people were asked their opinion of the following situation: "A hardware store has been selling snow shovels for US$15. The morning after a large snowstorm, the store raises the price to US$20." Eighty-two percent of those surveyed responded that they considered the hardware store's actions to be unfair. Kahneman, Knetsch, and Thaler have concluded that firms may sometimes not raise their prices even when the quantity demanded of their product is greater than the quantity supplied out of fear that in the long run, they will lose customers who believe the price increases were unfair.

These explanations share the same basic idea: Sometimes firms will give up some profits in the short run to keep their customers happy and increase their profits in the long run.

Making the Connection | How can we explain the long lines at Al-Baik Restaurant?

Al-Baik is one of the popular fast-food restaurants in the west part of Saudi Arabia. Its 24 branches are mainly located in the cities of Mecca, Madina, and Jeddah, and most of the time consumers have to wait in long queues to order their meals. Is this because of the low price of a typical meal or the high quality of food? The answer is: it is the relatively cheap price of Al-Baik meals. In general, Al Baik's prices are lower than similar international fast-food chains such as Hardee's, McDonald's, and KFC by around 30 percent (it costs you 11 Saudi riyals on average—about US$3—to get a meal from Al-Baik, while the average price of a similar meal from its competitors is around 15 Saudi riyals, or US$4.) Now we get back to the same question: if the market equilibrium price of that type of fast-food meals is 15 Saudi riyals, why does Al-Baik charge less than the equilibrium price? From Al-Baik company's point of view, it is the fairness explanation that made them not increase the price level although there is a high demand on their products. The following statement by Al-Baik company explains their strategy: "We understand very well that customers always expect and appreciate great tasting high quality food that they can trust, served courteously and fast, in sparkling clean and comfortable restaurants and *at fair and affordable prices*." But think about Kahneman, Knetsch, and Thaler's explanation above, that is: if Al-Baik decided to increase its prices to eliminate the long lines, it might also eliminate its popularity as well. Whatever explanation you choose to believe, the result is the same: Al-Baik prices are significantly cheaper than its competitors.

Should Al-Baik increase its prices?

YOUR TURN: Test your understanding by doing related problems 3.11 and 3.12 on page 203 at the end of this chapter.

6.4 | Describe the behavioral economics approach to understanding decision making.

Behavioral Economics: Do People Make Their Choices Rationally?

When economists say that consumers and firms are behaving 'rationally,' they mean that consumers and firms are taking actions that are appropriate to reach their goals, given the information available to them. In recent years, some economists have begun studying situations in which people do not appear to be making choices that are economically rational. This new area of economics is called **behavioral economics**. Why might consumers or businesses not act rationally? The most obvious reason would be that they do not realize that their actions are inconsistent with their goals. As we discussed in Chapter 1, one of the objectives of economics is to suggest ways to make better decisions. In this section, we discuss ways in which consumers can improve their decisions by avoiding some common pitfalls.

Consumers commonly commit the following three mistakes when making decisions:

- They take into account monetary costs but ignore nonmonetary opportunity costs.
- They fail to ignore sunk costs.
- They are overly optimistic about their future behavior.

Behavioral economics The study of situations in which people make choices that do not appear to be economically rational.

Opportunity cost The highest-valued alternative that must be given up to engage in an activity.

Ignoring Nonmonetary Opportunity Costs

Remember from Chapter 2 that the **opportunity cost** of any activity is the highest-valued alternative that must be given up to engage in that activity. For example, if you own something you could sell, using it yourself involves an opportunity cost. It is often difficult for people to think of opportunity costs in these terms.

Consider the following study carried out by Alan Krueger, a Professor of Economics and Public Affairs at Princeton University in the U.S.: Some of the fans at the 2001 Super Bowl, the championship game of the U.S. National Football League (NFL), participated in a lottery run by the NFL that allowed the winners to purchase tickets at their face value, which was either US$325 or US$400, depending on where in the stadium the seats were located. Krueger surveyed the lottery winners, asking them two questions:

Question 1: If you had not won the lottery, would you have been willing to pay US$3,000 for your ticket?
Question 2: If after winning your ticket (and before arriving in Florida for the Super Bowl) someone had offered you US$3,000 for your ticket, would you have sold it?

In answer to the first question, 94 percent said that if they had not won the lottery, they would not have paid US$3,000 for a ticket. In answer to the second question, 92 percent said they would not have sold their ticket for US$3,000. But these answers are contradictory! If someone offers you US$3,000 for your ticket, then by using the ticket rather than selling it, you incur an opportunity cost of US$3,000. There really is a US$3,000 cost involved in using that ticket, even though you do not pay US$3,000 in cash. The alternatives of either paying US$3,000 or not receiving US$3,000 amount to exactly the same thing.

If the ticket is really not worth US$3,000 to you, you should sell it. If it is worth US$3,000 to you, you should be willing to pay US$3,000 in cash to buy it. Not being willing to sell a ticket you already own for US$3,000, while at the same time not being willing to buy a ticket for US$3,000 if you didn't already own one is inconsistent behavior. The inconsistency comes from a failure to take into account nonmonetary opportunity costs. Behavioral economists believe this inconsistency is caused by the **endowment effect**, which is the tendency of people to be unwilling to sell a good they already own even if they are offered a price that is greater than the price they would be willing to pay to buy the good if they didn't already own it.

Endowment effect The tendency of people to be unwilling to sell a good they already own even if they are offered a price that is greater than the price they would be willing to pay to buy the good if they didn't already own it.

The failure to take into account opportunity costs is a very common error in decision making. Suppose, for example, that a friend is in a hurry to have his room cleaned—it's just the day before his parents arrive to visit him in the dormitory—and he offers you US$50 to do it for him. You turn him down and spend the time cleaning your own room, even though you know somebody down the hall who would be willing to clean your room for US$20. Leave aside complicating details—the guy who asked you to clean his room is a real slob, or you don't want the person who offered to clean your room for US$20 to go through your stuff—and you should see the point we are making. The opportunity cost of cleaning your own room is US$50—the amount your friend offered to pay you to clean his room. It is inconsistent to turn down an offer from someone else to clean your room for US$20 when you are doing it for yourself at a cost of US$50. The key point here is this: *Nonmonetary opportunity costs are just as real as monetary costs and should be taken into account when making decisions.*

Business Implications of Consumers Ignoring Nonmonetary Opportunity Costs

Behavioral economist Richard Thaler has studied several examples of how businesses make use of consumers' failure to take into account opportunity costs. Whenever you buy something with a credit card, the credit card company charges the merchant a fee to process the bill. Credit card companies generally do not allow stores to charge higher prices to customers who use credit cards. A bill was introduced in the U.S. Congress that would have made it illegal for credit card companies to enforce this rule. The credit card industry was afraid that if this law passed, credit card usage would drop because stores might begin charging a fee to credit card users. They attempted to have the law amended so that stores would be allowed to give a cash discount to people not using credit cards but would not be allowed to charge a fee to people using credit cards. There really is no difference in terms of opportunity cost between being charged a fee and not receiving a discount. The credit card industry was relying on the fact that *not* receiving a discount is a nonmonetary opportunity cost—and, therefore, likely to be ignored by consumers—but a fee is a monetary cost that people do take into account.

Film processing companies provide another example. Many of these companies have a policy of printing every picture on a roll of film, even if the picture is very fuzzy. Customers are allowed to ask for refunds on pictures they don't like. Once again, the companies are relying on the fact that passing up a refund once you have already paid for a picture is a nonmonetary opportunity cost rather than a direct monetary cost. In fact, customers rarely ask for refunds.

Making *the* **Connection** | **Why Do Hilton Hotels and other Firms Hide Their Prices?**

Economists recently began to use ideas from behavioral economics to understand a puzzling aspect of how some businesses price their products. David Laibson of Harvard University and Xavier Gabaix of New York University note that some products consist of a "base good" and "add-ons." For instance, to use a printer, you buy the printer itself—the base good—and replacement ink cartridges—the add-on. Typically, firms compete on the price of the base good but do their best to hide the prices of the add-ons. Because consumers sometimes spend more on the add-ons than on the base good, it may seem surprising that firms are able to successfully hide the prices of add-ons. For instance, over the life of a printer, consumers spend, on average, 10 times the price of the printer in buying ink cartridges. Yet one survey indicates that only 3 percent of consumers know the true cost of using a printer, including the cost of the ink cartridges. Similarly, many consumers are unaware of the add-on charges

(Continued)

from using a checking account, such as ATM fees, returned check charges, and minimum balance fees. Many consumers making a hotel reservation are unaware of the hotel's charges for Internet access, for breakfast at the hotel restaurant, for local phone calls, or for ordering room service.

How are firms able to hide the prices of add-ons? Why doesn't competition lead some firms to offer lower-priced add-ons and advertise that their competitors' add-ons are higher priced? Laibson and Gabaix explain this puzzle by arguing that there are two types of consumers: sophisticated consumers, who pay attention to prices of add-ons, and myopic consumers, who ignore the prices of add-ons. It turns out that using advertising to convert myopic consumers into sophisticated consumers is not a profitable strategy. Consider the following example: Suppose that Hilton Hotels charges US$80 per night for a room and the typical myopic consumer also spends US$20 per night on local phone calls, food from the minibar, high-priced breakfasts, and other add-ons. Could a competing hotel, such as Marriott, attract Hilton's customers by advertising that Marriott's add-ons were more fairly priced than Hilton's? Laibson and Gabaix argue that this strategy would not work because its main effect would be to turn myopic consumers into sophisticated consumers. Once Hilton's customers become sophisticated, they will avoid the add-on fees, by, for instance, using their cellphones rather than the hotel phones to make calls or by eating breakfast in nearby restaurants rather than in the hotel. According to Laibson and Gabaix, Marriott's advertising campaign, "hurts Hilton—which sells fewer add-ons—but helps Hilton's customers, who are taught to substitute away from add-ons." But these sophisticated consumers are no more likely to switch from Hilton to Marriott than they were before Marriott incurred the cost of its advertising campaign. Exposing a competitor's hidden costs, say Laibson and Gabaix, "is good for the consumer and bad for both firms. Neither firm has an incentive to do it." As a result, many consumers remain unaware of the true prices of some of the products they purchase.

Sources: Christopher Shay, "The Hidden-Fee Economy," *New York Times*, December 10, 2006; and Xavier Gabaix and David Laibson, "Shrouded Attributes, Consumer Myopia, and Information Suppression in Competitive Markets," *Quarterly Journal of Economics* Vol. 121, No. 2, May 2006, pp. 351–397.

YOUR TURN: Test your understanding by doing related problem 4.6 on page 203 at the end of this chapter.

Failing to Ignore Sunk Costs

Sunk cost A cost that has already been paid and cannot be recovered

A **sunk cost** is a cost that has already been paid and cannot be recovered. Once you have paid money and can't get it back, you should ignore that money in any later decisions you make. Consider the following two situations:

Situation 1: You bought a ticket to a play for US$75. The ticket is nonrefundable and must be used on Tuesday night, which is the only night the play will be performed. On Monday, a friend calls and invites you to a football game between Al-Ahly of Egypt and Al-Hilal of Saudi Arabia, which also takes place in your town on Tuesday night. Your friend offers to pay the cost of attending the football game.

Situation 2: It's Monday night, and you are about to buy a ticket for the Tuesday night performance of the same play as in situation 1. As you are leaving to buy the ticket, your friend calls and invites you to the football game.

Would your decision to go to the play or to the football game be different in situation 1 than in situation 2? Most people would say that in situation 1, they would go to the play, because otherwise they would lose the US$75 they had paid for the ticket. In fact, though, the US$75 is 'lost' no matter what you do because the ticket is not refundable. The only real issue for you to decide is whether you would prefer to see the play or prefer to go with your friend to the football game. If you would prefer to go to the football game, the fact that you have already paid US$75 for the ticket to the play is irrelevant. Your decision should be the same in situation 1 and situation 2.

Psychologists Daniel Kahneman and Amos Tversky explored the tendency of consumers to not ignore sunk costs by asking two samples of people the following questions:

Question 1: One sample of people was asked the following question: "Imagine that you have decided to see a play and have paid the admission price of US$10 per ticket. As you enter the theater, you discover that you have lost the ticket. The seat was not marked, and the ticket cannot be recovered. Would you pay US$10 for another ticket?" Of those asked, 46 percent answered "yes," and 54 percent answered "no."

Question 2: A different sample of people was asked the following question: "Imagine that you have decided to see a play where admission is US$10 per ticket. As you enter the theater, you discover that you have lost a US$10 bill. Would you still pay US$10 for a ticket to the play?" Of those asked, 88 percent answered "yes," and 12 percent answered "no."

The situations presented in the two questions are actually the same and should have received the same fraction of yes and no responses. Many people, though, have trouble seeing that in question 1, when deciding whether to see the play, they should ignore the US$10 already paid for a ticket because it is a sunk cost.

Being Unrealistic about Future Behavior

Studies made by the World Health Organization have shown that Saudi Arabia, the United Arab Emirates, Bahrain, and Kuwait, along with the United States, are among the top countries with adult obesity worldwide. Why do many people choose to eat too much? One possibility is that they receive more utility from eating too much than they would from being thin. Another explanation, however, is that many people eat a lot today because they expect to eat less tomorrow (because they will start a diet tomorrow or next week for example.) But they never do eat less, and so they end up overweight. (Of course, some people also suffer from medical problems that lead to weight gain.) Similarly, some people continue smoking today because they expect to be able to give it up sometime in the future. Unfortunately, for many people that time never comes, and they suffer the health consequences of prolonged smoking. In both these cases, people are overvaluing the utility from current choices—eating chocolate cake or smoking—and undervaluing the utility to be received in the future from being thin or not getting lung cancer.

Economists who have studied this question argue that many people have preferences that are not consistent over time. In the long run, you would like to be thin or give up smoking or achieve some other goal, but each day, you make decisions (such as to eat too much or to smoke) that are not consistent with this long-run goal. If you are unrealistic about your future behavior, you underestimate the costs of choices—like overeating or smoking—that you make today. A key way of avoiding this problem is to be realistic about your future behavior.

Making *the* **Connection** | **Why Don't Students Study More?**

Government statistics in the U.S. show that students who do well in college earn at least US$10,000 more per year than students who fail to graduate or who graduate with low grades. So, over the course of a career of 40 years or more, students who do well in college will have earned upwards of US$400,000 more than students who failed to graduate or who received low grades. Most colleges advise that students study at least two hours

(Continued)

If the payoff for studying is so high, why don't students study more?

outside of class for every hour they spend in class. Surveys show that students often ignore this advice.

If the opportunity cost of not studying is so high, why do many students choose to study relatively little? Some students have work or family commitments that limit the amount of time they can study such as the case of young Egyptian students helping their parents in farming. But many other students study less than they would if they were more realistic about their future behavior. On any given night, a student has to choose between studying and other activities—like watching television, going to the movies, or meeting up with friends—that may seem to provide higher utility in the short run. Many students choose one of these activities over studying because they expect to study tomorrow or the next day, but tomorrow they face the same choices and make similar decisions. As a result, they do not study enough to meet their long-run goal of graduating with high grades. If they were more realistic about their future behavior, they would not make the mistake of overvaluing the utility from activities like watching television or socializing because they would realize that those activities can endanger their long-run goal of graduating with honors.

YOUR TURN: Test your understanding by doing related problem 4.9 on page 204 at the end of this chapter.

Solved Problem | 6-4

How Do You Get People to Save More of Their Income?

Many people do not put away enough savings for their retirement. People seem unwilling to save for their retirement and would rather spend the money they have now. However, if you ask people to commit now to saving more in the future, you'll find that people are more willing to do this.

Why would people refuse to increase their savings now but agree to increase their savings in the future?

Source: Louis Uchitelle, "Why It Takes Psychology to Make People Save," *New York Times*, January 13, 2002.

SOLVING THE PROBLEM:

Step 1: **Review the chapter material.** This problem is about how people are not always realistic about their future behavior, so you may want to review the section "Being Unrealistic about Future Behavior," which begins on page 195.

Step 2: **Use your understanding of consumer decision making to show that this plan may work.** We have seen that many people are unrealistic about their future behavior. They spend money today that they should be saving for retirement, partly because they expect to increase their saving in the future. A savings plan that gets people to commit today to saving in the future takes advantage of people's optimism about their future behavior. They agree to save more in the future because they expect to be doing that anyway. In fact, without being part of a plan that automatically saves their next raise, they probably would not have increased their savings.

YOUR TURN: For more practice, do related problems 4.7 and 4.8 on page 204 at the end of this chapter.

>> End Solved Problem 6-4

Taking into account nonmonetary opportunity costs, ignoring sunk costs, and being more realistic about future behavior are three ways in which consumers are able to improve the decisions they make.

>> Continued from page 175

Economics in YOUR Life!

At the beginning of the chapter, we asked you to consider a situation in which you had paid US$75 for a concert ticket, which is the most you would be willing to pay. Just before you enter the concert hall, someone offers you US$90 for the ticket. We posed two questions: would you sell the ticket? and would an economist think it is rational to sell the ticket? If you answered that you would sell, then your answer is rational in the sense in which economists use the term. The cost of going to see the concert is what you have to give up for the ticket. Initially, the cost was just US$75—the dollar price of the ticket. This amount was also the most you were willing to pay. However, once someone offers you US$90 for the ticket, the cost of seeing the concert rises to US$90. The reason the cost of the concert is now US$90 is that once you turn down an offer of US$90 for the ticket you have incurred a nonmonetary opportunity cost of US$90 if you use the ticket yourself. The endowment effect explains why some people would not sell the ticket. People seem to value things that they have more than things that they do not have. Therefore, a concert ticket you already own may be worth more to you than a concert ticket you have yet to purchase. Behavioral economists study situations like this where people make choices that do not appear to be economically rational.

Conclusion

In a market system, consumers are in the driver's seat. Goods are produced only if consumers want them to be. Therefore, how consumers make their decisions is an important area for economists to study, a fact that was highlighted when Daniel Kahneman—whose research was mentioned several times in this chapter—shared the Nobel Prize in Economics. Economists expect that consumers will spend their incomes so that the last dollar spent on each good provides them with equal additional amounts of satisfaction, or utility. In practice, there are significant social influences on consumer decision making, particularly when a good or service is consumed in public. Fairness also seems to be an important consideration for most consumers. Finally, many consumers could improve the decisions they make if they would take into account nonmonetary opportunity costs and ignore sunk costs.

In this chapter, we studied consumers' choices. In the next several chapters, we will study firms' choices. Before moving on to the next chapter, read *An Inside Look* on the next page for a discussion of why Nokia chose Mohamed Hamaki to endorse its "Comes with Music" service in the Middle East and Africa.

Was Nokia Right to Choose Mohamed Hamaki to Endorse Its New Music Service?

AMEINFO.COM, APRIL 14, 2010

Nokia Cooperates with Popular Singer Mohamed Hamaki to Promote 'Comes With Music'

ⓐ Nokia in the Middle East and Africa announced that it will be cooperating with Mohamed Hamaki, one of the Middle East's most popular young artists, in promoting its new "Comes with Music" service in the region. "Comes with Music" is a revolutionary service from Nokia which gives people a year of unlimited access to over four million tracks that can be downloaded for free.

ⓑ As one of today's most respected and popular artists, Hamaki will be participating in television and radio spots where he introduces the "Comes with Music" service and highlights to consumers its use and great benefits. The cooperation will also see him making special appearances at selected Nokia stores across the Middle East. "Hamaki is one of the region's leading recording artists with huge appeal and fans across the Middle East. He is young and has an exciting music career ahead of him, and his popularity and great appeal amongst young consumers will support Nokia in spreading the word on this first of its kind and revolutionary service," said Steve Lewis, Head of Marketing, Nokia, Middle East and Africa.

Hamaki said, "I'm very excited to be cooperating with Nokia in getting people to get to know the 'Comes with Music' service better. It is a truly amazing service in that it gives consumers access to millions and millions of tracks in a simple way, and for free. From an artist's standpoint, this service is also a great way for us to distribute our music legally and to reach an even larger audience."

Mohamed Hamaki, known to his fans as Hamaki, is an Egyptian singer who has achieved the status of superstar in the Middle East. He has attained great commercial success with the release of three albums, with the fourth due to be released early this summer. His hits include singles such as "Whada whada," "Ahla haga feeki," "Bahebak kul yom aktar," "Naweeha," and "Iftakart." Hamaki is signed on to Delta Sound label.

Key Points in the Article

This article discusses how firms benefit from using celebrity endorsements in their advertising. Steve Lewis clearly believes that hiring Mohamed Hamaki to endorse Nokia's new music service, which works with specific Nokia phones, will pay off financially. The firm believes that because Hamaki is a popular celebrity, some of that popularity will be transferred to the new Nokia products and services. Essentially, Nokia is betting that a large number of consumers will see Hamaki's endorsement and purchase new Nokia cellphones because of that endorsement. Consumers may purchase Nokia phones to be like Mohamed Hamaki or just to signal that they like Mohamed Hamaki. However, celebrity endorsements sometimes come with risks. For example, some young Arabs created groups on Facebook that were against the popular singer Tamer Hosny (the new Pepsi-Cola star), after the release of some

of his video clips and movies which contained what they held to be offensive and bold scenes. Of course, Pepsi-Cola company managers were not at all happy with the "anti-Tamer Hosny" groups. Once a firm hires a celebrity, consumers associate the product with the celebrity. This association can be a good or a bad thing depending on the celebrity's actions.

Analyzing the News

(a) Nokia hired Hamaki because it believes doing so will increase its profits. His endorsement could lead to higher demand and thus, a greater quantity of new phones sold, but the firm's profits will increase only if its increase in revenue is greater than the required payments to Hamaki and the cost of the advertisement.

We saw in Chapter 3 that when consumers' taste for a product increases, the demand curve will shift to the right, and when consumers' taste for a product decreases, the demand curve for the product will shift to the left. When a firm hires a celebrity to endorse its products, it is hoping to increase consumers' taste for its product. The figure shows that if the endorsement is successful, the demand curve for Nokia new phones shifts from D_1 to D_2. The increase in demand allows the firm to sell more phones at every price. For example, at a

price of P_1 it could sell Q_1 phones without the endorsement but Q_2 phones with the endorsement.

(b) Nokia knows exactly to whom it wants to sell its products: Arab teenagers. That is why Steve Lewis chose a singer who is popular with this segment of consumers, and one who is perceived by many young Arabs as a respectful singer. This helps Nokia avoid the risk of hiring a controversial celebrities whose actions might not be satisfying Nokia consumers.

Thinking Critically

1. Celebrity endorsements may be rewarding to firms, but they can also be risky. Nokia has committed a significant amount of money to hiring Mohamed Hamaki and developing the new music service that he endorses. What do you think would happen to the demand curve for Nokia new phones if Mohamed Hamaki gets involved in an embarrassing scandal?

2. Celebrity endorsements are also expensive. Should a firm whose celebrity endorser has just been arrested base its decision on whether or not to cancel its ad campaign on the amount it has already spent on making the ads? Briefly explain.

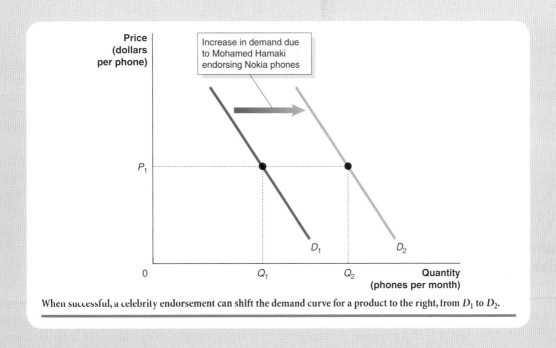

When successful, a celebrity endorsement can shift the demand curve for a product to the right, from D_1 to D_2.

Key Terms

Summary

Utility and Consumer Decision Making

Utility is the enjoyment or satisfaction that people receive from consuming goods and services. The goal of a consumer is to spend available income so as to maximize utility. Marginal utility is the change in total utility a person receives from consuming one additional unit of a good or service. The law of diminishing marginal utility states that consumers receive diminishing additional satisfaction as they consume more of a good or service during a given period of time. The budget constraint is the amount of income consumers have available to spend on goods and services. To maximize utility, consumers should make sure they spend their income so that the last dollar spent on each product gives them the same marginal utility. The income effect is the change in the quantity demanded of a good that results from the effect of a change in the price on consumer purchasing power. The substitution effect is the change in the quantity demanded of a good that results from a change in price making the good more or less expensive relative to other goods, holding constant the effect of the price change on consumer purchasing power.

Where Demand Curves Come From

When the price of a good declines, the ratio of the marginal utility to price rises. This leads consumers to buy more of that good. As a result, whenever the price of a product falls, the quantity demanded increases. We saw in Chapter 3 that this is known as the *law of demand*. The market demand curve can be constructed from the individual demand curves for all the consumers in the market.

Social Influences on Decision Making

Social factors can have an influence on consumption. For example, the amount of utility people receive from consuming a good often depends on how many other people they know who also consume the good. There is a network externality in the consumption of a product if the usefulness of the product increases with the number of consumers who use it. There is also evidence that people like to be treated fairly and that they usually attempt to treat others fairly, even if doing so makes them worse off financially. This result has been demonstrated in laboratory experiments, such as the ultimatum game. When firms set prices, they take into account consumers' preference for fairness. For example, hardware stores often do not increase the price of snow shovels to take advantage of a temporary increase in demand following a snowstorm.

Behavioral Economics: Do People Make Their Choices Rationally?

Behavioral economics is the study of situations in which people act in ways that are not economically rational. Opportunity cost is the highest-value alternative that must be given up to engage in an activity. People would improve their decision making if they took into account nonmonetary opportunity costs. People sometimes ignore nonmonetary opportunity costs because of the *endowment effect*. The endowment effect is the tendency of people to be unwilling to sell something they already own even if they are offered a price that is greater than the price they would be willing to pay to buy the good if they didn't already own it. People would also improve their decision making if they ignored *sunk costs*. A sunk cost is a cost that has already been paid and cannot be recovered. Finally, people would improve their decision making if they were more realistic about their future behavior.

Review, Problems and Applications

6.1 LEARNING OBJECTIVE   Define utility and explain how consumers choose goods and services to maximize their utility, **pages 176–184.**

Review Questions

1.1 What is the economic definition of utility? Is utility measurable?

1.2 What is the definition of marginal utility? What is the law of diminishing marginal utility? Why is marginal utility more useful than total utility in consumer decision making?

1.3 What is meant by a consumer's budget constraint? What is the rule of equal marginal utility per dollar spent?

Problems and Applications

1.4 Does the law of diminishing marginal utility hold true in every situation? Is it possible to think of goods for which consuming additional units will result in increasing marginal utility?

1.5 If consumers should allocate their income so that the last dollar spent on every product gives them the same amount of additional utility, how should they decide the amount of their income to save?

1.6 You have six hours to study for two exams tomorrow. The relationship between hours of study and test scores is shown in the following table.

ECONOMICS		ACCOUNTING	
HOURS	SCORE	HOURS	SCORE
0	54	0	54
1	62	1	62
2	69	2	69
3	75	3	75
4	80	4	80
5	84	5	84
6	87	6	87

a. Use the rule for determining optimal purchases to decide how many hours you should study each subject. Treat each point on an exam like 1 unit of utility and assume that you are equally interested in doing well in economics and accounting.

b. Now suppose that you are an accounting major, and that you value each point you earn on an accounting exam as being worth three times as much as each point you earn on an economics exam. Now how many hours will you study each subject?

1.7 (Related to *Solved problem 6-1* on page 181) Farida has US$16 to spend on Twinkies and Ho-Hos. Twinkies have a price of US$1 per pack, and Ho-Hos have a price of US$2 per pack. Use the information in the graphs provided to determine the number of Twinkies packs and the number of Ho-Hos packs Farida should buy to maximize her utility. Briefly explain your reasoning.

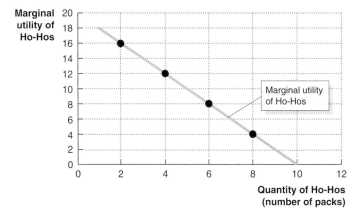

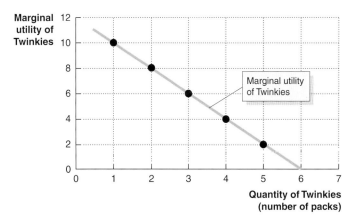

1.8 (Related to *Solved problem 6-1* on page 181) Farida has US$55 to spend on apples and oranges. Given the information in the following table, is Farida maximizing utility? Briefly explain.

PRODUCT	PRICE	QUANTITY	TOTAL UTILITY	MARGINAL UTILITY OF LAST UNIT
Apples	$0.50	50	1,000	20
Oranges	$0.75	40	500	30

1.9 Suppose the price of a bag of Frito's corn chips declines from US$0.69 to US$0.59. Which is likely to be larger: the income effect or the substitution effect? Briefly explain.

1.10 Hala is buying corn chips and soda. She has four bags of corn chips and five bottles of soda in her shopping cart. The marginal utility of the fourth bag of corn chips is 10, and the marginal utility of the fifth bottle of soda is also 10. Is Hala maximizing utility? Briefly explain.

1.11 When the price of pizza falls in the Final game of the African Cup of Nations example on page 178, both the income and the substitution effect cause you to want to consume more pizza. If pizza were an inferior good, how would the analysis be changed? In this case, is it possible that a lower price of pizza might lead you to buy less pizza? Briefly explain.

6.2 LEARNING OBJECTIVE   Use the concept of utility to explain the law of demand, **pages 184–186.**

Review Questions

2.1 Explain how a downward-sloping demand curve results from consumers adjusting their consumption choices to changes in price.

2.2 What would need to be true for a demand curve to be upward sloping?

Problems and Applications

2.3 Considering only the income effect, if the price of an inferior good declines, would a consumer want to buy a larger quantity or a smaller quantity of the good? Does this mean that the demand curves for inferior goods should slope upward? Briefly explain.

2.4 The chapter states that "when the price of an inferior good falls, the income and substitution effects work in opposite directions." Explain what this statement means.

2.5 Suppose the market for ice cream cones is made up of three consumers: Khaled, Ayman, and Housam. Use the information in the following table to construct the market demand curve for ice cream cones. Show the information in a table and in a graph.

PRICE	KHALED QUANTITY DEMANDED (CONES PER WEEK)	AYMAN QUANTITY DEMANDED (CONES PER WEEK)	HOUSAM QUANTITY DEMANDED (CONES PER WEEK)
$1.75	2	1	0
1.50	4	3	2
1.25	6	4	3
1.00	7	6	4
0.75	9	7	5

2.6 Suppose the wage you are being paid increases. Is there an income and substitution effect involved? If so, what is being substituted for what?

6.3 LEARNING OBJECTIVE   Explain how social influences can affect consumption choices, **pages 186–191.**

Review Questions

3.1 In which of the following situations are social influences on consumer decision making likely to be greater: choosing a restaurant for dinner or choosing a brand of toothpaste to buy? Briefly explain.

3.2 Why do consumers pay attention to celebrity endorsements of products?

3.3 What are network externalities? For what types of products are network externalities likely to be important? What is path dependence?

3.4 What is the ultimatum game? What insight does it provide into consumer decision making?

3.5 How does the fact that consumers apparently value fairness affect the decisions that businesses make?

Problems and Applications

3.6 Which of the following products are most likely to have significant network externalities? Explain.
  a. Fax machines
  b. Dog food
  c. Board games
  d. Conventional (CRT) television sets
  e. Plasma television sets

3.7 Linux is a computer operating system that is an alternative to Microsoft's Windows system. According to a newspaper article:

> The dominance of the Windows operating system, which runs 95 per cent of the world's PCs, is coming under greater

attack in Asia than in any other part of the world, analysts say. Linux for PCs sold three times as many copies in Asia as in the U.S. last year.... "In emerging markets such as India and China, where PC growth rates are the highest, Linux's momentum seems to be accelerating," said Robert Stimson, a Bank of America analyst in San Francisco.

If network externalities are important in choosing a computer operating system, why might Linux be more successful in Asia than in the United States?

Source: "Gates Blitzes Asia to Stem Linux Threat," *New Zealand Herald*, June 29, 2004.

3.8 (Related to the *Chapter Opener* on page 174) Think of some firms that don't use celebrities to endorse their products. Why do some firms, like Coca-Cola, use celebrity endorsers, while other firms don't?

3.9 (Related to the *Making the Connection* on page 187) Mohamed Aboutrika is a professional footballer who knows more about football and football-related products than most consumers. However, this is not necessarily the case in respect of telecommunications and dairy products. Consider the model of utility maximizing behavior described in this chapter. For the Best Cheese company's use of Mohamed Aboutrika as a celebrity endorser to make economic sense, how must Aboutrika's endorsement affect the marginal utility that at least some consumers receive from buying its Teama cheese? What will this do to the demand curve for Teama Cheese?

3.10 An article in the *New York Times* published during the 2002 Winter Olympics held in Utah indicated that

many businesses raised prices during the two-week event. The article described one incident as follows:

Susanne and Heather McDonald, sisters from the northwest Wyoming town of Moose, said a friend was having sushi at a restaurant in Park City, where skiing events are held, and the waiter was adding US$3 for every side dish until the man identified himself as a local resident. "Then he got them for free," Susanne McDonald said.

When setting the price for a meal, why would it matter to the restaurant whether the customer was a local resident?

Source: Michael Janofsky, "Olympic Boom Leaves Visitors Feeling Busted," *New York Times*, February 19, 2002.

3.11 (Related to the *Making the Connection* on page 191) Suppose that the Lebanese singer Wael Kfoury can sell out a concert with tickets priced at US$45. Kfoury's manager estimates that they could still sell out a very big station venve at US$85 per ticket. Why might Wael Kfoury and his manager want to keep ticket prices at US$45?

3.12 (Related to the *Making the Connection* on page 191) Suppose that *Spider-Man 4* comes out, and hundreds of people arrive at a theater and discover that the movie is already sold out. Meanwhile, the theater is also showing a boring movie in its third week of release in a mostly empty theater. Why would this firm charge the same US$7.50 for a ticket to either movie, when the quantity of tickets demanded is much greater than the quantity supplied for one movie, and the quantity of tickets demanded is much less than the quantity supplied for the other?

6.4 LEARNING OBJECTIVE Describe the behavioral economics approach to understanding decision making, **pages 192–197.**

Review Questions

4.1 What does it mean to be economically rational?

4.2 Define behavioral economics and give an example of three common mistakes that consumers often make

Problems and Applications

4.3 Suppose your younger brother tells you on Tuesday that one of his friends offered him US$50 for his Al-Ahly club T-shirt, but your brother decided not to sell the T-shirt. On Wednesday, your brother loses the T-shirt. Your parents feel sorry for him and give him US$50 to make up the loss. Instead of buying another T-shirt with the money (which we will assume he could have done), your brother uses the money to go to the movies and dine out with his friends. Explain your brother's actions by using the concepts in this chapter.

4.4 You have tickets to see Ragheb Alama in concert at a stadium 50 km away. A severe thunderstorm on the night of the concert makes driving hazardous. Will your decision to attend the concert be different if you had paid US$70 for the tickets than if you had received the tickets for free? Explain your answer.

4.5 After owning a used car for two years, you start having problems with it. You take it into a mechanic, and the mechanic tells you that repairs will cost US$4,000. What factors will you take into account in deciding whether to have the repairs done or to sell the car and buy another one? Will the price you paid for the car be one of those factors? Briefly explain.

4.6 (Related to the *Making the Connection* on page 193) Consumers tend to ignore the prices of "add-on" goods like ATM fees for checking accounts. Does this mean that if the government were to ban ATM fees that consumers would benefit?

4.7 (Related to *Solved problem 6-4* on page 196) In an article in the *Quarterly Journal of Economics*, Ted O'Donoghue and Matthew Rabin make the following observation: "People have self-control problems caused by a tendency to pursue immediate gratification in a way that their 'long-run selves' do not appreciate." What do they mean by a person's "long-run self"? Give two examples of people pursuing immediate gratification that their long-run selves would not appreciate.

Source: Ted O'Donoghue and Matthew Rabin, "Choice and Procrastination," *Quarterly Journal of Economics*, February 2001, pp. 125–126.

4.8 (Related to *Solved problem 6-4* on page 196) Data from health clubs show that members who choose a contract with a flat monthly fee over US\$70 attend, on average, 4.8 times per month. They pay a price per expected visit of more than US\$14, even though a US\$10-per-visit fee is also available. Why would these consumers choose a monthly contract when they lose money on it?

4.9 (Related to the *Making the Connection* on page 195) Briefly explain whether you agree or disagree with the following statement: "If people were more realistic about their future behavior, the demand curve for potato chips would shift to the left."

Appendix

Using Indifference Curves and Budget Lines to Understand Consumer Behavior

LEARNING OBJECTIVE

Use indifference curves and budget lines to understand consumer behavior.

Consumer Preferences

In this chapter, we analyzed consumer behavior, using the assumption that satisfaction, or *utility*, is measurable in utils. Although this assumption made our analysis easier to understand, it is unrealistic. Instead, we can use the more realistic assumption that consumers are able to *rank* different combinations of goods and services in terms of how much utility they provide. In other words, a consumer is able to determine whether he or she prefers 2 slices of pizza and 1 can of Coke or 1 slice of pizza and 2 cans of Coke, even if the consumer is unsure exactly how much utility he or she would receive from consuming these goods. This approach has the advantage that it allows us to actually draw a map of a consumer's preferences.

To begin with, suppose that a consumer is presented with the following alternatives, or *consumption bundles*:

CONSUMPTION BUNDLE A	CONSUMPTION BUNDLE B
2 slices of pizza and 1 can of Coke	1 slice of pizza and 2 cans of Coke

We assume that the consumer will always be able to decide which of the following is true:

- The consumer prefers bundle A to bundle B.
- The consumer prefers bundle B to bundle A.
- The consumer is indifferent between bundle A and bundle B; that is, the consumer receives equal utility from the two bundles.

For consistency, we also assume that the consumer's preferences are *transitive*. For example, if a consumer prefers cheese pizza to mushroom pizza and prefers mushroom pizza to anchovy pizza, the consumer must prefer cheese pizza to anchovy pizza.

Indifference Curves

Given the assumptions in the preceding section, we can draw a map of a consumer's preferences by using indifference curves. An **indifference curve** shows combinations of consumption bundles that give the consumer the same utility. In reality, consumers choose among consumption bundles containing many goods and services, but to make

Indifference curve A curve that shows the combinations of consumption bundles that give the consumer the same utility.

Figure 6A-1

Every possible combination of pizza and Coke will have an indifference curve passing through it, although in the graph we show just four of Ahmed's indifference curves. Ahmed is indifferent among all the consumption bundles that are on the same indifference curve. So, he is indifferent among bundles *E*, *B*, and *F* because they all lie on indifference curve *I₃*. Moving to the upper right in the graph increases the quantities of both goods available for Ahmed to consume. Therefore, the further to the upper right the indifference curve is, the greater the utility Ahmed receives.

Consumption Bundle	Slices of Pizza	Cans of Coke
A	1	2
B	3	4
C	4	5
D	1	6
E	2	8
F	5	2

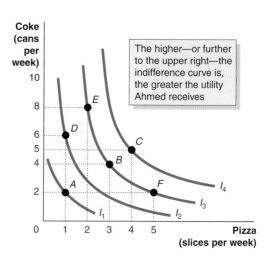

The higher—or further to the upper right—the indifference curve is, the greater the utility Ahmed receives

the discussion easier to follow, we will assume that only two goods are involved. Nothing important would change if we expanded the discussion to include many goods instead of just two.

The table in Figure 6A-1 gives Ahmed's preferences for pizza and Coke. The graph plots the information from the table. Every possible combination of pizza and Coke will have an indifference curve passing through it, although in the figure we have shown only four of Ahmed's indifference curves. Ahmed is indifferent among all the consumption bundles that are on the same indifference curve. So, he is indifferent among bundles *E*, *B*, and *F*, because they all lie on indifference curve *I₃*. Even though Ahmed has 4 fewer cans of Coke with bundle *B*, than with bundle *E*, the additional slice of pizza he has in bundle *B*, means he has the same amount of utility at both points.

Even without looking at Ahmed's indifference curves, we know he will prefer consumption bundle *D* to consumption bundle *A* because in *D* he receives the same quantity of pizza as in *A* but 4 additional cans of Coke. But we need to know Ahmed's preferences, as shown by his indifference curves, to know how he will rank bundle *B* and bundle *D*. Bundle *D* contains more Coke but less pizza than bundle *B*, so Ahmed's ranking will depend on how much pizza he would be willing to give up to receive more Coke. The higher the indifference curve—that is, the further to the upper right on the graph—the greater the amounts of both goods that are available for Ahmed to consume and the greater his utility. In other words, Ahmed receives more utility from the consumption bundles on indifference curve *I₂* than from the consumption bundles on indifference curve *I₁*, more utility from the bundles on *I₃* than from the bundles on *I₂*, and so on.

The Slope of an Indifference Curve

Remember that the slope of a curve is the ratio of the change in the variable on the vertical axis to the change in the variable on the horizontal axis. Along an indifference curve, the slope tells us the rate at which the consumer is willing to trade off one product for another while keeping the consumer's utility constant. The slope of an indifference curve is referred to as the **marginal rate of substitution** (*MRS*).

Marginal rate of substitution (MRS) The slope of an indifference curve, which represents the rate at which a consumer would be willing to trade off one good for another.

We expect that the *MRS* will change as we move down an indifference curve. In Figure 6A-1, at a point like *E* on indifference curve *I₃*, Ahmed's indifference curve is relatively steep. As we move down the curve, it becomes less steep until it becomes relatively flat at a point like *F*. This is the usual shape of indifference curves: they are bowed in, or convex. A consumption bundle like *E* contains a lot of Coke and not much pizza. We would expect that Ahmed could give up a significant quantity of Coke for a smaller quantity of additional pizza and still have the same level of utility. Thus, the *MRS* will be high. As we move down the indifference curve, Ahmed moves to bundles, like *B* and *F*, that have more pizza and less Coke. As a result, Ahmed is willing to trade less Coke for pizza, and the *MRS* declines.

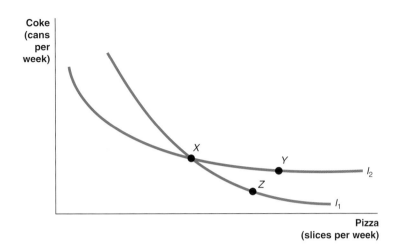

Figure 6A-2

Indifference Curves Cannot Cross

Because bundle X and bundle Z are both on indifference curve I_1, Ahmed must be indifferent between them. Similarly, because bundle X and bundle Y are on indifference curve I_2, Ahmed must be indifferent between them. The assumption of transitivity means that Ahmed should also be indifferent between bundle Z and bundle Y. We know that this is not true, however, because bundle Y contains more pizza and more Coke than bundle Z. So Ahmed will definitely prefer bundle Y to bundle Z, which violates the assumption of transitivity. *Therefore, none of Ahmed's indifference curves can cross.*

Can Indifference Curves Ever Cross?

Remember that we assume that consumers have transitive preferences. That is, if Ahmed prefers consumption bundle X to consumption bundle Y and he prefers consumption bundle Y to consumption bundle Z, he must prefer bundle X to bundle Z. If indifference curves cross, this assumption is violated. To understand why, look at Figure 6A-2, which shows two of Ahmed's indifference curves crossing.

Because bundle X and bundle Z are both on indifference curve I_1, Ahmed must be indifferent between them. Similarly, because bundle X and bundle Y are on indifference curve I_2, Ahmed must be indifferent between them. The assumption of transitivity means that Ahmed should also be indifferent between bundle Z and bundle Y. We know that this is not true, however, because bundle Y contains more pizza and more Coke than bundle Z. So, Ahmed will definitely prefer bundle Y to bundle Z, which violates the assumption of transitivity. Therefore, none of Ahmed's indifference curves can cross.

The Budget Constraint

Remember that a consumer's *budget constraint* is the amount of income he or she has available to spend on goods and services. Suppose that Ahmed has US$10 per week to spend on pizza and Coke. The table in Figure 6A-3 shows the combinations that he can afford to buy if the price of pizza is US$2 per slice and the price of Coke is US$1 per can. As you can see, all the points lie on a straight line. This line represents Ahmed's budget constraint. The line intersects the vertical axis at the maximum number of cans of Coke Ahmed can afford to buy with US$10, which is consumption bundle G. The line intersects the horizontal axis at the maximum number of slices of pizza Ahmed can afford to buy with US$10, which is consumption bundle L. As he moves down his budget constraint from bundle G, he gives up 2 cans of Coke for every slice of pizza he buys.

Any consumption bundle along the line or inside the line is *affordable* for Ahmed because he has the income to buy those combinations of pizza and Coke. Any bundle that lies outside the line is *unaffordable* because those bundles cost more than the income Ahmed has available to spend.

The slope of the budget constraint is constant because the budget constraint is a straight line. The slope of the line equals the change in the number of cans of Coke divided by the change in the number of slices of pizza. In this case, moving down the budget constraint from one point to another point, the change in the number of cans of Coke equals −2, and the change in the number of slices of pizza equals 1, so the slope equals −2/1, or −2. Notice that with the price of pizza equal to US$2 per slice and the price of Coke equal to US$1 per can, the slope of the budget constraint is equal to the ratio of the price of pizza to the price of Coke (multiplied by −1). In fact,

Figure 6A-3

Ahmed's Budget Constraint

Ahmed's budget constraint shows the combinations of slices of pizza and cans of Coke he can buy with US$10. The price of Coke is US$1 per can, so if he spends all of his US$10 on Coke, he can buy 10 cans (bundle *G*). The price of pizza is US$2 per slice, so if he spends all of his US$10 on pizza, he can buy 5 slices (bundle *L*). As he moves down his budget constraint from bundle *G*, he gives up 2 cans of Coke for every slice of pizza he buys. Any consumption bundles along the line or inside the line are affordable. Any bundles that lie outside the line are unaffordable.

Combinations of Pizza and Coke Ahmed Can Buy with $10			
Consumption Bundle	Slices of Pizza	Cans of Coke	Total Spending
G	0	10	$10.00
H	1	8	10.00
I	2	6	10.00
J	3	4	10.00
K	4	2	10.00
L	5	0	10.00

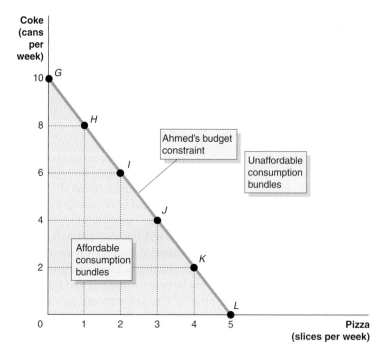

this result will always hold: *The slope of the budget constraint is equal to the ratio of the price of the good on the horizontal axis divided by the price of the good on the vertical axis, multiplied by −1.*

Choosing the Optimal Consumption of Pizza and Coke

Ahmed would like to be on the highest possible indifference curve because higher indifference curves represent more pizza and more Coke. But Ahmed can only buy the bundles that lie on or inside his budget constraint. In other words, *to maximize utility, a consumer needs to be on the highest indifference curve, given his budget constraint.*

Figure 6A-4 plots the consumption bundles from Figure 6A-1 along with the budget constraint from Figure 6A-3. The figure also shows the indifference curves that pass through each consumption bundle. In Figure 6A-4, the highest indifference curve shown is I_4. Unfortunately, Ahmed lacks the income to purchase consumption bundles—like *C*—that lie on I_4. He has the income to purchase bundles like *A* and *D*, but he can do better. If he consumes bundle *B*, he will be on the highest indifference curve he can reach, given his budget constraint of US$10. The resulting combination of 3 slices of pizza and 4 cans of Coke represents optimal consumption of pizza and Coke, given Ahmed's preferences and given his budget constraint. Notice that at point *B*, Ahmed's budget constraint just touches—or is *tangent* to—I_3. In fact, bundle *B* is the only bundle on I_3 that Ahmed is able to purchase for US$10.

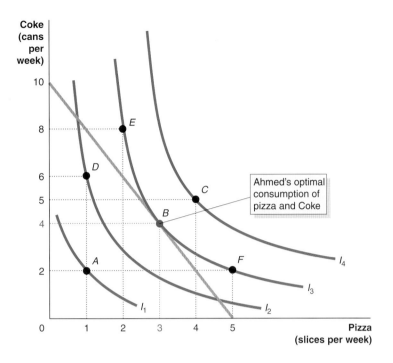

Figure 6A-4

Finding Optimal Consumption

Ahmed would like to be on the highest possible indifference curve, but he cannot reach indifference curves like I_4 that are outside his budget constraint. Ahmed's optimal combination of slices of pizza and cans of Coke comes at point B, where his budget constraint just touches—or is *tangent* to—the highest indifference curve he can reach. At point B, he buys 3 slices of pizza and 4 cans of Coke.

Making the Connection

Dell Determines the Optimal Mix of Products

Consumers have different preferences, which helps explain why many firms offer products with a variety of characteristics. For example, Dell sells laptop computers with different screen sizes, processor speeds, hard drive sizes, graphics cards, and so on. We can use the model of consumer choice to analyze a simplified version of the situation Dell faces in deciding which features to offer consumers.

Assume that consumers have US$1,000 each to spend on laptops and that they are concerned with only two laptop characteristics: screen size and processor speed. Because larger screens and faster processors increase Dell's cost of producing laptops, consumers face a trade-off: the larger the screen, the slower the processor speed. Consumers in panel (a) of the figure prefer screen size to processor speed. For this group, the point of tangency between a typical consumer's indifference curve and the

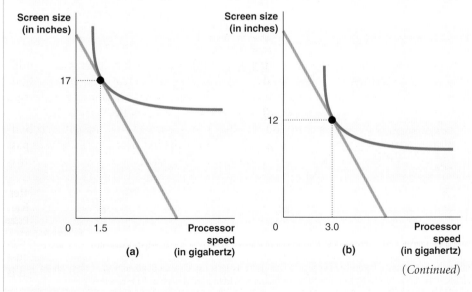

(Continued)

budget constraint shows an optimal choice of a 17-inch screen and a 1.5-gigahertz processor. Consumers in panel (b) prefer processor speed to screen size. For this group, the point of tangency between a typical consumer's indifference curve and the budget constraint shows an optimal choice of a 12-inch screen and 3.0-gigahertz processor.

Companies like Dell use surveys and other means to gather information about consumer preferences. With knowledge of consumers' preferences and data on the costs of producing different laptop components, Dell can determine the mix of components to offer consumers.

YOUR TURN: Test your understanding by doing related problem 6A.8 on page 218 at the end of this appendix.

How a Price Change Affects Optimal Consumption

Suppose the price of pizza falls from US$2 per slice to US$1 per slice. How will this affect Ahmed's decision about which combination of pizza and Coke is optimal? First, notice what happens to Ahmed's budget constraint when the price of pizza falls. As Figure 6A-5 shows, when the price of pizza is US$2 per slice, the maximum number of slices Ahmed can buy is 5. After the price of pizza falls to US$1 per slice, Ahmed can buy a maximum of 10 slices. His budget constraint rotates outward from point *A* to point *B* to represent this. (Notice that the fall in the price of pizza does not affect the maximum number of cans of Coke Ahmed can buy with his US$10.)

When his budget constraint rotates outward, Ahmed is able to purchase consumption bundles that were previously unaffordable. Figure 6A-6 shows that the combination of 3 slices of pizza and 4 cans of Coke was optimal when the price of pizza was US$2 per slice, but the combination of 7 slices of pizza and 3 cans of Coke is optimal when the price of pizza falls to US$1. The lower price of pizza causes Ahmed to consume more pizza and less Coke and to end up on a higher indifference curve.

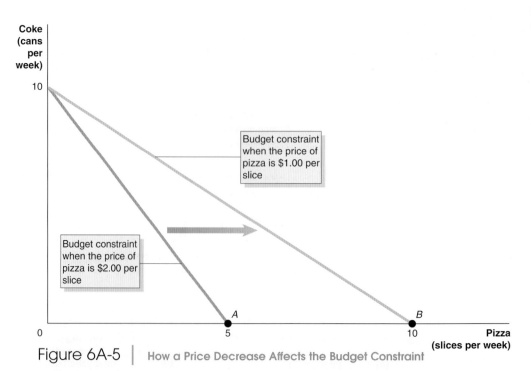

Figure 6A-5 | How a Price Decrease Affects the Budget Constraint

A fall in the price of pizza from US$2 per slice to US$1 per slice increases the maximum number of slices Ahmed can buy with US$10 from 5 to 10. The budget constraint rotates outward from point *A* to point *B* to show this.

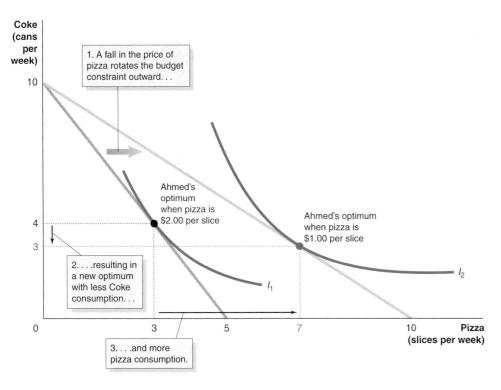

How a Price Change Affects Optimal Consumption

A fall in the price of pizza results in Ahmed consuming less Coke and more pizza.
1. A fall in the price of pizza rotates the budget constraint outward because Ahmed can now buy more pizza with his $10.
2. In the new optimum on indifference curve I_2, Ahmed changes the quantities he consumes of both goods. His consumption of Coke falls from 4 cans to 3 cans.
3. In the new optimum, Ahmed's consumption of pizza increases from 3 slices to 7 slices.

Solved Problem | 6A-1

When Does a Price Change Make a Consumer Better Off?

Ahmed has US$300 to spend each month on DVDs and CDs. DVDs and CDs both currently have a price of US$10, and Ahmed is maximizing his utility by buying 20 DVDs and 10 CDs. Suppose Ahmed still has US$300 to spend, but the price of CDs rises to US$20, while the price of DVDs drops to US$5. Is Ahmed better or worse off than he was before the price change? Use a budget constraint–indifference curve graph to illustrate your answer.

SOLVING THE PROBLEM:

Step 1: **Review the chapter material.** This problem concerns the effect of price changes on optimal consumption, so you may want to review the section "How a Price Change Affects Optimal Consumption," which begins on page 210.

Step 2: **Answer the problem by drawing the appropriate graph.** We begin by drawing the budget constraint, indifference curve, and point of optimal consumption for the original prices:

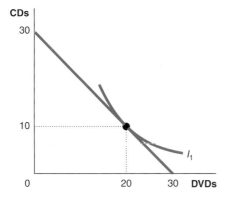

Now draw a graph that shows the results of the price changes. Notice that in this problem, the prices of *both* goods change. However, you can determine the position of the new budget constraint by calculating the maximum quantity of DVDs and CDs Ahmed can buy after the price changes. You should also note that after the price changes, Ahmed can still buy his original optimal consumption bundle—20 DVDs and 10 CDs—by spending all of his US$300, so his new budget constraint must pass through this point.

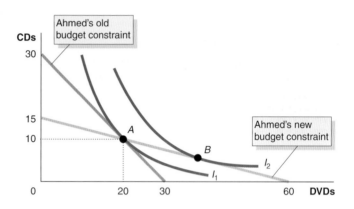

At the new prices, Ahmed can buy a maximum of 60 DVDs or 15 CDs. Both his old and his new budget constraints pass through the consumption bundle at point A. This consumption bundle is no longer optimal, however, because with the new prices, it is possible for him to reach an indifference curve that is higher than I_1. We can draw in the new highest indifference curve he can reach—I_2—and show the new optimal consumption bundle—point B.

Because Ahmed can now reach a higher indifference curve, we can conclude that he is better off as a result of the price change.

>> End Solved Problem 6A-1   **YOUR TURN:** For more practice, do related problem 6A.10 on page 218 at the end of this appendix.

Deriving the Demand Curve

The change in Ahmed's optimal consumption of pizza as the price changes explains why demand curves slope downward. Ahmed adjusted his consumption of pizza as follows:

Price of pizza = US$2 per slice ⟹ Quantity of pizza demanded = 3 slices

Price of pizza = US$1 per slice ⟹ Quantity of pizza demanded = 7 slices

In panel (a) of Figure 6A-7, we plot the two points of optimal consumption. In panel (b) of Figure 6A-7, we draw a line connecting the points. This downward-sloping line is Ahmed's demand curve for pizza. We could find more points on the demand curve by changing the price of pizza and finding the new optimal number of slices of pizza Ahmed would demand.

Remember that according to the law of demand, demand curves always slope downward. We have just shown that the law of demand results from the optimal adjustment by consumers to changes in prices. A fall in the price of a good will rotate *outward* the budget constraint and make it possible for a consumer to reach higher indifference curves. As a result, the consumer will increase the quantity of the good demanded. An increase in price will rotate *inward* the budget constraint and force the consumer to a lower indifference curve. As a result, the consumer will decrease the quantity of the good demanded.

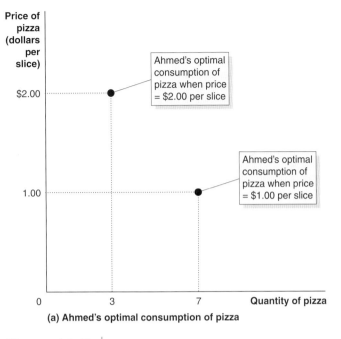

(a) Ahmed's optimal consumption of pizza

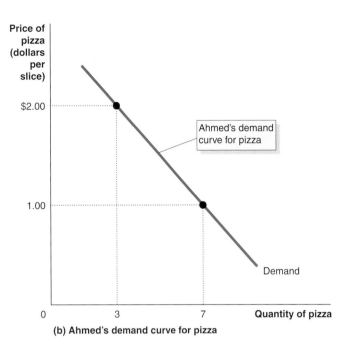

(b) Ahmed's demand curve for pizza

Figure 6A-7 | Deriving a Demand Curve

Ahmed responds optimally to the fall in the price of a product by consuming more of that product. In panel (a), the price of pizza falls from US$2 per slice to US$1, and the optimal quantity of slices consumed rises from 3 to 7. When we graph this result in panel (b), we have Ahmed's demand curve for pizza.

The Income Effect and the Substitution Effect of a Price Change

We saw in this chapter that a price change has two effects on the quantity of a good consumed: the *income effect* and the *substitution effect*. The income effect is the change in the quantity demanded of a good that results from the effect of a change in price on consumer purchasing power, holding all other factors constant. The substitution effect is the change in the quantity demanded of a good that results from a change in price making the good more or less expensive relative to other goods, holding constant the effect of the price change on consumer purchasing power. We can use indifference curves and budget constraints to analyze these two effects more exactly.

Figure 6A-8 illustrates the same situation as Figure 6A-7: the price of pizza has fallen from US$2 per slice to US$1 per slice, and Ahmed's budget constraint has rotated outward. As before, Ahmed's optimal consumption of pizza increases from 3 slices (point A in Figure 6A-8) per week to 7 slices per week (point C). We can think of this movement from point A to point C as taking place in two steps: the movement from point A to point B represents the substitution effect, and the movement from point B to point C represents the income effect. To isolate the substitution effect, we have to hold constant the effect of the price change on Ahmed's income. We do this by changing the price of pizza relative to the price of Coke *but at the same time holding his utility constant by keeping Ahmed on the same indifference curve.* In Figure 6A-8, in moving from point A to point B, Ahmed remains on indifference curve I_1. Point A is a point of tangency between I_1 and Ahmed's original budget constraint. Point B is a point of tangency between I_1 and a new, *hypothetical* budget constraint that has a slope equal to the new ratio of the price of pizza to the price of Coke. At point B, Ahmed has increased his consumption of pizza from 3 slices to 5 slices. Because we are still on indifference curve I_1, we know that this

Figure 6A-8

Income and Substitution Effects of a Price Change

Following a decline in the price of pizza, Ahmed's optimal consumption of pizza increases from 3 slices (point *A*) per week to 7 slices per week (point *C*). We can think of this movement from point *A* to point *C* as taking place in two steps: The movement from point *A* to point *B* along indifference curve *I*₁ represents the substitution effect, and the movement from point *B* to point *C* represents the income effect. Ahmed increases his consumption of pizza from 3 slices per week to 5 slices per week because of the substitution effect of a fall in the price of pizza and from 5 slices per week to 7 slices per week because of the income effect.

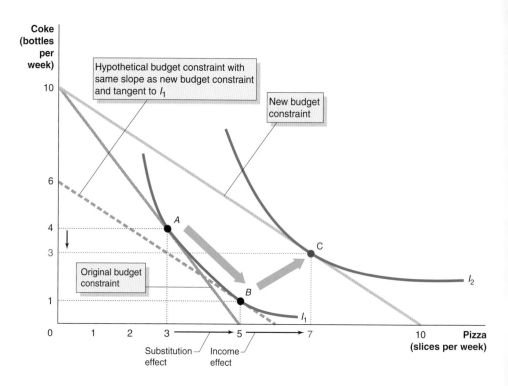

increase is Ahmed's response only to the change in the relative price of pizza and, therefore, that the increase represents the substitution effect of the fall in the price of pizza.

At point *B*, Ahmed has not spent all his income. Remember that the fall in the price of pizza has increased Ahmed's purchasing power. In Figure 6A-8, we illustrate the additional pizza Ahmed consumes because of the income effect of increased purchasing power by the movement from point *B* to point *C*. Notice that in moving from point *B* to point *C*, the price of pizza relative to the price of Coke is constant because the slope of the new budget constraint is the same as the slope of the hypothetical budget constraint that is tangent to *I*₁ at point *B*.

We can conclude that Ahmed increases his consumption of pizza from 3 slices per week to 5 slices per week because of the substitution effect of a fall in the price of pizza and from 5 slices per week to 7 slices per week because of the income effect. Recall from our discussion of income and substitution effects in this chapter that the income effect of a price decline causes consumers to buy more of a normal good and less of an inferior good. Because the income effect causes Ahmed to increase his consumption of pizza, pizza must be a normal good for him.

How a Change in Income Affects Optimal Consumption

Suppose that the price of pizza remains at US$2 per slice, but the income Ahmed has to spend on pizza and Coke increases from US$10 to US$20. Figure 6A-9 shows how this affects his budget constraint. With an income of US$10, Ahmed could buy a maximum of 5 slices of pizza or 10 cans of Coke. With an income of US$20, he can buy 10 slices of pizza or 20 cans of Coke. The additional income allows Ahmed to increase his consumption of both pizza and Coke and to move to a higher indifference curve. Figure 6A-10 shows Ahmed's new optimum. Ahmed is able to increase his consumption of pizza from 3 slices per week to 7 and his consumption of Coke from 4 cans per week to 6.

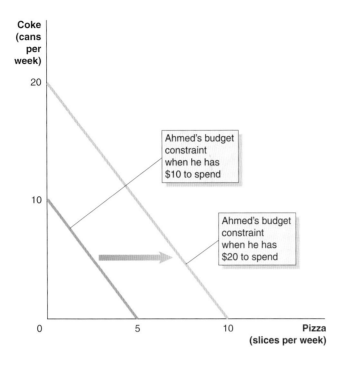

Figure 6A-9

How a Change in Income Affects the Budget Constraint

When the income Ahmed has to spend on pizza and Coke increases from U$10 to U$20, his budget constraint shifts outward. With U$10, Ahmed could buy a maximum of 5 slices of pizza or 10 cans of Coke. With U$20, he can buy a maximum of 10 slices of pizza or 20 cans of Coke.

The Slope of the Indifference Curve, the Slope of the Budget Line, and the Rule of Equal Marginal Utility per Dollar Spent

In this chapter, we saw that consumers maximize utility when they consume each good up to the point where the marginal utility per dollar spent is the same for every good. This condition seems different from the one we stated earlier in this appendix that to maximize utility, a consumer needs to be on the highest indifference curve, given his

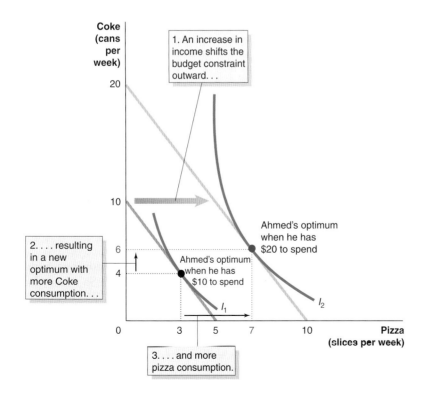

Figure 6A-10

How a Change in Income Affects Optimal Consumption

An increase in income leads Ahmed to consume more Coke and more pizza.
1. An increase in income shifts Ahmed's budget constraint outward because he can now buy more of both goods.
2. In the new optimum on indifference curve I_2, Ahmed changes the quantities he consumes of both goods. His consumption of Coke increases from 4 cans to 6 cans.
3. In the new optimum, Ahmed's consumption of pizza increases from 3 slices to 7 slices.

Figure 6A-11

At the Optimum Point, the Slopes of the Indifference Curve and Budget Constraint Are the Same

At the point of optimal consumption, the marginal rate of substitution is equal to the ratio of the price of the product on the horizontal axis to the price of the product on the vertical axis.

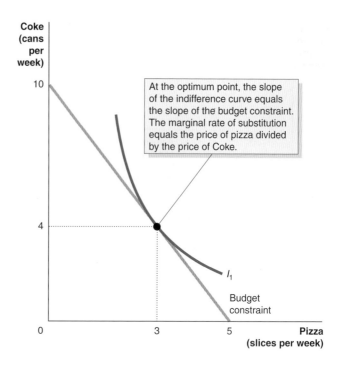

At the optimum point, the slope of the indifference curve equals the slope of the budget constraint. The marginal rate of substitution equals the price of pizza divided by the price of Coke.

budget constraint. In fact, though, the two conditions are equivalent. To see this, begin by looking at Figure 6A-11, which again combines Ahmed's indifference curve and budget constraint. Remember that at the point of optimal consumption, the indifference curve and the budget constraint are tangent, so they have the same slope. Therefore: *At the point of optimal consumption, the marginal rate of substitution* (MRS) *is equal to the ratio of the price of the product on the horizontal axis to the price of the product on the vertical axis.*

The slope of the indifference curve tells us the rate at which a consumer is *willing* to trade off one good for the other. The slope of the budget constraint tells us the rate at which a consumer is *able* to trade off one good for the other. Only at the point of optimal consumption is the rate at which a consumer is willing to trade off one good for the other equal to the rate at which he can trade off one good for the other.

The Rule of Equal Marginal Utility per Dollar Spent Revisited

Recall from this chapter the *rule of equal marginal utility per dollar*, which states that to maximize utility, consumers should spend their income so that the last dollar spent on each product gives them the same marginal utility. We can use our indifference curve and budget constraint analysis to see why this rule holds. When we move from one point on an indifference curve to another, we end up with more of one product and less of the other product but the same amount of utility. For example, as Ahmed moves down an indifference curve, he consumes less Coke and more pizza, but he has the same amount of utility.

Remember that marginal utility (MU) tells us how much additional utility a consumer gains (or loses) from consuming more (or less) of a good. So when Ahmed consumes less Coke by moving down an indifference curve, he loses utility equal to:

$$-\text{Change in the quantity of Coke} \times MU_{Coke}$$

but he consumes more pizza, so he gains utility equal to:

$$\text{Change in the quantity of pizza} \times MU_{Pizza}$$

We know that the gain in utility from the additional pizza is equal to the loss from the smaller quantity of Coke because Ahmed's total utility remains the same along an indifference curve. Therefore we can write:

$$-(\text{Change in the quantity of Coke} \times MU_{Coke}) = (\text{Change in the quantity of pizza} \times MU_{Pizza})$$

Loss in utility from consuming less Coke

Gain in utility from consuming more pizza

If we rearrange terms, we have:

$$\frac{-\text{Change in the quantity of Coke}}{\text{Change in the quantity of pizza}} = \frac{MU_{pizza}}{MU_{Coke}}$$

because the

$$\frac{-\text{Change in the quantity of Coke}}{\text{Change in the quantity of pizza}}$$

is the slope of the indifference curve, or the marginal rate of substitution, we can write:

$$\frac{-\text{Change in the quantity of Coke}}{\text{Change in the quantity of pizza}} = MRS = \frac{MU_{pizza}}{MU_{Coke}}$$

The slope of Ahmed's budget constraint equals the price of pizza divided by the price of Coke. At the point of optimal consumption, the slope of the indifference curve is equal to the slope of the budget line. Therefore:

$$\frac{MU_{Pizza}}{MU_{Coke}} = \frac{P_{Pizza}}{P_{Coke}}$$

We can rewrite this to show that at the point of optimal consumption:

$$\frac{MU_{Pizza}}{P_{Pizza}} = \frac{MU_{Coke}}{P_{Coke}}$$

This last expression is the rule of equal marginal utility per dollar that we first developed in this chapter. So we have shown how this rule follows from the indifference curve and budget constraint approach to analyzing consumer choice.

Key Terms

Indifference curve, p. 205

Marginal rate of substitution (*MRS*), p. 206

Review, Problems and Applications

myeconlab Visit www.pearsoned.co.uk/awe/hubbard to complete these exercises online and get instant feedback.
Get Ahead of the Curve

LEARNING OBJECTIVE   Use indifference curves and budget lines to understand consumer behavior, **pages 205–215.**

Review Questions

6A.1 What are the two assumptions economists make about consumer preferences?

6A.2 What is an indifference curve? What is a budget constraint?

6A.3 How do consumers choose the optimal consumption bundle?

Problems and Applications

6A.4 Yousif receives an allowance of US$5 per week. He spends all his allowance on ice cream cones and cans of Lemon Fizz soda.

a. If the price of ice cream cones is US$0.50 per cone and the price of Lemon Fizz is US$1 per can, draw a graph showing Yousif's budget constraint. Be sure to indicate on the graph the maximum number of ice cream cones and the maximum number of cans of Lemon Fizz that Yousif can buy.

b. Yousif buys 8 cones and 1 can of Lemon Fizz. Draw an indifference curve representing Yousif's choice, assuming that he has chosen the optimal combination.

c. Suppose that the price of ice cream cones rises to US$1 per cone. Draw in Yousif's new budget constraint and his new optimal consumption of ice cream cones and Lemon Fizz.

6A.5 Suppose that Yousif's allowance in problem 6A.4 climbs from US$5 per week to US$10 per week.

a. Show how the increased allowance alters Yousif's budget constraint.

b. Draw a set of indifference curves showing how Yousif's choice of cones and Lemon Fizz changes when his allowance increases. Assume that both goods are normal.

c. Draw a set of indifference curves showing how Yousif's choice of cones and Lemon Fizz changes when his allowance increases. Assume that Lemon Fizz is normal but cones are inferior.

6A.6 Suppose that Yousif considers Pepsi and Coke to be perfect substitutes. They taste the same to him, and he gets exactly the same amount of enjoyment from drinking a can of Pepsi or a can of Coke.

a. Will Yousif's indifference curves showing his trade-off between Pepsi and Coke have the same curvature as the indifference curves drawn in the figures in this appendix? Briefly explain.

b. How will Yousif decide whether to buy Pepsi or to buy Coke?

6A.7 In the following budget constraint–indifference curve graph, Hala has US$200 to spend on blouses and skirts.

a. What is the price of blouses? What is the price of skirts?

b. Is Hala making the optimum choice if she buys 4 blouses and 2 skirts? Explain how you know this.

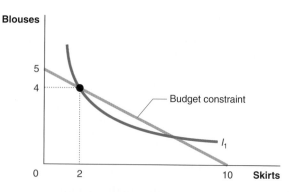

6A.8 (Related to the *Making the Connection* on page 209) Abdullah and Maziad both purchase milk and doughnuts at the same Quik Mart. They have different tastes for milk and doughnuts and different incomes. They both buy some milk and some doughnuts, but they buy considerably different quantities of the two goods. Can we conclude that their marginal rate of substitution between milk and doughnuts is the same? Draw a graph showing their budget constraints and indifference curves and explain.

6A.9 Almarai company decides that peach juice has a bad image problem, so it launches a slick advertising campaign to convince young people that peach juice is very healthy. They hire footballers Emad Meteab and Yaser Al-Qahtani to market their product. The campaign works! Peach juice sales soar, even though Almarai hasn't cut the price. Draw a budget constraint and indifference curve diagram with Almarai Peach Juice on one axis and other drinks on the other axis and show how the celebrity endorsements have changed things.

6A.10 (Related to *Solved problem 6A-1* on page 211) Ahmed has US$300 to spend each month on DVDs and CDs. DVDs and CDs both currently have a price of US$10, and Ahmed is maximizing his utility by buying 20 DVDs and 10 CDs. Suppose Ahmed still has US$300 to spend, but the price of DVDs rises to US$12, while the price of CDs drops to US$6. Is Ahmed better or worse off than he was before the price change? Use a budget constraint–indifference curve graph to illustrate your answer.

>> **End Appendix Learning Objective**

Chapter 7

Technology, Production, and **Costs**

Sony Uses a Cost Curve to Determine the Price of Radios

In consumer electronics, rapid technological change leads to new products and lower cost ways of manufacturing existing products. How do firms take costs into account when setting prices? This is an important question that we will explore in the next few chapters and it is a question that Sony Corporation, the Japanese electronics giant, must answer every day. Sony manufactures televisions, computers, satellite systems, semiconductors, telephones, and flat-screen televisions, among other products.

Like most firms, Sony started small. Its early success resulted from the vision and energy of two young entrepreneurs, Akio Morita and Masaru Ibuka.

In 1953, Sony purchased a license that allowed it to use transistor technology developed in the United States at Western Electric's Bell Laboratories. Sony used the technology to develop a transistor radio that was small enough

to fit in a shirt pocket and far smaller than any other radio then available. In 1955, Akio Morita, Sony's chairman, arrived in New York, hoping to convince one of the U.S. department store chains to carry the Sony radios.

Morita offered to sell one department store chain 5,000 radios at a price of US$29.95 each. If the chain wanted more than 5,000 radios, the price would change. As Morita described it later:

I sat down and drew a curve that looked something like a lopsided letter U. The price for five thousand would be our regular price. That would be the beginning of the curve. For ten thousand there would be a discount, and that was at the bottom of the curve. For thirty thousand the price would begin to climb. For fifty thousand the price per unit would be higher than for five thousand, and for one hundred thousand units the price per unit would have to be much higher than for the first five thousand.

Why would the prices Morita offered the department store follow a U shape? Because Sony's cost per unit, or *average cost*, of manufacturing the radios would have the same shape. Curves that show the relationship between the level of output and per-unit cost are called *average total cost curves*. Average total cost curves typically have the U shape of Morita's curve. As we explore the relationship between production and costs in this chapter, we will see why average total cost curves have this shape.

Today, Sony is one of the largest electronics firms in the world, but more than 50 years ago, when it was a small, struggling company, Akio Morita used a simple economic tool—the average cost curve—to help make an important business decision. Every day, in companies large and small, managers use economic tools to make decisions. **AN INSIDE LOOK** on **page 242** discusses the effect of lower manufacturing costs on the prices of flat-panel televisions.

Source: Akio Morita, with Edwin M. Reingold and Mitsuko Shimomura, *Made in Japan: Akio Morita and Sony*, New York: Signet Books, 1986, p. 94.

Economics in YOUR Life!

Using Cost Concepts in Your Own Business

Suppose that you have the opportunity to open a store selling recliners. You learn that you can purchase the recliners from the manufacturer for US$300 each. Assume that Eyad's Big Chairs is an existing store that is the same size as your new store will be. Eyad's sells the same recliners you plan to sell and also buys them from the manufacturer for US$300 each. Your plan is to sell the recliners for a price of US$500. After studying how Eyad's is operated, you find that they are selling more recliners per month than you expect to be able to sell and that they are selling them for US$450. You wonder how Eyad's makes a profit at the lower price. Are there any reasons to expect that because Eyad's sells more recliners per month, its costs will be lower than your store's costs? You can check your answer against the one we provide at the end of the chapter. **>> Continued on page 240**

I n Chapter 6, we looked behind the demand curve to better understand consumer decision making. In this chapter, we look behind the supply curve to better understand firm decision making. Earlier chapters showed that supply curves are upward sloping because marginal cost increases as firms increase the quantity of a good that they supply. In this chapter, we look more closely at why this is true. In the appendix to this chapter, we extend the analysis by using isoquants and isocost lines to understand the relationship between production and costs. Once we have a good understanding of production and cost, we can proceed in the following chapters to understand how firms decide what level of output to produce and what price to charge.

7.1 LEARNING OBJECTIVE

7.1 | Define technology and give examples of technological change.

Technology: An Economic Definition

The basic activity of a firm is to use *inputs*, such as workers, machines, and natural resources, to produce *outputs* of goods and services. A pizza parlor, for example, uses inputs such as pizza dough, pizza sauce, cooks, and ovens to produce pizza. A firm's **technology** is the processes it uses to turn inputs into outputs of goods and services. Notice that this economic definition of technology is broader than the everyday definition. When we use the word *technology* in everyday language, we usually refer only to the development of new products. In the economic sense, a firm's technology depends on many factors, such as the skill of its managers, the training of its workers, and the speed and efficiency of its machinery and equipment. The technology of pizza production, for example, includes not only the capacity of the pizza ovens and how quickly they bake the pizza but also how quickly the cooks can prepare the pizza for baking, how well the manager motivates the workers, and how well the manager has arranged the facilities to allow the cooks to quickly prepare the pizzas and get them in the ovens.

Whenever a firm experiences positive **technological change**, it is able to produce more output using the same inputs or the same output using fewer inputs. Positive technological change can come from many sources. The firm's managers may rearrange the factory floor or the layout of a retail store, thereby increasing production and sales. The firm's workers may go through a training program. The firm may install faster or more reliable machinery or equipment. It is also possible for a firm to experience negative technological change. If a firm hires less-skilled workers or if a hurricane damages its facilities, the quantity of output it can produce from a given quantity of inputs may decline.

Technology The processes a firm uses to turn inputs into outputs of goods and services.

Technological change A change in the ability of a firm to produce a given level of output with a given quantity of inputs.

Making the Connection | Improving Inventory Control at Wal-Mart and Bread Quality at Carrefour

Inventories are goods that have been produced but not yet sold. For a retailer such as Wal-Mart, the largest retailer in the world in terms of revenue, and Carrefour, the second largest in the world, inventories at any point in time include the goods on the store shelves as well as goods in warehouses. Inventories are an input into the retailer's output of goods sold to consumers. Having money tied up in holding inventories is costly, so there is incentive for stores to hold as few inventories as possible and to *turn over* their inventories as rapidly as possible by ensuring that goods do not remain on the shelves long. Holding too few inventories, however, results in *stockouts*—that is, sales being lost because the goods that consumers want to buy are not on the shelves.

Improvements in inventory control meet the economic definition of positive technological change because they allow firms to produce the same output with fewer inputs. In recent years, many firms have adopted *just-in-time* inventory systems in which firms accept shipments from suppliers as close as possible to the time they will be needed. The just-in-time system was pioneered by Toyota, which used it to reduce the inventories of parts in its automobile assembly plants. Wal-Mart has been a pioneer in using similar inventory control systems in its stores.

Wal-Mart actively manages its *supply chain*, which stretches from the manufacturers of the goods it sells to its retail stores. Entrepreneur Sam Walton, the company founder, built a series of distribution centers across the U.S. to supply goods to the retail stores. As goods are sold in the stores, this *point-of-sale* information is sent electronically to the firm's distribution centres to help managers determine what products will be shipped to each store overnight. This distribution system allows Wal-Mart to minimize its inventory holdings without running the risk of many stock-outs. For example, a company such as Procter & Gamble, which is one of the world's largest manufacturers of toothpaste, laundry detergent, and other products, receives Wal-Mart's point-of-sale and inventory information electronically. Procter & Gamble uses that information to help determine its production schedules and the quantities it should ship to Wal-Mart's distribution centres.

On the other hand, Carrefour used the e-learning technology to train bakers across 17 hypermarkets in France to produce identical quality bread. By installing a *pilot e-learning solution* in the bakery/pastry outlets, Carrefour managers are able to efficiently transfer bread making skills and know-how between different bakers in a timely manner without having to force bakers to attend a training course, which would affect the production process negatively.

Technological change has been key to Wal-Mart and Carrefour joining the ranks of the largest firms in the world: Wal-Mart with 2.1 million employees and revenue of more than US$408 billion in 2009, and Carrefour with 495,000 employees and revenue of around US$112 billion in the same year.

Sources: "Carrefour: On Demand E-Learning in the Bakery, On Demand Business Solution," IBM Business Consulting Services, 2004, www-935.ibm.com/services/us/imc/pdf/cs-carrefour-english.pdf,www.carrefour.net; and "The Global 2000," www.forbes.com.

YOUR TURN: Test your understanding by doing related problem 1.5 on page 245 at the end of this chapter.

7.2 | Distinguish between the economic short run and the economic long run.

The Short Run and the Long Run in Economics

When firms analyze the relationship between their level of production and their costs, they separate the time period involved into the short run and the long run. In the **short run**, at least one of the firm's inputs is fixed. In particular, in the short run, the firm's technology and the size of its physical plant—its factory, store, or office—are both fixed, while the number of workers the firm hires is variable. In the **long run**, the firm is able to vary all its inputs and can adopt new technology and increase or decrease the size of its physical plant. Of course, the actual length of calendar time in the short run will be different from firm to firm. A pizza parlor may be able to increase its physical plant by adding another pizza oven and some tables and chairs in just a few weeks. BMW, in contrast, may take more than a year to increase the capacity of one of its automobile assembly plants by installing new equipment.

Short run The period of time during which at least one of a firm's inputs is fixed.

Long run The period of time in which a firm can vary all its inputs, adopt new technology, and increase or decrease the size of its physical plant.

The Difference between Fixed Costs and Variable Costs

Total cost The cost of all the inputs a firm uses in production.

Variable costs Costs that change as output changes.

Fixed costs Costs that remain constant as output changes.

Total cost is the cost of all the inputs a firm uses in production. We have just seen that in the short run, some inputs are fixed and others are variable. The costs of the fixed inputs are *fixed costs*, and the costs of the variable inputs are *variable costs*. We can also think of **variable costs** as the costs that change as output changes. Similarly, **fixed costs** are costs that remain constant as output changes. A typical firm's variable costs include its labor costs, raw material costs, and costs of electricity and other utilities. Typical fixed costs include lease payments for factory or retail space, payments for fire insurance, and payments for newspaper and television advertising. All of a firm's costs are either fixed or variable, so we can state the following:

Total cost = Fixed Cost + Variable Cost

or, using symbols:

$$TC = FC + VC$$

Making the Connection	**Fixed Costs in the Publishing Industry**

An editor at Cambridge University Press gives the following estimates of the annual fixed cost for a medium-size academic book publisher.

COST	AMOUNT
Salaries and benefits	$437,500
Rent	75,000
Utilities	20,000
Supplies	6,000
Postage	4,000
Travel	8,000
Subscriptions, etc.	4,000
Miscellaneous	5,000
Total	$559,500

Academic book publishers hire editors, designers, and production and marketing managers who help prepare books for publication. Because these employees work on several books simultaneously, the number of people the company hires does not go up and down with the quantity of books the company publishes during any particular year. Publishing companies therefore consider the salaries and benefits of people in these job categories as fixed costs.

In contrast, for a company that *prints* books, the quantity of workers varies with the quantity of books printed. The wages and benefits of the workers operating the printing presses, for example, would be a variable cost.

The other costs listed in the preceding table are typical of fixed costs at many firms.

Source: Beth Luey, *Handbook for Academic Authors*, 4th ed., Cambridge, U.K.: Cambridge University Press, 2002, p. 244.

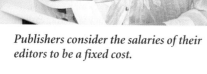

Publishers consider the salaries of their editors to be a fixed cost.

YOUR TURN: Test your understanding by doing related problems 2.3, 2.4, and 2.5 on page 246 at the end of this chapter.

Pizza dough, tomato sauce, and other ingredients	$20,000
Wages	48,000
Interest payments on loan to buy pizza ovens	10,000
Electricity	6,000
Lease payment for store	24,000
Foregone salary	30,000
Foregone interest	3,000
Economic depreciation	10,000
Total	$151,000

TABLE 7-1

Salma's Costs Per Year

Implicit Costs versus Explicit Costs

It is important to remember that economists always measure costs as *opportunity costs*. The **opportunity cost** of any activity is the highest-valued alternative that must be given up to engage in that activity. Economists also classify costs into either *explicit* or *implicit*. When a firm spends money, it incurs an **explicit cost**. When a firm experiences a nonmonetary opportunity cost, it incurs an **implicit cost**.

For example, suppose that Salma owns a pizza restaurant. In operating her store, Salma has explicit costs, such as the wages she pays her workers and the payments she makes for rent and electricity. But some of Salma's most important costs are implicit. Before opening her own restaurant, Salma earned a salary of US$30,000 per year managing a restaurant for someone else. To start her restaurant, Salma quit her job, withdrew US$50,000 from her bank account—where it earned her interest of US$3,000 per year—and used the funds to equip her restaurant with tables, chairs, a cash register, and other equipment. To open her own business, Salma had to give up the US$30,000 salary and the US$3,000 in interest. This US$33,000 is an implicit cost because it does not represent payments that Salma has to make. All the same, giving up this US$33,000 per year is a real cost to Salma. In addition, during the course of the year, the US$50,000's worth of tables, chairs, and other physical capital in Salma's store will lose some of its value due partly to wear and tear and partly to better furniture, cash registers, and so forth becoming available. *Economic depreciation* is the difference between what Salma paid for her capital at the beginning of the year and what she could sell the capital for at the end of the year. If Salma could sell the capital for US$40,000 at the end of the year, then the US$10,000 in economic depreciation represents another implicit cost. (Note that the whole US$50,000 she spent on the capital is not a cost because she still has the equipment at the end of the year, although it is now worth only US$40,000.)

Table 7-1 lists Salma's costs. The entries in red are explicit costs, and the entries in blue are implicit costs. Generally, the rules of accounting require that only explicit costs be used for purposes of keeping the company's financial records and for paying taxes. Therefore, explicit costs are sometimes called *accounting costs*. *Economic costs* include both accounting costs and implicit costs.

Opportunity cost The highest-valued alternative that must be given up to engage in an activity.

Explicit cost A cost that involves spending money.

Implicit cost A nonmonetary opportunity cost.

The Production Function

Let's look at the relationship between the level of production and costs in the short run for Salma's restaurant. To keep things simpler than in the more realistic situation in Table 7-1, let's assume that Salma uses only labor—workers—and one type of capital—pizza ovens—to produce a single good: pizzas. Many firms use more than two inputs and produce more than one good, but it is easier to understand the relationship between output and cost by focusing on the case of a firm using only two inputs and producing only one good. In the short run, Salma doesn't have time to build a larger restaurant, install additional pizza ovens, or redesign the layout of her restaurant. So, in the short run, she can increase or decrease the quantity of pizzas she produces only by increasing or decreasing the quantity of workers she employs.

TABLE 7-2 | **Short-Run Production and Cost at Salma's Restaurant**

QUANTITY OF WORKERS	QUANTITY OF PIZZA OVENS	QUANTITY OF PIZZAS PER WEEK	COST OF PIZZA OVENS (FIXED COST)	COST OF WORKERS (VARIABLE COST)	TOTAL COST OF PIZZAS	COST PER PIZZA (AVERAGE TOTAL COST)
0	2	0	$800	$0	$800	—
1	2	200	800	650	1,450	$7.25
2	2	450	800	1,300	2,100	4.67
3	2	550	800	1,950	2,750	5.00
4	2	600	800	2,600	3,400	5.67
5	2	625	800	3,250	4,050	6.48
6	2	640	800	3,900	4,700	7.34

Production function The relationship between the inputs employed by a firm and the maximum output it can produce with those inputs.

The first three columns of Table 7-2 show the relationship between the quantity of workers and ovens Salma uses each week and the quantity of pizzas she can produce. The relationship between the inputs employed by a firm and the maximum output it can produce with those inputs is called the firm's **production function**. Because a firm's technology is the processes it uses to turn inputs into output, the production function represents the firm's technology. In this case, Table 7-2 shows Salma's *short-run* production function because we are assuming that the time period is too short for Salma to increase or decrease the quantity of ovens she is using.

A First Look at the Relationship between Production and Cost

Table 7-2 gives us information on Salma's costs. We can determine the total cost of producing a given quantity of pizzas if we know how many workers and ovens are required to produce that quantity of pizzas and what Salma has to pay for those workers and pizzas. Suppose Salma has taken out a bank loan to buy two pizza ovens. The cost of the loan is US$800 per week. Therefore, her fixed costs are US$800 per week. If Salma pays US$650 per week to each worker, her variable costs depend on how many workers she hires. In the short run, Salma can increase the quantity of pizzas she produces only by hiring more workers. The table shows that if she hires 1 worker, she produces 200 pizzas during the week; if she hires 2 workers, she produces 450 pizzas; and so on. For a particular week, Salma's total cost of producing pizzas is equal to the US$800 she pays on the loan for the ovens plus the amount she pays to hire workers. If Salma decides to hire 4 workers and produce 600 pizzas, her total cost is US$3,400: US$800 to lease the ovens and US$2,600 to hire the workers. Her cost per pizza is equal to her total cost of producing pizzas divided by the quantity of pizzas produced. If she produces 600 pizzas

Average total cost Total cost divided by the quantity of output produced.

at a total cost of US$3,400, her cost per pizza, or *average total cost*, is US$3,400/600 = US$5.67. A firm's **average total cost** is always equal to its total cost divided by the quantity of output produced.

Panel (a) of Figure 7-1 uses the numbers in the next-to-last column of Table 7-2 to graph Salma's total cost. Panel (b) uses the numbers in the last column to graph her average total cost. Notice in panel (b) that Salma's average cost has roughly the same U shape as the average cost curve we saw Akio Morita calculate for Sony transistor radios at the beginning of this chapter. As production increases from low levels, average cost falls. Average cost then becomes fairly flat, before rising at higher levels of production. To understand why average cost has this U shape, we first need to look more closely at the technology of producing pizzas, as shown by the production function for Salma's restaurant. Then we need to look at how this technology determines the relationship between production and cost.

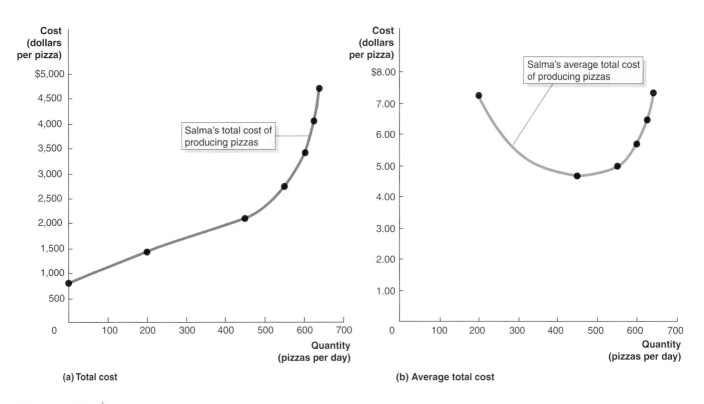

Figure 7-1 | Graphing Total Cost and Average Total Cost at Salma's Restaurant

We can use the information from Table 7-2 to graph the relationship between the quantity of pizzas Salma produces and her total cost and average total cost. Panel (a) shows that total cost increases as the level of production increases. In panel (b), we see that the average total cost is roughly U-shaped: as production increases from low lev-els, average cost falls before rising at higher levels of production. To understand why average cost has this shape, we must look more closely at the technology of producing pizzas, as shown by the production function.

7.3 | Understand the relationship between the marginal product of labor and the average product of labor.

The Marginal Product of Labor and the Average Product of Labor

To better understand the choices Salma faces, given the technology available to her, think first about what happens if she hires only one worker. That one worker will have to perform several different activities, including taking orders from customers, baking the pizzas, bringing the pizzas to the customers' tables, and ringing up sales on the cash register. If Salma hires two workers, some of these activities can be divided up: One worker could take the orders and ring up the sales, and one worker could bake the pizzas. With this division of tasks, Salma will find that hiring two workers actually allows her to produce more than twice as many pizzas as she could produce with just one worker.

The additional output a firm produces as a result of hiring one more worker is called the **marginal product of labor**. We can calculate the marginal product of labor by determining how much total output increases as each additional worker is hired. We do this for Salma's restaurant in Table 7-3.

When Salma hires only 1 worker, she produces 200 pizzas per week. When she hires 2 workers, she produces 450 pizzas per week. Hiring the second worker increases her production by 250 pizzas per week. So, the marginal product of labor for 1 worker is

Marginal product of labor The additional output a firm produces as a result of hiring one more worker.

TABLE 7-3

The Marginal Product of Labor at Salma's Restaurant

QUANTITY OF WORKERS	QUANTITY OF PIZZA OVENS	QUANTITY OF PIZZAS	MARGINAL PRODUCT OF LABOR
0	2	0	—
1	2	200	200
2	2	450	250
3	2	550	100
4	2	600	50
5	2	625	25
6	2	640	15

200 pizzas. For 2 workers, the marginal product of labor rises to 250 pizzas. This increase in marginal product results from the *division of labor* and from *specialization*. By dividing the tasks to be performed—the division of labor—Salma reduces the time workers lose moving from one activity to the next. She also allows them to become more specialized at their tasks. For example, a worker who concentrates on baking pizzas will become skilled at doing so quickly and efficiently.

The Law of Diminishing Returns

Law of diminishing returns The principle that, at some point, adding more of a variable input, such as labor, to the same amount of a fixed input, such as capital, will cause the marginal product of the variable input to decline.

In the short run, the quantity of pizza ovens Salma leases is fixed, so as she hires more workers, the marginal product of labor eventually begins to decline. This happens because at some point, Salma uses up all the gains from the division of labor and from specialization and starts to experience the effects of the **law of diminishing returns**. This law states that adding more of a variable input, such as labor, to the same amount of a fixed input, such as capital, will eventually cause the marginal product of the variable input to decline. For Salma, the marginal product of labor begins to decline when she hires the third worker. Hiring three workers raises the quantity of pizzas she produces from 450 per week to 550. But the increase in the quantity of pizzas—100—is less than the increase when she hired the second worker—250.

If Salma kept adding more and more workers to the same quantity of pizza ovens, eventually workers would begin to get in each other's way, and the marginal product of labor would actually become negative. When the marginal product is negative, the level of total output declines. No firm would actually hire so many workers as to experience a negative marginal product of labor and falling total output.

Graphing Production

Panel (a) in Figure 7-2 shows the relationship between the quantity of workers Salma hires and her total output of pizzas, using the numbers from Table 7-3. Panel (b) shows the marginal product of labor. In panel (a), output increases as more workers are hired, but the increase in output does not occur at a constant rate. Because of specialization and the division of labor, output at first increases at an increasing rate, with each additional worker hired causing production to increase by a *greater* amount than did the hiring of the previous worker. But after the second worker has been hired, hiring more workers while keeping the quantity of ovens constant results in diminishing returns. When the point of diminishing returns is reached, production increases at a decreasing rate. Each additional worker hired after the second worker causes production to increase by a *smaller* amount than did the hiring of the previous worker. In panel (b), the marginal product of labor curve rises initially because of the effects of specialization and division of labor, and then it falls due to the effects of diminishing returns.

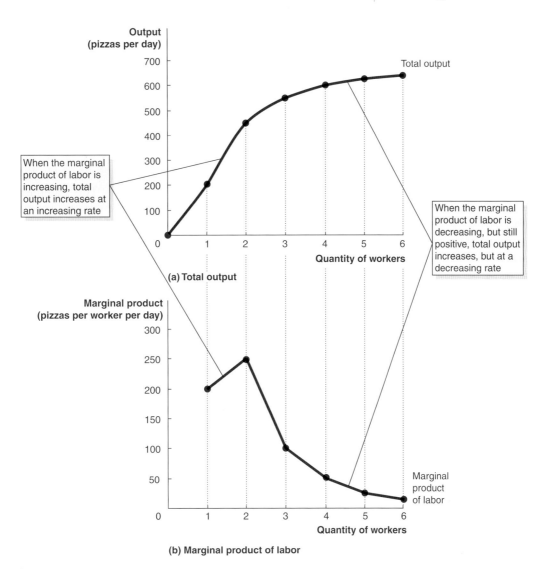

Figure 7-2 | Total Output and the Marginal Product of Labor

In panel (a), output increases as more workers are hired, but the increase in output does not occur at a constant rate. Because of specialization and the division of labor, output at first increases at an increasing rate, with each additional worker hired causing production to increase by a *greater* amount than did the hiring of the previous worker. After the third worker has been hired, hiring more workers while keeping the number of pizza ovens constant results in diminishing returns. When the point of diminishing returns is reached, production increases at a decreasing rate. Each additional worker hired after the third worker causes production to increase by a *smaller* amount than did the hiring of the previous worker. In panel (b), the *marginal product of labor* is the additional output produced as a result of hiring one more worker. The marginal product of labor rises initially because of the effects of specialization and division of labor, and then it falls due to the effects of diminishing returns.

The Relationship between Marginal and Average Product

The marginal product of labor tells us how much total output changes as the quantity of workers hired changes. We can also calculate how many pizzas workers produce on average. The **average product of labor** is the total output produced by a firm divided by the quantity of workers. For example, using the numbers in Table 7-3, if Salma hires 4 workers to produce 600 pizzas, the average product of labor is 600/4 = 150.

We can state the relationship between the marginal and average products of labor this way: *The average product of labor is the average of the marginal products of labor.* For example, the numbers from Table 7-3 show that the marginal product of the first worker Salma hires is 200, the marginal product of the second worker is 250, and the marginal product of the third worker is 100. Therefore, the average product of labor for three workers is 183.3:

Average product of labor The total output produced by a firm divided by the quantity of workers.

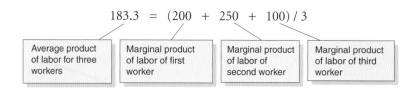

$$183.3 = (200 + 250 + 100) / 3$$

| Average product of labor for three workers | Marginal product of labor of first worker | Marginal product of labor of second worker | Marginal product of labor of third worker |

By taking the average of the marginal products of the first three workers, we have the average product of the three workers.

Whenever the marginal product of labor is greater than the average product of labor, the average product of labor must be increasing. This statement is true for the same reason that a person who is 186 centimeter tall entering a room where the average height is 175 centimeter raises the average height of people in the room. Whenever the marginal product of labor is less than the average product of labor, the average product of labor must be decreasing. The marginal product of labor equals the average product of labor for the quantity of workers where the average product of labor is at its maximum.

The gains from division of labor and specialization are as important to firms today as they were in the eighteenth century, when Adam Smith first discussed them.

Making the Connection | Adam Smith's Famous Account of the Division of Labor in a Pin Factory

In *The Wealth of Nations*, Adam Smith uses production in a pin factory as an example of the gains in output resulting from the division of labor. The following is an excerpt from his account of how pin making was divided into a series of tasks:

> One man draws out the wire, another straightens it, a third cuts it, a fourth points it, a fifth grinds it at the top for receiving the head; to make the head requires two or three distinct operations; to put it on is a [distinct operation], to whiten the pins is another; it is even a trade by itself to put them into the paper; and the important business of making a pin is, in this manner, divided into eighteen distinct operations.

Because the labor of pin making was divided up in this way, the average worker was able to produce about 4,800 pins per day. Smith speculated that a single worker using the pin-making machinery alone would make only about 20 pins per day. This lesson from more than 225 years ago, showing the tremendous gains from division of labor and specialization, remains relevant to most business situations today.

Source: Adam Smith, *An Inquiry into the Nature and Causes of the Wealth of Nations*, Vol. I, Oxford, U.K.: Oxford University Press edition, 1976, pp. 14–15.

YOUR TURN: Test your understanding by doing related problem 3.6 on page 247 at the end of this chapter.

An Example of Marginal and Average Values: College Grades

The relationship between the marginal product of labor and the average product of labor is the same as the relationship between the marginal and average values of any variable. To see this more clearly, think about the familiar relationship between a student's grade point average (GPA) in one semester and his overall, or cumulative, GPA. The table in

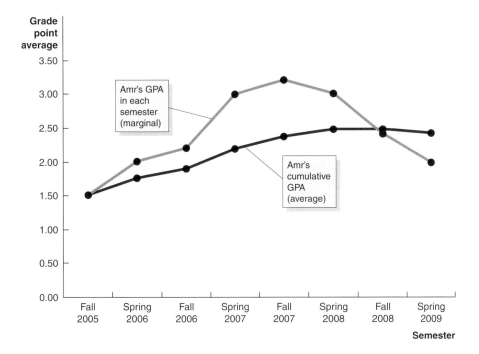

	Semester GPA (Marginal) GPA	Cumulative GPA (Average) GPA
Freshman Year		
Fall	1.50	1.50
Spring	2.00	1.75
Sophomore Year		
Fall	2.20	1.90
Spring	3.00	2.18
Junior Year		
Fall	3.20	2.38
Spring	3.00	2.48
Senior Year		
Fall	2.40	2.47
Spring	2.00	2.41

Average GPA continues to rise, although marginal GPA falls

With the marginal GPA below the average, the average GPA falls

Amr's GPA in each semester (marginal)

Amr's cumulative GPA (average)

Figure 7-3

Marginal and Average GPAs

The relationship between marginal and average values for a variable can be illustrated using GPAs. We can calculate the GPA Amr earns in a particular semester (his 'marginal GPA'), and we can calculate his cumulative GPA for all the semesters he has completed so far (his 'average GPA'). Amr's GPA is only 1.50 in the fall semester of his freshman year. In each following semester through fall of his junior year, his GPA for the semester increases—raising his cumulative GPA. In Amr's junior year, even though his semester GPA declines from fall to spring, his cumulative GPA rises. Only in the fall of his senior year, when his semester GPA drops below his cumulative GPA, does his cumulative GPA decline.

Figure 7-3 shows Amr's college grades for each semester, beginning with fall 2005. The graph in Figure 7-3 plots the grades from the table. Just as each additional worker hired adds to a firm's total production, each additional semester adds to Amr's total grade points. We can calculate what each individual worker hired adds to total production (marginal product), and we can calculate the average production of the workers hired so far (average product).

Similarly, we can calculate the GPA Amr earns in a particular semester (his 'marginal GPA'), and we can calculate his cumulative GPA for all the semesters he has completed so far (his 'average GPA'). As the table shows, Amr gets off to a weak start in the fall semester of his freshman year, earning only a 1.50 GPA. In each subsequent semester through the fall of his junior year, his GPA for the semester increases from the previous semester—raising his cumulative GPA. As the graph shows, however, his cumulative GPA does not increase as rapidly as his semester-by-semester GPA because his cumulative GPA is held back by the low GPAs of his first few semesters. Notice that in Amr's junior year, even though his semester GPA declines from fall to spring, his cumulative GPA rises. Only in the fall of his senior year, when his semester GPA drops below his cumulative GPA, does his cumulative GPA decline.

7.4 | Explain and illustrate the relationship between marginal cost and average total cost.

The Relationship between Short-Run Production and Short-Run Cost

We have seen that technology determines the values of the marginal product of labor and the average product of labor. In turn, the marginal and average products of labor affect the firm's costs. Keep in mind that the relationships we are discussing are *short-run* relationships: we are assuming that the time period is too short for the firm to change its technology or the size of its physical plant.

At the beginning of this chapter, we saw how Akio Morita used an average total cost curve to determine the price of radios. The average total cost curve Morita used and the average total cost curve in Figure 7-1 for Salma's restaurant both have a U shape. As we will soon see, the U shape of the average total cost curve is determined by the shape of the curve that shows the relationship between *marginal cost* and the level of production.

Marginal Cost

Marginal cost The change in a firm's total cost from producing one more unit of a good or service.

As we saw in Chapter 1, one of the key ideas in economics is that optimal decisions are made at the margin. Consumers, firms, and government officials usually make decisions about doing a little more or a little less. As Salma considers whether to hire additional workers to produce additional pizzas, she needs to consider how much she will add to her total cost by producing the additional pizzas. **Marginal cost** is the change in a firm's total cost from producing one more unit of a good or service. We can calculate marginal cost for a particular increase in output by dividing the change in cost by the change in output. We can express this idea mathematically (remembering that the Greek letter delta, Δ, means 'change in'):

$$MC = \frac{\Delta TC}{\Delta Q}$$

In the table in Figure 7-4, we use this equation to calculate Salma's marginal cost of producing pizzas.

Why Are the Marginal and Average Cost Curves U-Shaped?

Notice in the graph in Figure 7-4 that Salma's marginal cost of producing pizzas declines at first and then increases, giving the marginal cost curve a U shape. The table in Figure 7-4 also shows the marginal product of labor. This table helps us see the important relationship between the marginal product of labor and the marginal cost of production: The marginal product of labor is *rising* for the first two workers, but the marginal cost of the pizzas produced by these workers is *falling*. The marginal product of labor is *falling* for the last four workers, but the marginal cost of pizzas produced by these workers is *rising*. To summarize this point: *When the marginal product of labor is rising, the marginal cost of output is falling. When the marginal product of labor is falling, the marginal cost of production is rising.*

One way to understand why this point is true is first to notice that the only additional cost to Salma from producing more pizzas is the additional wages she pays to hire more workers. She pays each new worker the same US$650 per week. So the marginal cost of the additional pizzas each worker makes depends on that worker's additional output, or marginal product. As long as the additional output from each new worker is rising, the marginal cost of that output is falling. When the additional output from each new worker is falling, the marginal cost of that output is rising. We can conclude that the marginal cost of production falls and then rises—forming a U shape—because the marginal product of labor rises and then falls.

Quantity of Workers	Quantity of Ovens	Marginal Product of Labor	Total Cost of Pizzas	Marginal Cost of Pizzas	Average Total Cost of Pizzas
0	0	–	$800	–	–
1	200	200	1,450	$3.25	$7.25
2	450	250	2,100	2.60	4.67
3	550	100	2,750	6.50	5.00
4	600	50	3,400	13.00	5.67
5	625	25	4,050	26.00	6.48
6	640	15	4,700	43.33	7.34

Figure 7-4

Salma's Marginal Cost and Average Total Cost of Producing Pizzas

We can use the information in the table to calculate Salma's marginal cost and average total cost of producing pizzas. For the first two workers hired, the marginal product of labor is increasing. This increase causes the marginal cost of production to fall. For the last four workers hired, the marginal product of labor is falling. This causes the marginal cost of production to increase. Therefore, the marginal cost curve falls and then rises—that is, has a U shape—because the marginal product of labor rises and then falls. As long as marginal cost is below average total cost, average total cost will be falling. When marginal cost is above average total cost, average total cost will be rising. The relationship between marginal cost and average total cost explains why the average total cost curve also has a U shape.

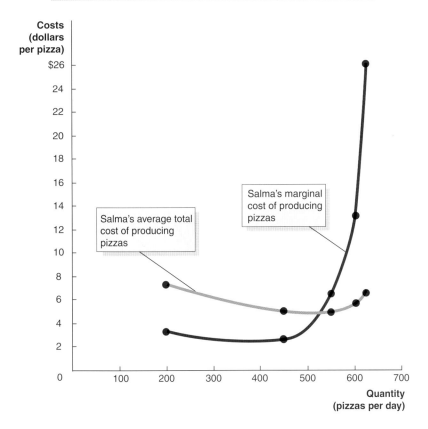

The relationship between marginal cost and average total cost follows the usual relationship between marginal and average values. As long as marginal cost is below average total cost, average total cost falls. When marginal cost is above average total cost, average total cost rises. Marginal cost equals average total cost when average total cost is at its lowest point. Therefore, the average total cost curve has a U shape because the marginal cost curve has a U shape.

Solved Problem | **7-4**

The Relationship between Marginal Cost and Average Cost

Is Salma right or wrong when she says the following? "I am currently producing 10,000 pizzas per month at a total cost of US$500.00. If I produce 10,001 pizzas, my total cost will rise to US$500.11. Therefore, my marginal cost of producing pizzas must be increasing." Draw a graph to illustrate your answer.

SOLVING THE PROBLEM:

Step 1: **Review the chapter material.** This problem requires understanding the relationship between marginal and average cost, so you may want to review the section "Why Are the Marginal and Average Cost Curves U-Shaped?" which begins on page 232.

Step 2: **Calculate average total cost and marginal cost.** Average total cost is total cost divided by total output. In this case, average total cost is US$500.11/10,001 = US$0.05. Marginal cost is the change in total cost divided by the change in output. In this case, marginal cost is US$0.11/1 = US$0.11.

Step 3: **Use the relationship between marginal cost and average total cost to answer the question.** When marginal cost is greater than average total cost, marginal cost must be increasing. You have shown in Step 2 that marginal cost is greater than average total cost. Therefore, Salma is right: Her marginal cost of producing pizzas must be increasing.

Step 4: **Draw the graph.**

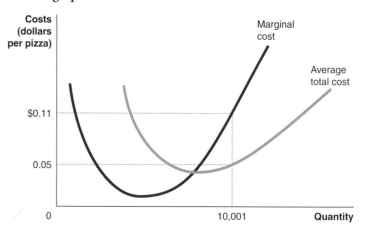

YOUR TURN: For more practice, do related problems 4.5 and 4.6 on page 247 at the end of this chapter.

>> **End Solved Problem 7-4**

7.5 LEARNING OBJECTIVE

7.5 | Graph average total cost, average variable cost, average fixed cost, and marginal cost.

Graphing Cost Curves

We have seen that we calculate average total cost by dividing total cost by the quantity of output produced. Similarly, we can calculate **average fixed cost** by dividing fixed cost by the quantity of output produced. And we can calculate **average variable cost** by dividing variable cost by the quantity of output produced. Or, mathematically, with Q being the level of output, we have:

Average fixed cost Fixed cost divided by the quantity of output produced.

Average variable cost Variable cost divided by the quantity of output produced.

$$\text{Average total cost} = ATC = \frac{TC}{Q}$$

$$\text{Average fixed cost} = AFC = \frac{FC}{Q}$$

$$\text{Average variable cost} = AVC = \frac{VC}{Q}$$

Finally, notice that average total cost is the sum of average fixed cost plus average variable cost:

$$ATC = AFC + AVC$$

Quantity of Workers	Quantity of Ovens	Quantity of Pizzas	Cost of Ovens (Fixed Cost)	Cost of Workers (Variable Cost)	Total Cost of Pizzas	ATC	AFC	AVC	MC
0	2	0	$800	$0	$800	–	–	–	–
1	2	200	800	650	1,450	$7.25	$4.00	$3.25	$3.25
2	2	450	800	1,300	2,100	4.67	1.78	2.89	2.60
3	2	550	800	1,950	2,750	5.00	1.45	3.55	6.50
4	2	600	800	2,600	3,400	5.67	1.33	4.33	13.00
5	2	625	800	3,250	4,050	6.48	1.28	5.2	26.00
6	2	640	800	3,900	4,700	7.34	1.25	6.09	43.33

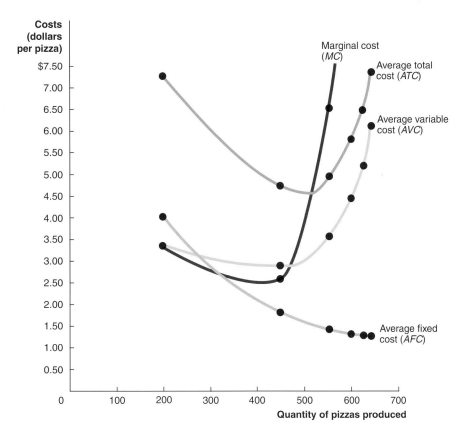

Figure 7-5

Costs at Salma's Restaurant

Salma's costs of making pizzas are shown in the table and plotted in the graph. Notice three important facts about the graph: (1) The marginal cost (*MC*), average total cost (*ATC*), and average variable cost (*AVC*) curves are all U-shaped, and the marginal cost curve intersects both the average variable cost curve and average total cost curve at their minimum points. (2) As output increases, average fixed cost (*AFC*) gets smaller and smaller. (3) As output increases, the difference between average total cost and average variable cost decreases. Make sure you can explain why each of these three facts is true. You should spend time becoming familiar with this graph because it is one of the most important graphs in microeconomics.

The only fixed cost Salma incurs in operating her restaurant is the US$800 per week she pays on the bank loan for her pizza ovens. Her variable costs are the wages she pays her workers. The table and graph in Figure 7-5 show Salma's costs.

We will use graphs like the one in Figure 7-5 in the next several chapters to analyze how firms decide the level of output to produce and the price to charge. Before going further, be sure you understand the following three key facts about Figure 7-5:

1 The marginal cost (*MC*), average total cost (*ATC*), and average variable cost (*AVC*) curves are all U-shaped, and the marginal cost curve intersects the average variable cost and average total cost curves at their minimum points. When marginal cost is less than either average variable cost or average total cost, it causes them to decrease. When marginal cost is above average variable cost or average total cost, it causes them to increase. Therefore, when marginal cost equals average variable cost or average total cost, they must be at their minimum points.

2 As output increases, average fixed cost gets smaller and smaller. This happens because in calculating average fixed cost, we are dividing something that gets larger and larger—output—into something that remains constant—fixed cost. Firms

often refer to this process of lowering average fixed cost by selling more output as 'spreading the overhead.' By 'overhead' they mean fixed costs.

3 As output increases, the difference between average total cost and average variable cost decreases. This happens because the difference between average total cost and average variable cost is average fixed cost, which gets smaller as output increases.

7.6 | Understand how firms use the long-run average cost curve in their planning.

Costs in the Long Run

The distinction between fixed cost and variable cost that we just discussed applies to the short run but *not* to the long run. For example, in the short run, Salma has fixed costs of US$800 per week because she signed a loan agreement with a bank when she bought her pizza ovens. In the long run, the cost of purchasing more pizza ovens becomes variable because Salma can choose whether to expand her business by buying more ovens. The same would be true of any other fixed costs a company like Salma's might have. Once a company has purchased a fire insurance policy, the cost of the policy is fixed. But when the policy expires, the company must decide whether to renew it, and the cost becomes variable. The important point here is this: *In the long run, all costs are variable. There are no fixed costs in the long run.* In other words, in the long run, total cost equals variable cost, and average total cost equals average variable cost.

Managers of successful firms simultaneously consider how they can most profitably run their current store, factory, or office and also whether in the long run they would be more profitable if they became larger or, possibly, smaller. Salma must consider how to run her current restaurant, which has only two pizza ovens, and she must also plan what to do when her current bank loan is paid off and the lease on her store ends. Should she buy more pizza ovens? Should she lease a larger restaurant?

Economies of Scale

Long-run average cost curve A curve showing the lowest cost at which a firm is able to produce a given quantity of output in the long run, when no inputs are fixed.

Economies of scale The situation when a firm's long-run average costs fall as it increases output.

Short-run average cost curves represent the costs a firm faces when some input, such as the quantity of machines it uses, is fixed. The **long-run average cost curve** shows the lowest cost at which a firm is able to produce a given level of output in the long run, when no inputs are fixed. Many firms experience **economies of scale**, which means the firm's long-run average costs fall as it increases the quantity of output it produces. We can see the effects of economies of scale in Figure 7-6, which shows the relationship between short-run and long-run average cost curves. Managers can use long-run average cost curves for planning because they show the effect on cost of expanding output by, for example, building a larger factory or store.

Long-Run Average Total Cost Curves for Bookstores

Figure 7-6 shows long-run average cost in the retail bookstore industry. If a small bookstore expects to sell only 1,000 books per month, then it will be able to sell that quantity of books at the lowest average cost of US$22 per book if it builds the small store represented by the *ATC* curve on the left of the figure. A much larger bookstore, such as a national chain like Jarir Bookstore, will be able to sell 20,000 books per month at a lower average cost of US$18 per book. This decline in average cost from US$22 to US$18 represents the economies of scale that exist in bookselling. Why would the larger bookstore have lower average costs? One important reason is that Jarir is selling 20 times as many books per month as the small store but might need only six times as many workers. This saving in labor cost would reduce Jarir's average cost of selling books.

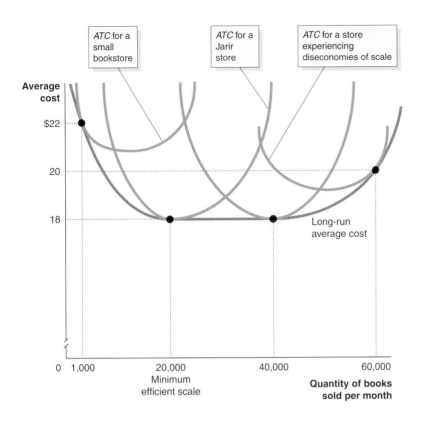

Figure 7-6

The Relationship between Short-Run Average Cost and Long-Run Average Cost

If a small bookstore expects to sell only 1,000 books per month, then it will be able to sell that quantity of books at the lowest average cost of US$22 per book if it builds the small store represented by the *ATC* curve on the left of the figure. A larger bookstore will be able to sell 20,000 books per month at a lower cost of US$18 per book. A bookstore selling 20,000 books per month and a bookstore selling 40,000 books per month will experience constant returns to scale and have the same average cost. A bookstore selling 20,000 books per month will have reached minimum efficient scale. Very large bookstores will experience diseconomies of scale, and their average costs will rise as sales increase beyond 40,000 books per month.

Firms may experience economies of scale for several reasons. First, as in the case of Jarir, the firm's technology may make it possible to increase production with a smaller proportional increase in at least one input. Second, both workers and managers can become more specialized, enabling them to become more productive, as output expands. Third, large firms, like Jarir, Carrefour, and Aramco (the largest oil company in the world), may be able to purchase inputs at lower costs than smaller competitors. In fact, as Carrefour expanded, its bargaining power with its suppliers increased, and its average costs fell. Finally, as a firm expands, it may be able to borrow money more inexpensively, thereby lowering its costs.

Economies of scale do not continue forever. The long-run average cost curve in most industries has a flat segment that often stretches over a substantial range of output. As Figure 7-6 shows, a bookstore selling 20,000 books per month and a bookstore selling 40,000 books per month have the same average cost. Over this range of output, firms in the industry experience **constant returns to scale**. As these firms increase their output, they have to increase their inputs, such as the size of the store and the quantity of workers, proportionally. The level of output at which all economies of scale are exhausted is known as **minimum efficient scale**. A bookstore selling 20,000 books per month has reached minimum efficient scale.

Very large bookstores experience increasing average costs as managers begin to have difficulty coordinating the operation of the store. Figure 7-6 shows that for sales above 40,000 books per month, firms in the industry experience **diseconomies of scale**. Toyota ran into diseconomies of scale in assembling automobiles. The firm found that as it expanded production at its Georgetown, Kentucky, plant and its plants in China, its managers had difficulty keeping costs from rising. The president of Toyota's Georgetown plant was quoted as saying, "Demand for...high volumes saps your energy. Over a period of time, it eroded our focus...[and] thinned out the expertise and knowledge we painstakingly built up over the years." One analysis of the problems Toyota faced in expanding production concluded: "It is the kind of paradox many highly successful companies face: getting bigger doesn't always mean getting better."

Constant returns to scale The situation when a firm's long-run average costs remain unchanged as it increases output.

Minimum efficient scale The level of output at which all economies of scale are exhausted.

Diseconomies of scale The situation when a firm's long-run average costs rise as the firm increases output.

Solved Problem | 7-6

Using Long-Run Average Cost Curves to Understand Business Strategy

In fall 2002, Motorola and Siemens were each manufacturing both mobile phone handsets and wireless infrastructure—the base stations needed to operate a wireless communications network. The firms discussed the following arrangement: Motorola would give Siemens its wireless infrastructure business in exchange for Siemens giving Motorola its mobile phone handsets business. The main factor motivating the trade was the hope of taking advantage of economies of scale in each business. Use long-run average total cost curves to explain why this trade might make sense for Motorola and Siemens.

SOLVING THE PROBLEM:

Step 1:   **Review the chapter material.** This problem is about the long-run average cost curve, so you may want to review the material in the section "Costs in the Long Run," which begins on page 236.

Step 2:   **Draw long-run average cost graphs for Motorola and Siemens.** The question does not provide us with the details of the quantity of each product each firm is producing before the trade or the firms' average costs of production. If economies of scale were an important reason for the trade, we can assume that Motorola and Siemens were not yet at minimum efficient scale in the wireless infrastructure and phone handset businesses. Therefore, we can draw the following graphs:

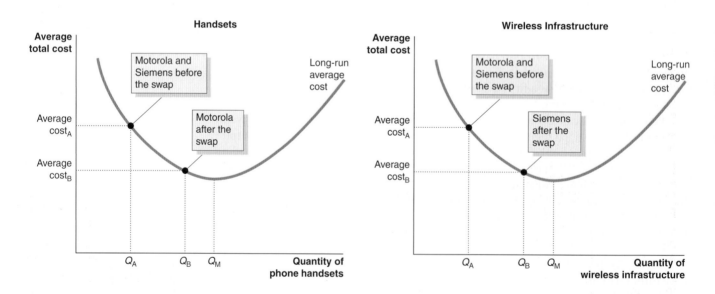

Step 3:   **Explain the curves in the graphs.** Before the proposed trade, Motorola and Siemens are producing both products at less than the minimum efficient scale, which is Q_M in both graphs. After the trade, Motorola's production of handsets will increase, moving it from Q_A to Q_B in the first graph. This increase in production will allow it to take advantage of economies of scale and reduce its average cost from Average Cost$_A$ to Average Cost$_B$. Similarly, production of wireless infrastructure by Siemens will increase from Q_A to Q_B, lowering its average cost from Average Cost$_A$ to Average Cost$_B$. As drawn, the graphs show that both firms will still be short of minimum efficient scale after the trade, although their average costs will have fallen.

EXTRA CREDIT: These were new technologies at the time Motorola and Siemens discussed the trade. As a result, companies making these products were only beginning to understand how large minimum efficient scale was. To survive in the industry, the managements of both companies wanted to lower their costs by taking advantage of economies of scale. As one industry analyst put it: "Motorola and Siemens may be driven by the conviction that they have little choice. Most observers believe consolidation in both the [wireless] networking and handset areas is inevitable."

Source for quote: Ray Hegarty, *Rumored Motorola–Siemens Business Unit Swap? A Compelling M&A Story*, www.thefeature.com.

YOUR TURN: For more practice, do related problems 6.4, 6.5, 6.6, and 6.7 on pages 249–250 at the end of this chapter.

>> End Solved Problem 7-6

Over time, most firms in an industry will build factories or stores that are at least as large as the minimum efficient scale but not so large that diseconomies of scale occur. In the bookstore industry, stores will sell between 20,000 and 40,000 books per month. However, firms often do not know the exact shape of their long-run average cost curves. As a result, they may mistakenly build factories or stores that are either too large or too small.

| Making the Connection | **Economies and Diseconomies of Scale in the Car Industry** |

GB Auto Ghabbour, founded in 1960, is a leading Egyptian automotive assembler, importer, and distributor in the Middle East and North Africa, with a market share of around 25 percent of Egypt's transportation market. The company assembles and distributes passenger cars under the Hyundai brand, as well as buses and trucks under the Volvo, Mitsubishi, Hyundai, and Ghabbour brands. Until 2004, the company was not able to benefit from its economies of scale for two main reasons. First, the Egyptian automotive market is considered small by international standards, which makes it difficult to establish economies of scale for manufacturing. Second, Egypt was hit by a recession in the late 1990s, which significantly affected demand for cars, from a peak of 72,000 units in 1998 to a low of 47,000 units in 2002. The year 2004 was a turning point in the automotive market in Egypt, when the Egyptian government implemented an economic reform program that led to a sharp reduction in tariffs on imported cars (up to 1600 CC) from 105 percent to 40 percent. This dramatic reduction in customs duties on both imported cars and also car parts resulted in a sharp increase in demand on passenger cars by 323 percent in only 3 years (2005–07). This helped GB Auto to increase its production and generate economies of scale. The company's revenue increased by 108.7 percent, 50.2 percent, and 57.3 percent in the three years following the economic reform.

In another trend, when Henry Ford started the Ford Motor Company in Detroit, USA, in 1903, he introduced two new ideas that allowed him to take advantage of economies of scale. First, Ford used identical—or, interchangeable—parts so that unskilled workers could assemble the cars. Second, instead of having groups of workers moving from one stationary automobile to the next, he had the workers remain stationary while the automobiles moved along an assembly line. Ford built a large factory where he used these ideas to produce the famous Model T at an average cost well below what his competitors could match using older production methods in smaller factories.

Ghabbour Auto, the Egyptian motor manufacturer, has a major strategic partnership with Hyundai.

(Continued)

Ford believed that he could produce automobiles at an even lower average cost by building a still larger plant along the River Rouge, in the U.S. State of Michigan. Unfortunately, Ford's River Rouge plant was too large and suffered from diseconomies of scale. Ford's managers had great difficulty coordinating the production of automobiles in such a large plant.

Beginning in 1927, Ford produced the Model A at the River Rouge plant. Ford failed to achieve economies of scale and actually *lost money* on each of the four Model A body styles.

Ford could not raise the price of the Model A to make it profitable because, the car could not compete with similar models produced by competitors. He eventually reduced the cost of making the Model A by constructing smaller factories spread out across the country.

Sources: Menatalla Sadek and Tarek Shahin, "GB Auto 'Ghabbour'", Automotive Industry Egypt," http://ae.zawya .com, May 24, 2007; Lubna El-Elaimy, "Automotive in Egypt: Drive to Succeed", German–Arab Chamber of Industry and Commerce, Sept./Oct. 2008, http://aegypten.ahk.de/index.php.

YOUR TURN: Test your understanding by doing related problem 6.8 on page 250 at the end of this chapter.

>> Continued from page 221

Economics in YOUR Life!

At the beginning of the chapter, we asked you to consider a situation in which you are about to open a store to sell recliners. Both you and a competing store, Eyad's Big Chairs, can buy recliners from the manufacturer for US$300 each. But because Eyad's sells more recliners per month than you expect to be able to, his costs per recliner are lower than yours. We asked you to think about why this might be true. In this chapter, we have seen that firms often experience declining average costs as the quantity they sell increases. One significant reason Eyad's average cost might be lower than yours has to do with fixed costs. Because your stores are the same size, you may be paying about the same amount to lease the store space. You may also be paying about the same amounts for utilities, insurance, and advertising. All these are fixed costs because they do not change as the quantity of recliners you sell changes. Because Eyad's fixed costs are the same as yours, but he is selling more recliners, his average fixed costs are lower than yours, and, therefore, so are his average total costs. With lower average total costs, he can sell his recliners for a lower price than you do and still make a profit.

Conclusion

In this chapter, we discussed the relationship between a firm's technology, production, and costs. In the discussion, we encountered a number of definitions of costs. Because we will use these definitions in later chapters, it is useful to bring them together in Table 7-4 for you to review.

We have seen the important relationship between a firm's level of production and its costs. Just as this information was vital to Akio Morita in deciding which price to charge for his transistor radios, so it remains vital today to all firms as they attempt to decide the optimal level of production and the optimal prices to charge for their products. We will explore this point further in Chapter 8. Before moving on to that chapter, read *An Inside Look* on the next page to see how we can use long-run average cost curves to understand the effect of lower costs of production on the pricing of flat-panel TVs.

TABLE 7-4

A Summary of Definitions of Cost

TERM	DEFINITION	SYMBOLS AND EQUATIONS
Total cost	The cost of all the inputs used by a firm, or fixed cost plus variable cost	TC
Fixed cost	Costs that remain constant when a firm's level of output changes	FC
Variable cost	Costs that change when the firm's level of output changes	VC
Marginal cost	Increase in total cost resulting from producing another unit of output	$MC = \dfrac{\Delta TC}{\Delta Q}$
Average total cost	Total cost divided by the quantity of output produced	$ATC = \dfrac{TC}{Q}$
Average fixed cost	Fixed cost divided by the quantity of output produced	$AFC = \dfrac{FC}{Q}$
Average variable cost	Variable cost divided by the quantity of output produced	$AVC = \dfrac{VC}{Q}$
Implicit cost	A nonmonetary opportunity cost	—
Explicit cost	A cost that involves spending money	—

Lower Manufacturing Costs Push Down the Price of Flat-Panel TVs

WALL STREET JOURNAL, APRIL 15, 2006

Flat-Panel TVs, Long Touted, Finally Are Becoming the Norm

After years as the Next Big Thing in consumer electronics, flat-panel TVs are finally becoming the mainstream standard...

Last year, flat-screen TVs for the first time accounted for the majority of TVs bought in Japan, Hong Kong and Singapore. That crossover will happen this year or next in the U.S. and most European countries, industry watchers say, and at least one company has already stopped shipping tube TVs in the U.S. "It's happening faster than the most optimistic targets," says Ross Young, president of DisplaySearch, an Austin, Texas, market-research firm.

World-wide, sales this year of liquid-crystal display and plasma flat-panel TVs are on track to total about 44 million units, valued at as much as US$54 billion, out of an overall market of 185 million TVs, according to market research firms. In the U.S., sales are expected to reach between 12 million and 14 million flat-panel TVs, or roughly half of all TVs sold. Last year, world-wide sales of flat-panel TVs totaled 25 million units.

Consumers like the thin form and light weight of flat-panel TVs, but until recently, many considered them too expensive. Two years ago, a 30-inch, LCD-TV cost US$3,500 to US$4,000. Since then, more than a dozen factories producing critical glass and screen components have opened, which has pushed down manufacturing costs, allowing for lower prices.

Competition between LCD and plasma technologies is pushing down prices, too. Plasma models use electricity to light individual points of gas on a screen; in LCDs, a layer of liquid crystal filters a bright light. LCD beat plasma about 15 years ago as the flat-panel of choice in notebook computers. From there, plasma developers jumped to big size screens, where they have since been most cost effective, while technical challenges long limited the size of LCDs...

Increased production is likely to help prices continue to fall throughout the year. Seven new factories are under construction in Asia that will make LCD panels 40 inches or larger, and three new factories for plasma screens are under construction. Several are being optimized for screens that are 50 inches or larger. By late next year, prices of 40-inch models will be closing in on US$1,000 as production ramps up...

Japan's Matsushita Electric Industrial Co., maker of Panasonic products, has stopped shipping tube TVs altogether to the U.S., where it expects to sell about 1.5 million plasma-screen TVs this year. Just two years ago, it sold one million tube TVs and 150,000 plasma models in the U.S. Flat-panel TVs of all types have become an easier sell as popular television shows such as "CSI" and "Lost" adopt the widescreen, high-definition look of movies. The U.S. and several other countries are shifting their broadcast systems to digital signals that promise to broaden the availability of HDTV content. Higher-definition DVDs that are emerging this year may also fuel demand...

To meet demand, manufacturers are in a mad dash to build new factories, or change existing ones, to accommodate flat-panel TVs. In one week last month, Sony, LG Electronics Co. and China's Changhong Group announced new factories in Eastern Europe to assemble flat-panel models for the European market. Just this week, Sony and Samsung Electronics Co. said they would expand their LCD-panel joint venture by spending US$2 billion on what, for the moment, will be the industry's largest factory. Hitachi Corp. a week earlier said it's considering building factories to quadruple its annual output of LCD-TVs to more than five million annually...

Source: Evan Ramstad, "Flat-Panel TVs, Long Touted, Finally Are Becoming the Norm," *Wall Street Journal*, April 15, 2006, p. A1. Reprinted by permission. Copyright © 2006 Dow Jones & Company, Inc. All Rights Reserved Worldwide. License number 2744221405368.

Key Points in the Article

This article illustrates how several firms are racing to expand production of flat-panel televisions. The article discusses long-run decisions firms make, such as what plant size to build. It also discusses how the costs of inputs into flat-panel televisions have been declining. Lower costs of production have resulted in sharply lower prices of flat-panel televisions.

Analyzing the News

a As more factories open to produce components to make flat-panel televisions, the price of the components should fall. As a result, the marginal and average cost of producing flat-panel televisions should decline. In Figure 1, we see that more factories producing components for flat-panel TVs increases the supply of components from S_1 to S_2. The increased supply causes the price of components to fall from P_1 to P_2, while the

quantity of components sold increases from Q_1 to Q_2.

Because these components are inputs in production of flat-panel TVs, as the price of components falls, the costs of producing flat-panel TVs also fall. This is seen in Figure 2, where the marginal cost curve of TVs falls from MC_1 to MC_2 and the average cost curve falls from ATC_1 to ATC_2.

Falling costs, make it possible for firms like Sony to sell TVs at lower prices and still cover their costs. You can see in Figure 2 that prior to the decrease in input prices a firm would need to receive ATC_1 dollars per TV to cover the cost of producing Q_1 TVs. After the reduction in input prices, the average cost of producing Q_1 TVs falls to ATC_2 dollars and the firm is able to cover its costs at lower prices.

b Increased production moves a firm further to the right on its cost curve. For goods like flat-panel TVs, fixed costs tend to be high relative to marginal costs, because the factories that produce the televisions are expensive to build. So, average cost will decline over large ranges of output, which makes it possible for Sony and other manufacturers to offer the televisions for sale at lower prices.

c Firms use the long-run average cost curve when choosing what size manufacturing plant to build. The long-run

average cost curve shows the minimum cost of producing at each output level. Choosing the best point to be on the long-run average cost curve requires firms to forecast future sales. In this case, firms are expecting continuing rapid increases in demand for flat-panel televisions and are building increasingly larger plants. They are expecting that economies of scale will make the average costs of production in the larger plants lower than the average costs of production in smaller plants. But as the example of Ford's River Rouge plant discussed on page 24 shows, when a new industry is rapidly expanding, it is not unusual for at least one firm to build a plant that is too large and to begin experiencing diseconomies of scale. With diseconomies of scale, the average cost of production in a larger plant is actually *higher* than in a smaller plant.

Thinking Critically

1. Suppose you are a manager at Sony and you are asked to determine what size manufacturing plants for flat-panel televisions the firm should be planning to build. What information would you need to gather in order to determine the optimal sized plant?

2. Use the concepts from this chapter to explain why the long-run supply of flat-panel TVs is more elastic than the short-run supply of flat-panel TVs.

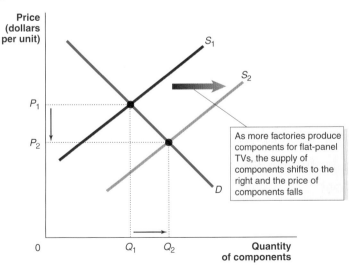

Figure 1. An increased supply of flat-panel television components leads to a lower price.

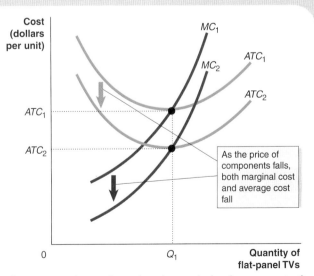

Figure 2. Lower input prices reduce the marginal and average costs of producing flat-panel televisions.

Key Terms

Summary

7.1 LEARNING OBJECTIVE

Define technology and give examples of technological change, **pages 222–223.**

Technology: An Economic Definition

The basic activity of a firm is to use inputs, such as workers, machines, and natural resources, to produce goods and services. The firm's **technology** is the processes it uses to turn inputs into goods and services. **Technological change** refers to a change in the ability of a firm to produce a given level of output with a given quantity of inputs.

7.2 LEARNING OBJECTIVE

Distinguish between the economic short run and the economic long run, **pages 223–227.**

The Short Run and the Long Run in Economics

In the **short run**, a firm's technology and the size of its factory, store, or office are fixed. In the **long run**, a firm is able to adopt new technology and to increase or decrease the size of its physical plant. **Total cost** is the cost of all the inputs a firm uses in production. Variable costs are costs that change as output changes. Fixed costs are costs that remain constant as output changes. Opportunity cost is the highest-valued alternative that must be given up to engage in an activity. An explicit cost is a cost that involves spending money. An implicit cost is a nonmonetary opportunity cost. The relationship between the inputs employed by a firm and the maximum output it can produce with those inputs is called the firm's **production function**.

7.3 LEARNING OBJECTIVE

Understand the relationship between the marginal product of labor and the average product of labor, **pages 227–231.**

The Marginal Product of Labor and the Average Product of Labor

The **marginal product of labor** is the additional output produced by a firm as a result of hiring one more worker. Specialization and division of labor cause the marginal product of labor to rise for the first few workers hired. Eventually, the **law of diminishing returns** causes the marginal product of labor to decline. The **average product of labor** is the total amount of output produced by a firm divided by the quantity of workers hired. When the marginal product of labor is greater than the average product of labor, the average product of labor increases. When the marginal product of labor is less than the average product of labor, the average product of labor decreases.

7.4 LEARNING OBJECTIVE

Explain and illustrate the relationship between marginal cost and average total cost, **pages 232–234.**

The Relationship between Short-Run Production and Short-Run Cost

The **marginal cost** of production is the increase in total cost resulting from producing another unit of output. The marginal cost curve has a U shape because when the marginal product of labor is rising, the marginal cost of output is falling. When the marginal product of labor is falling, the marginal cost of output is rising. When marginal cost is less than average total cost, average total cost falls. When marginal cost is greater than average total cost, average total cost rises.

Graphing Cost Curves

Average fixed cost is equal to fixed cost divided by the level of output. **Average variable cost** is equal to variable cost divided by the level of output. Figure 7-5 on page 235 shows the relationship among marginal cost, average total cost, average variable cost, and average fixed cost. It is one of the most important graphs in microeconomics.

7.5 LEARNING OBJECTIVE

Graph average total cost, average variable cost, average fixed cost, and marginal cost, **pages 234–236.**

Costs in the Long Run

The **long-run average cost curve** shows the lowest cost at which a firm is able to produce a given level of output in the long run. For many firms, the long-run average cost curve falls as output expands because of **economies of scale**. **Minimum efficient scale** is the level of output at which all economies of scale have been exhausted. After economies of scale have been exhausted, firms experience **constant returns to scale**, where their long-run average cost curve is flat. At high levels of output, the long-run average cost curve turns up as the firm experiences **diseconomies of scale**.

7.6 LEARNING OBJECTIVE

Understand how firms use the long-run average cost curve in their planning, **pages 236–241.**

Review, Problems and Applications

myeconlab Visit www.pearsoned.co.uk/awe/hubbard to complete these exercises online and get instant feedback.

Get Ahead of the Curve

7.1 LEARNING OBJECTIVE | Define technology and give examples of technological change, **pages 222–223.**

Review Questions

1.1 What is the difference between technology and technological change?

1.2 Is it possible for technological change to be negative? If so, give an example.

Problems and Applications

1.3 Briefly explain whether you agree with the following observation: "Technological change refers only to the introduction of new products, so it is not relevant to the operations of most firms."

1.4 Which of the following are examples of a firm experiencing positive technological change?
  a. A firm is able to cut each worker's wage rate by 10 percent and still produce the same level of output.
  b. A training program makes a firm's workers more productive.

  c. An exercise program makes a firm's workers more healthy and productive.
  d. A firm cuts its workforce and is able to maintain its initial level of output.
  e. A firm rearranges the layout of its factory and finds that by using its initial set of inputs, it can produce exactly as much as before.

1.5 (Related to the *Making the Connection* on page 222) The Carrefour chain of stores in the United Arab Emirates reorganized its system for supplying its stores with food. This led to a sharp reduction in the number of trucks the company had to use, while increasing the amount of fresh food on store shelves. Someone discussing Carrefour's new system argues: "This is not an example of technological change because it did not require the use of new machinery or equipment." Briefly explain whether you agree with this argument.

7.2 LEARNING OBJECTIVE | Distinguish between the economic short run and the economic long run,

pages 223–227.

Review Questions

2.1 What is the difference between the short run and the long run? Is the amount of time that separates the short run from the long run the same for every firm?

2.2 What are implicit costs? How are they different from explicit costs?

Problems and Applications

2.3 **(Related to the *Making the Connection* on page 224)** Many firms consider their wage costs to be variable costs. Why do publishers usually consider their wage and salary costs to be fixed costs? Are the costs of utilities always fixed, always variable, or can they be both? Briefly explain?

2.4 **(Related to the *Making the Connection* on page 224)** For Salma's pizza restaurant, explain whether each of the following is a fixed cost or a variable cost.

a. The payment she makes on her fire insurance policy

b. The payment she makes to buy pizza dough

c. The wages she pays her workers

d. The lease payment she makes to her landlord who owns the building where her store is located

e. The US$300-per-month payment she makes to her local newspaper for running her weekly advertisements

2.5 **(Related to the *Making the Connection* on page 224)** The *National Accounts of Saudi Arabia* is a book published each year by the Saudi Arabian Central Department of Statistics and Information. It provides data on income, consumption, saving, and government budget. Suppose that it is available at a price of US$35.00 but that government documents are not copyrighted, meaning that anyone can print copies of the *National Accounts* book and sell them. Assume that one or two companies will print and sell copies of that book for a significantly lower price than the Government Printing Office does. The copies of the *National Accounts* that these companies sell are usually identical to those sold by the government, except they have different covers. How can these companies sell the same book for a lower price than the government and still cover their costs?

2.6 Suppose Salma operates her pizza restaurant in a building she owns in the center of the city of Doha.

Similar buildings in the neighborhood rent for US$4,000 per month. Salma is considering selling her building and renting space in the suburbs for US$3,000 per month. Salma decides not to make the move. She reasons, "I would like to have a restaurant in the suburbs, but I pay no rent for my restaurant now, and I don't want to see my costs rise by US$3,000 per month." What do you think of Salma's reasoning?

2.7 When the DuPont chemical company first attempted to enter the paint business, it was not successful. According to a company report, in one year it "lost nearly US$500,000 in actual cash in addition to an expected return on investment of nearly US$500,000, which made a total loss of income to the company of nearly a million." Why did this report include as part of the company's loss the amount it had expected to earn—but didn't—on its investment in manufacturing paint?

Source: Alfred D. Chandler, Jr., Thomas K. McCraw, and Richard Tedlow, *Management Past and Present*, Cincinnati: South-Western, 2000, pp. 3–92.

2.8 An account of the life of Benjamin Franklin, one of the Founding Fathers of the United States, notes that he started his career as a printer and publisher of the newspaper the *Pennsylvania Gazette*. He also opened a store where he sold stationery, books, and food. According to this account, "He could without expense apprise the public of items on hand by advertisements in his *Gazette*." Is the author correct that Franklin did not incur a cost when he used space in his newspaper to run advertisements for his store? Briefly explain.

Source: Richard Tedlow, "Benjamin Franklin and the Definition of American Values," in Alfred D. Chandler, Jr., Thomas K. McCaw, and Richard S. Tedlow, *Management Past and Present: A Casebook on the History of American Business*, Cincinnati: South-Western College Publishing, 2000.

7.3 LEARNING OBJECTIVE   Understand the relationship between the marginal product of labor and the average product of labor, **pages 227–231.**

Review Questions

3.1 Draw a graph showing the usual relationship between the marginal product of labor and the average product of labor. Why do the marginal product of labor and the average product of labor have the shapes you drew?

3.2 What is the law of diminishing returns? Does it apply in the long run?

Problems and Applications

3.3 Fill in the missing values in the following table.

QUANTITY OF WORKERS	TOTAL OUTPUT	MARGINAL PRODUCT OF LABOR	AVERAGE PRODUCT OF LABOR
0	0		
1	400		
2	900		
3	1,500		
4	1,900		
5	2,200		
6	2,400		
7	2,300		

3.4 Use the numbers from problem 3.3 to draw one graph showing how total output increases with the quantity of workers hired and a second graph showing the marginal product of labor and the average product of labor.

3.5 A student looks at the data in Table 7-3 on page 228 and draws this conclusion: "The marginal product of labor is increasing for the first two workers hired, and then it declines for the next four workers. I guess each of the first two workers must have been hard workers. Then Salma must have had to settle for increasingly poor workers." Do you agree with the student's analysis? Briefly explain.

3.6 (Related to the *Making the Connection* on page 230) Briefly explain whether you agree or disagree with the following argument: Adam Smith's idea of the gains to firms from the division of labor makes a lot of sense when the good being manufactured is something complex like automobiles or computers, but it doesn't apply in the manufacturing of less complex goods or in other sectors of the economy, such as retail sales.

3.7 Sally looks at her college transcript and says to Samy, "How is this possible? My grade point average for this semester's courses is higher than my grade point average for last semester's courses, but my cumulative grade point average still went down from last semester to this semester." Explain to Sally how this is possible.

3.8 Is it possible for a firm to experience a technological change that would increase the marginal product of labor while leaving the average product of labor unchanged? Explain.

7.4 LEARNING OBJECTIVE Explain and illustrate the relationship between marginal cost and average total cost, pages 232–234.

Review Questions

4.1 If the marginal product of labor is rising, is the marginal cost of production rising or falling? Briefly explain.

4.2 Explain why the marginal cost curve intersects the average total cost curve at the level of output where average total cost is at a minimum.

Problems and Applications

4.3 Is it possible for average total cost to be decreasing over a range of output where marginal cost is increasing? Briefly explain.

4.4 Suppose a firm has no fixed costs, so all of its costs are variable, even in the short run.
   a. If the firm's marginal costs are continually increasing (that is, marginal cost is increasing from the first unit of output produced) will the firm's average total cost curve have a U shape?
   b. If the firm's marginal costs are US$5 at every level of output, what shape will the firm's average total cost have?

4.5 (Related to *Solved Problem 7-4* on page 233) Is Salma right or wrong when she says the following: "Currently, I am producing 20,000 pizzas per month at a total cost of US$750.00. If I produce 20,001 pizzas, my total cost will rise to US$750.02.

Therefore, my marginal cost of producing pizzas must be increasing." Illustrate your answer with a graph.

4.6 (Related to *Solved Problem 7-4* on page 233) The following problem is somewhat advanced. Using symbols, we can write that the marginal product of labor is equal to $\Delta Q/\Delta L$. Marginal cost is equal to $\Delta TC/\Delta Q$. Because fixed costs by definition don't change, marginal cost is also equal to $\Delta VC/\Delta Q$. If Salma's only variable cost is labor cost, then her variable cost is just the wage multiplied by the quantity of workers hired, or wL.
   a. If the wage Salma pays is constant, then what is ΔVC in terms of w and L?
   b. Use your answer to question (a) and the expressions given above for the marginal product of labor and the marginal cost of output to find an expression for marginal cost, $\Delta TC/\Delta Q$, in terms of the wage, w, and the marginal product of labor, $\Delta Q/\Delta L$.
   c. Use your answer to question (b) to determine Salma's marginal cost of producing pizzas if the wage is US$750 per week and the marginal product of labor is 150. If the wage falls to US$600 per week and the marginal product of labor is unchanged, what happens to Salma's marginal cost? If the wage is unchanged at US$750 per week and the marginal product rises to 250, what happens to Salma's marginal cost?

7.5 LEARNING OBJECTIVE Graph average total cost, average variable cost, average fixed cost, and marginal cost, **pages 234–236.**

Review Questions

5.1 As the level of output increases, what happens to the value of average fixed cost?

5.2 As the level of output increases, what happens to the difference between the value of average total cost and average variable cost?

Problems and Applications

5.3 Suppose the total cost of producing 10,000 tennis balls is US$30,000, and the fixed cost is US$10,000.
 a. What is the variable cost?
 b. When output is 10,000, what are the average variable cost and the average fixed cost?
 c. Assuming that the cost curves have the usual shape, is the dollar difference between the average total cost and the average variable cost greater when the output is 10,000 tennis balls or when the output is 30,000 tennis balls? Explain.

5.4 One description of the costs of operating a railroad makes the following observation: "The fixed… expenses which attach to the operation of railroads… are in the nature of a tax upon the business of the road; the smaller the [amount of] business, the larger the tax." Briefly explain why fixed costs are like a tax. In what sense is this tax smaller when the amount of business is larger?
 Source: Alfred D. Chandler, Jr., Thomas K. McCraw, and Richard Tedlow, *Management Past and Present*, Cincinnati: South-Western, 2000, pp. 2–27.

5.5 In the ancient world, a book could be produced either on a scroll or as a codex, which was made of folded sheets glued together, something like a modern book. One scholar has estimated the following variable costs (in Greek drachmas) of the two methods:

	SCROLL	CODEX
Cost of writing (wage of a scribe)	11.33 drachmas	11.33 drachmas
Cost of paper	16.50 drachmas	9.25 drachmas

Another scholar points out that a significant fixed cost was involved in producing a codex:

> In order to copy a codex…the amount of text and the layout of each page had to be carefully calculated in advance to determine the exact number of sheets… needed. No doubt, this is more time-consuming and calls for more experimentation than the production of a scroll would. But for the next copy, these calculations would be used again.

 a. Suppose that the fixed cost of preparing a codex was 58 drachmas and that there was no similar fixed cost for a scroll. Would an ancient book publisher who intended to sell 5 copies of a book be likely to publish it as a scroll or as a codex? What if he intended to sell 10 copies? Briefly explain.
 b. Although most books were published as scrolls in the first century A.D., by the third century, most were published as codices. Considering only the factors mentioned in this problem, explain why this change may have taken place.

Sources: T. C. Skeat, "The Length of the Standard Papyrus Roll and the Cost-Advantage of the Codex," *Zeitschrift fur Papyrologie and Epigraphik*, 1982, p. 175; and David Trobisch, *The First Edition of the New Testament*, New York: Oxford University Press, 2000, p. 73.

5.6 Use the information in the following graph to find the values for the following at an output level of 1,000.
 a. Marginal cost
 b. Total cost
 c. Variable cost
 d. Fixed cost

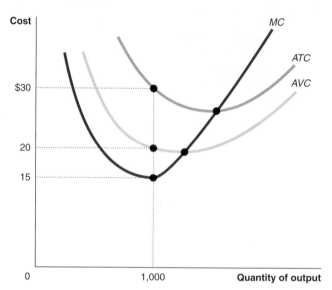

5.7 List the errors in the following graph. Carefully explain why the curves drawn this way are wrong. In other words, why can't these curves be as they are shown in the graph?

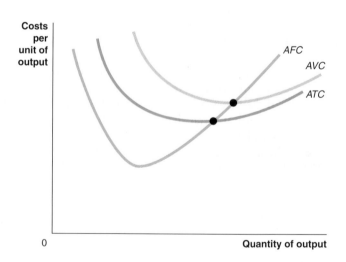

5.8 Explain how the listed events (a–d) would affect the following at Ford Motor Company:
 i. Marginal cost
 ii. Average variable cost
 iii. Average fixed cost
 iv. Average total cost

a. Ford signs a new contract with the United Automobile Workers union that requires the company to pay higher wages.

b. The federal government starts to levy a US$1,500-per-vehicle tax on sport utility vehicles.

c. Ford decides to give its senior executives a one-time US$100,000 bonus.

d. Ford decides to increase the amount it spends on designing new car models.

7.6 LEARNING OBJECTIVE   Understand how firms use the long-run average cost curve in their planning,

pages 236–240.

Review Questions

6.1 What is the difference between total cost and variable cost in the long run?

6.2 What is minimum efficient scale? What is likely to happen in the long run to firms that do not reach minimum efficient scale?

6.3 What are economies of scale? What are diseconomies of scale? What is the main reason that firms eventually encounter diseconomies of scale as they keep increasing the size of their store or factory?

Problems and Applications

6.4 **(Related to *Solved Problem 7-6* on page 238)** Suppose that Salma has to choose between building a smaller restaurant and a larger restaurant. In the following graph, the relationship between costs and output for the smaller restaurant is represented by the curve ATC_1, and the relationship between costs and output for the larger restaurant is represented by the curve ATC_2.

a. If Salma expects to produce 5,100 pizzas per week, should she build a smaller restaurant or a larger restaurant? Briefly explain.

b. If Salma expects to produce 6,000 pizzas per week, should she build a smaller restaurant or a larger restaurant? Briefly explain.

c. A student asks, "If the average cost of producing pizzas is lower in the larger restaurant when Salma produces 7,500 pizzas per week, why isn't it also lower when Salma produces 5,200 pizzas per week?" Give a brief answer to the student's question.

6.5 **(Related to *Solved Problem 7-6* on page 238)** Consider the following description of U.S. manufacturing in the late nineteenth century:

> When…Standard Oil…reorganized its refinery capacity in 1883 and concentrated almost two-fifths of the nation's refinery production in three huge refineries, the unit cost dropped from 1.5 cents a gallon to 0.5 cents. A comparable concentration of two-fifths of the nation's output of textiles or shoes in three plants would have been impossible, and in any case would have brought huge diseconomies of scale and consequently higher prices.

a. Use this information to draw a long-run average cost curve for an oil-refining firm and a long-run average cost curve for a firm manufacturing shoes.

b. Is it likely that there were more oil refineries or more shoe factories in the United States in the late nineteenth century? Briefly explain.

c. Why would concentrating two-fifths of total shoe output in three factories have led to higher shoe prices?

Source: Alfred D. Chandler, Jr., Thomas K. McCraw, and Richard Tedlow, *Management Past and Present*, Cincinnati: South-Western, 2000, pp. 4–53.

6.6 **(Related to *Solved Problem 7-6* on page 238)** The company eToys sold toys on the Internet. In 1999, the total value of the company was about US$7.7 billion, but by early 2001, the company was in deep financial trouble, and it eventually closed. One of the company's key mistakes was the decision in 2000 to build a large distribution center from which it would ship toys throughout the United States. The following description of this decision appeared in an article in the *Wall Street Journal*:

> [eToys built] a giant automated distribution center in Virginia…. Although many analysts agreed that the costly move was a sound decision for the long run… [the] decision meant eToys needed to generate much higher sales to justify its costs…. Despite a spiffy TV ad campaign and an expanded line of goods, there weren't enough customers.

What does the author mean when she says that eToys "needed to generate much higher sales to justify its

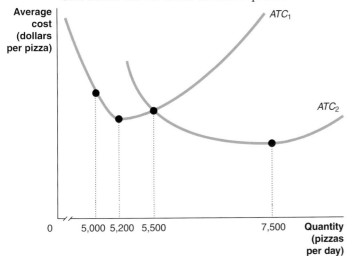

Average cost (dollars per pizza)

ATC_1

ATC_2

0   5,000 5,200 5,500   7,500   **Quantity (pizzas per day)**

costs"? Use a graph like Figure 7-6 to illustrate your answer.

Source: Lisa Bannon, "The eToys Saga: Costs Kept Rising but Sales Slowed," *Wall Street Journal*, January 22, 2001.

6.7 **(Related to *Solved Problem 7-6* on page 238)** In 2003, Time Warner and the Walt Disney Company discussed merging their news operations. Time Warner owns the Cable News Network (CNN), and Disney owns ABC News. After analyzing the situation, the companies decided that a combined news operation would have higher average costs than either CNN or ABC News had separately. Use a long-run average cost curve graph to illustrate why the companies did not merge their news operations.

Source: Martin Peers and Joe Flint, "AOL Calls Off CNN–ABC Deal, Seeing Operating Difficulties," *Wall Street Journal*, February 14, 2003.

6.8 **(Related to the *Making the Connection* on page 239)** Suppose that GB Auto Ghabbour of Egypt experienced increasing returns to scale, no matter how large an automobile factory they built. Discuss what the implications of this would have been for the automobile industry.

6.9 One scholar has made the following comment on the publishing industry: "If publishers were able to determine exactly what sells a book, they all would feature fewer titles and produce them in larger numbers." What must be true about the costs of publishing books for this statement to be correct? Briefly explain.

Source: David Trobisch, *The First Edition of the New Testament*, New York: Oxford University Press, 2000, p. 75.

6.10 Explain whether you agree or disagree with the following statement: "Henry Ford expected to be able to produce cars at a lower average cost at his River Rouge plant. Unfortunately, because of diminishing returns, his costs were actually higher."

6.11 **(Related to the *Chapter Opener* on page 220)** Review the discussion at the beginning of the chapter of Akio Morita selling transistor radios in the United States. Suppose that Morita became convinced that Sony would be able to sell more than 75,000 transistor radios each year in the United States. What steps would he have taken?

6.12 Michael Korda was for many years editor-in-chief at the Simon & Schuster book publishing company. He has described how during the 1980s many publishing companies merged together to form larger firms. He claims that publishers hoped to take advantage of economies of scale. But, he concludes, "sheer size did not make publishing necessarily more profitable, and most of these big publishing monoliths would continue to disappoint their corporate owners in terms of earnings." On the basis of this information, draw a long-run average cost curve for a publishing firm that reflects the economies of scale expected to result from the mergers. Draw another long-run average cost curve that reflects the actual results experienced by the new larger publishing firms.

Source: Michael Korda, *Making the List: A Cultural History of the American Bestseller, 1900–1999*, New York: Barnes & Noble Books, 2001, p. 166.

Appendix

Using Isoquants and Isocosts to Understand Production and Cost

LEARNING OBJECTIVE

Use isoquants and isocost lines to understand production and cost.

Isoquants

In this chapter, we studied the important relationship between a firm's level of production and its costs. In this appendix, we will look more closely at how firms choose the combination of inputs to produce a given level of output. Firms usually have a choice of how they will produce their output. For example, Salma is able to produce 5,000 pizzas per week using 10 workers and 2 ovens or using 6 workers and 3 ovens. We will see that firms search for the *cost-minimizing* combination of inputs that will allow them to produce a given level of output. The cost-minimizing combination of inputs depends on two factors: technology—which determines how much output a firm receives from employing a given quantity of inputs—and input prices—which determine the total cost of each combination of inputs.

An Isoquant Graph

We begin by graphing the levels of output that Salma can produce using different combinations of two inputs: labor—the quantity of workers she hires per week—and capital—the quantity of ovens she uses per week. In reality, of course, Salma uses more than just these two inputs to produce pizzas, but nothing important would change if we expanded the discussion to include many inputs instead of just two. Figure 7A-1 measures capital along the vertical axis and labor along the horizontal axis. The curves in the graph are **isoquants**, which show all the combinations of two inputs, in this case capital and labor, that will produce the same level of output.

Isoquant A curve that shows all the combinations of two inputs, such as capital and labor, that will produce the same level of output.

The isoquant labeled $Q = 5,000$ shows all the combinations of workers and ovens that enable Salma to produce that quantity of pizzas per week. For example, at point A, she produces 5,000 pizzas using 6 workers and 3 ovens, and at point B, she produces the same output using 10 workers and 2 ovens. With more workers and ovens, she can move to a higher isoquant. For example, with 12 workers and 4 ovens, she can produce at point C on the isoquant $Q = 10,000$. With even more workers and ovens, she could move to the isoquant $Q = 13,000$. The higher the isoquant—that is, the further to the upper right on the graph—the more output the firm produces. Although we have shown only three isoquants in this graph, there are, in fact, an infinite number of isoquants—one for every level of output.

The Slope of an Isoquant

Remember that the slope of a curve is the ratio of the change in the variable on the vertical axis to the change in the variable on the horizontal axis. Along an isoquant, the slope

Figure 7A-1

Isoquants show all the combinations of two inputs, in this case capital and labor, that will produce the same level of output. For example, the isoquant labeled $Q = 5,000$ shows all the combinations of ovens and workers that enable Salma to produce that quantity of pizzas per week. At point A, she produces 5,000 pizzas using 3 ovens and 6 workers, and at point B, she produces the same output using 2 ovens and 10 workers. With more ovens and workers, she can move to a higher isoquant. For example, with 4 ovens and 12 workers, she can produce at point C on the isoquant $Q = 10,000$. With even more ovens and workers, she could move to the isoquant $Q = 13,000$.

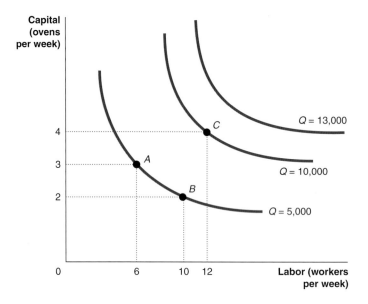

Marginal rate of technical substitution *(MRTS)* The slope of an isoquant, or the rate at which a firm is able to substitute one input for another while keeping the level of output constant.

tells us the rate at which a firm is able to substitute one input for another while keeping the level of output constant. The slope of an isoquant is called the **marginal rate of technical substitution (*MRTS*)**.

We expect that the *MRTS* will change as we move down an isoquant. In Figure 7A-1, at a point like *A* on isoquant $Q = 5,000$, the isoquant is relatively steep. As we move down the curve, it becomes less steep at a point like *B*. This shape is the usual one for isoquants: they are bowed in, or convex. The reason isoquants have this shape is that as we move down the curve, we continue to substitute labor for capital. As the firm produces the same quantity of output using less capital, the additional labor it needs increases because of diminishing returns. Remember from the chapter that, as a consequence of diminishing returns, for a given decline in capital, increasing amounts of labor are necessary to produce the same level of output. Because the *MRTS* is equal to the change in capital divided by the change in labor, it will become smaller (in absolute value) as we move down an isoquant.

Isocost Lines

Any firm wants to produce a given quantity of output at the lowest possible cost. We can show the relationship between the quantity of inputs used and the firm's total cost by using an *isocost* line. An **isocost line** shows all the combinations of two inputs, such as capital and labor, that have the same total cost.

Isocost line All the combinations of two inputs, such as capital and labor, that have the same total cost.

Graphing the Isocost Line

Suppose Salma has US$6,000 per week to spend on capital and labor. Suppose, to simplify the analysis, that Salma can rent pizza ovens by the week. The table in Figure 7A-2 shows the combinations of capital and labor available to her if the rental price of ovens is US$1,000 per week and the wage rate is US$500 per week. The graph uses the data in the table to construct an isocost line. The isocost line intersects the vertical axis at the maximum number of ovens Salma can rent per week, which is shown by point *A*. The line intersects the horizontal axis at the maximum number of workers Salma can hire per week, which is point *G*. As Salma moves down the isocost line from point *A*, she gives up renting 1 oven for every 2 workers she hires. Any combination of inputs along the line or inside the line can be purchased with US$6,000. Any combination that lies outside the line cannot be purchased because it would have a total cost to Salma of more than US$6,000.

Combinations of Workers and Ovens with a Total Cost of $6,000			
Point	Ovens	Workers	Total Cost
A	6	0	(6 x $1,000) + (0 x $500) = $6,000
B	5	2	(5 x $1,000) + (2 x $500) = 6,000
C	4	4	(4 x $1,000) + (4 x $500) = 6,000
D	3	6	(3 x $1,000) + (6 x $500) = 6,000
E	2	8	(2 x $1,000) + (8 x $500) = 6,000
F	1	10	(1 x $1,000) + (10 x $500) = 6,000
G	0	12	(0 x $1,000) + (12 x $500) = 6,000

Figure 7A-2

An Isocost Line

The isocost line shows the combinations of inputs with a total cost of US$6,000. The rental price of ovens is US$1,000 per week, so if Salma spends the whole US$6,000 on ovens, she can rent 6 ovens (point A). The wage rate is US$500 per week, so if Salma spends the whole US$6,000 on workers, she can hire 12 workers. As she moves down the isocost line, she gives up renting 1 oven for every 2 workers she hires. Any combinations of inputs along the line or inside the line can be purchased with US$6,000. Any combinations that lie outside the line cannot be purchased with US$6,000.

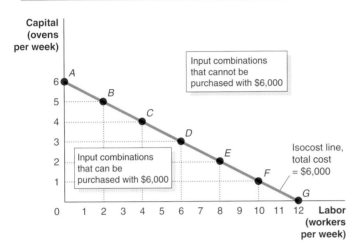

The Slope and Position of the Isocost Line

The slope of the isocost line is constant and equals the change in the quantity of ovens divided by the change in the quantity of workers. In this case, in moving from any point on the isocost line to any other point, the change in the quantity of ovens equals –1, and the change in the quantity of workers equals 2, so the slope equals –1/2. Notice that with a rental price of ovens of US$1,000 per week and a wage rate for labor of US$500 per week, the slope of the isocost line is equal to the ratio of the wage rate divided by the rental price of capital, multiplied by –1: –US$500/US$1,000 = –1/2. In fact, this result will always hold, whatever inputs are involved and whatever their prices may be: *The slope of the isocost line is equal to the ratio of the price of the input on the horizontal axis divided by the price of the input on the vertical axis, multiplied by –1.*

The position of the isocost line depends on the level of total cost. Higher levels of total cost shift the isocost line outward, and lower levels of total cost shift the isocost line inward. This can be seen in Figure 7A-3, which shows isocost lines for total costs of US$3,000, US$6,000, and US$9,000. We have shown only three isocost lines in the graph, but there are, in fact, an infinite number of isocost lines—one for every level of total cost.

Choosing the Cost-Minimizing Combination of Capital and Labor

Suppose Salma wants to produce 5,000 pizzas per week. Figure 7A-1 shows that there are many combinations of ovens and workers that will allow Salma to produce this level of output. There is only one combination of ovens and workers, however, that will allow her to produce 5,000 pizzas *at the lowest total cost*. Figure 7A-4 shows the isoquant Q = 5,000 along with three isocost lines. Point B is the lowest-cost combination of inputs shown in the graph, but this combination of 1 oven and 4 workers will produce fewer than the

Figure 7A-3

The Position of the Isocost Line

The position of the isocost line depends on the level of total cost. As total cost increases from US$3,000 to US$6,000 to US$9,000 per week, the isocost line shifts outward. For each isocost line shown, the rental price of ovens is US$1,000 per week, and the wage rate is US$500 per week.

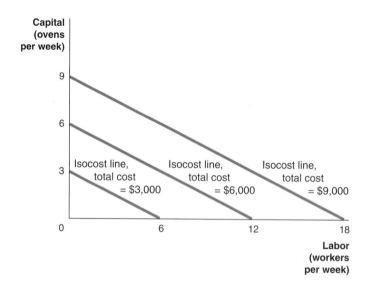

5,000 pizzas needed. Points *C* and *D* are combinations of ovens and workers that will produce 5,000 pizzas, but their total cost is US$9,000. The combination of 3 ovens and 6 workers at point *A* produces 5,000 pizzas at the lowest total cost of US$6,000.

The graph shows that moving to an isocost line with a total cost of less than US$6,000 would mean producing fewer than 5,000 pizzas. Being at any point along the isoquant $Q = 5,000$ other than point *A* would increase total cost above US$6,000. In fact, the combination of inputs at point *A* is the only one on isoquant $Q = 5,000$ that has a total cost of US$6,000. All other input combinations on this isoquant have higher total costs. Notice also that at point *A*, the isoquant and the isocost lines are tangent, so the slope of the isoquant is equal to the slope of the isocost line at that point.

Different Input Price Ratios Lead to Different Input Choices

Salma's cost-minimizing choice of 3 ovens and 6 workers is determined jointly by the technology available to her—as represented by her firm's isoquants—and by input prices—as represented by her firm's isocost lines. If the technology of making pizzas changes, perhaps because new ovens are developed, her isoquants will be affected, and

Figure 7A-4

Choosing Capital and Labor to Minimize Total Cost

Salma wants to produce 5,000 pizzas per week at the lowest total cost. Point *B* is the lowest-cost combination of inputs shown in the graph, but this combination of 1 oven and 4 workers will produce fewer than the 5,000 pizzas needed. Points *C* and *D* are combinations of ovens and workers that will produce 5,000 pizzas, but their total cost is US$9,000. The combination of 3 ovens and 6 workers at point *A* produces 5,000 pizzas at the lowest total cost of US$6,000.

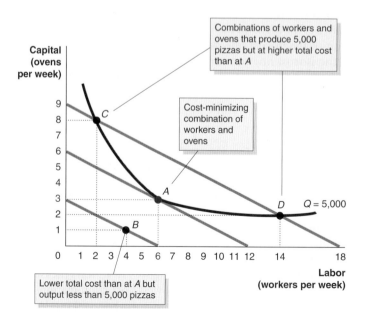

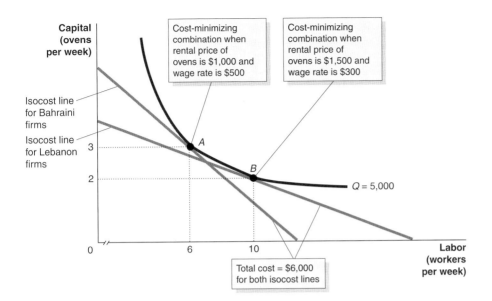

Figure 7A-5

Changing Input Prices Affects the Cost-Minimizing Input Choice

As the graph shows, the input combination at point *A*, which was optimal for Salma, is not optimal for a businessperson in Lebanon. Using the input combination at point *A* would cost businesspeople in Lebanon more than US$6,000. Instead, the Lebanese isocost line is tangent to the isoquant at point *B*, where the input combination is 2 ovens and 10 workers. Because ovens cost more in Lebanon but workers cost less, a Lebanese firm will use fewer ovens and more workers than a Bahraini firm, even if it has the same technology as the Bahraini firm.

her choice of inputs may change. If her isoquants remain unchanged but input prices change, then her choice of inputs may also change. This fact can explain why firms in different countries that face different input prices may produce the same good using different combinations of capital and labor, even though they have the same technology available.

For example, suppose that in Lebanon, pizza ovens are higher priced and labor is lower priced than in Bahrain. In our example, Salma—who operates her business in Bahrain—pays US$1,000 per week to rent pizza ovens and US$500 per week to hire workers. Suppose a businessperson in Lebanon must pay a price of US$1,500 per week to rent the identical pizza ovens but can hire Lebanese workers who are as productive as Bahraini workers at a wage of US$300 per week. Figure 7A-5 shows how the cost-minimizing input combination for the businessperson in Lebanon differs from Salma's.

Remember that the slope of the isocost line equals the wage rate divided by the rental price of capital, multiplied by –1. The slope of the isocost line that Salma and other Bahraini firms face is –US$500/US$1,000, or –1/2. Firms in Lebanon, however, face an isocost line with a slope of –US$300/US$1,500, or –1/5. As the graph shows, the input combination at point *A*, which was optimal for Salma, is not optimal for a firm in Lebanon. Using the input combination at point *A* would cost a firm in China more than US$6,000. Instead, the Lebanese isocost line is tangent to the isoquant at point *B*, where the input combination is 2 ovens and 10 workers. This result makes sense: because ovens cost more in Lebanon, but workers cost less, a Lebanese firm will use fewer ovens and more workers than a Bahraini firm, even if it has the same technology as the Bahraini firm.

Making the Connection | The Changing Input Mix in Walt Disney Film Animation

The inputs used to make feature-length animated films have changed dramatically in the past 15 years. Prior to the early 1990s, the Walt Disney Company dominated the market for animated films. Disney's films were produced using hundreds of animators drawing most of the film by hand. Each film would contain as many as 170,000 individual drawings. Then, two developments dramatically affected how animated films are produced.

(Continued)

First, in 1994, Disney had a huge hit with *The Lion King*, which cost only US$50 million but earned the company more than US$1 billion in profit. As a result of this success, Disney and other film studios began to produce more animated films, increasing the demand for animators and more than doubling their salaries. The second development came in 1995, when Pixar Animation Studios released the film *Toy Story*. This was the first successful feature-length film produced using computers, with no hand-drawn animation. In the following years, technological advance continued to reduce the cost of the computers and software necessary to produce an animated film.

As a result of these two developments, the price of capital—computers and software—fell relative to the price of labor—animators. As the figure shows, the change in the price of computers relative to animators changed the slope of the isocost line and resulted in film studios now producing animated films using many more computers and many fewer animators than in the early 1990s.

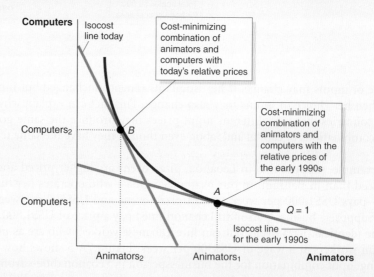

Based on Bruce Orwall, "Disney Delivers 'Lilo and Stitch' on Competition-Driven Budget," *Wall Street Journal*, June 18, 2002, p. A1.

Another Look at Cost Minimization

In Chapter 6, we saw that consumers maximize utility when they consume each good up to the point where the marginal utility per dollar spent is the same for every good. We can derive a very similar cost-minimization rule for firms. Remember that at the point of cost minimization, the isoquant and the isocost line are tangent, so they have the same slope. Therefore, *at the point of cost minimization, the marginal rate of technical substitution* (MRTS) *is equal to the wage rate divided by the rental price of capital.*

The slope of the isoquant tells us the rate at which a firm is able to substitute labor for capital, *given existing technology*. The slope of the isocost line tells us the rate at which a firm is able to substitute labor for capital, *given current input prices*. Only at the point of cost minimization are these two rates the same.

When we move from one point on an isoquant to another, we end up using more of one input and less of the other input, but the level of output remains the same. For example, as Salma moves down an isoquant, she uses fewer ovens and more workers but produces the same quantity of pizzas. In this chapter, we defined the *marginal product of labor* (MP_L) as the additional output produced by a firm as a result of hiring one more worker. Similarly, we can define the *marginal product of capital* (MP_K) as the additional output produced by a firm as a result of using one more machine. So, when Salma uses fewer ovens by moving down an isoquant, she loses output equal to:

$$-\text{Change in the quantity of ovens} \times MP_K$$

But she uses more workers, so she gains output equal to:

$$\text{Change in the quantity of workers} \times MP_L$$

We know that the gain in output from the additional workers is equal to the loss from the smaller quantity of ovens because total output remains the same along an isoquant. Therefore, we can write:

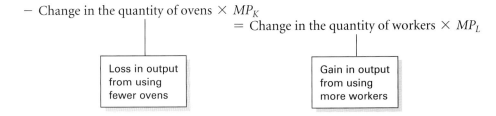

$$-\text{Change in the quantity of ovens} \times MP_K$$
$$= \text{Change in the quantity of workers} \times MP_L$$

Loss in output from using fewer ovens

Gain in output from using more workers

If we rearrange terms, we have the following:

$$\frac{-\text{Change in the quantity of ovens}}{\text{Change in the quantity of workers}} = \frac{MP_L}{MP_K}$$

Because the

$$\frac{-\text{Change in the quantity of ovens}}{\text{Change in the quantity of workers}}$$

is the slope of the isoquant, or the marginal rate of technical substitution (*MRTS*), we can write:

$$\frac{-\text{Change in the quantity of ovens}}{\text{Change in the quantity of workers}} = MRTS = \frac{MP_L}{MP_K}$$

The slope of the isocost line equals the wage rate (w) divided by the rental price of capital (r). At the point of cost minimization, the slope of the isoquant is equal to the slope of the isocost line. Therefore:

$$\frac{MP_L}{MP_K} = \frac{w}{r}$$

We can rewrite this to show that at the point of cost minimization:

$$\frac{MP_L}{w} = \frac{MP_K}{r}$$

This last expression tells us that to minimize cost, a firm should hire inputs up to the point where the last dollar spent on each input results in the same increase in output. If this equality did not hold, a firm could lower its costs by using more of one input and less of the other. For example, if the left-hand side of the equation were greater than the right-hand side, a firm could rent fewer ovens, hire more workers, and produce the same output at lower cost.

Solved Problem | 7A-1

Determining the Optimal Combination of Inputs

Consider the information in the following table for Salma's restaurant:

Marginal product of capital	3,000 pizzas
Marginal product of labor	1,200 pizzas
Wage rate	US$300 per week
Rental price of ovens	US$600 per week

Briefly explain whether Salma is minimizing costs. If she is not minimizing costs, explain whether she should rent more ovens and hire fewer workers or rent fewer ovens and hire more workers.

SOLVING THE PROBLEM:

Step 1: **Review the chapter material.** This problem is about determining the optimal choice of inputs by comparing the ratios of the marginal products of inputs to their prices, so you may want to review the section "Another Look at Cost Minimization," which begins on page 256.

Step 2: **Compute the ratios of marginal product to input price to determine whether Salma is minimizing costs.** If Salma is minimizing costs, the following relationship should hold:

$$\frac{MP_L}{w} = \frac{MP_K}{r}$$

In this case, we have:

$$MP_L = 1,200$$
$$MP_K = 3,000$$
$$w = \$300$$
$$r = \$600$$

So:

$$\frac{MP_L}{w} = \frac{1,200}{\$300} = 4 \text{ pizzas per dollar}$$

$$\text{and } \frac{MP_K}{r} = \frac{3,000}{\$600} = 5 \text{ pizzas per dollar}$$

Because the two ratios are not equal, Salma is not minimizing cost.

Step 3: **Determine how Salma should change the mix of inputs she uses.** Salma produces more pizzas per dollar from the last oven than from the last worker. This indicates that she has too many workers and too few ovens. Therefore, to minimize cost, Salma should use more ovens and hire fewer workers.

YOUR TURN: For more practice, do related problems 7A.6 and 7A.7 on page 260 at the end of this appendix.

>> End Solved Problem 7A-1

The Expansion Path

We can use isoquants and isocost lines to examine what happens as a firm expands its level of output. Figure 7A-6 shows three isoquants for a firm that produces bookcases. The isocost lines are drawn, assuming that the machines used in producing bookcases

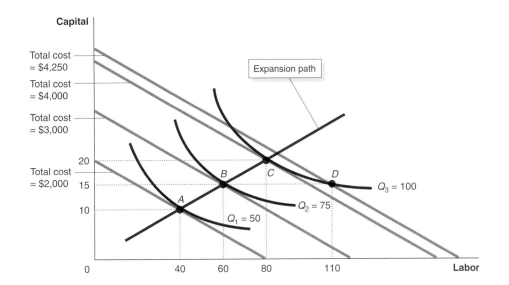

Figure 7A-6

The Expansion Path

The tangency points A, B, and C lie along the firm's expansion path, which is a curve that shows the cost-minimizing combination of inputs for every level of output. In the short run, when the quantity of machines is fixed, the firm can expand output from 75 bookcases per day to 100 bookcases per day at the lowest cost only by moving from point B to point D and increasing the number of workers from 80 to 110. In the long run, when it can increase the quantity of machines it uses, the firm can move from point D to point C, thereby reducing its total costs of producing 100 bookcases per day from US$4,250 to US$4,000.

can be rented for US$100 per day and the wage rate is US$25 per day. The point where each isoquant is tangent to an isocost line determines the cost-minimizing combination of capital and labor for producing that level of output. For example, 10 machines and 40 workers is the cost-minimizing combination of inputs for producing 50 bookcases per day. The cost-minimizing points A, B, and C lie along the firm's **expansion path**, which is a curve that shows the cost-minimizing combination of inputs for every level of output.

An important point to note is that the expansion path represents the least-cost combination of inputs to produce a given level of output *in the long run*, when the firm is able to vary the levels of all of its inputs. We know, though, that in the short run, at least one input is fixed. We can use Figure 7A-6 to show that as the firm expands in the short run, its costs will be higher than in the long run. For example, suppose that the firm is currently at point B, using 15 machines and 60 workers to produce 75 bookcases per day. The firm wants to expand its output to 100 bookcases per day, but in the short run, it is unable to increase the quantity of machines it uses. Therefore, to expand output, it must hire more workers. The figure shows that in the short run, to produce 100 bookcases per day using 15 machines, the lowest costs it can attain are at point D, where it employs 110 workers. With a rental price of machines of US$100 per day and a wage rate of US$25 per day, in the short run, the firm will have total costs of US$4,250 to produce 100 bookcases per day. In the long run, though, the firm can increase the number of machines it uses from 15 to 20 and reduce the number of workers from 110 to 80. This change allows it to move from point D to point C on its expansion path and to lower its total costs of producing 100 bookcases per day from US$4,250 to US$4,000. The firm's minimum total costs of production are lower in the long run than in the short run.

Expansion path A curve that shows a firm's cost-minimizing combination of inputs for every level of output.

Key Terms

Review, Problems and Applications

LEARNING OBJECTIVE 7A Use isoquants and isocost lines to understand production and cost, **pages 251–259.**

Review Questions

7A.1 What is an isoquant? What is the slope of an isoquant?

7A.2 What is an isocost line? What is the slope of an isocost line?

7A.3 How do firms choose the optimal combination of inputs?

Problems and Applications

7A.4 Draw an isoquant–isocost line graph to illustrate the following situation: Salma can rent pizza ovens for US$400 per week and hire workers for US$200 per week. She is currently using 5 ovens and 10 workers to produce 20,000 pizzas per week and has total costs of US$4,000. Make sure to label your graph showing the cost-minimizing input combination and the maximum quantity of labor and capital she can use with total costs of US$4,000.

7A.5 Use the following graph to answer the questions.

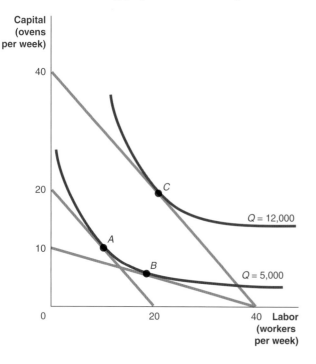

a. If the wage rate and the rental price of machines are both US$100 and total cost is US$2,000, is the cost-minimizing point A, B, or C? Briefly explain.

b. If the wage rate is US$25, the rental price of machines is US$100, and total cost is US$1,000, is the cost-minimizing point A, B, or C? Briefly explain.

c. If the wage rate and the rental price of machines are both US$100 and total cost is US$4,000, is the cost-minimizing point A, B, or C? Briefly explain.

7A.6 (Related to *Solved Problem 7A-1* on page 258) Consider the information in the following table for Salma's restaurant.

Marginal product of capital	4,000
Marginal product of labor	100
Wage rate	$10
Rental price of pizza ovens	$500

Briefly explain whether Salma is minimizing costs. If she is not minimizing costs, explain whether she should rent more ovens and hire fewer workers or rent fewer ovens and hire more workers.

7A.7 (Related to *Solved Problem 7A-1* on page 258) Draw an isoquant–isocost line graph to illustrate the following situation: Salma can rent pizza ovens for US$200 per week and hire workers for US$100 per week. Currently, she is using 5 ovens and 10 workers to produce 20,000 pizzas per week and has total costs of US$2,000. Salma's marginal rate of technical substitution (*MRTS*) equals –1. Explain why this means that she's not minimizing costs and what she could do to minimize costs.

7A.8 Draw an isoquant–isocost line graph to illustrate the following situation and the change that occurs: Salma can rent pizza ovens for US$2,000 per week and hire workers for US$1,000 per week. Currently, she is using 5 ovens and 10 workers to produce 20,000 pizzas per week and has total costs of US$20,000. Then Salma reorganizes the way things are done in her business and achieves positive technological change.

7A.9 Use the following graph to answer the following questions about Salma's isoquant curve.

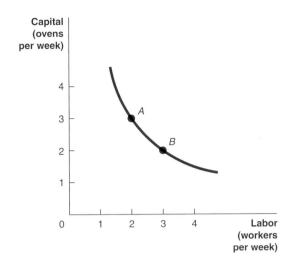

a. Which combination of inputs yields more output: combination *A* (3 ovens and 2 workers) or combination *B* (2 ovens and 3 workers)?

b. What will determine whether Salma selects *A*, *B*, or some other point along this isoquant curve?

c. Is the marginal rate of technical substitution (*MRTS*) greater at point *A* or point *B*?

7A.10 Draw an isoquant–isocost line graph to illustrate the following situation: Salma can rent pizza ovens for US$2,000 per week and hire workers for US$1,000 per week. She can minimize the cost of producing 20,000 pizzas per week by using 5 ovens and 10 workers, at a total cost of US$20,000. She can minimize the cost of producing 45,000 pizzas per week by using 10 ovens and 20 workers, at a total cost of US$40,000. And she can minimize the cost of producing 60,000 pizzas per week by using 15 ovens and 30 workers, at a total cost of US$60,000. Now draw Salma's long-run average cost curve and discuss its economies and diseconomies of scale.

7A.11 In Egypt, a garden of oranges is picked using 20 workers, ladders, and baskets. In France, a garden of oranges is picked using 1 worker and a machine that shakes the oranges off the trees and scoops up the fallen oranges. Using an isoquant–isocost line graph, illustrate why these two different methods are used to pick the same number of oranges per day in these two locations.

7A.12 Salma is minimizing the costs of producing pizzas. The rental price of one of her ovens is US$2,000 per week, and the wage rate is US$600 per week. The marginal product of capital in her business is 12,000 pizzas. What must be the marginal product of her workers?

≫ End Appendix Learning Objective

Market Structure and Firm Strategy

Chapter 8

Firms in Perfectly Competitive Markets

Perfect Competition in the Retail Market for Mobile Phones

How many shops in your city are selling mobile phones? How many of them existed 15 years ago (when mobile phones started to penetrate the Arab world)? Your estimated answer to the first question may well be much bigger than your answer to the second question. The main reason for this drastic increase in mobile phones shops is the large increase in the number of cellular phone subscribers in the Arab world. Let us see some examples. According to the World Development indicators, 2010, the percentage of mobile phone subscribers per 100 people rose from as low as 0.01–3 percent in most of the Arab countries in 1995, to as high as 210 percent in the United Arab Emirates, 190 percent in Bahrain, 110 percent in Kuwait, 150 percent in Saudi Arabia, and 77 percent in Egypt, in 2009. These percentages indicate that sales of mobile phone devices have also

grown dramatically during the same period. How did this increase in supply of mobile phones affect their prices? If you ask someone what they paid for a mobile phone they bought 15 years ago, which would have had very limited features compared with those available today, they'd tell you it cost them more than US$1,300. Nowadays, the latest and most impressive mobile phones, such as the iPhone 4, cost only US$500 to US$700. The secret word that largely explains this price reduction, alongside advances in technology and the outsourcing of mobile phone production to countries with low cost of labor, such as China, is: *competition*. In the 1990s, very few mobile phone shops could be found in one city, and those that did exist would only be selling two brands, Nokia and Motorola. At that time, the price of mobile phones, and also the sellers' profit was high. Now, with tens of mobile phone shops to be found in any single street of one city, such as King Fahd Street in the city of Khobar, Saudi Arabia, and with each selling dozens of brands and models, the price of a mobile phone

has become very *competitive*. Many entrepreneurs found great economic opportunities in selling mobile phones in the 1990s, but as more entrepreneurs enter the mobile market, fewer economic opportunities are found. In other words, economic opportunities are exhausted because the additional supply of mobile phones forced down prices and decreased the profit margin of existing sellers and, of course, new potential entrants. AN **INSIDE LOOK** on **page 292** discusses how a well-established industry might be endangered because of foreign competition.

What mobile phones sellers in the Arab world experienced is not unique to the telecommunication market. Throughout the economy, entrepreneurs are continually introducing new products, which—when successful—enable them to earn economic profits in the short run. But in the long run, competition among firms force prices to the level where they just cover the costs of production. This process of competition is at the heart of the market system and is the focus of this chapter.

LEARNING Objectives

After studying this chapter, you should be able to:

8.1 Define a **perfectly competitive market** and explain why a perfect competitor faces a horizontal demand curve, page 267.

8.2 Explain how a **firm maximizes profits** in a perfectly competitive market, page 269.

8.3 Use **graphs** to show a firm's **profit or loss**, page 273.

8.4 Explain why firms may **shut down temporarily**, page 278.

8.5 Explain how **entry** and **exit** ensure that perfectly competitive firms earn **zero economic profit** in the long run, page 281.

8.6 Explain how **perfect competition** leads to **economic efficiency**, page 287.

Economics in YOUR Life!

Are You an Entrepreneur?

Were you an entrepreneur during your high school years? Perhaps you didn't have your own store, but you may have worked as a babysitter, or perhaps as a cashier in a nearby supermarket. While you may not think of these jobs as being small businesses, that is exactly what they are. How did you decide what price to charge for your services? You may have wanted to charge US$25 per hour to babysit or to work as a cashier, but you probably charged much less. As you read the chapter, think about the competitive situation you faced as a teenage entrepreneur and try to determine why the prices received by most people who babysit and work at supermarkets are so low. You can check your answers against those we provide at the end of the chapter. **>> Continued on page 290**

S hops selling mobile phones are an example of a *perfectly competitive* market. Firms in perfectly competitive industries are unable to control the prices of the products they sell and are unable to earn an economic profit in the long run. There are two main reasons for this result: firms in these industries sell identical products, and it is easy for new firms to enter these industries. Studying how perfectly competitive industries operate is the best way to understand how markets answer the fundamental economic questions discussed in Chapter 1:

- What goods and services will be produced?
- How will the goods and services be produced?
- Who will receive the goods and services produced?

In fact, though, most industries are not perfectly competitive. In most industries, firms do *not* produce identical products, and in some industries, it may be difficult for new firms to enter. Although in some ways each industry is unique, industries share enough similarities that economists group them into four market structures. In particular, any industry has three key characteristics:

- The number of firms in the industry
- The similarity of the good or service produced by the firms in the industry
- The ease with which new firms can enter the industry.

Economists use these characteristics to classify industries into the four market structures listed in Table 8-1.

Many industries, including restaurants, hardware stores, and other retailers, have a large number of firms selling products that are differentiated, rather than identical, and fall into the category of *monopolistic competition*. Some industries, such as computers and automobiles, have only a few firms and are *oligopolies*. Finally, a few industries, such as the delivery of first-class mail by the Postal Service in some cities, have only one firm and are *monopolies*. After discussing perfect competition in this chapter, we will devote a chapter to each of these other market structures.

TABLE 8-1 | **The Four Market Structures**

CHARACTERISTIC	MARKET STRUCTURE			
	PERFECT COMPETITION	**MONOPOLISTIC COMPETITION**	**OLIGOPOLY**	**MONOPOLY**
Number of firms	Many	Many	Few	One
Type of product	Identical	Differentiated	Identical or differentiated	Unique
Ease of entry	High	High	Low	Entry blocked
Examples of industries	• Wheat • Apples	• Selling DVDs • Restaurants	• Manufacturing computers • Manufacturing automobiles	First-class mail delivery Tap water

8.1 | Define a perfectly competitive market and explain why a perfect competitor faces a horizontal demand curve.

Perfectly Competitive Markets

Why are firms in a **perfectly competitive market** unable to control the prices of the goods they sell, and why are the owners of these firms unable to earn economic profits in the long run? We can begin our analysis by listing the three conditions that make a market perfectly competitive:

1 There must be many buyers and many firms, all of whom are small relative to the market.

2 The products sold by all firms in the market must be identical.

3 There must be no barriers to new firms entering the market.

All three of these conditions hold in the mobile phone retail market in most of the Arab countries. No single consumer or seller of mobile phones buys or sells more than a tiny fraction of the total mobile phones sales. Mobile phones of a specific model sold in the retail market are identical in all shops (Nokia 5800 express music sold at *i2* mobile store is identical to that sold at any other mobile phone store), and there are no barriers to a new shop entering the mobile phones market. As we will see, it is the existence of many shops, all selling the same good, that keeps any single dealer from affecting the price of mobile phones.

Although the market for mobile phones meets the conditions for perfect competition, the markets for most goods and services do not. In particular, the second and third conditions are very restrictive. In most markets that have many buyers and sellers, firms do not sell identical products. For example, not all restaurant meals are the same, nor is all women's clothing the same. In Chapter 9, we will explore the common situation of monopolistic competition where many firms are selling similar but not identical products. In Chapters 10 and 11, we will analyze industries that are oligopolies or monopolies, where it is difficult for new firms to enter. In this chapter, we concentrate on perfectly competitive markets so we can use as a benchmark the situation in which firms are facing the maximum possible competition.

Perfectly competitive market
A market that meets the conditions of (1) many buyers and sellers, (2) all firms selling identical products, and (3) no barriers to new firms entering the market.

A Perfectly Competitive Firm Cannot Affect the Market Price

Prices in perfectly competitive markets are determined by the interaction of demand and supply. The actions of any single consumer or any single firm have no effect on the market price. Consumers and firms have to accept the market price if they want to buy and sell in a perfectly competitive market.

Because a firm in a perfectly competitive market is very small relative to the market and because it is selling exactly the same product as every other firm, it can sell as much as it wants without having to lower its price. But if a perfectly competitive firm tries to raise its price, it won't sell anything at all because consumers will switch to buying from the firm's competitors. Therefore, the firm will be a **price taker** and will have to charge the same price as every other firm in the market. Although we don't usually think of firms as being too small to affect the market price, consumers are often in the position of being price takers. For instance, suppose your local supermarket is selling bread for US\$1.50 per pack of bread. You can load up your shopping cart with 10 packs of bread, and the supermarket will gladly sell them all to you for US\$1.50 per pack. But if you go to the cashier and offer to buy the bread for US\$1.49 per pack, he or she will not sell it to you. As a buyer, you are too small relative to the bread market to have any effect on the equilibrium price. Whether you leave the supermarket and buy no bread or you buy 10 packs, you are unable to change the market price of bread by even 1 cent.

Price taker A buyer or seller that is unable to affect the market price.

Figure 8-1

A Perfectly Competitive Firm Faces a Horizontal Demand Curve

A firm in a perfectly competitive market is selling exactly the same product as many other firms. Therefore, it can sell as much as it wants at the current market price, but it cannot sell anything at all if it raises the price by even 1 cent. As a result, the demand curve for a perfectly competitive firm's output is a horizontal line. In the figure, whether the orange farmer sells 3,000 kilos per year or 7,500 kilos has no effect on the market price of US$4.

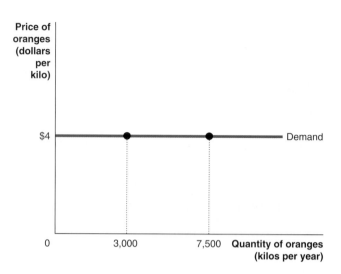

The situation you face as a bread buyer is the same one an orange farmer faces as an orange seller. Hundreds of farmers grow citrus product in Lebanon. The market price of oranges, for example, is determined not by any individual orange farmer but by the interaction in the orange market of all the buyers and all the sellers. If any *one* orange farmer has the best crop the farmer has ever had, or if any *one* orange farmer stops growing oranges altogether, the market price of oranges will not be affected *because the market supply curve for oranges will not shift by enough to change the equilibrium price by even 1 cent.*

The Demand Curve for the Output of a Perfectly Competitive Firm

Suppose Farmer Khouri grows oranges on a 250-acre farm in Maghdousheh, the orange blossom capital of Lebanon. Farmer Khouri is selling oranges in a perfectly competitive market, so he is a price taker. Because he can sell as many oranges as he chooses at the market price—but can't sell any oranges at all at a higher price—the demand curve for his oranges has an unusual shape: it is horizontal, as shown in Figure 8-1. With a horizontal demand curve, Farmer Khouri must accept the market price, which in this case is US$4. Whether Farmer Khouri sells 3,000 kilo per year or 7,500 has no effect on the market price.

The demand curve for Farmer Khouri's oranges is very different from the market demand curve for oranges. Panel (a) of Figure 8-2 shows the market for oranges. The demand curve in panel (a) is the *market demand curve for oranges* and has the normal downward slope we are familiar with from the market demand curves in Chapter 3. Panel (b) of Figure 8-2 shows the demand curve for Farmer Khouri's oranges, which is a horizontal line. By viewing these graphs side by side, you can see that the price Farmer Khouri receives for his oranges in panel (b) is determined by the interaction of all sellers and all buyers of oranges in the orange market in panel (a). Keep in mind, however, that the scales on the horizontal axes in the two panels are very different. In panel (a), the equilibrium quantity of oranges is 2 *billion* kilos. In panel (b), Farmer Khouri is producing only 7,500 kilos, or less than 0.0004 percent of market output. We need to use different scales in the two panels so we can display both of them on one page. Keep in mind the key point: Farmer Khouri's output of oranges is very small relative to the total market output.

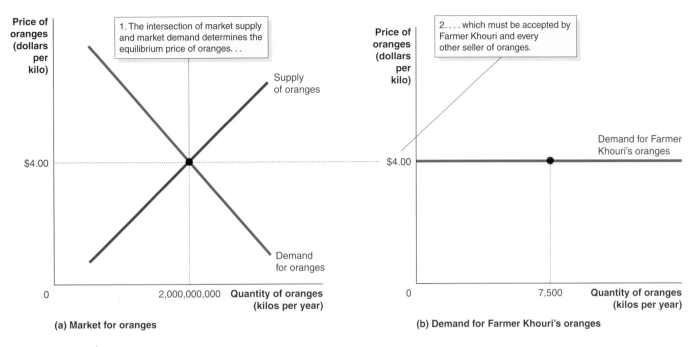

Figure 8-2 | The Market Demand for Oranges versus the Demand for One Farmer's Oranges

In a perfectly competitive market, price is determined by the intersection of market demand and market supply. In panel (a), the demand and supply curves for oranges intersect at a price of US$4 per kilo. An individual orange farmer like Farmer Khouri has no ability to affect the market price for oranges. Therefore, as panel (b) shows, the demand curve for Farmer Khouri's oranges is a horizontal line. To understand this figure, it is important to notice that the scales on the horizontal axes in the two panels are very different. In panel (a), the equilibrium quantity of oranges is 2 billion kilos, and in panel (b), Farmer Khouri is producing only 7,500 kilos of oranges.

8.2 | Explain how a firm maximizes profits in a perfectly competitive market.

How a Firm Maximizes Profit in a Perfectly Competitive Market

We have seen that Farmer Khouri cannot control the price of his oranges. In this situation, how does he decide how many oranges to produce? We assume that Farmer Khouri's objective is to maximize profits. This is a reasonable assumption for most firms, most of the time. Remember that **profit** is the difference between total revenue (*TR*) and total cost (*TC*):

Profit Total revenue minus total cost.

$$\text{Profit} = TR - TC$$

To maximize his profit, Farmer Khouri should produce the quantity of oranges where the difference between the total revenue he receives and his total cost is as large as possible.

Revenue for a Firm in a Perfectly Competitive Market

To understand how Farmer Khouri maximizes profits, let's first consider his revenue. To keep the numbers simple, we will assume that he owns a very small farm and produces at most 10 kilos of oranges per year. Table 8-2 shows the revenue Farmer Khouri will earn from selling various quantities of oranges if the market price for oranges is US$4.

TABLE 8-2

Farmer Khouri's Revenue from Orange Farming

NUMBER OF KILOS (Q)	MARKET PRICE (PER KILO) (P) IN US$	TOTAL REVENUE (TR) IN US$	AVERAGE REVENUE (AR) IN US$	MARGINAL REVENUE (MR) IN US$
0	4	0	—	—
1	4	4	4	4
2	4	8	4	4
3	4	12	4	4
4	4	16	4	4
5	4	20	4	4
6	4	24	4	4
7	4	28	4	4
8	4	32	4	4
9	4	36	4	4
10	4	40	4	4

Average revenue (AR) Total revenue divided by the quantity of the product sold.

The third column in Table 8-2 shows that Farmer Khouri's *total revenue* rises by US$4 for every additional kilo he sells because he can sell as many kilos as he wants at the market price of US$4 per kilo. The fourth and fifth columns in the table show Farmer Khouri's *average revenue* and *marginal revenue* from selling oranges. His **average revenue** (*AR*) is his total revenue divided by the quantity of kilos he sells. For example, if he sells 5 kilos for a total of US$20, his average revenue is US$20/5 = US$4. Notice that his average revenue is also equal to the market price of US$4. In fact, for any level of output, a firm's average revenue is always equal to the market price. One way to see this is to note that total revenue equals price times quantity ($TR = P - Q$), and average revenue equals total revenue divided by quantity ($AR = TR/Q$). So, $AR = TR/Q = (P - Q)/Q = P$.

Marginal revenue (MR) Change in total revenue from selling one more unit of a product.

Farmer Khouri's **marginal revenue** (*MR*) is the change in his total revenue from selling one more kilo:

$$\text{Marginal Revenue} = \frac{\text{Change in total revenue}}{\text{Change in quantity}} \quad \text{or } MR = \frac{\Delta TR}{\Delta Q}$$

Because for each additional kilo sold he always adds US$4 to his total revenue, his marginal revenue is US$4. Farmer Khouri's marginal revenue is US$4 per kilo because he is selling oranges in a perfectly competitive market and can sell as much as he wants at the market price. In fact, Farmer Khouri's marginal revenue and average revenue are both equal to the market price. This is an important point: *For a firm in a perfectly competitive market, price is equal to both average revenue and marginal revenue.*

Determining the Profit-Maximizing Level of Output

To determine how Farmer Khouri can maximize profit, we have to consider his costs as well as his revenue. An orange farmer has many costs, including seed, fertilizer, and the wages of farm workers. In Table 8-3, we bring together the revenue data from Table 8-1 with cost data for Farmer Khouri's farm. Recall from Chapter 6 that a firm's *marginal cost* is the increase in total cost resulting from producing another unit of output.

We calculate profit in the fourth column by subtracting total cost in the third column from total revenue in the second column. The fourth column shows that

QUANTITY (KILOS) (Q)	TOTAL REVENUE (TR) IN US$	TOTAL COST (TC) IN US$	PROFIT (TR–TC) IN US$	MARGINAL REVENUE (MR) IN US$	MARGINAL COST (MC) IN US$
0	0.00	1.00	1.00	—	—
1	4.00	4.00	0.00	4.00	3.00
2	8.00	6.00	2.00	4.00	2.00
3	12.00	7.50	4.50	4.00	1.50
4	16.00	9.50	6.50	4.00	2.00
5	20.00	12.00	8.00	4.00	2.50
6	24.00	15.00	9.00	4.00	3.00
7	28.00	19.50	8.50	4.00	4.50
8	32.00	25.50	6.50	4.00	6.00
9	36.00	32.50	3.50	4.00	7.00
10	40.00	40.50	–0.50	4.00	8.00

TABLE 8-3

Farmer Khouri's Profits from Orange Farming

as long as Farmer Khouri produces between 2 and 9 kilos of oranges, he will earn a profit. His maximum profit is US$9.00, which he will earn by producing 6 kilos of oranges. Because Farmer Khouri wants to maximize his profits, we would expect him to produce 6 kilos of oranges. Producing more than 6 kilos reduces his profit. For example, if he produces 7 kilos of oranges, his profit will decline from US$9.00 to US$8.50. The values for marginal cost given in the last column of the table help us understand why Farmer Khouri's profits will decline if he produces more than 6 kilos of oranges. After the sixth kilo of oranges, rising marginal cost causes Farmer Khouri's profits to fall.

In fact, comparing the marginal cost and marginal revenue at each level of output is an alternative method of calculating Farmer Khouri's profits. We illustrate the two methods of calculating profits in Figure 8-3. We show the total revenue and total cost approach in panel (a) and the marginal revenue and marginal cost approach in panel (b). Total revenue is a straight line on the graph in panel (a) because total revenue increases at a constant rate of US$4 for each additional kilo sold. Farmer Khouri's profits are maximized when the vertical distance between the line representing total revenue and the total cost curve is as large as possible. Just as we saw in Table 8-3, this occurs at an output of 6 kilos.

The last two columns of Table 8-3 provide information on the marginal revenue (MR) Farmer Khouri receives from selling another kilo of oranges and his marginal cost (MC) of producing another kilo of oranges. Panel (b) is a graph of Farmer Khouri's marginal revenue and marginal cost. Because marginal revenue is always equal to US$4, it is a horizontal line at the market price. We have already seen that the demand curve for a perfectly competitive firm is also a horizontal line at the market price. *Therefore, the marginal revenue curve for a perfectly competitive firm is the same as its demand curve.* Farmer Khouri's marginal cost of producing oranges first falls and then rises, following the usual pattern we discussed in Chapter 9.

We know from panel (a) that profit is at a maximum at 6 kilos of oranges. In panel (b), profit is also at a maximum at 6 kilos of oranges. To understand why profit is maximized at the level of output where marginal revenue equals marginal cost, remember a key economic principle that we discussed in Chapter 1: *Optimal decisions are made at the margin.* Firms use this principle to decide the quantity of a good to produce. For example, in deciding how many oranges to produce, Farmer Khouri needs to compare the marginal revenue he earns from selling another kilo of oranges with the marginal cost of producing that kilo. The difference between

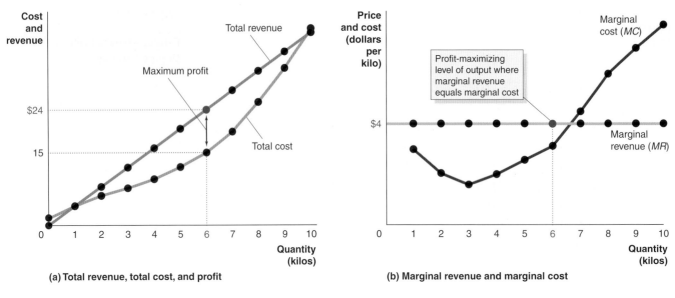

(a) Total revenue, total cost, and profit

(b) Marginal revenue and marginal cost

Figure 8-3 | The Profit-Maximizing Level of Output

In panel (a), Farmer Khouri maximizes his profit where the vertical distance between total revenue and total cost is the largest. This happens at an output of 6 kilos. Panel (b) shows that Farmer Khouri's marginal revenue (*MR*) is equal to a constant US$4 per kilo. Farmer Khouri maximizes profits by producing oranges up to the point where the marginal revenue of the last kilo produced is equal to its marginal cost, or *MR* = *MC*. In this case, at no level of output does marginal revenue exactly equal marginal cost. The closest Farmer Khouri can come is to produce 6 kilos of oranges. He will not want to continue to produce once marginal cost is greater than marginal revenue because that would reduce his profits. Panels (a) and (b) show alternative ways of thinking about how Farmer Khouri can determine the profit-maximizing quantity of oranges to produce.

the marginal revenue and the marginal cost is the additional profit (or loss) from producing one more kilo. As long as marginal revenue is greater than marginal cost, Farmer Khouri's profits are increasing, and he will want to expand production. For example, he will not stop producing at 5 kilos of oranges because producing and selling the sixth kilo adds US$4 to his revenue but only US$3 to his cost, so his profit increases by US$1. He wants to continue producing until the marginal revenue he receives from selling another kilo is equal to the marginal cost of producing it. At that level of output, he will make no *additional* profit by selling another kilo, so he will have maximized his profits.

By inspecting the table, we can see that at no level of output does marginal revenue exactly equal marginal cost. The closest Farmer Khouri can come is to produce 6 kilos of oranges. He will not want to continue to produce once marginal cost is greater than marginal revenue because that would reduce his profits. For example, the seventh kilo of oranges adds US$4.50 to his cost but only US$4.00 to his revenue, so producing the seventh kilo *reduces* his profit by US$0.50.

From the information in Table 8-3 and Figure 8-3, we can draw the following conclusions:

1 The profit-maximizing level of output is where the difference between total revenue and total cost is the greatest.

2 The profit-maximizing level of output is also where marginal revenue equals marginal cost, or *MR* = *MC*.

Both these conclusions are true for any firm, whether or not it is in a perfectly competitive industry. We can draw one other conclusion about profit maximization that is true only of firms in perfectly competitive industries: for a firm in a perfectly competitive industry, price is equal to marginal revenue, or *P* = *MR*. So, we can restate the *MR* = *MC* condition as *P* = *MC*.

8.3 | Use graphs to show a firm's profit or loss.

Illustrating Profit or Loss on the Cost Curve Graph

We have seen that profit is the difference between total revenue and total cost. We can also express profit in terms of *average total cost* (*ATC*). This allows us to show profit on the cost curve graph we developed in Chapter 6.

To begin, we need to work through the several steps necessary to determine the relationship between profit and average total cost. Because profit is equal to total revenue minus total cost (*TC*) and total revenue is price times quantity, we can write the following:

$$\text{Profit} = (P \times Q) - TC$$

If we divide both sides of this equation by Q, we have:

$$\frac{\text{Profit}}{Q} = \frac{(P \times Q)}{Q} - \frac{TC}{Q}$$

or:

$$\frac{\text{Profit}}{Q} = P - ATC$$

because TC/Q equals ATC. This equation tells us that profit per unit (or average profit) equals price minus average total cost. Finally, we obtain the expression for the relationship between total profit and average total cost by multiplying again by Q:

$$\text{Profit} = (P - ATC) \times Q$$

This expression tells us that a firm's total profit is equal to the quantity produced multiplied by the difference between price and average total cost.

Showing a Profit on the Graph

Figure 8-4 shows the relationship between a firm's average total cost and its marginal cost that we discussed in Chapter 7. In this figure, we also show the firm's marginal revenue curve (which is the same as its demand curve) and the area representing total profit. Using the relationship between profit and average total cost that we just determined, we can say that the area representing total profit has a height equal to $(P - ATC)$ and a base equal to Q. This area is shown by the green-shaded rectangle.

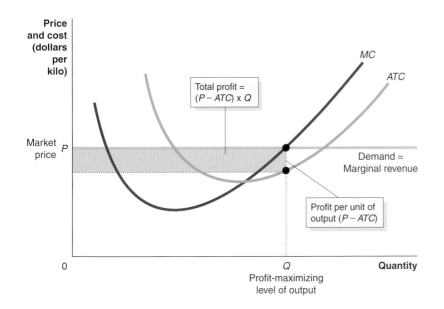

Figure 8-4

The Area of Maximum Profit

A firm maximizes profit at the level of output at which marginal revenue equals marginal cost. The difference between price and average total cost equals profit per unit of output. Total profit equals profit per unit multiplied by the number of units produced. Total profit is represented by the area of the green-shaded rectangle, which has a height equal to $(P–ATC)$ and a width equal to Q.

Solved Problem | 8-3

Determining Profit-Maximizing Price and Quantity

Suppose that Mustafa sells footballs in the perfectly competitive football market. His output per day and his costs are as follows:

OUTPUT PER DAY	TOTAL COST
0	$10.00
1	15.00
2	17.50
3	22.50
4	30.00
5	40.00
6	52.50
7	67.50
8	85.00
9	105.00

a. If the current equilibrium price in the football market is US$12.50, to maximize profits, how many footballs will Mustafa produce, what price will he charge, and how much profit (or loss) will he make? Draw a graph to illustrate your answer. Your graph should be labeled clearly and should include Mustafa's demand, *ATC*, *AVC*, *MC*, and *MR* curves; the price he is charging; the quantity he is producing; and the area representing his profit (or loss).

b. Suppose the equilibrium price of footballs falls to US$5.00. Now how many footballs will Mustafa produce, what price will he charge, and how much profit (or loss) will he make? Draw a graph to illustrate this situation, using the instructions in question (a).

SOLVING THE PROBLEM:

Step 1: **Review the chapter material.** This problem is about using cost curve graphs to analyze perfectly competitive firms, so you may want to review the section "Illustrating Profit or Loss on the Cost Curve Graph," which begins on page 273.

Step 2: **Calculate Mustafa's marginal cost, average total cost, and average variable cost.** To maximize profits, Mustafa will produce the level of output where marginal revenue is equal to marginal cost. We can calculate marginal cost from the information given in the table. We can also calculate average total cost and average variable cost in order to draw the required graph. Average total cost (*ATC*) equals total cost (*TC*) divided by the level of output (*Q*). Average variable cost (*AVC*) equals variable cost (*VC*) divided by output (*Q*). To calculate variable cost, recall that total cost equals variable cost plus fixed cost. When output equals zero, total cost equals fixed cost. In this case, fixed cost equals US$10.00.

OUTPUT PER DAY (*Q*) IN US$	TOTAL COST (*TC*) IN US$	FIXED COST (*FC*) IN US$	VARIABLE COST (*VC*) IN US$	AVERAGE TOTAL COST (*ATC*) IN US$	AVERAGE VARIABLE COST (*AVC*) IN US$	MARGINAL COST (*MC*) IN US$
0	10.00	10.00	0.00	—	—	—
1	15.00	10.00	5.00	15.00	5.00	5.00
2	17.50	10.00	7.50	8.75	3.75	2.50
3	22.50	10.00	12.50	7.50	4.17	5.00
4	30.00	10.00	20.00	7.50	5.00	7.50
5	40.00	10.00	30.00	8.00	6.00	10.00
6	52.50	10.00	42.50	8.75	7.08	12.50
7	67.50	10.00	57.50	9.64	8.21	15.00
8	85.00	10.00	75.00	10.63	9.38	17.50
9	105.00	10.00	95.00	11.67	10.56	20.00

Step 3: **Use the information from the table in Step 2 to calculate how many footballs Mustafa will produce, what price he will charge, and how much profit he will earn if the market price of footballs is US$12.50.** Mustafa's marginal revenue is equal to the market price of US$12.50. Marginal revenue equals marginal cost when Mustafa produces 6 footballs per day. So, Mustafa will produce 6 footballs per day and charge a price of US$12.50 per football. Mustafa's profits are equal to his total revenue minus his total costs. His total revenue equals the 6 footballs he sells multiplied by the US$12.50 price, or US$75.00. So, his profits equal US$75.00 – US$52.50 = US$22.50.

Step 4: **Use the information from the table in step 2 to illustrate your answer to question (a) with a graph.**

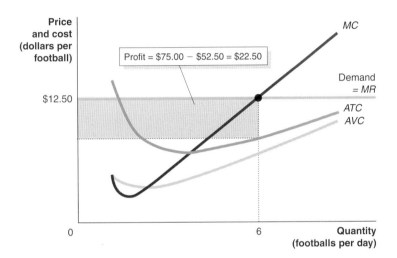

Step 5: **Calculate how many footballs Mustafa will produce, what price he will charge, and how much profit he will earn when the market price of footballs is US$5.00.** Referring to the table in Step 2, we can see that marginal revenue equals marginal cost when Mustafa produces 3 footballs per day. He charges the market price of US$5.00 per football. His total revenue is only US$15.00, while his total costs are US$22.50, so he will have a loss of US$7.50. (Can we be sure that Mustafa will continue to produce even though he is operating at a loss? We answer this question in the next section.)

Step 6: **Illustrate your answer to question (b) with a graph.**

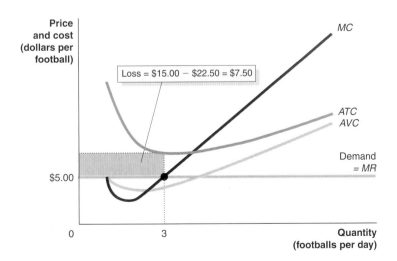

YOUR TURN: For more practice, do related problems 3.3 and 3.4 on page 296 at the end of this chapter.   **>> End Solved Problem 8-3**

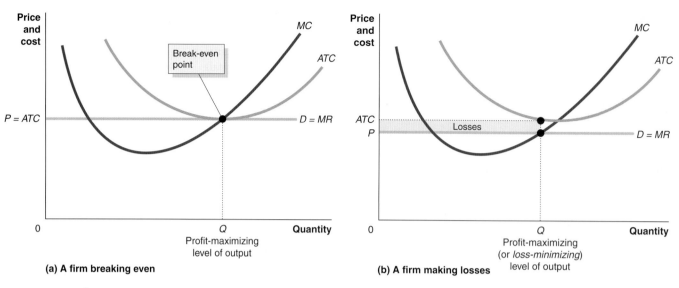

(a) A firm breaking even

(b) A firm making losses

Figure 8-5 | A Firm Breaking Even and a Firm Experiencing Losses

In panel (a), price equals average total cost, and the firm breaks even because its total revenue will be equal to its total cost. In this situation, the firm makes zero economic profit. In panel (b), price is below average total cost, and the firm experiences a loss.

The loss is represented by the area of the red-shaded rectangle, which has a height equal to ($ATC - P$) and a width equal to Q.

Illustrating When a Firm Is Breaking Even or Operating at a Loss

We have already seen that to maximize profits, a firm produces the level of output where marginal revenue equals marginal cost. But will the firm actually make a profit at that level of output? It depends on the relationship of price to average total cost. There are three possibilities:

1 $P > ATC$, which means the firm makes a profit.

2 $P = ATC$, which means the firm *breaks even* (its total cost equals its total revenue).

3 $P < ATC$, which means the firm experiences losses.

Figure 8-4 shows the first possibility, where the firm makes a profit. Panels (a) and (b) of Figure 8-5 show the situations where a firm experiences losses or breaks even. In panel (a) of Figure 8-5, at the level of output at which $MR = MC$, price is equal to average total cost. Therefore, total revenue is equal to total cost, and the firm will break even, making zero economic profit. In panel (b), at the level of output at which $MR = MC$, price is less than average total cost. Therefore, total revenue is less than total cost, and the firm has losses. In this case, maximizing profits amounts to *minimizing* losses.

Making	The Medical Screening
the	**Industry: When to Make Money**
Connection	**and When to Lose**

Making *the* **Connection** | **The Medical Screening Industry: When to Make Money and When to Lose**

In a market system, a good or service becomes available to consumers only if an entrepreneur brings the product to market. Each new business represents an entrepreneur risking his or her funds trying to earn a profit by offering a good or service to consumers. Of course, there are no guarantees of success, and many new businesses experience losses rather than earn the profits their owners hoped for.

In the early 2000s, technological advance reduced the price of computed tomography (CT) scanning equipment. For years, doctors and hospitals had prescribed CT scans to diagnose patients showing symptoms of heart disease, cancer, and other disorders. The declining price of CT scanning equipment convinced many entrepreneurs that it would be profitable to offer preventive body scans to apparently healthy people. The idea was that the scans would provide early detection of diseases before the customers had begun experiencing symptoms. Unfortunately, the new firms offering this service in the U.S. ran into several difficulties: first, because the CT scan was a voluntary procedure, it was not covered under most medical insurance plans; second, very few consumers used the service more than once, so there was almost no repeat business; finally, as with any other medical test, some false positives occurred, where the scan appeared to detect a problem that did not actually exist. Negative publicity from people who had expensive additional—and unnecessary—medical procedures as a result of false-positive CT scans also hurt these new businesses.

As a result of these difficulties, the demand for CT scans was less than most of these entrepreneurs had expected, and the new businesses operated at a loss. For example, the owner of California HeartScan would have broken even if the market price had been US$495 per heart scan, but it suffered losses because the actual market price was only US$250. The following graphs show the owner's situation.

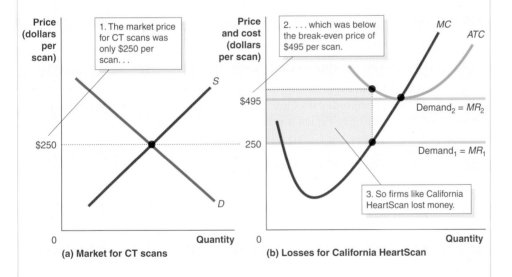

(a) Market for CT scans

(b) Losses for California HeartScan

Why didn't California HeartScan just raise the price to the level they needed to break even? We have already seen that any firm that tries to raise the price it charges above the market price loses customers to competing firms.

In contrast, the CT scan industry seems profitable in Saudi Arabia for the following reasons: first, most health insurance plans cover the cost of a CT scan; second, the number of diagnostic imaging centres is low compared with the population of Saudi Arabia. A news report from AME Info indicated that

> With a population of around 25 million, Saudi Arabia is the largest healthcare market in the GCC. Healthcare spending in Saudi Arabia has increased by 18 percent in 2009, according to the Economist Intelligence Unit (EIU) estimates, reaching US$20bn. It is expected to continue on this trajectory as a result of aging population, alleviated health awareness, increased incomes, and higher incidences of lifestyle diseases.

(Continued)

> For example, the leading medical diagnostic imaging company in Saudi Arabia, TechnoGroup, will be operating only 17 diagnostic centres that serve around 110 million people in both Saudi Arabia and Egypt, by the end of 2010. Now think about the necessary changes in the previous two graphs to present the case of TechnoGroup in Saudi Arabia.
>
> Sources: Patricia Callahan, "Scanning for Trouble," *Wall Street Journal*, September 11, 2003, p. B1; Rana Mesbah, "Gulf Capital Acquires Leading Medical Diagnostic Imaging Company in Saudi Arabia," www .AMEinfo.com, June 15, 2010.
>
> **YOUR TURN:** Test your understanding by doing related problem 3.7 on page 296 at the end of this chapter.

8.4 LEARNING OBJECTIVE

8.4 | Explain why firms may shut down temporarily.

Deciding Whether to Produce or to Shut Down in the Short Run

In panel (b) of Figure 8-5, we assumed that the firm would continue to produce, even though it was operating at a loss. In fact, in the short run, a firm suffering losses has two choices:

1 Continue to produce

2 Stop production by shutting down temporarily.

In many cases, a firm experiencing losses will consider stopping production temporarily. Even during a temporary shutdown, however, a firm must still pay its fixed costs. For example, if the firm has signed a lease for its building, the landlord will expect to receive a monthly rent payment, even if the firm is not producing anything that month. Therefore, if a firm does not produce, it will suffer a loss equal to its fixed costs. This loss is the maximum the firm will accept. If, by producing, the firm would lose an amount greater than its fixed costs, it will shut down.

A firm will be able to reduce its loss below the amount of its total fixed cost by continuing to produce, provided the total revenue it receives is greater than its variable cost. A firm can use the revenue over and above variable cost to cover part of its fixed cost. In this case, the firm will have a smaller loss by continuing to produce than if it shut down.

Sunk cost A cost that has already been paid and that cannot be recovered.

In analyzing the firm's decision to shut down, we are assuming that its fixed costs are *sunk costs*. Remember from Chapter 6 that a **sunk cost** is a cost that has already been paid and cannot be recovered. We assume, as is usually the case, that the firm cannot recover its fixed costs by shutting down. For example, if a farmer has taken out a loan to buy land, the farmer is legally required to make the monthly loan payment whether he grows any oranges that season or not. The farmer has to spend those funds and cannot get them back, so the farmer should treat his sunk costs as irrelevant to his decision making. For any firm, whether total revenue is greater than or less than *variable costs* is the key to deciding whether to shut down. As long as a firm's total revenue is greater than its variable costs, it should continue to produce no matter how large or small its fixed costs are.

One option not available to a firm with losses in a perfectly competitive market is to raise its price. If the firm did raise its price, it would lose all its customers, and its sales would drop to zero. For example, suppose that the price of oranges in Jordan is 0.5 Jordanian dinars per kilo (around 0.7 U.S. dollars). At that price, the Jordanian farmers with high cost of production are expected to lose JD9,500 (US$13,400). At a price of about JD0.7 per kilo, those farmers would have broken even. But any farmer who tries to raise his price to JD0.7 per kilo of oranges would have seen his sales quickly disappear because buyers could purchase all the oranges they wanted at JD0.5 per kilo from the many other orange farmers.

The Supply Curve of a Firm in the Short Run

Remember that the supply curve for a firm tells us how many units of a product the firm is willing to sell at any given price. Notice that the marginal cost curve for a firm in a perfectly competitive market tells us the same thing. The firm will produce at the level of output where $MR = MC$. Because price equals marginal revenue for a firm in a perfectly competitive market, the firm will produce where $P = MC$. For any given price, we can determine from the marginal cost curve the quantity of output the firm will supply. *Therefore, a perfectly competitive firm's marginal cost curve also is its supply curve.* There is, however, an important qualification to this. We have seen that if a firm is experiencing losses, it will shut down if its total revenue is less than its variable cost:

$$\text{Total revenue} < \text{Variable cost}$$

or, in symbols:

$$P \times Q < VC$$

If we divide both sides by Q, we have the result that the firm will shut down if:

$$P < AVC$$

If the price drops below average variable cost, the firm will have a smaller loss if it shuts down and produces no output. *So, the firm's marginal cost curve is its supply curve only for prices at or above average variable cost.* The red line in Figure 8-6 shows the supply curve for the firm in the short run.

Recall that the marginal cost curve intersects the average variable cost where the average variable cost curve is at its minimum point. Therefore, the firm's supply curve is its marginal cost curve above the minimum point of the average variable cost curve. For prices below minimum average variable cost (P_{MIN}), the firm will shut down, and its output will fall to zero. The minimum point on the average variable cost curve is called the **shutdown point** and occurs in Figure 8-6 at output level Q_{SD}.

Shutdown point The minimum point on a firm's average variable cost curve; if the price falls below this point, the firm shuts down production in the short run.

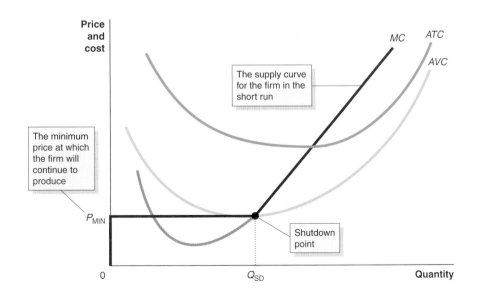

Price and cost

MC   ATC

AVC

The supply curve for the firm in the short run

The minimum price at which the firm will continue to produce

P_{MIN}

Shutdown point

0   Q_{SD} **Quantity**

Figure 8-6

The Firm's Short-Run Supply Curve

The firm will produce at the level of output at which $MR = MC$. Because price equals marginal revenue for a firm in a perfectly competitive market, the firm will produce where $P = MC$. For any given price, we can determine the quantity of output the firm will supply from the marginal cost curve. In other words, the marginal cost curve is the firm's supply curve. But remember that the firm will shut down if the price falls below average variable cost. The marginal cost curve crosses the average variable cost at the firm's shutdown point. This point occurs at output level Q_{SD}. For prices below P_{MIN}, the supply curve is a vertical line along the price axis, which shows that the firm will supply zero output at those prices. The red line in the figure is the firm's short-run supply curve.

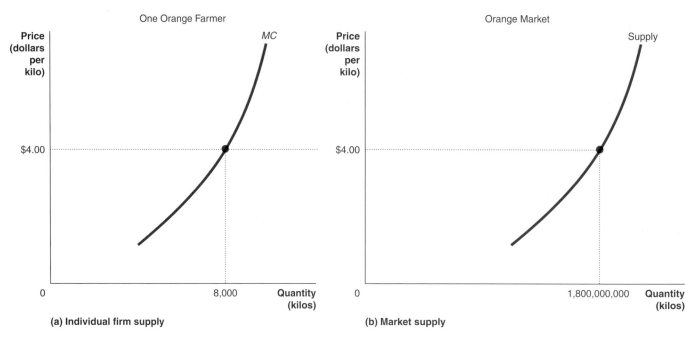

Figure 8-7 | Firm Supply and Market Supply

We can derive the market supply curve by adding up the quantity that each firm in the market is willing to supply at each price. In panel (a), one orange farmer is willing to supply 8,000 kilos of oranges at a price of US$4 per kilo. If every orange farmer supplies the same amount of oranges at this price and if there are 225,000 orange farmers, the total amount of oranges supplied at a price of US$4 will equal 8,000 kilos per farmer × 225,000 farmers = 1.8 billion kilos of oranges. This is one point on the market supply curve for oranges shown in panel (b). We can find the other points on the market supply curve by seeing the amount of oranges each farmer is willing to supply at each price.

The Market Supply Curve in a Perfectly Competitive Industry

We saw in Chapter 6 that the market demand curve is determined by adding up the quantity demanded by each consumer in the market at each price. Similarly, the market supply curve is determined by adding up the quantity supplied by each firm in the market at each price. Each firm's marginal cost curve tells us how much that firm will supply at each price. So, the market supply curve can be derived directly from the marginal cost curves of the firms in the market. Panel (a) of Figure 8-7 shows the marginal cost curve for one orange farmer.

At a price of US$4, this orange farmer supplies 8,000 kilos of oranges. If every orange farmer supplies the same amount of oranges at this price and if there are 225,000 orange farmers, the total amount of oranges supplied at a price of US$4 will be:

$$8000 \text{ kilos per farmer} \times 225{,}000 \text{ farmers} = 1.8 \text{ billion kilos of oranges}$$

Panel (b) shows a price of US$4 and a quantity of 1.8 billion kilos as a point on the market supply curve for oranges. In reality, of course, not all orange farms are alike. Some orange farms supply more at the market price than the typical farm; other orange farms supply less. The key point is that we can derive the market supply curve by adding up the quantity that each firm in the market is willing to supply at each price.

8.5 | Explain how entry and exit ensure that perfectly competitive firms earn zero economic profit in the long run.

"If Everyone Can Do It, You Can't Make Money at It": The Entry and Exit of Firms in the Long Run

In the long run, unless a firm can cover all its costs, it will shut down and exit the industry. In a market system, firms continually enter and exit industries. In this section, we will see how profits and losses provide signals to firms that lead to entry and exit.

Economic Profit and the Entry or Exit Decision

To begin, let's look more closely at how economists characterize the profits earned by the owners of a firm. Suppose Aliaa Adel decides to start her own business. After considering her interests and preparing a business plan, she decides to start an organic apple farm rather than open a restaurant or gift shop. After 10 years of effort, Aliaa has saved US$100,000 and borrowed another US$900,000 from a bank. With these funds, she has bought the land, apple trees, and farm equipment necessary to start her organic apple business. As we saw in Chapter 6, when someone invests her own funds in her firm, the opportunity cost to the firm is the return the funds would have earned in their best alternative use. If Farmer Aliaa Adel could have earned a 10 percent return on her US$100,000 in savings in their best alternative use—which might have been, for example, to buy a small restaurant—then her apple business incurs a US$10,000 opportunity cost. We can also think of this US$10,000 as being the minimum amount that Farmer Aliaa needs to earn on her US$100,000 investment in her farm to remain in the industry in the long run.

Table 8-4 lists Farmer Aliaa Adel's costs. In addition to her explicit costs, we assume that she has two implicit costs: the US$10,000, which represents the opportunity cost of the funds she invested in her farm, and the US$30,000 salary she could have earned managing someone else's farm instead of her own. Her total costs are US$125,000. If the market price of organic apples is US$15 per box and Farmer Aliaa sells 10,000 boxes, her total revenue will be US$150,000 and her economic profit will be US$25,000 (total revenue of US$150,000 minus total of US$125,000). **Economic profit** is calculated as the firm's revenues minus all of its explicit and implicit costs. This is different from the **accounting profit**, which is defined as a firm's net income measured by revenue minus operating expenses and taxes paid. Accounting profit provides information on a firm's

Economic profit A firm's revenues minus all its costs, implicit and explicit.

Accounting profit A firm's net income measured by revenue minus operating expenses and taxes paid.

TABLE 8-4

Farmer Aliaa's Costs per Year

EXPLICIT COSTS	
Water	US$10,000
Wages	$15,000
Organic fertilizer	$10,000
Electricity	$5,000
Payment on bank loan	$45,000
IMPLICIT COSTS	
Foregone salary	US$30,000
Opportunity cost of the US$100,000 she has invested in her farm	$10,000
Total cost	$125,000

Implicit cost A nonmonetary opportunity cost.

Explicit cost A cost that involves spending money.

current net income measured according to accepted accounting standards. Accounting profit is not, however, the ideal measure of a firm's profits because it neglects some of the firm's costs. By taking into account all costs, economic profit provides a better indication than accounting profit of how successful a firm is. So, Farmer Aliaa is covering the US$10,000 opportunity cost of the funds invested in her firm, and she is also earning an additional US$25,000 in economic profit.

Economic Profit Leads to Entry of New Firms Unfortunately, Farmer Aliaa is unlikely to earn an economic profit for very long. Suppose other apple farmers are just breaking even by growing apples using conventional methods. In that case, they will have an incentive to convert to organic growing methods so they can begin earning an economic profit. Remember that the more firms there are in an industry, the further to the right the market supply curve is. Panel (a) of Figure 8-8 shows that more farmers entering the market for organically grown apples will cause the market supply curve to shift to the right. Farmers will continue entering the market until the market supply curve has shifted from S1 to S2.

With the supply curve at S_2, the market price will have fallen to US$10 per box. Panel (b) shows the effect on Farmer Aliaa, whom we assume has the same costs as other organic apple farmers. As the market price falls from US$15 to US$10 per box, Farmer Aliaa's demand curve shifts down, from D_1 to D_2. In the new equilibrium, Farmer Aliaa is selling 8,000 boxes at a price of US$10 per box. She and the other organic apple growers are no longer earning any economic profit. They are just breaking even, and the return on their investment is just covering the opportunity cost of these funds. New farmers will stop entering the market for organic apples because the rate of return is no better than they can earn elsewhere.

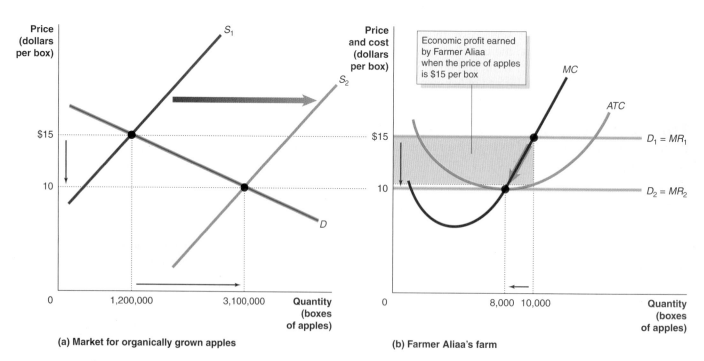

(a) Market for organically grown apples

(b) Farmer Aliaa's farm

Figure 8-8 | The Effect of Entry on Economic Profits

We assume that Farmer Aliaa's costs are the same as the costs of other organic apple growers. Initially, she and other producers of organically grown apples are able to charge US$15 per box and earn an economic profit. Farmer Aliaa's economic profit is represented by the area of the green box. Panel (a) shows that as other farmers begin to grow apples using organic methods, the market supply curve shifts to the right, from S_1 to S_2, and the market price drops to US$10 per box. Panel (b) shows that the falling price causes Farmer Aliaa's demand curve to shift down from D_1 to D_2, and she reduces her output from 10,000 boxes to 8,000. At the new market price of US$10 per box, organic apple growers are just breaking even: Their total revenue is equal to their total cost, and their economic profit is zero. Notice the difference in scale between the graph in panel (a) and the graph in panel (b).

Will Farmer Aliaa continue to grow organic apples even though she is just break-ing even? She will, because growing organic apples earns her as high a return on her investment as she could earn elsewhere. It may seem strange that new firms will con-tinue to enter a market until all economic profits are eliminated and that established firms remain in a market despite not earning any economic profit. It only seems strange because we are used to thinking in terms of accounting profits, rather than *economic* profits. Remember that accounting rules generally require that only explicit costs be included on a firm's financial statements. The opportunity cost of the funds Farmer Aliaa invested in her firm—US$10,000—and her foregone salary—US$30,000—are economic costs, but neither is an accounting cost. So, although an accountant would see Farmer Aliaa as earning a profit of US$40,000, an economist would see her as just breaking even. Farmer Aliaa must pay attention to her accounting profit when prepar-ing her financial statements and when paying her income tax. But because economic profit takes into account all her costs, it gives a truer indication of the financial health of her farm.

Economic Losses Lead to Exit of Firms Suppose some consumers decide there are no important benefits from eating organically grown apples and they switch back to buying conventionally grown apples. Panel (a) of Figure 8-9 shows that the demand curve for organically grown apples will shift to the left, from D_1 to D_2, and the market price will fall from US$10 per box to US$7. Panel (b) shows that as the price falls, a typi-cal organic apple farmer, like Aliaa Adel, will move down her marginal cost curve to a lower level of output. At the lower level of output and lower price, she will be suffering an **economic loss** because she will not cover all her costs. As long as price is above average variable cost, she will continue to produce in the short run, even when suffering losses. But in the long run, firms will exit an industry if they are unable to cover all their costs. In this case, some organic apple growers will switch back to growing apples using con-ventional methods.

> **Economic loss** The situation in which a firm's total revenue is less than its total cost, including all implicit costs.

Panel (c) of Figure 8-9 shows that firms exiting the organic apple industry will cause the market supply curve to shift to the left. Firms will continue to exit, and the supply curve will continue to shift to the left until the price has risen back to US$10 and the market supply curve is at S_2. Panel (d) shows that when the price is back to US$10, the remaining firms in the industry will be breaking even.

Long-Run Equilibrium in a Perfectly Competitive Market

We have seen that economic profits attract firms to enter an industry. The entry of firms forces down the market price until the typical firm is breaking even. Economic losses cause firms to exit an industry. The exit of firms forces up the equilibrium mar-ket price until the typical firm is breaking even. This process of entry and exit results in *long-run competitive equilibrium*. In **long-run competitive equilibrium**, entry and exit have resulted in the typical firm breaking even. The *long-run equilibrium market price* is at a level equal to the minimum point on the typical firm's average total cost curve.

> **Long-run competitive equilibrium** The situation in which the entry and exit of firms has resulted in the typical firm breaking even.

The long run in the organic apple market is three to four years, which is the amount of time it takes farmers to convert from conventional growing methods to organic grow-ing methods.

Firms in perfectly competitive markets are in a constant struggle to stay one step ahead of their competitors. They are always looking for new ways to provide a product, such as growing apples organically. It is possible for firms to find ways to earn an economic profit for a while, but as we mentioned in the beginning if this chapter, as more people are entering this profitable industry, economic opportuni-ties will eventually be exhausted after few years. This observation is not restricted to agriculture. In any perfectly competitive market, an opportunity to make eco-nomic profits never lasts long. As Sharon Oster, an economist at Yale University, has put it, "If everyone can do it, you can't make money at it."

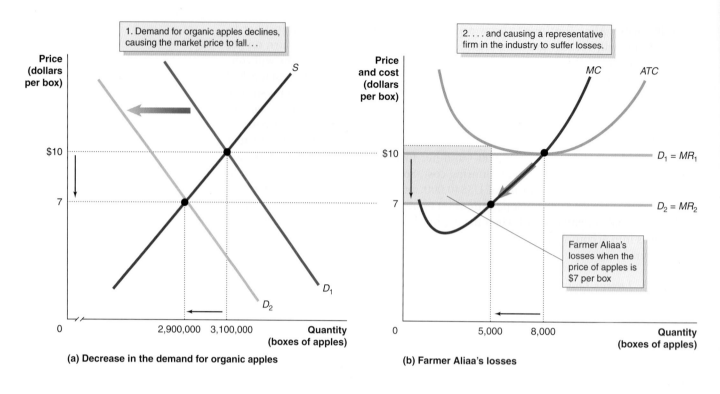

(a) Decrease in the demand for organic apples

(b) Farmer Aliaa's losses

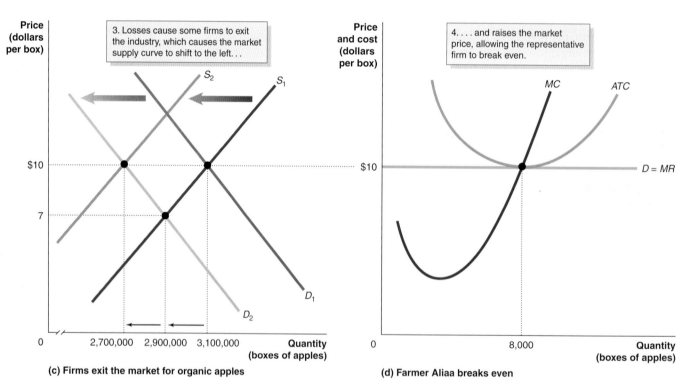

(c) Firms exit the market for organic apples

(d) Farmer Aliaa breaks even

Figure 8-9 | The Effect of Exit on Economic Losses

When the price of apples is US$10 per box, Farmer Aliaa Adel and other producers of organically grown apples are breaking even. A total quantity of 3,100,000 boxes is sold in the market. Farmer Aliaa sells 8,000 boxes. Panel (a) shows a decline in the demand for organically grown apples from D_1 to D_2 that reduces the market price to US$7 per box. Panel (b) shows that the falling price causes Farmer Aliaa's demand curve to shift down from D_1 to D_2 and her output to fall from 8,000 to 5,000 boxes. At a market price

of US$7 per box, farmers have economic losses, represented by the area of the red box. As a result, some farmers will exit the market, which shifts the market supply curve to the left. Panel (c) shows that exit continues until the supply curve has shifted from S_1 to S_2 and the market price has risen from US$7 back to US$10. Panel (d) shows that with the price back at US$10, Farmer Aliaa will break even. In the new market equilibrium, total production of organic apples has fallen from 3,100,000 to 2,700,000 boxes.

The Long-Run Supply Curve in a Perfectly Competitive Market

If the typical organic apple grower breaks even at a price of US$10 per box, in the long run, the market price will always return to this level. If an increase in demand causes the market price to rise above US$10, farmers will be earning economic profits. This profit will attract additional farmers into the market, and the market supply curve will shift to the right until the price is back to US$10. Panel (a) in Figure 8-10 illustrates the long-run effect of an increase in demand. An increase in demand from D_1 to D_2 causes the market price to temporarily rise from US$10 per box to US$15. At this price, farmers are making economic profits growing organic apples, but these profits attract entry of new farmers' organic apples. The result is an increase in supply from S_1 to S_2, which forces the price back down to US$10 per box and eliminates the economic profits.

Similarly, if a decrease in demand causes the market price to fall below US$10, farmers will experience economic losses. These losses will cause some farmers to exit the market, the supply curve will shift to the left, and the price will return to US$10. Panel (b) in Figure 8-10 illustrates the long-run effect of a decrease in demand. A decrease in demand from D_1 to D_2 causes the market price to fall temporarily from US$10 per box to US$7. At this price, farmers are suffering economic losses growing organic apples, but these losses cause some farmers to exit the market for organic apples. The result is a decrease in supply from S_1 to S_2, which forces the price back up to US$10 per box and eliminates the losses.

The **long-run supply curve** shows the relationship in the long run between market price and the quantity supplied. In the long run, the price in the organic apple market will be US$10 per box, no matter how many boxes of apples are produced. So, as Figure 8-10 shows, the long-run supply curve (S_{LR}) for organic apples is a horizontal line at a price of US$10. Remember that the reason the price returns to US$10 in the long run is that this is

Long-run supply curve A curve that shows the relationship in the long run between market price and the quantity supplied.

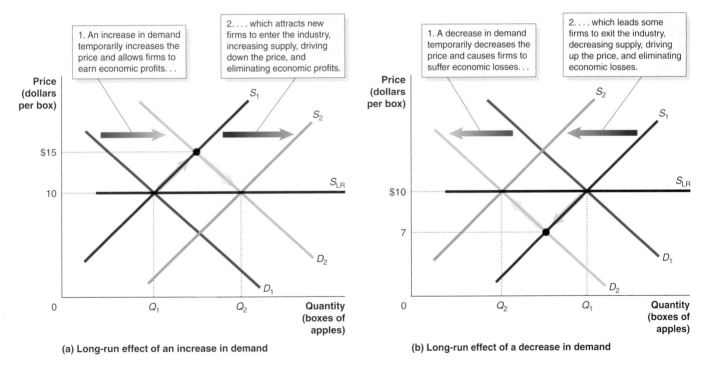

(a) Long-run effect of an increase in demand

(b) Long-run effect of a decrease in demand

Figure 8-10 | The Long-Run Supply Curve in a Perfectly Competitive Industry

Panel (a) shows that an increase in demand for organic apples will lead to a temporary increase in price from US$10 to US$15 per box, as the market demand curve shifts to the right, from D_1 to D_2. The entry of new firms shifts the market supply curve to the right, from S_1 to S_2, which will cause the price to fall back to its long-run level of US$10. Panel (b) shows that a decrease in demand will lead to a temporary decrease in price from US$10 to US$7 per box, as the market demand curve shifts to the left, from D_1 to D_2. The exit of firms shifts the market supply curve to the left, from S_1 to S_2, which causes the price to rise back to its long-run level of US$10. The long-run supply curve (S_{LR}) shows the relationship between market price and the quantity supplied in the long run. In this case, the long-run supply curve is a horizontal line.

the price at which the typical firm in the industry just breaks even. The typical firm breaks even at this price because it is at the minimum point on the firm's average total cost curve. We can draw the important conclusion that *in the long run, a perfectly competitive market will supply whatever amount of a good consumers demand at a price determined by the minimum point on the typical firm's average total cost curve.*

Because the position of the long-run supply curve is determined by the minimum point on the typical firm's average total cost curve, anything that raises or lowers the costs of the typical firm in the long run will cause the long-run supply curve to shift. For example, if a disease infects apple trees and the costs of treating the disease adds US$2 per box to the cost of producing apples, the long-run supply curve will shift up by US$2.

Making the Connection | Easy Entry Makes the Long Run Pretty Short in the Apple iPhone Apps Store

Apple introduced the first version of the iPhone in June 2007. Although popular, the original iPhone had some drawbacks, including a slow connection to the Internet and an inability to run any applications except those written by Apple. The iPhone 3G, released in July 2008, could connect to the Internet more quickly and easily, had a faster processor, and had a larger capacity. Apple announced that a section of its hugely popular iTunes music and video store would be devoted to applications (or 'apps') for the iPhone. Independent software programmers would write these iPhone apps. Apple would approve the apps and make them available in the iTunes app store in exchange for receiving 3 percent of the purchase price. Major software companies, as well as individuals writing their first software programs, have posted games, calendars, dictionaries, and many other types of apps to the iPhone store.

Apple sold more than 3 million iPhones within a month of launching the iPhone 3G. Demand for apps from the iTunes store soared along with the sales of the iPhone. Ethan Nichols, who in August 2008 was a programmer at Sun Microsystems but had never written a game before, decided to teach himself the coding language used in iPhone apps. His game, iShoot, with an initial price of US$4.99, was a great success. Within five months, enough people had downloaded iShoot to earn Nichols US$800,000.

But could Nichols's success last? As we have seen, when firms earn economic profits in a market, other firms have a strong economic incentive to enter that market. This is exactly what happened with iPhone apps, and by April 2009, more than 25,000 apps were available in the iTunes store. The cost of entering this market was very small. Anyone with the programming skills and the available time to write an app could have it posted in the store. As a result of this enhanced competition, the ability to get rich quick with a killer app was quickly fading. As an article in the *New York Times* put it: "The chances of hitting the iPhone jackpot keeps getting slimmer: the Apple store is already crowded with look-alike games…and fresh inventory keeps arriving daily. Many of the simple but clever concepts that sell briskly…are already taken."

To try to maintain sales, Ethan Nichols was forced to drop the price of iShoot from US$4.99 in October 2008 to US$2.99 in April 2009 and to US$1.99 in May 2009. But his profits from the game continued to decline. In a competitive market, earning an economic profit in the long run is extremely difficult. And the ease of entering the market for iPhone apps has made the long run pretty short.

Sources: Jenna Wortham, "The iPhone Gold Rush," *New York Times*, April 5 2009; and Bruce X. Chen, "Coder's Half-Million-Dollar Baby Proves iPhone Gold Rush Is Still On," www.wired.com, February 12, 2009.

YOUR TURN: Test your understanding by doing related problem 6.4 on page 298 at the end of this chapter.

Increasing-Cost and Decreasing-Cost Industries

Any industry in which the typical firm's average costs do not change as the industry expands production will have a horizontal long-run supply curve, like the one in Figure 8-10. Industries, like the apple industry, where this holds true are called *constant-cost industries*. It's possible, however, for the typical firm's average costs to change as an industry expands.

For example, if an input used in producing a good is available in only limited quantities, the cost of the input will rise as the industry expands. If only a limited amount of land is available on which to grow peaches to make a certain variety of jam, an increase in demand for jam made from these peaches will result in competition for the land and will drive up its price. As a result, more of jam will be produced in the long run only if the price rises to cover the higher average costs of the typical firm. In this case, the long-run supply curve will slope upward. Industries with upward-sloping long-run supply curves are called *increasing-cost industries*.

Finally, in some cases, the typical firm's costs may fall as the industry expands. Suppose that someone invents a new microwave that uses as an input a specialized memory chip that is currently produced only in small quantities. If demand for the microwave increases, firms that produce microwaves will increase their orders for the memory chip. We saw in Chapter 7 that if there are economies of scale in producing a good, its average cost will decline as output increases. If there are economies of scale in producing this memory chip, the average cost of producing it will fall, and competition will result in its price falling as well. This price decline, in turn, will lower the average cost of producing the new microwave. In the long run, competition will force the price of the microwave to fall to the level of the new lower average cost of the typical firm. In this case, the long-run supply curve will slope downward. Industries with downward-sloping long-run supply curves are called *decreasing-cost industries*.

8.6 LEARNING OBJECTIVE

8.6 | Explain how perfect competition leads to economic efficiency.

Perfect Competition and Efficiency

Notice how powerful consumers are in a market system. If consumers want more organic apples, the market will supply them. This happens not because a government bureaucrat, or an official in an apple growers' association gives orders. The additional apples are produced because an increase in demand results in higher prices and a higher rate of return on investments in organic growing techniques. Apple growers, trying to get the highest possible return on their investment, begin to switch from using conventional growing methods to using organic growing methods. If consumers lose their taste for organic apples and demand falls, the process works in reverse.

Making the Connection | **"Lose Money But Do Not Lose the Market Share"**

In recent years, Egyptian apparel producers faced unfavourable economic conditions for two main reasons. First, the Egyptian government has applied economic reform programs aiming at liberalizing its economic policies and trade. One result of these programs is the reduction of tariffs on apparel from 22 percent to 10 percent in 2007. Although this is good news for Egyptian consumers of apparel, it is not good for domestic producers because it simply means that imported clothes will enter the Egyptian market at a cheaper price. Second, the 2008 financial crisis resulted in a decline in the international demand for the Egyptian apparel. These two economic events affected the profit of apparel producers negatively.

Alaa Arafa, the chairman and chief executive officer of Arafa Holding, an Egyptian manufacturer specializing in apparel production, advised other manufacturers to cut

(Continued)

their prices and keep factories running even at a loss. "The ball has to keep rolling even at a loss of profitability. Lose money but do not lose the market share," said Arafa. How can we explain Arafa's view? And what time scale is he talking about? It is clear that Arafa is advising others to keep producing, and not to shut down, as long as the market price covers the average variable cost in order to keep their market share. This could only be done in the short run when manufacturers are expecting that these adverse market conditions will not last for long, or they will be able to decrease their average total cost in the long run, in response to the foreign competition, so that they will eventually break even.

Source: "The Year the Bubble Burst," *Al-Ahram Weekly*, 1–6 January 2009, Issue No. 928.

Productive Efficiency

Productive efficiency The situation in which a good or service is produced at the lowest possible cost.

In the market system, consumers get as many apples as they want, produced at the lowest average cost possible. The forces of competition will drive the market price to the minimum average cost of the typical firm. **Productive efficiency** refers to the situation in which a good or service is produced at the lowest possible cost. As we have seen, perfect competition results in productive efficiency.

The managers of every firm strive to earn an economic profit by reducing costs. But in a perfectly competitive market, other firms quickly copy ways of reducing costs, so that in the long run, only the consumer benefits from cost reductions.

Solved Problem | 8-6

How Productive Efficiency Benefits Consumers

Writing in the *New York Times* on the technology boom of the late 1990s, Michael Lewis argues: "The sad truth, for investors, seems to be that most of the benefits of new technologies are passed right through to consumers free of charge."

a. What do you think Lewis means by the benefits of new technology being "passed right through to consumers free of charge"? Use a graph like Figure 8-8 illustrate your answer.

b. Explain why this result is a "sad truth" for investors.

SOLVING THE PROBLEM:

Step 1: **Review the chapter material.** This problem is about perfect competition and efficiency, so you may want to review the section "Perfect Competition and Efficiency," which begins on page 287.

Step 2: **Use the concepts from this chapter to explain what Lewis means.** By "new technologies," Lewis means new products—like cellphones or plasma television sets—or lower-cost ways of producing existing products. In either case, new technologies will allow firms to earn economic profits for a while, but these profits will lead new firms to enter the market in the long run.

Step 3: **Use a graph like Figure 8-8 to illustrate why the benefits of new technologies are "passed right through to consumers free of charge."** Figure 8-8 shows the situation in which a firm is making economic profits in the short run but has these profits eliminated by entry in the long run. We can draw a similar graph to analyze what happens in the long run in the market for plasma televisions:

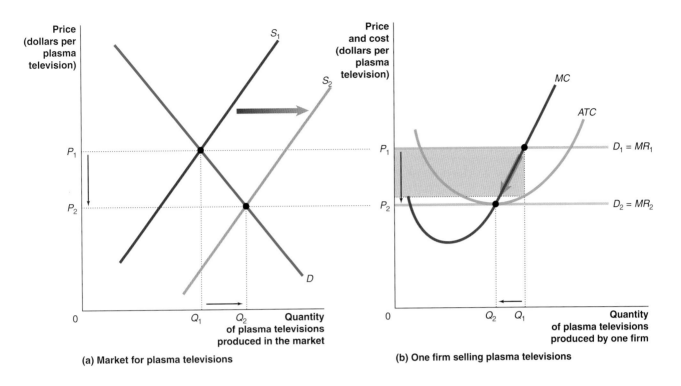

(a) Market for plasma televisions

(b) One firm selling plasma televisions

When plasma televisions were first introduced, prices were high, and only a few firms were in the market. Panel (a) shows that the initial equilibrium price in the market for plasma televisions is P_1. Panel (b) shows that at this price, the typical firm in the industry is earning an economic profit, which is shown by the green-shaded box. The economic profit attracts new firms into the industry. This entry shifts the market supply curve from S_1 to S_2 in panel (a) and lowers the equilibrium price from P_1 to P_2. Panel (b) shows that at the new market price, P_2, the typical firm is breaking even. Therefore, plasma televisions are being produced at the lowest possible cost, and productive efficiency is achieved. Consumers receive the new technology "free of charge" in the sense that they only have to pay a price equal to the lowest possible cost of production.

Step 4: **Answer question (b) by explaining why the result in question (a) is a "sad truth" for investors.** We have seen in answering question (a) that in the long run, firms only break even on their investment in producing high-technology goods. That result implies that investors in these firms are also unlikely to earn an economic profit in the long run.

EXTRA CREDIT: Lewis is using a key result from this chapter: in the long run, entry of new firms competes away economic profits. We should notice that, strictly speaking, the high-technology industries Lewis is discussing are not perfectly competitive. Plasma televisions models, for instance, are not identical, and each TV company produces a quantity large enough to affect the market price. However, as we will see in Chapter 9, these deviations from perfect competition do not change the important conclusion that the entry of new firms benefits consumers by forcing prices down to the level of average cost. In fact, the price of plasma televisions dropped by more than 75 percent within five years of their first becoming widely available.

Source: Michael Lewis, "In Defense of the Boom," *New York Times*, October 27, 2002.

YOUR TURN: For more practice, do related problems 6.5 and 6.6 on pages 298–299 at the end of this chapter.

>> End Solved Problem 8-6

Allocative Efficiency

Not only do perfectly competitive firms produce goods and services at the lowest possible cost, they also produce the goods and services that consumers value most. Firms will produce a good up to the point where the marginal cost of producing another unit is equal to the marginal benefit consumers receive from consuming that unit. In other words, firms will supply all those goods that provide consumers with a marginal benefit at least as great as the marginal cost of producing them. We know this is true because:

1 The price of a good represents the marginal benefit consumers receive from consuming the last unit of the good sold.

2 Perfectly competitive firms produce up to the point where the price of the good equals the marginal cost of producing the last unit.

3 Therefore, firms produce up to the point where the last unit provides a marginal benefit to consumers equal to the marginal cost of producing it.

Allocative efficiency A state of the economy in which production represents consumer preferences; in particular, every good or service is produced up to the point where the last unit provides a marginal benefit to consumers equal to the marginal cost of producing it.

These statements are another way of saying that entrepreneurs in a market system efficiently *allocate* labor, machinery, and other inputs to produce the goods and services that best satisfy consumer wants. In this sense, perfect competition achieves **allocative efficiency**. As we will explore in the next few chapters, many goods and services sold in the Arab economies are not produced in perfectly competitive markets. Nevertheless, productive efficiency and allocative efficiency are useful benchmarks against which to compare the actual performance of the economy.

Economics in YOUR Life!

≫ **Continued from page 265**

At the beginning of the chapter, we asked you to think about why you can charge only a relatively low price for performing services such as babysitting or working as a cashier. In this chapter, we saw that firms selling products in competitive markets are unable to charge prices higher than those being charged by competing firms. The market for babysitting and cashiering is very competitive. In most neighborhoods, there are a lot of teenagers willing to supply these services. The price you can charge for babysitting may not be worth your while at age 20, but is enough to cover the opportunity cost of a 14-year-old eager to enter the market. (Or, as we put it in Table 8-1 on page 266, the ease of entry into babysitting and cashiering is high.) So, in your career as a teenage entrepreneur, you may have become familiar with one of the lessons of this chapter. A firm in a competitive market has no control over price.

Conclusion

The competitive forces of the market impose constant pressure on firms to produce new and better goods and services at the lowest possible cost. Firms that fail to adequately anticipate changes in consumer tastes or that fail to adopt the latest and most efficient technology do not survive in the long run. In the nineteenth century, the biologist Charles Darwin developed a theory of evolution based on the idea of the 'survival of the fittest.' Only those plants and animals that are best able to adapt to the demands of their environment are able to survive. Darwin first realized the important role that the struggle for existence plays in the natural world after reading early nineteenth-century economists' descriptions of the role it plays in the economic world. Just as 'survival of the fittest' is the rule in nature, so it is in the economic world.

At the start of this chapter, we saw that there are four market structures: perfect competition, monopolistic competition, oligopoly, and monopoly. Now that we have studied perfect competition, in the following chapters we move on to the other three market structures. Before turning to those chapters, read *An Inside Look* on the next page to learn how a well-established industry might be endangered because of foreign competition.

Egyptian Lantern Makers Face Tough Competition from Chinese Exporters

AL-SHORFA.COM, SEPTEMBER 27, 2008

An industry based on a thousand-year old tradition faces collapse

(a) The entire country of Egypt is filled with excitement over the festivities of the holy month of Ramadan. The houses and streets are decorated with Ramadan lanterns that light up the night with bright colours. Nevertheless, Ramadan's lantern industry is facing collapse due to the Chinese invasion of the industry.

In Egypt, the Ramadan lantern is revered as a beloved and important symbol that reflects the region's culture and heritage. However, the lantern industry in Egypt is showing signs of recession. Ramadan lanterns are being imported from abroad—especially from China. This foreign invasion of the market has caused many lantern workshops to go bankrupt recently.

Ismail Mohamed Saeed, a lantern salesman from the Al-Sayeda Zeinab area, says, "The Egyptian workshop owners still utilize primitive techniques, which were handed down from generation to generation, to build Ramadan lanterns. They use soldering irons, scissors, hammers, and their lanterns are made of cast iron.

(b) "Now that China has invaded the industry, they recreate the traditional Ramadan lantern shape every year. Even worse, they make plastic Ramadan lanterns that play the music of the latest pop songs!" Mahmoud Al Masry, an owner of a lantern shop in the Al-Hussein neighbourhood, warns, "The Egyptian Ramadan lantern workshops are in danger of collapse and bankruptcy. They simply cannot compete with the Chinese Ramadan lanterns which are distinctive, come in different shapes and sizes, and are very inexpensive. The price and the shape of the Chinese Ramadan lanterns are the most important elements in attracting adults and youngsters alike."

Masry adds, "The Chinese lanterns are sold in Egypt for anywhere from 10 to 60 pounds [EGP]. The Egyptian lanterns are sold for anywhere from 40 to 300 pounds—this is because of their size, shape, and the quality of their construction. However, the consumers usually prefer buying the cheaper lanterns, overlooking quality."

Workshop owner, Ahmad Ali, says, "The Chinese use modern methods in their production of Ramadan lanterns that the Egyptian lantern makers simply do not have. When Egyptian workshops tried to compete and modernise, they asked for the Alumni of the College of Fine Arts to assist by drawing pictures and beautiful shapes on the glass of their lanterns. Then the Chinese surprised us all and came up with the idea of making lanterns that look like puppets and airplanes that walk and sing. They even work by remote control—to top that off they are still cheap!" Ali implores, "The Egyptian government, which is represented by the Ministry of Trade and Industry, needs to take an interest in the Egyptian Ramadan lantern industry and help modernize it. Most importantly, the government should regulate Chinese imports and enforce specific stipulations concerning imported goods."

Mohamed Abdul Aziz, an accountant, declares, "I buy the original Egyptian-made Ramadan lantern every year. However, I can see how the overinflated prices of these lanterns force many consumers to opt for buying the imported ones because they simply cannot afford the Egyptian ones."

Mohsen Khalil Rakha, an employee, says, "The present economic crisis stops people from being able to afford the Egyptian-made lanterns. Personally, I buy the Chinese lanterns for my children—they like the songs coming from them."

In an exclusive interview, Dr. Salah Edin Fahmy, Professor of Economics at the American University in Cairo, says, "The cost of importing the Ramadan Lantern from China last month reached 2.5 million Egyptian pounds. This is just one episode from a series of Chinese invasions of our Egyptian market. Can you believe they also produce the cakes we eat during Eid? They were sold in our markets—and they are cheaper than the Egyptian cakes!"

He warns, "The industry is a source of income for thousands. They've begun to export their goods to other countries in the Arab world and to some counties in Europe, like Germany. The Egyptian lantern makers are faced with tough choices: they can either ration their budgets between the high cost of raw materials and the rise of wages for their employees, or sell competitively to counteract the low prices of the Chinese Ramadan lanterns—any way you cut it, it is a huge loss."

Source: "An Industry Based on a Thousand-year-old Tradition Faces Collapse," Al-Shorfa.com, September 27, 2008.

Key Points in the Article

The popularity of the historical Egyptian lanterns has caught the attention of Chinese producers to penetrate the Egyptian market and take advantage of the huge seasonal demand for lanterns. In recent years, many Egyptian lantern-makers find it difficult to compete with the Chinese-imported lanterns because of the low cost of production in China that made the Chinese lanterns cheaper than the Egyptian traditional ones. This price difference made many Egyptian families prefer to buy the Chinese lanterns. The diversion in demand from the Egyptian traditional lanterns to the Chinese lanterns over the years has increased the probability of making Egyptian-made lanterns an extinct industry. In the long run, if the Chinese lanterns become identical to the Egyptian traditional lanterns, and the Egyptian government keeps the lanterns' market free for entry, then the only way for Egyptian producers to compete with the Chinese is by lowering their average total cost so that they can make a profit and survive in the market.

Analyzing the News

a One of the key points of this chapter is that, ultimately, it is consumers who decide which goods will be produced (or imported).

Since Egyptian families have a steady demand for Ramadan lanterns, some producers, local and foreign, would find it profitable to direct factors of production toward producing lanterns. For many Egyptian families, the demand for lanterns is highly inelastic. Their demand is mainly determined by the number of children in the family. This means that there is a high potential to make a profit from selling lanterns in the short run.

In fact, it is those profits that signal to entrepreneurs that demand for lanterns might be increased due to the increase in the number of children in Egypt. We know from the analysis in this chapter, though, that these profits will not persist in the long run. Figure 1 shows that an increase in demand for lanterns, due to the high population growth rate in Egypt, raises the price from P_1 to P_2, which results in the typical producer, local or foreign, earning economic profits. Figure 2 shows the long-run result. The economic profit earned by producing lanterns will attract additional firms to enter the industry.

b Until recently, Chinese lanterns were somewhat different from the Egyptian traditional lanterns. This means that the lantern market was not a perfectly competitive market; rather, it is monopolistically competitive. Surprisingly, the situation changed in 2010 when Chinese lantern producers realized that some Egyptian families still like

to buy the traditional lanterns. The Chinese decided to produce lanterns that are identical to the Egyptian traditional lanterns. Now with many sellers and buyers of identical traditional lanterns, and free entry and exit to the market, the traditional lanterns' market is going to be perfectly competitive. This increases the threat to the Egyptian lanterns industry since the Chinese competitors are producing at a lower average cost, meaning they can sell lanterns at a cheaper price. As we mentioned earlier, Egyptian lantern producers have to decrease their average total cost in order to be able to compete in the lanterns market.

Thinking Critically

1. Use a demand and supply graph and a cost curve graph to show what would happen if the Egyptian government imposed high tariffs on imported Chinese lanterns.

2. In a free lanterns' market, suppose that Egyptian lantern-makers protest to their parliament as prices of lanterns decline. Use a demand and supply graph to show the impact on the market if parliament decides to impose a price floor above the equilibrium price. What happens to consumer surplus and producer surplus as a result of the price floor?

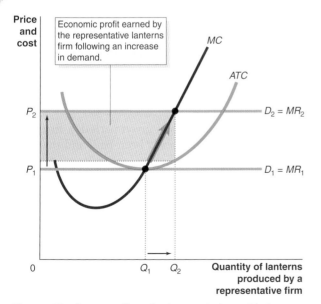

Figure 1. The short-run effects of an increase in demand for lanterns.

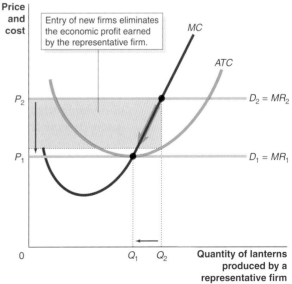

Figure 2. The long-run effects of an increase in demand for lanterns.

Key Terms

Summary

8.1 LEARNING OBJECTIVE

Define a perfectly competitive market and explain why a perfect competitor faces a horizontal demand curve, **pages 267-269.**

Perfectly Competitive Markets

A **perfectly competitive market** must have many buyers and sellers, firms must be producing identical products, and there must be no barriers to entry of new firms. The demand curve for a good or service produced in a perfectly competitive market is downward sloping, but the demand curve for the output of one firm in a perfectly competitive market is a horizontal line at the market price. Firms in perfectly competitive markets are **price takers** and see their sales drop to zero if they attempt to charge more than the market price.

8.2 LEARNING OBJECTIVE

Explain how a firm maximizes profits in a perfectly competitive market, **pages 269-272.**

How a Firm Maximizes Profit in a Perfectly Competitive Market

Profit is the difference between total revenue (TR) and total cost (TC). **Average revenue** (AR) is total revenue divided by the quantity of the product sold. A firm maximizes profit by producing the level of output where the difference between revenue and cost is the greatest. This is the same level of output where marginal revenue is equal to marginal cost. **Marginal revenue** is the change in total revenue from selling one more unit.

8.3 LEARNING OBJECTIVE

Use graphs to show a firm's profit or loss, **pages 273-278.**

Illustrating Profit or Loss on the Cost Curve Graph

From the definitions of profit and average total cost, we can develop the following expression for the relationship between total profit and average total cost: Profit = $(P - ATC) \times Q$. Using this expression, we can determine the area showing profit or loss on a cost-curve graph: the area of profit or loss is a box with a height equal to price minus average total cost (for profit) or average total cost minus price (for loss) and a base equal to the quantity of output.

8.4 LEARNING OBJECTIVE

Explain why firms may shut down temporarily, **pages 278-280.**

Deciding Whether to Produce or to Shut Down in the Short Run

In deciding whether to shut down or produce during a given period, a firm should ignore its *sunk costs*. A **sunk cost** is a cost that has already been paid and that cannot by recovered. In the short run, a firm continues to produce as long as its price is at least equal to its average variable cost. A perfectly competitive firm's **shutdown point** is the minimum point on the firm's average variable cost curve. If price falls below average variable cost, the firm shuts down in the short run. For prices above the shutdown point, a perfectly competitive firm's marginal cost curve is also its supply curve.

8.5 LEARNING OBJECTIVE

Explain how entry and exit ensure that perfectly competitive firms earn zero economic profit in the long run, **pages 281-287.**

"If Everyone Can Do It, You Can't Make Money at It": The Entry and Exit of Firms in the Long Run

Economic profit is a firm's revenues minus all its costs, implicit and explicit. **Economic loss** is the situation in which a firm's total revenue is less than its total cost, including all implicit costs. If firms make economic profits in the short run, new firms enter the industry until the market price has fallen enough to wipe out the profits. If firms make economic losses, firms exit the industry until the market price has risen enough to wipe out the losses. **Long-run competitive equilibrium** is the situation in which the entry and exit of firms has resulted in the typical firm breaking even. The **long-run supply curve** shows the relationship between market price and the quantity supplied.

Perfect Competition and Efficiency

Perfect competition results in **productive efficiency**, which means that goods and services are produced at the lowest possible cost. Perfect competition also results in **allocative efficiency**, which means the goods and services are produced up to the point where the last unit provides a marginal benefit to consumers equal to the marginal cost of producing it.

8.6 LEARNING OBJECTIVE

Explain how perfect competition leads to economic efficiency, **pages 287–291.**

Review, Problems and Applications

myeconlab
Get Ahead of the Curve
Visit www.pearsoned.co.uk/awe/hubbard to complete these exercises online and get instant feedback.

8.1 LEARNING OBJECTIVE   Define a perfectly competitive market and explain why a perfect competitor faces a horizontal demand curve, **pages 267–269.**

Review Questions

1.1 What are the three conditions for a market to be perfectly competitive?
1.2 What is a price taker? When are firms likely to be price takers?
1.3 Draw a graph showing the market demand and supply for corn and the demand for the corn produced by one corn farmer. Be sure to indicate the market price and the price received by the corn farmer.

Problems and Applications

1.4 Explain whether each of the following is a perfectly competitive market. For each market that is not perfectly competitive, explain why it is not.
  a. Corn farming
  b. Retail bookselling
  c. Automobile manufacturing
  d. New home construction
1.5 Why are consumers usually price takers when they buy most goods and services, while relatively few firms are price takers?

1.6 The financial writer Andrew Tobias has described an incident when he was a student at the Harvard Business School: each student in the class was given large amounts of information about a particular firm and asked to determine a pricing strategy for the firm. Most of the students spent hours preparing their answers and came to class carrying many sheets of paper with their calculations. Tobias came up with the correct answer after just a few minutes and without having made any calculations. When his professor called on him in class for an answer, Tobias stated, "The case said the XYZ Company was in a very competitive industry…and the case said that the company had all the business it could handle." Given this information, what price do you think Tobias argued the company should charge? Briefly explain. (Tobias says the class greeted his answer with "thunderous applause.")
Source: Andrew Tobias, *The Only Investment Guide You'll Ever Need*, San Diego: Harcourt, 2005, pp. 6–8.

8.2 LEARNING OBJECTIVE   Explain how a firm maximizes profits in a perfectly competitive market, **pages 269–272.**

Review Questions

2.1 Explain why it is true that for a firm in a perfectly competitive market that $P = MR = AR$.
2.2 Explain why it is true that for a firm in a perfectly competitive market, the profit-maximizing condition $MR = MC$ is equivalent to the condition $P = MC$.

Problems and Applications

2.3 A student argues: "To maximize profit, a firm should produce the quantity where the difference between marginal revenue and marginal cost is the greatest. If

it produces more than this quantity, then the profit made on each additional unit will be falling." Briefly explain whether you agree with this reasoning.
2.4 Why don't firms maximize revenue rather than profit? If a firm decided to maximize revenue, would it be likely to produce a smaller or a larger quantity than if it were maximizing profit? Briefly explain.
2.5 Refer to Table 8-2 on page 270 and Table 8-3 on page 271. Suppose that the price of oranges rises to US$6.00 per kilo. How many kilos of oranges will Farmer Khouri produce, and how much profit will he make? Briefly explain.

2.6 Refer to Table 8-2 and Table 8-3. Suppose that the marginal cost of oranges is US$0.50 higher for every kilo of oranges produced. For example, the marginal cost of producing the eighth kilo of oranges is now US$6.50. Assume that the price of oranges remains US$4 per kilo. Will this increase in marginal cost change the profit-maximizing level of production for Farmer Khouri? Briefly explain. How much profit will Farmer Khouri make now?

8.3 LEARNING OBJECTIVE   Use graphs to show a firm's profit or loss, **pages 273–278.**

Review Questions

3.1 Draw a graph showing a firm in a perfectly competitive market that is making a profit. Be sure your graph includes the firm's demand curve, marginal revenue curve, marginal cost curve, average total cost curve, and average variable cost curve and make sure to indicate the area representing the firm's profits.

3.2 Draw a graph showing a firm in a perfectly competitive market that is operating at a loss. Be sure your graph includes the firm's demand curve, marginal revenue curve, marginal cost curve, average total cost curve, and average variable cost curve and make sure to indicate the area representing the firm's losses.

Problems and Applications

3.3 **(Related to Solved Problem 8-3 on page 274)** Frances sells earrings in the perfectly competitive earring market. Her output per day and costs are as follows:

OUTPUT PER DAY	TOTAL COST
0	$1.00
1	2.50
2	3.50
3	4.20
4	4.50
5	5.20
6	6.80
7	8.70
8	10.70
9	13.00

a. If the current equilibrium price in the earring market is US$1.80, how many earrings will Frances produce, what price will she charge, and how much profit (or loss) will she make? Draw a graph to illustrate your answer. Your graph should be clearly labeled and should include Frances's demand, *ATC, AVC, MC,* and *MR* curves; the price she is charging; the quantity she is producing; and the area representing her profit (or loss).

b. Suppose the equilibrium price of earrings falls to US$1.00. Now how many earrings will Frances produce, what price will she charge, and how much profit (or loss) will she make? Show your work. Draw a graph to illustrate this situation, using the instructions in question (a).

c. Suppose the equilibrium price of earrings falls to US$0.25. Now how many earrings will Frances produce, what price will she charge, and how much profit (or loss) will she make?

3.4 **(Related to Solved Problem 8-3 on page 274)** Review Solved Problem 8-3 and then answer the following: suppose the equilibrium price of footballs falls to US$2.50. Now how many footballs will Mustafa produce? What price will he charge? How much profit (or loss) will he make?

3.5 According to a report in the *Wall Street Journal*, during the fourth quarter of 2003, the profits of British Airways rose to £83 million, from £13 million one year earlier. At the same time, "the average amount the airline makes on each paying passenger fell 0.8 percent." If profit per passenger fell, how could total profits rise? Illustrate your answer with a graph. Be sure to indicate profit per passenger and total profit on the graph.
Source: Emma Blak.e, "British Airways Reports Sharp Jump in Net Profits," *Wall Street Journal*, February 9, 2004.

3.6 Suppose that a HyperPanda supermarket manager in the eastern province of Saudi Arabia decided to shut down one the branches of the supermarket (branch no. 5) because the landlord asked for a 20 percent increase in the annual rent, and workers asked for 10 percent wage increase. Assuming the branch is specializing in selling meat, draw a graph showing HyperPanda earning a profit before the increase in the annual rent and wages. Draw a second graph showing why the HyperPanda manager shut down branch no. 5, following the increase in annual rent and wage costs.

3.7 **(Related to the Making the Connection on page 276)** Suppose the medical screening firms had run an effective advertising campaign which convinced a large number of people that yearly CT scans were critical for good health. How would this have changed the fortunes of these firms? Illustrate your answer with a graph showing the situation for a representative firm in the industry. Be sure your graph includes the firm's demand curve, marginal revenue curve, marginal cost curve, and average total cost curve.

Review Questions

4.1 What is the difference between a firm's shutdown point in the short run and in the long run? Why are firms willing to accept losses in the short run but not in the long run?

4.2 What is the relationship between a perfectly competitive firm's marginal cost curve and its supply curve?

Problems and Applications

4.3 Zeyad Galal produces table lamps in the perfectly competitive desk lamp market.
  a. Fill in the missing values in the table.

OUTPUT PER WEEK	TOTAL COSTS	AFC	AVC	ATC	MC
0	$100				
1	150				
2	175				
3	190				
4	210				
5	240				
6	280				
7	330				
8	390				
9	460				
10	540				

  b. Suppose the equilibrium price in the desk lamp market is US$50. How many table lamps should Zeyad produce, and how much profit will he make?
  c. If next week the equilibrium price of desk lamps drops to US$30, should Zeyad shut down? Explain.

4.4 The graph in the next column represents the situation of a perfectly competitive firm.

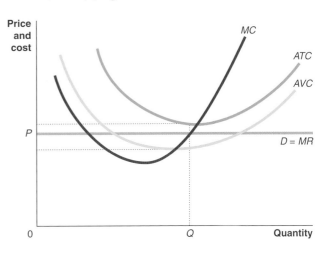

Indicate on the graph the areas that represent the following:
  a. Total cost
  b. Total revenue
  c. Variable cost
  d. Profit or loss
Briefly explain whether the firm will continue to produce in the short run.

4.5 Suppose you decide to open a copy store. You rent store space (signing a one-year lease to do so), and you take out a loan at a local bank and use the money to purchase 10 copiers. Six months later, a large chain opens a copy store two blocks away from yours. As a result, the revenue you receive from your copy store, while sufficient to cover the wages of your employees and the costs of paper and utilities, doesn't cover all your rent and the interest and repayment costs on the loan you took out to purchase the copiers. Should you continue operating your business?

Review Problems

5.1 When are firms likely to enter an industry? When are they likely to exit an industry?

5.2 Would a firm earning zero economic profit continue to produce, even in the long run?

5.3 Discuss the shape of the long-run supply curve in a perfectly competitive market. Suppose that a perfectly competitive market is initially at long-run equilibrium and then there is a permanent decrease in the demand for the product. Draw a graph showing how the market adjusts in the long run.

Problems and Applications

5.4 Suppose an assistant professor of economics is earning a salary of US$65,000 per year. One day she quits her job, sells US$100,000 worth of bonds that had been earning 5 percent per year, and uses the funds to open a bookstore. At the end of the year, she shows an accounting profit of US$80,000 on her income tax return. What is her economic profit?

5.5 Suppose that you and your sister both decide to open copy stores. Your parents always liked your sister better than you, so they purchase and give to her free of charge the three copiers she needs to operate her store. You, however, have to rent your copiers for US$1,500 per month each. Does your sister have lower costs in operating her copy store than you have in operating your copy store because of this? Explain.

5.6 Consider the following statement: "The products for which demand is the greatest will also be the products that are most profitable to produce." Briefly explain whether you agree with this statement.

5.7 In panel (b) of Figure 8-9 on page 284, Aliaa Adel reduces her output from 8,000 to 5,000 boxes of apples when the price falls to US$7. At this price and this output level, she is operating at a loss. Why doesn't she just continue charging the original US$10 and continue producing 8,000 boxes of apples?

5.8 The following statement appeared in a U.S. Congressional analysis of the airline industry: "In lean times, airlines can operate for extended periods of time [while making losses]...because revenues will cover a large part of their costs (Pan Am lost money for about a decade before finally closing down)." Why would Pan Am—or any other airline—continue losing money for 10 years rather than shut down immediately? In the statement "revenues will cover a large part of their costs," does it matter if the costs being referred to are fixed costs or variable costs? Briefly explain.

Source: Joint Economic Committee, Democratic Staff, "Assessing Losses for the Airline Industry and Its Workers in the Aftermath of the Terrorist Attacks," October 3, 2001.

5.9 A student in a principles of economics course makes the following remark: "The economic model of perfectly competitive markets is fine in theory but not very realistic. It predicts that in the long run, a firm in a perfectly competitive market will earn no profits. No firm in the real world would stay in business if it earned zero profits." Do you agree with this remark?

5.10 Suppose that the laptop computer industry is perfectly competitive and that the firms that assemble laptops do not also make the displays, or screens, for them. Suppose that the laptop display industry is also perfectly competitive. Finally, suppose that because the demand for laptop displays is currently relatively small, firms in the laptop display industry have not been able to take advantage of all the economies of scale in laptop display production. Use a graph of the laptop computer market to illustrate the long-run effects on equilibrium price and quantity in the laptop computer market of a substantial and sustained increase in the demand for laptop computers. Use another graph to show the impact on the cost curves of a typical firm in the laptop computer industry. Briefly explain your graphs. Do your graphs indicate that the laptop computer industry is a constant-cost industry, an increasing-cost industry, or a decreasing-cost industry?

5.11 If in the long run apple growers who use organic methods of cultivation make no greater rate of return on their investment than apple growers who use conventional methods, why did a significant number of apple growers switch from conventional to organic methods in the first place?

8.6 LEARNING OBJECTIVE   Explain how perfect competition leads to economic efficiency, **pages 287–291.**

Review Questions

6.1 What is meant by allocative efficiency? What is meant by productive efficiency? Briefly discuss the difference between these two concepts.

6.2 How does perfect competition lead to allocative and productive efficiency?

Problems and Applications

6.3 The chapter states, "Firms will supply all those goods that provide consumers with a marginal benefit at least as great as the marginal cost of producing them." A student objects to this statement by making the following argument: "I doubt that firms will really do this. After all, firms are in business to make a profit; they don't care about what is best for consumers." Evaluate the student's argument.

6.4 **(Related to *Making the Connection* on page 285)** Ethan Nichols developed his first game while still working at Sun Microsystems. After his first game was a success, he quit Sun to form his own company—with himself as the only employee. How did Nichols' quitting Sun to work full-time for himself affect the cost to him of developing games?

Source: Jenna Wortham,"The iPhone Gold Rush," *New York Times*, April 5, 2009.

6.5 **(Related to *Solved Problem 8-6* on page 288)** Discuss the following statement: "In a perfectly competitive market, in the long run consumers benefit from reductions in costs, but firms don't." Don't firms also benefit from cost reductions because they are able to earn greater profits?

6.6 (Related to *Solved Problem 8-6* on page **288**) In early 2007, Pioneer and JVC, two Japanese electronics firms, each announced that their profits would be lower than expected because they had been forced to cut prices for LCD and plasma television sets. Given the strong consumer demand for plasma television sets, shouldn't firms have been able to raise prices and increase their profits? Briefly explain.

Source: Hiroyuki Kachi, "Pioneer's Net Rises 74 percent, JVC Posts Loss," *Wall Street Journal*, February 1, 2007.

6.7 Suppose a nutritionist develops a revolutionary new diet that involves eating 10 oranges per day. The new diet becomes wildly popular. What effect is the new diet likely to have on the number of orange gardens within 100 km of Maghdousheh town in Lebanon? What effect is the diet likely to have on housing prices in Maghdousheh?

Monopolistic Competition: The Competitive Model in a More Realistic Setting

Costa Coffee Expansion in the Middle East: Growth through Product Differentiation

Today, you can observe that a significant consumer demand exists for coffeehouses where customers can sit, relax, read newspapers, browse the Internet, and drink higher-quality coffee than was typically served in traditional coffee shops. How many times have you seen a Costa print or television ad? Costa Coffee, the U.K.'s authentic Italian-branded coffee franchise, is one of the largest coffee-shop brands in the world after Starbucks, its U.S. competitor. Today, Costa serves 108 million cups of coffee around the world each year, and seems to have stores in almost every mall and airport in the Arab world.

Instead of advertising and marketing campaigns, Costa owes its success to the 'perfect combination,' referring to a distinctive in-store experience and good product differentiation. Costa's website reads: "When you walk into a Costa store you'll notice…First of all, there's the warm and welcoming atmosphere. Then the great range of authentic coffee drinks.

Next, the Ferrari of coffee machines; and finally, the most passionate and well-trained baristas around. It's this unique combination that makes us stand out from the others…." When asked about the key to the success of the Costa brand, the UAE general manager, Eric Hughes, answered:

Our master roasters, based in the U.K., source the world's best beans and then [we] carefully slow-roast them for a fuller, smoother flavor to create our special Mocha Italia blend. Once in our shops, our highly trained baristas hand craft coffee in the authentic Italian way, with true attention to detail: freshly ground beans and coffees made one cup at a time…We also make sure our stores are as welcoming and hospitable as possible to ensure our guests always feel relaxed, comfortable and cared for.

Like many other large, global firms, Costa started small. In 1971, the Costa brothers, Sergio and Bruno, opened the first Costa store at 9 Newport Street, London. After the acquisition of Costa Coffee by Whitbread in 1995, the company experienced strong growth, making it the U.K.'s largest coffee retailer and one of the largest worldwide today. The brand operates more than 1,100 stores in the U.K. alone, and more than 600 stores around the world.

Costa decided to expand in the Middle East at the beginning of the 2000s because the region has a very strong coffee culture, with a large percentage of the population already being habitual coffee drinkers. Costa opened its first international store in Dubai, at the Aviation Club, at the end of 1999. It appointed its first Middle East franchise director, operating from Dubai, in 2004. By that time Costa had only 40 stores in the region. By 2008, Costa celebrated the opening of its 200th store in Mohandeseen, Cairo, Egypt. In the following two years it added at least 25 more stores. Today it has over 70 outlets in the UAE alone.

Still, Costa is *not* unique: You probably know of three or more coffeehouses in your neighborhood. The coffeehouse market is competitive because it is inexpensive to open a new store by leasing store space and buying espresso machines. Hundreds of firms in the Arab world operate coffeehouses. Some firms are large international chains, such as Starbucks and Caribou Coffee, which have hundreds of stores. Others are regional chains, such as Cilantro Coffee, which operates over 50 stores in Egypt alone. Still others are small firms that operate only one store.

In the previous chapter, we discussed the situation of firms in perfectly competitive markets. These markets share three key characteristics:

1 There are many firms.
2 All firms sell identical products.
3 There are no barriers to new firms entering the industry.

The market Costa competes in shares two of these characteristics: there are many other coffeehouses—with the number increasing all the time—and the barriers to entering the market are very low. But consumers do not view the products sold by coffeehouses as being identical. The coffee at Costa, as well as the muffins and other snacks, are not identical to what competing coffeehouses offer. Selling coffee in coffeehouses is not like selling wheat: the products that Costa and its competitors sell are *differentiated* rather than identical. So, the coffeehouse market is *monopolistically competitive* rather than perfectly competitive. **AN INSIDE LOOK** on **page 320** shows how a growing coffee culture in the Middle East is fueling more competition in the coffeehouse business.

Source: "Costa Building on Middle East Success," www
.HotelierMiddleEast.com, January 4, 2010; "Costa Continues Its Unique
Coffee Experience as It Opens Its 200th Store within the Region,"
AMEinfo.com, August 10, 2008; "Costa Coffee Appoints First Middle East
Regional Director," AMEinfo.com, July 08, 2004; www.costacoffee.com.

LEARNING Objectives

After studying this chapter, you should be able to:

9.1 Explain why a **monopolistically competitive firm** has downward-sloping **demand and marginal revenue curves**, page 302.

9.2 Explain how a monopolistically competitive firm **maximizes profits** in the **short run**, page 305.

9.3 Analyze the situation of a monopolistically competitive firm in the **long run**, page 307.

9.4 Compare the **efficiency** of monopolistic competition and perfect competition, page 314.

9.5 Define **marketing** and explain how firms use it to differentiate their products, page 315.

9.6 Identify the **key factors** that determine a **firm's success**, page 317.

Economics in YOUR Life!

Opening Your Own Restaurant

After you graduate, you plan to realize your dream of opening your own Lebanese restaurant. You are confident that many people will enjoy the fattoush prepared with your grandmother's secret dressing. Although your hometown already has three Lebanese restaurants, you are convinced that you can enter this market and make a profit.

You have many choices to make in operating your restaurant. Will it be 'family style,' with sturdy but inexpensive furniture, where families with small—and noisy!—children will feel welcome, or will it be more elegant, with nice furniture, tablecloths, and candles? Will you offer a full menu or concentrate on famous dishes that use your grandmother's secret recipes? These and other choices you make will distinguish your restaurant from other competing restaurants. What's likely to happen in the restaurant market in your hometown after you open? How successful are you likely to be? See if you can answer these questions as you read this chapter. You can check your answers against those we provide at the end of the chapter. > **Continued on page 319**

Monopolistic competition A market structure in which barriers to entry are low and many firms compete by selling similar, but not identical, products.

Many markets in the Arab-world economy are similar to the coffeehouse market: they have many buyers and sellers, and the barriers to entry are low, but the goods and services offered for sale are differentiated rather than identical. Examples of these markets include consumer electronics stores, restaurants, movie theaters, supermarkets, and manufacturers of men's and women's clothing. In fact, the majority of the firms you patronize are competing in **monopolistically competitive** markets.

In the previous chapter, we saw how perfect competition benefits consumers and results in economic efficiency. Will these same desirable outcomes also hold for monopolistically competitive markets? This question, which we explore in this chapter, is important because monopolistically competitive markets are so common.

9.1 LEARNING OBJECTIVE

9.1 | Explain why a monopolistically competitive firm has downward-sloping demand and marginal revenue curves.

Demand and Marginal Revenue for a Firm in a Monopolistically Competitive Market

If the Costa coffeehouse located one mile from your house raises the price for a cafè latte from US$3.00 to US$3.25, it will lose some, but not all, of its customers. Some customers will switch to buying their coffee at another store, but other customers will be willing to pay the higher price for a variety of reasons: this store may be closer to them, or they may prefer Costa cafè lattes to similar coffees at competing stores. Because changing the price affects the quantity of cafè lattes sold, a Costa store will face a downward-sloping demand curve rather than the horizontal demand curve that an orange farmer faces.

The Demand Curve for a Monopolistically Competitive Firm

Figure 9-1 shows how a change in price affects the quantity of cafè lattes that Costa sells. The increase in the price from US$3.00 to US$3.25 decreases the quantity of cafè lattes sold from 3,000 per week to 2,400 per week.

Figure 9-1

The Downward-Sloping Demand for Cafè Lattes at Costa

If Costa increases the price of cafè lattes, it will lose some, but not all, of its customers. In this case, raising the price from US$3.00 to US$3.25 reduces the quantity of cafè lattes sold from 3,000 to 2,400. Therefore, unlike a perfect competitor, a Costa store faces a downward-sloping demand curve.

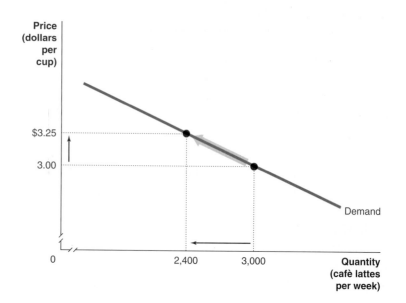

Marginal Revenue for a Firm with a Downward-Sloping Demand Curve

Recall that for a firm in a perfectly competitive market, the demand curve and the marginal revenue curve are the same. A perfectly competitive firm faces a horizontal demand curve and does not have to cut the price to sell a larger quantity. A monopolistically competitive firm, however, must cut the price to sell more, so its marginal revenue curve will slope downward and will be below its demand curve.

The data in Table 9-1 illustrate this point. To keep the numbers simple, let's assume that your local Costa coffeehouse is very small and sells at most 10 cafè lattes per week. If Costa charges a price of US$6.00 or more, all of its potential customers will buy their coffee somewhere else. If it charges US$5.50, it will sell 1 cafè latte per week. For each additional US$0.50 Costa reduces the price, it increases the number of cafè lattes it sells by 1. The third column in the table shows how the firm's *total revenue* changes as it sells more cafè lattes. The fourth column shows the firm's revenue per unit, or its *average revenue*. Average revenue is equal to total revenue divided by quantity. Because total revenue equals price multiplied by quantity, dividing by quantity leaves just price. Therefore, *average revenue is always equal to price*. This result will be true for firms selling in any of the four market structures we discussed in the previous chapter.

The last column shows the firm's marginal revenue, or the amount that total revenue changes as the firm sells 1 more cafè latte. For a perfectly competitive firm, the additional revenue received from selling 1 more unit is just equal to the price. That will not be true for Costa because to sell another cafè latte, it has to reduce the price. When the firm cuts the price by US$0.50, one good thing and one bad thing happen:

- **The good thing.** It sells one more cafè latte; we can call this the *output effect.*
- **The bad thing.** It receives US$0.50 less for each cafè latte that it could have sold at the higher price; we can call this the *price effect.*

Figure 9-2 illustrates what happens when the firm cuts the price from US$3.50 to US$3.00. Selling the sixth cafè latte adds the US$3.00 price to the firm's revenue; this is the output effect. But Costa now receives a price of US$3.00, rather than US$3.50, on the first 5 cafè lattes sold; this is the price effect. As a result of the price effect, the firm's revenue on these 5 cafè lattes is US$2.50 less than it would have been if the price had remained at US$3.50. So, the firm has gained US$3.00 in revenue on the sixth cafè latte and lost US$2.50 in revenue on the first 5 cafè lattes, for a net change in revenue

TABLE 9-1

Demand and Marginal Revenue at a Costa

CAFÈ LATTES SOLD PER WEEK (Q)	PRICE (P)	TOTAL REVENUE ($TR = P \times Q$)	AVERAGE REVENUE ($AR = \dfrac{TR}{Q}$)	MARGINAL REVENUE ($MR = \dfrac{\Delta TR}{\Delta Q}$)
0	$6.00	$0.00	—	—
1	5.50	5.50	$5.50	$5.50
2	5.00	10.00	5.00	4.50
3	4.50	13.50	4.50	3.50
4	4.00	16.00	4.00	2.50
5	3.50	17.50	3.50	1.50
6	3.00	18.00	3.00	0.50
7	2.50	17.50	2.50	–0.50
8	2.00	16.00	2.00	–1.50
9	1.50	13.50	1.50	–2.50
10	1.00	10.00	1.00	–3.50

Figure 9-2

How a Price Cut Affects a Firm's Revenue

If the local Costa reduces the price of a cafè latte from US$3.50 to US$3.00, the number of cafè lattes it sells per week will increase from 5 to 6. Its marginal revenue from selling the sixth cafè latte will be US$0.50, which is equal to the US$3.00 additional revenue from selling 1 more cafè latte (the area of the green box) minus the US$2.50 loss in revenue from selling the first 5 cafè lattes for US$0.50 less each (the area of the red box).

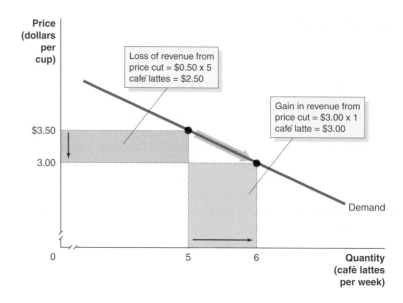

of US$0.50. Marginal revenue is the change in total revenue from selling one more unit. Therefore, the marginal revenue of the sixth cafè latte is US$0.50. Notice that the marginal revenue of the sixth unit is far below its price of US$3.00. In fact, for each additional cafè latte Costa sells, marginal revenue will be less than price. There is an important general point: *Every firm that has the ability to affect the price of the good or service it sells will have a marginal revenue curve that is below its demand curve.* Only firms in perfectly competitive markets, which can sell as many units as they want at the market price, have marginal revenue curves that are the same as their demand curves.

Figure 9-3 shows the relationship between the demand curve and the marginal revenue curve for the local Costa. Notice that after the sixth cafè latte, marginal revenue

Figure 9-3

The Demand and Marginal Revenue Curves for a Monopolistically Competitive Firm

Any firm that has the ability to affect the price of the product it sells will have a marginal revenue curve that is below its demand curve. We plot the data from Table 9-1 to create the demand and marginal revenue curves. After the sixth cafè latte, marginal revenue becomes negative because the additional revenue received from selling 1 more cafè latte is smaller than the revenue lost from receiving a lower price on the cafè lattes that could have been sold at the original price.

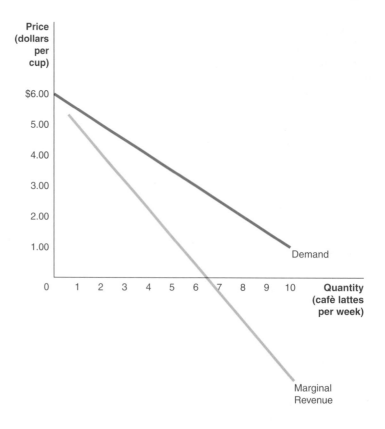

becomes negative. Marginal revenue is negative because the additional revenue received from selling 1 more cafè latte is smaller than the revenue lost from receiving a lower price on the cafè lattes that could have been sold at the original price.

9.2 LEARNING OBJECTIVE

9.2 | Explain how a monopolistically competitive firm maximizes profits in the short run.

How a Monopolistically Competitive Firm Maximizes Profits in the Short Run

All firms use the same approach to maximize profits: they produce where marginal revenue is equal to marginal cost. For the local Costa, this means selling the quantity of cafè lattes for which the last cafè latte sold adds the same amount to the firm's revenue as to its costs. To begin our discussion of how monopolistically competitive firms maximize profits, let's consider the situation the local Costa faces in the short run. Recall from Chapter 7 that in the short run, at least one factor of production is fixed and there is not enough time for new firms to enter the market. A Costa has many costs, including the cost of purchasing the ingredients for its cafè lattes and other coffees, the electricity it uses, and the wages of its employees. Recall that a firm's *marginal cost* is the increase in total cost resulting from producing another unit of output. We have seen that for many firms, marginal cost has a U shape. We will assume that the Costa's marginal cost has this usual shape.

In the table in Figure 9-4, we bring together the revenue data from Table 9-1 with the cost data for Costa. The graphs in Figure 9-4 plot the data from the table. In panel (a), we see how Costa can determine its profit-maximizing quantity and price. As long as the marginal cost of selling one more cafè latte is less than the marginal revenue, the firm should sell additional cafè lattes. For example, increasing the quantity of cafè lattes sold from 3 per week to 4 per week increases marginal cost by US$1.00 but increases marginal revenue by US$2.50. So, the firm's profits are increased by US$1.50 as a result of selling the fourth cafè latte.

As Costa sells more cafè lattes, rising marginal cost eventually equals marginal revenue, and the firm sells the profit-maximizing quantity of cafè lattes. Marginal cost equals marginal revenue with the fifth cafè latte, which adds US$1.50 to the firm's costs and US$1.50 to its revenues—point *A* in panel (a) of Figure 9-4. The demand curve tells us the price at which the firm is able to sell 5 cafè lattes per week. In Figure 9-4, if we draw a vertical line from 5 cafè lattes up to the demand curve, we can see that the price at which the firm can sell 5 cafè lattes per week is US$3.50 (point *B*). We can conclude that for Costa the profit-maximizing quantity is 5 cafè lattes, and its profit-maximizing price is US$3.50. If the firm sells more than 5 cafè lattes per week, its profits fall. For example, selling a sixth cafè latte adds US$2.00 to its costs and only US$0.50 to its revenues. So, its profit would fall from US$5.00 to US$3.50.

Panel (b) adds the average total cost curve for Costa. The panel shows that the average total cost of selling 5 cafè lattes is US$2.50. Recall from Chapter 8 that:

$$\text{Profit} = (P - ATC) \times Q$$

In this case, profit = (US$3.50 − US$2.50) × 5 = US$5.00. The green box in panel (b) shows the amount of profit. The box has a base equal to *Q* and a height equal to (*P* − *ATC*), so its area equals profit.

Notice that, unlike a perfectly competitive firm, which produces where $P = MC$, a monopolistically competitive firm produces where $P > MC$. In this case, Costa is charging a price of US$3.50, although marginal cost is US$1.50. For the perfectly competitive firm, price equals marginal revenue, $P = MR$. Therefore, to fulfill the $MR = MC$ condition for profit maximization, a perfectly competitive firm will produce where $P = MC$. Because $P > MR$ for a monopolistically competitive firm—which results from the marginal revenue curve being below the demand curve—a monopolistically competitive firm will maximize profits where $P > MC$.

Café Lattes Sold per Week (Q)	Price (P)	Total Revenue (TR)	Marginal Revenue (MR)	Total Cost (TC)	Marginal Cost (MC)	Average Total Cost (ATC)	Profit
0	$6.00	$0.00	–	$5.00	–	–	–$5.00
1	5.50	5.50	$5.50	8.00	$3.00	$8.00	–2.50
2	5.00	10.00	4.50	9.50	1.50	4.75	0.50
3	4.50	13.50	3.50	10.00	0.50	3.33	3.50
4	4.00	16.00	2.50	11.00	1.00	2.75	5.00
5	3.50	17.50	1.50	12.50	1.50	2.50	5.00
6	3.00	18.00	0.50	14.50	2.00	2.42	3.50
7	2.50	17.50	–0.50	17.00	2.50	2.43	0.50
8	2.00	16.00	–1.50	20.00	3.00	2.50	–4.00
9	1.50	13.50	–2.50	23.50	3.50	2.61	–10.00
10	1.00	10.00	–3.50	27.50	4.00	2.75	–17.50

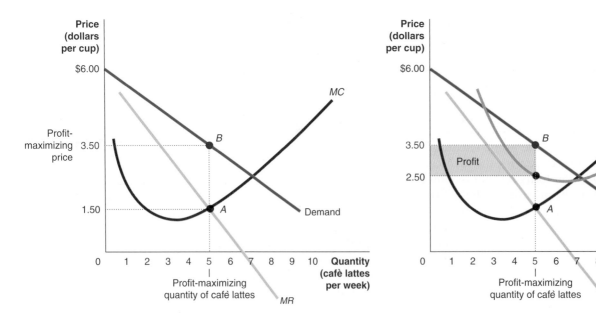

(a) Profit-maximizing quantity and price for a monopolistic competitor

(b) Short-run profits for a monopolistic competitor

Figure 9-4 | Maximizing Profit in a Monopolistically Competitive Market

To maximize profit, a Costa coffeehouse wants to sell café lattes up to the point where the marginal revenue from selling the last café latte is just equal to the marginal cost. As the table shows, this happens with the fifth café latte—point A in panel (a)—which adds US$1.50 to the firm's costs and US$1.50 to its revenues. The firm then uses the demand curve to find the price that will lead consumers to buy this quantity of café lattes (point B). In panel (b), the green box represents the firm's profits. The box has a height equal to US$1.00, which is the price of US$3.50 minus the average total cost of US$2.50, and a base equal to the quantity of 5 café lattes. So, Costa profit equals US$1 × 5 = US$5.00.

Solved Problem | 9-2

How Not to Maximize Profits at Dar Al-Shorouk Publishing Company

Lebanon is famous for its publishing houses. When Dar Al-Shorouk, the Beirut-based publishing company, decides whether to print one more copy of a given, already published book, they need to decide if it is a profitable to do so. Managers at Dar Al-Shorouk begin by calculating the cost of printing one additional copy. In their calculations, these managers include all the other expenses associated with a book, including the overheads like rent and editors' salaries, and then dividing by the number of copies. Will this give an accurate estimate of marginal cost? If you were a manager at Dar Al-Shorouk, how would you determine whether producing one more copy of a book will increase your profits?

SOLVING THE PROBLEM:

Step 1: **Review the chapter material.** This problem is about how monopolistically competitive firms maximize profits, so you may want to review the section "How a Monopolistically Competitive Firm Maximizes Profits in the Short Run," which begins on page 305.

Step 2: **Analyze the costs described in the problem.** We have seen that to maximize profits, firms should produce up to the point where marginal revenue equals marginal cost. Marginal cost is the increase in total cost that results from producing another unit of output. Rent and editors' salaries are part of a publishing company's fixed costs because they do not change as the company increases its output of books. Therefore, managers at Dar Al-Shorouk should not include them in calculating marginal cost.

Step 3: **Explain how a manager at Dar Al-Shorouk publishing firm should decide whether to publish one more copy of a book.** To determine whether producing one more copy of a book will increase your profits, you need to compare the marginal revenue received from selling the book with the marginal cost of producing it. If the marginal revenue is greater than the marginal cost, producing the book will increase your profits.

YOUR TURN: For more practice, do related problem 2.9 on page 324 at the end of this chapter.

>> **End Solved Problem 9-2**

9.3 LEARNING OBJECTIVE

9.3 | Analyze the situation of a monopolistically competitive firm in the long run.

What Happens to Profits in the Long Run?

Remember that a firm makes an economic profit when its total revenue is greater than all of its costs, including the opportunity cost of the funds invested in the firm by its owners. Because cost curves include the owners' opportunity costs, the Costa coffeehouse represented in Figure 9-4 is making an economic profit. This economic profit gives entrepreneurs an incentive to enter this market and establish new firms. If a Costa is earning economic profit selling cafè lattes, new coffeehouses are likely to open in the same area.

How Does the Entry of New Firms Affect the Profits of Existing Firms?

As new coffeehouses open near the local Costa, the firm's demand curve will shift to the left. The demand curve will shift because Costa will sell fewer cafè lattes at each price when there are additional coffeehouses in the area selling similar drinks. The

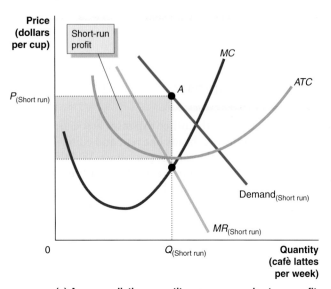

(a) A monopolistic competitor may earn a short-run profit

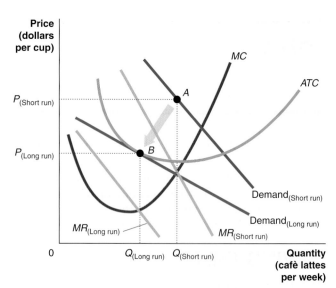

(b) A monopolistic competitor's profits are eliminated in the long run

Figure 9-5 | How Entry of New Firms Eliminates Profits

In the short run—panel (a)—the local Costa faces the demand and marginal revenue curves labeled "Short run." With this demand curve, Costa can charge a price above average total cost (point *A*) and make a profit, shown by the green rectangle. But this profit attracts new firms to enter the market, which shifts the demand and marginal revenue curves to the ones labeled "Long run" in panel (b). Because price is now equal to average total cost (point *B*), Costa breaks even and no longer earns an economic profit.

demand curve will also become more elastic because consumers have additional coffeehouses from which to buy coffee, so Costa will lose more sales if it raises its prices. Figure 9-5 shows how the demand curve for the local Costa shifts as new firms enter its market.

In panel (a) of Figure 9-5, the short-run demand curve shows the relationship between the price of café lattes and the quantity of café lattes Costa sells per week before the entry of new firms. With this demand curve, Costa can charge a price above average total cost—shown as point *A* in panel (a)—and make a profit. But this profit attracts additional coffeehouses to the area and shifts the demand curve for the Costa café lattes to the left. As long as Costa is making an economic profit, there is an incentive for additional coffeehouses to open in the area, and the demand curve will continue shifting to the left. As panel (b) shows, eventually the demand curve will have shifted to the point where it is just touching—or tangent to—the average cost curve.

In the long run, at the point at which the demand curve is tangent to the average cost curve, price is equal to average total cost (point *B*), the firm is breaking even, and it no longer earns an economic profit. In the long run, the demand curve is also more elastic because the more coffeehouses there are in the area, the more sales Costa will lose to other coffeehouses if it raises its price.

Of course, it is possible that a monopolistically competitive firm will suffer economic losses in the short run. As a consequence, the owners of the firm will not be covering the opportunity cost of their investment. We expect that, in the long run, firms will exit an industry if they are suffering economic losses. If firms exit, the demand curve for the output of a remaining firm will shift to the right. This process will continue until the representative firm in the industry is able to charge a price equal to its average cost and break even. Therefore, in the long run, monopolistically competitive firms will experience neither economic profits nor economic losses. Table 9-2 summarizes the short run and the long run for a monopolistically competitive firm.

TABLE 9-2 | The Short Run and the Long Run for a Monopolistically Competitive Firm

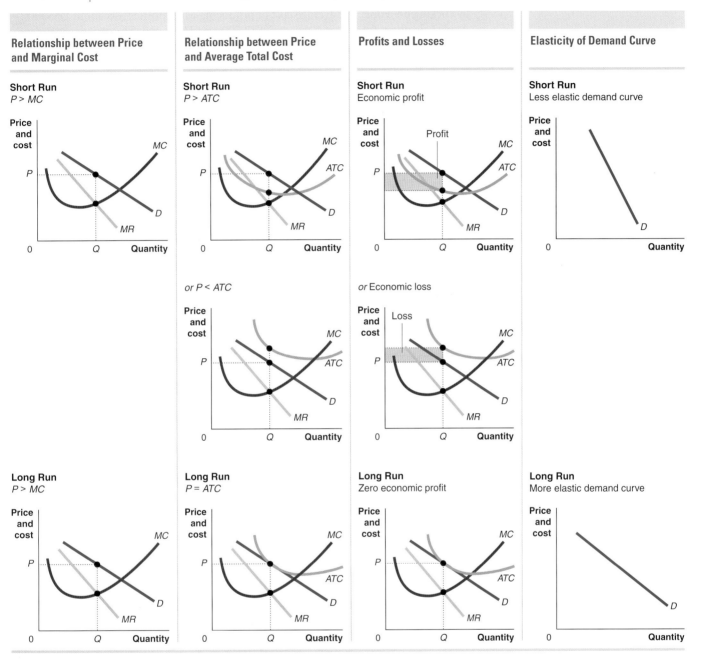

Making the Connection

The Rise and Fall of Apple's Macintosh Computer

In 1983, there were more than 15 firms selling personal computers, as well as many smaller firms in local markets selling computers assembled from purchased components. None of these personal computers operated using the current system of clicking on icons with a mouse. Instead, users had to type in commands to call up word processing, spreadsheet, and other software programs. This awkward system required users to memorize many commands or constantly consult computer manuals. In January 1984, Apple

(Continued)

Computer introduced the Macintosh, which used a mouse and could be operated by clicking on icons. The average cost of producing Macintoshes was about US$500. Apple sold them for prices between US$2,500 and US$3,000. This price was more than twice that of comparable personal computers sold by IBM and other companies, but the Macintosh was so easy to use that it was able to achieve a 15 percent share of the market. Apple had successfully introduced a personal computer that was strongly differentiated from its competitors. One journalist covering the computer industry has gone so far as to call the Macintosh "the most important consumer product of the last half of the twentieth century."

Microsoft produced the operating system known as MS-DOS (for Microsoft disk operating system), which most non-Apple computers used. The financial success of the Macintosh led Microsoft to develop an operating system that would also use a mouse and icons. In 1992, Microsoft introduced the operating system Windows 3.1, which succeeded in reproducing many of the key features of the Macintosh. By August 1995, when Microsoft introduced Windows 95, non-Apple computers had become as easy to use as Macintosh computers. By that time, most personal computers operated in a way very similar to the Macintosh, and Apple was no longer able to charge prices that were significantly above those that its competitors charged. The Macintosh had lost its differentiation. However, the Macintosh (which has since evolved into the iMac, MacBook, and most recently the iPad) continues to have a loyal following, and has experienced strong sales growth in recent years, in part because of the popularity of the iPod and iPhone. Apple is now leading the way in tablet sales with its iPad, and if iPad sales are included, Apple is now the third largest PC seller in the world, with a market share of 10.8% in 2010. But Apple's competitors are hot on its heels: Blackberry has brought out PlayBook, HP has launched TouchPad, and many more tablets are evolving. Apple could once again be at risk of losing its differentiation.

Macintosh lost some of its differentiation when competitors started producing similar products, but still has a loyal following.

Source for quote: Steven Levy, *Insanely Great: The Life and Times of Macintosh, the Computer that Changed Everything*, New York: Viking, 1994, p. 7.

YOUR TURN: Test your understanding by doing related problem 3.4 on page 326 at the end of this chapter.

Solved Problem | 9-3

The Short Run and the Long Run for the Macintosh

Use the information in *Making the Connection* on page 309 to draw a graph that shows changes in the market for Macintosh computers between 1984 and 1995.

SOLVING THE PROBLEM:

Step 1: **Review the chapter material.** This problem is about how the entry of new firms affected the market for the Macintosh, so you may want to review the section "How Does the Entry of New Firms Affect the Profits of Existing Firms?" which begins on page 307.

Step 2: **Draw the graph.** The *Making the Connection* about Apple indicates that in 1984, when the Macintosh was first introduced, its differentiation from other computers allowed Apple to make a substantial economic profit. In 1995, the release of Windows 95 meant that non-Macintosh computers were as easy to use as Macintosh computers. Apple's product differentiation was eliminated, as was its ability to earn economic profits. The change over time in Apple's situation is shown in the following graph, which combines panels (a) and (b) from Figure 9-5 in one graph.

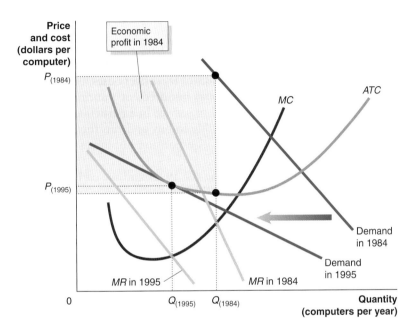

Between 1984 and 1995, Microsoft's development of the Windows operating system eliminated Macintosh's product differentiation. The demand curve for Macintosh shifted to the left and became more elastic throughout the relevant range of prices.

EXTRA CREDIT: Note that this analysis is simplified. The Macintosh of 1995 was a different—and better—computer than the Macintosh of 1984. Apple has made changes to the Macintosh, such as the introduction of the colorful iMac computer in 1999, that have sometimes led to increases in sales. The great success of the Apple iPod has also lead some consumers to switch to Apple computers.

>> End Solved Problem 9-3

Is Zero Economic Profit Inevitable in the Long Run?

The economic analysis of the long run shows the effects of market forces over time. In the case of Costa, the effect of market forces is to eliminate the economic profit earned by a monopolistically competitive firm. Owners of monopolistically competitive firms, of course, do not have to passively accept this long-run result. The key to earning economic profits is either to sell a differentiated product or to find a way of producing an existing product at a lower cost. If a monopolistically competitive firm selling a differentiated product is earning profits, these profits will attract the entry of additional firms, and the entry of those firms will eventually eliminate the firm's profits. If a firm introduces new technology that allows it to sell a good or service at a lower cost, competing firms will eventually be able to duplicate that technology and eliminate the firm's profits. *But this result holds only if the firm stands still and fails to find new ways of differentiating its product or fails to find new ways of lowering the cost of producing its product.* Firms continually struggle to find new ways of differentiating their products as they try to stay one step ahead of other firms that are attempting to copy their success. As new coffeehouses enter the area served by the Costa coffeehouse, the owners can expect to see their economic profits competed away, unless they can find ways to differentiate their product.

Costa has used various strategies to differentiate itself from competing coffeehouses. The brand coffeehouse has continued to be very responsive to its customers' preferences. Costa started serving breakfast sandwiches and made its stores appear similar to other fast-food restaurants. Although at one time Costa had been able to maintain greater control over the operations of its coffeehouses, because all of its coffeehouses were company owned, it now has hundreds of *franchises.* A franchise is a business with the legal right to sell a good or service in a particular area. When a firm uses franchises, local businesspeople are able to buy and run the stores in their area. This makes it easier for a firm to finance its expansion but forces the firm to give up some control over its stores.

Costa experienced great success during the 1990s and the early 2000s, but history shows that in the long run competitors will be able to duplicate most of what it does. In the face of that competition, it will be very difficult for Costa to continue earning economic profits.

The shadow of the end of their profits haunts owners of every firm. Firms try to avoid losing profits by reducing costs, by improving their products, or by convincing consumers their products are indeed different from what competitors offer. To stay one step ahead of its competitors, a firm has to offer consumers goods or services that they perceive to have greater *value* than those offered by competing firms. Value can take the form of product differentiation that makes the good or service more suited to consumers' preferences, or it can take the form of a lower price.

Making the **Connection** │ **A Regional Brand on a Global Mission: Aramex to Join the 'Big Four': UPS, DHL, FedEx, and TNT**

In 1982, Fadi Ghandour, a Jordanian entrepreneur, founded Aramex as an express wholesale delivery provider for American companies such as FedEx in the Middle East and North Africa (MENA). The new company then had only two offices: one in Amman and the other in New York. At its start, Aramex had only one major competitor in the region, DHL. Over the years, the company evolved from being an express wholesale delivery provider to a worldwide provider of integrated supply-chain solutions, offering services such as express delivery, freight forwarding and warehousing, in addition to value-added services such as document management. Aramex serves a diverse base of global customers across all industries. It now operates in the Middle East, Europe, South Asia, and United States, and has 307 offices in 195 cities, employing over 7,000 employees, and with main hubs in Dubai, Hong Kong, Liege, London, New York, and Singapore. The chart shows Aramex's geographic concentration of revenues. It reveals an increasing share of Europe in total revenues, indicating a fast expansion in Europe in the past few years.

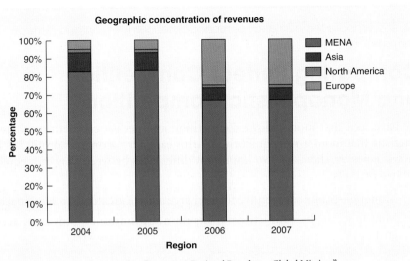

Source: K. Murad and R. Hamdan, "Aramex: A Regional Brand on a Global Mission," equity research report, SHUAA Capital, www.gulfbase.com.

Today, Aramex has become the dominant regional brand with global ambitions. The company is growing strongly enough soon to join the 'big four'—UPS, DHL, FedEX, and TNT— to become the fifth largest express-delivery provider worldwide. In addition to offering tough competition on the global scale, the big four have established alliances with regional players to bring this competition closer to home for Aramex. Examples include SMSA Express, FedEx, and SNAS DHL Worldwide Express in Saudi Arabia. Since, the MENA region has above-average growth potential, regional companies such as Aramex have an opportunity to leverage the first mover advantage despite the increasing presence of global majors. In addition to facing fierce competition from the international players, Aramex is also facing regional competitors such as Emirates Post, Jordan Post Company, Egypt Post, and Al-Futtaim Logistics (a UAE-based logistics services provider).

The competitive advantage of Aramex lies within the MENA region, with its widespread presence and partial dominance of the express and postal market giving it an edge over other players. Realizing this, Aramex is upgrading its extensive land network by including additional routes to link Dubai to Muscat, Manama, Doha, and some regions in Saudi Arabia.

The formula for the success of Aramex's growth has been twofold: (a) expanding its geographical reach through successful acquisitions; (b) the expansion of its existing product portfolio to stay ahead in the differentiation and branding race. Aramex has been enhancing its existing infrastructure on different levels, such as: new products and services to fill gaps in delivery schedules; new facilities and warehouses to meet the increasing demand both globally and regionally for freight forwarding and logistics services; and upgraded IT infrastructure to better connect with its suppliers, customers, and employees. In addition, the company has built a strong reputation for having a customer-focused culture and operations. With the increased popularity of online shopping in the Arab world, Aramex's business is growing at 15 percent despite the continued volatility in the global economy. Despite its latest large expansion, to keep an edge over its competitors, Aramex's business model is determined to maintain the 'asset light' nature of its operations.

Source: K. Murad and R. Hamdan, "Aramex: A Regional Brand on a Global Mission," equity research report, SHUAA Capital, www.gulfbase.com.

YOUR TURN: Test your understanding by doing related problem 3.6 on page 326 at the end of this chapter.

9.4 | Compare the efficiency of monopolistic competition and perfect competition.

Comparing Perfect Competition and Monopolistic Competition

We have seen that monopolistic competition and perfect competition share the characteristic that in long-run equilibrium, firms earn zero economic profits. As Figure 9-6 shows, however, there are two important differences between long-run equilibrium in the two markets:

* Monopolistically competitive firms charge a price greater than marginal cost.
* Monopolistically competitive firms do not produce at minimum average total cost.

Excess Capacity under Monopolistic Competition

Recall that a firm in a perfectly competitive market faces a perfectly elastic demand curve that is also its marginal revenue curve. Therefore, the firm maximizes profit by producing where price equals marginal cost. As panel (a) of Figure 9-6 shows, in long-run equilibrium, a perfectly competitive firm produces at the minimum point of its average total cost curve.

Panel (b) of Figure 9-6 shows that the profit-maximizing level of output for a monopolistically competitive firm comes at a level of output where price is greater than marginal cost and the firm is not at the minimum point of its average total cost curve. A monopolistically competitive firm has *excess capacity*: if it increased its output, it could produce at a lower average cost.

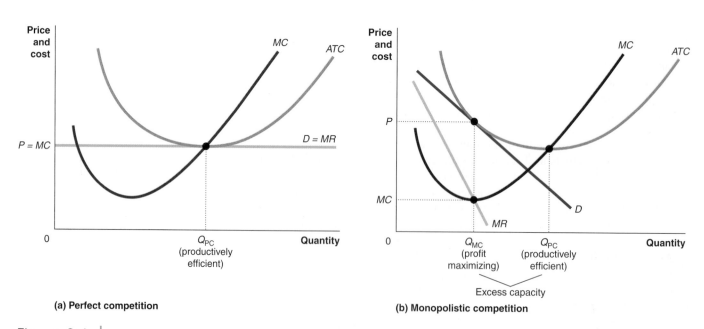

Figure 9-6 | Comparing Long-Run Equilibrium under Perfect Competition and Monopolistic Competition

In panel (a), the perfectly competitive firm in long-run equilibrium produces at Q_{PC}, where price equals marginal cost, and average total cost is at a minimum. The perfectly competitive firm is both allocatively efficient and productively efficient. In panel (b), the monopolistically competitive firm produces at Q_{MC}, where price is greater than marginal cost, and average total cost is not at a minimum. As a result,

the monopolistically competitive firm is neither allocatively efficient nor productively efficient. The monopolistically competitive firm has excess capacity equal to the difference between its profit-maximizing level of output and the productively efficient level of output.

Is Monopolistic Competition Inefficient?

In the previous chapter, we discussed *productive efficiency* and *allocative efficiency*. Productive efficiency refers to the situation where a good is produced at the lowest possible cost. Allocative efficiency refers to the situation where every good or service is produced up to the point where the last unit provides a marginal benefit to consumers equal to the marginal cost of producing it. For productive efficiency to hold, firms must produce at the minimum point of average total cost. For allocative efficiency to hold, firms must charge a price equal to marginal cost. In a perfectly competitive market, both productive efficiency and allocative efficiency are achieved, but in a monopolistically competitive market, neither is achieved. Does it matter? Economists have debated whether monopolistically competitive markets being neither productively nor allocatively efficient results in a significant loss of well-being to society in these markets compared with perfectly competitive markets.

How Consumers Benefit from Monopolistic Competition

Looking again at Figure 9-6, you can see that the only difference between the monopolistically competitive firm and the perfectly competitive firm is that the demand curve for the monopolistically competitive firm slopes downward, whereas the demand curve for the perfectly competitive firm is a horizontal line. The demand curve for the monopolistically competitive firm slopes downward because the good or service the firm is selling is differentiated from the goods or services being sold by competing firms. The perfectly competitive firm is selling a good or service identical to those being sold by its competitors. A key point to remember is that *firms differentiate their products to appeal to consumers*. When Costa coffeehouses began offering new flavors of coffee, when FedEX was the first to introduce overnight delivery, when Aramex offered Arab consumers the option to shop online and send their purchases to an address in the U.K. or U.S., or when PepsiCo introduced caffeine-free Diet Pepsi, they were all attempting to attract and retain consumers through product differentiation. The success of these product differentiation strategies indicates that some consumers find these products preferable to the alternatives. Consumers, therefore, are better off than they would have been had these companies not differentiated their products.

We can conclude that consumers face a trade-off when buying the product of a monopolistically competitive firm: they are paying a price that is greater than marginal cost, and the product is not being produced at minimum average cost, but they benefit from being able to purchase a product that is differentiated and more closely suited to their tastes.

9.5 | Define marketing and explain how firms use it to differentiate their products.

9.5 LEARNING OBJECTIVE

How Marketing Differentiates Products

Firms can differentiate their products through marketing. **Marketing** refers to all the activities necessary for a firm to sell a product to a consumer. Marketing includes activities such as determining which product to produce, designing the product, advertising the product, deciding how to distribute the product—for example, in retail stores or through a website—and monitoring how changes in consumer tastes are affecting the market for the product. Peter F. Drucker, a leading business strategist, describes marketing as follows: "It is the whole business seen from the point of view of its final result, that is, from the consumer's point of view.... True marketing...does not ask, 'What do we want to sell?' It asks, 'What does the consumer want to buy?'"

Marketing All the activities necessary for a firm to sell a product to a consumer.

As we have seen, for monopolistically competitive firms to earn economic profits and to defend those profits from competitors, they must differentiate their products. Firms use two marketing tools to differentiate their products: brand management and advertising.

Brand Management

Brand management The actions of a firm intended to maintain the differentiation of a product over time.

Once a firm has succeeded in differentiating its product, it must try to maintain that differentiation over time through **brand management**. As we have seen, whenever a firm successfully introduces a new product or a significantly different version of an old product, it earns economic profits in the short run. But the success of the firm inspires competitors to copy the new or improved product and, in the long run, the firm's economic profits will be competed away. Firms use brand management to postpone the time when they will no longer be able to earn economic profits.

Advertising

An innovative advertising campaign can make even long-established and familiar products, such as Coke or McDonald's Big Mac hamburgers, seem more desirable than competing products. When a firm advertises a product, it is trying to shift the demand curve for the product to the right and to make it more inelastic. If the firm is successful, it will sell more of the product at every price, and it will be able to increase the price it charges without losing as many customers. Of course, advertising also increases a firm's costs. If the increase in revenue that results from the advertising is greater than the increase in costs, the firm's profits will rise. Needless to say, advertising campaigns are not always successful. Huge advertising campaigns still may fail to make a product successful.

Defending a Brand Name

Once a firm has established a successful brand name, it has a strong incentive to defend it. A firm can apply for a *trademark*, which grants legal protection against other firms using its product's name.

One threat to a trademarked name is the possibility that it will become so widely used for a type of product that it will no longer be associated with the product of a specific company. For example, 'aspirin' was originally a brand name of the product of a particular firm, but it became so widely used to refer to painkillers that it did not remain a legally protected brand name. Firms spend substantial amounts of money trying to make sure that this does not happen to them. Coca-Cola, for example, employs workers to travel around the country stopping at restaurants and asking to be served a 'Coke' with their meal. If the restaurant serves Pepsi or some other cola, rather than Coke, Coca-Cola's legal department sends the restaurant a letter reminding that 'Coke' is a trademarked name and not a generic name for any cola. Similarly, Xerox Corporation spends money on advertising to remind the public that 'Xerox' is not a generic term for making photocopies. Legally enforcing trademarks can be difficult. Firms lose hundreds of billions of dollars in sales worldwide as a result of unauthorized use of their trademarked brand names. Although it is often difficult to enforce their trademarks in the courts of some foreign countries, the World Trade Organization's Agreement on Trade-Related Aspects of Intellectual Property Rights (TRIPS), which was signed by most developed and developing nations in 1995, has increased the legal protection for trademarks.

Firms that sell their products through franchises rather than through company-owned stores encounter the problem that if a franchisee does not run his or her business well, the firm's brand may be damaged. Automobile firms send 'roadmen' to visit their dealers to make sure the dealerships are clean and well maintained and that the service departments employ competent mechanics and are well equipped with spare parts. Similarly, McDonald's sends employees from corporate headquarters to visit McDonald's franchises to make sure the bathrooms are clean and the French fries are hot.

Making *the* Connection | **Can Dunkin' Donuts' Marketing Strategy Help it Compete with Starbucks?**

You may have noticed that Dunkin' Donuts' stores, like Starbucks, are also scattered in all large malls in the Arab gulf countries. While customers at Dunkin' Donuts and Starbucks are looking for similar products—coffee and food—there are important differences between the customers that cause them to shop at one coffee shop over another. In 2005, Dunkin' Donuts paid dozens of faithful customers US$100 a week to buy coffee at Starbucks instead. At the same time, they paid Starbucks customers to make the opposite switch. This Dunkin' Donuts marketing effort was an attempt to appeal to some of Starbucks' customers. As we see in this chapter, when a firm successfully differentiates its product, its competitors do their best to copy it. Starbucks has experienced great success by reinventing the coffeehouse. As Dunkin' Donuts begins to expand, it is redesigning its stores to make them more like Starbucks.

Is it a good marketing strategy for Dunkin' Donuts to imitate Starbucks' style?

As this chapter has shown, once consumers show they want a particular good or service, firms will compete to offer it to them. Dunkin' Donuts is trying to capture the feel of a Starbucks' store in order to attract customers who may like some of the elements of Starbucks, but who may also like some of the elements of Dunkin' Donuts. Dunkin' Donuts' marketing strategy may never succeed in attracting loyal Starbucks' customers who see Dunkin' Donuts stores as 'unoriginal.' However, it can attract customers who like some features about Starbucks but who may prefer a different environment and food selection.

Early research showed that Dunkin' Donuts customers wanted nicer, upscale stores, but it revealed a potential problem: the loyal Dunkin' customer was turned off by the atmosphere at Starbucks. They often complained that crowds of laptop-users made it difficult to find a seat, Dunkin' says. They didn't like Starbucks' "tall," "grande," and "venti" lingo for small, medium and large coffees. And, Dunkin' says, they couldn't understand why anyone would pay as much as US$4 for a cup of coffee. So, going upscale without alienating that loyal base is proving tricky. Dunkin', in its expansion strategy, is trying to strike the balance between appealing to some Starbucks customers and maintaining their loyal base.

Based on Janet Adamy, "Brewing Battle: Dunkin' Donuts Tries to Go Upscale, But Not Too Far," *Wall Street Journal*, April 8, 2006.

9.6 | Identify the key factors that determine a firm's success.

What Makes a Firm Successful?

A firm's owners and managers control some of the factors that make a firm successful and allow it to earn economic profits. The most important of these are the firm's ability to differentiate its product and to produce its product at a lower average cost than competing firms. A firm that successfully does these things creates *value* for its customers. Consumers will buy a product if they believe it meets a need not met by competing products or if its price is below that of competitors.

Some factors that affect a firm's profitability are not directly under the firm's control. Certain factors will affect all the firms in a market. For example, rising prices for jet fuel will reduce the profitability of all airlines. If consumers decide that they would

Figure 9-7

What Makes a Firm Successful?

The factors under a firm's control—the ability to differentiate its product and the ability to produce it at lower cost—combine with the factors beyond its control to determine the firm's profitability.
Source: Adapted from Figure 11.3 in David Besanko, David Dranove, Mark Shanley, and Scott Schaefer, *The Economics of Strategy*, 4th ed., New York: Wiley, 2007.

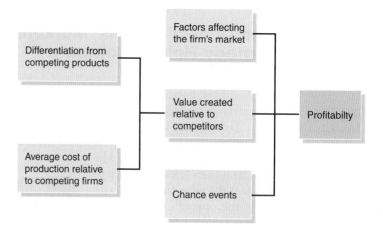

rather watch pay-for-view movies delivered to their homes by cable or satellite than buy DVDs, the profitability of all stores selling DVDs will be reduced.

Sheer chance also plays a role in business, as it does in all other aspects of life. A struggling McDonald's franchise may see profits increase dramatically after an unexpected decision to build a new road nearby. Many businesses in New York City, including restaurants, hotels, and theaters, experienced a marked drop in customers and profits following the September 11, 2001, terrorist attacks. Figure 9-7 illustrates the important point that factors within the firm's control and factors outside the firm's control interact to determine the firm's profitability.

Making the Connection | Is Being the First Firm in the Market a Key to Success?

Some business analysts argue that the first firm to enter a market can have important *first-mover advantages*. By being the first to sell a particular good, a firm may find its name closely associated with the good in the public's mind, as, for instance, Amazon is closely associated with ordering books online or eBay is associated with online auctions. This close association may make it more difficult for new firms to enter the market and compete against the first mover.

Surprisingly, though, recent research has shown that the first firm to enter a market often does *not* have a long-lived advantage over later entrants. Consider, for instance, the market for pens. Until the 1940s, the only pens available were fountain pens that had to be refilled frequently from an ink bottle and used ink that dried slowly and smeared easily. In October 1945, entrepreneur Milton Reynolds introduced the first ballpoint pen, which never needed to be refilled. When it went on sale at Gimbel's department store in New York City, it was an instant success. Although the pen had a price of US$12.00—the equivalent of about US$135.00 at today's prices—hundreds of thousands were sold, and Milton Reynolds became a millionaire. Unfortunately, it didn't last. Although Reynolds had guaranteed that his pen would write for two years—later raised to five years—in fact, the pen often leaked and frequently stopped writing after only limited use. Sales began to collapse, the flood of pens returned under the company's guarantee wiped out its profits, and within a few years, Reynolds International Pen Company stopped selling pens in the United States. By the late 1960s, firms such as Bic selling inexpensive—but reliable—ballpoint pens dominated the market.

What happened to the Reynolds International Pen Company turns out to be more the rule than the exception. For example, Apple's iPod was not the

Although not first to market, Bic ultimately was more successful than the firm that pioneered ballpoint pens.

first digital music player to appear in the market. The PMP300 was released in 1998, three years before the iPod. Similarly, although Hewlett-Packard currently dominates the market for laser printers it did not invent the laser printer. Xerox invented the laser printer, and IBM sold the first commercial laser printers. Nor was Procter & Gamble the first firm to sell disposable diapers when it introduced Pampers in 1961. Microsoft's Internet Explorer was not the first web browser: before Internet Explorer, there was Netscape; before Netscape, there was Mosaic; and before Mosaic, there were several other browsers that for a time looked as if they might dominate the market. In all these cases, the firms that were first to introduce a product ultimately lost out to latecomers who did a better job of providing consumers with products that were more reliable, less expensive, more convenient, or otherwise provided greater value.

Sources: Steven P. Schnaars, *Managing Imitation Strategies: How Later Entrants Seize Markets from Pioneers*, New York: The Free Press, 1994; and Gerard J. Tellis and Peter N. Golder, *Will and Vision: How Latecomers Grow to Dominate Markets*, Los Angeles: Figueroa Press, 2002.

YOUR TURN: Test your understanding by doing related problem 6.5 on page 327 at the end of this chapter.

>> **Continued from page 301**

Economics in YOUR Life!

At the beginning of the chapter, we asked you to think about how successful you are likely to be in opening a Lebanese restaurant in your hometown. As you learned in this chapter, if your restaurant is successful, other people are likely to open competing restaurants, and all your economic profits will eventually disappear. This occurs because economic profits attract entry of new firms into a market. The new restaurants will sell Lebanese food, but it won't be exactly like your Lebanese food—after all, they don't have your grandmother's secret recipes! Each restaurant will have its own ideas on how best to appeal to people who like Lebanese food. Unless your food is so different from the food offered by competing restaurants that your consumers will continue to pay higher prices for your food, you probably won't earn an economic profit in the long run.

In a monopolistically competitive market, free entry will lead to zero economic profits in the long run. But competition will also lead firms to offer somewhat different versions of the same product; for example, two Lebanese restaurants will rarely be exactly alike.

Conclusion

In this chapter, we have applied many of the ideas about competition we developed in the previous chapter to the more common market structure of monopolistic competition. We have seen that these ideas apply to monopolistically competitive markets, just as they do to perfectly competitive markets. At the end of the previous chapter, we concluded that "The competitive forces of the market impose relentless pressure on firms to produce new and better goods and services at the lowest possible cost. Firms that fail to adequately anticipate changes in consumer tastes or that fail to adopt the latest and most efficient production technology do not survive in the long run." These conclusions are as true for coffeehouses and firms in other monopolistically competitive markets as they are for wheat farmers or apple growers.

In Chapters 10 and 11, we discuss the remaining market structures: oligopoly and monopoly. Before moving on to those chapters, read *An Inside Look* on the next page for a discussion of how the new coffeehouse culture in the Arab world ignited a fierce competition among coffeehouse companies.

ARROYA.COM, JUNE 29, 2010

Coffee Culture Thrives in the Middle East

A Euromonitor International survey has suggested that the regional coffee industry continues to thrive despite the recent economic downturn, which saw most consumers cutting back costs on non-basic commodities.

Michael Schaefer, consumer food service analyst at Euromonitor, says the Middle East coffee sector, including that of the North African region, is now a multi-million dollar industry that has not shown any let-up in its annual growth performance....Schaefer added that since 2004, overall coffee consumption in the region has posted steady increase with UAE growing by a massive 85 percent, Morocco and Saudi Arabia by over 30 percent, and Egypt by a healthy 20 percent. The figures, he said, indicate a "strong demand for both at-home and on-the-go coffee drinking opportunities."

The Euromonitor analyst added that while coffee consumption and the presence of coffee shops are not new to the region, it has evolved into a more socially oriented business that attracts people of various age, gender, and cultural background.

"There is no question that the modern coffee-shop sector represents something new, providing a social outlet for women, students, and other young people in stark contrast to the male-dominated traditional café sector. Particularly in more conservative markets like Saudi Arabia, where alcoholic drinks are banned and social opportunities of any kind are limited, coffee shops have emerged as a major nighttime gathering place," he said.

The Euromonitor study focused on the region's surging young demographics—in the GCC, for instance, where the median age is 26—as one of the factors driving the coffee industry to post significant revenues. "One of the key drivers behind [the coffee industry's] expansion is a soaring youth population—students and young people are a key demographic for coffee chains the world over, and many of the Middle East's most important markets boast very young populations indeed," says Schaefer.

Saudi Arabia, one of the largest markets in the Gulf region, enjoys a population of 15 million consumers under the age of 30, while Egypt is home to over 45 million consumers under the age of 30 years old, according to Euromonitor statistics. These brand-savvy young consumers, the report noted, have been key to transforming coffee shops into a place to socialize. Consequently, coffee shops have also transformed their recipes to cater to their "hip" clientele in the region by offering a wide array of hot and cold concoctions. Starbucks, for instance, sells over 30 blends of coffee, espresso, blended drinks, teas, and the Frappuccino range. According to the chain's spokesperson, they currently offer a whopping list of 87,000 beverage combinations, which include low-fat/skimmed milk and decaf, and different types of milk, syrups, and sugar.

With its huge client base, the Middle East has become a favorite destination for globally recognized coffee brands such as U.S. giant Starbucks, UK's Costa Coffee, and Canada's Second Cup, to name a few. In an earlier interview with Arroya.com, a Starbucks spokesperson for the Middle East region, said the coffee chain has been operating 300 stores in Kuwait, Saudi Arabia, UAE, Egypt, Lebanon, Jordan, Qatar, Oman, and Bahrain. About 90 of these stores are located in the UAE—60 of which are based in Dubai...."We are comfortable with our performance and growth plans in the region. Last year we opened over 26 stores across the Middle East region, with 17 stores in UAE alone, and we believe there is plenty of potential for more new stores. We see a significant growth opportunity in the UAE, and across the region, and we continue to invest in the market," the Starbucks spokesperson said.

In addition to these international brands, Schaefer said local operators have contributed to the vibrancy of the coffee business in the region. "Multiple local chains continue to hold their own—Egypt's Cilantro [which caters to the high-end market], for instance, now operates 56 branches there, more than Starbucks and Costa combined, while in Saudi Arabia a number of local [stores] enjoy a brisk business," he said. Fierce competition, Schaefer mentioned, has "helped fuel an accelerating process of segmentation, as chains look to differentiate their offerings."

Source: Criselda E. Diala, "Coffee Culture Thrives in Middle East," Arroya.com, June 29, 2010.

Key Points in the Article

The article discusses the impact of the demographic characteristics of the Arab World on the booming coffee industry. The surging young population in countries such as Kuwait, Saudi Arabia, the UAE, Oman, Qatar, Bahrain, Egypt, Jordan, and Lebanon, led to a significant change in the coffee industry. New habits emerged since these young people found coffee shops a good place to socialize. The strong growing demand attracts large international coffee chains, each trying to differentiate its products.

Analyzing the News

(a) Coffee shops are transformed into a new social phenomenon where people of all ages and backgrounds socialize. The idea is old in the Arab world, but it took a new turn when women became part of that growing phenomenon.

(b) The Middle East is offering a very unique opportunity for chains such as Costa to expand in the region due to a soaring demand from young population. Many coffee chains have transformed their products to meet the tastes of these young customers.

(c) The region attracts international coffee chains because the potential of the market is so huge that it can absorb hundreds of new branches while maintaining a large profit edge. So, currently, coffeehouses like Costa are earning an economic profit. This would suggest that an existing firm could be represented by point A in the figure selling Q_1 cups of coffee and charging a price of P_1 dollars. The profit-maximizing quantity is found at the point where the marginal revenue curve MR_1 intersects the marginal cost curve MC. The price is determined by the demand curve. The firm is earning economic profits equal to the shaded area. The economic profits earned by coffeehouses like Costa explain why other international chains are seeking to expand in the Arab region as well.

As the figure shows, new entrants in a market will take some demand away from current firms in the market. This causes the demand curve to shift to the left from demand curve D_1 to demand curve D_2. The marginal revenue curve also shifts to the left (from MR_1 to MR_2). The profit-maximizing level of output is now Q_2, where the new marginal revenue curve intersects the marginal cost curve, MC. The new profit maximizing price is P_2. Notice that at this point the demand curve D_2 is tangent to the average total cost curve ATC and the firm is earning zero profits. At equilibrium, all firms in the market will earn zero profits. This is shown as point E in the figure.

Thinking Critically

1. Suppose that the government restricts the total number of new branches that can be opened by all chains. How would this affect the equilibrium price and chains profits?
2. How can Costa ensure maintaining a profit margin over its competitors for a longer period of time before economic profits becomes zero?

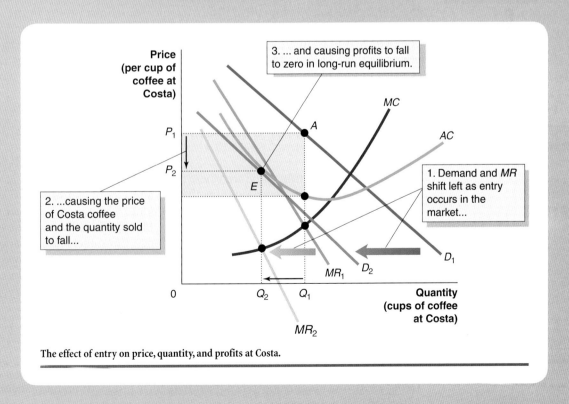

The effect of entry on price, quantity, and profits at Costa.

Key Terms

Summary

9.1 LEARNING OBJECTIVE

Explain why a monopolistically competitive firm has downward-sloping demand and marginal revenue curves, **pages 302–305.**

Demand and Marginal Revenue for a Firm in a Monopolistically Competitive Market

A firm competing in a **monopolistically competitive** market sells a differentiated product. Therefore, unlike a firm in a perfectly competitive market, it faces a downward-sloping demand curve. When a monopolistically competitive firm cuts the price of its product, it sells more units but must accept a lower price on the units it could have sold at the higher price. As a result, its marginal revenue curve is downward sloping. Every firm that has the ability to affect the price of the good or service it sells will have a marginal revenue curve that is below its demand curve.

9.2 LEARNING OBJECTIVE

Explain how a monopolistically competitive firm maximizes profits in the short run, **pages 305–307.**

How a Monopolistically Competitive Firm Maximizes Profits in the Short Run

A monopolistically competitive firm maximizes profits at the level of output where marginal revenue equals marginal cost. Price equals marginal revenue for a perfectly competitive firm, but price is greater than marginal revenue for a monopolistically competitive firm. Therefore, unlike a perfectly competitive firm, which produces where $P = MC$, a monopolistically competitive firm produces where $P > MC$.

9.3 LEARNING OBJECTIVE

Analyze the situation of a monopolistically competitive firm in the long run, **pages 307–313.**

What Happens to Profits in the Long Run?

If a monopolistically competitive firm is earning economic profits in the short run, entry of new firms will eliminate those profits in the long run. If a monopolistically competitive firm is suffering economic losses in the short run, exit of existing firms will eliminate those losses in the long run. Monopolistically competitive firms continually struggle to find new ways of differentiating their products as they try to stay one step ahead of other firms that are attempting to copy their success.

9.4 LEARNING OBJECTIVE

Compare the efficiency of monopolistic competition and perfect competition, **pages 314–315.**

Comparing Perfect Competition and Monopolistic Competition

Perfectly competitive firms produce where price equals marginal cost and at minimum average total cost. Perfectly competitive firms achieve both allocative and productive efficiency. Monopolistically competitive firms produce where price is greater than marginal cost and above minimum average total cost. Monopolistically competitive firms do not achieve either allocative or productive efficiency. Consumers face a trade-off when buying the product of a monopolistically competitive firm: they are paying a price that is greater than marginal cost, and the product is not being produced at minimum average cost, but they benefit from being able to purchase a product that is differentiated and more closely suited to their tastes.

9.5 LEARNING OBJECTIVE

Define marketing and explain how firms use it to differentiate their products, **pages 315–317.**

How Marketing Differentiates Products

Marketing refers to all the activities necessary for a firm to sell a product to a consumer. Firms use two marketing tools to differentiate their products: brand management and advertising. **Brand management** refers to the actions of a firm intended to maintain the differentiation of a product over time. When a firm has established a successful brand name, it has a strong incentive to defend it. A firm can apply for a *trademark*, which grants legal protection against other firms using its product's name.

What Makes a Firm Successful?

A firm's owners and managers control some of the factors that determine the profitability of the firm. Other factors affect all the firms in the market or are the result of chance, so they are not under the control of the firm's owners. The interactions between factors the firm controls and factors it does not control determine its profitability.

9.6 LEARNING OBJECTIVE

Identify the key factors that determine a firm's success, **pages 317–319.**

Review, Problems and Applications

 Visit www.pearsoned.co.uk/awe/hubbard to complete these exercises online and get instant feedback.
Get Ahead of the Curve

9.1 LEARNING OBJECTIVE Explain why a monopolistically competitive firm has downward-sloping demand and marginal revenue curves, **pages 302–305.**

Review Questions

1.1 What are the most important differences between perfectly competitive markets and monopolistically competitive markets? Give two examples of products sold in perfectly competitive markets and two examples of products sold in monopolistically competitive markets.

1.2 Why does the local McDonald's face a downward-sloping demand curve for Big Macs? If it raises the price it charges for Big Macs above the prices charged by other McDonald's stores, won't it lose all its customers?

1.3 Explain the differences between total revenue, average revenue, and marginal revenue.

Problems and Applications

1.4 Complete the following table:

1.5 A student makes the following argument:

> When a firm sells another unit of a good, the additional revenue the firm receives is equal to the price: if the price is US\$10, then the additional revenue is also US\$10. Therefore, this chapter is incorrect when it says that marginal revenue is less than price for a monopolistically competitive firm.

Briefly explain whether you agree with this argument.

1.6 There are many wheat farms in the world, but there are also many Costa coffeehouses. Why, then, does a Costa coffeehouse face a downward-sloping demand curve when a wheat farmer faces a horizontal demand curve?

1.7 Is it possible for marginal revenue to be negative for a firm selling in a perfectly competitive market? Would a firm selling in a monopolistically competitive market ever produce where marginal revenue is negative?

DVDS RENTED PER WEEK (Q)	PRICE (P)	TOTAL REVENUE (TR = P × Q)	AVERAGE REVENUE (AR = TR/Q)	MARGINAL REVENUE (MR = $\Delta TR/\Delta Q$)
0	$8.00			
1	7.50			
2	7.00			
3	6.50			
4	6.00			
5	5.50			
6	5.00			
7	4.50			
8	4.00			

9.2 LEARNING OBJECTIVE   Explain how a monopolistically competitive firm maximizes profits in the short run,
pages 305–307.

Review Questions

2.1 Sally runs a McDonald's franchise. She is selling 350 Big Macs per week at a price of US$3.25. If she lowers the price to US$3.20, she will sell 351 Big Macs. What is the marginal revenue of the 351st Big Mac?

2.2 Sami runs a Video store. Sami is currently renting 3,525 DVDs per week. If instead of renting 3,525 DVDs, he rents 3,526 DVDs, he will add US$2.95 to his costs and US$2.75 to his revenues. What will be the effect on his profits of renting 3,526 DVDs instead of 3,525 DVDs?

2.3 Should a monopolistically competitive firm take into account its fixed costs when deciding how much to produce? Briefly explain.

Problems and Applications

2.4 If Ahmed sells 350 Big Macs at a price of US$3.25, and his average cost of producing 350 Big Macs is US$3.00, what is his profit?

2.5 Huda manages a video store and has the following information on demand and costs:

DVDS RENTED PER WEEK (Q)	PRICE (P)	TOTAL COST (TC)
0	$6.00	$3.00
1	5.50	7.00
2	5.00	10.00
3	4.50	12.50
4	4.00	14.50
5	3.50	16.00
6	3.00	17.00
7	2.50	18.50
8	2.00	21.00

a. To maximize profit, how many DVDs should Huda rent, what price should she charge, and how much profit will she make?

b. What is the marginal revenue received by renting the profit-maximizing DVD? What is the marginal cost of renting the profit-maximizing DVD?

2.6 A trucking company investigates the relationship between the gas mileage of its trucks and the average speed at which the trucks are driven on the highway. The company finds the relationship shown in the following graph:

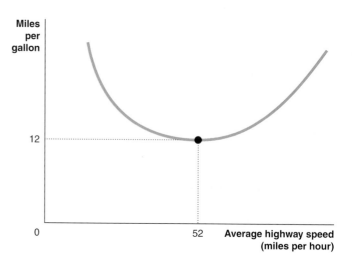

Will the firm maximize profits if it instructs its drivers to maintain an average speed of 52 miles per hour? Briefly explain.

2.7 Krispy Kreme Doughnuts Inc. reported its profit fell 56 percent in its second quarter despite an 11 percent increase in revenue. Briefly explain how it is possible for a firm's revenue to increase at the same time its profits decrease.

2.8 During 2003, General Motors cut the prices of most of its car models. As a result, GM earned a profit of only US$184 per car, compared to the profit of US$555 per car it had earned in 2002. Does the decline in GM's profits per car indicate that cutting prices was not a profit-maximizing strategy? Briefly explain.
Source: Karen Lundergaard and Sholnn Freeman, "Detroit's Challenge: Weaning Buyers from Years of Deals," *Wall Street Journal*, January 6, 2004.

2.9 **(Related to *Solved Problem 9-2* on page 307)** William Germano is vice president and publishing director at the Routledge publishing company. He has given the following description of how a publisher might deal with an unexpected increase in the cost of publishing a book:

It's often asked why the publisher can't simply raise the price [if costs increase].... It's likely that the editor [is already]... charging as much as the market will bear.... In other words, you might be willing to pay US$50.00 for a...book on the Brooklyn Bridge, but if...production costs [increase] by 25 percent, you might think US$62.50 is too much to pay, though that would be what the publisher needs to charge. And indeed the publisher may determine that US$50.00 is this book's ceiling—the most you would pay before deciding to rent a movie instead.

According to what you have learned in this chapter, how do firms adjust the price of a good when there is an increase in cost? Use a graph to illustrate your answer. Does the model of monopolistic competition seem to fit Germano's description? If a publisher does not raise the price of a book following an increase in its production cost, what will be the result?

Source: William Germano, *Getting It Published: A Guide to Scholars and Anyone Else Serious about Serious Books*, Chicago: University of Chicago Press, 2001, pp. 110–11.

2.10 To overcome a period of sales stagnation, Amazon.com boosted sales through cutting the prices of books and offering free shipping.

a. If Amazon.com's revenue increased after it cut the price of books, what must be true about the price elasticity of demand for ordering books online?

b. Suppose that before the price cut, Amazon.com was not selling the profit-maximizing quantity of books, but after the price cut, it was. Draw a graph that shows Amazon's situation before and after the price cut. (For simplicity, assume that Amazon charges the same price for all books.) Be sure your graph includes the price Amazon was charging and the quantity of books it was selling before the price cut;

the price and quantity after the price cut; Amazon's demand, marginal revenue, average total cost, and marginal cost curves; and the areas representing Amazon's profits before and after the price cut.

2.11 In 1916, the Ford Motor Company produced 500,000 Model T Fords at a price of US$440 each. The company made a profit of US$60 million that year. Henry Ford told a newspaper reporter that he intended to reduce the price of the Model T to US$360, and he expected to sell 800,000 cars at that price. Ford said, "Less profit on each car, but more cars, more employment of labor, and in the end we get all the total profit we ought to make."

a. Did Ford expect the total revenue he received from selling Model Ts to rise or fall following the price cut?

b. Use the information given above to calculate the price elasticity of demand for Model Ts. Use the midpoint formula to make your calculation. See Chapter 5, page 142.

c. What would the average total cost of producing 800,000 Model Ts have to be for Ford to make as much profit selling 800,000 Model Ts as it made selling 500,000 Model Ts? Is this smaller or larger than the average total cost of producing 500,000 Model Ts?

d. Assume that Ford would make the same total profit when selling 800,000 cars as when selling 500,000 cars. Was Henry Ford correct in saying he would make less profit per car when selling 800,000 cars than when selling 500,000 cars?

9.3 LEARNING OBJECTIVE Analyze the situation of a monopolistically competitive firm in the long run,

pages 307-313.

Review Problems

3.1 What effect does the entry of new firms have on the economic profits of existing firms?

3.2 What is the difference between zero accounting profit and zero economic profit.

Problems and Applications

3.3 Use this graph to answer the questions that follow.

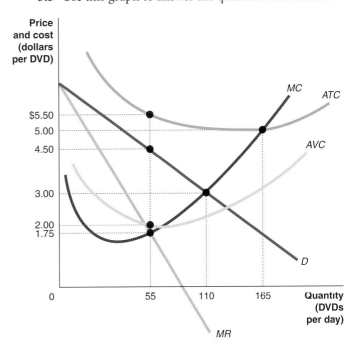

a. If the owner of this video store wants to maximize profits, how many DVDs should she rent per day, and what rental price should she charge? Briefly explain your answer.

b. How much economic profit (or loss) is she making? Briefly explain.

c. Is the owner likely to continue renting this number of DVDs in the long run? Briefly explain.

3.4 (Related to the *Making the Connection* on page 309) Writing in the *Wall Street Journal*, Walter Mossberg argues:

> But the new popularity of the [Macintosh computer] is also partly due to the fact that it can now run Windows along with Apple's superior Mac OS X operating system. That means that if there's a program you need that comes only in a Windows version, you can run it on any current Mac model, speedily and with all its features.

If it is an advantage to Apple that the Macintosh can now run Windows as well as the Mac operating system, would Apple be even better off if it abandoned its own operating system and installed only Windows on the computers it sells?

Source: Walter S. Mossberg, "Fusion Is the Latest Way for Macs to Run Windows. PC Software," *Wall Street Journal*, August 2, 2007.

3.5 According to an article in *Fortune* magazine, "The big question for [Starbucks' chairman] Howard Schultz is whether Starbucks can keep it up. There are those on Wall Street who say that Starbucks' game is almost over." What do you think the article means by "Starbucks' game is almost over"? Why would some people on Wall Street be making this prediction about a firm that was making substantial economic profits at the time the article was written?

Source: Andy Serwer, "Hot Starbucks to Go," *Fortune*, January 12, 2004.

3.6 (Related to the *Making the Connection* on page 312) Aramex, the giant logistics company, devotes significant resources to developing new products and services and differentiating them from those of its competitors. Suppose it did not do that. What would be the effect on its profits in the short run? What would be the effect on its profits in the long run?

9.4 LEARNING OBJECTIVE   Compare the efficiency of monopolistic competition and perfect competition, **pages 314–315.**

Review Questions

4.1 What are the differences between the long-run equilibrium of a perfectly competitive firm and the long-run equilibrium of a monopolistically competitive firm?

4.2 Does the fact that monopolistically competitive markets are not allocatively or productively efficient mean that there is a significant loss in economic well-being to society in these markets? In your answer, be sure to define what you mean by 'economic well-being.'

Problems and Applications

4.3 A student asks the following question:

> I can understand why a perfectly competitive firm will not earn profits in the long run because a perfectly competitive firm charges a price equal to marginal cost. But a monopolistically competitive firm can charge a price greater than marginal cost, so why can't it continue to earn profits in the long run?

How would you answer this question?

4.4 Consider the following graph.

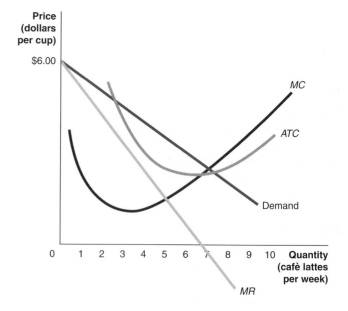

a. Is it possible to say whether this firm is a perfectly competitive firm or a monopolistically competitive firm? If so, explain how you are able to say this.

b. Does the graph show a short-run equilibrium or a long-run equilibrium? Briefly explain.

c. What quantity on the graph represents long-run equilibrium if the firm were perfectly competitive?

4.5 Juicy Couture has been successful in selling women's clothing using an unusual strategy. The key to the firm's strategy is to limit the distribution of its products to only a few high-end department stores, even if that means sacrificing sales—a brand-management technique once used only for luxury brands. Although Juicy was originally known mainly for the fashion tracksuits it sold, with its edgy contemporary sportswear and accessories, Juicy Couture has become a lifestyle brand for women, men, and kids.

a. Why would limiting the number of stores your product was sold in be a successful strategy for a clothing firm? What would be likely to happen to Juicy's sales if it began to sell its clothes at regular and cheaper stores?

b. Compared with the situation Apple Computer faced during the mid-1980s, is Juicy more or less likely to be able to maintain its product differentiation over a long period of time?

9.5 LEARNING OBJECTIVE   Define marketing and explain how firms use it to differentiate their products, pages 315–317.

Review Questions

5.1 Define marketing. Is marketing just another name for advertising?

5.2 Why are many companies so concerned about brand management?

Problems and Applications

5.3 Draw a graph that shows the impact on a firm's profits when it increases spending on advertising and the increased advertising has *no* effect on the demand for the firm's product.

5.4 A skeptic says, "Marketing research and brand management are redundant. If a company wants to find out what customers want, it should simply look at what they're already buying." Do you agree with this comment? Explain.

5.5 Some companies have done a poor job protecting their products' images. Think of cases where companies have failed to protect their brand names. What can they do about it now? Should they re-brand their products?

9.6 LEARNING OBJECTIVE   Identify the key factors that determine a firm's success, **pages 317–319.**

Review Questions

6.1 What are the key factors that determine the profitability of a firm in a monopolistically competitive market?

6.2 How might a monopolistically competitive firm continually earn economic profit greater than zero?

Problems and Applications

6.3 Businesses usually worry the most about competition and consider it the greatest risk to any business. In what sense is competition a 'risk' to a business? Why would a company in the retail business need to be particularly aware of competition?

6.4 Large chain stores such as Carrefour sometimes decide to buy large, well-run stores in the markets they want to newly enter. What advantages does Carrefour gain from buying large retail chains, rather than small chains?

6.5 **(Related to the *Making the Connection* on page 318)** A firm that is first to the market with a new product frequently discovers that there are design flaws or problems with the product that were not anticipated. For example, the ballpoint pens made by the Reynolds International Pen Company often leaked. What effect do these problems have on the innovating firm and how do these unexpected problems open up possibilities for other firms to enter the market?

Chapter 10

Oligopoly: Firms in Less Competitive Markets

Competing with Carrefour

In the past two decades, consumers in the Arab world have embraced the hypermarket culture of large-scale shopping and buying all their needs from one store at discounted prices. There are some important retailers emerging as leaders in the region such as Carrefour, Casino, Panda, and the Emke Group, which operates LuLu hypermarkets. These retailers have had ambitious plans for rapid expansion in the Arab world. Since 2007, Carrefour, the French retailer, sealed the deal and became the Arab world's top hypermarket operator in the latest ranking of Top 30 Middle Eastern and African retailers.

An industry with only a few firms is an *oligopoly*. In an oligopoly, a firm's profitability depends on its interactions with other firms. In these industries, firms must develop *business strategies*, which involve not just deciding what price to charge and how many units to produce but also how much to advertise, which new technologies to adopt, how to manage relations with suppliers, and which new markets to enter.

Carrefour was founded in France in 1959, and in 1963 the group opened its first hypermarket, which paved the way for the retailer's eventual success. In 1977, the company decided to expand internationally and opened its first hypermarket in Belgium. This expansion was followed by worldwide hypermarkets. Carrefour used extremely low prices as one of its strategies to compete and buy out other chains.

The way Carrefour pioneered the concept of global hypermarkets gave it a significant edge over its competitors. Currently, Carrefour is the second largest hypermarket-chain worldwide, behind Wal-Mart, and the largest in Europe and the Arab world, with more than 15,000 stores worldwide. By 1995, Carrefour had developed significant First Mover Advantages in having been the first to enter into many emerging markets. That year, Carrefour considered the first entry in the Arab world; in particular it had its eyes on Dubai as a starting point. None of Carrefour's competitors such as Wal-Mart, Tesco, Auchuan, Casino, and E. Leclerc had any presence in that market at the time.

The French retailer partnered in a joint venture with Majid Al-Futtaim, a pan-regional investor with retail operations throughout the entire Arab world. This partnership allowed Carrefour to expand later into other countries in the Arab world, in particular Egypt. The venture was successful for Carrefour, which increased the number of its stores in Dubai and expanded to the rest of the UAE and nearby countries.

A key part of Al-Futtaim business strategy for Carrefour involved placing stores in big malls that were mainly operated by the Al-Futtaim Group itself. That prevented competitors from having the same advantage; hence the main competition was from small, locally owned stores. Carrefour adapted its food to the socio-cultural norms of the Arab world and promoted mostly non-food items because of their higher profit margins. In addition, a key ingredient in Carrefour's success was the expansion of the production of the Carrefour private-label line. One important milestone was the shift from importing them from France or other markets to producing them locally under the "No. 1" economy-label line, which enabled Carrefour to offer lower prices in a market that suffers from high inflation. The shift was a clear sign of Carrefour's having a grip on the market and establishing a long-term commitment in the Arab world.

Carrefour has been successful because it developed a first mover advantage in the Arab world and thoroughly adapted to the extent that it did not feel foreign to many consumers. The joint venture has also been successful in identifying and aggressively pursuing growth opportunities in the region as soon as they occurred. **AN INSIDE LOOK** on **page 348** discusses how LuLu hypermarket is expanding in the Arab world to cope with Carrefour's expansion.

Source: SIS International Research report, "Carrefour's Market Entry into Dubai in 1995," February 2, 2009, www.marketintelligences.com; Arvind Nair, "Carrefour Heads Arab world Ranking," Gulf Times, September 24, 2007.

LEARNING Objectives

After studying this chapter, you should be able to:

10.1 Show how **barriers to entry** explain the existence of **oligopolies**, page 330.

10.2 Use **game theory** to analyze the strategies of oligopolistic firms, page 332.

10.3 Use **sequential games** to analyze business strategies, page 341.

10.4 Use the **five competitive forces model** to analyze competition in an industry, page 344.

Economics in YOUR Life!

Why Can't You Find a Cheap PlayStation 3?

It is summer time, and you and your friend decided to treat yourselves to a PlayStation 3 game system—provided that you can find one that has a relatively low price. First you check Carrefour and find a price of US$499.99. Then you check Géant, but the price is also equivalent to US$499.99. Then you check LuLu hypermarket: US$499.99 again! Finally, you check Panda, and you find a lower price: US$499.*82*—a whopping discount of US$0.17. Why isn't one of these big retailers willing to charge a lower price? What happened to price competition? As you read the chapter, see if you can answer these questions. You can check your answers against those we provide at the end of the chapter. **>** Continued on page 347

Oligopoly A market structure in which a small number of interdependent firms compete.

I n Chapters 8 and 9, we studied perfectly competitive and monopolistically competitive industries. Our analysis focused on the determination of a firm's profit-maximizing price and quantity. We concluded that firms maximize profit by producing where marginal revenue equals marginal cost. To determine marginal revenue and marginal cost, we used graphs that included the firm's demand, marginal revenue, and marginal cost curves. In this chapter, we will study **oligopoly**, a market structure in which a small number of interdependent firms compete. In analyzing oligopoly, we cannot rely on the same types of graphs we used in analyzing perfect competition and monopolistic competition—for two reasons.

First, we need to use economic models that allow us to analyze the more complex business strategies of large oligopoly firms. Second, even in determining the profit-maximizing price and output of an oligopoly firm, demand curves and cost curves are not as useful as in the cases of perfect competition and monopolistic competition. We are able to draw the demand curves for competitive firms by assuming that the prices these firms charge have no impact on the prices other firms in their industries charge. This assumption is realistic when each firm is small relative to the market. It is not a realistic assumption, however, for firms that are as large relative to their markets as Microsoft, Dell, or Carrefour.

When large firms cut their prices, their rivals in the industry often—but not always—respond by also cutting their prices. Because we don't know for sure how other firms will respond to a price change, we don't know the quantity an oligopolist will sell at a particular price. In other words, it is difficult to know what an oligopolist's demand curve will look like. As we have seen, a firm's marginal revenue curve depends on its demand curve. If we don't know what an oligopolist's demand curve looks like, we also don't know what its marginal revenue curve looks like. Not knowing marginal revenue, we can't calculate the profit-maximizing level of output and the profit-maximizing price the way we did for competitive firms.

The approach we use to analyze competition among oligopolists is called *game theory*. Game theory can be used to analyze any situation in which groups or individuals interact. In the context of economic analysis, game theory is the study of the decisions of firms in industries where the profits of each firm depend on its interactions with other firms. It has been applied to strategies for nuclear war, for international trade negotiations, and for political campaigns, among many other examples. In this chapter, we use game theory to analyze the business strategies of large firms.

10.1 LEARNING OBJECTIVE

10.1 | Show how barriers to entry explain the existence of oligopolies.

Oligopoly and Barriers to Entry

Oligopolies are industries with only a few firms. This market structure lies between the competitive industries, which have many firms, and the monopolies which have only a single firm as we will see in the following chapters. One measure of the extent of competition in an industry is the *concentration ratio*. Most economists believe that a four-firm concentration ratio of greater than 40 percent indicates that an industry is an oligopoly.

The concentration ratio has some flaws as a measure of the extent of competition in an industry. For example, concentration ratios do not include sales in a country by foreign firms. In addition, concentration ratios are calculated for the national market, even though the competition in some industries, such as restaurants or college bookstores, is mainly local. Finally, competition sometimes exists between firms in different industries. For example, LuLu hypermarket is included in the discount department stores industry but also competes with firms in the supermarket industry and the retail toy store industry. As we will see later, some economists prefer another measure of competition, known as the *Herfindahl-Hirschman Index*. Despite their shortcomings, concentration ratios can be useful in providing a general idea of the extent of competition in an industry.

Barriers to Entry

Why do oligopolies exist? Why aren't there many more firms in the discount department store industry, the telecommunication industry, or the automobile industry? Recall that new firms will enter industries where existing firms are earning economic profits. But new firms often have difficulty entering an oligopoly. Anything that keeps new firms from entering an industry in which firms are earning economic profits is called a **barrier to entry**. Three barriers to entry are economies of scale, ownership of a key input, and government-imposed barriers.

Economies of Scale The most important barrier to entry is economies of scale. As we saw when we studied production technology, **economies of scale** exist when a firm's long-run average costs fall as it increases output. The greater the economies of scale, the fewer the number of firms that will be in the industry. Figure 10-1 illustrates this point.

If economies of scale are relatively unimportant in the industry, the typical firm's long-run average cost curve (*LRAC*) will reach a minimum at a level of output (Q_1 in Figure 10-1) that is a small fraction of total industry sales. The industry will have room for a large number of firms and will be competitive. If economies of scale are significant, the typical firm will not reach the minimum point on its long-run average cost curve (Q_2 in Figure 10-1) until it has produced a large fraction of industry sales. Then the industry will have room for only a few firms and will be an oligopoly.

Economies of scale can explain why there is much more competition in the restaurant industry than in the discount department store industry. Because very large restaurants do not have lower average costs than smaller restaurants, the restaurant industry has room for many firms. In contrast, large discount department stores, such as Carrefour, have much lower average costs than small discount department stores, for the reasons we discussed in the chapter opener. As a result, just four firms—Carrefour, LuLu, Géant, and Panda—account for about 95 percent of all sales in this industry in the Gulf countries.

Ownership of a Key Input If production of a good requires a particular input, then control of that input can be a barrier to entry. For many years, the Aluminum Company of America (Alcoa) controlled most of the world's supply of high-quality bauxite, the

Barrier to entry Anything that keeps new firms from entering an industry in which firms are earning economic profits.

Economies of scale The situation when a firm's long-run average costs fall as it increases output.

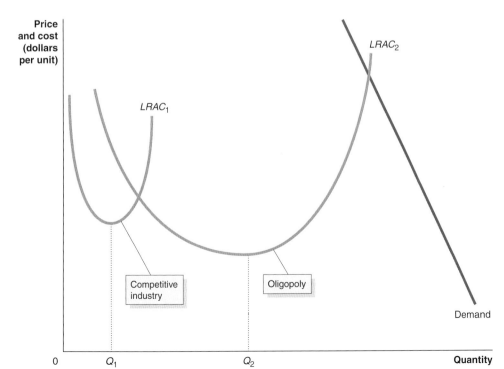

Figure 10-1

Economies of Scale Help Determine the Extent of Competition in an Industry

An industry will be competitive if the minimum point on the typical firm's long-run average cost curve (*LRAC*₁) occurs at a level of output that is a small fraction of total industry sales, like Q_1. The industry will be an oligopoly if the minimum point comes at a level of output that is a large fraction of industry sales, like Q_2.

mineral needed to produce aluminum. The only way other companies could enter the industry to compete with Alcoa was to recycle aluminum. The De Beers Company of South Africa was able to block competition in the diamond market by controlling the output of most of the world's diamond mines.

Government-Imposed Barriers Firms sometimes try to have the government impose barriers to entry. Many large firms employ *lobbyists* to convince state legislators and members of the U.S. Congress to pass laws favorable to the economic interests of the firms. Examples of government-imposed barriers to entry are patents, licensing requirements, and barriers to international trade. A **patent** gives a firm the exclusive right to a new product for a period of 15 to 25 years from the date the product is invented. Governments use patents to encourage firms to carry out research and development of new and better products and better ways of producing existing products. Output and living standards increase faster when firms devote resources to research and development, but a firm that spends money to develop a new product may not earn much profit if other firms can copy the product. For example, the U.S. pharmaceutical company Merck spends more than US$3 billion per year to develop new prescription drugs. If rival companies could freely produce these new drugs as soon as Merck developed them, most of the firm's investment would be wasted. Because Merck can patent a new drug, the firm can charge higher prices during the years the patent is in force and make an economic profit on its successful innovation.

The government also restricts competition through *occupational licensing*. For example, doctors and dentists need licenses to practice. The justification for the laws is to protect the public from incompetent practitioners, but by restricting the number of people who can enter the licensed professions, the laws also raise prices.

Government also imposes barriers to entering some industries by imposing tariffs and quotas on foreign competition. A *tariff* is a tax on imports, and a *quota* limits the quantity of a good that can be imported into a country, as we will see latter.

In summary, to earn economic profits, all firms would like to charge a price well above average cost, but earning economic profits attracts new firms to enter the industry. Eventually, the increased competition forces price down to average cost, and firms just break even. In an oligopoly, barriers to entry prevent—or at least slow down—entry, which allows firms to earn economic profits over a longer period.

Patent The exclusive right to a product for a period of 20 years from the date the product is invented.

10.2 LEARNING OBJECTIVE

10.2 | Use game theory to analyze the strategies of oligopolistic firms.

Using Game Theory to Analyze Oligopoly

As we noted at the beginning of the chapter, economists analyze oligopolies using *game theory*, which was developed during the 1940s by the mathematician John von Neumann and the economist Oskar Morgenstern. **Game theory** is the study of how people make decisions in situations in which attaining their goals depends on their interactions with others. In oligopolies, the interactions among firms are crucial in determining profitability because the firms are large relative to the market.

In all games—whether poker, chess, or Monopoly—the interactions among the players are crucial in determining the outcome. In addition, games share three key characteristics:

1 *Rules* that determine what actions are allowable

2 *Strategies* that players employ to attain their objectives in the game

3 *Payoffs* that are the results of the interaction among the players' strategies.

In business situations, the rules of the 'game' include not just laws that a firm must obey but also other matters beyond a firm's control—at least in the short run—such as its production function. A **business strategy** is a set of actions that a firm takes to achieve a goal, such as maximizing profits. The *payoffs* are the profits earned as a result of a firm's strategies interacting with the strategies of the other firms. The best way to understand the game theory approach is to look at an example.

Game theory The study of how people make decisions in situations in which achieving their goals depends on their interactions with others; in economics, the study of the decisions of firms in industries where the profits of each firm depend on its interactions with other firms.

Business strategy Actions taken by a firm to achieve a goal, such as maximizing profits.

A Duopoly Game: Price Competition between Two Firms

In this simple example, we use game theory to analyze price competition in a *duopoly*—an oligopoly with two firms. Suppose that an isolated town in Kuwait has only two stores: Carrefour and LuLu hypermarket. Both stores sell the Sony PlayStation 3 (PS3). For simplicity, let's assume that no other stores stock the PS3 and that consumers in the town can't buy it on the Internet or through mail-order catalogs. The manager of each store decides whether to charge US$400 or US$600 for the PS3. Which price will be more profitable depends on the price the other store charges. The decision regarding what price to charge is an example of a business strategy. In Figure 10-2, we organize the possible outcomes that result from the actions of the two firms into a *payoff matrix*. A **payoff matrix** is a table that shows the payoffs that each firm earns from every combination of strategies by the firms.

Carrefour's profits are shown in blue, and LuLu's profits are shown in red. If Carrefour and LuLu both charge US$600 for the PlayStation, each store will make a profit of US$10,000 per month from sales of the game console. If Carrefour charges the lower price of US$400, while LuLu charges US$600, Carrefour will gain many of LuLu's customers. Carrefour's profits will be US$15,000, and LuLu's will be only US$5,000. Similarly, if Carrefour charges US$600, while LuLu is charging US$400, Carrefour's profits will be only US$5,000, while LuLu's profits will be US$15,000. If both stores charge US$400, each will earn profits of US$7,500 per month.

Clearly, the stores will be better off if they both charge US$600 for the PlayStation. But will they both charge this price? One possibility is that the manager of the Carrefour and the manager of the LuLu will get together and *collude* by agreeing to charge the higher price. **Collusion** is an agreement among firms to charge the same price or otherwise not to compete. Unfortunately, for Carrefour and LuLu—but fortunately for their customers— collusion is against the law in many countries, especially in the developed world. The government can fine companies that collude and send the managers involved to prison.

The manager of the Carrefour store legally can't discuss his pricing decision with the manager of the LuLu store, so he has to predict what the other manager will do. Suppose the Carrefour manager is convinced that the LuLu manager will charge US$600 for the PlayStation. In this case, the Carrefour manager will definitely charge US$400 because that will increase his profit from US$10,000 to US$15,000. But suppose, instead, the Carrefour manager is convinced that the LuLu manager will charge US$400. Then the Carrefour manager also will charge US$400 because that will increase his profit from US$5,000 to US$7,500. In fact, whichever price the LuLu manager decides to charge, the Carrefour manager is better off charging US$400. So, we know that the Carrefour manager will choose a price of US$400 for the PlayStation.

Now consider the situation of the LuLu manager. The LuLu manager is in the identical position to the Carrefour manager, so we can expect her to make the same decision to charge US$400 for the PlayStation. In this situation, each manager has a *dominant strategy*. A **dominant strategy** is the best strategy for a firm, no matter what strategies other firms use. The result is an equilibrium where both managers charge US$400 for the PlayStation. This situation is an equilibrium because each manager is maximizing profits, *given the price chosen by the other manager*. In other words, neither firm can

Payoff matrix A table that shows the payoffs that each firm earns from every combination of strategies by the firms.

Collusion An agreement among firms to charge the same price or otherwise not to compete.

Dominant strategy A strategy that is the best for a firm, no matter what strategies other firms use.

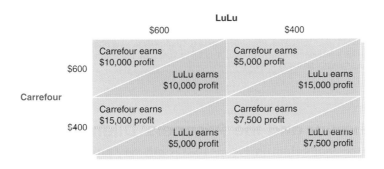

Figure 10-2

A Duopoly Game

Carrefour's profits are in blue, and LuLu's profits are in red. Carrefour and LuLu would each make profits of US$10,000 per month on sales of PlayStation 3 if they both charged US$600. However, each store manager has an incentive to undercut the other by charging a lower price. If both charge US$400, they would each make a profit of only US$7,500 per month.

Nash equilibrium A situation in which each firm chooses the best strategy, given the strategies chosen by other firms.

increase its profits by changing its price, given the price chosen by the other firm. An equilibrium where each firm chooses the best strategy, given the strategies chosen by other firms, is called a **Nash equilibrium**, named after the Nobel laureate John Nash, of Princeton University, a pioneer in the development of game theory.

Making *the* Connection | **The Price War Is Escalating between Qatar's Two Telecom Operators**

As we saw above, in a duopoly the decisions of one firm affects the profitability of the other. Each firm is trying to set its strategy based on the move it expects from the other firm in the industry. This may lead to a situation where each firm is trying to undercut the price of the other, entering into a price war.

In the beginning of 2009, Vodafone started operating as the second telecom operator in Qatar. Qatar Telecom (Qtel) used to be the exclusive telecommunication provider in Qatar and is one of the country's largest public companies since its successful launch in 1998. In January 2010, shortly after announcements of call-tariff reductions, Vodafone Qatar and Qtel both announced new offers for its customers. The price war between the two telecom companies escalated with both the players coming up with one attractive offer after another.

In 2009, Qtel launched a strong promotion program and announced many value pack packages that were loaded with cheap international calling at as low as 0.29 Qatari riyals and almost free domestic minutes. By the end of 2009, it was clear that thousands of consumers switched back to Qtel to enjoy the cheap offers.

In response, after a series of offerings, Vodafone Qatar allowed 2,010 bonus minutes, which can be used for domestic calls within the Vodafone network. This was in addition to the value included in their Flexi plans. Vodafone Qatar announced that this gift of 2,010 domestic call minutes was for all its customers who maintain an active account and new subscribers, until the end of February 2010. This giveaway of free minutes, good to use only during 2010, did not even require activation. "Ever since Vodafone entered the market with our innovative Flexi plans, we've made it a point to always offer the customer more and more value," said the chief marketing officer of Vodafone Qatar, Michael Portz. A long-standing feature of Vodafone's Flexi plans since their introduction has been that customers automatically receive more value than the money they pay, which can be used for calling, text-messaging, international, roaming, mobile data, and more—any of the services currently on offer from Vodafone.

Qtel, on the other hand, responded by extending the Dawli MENA and Dawli Asia International Calling Cards promotion until February 2010, so that callers could make cheap international calls to Asia or the Middle East and North Africa. The rival company then announced that many other promotions were on the way.

Source: MENAFN Press, "Value Pack Promotion Attracts Thousands to Switch to Qtel's Shahry," August 6, 2009, MENA Financial Network: www.menafn.com; Asif Iqbal, "Qtel, Vodafone Announce New Offers; Price War Escalates," *Qatar Tribune*, January 17, 2010.

Firm Behavior and the Prisoners' Dilemma

Notice that the equilibrium in Figure 10-2 is not very satisfactory for either firm. The firms earn US$7,500 profit each month by charging US$400, but they could have earned US$10,000 profit if they had both charged US$600. By 'cooperating' and charging the higher price, they would have achieved a *cooperative equilibrium*. In a **cooperative equilibrium**, players cooperate to increase their mutual payoff. We have seen, though, that the outcome of this game is likely to be a **noncooperative equilibrium**, in which each firm pursues its own self-interest.

A situation like this, in which pursuing dominant strategies results in noncooperation that leaves everyone worse off, is called a **prisoners' dilemma**. The game gets its name from the problem faced by two suspects the police arrest for a crime. If the police lack other evidence, they may separate the suspects and offer each a reduced prison sentence in exchange for confessing to the crime and testifying against the other criminal. Because each suspect now believes he would get a harsher sentence if he remains silent while the other one confesses to the crime, they both would have a dominant strategy to confess to the crime. Each suspect would believe that if he confesses he will be better off because he will get a shorter prison sentence. This is clearly better than if he does not confess while the other does, as in such a case he will end up serving a longer term. So, they will end up both choosing to confess to the crime and serve a prison term, even though they would have gone free if they had both remained silent. They don't go free, however, because they did not cooperate in the game and there was no commitment by both to remaining silent.

Cooperative equilibrium An equilibrium in a game in which players cooperate to increase their mutual payoff.

Noncooperative equilibrium An equilibrium in a game in which players do not cooperate but pursue their own self-interest.

Prisoners' dilemma A game in which pursuing dominant strategies results in noncooperation that leaves everyone worse off.

Solved Problem | 10-2

Is Advertising a Prisoners' Dilemma for Coca-Cola and Pepsi?

Coca-Cola and Pepsi both advertise aggressively, but would they be better off if they didn't? Their commercials are not designed to convey new information about the products. Instead, they are designed to capture each other's customers. Construct a payoff matrix using the following hypothetical information:

- If neither firm advertises, Coca-Cola and Pepsi both earn profits of US$750 million per year.

- If both firms advertise, Coca-Cola and Pepsi both earn profits of US$500 million per year.

- If Coca-Cola advertises and Pepsi doesn't, Coca-Cola earns profits of US$900 million and Pepsi earns profits of US$400 million.

- If Pepsi advertises and Coca-Cola doesn't, Pepsi earns profits of US$900 million and Coca-Cola earns profits of US$400 million.

a. If Coca-Cola wants to maximize profit, will it advertise? Briefly explain.

b. If Pepsi wants to maximize profit, will it advertise? Briefly explain.

c. Is there a Nash equilibrium to this advertising game? If so, what is it?

SOLVING THE PROBLEM:

Step 1: **Review the chapter material.** This problem uses payoff matrixes to analyze a business situation, so you may want to review the section "A Duopoly Game: Price Competition between Two Firms," which begins on page 333.

Step 2: **Construct the payoff matrix.**

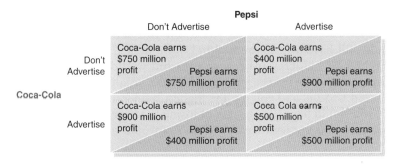

Step 3: Answer question (a) by showing that Coca-Cola has a dominant strategy of advertising. If Pepsi doesn't advertise, then Coca-Cola will make US$900 million if it advertises but only US$750 million if it doesn't. If Pepsi advertises, then Coca-Cola will make US$500 million if it advertises but only US$400 million if it doesn't. Therefore, advertising is a dominant strategy for Coca-Cola.

Step 4: Answer question (b) by showing that Pepsi has a dominant strategy of advertising. Pepsi is in the same position as Coca-Cola, so it also has a dominant strategy of advertising.

Step 5: Answer question (c) by showing that there is a Nash equilibrium for this game. Both firms advertising is a Nash equilibrium. Given that Pepsi is advertising, Coca-Cola's best strategy is to advertise. Given that Coca-Cola is advertising, Pepsi's best strategy is to advertise. Therefore, advertising is the optimal decision for both firms, *given the decision by the other firm.*

EXTRA CREDIT: This is another example of the prisoners' dilemma game. Coca-Cola and Pepsi would be more profitable if they both refrained from advertising, thereby saving the enormous expense of television and radio commercials and newspaper and magazine ads. Each firm's dominant strategy is to advertise, however, so they end up in an equilibrium where both advertise, and their profits are reduced.

YOUR TURN: For more practice, do related problems 2.9 and 2.10 on page 352 at the end of this chapter.

>> **End Solved Problem 10-2**

Making the Connection

Is There a Dominant Strategy for Bidding on Souq.com?

An auction is a game in which bidders compete to buy a product. The payoff in winning an auction is equal to the difference between the subjective value you place on the product being auctioned and the amount of the winning bid.

Souq.com is run as a *price auction*, where the winning bidder pays the highest bidder price. If the high bidder on a DVD of *Spider-Man 3* bids US$15, and the second bidder bids US$10, the high bidder wins the auction and pays US$15. It may seem that your best strategy when bidding on Souq.com is to place a bid well below the subjective value you place on the item in the hope of winning it at a low price. In fact, bidders on Souq.com have a dominant strategy of entering a bid equal to the maximum value they place on the item. For instance, suppose you are looking for a present for your parents' anniversary. They are Amr Diab fans, and someone is auctioning a pair of Amr Diab concert tickets. If the maximum value you place on the tickets is US$200, that should be your bid. To see why, consider the results of strategies of bidding more or less than US$200.

There are two possible outcomes of the auction: either someone else bids more than you do, or you are the highest bidder. First, suppose you bid US$200 but someone else bids more than you do. If you had bid less than US$200, you would still have lost. If you had bid more than US$200, you might have been the highest bidder, but because your bid would be for more than the value you place on the tickets, you would have a negative payoff. Second, suppose you bid US$200 and you are the highest bidder. If you had bid less than US$200, you would have run the risk of losing the tickets to someone who had bid more than you but less than US$200. You would be worse off than if you had bid US$200 and won. If you had bid more than US$200, you would not have affected the price you ended up paying—which, remember, is equal to the amount bid by the second-highest bidder. Therefore, a strategy of bidding US$200—the maximum value you place on the tickets—dominates bidding more or less than US$200.

Even though making your first bid your highest bid is a dominant strategy on Souq.com, many bidders don't use it. After an auction is over, a link leads to a web page showing all the bids. In many auctions, the same bidder bids several times, showing that the bidder had not understood his or her dominant strategy.

YOUR TURN: Test your understanding by doing related problem 2.12 on page 353 at the end of this chapter.

Can Firms Escape the Prisoners' Dilemma?

Although the prisoners' dilemma game seems to show that cooperative behavior always breaks down, we know it doesn't. People often cooperate to achieve their goals, and firms find ways to cooperate by not competing on price. The reason the basic prisoners' dilemma story is not always applicable is that it assumes the game will be played only once. Most business situations, however, are repeated over and over. Each month, LuLu and Carrefour managers will decide again what price they will charge for a PlayStation 3. In the language of game theory, the managers are playing a *repeated game*. In a repeated game, the losses from not cooperating are greater than in a game played once, and players can also employ *retaliation strategies* against those who don't cooperate. As a result, we are more likely to see cooperative behavior.

Figure 10-2 shows that Carrefour and LuLu are earning US$2,500 less per month by both charging US$400 instead of US$600 for the PS3. Every month that passes with both stores charging US$400 increases the total amount lost: two years of charging US$400 will cause each store to lose US$60,000 in profit. This lost profit increases the incentive for the store managers to cooperate by *implicitly* colluding. Remember that *explicit* collusion—such as the managers meeting and agreeing to charge US$600—is illegal. But if the managers can find a way to signal to each other that they will charge US$600, they may be within the law.

Suppose, for example, that Carrefour and LuLu hypermarket both advertise that they will match the lowest price offered by any competitor—in our simple example, they are each other's only competitor. These advertisements are signals to each other that they intend to charge US$600 for the PlayStation. The signal is clear because each store knows that if it charges US$400, the other store will automatically retaliate by also lowering its price to US$400. The offer to match prices is a good *enforcement mechanism* because it guarantees that if either store fails to cooperate and charges the lower price, the competing store will automatically punish that store by also charging the lower price. As Figure 10-3 shows, the stores have changed the payoff matrix they face.

With the original payoff matrix (a), there is no matching offer, and each store makes more profit if it charges US$400 when the other charges US$600. The matching offer changes the payoff matrix to (b). Now the stores can charge US$600 and receive a profit of US$10,000 per month, or they can charge US$400 and receive a profit of US$7,500 per month. The equilibrium shifts from the prisoners' dilemma result of both stores charging the low price and receiving low profits to a result where both stores charge the high price and receive high profits. An offer to match competitors' prices might seem to benefit consumers, but game theory shows that it actually may hurt consumers by helping to keep prices high.

Figure 10-3

Changing the Payoff Matrix in a Repeated Game

Carrefour and LuLu can change the payoff matrix by advertising that they will match their competitor's price. This retaliation strategy provides a signal that one store charging a lower price will be met automatically by the other store charging a lower price. In payoff matrix (a), there is no matching offer, and each store benefits if it charges US$400 when the other charges US$600. In payoff matrix (b), with the matching offer, the companies have only two choices: they can charge US$600 and receive a profit of US$10,000 per month, or they can charge US$400 and receive a profit of US$7,500 per month. The equilibrium shifts from the prisoners' dilemma result of both stores charging the low price and receiving low profits to both stores charging the high price and receiving high profits.

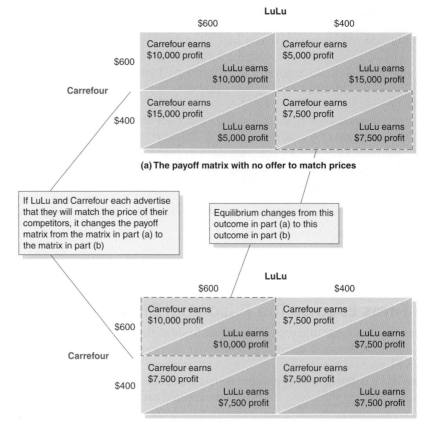

(a) The payoff matrix with no offer to match prices

If LuLu and Carrefour each advertise that they will match the price of their competitors, it changes the payoff matrix from the matrix in part (a) to the matrix in part (b)

Equilibrium changes from this outcome in part (a) to this outcome in part (b)

(b) The payoff matrix with an offer to match prices

Price leadership A form of implicit collusion where one firm in an oligopoly announces a price change, which is matched by the other firms in the industry.

One form of implicit collusion occurs as a result of *price leadership*. With **price leadership**, one firm takes the lead in announcing a price change, which is then matched by the other firms in the industry. In some cases, such as the telecom industry, firms have attempted to act as price leaders, but failed when other firms in the industry declined to cooperate.

Making the Connection

Du's Decision Not to Indulge in a Price War with Etisalat, UAE's Former Telecom Monopoly

Coordinating prices is easier in some industries than in others. Fixed costs in the telecom industry are very large, and marginal costs are very small. The marginal cost of adding one more subscriber is fairly low. As a result, after a certain number of subscribers, telecom providers often engage in last-minute price cutting to subscription renewal. In addition, providers usually have very cheap offers valid only for new subscribers. Even low priced calling-minutes will increase marginal revenue more than marginal cost. As with other oligopolies, if all telecom operators cut prices, industry profits would decline. Providers, therefore, continually adjust their prices while at the same time monitoring their rivals' prices and retaliating against them for either cutting prices or failing to go along with price increases.

Etisalat and du, the UAE's telecom operators, are good examples of a duopoly that is trying to avoid a price war. Du started operations in 2006, and by 2010 became a second telecom, Internet, and cable TV services provider, an alternative to the long-established Etisalat. Du's CEO, Osman Sultan, who launched the highly successful MobiNil in Egypt in 1998, discusses how du is approaching competition with its rival, Etisalat, and how du will differentiate itself. "One thing we will not do is offer the same services as Etisalat's, but cheaper. A price war would result in a destruction of value, and our purpose is to create value," says Sultan. Du is planning to compete by providing a service with a better value and quality to the consumer and by being ahead of the game in that fast growing market.

Du pledges to be the first to provide new applications before its competitor, Etisalat. "Telecom today is no longer about just making telephone calls or sending SMSs or even accessing the Internet. It is about carrying our entire environment with us everywhere. We want to carry our office, our music, our entertainment, our bank, our school, our whole lifestyle with us at all times wherever we are," says Sultan, du's CEO.

Since du started operating, the UAE has not really seen a trend of falling prices with the increased competition in the telecom sector as is often seen in other markets. It is not in Etisalat or du's long-term best interests to have a price war, so they have concentrated on promotions and new services to attract more customers.

Source: "Introducing Competition to a Long-Standing Monopoly," August 25, 2010, *Wall Street Market Research*, www.wallstreet-mr.com/ceo_du.php.

Cartels: The Case of OPEC

In developed countries, as well as in some Arab countries such as Egypt, firms cannot legally meet to agree on what prices to charge and how much to produce. But suppose they could. Would this be enough to guarantee that their collusion would be successful? The example of the Organization of Petroleum Exporting Countries (OPEC) indicates that the answer to this question is "no." OPEC has 11 members, including Saudi Arabia, Kuwait, and other Arab countries, as well as Iran, Venezuela, Nigeria, and Indonesia. Together, these countries own 75 percent of the world's proven oil reserves, although they pump a smaller share of the total oil sold each year. OPEC operates as a **cartel**, which is a group of firms that collude to restrict output to increase prices and profits. The members of OPEC meet periodically and agree on quotas, quantities of oil that each country agrees to produce. The quotas are intended to reduce oil production well below the competitive level, to force up the price of oil, and to increase the profits of member countries.

Figure 10-4 shows oil prices from 1972 to 2010. The blue line shows the price of a barrel of oil in each year. Prices in general have risen since 1972, which has reduced the amount of goods and services that consumers can purchase with a dollar. The red line corrects for general price increases by measuring oil prices in terms of the U.S. dollar's purchasing power in 2000. Although political unrest in the Middle East and other factors also affect the price of oil, the figure shows that OPEC had considerable success in raising the price of oil during the mid-1970s and early 1980s. Oil prices, which had been below US$3 per barrel in 1972, rose to more than US$39 per barrel in 1980, which was almost US$66 measured in dollars of 2000 purchasing power. The figure also shows that OPEC has had difficulty sustaining the high prices of 1980 in later years, although beginning in 2004, oil prices rose, in part due to increasing demand from China and India. The sharp decline in oil prices in 2008 was due to the global financial crises and a weak demand for oil by most industrial countries. Oil prices started to pick up again in 2010 due to stronger global demand and signs of a subsiding world recession.

Cartel A group of firms that collude by agreeing to restrict output to increase prices and profits.

Figure 10-4

The blue line shows the price of a barrel of oil in each year. The red line measures the price of a barrel of oil in terms of the purchasing power of the U.S. dollar in 2000. By reducing oil production, the Organization of Petroleum Exporting Countries (OPEC) was able to raise the world price of oil in the mid-1970s and early 1980s. Sustaining high prices has been difficult over the long run, however, because members often exceed their output quotas.
Source: International Financial Statistics, IMF.

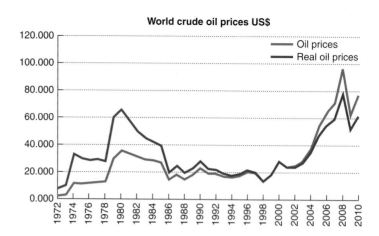

Game theory helps us understand why oil prices have fluctuated. If every member of OPEC cooperates and produces the low output level dictated by its quota, prices will be high, and the cartel will earn large profits. Once the price has been driven up, however, each member has an incentive to stop cooperating and to earn even higher profits by increasing output beyond its quota. But if no country sticks to its quota, total oil output will increase, and profits will decline. In other words, OPEC is caught in a prisoners' dilemma.

If the members of OPEC always exceeded their production quotas, the cartel would have no effect on world oil prices. In fact, the members of OPEC periodically meet and assign new quotas that, at least for a while, enable them to restrict output enough to raise prices. OPEC's occasional success at behaving as a cartel can be explained by two factors. First, the members of OPEC are participating in a repeated game. As we have seen, this increases the likelihood of a cooperative outcome. Second, Saudi Arabia has far larger oil reserves than any other member of OPEC. Therefore, it has the most to gain from high oil prices and a greater incentive to cooperate. To see this, consider the payoff matrix shown in Figure 10-5. To keep things simple, let's assume that OPEC has only two members: Saudi Arabia and Nigeria. In Figure 10-5, "low output" corresponds to cooperating with the OPEC-assigned output quota, and "high output" corresponds to producing at maximum capacity. The payoff matrix shows the profits received per day by each country.

We can see that Saudi Arabia has a strong incentive to cooperate and maintain its low output quota. By keeping output low, Saudi Arabia can by itself significantly raise the world price of oil, increasing its own profits as well as those of other members of OPEC. Therefore, Saudi Arabia has a dominant strategy of cooperating with the quota and producing a low output. Nigeria, however, cannot by itself have much effect on the price of oil. Therefore, Nigeria has a dominant strategy of not cooperating and producing a high output. The equilibrium of this game will occur with Saudi Arabia producing

Figure 10-5

Because Saudi Arabia can produce so much more oil than Nigeria, its output decisions have a much larger effect on the price of oil. In the figure, "low output" corresponds to cooperating with the OPEC-assigned output quota, and "high output" corresponds to producing at maximum capacity. Saudi Arabia has a dominant strategy to cooperate and produce a low output. Nigeria, however, has a dominant strategy not to cooperate and produce a high output. Therefore, the equilibrium of this game will occur with Saudi Arabia producing a low output and Nigeria producing a high output.

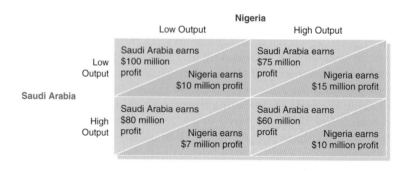

a low output and Nigeria producing a high output. In fact, OPEC often operates in just this way. Saudi Arabia will cooperate with the quota, while the other 10 members produce at capacity. Because this is a repeated game, however, Saudi Arabia will occasionally produce more oil than its quota to intentionally drive down the price and retaliate against the other members for not cooperating.

10.3 LEARNING OBJECTIVE

10.3 | Use sequential games to analyze business strategies.

Sequential Games and Business Strategy

We have been analyzing games in which both players move simultaneously. In many business situations, however, one firm will act first, and then other firms will respond. These situations can be analyzed using *sequential games*. We will use sequential games to analyze two business strategies: deterring entry and bargaining between firms. To keep things simple, we consider situations that involve only two firms.

Deterring Entry

We saw earlier that barriers to entry are a key to firms continuing to earn economic profits. Can firms create barriers to deter new firms from entering an industry? Some recent research in game theory has focused on this question. To take a simple example, suppose a town in Cairo currently has no discount department stores. Executives at Carrefour decide to enter the market and are considering what size store to build. To break even by covering the opportunity cost of the funds involved, the store must provide a minimum rate of return of 15 percent on the firm's investment. If Carrefour builds a small store in the town, it will earn economic profits by receiving a return of 30 percent. If Carrefour builds a large store, its costs will be somewhat higher, and it will receive a return of only 22 percent.

It seems clear that Carrefour should build the small store, but the executives are worried that LuLu may also build a store in this market. If Carrefour builds a small store and LuLu enters the market, both firms will earn an 18 percent return on their investment in this market. If Carrefour builds a large store and LuLu enters, the stores will have to cut prices, and the firms will each earn only a 10 percent return on their investments, which is below the 15 percent return necessary for either firm to break even.

We can analyze a sequential game by using a *decision tree*, like the one shown in Figure 10-6. The boxes in the figure represent *decision nodes*, which are points when the firms must make the decisions contained in the boxes. At the left, Carrefour makes the initial decision of what size store to build, and then LuLu responds by either entering the

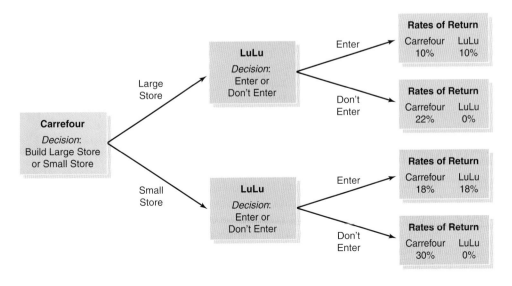

Figure 10-6

The Decision Tree for an Entry Game

Carrefour earns its highest return if it builds a small store and LuLu doesn't enter the market. If Carrefour builds a small store, LuLu will enter because it will earn economic profit by receiving an 18 percent return on its investment. Therefore, the best decision for Carrefour is to build a large store to deter LuLu's entry. Once Carrefour has built a large store, LuLu knows that if it enters this market, it will earn only 10 percent on its investment, which represents an economic loss, so it won't enter the market.

market or not. The decisions made are shown beside the arrows. The *terminal nodes* at the right side of the figure show the resulting rates of return.

Let's start with Carrefour's initial decision. If Carrefour builds a large store, then the arrow directs us to the upper red decision node for LuLu. If LuLu decides to enter, it will earn only a 10 percent rate of return on its investment, which represents an economic loss because it is below the opportunity cost of the funds involved. If LuLu doesn't enter, Carrefour will earn 22 percent, and LuLu will not earn anything in this market. Carrefour executives can conclude that if they build a large store, LuLu will not enter, and Carrefour will earn 22 percent on its investment.

If Carrefour decides to build a small store, then the arrow directs us to the lower red decision node for LuLu. If LuLu decides to enter, it will earn an 18 percent rate of return. If it doesn't enter, Carrefour will earn 30 percent, and LuLu will not earn anything in this market. Carrefour executives can conclude that if they build a small store, LuLu will enter, and Carrefour will earn 18 percent on its investment.

This analysis should lead Carrefour executives to conclude that they can build a small store and earn 18 percent—because LuLu will enter—or they can build a large store and earn 22 percent by deterring LuLu's entry.

Solved Problem | 10-3

Is Deterring Entry Always a Good Idea?

Whether deterring entry makes sense depends on how costly it is to the firm doing the deterring. Use the following decision tree to decide whether Carrefour should deter LuLu from entering this market. Assume that each firm must earn a 15 percent return on its investment to break even.

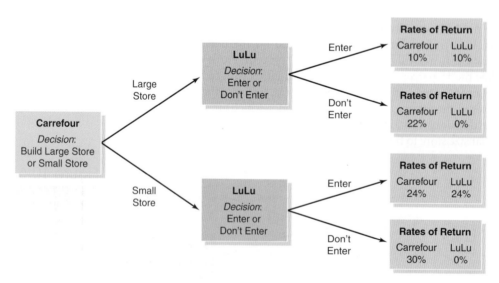

SOLVING THE PROBLEM:

Step 1: **Review the chapter material.** This problem is about sequential games, so you may want to review the section "Deterring Entry," which begins on page 341.

Step 2: **Determine how LuLu will respond to Carrefour's decision.** If Carrefour builds a large store, LuLu will not enter this market because the return on its investment represents an economic loss. If Carrefour builds a small store, LuLu will enter because it will earn a return that represents an economic profit.

Step 3: **Given how LuLu will react, determine which strategy maximizes profits for Carrefour.** If Carrefour builds the large store, it will have deterred LuLu's entry, and the rate of return on its investment will be 22 percent. If it builds the small store, LuLu will enter, but Carrefour will actually earn a higher return of 24 percent.

Step 4: **State your conclusion.** Like any other business strategy, deterrence is worth pursuing only if its costs are not too high. In this case, the high cost of building a large store lowers Carrefour's economic profits below what it earns by building a small store, even given that LuLu will enter the market.

YOUR TURN: For more practice, do related problem 3.3 on page 354 at the end of this chapter. >> **End Solved Problem 10-3**

Bargaining

The success of many firms depends on how well they bargain with other firms. For example, firms often must bargain with their suppliers over the prices they pay for inputs. Suppose that Al-Huda is a small firm, which has developed software that improves how pictures from a digital camera are displayed on computer screens. Al-Huda currently sells its software only on its website and earns profits of US$2 million per year. Dell Computer informs Al-Huda that it is considering installing the software on every new computer Dell sells. Dell expects to sell more computers at a higher price if it can install Al-Huda's software on its computers. The two firms begin bargaining over what price Dell will pay Al-Huda for its software.

The decision tree in Figure 10-7 illustrates this bargaining game. At the left, Dell makes the initial decision on what price to offer Al-Huda for its software, and then Al-Huda responds by either accepting or rejecting the contract offer. First, suppose that Dell offers Al-Huda a contract price of US$30 per copy for its software. If Al-Huda accepts this contract, its profits will be US$5 million per year, and Dell will earn US$10 million in additional profits. If Al-Huda rejects the contract, its profits will be the US$2 million per year it earns selling its software on its website, and Dell will earn zero additional profits.

Now, suppose Dell offers Al-Huda a contract price of US$20 per copy. If Al-Huda accepts this contract, its profits will be US$3 million per year, and Dell will earn US$15 million in additional profits. If Al-Huda rejects this contract, its profits will be the US$2 million it earns selling its software on its website, and Dell will earn zero additional profits. Clearly, for Dell, a contract of US$20 per copy is more profitable, while for Al-Huda, a contract of US$30 per copy is more profitable.

Suppose Al-Huda attempts to obtain a favorable outcome from the bargaining by telling Dell that it will reject a US$20-per-copy contract. If Dell believes this threat,

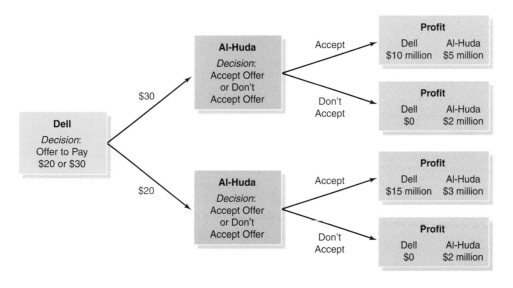

Figure 10-7

The Decision Tree for a Bargaining Game

Dell earns the highest profit if it offers a contract price of US$20 per copy and Al-Huda accepts the contract. Al-Huda earns the highest profit if Dell offers it a contract of US$30 per copy and it accepts the contract. Al-Huda may attempt to bargain by threatening to reject a US$20-per-copy contract. But Dell knows this threat is not credible because once Dell has offered a US$20-per-copy contract, Al-Huda's profits are higher if it accepts the contract than if it rejects it.

then it will offer Al-Huda a US$30-per-copy contract because Dell is better off with the US$10 million profit that will result from Al-Huda accepting the contract than with the zero profits Dell will earn if Al-Huda rejects the US$20-per-copy contract. This result is a Nash equilibrium because neither firm can increase its profits by changing its choice—*provided that Dell believes Al-Huda's threat.* But is Al-Huda's threat credible? Once Dell has offered Al-Huda the US$20 contract, Al-Huda's choices are to accept the contract and earn US$3 million or reject the contract and earn only US$2 million. Because rejecting the contract reduces Al-Huda's profits, Al-Huda's threat to reject the contract is not credible, and Dell should ignore it.

As a result, we would expect Dell to use the strategy of offering Al-Huda a US$20-per-copy contract and Al-Huda to use the strategy of accepting the contract. Dell will earn additional profits of US$15 million per year, and Al-Huda will earn profits of US$3 million per year. This outcome is called a *subgame-perfect equilibrium.* A subgame-perfect equilibrium is a Nash equilibrium in which no player can make himself better off by changing his decision at any decision node. In our simple bargaining game, each player has only one decision to make. As we have seen, Dell's profits are highest if it offers the US$20-per-copy contract, and Al-Huda's profits are highest if it accepts the contract. Typically, in sequential games of this type, there is only one subgame-perfect equilibrium.

Managers use decision trees like those in Figures 10-6 and 10-7 in business planning because they provide a systematic way of thinking through the implications of a strategy and of predicting the reactions of rivals. We can see the benefits of decision trees in the simple examples we considered here. In the first example, Carrefour managers can conclude that building a large store is more profitable than building a smaller store. In the second example, Dell managers can conclude that Al-Huda's threat to reject a US$20-per-copy contract is not credible.

10.4 LEARNING OBJECTIVE   10.4 | Use the five competitive forces model to analyze competition in an industry.

The Five Competitive Forces Model

We have seen that the number of competitors in an industry affects a firm's ability to charge a price above average cost and earn an economic profit. The number of firms is not the only determinant of the level of competition in an industry, however. Michael Porter of Harvard Business School has drawn on the research of a number of economists to develop a model that shows how five competitive forces determine the overall level of competition in an industry. Figure 10-8 illustrates Porter's model.

Figure 10-8

The Five Competitive Forces Model

Michael Porter's model identifies five forces that determine the level of competition in an industry: (1) competition from existing firms, (2) the threat from new entrants, (3) competition from substitute goods or services, (4) the bargaining power of buyers, and (5) the bargaining power of suppliers.

Source: The Free Press (Porter, Michael E. 1998) Reprinted with the permission of The Free Press, a Division of Simon & Schuster, Inc., Copyright © 1980, 1998 by The Free Press. All rights reserved.

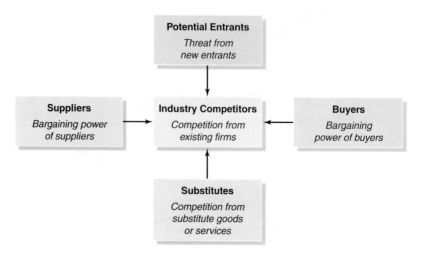

We now look at each of the five competitive forces: (1) competition from existing firms, (2) the threat from potential entrants, (3) competition from substitute goods or services, (4) the bargaining power of buyers, and (5) the bargaining power of suppliers.

Competition from Existing Firms

We have already seen that competition among firms in an industry can lower prices and profits. As we saw earlier in this chapter, when there are only a few firms in a market, it is easier for them to implicitly collude and to charge a price close to the monopoly price.

Competition in the form of advertising, better customer service, or longer warranties can also reduce profits by raising costs. For example, online booksellers usually compete by offering low-cost—or free—shipping, by increasing their customer service staffs, and by building more warehouses to provide faster deliveries. These activities have raised the booksellers' costs and reduced their profits.

The Threat from Potential Entrants

Firms face competition from companies that currently are not in the market but might enter. We have already seen how actions taken to deter entry can reduce profits. In our hypothetical example in the previous section, Carrefour built a larger store and earned less profit to deter LuLu's entry. Business managers often take actions aimed at deterring entry. Some of these actions include advertising to create product loyalty, introducing new products—such as slightly different cereals or toothpastes—to fill market niches, and setting lower prices to keep profits at a level that would make entry less attractive.

Competition from Substitute Goods or Services

Firms are always vulnerable to competitors introducing a new product that fills a consumer need better than their current product does. Consider the encyclopedia business. For decades, many parents bought expensive and bulky encyclopedias for their children attending high school or college. By the 1990s, computer software companies were offering electronic encyclopedias that sold for a small fraction of the price of the printed encyclopedias. Encyclopedia Britannica and the other encyclopedia publishers responded by cutting prices and launching advertising campaigns aimed at showing the superiority of printed encyclopedias. Still, profits continued to decline, and by the end of the 1990s, most printed encyclopedias had disappeared.

The Bargaining Power of Buyers

If buyers have enough bargaining power, they can insist on lower prices, higher-quality products, or additional services. Automobile companies, for example, have significant bargaining power in the tire market, which tends to lower tire prices and limit the profitability of tire manufacturers. Some retailers have significant buying power over their suppliers. For instance, a large retailer like Carrefour may require its suppliers to alter their distribution systems to accommodate Carrefour's need to control the stocks of goods in its stores.

The Bargaining Power of Suppliers

If many firms can supply an input and the input is not specialized, the suppliers are unlikely to have the bargaining power to limit a firm's profits. For instance, suppliers of paper napkins to McDonald's restaurants have very little bargaining power. With only a single or a few suppliers of an input, the purchasing firm may face a high price. During the 1930s and 1940s, for example, the Technicolor Company was the only producer of the cameras and film that studios needed to produce color movies. Technicolor charged the studios high prices to use its cameras, and it had the power to insist that only its technicians could operate the cameras. The only alternative for the movie studios was to make black-and-white movies.

As with other competitive forces, the bargaining power of suppliers can change over time. For instance, when IBM chose Microsoft to supply the operating system for its personal computers, Microsoft was a small company with very limited bargaining power. As Microsoft's Windows operating system became standard in more than 90 percent of personal computers, this large market share increased Microsoft's bargaining power.

Making the Connection | How Jordan's Fastlink (now Zain) Coped with the Threat of New Competition from Mobilcom in Early 2000

We saw earlier in this chapter that in an oligopoly firms respond to the announcement of entry by other competitors. They expect a reduction in profits caused by the increased new competition. When entry is confirmed, the best strategy by firms already operating in the market is to expand the market size and their base before the newcomer launches business.

For a number of years Fastlink was Jordan's sole mobile network operator. For nearly 6 months in the year 2000, Fastlink's offices in the heart of Amman were always busy with meetings, preparing for a strategy to face the new competition, which was going to end Fastlink's monopoly. The newcomer, Mobilcom, was a strong competitor backed by France Telecom, one of the world's largest operators. In 1999, Jordan's government decided to privatize Jordan Telecom (JT), the fixed-line monopoly, and reached a deal with France Telecom. As part of this deal, France Telecom was to buy 40 percent of JT, in addition to a mobile license as a bonus.

Fastlink had 100,000 subscribers at the end of 1999. In January 2000, it knew that within 8 months its monopoly would be over, so it had to act fast to increase the market base. It began to initiate competition and introduced several new products. By the end of the 8-month period, it had gained 80,000 new subscribers.

Meanwhile, almost 6 months prior to its launch, Mobilcom began an aggressive marketing campaign. Mobilcom raised expectations so high that ultimately it could never have met them. It also made a very costly offer. It offered 63 free minutes every month for a year to anyone who registered before launch, in addition to waiving the deposit on subscriptions. Mobilcom offered a flat tariff. This suited Fastlink very well since the latter had just lowered its on-net mobile-to-mobile tariffs, which stood at 0.08 dinars and 0.12 dinars per minute. If Mobilcom wanted to attract consumers, it had to match this figure. But they could simply not afford to lower their flat tariff without risking bankruptcy. Instead, Mobilcom positioned their tariff at about 0.25 dinars (about US$0.35) for prepaid and 0.10 (about US$0.70) dinars for post-paid.

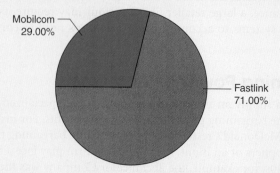

Source: *TeleGeography's GlobalComms,* March 1, 2005.

Mobilcom announced September 15, 2000 as the launch date. Fastlink made good use of this advance notice. Just a week before September 15, Fastlink launched two new schemes aimed at the prepaid and post-paid market, in an attempt to saturate the market just before Mobilcom came on stream. Both players ended 2000 with handsome gains. Fastlink had 250,000 subscribers; Mobilcom had 100,000. In little over 3 months, the two operators had managed to double the size of the market from 180,000 to 350,000. Before the end of 2001, it was clear that the game had been won by Fastlink. By July, Fastlink's subscription base increased to 850,000, while Mobilcom was way behind at 250,000. Fastlink was able to stand the competition, and used its market advantage to retain its grip on the industry.

Source: Ranvir Nayar, "The Fall of the Mideast Giants" www.mafhoum.com.

Economics in YOUR Life!

>> Continued from page 329

At the beginning of this chapter, we asked you to consider why the price of the PlayStation 3 game system is almost the same at every large retailer, from Carrefour to Panda. Why don't these retailers seem to compete on price for this type of product? In this chapter, we have seen that if big retailers were engaged in a one-time game of pricing PlayStations, they would be in a prisoner's dilemma and probably all charge a low price. However, we have also seen that pricing PlayStations is actually a repeated game because the retailers will be selling the game system in competition over a long period of time. In this situation, it is more likely that a cooperative equilibrium will be arrived at in which the retailers will all charge a high price. This is good news for the profits of the retailers but bad news for consumers! This is one of many insights that game theory provides into the business strategies of oligopolists.

Conclusion

Firms are locked in a never-ending struggle to earn economic profits. As noted in the two preceding chapters, competition erodes economic profits. Even in the oligopolies discussed in this chapter, firms have difficulty earning economic profits in the long run. We have seen that firms attempt to avoid the effects of competition in various ways. For example, they can stake out a secure niche in the market, they can engage in implicit collusion with competing firms, or they can attempt to have the government impose barriers to entry. Read *An Inside Look* on the next page for a discussion of the business strategy that the Emke group, the operators of LuLu hypermarket, uses to compete with Carrefour in expanding its market share.

Can LuLu Hypermarket Compete with Carrefour in the Middle East?

GULF NEWS, JUNE 22, 2010

LuLu Continues Oman Expansion

As part of the Lulu Hypermarket group's expansion plans, the seventh hypermarket in Oman's Wadi Kabir has opened, bringing the number of hypermarkets in Oman to seven.

(a) "We have always maintained that Oman is our biggest market outside the UAE and the most promising in our future growth plan. The response we have been getting from our loyal shoppers is tremendous and we intend to continue to give them a world-class shopping experience," said Yousuf Ali MA, managing director of the Lulu Hypermarket group.

This comes in line with the group's plan to open a string of new hypermarkets in the region.

New hypermarkets in Khaborah, Khasab, Salalah, and Nizwa will be operational this year [2010], taking the total store count up to 11 in Oman.

(b) "Oman is not a city-centric market and we intend to take our stores to different wilayats to be as close to the shoppers as possible rather than make them come to major cities to shop. It will be our constant endeavor to bring world-class shopping to the majority of residents of this great country," he said.

Currently the group employs more than 23,000 staff comprising 29 nationalities and has chalked out clear policy guidelines to generate employment opportunities for the Omani youth.

"We employ over 1,500 Omanis in our various operations and we intend to double this figure by the end of 2011. We also regularly send Omani staff to our stores in other countries for both training as well as for regular employment; this gives them a better exposure and enhanced knowledge about the international market," he said.

Despite challenges in the retail sector due to the economic climate, the group has enjoyed steady sales.

"We've experienced good sales in the country and as a hypermarket that doesn't fall into the luxury category, we don't see any slowdown in sales. For the last six years we have been continuously voted the number one hypermarket in the country," said Nanda Kumar, corporate communications manager of the Emke Group, which owns Lulu Hypermarket.

(c) The group, which currently operates 78 stores in the GCC and Yemen, holds more than 32 percent of the market in the organized grocery retail sector.

"We're also looking to expand the number of stores in the UAE, Bahrain, Qatar, Kuwait, and Saudi Arabia. We currently have 78 stores and plan to hit the 100 mark by 2012," said Kumar.

Outside the GCC region, the group has opened a store in Yemen and plans to open its first store in Cairo this year.

The group saw 18 percent growth last year with a Dh4.3 billion revenue. Over the next few years, it is looking for 15 to 20 percent growth year on year.

Source: Aya Lowe, "LuLu Continues Oman Expansion," *Gulf News*, June 22, 2010.

Key Points in the Article

This article illustrates the Emke Group's plan to match Carrefour's expansion in the Middle East and North Africa region. As we have seen in this chapter, when a market is an oligopoly, there are only a few firms. So, each firm must take into account the actions of its competitors. When a competitor opens new stores in a particular area, the other firms in the industry must decide how to react. In this case, the Emke group determined that its profits would be higher by expanding its dominance in the region by opening new LuLu stores in the region.

Analyzing the News

(a) In an oligopoly market, a firm responds to its rivals decisions. From LuLu's action, we can assume that it believes its profits will be higher when it expands to increase its share of the market, given that Carrefour is expanding as well. LuLu is increasing its stores across Oman to confirm its lead in that market, where it is most known and has 11 stores in different regions.

(b) Hypermarkets compete for larger segment of the retailing market, and hence concern themselves mostly with attracting new customers. Some areas are saturated when the consumer has many choices nearby to go to. Therefore, companies such as Emke believe that expanding the business in newly-growing areas is rewarding, since it will give LuLu hypermarket a first-mover-advantage, attracting the growing population of the area. This strategy is effective when the area has a good growth potential.

(c) Emke opened 78 Lulu hypermarkets in the Gulf Cooperation Council (GCC) area alone, which is almost double the number of stores Carrefour has in the region. The expansion strategy yielded a growth of 18 percent in 2010 (as opposed to only 8 percent for Carrefour), and it expects to maintain this growth in the coming few years.

Thinking Critically

1. Do you think LuLu's strategy to compete through opening more stores is enough to gain a larger market share, without having to compete on lowering prices?
2. What would happen if Carrefour decides to open new hypermarkets in the same areas where LuLu is expanding?

LuLu hypermarket is opening new stores across the Arab world to increase its dominance in the region and increase profits.

Key Terms

Summary

10.1 LEARNING OBJECTIVE

Show how barriers to entry explain the existence of oligopolies, **pages 330–332.**

Oligopoly and Barriers to Entry

An **oligopoly** is a market structure in which a small number of interdependent firms compete. **Barriers to entry** keep new firms from entering an industry. The three most important barriers to entry are economies of scale, ownership of a key input or raw material, and government barriers. Economies of scale are the most important barrier to entry. **Economies of scale** exist when a firm's long-run average costs fall as it increases output. Government barriers include patents, licensing, and barriers to international trade. A **patent** is the exclusive right to a product for a period of 20 years from the date the product is invented.

10.2 LEARNING OBJECTIVE

Use game theory to analyze the strategies of oligopolistic firms, **pages 332–341.**

Using Game Theory to Analyze Oligopoly

Because an oligopoly has only a few firms, interactions among those firms are particularly important. **Game theory** is the study of how people make decisions in situations in which attaining their goals depends on their interactions with others; in economics, it is the study of the decisions of firms in industries where the profits of each firm depend on its interactions with other firms. A **business strategy** refers to actions taken by a firm to achieve a goal, such as maximizing profits. Oligopoly games can be illustrated with a **payoff matrix**, which is a table that shows the payoffs that each firm earns from every combination of strategies by the firms. One possible outcome in oligopoly is **collusion**, which is an agreement among firms to charge the same price or otherwise not to compete. A **cartel** is a group of firms that collude by agreeing to restrict output to increase prices and profits. In a **cooperative equilibrium**, firms cooperate to increase their mutual payoff. In a **noncooperative equilibrium**, firms do not cooperate but pursue their own self-interest. A **dominant strategy** is a strategy that is the best for a firm, no matter what strategies other firms use. A **Nash equilibrium** is a situation in which each firm chooses the best strategy, given the strategies chosen by other firms. A situation in which pursuing dominant strategies results in noncooperation that leaves everyone worse off is called a **prisoners' dilemma**. Because many business situations are repeated games, firms may end up implicitly colluding to keep prices high. With **price leadership**, one firm takes the lead in announcing a price change, which is then matched by the other firms in the industry.

10.3 LEARNING OBJECTIVE

Use sequential games to analyze business strategies, **pages 341–344.**

Sequential Games and Business Strategy

Recent work in game theory has focused on actions firms can take to deter the entry of new firms into an industry. Deterring entry can be analyzed using a sequential game, where first one firm makes a decision and then another firm reacts to that decision. Sequential games can be illustrated using decision trees.

The Five Competitive Forces Model

Michael Porter of Harvard Business School argues that the state of competition in an industry is determined by five competitive forces: the degree of competition among existing firms, the threat from new entrants, competition from substitute goods or services, the bargaining power of buyers, and the bargaining power of suppliers.

10.4 LEARNING OBJECTIVE

Use the five competitive forces model to analyze competition in an industry, **pages 344–347.**

Review, Problems and Applications

 Visit www.pearsoned.co.uk/awe/hubbard to complete these exercises online and get instant feedback.
Get Ahead of the Curve

10.1 LEARNING OBJECTIVE   Show how barriers to entry explain the existence of oligopolies, **pages 330–332.**

Review Questions

1.1 What is an oligopoly? Give three examples of oligopolistic industries in the Arab world.

1.2 What do barriers to entry have to do with the extent of competition, or lack thereof, in an industry? What are the most important barriers to entry?

1.3 Give an example of a government-imposed barrier to entry. Why would the government be willing to erect barriers to entering an industry?

Problems and Applications

1.4 Michael Porter has argued, "The intensity of competition in an industry is neither a matter of coincidence nor bad luck. Rather, competition in an industry is rooted in its underlying economic structure." What does Porter mean by "economic structure"? What factors, other than economic structure, might be expected to determine the intensity of competition in an industry?
Source: Michael Porter, *Competitive Strategy: Techniques for Analyzing Industries and Competitors*, New York: The Free Press, 1980, p. 3.

1.5 Some entrepreneurs may try to create big businesses out of naturally small-scale operations. But that will not likely work. What advantage would entrepreneurs expect to gain from creating "big businesses"? Why would entrepreneurs fail to create big businesses with small-scale operations? Illustrate your answer with a graph showing long-run average costs.

1.6 The graph in the next column illustrates the average total cost curves for two automobile manufacturing firms: Little Auto and Big Auto. Under which of the following conditions would you expect to see the market composed of firms like Little Auto, and under

which conditions would you expect to see the market dominated by firms like Big Auto?

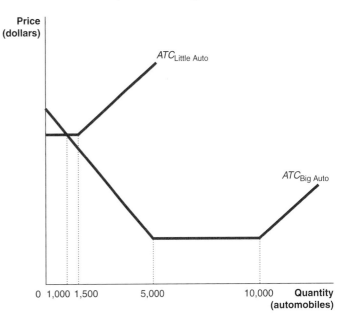

a. When the market demand curve intersects the quantity axis at less than 1,000 units

b. When the market demand curve intersects the quantity axis at more than 1,000 units but less than 10,000 units

c. When the market demand curve intersects the quantity axis at more than 10,000 units

1.7 The following graph contains two long-run average cost curves. Briefly explain which cost curve would most likely be associated with an oligopoly and which would most likely be associated with a perfectly competitive industry.

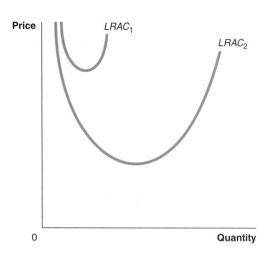

1.8 A historical account of the development of the cotton textile industry in England argues the following:

> The cotton textile industry was shaped by ruthless competition. Rapid growth in demand, low barriers to entry, frequent technological innovations, and a high rate of firm bankruptcy all combined to form an environment in which…oligopolistic competition became almost impossible.

Explain how each of the factors described here would contribute to making the cotton textile industry competitive rather than oligopolistic.

Source: Thomas K. McCraw, ed., *Creating Modern Capitalism*, Cambridge, MA: Harvard University Press, pp. 61–62.

10.2 LEARNING OBJECTIVE   Use game theory to analyze the strategies of oligopolistic firms, **pages 332–341.**

Review Questions

2.1 Give brief definitions of the following concepts.
  a. Game theory
  b. Cooperative equilibrium
  c. Noncooperative equilibrium
  d. Dominant strategy
  e. Nash equilibrium

2.2 Why do economists refer to the methodology for analyzing oligopolies as game theory?

2.3 Why do economists refer to the pricing strategies of oligopoly firms as a prisoners' dilemma game?

2.4 What is the difference between explicit collusion and implicit collusion? Give an example of each.

2.5 How is the prisoners' dilemma result changed in a repeated game?

Problems and Applications

2.6 Bob and Tom are two criminals who have been arrested for burglary. The police put Tom and Bob in separate cells. They offer to let Bob go free if he confesses to the crime and testifies against Tom. Bob also is told that he will serve a 15-year sentence if he remains silent while Tom confesses. If he confesses and Tom also confesses, they will each serve a 10-year sentence. Separately, the police make the same offer to Tom. Assume that if Bob and Tom both remain silent, the police have only enough evidence to convict them of a lesser crime, and they will both serve 3-year sentences.
  a. Use the information provided to write a payoff matrix for Bob and Tom.
  b. Does Bob have a dominant strategy? If so, what is it?
  c. Does Tom have a dominant strategy? If so, what is it?
  d. What sentences do Bob and Tom serve? How might they have avoided this outcome?

2.7 Explain how collusion makes firms better off. Given the incentives to collude, briefly explain why every industry doesn't become a cartel.

2.8 Baseball players who hit the most home runs *relative to other players* usually receive the highest pay. Beginning in the mid-1990s, the typical baseball player became significantly stronger and more muscular. As one baseball announcer put it, "The players of 20 years ago look like stick figures compared with the players of today." As a result, the average number of home runs hit each year increased dramatically. Some of the increased strength that baseball players gained came from more weight training and better conditioning and diet. As some players admitted, though, some of the increased strength came from taking steroids and other illegal drugs. Taking steroids can significantly increase the risk of developing cancer and other medical problems.
  a. In these circumstances, are baseball players in a prisoners' dilemma? Carefully explain.
  b. Suppose that Major League Baseball begins testing players for steroids and firing players who are caught using them (or other illegal muscle-building drugs). Will this testing make baseball players as a group better off or worse off? Briefly explain.

2.9 (Related to *Solved Problem 10-2* on page 335) Would a ban on advertising cigarettes on television be likely to increase or decrease the profits of cigarette companies? Briefly explain.

2.10 (Related to *Solved Problem 10-2* on page 335 and the *Chapter Opener* on page 328) Suppose that Carrefour and LuLu are independently deciding whether to stick with bar codes or switch to RFID tags to monitor the flow of products. Because many suppliers sell to both retailers, it is much less costly for suppliers to use one system or the other rather than to use both. The following payoff matrix shows the profits per year for each company resulting from the interaction of their strategies.

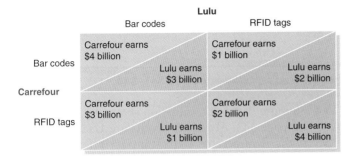

a. Briefly explain whether Carrefour has a dominant strategy.

b. Briefly explain whether LuLu has a dominant strategy.

c. Briefly explain whether there is a Nash equilibrium in this game.

2.11 A student argues, "The prisoners' dilemma game is unrealistic. Each player's strategy is based on the assumption that the other player won't cooperate. But if each player assumes that the other player *will* cooperate, the 'dilemma' disappears." Briefly explain whether you agree with this argument.

2.12 **(Related to the *Making the Connection* on page 336)** We made the argument that a bidder on a Souq.com auction has a dominant strategy of bidding only once, with that bid being the maximum the bidder would be willing to pay.

a. Is it possible that a bidder might receive useful information during the auction, particularly from the dollar amounts other bidders are bidding? If so, how does that change a bidder's optimal strategy?

b. Many people recommend the practice of 'sniping,' or placing your bid at the last second before the auction ends. Is there connection between sniping and your answer to part (a)?

2.13 Consider two oligopolistic industries. In the first industry, firms always match price changes by any other firm in the industry. In the second industry, firms always ignore price changes by any other firm. In which industry are firms likely to charge higher prices? Briefly explain.

2.14 Airlines often find themselves in price wars. Consider the following game: Etihad and Emirates airlines are the only two airlines flying the route from the UAE to the Philippines. Each firm has two strategies: charge a high price or charge a low price. The payoff matrix in the next column shows the profits for each airline resulting from the interaction of their strategies.

a. What (if any) is the dominant strategy for each firm?

b. Is this game a prisoner's dilemma?

c. How could repeated playing of the game change the strategy each firm uses?

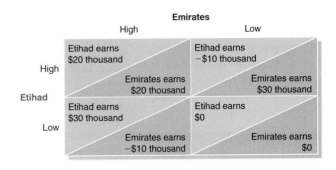

2.15 Suppose major airlines tried to raise fares per round-trip ticket between the UAE and Alexandria, Egypt, by US$20. The plan falls apart as one of the carriers, Egypt Air, refuses to go along. Shortly afterward, Egypt Air triggers a major round of discounting when it launches a sale on fares for late-summer travel. Most airlines then cut fares on nearly all routes. Briefly explain why airlines might be more likely to match price cuts than price increases.

2.16 Finding dominant strategies is often a very effective way of analyzing a game. Consider the following game: Microsoft and Apple are the two firms in the market for operating systems. Each firm has two strategies: charge a high price or charge a low price.

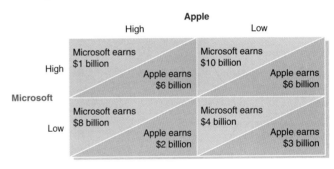

a. What (if any) is the dominant strategy for each firm?

b. Is there a Nash equilibrium? Briefly explain.

2.17 One day in October 2006, oil prices dropped 93 cents per barrel, to their lowest level in almost one year. The drop came as the Organization of Petroleum Exporting Countries said it was going to cut global production by one million barrels a day to boost prices, Nigerian oil minister and OPEC president Edmund Daukoru wondered: "Why would oil prices drop at the same time that OPEC was announcing a cut in production. Shouldn't lower production lead to higher prices?"

Source: Worth Civils, "Stocks Decline Amid Fed Minutes, Alcoa Earnings, Lower Oil Prices," *Wall Street Journal*, October 11, 2006.

2.18 In 2007, some countries that export natural gas discussed forming a cartel, modeled on the OPEC oil cartel. The head of Libya's energy sector was quoted as saying: "We are trying to strengthen the

cooperation among gas producers to avoid harmful competition."
a. What is a cartel?
b. What is "harmful competition"? Is competition typically harmful to consumers?

c. What factors would help the cartel succeed? What factors would reduce the cartel's chances for success?

Source: Ayesha Daya and James Herron, "Gas Exporters to Study Cartel," *Wall Street Journal*, April 10, 2007, p. A6.

10.3 LEARNING OBJECTIVE   Use sequential games to analyze business strategies, **pages 341–344.**

Review Questions

3.1 What is a sequential game?
3.2 How are decision trees used to analyze sequential games?

Problems and Applications

3.3 **(Related to *Solved Problem 10-3* on page 342)** A small town currently has no fast-food restaurants. McDonald's and Burger King are both considering entering this market. Burger King will wait until McDonald's has made its decision before deciding whether to enter. Use the following decision tree to decide the optimal strategy for each company. Does your answer depend on the rate of return that owners of fast-food restaurants must earn on their investments in order to break even? Briefly explain.

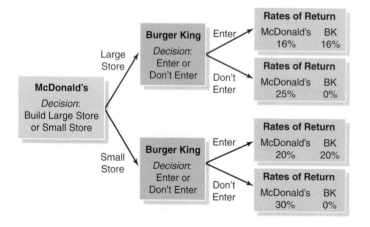

3.4 Suppose that in the situation shown in Figure 10-7 on page 343, Al-Huda's profits are US$1.5 million if the firm accepts Dell's contract offer of US$20 per copy. Now will Dell offer Al-Huda a contract of US$20 per copy or a contract of US$30 per copy? Briefly explain.

3.5 Refer to Figure 10-5 on page 340. Consider the entries in the row of the payoff matrix that correspond to Saudi Arabia choosing "low output." Suppose the numbers change so that Nigeria's profit is US$15 million when Nigeria chooses "low output" and US$10 million when it chooses "high output."

a. Create the payoff matrix for this new situation, assuming that Saudi Arabia and Nigeria choose their output levels simultaneously. Is there a Nash equilibrium to this game? If so, what is it?

b. Now draw the decision tree for this situation, (using the values from the payoff matrix you created in part a), assuming that Saudi Arabia and Nigeria make their decisions sequentially: first Saudi Arabia chooses its output level, and then Nigeria responds by choosing its output level. Is there a Nash equilibrium to this game? If so, what is it?

c. Compare your answers to parts a and b. Briefly explain the reason for any differences in the outcomes of these two games.

10.4 LEARNING OBJECTIVE   Use the five competitive forces model to analyze competition in an industry,

pages 344–347.

Review Questions

4.1 List the competitive forces in the five competitive forces model.
4.2 Does the strength of each of the five competitive forces remain constant over time? Briefly explain.

Problems and Applications

4.3 According to an article in the *Wall Street Journal*:

> The big car makers are pushing a wide array of new technology into production,

responding to relentless competitive pressure, rising energy prices and consumer demand for better safety. Once, side-curtain airbags were rare. Now they're becoming standard equipment on a growing number of vehicles. Car makers are racing to deploy fuel-saving technologies such as cylinder shutdown (variously known as "active fuel management" or "multi-displacement system"), six-speed transmissions and, of course, various kinds of gas-electric hybrid drives.

a. What does the article mean by "relentless competitive pressure"? Which of the five competitive forces is being referred to?

b. In the long run, will the car maker who first successfully incorporates these new technologies in its cars earn economic profits? Which group is likely to benefit the most from these innovations: the car companies or consumers?

Source: Joseph B. White, "Ford, GM Eye Shift in Buying Habits," *Wall Street Journal*, May 22, 2006.

4.4 In early 2004, Yahoo was set to challenge Google as the leading online search engine. Yahoo's strategy was not simply to match what Google does now but to add features its rival can't easily match. A senior vice president at Yahoo stated, "We're not going to beat the competition by being the competition." Briefly explain what the Yahoo executive means by "being the competition." Briefly discuss whether the strategy of "being the competition" ever makes sense.

Source: Mylene Mangalindan, "Yahoo Gets Set to Give Google a Run for Its Money," *Wall Street Journal*, January 6, 2004.

4.5 The following is from an article in the *Wall Street Journal*:

As US car makers continue to offer generous cash discounts and cut-rate financing to woo buyers, top Japanese manufacturers are taking a different pricing approach that seems to be working: Hold sticker prices steady but pack cars with alluring new features.

What happens to the profit a car company makes on each car sold if it cuts the price while holding the car's features constant? What happens to the company's profit per car if the company adds new features while holding the price constant? Briefly discuss how a car company might decide which of these strategies to use.

Source: Todd Zaun, "Japanese Battle US Discounts with Extras," *Wall Street Journal*, January 6, 2004.

Chapter 11

Monopoly and Antitrust Policy

Fixed-line Telecom Services: A Long-time Monopoly in the Middle East

Whenever you think of your home phone, how many telephone companies can you name serving your town? Unlike mobile carriers, you are likely to find only one fixed-line provider in your town, city, or even entire country. This is called a *monopoly*. It is a situation when only one firm supplies a good or a service to a particular market.

By the end of 2009, the total fixed-line subscribers of 20 operators in 15 Arab countries amounted to more than 27,824 million. Several fixed-lines markets are showing decline due to mobile substitution, particularly dramatically in Jordan with its very competitive mobile market. The fixed-line telecom sector has been the last to be opened to competition. All across the Arab world the first operator, the so called *incumbent*, remains the major or sole player in the fixed-line voice market. But change is underway. In many countries operators who began in the mobile sector are also moving into the fixed-line sector.

Having a quick look around the Arab world, we can draw a very similar picture. In Egypt, for example, Telecom Egypt started in 1854 with the first telegraph line. In 1998, it replaced the former National Telecommunication Organization. Now, the company has a fixed-line subscriber base of more than 12 million subscribers, which makes it the largest fixed-line provider in the Middle East and Africa. Despite the government's announcement to auction the license for a second fixed-line provider, in 2010, the highly profitable incumbent (Telecom Egypt) is still the sole provider of fixed-line.

Saudi Arabia, the largest telecommunications market in the Arabian Gulf, is one of the fastest growing in the Middle East. Until 2008, Saudi had its fixed lines solely provided by Saudi Telecom Co. The Saudi Arabian incumbent is the largest telecom company in the Middle East when measured by either revenue or by market capitalization.

The picture is not different in Jordan, despite a dynamic telecom sector. During 2005, Jordan's Telecommunication Regulatory Committee established the fixed telecommunications sub-sector liberalization program. Its ultimate goal was to end the fixed-service monopoly of Jordan Telecom as the sole fixed-line operator in Jordan. In spite of these efforts, Jordan Telecom Group remained a monopoly. The group lately rebranded its fixed-line services under the Orange trademark, the commercial brand of one of the world's leading telecommunication service operators, France Telecom Group (FTG). In Lebanon, fixed-line operator Ogero Telecom is a state monopoly. Efforts for privatization and liberalization have long been obstructed before implementation, leaving the monopoly fixed-line in government ownership.

Kuwait, on the other hand, does not have an independent telecom regulatory authority; the Ministry of Communications is both the regulatory entity and also the operating entity for fixed-line services. Plans were drafted for the establishment of a telecommunications regulatory authority in 2007, but have yet to come into existence.

In Bahrain, Bahrain Telecom Co. (Batelco) has been operating as the only provider for fixed lines and broadband connections up until 2008. In Oman, until 2009, the government had long been reluctant to end the state's monopoly over providing fixed-line telecom services via Omantel. Similarly, despite calls for liberalization, Qatar Telecom (Qtel) still has a monopoly over fixed lines and international telecommunication in Qatar. The company also was the sole mobile services provider in Qatar until early 2008. In the United Arab Emirates, Etisalat has maintained its monopoly over fixed lines, TV, and broadband services.

Few firms in the Arab world are monopolies, because in a market system, whenever a firm earns economic profits, other firms will enter its market. Therefore, it is very difficult for a firm to remain the only provider of a good or service. In this chapter, we will develop an economic model of monopoly that can help us analyze how such firms affect the economy. **AN INSIDE LOOK AT POLICY** on **page 380** explores how the government's non-independent communication regulatory authority is affecting market competition in Kuwait.

Economics in YOUR Life!

Why Can't I Watch Popular Movie Channels on Basic Cable TV Packages?

Are you a fan of movies? Would you like to watch more recent popular movies on television? Many do. There are many channels showing popular and classic movies on Orbit, Showtime, and ART Cable Networks. But, unfortunately for many movie fans, these movie channels will not be available to most households with regular basic cable television packages. Why do we expect that the largest cable TV systems will be unwilling to include the popular movie channels in their channel lineups? Why would some systems require customers who want these channels to upgrade to more expensive channel packages or digital services? As you read this chapter, see if you can answer these questions. You can check your answers against those we provide at the end of the chapter. **> Continued on page 378**

A
lthough few firms are monopolies, the economic model of monopoly can still be quite useful. As we saw in earlier chapters , even though perfectly competitive markets are rare, this market model provides a benchmark for how a firm acts in the most competitive situation possible: when it is in an industry with many firms that all supply the same product. Monopoly provides a benchmark for the other extreme, where a firm is the only one in its market and, therefore, faces no competition from other firms supplying its product. The monopoly model is also useful in analyzing situations in which firms agree to *collude*, or not compete, and act together as if they were a monopoly. As we will discuss in this chapter, collusion is illegal in the majority of countries, but it occasionally happens.

Monopolies also pose a dilemma for the government. Should the government allow monopolies to exist? Are there circumstances in which the government should actually promote the existence of monopolies? Should the government regulate the prices monopolies charge? If so, will such price regulation increase economic efficiency? In this chapter, we will explore these public policy issues.

11.1 LEARNING OBJECTIVE

11.1 | Define monopoly.

Is Any Firm Ever Really a Monopoly?

Monopoly A firm that is the only seller of a good or service that does not have a close substitute.

A **monopoly** is a firm that is the only seller of a good or service that does not have a close substitute. Because substitutes of some kind exist for just about every product, can any firm really be a monopoly? The answer is "yes," provided that the substitutes are not 'close' substitutes. But how do we decide whether a substitute is a close substitute? A narrow definition of monopoly that some economists use is that a firm has a monopoly if it can ignore the actions of all other firms. In other words, other firms must not be producing close substitutes if the monopolist can ignore the other firms' prices. For example, candles are a substitute for electric lights, but your local electric company can ignore candle prices because however low the price of candles falls, almost no customers will give up using electric lights and switch to candles. Therefore, your local electric company is clearly a monopoly.

Many economists, however, use a broader definition of monopoly. For example, suppose Ali owns the only pizza shop in a small town. (We will consider later the question of *why* a market may have only a single firm.) Does Ali have a monopoly? Substitutes for pizzas certainly exist. If the price of pizza is too high, people will switch to hamburgers or fried chicken or some other food instead. People do not have to eat at Ali's or starve. Ali is in competition with the local McDonald's and Kentucky Fried Chicken, among other firms. So, Ali does not meet the narrow definition of a monopoly. But many economists would still argue that it is useful to think of Ali as having a monopoly.

Although hamburgers and fried chicken are substitutes for pizza, competition from firms selling them is not enough to keep Ali from earning economic profits. We saw when we studied competition that when firms earn economic profits, we can expect new firms to enter the industry, and in the long run, the economic profits are competed away. Ali's profits will not be competed away as long as he is the *only* seller of pizza. Using the broader definition, Ali has a monopoly because there are no other firms selling a substitute close enough that his economic profits are competed away in the long run.

Making the Connection | Is Xbox 360 a Close Substitute for PlayStation 3?

In the early 2000s, Microsoft's Xbox and Sony's PlayStation 2 (PS2) were the best-selling video game consoles. When the two companies began work on the next generation of consoles, they had important decisions to make. In developing the Xbox, Microsoft had decided to include a hard disk and a version of the Windows computer operating system. As a result, the cost of producing the Xbox was much higher than the cost to Sony of producing the PS2. Microsoft was not concerned by the higher production cost because it believed it would be able to charge a higher price for Xbox than Sony charged for PS2. Unfortunately for Microsoft, consumers considered the Sony PS2 a close substitute for the Xbox. Microsoft was forced to charge the same price for the Xbox that Sony charged for the PS2. So, while Sony was able to make a substantial profit at that price, Microsoft initially lost money on the Xbox because of its higher costs.

In developing the next generation of video game consoles, both companies hoped to produce devices that could serve as multipurpose home-entertainment systems. To achieve this goal, the new systems needed to play DVDs as well as games. Sony developed a new type of DVD called Blu-ray. Blu-ray DVDs can store five times as much data as conventional DVDs and can play back high-definition (HD) video. Sony's decision to give the new PlayStation 3 (PS3) the capability to play Blu-ray DVDs was risky in two ways: first, it raised the cost of producing the consoles; second, because there is a competing second-generation standard for DVDs, called HD-DVD, the PS3 would not be capable of playing all available second-generation DVDs, thereby reducing its appeal to some consumers. Microsoft decided to sell its Xbox 360 with only the capability of playing older-format DVDs, while making available an add-on component that would play HD-DVDs.

To many gamers, PlayStation 3 is a close substitute for Xbox.

Early indications were that Microsoft may have made the better decision. Consumers seemed to consider the PS3 and the Xbox to be close substitutes. In that case, the fact that the PS3's price was US$200 higher than the Xbox 360's price was a significant problem for Sony. Ironically, Sony made the same mistake Microsoft made several years before when it launched the Xbox to compete with PS2.

Sources: Stephen H. Wildstrom, "PlayStation 3: It's Got Game," *Business Week*, December 4, 2006; and "Sony: Playing a Long Game," *The Economist*, November 16, 2006.

YOUR TURN: Test your understanding by doing related problem 1.6 on page 383 at the end of this chapter.

11.2 | Explain the four main reasons monopolies arise.

11.2 LEARNING OBJECTIVE

Where Do Monopolies Come From?

Because monopolies do not face competition, every firm would like to have a monopoly. But to have a monopoly, barriers to entering the market must be so high that no other firms can enter. *Barriers to entry* may be high enough to keep out competing firms for four main reasons:

1 Government blocks the entry of more than one firm into a market.

2 One firm has control of a key resource necessary to produce a good.

3 There are important *network externalities* in supplying the good or service.

4 Economies of scale are so large that one firm has a *natural monopoly*.

Entry Blocked by Government Action

As we will discuss later in this chapter, governments ordinarily try to promote competition in markets, but sometimes governments take action to block entry into a market. In the United States, government blocks entry in two main ways:

1 By granting a *patent* or *copyright* to an individual or firm, giving it the exclusive right to produce a product.

2 By granting a firm a *public franchise*, making it the exclusive legal provider of a good or service.

Patents and Copyrights Some Arab countries, such as Egypt, Saudi Arabia, and the UAE, give patents to firms that develop new products or new ways of making existing products. A **patent** gives a firm the exclusive right to a new product for a specific period of time, usually 20 years, from the date the product is invented. Because Microsoft has a patent on the Windows operating system, other firms cannot sell their own versions of Windows. The government grants patents to encourage firms to spend money on the research and development necessary to create new products. If other firms could have freely copied Windows, Microsoft is unlikely to have spent the money necessary to develop it. Sometimes firms are able to maintain a monopoly in the production of a good without patent protection, provided that they can keep secret how the product is made.

Patent protection is of vital importance to pharmaceutical firms as they develop new prescription drugs. Pharmaceutical firms start research and development work on a new prescription drug an average of 12 years before the drug is available for sale. A firm usually applies for a patent about 10 years before it begins to sell the product. The average 10-year delay between the government's granting a patent and the firm's actually selling the drug is due to the need to demonstrate that the drug is both safe and effective. Therefore, during the period before the drug can be sold, the firm will have substantial costs to develop and test the drug. If the drug does not make it successfully to market, the firm will have a substantial loss.

Once a drug is available for sale, the profits the firm earns from the drug will increase throughout the period of patent protection—which is usually about 10 years—as the drug becomes more widely known to doctors and patients. After the patent has expired, other firms are free to legally produce chemically identical drugs called *generic drugs*. Gradually, competition from generic drugs will eliminate the profits the original firm had been earning. For example, when patent protection expired for Glucophage, a diabetes drug manufactured by the U.S. pharmaceutical company Bristol-Myers Squibb, sales of the drug declined by more than US$1.5 billion in the first year. This was due to competition from 12 generic versions of the drug produced by other firms. Most economic profits from selling a prescription drug are eliminated 20 years after the drug is first offered for sale.

Patent The exclusive right to a product for a period of 20 years from the date the product is invented.

Making the Connection | The End of the Arab World's Mobile Telecom Monopolies

As we have seen in this chapter, monopolies last as long as barriers to entry exist. When barriers to entry are abolished, the market eventually moves closer to competition. As you read in the chapter opener, fixed lines are still a monopoly in most Arab countries, in many cases as a result of governments' blocking entry. The mobile sector, however, is a different story.

The last mobile monopoly in the Arab world ended when the British Vodafone started operating as a second mobile telecom provider in Qatar in 2009, ending a 20-year-long monopoly by Qtel. Towards the end of the 1990s, most Arab countries formed independent telecommunication regulatory authorities to overlook the telecom market structure and ensure a greater degree of competition in the telecom industry.

In Egypt, Click GSM (later to became Vodafone Egypt) was founded in 1998, as the second mobile phone operator in Egypt, competing with the then recently privatized operator Mobinil, which was formerly owned by the Egyptian National Telecommunication Authority (now Telecom Egypt). Etisalat Egypt, a subsidiary of Etisalat UAE, is the first 3.5G network operator in Egypt. Etisalat was granted the rights to develop Egypt's third mobile network, competing with existing service providers Vodafone and Mobinil.

Saudi became the most competitive mobile market with the arrival of a third mobile operator, Zain Saudi Arabia, which made its debut in August 2008. Mobile phones have significantly altered Saudi's telecommunications market. The explosion in services began in 1994 through the national telecoms provider, Saudi Telecommunications Company (STC), which monopolized the market until a second telecommunications company, Etihad-Etisalat (Mobily) launched its operations in 2006.

Jordan has one of the most dynamic and competitive mobile services sector in the Middle East. Reform in telecommunications and in information and communication technologies (ICT) in Jordan has been aggressively undertaken over the past few years. Today four operators share the market: Jordan Mobile Telephones Services—Zain; Mobile Petra Jordanian Telecommunications Company; MobileCom eXpress; and Mobile Umniah Company, which inaugurated its GSM network in June 2005.

The Arab consumer may now have more than one mobile carrier to combine the best offers of each.

Source: Tom Gara, "Vodaphone Qatar Entry to Break Monopoly," July 10, 2008, *The National*, UAE; BuddeCom telecommunications research and consultancy company, "Saudi Arabia – Telecoms, Mobile and Broadband," Report 2009, www.budde.com.

Just as the government grants a new product patent protection, books, films, and software receive **copyright** protection. If a product is copyrighted the creator of a book, film, or piece of music is given the exclusive right to use the creation during the creator's lifetime. The creator's heirs retain this exclusive right for a number of years can reach 70 or more years after the creator's death. In effect, copyrights create monopolies for the copyrighted items. Without copyrights, individuals and firms would be less likely to invest in creating new books, films, and software. Despite the fact that every country would have its own copyright laws, copyrights are now mostly protected through international agreements such as the WTO's TRIPS or the Anti-Counterfeiting Trade Agreement (ACTA).

Copyright A government-granted exclusive right to produce and sell a creation.

Public Franchises In some cases, the government grants a firm a **public franchise** that allows it to be the only legal provider of a good or service. For example, governments often designate one local or national company as the sole provider of electricity, natural gas, or water.

Public franchise A designation by the government that a firm is the only legal provider of a good or service.

Occasionally, the government may decide to provide certain services directly to consumers through a *public enterprise*. This is much more common in the Arab world than in the United States. For example, the governments in most Arab countries own the railroad systems. In the Arab world, many city governments provide water and sewage service themselves rather than rely on private firms.

Control of a Key Resource

Another way for a firm to become a monopoly is by controlling a key resource. This happens infrequently because most resources, including raw materials such as oil or iron ore, are widely available from a variety of suppliers. There are, however, a few prominent examples of monopolies based on control of a key resource, such as the Aluminum Company of America (Alcoa) and the International Nickel Company of Canada.

For many years until the 1940s, Alcoa either owned or had long-term contracts to buy nearly all of the available bauxite, the mineral needed to produce aluminum. Without access to bauxite, competing firms had to use recycled aluminum, which limited the amount of aluminum they could produce. Similarly, the International Nickel Company of Canada controlled more than 90 percent of available nickel supplies. Competition in the nickel market increased when the Petsamo nickel fields in northern Russia were developed after World War II.

Making the Connection | Are Diamond Profits Forever? The De Beers Diamond Monopoly

The most famous monopoly based on control of a raw material is the De Beers diamond mining and marketing company of South Africa. Before the 1860s, diamonds were extremely rare. Only a few pounds of diamonds were produced each year, primarily from Brazil and India. Then in 1870, enormous deposits of diamonds were discovered along the Orange River in South Africa. It became possible to produce thousands of pounds of diamonds per year, and the owners of the new mines feared that the price of diamonds would plummet. To avoid financial disaster, the mine owners decided in 1888 to merge and form De Beers Consolidated Mines, Ltd.

De Beers promoted the sentimental value of diamonds as a way to maintain its position in the diamond market.

De Beers became one of the most profitable and longest-lived monopolies in history. The company has carefully controlled the supply of diamonds to keep prices high. As new diamond deposits were discovered in Russia and Zaire, De Beers was able to maintain prices by buying most of the new supplies.

Because diamonds are rarely destroyed, De Beers has always worried about competition from the resale of stones. Heavily promoting diamond engagement and wedding rings with the slogan "A Diamond Is Forever" was a way around this problem. Because engagement and wedding rings have great sentimental value, they are seldom resold, even by the heirs of the original recipients. De Beers advertising has been successful even in some countries, such as Japan, that have had no custom of giving diamond engagement rings. As the populations in De Beers's key markets age, its advertising in recent years has focused on middle-aged men presenting diamond rings to their wives as symbols of financial success and continuing love and on professional women buying "right-hand rings" for themselves.

In the past few years, competition has finally come to the diamond business. By 2000, De Beers directly controlled only about 40 percent of world diamond production. The company became concerned about the amount it was spending to buy diamonds from other sources to keep them off the market. It decided to adopt a strategy of differentiating its diamonds by relying on its name recognition. Each De Beers diamond is now marked with a microscopic brand—a "Forevermark"—to reassure consumers of its high quality. Other firms, such as BHP Billiton, which owns mines in northern Canada, have followed suit by branding their diamonds. Sellers of Canadian diamonds stress that they are "mined under ethical, environmentally friendly conditions," as opposed to "blood diamonds," which are supposedly "mined under armed force in war-torn African countries and exported to finance military campaigns." Whether consumers will pay attention to brands on diamonds remains to be seen, although through 2006, the branding strategy had helped De Beers maintain its 40 percent share of the diamond market.

Sources: Edward Jay Epstein, "Have You Ever Tried to Sell a Diamond?" *Atlantic Monthly*, February 1982; Donna J. Bergenstock, Mary E. Deily, and Larry W. Taylor, "A Cartel's Response to Cheating: An Empirical Investigation of the De Beers Diamond Empire," *Southern Economic Journal*, Vol. 73, No. 1, July 2006, pp. 173–189; Bernard Simon, "Adding Brand Names to Nameless Stones," *New York Times*, June 27, 2002; Blythe Yee, "Ads Remind Women They Have Two Hands," *Wall Street Journal*, August 14, 2003; quote in last paragraph from Joel Baglole, "Political Correctness by the Carat," *Wall Street Journal*, April 17, 2003.

YOUR TURN: Test your understanding by doing related problem 2.8 on page 384 at the end of this chapter.

Network Externalities

There are **network externalities** in the consumption of a product if the usefulness of the product increases with the number of people who use it. If you owned the only cellphone in the world, for example, it would not be very valuable. The more cellphones there are in use, the more valuable they become to consumers.

Network externalities The situation where the usefulness of a product increases with the number of consumers who use it.

Some economists argue that network externalities can serve as barriers to entry. For example, in the early 1980s, Microsoft gained an advantage over other software companies by developing MS-DOS, the operating system for the first IBM personal computers. Because IBM sold more computers than any other company, software developers wrote many application programs for MS-DOS. The more people who used MS-DOS–based programs, the greater the usefulness to a consumer of using an MS-DOS–based program. Today, Windows, the program Microsoft developed to succeed MS-DOS, has a 95 percent share in the market for personal computer operating systems (although Windows has a much lower share in the market for operating systems for servers). If another firm introduced a competing operating system, some economists argue that relatively few people would use it initially, and few applications would run on it, which would limit the operating system's value to other consumers.

eBay was the first Internet site to attract a significant number of people to its online auctions. Once a large number of people began to use eBay to buy and sell collectibles, antiques, and many other products, it became a more valuable place to buy and sell. Yahoo.com, Amazon.com, Souq.com, and other Internet sites eventually started online auctions, but they found it difficult to attract buyers and sellers. On eBay, a buyer expects to find more sellers, and a seller expects to find more potential buyers than on Amazon or other auction sites.

As these examples show, network externalities can set off a *virtuous cycle*: if a firm can attract enough customers initially, it can attract additional customers because its product's value has been increased by more people using it, which attracts even more customers, and so on. With products such as computer operating systems and online auctions, it might be difficult for new firms to enter the market and compete away the profits being earned by the first firm in the market.

Economists engage in considerable debate, however, about the extent to which network externalities are important barriers to entry in the business world. Some economists argue that the dominant positions of Microsoft and eBay reflect the efficiency of those firms in offering products that satisfy consumer preferences more than the effects of network externalities. In this view, the advantages existing firms gain from network externalities would not be enough to protect them from competing firms offering better products. In other words, a firm entering the operating system market with a program better than Windows or a firm offering an Internet auction site better than eBay would be successful despite the effects of network externalities.

Figure 11-1

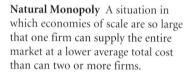

Average Total Cost Curve for a Natural Monopoly

With a natural monopoly, the average total cost curve is still falling when it crosses the demand curve (point *A*). If only one firm is producing electric power in the market and it produces where average cost intersects the demand curve, average total cost will equal US$0.04 per kilowatt-hour of electricity produced. If the market is divided between two firms, each producing 15 billion kilowatt-hours, the average cost of producing electricity rises to US$0.06 per kilowatt-hour (point *B*). In this case, if one firm expands production, it can move down the average total cost curve, lower its price, and drive the other firm out of business.

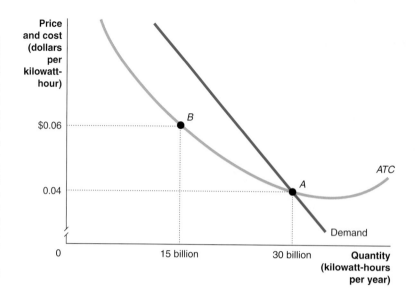

Natural Monopoly A situation in which economies of scale are so large that one firm can supply the entire market at a lower average total cost than can two or more firms.

Natural Monopoly

As we saw earlier, economies of scale exist when a firm's long-run average costs fall as it increases the quantity of output it produces. A **natural monopoly** occurs when economies of scale are so large that one firm can supply the entire market at a lower average total cost than two or more firms. In that case, there is really 'room' in the market for only one firm.

Figure 11-1 shows the average total cost curve for a firm producing electricity and the total demand for electricity in the firm's market. Notice that the average total cost curve is still falling when it crosses the demand curve at point *A*. If the firm is a monopoly and produces 30 billion kilowatt-hours of electricity per year, its average total cost of production will be US$0.04 per kilowatt-hour. Suppose instead that two firms are in the market, each producing half of the market output, or 15 billion kilowatt-hours per year. Assume that each firm has the same average total cost curve. The figure shows that producing 15 billion kilowatt-hours would move each firm back up its average cost curve so that the average cost of producing electricity would rise to US$0.06 per kilowatt-hour (point *B*). In this case, if one of the firms expands production, it will move down the average total cost curve. With lower average costs, it will be able to offer electricity at a lower price than the other firm can. Eventually, the other firm will be driven out of business, and the remaining firm will have a monopoly. Because a monopoly would develop automatically—or *naturally*—in this market, it is a natural monopoly.

Natural monopolies are most likely to occur in markets where fixed costs are very large relative to variable costs. For example, a firm that produces electricity must make a substantial investment in machinery and equipment necessary to generate the electricity and in wires and cables necessary to distribute it. Once the initial investment has been made, however, the marginal cost of producing another kilowatt-hour of electricity is relatively small.

11.3 | Explain how a monopoly chooses price and output.

How Does a Monopoly Choose Price and Output?

Like every other firm, a monopoly maximizes profit by producing where marginal revenue equals marginal cost. A monopoly differs from other firms in that *a monopoly's demand curve is the same as the demand curve for the product*. We saw earlier that the market demand curve for wheat was very different from the demand curve for the wheat produced by any one farmer. If, however, one farmer had a monopoly on wheat production, the two demand curves would be exactly the same.

Marginal Revenue Once Again

Recall that firms in perfectly competitive markets—such as a farmer in the wheat market—face horizontal demand curves. They are *price takers.* All other firms, including monopolies, are *price makers.* If price makers raise their prices, they will lose some, but not all, of their customers. Therefore, they face a downward-sloping demand curve and a downward-sloping marginal revenue curve as well. Let's review why a firm's marginal revenue curve slopes downward if its demand curve slopes downward.

Remember that when a firm cuts the price of a product, one good thing happens, and one bad thing happens:

- **The good thing.** It sells more units of the product.

- **The bad thing.** It receives less revenue from each unit than it would have received at the higher price.

For example, consider the table in Figure 11-2, which shows the demand curve in Abu Dhabi for Etisalat's eVision basic cable TV package. For simplicity, we assume that the market has only 10 potential subscribers. If Etisalat charges a price of US$60 per month, it won't have any subscribers. If it charges a price of US$57, it sells 1 subscription. At US$54, it sells 2, and so on. Etisalat's total revenue is equal to the number of subscriptions sold per month multiplied by the price. The firm's average revenue—or

Subscribers per Month (Q)	Price (P)	Total Revenue (TR = P x Q)	Average Revenue (AR = TR/Q)	Marginal Revenue (MR = ΔTR/ΔQ)
0	$60	$0	–	–
1	57	57	$57	$57
2	54	108	54	51
3	51	153	51	45
4	48	192	48	39
5	45	225	45	33
6	42	252	42	27
7	39	273	39	21
8	36	288	36	15
9	33	297	33	9
10	30	300	30	3

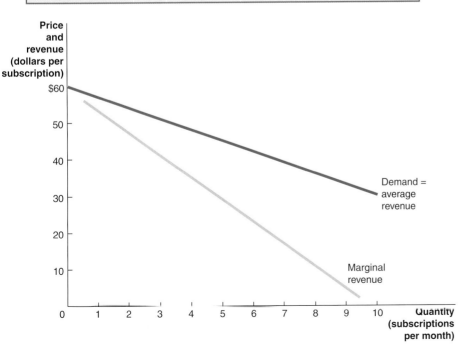

Figure 11-2

Calculating a Monopoly's Revenue

Etisalat faces a downward-sloping demand curve for subscriptions to basic cable. To sell more subscriptions, it must cut the price. When this happens, it gains the revenue from selling more subscriptions but loses revenue from selling at a lower price the subscriptions that it could have sold at a higher price. The firm's marginal revenue is the change in revenue from selling another subscription. We can calculate marginal revenue by subtracting the revenue lost as a result of a price cut from the revenue gained. The table shows that Etisalat's marginal revenue is less than the price for every subscription sold after the first subscription. Therefore, Etisalat's marginal revenue curve will be below its demand curve.

revenue per subscription sold—is equal to its total revenue divided by the quantity of subscriptions sold. Etisalat is particularly interested in marginal revenue because marginal revenue tells the firm how much revenue will increase if it cuts the price to sell one more subscription.

Notice that Etisalat's marginal revenue is less than the price for every subscription sold after the first subscription. To see why, think about what happens if Etisalat cuts the price of its basic cable package from US$42 to US$39, which increases its subscriptions sold from 6 to 7. Etisalat increases its revenue by the US$39 it receives for the seventh subscription. But it also loses revenue of US$3 per subscription on the first 6 subscriptions because it could have sold them at the old price of US$42. So, its marginal revenue on the seventh subscription is US$39 − US$18 = US$21, which is the value shown in the table. The graph in Figure 11-2 plots Etisalat's demand and marginal revenue curves, based on the information given in the table.

Profit Maximization for a Monopolist

Figure 11-3 shows how Etisalat combines the information on demand and marginal revenue with information on average and marginal costs to decide how many subscriptions to sell and what price to charge. We assume that the firm's marginal cost and average total cost curves have the usual U shapes we saw in previous chapters. In panel (a), we see how Etisalat can calculate its profit-maximizing quantity and price. As long as the marginal cost of selling one more subscription is less than the marginal revenue, the firm should sell additional subscriptions because it is adding to its profits. As Etisalat sells more cable subscriptions, rising marginal cost will eventually equal marginal revenue, and the firm will be selling the profit-maximizing quantity of subscriptions. This happens with the sixth subscription, which adds US$27 to the firm's costs and US$27 to its revenues (point A in panel (a) of Figure 11-3). The demand curve tells us that Etisalat can sell 6 subscriptions for a price of US$42 per month. We can conclude that

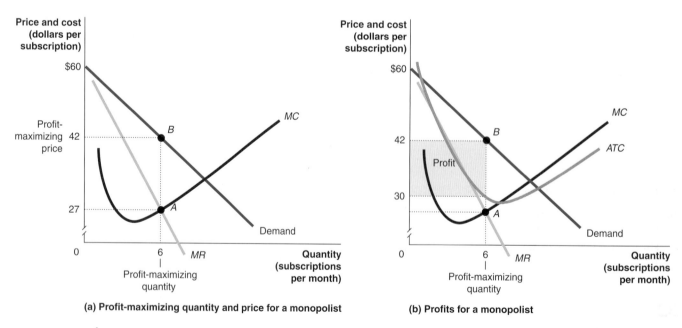

(a) Profit-maximizing quantity and price for a monopolist   (b) Profits for a monopolist

Figure 11-3 | Profit-Maximizing Price and Output for a Monopoly

Panel (a) shows that to maximize profit, Etisalat should sell subscriptions up to the point that the marginal revenue from selling the last subscription equals its marginal cost (point A). In this case, the marginal revenue from selling the sixth subscription and the marginal cost are both US$27. Etisalat maximizes profit by selling 6 subscriptions per

month and charging a price of US$42 (point B). In panel (b), the green box represents Etisalat's profits. The box has a height equal to US$12, which is the price of US$42 minus the average total cost of US$30, and a base equal to the quantity of 6 cable subscriptions. Etisalat's profit equals US$12 × 6 = US$72.

Etisalat's profit-maximizing quantity of subscriptions is 6 and its profit-maximizing price is US$42.

Panel (b) shows that the average total cost of 6 subscriptions is US$30 and that Etisalat can sell 6 subscriptions at a price of US$42 per month (point B on the demand curve). Etisalat is making a profit of US$12 per subscription—the price of US$42 minus the average cost of US$30. Its total profit is US$72 (6 subscriptions × US$12 profit per subscription), which is shown by the area of the green-shaded rectangle in the figure. We could also have calculated Etisalat's total profit as the difference between its total revenue and its total cost. Its total revenue from selling 6 subscriptions is US$252. Its total cost equals its average cost multiplied by the number of subscriptions sold, or US$30 × 6 = US$180. So, its profit is US$252 − US$180 = US$72.

It's important to note that even though Etisalat has been earning economic profits, new firms were *not* entering the market until du received its second operator license. However, because Etisalat is still the sole provider of cable TV, it will not face competition from other cable operators. Therefore, if du had not been able to secure the license, Etisalat would have been able to continue to earn economic profits, even in the long run.

Solved Problem | 11-3

Finding the Profit-Maximizing Price and Output for a Monopolist

Suppose that Etisalat still has a cable monopoly in Al Ain. The following table gives Etisalat's demand and costs per month for subscriptions to basic cable (for simplicity, we once again keep the number of subscribers artificially small).

PRICE IN US$	QUANTITY IN US$	TOTAL REVENUE IN US$	MARGINAL REVENUE $(MR = \Delta TR/\Delta Q)$ IN US$	TOTAL COST IN US$	MARGINAL COST $(MC = \Delta TC/\Delta Q)$ IN US$
17	3			56	
16	4			63	
15	5			71	
14	6			80	
13	7			90	
12	8			101	

a. Fill in the missing values in the table.

b. If Etisalat wants to maximize profits, what price should it charge and how many cable subscriptions per month should it sell? How much profit will Etisalat make? Briefly explain.

c. Suppose the local government imposes a US$2.50 per month tax on cable companies. Now what price should Etisalat charge, how many subscriptions should it sell, and what will its profits be?

SOLVING THE PROBLEM:

Step 1: **Review the chapter material.** This problem is about finding the profit-maximizing quantity and price for a monopolist, so you may want to review the section "Profit Maximization for a Monopolist," which begins on page 366.

Step 2: **Answer question (a) by filling in the missing values in the table.** Remember that to calculate marginal revenue and marginal cost, you must divide the change in total revenue or total cost by the change in quantity.

PRICE IN US$	QUANTITY IN US$	TOTAL REVENUE IN US$	MARGINAL REVENUE ($MR = \Delta TR/\Delta Q$) IN US$	TOTAL COST IN US$	MARGINAL COST ($MC = \Delta TC/\Delta Q$) IN US$
17	3	51	—	56	—
16	4	64	13	63	7
15	5	75	11	71	8
14	6	84	9	80	9
13	7	91	7	90	10
12	8	96	5	101	11

We don't have enough information from the table to fill in the values for marginal revenue or marginal cost in the first row.

Step 3: **Answer question (b) by determining the profit-maximizing quantity and price.** We know that Etisalat will maximize profits by selling subscriptions up to the point where marginal cost equals marginal revenue. In this case, that means selling 6 subscriptions per month. From the information in the first two columns, we know Etisalat can sell 6 subscriptions at a price of US$14 each. Etisalat's profits are equal to the difference between its total revenue and its total cost: Profit = US$84 − US$80 = US$4 per month.

Step 4: **Answer question (c) by analyzing the impact of the tax.** This tax is a fixed cost to Etisalat because it is a flat US$2.50, no matter how many subscriptions it sells. Because the tax has no impact on Etisalat's marginal revenue or marginal cost, the profit-maximizing level of output has not changed. So, Etisalat will still sell 6 subscriptions per month at a price of US$14, but its profits will fall by the amount of the tax from US$4.00 per month to US$1.50.

YOUR TURN: For more practice, do related problems 3.3 and 3.4 on page 384 at the end of this chapter.

>> **End Solved Problem 11-3**

11.4 LEARNING OBJECTIVE   11.4 | Use a graph to illustrate how a monopoly affects economic efficiency.

Does Monopoly Reduce Economic Efficiency?

We saw in Chapter 8 that a perfectly competitive market is economically efficient. How would economic efficiency be affected if instead of being perfectly competitive, a market were a monopoly? In Chapter 4, we developed the idea of *economic surplus*. Economic surplus provides a way of characterizing the economic efficiency of a perfectly competitive market: *Equilibrium in a perfectly competitive market results in the greatest amount of economic surplus, or total benefit to society, from the production of a good or service.* What happens to economic surplus under monopoly? We can begin the analysis by considering the hypothetical case of what would happen if the market for television sets begins as perfectly competitive and then becomes a monopoly. (In reality, the market for television sets is not perfectly competitive, but assuming that it is simplifies our analysis.)

Comparing Monopoly and Perfect Competition

Panel (a) in Figure 11-4 illustrates the situation if the market for televisions is perfectly competitive. Price and quantity are determined by the intersection of the demand and supply curves. Remember that none of the individual firms in a perfectly competitive industry has any control over price. Each firm must accept the price determined by the market. Panel (b) shows what happens if the television industry becomes a monopoly. We know that the monopoly will maximize profits by producing where marginal

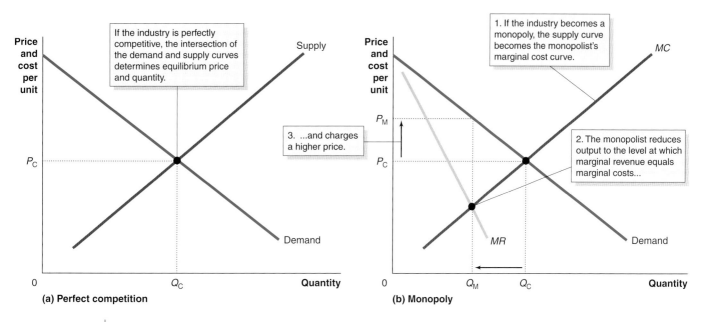

Figure 11-4 | What Happens If a Perfectly Competitive Industry Becomes a Monopoly?

In panel (a), the market for television sets is perfectly competitive, and price and quantity are determined by the intersection of the demand and supply curves. In panel (b), the perfectly competitive television industry became a monopoly. As a result, the equilibrium quantity falls, and the equilibrium price rises.

1. The industry supply curve becomes the monopolist's marginal cost curve.
2. The monopolist reduces output to where marginal revenue equals marginal cost, Q_M.
3. The monopolist raises the price from P_C to P_M.

revenue equals marginal cost. To do this, the monopoly reduces the quantity of televisions that would have been produced if the industry were perfectly competitive and increases the price. Panel (b) illustrates an important conclusion: *A monopoly will produce less and charge a higher price than would a perfectly competitive industry producing the same good.*

Measuring the Efficiency Losses from Monopoly

Figure 11-5 uses panel (b) from Figure 11-4 to illustrate how monopoly affects consumers, producers, and the efficiency of the economy. Recall from Chapter 4 that *consumer surplus* measures the net benefit received by consumers from purchasing a good or service. We measure consumer surplus as the area below the demand curve and above the market price. The higher the price, the smaller the consumer surplus. Because a monopoly raises the market price, it reduces consumer surplus. In Figure 11-5, the loss of consumer surplus is equal to rectangle *A* plus triangle *B*. Remember that *producer surplus* measures the net benefit to producers from selling a good or service. We measure producer surplus as the area above the supply curve and below the market price. The increase in price due to monopoly increases producer surplus by an amount equal to rectangle *A* and reduces it by an amount equal to triangle *C*. Because rectangle *A* is larger than triangle *C*, we know that a monopoly increases producer surplus compared with perfect competition.

Economic surplus is equal to the sum of consumer surplus plus producer surplus. By increasing price and reducing the quantity produced, the monopolist has reduced economic surplus by an amount equal to the areas of triangles *B* and *C*. This reduction in economic surplus is called *deadweight loss* and represents the loss of economic efficiency due to monopoly.

The best way to understand how a monopoly causes a loss of economic efficiency is to recall that price is equal to marginal cost in a perfectly competitive market. As a result, a consumer in a perfectly competitive market is always able to buy a good if she is willing to

Figure 11-5

The Inefficiency of Monopoly

A monopoly charges a higher price, P_M, and produces a smaller quantity, Q_M, than a perfectly competitive industry, which charges a price of P_C and produces at Q_C. The higher price reduces consumer surplus by the area equal to the rectangle A and the triangle B. Some of the reduction in consumer surplus is captured by the monopoly as producer surplus, and some becomes deadweight loss, which is the area equal to triangles B and C.

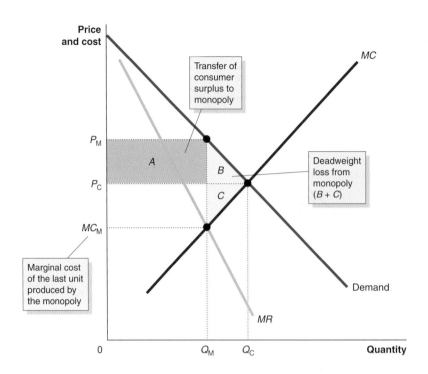

pay a price equal to the marginal cost of producing it. As Figure 11-5 shows, the monopolist stops producing at a point where the price is well above marginal cost. Consumers are unable to buy some units of the good for which they would be willing to pay a price greater than the marginal cost of producing them. Why doesn't the monopolist produce this additional output? Because the monopolist's profits are greater if it restricts output and forces up the price. A monopoly produces the profit-maximizing level of output but fails to produce the efficient level of output from the point of view of society.

We can summarize the effects of monopoly as follows:

1 Monopoly causes a reduction in consumer surplus.

2 Monopoly causes an increase in producer surplus.

3 Monopoly causes a deadweight loss, which represents a reduction in economic efficiency.

How Large Are the Efficiency Losses Due to Monopoly?

Market power The ability of a firm to charge a price greater than marginal cost.

We know that there are relatively few monopolies, so the loss of economic efficiency due to monopoly must be small. Many firms, though, have **market power**, which is the ability of a firm to charge a price greater than marginal cost. The analysis we just completed shows that some loss of economic efficiency will occur whenever a firm has market power and can charge a price greater than marginal cost, even if the firm is not a monopoly. The only firms that do *not* have market power are firms in perfectly competitive markets, who must charge a price equal to marginal cost. Because few markets are perfectly competitive, *some loss of economic efficiency occurs in the market for nearly every good or service.*

Is the total loss of economic efficiency due to market power large or small? It is possible to put a dollar value on the loss of economic efficiency by estimating for every industry the size of the deadweight loss triangle, as in Figure 11-5. The first economist to do this was Arnold Harberger of the University of Chicago, U.S. His estimates—largely confirmed by later researchers—indicated that the total loss of economic efficiency in the U.S. economy due to market power is small. According to his estimates, if every industry in the economy were perfectly competitive, so that price were equal to marginal cost in every market, the gain in economic efficiency would equal less than 1 percent of the value of total production in the United States, or about US$450 per person.

The loss of economic efficiency is this small primarily because true monopolies are very rare. In most industries, competition keeps price much closer to marginal cost than would be the case in a monopoly. The closer price is to marginal cost, the smaller the size of the deadweight loss.

Market Power and Technological Change

Some economists have raised the possibility that the economy may actually benefit from firms having market power. This argument is most closely identified with Joseph Schumpeter, an Austrian economist who spent many years as a professor of economics at Harvard. Schumpeter argued that economic progress depended on technological change in the form of new products. For example, the replacement of horse-drawn carriages by automobiles, the replacement of ice boxes by refrigerators, and the replacement of mechanical calculators by electronic computers all represent technological changes that significantly raised living standards. In Schumpeter's view, new products unleash a "gale of creative destruction" that drives older products—and, often, the firms that produced them—out of the market. Schumpeter was unconcerned that firms with market power would charge higher prices than perfectly competitive firms:

> It is not that kind of [price] competition which counts but the competition from the new commodity, the new technology, the new source of supply, the new type of organization ...competition which commands a decisive cost or quality advantage and which strikes not at the margins of the profits and outputs of the existing firms but at their foundations and their very lives.

Economists who support Schumpeter's view argue that the introduction of new products requires firms to spend funds on research and development. It is possible for firms to raise this money by borrowing from investors or from banks. But investors and banks are usually skeptical of ideas for new products that have not yet passed the test of consumer acceptance in the market. As a result, firms are often forced to rely on their profits to finance the research and development needed for new products. Because firms with market power are more likely to earn economic profits than are perfectly competitive firms, they are also more likely to carry out research and development and introduce new products. In this view, the higher prices firms with market power charge are unimportant compared with the benefits from the new products these firms introduce to the market.

Some economists disagree with Schumpeter's views. These economists point to the number of new products developed by smaller firms, including, for example, Steve Jobs and Steve Wozniak inventing the first Apple computer in Wozniak's garage, and Larry Page and Sergey Brin inventing the Google search engine as graduate students at Stanford. As we will see in the next section, government policymakers continue to struggle with the issue of whether, on balance, large firms with market power are good or bad for the economy.

11.5 | Discuss government policies toward monopoly.

11.5 LEARNING OBJECTIVE

Government Policy toward Monopoly

Because monopolies reduce consumer surplus and economic efficiency, most governments have policies that regulate their behavior. Recall that **collusion** refers to an agreement among firms to charge the same price or otherwise not to compete. In the United States, for example, government policies with respect to monopolies and collusion are embodied in the **antitrust laws**. These laws make illegal any attempts to form a monopoly or to collude. Governments also regulate firms that are natural monopolies, often by controlling the prices they charge.

As emerging markets, many Arab countries have realized the need to transform their economies into a more competitive and business friendly markets, ending years of state dominance and monopolies of major sectors in the economy. That necessitated devising anti-monopoly policies and in some cases taking the further step of passing antitrust laws.

Collusion An agreement among firms to charge the same price or otherwise not to compete.

Antitrust laws Laws aimed at eliminating collusion and promoting competition among firms

In Egypt, for example, the late 1990s witnessed some policies to reduce market barriers, such as reducing tariffs and privatizing long-time state monopolies. Finally, the government fully realized the need to adopt a total approach towards protecting competition and restricting antitrust acts. The following section describes the case of Egypt as an example from the Arab world.

Mergers: The Trade-off between Market Power and Efficiency

The government regulates business mergers because it knows that if firms gain market power by merging, they may use that market power to raise prices and reduce output. As a result, the government is most concerned with **horizontal mergers**, or mergers between firms in the same industry. Horizontal mergers are more likely to increase market power than **vertical mergers**, which are mergers between firms at different stages of the production of a good. An example of a vertical merger would be a merger between a company making personal computers and a company making computer hard drives.

Horizontal merger A merger between firms in the same industry.

Vertical merger A merger between firms at different stages of production of a good.

Making the Connection | An Example of Anti-Monopoly: Competition Law and Its Enforcement in Egypt

Until recently, the public sector in Egypt had default monopolies in most industries. Since the mid-1990s, Egypt, under structural reform programs, embarked on a wide privatization scheme that aimed at reducing government intervention and its leading role in the economy, and giving the lead to the private sector. To that end, creating a more competitive business-friendly environment became a necessity.

Towards the end of the 1990s, the Egyptian economy started witnessing a large number of mergers and acquisitions that could have had negative anti-competitive effects. The number of mergers and acquisitions reached more than 90 cases in different sectors of the economy, which was a cause for concern, given the new shift to a more free market economy.

As an integral part of this new policy shift, and to address these new merging trends, the Anti-Monopoly and Fair Competition Act was enacted in May 2005. Few months later, the Egyptian Competition Authority (ECA) was established to enforce the law.

The new law not only focuses on monopolies in absolute terms, but also prohibits monopolistic practices sometimes used by large companies to manipulate prices and supply in the market. Under the new law any company holding 25 percent or more of market share in a given industry or product line could be investigated for anti-competitive behavior after an initial complaint and appraisal process the ECA has devised. The ECA, as a research agency, also advises the government in matters related to price controls and malpractice.

Since its establishment, the ECA has investigated many cases where price fixing, colluding, and market power was suspected. In a case against cement producers, involving price fixing and limiting production among cement producers in Egypt, the court held that the ECA and prosecution did not need to prove the harm to the economy because the mere existence of the cartel agreement (colluding among large producers) was prohibited. Three criteria are essential for the enforcement of the law: a minimum threshold of 25 percent market share of the company involved; its ability to influence prices and production; and finally, the inability of the competitors to limit this influence. The three criteria determine the dominance of the firm on the market. Once dominance is established, the ECA looks at the practices of the firm.[1]

YOUR TURN: Test your understanding by doing related problems 5.9, 5.10, and 5.11 on page 386 at the end of this chapter.

Regulating horizontal mergers can be complicated by two factors. First, the 'market' that firms are in is not always clear. For example, if Cadbury (Egypt) wants to merge with Corona Inc., both makers of chocolate and other candies in Egypt, what is the relevant market? If the government looks just at the candy market, the newly merged company would have more than 70 percent of the market, a level at which the government would likely oppose the merger. What if the government looks at the broader market for 'snacks'? In this market, Cadbury and Corona compete with makers of potato chips, pretzels, peanuts, and, perhaps, even producers of fresh fruit. Of course, if the government looked at the very broad market for 'food,' then both Cadbury and Corona have very small market shares, and there would be no reason to oppose their merger. In practice, the government defines the relevant market on the basis of whether there are close substitutes for the products being made by the merging firms. In this case, potato chips and the other snack foods mentioned are not close substitutes for candy. So, the government would consider the candy market to be the relevant market and would oppose the merger on the grounds that the new firm would have too much market power.

The second factor that complicates merger policy is the possibility that the newly merged firm might be more efficient than the merging firms were individually. For example, one firm might have an excellent product but a poor distribution system for getting the product into the hands of consumers. A competing firm might have built a great distribution system but have an inferior product. Allowing these firms to merge might be good for both the firms and consumers. Or, two competing firms might each have an extensive system of warehouses that are only half full, but if the firms merged, they could consolidate their warehouses and significantly reduce their costs.

Most mergers are usually between large firms. For simplicity, let's consider a case where all the firms in a perfectly competitive industry want to merge to form a monopoly. As we saw in Figure 11-5, as a result of this merger, prices will rise and output will fall, leading to a decline in consumer surplus and economic efficiency. But what if the larger, newly merged firm actually is more efficient than the smaller firms had been? Figure 11-6 shows a possible result.

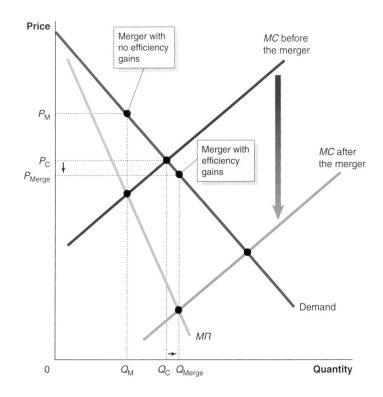

Figure 11-6

A Merger That Makes Consumers Better Off

This figure shows the result of all the firms in a perfectly competitive industry merging to form a monopoly. If costs are unaffected by the merger, the result is the same as in Figure 11-5 on page 370: price rises from P_C to P_M, quantity falls from Q_C to Q_M, consumer surplus declines, and a loss of economic efficiency results. If, however, the monopoly has lower costs than the perfectly competitive firms, as shown by the marginal cost curve shifting to MC after the merger, it is possible that the price will actually decline from P_C to P_{Merge} and output will increase from Q_C to Q_{Merge} following the merger.

If costs are unaffected by the merger, we get the same result as in Figure 11-5: price rises from P_C to P_M, quantity falls from Q_C to Q_M, consumer surplus is lower, and a loss of economic efficiency results. If the monopoly has lower costs than the competitive firms, it is possible for price to decline and quantity to increase. In Figure 11-6, to find the new profit-maximizing quantity, note where MR crosses MC after the merger. This new profit-maximizing quantity is Q_{Merge}. The demand curve shows that the monopolist can sell this quantity at a price of P_{Merge}. Therefore, the price declines after the merger from P_C to P_{Merge} and quantity increases from Q_C to Q_{Merge}. We have the following seemingly paradoxical result: *Although the newly merged firm has a great deal of market power, because it is more efficient, consumers are better off and economic efficiency is improved.* Of course, sometimes a merged firm will be more efficient and have lower costs, and other times it won't. Even if a merged firm is more efficient and has lower costs, that may not offset the increased market power of the firm enough to increase consumer surplus and economic efficiency.

As you might expect, whenever large firms propose a merger, they claim that the newly merged firm will be more efficient and have lower costs. They realize that without these claims, it is unlikely that the government will approve their merger. The merits of such claims are usually assessed by the government body in charge of the enforcement of the antitrust laws, along with the court system.

Anti-Monopoly Law Enforcement and Merger Guidelines

An important aspect of enforcing an anti-monopoly law is to develop some general guidelines to determine the effect of a merger on market power in order to conclude whether a merger will have a monopolistic effect on the market or that its impact can be tolerated. The analysis usually starts by deciding the dominance of the new entity after merger, and evaluates whether it can exert monopoly power that would be in violation of the anti-monopoly law.

Economists usually play a major role in the development of merger guidelines. The guidelines make it easier for firms considering a merger to understand whether the government is likely to allow the merger or to oppose it. The guidelines usually have three main parts:

1 Market definition

2 Measure of concentration

3 Merger standards.

Market Definition A market consists of all firms making products that consumers view as close substitutes. We can identify close substitutes by looking at the effect of a price increase. If our definition of a market is too narrow, a price increase will cause firms to experience a significant decline in sales—and profits—as consumers switch to buying close substitutes.

Identifying the relevant market involved in a proposed merger begins with a narrow definition of the industry. Consider the hypothetical merger of Cadbury (Egypt) and Corona, and we might start with the candy industry. If all firms in the candy industry increased price by 5 percent, would their profits increase or decrease? If profits would increase, the market is defined as being just these firms. If profits would decrease, we would try a broader definition—say, by adding in potato chips and other snacks. Would a price increase of 5 percent by all firms in the broader market raise profits? If profits increase, the relevant market has been identified. If profits decrease, we consider a broader definition. We continue this procedure until a market has been identified.

Measure of Concentration A market is *concentrated* if a relatively small number of firms have a large share of total sales in the market. A merger between firms in a market that is already highly concentrated is very likely to increase market power. A merger between firms in an industry that has a very low concentration is unlikely to increase market power and can be ignored. Let's look at one method to calculate market concentration: the *Herfindahl-Hirschman Index (HHI)* of concentration, which squares the market shares of each firm in the industry and adds up the values of the squares. The following are some examples of calculating a Herfindahl-Hirschman Index:

- 1 firm, with 100% market share (a monopoly):

$$\text{HHI} = 100^2 = 10,000$$

- 2 firms, each with a 50% market share:

$$\text{HHI} = 50^2 + 50^2 = 5,000$$

- 4 firms, with market shares of 30%, 30%, 20%, and 20%:

$$\text{HHI} = 30^2 + 30^2 + 20^2 + 20^2 = 2,600$$

- 10 firms, each with market shares of 10%:

$$\text{HHI} = 10\,(10^2) = 1,000$$

Merger Standards The institution responsible for enforcing anti-monopoly laws in a country can, then, use the HHI calculation for a market to evaluate proposed horizontal mergers according to specific standards or thresholds; for example:

- **Post-merger HHI below 1,000.** These markets are not concentrated, so mergers in them are not challenged.
- **Post-merger HHI between 1,000 and 1,800.** These markets are moderately concentrated. Mergers that raise the HHI by less than 100 probably will not be challenged. Mergers that raise the HHI by more than 100 may be challenged.
- **Post-merger HHI above 1,800.** These markets are highly concentrated. Mergers that increase the HHI by less than 50 points will not be challenged. Mergers that increase the HHI by 50 to 100 points may be challenged. Mergers that increase the HHI by more than 100 points will be challenged.

Making the Connection | Is Egypt's Steel Industry a Monopoly? The Case of Ezz-Dekhela

In October 1999, Al-Ezz Rebars acquired a controlling stake (28 percent) of the state-controlled Alexandria National Iron and Steel Company, the largest steel producer in Egypt. Shortly after the merger, the Alexandria National Iron and Steel Company's board of directors appointed Ahmed Ezz as the joint chairman and managing director of Al-Ezz Steel and Alexandria National Iron and Steel Company. The move fully consolidated both companies and the products of the two companies were rebranded as Ezz-Dekhela; a brand known for high quality, which justifies a higher price than its competitors.

The table on the following page lists the market shares in the Egyptian steel industry in the year 2000, shortly after the merger took place. In this chapter, we have learned how to calculate the Hirschman-Herfindahl Index (HHI) to determine market concentration. Applying this index to the market shares appearing in the table returns the market concentration in the Egyptian steel industry, which is calculated as 3,822. Remember that a perfectly competitive market has a zero HHI index while a complete monopoly has an HHI of 10,000. The calculated

(continued)

monopolistic performance of the entire Egyptian steel industry appears to exceed one-third the scale of monopoly power. The table also reveals that the Ezz-Dekhela partnership resulted in a combined market share and company concentration ratio of 60.7 percent; seven times the market share of its next competitor (Kouta Group). This implies that the merger duopoly partnership (Ezz-Dekhela) has an excessively dominant monopoly power in the steel markets, despite a fairly large number of players at the time.

MARKET SHARE OF LOCAL STEEL REBAR PRODUCERS, 2000		
SUPPLIER	PRODUCTION (MILLION TONS)	MARKET SHARE
Ezz Steel	1147	27.5%
Alexandria National Iron and Steel	1375	33.2%
Ezz-Dekhela	**2522**	**60.7%**
Kouta Group	360	8.6%
Int'l St. R. M.- Beshai	275	6.6%
Delta Steel	91.8	2.2%
Suez Co. Al-Koumy	82	2.0%
Egyptian Metal Hatem	80	1.9%
Egyptian Iron and Steel	56.2	1.3%
Al-Said Steel	50	1.2%
Menouefya Steel	46	1.1%
Ayaad Rolling	36	0.9%
Egyptian Copper Wk	34.2	0.8%
Al-Arabi Planet Sharkawi	33	0.8%
Misr Iron and Steel	24	0.6%
Al-Temsah Steel	24	0.6%
National Metal Ind.	16.9	0.4%
Sarhan Steel	<3.7	<0.1%
Total	**3731**	**89.7%**
Imports	440	10.3%

Source: Tarek H. Selim, "Monopoly: The Case of Egyptian Steel," *Journal of Business Case Studies,* Vol. 2(3), p. 87, 2006.

The new merger has had implications for the steel industry's entry barriers in Egypt. Three barriers can be identified: (i) quality steel production requires sizeable capital; (ii) local production capacity (supply of steel) exceeded its consumption in 2000; (iii) the new merger led to a single company controlling more than 60 percent of the total local market, which seriously discourages new players from attempting to enter the market. By 2006, the prices of steel had dramatically increased, which prompted a request from the Minister of Trade and Industry to the Egyptian Competition Authority (ECA) to look into whether such increase was due to anti-competitive practice.

After carefully studying the market, the ECA proved that the Ezz Group had violated Article 8(c) of the anti-monopoly law. That Article stipulates that a dominant person is prohibited from: "undertaking an act that limits distribution of a specific product, on the basis of geographic areas, distribution centers, clients, seasons or periods of time among persons with vertical relationships."

After inspection, the ECA concluded that the Ezz Group satisfied the three conditions of the prohibition. First, the Ezz Group undertook an act that would lead to the distribution of a specific product (and refraining from distributing others). The distribution contracts that the Ezz Group signed with the distributors included a quota system. Second, the ECA proved that this system would force the distributors to favor buying and distributing steel bars from the Ezz Group over its competitors in order to maintain the distributor's quota. Finally, there was a vertical relationship between the Ezz Group and the distributor. All three conditions of Article 8(c) were met and so it was clear that the Ezz Group had violated the law.

Despite the clear violation of Article 8(c) of the law, and after evaluating the effect of Ezz's practices on the market, the ECA decided that it did not affect the sales of the Ezz Group's rivals. Therefore, the board finally decided that Ezz Group was dominant in the market of steel bars but had not abused its dominant position. This decision was inconsistent with previous strict applications of the same prohibition in other cases, which certainly had a negative effect on the credibility of the ECA.

Sources: Tarek H. Selim, "Monopoly: The Case Of Egyptian Steel," *Journal of Business Case Studies*, Vol 2(3), pp. 85–92, 2006; Ahmed F. Ghoneim, "Competition Law and Competition Policy: What Does Egypt Really Need?" ERF Working Paper 0239, 2006; M. El-Far, "Enforcement Policy of the Egyptian Competition Law," *Competition Law International*, April 2010, http://ssrn.com/abstract=1580056.

Regulating Natural Monopolies

If a firm is a natural monopoly, competition from other firms will not play its usual role of forcing price down to the level where the company earns zero economic profit. As a result, local or state *regulatory commissions* usually set the prices for natural monopolies, such as firms selling natural gas or electricity. What price should these commissions set? Recall that economic efficiency requires the last unit of a good or service produced to provide an additional benefit to consumers equal to the additional cost of producing it. We can measure the additional benefit consumers receive from the last unit by the price and the additional cost to the monopoly of producing the last unit by marginal cost. Therefore, to achieve economic efficiency, regulators should require that the monopoly charge a price equal to its marginal cost. There is, however, an important drawback to doing so, which is illustrated in Figure 11-7. This figure shows the situation of a typical regulated natural monopoly.

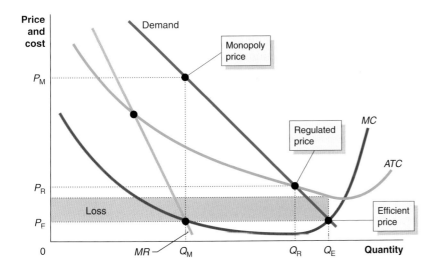

Figure 11-7

Regulating a Natural Monopoly

A natural monopoly that is not subject to government regulation will charge a price equal to P_M and produce Q_M. If government regulators want to achieve economic efficiency, they will set the regulated price equal to P_E, and the monopoly will produce Q_E. Unfortunately, P_E is below average cost, and the monopoly will suffer a loss, shown by the shaded rectangle. Because the monopoly will not continue to produce in the long run if it suffers a loss, government regulators set a price equal to average cost, which is P_R in the figure.

Remember that with a natural monopoly, the average total cost curve is still falling when it crosses the demand curve. If unregulated, the monopoly will charge a price equal to P_M and produce Q_M. To achieve economic efficiency, regulators should require the monopoly to charge a price equal to P_E. The monopoly will then produce Q_E. But here is the drawback: P_E is less than average total cost, so the monopoly will be suffering a loss, shown by the area of the red-shaded rectangle. In the long run, the owners of the monopoly will not continue in business if they are experiencing losses. Realizing this, most regulators will set the regulated price, P_R, equal to the level of average total cost at which the demand curve intersects the *ATC* curve. At that price, the owners of the monopoly are able to break even on their investment by producing the quantity Q_R.

Economics in YOUR Life!

>> Continued from page 357

At the beginning of the chapter, we asked why many cable systems won't carry popular movie channels on networks such as ART, Orbit, or Showtime. You might think that the cable systems would want to televise the most popular, recent movies. In most cities, a customer of a cable system can't switch to a competing cable system, so in many areas cable systems can be the sole source of many programs. (Although some consumers have the option of switching to satellite television.) As a result, a cable system can increase its profits by, for example, not offering popular programming such as the ART Network channels as part of its normal programming package, requiring instead that consumers upgrade to digital programming at a higher price.

Conclusion

The more intense the level of competition among firms, the better a market works. In this chapter, we have seen that with monopoly—where competition is entirely absent—price is higher, output is lower, and consumer surplus and economic efficiency decline compared with perfect competition. Fortunately, true monopolies are rare. Even though most firms resemble monopolies in being able to charge a price above marginal cost, most markets have enough competition to keep the efficiency losses from market power quite low.

We've seen that barriers to entry are an important source of market power. Read *An Inside Look at Policy* on the next page for a discussion of how a non-independent regulator in Kuwait affects the level of competition and the structure of the telecom market.

Kuwait—Telecoms, Mobile, Broadband and Forecasts

BUDDE.COM TELECOMMUNICATIONS RESEARCH AND CONSULTANCY COMPANY, 2009

Not only does Kuwait not have an independent regulator, but the Ministry of Communications is both the regulatory entity and also the operating entity for fixed-line services. Plans were drafted for the establishment of a telecommunications regulatory authority in 2007 but are yet to come [into effect].

(a) The Ministry does not charge customers for calls made from fixed lines to mobile phones. It also controls the international gateway and does not have an interconnection system with any of the mobile operators. As the Ministry controls all international charges, this prevents local mobile operators from offering promotions and discounts on overseas calls. It has also prevented mobile operator Zain from extending its "One Network" service, which gives free voice and data-roaming for subscribers across most of its network, to its subscribers in its home base of Kuwait.

A further problem with the lack of independence and corporatization in the fixed-line sector is a lack of available information on the sector.

(b) Competition does exist in the Internet provision sector, with four major Internet Service Providers, but again it is limited. In July 2009 the Ministry of Communications stated that it would suspend the licenses of a number of ISPs…

Kuwait's mobile sector presents a different picture to its fixed-lines sector. For many years two very strong operators have shared a comfortable duopoly. They have enjoyed high tariffs in their home market and have used this base to extend internationally. MTC, known as Zain, had extended its operations to 24 countries by mid-2009. However, its profits from its Kuwaiti operations still made up around 50 percent of its total Group profit at end-2008. In March 2010 it sold its African operations, with the exception of those in Sudan and Morocco, to Bharti Airtel of India, leaving it with operations in just 9 countries.

(c) Zain's competitor Wataniya, now a subsidiary itself of Qtel of Qatar, has extended into six countries in total but its Kuwaiti profits were slightly higher than its Group profits at end-2009. The two incumbent mobile operators, who have shared the market for the past ten years, were joined in December 2008 by a third operator, Kuwait Telecom Company—known as Viva, with Saudi Telecom Company as a major investor. All three mobile operators have the government as a major shareholder, owning approximately 25 percent in each case.

By end-2009 Viva would appear to have gained a market share of over 10 percent. Based on numbers reported by Zain and Wataniya, Viva's gain would appear to have come mostly at Zain's expense. The introduction of more competition has had a substantial effect on reducing ARPU (Average Revenue Per Unit) levels.

Source: Budde.com telecommunications research and consultancy company, "Kuwait – Telecoms, Mobile, Broadband and Forecasts," 2009 report, www.budde.com.

Key Points in the Article

This article discusses the effect of not having an independent telecom regulatory authority in Kuwait and how the monopoly of the Ministry of Communications as the regulatory authority and the operating entity for fixed-line services is hindering competition in the telecom sector. It also describes the process of how a once monopoly market is gradually turning into a more competitive market. Despite starting as monopolies, the Internet and mobile markets of Kuwait have become more competitive over time. As barriers fall, an increasing number of competitors has entered the market and the face of the industry has entirely changed.

Analyzing the News

c The Ministry of Communications in Kuwait is playing the roles of both the regulatory entity and also the operating entity for fixed-line services. That has

resulted in blocking competition in the fixed-line segment of the market. In addition, the Ministry controles the gateway to international calls, preventing competitors in the mobile market to compete on international phone rates. The Ministry also blocked Zain from extending its "One Network" service, which hurt consumers who travel from Kuwait to different Arab countries where Zain is operating. They lost the advantage of having a free roaming service among Zain subscribers in these countries.

b The Ministry of Communications allowed competition in the other two segments of the market: the Internet and mobile services. The competition is intensifying as more newcomers enter the market. By the end of 2008, the mobile market, which for a long time had been a duopoly between Zain and Wataniya, had a new, fierce competitor: Viva. The two existing players Zain and Wataniya had enjoyed large profit margins before the new market entry come into operation in 2009.

c Entry, of course, will reduce the economic profit existing firms earn. The figure illustrates what happens as entry occurs and the market becomes competitive. For

simplicity, we assume that the marginal cost of providing mobile phone services is constant, so the marginal cost curve is a horizontal line. Notice that output increases from Q_M to Q_C, and price falls from P_M to P_C. You can also see that consumer surplus increases from areas $A + E$ to areas $A + E + B + C + D$, and the deadweight loss in the market (area D) disappears and becomes consumer surplus. In this figure, what were profits to the monopoly (areas $B + C$) are redistributed to consumers as consumer surplus. Economic profits fall to zero.

Thinking Critically About Policy

1. What is the most a firm would be willing to spend to remain the sole provider of mobile phone services in a market?

2. Even with a countrywide franchise, what might prevent new mobile firms from entering local markets?

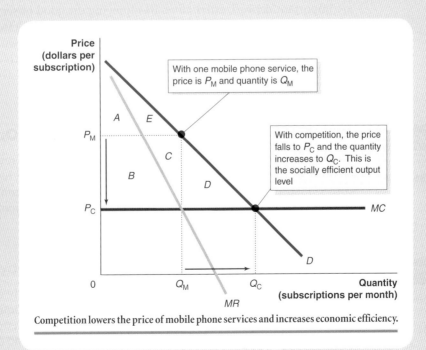

Competition lowers the price of mobile phone services and increases economic efficiency.

Key Terms

Summary

11.1 LEARNING OBJECTIVE

Define monopoly, **pages 358–359.**

Is Any Firm Ever Really a Monopoly?

A **monopoly** exists only in the rare situation in which a firm is producing a good or service for which there are no close substitutes. A narrow definition of monopoly that some economists use is that a firm has a monopoly if it can ignore the actions of all other firms. Many economists favor a broader definition of monopoly. Under the broader definition, a firm has a monopoly if no other firms are selling a substitute close enough that the firm's economic profits are competed away in the long run.

11.2 LEARNING OBJECTIVE

Explain the four main reasons monopolies arise, **pages 359–364.**

Where Do Monopolies Come From?

To have a monopoly, barriers to entering the market must be so high that no other firms can enter. Barriers to entry may be high enough to keep out competing firms for four main reasons: (1) government blocks the entry of more than one firm into a market by issuing a **patent**, which is the exclusive right to a product for 20 years, or a **copyright**, which is the exclusive right to produce and sell a creation, or giving a firm a **public franchise**, which is the right to be the only legal provider of a good or service (2) one firm has control of a key raw material necessary to produce a good, (3) there are important *network externalities* in supplying the good or service, or (4) economies of scale are so large that one firm has a *natural monopoly*. **Network externalities** refer to the situation where the usefulness of a product increases with the number of consumers who use it. A **natural monopoly** is a situation in which economies of scale are so large that one firm can supply the entire market at a lower average cost than two or more firms.

11.3 LEARNING OBJECTIVE

Explain how a monopoly chooses price and output, **pages 364–368.**

How Does a Monopoly Choose Price and Output?

Monopolists face downward-sloping demand and marginal revenue curves and, like all other firms, maximize profit by producing where marginal revenue equals marginal cost. Unlike a perfect competitor, a monopolist that earns economic profits does not face the entry of new firms into the market. Therefore, a monopolist can earn economic profits, even in the long run.

11.4 LEARNING OBJECTIVE

Use a graph to illustrate how a monopoly affects economic efficiency, **pages 368–371.**

Does Monopoly Reduce Economic Efficiency?

Compared with a perfectly competitive industry, a monopoly charges a higher price and produces less, which reduces consumer surplus and economic efficiency. Some loss of economic efficiency will occur whenever firms have **market power** and can charge a price greater than marginal cost. The total loss of economic efficiency due to market power is small, however, because true monopolies are very rare. In most industries, competition will keep price much closer to marginal cost than would be the case in a monopoly.

Government Policy toward Monopoly

Because monopolies reduce consumer surplus and economic efficiency, most governments regulate monopolies. Firms that are not monopolies have an incentive to avoid competition by **colluding**, or agreeing to charge the same price, or otherwise not to compete. In the United States, **antitrust laws** are aimed at deterring monopoly, eliminating collusion, and promoting competition among firms. We looked at the example of the **Egyptian Competition Authority** (ECA) which is responsible for enforcing the Anti-Monopoly and Fair Competition Act. A **horizontal merger** is a merger between firms in the same industry. A **vertical merger** is a merger between firms at different stages of production of a good. Local governments regulate the prices charged by natural monopolies.

> **11.5 LEARNING** OBJECTIVE
>
> Discuss government policies toward monopoly, **pages 371–378.**

Review, Problems and Applications

 Visit www.pearsoned.co.uk/awe/hubbard to complete these exercises online and get instant feedback.
Get Ahead of the Curve

11.1 LEARNING OBJECTIVE   Define monopoly, **pages 358–359.**

Review Questions

1.1 What is a monopoly? Can a firm be a monopoly if close substitutes for its product exist?

1.2 If you own the only hardware store in a small town, do you have a monopoly?

Problems and Applications

1.3 Is 'monopoly' a good name for the game *Monopoly*? What aspects of the game involve monopoly? Explain briefly, using the definition of monopoly.

1.4 Are there any products for which there are no substitutes? Are these the only products for which it would be possible to have a monopoly? Briefly explain.

1.5 An economist argues, "No firm can remain a monopoly for long in the face of technological change." Do you agree?

1.6 **(Related to the *Making the Connection* on page 358)** Microsoft thought that the initial Xbox was sufficiently different from PS2 that it could charge a significantly higher price for the Xbox than Sony could charge for PS2. As it turns out, Microsoft was wrong. Draw the average total cost and marginal cost curves for Microsoft's Xbox. Now draw the demand curve Microsoft thought would exist for Xbox and the demand curve that actually existed. Why were the two demand curves different? Show on your graph the profits Microsoft would earn with each demand curve.

11.2 LEARNING OBJECTIVE   Explain the four main reasons monopolies arise, **pages 359–364.**

Review Questions

2.1 What are the four most important ways a firm becomes a monopoly?

2.2 If patents reduce competition, why does the federal government grant them?

2.3 What is a public franchise? Are all public franchises natural monopolies?

2.4 What is "natural" about a natural monopoly?

Problems and Applications

2.5 The UAE Postal Service (EmPost) is a monopoly because the UAE government has blocked entry into the market for delivering first-class mail. Is it also a natural monopoly? How can we tell? What would

happen if the law preventing competition in this market were removed?

2.6 Patents are granted for 20 years, but pharmaceutical companies can't use their patent-guaranteed monopoly powers for anything liker this long because it takes several years to acquire an approval of drugs. Should the life of drug patents be extended to 20 years *after* the final approval? What would be the costs and benefits of this extension?

2.7 The German company Koenig & Bauer has 90 percent of the world market for presses that print currency. Discuss the factors that would make it difficult for new companies to enter this market.

2.8 (Related to the *Making the Connection* on page 362) Why was De Beers worried that people might resell their old diamonds? How did De Beers attempt to convince consumers that used diamonds were not good substitutes for new diamonds? How did De Beers' strategy affect the demand curve for new diamonds? How were De Beers' profits affected?

2.9 Suppose that the quantity demanded per day for a product is 90 when the price is US$35. The following table shows costs for a firm with a monopoly in this market:

QUANTITY (PER DAY)	TOTAL COST
30	$1,200
40	1,400
50	2,250
60	3,000

Briefly explain whether this firm has a natural monopoly in this market.

11.3 LEARNING OBJECTIVE　　Explain how a monopoly chooses price and output, **pages 364–368.**

Review Questions

3.1 What is the relationship between a monopolist's demand curve and the market demand curve? What is the relationship between a monopolist's demand curve and its marginal revenue curve?

3.2 Draw a graph that shows a monopolist that is earning a profit. Be sure your graph includes the monopolist's demand, marginal revenue, average total cost, and marginal cost curves. Be sure to indicate the profit-maximizing level of output and price.

Problems and Applications

3.3 (Related to *Solved Problem 11-3* on page 367) Alaa Al-Ayman has acquired a monopoly on the production of footballs, and faces the demand and cost situation given in the following table:

PRICE	QUANTITY (PER WEEK)	TOTAL REVENUE	MARGINAL REVENUE	TOTAL COST	MARGINAL COST
$20	15,000			$330,000	
19	20,000			365,000	
18	25,000			405,000	
17	30,000			450,000	
16	35,000			500,000	
15	40,000			555,000	

a. Fill in the remaining values in the table.

b. If Al-Ayman wants to maximize profits, what price should he charge and how many footballs should he sell? How much profit will he make?

c. Suppose the government imposes a tax of US$50,000 per week on football production. Now what price should Al-Ayman charge, how many footballs should he sell, and what will his profits be?

3.4 (Related to *Solved Problem 11-3* on page 367) Use the information in Solved Problem 11-2 to answer the following questions.

a. What will Etisalat do if the tax is US$6.00 per month instead of US$2.50? (*Hint:* Will its decision be different in the long run than in the short run?)

b. Suppose that the flat per-month tax is replaced with a tax on the firm of US$0.50 per cable subscriber. Now how many subscriptions should Etisalat sell if it wants to maximize profit? What price does it charge? What are its profits? (Assume that Etisalat will sell only the quantities listed in the table.)

3.5 Before inexpensive pocket calculators were developed, many science and engineering students used slide rules to make numeric calculations. Slide rules are no longer produced, which means nothing prevents you from establishing a monopoly in the slide rule market. Draw a graph showing the situation your slide rule firm would be in. Be sure to include on your graph your demand, marginal revenue, average total cost, and marginal cost curves. Indicate the price you would charge and the quantity you would produce. Are you likely to make a profit or a loss? Show this area on your graph.

3.6 Does a monopolist have a supply curve? Briefly explain. (*Hint:* Look again at the definition of a supply curve in Chapter 3 and consider whether this applies to a monopolist.)

3.7 A student argues, "If a monopolist finds a way of producing a good at lower cost, he will not lower his price. Because he is a monopolist, he will keep the price and the quantity the same and just increase his profit." Do you agree? Use a graph to illustrate your answer.

3.8 Discuss whether you agree or disagree with the following statement: "A monopolist maximizes profit by charging the highest price at which it can sell any of the good at all."

3.9 When homebuilders construct a new housing development, they usually sell the rights to lay cable to a single cable television company. As a result, anyone buying a home in that development is not able to choose between competing cable companies. Some cities have begun to ban such exclusive agreements and have decided to allow any cable company to lay cable in the utility trenches of new housing developments. In a situation in which the consumers in a housing development have only one cable company available, is the price really at the whim of the company?

Would a company in this situation be likely to charge, say, US$500 per month for basic cable services? Briefly explain why or why not.

3.10 Will a monopoly that maximizes profit also be maximizing revenue? Will it be maximizing production? Briefly explain.

11.4 LEARNING OBJECTIVE   Use a graph to illustrate how a monopoly affects economic efficiency, **pages 368–371.**

Review Questions

4.1 Suppose that a perfectly competitive industry becomes a monopoly. Describe the effects of this change on consumer surplus, producer surplus, and deadweight loss.

4.2 Explain why market power leads to a deadweight loss. Is the total deadweight loss from market power for the economy large or small?

Problems and Applications

4.3 Review Figure 11-5 on page 370 on the inefficiency of monopoly. Will the deadweight loss due to monopoly be larger if the demand is elastic or if it is inelastic? Briefly explain.

4.4 Economist Harvey Leibenstein argued that the loss of economic efficiency in industries that are not perfectly competitive has been understated. He argues that when competition is weak, firms are under less pressure to adopt the best techniques or to hold down their costs. He refers to this effect as "x-inefficiency." If x-inefficiency causes a firm's marginal costs to rise, show that the deadweight loss in Figure 11-5 understates the true deadweight loss caused by a monopoly.

4.5 In most cities, the city owns the water system that provides water to homes and businesses. Some cities charge a flat monthly fee, while other cities charge by the gallon. Which method of pricing is more likely to result in economic efficiency in the water market? Be sure to refer to the definition of economic efficiency in your answer. Why do you think the same method of pricing isn't used by all cities?

11.5 LEARNING OBJECTIVE   Discuss government policies toward monopoly, **pages 371–378.**

Review Problems

5.1 What is the purpose of the antitrust laws? Who is in charge of enforcing them?

5.2 What is the difference between a horizontal merger and a vertical merger? Which type of merger is more likely to increase the market power of a newly merged firm?

5.3 Why would it be economically efficient to require a natural monopoly to charge a price equal to marginal cost? Why do most regulatory agencies require natural monopolies to charge a price equal to average cost instead?

Problems and Applications

5.4 Use the following graph for a monopoly to answer the questions.
   a. What quantity will the monopoly produce, and what price will the monopoly charge?

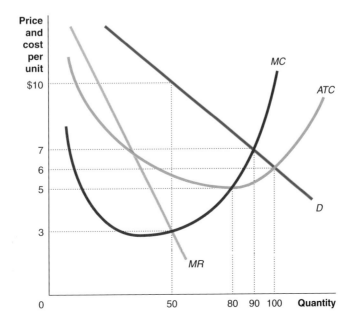

b. Suppose the monopoly is regulated. If the regulatory agency wants to achieve economic efficiency, what price should it require the monopoly to charge? How much output will the monopoly produce at this price? Will the monopoly make a profit if it charges this price? Briefly explain.

5.5 Use the following graph for a monopoly to answer the questions.
   a. What quantity will the monopoly produce, and what price will the monopoly charge?
   b. Suppose the government decides to regulate this monopoly and imposes a price ceiling of US$18 (in other words, the monopoly can charge less than US$18 but can't charge more). Now what quantity will the monopoly produce, and what price will the monopoly charge? Will every consumer who is willing to pay this price be able to buy the product? Briefly explain.

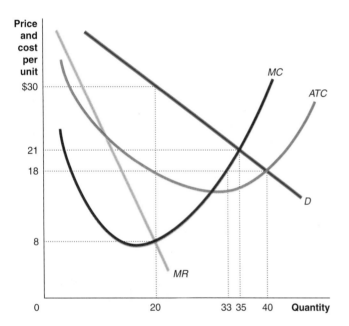

5.6 Suppose that Emirates airline and Etihad airline announced that they had called off their proposed merger after an antitrust lawsuit was filed to block the US$4 billion deal, calling it 'anti-competitive.' Why would the government care if two airlines merge? What is 'anti-competitive' about two airlines merging?

5.7 A marketing textbook observes, "Pricing actions that violate laws can land executives in jail." Why would executives be thrown in jail because of the prices they charge? Which laws are they likely to have violated?
Source: David W. Cravens, *Strategic Marketing*, 5th ed., Boston: Irwin McGraw-Hill, 1997, p. 343.

5.8 Draw a graph like Figure 11-6 on page 373. On your graph, show producer surplus and consumer surplus before a merger and consumer surplus and producer surplus after a merger.

5.9 (Related to the *Making the Connection* on page 372) Evaluate the following situations.
   a. A market initially has 20 firms, each with a 5 percent market share. Of the firms, 4 propose to merge, leaving a total of 17 firms in the industry. Is the government likely to oppose the merger? Briefly explain.
   b. A market initially has 5 firms, each with a 20 percent market share. Of the firms, 2 propose to merge, leaving a total of 4 firms in the industry. Is the government likely to oppose the merger? Briefly explain.

5.10 (Related to the *Making the Connection* on page 372) Industrial gases are used in the electronics industry. For example, nitrogen trifluoride is used for cleaning semiconductor wafers. The following table shows the market shares for the companies in this industry.

COMPANY	MARKET SHARE
Air Products	29%
Air Liquide	22
BOC Gases	21
Nippon Sanso	17
Praxzir	8
Other	3

Air Products discussed a merger with BOC Gases. Use the information in the section "Anti-Monopoly Law Enforcement and Merger Guidelines" that begins on page 374 to predict whether the government would oppose this merger. Assume that "Other" in the table consists of three firms, each of which has a 1 percent share of the market.
Source for market share data: Dan Shope, "Air Products Turns a Corner", (Allentown, Pennsylvania) *Morning Call*, July 29, 2001.

5.11 (Related to the *Making the Connection* on page 372) The following table gives the market shares of the companies forming the carbonated soft drink industry.

COMPANY	MARKET SHARE
Coca-Cola	37%
PepsiCo	35
Cadbury Schweppes	17
Other	11

Use the information in the section "Anti-Monopoly Law Enforcement and Merger Guidelines" that begins on page 374 to predict whether the government would be likely to approve a merger between any two of the first three companies listed. Does your answer depend on how many companies are included in the "Other" category? Briefly explain.
Source: PepsiCo, *Annual Report*, 2003

5.13 According to a column in the *New York Times* by Austan Goolsbee of the University of Chicago, the French National Assembly approved a bill:

> …that would require Apple Computer to crack open the software codes of its iTunes music store and let the files work on players other than the iPod…. If the French gave away the codes, Apple would lose much of its rationale for improving iTunes.

a. Why would Apple no longer want to improve iTunes if its software codes were no longer secret?

b. Why would the French government believe it was a good idea to require Apple to make the codes public?

Source: Austan Goolsbee, "In iTunes War, France Has Met the Enemy. Perhaps It Is France," *New York Times*, April 27, 2006.

Chapter 12

Pricing Strategy

Getting into Dream Park: One Price Does Not Fit All

When you visit Dream Park, the leading amusement park in Egypt and the Middle East, in 6th of October city, your age, home address, and occupation can determine how much you pay for admission. In the summer of 2010, the price for a one-day ticket for an adult was 49.99 Egyptian pounds (EGP) (around US\$8.66); the same ticket for a child under three was free; 6th of October city residents paid EGP32; handicapped people paid EGP28; active members of the military paid EGP40. Why does Dream Park charge so many different prices for the same product?

In previous chapters, we assumed that firms charge all consumers the same price for a given product. In reality, many firms charge customers different prices, based on differences in their willingness to pay for the product. Firms often face complicated pricing problems. For example, Dream Park Company faces the problem of determining the profit-maximizing prices to charge different groups of consumers for admission to its theme park.

Dream Park was established in 1999 and designed by FORREC, the international firm that designed Universal Studios and the Mall of America. The park management decided to follow the same pricing strategy that is applied now in many theme parks worldwide, which is: instead of charging a low admission price and a separate charge for each ride, charging a high price for admission to the park but, once a customer has paid to enter the park, the rides are free. This pricing system was first introduced by the Walt Disney Company for admission to Disneyland (California) and Walt Disney World (Florida) in the early 1980s.

Why did Disney, followed by many theme parks, change its pricing strategy? In this chapter, we will study some common pricing strategies, and we will see how Dream Park and other firms use these strategies to increase their profits. **AN INSIDE LOOK** on **page 408** discusses how governments also charge different prices to different electric-energy users.

Sources: Harrison Price, *Walt's Revolution! By the Numbers*, Ripley Entertainment Inc., 2004, p. 31; and Bruce Gordon and David Mumford, *Disneyland: The Nickel Tour*, Santa Clarita, CA: Camphor Tree Publishers, 2000, pp. 174– 5; Dream Park Website, http://www.dreamparkegypt.com.

LEARNING Objectives

After studying this chapter, you should be able to:

12.1 Define the **law of one price** and explain the role of **arbitrage**, page 390.

12.2 Explain how a firm can increase its profits through **price discrimination**, page 392.

12.3 Explain how some firms increase their profits through the use of **odd pricing, cost-plus pricing** and **two-part tariffs**, page 401.

Economics in YOUR Life!

Why So Many Prices to Visit a Museum or See a Movie?

Think about museums in your area. How much do you, as a student, pay to get into the museum? Would your parents pay the same amount? How about your little brother or sister? Is the price the same at night as in the afternoon? Why do you suppose museums charge different prices to different groups of consumers? In some countries, movie theaters also charge different prices to different groups of people according to their age and whether they are still in education or not.

If you buy a water bottle in the museum or popcorn at the movie theater, you pay the same price as everyone else. Why do you suppose people in certain age groups get a discount on museum and movie admission but not on movie popcorn? As you read the chapter, see if you can answer these questions. You can check your answers against those we provide at the end of the chapter. **>> Continued on page 406**

I n previous chapters, we saw that entrepreneurs continually seek out economic profit. Pricing strategies are one way firms can attempt to increase their economic profit. One of these strategies is called *price discrimination*. It involves firms setting different prices for the same good or service, as Dream Park does when setting admission prices at the theme park. In Chapter 11, we analyzed the situation of a monopolist who sets a single price for its product. In this chapter, we will see how a firm can increase its profits by charging a higher price to consumers who value the good more and a lower price to consumers who value the good less.

We will also analyze the widely used strategies of *odd pricing* and *cost-plus pricing*. Finally, we will analyze situations in which firms are able to charge consumers one price for the right to buy a good and a second price for each unit of the good purchased. The ability of Dream Park to charge for admission to the park and also to charge for each ride is an example of this situation, which economists call a *two-part tariff*.

12.1 LEARNING OBJECTIVE

12.1 | Define the law of one price and explain the role of arbitrage.

Pricing Strategy, the Law of One Price, and Arbitrage

We saw in the opening to this chapter that sometimes firms can increase their profits by charging different prices for the same good. In fact, many firms rely on economic analysis to practice *price discrimination* by charging higher prices to some customers and lower prices to others. Firms use technology to gather information on the preferences of consumers and their responsiveness to changes in prices. Managers use the information to rapidly adjust the prices of their goods and services. This practice of rapidly adjusting prices, called *yield management*, has been particularly important to airlines and hotels. There are limits, though, to the ability of firms to charge different prices for the same product. The key limit is the possibility in some circumstances that consumers who can buy a good at a low price will resell it to consumers who would otherwise have to buy at a high price.

Arbitrage

According to the *law of one price*, identical products should sell for the same price everywhere. Let's explore why the law of one price usually holds true. Suppose that a Sony Playstation Portable (PSP) handheld video game in Saudi Arabia sells for US$249 in stores in Jeddah, and for US$199 in Riyadh. Anyone who lives in Riyadh could buy PSPs for US$199 and resell them for US$249 in Jeddah. They could sell them on ewaseet.com or ship them to someone they know in Jeddah who could sell them in local flea markets. Buying a product in one market at a low price and reselling it in another market at a high price is referred to as *arbitrage*. The profits received from engaging in arbitrage are referred to as *arbitrage profits*.

As the supply of PSPs in Jeddah increases, the price of PSPs in Jeddah will decline, and as the supply of PSPs in Riyadh decreases, the price of PSPs in Riyadh will rise. Eventually the arbitrage process will eliminate most, but not all, of the price difference. Some price difference will remain because sellers must pay to list PSPs on ewaseet.com and to ship them to Jeddah. The costs of carrying out a transaction—by, for example, listing items on ewaseet.com and shipping them across the country—are called **transactions costs**. The law of one price holds exactly *only if transactions costs are zero*. As we shall see, in cases in which it is impossible to resell a product, the law of one price will not hold, and firms will be able to price discriminate. Apart from this important qualification, we expect that arbitrage will result in a product selling for the same price everywhere.

Transactions costs The costs in time and other resources that parties incur in the process of agreeing to and carrying out an exchange of goods or services.

Solved Problem | **12-1**

Is Arbitrage Just a Rip-off?

People are often suspicious of arbitrage. Buying something at a low price and reselling it at a high price exploits the person buying at the high price. Or does it? Is this view correct? If so, do the auctions on souq.com or eBay.com serve any useful economic purpose?

SOLVING THE PROBLEM:

Step 1: **Review the chapter material**. This problem is about arbitrage, so you may want to review the section "Arbitrage," which begins on page 390. If necessary, also review the discussion of the benefits from trade in Chapter 2.

Step 2: **Use the discussion of arbitrage and the discussion in earlier chapters of the benefits from trade to answer the questions**. Many of the goods on Souq and eBay have been bought at a low price and are being resold at a higher price. In fact, some people supplement their incomes by buying collectibles and other goods at garage sales and reselling them on Souq or eBay. Do Souq or eBay serve a useful economic purpose? Economists would say that they do. Consider the case of Mostafa, who buys collectible movie posters and resells them on Souq.com. Suppose Mostafa buys a *Spider-Man 3* poster at a garage sale for US$30 and resells it on Souq.com for US$60. Both the person who sold to Mostafa at the garage sale and the person who bought from him on Souq must have been made better off by the deals *or they would not have made them*. Mostafa has performed the useful service of locating the poster and making it available for sale on Souq. In carrying out this service, Mostafa has incurred costs, including the opportunity cost of his time spent searching garage sales, the opportunity cost of the funds he has tied up in posters he has purchased but not yet sold, and the cost of the fees Souq charges him. It is easy to sell goods on Souq, so over time, competition among Mostafa and other movie poster dealers should cause the difference between the prices of posters sold at garage sales and the prices on Souq to shrink until they are equal to the dealers' costs of reselling the posters.

YOUR TURN: For more practice, do related problems 1.5 on page 411 at the end of this chapter.

>> **End Solved Problem 12-1**

Why Don't All Firms Charge the Same Price?

The law of one price may appear to be violated even where transactions costs are zero and a product can be resold. For example, different websites may sell what seem to be identical products for different prices. We can resolve this apparent contradiction if we look more closely at what 'product' an website—or other business—actually offers for sale.

Suppose you want to buy an electronic copy of the book *Harry Potter and the Deathly Hallows*. You use a search engine to compare the book's price on various websites. You get the results shown in Table 12-1.

Would you automatically buy the book from one of the last two sites listed rather than from Amazon.com or BarnesandNoble.com? We can think about why you might not. Consider what product is being offered for sale. Suppose that Amazon.com is offering *Harry Potter and the Deathly Hallows* delivered to you in several digital formats that are compatible with free ebook reader software, such as Microsoft reader, Mobipocket, and Adobe reader. In addition, Amazon charges your credit card using a secure method that keeps your credit card number safe from computer hackers. As we discussed in

TABLE 12-1

Which Internet Bookseller Would You Buy From?

PRODUCT: *HARRY POTTER AND THE DEATHLY HALLOWS*	
COMPANY	PRICE
Amazon.com	$7.48
BarnesandNoble.com	10.79
PleaseBuyFromMe.com	5.86
KetabySadeqy.com	4.58

Chapter 9, firms differentiate the products they sell in many ways. One way is by providing easier, faster, and more reliable delivery than competitors.

Amazon.com and BarnesandNoble.com have built reputations for fast and reliable service. New Internet booksellers who lack that reputation will have to differentiate their products on the basis of price, as the last two fictitious firms in the table above have done. So, the difference in the prices of products offered on websites does *not* violate the law of one price. A book Amazon.com offers for sale is not the same product as a book PleaseBuyFromMe.com offers for sale.

12.2 LEARNING OBJECTIVE

12.2 | Explain how a firm can increase its profits through price discrimination.

Price Discrimination: Charging Different Prices for the Same Product

We saw at the beginning of this chapter that Dream Park charges different prices for the same product: admission to the theme park. Charging different prices to different customers for the same good or service when the price differences are not due to differences in cost is called **price discrimination**. But doesn't price discrimination contradict the law of one price? Why doesn't the possibility of arbitrage profits lead people to buy at the low price and resell at the high price?

Price discrimination Charging different prices to different customers for the same product when the price differences are not due to differences in cost.

The Requirements for Successful Price Discrimination

A successful strategy of price discrimination has three requirements:

1 A firm must possess market power.

2 Some consumers must have a greater willingness to pay for the product than other consumers, and the firm must be able to know what prices customers are willing to pay.

3 The firm must be able to divide up—or *segment*—the market for the product so that consumers who buy the product at a low price are not able to resell it at a high price. In other words, price discrimination will not work if arbitrage is possible.

Note that a firm selling in a perfectly competitive market cannot practice price discrimination because it can only charge the market price. But because most firms do not sell in perfectly competitive markets, they have market power and can set the price of the good they sell. Many firms may also be able to determine that some customers have a greater willingness to pay for the product than others. However, the third requirement—that markets be segmented so that customers buying at a low price will not be able to resell the product—can be difficult to fulfill. For example, some people really love Big Macs and would be willing to pay US$10 rather than do without one. Other people would not be willing to pay a penny more than US$1 for one. Even if McDonald's could identify differences in the willingness of its customers to pay for Big Macs, it would not be able to charge them different prices. Suppose McDonald's knows that Yamen is willing to pay US$10, whereas Yaser will pay only US$1. If McDonald's tries to charge Yamen US$10, he will just have Yaser buy his Big Mac for him.

Only firms that can keep consumers from reselling a product are able to practice price discrimination. Because buyers cannot resell the product, the law of one price does not hold. For example, movie theaters know that many people are willing to pay more to see a movie at night than during the afternoon. As a result, theaters usually charge higher prices for tickets to night showings than for tickets to afternoon showings. They keep these markets separate by making the tickets to afternoon showings a different color or by having the time printed on them, and by having a ticket taker examine the tickets. That makes it difficult for someone to buy a lower-priced ticket in the afternoon and use the ticket to gain admission to an evening showing.

Figure 12-1 illustrates how the owners of movie theaters use price discrimination to increase their profits. The marginal cost to the movie theater owner from another person attending a showing is very small: a little more wear on a theater seat and a few more pieces of popcorn to be swept from the floor. In previous chapters, we assumed that marginal cost has a U shape. In Figure 12-1, we assume for simplicity that marginal cost is a constant US$0.50, shown as a horizontal line. Panel (a) shows the demand for afternoon showings. In this segment of its market, the theater should maximize profit by selling the number of tickets for which marginal revenue equals marginal cost, or 450 tickets. We know from the demand curve that the theater can sell 450 tickets at a price of US$4.50 per ticket. Panel (b) shows the demand for night showings. Notice that charging US$4.50 per ticket would *not* be profit maximizing in this market. At a price of US$4.50, the theater sells 850 tickets, which is 225 more tickets than the profit-maximizing number of 625. By charging US$4.50 for tickets to afternoon showings and US$6.75 for tickets to night showings, the theater has maximized profits.

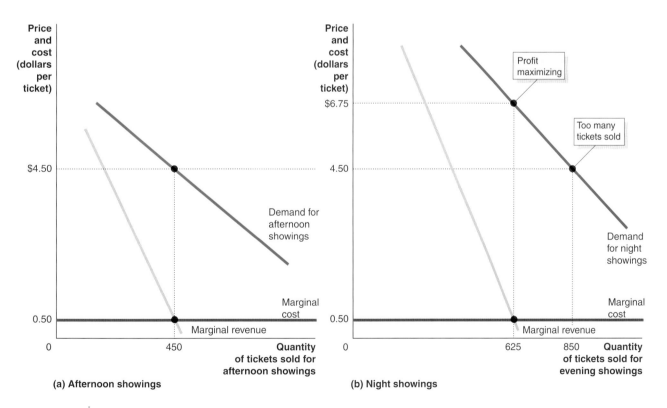

(a) Afternoon showings

(b) Night showings

Figure 12-1 | Price Discrimination by a Movie Theater

Fewer people want to go to the movies in the afternoon than in the evening. In panel (a), the profit-maximizing price for a ticket to an afternoon showing is US$4.50. Charging this same price for night showings would not be profit maximizing, as panel (b) shows. At a price of US$4.50, 850 tickets would be sold to night showings, which is more than the profit-maximizing number of 625 tickets. To maximize profits, the theater should charge US$6.75 for tickets to night showings.

Figure 12-1 also illustrates another important point about price discrimination: when firms can price discriminate, they will charge customers who are less sensitive to price—those whose demand for the product is *less elastic*—a higher price and charge customers who are more sensitive to price—those whose demand is *more elastic*—a lower price. In this case, the demand for tickets to night showings is less elastic, so the price charged is higher, and the demand for tickets to afternoon showings is more elastic, so the price charged is lower.

Solved Problem | **12-2**

How the Jordanian Government Uses Price Discrimination to Increase Revenue

According to an article in the *Global Water Intelligence* magazine, "When some customers in Jordan get their first water bill of 2011, they might not be too pleased to see that it has gone up.... Consumers who use less than 60 liters a day—around 60 percent of homes nationwide—will not see bills rise at all, while the remainder will see an average rise of 9 percent from the start of 2011." Why would the Jordanian government charge different prices for water consumption, depending on the consumption level of water? Draw a graph to illustrate your answer. For simplicity, assume that consumers with a consumption level less than 60 liters per day pay 0.12 Jordanian Dinars (JD) per cubic meter of water while consumers with more than 60 liters per day pay an extra 9 percent per each cubic meter of water they consume.

SOLVING THE PROBLEM:

Step 1: **Review the chapter material.** This problem is about using price discrimination to increase government revenue, so you may want to review the section "Price Discrimination: Charging Different Prices for the Same Product," which begins on page 392.

Step 2: **Explain why charging different prices to different customers, according to the level of water consumption, will increase the government revenue.** It makes sense for the government to charge different prices if low-income customers, those who consume low quantity of water, have a different price elasticity of demand than do high-income customers, the group of people who consume high quantity of water (think about rich people who have a garden and/or a swimming pool). In that case, the Jordanian government will charge the market segment with the, relatively, less elastic demand a higher price and the market segment with the more elastic demand a lower price. Because high-income customers are being charged the higher price, they must have a less elastic demand than low-income customers. (This pricing strategy has also a social reasoning: rich people must pay more than the poor.)

Step 3: **Draw a graph to illustrate your answer.** Your graph should look like the one below. As in the case of movie theaters, you can assume for simplicity that the marginal cost is constant; in the graph we assume that marginal cost is JD0.10, and that the government—as a monopolist—aims at maximizing its profits.

The graph shows that in the low-income customers segment of the market, marginal revenue equals marginal cost at a hypothetical quantity of 400 million cubic meter of water sold. Therefore, the government charges a price of JD0.12 to maximize profits. But if the government also charges JD0.12 in the high-income customers segment of the market, it would sell 700 million cubic meters, which is more than the profit-maximizing quantity. By charging

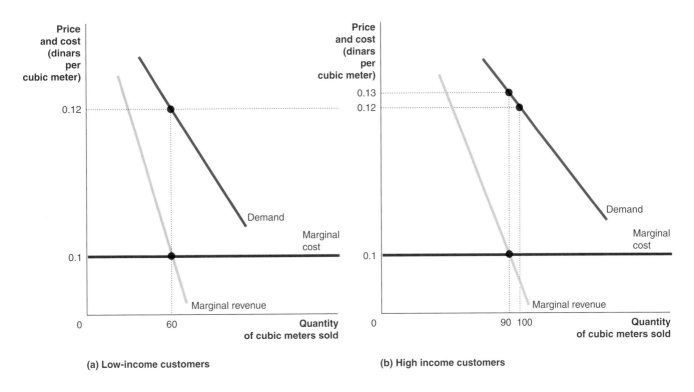

(a) Low-income customers

(b) High income customers

JD0.13 to high-income customers, the government will sell 600 million cubic meters, the profit-maximizing quantity. We have shown that the government maximizes its profits by charging high-income customers a higher price than low-income customers.

Source: "Jordanian ministry celebrates tariff rise," *Global Water Intelligence*, Volume 11, Issue 11, November 2010.

YOUR TURN: For more practice, do problem 2.11 on page 412 at the end of this chapter.

>> End Solved Problem 12-2

Airlines: The Kings of Price Discrimination

Airline seats are a perishable product. Once a plane has taken off from Beirut to Dubai any seat that has not been sold on that particular flight will never be sold. In addition, the marginal cost of flying one additional passenger is low. This situation gives airlines a strong incentive to manage prices so that as many seats as possible are filled on each flight.

Airlines divide their customers into two main categories: business travelers and leisure travelers. Business travelers often have inflexible schedules, can't commit until the last minute to traveling on a particular day, and, most importantly, are not very sensitive to changes in price. The opposite is true for leisure travelers: they are flexible about when they travel, willing to buy their tickets well in advance, and sensitive to changes in price. Based on what we discussed earlier in this chapter, you can see that airlines will maximize profits by charging business travelers higher ticket prices than leisure travelers, but they need to determine who is a business traveler and who is a leisure traveler. Some airlines do this by requiring people who want to buy a ticket at the leisure price to buy 14 days in advance and to stay at their destination over a Saturday night. Anyone unable to meet these requirements must pay a much higher price. Because business travelers often cannot make their plans 14 days in advance of their flight and don't want to stay over a weekend, they end up paying the higher ticket price. The gap between leisure fares and business fares is often very substantial. For example, in November 2010, the price of a leisure-fare ticket between Jeddah, Saudi Arabia, and Alexandria, Egypt, on Saudi Airlines was 2,135 Saudi riyals (SR) (around US$570). The price of a business-fare ticket was SR4320 (around US$1,150).

The airlines go well beyond a single leisure fare and a single business fare in their pricing strategies. Although they ordinarily charge high prices for tickets sold only a few days in advance, they are willing to reduce prices for seats that they expect will not be sold at existing prices. Since the late 1980s, airlines have employed economists and mathematicians to construct computer models of the market for airline tickets. To calculate a suggested price each day for each seat, these models take into account factors that affect the demand for tickets, such as the season of the year, the length of the route, the day of the week, and whether the flight typically attracts primarily business or leisure travelers. This practice of continually adjusting prices to take into account fluctuations in demand is called *yield management.*

Since the late 1990s, Internet sites such as Priceline.com have helped the airlines to implement yield management. On Priceline.com, buyers commit to paying a price of their choosing for a ticket on a particular day and agree that they will fly at any time on that day. This gives airlines the opportunity to fill seats that otherwise would have gone empty, particularly on late night or early morning flights, even though the price may be well below the normal leisure fare. In 2001, several airlines combined to form the Internet site Orbitz, which became another means of filling seats at discount prices. In fact, in the past few years, the chance that you paid the same price for your airline ticket as the person sitting next to you has become quite small.

Making the Connection | How Colleges Use Yield Management

Traditionally, college students admitted to public universities in the Arab countries pay a minimal tuition fee or no tuition fees at all. Furthermore, some students get a monthly financial reward if their GPA exceeds a specific level, as in the GCC countries. But this is not the case in the rest of the world or in private universities in the Arab countries. For example, in North America, students in higher education pay a significant amount of money in tuition fees per credit hour they register in, and few students get financial aid from colleges. This financial aid used to be based only on the incomes of prospective students. In recent years, however, many colleges have started using yield management techniques, first developed for the airlines, to determine the amount of financial aid they offer different students. Colleges typically use a name like 'financial aid engineering' or 'student enrollment management' rather than 'yield management' to describe what they are doing. There is an important difference between the airlines and colleges: colleges are interested not just in maximizing the revenue they receive from student tuition but also in increasing the academic quality of the students who enroll.

The 'price' of a college education equals the tuition charged minus any financial aid received. When colleges use yield management techniques, they increase financial aid offers to students likely to be more price sensitive, and they reduce financial aid offers to students likely to be less price sensitive. The same idea applies to scholarships offered by universities to gifted students. For instance, let us think of two different students: a smart student with a final percentage grade in the high school of 100 percent and a high SAT score, and an average student with a final percentage grade of 80 percent and an average SAT score. Of course the first one is likely to be offered a college scholarship because simply he or she has many alternative colleges to enroll in, while the second one will have few alternatives. Speaking in terms of elasticity, the first one is more price sensitive, that is, it has more elastic demand, compared with the second one. As Stanford economist Caroline Hoxby puts it, "Universities are trying to find the people whose decisions will be changed by these [financial aid] grants." Some of the factors colleges use to judge how sensitive to price students are likely to be include whether they applied for early admission, whether they came for an on-campus interview, their intended major, their home city, and the level of their family's income. Focusing on one of these factors, William F. Elliot, vice president for enrollment management at Carnegie Mellon University (a reputable university located in Pennsylvania, USA) advises, "If finances are a concern, you shouldn't be applying to any place [for] early decision" because you are less likely to receive a large financial aid or for offer.

Many students (and their parents) are critical of colleges that use yield management techniques in allocating financial aid. Colleges usually defend this practice on the grounds that it allows them to recruit the best students at a lower cost in financial aid. The following table shows the tuition fees charged by the German University in Cairo for the academic year 2010/2011. The first two categories of students, A and B, are charged less than category C since their GPA is higher than 3.5.

The German University in Cairo charges different tuition fees for different students according to their GPA.

TUITION FEES AT THE GERMAN UNIVERSITY IN CAIRO (2010/2011)			
STUDY GROUP	CATEGORY A	CATEGORY B	CATEGORY C
Engineering, Biological Sciences, and Management	EGP17,650	EGP21,400	EGP27,925

Sources: Jane J. Kim and Anjali Athavaley, "Colleges Seek to Address Affordability," *Wall Street Journal*, May 3, 2007; Albert B. Crenshaw, "Price Wars on Campus: Colleges Use Discounts to Draw Best Mix of Top Students, Paying Customers," *Washington Post*, October 15, 2002; Steve Stecklow, "Expensive Lesson: Colleges Manipulate Financial-Aid Offers, *Wall Street Journal*, April 1, 1996; The German University in Cairo website: www.guc.edu.eg.

YOUR TURN: Test your understanding by doing related problem 2.13 on page 412 at the end of this chapter.

Perfect Price Discrimination

If a firm knew every consumer's willingness to pay—and could keep consumers who bought a product at a low price from reselling it—the firm could charge every consumer a different price. In this case of *perfect price discrimination*—also known as *first-degree price discrimination*—each consumer would have to pay a price equal to the consumer's willingness to pay and, therefore, would receive no consumer surplus. To see why, remember that consumer surplus is the difference between the highest price a consumer is willing to pay for a product and the price the consumer actually pays. But if the price the consumer pays is the maximum the consumer would be willing to pay, there is no consumer surplus.

Figure 12-2 shows the effects of perfect price discrimination. To simplify the discussion, we assume that the firm is a monopoly and that it has constant marginal and average costs. Panel (a) should be familiar from Chapter 11. It shows the case of a monopolist who cannot price discriminate and, therefore, can charge only a single price for its product. The monopolist maximizes profits by producing the level of output where marginal revenue equals marginal cost. Recall that the economically efficient level of output occurs where price is equal to marginal cost, which is the level of output in a perfectly competitive market. Because the monopolist produces where price is greater than marginal cost, it causes a loss of economic efficiency equal to the area of the deadweight loss triangle in the figure.

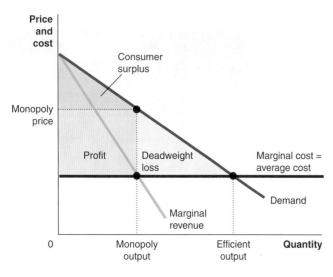

(a) A monopolist who cannot practice price discrimination

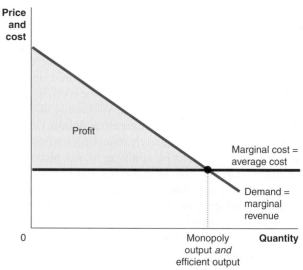

(b) A monopolist practicing perfect price discrimination

Figure 12-2 | Perfect Price Discrimination

Panel (a) shows the case of a monopolist who cannot price discriminate and, therefore, can charge only a single price for its product. The graph, like those in Chapter 11, shows that to maximize profits, the monopolist will produce the level of output where marginal revenue equals marginal cost. The resulting profit is shown by the area of the green rectangle. Given the monopoly price, the amount of consumer surplus in this market is shown by the area of the blue triangle. The economically effi-

cient level of output occurs where price equals marginal cost. Because the monopolist stops production at a level of output where price is above marginal cost, there is a deadweight loss equal to the area of the yellow triangle. In panel (b), the monopolist is able to perfectly price discriminate by charging a different price to each consumer. The result is to convert both the consumer surplus *and* the deadweight loss from panel (a) into profit.

Panel (b) shows the situation of a monopolist practicing perfect price discrimination. Because the firm can now charge each consumer the maximum the consumer is willing to pay, its marginal revenue from selling one more unit is equal to the price of that unit. Therefore, the monopolist's marginal revenue curve becomes equal to its demand curve, and the firm will continue to produce up to the point where price is equal to marginal cost. It may seem like a paradox, but the ability to perfectly price discriminate causes the monopolist to produce the efficient level of output. By doing so, it converts into profits what in panel (a) had been consumer surplus *and* what had been deadweight loss. In both panel (a) and panel (b), the profit shown is also producer surplus.

Even though the result in panel (b) is more economically efficient than the result in panel (a), consumers clearly are worse off because the amount of consumer surplus has been reduced to zero. We probably will never see a case of perfect price discrimination in the real world because firms typically do not know how much each consumer is willing to pay and therefore cannot charge each consumer a different price. Still, this extreme case helps us to see the two key results of price discrimination:

1 Profits increase

2 Consumer surplus decreases.

With perfect price discrimination, economic efficiency is improved. Can we also say that this will be the case if price discrimination is less than perfect? Often, less-than-perfect price discrimination will improve economic efficiency. But under certain circumstances, it may actually reduce economic efficiency, so we can't draw a general conclusion.

Price Discrimination across Time

Firms are sometimes able to engage in price discrimination over time. With this strategy, firms charge a higher price for a product when it is first introduced and a lower price later. Some consumers are *early adopters* who will pay a high price to be among the first to own certain new products. This pattern helps explain why DVD players, digital cameras, and flat-screen plasma televisions all sold for very high prices when they were first introduced. After the demand of the early adopters was satisfied, the companies reduced prices to attract more price-sensitive customers. For example, the price of DVD players dropped by 95 percent within five years of their introduction. Some of the price reductions over time for these products was also due to falling costs as companies took advantage of economies of scale, but some represented price discrimination across time.

Book publishers routinely use price discrimination across time to increase profits. Hardcover editions of novels have much higher prices and are published months before paperback editions. For example, the hardcover edition of *The Yacoubian Building* by Alaa Al-Aswany was published in March 2005 at a price of US$21.33. The paperback edition was published in August 2006 for US$10.07. Although this difference in price might seem to reflect the higher costs of hardcover books, in fact, it does not. The marginal cost of printing another copy of the hardcover is about US$1.50. The marginal cost of printing another copy of the paperback edition is only slightly less, about US$1.25. So, the difference in price between the hardcover and paperback is driven primarily by differences in demand. Alaa Al-Aswany's most devoted fans want to read his next book at the earliest possible moment and are not too sensitive to price. Many casual readers are also interested in Al-Aswany's books but will read something else if the price is too high.

As Figure 12-3 shows, a publisher will maximize profits by segmenting the market—in this case across time—and by charging a higher price to the less elastic market segment and a lower price to the more elastic segment. (This example is similar to our earlier analysis of movie tickets in Figure 12-1 on page 393.) If the publisher had skipped the hardcover and issued only the paperback version at a price of US$10.07 when the

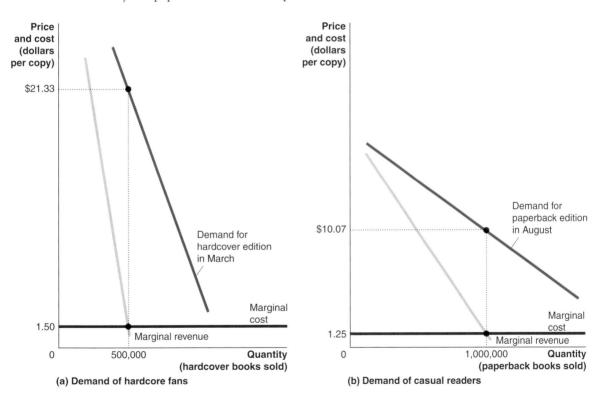

Figure 12-3 | Price Discrimination across Time

Publishers issue most novels in hardcover at high prices to satisfy the demand of the novelists' most devoted fans. Later, they publish paperback editions at much lower prices to capture sales from casual readers. In panel (a), with a marginal cost of US$1.50 per copy for a hardcover, the profit-maximizing level of output is 500,000 copies, which can be sold at a price of US$21.33. In panel (b), the more elastic demand of casual readers and the slightly lower marginal cost result in a profit-maximizing output of 1,000,000 for the paperback edition, which can be sold at a price of US$10.07

book was first published in March 2005, its revenue would have dropped by the number of readers who bought the hardcover multiplied by the difference between the price of the hardcover and the price of the paperback, or 500,000 × (US$21.33 − 10.07) = US$5,630,000.

Can Price Discrimination Be Illegal?

Price discrimination may be illegal if its effect is to reduce competition in an industry. To encourage competition in the Arab markets, some Arab countries established governmental agencies that aim at protecting the markets from monopolistic practices. For example, in 2004 Jordan issued the Competition Law. The Law established the Committee for Competition Matters, which is responsible for presenting opinions and advice on the general plan for competition. Egypt also established The Egyptian Competition Authority (ECA) in 2005 to promote a competitive economic environment, based on the principles of free and fair competition, through the effective implementation of the Law on the Protection of Competition and the Prohibition of Monopolistic Practices. This law was passed by the Egyptian parliament in February 2005 and amended in 2008. In November 2008, Egypt's Ministry of Trade referred the state-owned, and monopolist, Sugar and Integrated Industries Company (SIIC) to the general prosecutor on price-discrimination charges in violation of the anti-monopoly law. The story started in 2006 when the Egyptian-Belgium Industrial Investment Company, a buyer of molasses from the SIIC, filed a complaint to the Trade Ministry claiming it suffered losses due to price-discrimination practices from the SIIC. According to the complaint, SIIC used to sell molasses to the Egyptian-Belgium Industrial Investment Company at a higher price than the price charged to other buyers (competitors). The ECA investigated the compliant and affirmed the price discrimination practice conducted by SIIC which is a clear violation of the aforesaid law. The government-owned company was asked to stop any price-discrimination practice within 30 days of notifying the company with the decision of the ECA.

Making the Connection | **Price Discrimination at Foreign Restaurants in the Gulf Countries**

Price discrimination usually refers to charging different prices to different consumers for the same good or service or charging the same price for goods or services of different quality. Many American and Indian restaurants in Gulf countries have apparently engaged in the first form of price discrimination. For example, if you visit Bahrain, you have might noticed that the famous Australian casual restaurant The Crepe Café is offering a lunch menu that has exactly the same meals as the dinner menu but at much lower prices. The regular dinner main course costs on average 3.2 Bahrain dinars (BHD) (US$1 = 0.377), with an additional BHD1.2 for a salad and a soft drink. But if you go to The Crepe Café at lunchtime, between 11 and 3, you will get the same main course, a salad, and a soft drink for only BHD2.9. The same pricing strategy is applied by Applebees, Steak House, and some Indian restaurants across the Gulf region. Some of these restaurants apply the discounted lunch-pricing strategy on business days only and not at the weekend.

Why would these restaurants offer their products and services to customers who go for lunch at a discounted price? The answer is simple: first, most people are free after 5 p.m., so the probability that they dine out is much higher after 5 p.m. (dinner-time) compared with lunch-time; second, customers who go for dinner are likely to have less elastic demand compared with those who go for lunch. Customers who usually go for dinner are usually the fans of these restaurants, so they would go at dinner-time even though the price is higher than at lunch-time. In contrast, customers who only go for lunch are those who have high elasticity of demand, and the one way to attract their demand is by offering them a discounted price for the same goods and services. As we have seen in this chapter, firms can increase their profits by charging higher prices to consumers with less elastic demand and lower prices to consumers with more elastic demand.

But this strategy works only if firms have a reliable way of separating consumers into groups on the basis of how elastic their demand is. Restaurants can gather information on which group of customers you belong to by either asking you to fill out a card stating your name, age, the time of your visit to the restaurant, and how often you go to that particular restaurant monthly (Steak House usually follows this strategy), or by offering you a reward card which will be stamped or scanned each time you visit the restaurant, as in the case of The Crepe Café. After a few months of observing a customer's pattern of eating, these restaurants have enough information to determine whether the customer's demand is more or less elastic, and are able to apply the suitable price discrimination policy that aims at maximizing the restaurant's profit.

Sources: Sherine El-Madany, "Sugar Company Referred to Prosecution for Price-Discrimination," *The Daily News Egypt*, November 17, 2008; The Egyptian Competition Authority website: www.eca.org.eg/ECA/Default.aspx.

12.3 | Explain how some firms increase their profits through the use of odd pricing, cost-plus pricing, and two-part tariffs.

Other Pricing Strategies

In addition to price discrimination, firms use many different pricing strategies, depending on the nature of their products, the level of competition in their markets, and the characteristics of their customers. In this section, we consider three important strategies: odd pricing, cost-plus pricing, and two-part tariffs.

Odd Pricing: Why Is the Price US$2.99 Instead of US$3.00?

Many firms use what is called *odd pricing*—for example, charging US$4.95 instead of US$5.00, or US$199 instead of US$200. Surveys show that 80 percent to 90 percent of the products sold in supermarkets have prices ending in "9" or "5" rather than "0." Odd pricing has a long history. In the early nineteenth century, most goods in the United States were sold in general stores and did not have fixed prices. Instead, prices were often determined by haggling, much as prices of new cars are often determined today by haggling on dealers' lots. Later in the nineteenth century, when most products began to sell for a fixed price, odd pricing became popular.

Different explanations have been given for the origin of odd pricing. One explanation is that it began because goods imported from Great Britain had a reputation for high quality. When the prices of British goods in British currency—the pound—were translated into U.S. dollars, the result was an odd price. Because customers connected odd prices with high-quality goods, even sellers of domestic goods charged odd prices. Another explanation is that odd pricing began as an attempt to guard against employee theft. An odd price forced an employee to give the customer change, which reduced the likelihood that the employee would simply pocket the customer's money without recording the sale.

Whatever the origins of odd pricing, why do firms still use it today? The most obvious answer is that an odd price, say US$9.99, seems somehow significantly—more than a penny—cheaper than US$10.00. But do consumers really have this illusion? To find out, three market researchers conducted a study. We saw in Chapter 3 that demand curves can be estimated statistically. If consumers have the illusion that US$9.99 is significantly cheaper than US$10.00, they will demand a greater quantity of goods at US$9.99—and other odd prices—than the estimated demand curve predicts. The researchers surveyed consumers about their willingness to purchase six different products—ranging from a block of cheese to an electric blender—at a series of prices. Ten of the prices were either odd cent prices—99 cents or 95 cents—or odd dollar prices—US$95 or US$99. Nine of these 10 odd prices resulted in an odd-price effect, with the quantity demanded being greater than predicted using the estimated demand curve. The study was not conclusive because it relied on surveys rather than on observing actual purchasing behavior and because it used only a small group of products, but it does provide some evidence that using odd prices makes economic sense.

Why Do Firms Use Cost-Plus Pricing?

Many firms use *cost-plus pricing*, which involves adding a percentage *markup* to average cost. With this pricing strategy, the firm first calculates average cost at a particular level of production, usually equal to the firm's expected sales. It then increases average cost by a percentage amount, say 30 percent, to arrive at the price. For example, if average cost is US$100 and the percentage markup is 30 percent, the price will be US$130. In a firm selling multiple products, the markup is intended to cover all costs, including those that the firm cannot assign to any particular product. Most firms have costs that are difficult to assign to one particular product. For example, the work performed by the employees in McDonald's accounting and finance departments applies to all of McDonald's products and can't be assigned directly to Big Macs or Happy Meals.

Making **the** **Connection** | **Cost-Plus Pricing in the Publishing Industry**

Book publishing companies incur substantial costs for editing, designing, marketing, and warehousing books. These costs are difficult to assign directly to any particular book. Most publishers arrive at a price for a book by applying a markup to their production costs, which are usually divided into plant costs and manufacturing costs. Plant costs include typesetting the manuscript and preparing graphics or artwork for printing. Manufacturing costs include the costs of printing, paper, and binding the book.

Consider the following example for the hypothetical new book by Adam Smith, *How to Succeed at Economics without Really Trying*. We will assume that the book is 250 pages long, the publisher expects to sell 5,000 copies, and plant and manufacturing costs are as given in the following table:

PLANT COST		
	Typesetting	$3,500
	Other plant costs	2,000
MANUFACTURING COST		
	Printing	$5,750
	Paper	6,250
	Binding	5,000
TOTAL PRODUCTION COST		
		$22,500

With total production cost of US$22,500 and production of 5,000 books, the per-unit production cost is US$22,500/5,000 = US$4.50. Many publishers multiply the unit production cost number by 7 or 8 to arrive at the retail price they will charge customers in bookstores. In this case, multiplying by 7 results in a price of US$31.50 for the book. The markup seems quite high, but publishers typically sell books to bookstores at a 40 percent discount. Although a customer in a bookstore will pay US$31.50 for the book—or less, of course, if it is purchased from a bookseller that discounts the retail price—the publisher receives only US$18.90. The difference between the US$18.90 received from the bookstore and the US$4.50 production cost equals the cost of editing, marketing, warehousing, and all other costs, including the opportunity cost of the investment in the firm by its owners, plus any economic profit received by the owners.

Source: Beth Luey, *Handbook for Academic Authors*, 4th ed., New York: Cambridge University Press, 2002.

YOUR TURN: Test your understanding by doing related problem 3.8 on page 413 at the end of this chapter.

A difficulty that firms face when using cost-plus pricing should be obvious to you. In this chapter, as in the previous four chapters, we have emphasized that firms maximize profit by producing the quantity where marginal revenue equals marginal cost and charging a price that will cause consumers to buy this quantity. The cost-plus approach doesn't appear to maximize profits unless the cost-plus price turns out to be the same as the price that will cause the quantity sold to be where marginal revenue is equal to marginal cost. Economists have two views of cost-plus pricing. One is that cost-plus pricing is simply a mistake that firms should avoid. The other view is that cost-plus pricing is a good way to come close to the profit-maximizing price when either marginal revenue or marginal cost is difficult to calculate.

Small firms often like cost-plus pricing because it is easy to use. Unfortunately, these firms can fall into the trap of mechanically applying a cost-plus pricing rule, which can result in charging prices that do not maximize profits. The most obvious problems with cost-plus pricing are that it ignores demand and focuses on average cost rather than marginal cost. If the firm's marginal cost is significantly different from its average cost at its current level of production, cost-plus pricing is unlikely to maximize profits.

Despite these problems, cost-plus pricing is used by some large firms, such as General Motors, that clearly have the knowledge and resources to devise a better method of pricing if cost-plus pricing fails to maximize profits. Economists conclude that cost-plus pricing may be the best way to determine the optimal price in two situations:

1 When marginal cost and average cost are roughly equal

2 When the firm has difficulty estimating its demand curve.

In fact, most large firms that use cost-plus pricing do not just mechanically apply a markup to their estimate of average cost. Instead, they adjust the markup to reflect their best estimate of current demand. At General Motors, for example, a pricing policy committee adjusts prices to reflect its views of the current state of competition in the industry and the current state of the economy. If competition is strong in a weak economy, the pricing committee may decide to set price significantly below the cost-plus price—perhaps by offering buyers a rebate.

In general, firms that take demand into account will charge lower markups on products that are more price elastic and higher markups on products that are less elastic. Supermarkets, where cost plus pricing is widely used, have markups in the 5 percent to 10 percent range for products with more elastic demand, such as soft drinks and breakfast cereals, and markups in the 50 percent range for products with less elastic demand, such as fresh fruits and vegetables.

Pricing with Two-Part Tariffs

Some firms can require consumers to pay an initial fee for the right to buy their product and an additional fee for each unit of the product purchased. For example, many golf, tennis, and social clubs require members to buy an annual membership in addition to paying a fee each time they use the tennis court or golf course. The first wholesale store in Egypt, Makro, requires customers to pay a membership fee before shopping at its stores. Mobile phone companies charge a monthly fee and then have a per-minute charge after a certain number of minutes have been used. Economists refer to this situation as a **two-part tariff**.

Two-part tariff A situation in which consumers pay one price (or tariff) for the right to buy as much of a related good as they want at a second price.

Dream Park is in a position to use a two-part tariff by charging consumers for admission to the theme park and also charging them to use the rides in the park. As mentioned at the beginning of this chapter, at one time, the admission price to many theme parks worldwide was low, but people had to purchase tickets to go on the rides. Today, you must pay a high price for admission to most of the large, well-known famous theme parks, but the rides are free once you're in the park. Figure 12-4 helps us understand which of these pricing strategies is more profitable for Dream Park. The numbers in the figure are simplified to make the calculations easier.

Once visitors are inside the park, Dream Park is in the position of a monopolist—no other firm is operating rides in Dream Park. So, we can draw panel (a) in Figure 12-4 to represent the market for rides at Dream Park. This graph looks like the standard monopoly graph from Chapter 11. (Note that the marginal cost of another ride is quite low. We can assume that it is a constant LE2 (and equal to the average cost.) It seems obvious—but it will turn out to be wrong!—that Dream Park should determine the profit-maximizing quantity of ride tickets by setting marginal revenue equal to marginal cost. In this case, that would lead to 20,000 ride tickets sold per day at a price of LE26 per ride. Dream Park's profit from selling *ride tickets* is shown by the area of the light-green rectangle, *B*. It equals the difference between the LE26 price and the average cost of LE2, multiplied by the 20,000 tickets sold, or $(26 - 2) \times 20,000 = LE480,000$. Dream Park also has a second source of profit from selling *admission tickets* to the park. Given the LE26 price for ride tickets, what price would Dream Park be able to charge for admission tickets?

Let's assume the following for simplicity: The only reason people want admission to Dream Park is to go on the rides, all consumers have the same individual demand curve for rides, and Dream Park managers know what this demand curve is. This last assumption allows Dream Park to be able to practice perfect price discrimination. More realistic assumptions would make the outcome of the analysis somewhat different but would not affect the main point of how Dream Park uses a two-part tariff to increase its profits. With these assumptions, we can use the concept of consumer surplus to calculate the maximum total amount consumers would be willing to pay for admission. Remember that consumer surplus is equal to the area below the demand curve and above the price line, shown by the dark-green triangle, *A*, in panel (a). The area represents the benefit to buyers from consuming the product. In this case, consumers would not be willing to pay more for admission to the park than the consumer surplus they receive from the rides. In panel (a) of Figure 12-4, the total consumer surplus when Dream Park charges a price of LE26 per ride is LE240,000. (This number is easy to calculate if you remember that the formula for the area of a triangle is $1/2 \times$ base $\times$ height, or $1/2 \times 20,000 \times LE24$.) Dream can set the price of admission tickets so that the *total* amount spent by buyers would be LE240,000. In other words, Dream Park can set the price of admission to capture the entire consumer surplus from the rides. So, Dream Park's total profit would be the LE240,000 it receives from admission tickets plus the LE480,000 in profit from the rides, or LE720,000 per day.

Is this the most profit Dream Park can earn from selling admission tickets and ride tickets? The answer is "no." The key to seeing why is to notice that *the lower the price Dream Park charges for ride tickets, the higher the price it can charge for admission tickets.* Lower-priced ride tickets increase consumer surplus from the rides and, therefore, increase the willingness of buyers to pay a higher price for admission tickets. In panel

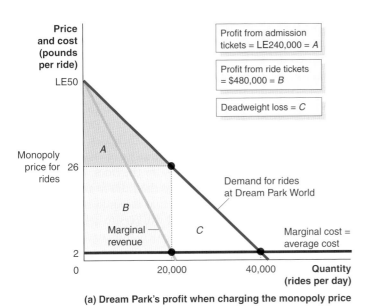

(a) Dream Park's profit when charging the monopoly price

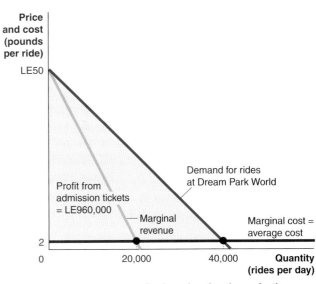

(b) Dream Park's profit when charging the perfectly competitive price

Figure 12-4 | Two-Part Tariff at Dream Park

In panel (a), Dream Park charges the monopoly price of LE26 per ride ticket and sells 20,000 ride tickets. Its profit from *ride tickets* is shown by the area of the light-green rectangle, *B*, LE480,000. If Dream Park is in the position of knowing every consumer's willingness to pay, it can also charge a price for *admission tickets* that would result in the total amount paid for admission tickets being equal to total consumer surplus from the rides. Total consumer surplus from the rides equals the area of the dark-green triangle, *A*, or LE240,000. So, when charging the monopoly price, Dream Park's total profit equals LE480,000 + LE240,000, or LE720,000. In panel (b), Dream Park charges the perfectly competitive price of LE2, where marginal revenue equals marginal cost, and sells 40,000 ride tickets. At the lower ride ticket price, Dream Park can charge a higher price for admission tickets, which will increase its total profits from operating the park to the area of the light-green triangle, or LE960,000.

(b) of Figure 12-4, we assume that Dream Park acts as it would in a perfectly competitive market and charges a price for ride tickets that is equal to marginal cost, or LE2. Charging this price increases consumer surplus—*and* the maximum total amount that Dream Park can charge for admission tickets—from LE240,000 to LE960,000. (Once again, we use the formula for the area of a triangle to calculate the light-green area in panel (b): $1/2 \times 40,000 \times 48 \times$ LE960,000.) Dream Park's profits from the rides will decline to zero because it is now charging a price equal to average cost, *but its total profit from Dream Park will rise from LE720,000 per day to LE960,000.* Table 12-2 summarizes this result.

What is the source of Dream Park's increased profit from charging a price equal to marginal cost? The answer is that Dream Park has converted what was deadweight loss when the monopoly price was charged—the area of triangle *C* in panel (a)—into consumer surplus. It then turns this consumer surplus into profit by increasing the price of admission tickets.

It is important to note the following about the outcome of a firm using an optimal two-part tariff:

1 Because price equals marginal cost at the level of output supplied, the outcome is economically efficient.

2 All of consumer surplus is transformed into profit.

	MONOPOLY PRICE FOR RIDES	COMPETITIVE PRICE FOR RIDES	
PROFITS FROM ADMISSION TICKETS	LE240,000	LE960,000	
PROFITS FROM RIDE TICKETS	480,000	0	
TOTAL PROFIT	720,000	960,000	

TABLE 12-2

Dream Park's Profits per Day from Different Pricing Strategies

Notice that, in effect, Dream Park is practicing perfect price discrimination. As we noted in our discussion of perfect price discrimination on page 397, Dream Park's use of a two-part tariff has increased the amount of the product—in this case, rides at Dream Park—consumers are able to purchase, but has eliminated consumer surplus. Although it may seem paradoxical, consumer surplus was actually higher when consumers were being charged the monopoly price for the rides. The solution to the paradox is that although consumers pay a lower price for the rides when Dream Park employs a two- part tariff, the overall amount they pay to be at Dream Park increases.

Dream Park actually does follow the profit-maximizing strategy of charging a high price for admission to the park and a very low price—zero—for the rides. It seems that Dream Park could increase its profits by raising the price for the rides from zero to the marginal cost of the rides. But the marginal cost is so low that it would not be worth the expense of printing ride tickets and hiring additional workers to sell the tickets and collect them at each ride. Finally, note that because the demand curves of Dream Park's customers are not all the same, and because Dream Park managers do not actually know precisely what these demand curves are, Dream Park is not able to convert all of consumer surplus into profit.

Economics in YOUR Life!

>> **Continued from page 389**

At the beginning of the chapter, we asked you to think about what you pay for a museum ticket and what people in other age groups pay. A museum will try to charge different prices to different consumers based on their willingness to pay. If you have two otherwise identical people, one a student and one not, you might assume that the student has less income, and thus a lower willingness to pay, than the non-student, and the museum would like to charge the student a lower price. The museum employee can ask to see a student ID to ensure that the museum is giving the discount to a student.

But why don't museums, and movie theaters, practice price discrimination at the concession stand? It is likely that a student will also have a lower willingness to pay for a water bottle or popcorn, and the museum employee can check for a student ID at the time of purchase; but unlike the case of the entry ticket, the museum employee would have a hard time preventing the student from giving the water bottle to a non-student once inside the museum. Since it is easier to limit resale in museum admissions, we often see different prices for different groups. Since it is difficult to limit resale of water bottles and other museum concessions, all groups will typically pay the same price.

Conclusion

Firms in perfectly competitive industries must sell their products at the market price. For firms in other industries—which means, of course, the vast majority of firms—pricing is an important part of the strategy used to maximize profits. We have seen in this chapter, for example, that if firms can successfully segment their customers into different groups on the basis of willingness to pay, they can increase their profits by charging different segments different prices.

Read *An Inside Look* on the next page for a discussion of why governments do not charge all electric-energy users the same price.

Electricity Bills: One Price Does Not Fit All Users

ARTICLE 1: DAILY NEWS EGYPT, JULY 1, 2008

Industrial Sector Sees Increases in Electricity Prices

The government is expected to introduce increases to the price of electricity for the industrial sector, according to press reports. Minister Rachid Mohamed Rachid said the decree will be issued on Wednesday, reported *Al-Mal* newspaper, in line with plans to gradually eliminate subsidies granted to energy-intensive industries. The Ministry of Electricity and Energy says the new prices were decided upon by industrial authorities who outlined price increases of energy and natural gas for energy-intensive industries last year.

In August 2007, Rachid said price increases—61 percent for electricity and 110 percent for gas spread over three years—will be applied to Egypt's iron, cement, aluminium, and fertilizer industries. Energy-intensive industries were identified as those consuming over 50 million KWHr or 66 million cubic meters of natural gas annually. The first price increase to electricity and natural gas was applied in October 2007, as part of a three-year plan. However, the government's decision to raise the price of natural gas for energy-intensive industries on May 5 necessitated another rise in electricity prices.

...Responding to industry claims that energy prices are now "unfair" for businessmen, Petroleum Minister Sameh Fahmi announced that the ministry is currently studying an initiative to allow businessmen to buy natural gas directly from private companies operating in Egypt, said the Ministry.

Private companies will set their selling price, and industries are free to accept or refuse them. This initiative is expected to create a free natural gas market.

Source: Reem Nafie, "Industrial Sector Sees Increases in Electricity Prices," *Daily News Egypt*, July 1, 2008.

ARTICLE 2: THE JORDAN TIMES, NOVEMBER 14, 2010

New Fuel Price Surcharge To Appear On Electricity Bills

The Electricity Regulatory Commission (ERC) has added a new surcharge to electricity bills to account for changes in fuel prices, according to an ERC official. The commission said its decision to link electricity tariffs with fuel prices, which went into effect this month, seeks to address the increasing cost of power generation.

According to ERC Chief Commissioner Suleiman Hafez, the fuel surcharge will be listed in citizens' electricity bills as "the difference in fuel prices" and updated every three months according to fluctuations on international oil markets.

...The ERC official said the commission is still working to develop a mechanism to calculate the new surcharge, which is designed to "address instability in oil prices" that affects the cost of electricity generation.

...The decision, which was endorsed by the government on August 11, 2009, increased the annual fees for those who reside in larger municipalities from JD20 to JD24, and from JD10 to JD15 for those who reside in medium-sized municipalities, according to Ahmad Al Ghazou, secretary general of the Ministry of Municipal Affairs. The official added that those who reside in small municipalities such as villages, will pay JD8 annually instead of JD6 per year. He stressed that the fee hikes seek to improve municipalities' garbage collection services.

Source: Omar Obeidat, "New Fuel Price Surcharge to Appear on Electricity Bills," *The Jordan Times*, November 14, 2010.

Key Points in the Articles

These articles highlight the increase in energy prices and the differential treatment of different sectors in Jordan and Egypt, in terms of electricity prices. In particular, both governments divide electricity users into groups or sectors, according to some economic and social criteria, and set a different price for each sector or group. The price elasticity of demand on electricity and the income level play an important rule in determining the price charged to each group.

Analyzing the News

ⓐ The Egyptian and Jordanian governments monopolize the electricity sector. This means that electricity users (industrial, commercial, and residential sectors) have no alternative but to buy electricity from the government. Since there are no substitutes to the government as a provider of energy, the demand for electricity is expected to be inelastic for many electricity users. In addition, according to several studies, the response of the business sector (industrial and commercial) to changes in electricity prices is found to be lower than that of the residential sector. Thus, consumers with more elastic demands tend to pay lower price for electricity.

ⓑ Charging energy-intensive industries (with high demand for electricity) a higher price per kilowatt-hour compared with the price charged to less energy-intensive industries (with low demand) is a clear form of price discrimination. The figure shows the price discrimination policy applied by a natural monopolist, the electricity provider in Egypt or in Jordan. As we discussed in Chapter 11, the average total cost curve (ATC) of a natural monopolist is falling when it crosses the demand curve, at point A, because of the large economies of scale. The marginal cost curve (MC) in a natural monopoly also falls as the production of electricity increases and is located below the ATC curve. If the government regulates the electricity company and imposes the marginal cost pricing ($P = MC$), to make the price close to that in a competitive market, the electricity company will realize losses since the price will fall short of the ATC. The total loss of the company would be equal to the area $AGMP_{L1}$. To balance this loss, many governments apply a price dis-

crimination policy and set a high price for energy-intensive users and a low price for less energy-intensive users. In doing so, the government applies the profit maximization rule ($MR = MC$) on energy-intensive industries and charges them the monopoly price P_I per kilowatt-hour. The total kilowatt-hours sold to energy-intensive industries would be Q_I. The less energy-intensive industries will be charged a price that is equal to the average cost ($P = ATC$), P_L, which is significantly lower than the profit maximizing price and allows industries with a relatively low demand on electricity to consume the quantity ($Q_L - Q_I$) kilowatt-hours. This pricing method is called the average cost pricing.

The Jordanian government is also applying a price discrimination policy by classifying electricity users in the residential sector into three groups according to the geographic location. This classification reflects differences in demand, price elasticity of demand, and income level in each group of users. For example, those who live in large municipalities are expected to have high demand for electricity, low price elasticity of demand, and a high level of income, while those who live in villages are expected to have low demand for electricity, relatively higher elasticity of demand, and a low income level. Since many Arab governments subsidize electricity for specific groups of users, such as people living in villages in Jordan, those governments can benefit from applying the price

discrimination method to fund the electricity subsidy. Assuming that the Jordanian government is subsidizing electricity for people who live in villages, it is expected that it applies the marginal cost pricing and charges them a price of P_{L1} per kilowatt-hour (equivalent to JD8 per year) and sells Q_{L1} kilowatt-hours. As we mentioned in the previous point, this pricing method will generate losses, the area $AGMP_{L1}$, since the price does not cover the ATC at Q_{L1} level of output. The Jordanian government covers this loss (subsidy) by charging people who live in large municipalities the profit maximizing price of P_I per kilowatt-hour (equivalent to JD24 per year) which exceeds the ATC at the quantity Q_I. This pricing method generates a total profit equals to the area $P_I JKH$ which helps the government fund the subsidy given to people who live in villages.

Thinking Critically

1. If increasing energy prices to some sectors increases the government's revenue, why don't governments just increase energy prices for all sectors?

2. If, in general, customers with less elastic demands will pay more for a product when firms can price discriminate, would you expect to see a newly married couple or a family of five with three children of school age pay a higher energy price in your neighborhood? Why?

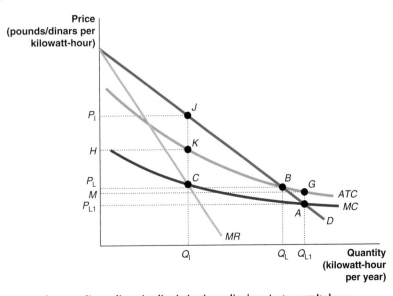

A natural monopolist applies price discrimination policy in order to cover its losses.

Key Terms

Price discrimination, p. 392   Transactions costs, p. 390   Two-part tariff, p. 404

Summary

12.1 LEARNING OBJECTIVE

Define the law of one price and explain the role of arbitrage, **pages 390–392.**

Pricing Strategy, the Law of One Price, and Arbitrage

According to the *law of one price*, identical products should sell for the same price everywhere. If a product sells for different prices, it will be possible to make a profit through *arbitrage*: buying a product at a low price and reselling it at a high price. The law of one price will hold as long as arbitrage is possible. Arbitrage is sometimes blocked by high **transactions costs**, which are the costs in time and other resources incurred to carry out an exchange, or because the product cannot be resold. Another apparent exception to the law of one price occurs when companies offset the higher price they charge for a product by providing superior or more reliable service to customers.

12.2 LEARNING OBJECTIVE

Explain how a firm can increase its profits through price discrimination, **pages 392–401.**

Price Discrimination: Charging Different Prices for the Same Product

Price discrimination occurs if a firm charges different prices for the same product when the price differences are not due to differences in cost. Three requirements must be met for a firm to successfully price discriminate: (1) A firm must possess market power. (2) Some consumers must have a greater willingness to pay for the product than other consumers, and firms must be able to know what customers are willing to pay. (3) Firms must be able to divide up—or segment—the market for the product so that consumers who buy the product at a low price cannot resell it a high price. In the case of *perfect price discrimination*, each consumer pays a price equal to the consumer's willingness to pay.

12.3 LEARNING OBJECTIVE

Explain how some firms increase their profits through the use of odd pricing, cost-plus pricing, and two-part tariffs, **pages 401–407.**

Other Pricing Strategies

In addition to price discrimination, firms also use odd pricing, cost-plus pricing, and two-part tariffs as pricing strategies. Firms use *odd pricing*—for example, charging US$1.99 rather than US$2.00—because consumers tend to buy more at odd prices than would be predicted from estimated demand curves. With *cost-plus pricing*, firms set the price for a product by adding a percentage markup to average cost. Cost-plus pricing may be a good way to come close to the profit-maximizing price when marginal revenue or marginal cost is difficult to measure. Some firms can require consumers to pay an initial fee for the right to buy their product and an additional fee for each unit of the product purchased. Economists refer to this situation as a **two-part tariff**. Makro wholesale store, mobile phone companies, and many golf and tennis clubs use two-part tariffs in pricing their products.

Review, Problems and Applications

 Visit www.pearsoned.co.uk/awe/hubbard to complete these exercises online and get instant feedback.

12.1 LEARNING OBJECTIVE   Define the law of one price and explain the role of arbitrage, **pages 390–392.**

Review Questions

1.1 What is the law of one price? What is arbitrage?

1.2 Does a product always have to sell for the same price everywhere? Briefly explain.

Problems and Applications

1.3 The following are two real-life examples of people benefiting from price differences between neighboring countries:

> First, until the late 1990s, retailers from Alexandria, in Egypt, have played a game of retail arbitrage, traveling to Benghazi, in Libya—where prices of electronics are cheap because of the low customs duties in Libya—to buy different kinds of electronic devices in order to sell them to households in Alexandria and make a profit.
>
> Second, many shoppers from Bahrain and Qatar go almost every weekend to the eastern province of Saudi Arabia to take advantage of retail arbitrage and buy traditional food, which is cheaper in Saudi's markets. Even accounting for tolls, gas, and time, shoppers can save money by visiting Dammam, Al-Khobar, and Al-Ehsaa markets.

Do these two real life examples use the word *arbitrage* correctly? Briefly explain.

1.4 The following table contains the prices charged by four different stores for a DVD of the movie *Asal Eswed of Ahmed Helmy*.

Extra	$22.19
Carrefour	$15.87
Rotana	$17.21
Souq	$15.99

Briefly explain whether the information in this table contradicts the law of one price.

1.5 **(Related to *Solved Problem 12-1* on page 391)** Al-Ehsaa city in Saudi Arabia has many palm trees, and the price of dates there is low. Dammam city has few palm trees, and the price of dates there is high. Hassan buys low-priced Al-Ehsaa dates and ships them to Dammam, where he resells them at a high price. Is Hassan exploiting Dammam consumers by doing this? Is he likely to earn economic profits in the long run? Briefly explain.

12.2 LEARNING OBJECTIVE   Explain how a firm can increase its profits through price discrimination,
pages 392–401.

Review Questions

2.1 What is price discrimination? Under what circumstances can a firm successfully practice price discrimination?

2.2 During a particular week, Nas airlines, a Saudi private airline, charged US$200 for a round-trip ticket on a flight from Riyadh to Jeddah, provided that the ticket was purchased at least 10 days in advance and the ticket buyer was willing to stay over a Saturday night. If the buyer did not meet these conditions, the price for the ticket was US$500. Why does Nas airlines use this pricing strategy?

2.3 What is yield management? Give an example of a firm using yield management to increase profits.

2.4 What is perfect price discrimination? Is it likely to ever occur? Explain. Is perfect price discrimination economically efficient? Explain.

2.5 Is it possible to price discriminate across time? Briefly explain.

Problems and Applications

2.6 Ponderosa restaurant in Bahrain usually offers a special price for lunch during business days and not at weekends. Why would it be profitable for Ponderosa to charge a discounted price for lunch on business days? Wouldn't the restaurant's revenues be higher if it charged the regular—higher—price all week long? Briefly explain.

2.7 An article on how prices in Mecca, Saudi Arabia, rise during *Hajj* contained the following:

> Demand is expected to be higher this Hajj pilgrimage season, raising Mecca's hotel rooms off-season prices for almost 10 times this November, the UAE-based *The National* reports. Last year Mecca received lesser numbers of pilgrims as fears of the swine flu overwhelmed the world, but this year's soaring hotel prices suggest hoteliers are expecting visitors in record droves. Hotels like Moevenpick and Residence Hajar Tower Makkah are charging approximately between US$12,000 and US$17,332 for 13 nights during the Hajj season, translating into US$923 to US$1333 per night. In September, a non-happening month, a hotel room can cost as little as US$1715 for 13 nights or US$131 per night.

Is this an example of price discrimination? Briefly explain.

Source: "Hotel Prices up Tenfold This Hajj Season," *Al-Arabiya*, August 24, 2010.

2.8 Political columnist Michael Kinsley writes, "The infuriating [airline] rules about Saturday night stayovers and so on are a crude alternative to administering truth serum and asking, 'So how much are you really willing to pay?'" Would a truth serum—or some other way of knowing how much people would be willing to pay for an airline ticket—really be all the airlines need to price discriminate? Briefly explain.

Source: Michael Kinsley, "Consuming Gets More Complicated," *Slate*, November 21, 2001.

2.9 In a column in the *Wall Street Journal*, Walter Mossberg offered the following opinion:

> There's a sucker in the software business today, and if you're in an average family with a couple of PCs, that sucker is you…. Families constitute the only significant customer group not getting a discount on [Microsoft] Office when upgrading multiple PCs. Big corporations, organizations and government agencies get a discount, called a "site license." College students get a discount. Small and medium-size businesses get a discount. But not families.

Why might Microsoft charge families a higher price for Office than it charges the other groups Mossberg mentions?

Source: Walter Mossberg, "Microsoft Should Offer Families a Deal with Its Office Program," *Wall Street Journal*, July 18, 2002.

2.10 According to an article in *The Economist*, "The PS3 [PlayStation 3] is available in two configurations, costing US$500 and US$600 in America, and ¥50,000 (US$425) and ¥60,000 (US$510) in Japan." Based on this information, does Sony consider the demand of US consumers for the PS3 to be more elastic or less elastic than the demand of Japanese consumers? Briefly explain.

Source: "Playing a Long Game," *The Economist*, November 16, 2006.

2.11 (Related to *Solved Problem 12-2* on page 394) Use the graphs here to answer the following questions.
   a. If the firm wants to maximize profits, what price will it charge in Market 1, and what quantity will it sell?

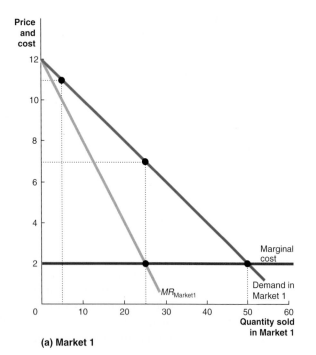

(a) Market 1

b. If the firm wants to maximize profits, what price will it charge in Market 2, and what quantity will it sell?

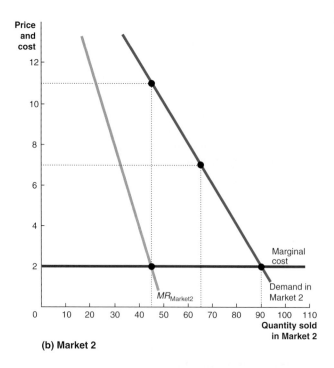

(b) Market 2

2.12 When a firm offers a rebate on a product, the buyer normally has to fill out a form and mail it in to receive a rebate check in the mail. A financial columnist argues:

> When a manufacturer offers a rebate, you needn't be too suspicious. The manufacturer wants to lower the price temporarily (to move an old product or combat a competitor's new low price), but doesn't have faith that the retailer will pass on the savings.

But suppose that a manufacturer wants to engage in price discrimination. Would offering rebates be a way of doing this? Briefly explain.

Source: Carol Vinzant, "The Great Rebate Scam," *Slate*, June 10, 2003.

2.13 (Related to the *Making the Connection* on page 396) Assume that the marginal cost of admitting one more student is constant for every university. Also assume that the demand for places in the freshmen class is downward sloping at every university. Now suppose that the public becomes upset that universities charge different prices to different students. Responding to these concerns, the government requires universities to charge the same price to each student. Who would gain and who would lose?

2.14 (Related to the *Chapter Opener* on page 388) Why does Dream Park charge a lower admission price for students than for adults? Why does it admit children under 3 for free? Why does it charge residents of 6th of October city a lower price than residents of other cities?

2.15 Eric Orkin, the president of Opus 2 Revenue Technologies, Inc., which sells yield management systems to hotels, argues, "The price-sensitive person gets what he wants as long as he's willing to have some flexibility." Why would a yield management system for hotels result in lower prices for "price-sensitive" customers than the alternative of charging one price for all customers? Why would a price-sensitive person need to be "flexible" to receive a lower price?

Source: Neal Templin, "Property Report: Your Room Costs US$250… No! US$200 … No …," *Wall Street Journal*, May 5, 1999.

2.16 Draw a graph that shows producer surplus, consumer surplus, and deadweight loss (if any) in a market where the seller practices perfect price discrimination. Profit-maximizing firms select an output at which marginal cost equals marginal revenue. Where is the marginal revenue curve in this graph?

12.3 LEARNING OBJECTIVE   Explain how some firms increase their profits through the use of odd pricing, cost-plus pricing, and two-part tariffs, **pages 401–407.**

Review Questions

3.1 What is odd pricing?

3.2 What is cost-plus pricing? Is using cost-plus pricing consistent with a firm maximizing profits?

3.3 Give an example of a firm using a two-part tariff as part of its pricing strategy.

3.4 Why do you think Dream Park chose to charge for admission to the park without charging for the rides, rather than charging for admission and charging for the rides?

3.5 One leading explanation for odd pricing is that it allows firms to trick buyers into the illusion that they're paying less than they really are. If this is true, in what types of markets and among what groups of consumers would you be mostly likely to find odd pricing? Should the government ban this practice and force companies to round up their prices to the nearest dollar?

3.6 Discuss the factors that would lead a typical firm to charge a price higher than the cost-plus price.

Problems and Applications

3.7 Consider the following hypothetical situation: Company X managers are calculating how much it cost to make and deliver refrigerators and then add a flat percentage of 30% on top of the cost.

Is it likely that this system of pricing maximized the company's profits? Briefly explain.

3.8 **(Related to the *Making the Connection* on page 402)** Would you expect a publishing company to use a strict cost-plus pricing system for all of its books? How might you find some indication whether a publishing company actually was using cost-pull pricing for all of its books?

3.9 Suppose that some professional sports teams charge fans a one-time lump sum for a "personal seat license." The personal seat license allows a fan the right to buy season tickets each year. No one without a personal seat license can buy season tickets. After the original purchase from the team, the personal seat licenses usually can be bought and sold by fans— whoever owns the seat license in a given year can buy season tickets—but the team does not earn any additional revenue from this buying and selling. Suppose a new sports stadium has been built, and the team is trying to decide on the price to charge for season tickets.

a. Will the team make more profit from the combination of selling personal seat licenses and season tickets if it keeps the prices of the season tickets low or if it charges the monopoly price? Briefly explain.

b. After the first year, is the team's strategy for pricing season tickets likely to change?

c. Will it make a difference in the team's pricing strategy for season tickets if all the personal seat licenses are sold in the first year?

Special Topics: The Need for the Government and International Trade

Externalities, Environmental Policy, and Public Goods

Economic Policy and the Environment

You must have heard the words 'global warming' or 'the greenhouse effect' before. Environmentalists believe that the world is on the brink of an environmental crisis as a result of fast-growing levels of pollution. Pollution is a part of economic life. Consumers create air pollution by burning gasoline to power their cars and natural gas to heat their homes. Firms create air pollution when they produce electricity, pesticides, or plastics, among other products. Utilities produce sulfur dioxide when they burn coal to generate electricity. Sulfur dioxide contributes to acid rain, which can damage trees, crops, and buildings. The burning of fossil fuels generates carbon dioxide and other greenhouse gases that can increase global warming.

In the Arab world, pollution is a pressing issue. The Arab Human Development Report, published by the UN in 2009, identifies the major environmental hazards facing the Arab world. It considers increasing population and demographic pressures major causes of many threats to the environment, such as water shortage and climate change. With the fast-growing population, water,

air, and soil pollution are increasingly becoming a concern to policymakers in the Arab region. Water pollution in Egypt, for example, is primarily attributed to industrial wastewater and the increased use of chemical fertilizers and pesticides. The report mentions that the ratio of pollution per worker in the Arab world is relatively higher than that in industrialized countries.

How should government policy deal with the problem of pollution? Can economic analysis help in formulating more efficient pollution policies? In the past, many countries frequently employed policies that ordered firms to use particular methods to reduce pollution. But many economists are critical of this approach—known as *command and control*—because some companies are able to reduce their emissions much more inexpensively if they are allowed to choose the method. To deal with reducing sulfur dioxide emissions in the most efficient way, economists recommended a *market-based approach* called *tradable emissions allowances*.

This mechanism has been adopted in developed economies, but not yet in the Arab world. Under this system, the government gives utility companies allowances to produce a target amount of sulfur dioxide emissions. Utilities are free to buy and sell allowances,

although they must end up with allowances equal to the amount of sulfur dioxide they wish to emit: one allowance for every ton of sulfur dioxide emitted. Utilities that initially lack sufficient allowances either must reduce the amount of sulfur dioxide they emit or buy allowances from other utilities that are polluting less.

For example, in an electric utility that already burns low-sulfur coal, reducing emissions of sulfur dioxide even further would be expensive. Many other electric utilities, however, burn high-sulfur coal, and their emissions can be reduced greatly by installing anti-pollution devices known as 'scrubbers.' As a result of installing these devises, these utilities can not only drastically reduce their own emissions but also have enough allowances left to sell to other low coal-burning utilities, for whom it is cheaper to buy the allowances than to install the device. According to company managers in charge of environmental compliance, reducing emissions of sulfur dioxide would cost a low coal-burning utility about US$300 per ton. But a relatively more polluting utility could reduce emissions for only about US$100 per ton. These utilities were willing to sell allowances to the former for US$200 each. As the managers put it, "They would make US$100, and the low-coal-burning utility would save US$100." Not only would the utilities gain, but sulfur dioxide emissions would be reduced at a lower total cost to the economy.

Some economists have advocated a similar program of tradable permits to reduce emissions of carbon dioxide from burning fossil fuels. Other economists have endorsed a carbon tax, which is a tax on energy sources that emit carbon dioxide. With a government carbon tax, the generation of power by burning gasoline, natural gas, coal, or other carbon-based fuels would be taxed. As we will see in this chapter, economic analysis can play a significant role in shaping environmental policies.

AN INSIDE LOOK AT POLICY on **page 444** discusses how the Arab oil-producing nations have a different perspective on carbon taxes.

Sources: Jeffrey Ball, "New Consensus: In Climate Controversy, Industry Cedes Ground," *Wall Street Journal*, January 23, 2007, p. A1; Daniel Altman, "Just How Far Can Trading of Emissions Be Extended?" *New York Times*, May 31, 2002; and Arab Human Development Report, 2009, Chapter 3, UN: New York.

LEARNING Objectives

After studying this chapter, you should be able to:

13.1 Identify examples of positive and negative **externalities** and use graphs to show how externalities affect **economic efficiency**, page 418.

13.2 Discuss the **Coase theorem** and explain how private bargaining can lead to economic efficiency in a market with an externality, page 423.

13.3 Analyze **government policies** to achieve economic efficiency in a market with an externality, page 427.

13.4 Explain how goods can be categorized on the basis of whether they are **rival or excludable**, and use graphs to illustrate the efficient quantities of **public goods** and **common resources**, page 432.

Economics in YOUR Life!

What's the 'Best' Level of Pollution?

Carbon taxes and carbon trading are alternative approaches for achieving the goal of reducing carbon dioxide emissions. But how do we know the 'best' level of carbon emissions? If carbon dioxide emissions hurt the environment, should the government take action to eliminate them completely? As you read the chapter, see if you can answer these questions. You can check your answers against those we provide at the end of the chapter. >> **Continued on page 442**

Externality A benefit or cost that affects someone who is not directly involved in the production or consumption of a good or service.

Pollution is just one example of an *externality*. An **externality** is a benefit or cost that affects someone who is not directly involved in the production or consumption of a good or service. In the case of air pollution, there is a *negative externality* because, for example, people with asthma may bear a cost even though they were not involved in the buying or selling of the electricity that caused the pollution. *Positive externalities* are also possible. For instance, medical research can provide a positive externality because people who are not directly involved in producing it or paying for it can benefit. A competitive market usually does a good job of producing the economically efficient amount of a good or service. This may not be true, though, if there is an externality in the market. When there is a negative externality, the market may produce a quantity of the good that is greater than the efficient amount. When there is a positive externality, the market may produce a quantity that is less than the efficient amount. In Chapter 4, we saw that government interventions in the economy—such as price floors on agricultural products or price ceilings on rents—can reduce economic efficiency. But when there are externalities, government intervention may actually increase economic efficiency and enhance the well-being of society. The way in which government intervenes is important, however. As the example of the program to reduce acid rain by reducing sulfur dioxide emissions shows, economists can help policymakers ensure that government programs are as efficient as possible.

In this chapter, we explore how best to deal with the problem of pollution and other externalities. We also look at *public goods*, which are goods that may not be produced at all unless the government produces them.

13.1 LEARNING OBJECTIVE

13.1 | Identify examples of positive and negative externalities and use graphs to show how externalities affect economic efficiency.

Externalities and Economic Efficiency

When you consume a Big Mac, only you benefit, but when you consume a college education, other people also benefit. College-educated people are less likely to commit crimes and, by being better-informed voters, more likely to contribute to better government policies. So, although you capture most of the benefits of your college education, you do not capture all of them.

When you buy a Big Mac, the price you pay covers all McDonald's costs of producing the Big Mac. When you buy electricity from a utility that burns coal and generates acid rain, the price you pay for the electricity does not cover the cost of the damage caused by the acid rain.

So, there is a *positive externality* in the production of college educations because people who do not pay for college educations will nonetheless benefit from them. There is a *negative externality* in the generation of electricity because, for example, people with homes on a lake from which fish and wildlife have disappeared because of acid rain have incurred a cost, even though they might not have bought their electricity from the polluting utility.

The Effect of Externalities

Private cost The cost borne by the producer of a good or service.

Social cost The total cost of producing a good or service, including both the private cost and any external cost.

Externalities interfere with the *economic efficiency* of a market equilibrium. We saw in Chapter 4 that a competitive market achieves economic efficiency by maximizing the sum of consumer surplus and producer surplus. *But that result holds only if there are no externalities in production or consumption.* An externality causes a difference between the *private cost* of production and the *social cost*, or the *private benefit* from consumption and the *social benefit*. The **private cost** is the cost borne by the producer of a good or service. The **social cost** is the private cost plus any external cost resulting from production, such as the cost of pollution. Unless there is an externality, the private cost and the social cost are equal. The **private benefit** is the benefit received by the consumer of a good or service. The **social benefit** is the private benefit plus any external benefit, such as the benefit to others resulting from your college education. Unless there is an externality, the private benefit and the social benefit are equal.

How a Negative Externality in Production Reduces Economic Efficiency

Consider first how a negative externality in production affects economic efficiency. In Chapters 3 and 4, we assumed that the producer of a good or service must bear all the costs of production. We now know that this observation is not always true. In producing electricity, some private costs are borne by the utility, but some external costs of acid rain are borne by farmers, fishermen, and the general public. The social cost of producing electricity is the sum of the private cost plus the external cost. Figure 13-1 shows the effect on the market for electricity of a negative externality in production.

S_1 is the market supply curve and represents only the private costs that utilities have to bear in generating electricity. As we saw in Chapter 4, firms will supply an additional unit of a good or service only if they receive a price equal to the additional cost of producing that unit, so a supply curve represents the *marginal cost* of producing a good or service. If utilities also had to bear the cost of acid rain, the supply curve would be S_2, which represents the true marginal social cost of generating electricity. The equilibrium with a price P_2 and quantity Q_2 is efficient. The equilibrium with a price P_1 and quantity Q_1 is not efficient. To see why, remember from Chapter 4 that an equilibrium is economically efficient if economic surplus—which is the sum of consumer surplus plus producer surplus—is at a maximum. When economic surplus is at a maximum, the net benefit to society from the production of the good or service is at a maximum. With an equilibrium quantity of Q_2, economic surplus is at a maximum, so this equilibrium is efficient. But with an equilibrium quantity of Q_1, economic surplus is reduced by the deadweight loss, shown in Figure 13-1 by the yellow triangle, and the equilibrium is not efficient. The deadweight loss occurs because the supply curve is above the demand curve for the production of the units of electricity between Q_2 and Q_1. That is, the additional cost—including the external cost—of producing these units is greater than the marginal benefit to consumers, as represented by the demand curve. In other words, because of the cost of the acid rain, economic efficiency would be improved if less electricity were produced.

We can conclude the following: *When there is a negative externality in producing a good or service, too much of the good or service will be produced at market equilibrium.*

Private benefit The benefit received by the consumer of a good or service.

Social benefit The total benefit from consuming a good or service, including both the private benefit and any external benefit.

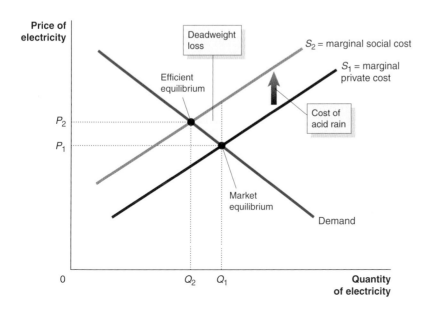

Figure 13-1

The Effect of Pollution on Economic Efficiency

Because utilities do not bear the cost of acid rain, they produce electricity beyond the economically efficient level. Supply curve S_1 represents just the marginal private cost that the utility has to pay. Supply curve S_2 represents the marginal social cost, which includes the costs to those affected by acid rain. The figure shows that if the supply curve were S_2, rather than S_1, market equilibrium would occur at a price of P_2 and a quantity of Q_2, the economically efficient level of output. But when the supply curve is S_1, the market equilibrium occurs at a price of P_1 and a quantity of Q_1 where there is a deadweight loss equal to the area of the yellow triangle. Because of the deadweight loss, this equilibrium is not efficient.

Making the Connection | The Importance of Adopting Industrial Energy-Efficiency Strategies in the Arab World

One of the negative externalities of industry is their negative impact on the environment due to so-called 'greenhouse gas emissions' (GHG). GHG emissions from industry include those resulting from burning fossil fuels, indirect emissions resulting from the use of electricity, and emissions related to certain industrial processes such as aluminum, steel, cement, and the food industry.

The industrial sector in many Arab economies, especially those richly endowed with oil and gas resources, is highly dependent on energy consumption. Energy-intensive industries, such as oil refining, metal extraction, chemicals, and petrochemicals, have been fast expanding in oil-producing countries since the 1970s. In 2006, almost half the Arab GDP was generated by these industries. In addition, the Gulf Corporation Council (GCC) region is home to many huge-capacity coal-dependent desalination plants. As a consequence, the energy and carbon intensities (i.e., energy units per a unit of output) of the *GCC countries* are ranked very high by international standards. For instance, in 2005, the energy intensity of *Bahrain* was more than double the world average and about seven times the Japanese intensity.

Greenhouse gas emissions from burning fossil fuels and using electricity in industry are negative externalities since they damage the environment.

Several technologies have been developed and used worldwide to improve industrial energy efficiency. Many Arab countries have adopted successful programs for improving industrial energy efficiency. In *Egypt*, for example, an energy-efficiency strategy has been adopted and promoted to conserve energy in the major energy-consuming sectors, including the industrial sector which consumes almost 36 percent of total electricity supplies. Industrial energy-efficiency measures included energy audits which showed an average potential saving of about 25 percent, mostly in the industrial sector. In the *UAE*, carbon emissions associated with electricity consumption in the industrial sector account for about 57 percent of all energy-related greenhouse gas emissions. Industrial energy consumption is expected to be reduced by 25 percent or more through a combination of energy-saving measures for industrial motors. These include proper motor sizing and use of high efficiency motors. The energy bill in *Jordan* is nearly 13 percent of GDP and 45 percent of exports. This shows the urgent need to devise and implement an energy-efficiency strategy. *Lebanon* is not an energy-producing country, and imported fossil fuel in Lebanon accounts for 97 percent of the country's energy bill, and about 7.5 percent of GDP. Energy consumption in Lebanon was responsible for approximately 15.3 million tons of carbon dioxide emissions in 2002. The Lebanese transport sector is the major energy consumer. Lebanon, with support from UNDP/GEF, started a project to reduce GHG emissions through the creation of a multi-purpose Lebanese Centre for Energy Conservation (LCEC). The LCEC provides energy-efficiency services to both public and private sectors, such as technical support, financial incentives, information dissemination, awareness programs, and policy design intended, for example, to improve the efficiency of the cement industry— the single largest source of Lebanese CO_2 emissions.

Sources: Ibrahim Abdel Gelil, "GHG Emissions: Mitigation Efforts in the Arab Countries," in *Arab Environment: Climate Change*, 2009 Report of the Arab Foundation for Environment and Development (AFED), Ch. 2, pp.14–30; and "Making Progress on Environmental Sustainability," 2006, UNDP, UN.

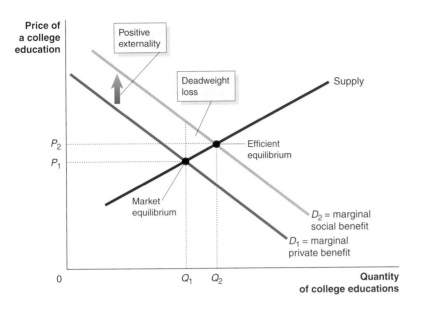

Figure 13-2

The Effect of a Positive Externality on Efficiency

People who do not consume college educations can still benefit from them. As a result, the marginal social benefit from a college education is greater than the marginal private benefit seen by college students. Because only the marginal private benefit is represented in the market demand curve D_1, the quantity of college educations produced, Q_1, is too low. If the market demand curve were D_2 instead of D_1, the level of college educations produced would be Q_2, which is the efficient level. At the market equilibrium of Q_1, there is a deadweight loss equal to the area of the yellow triangle.

How a Positive Externality in Consumption Reduces Economic Efficiency

We have seen that a negative externality interferes with achieving economic efficiency. The same holds true for a positive externality. In Chapters 3 and 4, we assumed that the demand curve represents all the benefits that come from consuming a good. But we have seen that a college education generates benefits that are not captured by the student receiving the education and so is not represented in the market demand curve for college education. Figure 13-2 shows the effect of a positive externality in consumption on the market for a college education.

If students receiving a college education could capture all its benefits, the demand curve would be D_2, which represents the marginal social benefits. The actual demand curve is D_1, however, which represents only the marginal private benefits received by students. The efficient equilibrium would come at price P_2 and quantity Q_2. At this equilibrium, economic surplus is maximized. The market equilibrium, at price P_1 and quantity Q_1, will not be efficient because the demand curve is above the supply curve for production of the units between Q_1 and Q_2. That is, the marginal benefit—including the external benefit—for producing these units is greater than the marginal cost. As a result, there is a deadweight loss equal to the area of the yellow triangle. Because of the positive externality, economic efficiency would be improved if more college educations were produced. We can conclude the following: *When there is a positive externality in consuming a good or service, too little of the good or service will be produced at market equilibrium.*

Making *the* Connection | Masdar: Building a Leading-Edge Clean Energy Technology in Abu Dhabi

Have you ever asked yourself why the development of clean energy is so important? Why is the government of Abu Dhabi investing heavily in resources to lead in the development of clean renewable energy? The short answer is that consuming renewable clean energy such as solar energy, instead of oil and coal, protects the environment and contributes to the reduction of greenhouse gas emissions.

Owing to a history of energy subsidies and price controls, the countries of the GCC make up one of the world's most

Construction started in the carbon neutral, 'green' technology city of Masdar.

(Continued)

energy-intensive regions. They have some of the world's worst environmental records in terms of carbon footprint per capita. In spite of a poor environmental record, however, the UAE has its eyes on a future beyond its vast oil and gas resources. The country seeks to double its electricity output through a combination of gas, nuclear, and renewable energy sources in the next 10 years. The UAE has pledged to obtain 7 percent of its energy needs from renewable sources by 2020, exploiting its plentiful endowment of sunshine for the generation of solar power.

Abu Dhabi, the emirate that controls 80 percent of the GCC countries' oil resources, is committed to becoming a global leader in renewable energy technology. Recognizing that the private sector would be reluctant to invest in large-scale research and development in renewable energy, the government took the upper hand and is devoting large public investments, using its extra petrodollars, to turning around the countries' environmental record. In 2006, Abu Dhabi launched Masdar, its renewable energy initiative, which is wholly owned by Mubadala, a government investment vehicle, with an initial capital of US$15bn.

Masdar is an integrated novel approach that combines acquiring strategic stakes in clean-tech companies to transfer technology to the Emirate, with profiting from the commercialization of renewable energy. Masdar City, known as the carbon-neutral, 'green' technology centre, is set to use state of the art clean-energy technology. However, the wider initiative has more tangible goals in the form of an investment arm that invests in renewable energy technology and a post-graduate research institute (Masdar Institute of Science and Technology) focusing on sustainable energy.

In the next few years, Masdar will invest US$2bn in solar power technology plants in its first facility, which is based in Germany, and in a second Abu Dhabi-based plant that began production in January 2011. In addition, it will invest between US$1.5bn and US$2bn in acquiring stakes in companies across the United States, Europe, and Asia. In 2009, Masdar announced its plans to launch a new clean-technology fund, with capital of at least US$250m, as it seeks out investment opportunities created by the global economic turmoil.

Sources: Simeon Kerr, "Abu Dhabi Seeks Renewable Advantage," *Financial Times*, January 20, 2008; Andrew England, "Masdar to Launch Clean-tech Fund," *Financial Times*, June 26, 2009; and James Drummond, "Desert City Grows into Living Laboratory," *Financial Times*, July 21, 2009.

Externalities May Result in Market Failure

Market failure A situation in which the market fails to produce the efficient level of output.

We have seen that because of externalities, the efficient level of output may not occur in either the market for electricity or the market for college educations. These are examples of **market failure**: situations in which the market fails to produce the efficient level of output. Later, we will discuss possible solutions to problems of externalities. But first we need to consider why externalities occur.

What Causes Externalities?

Property rights The rights individuals or businesses have to the exclusive use of their property, including the right to buy or sell it.

We saw in Chapter 2 that governments need to guarantee *property rights* for a market system to function well. **Property rights** refers to the rights individuals or businesses have to the exclusive use of their property, including the right to buy or sell it. Property can be tangible, physical property, such as a store or factory. Property can also be intangible, such as the right to an idea. Most of the time, the U.S. government and the governments of other high-income countries do a good job of enforcing property rights, but in certain situations, property rights do not exist or cannot be legally enforced.

Consider the following situation: Khalil owns land that includes a lake. A paper company wants to lease some of Khalil's land to build a pulp and paper mill. The paper mill will discharge pollutants into Khalil's lake. Because Khalil owns the lake, he can charge the paper company the cost of cleaning up the pollutants. The result is that the cost of the pollution is a private cost to the paper company and is included in the price of the paper it sells. There is no externality, the efficient level of paper is produced, and there is no market failure.

Now suppose that the paper company builds its paper mill on privately owned land on the banks of a lake that is owned by the state. In the absence of any government regulations, the company will be free to discharge pollutants into the lake. The cost of the pollution will be external to the company because it doesn't have to pay the cost of cleaning it up. More than the economically efficient level of paper will be produced, and a market failure will occur. Or, suppose that Khalil owns the lake, but the pollution is caused by acid rain generated by an electric utility hundreds of miles away. The law does not allow Khalil to charge the utility for the damage caused by the acid rain. Even though someone is damaging Khalil's property, the law does not allow him to enforce his property rights in this situation. Once again, there is an externality, and the market failure will result in too much electricity being produced.

Similarly, if you buy a house, the government will protect your right to exclusive use of that house. No one else can use the house without your permission. Because of your property rights in the house, your private benefit from the house and the social benefit are the same. When you buy a college education, however, other people are, in effect, able to benefit from your college education. You have no property right that will enable you to prevent them from benefiting or to charge them for the benefits they receive. As a result, there is a positive externality, and the market failure will result in too few college educations being supplied.

We can conclude the following: *Externalities and market failures result from incomplete property rights or from the difficulty of enforcing property rights in certain situations.*

13.2 | Discuss the Coase theorem and explain how private bargaining can lead to economic efficiency in a market with an externality.

Private Solutions to Externalities: The Coase Theorem

As noted at the beginning of this chapter, government intervention may actually increase economic efficiency and enhance the well-being of society when externalities are present. It is also possible, however, for people to find private solutions to the problem of externalities.

Can the market cure market failure? In an important article written in 1960, Ronald Coase of the University of Chicago, winner of the 1991 Nobel Prize in Economics, argued that under some circumstances, private solutions to the problem of externalities will occur. To understand Coase's argument, it is important to recognize that completely eliminating an externality usually is not economically efficient. Consider pollution, for example. There is, in fact, an *economically efficient level of pollution reduction*. At first, this seems paradoxical. Pollution is bad, and you might think the efficient amount of a bad thing is zero. But it isn't zero.

The Economically Efficient Level of Pollution Reduction

Chapter 1 introduced the important idea that the optimal decision is to continue any activity up to the point where the marginal benefit equals the marginal cost. This applies to reducing pollution just as much as to other activities. As sulfur dioxide emissions—or any other type of pollution—decline, society benefits: fewer trees die, fewer buildings are damaged, and fewer people suffer breathing problems. But a key point is that the additional benefit—that is, the *marginal benefit*—received from eliminating another ton of sulfur dioxide declines as sulfur dioxide emissions are reduced. To see why this is true, consider what happens with no reduction in sulfur dioxide emissions. In this situation, many smoggy days will occur in the cities. Even healthy people may experience breathing problems. As sulfur dioxide emissions are reduced, the number of smoggy days will fall, and healthy people will no longer experience breathing problems. Eventually, if emissions of sulfur dioxide fall to low levels, even people with asthma will no longer be affected. Further reductions in sulfur dioxide will have little additional benefit. The same will be true of the other benefits from reducing sulfur dioxide emissions: as the reductions increase, the additional benefits from fewer buildings and trees being damaged and lakes polluted will decline.

What about the marginal cost to electric utilities of reducing pollution? To reduce sulfur dioxide emissions, utilities have to switch from burning high-sulfur coal to burning more costly fuel, or they have to install pollution control devices, such as scrubbers. As the level of pollution falls, further reductions become increasingly costly. Reducing emissions or other types of pollution to very low levels can require complex and expensive new technologies. For example, Arthur Fraas of the Federal Office of Management and Budget United States' and Vincent Munley of Lehigh University in the United States, have shown that the marginal cost of removing 97 percent of pollutants from municipal wastewater is more than twice as high as the marginal cost of removing 95 percent.

The *net benefit* to society from reducing pollution is equal to the difference between the benefit of reducing pollution and the cost. To maximize the net benefit to society, sulfur dioxide emissions—or any other type of pollution—should be reduced up to the point where the marginal benefit from another ton of reduction is equal to the marginal cost. Figure 13-3 illustrates this point.

In Figure 13-3, we measure *reductions* in sulfur dioxide emissions on the horizontal axis. We measure the marginal benefit and marginal cost in dollars from eliminating another ton of sulfur dioxide emissions on the vertical axis. As reductions in pollution increase, the marginal benefit declines and the marginal cost increases. The economically efficient amount of pollution reduction occurs where the marginal benefit equals the marginal cost. The figure shows that in this case, the economically efficient reduction of sulfur dioxide emissions is 8.5 million tons per year. At that level of emission reduction, the marginal benefit and the marginal cost of the last ton of sulfur dioxide emissions eliminated are both US$200 per ton. Suppose instead that the emissions target were only 7.0 million tons. The figure shows that, at that level of reduction, the last ton of reduction has added US$250 to the benefits received by society, but it has added only

Figure 13-3

The Marginal Benefit from Pollution Reduction Should Equal the Marginal Cost

If the reduction of sulfur dioxide emissions is at 7.0 million tons per year, the marginal benefit of US$250 per ton is greater than the marginal cost of US$175 per ton. Further reductions in emissions will increase the net benefit to society. If the reduction of sulfur dioxide emissions is at 10.0 million tons, the marginal cost of US$225 per ton is greater than the marginal benefit of US$150 per ton. An increase in sulfur dioxide emissions will increase the net benefit to society. Only when the reduction is at 8.5 million tons is the marginal benefit equal to the marginal cost. This level is the economically efficient level of pollution reduction.

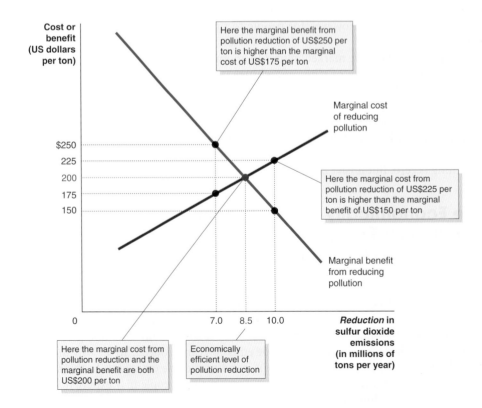

US$175 to the costs of utilities. There has been a net benefit to society from this ton of pollution reduction of US$75. In fact, the figure shows a net benefit to society from pollution reduction for every ton from 7.0 million to 8.5 million. Only when sulfur dioxide emissions are reduced by 8.5 million tons per year will marginal benefit fall enough and marginal cost rise enough that the two are equal.

Now suppose the government had set the target for sulfur dioxide emissions reduction at 10 million tons per year. The figure shows that the marginal benefit at that level of reduction has fallen to only US$150 per ton and the marginal cost has risen to US$225 per ton. The last ton of reduction has actually *reduced* the net benefit to society by US$75 per ton. In fact, every ton of reduction beyond 8.5 million reduces the net benefit to society.

To summarize: If the marginal benefit of reducing sulfur dioxide emissions is greater than the marginal cost, further reductions will make society better off. But if the marginal cost of reducing sulfur dioxide emissions is greater than the marginal benefit, reducing sulfur dioxide emissions will actually make society worse off.

The Basis for Private Solutions to Externalities

In arguing that private solutions to the problem of externalities were possible, Ronald Coase emphasized that when more than the optimal level of pollution is occurring, the benefits from reducing the pollution to the optimal level are greater than the costs. Figure 13-4 illustrates this point.

The marginal benefit curve shows the additional benefit from each reduction in a ton of sulfur dioxide emissions. The area under the marginal benefit curve between the two emission levels is the *total* benefit received from reducing emissions from one level to another. For instance, in Figure 13-4, the total benefit from increasing the reduction in sulfur dioxide emissions from 7.0 million tons to 8.5 million tons is the sum of the

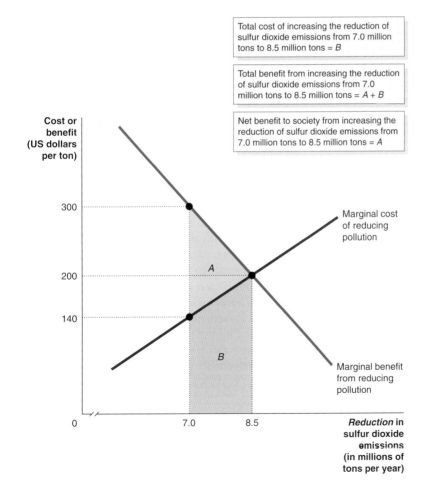

Total cost of increasing the reduction of sulfur dioxide emissions from 7.0 million tons to 8.5 million tons = B

Total benefit from increasing the reduction of sulfur dioxide emissions from 7.0 million tons to 8.5 million tons = A + B

Net benefit to society from increasing the reduction of sulfur dioxide emissions from 7.0 million tons to 8.5 million tons = A

Figure 13-4

The Benefits of Reducing Pollution to the Optimal Level Are Greater Than the Costs

Increasing the reduction in sulfur dioxide emissions from 7.0 million tons to 8.5 million tons results in total benefits equal to the sum of the areas A and B under the marginal benefits curve. The total cost of this decrease in pollution is equal to the area B under the marginal cost curve. The total benefits are greater than the total costs by an amount equal to the area of triangle A. Because the total benefits from reducing pollution are greater than the total costs, it's possible for those receiving the benefits to arrive at a private agreement with polluters to pay them to reduce pollution.

areas of *A* and *B*. The marginal cost curve shows the additional cost from each reduction in a ton of emissions. The *total* cost of reducing emissions from one level to another is the area under the marginal cost curve between the two emissions levels. The total cost from increasing the reduction in emissions from 7.0 million tons to 8.5 million tons is the area *B*. The net benefit from reducing emissions is the difference between the total cost and the total benefit, which is equal to the area of triangle *A*.

In Figure 13-4, the benefits from further reductions in sulfur dioxide emissions are much greater than the costs. In the appendix to Chapter 1, we reviewed the formula for calculating the area of a triangle, which is $1/2 \times$ base $\times$ height, and the formula for the area of a rectangle, which is base $\times$ height. Using these formulas, we can calculate the value of the total benefits from the reduction in emissions and the value of the total costs. The value of the benefits $(A + B)$ is US$375 million. The value of the costs (B) is US$255 million. If the people who would benefit from a reduction in pollution could get together, they could offer to pay the electric utilities US$255 million to reduce the pollution to the optimal level. After making the payment, they would still be left with a net benefit of US$120 million. In other words, a private agreement to reduce pollution to the optimal level is possible, without any need for government intervention.

Do Property Rights Matter?

In discussing the bargaining between the electric utilities and the people suffering the effects of the utilities' pollution, we assumed that the electric utilities were not legally liable for the damage they were causing. In other words, the victims of pollution could not legally enforce the right of their property not to be damaged, so they would have to pay the utilities to reduce the pollution. But would it make any difference if the utilities were legally liable for the damages? Surprisingly, as Coase was the first to point out, it does not matter for the amount of pollution reduction. The only difference would be that now the electric utilities would have to pay the victims of pollution for the right to pollute rather than the victims having to pay the utilities. Because the marginal benefits and marginal costs of pollution reduction would not change, the bargaining would still result in the efficient level of pollution reduction—in this case, 8.5 million tons.

In the absence of the utilities being legally liable, the victims of pollution have an incentive to pay the utilities to reduce pollution up to the point where the marginal benefit of the last ton of reduction is equal to the marginal cost. If the utilities are legally liable, they have an incentive to pay the victims of pollution to allow them to pollute up to the same point.

The Problem of Transactions Costs

Transactions costs The costs in time and other resources that parties incur in the process of agreeing to and carrying out an exchange of goods or services.

Unfortunately, there are frequently practical difficulties in the way of a private solution to the problem of externalities. In cases of pollution, for example, there are often both many polluters and many people suffering from the negative effects of pollution. Bringing together all those suffering from pollution with all those causing the pollution and negotiating an agreement often fails due to *transactions costs*. **Transactions costs** are the costs in time and other resources that parties incur in the process of agreeing to and carrying out an exchange of goods or services. In this case, the transactions costs would include the time and other costs of negotiating an agreement, drawing up a binding contract, purchasing insurance, and monitoring the agreement. Unfortunately, when many people are involved, the transactions costs are often higher than the net benefits from reducing the externality. Thus, the cost of transacting ends up exceeding the gain from the transaction. In such cases, a private solution to an externality problem is not feasible.

The Coase Theorem

Coase theorem The argument of economist Ronald Coase that if transactions costs are low, private bargaining will result in an efficient solution to the problem of externalities.

Coase's argument that private solutions to the problem of externalities are possible is summed up in the **Coase theorem**: If transactions costs are low, private bargaining will result in an efficient solution to the problem of externalities. We have seen the basis for the Coase theorem in the preceding example of pollution by electric utilities: because the benefits from reducing an externality are often greater than the costs, private bargaining can arrive at an efficient outcome. But we have also seen that this outcome will occur only if transactions costs are low, and in the case of pollution, they usually are not. In general, private bargaining is most likely to reach an efficient outcome if the number of parties bargaining is small.

In practice, we must add a couple of other qualifications to the Coase theorem. In addition to low transactions costs, private solutions to the problem of externalities will occur only if all parties to the agreement have full information about the costs and benefits associated with the externality, and all parties must be willing to accept a reasonable agreement. For example, if those suffering from the effects of pollution do not have information on the costs of reducing pollution, it is unlikely that the parties can reach an agreement. Unreasonable demands can also hinder an agreement. For instance, in the example of pollution by electric utilities, we saw that the total benefit of reducing sulfur dioxide emissions was US$375 million. Even if transactions costs are very low, if the utilities insist on being paid more than US$375 million to reduce emissions, no agreement will be reached because the amount paid exceeds the value of the reduction to those suffering from the emissions.

13.3 LEARNING OBJECTIVE

13.3 | Analyze government policies to achieve economic efficiency in a market with an externality.

Government Policies to Deal with Externalities

When private solutions to externalities are not feasible, how should the government intervene? The first economist to analyze market failure systematically was A. C. Pigou, a British economist at Cambridge University. Pigou argued that to deal with a negative externality in production, the government should impose a tax equal to the cost of the externality. The effect of such a tax is shown in Figure 13-5 which reproduces the negative externality from acid rain shown in Figure 13-1.

By imposing a tax equal to the cost of acid rain on the production of electricity, the government will cause electric utilities to *internalize* the externality. As a consequence, the cost of the acid rain will become a private cost borne by the utilities, and the supply curve for electricity will shift from S_1 to S_2. The result will be a decrease in the equilibrium output of electricity from Q_1 to the efficient level, Q_2. The price of electricity will rise from P_1—which does not include the cost of acid rain—to P_2—which does include the cost.

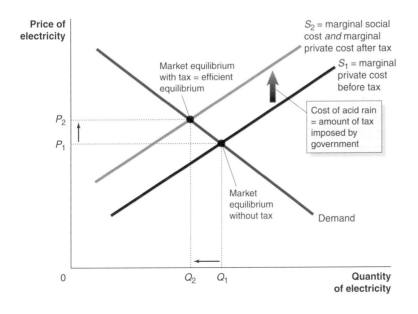

Figure 13-5

When There is a Negative Externality, a Tax Can Bring About the Efficient Level of Output

Because utilities do not bear the cost of acid rain, they produce electricity beyond the economically efficient level. If the government imposes a tax equal to the cost of acid rain, the utilities will internalize the externality. As a consequence, the supply curve will shift up from S_1 to S_2. The market equilibrium quantity changes from Q_1, where an inefficiently high level of electricity is produced, to Q_2, the economically efficient equilibrium quantity. The price of electricity will rise from P_1—which does not include the cost of acid rain—to P_2—which does include the cost.

Solved Problem | 13-3

Using a Tax to Deal with a Negative Externality

Companies that produce toilet paper bleach the paper to make it white. Some paper plants discharge the bleach into rivers and lakes, causing substantial environmental damage. Suppose the following graph illustrates the situation in the toilet paper market.

Explain how the government can use a tax on toilet paper to bring about the efficient level of production. What should the value of the tax be?

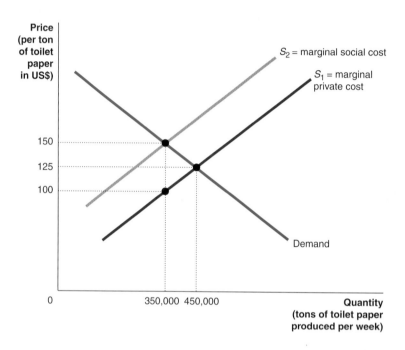

SOLVING THE PROBLEM:

Step 1: **Review the chapter material.** This problem is about the government using a tax to deal with a negative externality in production, so you may want to review the section "Government Policies to Deal with Externalities," which begins on page 427.

Step 2: **Use the information from the graph to determine the necessary tax.** The efficient level of toilet paper production will occur where the marginal social benefit from consuming toilet paper, as represented by the demand curve, is equal to the marginal social cost of production. The graph shows that this will occur at a price of US$150 per ton and production of 350,000 tons. In the absence of government intervention, the price will be US$125 per ton, and production will be 450,000 tons. It is tempting—but incorrect!—to think that the government could bring about the efficient level of production by imposing a per-ton tax equal to the difference between the price when production is at its optimal level and the current market price. But this would be a tax of only US$25. The graph shows that at the optimal level of production, the difference between the marginal private cost and the marginal social cost is US$50. Therefore, a tax of US$50 per ton is required to shift the supply curve up from S_1 to S_2.

>> End Solved Problem 13-3   **YOUR TURN:** For more practice, do related problem 3.7 on page 448 at the end of this chapter.

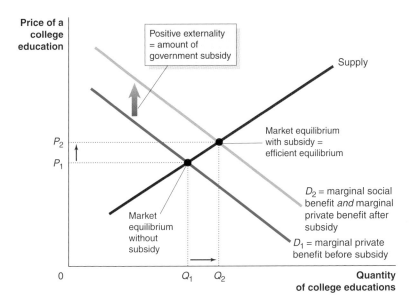

Price of a college education

Positive externality = amount of government subsidy

Supply

P_2

P_1

Market equilibrium with subsidy = efficient equilibrium

D_2 = marginal social benefit *and* marginal private benefit after subsidy

Market equilibrium without subsidy

D_1 = marginal private benefit before subsidy

0 Q_1 Q_2 **Quantity of college educations**

Figure 13-6

When There Is a Positive Externality, a Subsidy Can Bring about the Efficient Level of Output

People who do not consume college educations can benefit from them. As a result, the social benefit from a college education is greater than the private benefit seen by college students. If the government pays a subsidy equal to the external benefit, students will internalize the externality. The subsidy will cause the demand curve to shift up, from D_1 to D_2. The result will be that market equilibrium quantity shifts from Q_1, where an inefficiently low level of college educations is supplied, to Q_2, the economically efficient equilibrium quantity.

Pigou also argued that the government can deal with a positive externality in consumption by giving consumers a subsidy, or payment, equal to the value of the externality. The effect of the subsidy is shown in Figure 13-6, which reproduces the positive externality from college education shown in Figure 13-2.

By paying college students a subsidy equal to the external benefit from a college education, the government will cause students to *internalize* the externality. That is, the external benefit from a college education will become a private benefit received by college students, and the demand curve for college educations will shift from D_1 to D_2. The equilibrium number of college educations supplied will increase from Q_1 to the efficient level, Q_2. In fact, the government does heavily subsidize college educations. All states have government-operated universities that charge tuitions well below the cost of providing the education. The state and federal governments also provide students with grants and low-interest loans that subsidize college educations. The economic justification for these programs is that college educations provide an external benefit to society.

Because A. C. Pigou was the first economist to propose using government taxes and subsidies to deal with externalities, they are sometimes referred to as **Pigovian taxes and subsidies**. Note that a Pigovian tax eliminates deadweight loss and improves economic efficiency. This situation is the opposite of the one we saw in Chapter 4, in which we discussed how most taxes reduce consumer surplus and producer surplus and create a deadweight loss. In fact, one reason that economists support Pigovian taxes as a way to deal with negative externalities is that the government can use the revenues raised by Pigovian taxes to lower other taxes that reduce economic efficiency.

Pigovian taxes and subsidies Government taxes and subsidies intended to bring about an efficient level of output in the presence of externalities.

Command and Control versus Tradable Emissions Allowances

Although Arab governments have sometimes used taxes and subsidies to deal with externalities, in dealing with pollution, they have traditionally used a *command and control approach* with firms that pollute. A **command and control approach** to reducing pollution involves the government imposing quantitative limits on the amount of pollution firms are allowed to generate or requiring firms to install specific pollution control devices. Imagine, for example, a regulation by which the Egyptian government requires auto manufacturers to install catalytic converters to reduce auto emissions on all new automobiles, or one by which the UAE government requires petrochemical companies to install waste treatment facilities. Most governments around the world usually use different regulations to limit the amount of pollution.

Command and control approach An approach that involves the government imposing quantitative limits on the amount of pollution firms are allowed to emit or requiring firms to install specific pollution control devices.

Figure 13-7

Estimated Cost of the Acid Rain Program in 2010

The Edison Electric Institute estimated in 1989 that the program to reduce acid rain pollution would cost utilities a total of US$7.4 billion by 2010. The system of tradable emissions allowances used in the program resulted in the bulk of the reduction in pollution being carried out by the utilities that could do it at the lowest cost. As a result, the program is likely to cost US$870 million, which is almost 90 percent less than the original estimate. (*Note:* To correct for the effect of inflation, the costs are measured in dollars of 1990 purchasing power.)

Source: *Progress Report on the EPA Acid Rain Program,* November 1999, Figure 2.

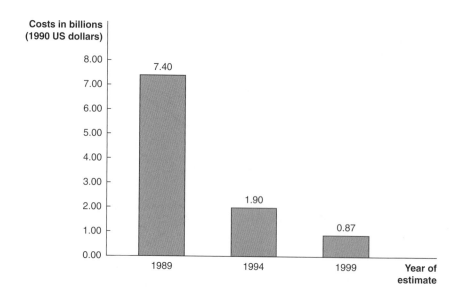

By the same token, the U.S. government could have used direct pollution-controls to deal with the problem of acid rain. To achieve its objective of a reduction of 8.5 million tons per year in sulfur dioxide emissions by 2012, the U.S. government could have required every utility to reduce sulfur dioxide emissions by a specified amount. However, this approach would not have been an economically efficient solution to the problem. As we saw at the beginning of this chapter, the costs for utilities of reducing sulfur dioxide emissions can be very different. Some utilities that already use low-sulfur coal can reduce emissions further only at a high cost. Other utilities, particularly high carbon-burning utilities, are able to reduce emissions at a lower cost.

Instead, the U.S. government decided to use a market-based approach to reducing sulfur dioxide emissions, by setting up a system of tradable emissions allowances. The federal government gave utilities allowances equal to the total amount of allowable sulfur dioxide emissions. The utilities were then free to buy and sell the allowances. Utilities that could reduce emissions at low cost did so and sold their allowances. Utilities that could only reduce emissions at high cost bought allowances. Using tradable emissions allowances to reduce acid rain has been a great success and has made it possible for utilities to meet Congress's emissions goal at a much lower cost than expected. As Figure 13-7 shows, just before Congress enacted the allowances program in 1990, the Edison Electrical Institute estimated that the cost to utilities of complying with the program would be US$7.4 billion by 2010. In practice, the cost appears likely to be almost 90 percent less than the initial estimate, or only about US$870 *million.* In developing countries, and the Arab world, however, the command approach is more heavily used than the market-based approach.

Are Tradable Emissions Allowances Licenses to Pollute?

Some environmentalists have criticized tradable emissions allowances, labeling them "licenses to pollute." They argue that just as the government does not issue licenses to rob banks or to drive under the influence of drugs, it should not issue licenses to pollute. But this criticism ignores one of the central lessons of economics: resources are scarce, and trade-offs exist. Resources that are spent reducing one type of pollution are not available to reduce other types of pollution or for any other use. Because reducing acid rain using tradable emissions allowances cost utilities US$870 million, rather than US$7.4 billion, as originally estimated, society saved more than US$6.5 billion.

<table>
<tr><td>Making
the
Connection</td><td>## Can Tradable Permits Reduce Global Warming?</td></tr>
</table>

In the past 25 years, the global surface temperature has increased about three-quarters of 1 degree Fahrenheit (or four-tenths of 1 degree Centigrade) compared with the average for the previous 30 years. The following graph shows changes in temperature over the years since 1880.

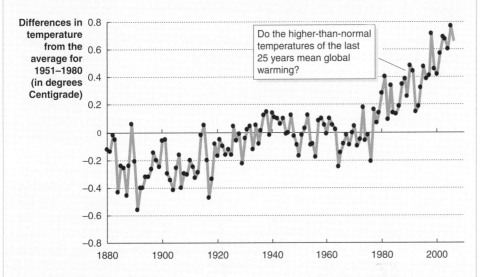

Global temperatures have gone through many periods of warming and cooling. In fact, the below-normal temperatures that prevailed before 1970 led some scientists to predict the eventual arrival of a new ice age. Nevertheless, many scientists are convinced that the recent warming is not part of the natural fluctuations in temperature but is instead due to the burning of fossil fuels, such as coal, natural gas, and petroleum. Burning these fuels releases CO_2 (carbon dioxide), which accumulates in the atmosphere as a 'greenhouse gas.' Greenhouse gases cause some of the heat released from the earth to be reflected back, increasing temperatures.

If greenhouse gases continue to accumulate in the atmosphere, according to some estimates, global temperatures could increase by 3 degrees Fahrenheit or more during the next 100 years. Such increases in temperature could lead to significant changes in climate, which might result in more storms and flooding as well as other problems. By 1995, a number of nations had concluded that the threat of global warming was significant enough to take steps toward reducing emissions of CO_2 and other greenhouse gases. The result was the 1997 Kyoto Treaty, which, if accepted, would have required the high-income countries to reduce their CO_2 emissions by more than 5 percent compared with their 1990 levels. However, President George W. Bush was not willing to commit the United States to the treaty. He argued that the costs to the United States of complying with the treaty were too high, particularly because some scientists were still skeptical that CO_2 emissions actually were causing the increase in temperature. Even scientists who believed that CO_2 emissions contribute to rising temperatures were skeptical that the Kyoto Treaty would have much effect on global warming. President Bush also argued that developing countries should be included in any agreement. Some developing countries, such as China and India, are experiencing rapid economic growth, which in turn has led to rapid increases in CO_2 emissions. European countries that ratified the Kyoto Treaty have had difficulty ful-

(Continued)

filling their commitments to reduce CO_2 emissions to the levels indicated by the treaty. Of the larger European countries, only Great Britain, where emissions have declined by more than 15 percent since 1990, seems likely to succeed in fulfilling its commitments by 2012.

The mechanism by which reductions in CO_2 emissions would occur has also been in dispute. The United States has favored a global system of tradable emission permits for CO_2 that would be similar to the system for sulfur dioxide discussed earlier in this chapter. As we have seen, this type of system has the potential to reduce CO_2 emissions at a lower cost. Most European countries, however, have been reluctant to fully accept such a system, preferring instead to require that each country reduce emissions by a specified amount. In recent years, though, support has grown in Europe for using tradable allowances, and an active market in these allowances has developed under the European Union Greenhouse Gas Emission Trading Scheme, which began operation in 2005.

In December 2009, the world's nations assembled in Copenhagen to discuss climate change and policies to increase carbon cuts. The Copenhagen conference ended without a unanimous agreement and resulted in a limited accord on areas of climate policy, such as cutting greenhouse gas emissions, and commitments by rich countries to provide financial aid to poor countries. The final accord was mainly a compromise negotiated between the U.S. government and developing nations, such as Brazil and Venezuela, disappointed at the failure of the conference to reach a forceful, fair commitment to emission reduction. The failure was a blow to the European Union's carbon-trading scheme. In the wake of the conference, prices for carbon permits, the benchmark for pricing European permits, dropped nearly 10 percent for December 2010 delivery.

So which countries did not participate in Copenhagen? Not surprisingly, leading Arab oil-producing nations showed an obvious lack of support to the cause by their absence. Among the no-shows were Saudi Arabia, Libya, the UAE, and several others, accounting for nearly half the world's proven oil reserves.

Sources: Juliet Eilperin and Steven Mufson, "Tax on Carbon Emissions Gains Support," *Washington Post*, April 1, 2007, p. A05; United Nations Framework Convention on Climate Change, *National Greenhouse Gas Inventory Data for the Period 1990–2004*, October 19, 2006; and (for data in the graph) NASA, Goddard Institute for Space Studies, http://data.giss.nasa.gov/gistemp/graphs, Fiona Harvey and Chris Flood, "Carbon Prices Drop in Wake of Climate Talks," *Financial Times*, December 21, 2009; Ed Crooks, Fiona Harvey and Andrew Ward, "Conference Diary," *Financial Times*, December 22, 2009.

13.4 LEARNING OBJECTIVE

13.4 | Explain how goods can be categorized on the basis of whether they are rival or excludable, and use graphs to illustrate the efficient quantities of public goods and common resources.

Four Categories of Goods

Rivalry The situation that occurs when one person's consuming a unit of a good means no one else can consume it.

Excludability The situation in which anyone who does not pay for a good cannot consume it.

We can explore further the question of when the market is likely to succeed in supplying the efficient quantity of a good by noting that goods differ on the basis of whether their consumption is *rival* and *excludable*. **Rivalry** occurs when one person's consuming a unit of a good means no one else can consume it. If you consume a Big Mac, for example, no one else can consume it. **Excludability** means that anyone who does not pay for a good cannot consume it. If you don't pay for a Big Mac, for example, MacDonald's can exclude you from consuming it. The consumption of a Big Mac is rival and excludable. The consumption of some goods, however, can be either *nonrival or nonexcludable*. Nonrival means that one person's consumption does not interfere with another person's consumption. Nonexcludable means that it is impossible to exclude others from consuming the good, whether they have paid for it or not. Figure 13-8 shows four possible categories into which goods can fall.

	Excludable	Nonexcludable
Rival	**Private Goods** *Examples:* *Big Macs* *Running shoes*	**Common Resources** *Examples:* *Tuna in the ocean* *Public pasture land*
Nonrival	**Quasi-Public Goods** *Examples:* *Cable TV* *Toll road*	**Public Goods** *Examples:* *National defense* *Court system*

Figure 13-8

Four Categories of Goods

Goods and services can be divided into four categories on the basis of whether people can be excluded from consuming them and whether they are rival in consumption. A good or service is rival in consumption if it can be consumed by only one person at the same time.

We next consider each of the four categories:

1 *Private goods.* A good that is both rival and excludable is a **private good**. Food, clothing, haircuts, and many other goods and services fall into this category. One person's consuming a unit of these goods precludes other people from consuming that unit, and anyone who does not buy these goods can't consume them. Although we didn't state it explicitly, when we analyzed the demand and supply for goods and services in Chapter 3, we assumed that the goods and services were all private goods.

2 *Public goods.* A **public good** is both nonrivalrous and nonexcludable. Public goods are often, although not always, supplied by a government rather than by private firms. The classic example of a public good is national defense. Your consuming national defense does not interfere with your neighbor's consuming it, so consumption is nonrivalrous. You also cannot be excluded from consuming it, whether you pay for it or not. No private firm would be willing to supply national defense because everyone can consume national defense without paying for it. The behavior of consumers in this situation is referred to as *free riding*. **Free riding** involves individuals benefiting from a good—in this case, the provision of national defense—without paying for it.

3 *Quasi-public goods.* Some goods are excludable but not rival. An example is cable television. People who do not pay for cable television do not receive it, but one person's watching it doesn't affect other people's watching it. The same is true of a toll road. Anyone who doesn't pay the toll doesn't get on the road, but one person using the road doesn't interfere with someone else using the road (unless so many people are using the road that it becomes congested). Goods that fall into this category are called *quasi-public goods*.

4 *Common resources.* If a good is rival but not excludable, it is a **common resource**. Forest land in many poor countries is a common resource. If one person cuts down a tree, no one else can use the tree. But if no one has a property right to the forest, no one can be excluded from using it. As we will discuss in more detail later, people often overuse common resources.

We discussed the demand and supply for private goods in Chapter 3. For the remainder of this chapter, we focus on the categories of public goods and common resources. To determine the optimal quantity of a public good, we have to modify the demand and supply analysis of Chapter 3 to take into account that a public good is both nonrivalrous and nonexcludable.

Private good A good that is both rival and excludable.

Public good A good that is both nonrivalrous and nonexcludable.

Free riding Benefiting from a good without paying for it.

Common resource A good that is rival but not excludable.

Making the Connection | Should the Government Run the Health Care System?

In many Arab countries, such as Egypt, Jordan, Kuwait, Qatar, and Saudi Arabia, among others, the government either supplies health care directly through running hospitals and employing doctors and nurses, or pays for most health care expenses, even if hospitals are not

(Continued)

government-owned and doctors are not government employees. In other countries, such as the United States, the federal government supplies health care to veterans of the armed forces, pays for the health care of people over age 65, and contributes to health care expenses for some poor people. Most medium- and large-size firms provide health insurance to their employees. Those individuals not covered by health insurance plans, and not eligible for government aid, must pay for their own health care bills out of pocket, just as they pay their other bills.

What should be the government's role in health care? Is health care a public good that government should supply—or, at least, pay for? Is it a private good, like food, clothing, or television sets, that private firms should supply and consumers should pay for without government aid? Should private firms supply most health care, subject to some government regulation? Economists differ in their answers to these questions because the delivery of health care involves a number of complex issues. But we can consider briefly some of the most important points. We have seen that a public good is both nonrivalrous and nonexcludable. In this sense, health care does not qualify as a public good. More than one person cannot simultaneously consume the same surgical operation, for example. And because there is nothing in the nature of health care that keeps people who do not pay for it from being excluded from consuming it, health care does not fit the definition of a public good.

There are aspects of the delivery of health care that have convinced some economists that government intervention is justified, however. For example, consuming certain types of health care generates positive externalities. In particular, being vaccinated against a communicable disease, such as influenza or chicken pox, not only reduces the chance that the person vaccinated will catch the disease but also reduces the probability that an epidemic of the disease will occur. Therefore, the market may supply an inefficiently small quantity of vaccinations unless vaccinations receive a government subsidy. Information problems can also be important in the market for private health insurance. Consumers as buyers of health insurance often know much more about the state of their health than do the companies selling health insurance. This information problem may raise costs to insurance companies when the pool of people being insured is small, making insurance companies less willing to offer health insurance to consumers the companies suspect may file too many claims. Economists debate how important information problems are in health care markets and whether government intervention is required to reduce them.

Many economists believe that market-based solutions are the best approach to improving the health care system. Currently, the U.S. health care system is a world leader in innovation in medical technology and prescription drugs. The market-oriented approach to reforming health care starts with the goal of preserving incentives for U.S. firms to continue with innovations in medical screening equipment, surgical procedures, and prescription drugs. Presently, markets are delivering inaccurate signals to consumers because when buying health care, unlike when buying most other goods and services, consumers pay a price well *below* the true cost of providing the service. Consumers usually pay less than the true cost of medical treatment because a third party—typically, an insurance company—often pays most of the bill. For example, consumers who have health insurance provided by their employers usually pay only a small amount—perhaps US$20—for a visit to a doctor's office, when the true cost of the visit might be US$80 or US$90. The result is that consumers demand a larger quantity of health care services than they would if they paid a price that better represented the cost of providing the services. Doctors and other health care providers also have a

Health care is almost free for nationals in many Gulf Arab countries through public insurance coverage.

reduced incentive to control costs because they know that an insurance company will pick up most of the bill.

Because health care is so important to consumers and because health care spending looms so large, the role of the government in the health care system is likely to be the subject of intense debate for some time to come.

To read more on the role of the government in the market for health care, see Sherman Folland, Allen C. Goodman, and Miron Stano, *The Economics of Health and Health Care*, 5th ed., Upper Saddle River, NJ: Prentice Hall, 2007, Chapter 19; and John F. Coogan, R. Glenn Hubbard, and Daniel P. Kessler, *Healthy, Wealthy, and Wise: Five Steps to a Better Health Care System*, Washington, DC: The AEI Press, 2005.

YOUR TURN: Test your understanding by doing related problem 4.9 on page 450 at the end of this chapter.

The Demand for a Public Good

We can determine the market demand curve for a good or service by adding up the quantity of the good demanded by each consumer at each price. To keep things simple, let's take the case of a market with only two consumers. Figure 13-9 shows that the market demand curve for hamburgers depends on the individual demand curves of Yusuf and Yusr.

At a price of US$4.00, Yusuf demands 2 hamburgers per week and Yusr demands 4. Adding horizontally, the combination of a price of US$4.00 per hamburger and a quantity demanded of 6 hamburgers will be a point on the market demand curve for hamburgers. Similarly, adding horizontally at a price of US$1.50, we have a price of US$1.50 and a quantity demanded of 11 as another point on the market demand curve. A consumer's demand curve for a good represents the marginal benefit the consumer receives from the good, so when we add together the consumers' demand curves, we not only have the market demand curve but also the marginal social benefit curve for this good, assuming that there is no externality in consumption.

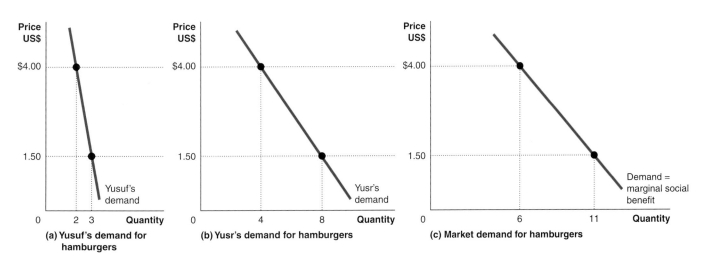

Figure 13-9 | Constructing the Market Demand Curve for a Private Good

The market demand curve for private goods is determined by adding horizontally the quantity of the good demanded at each price by each consumer. For instance, in panel (a), Yusuf demands 2 hamburgers when the price is US$4.00, and in

panel (b), Yusr demands 4 hamburgers when the price is US$4.00. So, a quantity of 6 hamburgers and a price of US$4.00 is a point on the market demand curve in panel (c).

How can we find the demand curve or marginal social benefit curve for a public good? Once again, for simplicity, assume that Yusuf and Yusr are the only consumers. Unlike with a private good, where Yusuf and Yusr can end up consuming different quantities, with a public good, they will consume *the same quantity*. Suppose that Yusuf owns a service station on an isolated rural road, and Yusr owns a car dealership next door. These are the only two businesses around for miles. Both Yusuf and Yusr are afraid that unless they hire a security guard at night, their businesses may be burgled. Like national defense, the services of a security guard are in this case a public good: once hired, the guard will be able to protect both businesses, so the good is nonrival. It also will not be possible to exclude either business from being protected, so the good is nonexcludable.

To arrive at a demand curve for a public good, we don't add quantities at each price, as with a private good. Instead, we add the price each consumer is willing to pay for each quantity of the public good. This value represents the total dollar amount consumers as a group would be willing to pay for that quantity of the public good. Put another way,

Figure 13-10

Constructing the Market Demand Curve for a Public Good

To find the demand curve for a public good, we add up the price at which each consumer is willing to purchase each quantity of the good. In panel (a), Yusuf is willing to pay US$8 per hour for a security guard to provide 10 hours of protection. In panel (b), Yusr is willing to pay US$10 for that level of protection. Therefore, in panel (c), the price of US$18 per hour and the quantity of 10 hours will be a point on the market demand curve for security guard services.

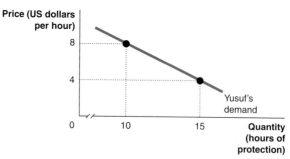

(a) Yusuf's demand for security guard services

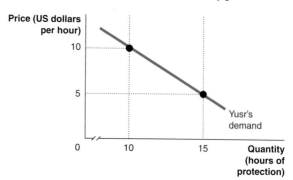

(b) Yusr's demand for security guard services

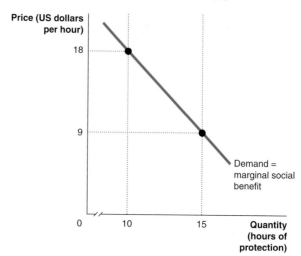

(c) Market demand for security guard services

to find the demand curve, or marginal social benefit curve, for a private good, we add the demand curves of individual consumers horizontally, while for public goods, we add individual demand curves vertically. Figure 13-10 shows how the marginal social benefit curve for security guard services depends on the individual demand curves of Yusuf and Yusr.

The figure shows that Yusuf is willing to pay US$8 per hour for the guard to provide 10 hours of protection per night. Yusr would suffer a greater loss from a burglary, so he is willing to pay US$10 per hour for the same amount of protection. Adding the dollar amount that each is willing to pay gives us a price of US$18 per hour and a quantity of 10 hours as a point on the marginal social benefit curve for security guard services. Because Yusuf is willing to spend US$4 per hour for 15 hours of guard services and Yusr is willing to pay US$5, a price of US$9 per hour and a quantity of 15 hours is also a point on the marginal social benefit curve for security guard services.

The Optimal Quantity of a Public Good

We know that to achieve economic efficiency, a good or service should be produced up to the point where the sum of consumer surplus and producer surplus is maximized, or, alternatively, where the marginal social cost equals the marginal social benefit. Therefore, the optimal quantity of security guard services—or any other public good—will occur where the marginal social benefit curve intersects the supply curve. As with private goods, in the absence of an externality in production, the supply curve represents the marginal social cost of supplying the good. Figure 13-11 shows that the optimal quantity of security guard services supplied is 15 hours, at a price of US$9 per hour.

Will the market provide the economically efficient quantity of security guard services? One difficulty is that the individual preferences of consumers, as shown by their demand curves, are not revealed in this market. This difficulty does not arise with private goods because consumers must reveal their preferences in order to purchase private goods. If the market price of Big Macs is US$4.00, Yusr either reveals he is willing to pay that much by buying it, or he does without it. In our example, neither Yusuf nor Yusr can be excluded from consuming the services provided by a security guard once either hires one, and, therefore, neither has an incentive to reveal his preferences. In this case, though, with only two consumers, it is likely that private bargaining will result in an efficient quantity of the public good. This outcome is not likely for a public good—such as national defense—that is supplied by the government to millions of consumers.

Governments sometimes use *cost–benefit analysis* to determine what quantity of a public good should be supplied. For example, before building a dam on a river, the government will attempt to weigh the costs against the benefits. The costs include the opportunity cost of other projects the government cannot carry out if it builds the dam. The benefits include improved flood control or new recreational

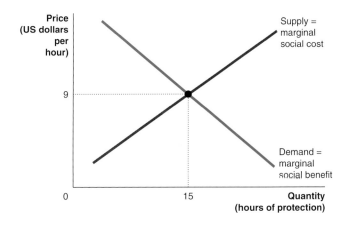

Figure 13-11

The Optimal Quantity of a Public Good

The optimal quantity of a public good is produced where the sum of consumer surplus and producer surplus is maximized, which occurs where the demand curve intersects the supply curve. In this case, the optimal quantity of security guard services is 15 hours at a price of US$9 per hour.

opportunities on the lake formed by the dam. However, for many public goods, including national defense, the government does not use a formal cost–benefit analysis. Even here, of course, you should realize that trade-offs are involved: the more resources used for national defense, the fewer resources available for other public goods or for private goods.

Solved Problem | 13-4

Determining the Optimal Level of Public Goods

Suppose, once again, that Yusuf and Yusr run isolated businesses that are next door to each other and in need of the services of a security guard. Their demand schedules for security guard services are as follows:

YUSR	
PRICE(DOLLARS PER HOUR) IN US$	QUANTITY (HOURS OF PROTECTION)
20	0
18	1
16	2
14	3
12	4
10	5
8	6
6	7
4	8
2	9

YUSUF	
PRICE (DOLLARS PER HOUR) IN US$	QUANTITY (HOURS OF PROTECTION)
20	1
18	2
16	3
14	4
12	5
10	6
8	7
6	8
4	9
2	10

The supply schedule for security guard services is as follows:

PRICE (DOLLARS PER HOUR) IN US$	QUANTITY (HOURS OF PROTECTION)
8	1
10	2
12	3
14	4
16	5
18	6
20	7
22	8
24	9

a. Draw a graph that shows the optimal level of security guard services. Be sure to label the curves on the graph.

b. Briefly explain why 8 hours of security guard protection is not an optimal quantity.

SOLVING THE PROBLEM:

Step 1: **Review the chapter material.** This problem is about the determination of the optimal level of public goods, so you may want to review the section "The Optimal Quantity of a Public Good," which begins on page 437.

Step 2: **Begin by deriving the demand curve or marginal social benefit curve for security guard services.** To calculate the marginal social benefit of guard services, we need to add the prices that Yusuf and Yusr are willing to pay at each quantity:

DEMAND OR MARGINAL SOCIAL BENEFIT	
PRICE (DOLLARS PER HOUR) IN US$	QUANTITY (HOURS OF PROTECTION)
38	1
34	2
30	3
26	4
22	5
18	6
14	7
10	8
6	9

Step 3: **Answer question (a) by plotting the demand (marginal social benefit) and supply (marginal social cost) curves.** The graph shows that the optimal level of security guard services is 6 hours.

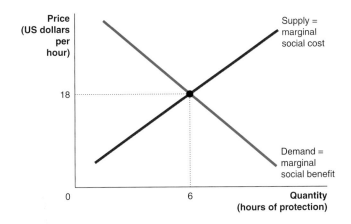

Step 4: **Answer question (b) by explaining why 8 hours of security guard protection is not an optimal quantity.** For each hour beyond 6, the supply curve is above the demand curve. Therefore, the marginal social benefit received will be less than the marginal social cost of supplying these hours. This results in a deadweight loss and a reduction in economic surplus.

YOUR TURN: For more practice, do related problem 4.4 on page 449 at the end of this chapter.

≫ End Solved Problem 13-4

Common Resources

In England during the Middle Ages, each village had an area of pasture, known as a *common*, on which any family in the village was allowed to graze its cows or sheep without charge. Of course, the grass one family's cow ate was not available for another family's cow, so consumption was rival. But every family in the village had the right to use the common, so it was nonexcludable. Without some type of restraint on usage, the common would end up overgrazed. To see why, consider the economic incentives facing a family that was thinking of buying another cow and grazing it on the common. The family would gain the benefits from increased milk production, but adding another cow to the common would create a negative externality by reducing the amount of grass available for the cows of other families. Because this family—and the other families in the village—did not take this negative externality into account when deciding whether to add another cow to the common, too many cows would be added. The grass on the common would eventually be depleted, and no family's cow would get enough to eat.

Figure 13-12

Overuse of a Common Resource

For a common resource such as wood from a forest, the efficient level of use, Q_2, is determined by the intersection of the demand curve—which represents the marginal benefit received by consumers—and S_2, which represents the marginal social cost of cutting the wood. Because each individual tree cutter ignores the external cost, the equilibrium quantity of wood cut is Q_1, which is greater than the efficient quantity. At the equilibrium level of output, there is a deadweight loss, as shown by the yellow triangle.

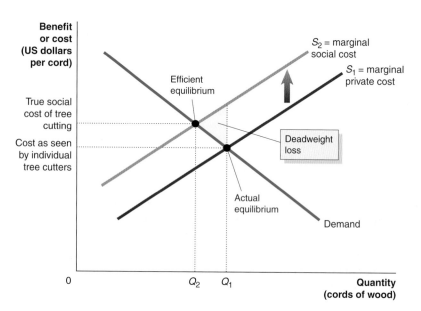

Tragedy of the commons The tendency for a common resource to be overused.

The Tragedy of the Commons The tendency for a common resource to be overused is called the **tragedy of the commons**. A modern example is the forests in many poor countries. When a family chops down a tree in a public forest, it takes into account the benefits of gaining firewood or wood for building, but it does not take into account the costs of deforestation. Haiti, for example, was once heavily forested. Today, 80 percent of the country's forests have been cut down, primarily to be burned to create charcoal, which is used for heating and cooking. Because the mountains no longer have tree roots to hold the soil, heavy rains lead to devastating floods. The following is from a newspaper account of tree cutting in Haiti:

> "No Tree Cutting" signs hang over the park entrance, but without money and manpower, there is no way to enforce that. Loggers make nightly journeys, hacking away at trees until they fall. The next day, they're on a truck out. Days later, they've been chopped up, burned and packaged in white bags offered for sale by soot-covered women. "This is the only way I can feed my four kids," said Vena Verone, one of the vendors. "I've heard about the floods and deforestation that caused them, but there's nothing I can do about that."

Figure 13-12 shows that with a common resource such as wood from a forest, the efficient level of use, Q_2, is determined by the intersection of the demand curve—which represents the marginal social benefit received by consumers—and S_2, which represents the marginal social cost of cutting the wood. As in our discussion of negative externalities, the social cost is equal to the private cost of cutting the wood plus the external cost. In this case, the external cost represents the fact that the more wood each person cuts, the less wood there is available for others, and the greater the deforestation, which increases the chances of floods. Because each individual tree cutter ignores the external cost, the equilibrium quantity of wood cut is Q_1, which is greater than the efficient quantity. At the equilibrium level of output, there is a deadweight loss, as shown in Figure 13-12 by the yellow triangle.

Making the Connection	**How Chefs and Chain Suppliers in the Arab World Are Dealing with Decreasing Seafood Stocks**

Overfishing is a worldwide problem that is bringing several sea species to near extinction. According to the UN's Food and Agriculture Organization (FAO), about 80 percent of the world's fish stocks are exploited, overexploited, depleted, or recovering from depletion. Emirates Wildlife Society, a UAE environmental non-governmental organization associated with the World Wildlife Fund (WWF), asserts that eight types of fish, popular to seafood lovers in the Gulf, are beyond their sustainable levels. The price of seafood in the Arab world, as in other areas in the world, has gone up significantly.

Chefs can have some influence on the problem since they decide what goes on their menus. Famous chefs in Dubai's luxurious seafood restaurants noted that wild-caught fish such as sea urchins and abalone became very expensive. Some seafood suppliers in the Arab world are partnered with WWF. They train fishermen and provide them with circle hooks, which help reduce accidental fish catches compared with regular J hooks. In addition, they do not supply certain endangered kinds of fish, such as bluefin tuna. Okku, a luxurious Japanese restaurant, has switched from bluefin to yellowfin tuna. According to Thushan Don, head chef of Aquara at Dubai Marina Yacht Club, the industry has not yet seen the full impact of depleted stocks. Despite seemingly available supplies, the stocks of hamour and other species in the same family, for example, have seen an overall decline of about 87 percent in the past 30 years.

Should these fishermen have unlimited access to the ocean?

The industry is aware of the problem of overfishing; some suppliers and restaurants are active in raising awareness to help save seafood stocks. According to Emirates Wildlife Society, the seafood market is changing worldwide, as in the Arab world. There is a rising demand for certified, sustainable, eco-friendly products, for example, those certified by the Marine Stewardship Council. Now more consumers and suppliers in the Arab world are aware of the impact of overfishing on species and on the environment.

Source: "Sustainable Seafood," Arabian Business, 7 May 2010, www.arabianbusiness.com/sustainable-seafood-182511.html.

Is There a Way Out of the Tragedy of the Commons? Notice that our discussion of the tragedy of the commons is very similar to our earlier discussion of negative externalities. The source of the tragedy of the commons is the same as the source of negative externalities: lack of clearly defined and enforced property rights. For instance, suppose that instead of being held as a collective resource, a piece of pastureland is owned by one person. That person will take into account the effect of adding another cow on the food available to cows already using the pasture. As a result, the optimal number of cows will be placed on the pasture. Over the years, most of the common lands in England were converted to private property. Most of the forest land in Haiti and other developing countries is actually the property of the government. The failure of the government to protect the forests against trespassers or convert them to private property is the key to their overuse.

In some situations, though, enforcing property rights is not feasible. An example is the oceans. Because no country owns the oceans beyond its own coastal waters, the fish and other resources of the ocean will remain a common resource. In situations in which enforcing property rights is not feasible, two types of solutions to the tragedy of the commons are possible. If the geographic area involved is limited and the number of people involved is small, access to the common can be restricted through community norms and laws. If the geographic area or the number of people involved is large, legal restrictions on access to the common is required. As an example of the first type of solution, the tragedy of the common was avoided in the Middle Ages by traditional limits on the number of animals each family was allowed to put on the common pasture. Although these traditions were not formal laws, they were usually enforced adequately by social pressure.

With the second type of solution, the government imposes restrictions on access to the common resources. These restrictions can take several different forms, of which taxes, quotas, and tradable permits are the most common. By setting a tax equal to the external cost, governments can ensure that the efficient quantity of a resource is used. Quotas, or legal limits, on the quantity of the resource that can be taken during a given time period have been used in the United States to limit access to pools of oil when the pool is beneath property owned by many different persons. The governments of Canada, New Zealand, and Iceland have used a system of tradable permits to restrict access to ocean fisheries. Under this system, a total allowable catch (TAC) limits the number of fish that fishermen can catch during a season. The fishermen are then assigned permits called Individual Transferable Quotas (ITQs) that are equal to the total allowable catch. This system operates like the tradable emissions allowances described earlier in this chapter. The fishermen are free to use the ITQs or to sell them, which ensures that the fishermen with the lowest costs use the ITQs. The use of ITQs has sometimes proven controversial, which has limited their use in managing fisheries along the coastal United States. Critics argue that allowing trading of ITQs can result in their concentration in the hands of a relatively few large commercial fishing firms. Such a concentration may, though, be economically efficient if these firms have lower costs than smaller, family-based firms.

Economics in YOUR Life!

>> Continued from page 417

At the beginning of the chapter, we asked you to think about what the 'best' level of carbon emissions is. Conceptually, this is a straightforward question to answer: the correct level of carbon emissions is the level for which the marginal benefit of reducing carbon emissions exactly equals the marginal cost of reducing carbon emissions. In practice, however, this is a very difficult question to answer. Scientists disagree about how much carbon emissions are contributing to the damage from climate change. In addition, the cost of reducing carbon emissions depends on the method of reduction used. As a result, neither the marginal cost curve nor the marginal benefit curve for reducing carbon emissions is known with certainty. This uncertainty makes it difficult for policymakers to determine the correct level of carbon emissions and is the source of much of the current debate. In any case, economists agree that the total cost of *completely* eliminating carbon emissions are much greater than the total benefits.

Conclusion

In Chapter 4, we saw that government intervention in the economy can reduce economic efficiency. In this chapter, however, we have seen that the government has an indispensable role to play in the economy when the absence of well-defined and enforceable property rights keeps the market from operating efficiently. Because no one has a property right for clean air, in the absence of government intervention, firms will produce too great a quantity of products that generate air pollution. We have also seen that public goods are nonrivalrous and nonexcludable and are, therefore, often supplied directly by the government.

Read *An Inside Look at Policy*, which begins on page 444, to learn about problems with carbon taxes and the prospective of oil-producing nations.

Oil-producing nations object to carbon taxes, calling them unfair

FINANCIAL TIMES, NOVEMBER 4, 2009

Oil-producing Nations Take a Different View on Carbon Taxes

Environmental policies such as a carbon tax, cap and trade and regulations to increase the efficiency of car engines, worry politicians from Qatar to Saudi Arabia, where national wealth depends largely on oil revenues. Recently, Saudi Arabia dusted off its arguments against climate change regulation. Though the effort was largely belittled by environmental groups, and laughed off by policy makers in countries that matter more than the Kingdom in determining whether December's climate summit in Copenhagen will be a success, it reveals a fundamental view shared by some—but not all—oil producers.

Saudi Arabia peddled its position that oil producers should be compensated for the demand drop at climate talks in Bangkok in October. Mohammad Al Sabban, the Saudi delegate, said: "Many politicians in the Western world think these climate change negotiations and the new agreement will provide them with a golden opportunity to reduce their dependence on imported oil.... That means

you will transfer the burden to developing countries, especially to those highly dependent on the exploitation of oil."

Environmental groups accused Saudi Arabia of delaying negotiations, pointing out that the revenue for the Organisation of Petroleum Exporting Countries (OPEC) would still increase US$23,000bn between 2008 and 2030 if countries enacted strong climate change legislation that cut oil use, according to the International Energy Agency, the consumers' watchdog. In addition richer Middle East countries have a relatively simple way to cut their carbon footprint: Reducing domestic oil consumption and pollution, by cutting their generous petrol subsidies.

Wael Hmaidan, executive director of IndyACT, a regional advocacy group, said in Bangkok: "Despite the variability in the region, the current Arab position is mainly focused around protecting the oil trade rather than saving the planet from the adverse impacts of climate change." OPEC—which sees itself as a champion of developing countries—is very sensitive to such criticism. This perhaps explains why Saudi Arabia found less traction from its ideas than it hoped when they were discussed at the group's September meeting in Vienna.

Nevertheless, OPEC's first comprehensive policy position, released shortly after the September OPEC meeting, notes: "We must ensure mitigation response measures and emission reduction commitments are fair and just, taking into account historical responsibility of [industrialized nations], the huge developmental needs of developing countries as well as the adverse impacts of climate change and of response measures, including the adverse impacts on fossil fuel exporting countries."

More recently, Shokri Ghanem, former oil minister of Libya, said any tax levied on carbon should be shared by the consuming and producing countries. "We don't think that oil-producing nations should be penalized and pay the price for improving the environment," he said in October, adding, "if you want a carbon tax imposed, ask us producers."

This may be a quickly dismissed notion, but it is not quite so farfetched a sentiment when one takes into account that the oil consuming countries looking to impose a carbon tax are the same governments that regularly warn OPEC not to increase oil prices by voluntarily withholding production.

Source: Carola Hoyos, "Oil-producing Nations Take a Different View on Carbon Taxes," *Financial Times*, November 4, 2009.

Key Points in the Article

The article discusses oil-producing countries' opposing stance and arguments against the industrial world's efforts to promote climate change regulations and carbon taxes. In short, oil-producing nations believe these regulations, if adopted by oil-importing countries, will be unfair to oil producers. A carbon tax will reduce the demand for oil, hurting oil-dependent economies' growth and developmental efforts. Some oil-producing nations go even further by suggesting that any carbon tax imposed in the developed world should be shared between these countries and oil producers.

Analyzing the News

(a) Oil-producing nations are opposing any climate change regulation to reduce carbon emissions that does not take into consideration the adverse effects on oil-producing countries. Any reduction in emission would mean that industries in oil-importing countries will have to reduce their use of oil. The combined reduction in demand by all countries will result in reducing world demand for oil, driving its prices down. The figure shows world demand for and world supply of oil; D_{oil} and S_{oil}. A world carbon tax will have the effect of a reducing world demand for oil, shifting the demand curve D_{oil1} to the left to D_{oil2}. This shift will result in a decline in the equilibrium quantity sold in international markets and a decline in world oil prices. Therefore, part of the costs of reducing carbon emissions in industrialized countries will be borne by oil producers.

(b) Industrialized nations in favor of the regulation respond to oil producers' claims by projecting that even if nations enacted legislations that will cut the use of oil, OPEC countries are still expected to have a surplus till 2030. They also suggest that oil countries may cut their generous subsidies to domestic oil uses. That will compensate some of the decline in revenues and meanwhile will help in the direction of reducing their carbon footprint.

(c) OPEC tried to dismiss the accusation that they care more about protecting oil trade than world climate change. They announced in their September 2009 meeting that they do not oppose a climate change regulation. Rather, they oppose an 'unjust or unfair' regulation that ignores the developmental needs of developing countries, the adverse impact on oil-producers, and the historical responsibility of developed nations in raising carbon emissions.

Thinking Critically About Policy

1. The world will gain from enacting a carbon tax that will lead to a reduction in the use of fossil fuels. Who are the gainers and who are the losers?
2. What could industrial nations do to compromise with developing countries and oil producers in order to provide better incentives for adopting a carbon tax, reducing world-wide carbon emissions?

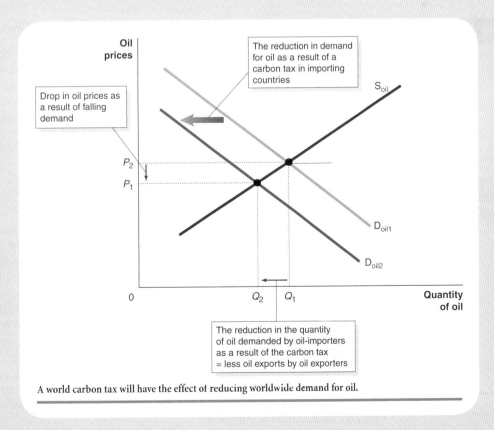

A world carbon tax will have the effect of reducing worldwide demand for oil.

Key Terms

Summary

13.1 LEARNING OBJECTIVE

Identify examples of positive and negative externalities and use graphs to show how externalities affect economic efficiency, **pages 418–423.**

Externalities and Economic Efficiency

An **externality** is a benefit or cost to parties who are not involved in a transaction. Pollution and other externalities in production cause a difference between the **private cost** borne by the producer of a good or services and the **social cost**, which includes any external cost, such as the cost of pollution. An externality in consumption causes a difference between the **private benefit** received by the consumer and the **social benefit**, which includes any external benefit. If externalities exist in production or consumption, the market will not produce the optimal level of a good or service. This outcome is referred to as **market failure**. Externalities arise when property rights do not exist or cannot be legally enforced. **Property rights** are the rights individuals or businesses have to the exclusive use of their property, including the right to buy or sell it.

13.2 LEARNING OBJECTIVE

Discuss the Coase theorem and explain how private bargaining can lead to economic efficiency in a market with an externality, **pages 423–427.**

Private Solutions to Externalities: The Coase Theorem

Externalities and market failures result from incomplete property rights or from the difficulty of enforcing property rights in certain situations. When an externality exists, and the efficient quantity of a good is not being produced, the total cost of reducing the externality is usually less than the total benefit. According to the **Coase theorem**, if **transactions costs** are low, private bargaining will result in an efficient solution to the problem of externalities.

13.3 LEARNING OBJECTIVE

Analyze government policies to achieve economic efficiency in a market with an externality, **pages 427–432.**

Government Policies to Deal with Externalities

When private solutions to externalities are unworkable, the government sometimes intervenes. One way to deal with a negative externality in production is to impose a tax equal to the cost of the externality. The tax causes the producer of the good to internalize the externality. The government can deal with a positive externality in consumption by giving consumers a subsidy, or payment, equal to the value of the externality. Government taxes and subsidies intended to bring about an efficient level of output in the presence of externalities are called **Pigovian taxes and subsidies**. Although the federal government has sometimes used subsidies and taxes to deal with externalities, in dealing with pollution, it has more often used a command and control approach. A **command and control approach** involves the government imposing quantitative limits on the amount of pollution allowed or requiring firms to install specific pollution control devices. Direct pollution controls of this type are not economically efficient, however. As a result, Congress decided to use a system of tradable emissions allowances to reduce sulfur dioxide emissions.

Four Categories of Goods

There are four categories of goods: private goods, public goods, quasi-public goods, and common resources. **Private goods** are both rival and excludable. **Rivalry** means that when one person consumes a unit of a good, no one else can consume that unit. **Excludability** means that anyone who does not pay for a good cannot consume it. **Public goods** are both nonrivalrous and nonexcludable. Private firms are usually not willing to supply public goods because of free riding. **Free riding** involves benefiting from a good without paying for it. **Quasi-public goods** are excludable but not rival. **Common resources** are rival but not excludable. The **tragedy of the commons** refers to the tendency for a common resource to be overused. The tragedy of the commons results from a lack of clearly defined and enforced property rights. We find the market demand curve for a private good by adding the quantity of the good demanded by each consumer at each price. We find the demand curve for a public good by adding vertically the price each consumer would be willing to pay for each quantity of the good. The optimal quantity of a public good occurs where the demand curve intersects the curve representing the marginal cost of supplying the good.

Review, Problems and Applications

 Visit www.pearsoned.co.uk/awe/hubbard to complete these exercises online and get instant feedback.

Get Ahead of the Curve

13.1 LEARNING OBJECTIVE   Identify examples of positive and negative externalities and use graphs to show how externalities affect economic efficiency, **pages 418–423.**

Review Questions

1.1 What is an externality? Give an example of a positive externality and give an example of a negative externality.

1.2 When will the private cost of producing a good differ from the social cost? Give an example. When will the private benefit from consuming a good differ from the social benefit? Give an example.

1.3 What is economic efficiency? How do externalities affect the economic efficiency of a market equilibrium?

1.4 What is market failure? When is market failure likely to arise?

1.5 Briefly discuss the relationship between property rights and the existence of externalities.

Problems and Applications

1.6 The chapter states that your consuming a Big Mac does not create an externality. But suppose you arrive at your favorite McDonald's at lunchtime and get in a long line to be served. By the time you reach the counter, there are 10 people in line behind you. Because you decided to have a Big Mac for lunch—instead of, say, a pizza—each of those 10 people must wait in line an additional 2 minutes. Or suppose that after a lifetime of consuming Big Macs, you develop heart disease. Because you are now over age 65, the government must pay most of your medical bills through the Medicare system. Is it still correct to say that your consuming a Big Mac created no externalities? Might there be a justification here for the government to intervene in the market for Big Macs? Explain.

1.7 The chapter discusses the cases of consumption generating a positive externality and production generating a negative externality. Is it possible for consumption to generate a negative externality? If so, give an example. Is it possible for production to generate a positive externality? If so, give an example.

1.8 Hassan and Saif are college students. Each of them will probably get married later and have two or three children. Each knows that if he studies more in college, he'll get a better job and earn more than if he doesn't study. Earning more means the ability to spend more on their future families—things like nice clothes, admission to an expensive college, and travel. Hassan thinks about the potential benefits to his potential children when he decides how much studying to do. Saif doesn't.
  a. What type of externality arises from studying?
  b. Draw a graph showing this externality, contrasting the responses of Hassan and Saif. Who studies more? Who acts more efficiently? Why?

1.9 A columnist for the *Wall Street Journal* observes: "No one collects money from those who benefit from the flood control a wetland provides, or the nutrient recycling a forest does…. In a nutshell, market failures help drive habitat loss." What does the columnist mean by *market failures*? What does she mean by *habitat loss*? Explain why she believes one is causing the other. Illustrate your argument with a graph showing the market for land to be used for development.

Source: Sharon Begley, "Furry Math? Market Has Failed to Capture True Value of Nature," *Wall Street Journal*, August 9, 2002, p. B1.

13.2 LEARNING OBJECTIVE   Discuss the Coase theorem and explain how private bargaining can lead to economic efficiency in a market with an externality, **pages 423–427.**

Review Questions

2.1 What do economists mean by "an economically efficient level of pollution"?

2.2 What is the Coase theorem? What are transactions costs? When are we likely to see private solutions to the problem of externalities?

Problems and Applications

2.3 Is it ever possible for an *increase* in pollution to make society better off? Briefly explain using a graph like Figure 13-3 on page 424.

2.4 If the marginal cost of reducing a certain type of pollution is zero, should all of that pollution be eliminated? Briefly explain.

2.5 Discuss the factors that determine the marginal cost of reducing crime. Discuss the factors that determine the marginal benefit of reducing crime. Would it be economically efficient to reduce the amount of crime to zero? Briefly explain.

2.6 Briefly explain whether you agree or disagree with the following statement: "Sulfur dioxide emissions cause acid rain and breathing difficulties for people with respiratory problems. The total benefit to society is greatest if we completely eliminate sulfur dioxide emissions. Therefore, the economically efficient level of emissions is zero."

2.7 In cleaning up oil spills, cleaning the first 90 percent is easy. But the tradeoffs for the remaining 10 percent are usually large. It is estimated that the last 1 percent of oil removed can cost seven times as much as the first 99 percent. Why should it be any more costly to clean up the last 1 percent of an oil spill than to clean up the first 1 percent? What do you think the trade-offs are?

2.8 Bees pollinate apple trees. We know that owners of apple orchards and owners of beehives are able to negotiate private agreements. Is it likely that as a result of these private agreements the market supplies the efficient quantities of apple trees and beehives? Are there any real-world difficulties that might stand in the way of achieving this efficient outcome?

13.3 LEARNING OBJECTIVE   Analyze government policies to achieve economic efficiency in a market with an externality, **pages 427–432.**

Review Questions

3.1 What is a Pigovian tax? At what level must a Pigovian tax be set to achieve efficiency?

3.2 Why do most economists prefer tradable emissions allowances rather than the command and control approach to pollution?

Problems and Applications

3.3 Why does the government subsidize the purchase of college educations but not the purchase of hamburgers?

3.4 Good new technologies have very large social benefits. Does this observation justify the government subsidizing the production of new technologies? If so, how might the government do this?

3.5 We saw in this chapter that market failure occurs when firms ignore the costs generated by pollution in deciding how much to produce. Government intervention is usually necessary to bring about a more efficient level of production. Before 1989, the Communist governments of Eastern Europe directly controlled the production of most goods and were free to choose how much of each good would be produced and what production process would be used. When these Communist governments collapsed, it was revealed that the countries of Eastern Europe suffered from very high levels of pollution, much higher than had existed in other high-income markets. Discuss reasons why the non-market Communist system generated more pollution than market economies.

3.6 Recall the definition of *normal good* given in Chapter 3. Is environmental protection a normal good? If so, is there any connection between this fact and the fact that more-developed nations are more concerned about the environment while less-developed countries are more concerned about economic development? Briefly explain. How do the marginal cost and marginal benefit of environmental protection change with economic development?

3.7 **(Related to *solved problem 13-3* on page 428)** The fumes from dry cleaners can contribute to air pollution. Suppose the following graph illustrates the situation in the dry cleaning market.

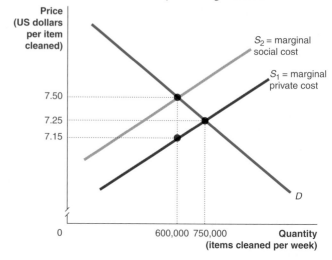

a. Explain how a government can use a tax on dry cleaning to bring about the efficient level of production. What should the value of the tax be?

b. How large is the deadweight loss (in u.s. dollars) from excessive dry cleaning, according to the figure?

3.8 The graph in the next column illustrates the situation in the dry cleaning market. In contrast to problem 3.7, the marginal social cost of the pollution rises as the quantity of items cleaned per week increases. In addition, there are two demand curves, one for a smaller city, D_S, the other for a larger city, D_L.

   a. Explain why the marginal social cost curve has a different slope than the marginal private cost curve.

   b. What tax per item cleaned will achieve economic efficiency in the smaller city? In the larger city? Explain why the efficient tax is different in the two cities.

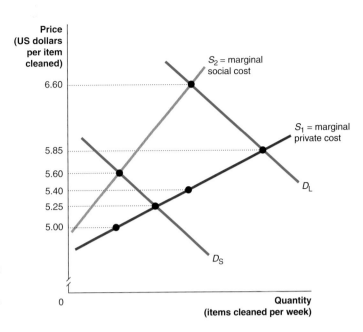

13.4 LEARNING OBJECTIVE

Explain how goods can be categorized on the basis of whether they are rival or excludable, and use graphs to illustrate the efficient quantities of public goods and common resources, **pages 432–443.**

Review Questions

4.1 Define rivalry and excludability and use these terms to discuss the four categories of goods.

4.2 What is a public good? What is free riding? How is free riding related to the tendency of a public good to create market failure?

4.3 What is the tragedy of the commons? How can it be avoided?

Problems and Applications

4.4 (Related to *Solved Problem 13-4* on page 438) Suppose that Yusuf and Yusr are the only two people in the small town of Andover. Andover has land available to build a park of no more than 9 acres. Yusuf and Yusr's demand schedules for the park are as follows:

YUSR	
PRICE PER ACRE IN US$	NUMBER OF ACRES
10	0
9	1
8	2
7	3
6	4
5	5
4	6
3	7
2	8
1	9

YUSEF	
PRICE PER ACRE IN US$	NUMBER OF ACRES
15	0
14	1
13	2
12	3
11	4
10	5
9	6
8	7
7	8
6	9

The supply curve is as follows:

PRICE IN US$	NUMBER OF ACRES
11	1
13	2
15	3
17	4
19	5
21	6
23	7
25	8
27	9

a. Draw a graph showing the optimal size of the park. Be sure to label the curves on the graph.

b. Briefly explain why a park of 2 acres is not optimal.

4.5 Commercial whaling has been described as a modern example of the tragedy of the commons. Briefly explain whether you agree or disagree.

4.6 According to an article in the *Wall Street Journal*, economist Paul Romer of Stanford University has argued: "The market mechanism and property rights are excellent at conserving scarce resources and putting them to the most profitable use.... They aren't so good at encouraging the production and distribution of new ideas, which are critical to progress." What characteristics of the production and distribution of new ideas might make it difficult for the market to produce the optimal amount?

Source: David Wessel, "Precepts from Professor Summers," *Wall Street Journal*, October 17, 2002.

4.7 The more frequently bacteria are exposed to antibiotics, the more quickly the bacteria will develop resistance to the antibiotics. Briefly discuss in what sense antibiotics can be considered a common resource.

4.8 Put each of these goods or services into one of the boxes in Figure 13-8 on page 433. That is, categorize them as private goods, public goods, quasi-public goods, or common resources.
a. A television broadcast of the World Cup
b. Home mail delivery
c. Education in a public school
d. Education in a private school
e. Hiking in a park surrounded by a fence
f. Hiking in a park not surrounded by a fence
g. An apple

4.9 (Related to the *Making the Connection* on page 433) Explain whether you agree or disagree with the following statement: "Providing health care is obviously a public good. If one person becomes ill and doesn't receive treatment, that person may infect many other people. If many people become ill, then the output of the economy will be negatively affected. Therefore, providing health care is a public good that should be supplied by the government."

Comparative Advantage and the Gains from International Trade

Trade Policy: Who Wins and Who Loses?

Trade is, simply, the act of buying or selling. Is there a difference between trade that takes place within a country and international trade? Within the United Arab Emirates, for example, domestic trade makes it possible for consumers in Abu Dhabi to eat chicken grown in Ras Al-Khaima or for consumers in Dubai to use furniture made in Sharjah. Similarly, international trade makes it possible for consumers in the UAE to drink milk from Saudi Arabia or use HD-DVD players from Japan. But one significant difference between domestic trade and international trade is that international trade is more controversial. To see this, think of 30 years ago when most of the TVs, shoes, clothing, and toys consumed in the Arab world were produced mainly by firms in other countries. Today, some of these goods are produced within the Arab world. This shift has benefited Arab workers because domestic firms were able to grow and hire more labor,

and hence more job opportunities were created. Not surprisingly, many Arab countries favor reducing international trade because they believe doing so would preserve domestic jobs. Arab consumers, on the other hand, are expected to lose because foreign-made goods, e.g., Chinese goods, have lower prices than the Arab-made goods.

But do restrictions on trade actually preserve jobs? In fact, restrictions on trade may preserve jobs in particular industries, but only at the cost of reducing jobs in other industries. Consider, for example, Egypt's car industry. Egypt imposes a 140 percent import duty (tariff) on fully built imported cars with an engine capacity larger than 1.6 liters. Smaller cars with engines in the range of 1.3 to 1.6 liters used to be subject to a 104 percent duty, until it was reduced to 40 percent in 2005. On the other hand, Egypt has international car brands assembled locally with at least 45 percent domestically manufactured component parts, as required by local laws designed to support the growth of the domestic parts and assembly industry. The imported proportion of the car parts falls under a considerably lower

tariff bracket than fully built cars. This difference in the tariff rate between fully built cars and car parts has had implications for the prices of cars in Egypt.

For example, in 2009, a 1.5L Korean-made imported Hyundai Matrix would on average cost the Egyptian consumer around US$15,000; this is relatively cheaper than the sale price of the same Egyptian assembled Matrix. However, after adding the 40 percent tariff to the import price of the Korean-made Hyundai Matrix it becomes far more expensive than its Egyptian-assembled counterpart. Therefore, based on this scenario, the Egyptian-assembled Hyundai car can only be sold in the market as long as the tariff stays. If the tariff is lifted or substantially reduced, it will be cheaper for the consumer to buy the Korean-made car. In that sense, the tariff protects the Egyptian producer by restricting imports and foreign competition. But is restricting international trade a good idea? Some would argue in favor of restrictions and some against.

The tariff helps Egyptian firms that produce car parts and Egyptian car assemblers, but at the same time it effectively increases transportation costs for all other Egyptian industries as a result of higher car prices. The higher transportation costs make other products more expensive, reducing sales and employment in the other industries. In addition, it hurts consumers as a result of higher car and other products prices. So, now the question is: Should Egypt have a tariff on imports of cars? The tariff creates winners and losers. In the former group, we find Egyptian producers of domestic car parts and assemblers are potential winners. In the latter group, we expect Egyptian companies that will have to buy more expensive cars, and their employees, to be among the losers. In addition, major losers are Egyptian consumers, who must pay higher prices for many goods that increased in price, and who are not able to buy the cheaper foreign cars and are stuck with the domestically assembled ones. In this chapter, we will explore who wins and who loses from international trade, and review the political debate over whether international trade should be restricted.

AN INSIDE LOOK AT POLICY on **page 482** discusses a recent trade agreement between the GCC countries and Singapore.

LEARNING Objectives

After studying this chapter, you should be able to:

14.1 Discuss the role of **international trade** in the **Arab world economy**, page 454.

14.2 Understand the difference between **comparative advantage** and **absolute advantage** in international trade, page 459.

14.3 Explain **how countries gain** from international trade, page 461.

14.4 Analyze the economic effects of **government policies** that restrict international **trade**, page 468.

14.5 Evaluate the arguments over **trade policy** and **globalization**, page 476.

Economics in YOUR Life!

Why Does Egypt Still Have a High Tariff on Imported Cars?

The rapid growth of the car industry puts more pressure on the government to keep a high tariff. Politicians often support restrictions on trade to convince people that they are working for their best interests. The workers in the industries protected by tariffs are likely to vote for these politicians because the workers think trade restrictions will protect their jobs. But these workers are just a small fraction of the population. The majority of people are not workers in the industries that benefit from the protection from foreign competition. Millions of consumers have had to pay higher prices not only for cars, but also for transportation in general. How, then, have car manufacturers convinced the Egyptian government to keep the tariff and why don't most people oppose it? As you read the chapter, see if you can answer this question. You can check your answers against those we provide at the end of the chapter. **> Continued on page 480**

M arkets for internationally traded goods and services can be analyzed using the tools of demand and supply that we developed in Chapter 3. We saw in Chapter 2 that trade in general—whether within a country or between countries—is based on the principle of comparative advantage. In this chapter, we look more closely at the role of comparative advantage in international trade. We also use the concepts of consumer surplus, producer surplus, and deadweight loss from Chapter 4 to analyze government policies that interfere with trade. With this background, we can return to the political debate over whether the Arab world benefits from international trade. We begin by looking at how large a role international trade plays in the Arab world economy.

14.1 | Discuss the role of international trade in the Arab World economy.

The Arab World in the International Economy

International trade has significantly grown over the past 50 years. The increase in trade is the result of the falling costs of shipping products around the world, the spread of inexpensive and reliable communications, and changes in government policies. Firms can use large container to send their products across the oceans at low cost. Business people today can travel to Europe or Asia using fast, inexpensive, and reliable air transportation. The Internet allows managers to communicate in seconds at a very low cost with customers and suppliers around the world. These and other improvements in transportation and communication have created a global marketplace that earlier generations of businesspeople could only dream of.

In addition, over the past 50 years, many governments have changed policies to encourage international trade. For example, tariff rates have fallen. A **tariff** is a tax imposed by a government on *imports* of a good into a country. **Imports** are goods and services bought domestically but produced in other countries. The average tariff rate has dramatically dropped in many countries. Today, for example, this rate is less than 2 percent in the U.S., 0.7 percent in Saudi Arabia, and 7 percent in Bahrain. Many countries around the world have signed free trade agreements, by which tariffs among signatory countries are eliminated or substantially reduced.

In North America, most tariffs between Canada, Mexico, and the United States were eliminated following the passage of the North American Free Trade Agreement (NAFTA) in 1994. Twenty-seven countries in Europe have formed the European Union, which has eliminated all tariffs among member countries, greatly increasing both imports and **exports**, which are goods and services produced domestically but sold to other countries. In the Arab-Gulf area, six Arab countries formed the Gulf Cooperation Council (GCC) in 1981, allowing free trade among the member countries. In 2008, the GCC announced a common market that will act as a unified bloc, after members unify their tariffs, when trading with other countries and blocs around the world. In 2005, 17 Arab countries in the MENA region, including the six GCC countries, signed the Greater Arab Free Trade Agreement (GAFTA) that aimed to encourage inter-Arab trade.

Tariff A tax imposed by a government on imports.

Imports Goods and services bought domestically but produced in other counties.

Exports Goods and services produced domestically but sold to other countries.

Making
the
Connection

Would the Greater Arab Free Trade Area Agreement (GAFTA) help Arabs Boost Exports?

Did you know that Arab countries began their first steps toward economic integration before European countries? This is a question that economics instructors in the Arab world often ask their students when they discuss regional trade agreements. Students usually answer, doubtfully, with a big "No." In fact, several attempts to promote regional economic integration among Arab countries have been made over the past 60 years (starting with the creation of the Arab League in 1945). Examples of these attempts are: (i) in 1953, six Arab countries signed the Agreement on Trade Flow and Transit Rules (Egypt, Iraq, Jordan, Lebanon, Saudi Arabia, and Syria), (ii) in 1964, Arab countries established the Arab Common Market (ACM) whose primary goal was to have full exemption from tariff and non-tariff barriers, and (iii) in 1981, the Economic and Social Council of the Arab League signed the Agreement on Trade Flow Facilitation and Development, which was a declaration of intent by the signatories to negotiate the full exemption of tariffs and nontariff measures for manufactured and semi-manufactured goods. The first two agreements created limited benefits to Arab countries as many of them did sign the agreements.[1]

Finally, in February 1997, the Arab Economic Union decided to create the Great Arab Free Trade Area (GAFTA) by the year 2008. For this purpose, the majority of the Arab League members signed a treaty aiming at the elimination of all trade barriers between them by gradually lowering by 10 percent each year the customs duties on their trade, gradually removing trade barriers in a process that started in February 1998. In September 2001, the Arab League's Economic and Social Council met in Riyadh and decided to move the deadline for the end of the transition period forward to early 2005.[2] As of 2009, there were 17 Arab countries in GAFTA: Jordan, the UAE, Bahrain, Tunisia, Saudi Arabia, Syria, Iraq, Oman, Palestine, Qatar, Kuwait, Sudan Lebanon, Libya, Egypt, Yemen, and Morocco.

Goods of Arab origin traded between GAFTA members should be treated the same as local imports, and therefore are fully exempted from customs duties.

The main privileges given to Arab countries are summarized as follows:[3]

1. Since 2005, goods of Arab origin and traded between GAFTA members are fully exempted from customs duties.

2. A preferential treatment is granted to the least developing Arab counties: Sudan and Yemen. These countries enjoy free access to the markets of GAFTA members while they are obligated to reduce customs duties on imports from GAFTA members by only a percentage of 16 percent to 20 percent.

3. Palestine is granted free access to the GAFTA markets with no obligation to give similar treatment to its imports from GAFTA members.

4. No additional taxes should be imposed on goods originated in GAFTA members.

5. Elimination of all non-tariff barriers such as: excessive technical barriers, excessive administrative barriers, and excessive financial barriers (transit fees).

6. GAFTA members should treat goods imported from each other the same as domestically produced goods.

Many economists are skeptical about the extent to which GAFTA has been successful in promoting trade among its members. For example, the 2008 World Bank Economic Developments and Prospects Report indicates that intraregional trade among GAFTA countries is low compared with its potential, and with levels achieved by economic blocs elsewhere in the world. For example, intraregional merchandise exports among GAFTA members are about 9 percent of total bloc exports, which is much less than the levels achieved by blocs such as the North American Free Trade Agreement (NAFTA) and the Association of Southeast Asian Nations (ASEAN). A very common explanation of these low levels of intraregional trade is because production and trade structures across the Arab world do not complement each other. The following table shows the level of trade with partners in several regional agreements within the Arab world.

(Continued)

Merchandise Imports and Exports with Partners as a Share of Total Merchandise Trade in 2007

AGREEMENT COUNTRY	AGADIR AGREEMENT*	ARAB MAGHREB UNION**	GCC***	GAFTA
Algeria	–	1.2	–	–
Bahrain			35	38.6
Egypt	1.5	–	–	13.6
Iraq	–	–	–	14.7
Jordan	3	–	–	35.7
Kuwait	–	–	4.5	7.4
Lebanon	–	–	–	30.6
Libya	–	2.7	–	5.1
Morocco	1.2	2.2	–	7.5
Oman	–	–	11	12.2
Qatar	–	–	6.4	7.5
Saudi Arabia	–	–	4.1	9.1
Syria	–	–	–	46.7
Tunisia	1.4	6.7	–	7.4
UAE	–	–	4.8	7.4
Yemen	–	–	–	24.5
Mauritania	–	2.8	–	–
Sudan	–	–	–	18.3

Sources: 2008 "MENA Economic Developments and Prospects: Regional Integration for Global Competitiveness," The World Bank, www.worldbank.org.

*Agadir Agreement is a free trade zone between the Arabic Mediterranean nations. It was signed in Rabat, Morocco, on February 25, 2004, and aims at establishing a free trade area between Jordan, Tunisia, Egypt, and Morocco.

**Arab Maghreb Union is a pan-Arab trade agreement aiming at establishing economic and political unity between North African countries, namely: Algeria, Libya, Mauritania, Morocco, and Tunisia.

***GCC, the Gulf Cooperation Council, is a trade bloc involving the six Arab countries of the Arab Gulf: Bahrain, Kuwait, Oman, Qatar, Saudi Arabia, and the UAE.

The percentages shown in the last column of the previous table indicate that, except for a few successful cases, such as Syria, Bahrain, and Jordan, the level of trade between Arab countries in the same free trade agreement is really low. This explains why many economists are raising doubts as to whether GAFTA and other Arab sub-regional free trade agreements can achieve their desired economic goals.

Source 1: "League of Arab States: Greater Arab Free Trade Agreement," The Institute for Domestic and International Affairs, Inc. (IDIA), Rutgers Model United Nations, 2007.
Source 2: "Arab Free Trade Area," European Institute for Research on Euro-Arab Cooperation, www.medea.be/en/themes/economy-and-trade/arab-free-trade-area-afta/.
Source 3: "The Great Arab Free Trade Area: An Explanatory Guide," The General Assembly of the Arab League (in Arabic), 2007.

The Importance of Trade to the Arab Economy

Arab consumers buy increasing quantities of goods and services produced in other countries. At the same time, businesses sell increasing quantities of goods and services to consumers in other countries. *Merchandise exports and imports* refer to internationally traded manufactured goods or raw materials such as cloths and petroleum. Also, countries trade commercial *services* such as telecommunication or financial and insurance services. The total exports of a country as a percentage of its gross domestic product reflects the importance of international trade in that particular economy.

Figure 14-1 shows the share of foreign trade in some selected Arab nations' incomes between 1995 and 2007. As major oil exporters, the GCC countries depend heavily on

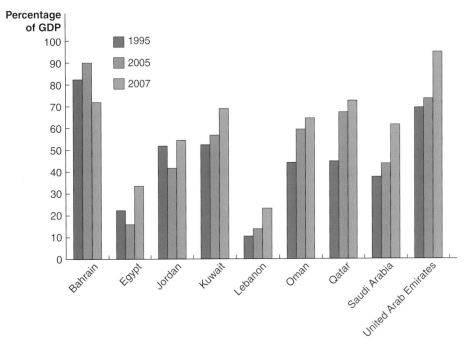

Figure 14-1

Exports of Goods and Services as a Percentage of GDP in Selected Arab Countries

Exports are increasing in importance for many Arab countries' incomes. Arab oil-producing countries experienced an increasing export share in 2007 due to the increase in oil prices.

Source: World Bank, World Development Indicators (WDI), 2009.

exports, which made up more than 50 percent of their incomes in 2007. In Jordan, due to increasing trade with other Arab countries and the promotion of free trade, international trade made up more than 50 percent of its income. Despite less dependence on international trade, the importance of exports in Egypt's and Lebanon's incomes almost doubled between 2000 and 2007. During the same period, the UAE depended on exports for 95 percent of its GDP; exceeding, by a large margin (more than 20 percent), Qatar, the next most dependent on exports among this group of Arab countries.

Figure 14-2 shows us that merchandise exports in major Arab countries have grown almost eightfold in value between 1998 and 2008. That reflects both increases in the volume of exports and the prices of major exports, mainly oil, petroleum products, and petrochemicals. Services in recent years have also seen important developments in the Arab world.

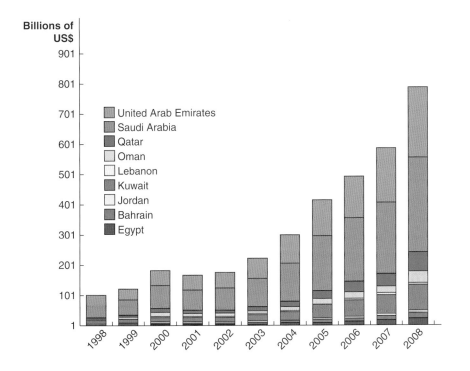

Figure 14-2

Merchandise Exports in Selected Arab Countries

Merchandise exports in major Arab countries have grown almost eightfold in value between 1998 and 2008.

Source: WTO, International Trade Statistics (ITS), 2009.

Figure 14-3

Inter-Arab Trade as a Percentage of Each Country's Total External Trade in 2006

Only four Arab countries - Jordan, Bahrain, Yemen, and Lebanon - depend on inter-Arab trade as more than 20% of their total external trade.
Source: ATFP, Arab Trade Financing Program 2006, www.atfp.org.ae.

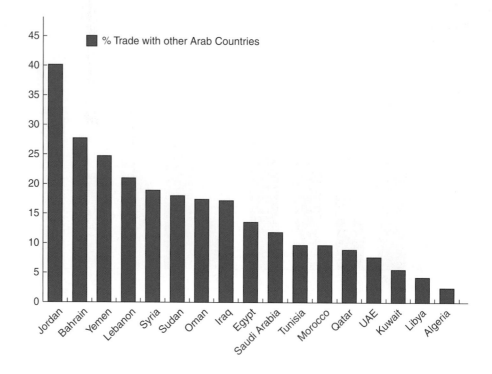

Since 2004, Kuwait has emerged as a new player in the telecommunications industry. The country has specialized in mobile communication services and its exports recorded rapid annual average growth of almost 156 percent. According to WTO 2007 statistics, Kuwait ranked fourth, after the EU, U.S., and Canada, as a major telecommunications services exporter worldwide.[4] In 2006, Kuwait tripled its telecommunications services' exports to US$3.4bn, and became the leading telecommunications provider in the Middle East. Kuwait connected an estimated 27 million mobile subscribers in neighboring Middle Eastern countries and in Sub-Saharan Africa. That amounts to about 40 percent of the total number of subscribers in the region. Egypt also showed a significant increase in its commercial services exports. The WTO 2007 report shows Egypt among the major worldwide exporters of construction and transportation services. Between 2000 and 2006, the exports of the two sectors were growing rapidly by an estimated annual growth rate of 24 percent and 13 percent, respectively.

Trading among Arab countries has gained momentum in recent years. An estimated 10 percent of total Arab countries' external trade takes place within the greater Arab area. The signing of the GAFTA by 17 Arab countries reflects the fact that Arabs are willing to take the necessary measures towards expanding inter-Arab trade. The importance of trading with other Arab nations is depicted in Figure 14-3, which shows trading with other Arab countries as a percentage of a country's total external trade.

By 2006, Jordan had by far the most dependent economy on Arab trade, with at least 40 percent of its total external trade being with Arab countries. As you saw earlier, exports in general make up more than 50 percent of Jordan's gross domestic product; hence trading with the Arab world makes almost one-fifth of Jordan's income. Following Jordan, Bahrain, Yemen, and Lebanon also rely on Arab trade for more than 20 percent of their total external trade.

The Importance of Arab Trade to the World Economy

In a world context, the Middle East's international trade is a relatively small fraction of the world trade, as shown by Figure 14-4. For the period 1948 to 2008, the percentage of Middle Eastern trade to total international trade ranged from 2 percent to about 6.8 percent. This share, however, grew steadily from 1948, to reach a peak around the

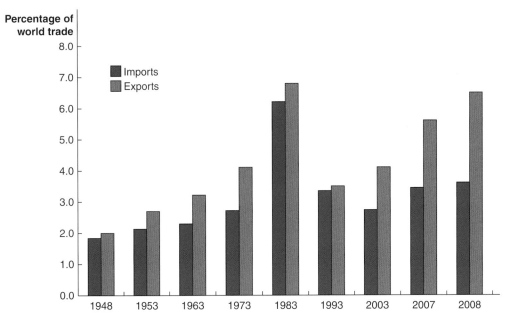

Figure 14-4

Middle East Trade as a Percentage of World Trade

During the period from 1948 to 2008, international trade in the Arab world accounted for a relatively small fraction of world trade. Source: WTO, World Trade Statistics, 2009.

mid-1980s. The increase in oil prices in the 1970s, known as the first and second oil shocks, has contributed to almost doubling that share between 1973 and 1983.

The sharp decline in oil prices around the mid-1980s and in the 1990s, two Gulf wars, growing political tensions in the region, and a world recession in the 80s, have contributed to a sharp decline in production[5] capacity and exports. However, from 2003 to 2008, the rebound of oil prices and a faster world growth resulted in a recovery in exports and an increase in the share of the Middle East international trade in world trade to almost 6.5 percent by 2008. In addition, efforts to diversify the oil economies to become less dependent on oil, the introduction of more free trade policies, the abandoning of high protection of local industries, and a growing trade among Arab countries have helped that recovery.

14.2 | Understand the difference between comparative advantage and absolute advantage in international trade.

14.2 LEARNING OBJECTIVE

Comparative Advantage In International Trade

Why have businesses around the world increasingly looked for markets in other countries? Why have consumers increasingly purchased goods and services made in other countries? People trade for one reason: trade makes them better off. Whenever a buyer and seller agree to a sale, they must both believe they are better off; otherwise, there would be no sale. This outcome must hold whether the buyer and seller live in the same city or in different countries. As we will see, governments are more likely to interfere with international trade than they are with domestic trade, but the reasons for the interference are more political than economic.

A Brief Review of Comparative Advantage

In Chapter 2, we discussed the key economic concept of *comparative advantage*. **Comparative advantage** is the ability of an individual, a firm, or a country to produce a good or service at a lower opportunity cost than competitors. Recall that **opportunity cost** is the highest-valued alternative that must be given up to engage in an activity. People, firms, and countries specialize in economic activities in which they have a comparative advantage. In trading, we benefit from the comparative advantage of other people (or firms or countries), and others benefit from our comparative advantage.

Comparative advantage The ability of an individual, a firm, or a country to produce a good or service at a lower opportunity cost than competitors.

Opportunity cost The highest-valued alternative that must be given up to engage in an activity.

A good way to think of comparative advantage is to recall the example in Chapter 2 of you and your neighbor picking fruit. Your neighbor is better at picking both apples and cherries than you are. Why, then, doesn't your neighbor pick both types of fruit? Because the opportunity cost to your neighbor of picking her own apples is very high: she is a particularly skilled cherry picker, and every hour spent picking apples is an hour taken away from picking cherries. You can pick apples at a much lower opportunity cost than your neighbor, so you have a comparative advantage in picking apples. Your neighbor can pick cherries at a much lower opportunity cost than you can, so she has a comparative advantage in picking cherries. Your neighbor is better off specializing in picking cherries, and you are better off specializing in picking apples. You can then trade some of your apples for some of your neighbor's cherries, and both of you will end up with more of each fruit.

Comparative Advantage in International Trade

The principle of comparative advantage can explain why people pursue different occupations. It can also explain why countries produce different goods and services. International trade involves many countries importing and exporting many different goods and services. Countries are better off if they specialize in producing the goods for which they have a comparative advantage. They can then trade for the goods for which other countries have a comparative advantage.

We can illustrate why specializing on the basis of comparative advantage makes countries better off with a simple example involving just two countries and two products. Suppose the United States and Japan produce only cellphones and digital music players, like Apple's iPod. Assume that each country uses only labor to produce each good, and that Japanese and U.S. cellphones and digital music players are exactly the same. Table 14-1 shows how much each country can produce of each good with one hour of labor.

Notice that Japanese workers are more productive than U.S. workers in making both goods. In one hour of work, Japanese workers can make six times as many cell- phones and one and a half times as many digital music players as U.S. workers. Japan has an *absolute advantage* over the United States in producing both goods. **Absolute advantage** is the ability to produce more of a good or service than competitors when using the same amount of resources. In this case, Japan can produce more of both goods using the same amount of labor as the United States.

It might seem at first that Japan has nothing to gain from trading with the United States because it has an absolute advantage in producing both goods. However, Japan should specialize and produce only cellphones. It can obtain the digital music players it needs by exporting cellphones to the United States in exchange for digital music players. The reason that Japan benefits from trade is that although it has an *absolute advantage* in the production of both goods, it has a *comparative advantage* only in the production of cellphones. The United States has a comparative advantage in the production of digital music players.

If it seems contrary to common sense that Japan should import digital music players from the United States even though Japan can produce more players per hour of work, think about the opportunity cost to each country of producing each good. If

Absolute advantage The ability to produce more of a good or service than competitors when using the same amount of resources.

TABLE 14-1

An Example of Japanese Workers Being More Productive than American Workers

	OUTPUT PER HOUR OF WORK	
	CELLPHONES	DIGITAL MUSIC PLAYERS
JAPAN	12	6
UNITED STATES	2	4

	OPPORTUNITY COSTS	
	CELLPHONES	**DIGITAL MUSIC PLAYERS**
JAPAN	0.5 digital music player	2 cellphones
UNITED STATES	2 digital music players	0.5 cellphone

TABLE 14-2

The Opportunity Costs of Producing Cellphones and Digital Music Players

The table shows the opportunity cost each country faces in producing cellphones and digital music players. For example, the entry in the first row and second column shows that Japan must give up 2 cellphones for every digital musicplayer it produces.

Japan wants to produce more digital music players, it has to switch labor away from cellphone production. Every hour of labor switched from producing cellphones to producing digital music players increases digital music player production by 6 and reduces cellphone production by 12. Japan has to give up 12 cellphones for every 6 digital music players it produces. Therefore, the opportunity cost to Japan of producing one more digital music player is 12/6, or 2 cellphones.

If the United States switches one hour of labor from cellphones to digital music players, production of cellphones falls by 2, and production of digital music players rises by 4. Therefore, the opportunity cost to the United States of producing one more digital music player is 2/4, or 0.5 cellphones. The United States has a lower opportunity cost of producing digital music players and, therefore, has a comparative advantage in making this product. By similar reasoning, we can see that Japan has a comparative advantage in producing cellphones. Table 14-2 summarizes the opportunity each country faces in producing these goods.

14.3 | Explain how countries gain from international trade.

How Countries Gain from International Trade

Can Japan really gain from producing only cellphones and trading with the United States for digital music players? To see that it can, assume at first that Japan and the United States do not trade with each other. A situation in which a country does not trade with other countries is called **autarky**. Assume that in autarky each country has 1,000 hours of labor available to produce the two goods, and each country produces the quantities of the two goods shown in Table 14-3. Because there is no trade, these quantities also represent consumption of the two goods in each country.

Autarky A situation in which a country does not trade with other countries.

Increasing Consumption through Trade

Suppose now that Japan and the United States begin to trade with each other. The **terms of trade** is the ratio at which a country can trade its exports for imports from other countries. For simplicity, let's assume that the terms of trade end up with Japan and the United States being willing to trade one cellphone for one digital music player.

Terms of trade The ratio at which a country can trade its exports for imports from other countries.

	PRODUCTION AND CONSUMPTION	
	CELLPHONES	**DIGITAL MUSIC PLAYERS**
JAPAN	9,000	1,500
UNITED STATES	1,500	1,000

TABLE 14-3

Production without Trade

Once trade has begun, the United States and Japan can exchange digital music players for cellphones or cellphones for digital music players. For example, if Japan specializes by using all 1,000 available hours of labor to produce cellphones, it will be able to produce 12,000. It then could export 1,500 cellphones to the United States in exchange for 1,500 digital music players. (Remember: We are assuming that the terms of trade are one cellphone for one digital music player.) Japan ends up with 10,500 cellphones and 1,500 digital music players. Compared with the situation before trade, Japan has the same number of digital music players but 1,500 more cellphones. If the United States specializes in producing digital music players, it will be able to produce 4,000. It could then export 1,500 digital music players to Japan in exchange for 1,500 cellphones. The United States ends up with 2,500 digital music players and 1,500 cellphones. Compared with the situation before trade, the United States has the same number of cellphones but 1,500 more digital music players. Trade has allowed both countries to increase the quantities of goods consumed. Table 14-4 summarizes the gains from trade for the United States and Japan.

By trading, Japan and the United States are able to consume more than they could without trade. This outcome is possible because world production of both goods increases after trade. (Remember that, in this example, our 'world' consists of just the United States and Japan.)

Why does total production of cellphones and digital music players increase when the United States specializes in producing digital music players and Japan specializes in producing cellphones? A domestic analogy helps to answer this question: if a company shifts production from an old factory to a more efficient modern factory, its output will increase. In effect, the same thing happens in our example. Producing digital music players in Japan and cellphones in the United States is inefficient. Shifting production to the more efficient country—the one with the comparative advantage—increases total production. The key point is this: *Countries gain from specializing in producing goods in which they have a comparative advantage and trading for goods in which other countries have a comparative advantage.*

TABLE 14-4

The Gains from Trade for Japan and the United States

WITHOUT TRADE

Production and Consumption

	CELLPHONES	MP3 PLAYERS
Japan	9,000	1,500
United States	1,500	1,000

WITH TRADE

	Production with Trade		Trade		Consumption with Trade	
	CELLPHONES	MP3 PLAYERS	CELLPHONES	MP3 PLAYERS	CELLPHONES	MP3 PLAYERS
Japan	12,000	0	Export 1,500	Import 1,500	10,500	1,500
United States	0	4,000	Import 1,500	Export 1,500	1,500	2,500

With trade, the United States and Japan specialize in the good they have a comparative advantage in producing . . .

. . . and export some of that good in exchange for the good the other country has a comparative advantage in producing.

GAINS FROM TRADE

Increased Consumption

| Japan | 1,500 Cellphones |
| United States | 1,500 MP3 Players |

The increased consumption made possible by trade represents the gains from trade.

Solved Problem | 14-3

The Gains from Trade

The first discussion of comparative advantage appears in *On the Principles of Political Economy and Taxation*, a book written by David Ricardo in 1817. The following example illustrates Ricardo's idea of gains from trade, using dairy products and cloth production in Kuwait and Syria. The following table shows the quantity of output per worker, per year, of cloth (measured in sheets) and dairy products (measured in kilos).

OUTPUT PER YEAR OF LABOR		
	CLOTH	DAIRY PRODUCTS
KUWAIT	100	150
SYRIA	90	60

a. Explain which country has an absolute advantage in the production of each good.

b. Explain which country has a comparative advantage in the production of each good.

c. Suppose that Kuwait and Syria currently do not trade with each other. Each country has 1,000 workers, so each has 1,000 years of labor time to use producing cloth and dairy products, and the countries are currently producing the amounts of each good shown in the table:

	CLOTH	DAIRY PRODUCTS
KUWAIT	18,000	123,000
SYRIA	63,000	18,000

d. Show that Kuwait and Syria can both gain from trade. Assume that the terms of trade are that one sheet of cloth can be traded for one kilo of dairy products.

SOLVING THE PROBLEM:

Step 1: **Review the chapter material.** This problem is about absolute and comparative advantage and the gains from trade, so you may want to review the section "Comparative Advantage in International Trade," which begins on page 461, and the section "How Countries Gain from International Trade," which begins on page 461.

Step 2: **Answer question (a) by determining which country has an absolute advantage.** Remember that a country has an absolute advantage over another country when it can produce more of a good using the same resources. The first table in the problem shows that Kuwait can produce more cloth *and* more dairy products with one year's worth of labor than can Syria. Thus, Kuwait has an absolute advantage in the production of both goods and, therefore, Syria does not have an absolute advantage in the production of either good.

Step 3: **Answer question (b) by determining which country has a comparative advantage.** A country has a comparative advantage when it can produce a good at a lower opportunity cost. To produce 100 sheets of cloth, Kuwait must give up 150 kilos of dairy products. Therefore, the opportunity cost to Kuwait of producing one sheet of cloth is 150/100, or 1.5 kilos of dairy products. Syria has to give up 60 kilos of dairy products to produce 90 sheets of cloth, so its opportunity cost of producing one sheet of cloth is 60/90, or 0.67 kilos of dairy products. The opportunity costs of producing dairy products can be calculated in the same way. The following table shows the opportunity cost to Kuwait and Syria of producing each good.

OPPORTUNITY COSTS		
	CLOTH	DAIRY PRODUCTS
KUWAIT	1.5 kilos of dairy products	0.67 sheets of cloth
SYRIA	0.67 kilos of dairy products	1.5 sheets of cloth

Kuwait has a comparative advantage in dairy products because its opportunity cost is lower. Syria has a comparative advantage in cloth because its opportunity cost is lower.

Step 4: **Answer question (c) by showing that both countries can benefit from trade.** By now it should be clear that both countries will be better off if they specialize where they have a comparative advantage and trade for the other product. The following table is very similar to Table 14-4 and shows one example of trade making both countries better off. (To test your understanding, construct another example.)

WITHOUT TRADE

	PRODUCTION AND CONSUMPTION	
	CLOTH	DAIRY PRODUCTS
KUWAIT	18,000	123,000
SYRIA	63,000	18,000

WITH TRADE

	PRODUCTION WITH TRADE		TRADE		CONSUMPTION WITH TRADE	
	CLOTH	DAIRY PRODUCTS	CLOTH	DAIRY PRODUCTS	CLOTH	DAIRY PRODUCTS
KUWAIT	0	150,000	Import 18,000	Export 18,000	18,000	132,000
SYRIA	90,000	0	Export 18,000	Import 18,000	72,000	18,000

GAINS FROM TRADE

	INCREASED CONSUMPTION
KUWAIT	9,000 dairy products
SYRIA	9,000 cloth

YOUR TURN: For more practice, do related problems 3.4 and 3.5 on page 486 at the end of this chapter.

>> End Solved Problem 14-3

Why Don't We See Complete Specialization?

In our example of two countries producing only two products, each country specializes in producing one of the goods. In the real world, many goods and services are produced in more than one country. For example, the United States and Japan both produce automobiles. We do not see complete specialization in the real world for three main reasons:

- *Not all goods and services are traded internationally.* Even if, for example, Japan had a comparative advantage in the production of medical services, it would be difficult for Japan to specialize in producing medical services and then export them. There is no easy way for U.S. patients who need operations to receive them from surgeons in Japan.

- *Production of most goods involves increasing opportunity costs.* Recall from Chapter 2 that production of most goods involves increasing opportunity costs. As a result, when the United States devotes more workers to producing digital music players, the opportunity cost of producing more digital music players will increase. At some point, the opportunity cost of producing digital music players in the United States may rise to the level of the opportunity cost of producing digital music players in Japan. When that happens, international trade will no longer push the United States further toward complete specialization. The same will be true of Japan: increasing opportunity cost will cause Japan to stop short of complete specialization in producing cellphones.

- *Tastes for products differ.* Most products are *differentiated.* Cellphones, digital music players, cars, and televisions—to name just a few products—come with a wide variety of features. When buying automobiles, some people look for reliability and good gasoline mileage, others look for room to carry seven passengers, and still others want styling and high performance. So, some car buyers prefer Toyota Prius hybrids, some prefer Chevy Suburbans, and others prefer BMWs. As a result, Japan, the United States, and Germany may each have a comparative advantage in producing different types of automobiles.

Does Anyone Lose as a Result of International Trade?

In our cellphone and digital music player example, consumption increases in both the United States and Japan as a result of trade. Everyone gains, and no one loses. Or do they? In our example, we referred repeatedly to "Japan" or the "United States" producing cellphones or digital music players. But countries do not produce goods—firms do. In a world without trade, there would be cellphone and digital music player firms in both Japan and the United States. In a world with trade, there would only be Japanese cellphone firms and U.S. digital music player firms. Japanese digital music player firms and U.S. cellphone firms would close. Overall, total employment will not change and production will increase as a result of trade. Nevertheless, the owners of Japanese digital music player firms, the owners of U.S. cellphone firms, and the people who work for them are worse off as a result of trade. The losers from trade are likely to do their best to convince the Japanese and U.S. governments to interfere with trade by barring imports of the competing products from the other country or by imposing high tariffs on them.

Making
the
Connection

The GCC Common Market: Are there Potential Gains? Who Wins and Who Loses?

In January 2008, the GCC countries took a major step towards their full regional economic integration when they launched a common market. The common market allows free labor and capital movements among the GCC states. GCC nationals will be able to pursue all economic, investment, and services activities in any of the member countries. The launching of the common market will also encourage harmony among member countries' laws and regulations.

According to the Doha Declaration of 2007, the common market would provide a number of advantages for its member countries, namely: (i) allowing GCC nationals to take full advantage of employment and investment opportunities available in the larger GCC economy, (ii) encouraging foreign and inter-GCC investments, (iii) maximizing the economic benefits resulting from large-scale economies, (iv) enhancing efficiency and encouraging the best use of resources, and (v) improving the GCC negotiating power with major economic blocs.

Despite these great expectations, some argue that the impact of the GCC common market would be modest due to the similar economic structure of the member countries and the relatively small volume of trade among them. The common market, however, is expected to bring some economic gains to the GCC member countries. These gains may not necessarily be evenly distributed; some countries may benefit more than others. Some countries may even end up losing.

Examining the GCC countries' economies, one can see that Saudi Arabia is the largest in terms of population and the size of its economy. Saudi nationals account for almost two-thirds of the total GCC population and its output is about half the GCC total production. Bahrain, on the other hand, is considered the smallest

(Continued)

economy. Qatar, the UAE, and Kuwait are the richest among GCC countries since they enjoy the largest per capita income; Saudi and Oman are at the other end of the scale. The UAE and Bahrain have the most diversified economies, with oil accounting for only one-third and a quarter of their respective GDPs. On the other side of the spectrum, Qatar and Saudi are the least diversified.

These differences will determine to a large extent who stands to win and who stands to lose. If national labor is allowed to move freely, Saudi and Oman would be the largest exporters of national labor. Labor will move to countries with the highest income per person. Indeed, a study by the Public Pension Agency in Saudi Arabia showed that the nationals of Saudi are, by a large number, those who accept the most jobs in other GCC countries, and that their preferred destination is Kuwait. In terms of capital flows, the direction of the flow will depend on the differences in business environment among the GCC economies and on the size of non-oil activities in a particular country. According to the World Bank's 2010 *Ease of Doing Business* report, Saudi Arabia followed by Bahrain and the UAE provide the most competitive business environment. Oman came at the end, behind Qatar and Kuwait. Oman and Kuwait are known to have more government controls, more regulations, and less competitive markets which could drive capital out. Oman also is the only GCC country that levies a relatively high corporate income tax rate of 15 percent on national corporations. On the other end, Qatar, Bahrain, and the UAE have no corporate taxes at all. The retail sector and local chain stores are also expected to seek expansion beyond the borders of their home countries. The main driving force would be the market size. Therefore, relatively larger markets such as Saudi and UAE are considered a potential target for retail business extension, enhancing more competition in the host countries.

In summary, the GCC common market may have few gains in terms of reducing national labor unemployment, attracting foreign capital, or improving the negotiating power of the GCC bloc in the global economy. Yet, some countries would end up net gainers in terms of exploiting better investment and employment opportunities. At the top of the list of expected gainers is Saudi Arabia as a net exporter of national labor and importer of national investments, especially in the retail sector. Oman, on the other hand, may be found at the bottom of the list, with its less diversified economy, less competitive markets, more regulations and government controls, and higher taxes. Both loose labor and capital may migrate, looking for better investment opportunities and a more business-friendly environment in other GCC countries, leaving Oman the ultimate loser.

Source: GCC Research Note: National Bank of Kuwait Economic Research, Kuwait, October 15, 2008.

YOUR TURN: Test your understanding by doing related problem 3.12 on page 486 at the end of this chapter.

Where Does Comparative Advantage Come From?

Among the main sources of comparative advantage are the following:

- *Climate and natural resources.* This source of comparative advantage is the most obvious. Because of geology, Saudi Arabia has a comparative advantage in the production of oil. Because of climate and soil conditions, Costa Rica has a comparative advantage in the production of bananas, and the United States has a comparative advantage in the production of wheat.

- *Relative abundance of labor and capital.* Some countries, such as the United States, have many highly skilled workers and a great deal of machinery. Other countries, such as China, have many unskilled workers and relatively little machinery. As a result, the United States has a comparative advantage in the production of goods that require highly skilled workers or sophisticated machinery to manufacture, such as aircraft, semiconductors, and computer software. China has a comparative advantage in the production of goods that require unskilled workers and small amounts of simple machinery, such as children's toys.

- *Technology.* Broadly defined, *technology* is the process firms use to turn inputs into goods and services. At any given time, firms in different countries do not all have access to the same technologies. In part, this difference is the result of past investments countries have made in supporting higher education or in providing support for research and development. Some countries are strong in *product technologies*, which involve the ability to develop new products. For example, firms in the United States have pioneered the development of such products as televisions, digital computers, airliners, and many prescription drugs. Other countries are strong in *process technologies*, which involve the ability to improve the processes used to make existing products. For example, firms in Japan, such as Toyota and Nissan, have succeeded by greatly improving the processes for designing and manufacturing automobiles.

- *External economies.* It is difficult to explain the location of some industries on the basis of climate, natural resources, the relative abundance of labor and capital, or technology. For example, why does Southern California have a comparative advantage in making movies or Switzerland in making watches or New York in providing financial services? The answer is that once an industry becomes established in an area, firms that locate in that area gain advantages over firms located elsewhere. The advantages include the availability of skilled workers, the opportunity to interact with other firms in the same industry, and being close to suppliers. These advantages result in lower costs to firms located in the area. Because these lower costs result from increases in the size of the industry in an area, economists refer to them as **external economies**.

External economies Reductions in a firm's costs that result from an increase in the size of an industry.

Comparative Advantage Over Time: The Rise and Fall—and Rise—of the U.S. Consumer Electronics Industry

A country may develop a comparative advantage in the production of a good, and then, as time passes and circumstances change, the country may lose its comparative advantage in producing that good and develop a comparative advantage in producing other goods. For several decades, the United States had a comparative advantage in the production of consumer electronic goods, such as televisions, radios, and stereos. The comparative advantage of the United States in these products was based on having developed most of the underlying technology, having the most modern factories, and having a skilled and experienced workforce. Gradually, however, other countries, particularly Japan, gained access to the technology, built modern factories, and developed skilled workforces. As mentioned earlier, Japanese firms have excelled in process technologies, which involve the ability to improve the processes used to make existing products. By the 1970s and 1980s, Japanese firms were able to produce many consumer electronic goods more cheaply and with higher quality than could U.S. firms. Japanese firms Sony, Panasonic, and Pioneer replaced U.S. firms Magnavox, Zenith, and RCA as world leaders in consumer electronics.

By 2007, however, as the technology underlying consumer electronics evolved, comparative advantage had shifted again, and several U.S. firms surged ahead of their Japanese competitors. For example, Apple Computer had developed the iPod and iPhone; Linksys, a division of Cisco Systems, took the lead in home wireless networking technology; and Kodak developed digital cameras with EasyShare software that made it easy to organize, enhance, and share digital pictures. As pictures and music converted to digital data, process technologies became less important than the ability to design and develop new products. These new consumer electronics products required skills similar to those in computer design and software writing, where the United States had long maintained a comparative advantage.

Once a country has lost its comparative advantage in producing a good, its income will be higher and its economy will be more efficient if it switches from producing the good to importing it, as the United States did when it switched from producing televisions to importing them. As we will see in the next section, however, there is often political pressure on governments to attempt to preserve industries that have lost their comparative advantage.

14.4 | Analyze the economic effects of government policies that restrict international trade.

Government Policies That Restrict International Trade

Free trade Trade between countries that is without government restrictions.

Free trade, or trade between countries that is without government restrictions, makes consumers better off. We can expand on this idea by using the concepts of consumer surplus and producer surplus from Chapter 4. Figure 14-5 shows the market for average-sized economic cars in Egypt, assuming autarky, where Egypt does not trade with other countries. The equilibrium price of a car is US$17,000 per car, and the equilibrium quantity is one million cars per year. The blue area represents consumer surplus, and the red area represents producer surplus.

Now suppose that Egypt begins importing cars from Korea and other countries that produce lower-priced average-sized cars, and that a car would sell for US$13,000 in these countries. Because the world market for average-sized cars is large, we will assume that Egypt can buy as many cars as it wants without causing the *world price* of US$13,000 per car to rise. Therefore, once imports of cars are permitted into Egypt, Egyptian firms will not be able to sell cars at prices higher than the world price of US$13,000, and Egypt's price will become equal to the world price.

Figure 14-6 shows the result of allowing imports of average-sized cars into Egypt. With the price lowered from US$17,000 to US$13,000, Egyptian consumers increase their purchases from one million cars to 1.5 million cars. Equilibrium moves from point *F* to point *G*. In the new equilibrium, Egyptian producers have reduced the quantity of cars they supply from one million cars to half a million cars. Imports will equal one million cars, which is the difference between Egypt's consumption and Egypt's production.

Under autarky, consumer surplus would be area *A* in Figure 14-6. With imports, the reduction in price increases consumer surplus, so it is now equal to the sum of areas

Figure 14-5

The Egyptian Market for Automobiles Under Autarky

This figure shows the market for average-sized economic cars in Egypt, assuming autarky, where Egypt does not trade with other countries. The equilibrium price of a car is US$17,000 per car, and the equilibrium quantity is one million cars per year. The blue area represents consumer surplus, and the red area represents producer surplus.

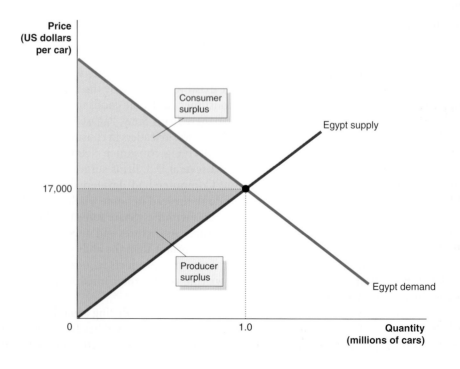

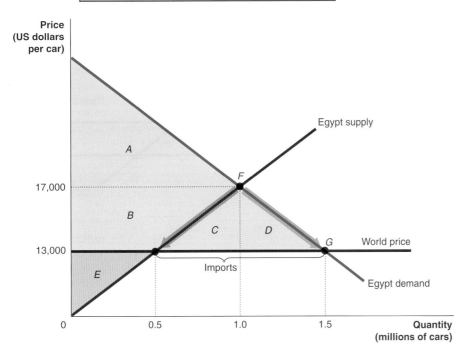

	Under Autarky	With Imports
Consumer Surplus	A	A + B + C + D
Producer Surplus	B + E	E
Economic Surplus	A + B + E	A + B + C + D + E

Figure 14-6

The Effect of Imports on Egypt's Automobile Market

When imports of cars are allowed into Egypt, the price of an average-size car falls from US$17,000 to US$13,000, Egyptian consumers increase their purchases from one million cars to 1.5 million cars. Equilibrium moves from point F to point G. In the new equilibrium, Egyptian producers have reduced the quantity of cars they supply from one million cars to half a million cars and imports will equal one million cars. Now consumer surplus will be the sum of areas A, B, C, and D, while the producer surplus will be decreased to the area E.

A, *B*, *C*, and *D*. Although the lower price increases consumer surplus, it reduces producer surplus. Under autarky, producer surplus was equal to the sum of the areas *B* and *E*. With imports, producer surplus is equal to only area *E*. Recall that economic surplus equals the sum of consumer surplus and producer surplus. Moving from autarky to allowing imports increases economic surplus in Egypt by an amount equal to the sum of areas *C* and *D*.

We can conclude that international trade helps consumers but hurts firms that are less efficient than foreign competitors. As a result, these firms and their workers are often strong supporters of government policies that restrict trade. These policies usually take one of two forms:

- Tariffs
- Quotas and voluntary export restraints.

Tariffs

The most common interferences with trade are *tariffs*, which are taxes imposed by a government on goods imported into a country. Like any other tax, a tariff increases the cost of selling a good. Figure 14-7 shows the impact of a tariff of US$3,000 per car. The tariff raises the price of cars in Egypt from the world price of US$13,000 per car to US$16,000 per car. At this higher price, Egypt's car producers increase the quantity they supply from half a million car to three quarters of a million cars. Egyptian consumers, though, cut back their purchases of cars from 1.5 million to 1.25 million cars. Imports decline from one million cars (1.5 million − 0.5 million) to half a million cars (1.25 million − 0.75 million). Equilibrium moves from point *G* to point *H*.

By raising the price of cars from US$13,000 to US$16,000, the tariff reduces consumer surplus by the sum of areas *A*, *T*, *C*, and *D*. Area *A* is the increase in producer surplus from the higher price. The government collects tariff revenue equal to the tariff of US$3,000 per car multiplied by the half million cars imported. Area *T* represents the government's tariff revenue. Areas *C* and *D* represent losses to Egyptian consumers

Figure 14-7

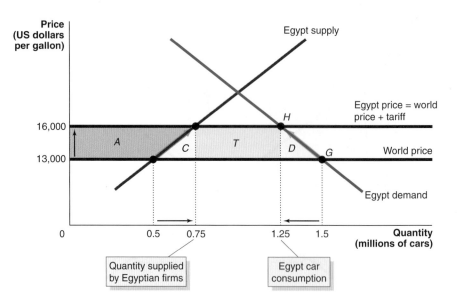

The Effects of a Tariff on Cars

Without a tariff on cars, Egyptian producers will sell 0.5 million cars, Egyptian consumers will purchase 1.5 million cars, and imports will be 1 million cars. The car price in Egypt will equal the world price of US$13,000 per car. The tariff raises the price of cars in Egypt from the world price of US$13,000 per car to US$16,000 per car. Egypt's car producers increase the quantity they supply from half a million car to three quarters of a million cars. Egyptian consumers cut back their purchases of cars from 1.5 million to 1.25 million cars. Imports decline from one million cars to half a million cars. Equilibrium moves from point G to point H. The tariff reduces consumer surplus by the sum of areas A, T, C, and D. Area A is the increase in producer surplus from the higher price. Area T represents the government's tariff revenue. Areas C and D represent deadweight loss.

that are not captured by anyone. They are deadweight loss that represents the decline in economic efficiency resulting from the car tariff. Area *C* shows the effect on Egyptian consumers of being forced to buy from Egyptian producers who are less efficient than foreign producers, and area *D* shows the effect of Egyptian consumers buying fewer cars than they would have at the world price. As a result of the tariff, economic surplus has been reduced by the sum of areas *C* and *D*. Recall from Chapter 4 that deadweight loss represents a loss of economic efficiency.

We can conclude that the tariff succeeds in helping Egypt's car producers but hurts Egyptian consumers and the efficiency of the Egyptian economy.

Quotas and Voluntary Export Restraints

Quota A numeric limit imposed by a government on the quantity of a good that can be imported into the country.

Voluntary export restraint (VER) An agreement negotiated between two countries that places a numeric limit on the quantity of a good that can be imported by one country from the other country.

A **quota** is a numeric limit on the quantity of a good that can be imported, and it has an effect similar to a tariff. A quota is imposed by the government of the importing country. A **voluntary export restraint (VER)** is an agreement negotiated between two countries that place a numeric limit on the quantity of a good that can be imported by one country from the other country. In the early 1980s, the United States and Japan negotiated a VER that limited the quantity of automobiles the United States would import from Japan. The Japanese government agreed to the VER primarily because it was afraid that if it did not, the United States would impose a tariff or quota on imports of Japanese automobiles. Quotas and VERs have similar economic effects.

The main purpose of most tariffs and quotas is to reduce the foreign competition that domestic firms face. Worth noting, the quota system is rarely used today in most Arab countries as part of the commitment to gradually reduce barriers to trade according to the WTO trade agreements. Let's assume a hypothetical quota that Egypt has imposed on its imports of sugar to protect domestic sugar producers. As shown in Figure 14-8, the effect of a quota is very similar to the effect of a tariff. By limiting imports, a quota forces the domestic price of a good above the world price. In this case, the sugar quota limits sugar imports to 1 million tons per year (shown by the bracket in Figure 14-8), forcing the domestic price of sugar up to US$700 per ton, or US$100 higher than the world price. The domestic price is above the world price because the quota keeps foreign sugar producers from selling the additional sugar in the Egyptian market, which would drive the price down to the world price.

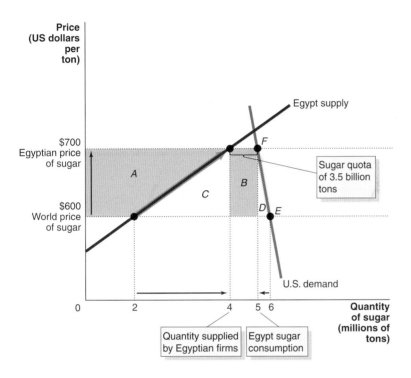

Loss of Consumer Surplus	=	Gain by Egyptian Sugar Producers	+	Gain to Foreign Sugar Producers	+	Deadweight Loss
A + C + B + D	=	A	+	B	+	C + D
US$2.24 billion	=	US$1.20 billion	+	US$0.35 billion	+	US$0.69 billion

Figure 14-8

The Economic Effect of the Sugar Quota

The sugar quota limits sugar imports to 1 million tons per year forcing the domestic price of sugar up to US$700 per ton. Egyptian producers increase the quantity of sugar they supply from 2 million tons to 4 million tons, and Egyptian consumers decrease their purchases of sugar from 6 million tons to 5 million tons. Equilibrium moves from point *E* to point *F*. The sugar reduces consumer surplus by the area *A* + *B* + *C* + *D*. Without a sugar quota, producer surplus would be equal to the area below the US$600 price line and above the supply curve. The higher domestic price resulting from the sugar quota increases the producer surplus of Egyptian sugar producers by an amount equal to area *A*.

At a price of US$700 per ton, Egyptian producers increased the quantity of sugar they supply from 2 million tons to 4 million tons, and the Egyptian consumers cut back their purchases of sugar from 6 million tons to 5 million tons. Equilibrium moves from point *E* to point *F*.

Measuring the Economic Effect of the Sugar Quota

Once again, we can use the concepts of consumer surplus, producer surplus, and dead-weight loss to measure the economic impact of the sugar quota. Without a sugar quota, the world price of US$600 per ton would also be the domestic price. In Figure 14-8, consumer surplus equals the area above the US$600 price line and below the demand curve. The sugar quota causes the domestic price to rise to US$700 a ton and reduces consumer surplus by the area *A* + *B* + *C* + *D*. Without a sugar quota, producer surplus received by Egyptian sugar producers would be equal to the area below the US$600 price line and above the supply curve. The higher domestic price resulting from the sugar quota increases the producer surplus of Egyptian sugar producers by an amount equal to area *A*.

A foreign producer must have a license from the Egyptian government to import sugar under the quota system. Therefore, a foreign sugar producer that is lucky enough to have an import license also benefits from the quota because it is able to sell sugar on the Egyptian market at US$700 per ton instead of US$600 per ton. The gain to foreign sugar producers is area *B*. Areas *A* and *B* represent transfers from Egyptian consumers of sugar to Egyptian and foreign producers of sugar. Areas *C* and *D* represent losses to Egyptian consumers that are not captured by anyone. They are deadweight losses and represent the decline in economic efficiency resulting from the sugar quota. Area *C* shows the effect of Egyptian consumers being forced to buy from Egyptian producers that are less efficient than foreign producers, and area *D* shows the effect of Egyptian consumers buying less sugar than they would have at the world price.

Figure 14-8 provides enough information to calculate the US dollar value of each of the four areas. The results of these calculations are shown in the table in the figure. The total loss to consumers from the sugar quota was US$550 million. About 53 percent of the loss to consumers, or US$291.5 million, was gained by Egyptian sugar producers as increased producer surplus. About 16 percent, or US$88 million, was gained by foreign sugar producers as increased producer surplus, and about 31 percent, or US$169.5 million, was a deadweight loss to the Egyptian economy. Eliminating the sugar quota would result in the loss of some jobs in the Egyptian sugar industry. On the other hand, eliminating the quota would result in new jobs being created, particularly in the candy industry. Egyptian candy companies will benefit from the decline in the sugar's price.

Solved Problem | 14-4

Measuring the Economic Effect of a Quota

Suppose that currently Lebanon both produces and imports apples. The Lebanese government then decides to restrict international trade in apples by imposing a quota that allows imports of only 20,000 boxes of apples into Lebanon each year. The figure shows the results of imposing the quota.

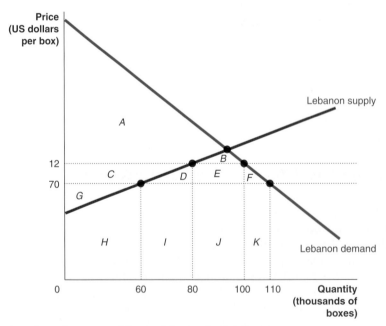

Fill in the following table, using the prices, quantities, and letters in the figure:

	WITHOUT QUOTA	WITH QUOTA
World price of apples	_____	_____
Price of apples in Lebanon	_____	_____
Quantity supplied by Lebanese firms	_____	_____
Quantity demanded by Lebanese consumers	_____	_____
Quantity imported	_____	_____
Area of consumer surplus	_____	_____
Area of producer surplus	_____	_____
Area of deadweight loss	_____	_____

SOLVING THE PROBLEM:

Step 1: Review the chapter material. This problem is about measuring the economic effects of a quota, so you may want to review the section "Quotas and Voluntary Export Restraints," which begins on page 471, and "Measuring the Economic Effect of the Sugar Quota," which begins on page 471.

Step 2: Fill in the table. After studying Figure 14-8, you should be able to fill in the table. Remember that consumer surplus is the area below the demand curve and above the market price.

	WITHOUT QUOTA IN US$	WITH QUOTA IN US$
World price of apples	10	10
Lebanese price of apples	10	12
Quantity supplied by Lebanese firms	60,000 boxes	80,000 boxes
Quantity demanded by Lebanese consumers	110,000 boxes	100,000 boxes
Quantity imported	50,000 boxes	20,000 boxes
Area of consumer surplus	A + B + C + D + E + F	A + B
Area of domestic producer surplus	G	G + C
Area of deadweight loss	No deadweight loss	D + F

YOUR TURN: For more practice, do related problem 4.11 on page 487 at the end of this chapter.

>> **End Solved Problem 14-4**

Making the Connection | Why the Egyptian Economy Is Compared with the South Korean Economy

Why is the Egyptian standard of living not as high as South Koreans? What went wrong? Whenever you discuss economic issues with ordinary Egyptians, you will find many of them hotly debating these questions. The main reason for this comparison goes back to the 1960s when both countries began setting their economic plans, with the common goal of achieving a high economic growth rate. What really surprises Egyptians these days is that Egypt and South Korea were almost at the same stage of development in the 1960s. In fact, economic indicators show that

Figure 1: GDP in Egypt and South Korea (1960–2008)

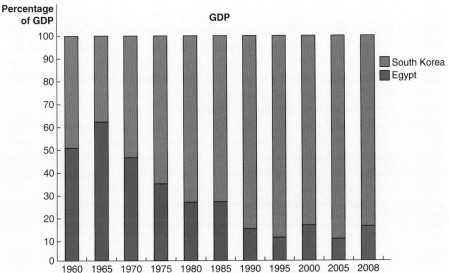

Source: World Bank: World Development Indicators (WDI).

(Continued)

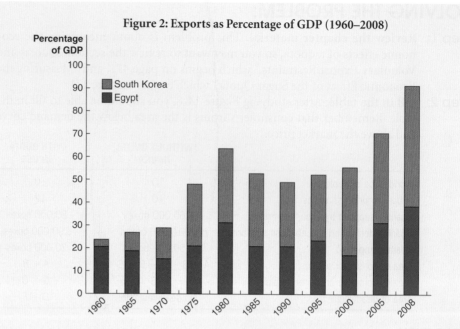

Figure 2: Exports as Percentage of GDP (1960–2008)

Source: World Bank: World Development Indicators (WDI).

the Egyptian economy is performing better than the South Korean economy, specifically, in terms of exports and aggregate output. Figures 1 and 2 show this fact.

In 1960, Egypt's gross domestic product (GDP) was US$4.144 billion compared with US$3.891 billion for South Korea. In addition, the percentage of exports to GDP in Egypt was 19.5, while it was only 3.1 for South Korea. Looking at the same indicators for 2008, we see an increase in Egyptian GDP to US$162.818 billion, while the South Korean GDP jumped to US$929.120 billion (more than five times the Egyptian GDP). The percentage of exports to GDP rose to 52.8 in South Korea compared with 37.6 in Egypt.

One explanation behind this dramatic difference in economic performance in both countries during the second half of the twentieth century is based on the trade policy adopted by each government in the 1960s. As pointed out by Paul Rivlin (2009), South Korea, and other East Asian Economies, started their economic development plan by implementing a *selective* import substitution policy that let private firms learn and achieve economies of scale (the so-called infant industry protection argument), followed by a policy of export incentives. It was obvious that the South Korean government believed that boosting exports would not be successful without reducing or eliminating import controls. This simply means that South Korea started to be integrated in the world economy in the 1960s. It is worth saying that the South Korean government used to penalize those firms that received government assistance if they failed to meet their export quota. The story was different in Egypt as the government played a central role in the economy by following the Soviet model of nationalizing private properties, and applying a policy of almost *complete* import substitution. This prevented the Egyptian economy from being integrated into the world economy and, thus, it lost the possible gains of open trading. During this socialist phase in the 1960s, the private sector was either eliminated or seriously weakened, so that it was unable to fill the economic gap left by the gradual withdrawal of the public sector, in the 1990s and the first decade of the twenty-first century, from several economic activities.

Source: www.worldbank.org; Paul Rivlin, *Arab Economies in the Twenty-First Century*, Cambridge, MA: Cambridge University Press, 2009.

Gains from Unilateral Elimination of Tariffs and Quotas

Some argue that eliminating tariffs and quotas would help the domestic economy only if other countries eliminated their tariffs and quotas in exchange. It is easier to gain political support for reducing or eliminating tariffs or quotas if it is done as part of an agreement with other countries that involves their eliminating some of their tariffs or quotas. But it is important to note that, as the example of the sugar quota shows, *the Egyptian economy would gain from the elimination of tariffs and quotas even if other countries do not reduce their tariffs and quotas.*

Making the Connection | **Qualified Industrial Zones and the Middle East Free Trade Area**

The United States has started to apply a new economic strategy that aims at integrating Arab economies into the world economy through a number of bilateral free trade agreements (FTA) between the U.S. and individual Arab countries, on one hand, and multilateral trade agreements between the U.S. and some Middle East economies, on the other hand. The later strategy began in 1996 when the U.S. Congress amended the Free Trade Area Implementation Act of 1975 with the goal of promoting peace, development, and trade in the Middle East—particularly in Egypt, Jordan, and Palestine—via the creation of Qualified Industrial Zones (QIZs) within those countries. QIZs are identified as designated geographic areas where companies located inside these zones enjoy free access status to the U.S. market, provided that they satisfy the agreed Israeli component (a minimum of 7 percent to 8 percent of the product price paid by the U.S. buyer in the U.S.–Jordan agreement) as per the pre-defined rules of origin. As a result of establishing QIZs in Jordan in 1997, Jordanian exports to the U.S. increased from US$2.4 million in 1998, to US$1.33 billion in 2007, of which 70 percent came from QIZs.[1]

In the same trend, the U.S. and Egypt signed a QIZ agreement in 2004. As indicated by Paul Rivlin (2009), QIZs in Egypt created 15,000 jobs, and Egyptian apparel exports to the U.S. rose by 5.3 percent in 2005 (from US$442 million in 2004, to US$444 million in 2005). This small percentage increase may seem disappointing; however, for some Egyptian government officials, it is a success, as it was expected that—without the QIZ agreement—the Egyptian garment exports to the U.S. would have decreased in 2005 under pressure from Chinese competition. Egyptian exports of textiles and textile products rose by 31 percent in 2006 (80 percent of QIZ companies produce textiles and clothing articles since Egypt has a comparative advantage in such industry). QIZs currently account for 33 percent of Egypt's total exports. In addition, the Egyptian government estimates that over the next few years, QIZ will create 300,000 new jobs.[2]

On the other hand, in 2003, the U.S. President, George W. Bush, created a plan aimed at enhancing the international trade with the Arab countries: first, by negotiating comprehensive free trade agreements with countries in the region bilaterally, and then, combining these into a single arrangement between the United States and the Middle East region as a whole. The strategy is known as the Middle East Free Trade Area (MEFTA). The U.S. administration began to implement this strategy by negotiating free trade agreements with Morocco, Oman, Bahrain, and the UAE. Several studies estimated the benefits of MEFTA on Arab economies and found that the economic impact is fairly small and that, in most Arab countries, imports from the U.S. increased by more than exports to the U.S. The main reason behind this result is that, in 2003, many Arab countries used to levy fairly high tariffs on U.S. exports, while the U.S. generally charges small duties on imports from Arab countries. So, when all tariffs between the U.S. and Arab countries are eliminated under the MEFTA, imports from the U.S. are expected to realize a significant increase relative to the increase in exports to the U.S. The estimated increase in welfare due to the MEFTA is far less than 1 percent of Arab countries' GDP.[3]

Source 1: Paul Rivlin, (2009), *Arab Economies in the Twenty-First Century*, Cambridge: Cambridge University Press.

Source 2: The American Chamber of Commerce in Egypt, www.amcham.org.eg; and the Egyptian Ministry of Trade and Industry, www.qizegypt.gov.eg.

Source 3: "The Arab World Competitiveness Review 2007," The World Economics Forum, www.weforum.org/en/initiatives/gcp/Arab%20World%20Competitiveness%20Report/index.htm.

Other Barriers to Trade

In addition to tariffs and quotas, governments sometimes erect other barriers to trade. For example, all governments require that imports meet certain health and safety requirements. Sometimes, however, governments use these requirements to shield domestic firms from foreign competition. This can be true when a government imposes stricter health and safety requirements on imported goods than on goods produced by domestic firms.

Many governments also restrict imports of certain products on national security grounds. The argument is that in time of war, a country should not be dependent on imports of critical war materials. Once again, these restrictions are sometimes used more to protect domestic companies from competition than to protect national security.

14.5 LEARNING OBJECTIVE   14.5 │ Evaluate the arguments over trade policy and globalization.

The Argument over Trade Policies and Globalization

The argument over whether governments should regulate international trade is very old. By the end of World War II in 1945, government officials in the United States and Europe were looking for a way to reduce tariffs and revive international trade. To help achieve this goal, they set up the General Agreement on Tariffs and Trade (GATT) in 1948. Countries that joined GATT agreed not to impose new tariffs or import quotas. In addition, a series of *multilateral negotiations*, called *trade rounds*, took place, in which countries agreed to reduce tariffs from the very high levels of the 1930s.

In the 1940s, most international trade was in goods, and the GATT agreement covered only goods. In the following decades, trade in services and in products incorporating *intellectual property*, such as software programs and movies, grew in importance. Many GATT members pressed for a new agreement that would cover services and intellectual property, as well as goods. A new agreement was negotiated, and in January 1995, GATT was replaced by the **World Trade Organization (WTO)**, headquartered in Geneva, Switzerland. More than 130 countries are currently members of the WTO.

World Trade Organization (WTO) An international organization that oversees international trade agreements.

Why do Some People Oppose the World Trade Organization?

During the years immediately after World War II, many low-income, or developing, countries erected high tariffs and restricted investment by foreign companies. When these policies failed to produce much economic growth, many of these countries decided during the 1980s to become more open to foreign trade and investment. This process became known as **globalization**. Most developing countries joined the WTO and began to follow its policies.

Globalization The process of countries becoming more open to foreign trade and investment.

During the 1990s, opposition to globalization began to increase. In 1999, this opposition took a violent turn at a meeting of the WTO in Seattle, Washington. The purpose of the meeting was to plan a new round of negotiations aimed at further reductions in trade barriers. A large number of protesters assembled in Seattle to meet the WTO delegates. Protests started peacefully but quickly became violent. Protesters looted stores and burned cars, and many delegates were unable to leave their hotel rooms.

Why would attempts to reduce trade barriers with the objective of increasing income around the world cause such a furious reaction? The opposition to the WTO comes from three sources. First, some opponents are specifically against the globalization process that began in the 1980s and became widespread in the 1990s. Second, other opponents have the same motivation as the supporters of tariffs in the 1930s—to erect trade barriers to protect domestic firms from foreign competition. Third, some critics of the WTO support globalization in principle but believe that the WTO favors the interests of the high-income countries at the expense of the low-income countries. Let's look more closely at the sources of opposition to the WTO.

Anti-Globalization Many people distrust globalization. Some believe that free trade and foreign investment destroy the distinctive cultures of many countries. As developing countries began to open their economies to imports from the United States and other high-income countries, these imports of food, clothing, movies, and other goods began to replace the equivalent local products. So, a teenager in a country like Saudi Arabia, Kuwait, or Qatar, which has its own national dress, might be sitting in a McDonald's restaurant, wearing Levi's jeans and a Ralph Lauren shirt, listening to a recording by U2 on his iPod, before going to the local movie theater to watch *Spider-Man 3*. Globalization has increased the variety of products available to consumers in developing countries, but some people argue that this is too high a price to pay for what they see as damage to local cultures.

Globalization has also allowed multinational corporations to relocate factories from high-income countries to low-income countries. These new factories in Indonesia, Egypt, Pakistan, and other countries pay much lower wages than are paid in the United States, Europe, and Japan and often do not meet the environmental or safety regulations that are imposed in high-income countries. Some factories use child labor, which is illegal in high-income countries. Some people have argued that firms with factories in developing countries should pay workers wages as high as those paid in the high-income countries. They also believe these firms should follow the health, safety, and environmental regulations that exist in the high-income countries.

The governments of most developing countries have resisted these proposals. They argue that when the currently rich countries were poor, they also lacked environmental or safety standards, and their workers were paid low wages. They argue that it is easier for rich countries to afford high wages and environmental and safety regulations than it is for poor countries. They also point out that many jobs that seem very poorly paid by high-income country standards are often better than the alternatives available to workers in low-income countries.

Making the Connection | The WTO Strategy for the Arab Region

In 2001, the United Nations Conference on Trade and Development (UNCTAD) organized the UNCTAD High-Level Meeting for Arab countries on WTO trade issues for representatives of Arab countries accredited to UNCTAD and WTO. The major items on the agenda included a review of the implementation of WTO agreements; future trade issues on international trade; and matters related to the accession to WTO. At that time, only 11 Arab countries were WTO members and 5 countries were observers.

The then WTO Director-General Mike Moore gave a speech delivering the WTO view toward the Arab world. The following extract is a part of his speech.

> We in the WTO are working on a Strategy for the Arab Region. There is a lot to do and it should have been done earlier. For the first time ever, we organized a meeting with Ambassadors from the Arab region to receive their advice on our strategy. We are also seeking guidance from other sources in the Arab region. The principal objectives of our strategy for the Arab region are:
>
> - **First, to raise awareness in the Arab world on WTO.** It is important to explain to the Arab world what the WTO is, what it does, and what to expect of its upcoming ministerial. Awareness must also be raised on the importance international trade for economic growth.
> - **Second, to facilitate the flow of information.** There is of course an undeniable language barrier confronting Arab members of WTO in the day-to-day work of the Organization. Another barrier to information flow is the dearth of Arab authors, and Arabic language publications, on WTO. These barriers must be overcome through improved information flow.

(Continued)

- **Third, to assist the Geneva-based missions of Arab delegations,** particularly small missions, in dealing with the very demanding work of WTO. The WTO is an organization in which large numbers of meetings can run simultaneously, and whose meetings require careful preparation as well as follow-up. Missions must be assisted in confronting this workload.

- **And, fourth, to prepare Arab countries for a potential round.** If a round is started, much work will be needed to help Arab countries seize the opportunities it provides.

Source: "The WTO and the Arab world: preparations for Doha," speech by Director-General Mike Moore at UNCTAD High-Level Meeting for Arab countries, Geneva, 20-21 June 2001. Transcript available at www.wto.org/english/news_e/spmm_e/spmm65_e.htm.

Note: As of 2009, 12 Arab countries became WTO members: Bahrain, Djibouti, Egypt, Jordan, Kuwait, Mauritania, Morocco, Oman, Qatar, Saudi Arabia, Tunisia, and the United Arab Emirates. The following five countries are observers: Algeria, Lebanon, Libya, Sudan, and Yemen, www.wto.org.

Protectionism The use of trade barriers to shield domestic firms from foreign competition.

'Old-Fashioned' Protectionism The anti-globalization argument against free trade and the WTO is relatively new. Another argument against free trade, called *protectionism*, has been around for centuries. **Protectionism** is the use of trade barriers to shield domestic firms from foreign competition. For as long as international trade has existed, governments have attempted to restrict it to protect domestic firms. As we saw with the hypothetical example of the sugar quota in Egypt, protectionism causes losses to consumers and eliminates jobs in the domestic industries that use the protected product. In addition, by reducing the ability of countries to produce according to comparative advantage, protectionism reduces incomes.

Why, then, does protectionism attract support? Most Arab countries adopted different protectionism measures in the past. Protectionism was justified on the basis of one of the following arguments:

- *Saving jobs.* Supporters of protectionism argue that free trade reduces employment by driving domestic firms out of business. It is true that when more-efficient foreign firms drive less-efficient domestic firms out of business, jobs are lost, but jobs are also lost when more-efficient domestic firms drive less-efficient domestic firms out of business. These job losses are rarely permanent. No economic study has ever found a long-term connection between the total number of jobs available and the level of tariff protection for domestic industries. In addition, trade restrictions destroy jobs in some industries at the same time that they preserve jobs in others. A sugar quota could have saved jobs in the Egyptian sugar industry, but it may also have destroyed some jobs in the Egyptian candy industry.

- *Protecting high wages.* Some people worry that firms in high-income countries will have to start paying much lower wages to compete with firms in developing countries. This fear is misplaced, however, because free trade actually raises living standards by increasing economic efficiency. When a country practices protectionism and produces goods and services it could obtain more inexpensively from other countries, it reduces its standard of living. In the 1970s, Saudi Arabia reduced imports of wheat and began growing it domestically. The government gave large subsidies to local producers to encourage growing wheat. By the late 1980s, Saudi became a net exporter of wheat. But this would entail a very high opportunity cost because growing wheat would require large amounts of water. Without the government's subsidy the wheat would have to sell for a very high price to cover these costs. By 2008, the government abolished the wheat self-sufficiency program after the 30-year-project almost depleted Saudi's water reserves. The Kingdom now aims at meeting the domestic demand totally through imports by 2016. Eliminating the subsidies to Saudi farmers at some future time would eliminate the jobs of Saudi wheat workers, but the standard of living in Saudi Arabia would rise as wheat prices declined and labor, machinery, and other resources moved out of wheat production and into production of goods and services for which Saudi has a comparative advantage.

- *Protecting infant industries.* It is possible that firms in a country may have a comparative advantage in producing a good, but because the country begins production of the good later than other countries, its firms initially have higher costs. In producing some goods and services, substantial 'learning by doing' occurs. As workers and firms produce more of the good or service, they gain experience and become more productive. Over time, costs and prices will fall. As the firms in the 'infant industry' gain experience, their costs will fall, and they will be able to compete successfully with foreign producers. Under free trade, however, they may not get the chance. The established foreign producers can sell the product at a lower price and drive domestic producers out of business before they gain enough experience to compete. To economists, this is the most persuasive of the protectionist arguments. It has a significant drawback, however. Tariffs used to protect an infant industry eliminate the need for the firms in the industry to become productive enough to compete with foreign firms. In the 1960s, the government of Egypt used the 'infant industry' argument to justify high tariff rates and lists of banned imports. Unfortunately, most of the infant industries never grew up, and they continued for years as inefficient drains on the economy.

- *Protecting national security.* As already discussed, a country should not rely on other countries for goods that are critical to its military defense. For example, Egypt would probably not want to import all its jet fighter engines from Iran.

Dumping

In recent years, some countries have extended protection to some domestic industries by using a provision in the WTO agreement that allows governments to impose tariffs in the case of *dumping.* **Dumping** is selling a product for a price below its cost of production. Although allowable under the WTO agreement, using tariffs to offset the effects of dumping is very controversial.

Dumping Selling a product for a price below its cost of production.

In practice, it is difficult to determine whether foreign companies are dumping goods because the true production costs of a good are not easy for foreign governments to calculate. As a result, the WTO allows countries to determine that dumping has occurred if a product is exported for a lower price than it sells for on the home market. There is a problem with this approach, however. Often there are good business reasons for a firm to sell a product for different prices to different consumers. For example, the airlines charge business travelers higher ticket prices than leisure travelers. Firms also use 'loss leaders'—products that are sold below cost, or even given away free—when introducing a new product or, in the case of retailing, to attract customers who will also buy full-price products. For example, when du started business and had to compete with Etisalat, the first company in the UAE telecom market, du gave the phone away free with every new subscription. During holydays, Carrefour offers toys at very cheap prices that could be in some cases below what they paid to the manufacturers. It's unclear why these normal business practices should be unacceptable when used in international trade.

Positive versus Normative Analysis (Once Again)

Economists emphasize the burden on the economy imposed by tariffs, quotas, and other government restrictions on free trade. Does it follow that these interferences are bad? Remember from Chapter 1 the distinction between *positive analysis* and *normative analysis.* Positive analysis concerns what *is.* Normative analysis concerns what *ought to be.* Measuring the impact of the sugar quota on the Egyptian economy is an example of positive analysis. Asserting that the sugar quota is bad public policy and should be eliminated is normative analysis. The sugar quota—like all other interferences with trade makes some people better off and some people worse off and it reduces total income and consumption. Whether increasing the profits of Egyptian sugar companies and the number of workers they employ justifies the costs imposed on consumers and the reduction in economic efficiency is a normative question.

Most economists do not support interferences with trade, such as the sugar quota. But the opposite view is certainly intellectually respectable. It is possible for someone to understand the costs of tariffs and quotas but still believe that tariffs and quotas are a good idea, perhaps because they believe unrestricted free trade would cause too much disruption to the economy.

The success of industries in getting the government to erect barriers to foreign competition depends partly on some members of the public knowing full well the costs of trade barriers but supporting them anyway. However, two other factors are also at work:

1 The costs tariffs and quotas impose on consumers are large in total but relatively small per person in a large country. In our hypothetical sugar quota example, the total burden of the quota spread across 80 million Egyptians would only be US$7 per person: too little to bother most people, even if they know that the burden exists. So, the burden of quotas and tariffs per person in a large country is usually too small for an individual person to worry about.

2 The jobs lost to foreign competition are easy to identify, but the jobs created by foreign trade are less easy to identify.

In other words, the industries that benefit from tariffs and quotas benefit a lot, whereas each consumer loses relatively little. This concentration of benefits and widely spread burdens makes it easy to understand why legislators are subject to strong pressure from some industries to enact tariffs and quotas and relatively little pressure from the general public to reduce them.

Economics in YOUR Life!

➤➤ **Continued from page 453**

At the beginning of the chapter, we asked you to consider how car companies have convinced the Egyptian government to keep the high tariff for years. In the chapter, we saw that the car tariff costs the Egyptian consumers as a result of higher domestic car prices. It also may have led several firms to eliminate domestic jobs and perhaps move their facilities to other countries as a result of higher transportation costs. This might seem to increase the mystery of why the government has kept the tariff; especially when it saves relatively few jobs in the Egyptian car industry. We have also seen that *per person*, the burden of the car tariff could be small per year. This cost is hidden and is not observable or directly linked to the car tariff for most consumers. Therefore, not too many people will be willing to take the time and effort to oppose the tariff. On the other hand, the Egyptian car industry's gains from the tariff are substantial, and hence car industry businessmen usually lobby hard to keep the tariff barriers high on fully made imported cars while reducing the tariff on parts. As a signatory of the General Agreement on Tariffs and Trade (GATT), the Egyptian government will have to gradually reduce the import tariff on vehicles by 2019.

Conclusion

There are few issues economists agree upon more than the economic benefits of free trade. However, there are few political issues as controversial as government policy toward trade. Many people who would be reluctant to see the government interfere with domestic trade are quite willing to see it interfere with international trade. The damage high tariffs inflicted on the world economy during the 1930s shows what can happen when governments around the world abandon free trade. Whether future episodes of that type can be avoided is by no means certain.

Read *An Inside Look at Policy* on the next page for a discussion of how eliminating tariffs benefits the GCC countries and Singapore.

The GCC-Singapore Free Trade Agreement

GULF NEWS, DECEMBER 15, 2008

First GCC Trade Accord Signed with Singapore

(a) Dubai: The six Gulf oil producers on Monday signed a free trade agreement (FTA) with Singapore, the first-ever FTA, a statement said.

"The Gulf Cooperation Council (GCC) Singapore FTA (GSFTA), the first-ever FTA for the GCC, is a key step forward for economic relations between Singapore and its 7th largest trading partner," the statement said.

The GCC and Singapore agreed to enhance cooperation in the air services sector. Such cooperation may include, among other things, concluding air services agreements between one or more of the GCC countries and Singapore.

The GCC currently accounts for 40 per cent of Singapore's oil imports. Bilateral trade with the GCC, comprising Saudi Arabia, the UAE, Qatar, Kuwait, Bahrain and Oman, reached a record high of US$42.4 billion (Dh105.45 billion) in 2007, a 127 per cent increase since 2002.

The agreement was signed in Doha between Singapore Prime Minister Lee Hsien Loong and his GCC counterparts, President-in-Office of the GCC Ministerial Council and Qatar Prime Minister Shaikh Hamad bin Jasem Al Thani, and GCC Secretary-General Abdul Rahman bin Hamad Al Attiyah.

(b) The GSFTA is a comprehensive free trade agreement covering areas including trade in goods, trade in services, investments, rules of origin, customs procedures, government procurement, electronic commerce, and economic cooperation.

(a) The agreement will grant tariff-free access for about 99 percent of Singapore's domestic exports, worth about US$3.1 billion in 2007. All GCC goods entering into Singapore will also be granted tariff-free access.

(b) The GSFTA will also encourage a greater recognition of Singapore's halal standards in the six-member Arab trade group. The GCC countries have committed to either recognize or begin talks to recognize the Singapore Muis Halal Standards (SMHS) as consistent and compliant with similar standards in their countries.

Recognition of SMHS by the GCC countries will not only facilitate trade in halal product exports to the GCC, but will also provide greater assurance to Gulf visitors that their dietary requirements will be met when they visit Singapore.

(c) The GSFTA allows Singapore-based companies and Singapore permanent residents to hold majority stakes in key sectors of the GCC markets. In particular, Singapore gained enhanced access in the UAE, Saudi Arabia, and Qatar for construction services, computer services, environmental services, and professional services.

GCC countries are committed to signing bilateral Investment Guarantee Agreements (IGAs) with Singapore in order to better protect the investments of our businessmen in each other's countries.

Source: Staff Report, *Gulf News*, December 15, 2008.

Key Points in the Article

The article discusses a recent trade agreement negotiated between the GCC countries and Singapore that will reduce restrictions on trade. Agreements to expand trade between two countries (or blocs) are known as *bilateral agreements*. Trade agreements, such as this one, that are worked out between more than two countries are *multilateral agreements*. In 2009, the agreement was endorsed by the legislatures of UAE, Qatar, and Oman, while Saudi Arabia, Kuwait, and Bahrain have not yet ratified it. However, if the legislatures of the three remaining countries do ratify the agreement, the GSFTA will strategically link the Gulf region and Singapore, and help promote and increase the flow of goods, services, and investment between the two economies.

Analyzing the News

(a) Free Trade Agreements can facilitate the flow of investments to the services sector, resulting in larger trade in services as well. Trade agreements can also encourage increasing bilateral and multilateral investment agreements, increasing capital flows.

(b) In this chapter, we saw that expanding trade raises living standards by increasing consumption and economic efficiency. Reducing tariffs on trade between Singapore and the GCC countries will aid consumers in both countries. The figure below shows the GCC market as a bloc following the elimination of the tariff on Singapore halal meat products. (For simplicity, we assume that there are no remaining GCC tariffs on meat products.) The price of halal processed meat in the GCC countries falls from P_1 to P_2, and equilibrium in the GCC processed meat market moves from point E to point F. GCC consumption of processed meat increases from Q_3 to Q_4, the quantity of processed meat supplied by GCC markets declines from Q_2 to Q_1, and imports increase from $Q_3 - Q_2$ to $Q_4 - Q_1$. Consumer surplus increases by the sum of areas A, B, C, and D. Area A represents a transfer from producer surplus under the tariff to consumer surplus. Areas C and D represent the conversion of deadweight loss to consumer surplus. Area B represents a conversion of government tariff revenue to consumer surplus. Eliminating the tariff reduces the cost to Singapore processed meat producers of selling their product in the GCC markets. GCC consumers purchase a larger quantity of Singaporean processed meat products at a lower price. The figure shows that eliminating the tariff on halal processed meat also eliminates the revenue the GCC governments had been collecting from this tariff. In developing oil-rich countries, such as the GCC countries, governments receive most of their revenues from royalties and oil sales. The tax base is generally weak, and tariff revenues are a very small percentage of all revenue received by the government. In more developed economies, the government mostly relies on taxes on personal and corporate income. But governments in low-income developing countries often have difficulty collecting income taxes, so they rely heavily on tariffs for revenue. In these countries, the government's need for revenue can pose a serious barrier to expanding international trade by reducing tariffs because governments have difficulty replacing the revenues lost from tariff reductions.

Note: Halal meat refers to Sharia compliant meat products from animals that have been slaughtered and processed according to Islamic Law.

Thinking Critically About Policy

1. Tariffs on Singaporean meat products imports save jobs for GCC nationals working in those industries. Do you support these tariffs? Why or why not?
2. In which goods mentioned in the article does the GCC have a comparative advantage? In which does Singapore have a comparative advantage? Explain your reasoning.

Increase in Consumer Surplus	=	Decrease in Producer Surplus	+	Decrease in Government Tariff Revenue	+	Decrease in Deadweight Loss
$A + C + B + D$		A		B		$C + D$

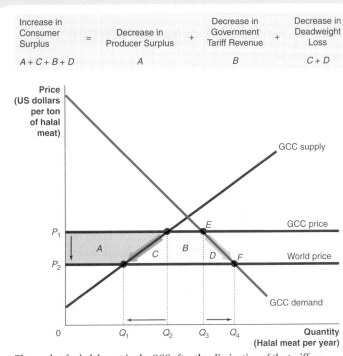

The market for halal meat in the GCC after the elimination of the tariff on Singapore halal meat products.

Key Terms

Summary

14.1 LEARNING OBJECTIVE

Discuss the role of international trade in the Arab world economy, **pages 454–459.**

The Arab World in the International Economy

International trade has been increasing in recent decades, in part because of reductions in *tariffs* and other barriers to trade. A **tariff** is a tax imposed by a government on imports. The quantity of goods and services the United States imports and exports has been continually increasing. **Imports** are goods and services bought domestically but produced in other countries. **Exports** are goods and services produced domestically but sold to other countries. Today, the United States is the leading exporting country in the world, and about 20 percent of U.S. manufacturing jobs depend on exports.

14.2 LEARNING OBJECTIVE

Understand the difference between comparative advantage and absolute advantage in international trade, **pages 459–461.**

Comparative Advantage in International Trade

Comparative advantage is the ability of an individual, a business, or a country to produce a good or service at the lowest **opportunity cost**. **Absolute advantage** is the ability to produce more of a good or service than competitors when using the same amount of resources. Countries trade on the basis of comparative advantage, not on the basis of absolute advantage.

14.3 LEARNING OBJECTIVE

Explain how countries gain from international trade, **pages 461–468.**

How Countries Gain from International Trade

Autarky is a situation in which a country does not trade with other countries. The **terms of trade** is the ratio at which a country can trade its exports for imports from other countries. When a country specializes in producing goods where it has a comparative advantage and trades for the other goods it needs, the country will have a higher level of income and consumption. We do not see complete specialization in production for three reasons: not all goods and services are traded internationally, production of most goods involves increasing opportunity costs, and tastes for products differ across countries. Although the population of a country as a whole benefits from trade, companies—and their workers—that are unable to compete with lower-cost foreign producers lose. Among the main sources of comparative advantage are climate and natural resources, relative abundance of labor and capital, technology, and *external economies*. **External economies** are reductions in a firm's cost that result from an increase in the size of an industry. A country may develop a comparative advantage in the production of a good, and then as time passes and circumstances change, the country may lose its comparative advantage in producing that good and develop a comparative advantage in producing other goods.

14.4 LEARNING OBJECTIVE

Analyze the economic effects of government policies that restrict international trade, **pages 468–476.**

Government Policies That Restrict International Trade

Free trade is trade between countries without government restrictions. Government policies that interfere with trade usually take the form of: *tariffs, quotas,* or *voluntary export restraints* (VERs). A **tariff** is a tax imposed by a government on imports to protect the domestic industry, save jobs, and raise revenue. A **quota** is a numeric limit imposed by a government on the quantity of a good that can be imported into the country. A **voluntary export restraint** (**VER**) is an agreement negotiated between two countries that places a numeric limit on the quantity of a good that can be imported by one country from the other country. Saving jobs by using tariffs and quotas is often very expensive since consumers of imported goods will pay higher price to enjoy consuming these goods.

The Argument over Trade Policies and Globalization

The **World Trade Organization** (**WTO**) is an international organization that enforces international trade agreements. The WTO has promoted **globalization**, the process of countries becoming more open to foreign trade and investment. Some critics of the WTO argue that globalization has damaged local cultures around the world. Other critics oppose the WTO because they believe in **protectionism**, which is the use of trade barriers to shield domestic firms from foreign competition. The WTO allows countries to use tariffs in cases of **dumping**, when an imported product is sold for a price below its cost of production. Economists can point out the burden imposed on the economy by tariffs, quotas, and other government interferences with free trade. But whether these policies should be used is a normative decision.

> **14.5 LEARNING** OBJECTIVE
>
> Evaluate the arguments over trade policy and globalization, **pages 476–481.**

Review, Problems and Applications

 Visit www.pearsoned.co.uk/awe/hubbard to complete these exercises online and get instant feedback.
Get Ahead of the Curve

> **14.1 LEARNING** OBJECTIVE   Discuss the role of international trade in the Arab world economy, **pages 454–459.**

Review Questions

1.1 Briefly explain whether you agree or disagree with the following statement: "International trade is more important to the Arab countries than some developed economies such as the U.S. economy."

Problems and Applications

1.2 If the United Arab Emirates were to stop trading goods and services with other countries, how this will affect the UAE economy? Briefly explain.

1.3 Briefly explain why you agree with the following statement: "Egypt and Lebanon exports to their GDP are much less than those of Saudi Arabia, Qatar, and Kuwait".

> **14.2 LEARNING** OBJECTIVE   Understand the difference between comparative advantage and absolute advantage in international trade, **pages 459–461.**

Review Questions

2.1 A World Trade Organization publication calls comparative advantage "arguably the single most powerful insight in economics." What is comparative advantage? What makes it such a powerful insight?
Source: World Trade Organization, *Trading into the Future*, April 1999.

2.2 What is the difference between absolute advantage and comparative advantage? Will a country always be an exporter of a good where it has an absolute advantage in production?

Problems and Applications

2.3 Why do the goods that countries import and export change over time? Use the concept of comparative advantage in your answer.

2.4 Briefly explain whether you agree with the following argument: "Unfortunately, Oman does not have a comparative advantage with respect to Jordan in the production of any good or service." (*Hint:* You do not need any specific information about the economies of Oman or Jordan to be able to answer this question.)

2.5 In 1987, an economic study showed that, on average, workers in the Japanese consumer electronics industry produced less output per hour than did U.S. workers producing the same goods. Despite this fact, Japan exported large quantities of consumer electronics to the United States. Briefly explain how this is possible.

Source: Study cited in Douglas A. Irwin, *Free Trade under Fire*, Princeton, NJ: Princeton University Press, 2002, p. 27.

14.3 LEARNING OBJECTIVE   Explain how countries gain from international trade, **pages 461–468.**

Review Questions

3.1 Briefly explain how international trade increases a country's consumption.

3.2 What is meant by a country specializing in the production of a good? Is it typical for countries to be completely specialized? Briefly explain.

3.3 What are the main sources of comparative advantage?

Problems and Applications

3.4 **(Related to *Solved Problem 14-3* on page 463)** The following table shows the hourly output per worker in two industries in Kuwait and Syria.

OUTPUT PER HOUR OF WORK		
	CLOTHES	DAIRY PRODUCTS
KUWAIT	8	6
SYRIA	1	2

a. Explain which country has an absolute advantage in the production of clothes and which country has an absolute advantage in the production of dairy products.

b. Explain which country has a comparative advantage in the production of clothes and which country has a comparative advantage in the production of dairy products.

c. Suppose that Kuwait and Syria currently do not trade with each other. Each has 1,000 hours of labor to use producing clothes and dairy products, and the countries are currently producing the amounts of each good shown in the following table.

	CLOTHES	DAIRY PRODUCTS
KUWAIT	7,200	600
SYRIA	600	800

Using this information, give a numeric example of how Kuwait and Syria can both gain from trade. Assume that after trading begins, one hat can be exchanged for one kilo of dairy products.

3.5 **(Related to *Solved Problem 14-3* on page 463)** A political commentator makes the following statement:

The idea that international trade should be based on the comparative advantage of each country is fine for rich countries like the United States and Japan. Rich countries have educated workers and large quantities of machinery and equipment. These advantages allow them to produce every product more efficiently than poor countries can. Poor countries like Kenya and Bolivia have nothing to gain from international trade based on comparative advantage.

Do you agree with this argument? Briefly explain.

3.6 Demonstrate how the opportunity costs of producing cellphones and digital music players in Japan and the United States were calculated in Table 14-2 on page 461.

3.7 Briefly explain whether you agree or disagree with the following statement: "Most countries exhaust their comparative advantage in producing a good or service before they reach complete specialization."

3.8 Is free trade likely to benefit a large, populous country, such as Egypt, more than a small country with fewer people, such as Qatar? Briefly explain.

3.9 Many Arabs could associate free trade with job losses rather than opportunities and a higher standard of living. Do you agree? Briefly explain.

Source: Surya Sen and Dan Wassmann, *The Great Trade Debate: From Rhetoric to Reality*, Federal Reserve Bank of Chicago, January 1999.

3.10 Hal Varian, an economist at the University of California, Berkeley, has made two observations about international trade:

a. Trade allows a country "to produce more with less."

b. There is little doubt who wins [from trade] in the long run: consumers.

Briefly explain whether you agree with either or both of these observations.

Source: Hal R. Varian, "The Mixed Bag of Productivity," *New York Times*, October 23, 2003.

3.11 Briefly explain whether you agree or disagree with the following statement: "I can't believe that anyone opposes expanding international trade. After all, when international trade expands, everyone wins."

3.12 **(Related to the *Making the Connection* on page 465)** Explain why there are advantages to a movie studio operating in Egypt, rather than in, say, Bahrain.

Review Questions

4.1 What is a tariff? What is a quota? Give an example of a non-tariff barrier to trade.

4.2 Who gains and who loses when a country imposes a tariff or a quota on imports of a good?

Problems and Applications

4.3 An editorial in *BusinessWeek* argued the following:

> [President] Bush needs to send a pure and clear signal that the U.S. supports free trade on its merits…. That means resisting any further protectionist demands by lawmakers. It could even mean unilaterally reducing tariffs or taking down trade barriers rather than erecting new ones. Such moves would benefit U.S. consumers while giving a needed boost to struggling economies overseas.

What does the editorial mean by "protectionist demands"? How would the unilateral elimination of U.S. trade barriers benefit both U.S. consumers and economies overseas?

Source: "The Threat of Protectionism," *BusinessWeek*, June 3, 2002.

4.4 Do you agree that a country benefits from free trade only if every other country also practices free trade? Briefly explain.

4.5 Saudi Arabia produces beef and also imports beef from other countries.
  a. Draw a graph showing the supply and demand for beef in Saudi Arabia. Assume that Saudi Arabia can import as much as it wants at the world price of beef without causing the world price of beef to increase. Be sure to indicate on the graph the quantity of beef imported.
  b. Now show on your graph the effect of Saudi Arabia imposing a tariff on beef. Be sure to indicate on your graph the quantity of beef sold by Saudi producers before and after the tariff is imposed, the quantity of beef imported before and after the tariff, and the price of beef in Saudi Arabia before and after the tariff.
  c. Discuss who benefits and who loses when Saudi Arabia imposes a tariff on beef.

4.6 When Congress was considering a bill to impose quotas on imports of textiles, shoes, and other products (the bill that affected the exports of Jordan, Morocco, and Egypt), Milton Friedman, a Nobel Prize-winning economist, made the following comment: "The consumer will be forced to spend several extra dollars to subsidize the producers [of these goods] by one dollar. A straight handout would be far cheaper." Why would a quota result in consumers paying much more than domestic producers receive? Where do the other dollars go? What does Friedman mean by a "straight handout"? Why would this be cheaper than a quota?

Source: Milton Friedman, "Free Trade," *Newsweek*, August 27, 1970.

4.7 In the 1980s, Saudi wheat farmers received large subsidies from the government. These payments resulted in Saudi farmers producing much more wheat than they otherwise would. That resulted in Saudi becoming a net wheat exporter. Why could it be the case that the subsidies paid to wheat farmers in Saudi will reduce the incomes of wheat farmers in Africa?

4.8 Suppose that the Egyptian government decided to impose a quota on steel imports in order to protect the domestic steel industry and save hundreds of jobs in the steel industry. Some opponents say that this procedure will result in losing jobs in other Egyptian industries. Why would a quota on steel imports cause employment to fall in other industries? Which other industries are likely to be most affected?

4.9 A student makes the following argument:

> Tariffs on imports of foreign goods into Jordan will cause the foreign companies to add the amount of the tariff to the prices they charge in Jordan for those goods. Instead of putting a tariff on imported goods, we should ban importing them. Banning imported goods is better than putting tariffs on them because Jordanian producers benefit from the reduced competition and Jordanian consumers don't have to pay the higher prices caused by tariffs.

Briefly explain whether you agree with the student's reasoning.

4.10 Suppose China decides to pay large subsidies to any Chinese company that exports goods or services to the GCC. As a result, these companies are able to sell products in the GCC at far below their cost of production. In addition, China decides to bar all imports from the GCC. The dollars that the GCC countries pay to import Chinese goods are left in banks in China. Will this strategy raise or lower the standard of living in China? Will it raise or lower the standard of living in the GCC? Briefly explain. Be sure to provide a definition of 'standard of living' in your answer.

4.11 **(Related to** *Solved Problem 14-4* **on page 472)** Suppose that Oman currently both produces cement and imports it. The government of Oman then decides to restrict international trade in cement by imposing a quota that allows imports of only one million tons of cement into Oman each year. The figure on the following page shows the results of imposing the quota.

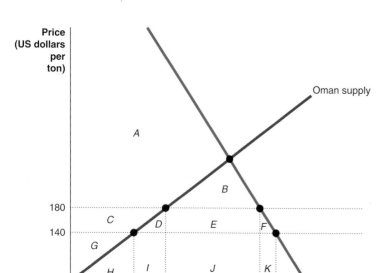

Fill in the table below using the letters in the figure:

	WITHOUT QUOTA	WITH QUOTA
World price of cement	_____	_____
Oman price of cement	_____	_____
Quantity supplied by Omani firms	_____	_____
Quantity demanded	_____	_____
Quantity imported	_____	_____
Area of consumer surplus	_____	_____
Area of domestic producer surplus	_____	_____
Area of deadweight loss	_____	_____

14.5 LEARNING OBJECTIVE   Evaluate the arguments over trade policy and globalization, **pages 476–481.**

Review Questions

5.1 What events led to the General Agreement on Tariffs and Trade? Why did the World Trade Organization eventually replace GATT?

5.2 What is globalization? Why are some people opposed to globalization?

5.3 What is protectionism? Who benefits and who loses from protectionist policies? What are the main arguments people use to justify protectionism?

5.4 What is dumping? Who benefits and who loses from dumping? What problems arise when implementing anti-dumping laws?

Problems and Applications

5.5 Steven Landsburg, an economist at the University of Rochester, wrote the following in an article in the *New York Times*:

> Free trade is not only about the right of American consumers to buy at the cheapest possible price; it's also about the right of foreign producers to earn a living. Steelworkers in West Virginia struggle hard to make ends meet. So do steelworkers in South Korea. To protect one at the expense of the other, solely because of where they happened to be born, is a moral outrage.

How does the U.S. government protect steelworkers in West Virginia at the expense of steelworkers in South Korea? Is Landsburg making a positive or a normative statement? A few days later, Tom Redburn published an article disagreeing with Landsburg:

> It is not some evil character flaw to care more about the welfare of people nearby than about that of those far away—it's human nature. And it is morally—and economically—defensible.... A society that ignores the consequences of economic disruption on those among its citizens who come out at the short end of the stick is not only heartless, it also undermines its own cohesion and adaptability.

Which of the two arguments do you find most convincing?

Sources: Steven E. Landsburg, "Who Cares if the Playing Field Is Level?" *New York Times*, June 13, 2001; and Tom Redburn, "Economic View: Of Politics, Free Markets, and Tending to Society," *New York Times*, June 17, 2001.

5.6 Do you agree that the negative effects of international trade are more visible than the positive effects? Briefly explain.

PART **5**

Macroeconomic Foundations

Chapter 15

GDP: Measuring Total Production and Income

Emirates Airline Feels the Impact of the Global Recession and the Fluctuations in GDP

Emirates Airline, based in Dubai in the United Arab Emirates, is the leading airliner in the Arab world and the Middle East. By the end of 2007 the carrier, known for its luxurious state of the art service, rose to be the seventh largest airliner in the world. It operates over 2,000 flights per week to nearly 100 destinations in 67 countries across the globe, using a fleet of aircrafts from both Boeing and its competitor, Airbus. Recently, Emirates has acquired the world's largest fleet of the Boeing 777 aircrafts.

At the beginning of 2009, Emirates Airline announced that it was slashing fares to cope with fierce competition from most international airliners. Later in the year, Emirates posted an 80 percent drop in full-year profit. In particular, net income fell to 982 million dirhams (US$267 million), from a record 5 billion dirhams a year earlier. What caused Emirates' problems during 2009? Emirates was experiencing the combined effects of rising costs of jet fuel and falling ticket sales due to the global financial crisis. Although until the

last quarter of 2008 it was uncertain whether the world economy had entered into a recession, economic activity had clearly slowed, with the airlines and many other industries experiencing declining demand. The 2009 recession was particularly tough for Emirates, because the economy of Dubai was the hardest hit by the global recession in the Arab Gulf and perhaps in the whole Arab world.

This decrease in demand and increase in costs resulted from factors outside Emirates' control. Emirates was experiencing the effects of the *business cycle*, which refers to the alternating periods of economic expansion and recession that occur in Dubai (UAE) and in other industrial economies around the world.

Although Emirates experienced several reductions in profits in 2009, these slips followed several years of spectacular increasing profits, which had resulted from the booming economy of Dubai in recent years. Airlines typically flourish during booms, as rising incomes, growing economic activity, and optimism usually have a direct impact on increasing the amount of both business and leisure travel. Conversely, airlines are the hardest hit during recessions, as falling incomes and uncertainty cause many leisure travelers to cancel pleasure trips and some firms to cut back on business travel.

Whether the general level of economic activity is increasing is not just important to firms like Emirates, as they decide whether to expand or contract their operations. It is also important to workers hoping for pay increases and to consumers wondering how rapidly prices will be increasing. College students are also affected by the state of the economy at the time they graduate. One recent study found that college students who graduate during a recession have to search longer to find a job and end up accepting jobs that, on average, pay 9 percent less than the jobs accepted by students who graduate during expansions. What's more, students who graduate during recessions will continue to earn less for 8 to 10 years after they graduate. The overall state of the economy is clearly important! AN INSIDE LOOK on page 512 discusses the fact that the latest global crisis hit almost all Arab countries in different ways and with various degrees of severity. Oil-exporting Arab countries, for example, suffered most from the decline in global demand for oil.

Sources: Maher Chmaytelli, "Emirates Airline Net Declines 80 Percent on Fuel Recession," *Bloomberg News*, May 21, 2009; Ivan Gale, "Emirates Is Now Seventh Biggest Airline," *Gulf News*, November 10, 2007; Philip Oreopoulos, Till von Wachter, and Andrew Heisz, "The Short-and-Long-Term Career Effects of Graduating in a Recession," National Bureau of Economic Research Paper 12159, April 2006.

LEARNING Objectives

After studying this chapter, you should be able to:

15.1 Explain how total production is measured, page 493.

15.2 Discuss whether GDP is a good measure of well-being, page 500.

15.3 Discuss the difference between real GDP and nominal GDP, page 503.

15.4 Become familiar with other measures of total production and total income, page 508.

Economics in YOUR Life!

What's the Best Country for You to Work In?

Suppose that an airline offers you a job after graduation. Because the firm has offices in Jordan and China, and because you are fluent in Arabic and Chinese, you get to choose the country in which you will work and live. Because gross domestic product (GDP) is a measure of an economy's total production of goods and services, one factor in your decision is likely to be the growth rate of GDP in each country. In 2009, the growth rate of GDP was 2.8 percent in Jordan and 8.7 percent in China. What effect do these two very different growth rates have on your decision to work and live in one country or the other? If China's much larger growth rate does not necessarily lead you to decide to work and live in China, why not? As you read this chapter, see if you can answer these questions. You can check your answers against those we provide at the end of the chapter. >> Continued on page 510

Microeconomics The study of how households and firms make choices, how they interact in markets, and how the government attempts to influence their choices.

Macroeconomics The study of the economy as a whole, including topics such as inflation, unemployment, and economic growth.

Business cycle Alternating periods of economic expansion and economic recession.

Expansion The period of a business cycle during which total production and total employment are increasing.

Recession The period of a business cycle during which total production and total employment are decreasing.

Economic growth The ability of an economy to produce increasing quantities of goods and services.

Inflation rate The percentage increase in the price level from one year to the next.

As we saw in Chapter 1, we can divide economics into the subfields of microeconomics and macroeconomics. **Microeconomics** is the study of how households and firms make choices, how they interact in markets, and how the government attempts to influence their choices. **Macroeconomics** is the study of the economy as a whole, including topics such as inflation, unemployment, and economic growth. In microeconomic analysis, economists generally study individual markets, such as the market for personal computers. In macroeconomic analysis, economists study factors that affect many markets at the same time. As we saw in the chapter opener, one important macroeconomic issue is the business cycle. The **business cycle** refers to the alternating periods of expansion and recession that any economy experiences over time. A business cycle **expansion** is a period during which total production and total employment are increasing. A business cycle **recession** is a period during which total production and total employment are decreasing. In the following chapters, we will discuss the causes of the business cycle and policies the government may use to reduce its effects.

Another important macroeconomic topic is **economic growth**, which refers to the ability of an economy to produce increasing quantities of goods and services. Economic growth is important because an economy that grows too slowly fails to raise living standards. In many countries in Africa, very little economic growth has occurred in the past 50 years, and many people remain in severe poverty. Macroeconomics analyzes both what determines the rate of economic growth within a country and the reasons growth rates differ so greatly across countries.

Macroeconomics also analyzes what determines the total level of employment in an economy. As we will see, the level of employment is affected significantly by the business cycle, but other factors also help determine the level of employment in the long run. A related issue is why some economies are more successful than others in maintaining high levels of employment over time. Another important macroeconomic issue is what determines the **inflation rate**, or the percentage increase in the average level of prices from one year to the next. As with employment, inflation is affected both by the business cycle and by other long-run factors. Finally, macroeconomics is concerned with the linkages among economies: international trade and international finance.

Macroeconomic analysis provides information that consumers and firms need in order to understand current economic conditions and to help predict future conditions. A family may be reluctant to buy a house if employment in the economy is declining because some family members may be at risk of losing their jobs. Similarly, firms may be reluctant to invest in building new factories or to undertake major new expenditures on information technology if they expect that future sales may be weak. For example, in 2010, Toyota announced plans to found an assembly plant in Egypt. The decision was made because macroeconomic forecasts indicated that consumer demand for cars is growing in Egypt. Macroeconomic analysis can also aid the government in designing policies that help the economy perform more efficiently.

In this chapter, we begin our study of macroeconomics by considering how best to measure key macroeconomic variables. As we will see, there are important issues involved in measuring macroeconomic variables. We start by considering measures of total production and total income in an economy.

15.1 | Explain how total production is measured.

Gross Domestic Product Measures Total Production

"India's GDP could double in seven years"

"UAE's GDP poised to exceed Dh1tr"

"Wall Street falls on weak GDP data"

"Stocks advance as GDP growth accelerates"

These headlines are from articles that appeared in the *Gulf News* in 2010. Why is GDP so often the focus of news stories? In this section, we explore what GDP is and how it is measured. We also explore why knowledge of GDP is important to consumers, firms, and government policymakers.

Measuring Total Production: Gross Domestic Product

Economists measure total production by **gross domestic product** (**GDP**). GDP is the market *value* of all *final* goods and services produced in a country during a period of time, typically one year. In Arab countries the Ministry of the Economy (statistics division) compiles the data needed to calculate GDP. Most Arab countries issue reports on the GDP every three months. GDP is a central concept in macroeconomics, so we need to consider its definition carefully.

Gross domestic product (GDP) The market value of all final goods and services produced in a country during a period of time, typically one year.

GDP Is Measured Using Market Values, Not Quantities The word *value* is important in the definition of GDP. In microeconomics, we measure production in quantity terms: the number of barrels of oil a country produces, the tons of wheat Saudi farmers grow, or the number of passengers flown by Emirates Airlines, etc. When we measure total production in the economy, we can't just add together the quantities of every good and service because the result would be a meaningless jumble. Tons of wheat would be added to gallons of milk, numbers of plane flights, and so on. Instead, we measure production by taking the *value*, in local currency terms (dirhams, dinars, pounds etc.), of all the goods and services produced.

GDP Includes Only the Market Value of Final Goods In measuring GDP, we include only the value of *final goods and services*. A **final good or service** is one that is purchased by its final user and is not included in the production of any other good or service. Examples of final goods are a hamburger purchased by a consumer and a computer purchased by a business. Some goods and services, though, are used in the production of other goods and services. For example, Almarai does not produce plastic bottles for its milk; it buys them from companies producing plastic containers. The containers are an **intermediate good**, while a bottle of Almarai milk is a final good. In calculating GDP, we include the value of the bottle of milk but not the value of the plastic container. If we included the value of the plastic container, we would be *double counting*: The value of the plastic container would be counted once when the plastic container company sold it to Almarai, and a second time when Almarai sold the bottle of milk to a consumer.

Final good or service A good or service purchased by a final user.

Intermediate good or service A good or service that is an input into another good or service, such as a tire on a truck.

GDP Includes Only Current Production GDP includes only production that takes place during the indicated time period. For example, GDP in 2010 includes only the goods and services produced during that year. In particular, GDP does *not* include the value of used goods. If you buy a DVD of *Iron Man* from Carrefour, the purchase is included in GDP. If six months later you resell that DVD on Souq.com, that transaction is not included in GDP.

Solved Problem | **15-1**

Calculating GDP

Suppose that a very simple economy produces only four goods and services: eye examinations, pizzas, textbooks, and paper. Assume that all the paper in this economy is used in the production of textbooks. Use the information in the following table to compute GDP for the year 2010.

PRODUCTION AND PRICE STATISTICS FOR 2010

(1) PRODUCT	(2) QUANTITY	(3) PRICE PER UNIT IN US$
Eye examinations	100	50.00
Pizzas	80	10.00
Textbooks	20	100.00
Paper	2,000	0.10

SOLVING THE PROBLEM:

Step 1: **Review the chapter material.** This problem is about gross domestic product, so you may want to review the section "Measuring Total Production: Gross Domestic Product," which begins on page 493.

Step 2: **Determine which goods and services listed in the table should be included in the calculation of GDP.** GDP is the value of all final goods and services. Therefore, we need to calculate the value of the final goods and services listed in the table. Eye examinations, pizzas, and textbooks are final goods. Paper would also be a final good if, for instance, a consumer bought it to use in a printer. However, here we are assuming that publishers purchase all the paper to use in manufacturing textbooks, so the paper is an intermediate good, and its value is not included in GDP.

Step 3: **Calculate the value of the three final goods and services listed in the table.** Value is equal to the quantity produced multiplied by the price per unit, so we multiply the numbers in column (1) by the numbers in column (2).

PRODUCT	(1) QUANTITY	(2) PRICE PER UNIT IN US$	(3) VALUE IN US$
Eye examinations	100	50	5,000
Pizzas	80	10	800
Textbooks	20	100	2,000

Step 4: **Add the value for each of the three final goods and services to find GDP.** GDP = Value of eye examinations produced + Value of pizzas produced + Value of textbooks produced = US$5,000 + US$800 + US$2,000 = US$7,800.

>> **End Solved Problem 15-1** | **YOUR TURN:** For more practice, do related problem 1.11 on page 515 at the end of this chapter.

Production, Income, and the Circular-Flow Diagram

When we measure the value of total production in the economy by calculating GDP, we are simultaneously measuring the value of total income. To see why the value of total production is equal to the value of total income, consider what happens to the money you spend on a single product. Suppose you buy an Apple iPod for US$250 at a City Center store. *All* of that US$250 must end up as someone's income. Apple and City Center mall will receive some of the US$250 as profits, workers at Apple will receive some as wages, the salesperson who sold you the iPod will receive some as salary, the firms that sell parts to Apple will receive some as profits, the workers for these firms will receive some as wages, and so on: every penny must end up as someone's income. (Note, though, that any sales tax on the iPod will be collected by the store and sent to the government without ending up as anyone's income.) Therefore, if we add up the value of every good and service sold in the economy, we must get a total that is exactly equal to the value of all of the income in the economy.

The circular-flow diagram in Figure 15-1 was introduced in Chapter 2 to illustrate the interaction of firms and households in markets. We use it here to illustrate the flow of spending and money in the economy. Firms sell goods and services to three groups: domestic households, foreign firms and households, and the government. Expenditures by foreign firms and households (shown as the Rest of the World in the diagram) on

GDP can be measured by total wages, interest, rent, and profits received by households.

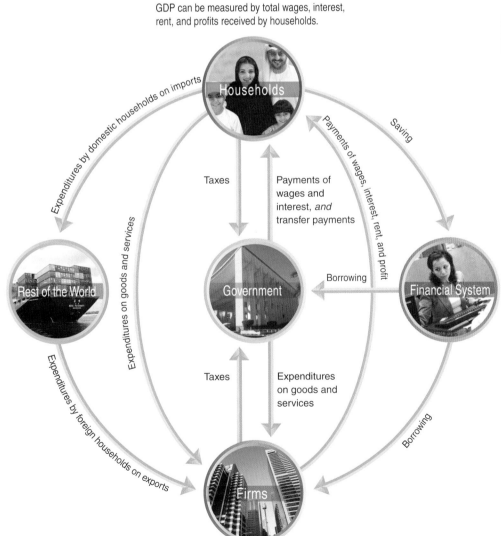

GDP can be measured by total expenditures on goods and services by households, firms, government, and the rest of the world.

Figure 15-1

The Circular Flow and the Measurement of GDP

The circular-flow diagram illustrates the flow of spending and money in the economy. Firms sell goods and services to three groups: domestic households, foreign firms and households, and the government. To produce goods and services, firms use factors of production: labor, capital, natural resources, and entrepreneurship. Households supply the factors of production to firms in exchange for income in the form of wages, interest, profit, and rent. Firms make payments of wages and interest to households in exchange for hiring workers and other factors of production. The sum of wages, interest, rent, and profit is total income in the economy. We can measure GDP as the total income received by households. The diagram also shows that households use their income to purchase goods and services, pay taxes, and save. Firms and the government borrow the funds that flow from households into the financial system. We can measure GDP either by calculating the total value of expenditures on final goods and services or by calculating the value of total income.

domestically produced goods and services are called *exports*. For example, Emirates Airlines sells many tickets to passengers in Europe and America. As we note at the bottom of Figure 15-1, we can measure GDP by adding up the total expenditures of these three groups on goods and services.

Firms use the *factors of production*—labor, capital, natural resources, and entrepreneurship—to produce goods and services. Households supply the factors of production to firms in exchange for income. We divide income into four categories: wages, interest, rent, and profit. Firms pay wages to households in exchange for labor services, interest for the use of capital, and rent for natural resources such as land. Profit is the income that remains after a firm has paid wages, interest, and rent. Profit is the return to entrepreneurs for organizing the other factors of production and for bearing the risk of producing and selling goods and services. As Figure 15-1 shows, governments make payments of wages and interest to households in exchange for hiring workers and other factors of production. Governments also make *transfer payments* to households. **Transfer payments** include Social Security payments to retired and disabled people and unemployment insurance payments to unemployed workers. These payments are not included in GDP because they are not received in exchange for production of a new good or service. The sum of wages, interest, rent, and profit is total income in the economy. As we note at the top of Figure 15-1, we can measure GDP as the total income received by households.

Transfer payments Payments by the government to individuals for which the government does not receive a new good or service in return.

The diagram also allows us to trace the ways that households use their income. Households spend some of their income on goods and services. Some of this spending is on domestically produced goods and services, and some is on foreign-produced goods and services. Spending on foreign-produced goods and services is known as *imports*. Households also use some of their income to pay taxes to the government. (Note that firms also pay taxes to the government.) Some of the income earned by households is not spent on goods and services or paid in taxes but is deposited in checking or savings accounts in banks or is used to buy stocks or bonds. Banks and stock and bond markets make up the *financial system*. The flow of funds from households into the financial system makes it possible for the government and firms to borrow. As we will see, the health of the financial system is of vital importance to an economy. Without the ability to borrow funds through the financial system, firms will have difficulty expanding and adopting new technologies. In fact, as we will discuss in Chapter 17, no country without a well-developed financial system has been able to sustain high levels of economic growth.

The circular-flow diagram shows that we can measure GDP either by calculating the total value of expenditures on final goods and services or by calculating the value of total income. We get the same dollar amount of GDP whichever approach we take.

Figure 15-2 shows 2009 GDP for some selected Arab countries. Saudi Arabia, the UAE, and Egypt have the largest gross domestic products in the region, while Bahrain seems to have the lowest GDP in the region. But do these figures mean that Bahrain is poorer than Egypt, for example? The answer is no. To see how affluent a nation is, what matters is how much each person receives on average. So, by dividing the GDP of a country by population size, we get average individual income in a particular country, known as the *income per capita*. This measure reflects an individual's average share of a country's GDP. Clearly, it is more relevant to addressing the question of whether a person is likely to be richer in Morocco or in Qatar, for example. Figure 15-3 rearranges countries according to their respective *per capita* GDP. We can clearly see that a person in Bahrain is likely to be more affluent than a person in Egypt, and a person in Morocco is likely to be far poorer than a person in Qatar. So, despite the fact that the size of GDP directly affects the well-being of individuals in a country, it may be misleading when trying to make international comparisons.

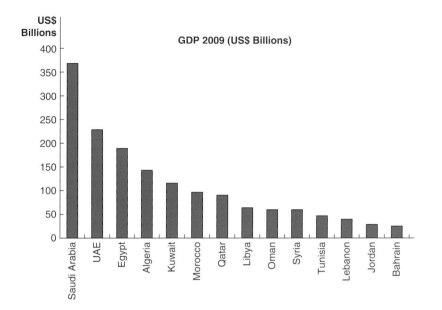

Figure 15-2

(2009) GDP for Selected Arab Countries

Saudi Arabia, the UAE, and Egypt have the largest gross domestic products in the region, while Bahrain seems to have the lowest GDP in the region. However, that does not mean that Bahrain is relatively less affluent than Egypt.
Source: IMF, World Economic Outlook, 2010.

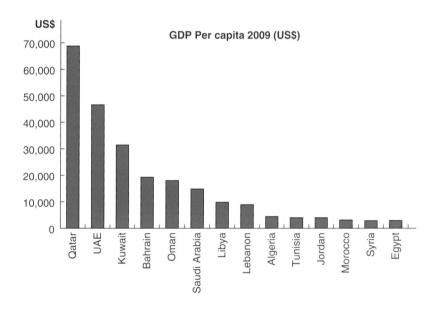

Figure 15-3

(2009) GDP Per Capita for Selected Arab Countries

Income per capita reflects an individual's average share of a country's GDP. Despite a smaller GDP in Bahrain than in Egypt, a person in Bahrain is likely to be more affluent than a person in Egypt.
Source: IMF, World Economic Outlook, 2010.

Components of GDP

The Ministry of the Economy or the statistical division responsible for the calculation of GDP divides its statistics on GDP into four major categories of expenditures. Economists use these categories to understand why GDP fluctuates and to forecast future GDP.

Personal Consumption Expenditures, or 'Consumption'

Consumption expenditures are made by households and are divided into expenditures on *services*, such as medical care, education, and haircuts; expenditures on *nondurable goods*, such as food and clothing; and expenditures on *durable goods*, such as automobiles

Consumption Spending by households on goods and services, not including spending on new houses.

and furniture. The spending by households on new houses is not included in consumption. Instead, spending on new houses is included in the investment category, which we discuss next.

Investment Spending by firms on new factories, office buildings, machinery, and additions to inventories, and spending by households on new houses.

Gross Private Domestic Investment, or 'Investment' Spending on *gross private domestic investment*, or simply **investment**, is divided into three categories: *Business fixed investment* is spending by firms on new factories, office buildings, and machinery used to produce other goods. *Residential investment* is spending by households and firms on new single-family and multi-unit houses. *Changes in business inventories* are also included in investment. Inventories are goods that have been produced but not yet sold. If Suzuki Egypt has US$200 million worth of unsold cars at the beginning of the year and US$350 million worth of unsold cars at the end of the year, then the firm has spent US$150 million on inventory investment during the year.

Government purchases Spending by federal, state, and local governments on goods and services.

Government Consumption and Gross Investment, or 'Government Purchases' **Government purchases** are spending by federal, state, and local governments on goods and services, such as teachers' salaries, highways, and aircraft carriers. Again, government spending on transfer payments is not included in government purchases because it does not result in the production of new goods and services.

Net exports Exports minus imports.

Net Exports of Goods and Services, or 'Net Exports' **Net exports** are equal to *exports* minus *imports*. Exports are goods and services produced in the United States but purchased by foreign firms, households, and governments. We add exports to our other categories of expenditures because otherwise we would not be including all spending on new goods and services produced in the country. For example, if a farmer in Jordan sells olives to Oman, the value of the olives is included in Jordan's GDP because it represents production in Jordan. Imports are goods and services produced in foreign countries but purchased by a country's firms, households, and governments. We subtract imports from total expenditures because otherwise we would be including spending that does not result in production of new goods and services in the country. For example, if Kuwaiti consumers buy US$100 million worth of furniture manufactured in China, that spending is included in consumption expenditures. But the value of those imports is subtracted from GDP because the imports do not represent production in Kuwait.

An Equation for GDP and Some Actual Values

A simple equation sums up the components of GDP:

$$Y = C + I + G + NX$$

The equation tells us that GDP (denoted as Y) equals consumption (C) plus investment (I) plus government purchases (G) plus net exports (NX). Figure 15-4 shows the values of the components of GDP for Lebanon in 2009. The graph in the figure highlights that consumption is by far the largest component of GDP. The table provides the detailed breakdown. Note that imports are greater than exports, so net exports are negative. Since Lebanon is a small open economy, this is typically the case. But what remains debatable is whether the size of such a trade balance deficit (–24 percent of GDP) is reasonable or not (compare for example to –6 percent in the U.S. for the same year).

Measuring GDP by the Value-Added Method

We have seen that GDP can be calculated by adding together all expenditures on final goods and services. An alternative way of calculating GDP is the *value-added method*. **Value added** refers to the additional market value a firm gives to a product and is

Value added The market value a firm adds to a product.

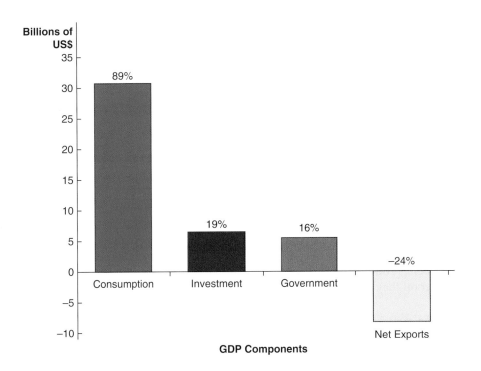

Figure 15-4

Lebanon's GDP Components in 2009

Consumption accounts for 89 percent of GDP, far more than any of the other components. In recent years, net exports typically have been negative, which reduces GDP.

Source: WDI, World Bank 2010.

equal to the difference between the price for which the firm sells a good and the price it paid other firms for intermediate goods. Table 15-1 gives a hypothetical example of the value added by each firm involved in the production of a shirt offered for sale at Carrefour.

Suppose a cotton farmer sells US$1 of raw cotton to a textile mill. If, for simplicity, we ignore any inputs the farmer may have purchased from other firms—such as cottonseed or fertilizer—then the farmer's value added is US$1. The textile mill then weaves the raw cotton into cotton fabric, which it sells to a shirt company for US$3. The textile mill's value added (US$2) is the difference between the price it paid for the raw cotton (US$1) and the price for which it can sell the cotton fabric (US$3). Similarly, the shirt company's value added is the difference between the price it paid for the cotton fabric (US$3) and the price it receives for the shirt from Carrefour. Carrefour's value added is the difference between the price it pays for the shirt (US$15) and the price for which it can sell the shirt (US$35). Notice that *the price of the shirt in* Carrefour *is exactly equal to the sum of the value added by each firm involved in the production of the shirt.* We can calculate GDP by adding up the market value of every

FIRM	VALUE OF PRODUCT IN US$	VALUE ADDED IN US$	
Cotton farmer	Value of raw cotton = 1	Value added by cotton farmer	= 1
Textile mill	Value of raw cotton woven into cotton fabric = 3	Value added by cotton textile mill = (3 − 1)	= 2
Shirt company	Value of cotton fabric made into a shirt = 15	Value added by shirt manufacturer = (15 − 3)	= 12
Carrefour	Value of shirt for sale in Carrefour = 35	Value added by Carrefour = (35 − 15)	= 20
	Total value added		**– 35**

TABLE 15-1

Calculating Value Added

final good and service produced during a particular period. Or, we can arrive at the same value for GDP by adding up the value added of every firm involved in producing those final goods and services.

15.2 | Discuss whether GDP is a good measure of well-being.

Does GDP Measure What We Want It to Measure?

Economists use GDP to measure total production in the economy. For that purpose, we would like GDP to be as comprehensive as possible, not overlooking any significant production that takes place in the economy. Most economists believe that GDP does a good—but not flawless—job of measuring production. GDP is also sometimes used as a measure of well-being. Although it is generally true that the more goods and services people have, the better off they are, we will see that GDP provides only a rough measure of well-being.

Shortcomings in GDP as a Measure of Total Production

GDP does not include two types of production: production in the home and production in the underground economy.

Household Production With only a couple of exceptions, the value of goods and services that are not bought and sold in markets are not included in GDP. If a carpenter makes and sells bookcases, the value of those bookcases will be counted in GDP. If the carpenter makes a bookcase for personal use, it will not be counted in GDP. *Household production* refers to goods and services people produce for themselves. The most important type of household production is the services a homemaker provides to the homemaker's family. If a person has been caring for children, cleaning the house, and preparing the family meals, the value of such services is not included in GDP. If the person then decides to work outside the home, enrolls the children in daycare, hires a cleaning service, and begins eating family meals in restaurants, the value of GDP will rise by the amount paid for daycare, cleaning services, and restaurant meals, even though production of these services has not actually increased.

The Underground Economy Individuals and firms sometimes conceal the buying and selling of goods and services, in which case their production isn't counted in GDP. Individuals and firms conceal what they buy and sell for three basic reasons: they are dealing in illegal goods and services, such as drugs or prostitution; they want to avoid paying taxes on the income they earn; or they want to avoid government regulations. This concealed buying and selling is referred to as the **underground economy**.

Underground economy Buying and selling of goods and services that is concealed from the government to avoid taxes or regulations or because the goods and services are illegal.

Is not counting household production or production in the underground economy a serious shortcoming of GDP? Most economists would answer "no" because the most important use of GDP is to measure changes in how the economy is performing over short periods of time, such as from one year to the next. For this purpose, omitting household production and production in the underground economy doesn't have much effect because there is not likely to be much change in the amounts of these types of production from one year to the next.

We also use GDP statistics to measure how production of goods and services grows over fairly long periods of a decade or more. For this purpose, omitting household production and production in the underground economy may be more important. For example, beginning in the 1970s, the number of women working outside the home increased dramatically. Some of the goods and services—such as childcare and restaurant meals—produced in the following years were not true additions to total production; rather, they were replacing what had been household production.

Making the Connection

Corruption and the Underground Economy: How Severe Is Corruption in the Arab World?

The underground economy in some developing countries may be more than 50 percent of measured GDP. In developing countries, the underground economy is often referred to as the *informal sector*, as opposed to the *formal sector* in which output of goods and services is measured. A large informal sector can be a sign of government policies that are retarding economic growth. The underground economy in Egypt, for example, may be more than half of measured GDP. Professor Ibrahim Oweiss of Georgetown University estimated the informal economy of Egypt in the 1980s to be more than the official GPD itself. Schneider and Enste (2000) estimated the informal sector in Egypt to be about three-quarters of the formal economy in the 90s. In other countries, such as Morocco and Tunisia, it could be as high as 40–45 percent of official GDP.

Because firms in the informal sector are acting illegally, they tend to be smaller and have less capital than firms acting legally. The entrepreneurs who start firms in the informal sector may be afraid that their firms could someday be closed or confiscated by the government, so they limit their investments in these firms. As a consequence, workers in these firms have less machinery and equipment to work with and so produce fewer and lower quality goods and services. Firms in the informal sector also have to pay the costs of avoiding government authorities, and in many countries have to pay substantial bribes to government officials to remain in business. Also, the informal sector is large in some developing economies because taxes are high and government regulations are extensive. Again, this induces widespread tax evasion and bribes.

This tendency by a large informal sector to survive outside of the official and regulated sector directly feeds into a culture of 'corruption.' Corruption itself is part of the informal economy such as bribes and favours. According to the World Bank Governance Indicators, the Arab world (with the exception of Qatar and the UAE) is by and large suffering from higher levels of corruption—compared with developed economies. However, the experience of Arab countries certainly varies. In the following two graphs we plot the control of corruption indicator that ranges from –2.5 (worst) to 2.5 (best) for selected Arab countries. In that sense, having a positive value indicates that the country is performing better than average, and vice versa.

In the first graph we see Arab countries with bad corruption records or those worsening to dip below zero in recent years. Syria, Lebanon, and Egypt are by far the worst in terms of corruption and the trend is getting even worse. Tunisia and Saudi Arabia, despite a relatively better performance, lately recorded a huge increase in the level of corruption. Algeria is the only improving economy among this group, with an increasing control of corruption across years. In the second graph, we see the group of countries that perform above average in terms of controlling corruption. Qatar and the UAE are the best performers by a wide margin. The other GCC countries, especially Kuwait, are recording worse corruption across years. Jordan, despite starting from higher levels of corruption compared with all GCC countries is notably improving.

In conclusion, many Arab countries have a larger informal sector than more developed economies. So, their official GDP is usually underestimated. This is particularly true in countries where corruption is rampant such as in Egypt, Lebanon, and Syria.

(Continued)

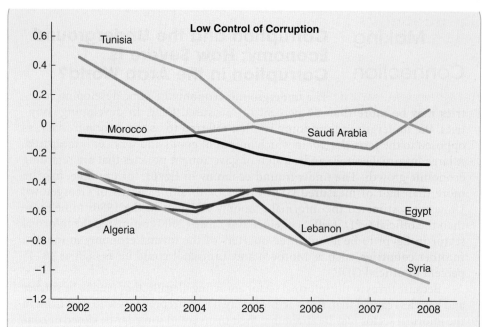

Source: World Governance Indicators (Control of Corruption), World Bank.

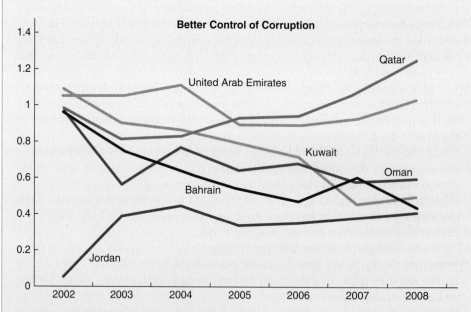

Source: World Governance Indicators (Control of Corruption), World Bank.

Sources: I. M. Oweiss, "Egypt's Economy: The Pressing Issues," in Ibrahim M. Oweiss (ed.) *The Political Economy of Contemporary Egypt*, Washington, DC: Center for Contemporary Arab Studies (Georgetown University), 1990; F. Schneider, and D. Enste, "Shadow Economies: Size, Causes, and Consequences," *Journal of Economic Literature*, 38, pp. 77–114, 2000; and "In the Shadows," *The Economist*, June 17, 2004.

YOUR TURN: Test your understanding by doing related problem 2.5 on page 516 at the end of this chapter.

Shortcomings of GDP as a Measure of Well-Being

The main purpose of GDP is to measure a country's total production. GDP is also frequently used, though, as a measure of well-being. For example, newspaper and magazine articles often include tables that show for different countries the levels of GDP per person, which is usually referred to as *real GDP per capita*. Real GDP per capita is calculated by dividing the value of real GDP for a country by the country's population. These articles imply that people in the countries with higher levels of real GDP per capita are better off. Although increases in GDP often do lead to increases in the well-being of the population, it is important to be aware that GDP is not a perfect measure of well-being for several reasons.

The Value of Leisure Is Not Included in GDP If an economic consultant decides to retire, GDP will decline even though the consultant may value increased leisure more than the income he or she was earning running a consulting firm. The consultant's well-being has increased, but GDP has decreased. Today, the typical person works fewer than 40 hours per week. But if one works 60 hours per week, GDP would be much higher than it is, but the well-being of the typical person would be lower because less time would be available for leisure activities.

GDP Is Not Adjusted for Pollution or Other Negative Effects of Production When a dry cleaner cleans and presses clothes, the value of this service is included in GDP. If chemicals the dry cleaner uses pollute the air or water, GDP is not adjusted to compensate for the costs of the pollution. Similarly, the value of cigarettes produced is included in GDP, with no adjustment made for the costs of the lung cancer that some smokers develop.

We should note, though, that increasing GDP often leads countries to devote more resources to pollution reduction. Developing countries often have higher levels of pollution than high-income countries because the lower GDPs of the developing countries make them more reluctant to spend resources on pollution reduction. Levels of pollution in Egypt or in North Africa in general are much higher than in the United States, Japan, or the countries of Western Europe. But as GDP continues to rise, it is likely to devote more resources to reducing pollution.

GDP Is Not Adjusted for Changes in Crime and Other Social Problems An increase in crime reduces well-being but may actually increase GDP if it leads to greater spending on police, security guards, and alarm systems. GDP is also not adjusted for changes in divorce rates, drug addiction, or other factors that may affect people's well-being.

GDP Measures the Size of the Pie but Not How the Pie Is Divided Up When a country's GDP increases, the country has more goods and services, but those goods and services may be very unequally distributed. Therefore, GDP may not provide good information about the goods and services consumed by the typical person.

To summarize, we can say that a person's well-being depends on many factors that are not taken into account in calculating GDP. Because GDP is designed to measure total production, it should not be surprising that it does an imperfect job of measuring well-being.

15.3 | Discuss the difference between real GDP and nominal GDP. **15.3 LEARNING** OBJECTIVE

Real GDP versus Nominal GDP

Because GDP is measured in value terms, we have to be careful about interpreting changes over time. To see why, consider interpreting an increase in the total value of heavy truck production from US$40 billion in 2009 to US$44 billion in 2010.

Can we be sure—because US$44 billion is 10 percent greater than US$40 billion—that the number of trucks produced in 2010 was 10 percent greater than the number produced in 2009? We can draw this conclusion only if the average price of trucks did not change between 2009 and 2010. In fact, when GDP increases from one year to the next, the increase is due partly to increases in production of goods and services and partly to increases in prices. Because we are interested mainly in GDP as a measure of production, we need a way of separating the price changes from the quantity changes.

Calculating Real GDP

Nominal GDP The value of final goods and services evaluated at current-year prices.

Real GDP The value of final goods and services evaluated at base-year prices.

National statistical agencies separate price changes from quantity changes by calculating a measure of production called *real GDP*. **Nominal GDP** is calculated by summing the current values of final goods and services. **Real GDP** is calculated by designating a particular year as the *base year* and then using the prices of goods and services in the base year to calculate the value of goods and services in all other years. For instance, if the base year is 2000, real GDP for 2009 would be calculated by using prices of goods and services from 2000. By keeping prices constant, we know that changes in real GDP represent changes in the quantity of goods and services produced in the economy.

Solved Problem | **15-3**

Calculating Real GDP

Suppose that a very simple economy produces only the following three final goods and services: eye examinations, pizzas, and textbooks. Use the information in the following table to compute real GDP for the year 2009. Assume that the base year is 2000.

	2000		2009	
PRODUCT	QUANTITY	PRICE IN US$	QUANTITY	PRICE IN US$
Eye examinations	80	40	100	50
Pizzas	90	11	80	10
Textbooks	15	90	20	100

SOLVING THE PROBLEM:

Step 1: **Review the chapter material.** This problem is about calculating real GDP, so you may want to review the section "Calculating Real GDP," which begins on page 504.

Step 2: **Calculate the value of the three goods and services listed in the table, using the quantities for 2009 and the prices for 2000.** The definition on this page tells us that real GDP is the value of all final goods and services, evaluated at base-year prices. In this case, the base year is 2000, and we are given information on the price of each product in that year.

PRODUCT	2009 QUANTITY	2000 PRICE IN US$	VALUE IN US$
Eye examinations	100	40	4,000
Pizzas	80	11	880
Textbooks	20	90	1,800

Step 3: **Add up the values for the three products to find real GDP.**

Real GDP for 2009 equals the sum of:

Quantity of eye examinations in 2009 × Price of eye exams in 2000 = US$4,000

+ Quantity of pizzas produced in 2009 × Price of pizzas in 2000 = US$880

+ Quantity of textbooks produced in 2009 × Price of textbooks in 2000 = US$1,800

or, US$6,680

EXTRA CREDIT: Notice that the quantities of each good produced in 2000 were irrelevant for calculating real GDP in 2009. Notice also that the value of US$6,680 for real GDP in 2009 is lower than the value of US$7,800 for nominal GDP in 2009 calculated in Solved Problem 15-1.

YOUR TURN: For more practice, do related problem 3.3 on page 517 at the end of this chapter.

>> **End Solved Problem 15-3**

One drawback of calculating real GDP using base-year prices is that, over time, prices may change relative to each other. For example, the price of cellphones may fall relative to the price of milk. Because this change is not reflected in the fixed prices from the base year, the estimate of real GDP is somewhat distorted. The further away the current year is from the base year, the worse the problem becomes.

By holding prices constant, the *purchasing power* of a dinar or a dirham remains the same from one year to the next. Ordinarily, the purchasing power of the dinar or the dirham falls every year, as price increases reduce the amount of goods and services that a dinar or a dirham can buy.

Comparing Real GDP and Nominal GDP

Real GDP holds prices constant, which makes it a better measure than nominal GDP of changes in the production of goods and services from one year to the next. In fact, growth in the economy is almost always measured as growth in real GDP.

We describe real GDP as being measured in 'base-year price.' Because, on average, prices rise from one year to the next, real GDP is greater than nominal GDP in years before the base year and less than nominal GDP for years after the base year. In the base year, real GDP and nominal GDP are the same because both are calculated for the base year using the same prices and quantities. Figure 15-5 on page 508 shows movements in nominal GDP and real GDP in Jordan, as one example, between 1990 and 2008. In the 1990s, prices were, on average, lower than in 2000, so nominal GDP was lower than real GDP. In 2000, nominal and real GDP were equal. Since 2000, prices have been, on average, higher than in 2000, so nominal GDP is higher than real GDP.

Making the Connection | The Global Financial Crisis and Arab Economies' Nominal and Real GDP

Most Arab economies are resource-based economies; that is, they depend on commodity exports such as oil and agricultural products for most of their income. All six GCC countries (Bahrain, Kuwait, Oman, Qatar, Saudi Arabia, and the UAE), Algeria, Libya, and Iraq are major world exporters of

(Continued)

oil and natural gas. Sudan and Syria are getting more dependent on oil resources as well in making their GDP. Jordan and Lebanon depend on agricultural exports, services, and workers' transfers from abroad. Egypt, as well, depends on three main sources: Suez Canal receipts, workers' transfers from abroad, and hydrocarbon resources (oil and natural gas). The contribution of the manufacturing sector is relatively small in all Arab economies.

With 2009 experiencing the largest decline in world trade in 80 years, all Arab countries seemed to suffer. But, the falling demand for oil and trade in advanced economies coupled with the drying up of trade finance have had severe implications on the Arab world's exports, especially oil. Looking at the data from the past decade, we see that the GCC economies, in particular, experienced the highest volatility in nominal GDP during the period (2000–2009). In fact, as the following graph shows, during the oil boom of 2007 and 2008 the surge in nominal GDP was so sharp that for some countries, such as Kuwait, Oman, and Qatar, the increase was more than 40 percent. Between 2008 and 2009 the drop was also severe in some countries like Kuwait, where nominal GDP declined by almost 30 percent.

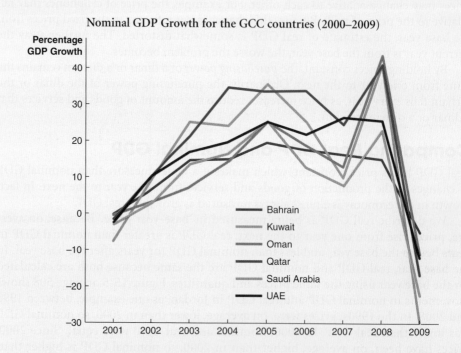

Nominal GDP Growth for the GCC countries (2000–2009)

Source: WDI, World Bank 2010.

The next graph compares nominal GDP 'losses' in the six GCC economies.

All the previous nominal growth rates do not tell much, except the fact that the GCC countries are subject to high income volatility or fluctuations. But are the changes in nominal GDP a good indicator of the growth of the economy? As we read earlier in the chapter, the answer is no. Growth is related to real GDP after correcting for price changes.

As we can see from the final graph, despite the fact that Kuwait's nominal GDP declined by 30 percent in 2009, the economy registered growth of more than 4 percent. By the same token, Saudi, which had a drop of income by more than 22 percent in 2009, had a spectacular growth of 9 percent in the same year. Among North African non-oil countries, Tunisia achieved very strong growth performance and tied with Saudi Arabia at 9 percent.

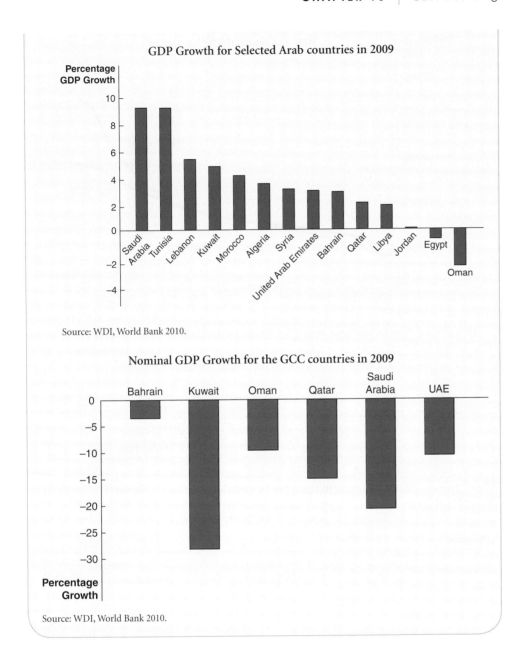

GDP Growth for Selected Arab countries in 2009

Source: WDI, World Bank 2010.

Nominal GDP Growth for the GCC countries in 2009

Source: WDI, World Bank 2010.

The GDP Deflator

Economists and policymakers are interested not just in the level of total production, as measured by real GDP, but also in the *price level*. The **price level** measures the average prices of goods and services in the economy. One of the goals of economic policy is a stable price level. We can use values for nominal GDP and real GDP to compute a measure of the price level called the *GDP deflator*. We can calculate the **GDP deflator** using this formula:

$$\text{GDP deflater} = \frac{\text{Norminal GDP}}{\text{Real GDP}} \times 100$$

Price level A measure of the average prices of goods and services in the economy.

GDP deflator A measure of the price level, calculated by dividing nominal GDP by real GDP and multiplying by 100.

To see why the GDP deflator is a measure of the price level, think about what would happen if prices of goods and services rose while production remained the same. In that case, nominal GDP would increase, but real GDP would remain constant, so the GDP deflator would increase. In reality, both prices and production increase each year, but the more prices increase relative to the increase in production, the more nominal GDP increases relative to real GDP, and the higher the value for the GDP deflator. Increases in the GDP deflator allow economists and policymakers to track increases in the price level over time.

Figure 15-5

Real and Nominal GDP for Jordan

Currently, the base year for calculating GDP is 2000. In the 1990s, prices were, on average, lower than in 2000, so nominal GDP was lower than real GDP. In 2000, nominal and real GDP were equal. After 2000, prices have been, on average, higher than in 2000, so nominal GDP is higher than real GDP.
Source: WDI, World Bank 2010.

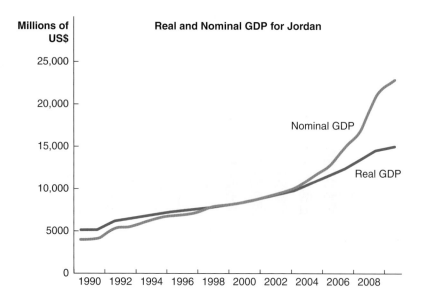

Remember that in the base year (2000), nominal GDP is equal to real GDP, so the value of the GDP price deflator will always be 100 in the base year. The following table gives the values for nominal and real GDP for Jordan in 2007 and 2008.

	2007 IN US$	**2008 IN US$**
NOMINAL GDP	17,006 million	21,217 million
REAL GDP	13,553 million	14,624 million

We can use the information from the table to calculate values for the GDP price deflator for 2007 and 2008:

FORMULA	APPLIED TO 2007	APPLIED TO 2008
$\text{GDP Deflator} = \dfrac{\text{Nominal GDP}}{\text{Real GDP}} \times 100$	$\dfrac{17{,}006 \; million}{13{,}553 \; million} \times 100 = 126$	$\dfrac{21{,}217 \; million}{14{,}624 \; million} \times 100 = 145$

From these values for the deflator, we can calculate that the price level increased in Jordan by 15 percent between 2007 and 2008:

$$\frac{145 - 126}{126} = 15\%$$

Later we will see that economists and policymakers also rely on another measure of the price level, known as the consumer price index. In addition, we will discuss the strengths and weaknesses of different measures of the price level.

15.4 LEARNING OBJECTIVE

15.4 | Become familiar with other measures of total production and total income.

Other Measures of Total Production and Total Income

We have already discussed the most important measure of total production and total income: gross domestic product (GDP). In addition to GDP, the national accounts of most countries usually include the following five measures of production and income: gross national income, net national product, national income, personal income, and disposable personal income.

Gross National Income (GNI)

We have seen that GDP is the value of final goods and services produced within a country. Gross national income (GNI) is the value of final goods and services produced by residents of that country, even if the production takes place *outside,* in other countries. For example, Qatari firms have facilities in foreign countries, and foreign firms have facilities in Qatar. For example, the Qatari government entities bought farms in Sri Lanka and Bangladesh to grow rice, pack it, and ship it back to Qatar. Qatar GNI thus includes the net value of the rice produced abroad, since it is produced by a Qatari firm, but excludes production in Qatar by foreign firms.

For some countries, such as the United States, for example, GNI is almost the same as GDP. As much as there are foreign companies in the United States, many U.S. companies are operating abroad. However, in most Arab countries and many countries around the world, they have more foreign companies producing inside, than national companies working abroad. In such a case, a significant percentage of domestic production takes place in foreign-owned facilities. For those countries, GDP is much larger than GNI. Figure 15-6 illustrates that Jordan's GDP is not only greater than its GNI, but also that the gap between the two concepts has become wider in recent years. This is mainly due to the fact that Jordan's economic policies became much more foreign-investment-friendly, attracting more foreign direct investment. So, for a country like Jordan, GDP is a more accurate measure of the level of production within the country's borders. As a result, many countries and international agencies have long preferred using GDP to using GNI.

Net National Income (NNI)

In producing goods and services, some machinery, equipment, and buildings wear out and have to be replaced. The value of this worn-out machinery, equipment, and buildings is *depreciation*. If we subtract this value from GNI, we are left with net national income (NNI).

In addition, when a consumer pays sales tax on a product, there is a difference between the amount the consumer has paid for the product and the amount the people who produced the product will receive as income. For instance, suppose you buy a TV that is priced at US$200. If the sales tax is 6 percent, you will actually pay US$212, but the seller will send the US$12 in tax directly to the government and it will never show

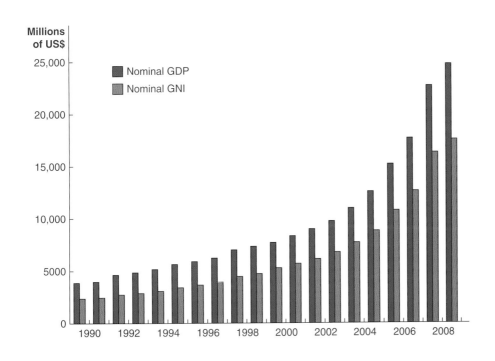

Figure 15-6

Comparing Jordan's GDP and GNI (1990–2009)

Jordan's GDP is not only greater than its GNI, but also the gap between the two has become wider in recent years.

Source: WDI, World Bank 2010.

up as anyone's income. Therefore, to calculate the total income actually received by a country's residents, the value of sales taxes has also to be subtracted.

In this chapter, we stressed that the value of total production is equal to the value of total income. This point is not strictly true if by 'value of total production' we mean GDP and by 'value of total income' we mean national income because national income will always be different from GDP. In practice, though, the difference between the value of GDP and value of national income does not matter for most macroeconomic issues.

Personal Income

Personal income is income received by households. To calculate personal income, we subtract the earnings that corporations retain rather than pay to shareholders in the form of dividends. We also add in the payments received by households from the government in the form of *transfer payments* or interest on government bonds.

Disposable Personal Income

Disposable personal income is equal to personal income minus personal tax payments, such as the federal personal income tax. It is the best measure of the income households actually have available to spend.

Economics in YOUR Life!

>> **Continued from page 491**

At the beginning of the chapter we posed two questions: What effect should Jordan's and China's two very different growth rates of GDP have on your decision to work and live in one country or the other? And if China's much higher growth rate does not necessarily lead you to decide to work and live in China, why not? This chapter has shown that although it is generally true that the more goods and services people have, the better off they are, GDP provides only a rough measure of well-being. That is to say, GDP does not include the value of leisure; nor is it adjusted for pollution and other negative effects of production or crime and other social problems. So, in deciding where to live and work you would need to balance China's much higher growth rate of GDP against these other considerations.

Conclusion

In this chapter, we have begun the study of macroeconomics by examining an important concept—how a nation's total production and income can be measured. Understanding GDP is important for understanding the business cycle and the process of long-run economic growth. In the next chapter, we discuss the issues involved in measuring two other key economic variables: the unemployment rate and the inflation rate.

Read *An Inside Look* on the next page for a discussion of why increasing government spending by oil exporters during the 2008 financial crisis reduced the impact of the crisis on the Middle East and North Africa countries.

The Government Spending Component of GDP Can Make up for the Decline in Other Components to Help Avoid a Recession

IMF SURVEY ONLINE, MAY 10, 2009

Middle East, North Africa Weathering Global Crisis

The global financial crisis has not spared the Middle East and North Africa region, but good economic fundamentals, appropriate policy responses, and sizeable currency reserves are helping to mitigate the impact of the shock, the IMF says in its latest assessment of conditions in the region.

"Given the global reach of the current economic crisis, countries in the Middle East and North Africa have also been impacted negatively. However, they are likely to fare better than countries in other regions of the world—in part because of prudent financial and economic management, but also because oil exporters in the region can draw upon their large reserves," said Masood Ahmed, Director of the IMF's Middle East and Central Asia Department, at a May 10 briefing in Dubai.

The Middle East's oil-exporting countries—Algeria, Bahrain, Iran, Iraq, Kuwait, Libya, Oman, Qatar, Saudi Arabia, Sudan, the United Arab Emirates, and Yemen—are feeling the impact mainly through the sharp fall in oil prices and the tightening of credit conditions.

Amid high oil prices and strong investor interest in the region, these countries grew by nearly 6 percent per year between 2004 and 2008. With lower global demand for oil, however, GDP growth rates are forecast to decline.

Despite the decline in oil revenues, however, most oil exporters in the region are maintaining government spending at a high level. This spending is providing an important stimulus to both domestic and global demand. In countries with less fiscal space—such as Iran, Sudan, and Yemen—governments will need to prioritize their expenditures, especially if oil prices remain at their current level.

Lower oil prices and high spending are expected to cause a turnaround in the oil exporters' external current account position from a surplus of US$400 billion last year to a deficit of nearly US$10 billion in 2009.

Middle Eastern oil importers—Afghanistan, Djibouti, Egypt, Jordan, Lebanon, Mauritania, Morocco, Pakistan, Syria, and Tunisia—have largely escaped the direct effects of the crisis, because of the positive impact of lower oil prices and their limited links to global financial markets. But as the worldwide recession has deepened, these countries face weaker prospects for exports, foreign direct investment, tourism, and remittances.

This group has mainly been affected by slowdown in their trading partners—Europe, the United States, and GCC countries—which has led to a fall in exports and foreign direct investment, according to the report. Tourism and remittances are also likely to be affected, although the data so far show them to be quite resilient.

Oil-importing countries that trade mainly with the GCC could be protected to some degree by oil exporters' continued spending. But a protracted recession in trading partners could have a significant impact on the growth of oil importers, and unemployment and poverty could rise, Ahmed said. Countries in this group represent a range of different economic structures and levels of development, and depend upon different types of foreign inflows. Some countries are better integrated with world financial markets (for example, Egypt, Jordan, Lebanon, and Pakistan), but others, such as Afghanistan, are more dependent on official development assistance.

Given the region's unique characteristics, economic policy should concentrate on the following key measures, Ahmed stressed:

- *Maintain or increase public spending where possible.* Countries where public debt levels are not a concern would do well to maintain or enhance public spending. This is true for most oil exporters, but also for countries like Morocco, Syria, and Tunisia.

- *Strengthen financial systems.* Countries should keep a close eye on their banking systems and, where appropriate, conduct "stress tests" to assess recapitalization needs and deal with troubled financial institutions.

- *Ease monetary policy as inflationary (pressures) fall.* As inflationary pressures recede, some countries will have more room for an easing of monetary policy to support investment and growth.
- *Strengthen social safety nets.* In this period of economic slowdown, it will be crucial to target government resources and develop policies to protect the poor and vulnerable segments of society.

Source: Regional Economic Outlook, "Middle East, North Africa Weathering Global Crisis," IMF Survey online, www.imf.org, May 10, 2009.

Key Points in the Article

This article discusses how the global financial crisis has affected the economies of the MENA countries. The sharp decline in global demand for oil that resulted in a large drop in oil prices has negatively reduced oil exporting countries income from exports; and hence their GDP. Such a slowing down affected the economies of oil importing countries in the region, mainly, through trade ties, foreign direct investment ties, and worker's transfers from abroad (remittances). Arab oil exporters became less able to import from other oil-importing Arab countries, less able to invest in these countries, and many workers who used to live and work and transfer their income to their countries stopped transferring. But, in general, this area of the world was able to weather the crisis better than many other countries in the world due to sound policies and responses to the (demand) shock.

Analyzing the News

(a) Arab oil exporting countries' GDP was directly hit by the crisis due to a decline in export income from oil. You can see from the figure how the Arab Gulf countries experienced a serious drop in their nominal GDP during 2009 as a result of a drop in oil exports. Note that the most hit by the net export decline were Kuwait and Saudi Arabia because they depend more on oil exports in making their GDPs. But, in order to keep their economies protected from such a significant drop in income, governments of these countries increased their spending. So, through maintaining high government spending, these countries were able to weather the crisis and compensate for the drop in export incomes. But, the combined effect of lower oil prices and higher government spending will mean lower foreign reserves after a period of mounting reserves (2004–2008).

(b) In the beginning, oil-importing (less rich) Arab countries were not greatly affected by the crisis because they benefitted from lower oil prices and because their financial systems are less tied to the international system. But when the crisis intensified, these economies' incomes were affected due to fewer exports, less demand for tourism, less direct foreign investment flows, and less income transferred from workers living and working abroad (remittances).

(c) The IMF sees that the policies protecting the Arab countries against such acrisis are maintaining high government spending in countries that have less external debt, strengthening the financial system, easing monetary policy to support growth and investment, and protecting the poor through more well-targeted social spending.

Thinking Critically

1. All Arab countries were affected by the crisis, but some did better than others in terms of coping with the crisis and not being severely hurt. Why did macroeconomic conditions in different Arab countries affect them differently?
2. In the past two years, the prices of oil declined. Has this trend been good news or bad news for Arab oil-exporting and -importing countries? How did this affect their response to the crisis?

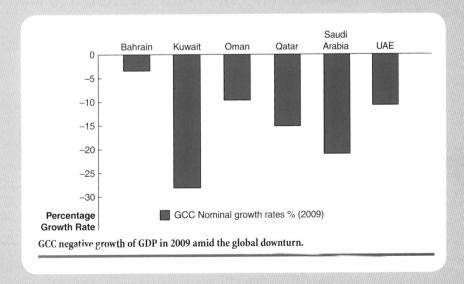

GCC negative growth of GDP in 2009 amid the global downturn.

Key Terms

Summary

15.1 LEARNING OBJECTIVE

Explain how total production is measured, **pages 493–500.**

Gross Domestic Product Measures Total Production

Economics is divided into the subfields of **microeconomics**—which studies how households and firms make choices—and **macroeconomics**—which studies the economy as a whole. An important macroeconomic issue is the **business cycle**, which refers to alternating periods of economic expansion and economic recession. An **expansion** is a period during which production and employment are increasing. A **recession** is a period during which production and employment are decreasing. Another important macroeconomic topic is **economic growth**, which refers to the ability of the economy to produce increasing quantities of goods and services. Macroeconomics also studies the **inflation rate**, or the percentage increase in the price level from one year to the next. Economists measure total production by **gross domestic product (GDP)**, which is the value of all *final goods and services* produced in an economy during a period of time. A **final good or service** is purchased by a final user. An **intermediate good or service** is an input into another good or service and is not included in GDP. When we measure the value of total production in the economy by calculating GDP, we are simultaneously measuring the value of total income. GDP is divided into four major categories of expenditures: **consumption, investment, government purchases, and net exports**. Government **transfer payments** are not included in GDP because they are payments to individuals for which the government does not receive a good or service in return. We can also calculate GDP by adding up the **value added** of every firm involved in producing final goods and services.

15.2 LEARNING OBJECTIVE

Discuss whether GDP is a good measure of well-being, **pages 500–503.**

Does GDP Measure What We Want It to Measure?

GDP does not include household production, which refers to goods and services people produce for themselves, nor does it include production in the **underground economy**, which consists of concealed buying and selling. The underground economy in some developing countries may be more than half of measured GDP. GDP is not a perfect measure of well-being because it does not include the value of leisure, it is not adjusted for pollution or other negative effects of production, and it is not adjusted for changes in crime and other social problems.

15.3 LEARNING OBJECTIVE

Discuss the difference between real GDP and nominal GDP, **pages 503–508.**

Real GDP versus Nominal GDP

Nominal GDP is the value of final goods and services evaluated at current-year prices. **Real GDP** is the value of final goods and services evaluated at *base-year* prices. By keeping prices constant, we know that changes in real GDP represent changes in the quantity of goods and services produced in the economy. When the **price level**, the average prices of goods and services in the economy, is increasing, real GDP is greater than nominal GDP in years before the base year and less than nominal GDP for years after the base year. The **GDP deflator** is a measure of the price level and is calculated by dividing nominal GDP by real GDP and multiplying by 100.

Other Measures of Total Production and Total Income

The most important measure of total production and total income is gross domestic product (GDP). The other measures of total production and total income are: gross national income (GNI), net national income (NNI), personal income, and disposable personal income.

15.4 LEARNING OBJECTIVE

Become familiar with other measures of total production and total income, **pages 508–510.**

Review, Problems and Applications

 Visit www.pearsoned.co.uk/awe/hubbard to complete these exercises online and get instant feedback.

Get Ahead of the Curve

15.1 LEARNING OBJECTIVE   Explain how total production is measured, **pages 493–500.**

Review Questions

1.1 Why in microeconomics can we measure production in terms of quantity, but in macroeconomics we measure production in terms of market value?

1.2 If the values of every good and service sold during the year are added up, would the total be larger or smaller than GDP?

1.3 In the circular flow of expenditure and income, why must the value of total production in an economy equal the value of total income?

1.4 Describe the four major components of expenditures in GDP and write the equation used to represent the relationship between GDP and the four expenditure components.

1.5 What is the difference between the value of a firm's final product and the value added by the firm to the final product?

Problems and Applications

1.6 Is the value of intermediate goods and services produced during the year included in GDP? For example, are computer chips produced and installed on a new PC included in GDP? (Note that this question does not ask whether the computer chips are directly counted in GDP but rather whether their production is included in GDP.)

1.7 Briefly explain whether each of the following transactions represents the purchase of a final good.
   a. The purchase of wheat from a wheat farmer by a bakery.
   b. The purchase of an aircraft carrier by the government.
   c. The purchase of French cheese by a consumer.
   d. The purchase of a new machine tool by a domestic company.

1.8 Briefly explain whether you agree or disagree with the following statement: "In years when people buy many shares of stock, investment will be high and, therefore, so will GDP."

1.9 **(Related to the *Chapter Opener* on page 490)** Which component of GDP will be affected by each of the following transactions involving Emirates

Airlines? If you do not believe any component of GDP will be affected by the transactions, briefly explain why.
   a. You purchase a ticket on an Emirates flight to Beirut to visit your uncle.
   b. Emirates purchases a new jetliner from Boeing.
   c. Emirates purchases new seats to be installed on a jetliner it already owns.
   d. Emirates purchases 100 million gallons of jet fuel.
   e. A person in France purchases a ticket to fly on an Emirates flight from Paris to Dubai.
   f. Dubai government agrees to spend funds to extend one of the runways at Dubai International Airport so that Emirates will be able to land larger jets.

1.10 Is the value of a house built in 2000 and resold in 2009 included in the GDP of 2009? Why or why not? Would the services of the real-estate agent who helped sell (or buy) the house in 2009 be counted in GDP for 2009? Why or why not?

1.11 **(Related to *Solved Problem 15-1* on page 494)** Suppose that a simple economy produces only the following four goods and services: textbooks, hamburgers, shirts, and cotton. Assume that all the cotton is used in the production of shirts. Use the information in the following table to calculate nominal GDP for 2009.

PRODUCTION AND PRICE STATISTICS FOR 2009		
PRODUCT	QUANTITY	PRICE IN US$
Textbooks	100	60.00
Hamburgers	100	2.00
Shirts	50	25.00
Cotton	8,000	0.60

1.12 For the total value of expenditures on final goods and services to equal the total value of income generated from producing those final goods and services, all the money that a business receives from the sale of its product must be paid out as income to the owners of the factors of production. How can a business make a profit if it pays out as income all the money it receives?

1.13 How does the value added of a business differ from the profits of a business?

1.14 It is reported that some state-owned firms in the former Soviet Union produced goods and services whose value was less than the value of the raw materials the firms used to produce their goods and services. If so, what would have been the value added

of these state-owned firms? Would such a firm be able to survive in a free-market economy?

1.15 An artist buys scrap metal from a local steel mill as a raw material for her metal sculptures. Last year, she bought US$5,000 worth of the scrap metal. During the year, she produced 10 metal sculptures that she sold for US$800 each to the local art store. The local art store sold all of them to local art collectors at an average price of US$1,000 each. For the 10 metal sculptures, what was the total value added of the artist and what was the total value added of the local art store?

15.2 LEARNING OBJECTIVE   Discuss whether GDP is a good measure of well-being, **pages 500–503.**

Review Questions

2.1 Why does the size of a country's GDP matter? How does it affect the quality of life of the country's people?

2.2 Why is GDP an imperfect measure of economic well-being? What types of production does GDP not measure? Even if GDP included these types of production, why would it still be an imperfect measure of economic well-being?

Problems and Applications

2.3 Which of the following are likely to increase measured GDP, and which are likely to reduce it?
   a. The fraction of women working outside the home increases.
   b. There is a sharp increase in the crime rate.
   c. Higher tax rates cause some people to hide more of the income they earn.

2.4 What would you expect to happen to household production as unemployment rises during a recession? What would you expect to happen to household production as unemployment falls during an expansion? Would you therefore expect the fluctuation in actual production—GDP plus household production—to be greater or less than the fluctuation in measured GDP?

2.5 **(Related to *Making the Connection* on page 506)** A report of the World Bank, includes the following statement: "Informal economic activities pose a particular measurement problem [in calculating GDP], especially in developing countries, where much economic activity may go unrecorded." What do they mean by "informal economic activities"? Why would these activities make it harder to measure GDP? Why might they make it harder to evaluate the standard of living in developing countries relative to the standard of living in more developed economies?

Source: The World Bank, *World Development Indicators*, Washington, DC: The World Bank, 2003, p. 189.

2.6 Each year, the United Nations publishes the Human Development Report, which provides information on the standard of living in nearly every country in the world. The report includes data on real GDP per person and also contains a broader measure of the standard of living called the Human Development Index (HDI). The HDI combines data on real GDP per person with data on life expectancy at birth, adult literacy, and school enrollment. The following table shows values for real GDP per person and the HDI for several countries. Prepare one list that ranks countries from highest real GDP per person to lowest and another list that ranks countries from highest HDI to lowest. Briefly discuss possible reasons for any differences in the rankings of countries in your two lists. (All values in the table are for the year 2005.)

COUNTRY	REAL GDP PER PERSON IN US$	HDI
Australia	31,794	0.962
China	6,757	0.777
Greece	23,381	0.926
Iran	7,968	0.759
Kuwait	22,070	0.915
Norway	41,420	0.968
Qatar	29,454	0.903
Saudi Arabia	9,816	0.837
United Arab Emirates	25,514	0.868
United States	41,890	0.951
Yemen	552	0.562

Source: United Nations Development Programme, *Human Development Report, 2007/2008*, New York: Palgrave Macmillan, 2007.

Review Questions

3.1 Why does inflation make nominal GDP a poor measure of the increase in total production from one year to the next?

3.2 What is the GDP deflator, and how is it calculated?

Problems and Applications

3.3 (Related to *Solved Problem 15-3* on page **504**) Suppose the information in the following table is for a simple economy that produces only the following four goods and services: textbooks, hamburgers, shirts, and cotton. Assume that all the cotton is used in the production of shirts.

PRODUCT	2000 STATISTICS QUANTITY	PRICE IN US$	2009 STATISTICS QUANTITY	PRICE IN US$	2010 STATISTICS QUANTITY	PRICE IN US$
Textbooks	90	50.00	100	60.00	100	65.00
Hamburgers	75	2.00	100	2.00	120	2.25
Shirts	50	30.00	50	25.00	65	25.00
Cotton	10,000	0.80	8,000	0.60	12,000	0.70

a. Use the information in the table to calculate real GDP for 2009 and 2010, assuming that the base year is 2000.

b. What is the growth rate of real GDP during 2010?

3.4 Assuming that inflation has occurred over time, what is the relationship between nominal GDP and real GDP in each of the following situations?
a. Years after the base year
b. In the base year
c. Years before the base year

3.5 If the quantity of final goods and services produced decreased, could real GDP increase? Could nominal GDP increase? If so, how?

3.6 Use the data in the following table to calculate the GDP deflator for each year (values are in billions of us dollars).

	NOMINAL GDP IN US$	REAL GDP IN US$
2003	10,961	10,301
2004	11,686	10,676
2005	12,434	11,003
2006	11,319	13,195
2007	13,841	11,567

Which year from 2004 to 2007 saw the largest percentage increase in the price level, as measured by changes in the GDP deflator? Briefly explain.

Review Questions

4.1 Under what circumstances would GDP be a better measure of total production and total income than GNI?

4.2 What are the differences in national income, personal income, and personal disposable income?

Problems and Applications

4.3 Suppose a country has many of its citizens temporarily working in other countries, and many of its firms have facilities in other countries. Furthermore, relatively few citizens of foreign countries are working in this country, and relatively few foreign firms have facilities in this country. In these circumstances, which would you expect to be larger for this country, GDP or GNI? Briefly explain.

4.4 Suppose the amount the government collects in personal income taxes increases, while the level of GDP remains the same. What will happen to the values of national income, personal income, and personal disposable income?

4.5 If you were attempting to forecast the level of consumption spending by households, which measure of total production or total income might be most helpful to you in making your forecast? Briefly explain.

Chapter 16

Unemployment and Inflation

Unemployment and Inflation: Two Persistent Problems in the Arab World

When we study macroeconomics, we are looking at the big picture: total production, total employment, and the price level. Of course, the big picture is determined by the decisions of millions of individual consumers and firms. Unemployment is always a big concern in the Arab countries, which have a population intensity of around 326 million people. An unemployment rate of 14 percent was announced in the 36th Arab Labor Conference, held in Amman, Jordan, in November 2010. This means the Arab region has one of the highest unemployment rates in the world. Of course the unemployment rate varies significantly between Arab countries. For example, the unemployment rate is as low as 0.5 percent in Qatar and as high as 19 percent in the West Bank, Palestine, and around 35 percent in Yemen, according to Index Mundi 2010 statistics. The low

quality of education, high illiteracy rate, low productivity, and economic instability are important factors that have led to this high unemployment rate in many Arab countries. As we'll discuss later in this chapter, more jobless people means less aggregate production and a slow economic growth. The connection between unemployment and production was pointed out by the Arab League's Assistant Secretary General for Economic Affairs, Mohammad Tuwaijri, when he mentioned that the overall gross domestic product (GDP) of all Arab countries stands at around US$1.47 trillion, which is modest compared with European countries such as Germany, whose GDP stands at US$3 trillion and has a population of around 82 million. But unemployment is not the only big concern among Arab citizens; it is also how much they have to pay for food, clothing, and housing this month compared with last month. In other words, how much extra money those citizens have to pay this month, to get the same amount of different consumer goods and services they used to buy in the past, to keep their

welfare level as it is. The increase in the overall price level, *inflation*, is another persistent problem in the Arab economies. According to the Inter-Arab Investment Guarantee Corporation (IAIGC) 2009 annual report, the average Arab inflation rate climbed to a record of 15 percent in 2008, before it dropped to 8.3 percent in 2009 due to the decline in the international prices of energy and food, and the drop in domestic demand as a result of the 2008 financial crisis.

In this chapter, we will focus on measuring changes in unemployment and changes in the price level, *inflation*. Because unemployment and inflation are both important macroeconomic problems, it is important to understand how they are measured. For an example of a newspaper discussion of three major problems faced by most of the Arab countries—the rise in food prices, housing prices, and unemployment among Arab youth—read AN INSIDE LOOK on page 542.

Sources: Hani Hazaimeh, "Rising Unemployment Threat to Arab World," *The Jordan Times*, November 28, 2010; and the Inter-Arab Investment Guarantee Corporation 2009 annual report.

Economics in YOUR Life!

Should You Change Your Career Plans if You Graduate During a Recession?

Suppose that you are about to graduate from college with a bachelor's degree in economics. You plan to seek a job in manufacturing. If the economy is currently in a recession and the unemployment rate is a relatively high 7 percent, should you change your career plans? Should you still try for a job in manufacturing, or should you try to enter another industry or, perhaps, stay in school to get a master's degree? As you read this chapter, see if you can answer these questions. You can check your answers against those we provide at the end of the chapter. >> **Continued on page 540**

Unemployment and inflation are the macroeconomic problems that are most often discussed in the media and during political campaigns. For many members of the general public, the state of the economy is summarized in just two measures: the unemployment rate and the inflation rate. In the 1960s, Arthur Okun, who was chairman of the U.S. Council of Economic Advisers, coined the term *misery index*, which adds together the inflation rate and the unemployment rate to give a rough measure of the state of the economy. As we will see in later chapters, although inflation and unemployment are important problems, the long-run success of an economy is best judged by its ability to generate high levels of real GDP per person. We devote this chapter to discussing how the government measures the unemployment and inflation rates. In particular, we will look closely at the statistics on unemployment and inflation that the government issues monthly or quarterly.

16.1 LEARNING OBJECTIVE

16.1 │ Define unemployment rate and labor force participation rate and understand how they are computed.

Measuring the Unemployment Rate and the Labor Force Participation Rate

Labor and National Accounts Departments in many Arab countries report their estimate of the unemployment rate in the previous quarter or year. If the unemployment rate is higher or lower than expected, investors are likely to change their views on the health of the economy. The announced unemployment rate might have an impact on the Stock Market. Good news about unemployment usually causes stock prices to rise, and bad news causes stock prices to fall. The unemployment rate is a key macroeconomic statistic. But how does the Department of Labor, or the National Accounts Departments, prepare its estimates of the unemployment rate, and how accurate are these estimates? We will explore the answers to these questions in this section.

How to Calculate the Unemployment Rate

People are considered *employed* if they are working during the quarter or the year at which the government is measuring the unemployment rate full-time or part-time, or if they were temporarily away from their job because they were ill, on vacation, on strike, or for other reasons. People are considered *unemployed* if they did not work during the period of estimating the unemployment rate, but were available for work and had actively looked for work at some point during that period. The **labor force** is the sum of the *employed* and the *unemployed*. The **unemployment rate** is the percentage of the labor force that is unemployed.

Labor force The sum of employed and unemployed workers in the economy.

Unemployment rate The percentage of the labor force that is unemployed.

People who do not have a job and who are not actively looking for a job are classified as *not in the labor force*. People not in the labor force include retirees, homemakers, full-time students, and people on active military service, in prison, or in mental hospitals. Also not in the labor force are people who are available for work and who have actively looked for a job at some point during the previous 12 months but who have not looked during the period of estimation. In developed economies, the unemployment rate is usually measured and announced each month; thus, people are considered not in the labor force if they were available for work and actively looked for a job during the previous 12 months but have stopped looking for a job in the previous four weeks (the period of estimating the unemployment rate). Some people have not actively looked for work lately for reasons such as transportation difficulties or childcare responsibilities. Other people who have not actively looked for work are called *discouraged workers*. **Discouraged workers** are available for work but have not looked for a job during the period of estimation because they believe no jobs are available for them.

Discouraged workers People who are available for work but have not looked for a job during the period of estimation because they believe no jobs are available for them.

Table 16-1 shows the employment status of the civilian working-age population in different Arab countries.

TABLE 16-1 | Labor Market Statistics for Arab Countries (Most Recent Year Available)

COUNTRY GROUPS	POPULATION	WORKING AGE POPULATION	LABOR FORCE (LF)	LF PARTICIPATION TOTAL %	LF PARTICIPATION M %	LF PARTICIPATION F %	CURRENTLY EMPLOYED	CURRENTLY UNEMPLOYED	UNEMPLOYED %	POPULATION EMPLOYED %
1) Labor Abundant; Resource Rich	**40,134,600**	**26,643,363**	**16,186,847**	**61**	**80**	**37**	**11,258,527**	**1,539,700**	**10%**	**28%**
Algeria	34,096,000	22,666,401	13,909,320	60	80	39	9,146,000	1,374,700	10%	27%
Libya	6,038,600	3,976,962	2,277,527	55	80	28	2,112,527	165,000	7%	35%
2) Labor Abundant; Resource Poor	**74,166,000**	**46,085,269**	**25,834,710**	**50**	**74**	**26**	**20,443,600**	**2,040,000**	**8%**	**28%**
Egypt	74,166,000	46,085,269	25,834,710	50	74	26	20,443,600	2,040,000	8%	28%
3) Labor Importing; Resource Rich	**34,633,420**	**23,061,951**	**15,626,139**	**68**	**85**	**29**	**14,972,270**	**653,869**	**4%**	**43%**
Bahrain	738,910	525,247	364,094	66	86	37	345,326	18,768	5%	47%
Kuwait	2,599,400	1,938,217	1,483,454	68	83	44	1,444,031	39,423	3%	56%
Oman	2,546,300	1,632,764	1,053,958	58	79	28	985,408	68,550	7%	39%
Qatar	821,310	633,805	860,975	81	91	43	851,475	9,500	1%	104%
Saudi Arabia	23,679,000	14,963,707	9,028,768	56	82	20	8,570,181	458,587	5%	36%
United Arab Emirates	4,248,500	3,368,211	|2,834,890	79	94	42	2,775,849	59,041	2%	65%
4) Labor Exporting	**69,891,700**	**46,399,341**	**24,810,237**	**53**	**80**	**25**	**20,550,516**	**3,407,344**	**14%**	**29%**
Jordan	5,537,600	3,333,746	1,726,433	46	74	17	1,123,780	184,220	11%	20%
Lebanon	4,227,000	2,791,000	1,506,990	54	82	28	1,340,000	178,756	12%	32%
Morocco	30,497,000	19,818,475	11,220,030	54	83	27	10,056,000	1,092,194	10%	33%
Syria	19,405,000	12,779,420	6,735,919	52	81	22	4,945,636	1,444,074	21%	25%
Tunisia	10,225,100	7,676,700	3,620,865	51	74	28	3,085,100	508,100	14%	30%
5) Poor Countries	**41,569,110**	**23,351,014**	**14,033,457**	**60**	**73**	**37**	**11,071,189**	**2,962,268**	**21%**	**27%**
Djibouti	818,510	483,723	359,667	70	80	61	211,767	147,900	41%	26%
Mauritania	3,043,600	1,714,795	1,330,970	72	81	63	1,116,602	214,368	16%	37%
Sudan	37,707,000	21,152,496	12,342,820	53	72	33	9,742,820	2,600,000	21%	26%
6) Conflict Countries	**41,110,255**	**38,961,802**	**11,562,201**	**30**	**77**	**27**	**7,952,529**	**3,562,570**	**31%**	**19%**
Iraq	28,945,657	16,846,372	7,253,015	44	71	15	5,041,699	2,211,316	30%	17%
Somalia	8,445,400	20,066,157	3,386,799	72	90	56	2,263,119	1,123,680	33%	27%
West Bank and Gaza	3,719,198	2,049,273	922,387	43	69	15	647,711	227,574	25%	17%
Total	**301,505,085**	**204,502,740**	**108,053,591**	**36**	**78**	**29**	**86,248,631**	**14,165,751**	**13%**	**29%**

Source. Jad Chaaban, "Job Creation in The Arab Economies: Navigating Through Difficult Waters", *Arab Human Development Report, Research Paper Series*, 2010.

Note: The demographic and labor market data used here are based on the latest available country-level official statistics as compiled by the Arab Labor Organization and the World Development Indicators. Mirkin (2010) provides recent UN demographic projections for the Arab countries, which might differ from the data reported here. For consistency purposes, we have relied on a single source of country-level estimates and opted not to use projection data from the ILO or the UN Population Division.

We can use the information in the table to calculate two important macroeconomic indicators:

- *The unemployment rate.* The unemployment rate measures the percentage of the labor force that is unemployed:

$$\frac{\text{Number of unemployed}}{\text{Labor force}} \times 100 = \text{Unemployment rate}$$

Using the numbers from Table 16-1, we can show how the unemployment rate for Lebanon is calculated using the previous formula:

$$\frac{178,756}{1,506,990} \times 100 = 12\% \, (approximately)$$

Labor force participation rate The percentage of the working-age population in the labor force.

- *The labor force participation rate.* The **labor force participation rate** measures the percentage of the working-age population that is in the labor force:

$$\frac{\text{Labor force}}{\text{Working-age population}} \times 100 = \text{Labor force participation rate}$$

For the same country, Lebanon, the labor force participation rate equals:

$$\frac{1,506,990}{2,791,000} \times 100 = 54\% \, (approximately)$$

Solved Problem | 16-1

What Happens if You Include the Military?

People on active military service are usually not included in the totals for employment, the labor force, or the working-age population. Suppose people in the military were included in these categories. How would the unemployment rate and the labor force participation rate change?

SOLVING THE PROBLEM:

Step 1: **Review the chapter material.** This problem is about calculating the unemployment rate and the labor force participation rate, so you may want to review the section "Measuring the Unemployment Rate and the Labor Force Participation Rate," which begins on page 520.

Step 2: **Show that including the military decreases the measured unemployment rate.** The unemployment rate is calculated as:

$$\frac{\text{Number of unemployed}}{\text{Labor force}} \times 100$$

Including people in the military would increase the number of people counted as being in the labor force but would leave unchanged the number of people counted as unemployed. Therefore, the unemployment rate would decrease.

Step 3: **Show that including the military increases the measured labor force participation rate.** The labor force participation rate is calculated as:

$$\frac{\text{Labor force}}{\text{Working-age population}} \times 100$$

Including people in the military would increase both the number of people in the labor force and the number of people in the working-age population by the same amount. This change would increase the labor force participation rate because adding the same number to both the numerator and the denominator of a fraction that is less than one increases the value of the fraction.

To see why this is true, consider the following simple example. Suppose that 100,000,000 people are in the working-age population and 50,000,000 are in the labor force, not counting people in the military. Suppose that 1,000,000 people are in the military. Then, the labor force participation rate excluding the military is:

$$\frac{50,000,000}{100,000,000} \times 100 = 50\%$$

and the labor force participation rate including the military is:

$$\frac{51,000,000}{101,000,000} \times 100 = 50.5\%$$

YOUR TURN: For more practice, do related problem 1.6 on page 546 at the end of this chapter.

>> **End Solved Problem 16-1**

Problems with Measuring the Unemployment Rate

In general, the unemployment rate announced by the labor or national accounts departments is not a perfect measure of the current state of joblessness in the economy. One problem that these departments confront is distinguishing between the unemployed and people who are not in the labor force. During an economic recession, for example, an increase in discouraged workers usually occurs, as people who have had trouble finding a job stop actively looking. Because these workers are not counted as unemployed, the unemployment rate as measured by the labor or national accounts departments may significantly understate the true degree of joblessness in the economy. The governmental departments also count people as being employed if they hold part-time jobs even though they would prefer to hold full-time jobs. In a recession, counting as 'employed' a part-time worker who wants to work full-time tends to understate the degree of joblessness in the economy and make the employment situation appear better than it is.

Not counting discouraged workers as unemployed and counting people as employed who are working part-time, although they would prefer to be working full-time, has a substantial effect on the measured unemployment rate.

There are other measurement problems, however, that cause the measured unemployment rate to *overstate* the true extent of joblessness. These problems arise because any unemployment survey does not verify the responses of people included in the survey. Some people who claim to be unemployed and actively looking for work may not be actively looking. If the government promises unemployed people with a subsidy, then some people might claim to be actively looking for a job to remain eligible for government payments to the unemployed. In this case, a person who is actually not in the labor force is counted as unemployed. Other people might be employed but engaged in illegal activity—such as drug dealing—or might want to conceal a legitimate job to avoid paying taxes. In these cases, individuals who are actually employed are counted as unemployed. These inaccurate responses to the survey bias the unemployment rate toward overstating the true extent of joblessness. We can conclude that, although the unemployment rate provides some useful information about the employment situation in the country, it is far from an exact measure of joblessness in the economy.

Trends in Labor Force Participation

The labor force participation rate is important because it determines the amount of labor that will be available to the economy from a given population. The higher the labor force participation rate, the more labor will be available and the higher a country's levels of GDP and GDP per person. Table 16-1 highlights three important trends in labor force participation rates of Arab countries: first, labor force participation rate for females is significantly lower than that of males. Second, the highest female labor participation rate is found in poor Arab countries. Third the highest total labor force participation rate exists in poor and oil-based Arab countries.

The labor force participation rate of females appears to be less than half of the labor force participation rate of males in 16 Arab countries. This is due to cultural, and sometimes religious, reasons and also the low quality of education received by females in some Arab countries. The relatively high female labor force participation rate in poor Arab countries is explained by the fact that the male's (household) monthly income in poor Arab countries, such as Djibouti, Mauritania, and Somalia, is too low to cover the family's necessary expenses. Female participation in the job market is therefore essential to secure an additional source of funding the family's needs.

Unemployment Rates for Demographic Groups

Different groups in the population can have very different unemployment rates. According to the Arab Human Development Report 2010, unemployment in the Arab world affects mainly three groups of people: youth, women, and individuals with mid- and higher-education attainment. For example, the International Labor Organization estimates the youth unemployment in the GCC countries to be, on average, 50 per cent of total unemployment. The Arab youth unemployment rate stands at 21.5 per cent and is among the highest in the world.

How Long Are People Typically Unemployed?

The longer a person is unemployed, the greater the hardship. During the Great Depression of the 1930s, some people were unemployed for years at a time. In modern developed economies, the typical unemployed person stays unemployed for a relatively brief period of time compared to developing economies. The important conclusion (mainly applied to developed economies), is that *except in severe recessions, the typical person who loses a job finds another one or is recalled to a previous job within a few months.* In developing countries, weak economies (low level of GDP), low quality of education, and the mismatch between workers' skills and the job market needs result in a longer period of unemployment for jobless people.

Job Creation and Job Destruction Over Time

One important fact about employment is not very well known: All economies create and destroy millions of jobs every year. For example, you might see the government announce that hundreds of thousands of jobs are created in a specific year and yet, the unemployment rate stays the same. This means that an equivalent number of jobs were destroyed. This degree of job creation and destruction is not surprising in a vibrant market system where new firms are constantly being started, some existing firms are expanding, some existing firms are contracting, and some firms are going out of business. The creation and destruction of jobs results from changes in consumer tastes, technological progress, and the success and failures of entrepreneurs in responding to the opportunities and challenges of shifting consumer tastes and technological change. The volume of job creation and job destruction helps explain why the typical person who loses a job is unemployed for a relatively brief period of time.

16.2 LEARNING OBJECTIVE

16.2 | Identify the three types of unemployment.

Types of Unemployment

Figure 16-1 illustrates the unemployment rates in three Arab countries: Egypt, Jordan, and Kuwat. Normally, unemployment rates are affected by the business cycle, i.e., rising during recessions and falling during expansions. For example, as you can see in Figure 16-1, many Arab countries realized an increase in the unemployment rate in 2003 as a result of the recession due to the Iraq invasion. In addition, there are other reasons that lead to an increase in the unemployment rate other than the fluctuations of the business cycle. Notice, though, that the unemployment rate never falls to zero. To understand why this is true, we need to discuss the three types of unemployment:

- Frictional unemployment
- Structural unemployment
- Cyclical unemployment

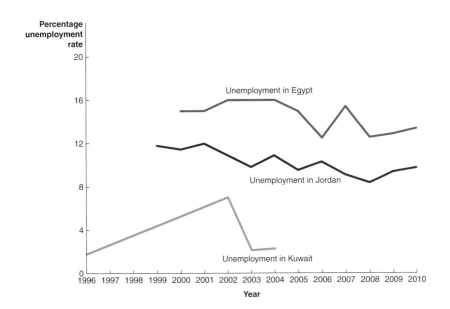

Figure 16-1

Unemployment Rates in Selected Arab Countries

The unemployment rate in Egypt and Jordan (non-oil-based economies) are significantly above the estimated natural rate of unemployment of 5 percent, while the unemployment rate in Kuwait (oil-based economy) is below it. The differences in population and wealth between the three countries explain the gap between the unemployment rates between the three countries.

Source: Index Mundi, www.indexmundi.com. Based on data from the CIA World Factbook.

Frictional Unemployment and Job Search

Workers have different skills, interests, and abilities, and jobs have different skill requirements, working conditions, and pay levels. As a result, a new worker entering the labor force or a worker who has lost a job probably will not find an acceptable job right away. Most workers spend at least some time engaging in *job search*, just as most firms spend time searching for a new person to fill a job opening. **Frictional unemployment** is short-term unemployment that arises from the process of matching workers with jobs. Some frictional unemployment is unavoidable. As we have seen, all economies create and destroy millions of jobs each year. The process of job search takes time, so there will always be some workers who are frictionally unemployed because they are between jobs and in the process of searching for new ones.

Some unemployment is due to seasonal factors, such as weather or fluctuations in demand for some products or services during different times of the year. For example, stores located in beach resorts in Beirut (Lebanon) and Alexandria (Egypt) reduce their hiring during the winter, and ski resorts, such as Mzaar (Lebanon) reduce their hiring during the summer. Some department stores increase their hiring during the month of Ramadan, Eid Al-Fitr, and Eid Al-Adha. In agricultural areas, employment increases during harvest season and declines thereafter. In countries with harsh climate conditions (abnormally hot weather), construction workers experience greater unemployment during the summer than during the winter. *Seasonal unemployment* refers to unemployment due to factors such as weather, variations in tourism, and other calendar-related events. Because seasonal unemployment can make the unemployment rate seem artificially high during some months and artificially low during other months, many developed countries report two unemployment rates each month—one that is *seasonally adjusted* and one that is not seasonally adjusted. The seasonally adjusted data eliminate the effects of seasonal unemployment. Economists and policymakers rely on the seasonally adjusted data as a more accurate measure of the current state of the labor market.

Would eliminating all frictional unemployment be good for the economy? No, because some frictional unemployment actually increases economic efficiency. Frictional unemployment occurs because workers and firms take the time necessary to ensure a good match between the attributes of workers and the characteristics of jobs. By devoting time to job search, workers end up with jobs they find satisfying and in which they can be productive. Of course, having more productive and better-satisfied workers is also in the best interest of firms.

Frictional unemployment Short-term unemployment that arises from the process of matching workers with jobs.

Structural Unemployment

By 2007, computer-generated three-dimensional animation, which was used in movies such as *Shrek* and *Ratatouille*, had become much more popular than traditional hand-drawn two-dimensional animation. Many people who were highly skilled in hand-drawn animation lost their jobs at Walt Disney Pictures, Dreamworks, and other movie studios. To become employed again, many of these people either became skilled in computer-generated animation or found new occupations. In the meantime, they were unemployed. Economists consider these animators *structurally unemployed*. **Structural unemployment** arises from a persistent mismatch between the job skills or attributes of workers and the requirements of jobs. While frictional unemployment is short term, structural unemployment can last for longer periods because workers need time to learn new skills. The mismatch between workers skills and the job market characteristics explains why some people stay unemployed although the government and/or the market create new job opportunities. Many firms would like to hire new workers but they might not be able to do so because simply they do not find the needed skills in the existing '*pool*' of unemployed workers. One solution to this problem is to retrain those workers so they can acquire the new skills needed in the job market, which usually takes quite a long time. The *Making the Connection* on page 527 describes how this is done in many Arab countries.

Some workers lack even basic skills, such as literacy, or have addictions to drugs or alcohol that make it difficult for them to perform adequately the duties of almost any job. These workers may remain structurally unemployed for years.

Structural unemployment
Unemployment arising from a persistent mismatch between the skills and characteristics of workers and the requirements of jobs.

Cyclical Unemployment

When the economy moves into recession, many firms find their sales falling and cut back on production. As production falls, they start laying off workers. Workers who lose their jobs because of a recession are experiencing **cyclical unemployment**. For example, because of the 2008 global financial crisis, around 100,000 Egyptian workers were laid off during the six months ending March 2009, according to the Arab Reform Initiative. It is expected that these workers will rejoin their work when the economy recovers into the upward trend of the business cycle. If this happens, then those 100,000 Egyptian workers will have experienced cyclical unemployment.

Cyclical unemployment
Unemployment caused by a business cycle recession.

Full Employment

As the economy moves through the expansion phase of the business cycle, cyclical unemployment will eventually drop to zero. The unemployment rate will not be zero, however, because of frictional and structural unemployment. As Figure 16-1 shows, the unemployment rate in the selected Arab countries is always positive. When the only remaining unemployment is structural and frictional unemployment, the economy is said to be at *full employment*.

Economists consider frictional and structural unemployment as the normal underlying level of unemployment in the economy. The fluctuations around this normal level of unemployment are mainly due to the changes in the level of cyclical unemployment. This normal level of unemployment, which is the sum of frictional and structural unemployment, is referred to as the **natural rate of unemployment**. Economists disagree on the exact value of the natural rate of unemployment, and there is good reason to believe it varies over time. Currently, most economists estimate the natural rate to be about 5 percent. The natural rate of unemployment is also sometimes called the *full-employment rate of unemployment*. It is obvious from Figure 16-1 that the unemployment rates in Egypt and Jordan are significantly above the estimated natural rate of unemployment of 5 percent, while the unemployment rate in Kuwait is below it. The differences in population and wealth between the three countries explain, to a great extent, the gap between the unemployment rates between the three countries.

Natural rate of unemployment The normal rate of unemployment, consisting of frictional unemployment plus structural unemployment.

Making the Connection

How Should We Classify Unemployment in the Arab Countries?

Which type of unemployment contributes the most to the high unemployment rate in many Arab countries: frictional unemployment, structural unemployment, or cyclical unemployment? Before answering this question, we should acknowledge that categorizing unemployment as frictional, structural, or cyclical is useful in understanding the sources of unemployment, but it can be difficult to apply these categories in a particular case, i.e. a particular firm or industry. Labor and national accounts departments, for instance, provide estimates of total unemployment but they usually do not classify it as frictional, structural, or cyclical. In addition, we should also address the dissimilarity between Arab economies, especially between oil-based and non-oil-based economies. So factors that might contribute to unemployment in one country, or in one group of Arab countries, might not be the main contributors to unemployment in other countries.

Many young unemployed Egyptians can usually be seen sitting in coffee shops for hours.

Despite these difficulties, we can infer the main type(s) of unemployment in the Arab countries by looking at the main causes of unemployment. According to the 2003 economic report of the Arab League, the main factors that cause the high unemployment rate in the Arab countries, especially non-oil-exporting Arab countries, are: lower development spending in most members, a rapid population growth, a surge in the workforce, and flawed economic and fiscal policies.

When adding to these factors a high illiteracy rate of around 30 percent in 10 Arab countries, with the rest having a rate of between 10 percent and 25 percent, we can say that frictional unemployment is unlikely to contribute much to the unemployment rate in the Arab countries. Rather, it is the structural unemployment that plays the major role in this matter. This conclusion is supported by the fact that unemployment is particularly affecting Arab youth (those who are between the age of 15 to 24) with mid-level education attainment, as we mentioned earlier. This means that youth skills do not match with the market needs. Also, the latest Arab Human Development Report (2010) states clearly: "High unemployment rates in the Arab countries are largely due to mismatches which seem to affect Arab labor markets."

In order to mitigate the structural unemployment problem, many Arab governments established training programs that aim to teach Arab youth the necessary skills to help them satisfy the job market's needs. For example, the Saudi Arabian Human Resources Development Fund established the 'Maher 12/12' program, which aims at addressing the needs of the Saudi work place and the knowledge and skills of a targeted group of students. The program then covers the knowledge and skills required by the work place, such as information technology, English, and software quality assurance, to young Saudis in two comprehensive, academic semesters. Other Arab countries benefit from the cooperation of some foreign non-for-profit organizations that help governments to establish training programs that give unemployed young people the specific skills to get and keep a job. The Education for Employment Foundation (EFE) is an example of such an organization, which operates in many countries in MENA region, such as Morocco, West Bank and Gaza, Egypt, Jordan, and Yemen.

Sources: Nadim Kawach, "Arab Unemployment Threatens to Surge," *Gulf News*, March 19, 2004; "Arab Human Development Report," United Nations Development Programme, 2010; and Education for Employment Foundation, www.efefoundation.org.

YOUR TURN: Test your understanding by doing related problem 2.4 on page 546 at the end of this chapter.

16.3 | Explain what factors determine the unemployment rate.

Explaining Unemployment

We have seen that some unemployment is caused by the business cycle. In later chapters, we will explore the causes of the business cycle, which will help us understand the causes of cyclical unemployment. In this section, we will look at what determines the levels of frictional and structural unemployment.

Government Policies and the Unemployment Rate

Workers search for jobs by sending out résumés, registering with Internet job sites such as gulfjobsites.com and monstergulf.com, and getting job referrals from friends and relatives. Firms fill job openings by advertising in newspapers, participating in job fairs, and recruiting on college campuses. Government policy can aid these private efforts. Governments can help reduce the level of frictional unemployment by pursuing policies that help speed up the process of matching unemployed workers with unfilled jobs. Governments can help reduce structural unemployment through policies that aid the retraining of workers, such as: the Textiles Merchandiser Training Program (MTP) in Egypt, which provides technical training in the fundamentals of textiles, the Teacher Training program in Jordan, which targets university graduates to train them to teach Arabic, English, and Information and Communications Technology, and the Sales Training Program in Morocco, which provides unemployed university graduates with training in cutting-edge business-to-consumer sales techniques.

Some government policies, however, can add to the level of frictional and structural unemployment. These government policies increase the unemployment rate either by increasing the time workers devote to searching for jobs, by providing disincentives to firms to hire workers, or by keeping wages above their market level.

Unemployment Insurance and Other Payments to the Unemployed Suppose you have been in the labor force for a few years but have just lost your job. You could probably find a low-wage job immediately if you needed to—perhaps at Carrefour or McDonald's. But you might decide to search for a better, higher-paying job by sending out resumes and responding to want ads and Internet job postings. Remember from Chapter 1 that the *opportunity cost* of any activity is the highest-valued alternative that you must give up to engage in that activity. In this case, the opportunity cost of continuing to search for a job is the salary you are giving up at the job you could have taken. The longer you search, the greater your chances of finding a better, higher-paying job, but the longer you search, the greater the opportunity cost of the salary you are giving up by not working.

In many countries in the world, especially industrial countries, the unemployed are eligible for *unemployment insurance payments* from the government. The unemployed spend more time searching for jobs because they receive these payments. This additional time spent searching raises the unemployment rate. Does this mean that the unemployment insurance program is a bad idea? Most economists would say no. The reason is that unemployed workers suffer large declines in their incomes, which led them to greatly reduce their spending. This reduced spending contributed to the severity of recessions. Unemployment insurance helps the unemployed maintain their income and spending, which lessens the personal hardship of being unemployed and also helps reduce the severity of recessions.

Few Arab countries apply an unemployment insurance program. Bahrain was the first Gulf country to introduce unemployment insurance in 2006. According to legislative decree no.(78) of the year 2006, a monthly unemployment compensation is paid at the rate of 60 percent of the insured's wage, based on his monthly wages during the 12-month period prior to his unemployment without exceeding a sum of BD500 and with a minimum of BD150 per month. For a Bahraini citizen to be eligible for the unemployment insurance, he/she has to meet several conditions such as:

- The unemployed worker shall not have left his employment by his free will.
- The unemployed worker shall be able to take up employment.

- The unemployed worker shall have the desire to work.
- The unemployed worker should be looking for a job.
- The unemployed worker should join a retraining program provided by the government.

If all conditions are met, the maximum period for payments of the unemployment compensation is 6 months. The unemployment insurance is funded by contributions made by the insured person and the employer (1 percent of the wage will be paid by each of them).

Algeria is applying a (relatively) more generous unemployment insurance program, in terms of duration, since the government sets the maximum duration of benefits at 36 months. The level of the monthly unemployment benefits is equal to half the worker's average monthly wage over the past 12 months, called the reference wage, plus the national minimum wage. Since unemployment insurance creates a disincentive to find a job, the Algerian government applies the unemployment benefits program in a regressive basis as follows:

- 100 percent of the reference wage for the first quarter of the entitlement period.
- 80 percent of the reference wage for the second quarter.
- 60 percent of the reference wage for the third quarter.
- 50 percent of the reference wage for the fourth quarter.

International Comparisons As we mentioned earlier, many governments in developed economies offer unemployed workers unemployment insurance payments. For example, in the United States, unemployed workers are typically eligible to receive unemployment insurance payments equal to about half their previous wage for only six months (the same period in the case of Bahrain). After that, the opportunity cost of continuing to search for a job rises. In Canada and most of the countries of Western Europe, workers are eligible to receive unemployment payments for a year or more, which is similar in Algeria, and the payments may equal 70 percent to 80 percent of their previous wage. In addition, many of these countries have generous *social insurance programs* that allow unemployed adults to receive some government payments even after their eligibility for unemployment insurance has ended. Although there are many reasons unemployment rates may differ across countries, most economists believe that because the opportunity cost of job search is lower in Canada and Western Europe, unemployed workers in those countries search longer for jobs and, therefore, the unemployment rates in those countries tend to be higher than in the United States.

Figure 16-2 shows the average yearly unemployment rate for the 10-year period from 1998 to 2007 for the United States, Canada, Japan, and several Western European countries. The United States and Japan provide unemployment insurance payments for only a short period of time, and their average unemployment rate during these years was

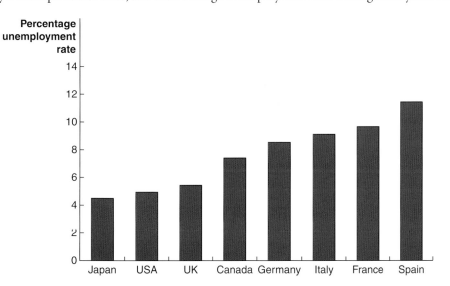

Figure 16-2

Average Unemployment Rates in the United States, Canada, Japan, and Europe, 1998–2007

The unemployment rate in the United States is usually lower than the unemployment rates in most other high-income countries, partly because the United States has tougher requirements for the unemployed to receive government payments. These requirements raise the costs of searching for a better job and lower the unemployment rate.

Based on data from Organization for Economics Cooperation and Development.

lower than for the other countries shown. Many European countries also have laws that make it difficult for companies to fire workers. These laws create a disincentive for firms to hire workers, which also contributes to a higher unemployment rate.

Minimum Wage Laws In contrast to the unemployment insurance programs, quite a good number of Arab countries apply minimum wages laws, such as Kuwait, Saudi Arabia, Jordan, Algeria, Libya, Syria, Iraq, Lebanon, and Tunisia. Some of these countries, such as Kuwait, apply the minimum wage law to workers in the public sector but not in the private sector. As we discussed in Chapter 4, if the minimum wage is set above the market wage determined by the demand and supply of labor, the quantity of labor supplied will be greater than the quantity of labor demanded. Some workers will be unemployed who would have been employed if there were no minimum wage. As a result, the unemployment rate will be higher than it would be without a minimum wage. There is no clear evidence on whether the minimum wage law is a major cause of unemployment in the Arab world. However, the existence of a minimum wage for working citizens, with no or very low minimum wage for foreign labor (low-skilled foreign labor in particular), could eventually create unemployment among the country's citizens. This could be the case for citizens working in the private sector in some Gulf countries such as Saudi Arabia. Some economists in the Gulf area suggest setting the wage of a foreign worker at the same level of that of a citizen. This will make the employment of foreign workers less attractive to private investors and, thus, the private sector will be more willing to hire the country's citizens (assuming an equal productivity).

Labor Unions

Labor unions are organizations of workers that bargain with employers for higher wages and better working conditions for their members. In unionized industries, the wage is usually above what otherwise would be the market wage. This above-market wage results in employers in unionized industries hiring fewer workers, but does it also increase the overall unemployment rate in the economy? Most economists would say the answer is "no" because labor unions in most of the Arab countries are not strong enough to enforce a higher wage.

Efficiency Wages

Efficiency wage A higher-than-market wage that a firm pays to increase worker productivity.

Many firms pay higher-than-market wages, not because the government requires them to or because they are unionized, but because they believe doing so will increase their profits. This link may seem like a paradox. Wages are the largest cost for many employers, so paying higher wages seems like a good way for firms to lower profits rather than to increase them. The key to understanding the paradox is that the level of wages can affect the level of worker productivity. Many studies have shown that workers are motivated to work harder by higher wages. An **efficiency wage** is a higher-than-market wage that a firm pays to motivate workers to be more productive. Can't firms ensure that workers work hard by supervising them? In some cases, they can. For example, a telemarketing firm can monitor workers electronically to ensure that they make the required number of phone calls per hour. In many business situations, however, it is much more difficult to monitor workers. Many firms must rely on workers being motivated enough to work hard. In fact, the following is the key to the efficiency wage: by paying a wage above the market wage, a firm raises the costs to workers of losing their jobs because most alternative jobs will pay only the market wage. The increase in productivity that results from paying the high wage can more than offset the cost of the wage, thereby lowering the firm's costs of production.

Because the efficiency wage is above the market wage, it results in the quantity of labor supplied being greater than the quantity of labor demanded, just as do minimum wage laws and unions. So, efficiency wages are another reason economies experience some unemployment even when cyclical unemployment is zero.

16.4 | Define price level and inflation rate and understand how they are computed.

Measuring Inflation

One of the facts of economic life is that the prices of most goods and services rise over time. As a result, the cost of living continually rises. In the beginning of this chapter, we learned how the government's employment and unemployment statistics are compiled in order to be able to interpret them. The same is true of the government's statistics on the cost of living and changes in the price level. The **price level** in an economy measures the average prices of goods and services in the economy. The **inflation rate** is the percentage increase in the price level from one year to the next. In Chapter 15, we introduced the *GDP deflator* as a measure of the price level. The GDP deflator is the broadest measure we have of the price level because it includes the price of every final good and service. But, for some purposes, it is too broad. For example, if we want to know the impact of inflation on the typical household, the GDP price deflator may be misleading because it includes the prices of products such as large electric generators and machine tools that are included in the investment component of GDP but are not purchased by the typical household. In this chapter, we will focus on measuring the inflation rate by changes in the *consumer price index* because changes in this index come closest to measuring changes in the cost of living as experienced by the typical household. We will also briefly discuss a third measure of inflation: the *producer price index.*

Price level A measure of the average prices of goods and services in the economy.

Inflation rate The percentage increase in the price level from one year to the next.

The Consumer Price Index

To obtain prices of a representative group of goods and services, the national accounts or a governmental statistical department in each country surveys thousands of households nationwide on their spending habits. It uses the results of this survey to construct a *market basket* of different types of goods and services purchased by typical households. For example, Figure 16-3 on the next page shows the goods and services in the market basket for a typical household in Saudi Arabia, grouped into eight broad categories: food, clothing, housing, home furniture, medical care, transportation and telecommunication, education and entertainment, and other expenses. The eight categories account for 406 different items of consumer goods and services. This categorization doesn't change much between countries, especially countries with the same traditions and consumption habits. For example, the consumer basket of a typical household in the United States has some items that do not appear in the consumer basket of a typical Arab household, such as alcoholic beverages and funeral expenses. But economists in each country usually set a different weight for each category. Each price in the consumer price index is given a weight equal to the fraction of the typical family's budget spent on that good or service. For example, according to the Household, Income, Expenditure and Consumption Survey (HIECS) 2004/2005 in Egypt, a typical Egyptian household spends around 48 percent of the budget on the food category. So the weight of the food group in the consumer basket in Egypt will be equal to 48 percent, while it is equal to 26 percent for a typical Saudi household, as indicated in Figure 16-3. The **consumer price index (CPI)** is an average of the prices of the goods and services purchased by the typical household. One year is chosen as the base year, and the value of the CPI is set equal to 100 for that year (for example, the base year in Saudi Arabia and Egypt is 1999). In any year other than the base year, the CPI is equal to the ratio of the sum of money necessary to buy the market basket of goods in that year divided by the sum of money necessary to buy the market basket of goods in the base year, multiplied by 100. Because the CPI measures the cost to the typical family to buy a representative basket of goods and services, it is sometimes referred to as the *cost-of-living index,* such as in the case of Saudi Arabia.

Consumer price index (CPI) An average of the prices of the goods and services purchased by the typical urban family of four.

A simple example can clarify how the CPI is constructed. For the purposes of this example, we assume that the market basket has only three products: diabetes examinations, rice, and chicken.

Figure 16-3

The Consumer Market Basket and Weights of Different Groups of Consumer Goods and Services in Saudi Arabia

The goods and services in the market basket for a typical household in Saudi Arabia are grouped into eight broad categories: food, clothing, housing, home furniture, medical care, transportation and telecommunication, education and entertainment, and other expenses. While these groups of goods and services do not change much between countries, the weight assigned to each group usually differs significantly.

Source: Saudi Arabian Central Department of Statistics and Information, Price Statistics & Indices Department, "Cost of Living Index," March 2009.

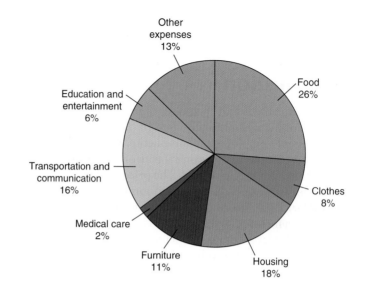

	BASE YEAR (1999)			2008		2009	
PRODUCT	**QUANTITY**	**PRICE IN US$**	**EXPENDITURES IN US$**	**PRICE IN US$**	**EXPENDITURES (ON BASE-YEAR QUANTITIES) IN US$**	**PRICE IN US$**	**EXPENDITURES (ON BASE-YEAR QUANTITIES) IN US$**
Diabetes examination	1	50.00	50.00	100.00	100.00	85.00	85.00
Rice	20	10.00	200.00	15.00	300.00	14.00	280.00
Chicken	20	25.00	500.00	25.00	500.00	27.50	550.00
Total			750.00		900.00		915.00

Suppose that during the base year of 1999, a survey determines that each month, the typical family purchases 1 diabetes examination, 20 kilos of rice, and 20 chickens. At 1999 prices, the typical family must spend US$750.00 to purchase this market basket of goods and services. The CPI for every year after the base year is determined by dividing the amount necessary to purchase the market basket in that year by the amount required in the base year, multiplied by 100. Notice that the quantities of the products purchased in 2008 and 2009 are irrelevant in calculating the CPI because *we are assuming that households buy the same market basket of products each month.* Using the numbers in the table, we can calculate the CPI for 2008 and 2009:

FORMULA	APPLIED TO 2008	APPLIED TO 2009
$CPI = \dfrac{\text{Expenditures in the current year}}{\text{Expenditures in the base year}} \times 100$	$\dfrac{US\$900}{US\$750} \times 100 = 120$	$\dfrac{US\$915}{US\$750} \times 100 = 122$

How do we interpret values such as 120 and 122? The first thing to recognize is that they are *index numbers*, which means they are not measured in dollars or any other units. *The CPI is intended to measure changes in the price level over time.* We can't use the CPI to tell us in an absolute sense how high the price level is, only how much it has changed over time. We measure the inflation rate as the percentage increase in the CPI from one year to the next. For our simple example, the inflation rate in 2009 would be the percentage change in the CPI from 2008 to 2009:

$$\left(\frac{122 - 120}{120} \right) \times 100 = 1.7\%$$

Because the CPI is designed to measure the cost of living, we can also say that the cost of living increased by 1.7 percent during 2009.

Is the CPI Accurate?

The CPI is the most widely used measure of inflation. Policymakers use the CPI to track the state of the economy. Businesses use it to help set the prices of their products and the wages and salaries of their employees. Each year, many governments, especially in developed economies, increase the Social Security payments made to retired workers by a percentage equal to the increase in the CPI during the previous year.

It is important that the CPI be as accurate as possible, but there are four biases that make changes in the CPI overstate the true inflation rate:

- *Substitution bias.* In constructing the CPI, the statistical department assumes that each month, consumers purchase the same amount of each product in the market basket. In fact, consumers are likely to buy fewer of those products that increase most in price and more of those products that increase least in price (or fall the most in price). For instance, if apple prices rise rapidly during the month while orange prices fall, consumers will reduce their apple purchases and increase their orange purchases. Therefore, the prices of the market basket consumers actually buy will rise less than the prices of the market basket the statistical department uses to compute the CPI.

- *Increase in quality bias.* Over time, most products included in the CPI improve in quality: automobiles become more durable and side air bags become standard equipment, computers become faster and have more memory, dishwashers use less water while getting dishes cleaner, and so on. Increases in the prices of these products partly reflect their improved quality and partly are pure inflation. The statistical department attempts to make adjustments so that only the pure inflation part of price increases is included in the CPI. These adjustments are difficult to make, so the recorded price increases overstate the pure inflation in some products.

- *New product bias.* Many statistical departments update the market basket of goods used in computing the CPI only every 10 years. That means that new products introduced between updates were not included in the market basket. For example, until 2008, the Saudi Arabian Central Department of Statistics and Information used to take 1988 as a base year. This means new products that came into the Saudi market during the period 1988 to 2009, such as mobile phones, are not included in the consumer basket when calculating the CPI, although these new products might take a significant portion of a typical household budget. In 2009, the Saudi Arabian Central Department of Statistics and Information updated its statistics and changed the base year to be 1999. In addition, the prices of many products, such as mobile phones, HD-DVD players, and computers, decrease in the years immediately after they are introduced. If the market basket is not updated frequently, these price decreases are not included in the CPI.

- *Outlet bias.* In developed economies, during the mid-1990s, many consumers began to increase their purchases from discount stores (big department stores that offer a discounted price since you have to buy in bulk, such as Makro in Egypt). By the late 1990s, the Internet began to account for a significant fraction of sales of some products. Because the statistical department continued to collect price statistics from traditional full-price retail stores, the CPI was not reflecting the prices some consumers actually paid.

Most economists believe these biases cause changes in the CPI to overstate the true inflation rate by one-half of a percentage point to one percentage point. That is, if the CPI indicates that the inflation rate was 3 percent, it is probably between 2 percent and 2.5 percent. So it is important that the statistical department takes steps to reduce the size of the bias by updating the market basket more frequently, rather than every 10 years, and by conducting a point-of-purchase survey to track where consumers actually make their purchases.

The Producer Price Index

Producer price index (PPI) An average of the prices received by producers of goods and services at all stages of the production process.

In addition to the GDP deflator and the CPI, the government also computes the **producer price index (PPI)**. Like the CPI, the PPI tracks the prices of a market basket of goods. But, whereas the CPI tracks the prices of goods and services purchased by the typical household, the PPI tracks the prices firms receive for goods and services at all stages of production. The PPI includes the prices of intermediate goods, such as flour, cotton, yarn, steel, and lumber, and raw materials, such as raw cotton, coal, and crude petroleum. If the prices of these goods rise, the cost to firms of producing final goods and services will rise, which may lead firms to increase the prices of goods and services purchased by consumers. Changes in the PPI therefore can give an early warning of future movements in the CPI.

16.5 LEARNING OBJECTIVE

16.5 | Use price indexes to adjust for the effects of inflation.

Using Price Indexes to Adjust for the Effects of Inflation

The typical college student today is likely to receive a much higher salary than the student's parents did 25 or more years ago; but prices 25 years ago were, on average, much lower than prices today. Put another way, the purchasing power of the dollar was much higher 25 years ago because the prices of most goods and services were much lower. Price indexes such as the CPI give us a way of adjusting for the effects of inflation so that we can compare dollar values from different years. For example, suppose your father received an annual salary of US$20,000 in 1980. By using the CPI, we can calculate what US$20,000 in 1980 is equivalent to in 2007. Suppose that the consumer price index is 82 for 1980 and 207 for 2007. Because 207/82 = 2.5, we know that, on average, prices were about 2.5 times as high in 2007 as in 1980. We can use this result to inflate a salary of US$20,000 received in 1980 to its value in current purchasing power:

$$\text{Value in 2007 dollars} = \text{Value in 1980 dollars} \times \frac{\text{CPI in 2007}}{\text{CPI in 1980}}$$

$$= \text{US\$20,000} \times (207/82) = \text{US\$50,488}$$

Our calculation shows that if you are paid a salary of US$50,488 today, you will be able to purchase roughly the same amount of goods and services that your father could have purchased with a salary of US$20,000 in 1980. Economic variables that are calculated in current-year prices are referred to as *nominal variables*. The calculation we have just made used a price index to adjust a nominal variable—your father's salary—for the effects of inflation.

For some purposes, we are interested in tracking changes in an economic variable over time rather than in seeing what its value would be in today's US dollars. In that case, to correct for the effects of inflation, we can divide the nominal variable by a price index and multiply by 100 to obtain a *real variable*. The real variable will be measured in US dollars of the base year for the price index.

Solved Problem | 16-5

Calculating Real Average Hourly Earnings

In addition to data on employment, the statistical departments gather data on average hourly earnings of production workers. Production workers are all workers, except for managers and professionals. Average hourly earnings are the wages or salaries earned by these workers per hour. Economists closely follow average hourly earnings because they are a broad measure of the typical worker's income. Using the following hypothetical data on nominal earnings and CPI, calculate the percentage change in real average hourly earnings between 2009 and 2010.

YEAR	NOMINAL AVERAGE HOURLY EARNINGS IN US$	CPI (1999 = 100)
2008	16.13	195.3
2009	16.76	201.6
2010	17.42	207.3

SOLVING THE PROBLEM:

Step 1: **Review the chapter material.** This problem is about using price indexes to correct for inflation, so you may want to review the section "Using Price Indexes to Adjust for the Effects of Inflation," which begins on page 534.

Step 2: **Calculate real average hourly earnings for each year.** To calculate real average hourly earnings for each year, divide nominal average hourly earnings by the CPI and multiply by 100. For example, real average hourly earnings for 2008 are equal to:

$$\frac{US\$16.13}{US\$195.3} \times 100 = \$8.26$$

These are the results for all the years:

YEAR	NOMINAL AVERAGE HOURLY EARNINGS IN US$	CPI (1999 = 100)	REAL AVERAGE HOURLY EARNINGS (1999 RIYALS) IN US$
2008	16.13	195.3	8.26
2009	16.76	201.6	8.31
2010	17.42	207.3	8.40

Step 3: **Calculate the percentage change in real average earnings from 2009 to 2010.** This percentage change is equal to:

$$\frac{US\$8.40 - US\$8.31}{US\$8.31} \times 100 = 1.1\%$$

We can conclude that both nominal average hourly earnings and real average hourly earnings increased between 2009 and 2010.

EXTRA CREDIT: The values we have computed for real average hourly earnings are in 1999 dollars. Because this period is more than 10 years ago, the values are somewhat difficult to interpret. We can convert the earnings to 2010 dollars using the method we used earlier to calculate your father's salary. But notice that, for purposes of calculating the *change* in the value of real average hourly earnings over time, the base year of the price index doesn't matter. The change from 2009 to 2010 would have still been 1.1 percent, no matter what the base year of the price index. If you don't see that this is true, test it by using the father's salary method to calculate real average hourly earnings for 2009 and 2010 in 2010 dollars. Then calculate the percentage change. Unless you make an arithmetic error, you should find the answer is still 1.1 percent.

YOUR TURN: For more practice, do related problems 5.3, 5.4, and 5.5 on pages 547–548 at the end of this chapter.

» End Solved Problem 16-5

16.6 LEARNING OBJECTIVE

16.6 | Distinguish between the nominal interest rate and the real interest rate.

Real versus Nominal Interest Rates

The difference between nominal and real values is important when money is being borrowed and lent. The terminology *interest rate* is used to describe the cost of borrowing funds, expressed as a percentage of the amount borrowed. If you lend someone

Nominal interest rate The stated interest rate on a loan.

Real interest rate The nominal interest rate minus the inflation rate.

1,000 Saudi riyals (SR) for one year and charge an interest rate of 6 percent, the borrower will pay back US$1,060, or 6 percent more than the amount you lent. But is US$1,060 received one year from now really 6 percent more than US$1,000 today? If prices rise during the year, you will not be able to buy as much with US$1,060 one year from now as you could with that amount today. Your true return from lending the US$1,000 is equal to the percentage change in your purchasing power after taking into account the effects of inflation.

The stated interest rate on a loan is the **nominal interest rate**. The **real interest rate** corrects the nominal interest rate for the effect of inflation on purchasing power. As a simple example, suppose that the only good you purchase is DVDs, and at the beginning of the year, the price of DVDs is US$10.00. With US$1,000, you can purchase 100 DVDs. If you lend the US$1,000 out for one year at an interest rate of 6 percent, you will receive US$1,060 at the end of the year. Suppose the inflation rate during the year is 2 percent, so that the price of DVDs has risen to US$10.20 by the end of the year. How has your purchasing power increased as a result of making the loan? At the beginning of the year, your US$1,000 could purchase 100 DVDs. At the end of the year, your US$1,060 can purchase US$1,060/US$10.20 = 103.92 DVDs. In other words, you can purchase almost 4 percent more DVDs. So, in this case the real interest rate you received from lending was a little less than 4 percent (actually, 3.92 percent). For low rates of inflation, a convenient approximation for the real interest rate is:

$$\text{Real interest rate } = \text{ Nominal interest rate } - \text{ Inflation rate.}$$

In our example, we can calculate the real interest rate by using this formula as 6 percent − 2 percent = 4 percent, which is close to the actual value of 3.92 percent. If the inflation rate during the year was 4 percent, the real interest rate would be only 2 percent. Holding the nominal interest rate constant, the higher the inflation rate, the lower the real interest rate. Notice that if the inflation rate turns out to be higher than expected, borrowers pay and lenders receive a lower real interest rate than either of them expected. For example, if both you and the person to whom you lent the US$1,000 expected the inflation rate to be 2 percent, you both expected the real interest rate on the loan to be 4 percent. If inflation actually turns out to be 4 percent, the real interest rate on the loan will be 2 percent: that's bad news for you but good news for your borrower.

For the economy as a whole, we can measure the nominal interest rate as the interest rate on banks' deposits. We can use inflation as measured by changes in the CPI to calculate the real interest rate on banks' deposits. Figure 16-4 shows the nominal and real interest rates along with the inflation rate for the years 1980 to 2008 in Egypt. The nominal interest rate is represented by the deposit interest rate. So, the real interest rate in Figure 16-4 is calculated from the depositors' perspective. Notice that when the inflation rate is low, as it was during the period 1997–2003, the gap between the nominal and real interest rates is small. When the inflation rate is high, as it was during the period 1986–1992, the gap between the nominal and real interest rates becomes large. In fact, a particular high nominal interest rate can be associated with a low, or negative, real interest rate, and a relatively low nominal interest rate can be associated with a high real interest rate. For example, in 1986, the nominal interest rate on deposits was about 11 percent, but because the inflation rate was 23.86 percent, the real interest rate was −12.86 percent. In 1996, the nominal interest rate was 10.54 percent, but because the inflation rate was only 7.18 percent, the real interest rate was 3.36 percent.

This example shows that it is impossible to know whether a particular nominal interest rate is 'high' or 'low.' It all depends on the inflation rate. *The real interest rate provides a better measure of the true cost of borrowing and the true return from lending (or depositing money in the bank) than does the nominal interest rate.* In the banking sector, the nominal lending interest rate is higher than the nominal deposit interest rate so that banks can make profits. This means that the real interest rate from the borrower perspective is different (higher) from that one calculated by a depositor. When a firm like Aramco is deciding whether to borrow the funds to buy an investment good, such as a

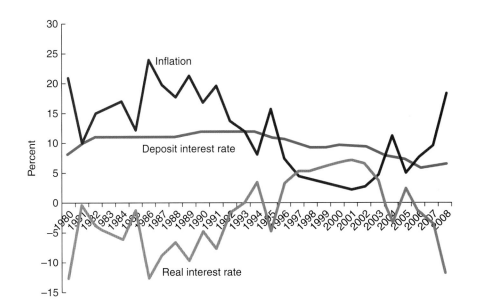

Figure 16-4

Nominal and Real Interest Rates in Egypt Based on Deposits Interest Rate (1980–2008)

When the inflation rate is low, as it was during the period 1997–2003, the gap between the nominal and real interest rates is small. When the inflation rate is high, as it was during the period 1986–1992, the gap between the nominal and real interest rates becomes large.

new factory, it will look at the real interest rate because the real interest rate measures the true cost to the firm of borrowing. A higher real interest rate means that the loan is more costly, which decreases the ability for investors to take loans.

Is it possible for the nominal interest rate to be less than the real interest rate? Yes, but only when the inflation rate is negative. A negative inflation rate is referred to as **deflation** and occurs on the rare occasions when the price level falls. During the years shown in Figure 16-4, the inflation rate as measured by changes in the CPI was never negative.

Deflation A decline in the price level.

16.7 | Discuss the problems that inflation causes.

16.7 LEARNING OBJECTIVE

Does Inflation Impose Costs on the Economy?

Imagine waking up tomorrow morning and finding that every price in the economy has doubled. The prices of food, gasoline, DVDs, computers, houses, and haircuts have all doubled. But suppose that all wages and salaries have also doubled. Will this doubling of prices and wages matter? Think about walking into Jarir expecting to find an iPod selling for US$250. Instead, you find it selling for US$500. Will you turn around and walk out? Probably not because your salary has also increased overnight from US$30,000 per year to US$60,000 per year. So, the purchasing power of your salary has remained the same, and you are just as likely to buy the iPod today as you were yesterday.

This hypothetical situation makes an important point: nominal incomes generally increase with inflation. We can think of the US$250 price of the iPod as representing either the value of the product or the value of all the income generated in producing the product. The two amounts are the same, whether the iPod sells for US$250 or US$500. When the price of the iPod rises from US$250 to US$500, that extra US$250 ends up as income that goes to the workers at Apple, the salespeople at Jarir, or the stockholders of Apple, just as the first US$250 did.

You might now think about what causes the price level in the economy to rise. In general, inflation might arise as a result of an increase in the cost of production (such as the cost of raw material and labor cost) or an increase in the quantity of GDP demanded by households, firms, and the government. The first type of inflation is called cost-push inflation: this means that the increase in the cost of production is transferred to consumers in the form of an increase in the price level. For example, if workers at a mobile phone manufacturer succeeded in 'pushing up' their wages, the prices of the mobile phones in question would increase. The second type of inflation is called demand-pull inflation. This arises when the economy operates at full employment while the quantity of GDP demanded is increasing (as we will discuss in Chapter 20). In this case, the economy will not be able to increase production enough to meet the increase in the quantity of GDP demanded; thus, inflation will increase.

It's tempting to think that the problem with inflation is that, as prices rise, consumers can no longer afford to buy as many goods and services, but our example shows that this is not the case. An expected inflation rate of 10 percent will raise the average price of goods and services by 10 percent, but it will also raise average incomes by 10 percent. Goods and services will be as affordable to the average consumer as they were before the inflation.

Inflation Affects the Distribution of Income

If inflation will not reduce the affordability of goods and services to the average consumer, why do people dislike inflation? One reason is that the argument in the previous section applies to the *average* person but not to every person. Some people will find their incomes rising faster than the rate of inflation, and so their purchasing power will rise. Other people will find their incomes rising slower than the rate of inflation—or not at all—and their purchasing power will fall. People on fixed incomes are particularly likely to be hurt by inflation. If a retired worker receives a pension fixed at US$2,000 per month, over time, inflation will reduce the purchasing power of that payment. In that way, inflation can change the distribution of income in a way that strikes many people as being unfair.

The extent to which inflation redistributes income depends in part on whether the inflation is *anticipated*—in which case consumers, workers, and firms can see it coming and can prepare for it—or *unanticipated*—in which case they do not see it coming and do not prepare for it.

The Problem with Anticipated Inflation

Like many of life's other problems, inflation is easier to manage if you see it coming. Suppose that everyone knows that the inflation rate for the next 10 years will be 10 percent per year. Workers know that unless their wages go up by at least 10 percent per year, the real purchasing power of their wages will fall. Businesses will be willing to increase workers' wages enough to compensate for inflation because they know that the prices of the products they sell will increase. Lenders will realize that the loans they make will be paid back with riyals that are losing 10 percent of their value each year, so they will charge a higher interest rate to compensate for this. Borrowers will be willing to pay these higher interest rates because they also know they are paying back these loans with dollars that are losing value. So far, there don't seem to be costs to anticipated inflation.

Even when inflation is perfectly anticipated, however, some individuals will experience a cost. Inevitably, there will be a redistribution of income, as some people's incomes fall behind even an anticipated level of inflation. In addition, firms and consumers have to hold some paper money to facilitate their buying and selling. Anyone holding paper money will find its purchasing power decreasing each year by the rate of inflation. To avoid this cost, workers and firms will try to hold as little paper money as possible, but they will have to hold some. In addition, firms that print catalogs listing the prices of their products will have to reprint them more frequently. Supermarkets and other stores that mark prices on packages or on store shelves will have to devote more time and labor to changing the marked prices. The costs to firms of changing prices are called **menu costs**. Although at moderate levels of anticipated inflation, menu costs are relatively small, at very high levels of inflation, such as are experienced in some developing countries, menu costs and the costs due to paper money losing value can become substantial. Finally, even anticipated inflation acts to raise the taxes paid by investors and raises the cost of capital for business investment. These effects arise because investors are taxed on the nominal payments they receive rather than on the real payments.

Menu costs The costs to firms of changing prices.

Making the Connection

Why a Lower Inflation Rate is Like a Tax Cut for Orascom Telecom Bondholders

Borrowers and lenders are interested in the real interest rate rather than the nominal interest rate. Therefore, if expected inflation increases, the nominal interest rate will rise, and if expected inflation decreases, the nominal interest rate will fall. Suppose that Orascom Telecom sells bonds to investors to raise funds to purchase investment goods. A bond is a contractual debt security between a borrower and a lender in which the borrower promises the lender to make periodic payments for a specified period of time (until the maturity date). Suppose also that Orascom Telecom (the borrower) is willing to pay, and investors (the lenders) are willing to receive, a real interest rate of 4 percent. If the inflation rate is expected to be 2 percent, the nominal interest rate on Orascom Telecom's bonds must be 6 percent for the real interest rate to be 4 percent. If the inflation rate is expected to be 6 percent, the nominal rate on the bond must rise to 10 percent for the real interest rate to be 4 percent. The following table summarizes this information, assuming that the bond has a principal, or face value, of US$1,000.

PRINCIPAL IN US$	REAL INTEREST RATE	INFLATION RATE	NOMINAL NTEREST RATE
1,000	4%	6%	10%
1,000	4%	2%	6%

With a nominal interest rate of 6 percent, the interest payment (also known as the *coupon payment*) on newly issued bonds is US$60. When the nominal interest rate rises to 10 percent, the interest payment on newly issued bonds is US$100.

Unfortunately for investors, the government taxes the nominal payment on bonds, with no adjustment for inflation. So, even though in this case, the increase in the interest payment from US$60 to US$100 represents only compensation for inflation, the whole US$100 is subject to the income tax. The following table shows the effect of inflation on an investor's real after-tax interest payment, assuming a tax rate of 25 percent.

INFLATION RATE	NOMINAL INTEREST PAYMENT IN US$	TAX PAYMENT IN US$	AFTER-TAX INTEREST PAYMENT IN US$	ADJUSTMENT FOR INFLATION IN US$	REAL AFTER-TAX INTEREST PAYMENT IN US$
6%	100	–25	= 75	–60	= 15
2%	60	–15	= 45	–20	= 25

The table shows that reducing the inflation rate from 6 percent to 2 percent will increase the real after-tax payment received by investors who purchase a US$1,000 Orascom Telecom bond from US$15 to US$25. By raising the after-tax reward to investors, lower inflation rates will increase the incentive for investors to lend funds to firms. The greater the flow of funds to firms, the greater the amount of investment spending that will occur.

YOUR TURN: Test your understanding by doing related problem 7.6 on page 549 at the end of this chapter.

The Problem with Unanticipated Inflation

In any advanced economy households, workers, and firms routinely enter into contracts that commit them to make or receive certain payments for years in the future. For example, many workers have a job on a contract basis. Once this contract is signed, the firm (employer) is committed to pay a specified wage for the duration of the contract to its workers. When people buy homes, sometimes they borrow a part of the amount they need from a bank. These loans, called *mortgage loans*, commit a borrower to make a fixed monthly payment for the length of the loan. Most mortgage loans are for long periods (as much as 30 years).

To make these long-term commitments, households, workers, and firms must forecast the rate of inflation. If a firm believes the inflation rate over the next three years will be 6 percent per year, signing a three-year contract with a unionized worker whose union calls for wage increases of 8 percent per year may seem reasonable because the firm may be able to raise its prices by at least the rate of inflation each year. If the firm believes that the inflation rate will be only 2 percent over the next three years, paying wage increases of 8 percent may significantly reduce its profits or even force it out of business.

When people borrow money or banks lend money, they must forecast the inflation rate so they can calculate the real rate of interest on a loan. In 1993, banks in Egypt were charging interest rates of 18.2 percent on loans. This rate seems very high compared with the 12.9 percent charged on loans in 1999, but the inflation rate in 1993 was around 12 percent, while it was only 3 percent in 1999. The inflation rate in 1994 dropped to 8 percent, so people who borrowed money for one year at the high interest rate of 1993 (18.2 percent) soon found that the real interest rate on their loans was much higher than they expected.

When the actual inflation rate turns out to be very different from the expected inflation rate, some people gain, and other people lose. This outcome seems unfair to most people because they are either winning or losing only because something unanticipated has happened. This apparently unfair redistribution is a key reason why people dislike unanticipated inflation.

Economics in YOUR Life!

>> Continued from page 519

At the beginning of this chapter, we posed a question: Should you change your career plans if you graduate during a recession when the unemployment rate is high? We have seen in this chapter that the high unemployment rates during a recession, although painful for people who lose their jobs, do not generally last very long. So, on the one hand, if you graduate with an economics degree and want a job in the banking sector, you may have some difficulty finding one during a recession, but you probably do not need to change your career plans. On the other hand, if you plan at some point to earn a master's degree, you might consider staying in school to ride out the temporary increases in unemployment caused by the recession. But if you are not sure that the reason why you are unemployed is the recession, i.e. your unemployment is not a cyclical one, then you have to consider joining any of the training programs that aim to retrain graduates in order for their skills to match the market needs. If this is the solution to your unemployment, then you are structurally unemployed.

Conclusion

Inflation and unemployment are key macroeconomic problems. Many economists would argue that, in the long run, maintaining high rates of growth of real GDP per person is the most important macroeconomic concern. Only when real GDP per person is increasing will a country's standard of living increase. We turn in the next chapter to discussing this important issue of economic growth.

Read *An Inside Look* on the next page for an example of a newspaper discussion of three major problems faced by most of the Arab countries: the rise in food prices, housing prices, and unemployment among Arab youth.

Food Prices, Housing Prices, and the 'Youthquake': Major Problems Facing the Arab World

ARTICLE 1: *ARAB TIMES*, SEPTEMBER 28, 2010

GCC Inflation Down; Rising Food Prices Need 'Attention': CBK Gov. Kuwait Inflation at 13-month High

Inflationary pressures in Gulf Arab countries have decreased significantly, but they must pay attention to rising global food prices, Kuwait's central bank governor said on Tuesday.

Kuwait's own inflation rose to a 13-month high of 4.0 percent year-on-year in July, according to data released on Tuesday, though it is expected to decelerate towards the end of the year....

(a) Price pressures are highest in Saudi Arabia, where inflation hit an 18-month high of 6.1 percent in August, mainly because of surging food costs and chronic housing shortages in the world's biggest crude exporter and the top Arab economy....

Oman's inflation, pressured this year by rising food and housing costs, eased slightly to 3.3 percent year-on-year in July after hitting a 13-month high the previous month....

Food prices, which account for 18 percent of the basket, jumped by 3.1 percent in July, following a 0.1 percent rise in the previous month.

"What drives food inflation is what happens to global commodities prices," said Daniel Kaye, senior economist at the National Bank of Kuwait. "The central bank will see this as something a little bit beyond its control," he said.

Housing prices, which have the largest weight of 27 percent in the overall basket, dropped 0.1 percent month on month after rising by 1.3 percent in June.

Central Bank Governor Sheikh Salem Abdul-Aziz al-Sabah said on Tuesday that inflation pressures in the Gulf Arab oil producing region had decreased significantly.

"If commodities prices stay more or less where they are now I suspect that food price inflation is probably close to its top. Hopefully towards the end of the year this will start to ease back again," Kaye said.

"Inflation will be a little bit lower from where it is now, edging down towards the 3 percent mark as the impact of this food inflation begins to decline a little bit," he added.

ARTICLE 2: *THE MAJILIS*, DECEMBER 22, 2009

26% youth unemployment in Arab world

The Arab Labor Organization (ALO) has a new report out on youth unemployment in Arab countries....

(b) The Middle East and North Africa have an average youth unemployment rate of 26 percent, the highest in the world. The situation is worst in Algeria, which stands at 46 percent; the United Arab Emirates has the lowest rate, just 6.3 percent. (The other Gulf states are not so successful. Bahrain is 27 percent; Saudi Arabia, 26 percent.)

Young people represent nearly half of the unemployed workers in Arab countries....

What's really striking—and this is a trend we've commented on before—is that high levels of unemployment persist despite positive macroeconomic trends in the region. Every single Arab country posted positive GDP growth in 2008; five states, including Qatar and the UAE, recorded 8 percent growth or higher.

But the macroeconomic gains simply do not filter down to a microeconomic level. The official poverty rate in the Arab world still stands at 40 percent, virtually unchanged since 1990. That means roughly 140 million people live in poverty, according to the report....

(c) The Middle East is going through a baby boom right now: Nearly 65 percent of the region's population is under the age of 30. If the ALO's numbers are correct, one-fourth of *that* population is unemployed. The policy implications of these numbers should be quite clear: Arab states can't hope to ever build stable, educated middle classes with one-quarter of their young people out of work.

Source: "GCC Inflation Down; Rising Food Prices Need 'Attention': CBK Gov. Kuwait Inflation at 13-month High," *Arab Times*, September 28, 2010;

and Gregg Carlstrom, "Report: 26 percent Youth Unemployment in Arab World", *The Majlis*, December 22, 2009.

Key Points in the Articles

The first article discusses the rise in food and housing prices as sources of inflation in many Arab countries. Until 2008, the international food prices were increasing significantly, which affected the inflation rates in the Arab countries since food accounts for a considerable weight in the consumer basket. In 2009, food prices started to drop, and that is why policymakers in the Gulf area revised their expectations and predicted a slight decline in the inflation rate. Countries with housing shortages, such as Saudi Arabia, still suffer from a high inflation rate since housing is the second largest item in a typical Saudi household basket.

The second article addresses another major problem in the Arab world: unemployment among young Arabs. This is a signal of a structural unemployment and a distortion in the education system that caused this mismatch between the graduates' skills and the market characteristics.

Analyzing the News

(a) Arab countries, especially Gulf countries, import different food items to satisfy their consumers' needs. So any increase in the international prices of food will also be imported to the Arab countries. In addition, food usually has a high weight in the consumer basket of an Arab household when calculating the CPI. But the weights differ from one country to another. Since the weights of food in the consumer basket is 18 percent in Kuwait and 26 percent in Saudi Arabia (as we discussed previously), the impact of a rise in food prices will have a larger impact on the inflation rate in Saudi Arabia compared with that of Kuwait. Of course, the impact of a rise (or a reduction) in food prices on the inflation rate would be much greater in a country like Egypt since the weight of food is close to 50 percent in the Egyptian consumer basket.

Housing is another major item in the household basket, but this time, its impact on the inflation rate in Kuwait will be greater than that of Saudi Arabia since housing accounts for 27 percent of the consumer basket in Kuwait and only 18 percent of the consumer basket in Saudi Arabia.

(b) This article addresses two main characteristics of unemployment in the Arab world: first, the average Arab youth unemployment rate is the highest in the world (the 'youthquake' phenomenon, as described by Isobel Coleman, a senior fellow for US foreign policy at the Council on Foreign Relations), and, second, the unemployment rate stayed high in 2008 although many Arab countries realized high economic growth rates. The later characteristic means that young Arabs are not benefiting much from the high economic growth rates and that the skills of the current pool of unemployed young workers do not match the characteristics of the new job opportunities that came along with the economic expansion. This explains why the unemployment rate and the poverty level in the Arab world did not change during 2008. This later feature could be used as evidence against the argument, voiced by some economists, that as economic growth increases, poverty level decreases. Current highly skilled workers and professional expatriates, especially in the Gulf countries, are among the main beneficiaries from the high economic growth rates. Again, the unemployed Arab youth, mainly those who have mid-level education, are classified as structurally unemployed.

(c) With one-fourth of young Arabs are currently unemployed, Arab countries have no chance but to apply dramatic changes in their educational system according to the market needs. Young Arabs should acquire many advanced skills, such as: leadership, critical thinking, problem solving, different languages, and computer and information technology skills, which cannot be obtained from the current way teaching. In addition, as we mentioned earlier in the chapter, intensive retraining programs should be implemented for the current unemployed graduates to help them change their career and get the required skills that match with the market needs.

Source: Jack Farchy, Heba Saleh, and Abeer Allam, "Ramadan Demand Prompts Rise in Food Prices," *Financial Times*, September 5, 2010.

Thinking Critically

1. Suppose that the unemployment rate in the Saudi Arabian construction industry in 2009 was 12 percent, which was more than 2 percentage points above the overall unemployment rate, since many companies delayed their projects because of the 2008 financial crisis. Some economists believed that beginning in 2009, housing construction entered a period of decline that might last for several years. If this assumption was true, how should we characterize unemployment in the Saudi Arabian construction industry: mainly frictional, mainly structural, mainly cyclical, or some combination of these types?

2. Suppose that you manage a used-book store in a college town. Your employees request a 3 percent wage increase for next year. Meanwhile, you expect inflation to be 4 percent next year. Should you agree to the 3 percent wage increase? Why or why not?

Youth unemployment rate is the highest in the Middle East and North Africa

- South Asia
- Latin America & the Caribbean
- Sub-Saharan Africa
- Middle East
- North Africa

Source: "Global Employment Trends for Youth," Labour Office, International Labour Organization, August 2010.

Key Terms

Summary

16.1 LEARNING OBJECTIVE

Define unemployment rate and labor force participation rate and understand how they are computed, **pages 520–524.**

Measuring the Unemployment Rate and the Labor Force Participation Rate

National Labor Statistics Departments uses the results of the household and firms' surveys to calculate the *unemployment rate* and the *labor force participation rate*. The **labor force** is the total number of people who have jobs plus the number of people who do not have jobs but are actively looking for them. The **unemployment rate** is the percentage of the labor force that is unemployed. **Discouraged workers** are people who are available for work but who are not actively looking for a job. Discouraged workers are not counted as unemployed. The **labor force participation rate** is the percentage of the working-age population in the labor force. Arabs youths with mid-level education are the most affected segment of the labor force when the unemployment rate rises. The typical unemployed person should find a new job or return to his or her previous job within a few months. Each year, hundreds of thousands of jobs are created and destroyed in the Arab world.

16.2 LEARNING OBJECTIVE

Identify the three types of unemployment, **pages 524–527.**

Types of Unemployment

There are three types of unemployment: frictional, structural, and cyclical. **Frictional unemployment** is short-term unemployment that arises from the process of matching workers with jobs. One type of frictional unemployment is *seasonal unemployment*, which refers to unemployment due to factors such as weather, variations in tourism, and other calendar-related events. **Structural unemployment** arises from a persistent mismatch between the job skills or attributes of workers and the requirements of jobs. **Cyclical unemployment** is caused by a business cycle recession. The **natural rate of unemployment** is the normal rate of unemployment, consisting of structural unemployment and frictional unemployment. The natural rate of unemployment is also sometimes called the *full-employment rate of unemployment*.

16.3 LEARNING OBJECTIVE

Explain what factors determine the unemployment rate, **pages 528–530.**

Explaining Unemployment

Government policies can reduce the level of frictional and structural unemployment by aiding the search for jobs and the retraining of workers. Some government policies, however, can add to the level of frictional and structural unemployment. Unemployment insurance payments can raise the unemployment rate by extending the time that unemployed workers search for jobs. Government policies have caused the unemployment rates in most industrial countries to be high. Wages above market levels can also increase unemployment. Wages may be above market levels because of the minimum wage, labor unions, and *efficiency wages*. An **efficiency wage** is a higher-than-market wage paid by a firm to increase worker productivity.

Measuring Inflation

The **price level** measures the average prices of goods and services. The **inflation rate** is equal to the percentage change in the price level from one year to the next. The federal government compiles statistics on three different measures of the price level: the consumer price index (CPI), the GDP price deflator, and the producer price index (PPI). The **consumer price index (CPI)** is an average of the prices of goods and services purchased by the typical urban family of four. Changes in the CPI are the best measure of changes in the cost of living as experienced by the typical household. Biases in the construction of the CPI cause changes in it to overstate the true inflation rate by one-half of a percentage point to one percentage point. The **producer price index (PPI)** is an average of prices received by producers of goods and services at all stages of production.

16.4 LEARNING OBJECTIVE

Define price level and inflation rate and understand how they are computed, **pages 531–534.**

Using Price Indexes to Adjust for the Effects of Inflation

Price indexes are designed to measure changes in the price level over time, not the absolute level of prices. To correct for the effects of inflation, we can divide a *nominal variable* by a price index and multiply by 100 to obtain a *real variable*. The real variable will be measured in monetary units of the base year for the price index.

16.5 LEARNING OBJECTIVE

Use price indexes to adjust for the effects of inflation, **pages 534–535.**

Real versus Nominal Interest Rates

The stated interest rate on a loan is the **nominal interest rate**. The **real interest rate** is the nominal interest rate minus the inflation rate. Because it is corrected for the effects of inflation, the real interest rate provides a better measure of the true cost of borrowing and the true return from lending than does the nominal interest rate. The nominal interest rate is always greater than the real interest rate unless the economy experiences *deflation*. **Deflation** is a decline in the price level.

16.6 LEARNING OBJECTIVE

Distinguish between the nominal interest rate and the real interest rate, **pages 535–537.**

Does Inflation Impose Costs on the Economy?

Inflation does not reduce the affordability of goods and services to the average consumer, but it still imposes costs on the economy. When inflation is anticipated, its main costs are that paper money loses some of its value and firms incur *menu costs*. **Menu costs** include the costs of changing prices on products and printing new catalogs. When inflation is unanticipated, the actual inflation rate can turn out to be different from the expected inflation rate. As a result, income is redistributed as some people gain and some people lose.

16.7 LEARNING OBJECTIVE

Discuss the problems that inflation causes, **pages 537–541.**

Review, Problems and Applications

myeconlab Visit www.pearsoned.co.uk/awe/hubbard to complete these exercises online and get instant feedback.
Get Ahead of the Curve

16.1 LEARNING OBJECTIVE Define unemployment rate and labor force participation rate and understand how they are computed, **pages 520–524.**

Review Questions

1.1 How is the unemployment rate calculated? Which groups tend to have above-average unemployment rates, and which groups tend to have below-average unemployment rates?

1.2 How is the labor force participation rate calculated?

1.3 How does the discouraged worker effect reduce the unemployment rate?

Problems and Applications

1.4 Fill in the missing values in the table of data collected in the following hypothetical household survey for the year 2007.

Working-age population	
Employment	146,047,000
Unemployment	
Unemployment rate	4.6%
Labor force	
Labor force participation rate	66.0%

1.5 What would be some general reasons a firm would lay off a substantial number of workers?

1.6 **(Related to *Solved Problem 16-1* on page 522)** Homemakers are not included in the employment or labor force totals compiled in the Labor Department Statistics. They are included in the working-age population totals. Suppose that homemakers were counted as employed and included in the labor force statistics. What would be the impact on the unemployment rate and the labor force participation rate?

1.7 Suppose that in 2008 there were 3.7 million job openings at businesses in the Arab world. At the same time, there were about 7.6 million people unemployed. Why didn't the unemployed workers accept these job openings, thereby reducing the total number of unemployed by almost 50 percent?

1.8 Suppose that between the first quarter of 2010 and the same quarter of 2011, the total number of people employed and the unemployment rate both fell. Briefly explain how this is possible.

1.9 Assume that the labor force participation rate fell by 1 percentage point over the past year. An economist commented on this reduction by saying: "The sharp decline [in the labor force participation rate] suggests that the published unemployment rate understates the damage to the labor market."

Why would a fall in the labor force participation rate indicate that the unemployment rate is not doing a good job reflecting labor market conditions?

Source: "Climbing Out of the Job Pool," *BusinessWeek*, February 25, 2002, p. 32.

1.10 In an article on the conditions in the labor market, two business reporters remarked that the unemployment rate "typically rises months after the economy rebounds." What do they mean by the phrase "the economy rebounds"? Why would the unemployment rate be rising if the economy is rebounding?

Source: Vince Golle and Terry Barrett, "Hiring Picks Up, Factories Expand," *Bloomberg News*, April 1, 2002.

16.2 LEARNING OBJECTIVE | Identify the three types of unemployment, **pages 524–527.**

Review Questions

2.1 What is the relationship between frictional unemployment and job search?

2.2 Why isn't the natural rate of unemployment equal to zero?

Problems and Applications

2.3 Macroeconomic conditions affect the decisions firms and families make. Why, for example, might a college student after graduation enter the job market during an economic expansion but apply for graduate school during a recession?

2.4 **(Related to *Making the Connection* page 527)** What advice for finding a job would you give someone who is frictionally unemployed? What advice would you give someone who is structurally unemployed? What advice would you give someone who is cyclically unemployed?

2.5 Recall from Chapter 3 the definitions of normal and inferior goods. During an economic expansion, would you rather be working in an industry that produces a normal good or in an industry that produces an inferior good? Why? During a recession, would you rather be working in an industry that produces a normal good or an inferior good? Why?

2.6 If Algeria eliminated the unemployment insurance system, what would be the effect on the level of frictional unemployment? What would be the effect on the level of real GDP? Would well-being in the economy be increased? Briefly explain.

16.3 LEARNING OBJECTIVE | Explain what factors determine the unemployment rate, **pages 528–530.**

Review Questions

3.1 What effect does the payment of government unemployment insurance have on the unemployment rate:

3.2 Discuss the effect of each of the following on the unemployment rate:

a. The minimum wage law
b. Labor unions
c. Efficiency wages

Problems and Applications

3.3 In 2007, Ségolène Royal, who was running unsuccessfully for president of France, proposed that workers who lost their jobs would receive unemployment payments equal to 90 percent of their previous wages during their first year of unemployment. If this proposal were enacted, what would likely be the effect on the unemployment rate in France? Briefly explain.

Source: Alessandra Galloni and David Gauthier-Villars, "France's Royal Introduces Platform Ahead of Election," *Wall Street Journal*, February 12, 2007, p. A.8.

3.4 Discuss the likely impact of each of the following on the unemployment rate:

a. The length of time workers are eligible to receive unemployment insurance payments doubles.

b. The minimum wage is abolished.

c. Most Arab workers join labor unions.

d. More companies make information on job openings easily available on Internet job sites.

3.5 An economic consultant studies the labor policies of a firm where it is difficult to monitor workers and prepares a report in which she recommends that the firm raise employee wages. At a meeting of the firm's managers to discuss the report, one manager makes the following argument: "I think the wages we are paying are fine. As long as enough people are willing to work here at the wages we are currently paying, why should we raise them?" What argument can the economic consultant make to justify her advice that the firm should increase its wages?

3.6 If Carrefour adopted an efficiency wage policy, what would likely happen to the number of workers employed by Carrefour? Is it likely that consumers would be better off or worse off?

16.4 LEARNING OBJECTIVE   Define price level and inflation rate and understand how they are computed,

pages 531–534.

Review Questions

4.1 Briefly describe the three major measures of the price level. Which measure is used most frequently?

4.2 What potential biases exist in calculating the consumer price index? What steps has the Statistical Department taken to reduce the size of the biases?

Problems and Applications

4.3 Briefly explain whether you agree or disagree with the following statement: "I don't believe the government price statistics. The CPI for 2007 was 207, but I know that the inflation rate couldn't have been as high as 107 percent in 2007."

4.4 Briefly explain whether you agree with the following statement: "If changes in the CPI were a more accurate measure of the inflation rate, the government would pay less in Social Security payments each year."

4.5 Consider a simple economy that produces only three products. Use the information in the following table to calculate the inflation rate for 2009 as measured by the consumer price index.

		PRICE IN US$		
PRODUCT	QUANTITY	BASE YEAR (1999)	2008	2009
Haircuts	2	10.00	11.00	16.20
Kabsah	10	2.00	2.45	2.40
DVDs	6	15.00	15.00	14.00

4.6 The *Wall Street Journal* publishes an index of the prices of luxury homes in various U.S. cities. The base year for the index is January 2000. Here are the indexes for December 2005 and December 2006.

CITY	DECEMBER 2005	DECEMBER 2006
New York	184.6	193.1
Los Angeles	223.9	226.7
Chicago	153.4	157.1
Seattle	147.4	159.1

a. In which city did the prices of luxury homes increase the most during this year?

b. Can you determine on the basis of these numbers which city had the most expensive luxury homes in December 2006? Briefly explain.

Source: "Luxury Home Index," *Wall Street Journal*, December 29, 2006.

16.5 LEARNING OBJECTIVE   Use price indexes to adjust for the effects of inflation, **pages 534–535.**

Review Questions

5.1 What is the difference between a nominal variable and a real variable?

5.2 Briefly explain how you can use data on nominal wages for 2002 to 2008 and data on the consumer price index for the same years to calculate the real wage for these years.

Problems and Applications

5.3 **(Related to *Solved Problem 16-5* on page 534)** Assume that in 1970, the Arab Contractors company paid its workers US$5 per day for an eight-hour day and the CPI was 10. In 2007, when the average wage paid by the same company was about US$30 per day, the CPI was 207. Were workers in 1970 or workers in 2007 paid more in real terms? Be sure to show your calculation.

5.4 **(Related to *Solved Problem 16-5* on page 534)** Use the hypothetical monetary figures and CPI in the following table to determine the percentage changes in the Jordanian and Kuwaiti real minimum wages between 1956 and 2007.

	JORDAN		KUWAIT	
YEAR	MINIMUM WAGE (DINARS PER HOUR)	CPI	MINIMUM WAGE (DINARS PER HOUR)	CPI
1956	1.00 dinars	27	0.19 dinars	10
2007	5.85 dinars	207	8.44 dinars	116

Does it matter for your answer that you have not been told the base year for the Jordanian CPI or the Kuwaiti CPI? Was the percentage increase in the price level greater in the Jordan or in Kuwait during these years?

5.5 **(Related to *Solved Problem 16-5* on page 534)** The Great Depression was the worst economic disaster in US history in terms of declines in real GDP and increases in the unemployment rate. Use the data in the following table to calculate the percentage decline in real GDP between 1929 and 1933.

YEAR	NOMINAL GDP (BILLIONS OF US DOLLARS)	GDP PRICE DEFLATOR (2000 = 100)
1929	103.6	11.9
1933	56.4	8.9

16.6 LEARNING OBJECTIVE   Distinguish between the nominal interest rate and the real interest rate, **pages 535–537.**

Review Questions

6.1 What is the difference between the nominal interest rate and the real interest rate?

6.2 If the inflation is expected to increase, what is likely to happen to the nominal interest rate? Briefly explain.

Problems and Applications

6.3 Suppose you heard in the news the following statement: "Inflation in Aleppo, Syria, during the last year was less than half the national inflation rate.... So, producers in Aleppo are scared of deflation—when prices decrease sharply, the CPI drops below zero." Do you agree with the reporter's definition of deflation? Briefly explain.

6.4 Suppose you were borrowing money to buy a car. Which of these situations would you prefer: the interest rate on your car loan is 20 percent and the inflation rate is 19 percent, or the interest rate on

your car loan is 5 percent and the inflation rate is 2 percent? Briefly explain.

6.5 Describing the situation in England in 1920, the historian Robert Skidelsky wrote the following: "Who would not borrow at 4 per cent a year, with prices going up 4 per cent a *month*?" What was the real interest rate paid by borrowers in this situation? (*Hint:* What is the annual inflation rate, if the monthly inflation rate is 4 percent?)

Source: Robert Skidelsky, *John Maynard Keynes: Volume 2, The Economist as Saviour, 1920–1937*, New York: The Penguin Press, 1992, p. 39, emphasis in original.

6.6 Suppose that the only good you purchase is rice and that at the beginning of the year, the price of one kilo of rice is US$2.00. Suppose you lend US$1,000 for one year at an interest rate of 5 percent. At the end of the year, one kilo of rice costs US$2.08. What was the real rate of interest you earned on your loan?

16.7 LEARNING OBJECTIVE   Discuss the problems that inflation causes, **pages 537–534.**

Review Questions

7.1 How can inflation affect the distribution of income?

7.2 Which is a greater problem: anticipated inflation or unanticipated inflation? Why?

Problems and Applications

7.3 What are menu costs? What affect has the Internet had on the size of menu costs?

7.4 Suppose that the inflation rate turns out to be much higher than most people expected. In that case, would

you rather have been a borrower or a lender? Briefly explain.

7.5 Suppose Hassan and Adam both retire this year. For income in retirement, Hassan will rely on a pension from his company that pays him a fixed US$2,500 per month for as long as he lives. Hassan hasn't saved anything for retirement. Adam has no pension but has saved a considerable amount, which he has invested in certificates of deposit (CDs) at his bank. Currently, Adam's CDs pay him interest of US$2,300 per month.

a. Ten years from now, is Hassan or Adam likely to have a higher real income? In your answer, be sure to define real income.

b. Now suppose that instead of being a constant amount, Hassan's pension increases each year by the same percentage as the CPI. For example, if the CPI increases by 5 percent in the first year after Hassan retires, then his pension in the second year equals US$2,500 + (US$2,500 × .05) = US$2,625. In this case, 10 years from now, is Hassan or Adam likely to have a higher real income?

7.6 **(Related to the *Making the Connection* on page 539)** Suppose that Orascom Telecom and the investors buying the firm's bonds both expect a 2 percent inflation rate for the year. Given that expectation, suppose the nominal interest rate on the bonds is 6 percent and the real interest rate is 4 percent. Suppose that a year after the investors have purchased the bonds, the inflation turns out to be 6 percent, rather than the 2 percent that had been expected. Who gains and who loses from the unexpectedly high inflation rate?

Economic Growth, the **Financial System,** and **Business Cycles**

Economic Growth in the Arab World: What Is Missing?

I would suggest that the rate at which countries grow is substantially determined by three things: their ability to integrate with the global economy through trade and investment; their capacity to maintain sustainable government finances and sound money; and their ability to put in place an institutional environment in which contracts can be enforced and property rights can be established. I would challenge anyone to identify a country that has done all three of these things and has not grown at a substantial rate.

Lawrence Summers, the Director of the U.S. National Economic Council.

Achieving high rates of economic growth is an essential goal for any government in order to guarantee, or maintain, a high standard of living for its citizens over the years. For this reason, economic growth is always considered a long-run process. In other words, an upward trend in a country's real GDP in the long run is what economists mean by economic growth. Around this upward trend, the economy faces short-run fluctuations (ups and downs) in real GDP. These short-run fluctuations form the business cycle in the economy. Many obstacles face the Arab countries, especially non-oil-based Arab countries, that decrease their ability to grow faster consistently, such as: lack of capital, youth unemployment, weak financial markets, low labor productivity, and economic instability that makes investment in these countries riskier than other developing countries. Oil-based Arab countries are in a better shape since they are rich in capital and enjoy a relatively higher degree of economic stability. But both types of Arab countries suffer from a lack of what Lawrence Summers calls "the institutional environment." Some Arab countries suffer from the nonexistence of laws and regulations that are needed to organize complex economic activities and provide a clear and strong system of property rights, and if these laws and regulations do exist, the ability of the government to enforce them is weak. In addition, during the discussions of "the Institutions and Economic Growth in the Arab Countries" seminar which was held in Abu Dhabi in 2006, Arab government officials (ministers and central bank governors) agreed that the poor institutional quality in the Arab countries dampened economic growth through its negative impact on productivity and capital accumulation. The main features of this poor institutional quality include: a high degree of bureaucracy, lack of accountability, and an excessively large public sector focused on the public provision of social services and some private goods, which resulted in crowding out private sector investment.

In this chapter, we will provide an overview of long-run growth and the business cycle and discuss their importance for individual firms, for consumers, and for the economy as a whole. As an example of the impact of business cycle fluctuations on economic growth, read AN INSIDE LOOK AT POLICY on page 557, where we discuss the relationship between economic growth and inflation in the Arab economies.

Source: "Institutions and Economic Growth in the Arab Countries," International Monetary Fund/Arab Monetary Fund High-Level Seminar, Abu Dhabi, UAE, December 20, 2006.

LEARNING Objectives

After studying this chapter, you should be able to:

17.1 Discuss the importance of long-run economic growth, page 552–560.

17.2 Discuss the role of the financial system in facilitating long-run economic growth, page 560–568.

17.3 Explain what happens during a business cycle, page 568–571.

Economics in YOUR Life!

If You Spend More, Will the Economy Grow More?

Suppose that, after a full day of unsuccessfully shopping for a pair of jeans, you decide to use the money you would have spent to open a savings account instead. When you return home empty handed, your roommate informs you that your decision to save instead of consume will reduce economic growth because consumption expenditures comprise over two-thirds of gross domestic product. How do you respond to your roommate's assertion? As you read this chapter, see if you can answer this question. You can check your answer against the one we provide at the end of the chapter. **>> Continued on page 571**

A key measure of the success of any economy is its ability to increase production of goods and services faster than the growth in population. Increasing production faster than population growth is the only way that the standard of living of the average person in a country can increase. Unfortunately, many economies around the world are not growing at all or are growing very slowly. In many countries in sub-Saharan Africa, living standards are barely higher, or in some cases are lower, than they were 50 years ago. Most people in these countries live in the same grinding poverty as their ancestors. In developed countries, however, living standards are much higher than they were 50 years ago. An important macroeconomic question is why some countries grow much faster than others.

As we will see, one determinant of economic growth is the ability of firms to expand their operations, buy additional equipment, train workers, and adopt new technologies. To carry out these activities, firms must acquire funds from households, either directly through financial markets—such as the stock and bond markets—or indirectly through financial intermediaries—such as banks. Financial markets and financial intermediaries together comprise the *financial system*. In this chapter, we will present an overview of the financial system and see how funds flow from households to firms through the *market for loanable funds*.

Business cycle Alternating periods of economic expansion and economic recession.

Economies of developed and developing countries experience periods of expanding production and employment followed by periods of recession during which production and employment decline. As we noted in Chapter 15, these alternating periods of expansion and recession are called the **business cycle**. The business cycle is not uniform: each period of expansion is not the same length, nor is each period of recession, but, historically speaking, every period of expansion has been followed by a period of recession, and every period of recession has been followed by a period of expansion.

In this chapter, we begin the exploration of two key aspects of macroeconomics—the long-run growth that steadily raise living standards and the short-run fluctuations of the business cycle.

17.1 | Discuss the importance of long-run economic growth.

Long-Run Economic Growth

Most people around the world, especially in developed countries, expect that over time, their standard of living will improve. They expect that year after year, firms will introduce new and improved products, new prescription drugs and better surgical techniques will overcome more diseases, and their ability to afford these goods and services will increase. For most people, these are reasonable expectations.

Long-run economic growth The process by which rising productivity increases the average standard of living.

When looking at historical time series of real GDP per capita in developed countries as a measure of the standard of living, we notice an upward trend of the measure. The process of **long-run economic growth** brought the typical citizen in developed economies from a low standard of living in the past to the standard of living of today. Real GDP per capita (per person) is known as the best measure of the standard of living in a country. So, we measure long-run economic growth by increases in real GDP per capita over long periods of time, generally decades or more. We use real GDP rather than nominal GDP to adjust for changes in the price level over time. Figure 17-1 shows the trends in real GDP per capita in selected Arab countries (oil-based: Saudi Arabia, Oman, United Arab Emirates, and non-oil-based: Egypt, Jordan, and Tunisia) from 1975 to 2009. The figure shows that real GDP per capita fluctuations are more noticeable in oil-based economies due to the fluctuations in the international price of oil. The sharp decline in real GDP per capita in the UAE and Saudi Arabia between 1981 and 1989 is caused by the drop in oil prices from around US$36 to around US$13 per barrel. Non-oil-based economies are very close to each other and have a very slow upward trend

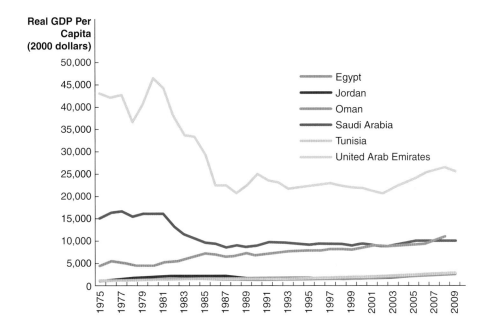

Figure 17-1

Real GDP per Capita in Selected Arab Countries from 1975 to 2009

Measured in constant 2000 US dollars, real GDP per capita in Oman grew from about US$4,504 in 1975 to about US$10,800 in 2009 while it declined in the UAE from US$42,854 to US$25, 606 in the same period. The average Omani citizen in the year 2009 could buy more than twice as many goods and services as the average Omani in the year 1975. An average citizen in the UAE is worse off in 2009 compared with the average citizen in the UAE in 1975 as the former could buy only about 60 percent of the goods and services that the later could buy. Non-oil-based Arab countries, Egypt, Jordan, and Tunisia, have a very slow upward trend in real GDP per capita.
Source: World Development Indicators, World Bank.

in real GDP per capita. This upward trend in real GDP per capita is what we focus on when discussing long-run economic growth.

The values in Figure 17-1 are measured in prices of the year 2000, so they represent constant dollar amounts of purchasing power (we use constant 2000 U.S. dollars for the sake of comparison between countries). Let us take two different examples: first, Oman. In 1975, real GDP per capita was about US$4,504 and it had risen gradually to about US$10,800 in 2009. This means that the average citizen in Oman in 2009 could purchase more than twice as many goods and services as the average citizen in 1975. Second, United Arab Emirates: in contrast, to Oman, real GDP per capita was about US$42,854 in 1975 but it dropped to US$25,606 in 2009. Again, this means that the average Emirati citizen in 2009 could purchase only about 60 percent of what he/she used to purchase in 1975. In other words, the standard of living for an average Emirati citizen has decreased.

In general, if countries enjoy an increase in real GDP per capita, this increase actually understates the true increase in the standard of living of citizens in recent years compared with 1975. Many of today's goods and services were not available in 1970. For example, if you lived in 1970 and became ill with a serious infection, you would have been unable to purchase antibiotics to treat your illness—no matter how high your income. You might have died from an illness for which even a very poor person in today's society could receive effective medical treatment. Of course, the quantity of goods and services that a person can buy is not a perfect measure of how happy or contented that person may be. The level of pollution, the level of crime, spiritual well-being, and many other factors ignored in calculating GDP contribute to a person's happiness. Nevertheless, economists rely heavily on comparisons of real GDP per capita because it is the best means of comparing the performance of one economy over time or the performance of different economies at any particular time.

Making the Connection | The Connection between Economic Prosperity and Health

We can see the direct impact of economic growth on living standards by looking at improvements in health in the high-income countries over the past 100 years. The research of Robert Fogel, winner of the Nobel Prize in Economics, has highlighted the close connection between economic growth, improvements in technology, and improvements in

(Continued)

human physiology. One important measure of health is life expectancy at birth. For example, as the following graph shows, in 1960 life expectancy was, on average, about 50 years in many Arab countries. Today, life expectancy is about 75 years, on average.

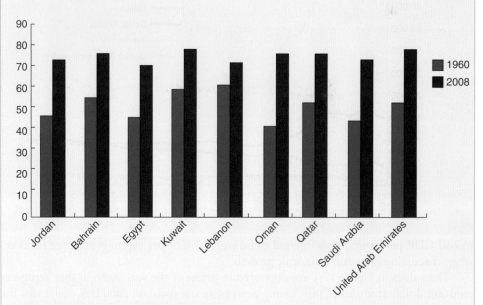

Source: World Development Indicators, World Bank.

Although life expectancies in the lowest-income countries remain very short, some countries that have begun to experience economic growth have seen dramatic increases in life expectancies. For example, life expectancy in India has more than doubled from 27 years in 1900 to 69 years today.

Many economists believe there is a link between health and economic growth. In the United States and Western Europe during the nineteenth century, improvements in agricultural technology and rising incomes led to dramatic improvements in the nutrition of the average person. The development of the germ theory of disease and technological progress in the purification of water in the late-nineteenth century led to sharp declines in sickness due to waterborne diseases. As people became taller, stronger, and less susceptible to disease, they also became more productive. In contrast, many Arab citizens these days, especially poor workers, believe that pollution in general, and the bad quality of water specifically, in addition to agricultural products that are full of toxic fertilizers, are responsible for the deterioration of their health and thus productivity. Today, economists studying economic development have put increasing emphasis on the need for low-income countries to reduce disease and increase nutrition if they are to experience economic growth.

Many researchers believe that the state of human physiology will continue to improve as technology advances. In high-income countries, life expectancy at birth is expected to rise from about 80 years today to about 90 years by the middle of the century. Technological advance will continue to reduce the average number of hours worked per day and the number of years the average person spends in the paid workforce. Individuals spend about 10 hours per day sleeping, eating, and bathing. Their remaining "discretionary hours" are divided between paid work and leisure. The following graph is based on estimates by Robert Fogel that contrast how individuals in the United States will divide their time in 2040 compared with 1880 and 1995.

Not only will technology and economic growth allow people in the near future to live longer lives, but a much smaller fraction of those lives will need to be spent at paid work.

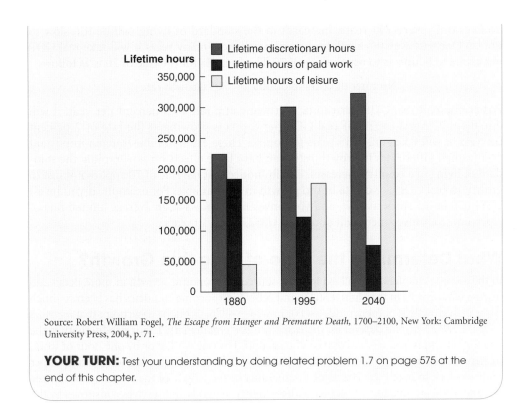

Source: Robert William Fogel, *The Escape from Hunger and Premature Death*, 1700–2100, New York: Cambridge University Press, 2004, p. 71.

YOUR TURN: Test your understanding by doing related problem 1.7 on page 575 at the end of this chapter.

Calculating Growth Rates and the Rule of 70

The growth rate of real GDP or real GDP per capita during a particular year is equal to the percentage change from the previous year. For example, measured in prices of the year 2000 (constant 2000 U.S. dollars), real GDP in Saudi Arabia equaled US$249,167 billion in 2008 and rose to US$249,539 billion in 2009, according to the World Development Indicators (WDI). We calculate the growth of real GDP in 2009 as:

$$\left[\frac{(US\$249{,}539 \text{ billion} - US\$249{,}167 \text{ billion})}{US\$249{,}167 \text{ billion}}\right] \times 100 = 0.15\%$$

For longer periods of time, we can use the *average annual growth rate*. For example, real GDP in Saudi Arabia was US$37,099 billion in 1968 and US$249,539 billion in 2009. To find the average annual growth rate during this 41-year period, we compute the annual growth rate that would result in US$37,099 billion increasing to US$249,539 billion over 41 years. In this case, the growth rate is 5.04 percent. That is, if US$37,099 billion grows at an average rate of 5.04 percent per year, after 41 years it will have grown to US$249,539 billion.

For shorter periods of time, we get approximately the same answer by averaging the growth rate for each year. For example, real GDP in the Saudi Arabia grew by 5.26 percent in 2004, 5.55 percent in 2005, and 3.15 percent in 2006. So, the average annual growth rate of real GDP for the period 2004–2006 was 4.65 percent, which is the average of the three annual growth rates:

$$\frac{(5.26\% + 5.55\% + 3.15\%)}{3} = 4.65\%$$

When discussing long-run economic growth, we usually shorten "average annual growth rate" to "growth rate."

We can judge how rapidly an economic variable is growing by calculating the number of years it would take to double. For example, if real GDP per capita in a country doubles, say, every 20 years, most people in the country will experience significant increases in their standard of living over the course of their lives. If real GDP per capita doubles only every 100 years, increases in the standard of living will be too slow to notice. One easy way to calculate approximately how many years it will take real GDP per capita to double is to use the *rule of 70*. The formula for the rule of 70 is as follows:

$$\text{Number of years to double} = 70/(\text{Growth rate})$$

For example, if real GDP per capita is growing at a rate of 5 percent per year, it will double in 70/5 = 14 years. If real GDP per capita is growing at the rate of 2 percent per year, it will take 70/2 = 35 years to double. These examples illustrate an important point: small differences in growth rates can have large effects on how rapidly the standard of living in a country increases. Finally, notice that the rule of 70 applies not just to growth in real GDP per capita but to growth in any variable. For example, if you invest US$1,000 in the stock market, and your investment grows at an average annual rate of 7 percent, your investment will double to US$2,000 in 10 years.

What Determines the Rate of Long-Run Growth?

In the coming chapters, we will explore the sources of economic growth in more detail and discuss why growth in the United States and other high-income countries has been so much faster than growth in poorer countries. For now, we will focus on the basic point that *increases in real GDP per capita depend on increases in labor productivity*. **Labor productivity** is the quantity of goods and services that can be produced by one worker or by one hour of work. In analyzing long-run growth, economists usually measure labor productivity as output per hour of work to avoid the effects of fluctuations in the length of the workday and in the fraction of the population employed. If the quantity of goods and services consumed by the average person is to increase, the quantity of goods and services produced per hour of work must also increase. Why, in recent years, is the average Arab citizen able to consume more of goods and services than the average Arab citizen in the past? Because the average Arab worker in recent times is more productive than the Arab worker in the past, *ceteris paribus*.

Labor productivity The quantity of goods and services that can be produced by one worker or by one hour of work.

If increases in labor productivity are the key to long-run economic growth, what causes labor productivity to increase? Economists believe two key factors determine labor productivity: the quantity of capital per hour worked and the level of technology. Therefore, economic growth occurs if the quantity of capital per hour worked increases and if technological change occurs.

Increases in Capital per Hour Worked Workers today in high-income countries have more physical capital available than workers in low-income countries or workers in the high-income countries of 100 years ago. Recall that **capital** refers to manufactured goods that are used to produce other goods and services. Examples of capital are computers, factory buildings, machine tools, warehouses, and trucks. The total amount of physical capital available in a country is known as the country's *capital stock*.

Capital Manufactured goods that are used to produce other goods and services.

As the capital stock per hour worked increases, worker productivity increases. A secretary with a personal computer can produce more documents per day than a secretary who has only a typewriter. A worker with a backhoe can excavate more earth than a worker who has only a shovel.

Human capital refers to the accumulated knowledge and skills workers acquire from education and training or from their life experiences. For example, workers with a college education generally have more skills and are more productive than workers who have only a high school degree. Increases in human capital are particularly important in stimulating economic growth.

Technological Change Economic growth depends more on *technological change* than on increases in capital per hour worked. Technology refers to the processes a firm uses to turn inputs into outputs of goods and services. Technological change is an increase in the quantity of output firms can produce using a given quantity of inputs. Technological change can come from many sources. For example, a firm's managers may rearrange a factory floor or the layout of a retail store to increase production and sales. Most technological change, however, is embodied in new machinery, equipment, or software.

A very important point is that just accumulating more inputs—such as labor, capital, and natural resources—will not ensure that an economy experiences economic growth unless technological change also occurs. For example, the Soviet Union failed to maintain a high rate of economic growth, even though it continued to increase the quantity of capital available per hour worked, because it experienced relatively little technological change.

In implementing technological change, *entrepreneurs* are of crucial importance. Recall from Chapter 2 that an entrepreneur is someone who operates a business, bringing together the factors of production—labor, capital, and natural resources—to produce goods and services. In a market economy, entrepreneurs make the crucial decisions about whether to introduce new technology to produce better or lower-cost products. Entrepreneurs also decide whether to allocate the firm's resources to research and development that can result in new technologies. One of the difficulties centrally planned economies have in sustaining economic growth is that managers employed by the government are usually much slower to develop and adopt new technologies than entrepreneurs in a market system.

Solved Problem | 17-1

The Role of Technological Change in Growth

Between 1960 and 1995, real GDP per capita in Singapore grew at an average annual rate of 6.2 percent. This very rapid growth rate results in the level of real GDP per capita doubling about every 11.5 years. In 1995, Alywn Young of the University of Chicago in the U.S. published an article in which he argued that Singapore's growth depended more on increases in capital per hour worked, increases in the labor force participation rate, and the transfer of workers from agricultural to nonagricultural jobs than on technological change. If Young's analysis was correct, predict what was likely to happen to Singapore's growth rate in the years after 1995.

SOLVING THE PROBLEM:

Step 1: **Review the chapter material.** This problem is about what determines the rate of long-run growth, so you may want to review the section "What Determines the Rate of Long-Run Growth?" which begins on page 556.

Step 2: **Predict what happened to the growth rate in Singapore after 1995.** As countries begin to develop, they often experience an increase in the labor force participation rate, as workers who are not part of the paid labor force respond to rising wage rates. Many workers also leave the agricultural sector—where output per hour worked is often low—for the nonagricultural sector. These changes increase real GDP per capita, but they are 'one-shot' changes that eventually come to an end, as the labor force participation rate and the fraction of the labor force outside agriculture both approach the levels found in high-income countries. Similarly, as we already noted, increases in capital per hour worked cannot sustain high rates of economic growth unless they are accompanied by technological change.

We can conclude that Singapore was unlikely to sustain its high growth rates in the years after 1995. In fact, from 1996 to 2007, the growth of real GDP per capita slowed to an average rate of 2.5 percent per year. Although this growth rate is comparable to those experienced in high-income countries, such as the United States, it leads to a doubling of real GDP per capita only every 28 years rather than every 11.5 years.

Source: Alwyn Young, "The Tyranny of Numbers: Confronting the Statistical Realities of the East Asian Growth Experience," *Quarterly Journal of Economics*, Vol. 110, No. 3, August 1995, pp. 641–680.

YOUR TURN: For more practice, do related problem 1.11 on page 575 at the end of this chapter.

>> **End Solved Problem 17-1**

Finally, an additional requirement for economic growth is that the government provides secure rights to private property. As we saw in Chapter 2, a market system cannot function unless rights to private property are secure. In addition, the government can help the market work and aid economic growth by establishing an independent court system that enforces contracts between private individuals. Many economists would also say the government has a role in facilitating the development of an efficient financial system, as well as systems of education, transportation, and communication. Economist Richard Sylla of New York University in the United States has argued that every country that has experienced economic growth first experienced a 'financial revolution.' Without supportive government policies, long-run economic growth is unlikely.

Making the Connection | What Explains Rapid Economic Growth in Botswana?

Economic growth in much of sub-Saharan Africa has been very slow. As desperately poor as most of these countries were in 1960, some are even poorer today. The growth rate in one country in this region stands out, however, as being exceptionally rapid. The following graph shows the average annual growth rate in real GDP per capita between 1960 and 2004 for Botswana and the six most populous sub-Saharan countries. Botswana's average annual growth rate over this 44-year period was four times as great as that of Tanzania and South Africa, which were the second-fastest-growing countries in the group. Botswana may seem an unlikely country to experience rapid growth because it has been hard hit by the HIV epidemic. Despite the disruptive effects of the epidemic, growth in real per capita GDP slowed only moderately to 4.7 percent in 2007.

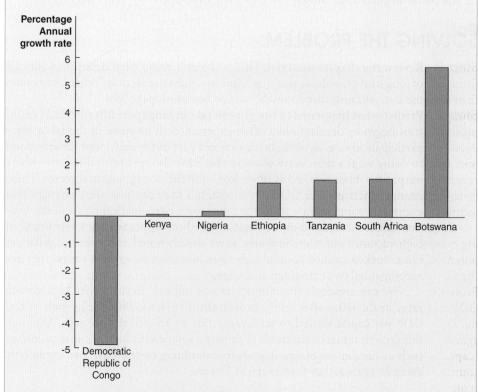

Note: Data for Democratic Republic of Congo are for 1970–2004.

Source: Authors' calculations from data in Alan Heston, Robert Summers, and Bettina Aten, *Penn World Table Version 6.2*, Center for International Comparisons of Production, Income and Prices at the University of Pennsylvania, September 2006.

What explains Botswana's rapid growth rate? Several factors have been important. Botswana avoided the civil wars that plagued other African countries during these years. The country also benefited from earnings from diamond exports. But many economists believe the pro-growth policies of its government are the most important reason for the country's success. Economists Shantayanan Devarajan of the World Bank, William Easterly of New York University, and Howard Pack of the University of Pennsylvania have summarized these policies:

> The government [of Botswana] made it clear it would protect private property rights. It was a "government of cattlemen" who were attuned to commercial interests…. The relative political stability and relatively low corruption also made Botswana a favorable location for investment. Botswana's relatively high level of press freedom and democracy (continuing a pre-colonial tradition that held chiefs responsible to tribal members) held the government responsible for any economic policy mistakes.
>
> These policies—protecting private property, avoiding political instability and corruption, and allowing press freedom and democracy—may seem a straightforward recipe for providing an environment in which economic growth can occur. However, in practice, these are policies many countries have difficulty implementing successfully.

Source: Shantayanan Devarajan, William Easterly, and Howard Pack, "Low Investment Is Not the Constraint on African Development," *Economic Development and Cultural Change*, Vol. 51, No. 3, April 2003, pp. 547–571.

YOUR TURN: Test your understanding by doing related problem 1.13 on page 575 at the end of this chapter.

Potential Real GDP

Because economists take a long-run perspective in discussing economic growth, the concept of *potential GDP* is useful. **Potential GDP** is the level of GDP attained when all firms are producing at capacity. The capacity of a firm is *not* the maximum output the firm is capable of producing. The BMW assembly plant in 6th of October City, Egypt, could operate 24 hours per day for 52 weeks per year and would be at its maximum production level. The plant's capacity, however, is measured by its production when operating on normal hours, using a normal workforce. If all firms in the economy were operating at capacity, the level of total production of final goods and services would equal potential GDP. Potential GDP will increase over time as the labor force grows, new factories and office buildings are built, new machinery and equipment are installed, and technological change takes place.

> **Potential GDP** The level of GDP attained when all firms are producing at capacity.

Since there are no statistics on potential GDP in the Arab countries, and in developing countries in general, let's look at some international examples on the gap between potential and actual real GDP in some developed economies such as Canada, Japan, the U.K., and the U.S. For example, the International Monetary Fund (IMF) World Economic Outlook Statistics shows that, in 2010, the output gap between potential real GDP and actual real GDP (as a percentage of potential GDP) is estimated to be –0.82 in the U.K., –3.64 in Canada, –5.67 in Japan, and –1.97 in the U.S. Notice that all percentages are negative, which means that these economies are producing below their potential (capacity). Japan is estimated to have the largest output gap among other developed countries under investigation, which is an indicator of a deeper recession in the Japanese economy compared with the other three developed economies in 2010. Generally speaking, potential GDP might exceed the actual GDP in some years and might be below it in some other years. For example, growth in potential real GDP in the United States is estimated to be about 3.5 percent per year. In other words, each year, the capacity of the economy to produce final goods and services expands by 3.5 percent. The *actual* level of

Figure 17-2

Actual and Potential Real GDP

Potential real GDP increases every year as the labor force and the capital stock grow and technological change occurs. The smooth light blue line represents potential real GDP, and the dark blue line represents actual real GDP. Because of the business cycle, actual real GDP has sometimes been greater than potential real GDP and sometimes less.

Source: Congressional Budget Office, *Spreadsheets for Selected Estimates and Projections*, January 2008; and U.S. Bureau of Economic Analysis.

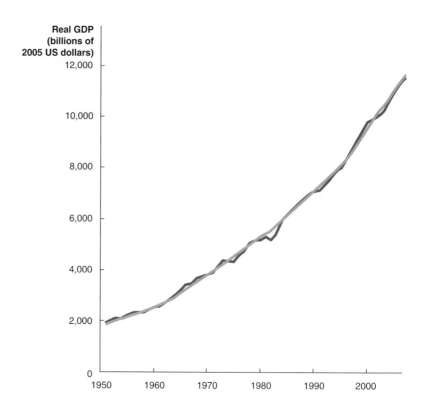

GDP may increase by more or less than 3.5 percent as the economy moves through the business cycle. Figure 17-2 above shows movements in actual and potential real GDP for the years since 1950. The smooth light blue line represents potential real GDP, and the dark blue line represents actual real GDP.

17.2 LEARNING OBJECTIVE

17.2 | Discuss the role of the financial system in facilitating long-run economic growth.

Saving, Investment, and the Financial System

Financial system The system of financial markets and financial intermediaries through which firms acquire funds from households.

The process of economic growth depends on the ability of firms to expand their operations, buy additional equipment, train workers, and adopt new technologies. Firms can finance some of these activities from *retained earnings*, which are profits that are reinvested in the firm rather than paid to the firm's owners. For many firms, retained earnings are not sufficient to finance the rapid expansion required in economies experiencing high rates of economic growth. Firms acquire funds from households, either directly through financial markets—such as the stock and bond markets—or indirectly through financial intermediaries—such as banks. Financial markets and financial intermediaries together comprise the **financial system**. Without a well-functioning financial system, economic growth is impossible because firms will be unable to expand and adopt new technologies. As we noted earlier, no country without a well-developed financial system has been able to sustain high levels of economic growth.

An Overview of the Financial System

Financial markets Markets where financial securities, such as stocks and bonds, are bought and sold.

The financial system channels funds from savers to borrowers and channels returns on the borrowed funds back to savers. In **financial markets**, such as the stock market or the bond market, firms raise funds by selling financial securities directly to savers. A financial security is a document—sometimes in electronic form—that states the terms under which funds pass from the buyer of the security—who is lending funds—to the seller. *Stocks* are financial securities that represent partial ownership of a firm. If you buy one share of stock in Orascom Telecom, you become one of millions of owners of that firm. *Bonds* are financial securities that represent promises to repay a fixed amount of funds. When Orascom Telecom sells a bond, the firm promises to pay the purchaser of the bond an interest payment each year for the term of the bond, as well as a final payment of the amount of the loan.

Financial intermediaries, such as banks, mutual funds, pension funds, and insurance companies, act as go-betweens for borrowers and lenders. In effect, financial intermediaries borrow funds from savers and lend them to borrowers. When you deposit funds in your checking account, you are lending your funds to the bank. The bank may lend your funds (together with the funds of other savers) to an entrepreneur who wants to start a business. Suppose Fatma wants to open a laundry. Rather than you lending money directly to Fatma's Laundry, the bank acts as a go-between for you and Fatma. Intermediaries pool the funds of many small savers to lend to many individual borrowers. The intermediaries pay interest to savers in exchange for the use of savers' funds, and earn a profit by lending money to borrowers and charging borrowers a higher rate of interest on the loans. For example, a bank might pay you as a depositor a 3 percent rate of interest, while it lends the money to Fatma's Laundry at a 6 percent rate of interest.

Banks, mutual funds, pension funds, and insurance companies also make investments in stocks and bonds on behalf of savers. For example, *mutual funds* sell shares to savers and then use the funds to buy a portfolio of stocks, bonds, mortgages, and other financial securities. Mutual funds are either closed-end or open-end funds. In closed-end mutual funds, the mutual fund company issues shares that investors may buy and sell in financial markets, like shares of stock issued by corporations. More common are open-end mutual funds, which issue shares that the mutual fund company will buy back—or redeem—at a price that represents the underlying value of the financial securities owned by the fund. Many banks have mutual fund operations in the Arab countries such as: the Arab African International Bank, The Arab Bank, The Arab National Bank, and HSBC. Some funds hold a wide range of stocks or bonds; others specialize in securities issued by a particular industry or sector, such as technology; and others invest as an index fund in a fixed-market basket of securities, such as shares of the Standard & Poor's 500 firms. Over the past 30 years, the role of mutual funds in the financial system has increased dramatically. By 2008, competition among hundreds of mutual fund firms gave investors thousands of funds from which to choose.

In addition to matching households that have excess funds with firms that want to borrow funds, the financial system provides three key services for savers and borrowers: risk sharing, liquidity, and information. *Risk* is the chance that the value of a financial security will change relative to what you expect. For example, you may buy a share of stock in Google at a price of US$450, only to have the price fall to US$100. Most individual savers are not gamblers and seek a steady return on their savings rather than erratic swings between high and low earnings. The financial system provides risk sharing by allowing savers to spread their money among many financial investments. For example, you can divide your money among a bank certificate of deposit, individual bonds, and a mutual fund.

Liquidity is the ease with which a financial security can be exchanged for money. The financial system provides the service of liquidity by providing savers with markets in which they can sell their holdings of financial securities. For example, savers can easily sell their holdings of the stocks and bonds issued by large corporations on the major stock and bond markets.

A third service that the financial system provides savers is the collection and communication of *information*, or facts about borrowers and expectations about returns on financial securities. For example, Fatma's Laundry may want to borrow US$10,000 from you. Finding out what Fatma intends to do with the funds and how likely she is to pay you back may be costly and time-consuming. By depositing US$10,000 in the bank, you are, in effect, allowing the bank to gather this information for you. Because

Financial intermediaries Firms, such as banks, mutual funds, pension funds, and insurance companies, that borrow funds from savers and lend them to borrowers.

banks specialize in gathering information on borrowers, they are able to do it faster and at a lower cost than can individual savers. The financial system plays an important role in communicating information. If you read a newspaper headline announcing that an automobile firm has invented a car with an engine that runs on water, how would you determine the effect of this discovery on the firm's profits? Financial markets do that job for you by incorporating information into the prices of stocks, bonds, and other financial securities. In this example, the expectation of higher future profits would boost the prices of the automobile firm's stock and bonds.

The Macroeconomics of Saving and Investment

As we have seen, the funds available to firms through the financial system come from saving. When firms use funds to purchase machinery, factories, and office buildings, they are engaging in investment. In this section, we explore the macroeconomics of saving and investment. A key point we will develop is that *the total value of saving in the economy must equal the total value of investment*. We saw in Chapter 15 that *national income accounting* refers to the methods the Bureau of Economic Analysis uses to keep track of total production and total income in the economy. We can use some relationships from national income accounting to understand why total saving must equal total investment.

We begin with the relationship between GDP (Y) and its components, consumption (C), investment (I), government purchases (G), and net exports (NX):

$$Y = C + I + G + NX$$

Remember that GDP is a measure of both total production in the economy and total income.

In an *open economy*, there is interaction with other economies in terms of both trading of goods and services and borrowing and lending. All economies today are open economies, although they vary significantly in the extent of their openness. In a *closed economy*, there is no trading or borrowing and lending with other economies. For simplicity, we will develop the relationship between saving and investment for a closed economy. This allows us to focus on the most important points in a simpler framework. We will consider the case of an open economy in Chapter 25.

In a closed economy, net exports are zero, so we can rewrite the relationship between GDP and its components as:

$$Y = C + I + G$$

If we rearrange this relationship, we have an expression for investment in terms of the other variables:

$$I = Y - C - G$$

This expression tells us that in a closed economy, investment spending is equal to total income minus consumption spending and minus government purchases.

We can also derive an expression for total saving. *Private saving* is equal to what households retain of their income after purchasing goods and services (C) and paying taxes (T). Households receive income for supplying the factors of production to firms. This portion of household income is equal to Y. Households also receive income from government in the form of *transfer payments* (TR). Recall that transfer payments include social security payments and unemployment insurance payments. We can write an expression for private saving ($S_{private}$):

$$S_{private} = Y + TR - C - T$$

The government also engages in saving. *Public saving* (S_{public}) equals the amount of tax revenue the government retains after paying for government purchases and making transfer payments to households:

$$S_{public} = T - G - TR$$

So, total saving in the economy (S) is equal to the sum of private saving and public saving:

$$S = S_{\text{private}} + S_{\text{public}}$$

or:

$$S = (Y + TR - C - T) + (T - G - TR)$$

or:

$$S = Y - C - G$$

The right-hand side of this expression is identical to the expression we derived earlier for investment spending. So, we can conclude that total saving must equal total investment:

$$S = I$$

When the government spends the same amount that it collects in taxes, there is a *balanced budget*. When the government spends more than it collects in taxes, there is a *budget deficit*. In the case of a deficit, T is less than $G + TR$, which means that public saving is negative. Negative saving is also known as *dissaving*. How can public saving be negative? When the government runs a budget deficit, the Department of the Treasury sells Treasury bonds to borrow the money necessary to fund the gap between taxes and spending. In this case, rather than adding to the total amount of saving available to be borrowed for investment spending, the government is subtracting from it. (Notice that if households borrow more than they save, the total amount of saving will also fall.) With less saving, investment must also be lower. We can conclude that, holding constant all other factors, there is a lower level of investment spending in the economy when there is a budget deficit than when there is a balanced budget.

When the government spends less than it collects in taxes, there is a *budget surplus*. A budget surplus increases public saving and the total level of saving in the economy. A higher level of saving results in a higher level of investment spending. Therefore, holding constant all other factors, there is a higher level of investment spending in the economy when there is a budget surplus than when there is a balanced budget.

Arab oil-based countries usually enjoy budget surplus during periods of high oil prices, such as the period 2005–2008, while non-oil-based countries are usually in deficit. This discrepancy between the two types of countries affected the magnitude of government expenditure programs. Oil-based Arab countries invested part of their budget surplus in huge projects that affected their citizens' well-being positively, such as building universities, industrial cities, and roads and highways. In addition, Gulf countries constructed Sovereign Wealth Funds (SWF), using oil revenues, for the purpose of protecting and stabilizing the government budget and the economy as a whole from excess volatility in revenues and exports due to the fluctuations in international oil prices. The Sovereign Wealth Fund Institute defines SWF as "a state-owned investment fund composed of financial assets such as stocks, bonds, real estate, or other financial instruments funded by foreign exchange assets. These assets can include: balance of payments surpluses, official foreign currency operations, the proceeds of privatizations, fiscal surpluses, and/or receipts resulting from commodity exports." Figure 17-3 shows the budget surplus/deficit in selected oil-based and non-oil-based Arab countries.

The Market for Loanable Funds

We have seen that the value of total saving must equal the value of total investment, but we have not yet discussed how this equality actually is brought about in the financial system. We can think of the financial system as being composed of many markets through which funds flow from lenders to borrowers: the market for certificates of deposit at banks, the market for stocks, the market for bonds, the market for mutual fund shares,

Figure 17-3

Government Budget Surplus/ Deficit in Selected Oil and Non-Oil-Based Arab Countries.

Arab oil-based countries usually enjoy budget surplus during periods of high oil prices, such as the period 2005–2008, while non-oil-based countries are usually in deficit. Oil-based Arab countries invested part of their budget surplus in huge projects that affected their citizens' well-being positively.

Source: Saudi Arabian Ministry of Finance Statistics, World Development Indicators, World Bank.

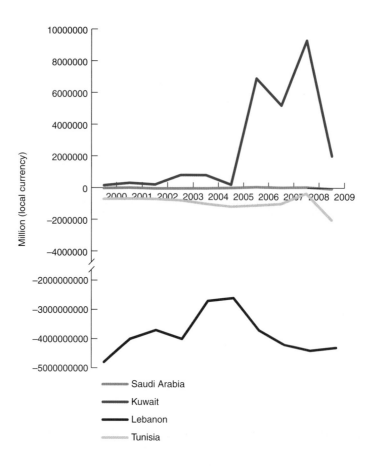

Market for loanable funds The interaction of borrowers and lenders that determines the market interest rate and the quantity of loanable funds exchanged.

and so on. For simplicity, we can combine these markets into a single market for *loanable funds*. In the model of the **market for loanable funds**, the interaction of borrowers and lenders determines the market interest rate and the quantity of loanable funds exchanged. Firms can also borrow from savers in other countries, but for the remainder of this chapter, we will assume that there are no interactions between households and firms inside a typical Arab country and those in other countries.

Demand and Supply in the Loanable Funds Market

The demand for loanable funds is determined by the willingness of firms to borrow money to engage in new investment projects, such as building new factories or carrying out research and development of new products. In determining whether to borrow funds, firms compare the return they expect to make on an investment with the interest rate they must pay to borrow the necessary funds. For example, if Carrefour is considering opening several new stores and expects to earn a return of 15 percent on its investment, the investment will be profitable if it can borrow the funds at an interest rate of 10 percent but will not be profitable if the interest rate is 20 percent. In Figure 17-4, the demand for loanable funds is downward sloping because the lower the interest rate, the more investment projects firms can profitably undertake, and the greater the quantity of loanable funds they will demand.

The supply of loanable funds is determined by the willingness of households to save and by the extent of government saving or dissaving. When households save, they reduce the amount of goods and services they can consume and enjoy today. The willingness of households to save rather than consume their incomes today will be determined in part by the interest rate they receive when they lend their savings. The higher the interest rate, the greater the reward to saving and the larger the amount of funds households will save. Therefore, the supply curve for loanable funds in Figure 17-4 is upward sloping because the higher the interest rate, the greater the quantity of saving supplied.

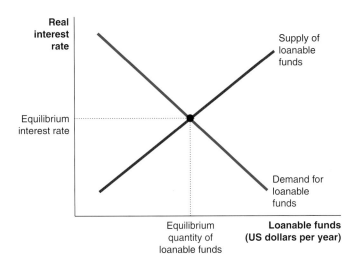

Figure 17-4

The Market for Loanable Funds

The demand for loanable funds is determined by the willingness of firms to borrow money to engage in new investment projects. The supply of loanable funds is determined by the willingness of households to save and by the extent of government saving or dissaving. Equilibrium in the market for loanable funds determines the real interest rate and the quantity of loanable funds exchanged.

In Chapter 16, we discussed the distinction between the *nominal interest rate* and the *real interest rate*. The nominal interest rate is the stated interest rate on a loan. The real interest rate corrects the nominal interest rate for the impact of inflation and is equal to the nominal interest rate minus the inflation rate. Because both borrowers and lenders are interested in the real interest rate they will receive or pay, equilibrium in the market for loanable funds determines the real interest rate rather than the nominal interest rate.

Explaining Movements in Saving, Investment, and Interest Rates Equilibrium in the market for loanable funds determines the quantity of loanable funds that will flow from lenders to borrowers each period. It also determines the real interest rate that lenders will receive and that borrowers must pay. We draw the demand curve for loanable funds by holding constant all factors, other than the interest rate, that affect the willingness of borrowers to demand funds. We draw the supply curve by holding constant all factors, other than the interest rate, that affect the willingness of lenders to supply funds. A shift in either the demand curve or the supply curve will change the equilibrium interest rate and the equilibrium quantity of loanable funds.

Suppose, for example, that the profitability of new investment increases due to technological change. Firms will increase their demand for loanable funds. Figure 17-5 shows the impact of an increase in demand in the market for loanable funds. As in the markets for goods and services we studied in Chapter 3, an increase in demand in the market for loanable funds shifts the demand curve to the right. In the new equilibrium, the interest rate increases from i_1 to i_2, and the equilibrium quantity of loanable funds increases from L_1 to L_2. Notice that an increase in the quantity of loanable funds means that both the quantity of saving by households and the quantity of investment by firms have increased. Increasing investment increases the capital stock and the quantity of capital per hour worked, helping to increase economic growth.

We can also use the market for loanable funds to examine the impact of a government budget deficit. Putting aside the effects of foreign saving—which we will consider in Chapter 25—recall that if the government begins running a budget deficit, it reduces the total amount of saving in the economy. Suppose the government increases spending, which results in a budget deficit. We illustrate the effects of the budget deficit in Figure 17-6 by shifting the supply of loanable funds to the left. In the new equilibrium, the interest rate is higher, and the equilibrium quantity of loanable funds is lower. Running a deficit has reduced the level of total saving in the economy and, by increasing the interest rate, has also reduced the level of investment spending by firms. By borrowing to finance its budget deficit, the government will have *crowded out* some firms that would otherwise have been able to borrow to finance investment. **Crowding out** refers to a decline in investment spending as a result of an increase in government purchases. In Figure 17-6, the decline in investment spending due to crowding out is shown by the movement from L_1 to L_2 on the demand

Crowding out A decline in private expenditures as a result of an increase in government purchases.

Figure 17-5

An Increase in the Demand for Loanable Funds

An increase in the demand for loanable funds increases the equilibrium interest rate from i_1 to i_2, and it increases the equilibrium quantity of loanable funds from L_1 to L_2. As a result, saving and investment both increase.

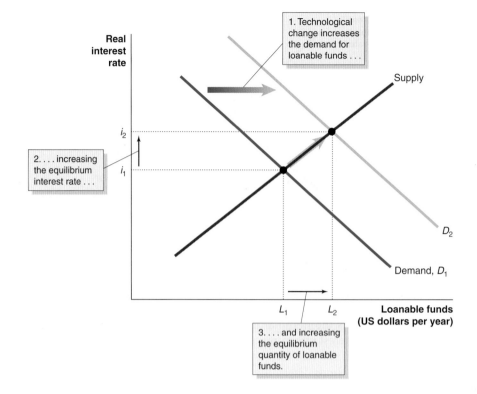

for loanable funds curve. Lower investment spending means that the capital stock and the quantity of capital per hour worked will not increase as much.

A government budget surplus would have the opposite effect of a deficit. A budget surplus increases the total amount of saving in the economy, shifting the supply of loanable funds to the right. In the new equilibrium, the interest rate will be lower, and the quantity of loanable funds will be higher. We can conclude that a budget surplus increases the level of saving and investment.

In practice, however, the impact of government budget deficits and surpluses on the equilibrium interest rate is relatively small. (This finding reflects in part the importance

Figure 17-6

The Effect of a Budget Deficit on the Market for Loanable Funds

When the government begins running a budget deficit, the supply of loanable funds shifts to the left. The equilibrium interest rate increases from i_1 to i_2, and the equilibrium quantity of loanable funds falls from L_1 to L_2. As a result, saving and investment both decline.

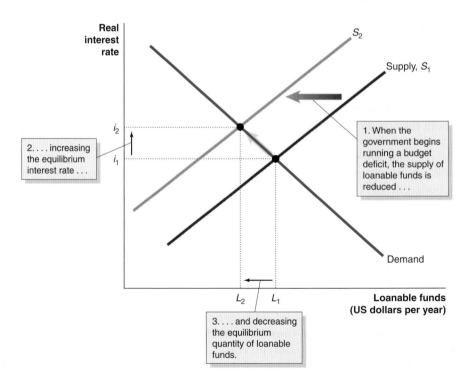

of global saving in determining the interest rate.) For example, a recent study found that increasing government borrowing by an amount equal to 1 percent of GDP would increase the equilibrium real interest rate by only about three one-hundredths of a percentage point. However, this small effect on interest rates does not imply that we can ignore the effect of deficits on economic growth. Paying off government debt in the future may require higher taxes, which can depress economic growth.

Solved Problem | 17-2

How Would a Consumption Tax Affect Saving, Investment, the Interest Rate, and Economic Growth?

Some economists and policymakers have suggested that governments should shift from relying on an income tax to relying on a *consumption tax.* Under the income tax, households pay taxes on all income earned. Under a consumption tax, households pay taxes only on the income they spend.

Households would pay taxes on saved income only if they spend the money at a later time. Use the market for loanable funds model to analyze the effect on saving, investment, the interest rate, and economic growth of switching from an income tax to a consumption tax.

SOLVING THE PROBLEM:

Step 1: **Review the chapter material.** This problem is about applying the market for loanable funds model, so you may want to review the section "Explaining Movements in Saving, Investment, and Interest Rates," which begins on page 565.

Step 2: **Explain the effect of switching from an income tax to a consumption tax.** Households are interested in the return they receive from saving after they have paid their taxes. For example, consider someone who puts his savings in a certificate of deposit at an interest rate of 4 percent and whose tax rate is 25 percent. Under an income tax, this person's after-tax return to saving is 3 percent $[4 \times (1 - 0.25)]$. Under a consumption tax, income that is saved is not taxed, so the return rises to 4 percent. We can conclude that moving from

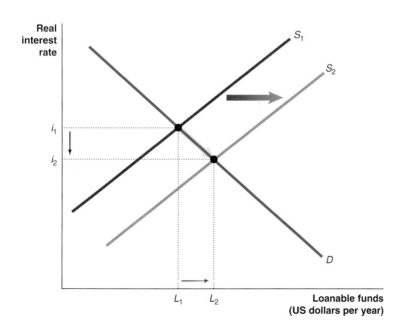

an income tax to a consumption tax would increase the return to saving, causing the supply of loanable funds to increase.

Step 3: **Draw a graph of the market for loanable funds to illustrate your answer.**
The supply curve for loanable funds will shift to the right as the after-tax return to saving increases under the consumption tax. The equilibrium interest rate will fall, and the levels of saving and investment will both increase. Because investment increases, the capital stock and the quantity of capital per hour worked will grow, and the rate of economic growth should increase. Note that the size of the fall in the interest rate and the increase in loanable funds shown in the graph are larger than the effects that most economists expect would actually result from the replacement of the income tax with a consumption tax.

>> End Solved Problem 17-2

YOUR TURN: For more practice, do related problem 2.16 on page 577 at the end of this chapter.

17.3 LEARNING OBJECTIVE

17.3 | Explain what happens during a business cycle.

The Business Cycle

Figure 17-1 on page 553 shows the increase in the standard of living of the average citizen in Oman and some other Arab countries. But close inspection of the figure reveals that real GDP per capita did not increase every year during the period of study (1975–2009). For example, during the 1980's in Oman, real GDP per capita *fell* for several years in a row. What accounts for these fluctuations in the long-run upward trend?

Some Basic Business Cycle Definitions

The fluctuations in real GDP per capita shown in Figure 17-1 reflect the underlying fluctuations in real GDP. Generally speaking, both developed and developing economies have experienced a business cycle that consists of alternating periods of expanding and contracting economic activity. Because real GDP is our best measure of economic activity, the business cycle is usually illustrated using movements in real GDP.

During the *expansion phase* of the business cycle, production, employment, and income are increasing. The period of expansion ends with a *business cycle peak*. Following the business cycle peak, production, employment, and income decline as the economy enters the *recession phase* of the cycle. The recession comes to an end with a *business cycle trough*, after which another period of expansion begins. Figure 17-7 illustrates the phases of the business cycle. Panel (a) shows an idealized business cycle with real GDP increasing smoothly in an expansion to a business cycle peak and then decreasing smoothly in a recession to a business cycle trough, which is followed by another expansion. Panel (b) shows the somewhat messier reality of an actual business cycle by plotting fluctuations in real GDP (constant local currency units) in Egypt during the period from 2006 to 2009. The figure shows that the expansion that began in 2006 continued through the beginning of 2008, until a business cycle peak was reached in the first quarter of 2008. The following recession was short, and a business cycle trough was reached in the third quarter of 2008, when the next expansion began and continued until the first quarter of 2009 (the peak of this expansion). The following recession was also short as it lasted for only two quarters, the second and third quarter of 2009, and then another expansion began in the fourth quarter of 2009.

What Happens during a Business Cycle?

Each business cycle is different. The lengths of the expansion and recession phases and which sectors of the economy are most affected are rarely the same in any two cycles. But most business cycles share certain characteristics, which we will discuss in this section. As the economy nears the end of an expansion, interest rates usually are rising, and

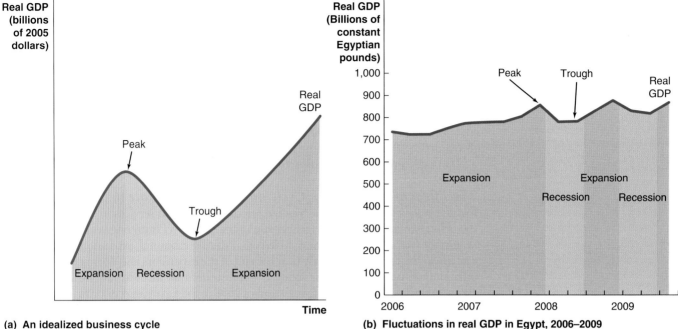

(a) An idealized business cycle

(b) Fluctuations in real GDP in Egypt, 2006–2009

Figure 17-7 | The Business Cycle

Panel (a) shows an idealized business cycle with real GDP increasing smoothly in an expansion to a business cycle peak and then decreasing smoothly in a recession to a business cycle trough, which is followed by another expansion. The periods of expansion are shown in green, and the period of recession is shown in red. In panel (b), the actual movements in real GDP in Egypt for 2006 to 2009 are shown. The Egyptian economy was expanding during the period 2006–2008 and reached the peak in the first quarter of 2008. The following recession was short, and a business cycle trough was reached in the third quarter of 2008, when the next expansion began and continued until the first quarter of 2009. The following recession was also short as it lasted for only two quarters, and then another expansion began in the fourth quarter of 2009.

Source: World Development Indicators, World Bank.

the wages of workers usually are rising faster than prices. As a result of rising interest rates and rising wages, the profits of firms will be falling. Typically, toward the end of an expansion, both households and firms will have substantially increased their debts. These debts are the result of the borrowing firms and households undertake to help finance their spending during the expansion.

A recession will often begin with a decline in spending by firms on capital goods, such as machinery, equipment, new factories, and new office buildings, or by households on new houses and consumer durables, such as furniture and automobiles. As spending declines, firms selling capital goods and consumer durables will find their sales declining. As sales decline, firms cut back on production and begin to lay off workers. Rising unemployment and falling profits reduce income, which leads to further declines in spending.

As the recession continues, economic conditions gradually begin to improve. The declines in spending eventually come to an end; households and firms begin to reduce their debt, thereby increasing their ability to spend; and interest rates decline, making it more likely that households and firms will borrow to finance new spending. Firms begin to increase their spending on capital goods as they anticipate the need for additional production during the next expansion. Increased spending by households on consumer durables and by businesses on capital goods will finally bring the recession to an end and begin the next expansion.

The Effect of the Business Cycle on Firms Durables are goods that are expected to last for three or more years. Consumer durables include furniture, appliances, and automobiles, and producer durables include machine tools, electric generators, and commercial airplanes. Durables are affected more by the business cycle than are nondurables—such as food and clothing—or services—such as haircuts and medical care. During a recession, workers reduce spending if they lose their jobs, fear losing their jobs, or suffer wage cuts. Because people can often continue to use their existing furniture, appliances, or automobiles, they are more likely to postpone spending on durables than spending on other goods. Similarly, when firms experience declining sales and profits during a recession, they often cut back on purchases of producer durables, jobs, and workers' monthly wages.

For example, Emaar Properties, one of the world's largest property developers based in Dubai, decided to cut jobs (about 250 jobs) in late 2008 due to the 2008 financial crisis. In addition, according to Gulf Base, Emaar slashed wages by around 20 to 30 percent in March 2009. The reason for this job cut and reduction in wages is clear: Emaar reported a 73.6 percent decline in its net profits to 236.54 million dirhams (approximately US$64.4 million) in the first quarter of 2009, compared to 896.21 million dirhams (US$244 million) in the first quarter of 2008. The drop in net income is due to a fall in sales amid the 2009 property slump in UAE.

The Effect of the Business Cycle on the Inflation Rate In Chapter 16, we saw that the *price level* measures the average prices of goods and services in the economy and the *inflation rate* is the percentage increase in the price level from one year to the next. An important fact about the business cycle is that during economic expansions, the inflation rate *usually* increases, particularly near the end of the expansion; and during recessions, the inflation rate *usually* decreases. Figure 17-8 illustrates that this was fairly true during the expansion of 2006–2008 and the recession of 2008 in the Egyptian economy.

Figure 17-8 shows that during the 2006–2008 expansion in the Egyptian economy, the inflation rate rose from about 7.6 percent to 18.3 percent (the significant increase in the international prices of food in 2008 is partially responsible for this dramatic jump in the inflation rate in Egypt, since food accounts for 43.9 percent of the consumer basket when calculating CPI, as we mentioned in the previous chapter). The recession that began in the second quarter of 2008 caused the inflation rate to fall back to 11.7 percent in 2009. Notice that there is a time lag between the beginning of the recession and the time when the inflation rate started to fall (the recession began in 2008 and the inflation rate declined in 2009). The impact of a business cycle on inflation is obvious. During a business cycle expansion, spending by businesses and households is strong, and producers of goods and services find it easier to raise prices. As spending declines during a recession, firms have a more difficult time selling their goods and services and are likely to increase prices less than they otherwise might have.

The Effect of the Business Cycle on the Unemployment Rate Recessions cause the inflation rate to fall, but they cause the unemployment rate to increase. As firms see their sales decline, they begin to reduce production and lay off workers. Figure 17-9 shows the impact of the business cycle on the unemployment rate. During the expansion of 2006–2008, the unemployment rate started to decrease from 10.6 percent in 2006 to 8.7 percent in 2008. When the recession began in 2008, the unemployment rate started to rise in 2009 and

Figure 17-8

The Impact of the 2008 Recession on the Inflation Rate in Egypt

During the 2006–2008 expansion, the inflation rate was rising. The recession that began in the second quarter of 2008, marked by the shaded vertical bar, caused the inflation rate to fall.

Source: World Development Indicators, World Bank.

Note: The points on the figure represent the annual inflation rate measured by the change in the CPI.

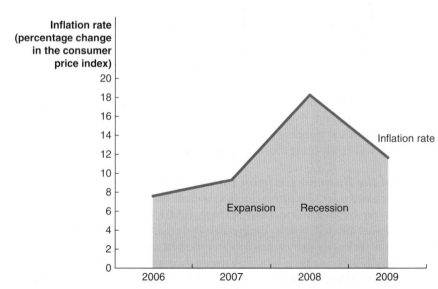

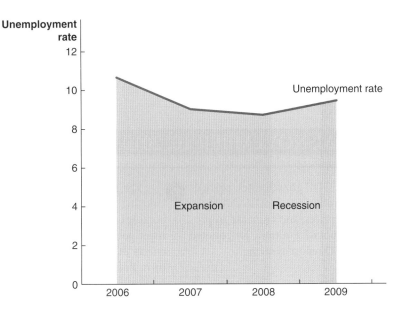

Figure 17-9

How the Recession of 2008 Affected the Unemployment Rate in Egypt

The reluctance of firms to hire new employees during the early stages of a recovery means that the unemployment rate usually continues to rise even after the recession has ended.
Source: World Development Indicators, World Bank.

reached 9.7 percent. Again, there is a noticeable time lag between the beginning of the recession and its impact on the unemployment rate. This pattern is typical and is due to two factors. First, during the business cycle, discouraged workers drop out of, and then return to, the labor force, as we discussed in Chapter 16. When discouraged workers drop out of the labor force during a recession, they keep the measured unemployment rate from increasing as much as it would if these workers were counted as unemployed. When discouraged workers return to the labor force as the recession ends, they increase the measured unemployment rate because they are now counted as being unemployed. Second, firms continue to operate well below their capacity even after a recession has ended and production has begun to increase. As a result, at first, firms may not hire back all the workers they have laid off and may even continue for a while to lay off more workers.

Economics in YOUR Life!

>> Continued from page 551

At the beginning of the chapter, we posed a question: How do you respond to your roommate's assertion that your decision to save instead of consume will reduce economic growth? In answering this question, this chapter has shown that consumption spending promotes the production of more consumption goods and services—such as jeans and haircuts—and fewer investment goods and services—such as physical capital and worker education. This is because saving—and, so, not consuming—is necessary to fund investment expenditure. Because an economy uses investment goods and services to produce other goods and services, your decision to save instead of consume will promote, rather than reduce, economic growth.

Conclusion

Productivity and technology advancement are the main engines of economic growth. In many Arab countries, the standard of living today is higher than that of the 1970s. But households and firms are still subject to the ups and downs of the business cycle.

Read *An Inside Look at Policy* on the next page to learn why economic growth and inflation are positively related in the Arab economies.

Economic Growth and the Inflation Rate: Are They Positively Related?

SUITE101.COM, NOVEMBER 10, 2010

Arab Economic Growth Predicted to Rebound after 2009 Drop

Economic growth across the Arab world fell in 2009. The IMF predicts recovery in 2010, but warns more jobs must be created. Real growth in the combined economies of Arab countries fell to around 1.5 percent in 2009, according to the annual report of the Abu Dhabi Department of Economic Development (ADDED) issued on November 10, 2010, and cited by the Dubai-based Emirates 24/7 website. This was much lower than the growth rate of 6.2 percent in 2008, when oil prices averaged as high as 95 US dollars a barrel and most Arab producers were pumping at near capacity, the ADDED report said. Except for Qatar, the world's top exporter of liquefied natural gas (LNG), all Arab states recorded single-digit growth in 2009.

ⓐ But ADDED, citing estimates by the Abu Dhabi-based Arab Monetary Fund (AMF), noted that the economic crisis also had positive effects, as it had pulled some Arab countries out of the throes of inflation that had hit record rates....

Outside the Gulf, growth in Egypt fell from seven to 4.7 percent, while it declined from 5.5 to four percent in Jordan, from 8.5 to seven percent in Lebanon, and from around 5.1 to three percent in Syria. "The real economy in the Arab countries, as in other nations, declined in 2009 as a result of vulnerability to international changes, and most countries in the region saw a decline in GDP growth rates, particularly oil-producing countries due to the fall of oil prices, and cutbacks in production quotas," Emirates 24/7 quoted the ADDED report as saying.

Inflation Down

ⓑ "After climbing to one of its highest levels in 2008, inflation in the region dipped to single-digit rates, mainly in the six-nation Gulf Cooperation Council (GCC)," the ADDED report said. According to estimates by the IMF and the GCC countries, the combined inflation rate in the GCC fell dramatically from 10.7 percent in 2008 to about 3.7 percent in 2009. Jordan, Egypt and other countries in the Middle East recorded falls in their inflation rates too. However, in August 2010 inflation in Saudi Arabia, the biggest Arab economy, climbed to an 18-month high of 6.1 percent, mainly because of rising food and housing costs.

IMF Forecasts Growth to Rise Again in 2010

In October 2010 the IMF forecast economic growth in the Gulf states of 4.5 percent in 2010, compared with a mere 0.4 percent in 2009. In North Africa, the IMF predicted growth of 5 percent. "With the rebound in crude oil prices and production, the oil-exporting countries of the Middle East and North Africa [MENA] will see visible improvements in their fiscal and external balances in 2010–11," the IMF said in its *Regional Economic Outlook: Middle East and Central Asia* report, released on October 24, 2010.

ⓒ The IMF said the Middle East was enjoying "a generally robust recovery," because of higher oil prices and government policies designed to mitigate the effects of the global economic downturn. But it said more had to be done to diversify economies and create more jobs in the private sector, particularly in countries such as Egypt, Jordan, and Syria with large youth populations and chronic unemployment. According to IMF estimates, the countries of the MENA region will have to create 18 million jobs in the next decade. High and sustained growth is a "precondition for such large-scale job creation and for raising incomes," said Masood Ahmed, director of the IMF's Middle East and Central Asia department, quoted by the *Financial Times* on November 8. 2010.

Source: Peter Feuilherade, "Arab Economic Growth Predicted to Rebound After 2009 Drop," suite101.com, November 10, 2010.

Peter Feuilherade, a former BBC World Service journalist, is a UK-based Middle East writer and analyst.

Key Points in the Article

This article discusses the impact of the recent business downturn on economic growth in the Arab economies during the period 2008–2010. The recession of 2009, caused by the international financial crisis, resulted in a slower economic expansion in the Arab countries compared with the expansion (growth) rates realized in 2008. The low economic growth rates were associated with low inflation rates too, but also with more jobless people. The increase in oil prices in 2010 and the ambitious government expenditure programs made many economic analysts predict a strong economic recovery in the Arab economies in the near future.

Analyzing the News

(a) Both oil-based and non-oil-based Arab economies suffered from a reduction in their economic growth rates in the year of 2009 as a result of the global recession in that year, which affected private investment negatively. But the recession hit the oil-based Arab economies more than the non-oil-based ones. The reason lies behind the sharp decline in oil prices in 2009 (around US$95 per barrel on average) compared with 2008 (around US$53 per barrel on Average). For example, according to the World Development Indicators, between 2008 and 2009, the economic growth rates dropped from 4.3 percent to 0.15 percent in Saudi Arabia, from 8.3 percent to 6.3 percent in Bahrain, from 5.1 percent to –0.7 in the UAE, and from 6.3 percent to –1.5 percent in Kuwait. As we can infer from the article, non-oil-based Arab economies were a little less affected by the global recession as they are less vulnerable to changes in oil prices (oil production accounts for a smaller portion of their GDP compared with oil-based economies).

(b) A lower inflation rate is the blessing of a low (or negative) economic growth rate. This statement appears to be true when we examine it in the Arab economies during the recent global economic crisis. People living in the Arab world enjoyed low inflation rates in 2009. Most Arab countries suffered from a two-digit inflation rate in 2008 due not only to the economic expansion in the period prior to 2008 but also to the increase in the international prices of food and oil, as we mentioned earlier in the chapter. The global recession resulted in a reduction in the aggregate demand, particularly investor and consumer demand, which drove inflation rates down.

(c) Following the same argument mentioned in part (a), the rebound in oil prices in 2010 resulted in a higher government revenues and GDP in oil-based Arab economies. In addition, as we mentioned earlier in this chapter, Arab governments conducted expansionary fiscal policies by increasing government expenditure on some mega projects such as building industrial cities, universities and schools, and the infrastructure in general, in order to mitigate the recession. These policies, along with the higher price of oil, led many economic analysts to predict a recovery in the Arab economies in the near future. The IMF recommendation to diversify Arab economies was intended to make Arab countries less vulnerable to fluctuations in the prices of natural resources in general, and of oil prices specifically. Notice that this rosy picture of economic recovery and higher economic growth rates is expected to be associated with higher inflation rates. This positive relationship between economic growth and inflation is well-known in economics, and reminds us of the *tradeoffs* that policymakers usually face: a higher economic growth rate usually makes people suffer from a higher inflation rate.

Thinking Critically About Policy

1. Many non-oil-based Arab governments applied expansionary fiscal policies to enhance economic growth during the period 2009-2010. What do you think the impact of these policies on the government budget in the short run and in the long run? *(Hint: non-oil-based economies usually rely on taxes to finance the government budget).* Will oil-based Arab economies realize the same impact? (Assume high oil prices).

2. Suppose that international oil prices fell significantly. How would oil-based Arab countries finance their mega projects? What would be the expected effect of the government finance on private investment?

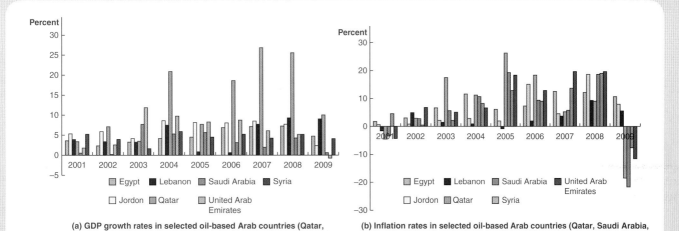

(a) **GDP growth rates in selected oil-based Arab countries (Qatar, Saudi Arabia, and the United Arab Emirates) and non-oil-based Arab countries (Egypt, Jordan, Lebanon, and Syria).**

(b) **Inflation rates in selected oil-based Arab countries (Qatar, Saudi Arabia, and the United Arab Emirates) and non-oil-based Arab countries (Egypt, Jordan, Lebanon, and Syria).**

Source: World Development indicators, the World Bank Group.

Key Terms

Business cycle, p. 552

Capital, p. 556

Crowding out, p. 566

Financial intermediaries, p. 561

Financial markets, p. 560

Financial system, p. 560

Labor productivity, p. 556

Long-run economic
   growth, p. 552

Market for loanable funds,
   p. 564

Potential GDP, p. 559

Summary

17.1 LEARNING OBJECTIVE

Discuss the importance of
long-run economic growth,
pages 552–560.

Long-Run Economic Growth

The Arab economies have experienced both *long-run economic growth* and the *business cycle*. The **business cycle** refers to alternating periods of economic expansion and economic recession. **Long-run economic growth** is the process by which rising productivity increases the standard of living of the typical person. Because of economic growth, many Arabs today can buy much more than they could in 1970. Long-run growth is measured by increases in real GDP per capita. Increases in real GDP per capita depend on increases in labor productivity. **Labor productivity** is the quantity of goods and services that can be produced by one worker or by one hour of work. Economists believe two key factors determine labor productivity—the quantity of capital per hour worked and the level of technology. **Capital** refers to manufactured goods that are used to produce other goods and services. *Human capital* is the accumulated knowledge and skills workers acquire from education training or their life experiences. Economic growth occurs if the quantity of capital per hour worked increases and if technological change occurs. Economists often discuss economic growth in terms of growth in **potential GDP**, which is the level of GDP attained when all firms are producing at capacity.

17.2 LEARNING OBJECTIVE

Discuss the role of the financial
system in facilitating long-run
economic growth, **pages 560–568.**

Saving, Investment, and the Financial System

Financial markets and financial intermediaries together comprise the **financial system**. A well-functioning financial system is an important determinant of economic growth. Firms acquire funds from households, either directly through financial markets—such as the stock and bond markets—or indirectly through financial intermediaries—such as banks. The funds available to firms come from *saving*. There are two categories of saving in the economy: *private saving* by households and *public saving* by the government. The value of total saving in the economy is always equal to the value of total investment spending. In the model of the **market for loanable funds**, the interaction of borrowers and lenders determines the market interest rate and the quantity of loanable funds exchanged.

17.3 LEARNING OBJECTIVE

Explain what happens during a
business cycle, **page 568–571.**

The Business Cycle

During the expansion phase of a business cycle, production, employment, and income are increasing. The period of expansion ends with a business cycle peak. Following the business cycle peak, production, employment, and income decline during the recession phase of the cycle. The recession comes to an end with a business cycle trough, after which another period of expansion begins. The inflation rate usually rises near the end of a business cycle expansion and then falls during a recession. The unemployment rate declines during the later part of an expansion and increases during a recession. The unemployment rate often continues to increase even after an expansion has begun. Economists have not found a method to predict when recessions will begin and end. Recessions are difficult to predict because they have more than one cause.

Review, Problems and Applications

17.1 LEARNING OBJECTIVE   Discuss the importance of long-run economic growth, **pages 552–560.**

Review Questions

1.1 By how much did real GDP per capita increase in Oman between 1975 and 2009? Discuss whether the increase in real GDP per capita is likely to be greater or smaller than the true increase in living standards.

1.2 What is the most important factor in explaining increases in real GDP per capita in the long run?

1.3 What two key factors cause labor productivity to increase over time?

1.4 What is potential real GDP? Does potential real GDP remain constant over time?

Problems and Applications

1.5 Briefly discuss whether you would rather live in the United Arab Emirates of 1965 with an income of Dh500,000 per year or the UAE of 2011 with an income of Dh140,000 per year. Assume that the incomes for both years are measured in constant 2000 dirhams (Dh).

1.6 Based on what you read about economic growth in this chapter, elaborate on the importance of growth in GDP, particularly real GDP per capita, to the quality of life of a country's citizens.

1.7 **(Related to the** *Making the Connection* **on page 553)** Think about the relationship between economic prosperity and life expectancy. What implications does this relationship have for the size of the health-care sector of the economy? In particular, is this sector likely to expand or contract in coming years?

1.8 Use the table to answer the following questions.

YEAR	REAL GDP OF QATAR (MILLIONS OF CONSTANT RIYALS)
2000	61,784,000
2001	63,840,000
2002	68,394,000
2003	70,781,000
2004	85,534,000

a. Calculate the growth rate of real GDP for each year from 2001 to 2004.

b. Calculate the average annual growth rate of real GDP for the period from 2001 to 2004.

1.9 Assume that GDP per capita in Qatar grew in the past at an average annual growth rate of 7 percent percent. If Qatar's economy continues to grow at this rate, how many years will it take for real GDP per capita to double?

1.10 The economy of China has boomed since the late 1970s, having periods during which real GDP per capita has grown at rates of 9 percent per year or more. At a 9 percent growth rate in real GDP per capita, how many years will it take to double?

1.11 **(Related to** *Solved Problem 17-1* **on page 557)** Two reasons for the rapid economic growth of China over the past two to three decades have been the massive movement of workers from agriculture to manufacturing jobs and the transformation of parts of its economy into a market system. In China, labor productivity in manufacturing substantially exceeds labor productivity in agriculture, and as many as 150 million Chinese workers will move from agriculture to manufacturing over the next decade or so. In 1978, China began to transform its economy into a market system, and today, nearly 40 percent of Chinese workers are employed in private firms (up from 0 percent in 1978). In the long run, which of these two factors—movement of workers from agriculture to manufacturing or transforming the economy into a market system—will be more important for China's economic growth? Briefly explain.

Source: "China: Awakening Giant," Federal Reserve Bank of Dallas, *Southwest Economy*, September/October 2003.

1.12 A newspaper story on labor productivity in the United States includes the following observation: "Productivity is the vital element needed to boost living standards." Briefly explain whether you agree. Make clear in your answer what you mean by living standards.

Source: Martin Crutsinger, "Productivity Rebounds in Fourth Quarter," Associated Press, February 8, 2007.

1.13 **(Related to the** *Making the Connection* **on page 558)** If the keys to Botswana's rapid economic growth seem obvious, why have other countries in the region had so much difficulty following them?

Review Questions

2.1 Why is the financial system of a country important for long-run economic growth? Why is it essential for economic growth that firms have access to adequate sources of funds?

2.2 How does the financial system—either financial markets or financial intermediaries—provide risk sharing, liquidity, and information for savers and borrowers?

2.3 Briefly explain why the total value of saving in the economy must equal the total value of investment.

2.4 What are loanable funds? Why do businesses demand loanable funds? Why do households supply loanable funds?

Problems and Applications

2.5 Suppose you can receive an interest rate of 3 percent on a certificate of deposit at a bank that is charging borrowers 7 percent on new car loans. Why might you be unwilling to loan money directly to someone who wants to borrow from you to buy a new car, even if that person offers to pay you an interest rate higher than 3 percent?

2.6 An article argues that a main barrier to continued rapid economic growth in China is "its fragile banking system." Why might a weak banking system make economic growth difficult?

Source: "The Real Great Leap Forward," *The Economist*, September 30, 2004.

2.7 According to World Development Indicators (WDI), the government of Tunisia realized an increase in its budget deficit from 0.6 percent of GDP in 2008 to 3.8 percent in 2009. Assuming that other factors that affect the demand and supply of loanable funds remain the same, what would be the effect of this larger budget deficit on the equilibrium real interest rate and the quantity of loanable funds? What would be the effect on the equilibrium quantity of saving and investment? Illustrate your answer using a graph showing the market for loanable funds in Tunisia.

Source: www.worldbank.org.

2.8 Consider the following data for a closed economy:

$Y =$ US$11 trillion
$C =$ US$8 trillion
$I =$ US$2 trillion
$TR =$ US$1 trillion
$T =$ US$3 trillion

Use the data to calculate the following.

a. Private saving
b. Public saving
c. Government purchases
d. The government budget deficit or budget surplus

2.9 Consider the following data for a closed economy:

$Y =$ US$12 trillion
$C =$ US$8 trillion
$G =$ US$2 trillion
$S_{public} =$ −US$0.5 trillion
$T =$ US$2 trillion

Use the data to calculate the following.

a. Private saving
b. Investment spending
c. Transfer payments
d. The government budget deficit or budget surplus

2.10 In problem 2.9, suppose that government purchases increase from US$2 trillion to US$2.5 trillion. If the values for Y and C are unchanged, what must happen to the values of S and I? Briefly explain.

2.11 Use the graph to answer the following questions.

a. Does the shift from S_1 to S_2 represent an increase or a decrease in the supply of loanable funds?
b. With the shift in supply, what happens to the equilibrium quantity of loanable funds?
c. With the change in the equilibrium quantity of loanable funds, what happens to the quantity of saving? What happens to the quantity of investment?

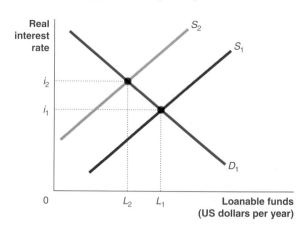

2.12 Use the graph on the next page to answer the following questions.

a. With the shift in the demand for loanable funds, what happens to the equilibrium real interest rate and the equilibrium quantity of loanable funds?
b. How can the equilibrium quantity of loanable funds increase when the real interest rate increases? Doesn't the quantity of loanable funds demanded decrease when the interest rate increases?
c. How much would the quantity of loanable funds demanded have increased if the interest rate had remained at i_1?
d. How much does the quantity of loanable funds supplied increase with the increase in the interest rate from i_1 to i_2?

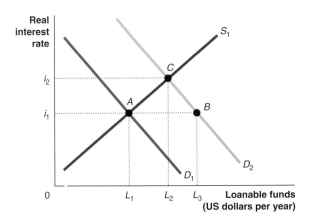

2.13 Suppose that the economy is currently in a recession and that economic forecasts indicate that the economy will soon enter an expansion. What is the likely effect of the expansion on the expected profitability of new investment in plant and equipment? In the market for loanable funds, graph and explain the effect of the forecast of an economic expansion, assuming that borrowers and lenders believe the forecast is accurate. What happens to the equilibrium real interest rate and the quantity of loanable funds? What happens to the quantity of saving and investment?

2.14 Firms care about their after-tax rate of return on investment projects. In the market for loanable funds, graph and explain the effect of an increase in taxes on business profits. (For simplicity, assume no change in the government budget deficit or budget surplus.) What happens to the equilibrium real interest rate and the quantity of loanable funds? What will be the effect on the quantity of investment by firms and the economy's capital stock in the future?

2.15 Use a market for loanable funds graph to illustrate the effect of the budget surpluses in the mid-2000s in Saudi Arabia. What happens to the equilibrium real interest rate and the quantity of loanable funds? What happens to the quantity of saving and investment?

2.16 (Related to *Solved Problem 17-2* on page 567) As discussed in Chapter 16, savers are taxed on the nominal interest payments they receive rather than the real interest payments. Suppose the government shifted from taxing nominal interest payments to taxing only real interest payments. Use a market for loanable funds graph to analyze the effects of this change in tax policy. What happens to the equilibrium real interest rate and the equilibrium quantity of loanable funds? What happens to the quantity of saving and investment?

17.3 LEARNING OBJECTIVE   Explain what happens during a business cycle, **pages 568–571.**

Review Questions

3.1 What are the names of the following events in a business cycle?
  a. The high point of economic activity
  b. The low point of economic activity
  c. The period between the high point of economic activity and the following low point
  d. The period between the low point of economic activity and the following high point

3.2 Briefly describe the effect of the business cycle on the inflation rate and the unemployment rate.

Problems and Applications

3.3 Briefly explain whether production of each of the following goods is likely to fluctuate more or less than real GDP does during the business cycle.

  a. Ford F-150 trucks
  b. McDonald's Big Macs
  c. Kenmore refrigerators
  d. Huggies diapers
  e. Caterpillar industrial tractors

3.4 "Real GDP in Bahrain in 2008 was 4,871,765 billion dinars. This value is a large number. Therefore, economic growth must have been high during 2008." Briefly explain whether you agree or disagree with this statement.

3.5 Imagine you own a business and that during the next recession you lay off 20 percent of your workforce. When economic activity picks up and your sales begin to increase, why might you not immediately start rehiring workers?

PART 6

Markets for Factors of Production and Short-Run Fluctuations

Chapter 18

The **Markets** for **Labor** and **Other Factors** of **Production**

Why is Real Madrid Paying Cristiano Ronaldo US$17 Million per Year?

Few businesses arouse in their customers the level of passion that sports teams do. Unlike most other industries, the sports industry has an entire section devoted to it in most newspapers. Of course, among the best-known people are football (soccer) players.

Sports fans admire the skills of star athletes, but many are also fascinated by their high salaries. How is it, fans often wonder, that some athletes are paid salaries of millions of US dollars "just for playing a game"? Many football fans also wonder why a few teams, such as Real Madrid, Barcelona, and Manchester United, are able to pay higher salaries than other teams. In the Arab world you can observe the same phenomenon with, for example, Al-Ahly of the UAE and Zamalek of Egypt.

In June 2009, Real Madrid signed a historic deal with Manchester United for a total sum of US$132 million to finalize the transfer of Cristiano Ronaldo to Real Madrid. The deal made Ronaldo the most expensive football player in history. In addition, Real Madrid agreed to pay Ronaldo US$17 million per year over the following six years. This represented a significant raise from the US$8 million that Manchester United, his previous team, had paid him the year before. This salary put Ronaldo on top of the worldwide highest-paid football players' list. University professors in the U.S. and Europe earn an average salary of US$50,000 to US$80,000. Why is Real Madrid willing to pay football player so much more than universities are willing to pay a professor?

The key to answering these questions is to understand that wages are determined in the labor market by the demand and supply of labor, just as the price of apples is determined by the demand and supply of apples and the price of DVDs is determined by the demand and supply of DVDs. In Chapter 3, we developed a model for analyzing the demand and supply of goods and services. We will use some of the same concepts in this chapter to analyze the demand and supply of labor and other factors of production. But there are important ways in which the markets for factors of production are not like markets for goods. The most obvious difference is that in factor markets, firms are demanders, and households are suppliers.

Another difference between the labor market and the markets for goods and services is that concepts of fairness arise more frequently in labor markets. When a sportsman like Cristiano Ronaldo signs a contract for millions of dollars, people often wonder "Why should someone playing a game get paid so much more than teachers, nurses, and other people doing more important jobs?" Because people typically earn most of their income from wages and salaries, they often view the labor market as being the most important market they participate in. **AN INSIDE LOOK** on **page 608** discusses how flexible employment terms may increase labor market and business efficiency in the Arab countries of the Gulf.

LEARNING Objectives

After studying this chapter, you should be able to:

18.1 Explain how firms choose the **profit-maximizing quantity of labor** to employ, page 582.

18.2 Explain how people choose the quantity of **labor** to **supply**, page 586.

18.3 Explain how **equilibrium wages are determined in labor markets**, page 589.

18.4 Use demand and supply analysis to explain how **compensating differentials, discrimination** and **labor unions** cause wages to differ, page 592.

18.5 Discuss the role **personnel economics** can play in helping firms deal with human resources issues, page 602.

18.6 Show how equilibrium prices are determined in the markets for **capital** and **natural resources**, page 604.

Economics in YOUR Life!

Why is it so Hard to Get a Raise?

Imagine that you have worked for a local sandwich shop for over a year and are preparing to ask for a raise. You might tell the manager that you are a good employee, with a good attitude and work ethic. You might also explain that you have learned more about your job and are now able to make sandwiches quicker, track inventory more accurately, and work the cash register more effectively than when you were first hired. Will this be enough to convince your manager to give you a raise? How can you convince your manager that you are worth more money than you are currently being paid? As you read this chapter, see if you can answer these questions. You can check your answers against those we provide at the end of the chapter. **➤ Continued on page 607**

Factors of production Labor, capital, natural resources, and other inputs used to produce goods and services.

Firms use **factors of production**—such as labor, capital, and natural resources—to produce goods and services. For example, Alhilal Saudi uses labor (football players), capital (football pitches), and natural resources (the land on which the pitches sit) to produce football games. In this chapter, we will explore how firms choose the profit-maximizing quantity of labor and other factors of production. The interaction between firm demand for labor and household supply of labor determines the equilibrium wage rate.

Because there are many different types of labor, there are many different labor markets. The equilibrium wage in the market for football players is much higher than the equilibrium wage in the market for college professors. We will explore why this is true. We will also explore how factors such as discrimination, unions, and compensation for dangerous or unpleasant jobs help explain differences among wages. We will then look at *personnel economics*, which is concerned with how firms can use economic analysis to design their employee compensation plans. Finally, we will analyze the markets for other factors of production.

18.1 LEARNING OBJECTIVE

18.1 | Explain how firms choose the profit-maximizing quantity of labor to employ.

The Demand for Labor

Up until now we have concentrated on consumer demand for final goods and services. The demand for labor is different from the demand for final goods and services because it is a *derived demand*. A **derived demand** is the demand for a factor of production that is based on the demand for the good the factor produces. You demand an Apple iPod because of the utility you receive from listening to music. Apple's demand for the labor to make iPods is derived from the underlying consumer demand for iPods. As a result, we can say that Apple's demand for labor depends primarily on two factors:

Derived demand The demand for a factor of production that is derived from the demand for the good the factor produces.

1 The additional iPods Apple will be able to produce if it hires one more worker

2 The additional revenue Apple receives from selling the additional iPods

The Marginal Revenue Product of Labor

Consider the following hypothetical example. To keep the main point clear, let's assume that in the short run, Apple can increase production of iPods only by increasing the quantity of labor it employs. The table in Figure 18-1 shows the relationship between the quantity of workers Apple hires, the quantity of iPods it produces, the additional revenue from selling the additional iPods, and the additional profit from hiring each additional worker.

For simplicity, we are keeping the scale of Apple's factory very small. We will also assume that Apple is a perfect competitor both in the market for selling digital music players and in the market for hiring labor. This means that Apple is a *price taker* in both markets. Although this is not realistic, the basic analysis would not change if we assumed that Apple can affect the price of digital music players and the wage paid to workers. Given these assumptions, suppose that Apple can sell as many iPods as it wants at a price of US$200 and can hire as many workers as it wants at a wage of US$600 per week. You saw earlier that the additional output a firm produces as a result of hiring one more worker is called the **marginal product of labor**. In the table, we calculate the marginal product of labor as the change in total output as each additional worker is hired. As we saw before, because of *the law of diminishing returns*, the marginal product of labor declines as a firm hires more workers.

When deciding how many workers to hire, a firm is not interested in how much *output* will increase as it hires another worker but in how much *revenue* will increase as it hires another worker. In other words, what matters is how much the firm's revenue

Marginal product of labor The additional output a firm produces as a result of hiring one more worker.

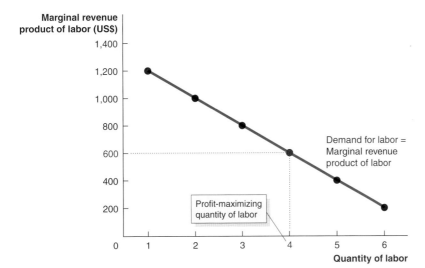

Number of Workers	Output of iPods per Week	Marginal Product of Labor (iPods per week)	Product Price	Marginal Revenue Product of Labor (US dollars per week)	Wage (US dollars per week)	Additional Profit from Hiring One More Worker (US dollars per week)
L	Q	MP	P	MRP = P x MP	W	MRP − W
0	0	—	US$200	—	US$600	—
1	6	6	200	US$1,200	600	US$600
2	11	5	200	1,000	600	400
3	15	4	200	800	600	200
4	18	3	200	600	600	0
5	20	2	200	400	600	−200
6	21	1	200	200	600	−400

Figure 18-1

The Marginal Revenue Product of Labor and the Demand for Labor

The marginal revenue product of labor equals the marginal product of labor multiplied by the price of the good. The marginal revenue product curve slopes downward because diminishing returns cause the marginal product of labor to decline as more workers are hired. A firm maximizes profits by hiring workers up to the point where the wage equals the marginal revenue product of labor. The marginal revenue product of labor curve is the firm's demand curve for labor because it tells the firm the profit-maximizing quantity of workers to hire at each wage. For example, using the demand curve shown in this figure, if the wage is US$600, the firm will hire 4 workers.

will rise when it sells the additional output it can produce by hiring one more worker. We can calculate this amount by multiplying the additional output produced by the product price. This amount is called the **marginal revenue product of labor** (MRP). For example, consider what happens if Apple increases the number of workers hired from 2 to 3. The table in Figure 18-1 shows that hiring the third worker allows Apple to increase its weekly output of iPods from 11 to 15, so the marginal product of labor is 4 iPods. The price of the iPods is US$200, so the marginal revenue product of the third worker is 4 × US$200, or US$800. In other words, Apple adds US$800 to its revenue as a result of hiring the third worker. In the graph, we plot the values of the marginal revenue product of labor at each quantity of labor.

To decide how many workers to hire, Apple must compare the additional revenue it earns from hiring another worker to the increase in its costs from paying that worker. The difference between the additional revenue and the additional cost is the additional profit (or loss) from hiring one more worker. This additional profit is shown in the last column of the table in Figure 18-1 and is calculated by subtracting the wage from the marginal revenue product of labor. As long as the marginal revenue product of labor is greater than the wage, Apple's profits are increasing, and it should continue to hire more workers. When the marginal revenue product of labor is less than the wage, Apple's profits are falling, and it should hire fewer workers. When the marginal revenue product of labor is equal to the wage, Apple has maximized its profits by hiring the optimal number of workers. The values in the table show that Apple should hire 4 workers. If the company hires a fifth worker, the marginal revenue product of US$400 will be less than the wage of US$600, and its profits will fall by US$200. Table 18-1 summarizes the relationship between the marginal revenue product of labor and the wage.

Marginal revenue product of labor (**MRP**) The change in a firm's revenue as a result of hiring one more worker.

TABLE 18-1

The Relationship between the Marginal Revenue Product of Labor and the Wage

WHEN...	THEN THE FIRM...
MRP > W,	Should hire more workers to increase profits.
MRP < W,	Should hire fewer workers to increase profits.
MRP = W,	Is hiring the optimal number of workers and is maximizing profits.

We can see from Figure 18-1 that if Apple has to pay a wage of US$600 per week, it should hire 4 workers. If the wage were to rise to US$1,000, then applying the rule that profits are maximized where the marginal revenue product of labor equals the wage, Apple should hire only 2 workers. Similarly, if the wage is only US$400 per week, Apple should hire 5 workers. In fact, the marginal revenue product curve tells a firm how many workers it should hire at any wage rate. In other words, *the marginal revenue product of labor curve is the demand curve for labor.*

Solved Problem | **18-1**

Hiring Decisions by a Firm that is a Price Maker

We have assumed that Apple can sell as many iPods as it wants without having to cut the price. Recall from Chapter 8 that this is the case for firms in perfectly competitive markets. These firms are *price takers.* Suppose instead that a firm has market power and is a *price maker,* so that to increase sales, it must reduce the price.

Suppose Apple faces the situation shown in the following table. Fill in the blanks and then determine the profit-maximizing number of workers for Apple to hire. Briefly explain why hiring this number of workers is profit maximizing.

(1) QUANTITY OF LABOR	(2) OUTPUT OF IPODS PER WEEK	(3) MARGINAL PRODUCT OF LABOR	(4) PRODUCT PRICE IN US$	(5) TOTAL REVENUE	(6) MARGINAL REVENUE PRODUCT OF LABOR	(7) WAGE IN US$	(8) ADDITIONAL PROFIT FROM HIRING ONE ADDITIONAL WORKER
0	0	—	200		—	500	—
1	6	6	180			500	
2	11	5	160			500	
3	15	4	140			500	
4	18	3	120			500	
5	20	2	100			500	
6	21	1	80			500	

SOLVING THE PROBLEM:

Step 1: **Review the chapter material.** This problem is about determining the profit-maximizing quantity of labor for a firm to hire, so you may want to review the section "The Demand for Labor," which begins on page 582.

Step 2: **Fill in the blanks in the table.** As Apple hires more workers, it sells more iPods and earns more revenue. You can calculate how revenue increases by multiplying the number of iPods produced—shown in column 2—by the price—shown in column 4. Then you can calculate the marginal revenue product of labor as the change in revenue as each additional worker is hired. (Notice that in this case marginal revenue product is *not* calculated by multiplying the marginal product by the product price. Because Apple is a price maker, its marginal revenue from selling additional iPods is less than the price of iPods.) Finally, you can calculate the additional profit from hiring one more worker by subtracting the wage—shown in column 7—from each worker's marginal revenue product.

(1) QUANTITY OF LABOR	(2) OUTPUT OF IPODS PER WEEK	(3) MARGINAL PRODUCT OF LABOR	(4) PRODUCT PRICE IN US$	(5) TOTAL REVENUE IN US$	(6) MARGINAL REVENUE PRODUCT OF LABOR IN US$	(7) WAGE IN US$	(8) ADDITIONAL PROFIT FROM HIRING ONE ADDITIONAL WORKER IN US$
0	0	—	200	0	—	500	—
1	6	6	180	1,080	1,080	500	580
2	11	5	160	1,760	680	500	180
3	15	4	140	2,100	340	500	−160
4	18	3	120	2,160	60	500	−440
5	20	2	100	2,000	−160	500	−660
6	21	1	80	1,680	−320	500	−820

Step 3: **Use the information in the table to determine the profit-maximizing quantity of workers to hire.** To determine the profit-maximizing quantity of workers to hire, you need to compare the marginal revenue product of labor with the wage. Column 8 does this by subtracting the wage from the marginal revenue product. As long as the values in column 8 are positive, the firm should continue to hire workers. The marginal revenue product of the second worker is US$680, and the wage is US$500, so column 8 shows that hiring the second worker will add US$180 to Apple's profits. The marginal revenue product of the third worker is US$340, and the wage is US$500, so hiring the third worker would reduce Apple's profits by US$160. Therefore, Apple will maximize profits by hiring 2 workers.

YOUR TURN: For more practice, do problem 1.5 on page 611 at the end of this chapter.

>> End Solved Problem 18-1

The Market Demand Curve for Labor

We can determine the market demand curve for labor in the same way we determine a market demand curve for a good. We saw earlier that the market demand curve for a good is determined by adding up the quantity of the good demanded by each consumer at each price. Similarly, the market demand curve for labor is determined by adding up the quantity of labor demanded by each firm at each wage, holding constant all other variables that might affect the willingness of firms to hire workers.

Factors That Shift the Market Demand Curve for Labor

In constructing the demand curve for labor, we held constant all variables that would affect the willingness of firms to demand labor—except for the wage. An increase or a decrease in the wage causes *an increase or a decrease in the quantity of labor demanded*, which we show by a movement along the demand curve. If any variable other than the wage changes, the result is *an increase or a decrease in the demand for labor*, which we show by a shift of the demand curve. The five most important variables that cause the labor demand curve to shift are the following:

- **Increases in human capital.** **Human capital** represents the accumulated training and skills that workers possess. For example, a worker with a college education generally has more skills and is more productive than a worker who has only a high

Human capital The accumulated training and skills that workers possess.

school diploma. If workers become more educated and are therefore able to produce more output per day, the demand for their services will increase, shifting the labor demand curve to the right.

- ***Changes in technology.*** As new and better machinery and equipment are developed, workers become more productive. This effect causes the labor demand curve to shift to the right over time.

- ***Changes in the price of the product.*** The marginal revenue product of labor depends on the price a firm receives for its output. A higher price increases the marginal revenue product and shifts the labor demand curve to the right. A lower price shifts the labor demand curve to the left.

- ***Changes in the quantity of other inputs.*** Workers are able to produce more if they have more machinery and other inputs available to them. The marginal product of labor is higher in countries that provide workers with more machinery and equipment. Over time, workers have had increasing amounts of other inputs available to them, and that has increased their productivity and caused the demand for labor to shift to the right.

- ***Changes in the number of firms in the market.*** If new firms enter the market, the demand for labor will shift to the right. If firms exit the market, the demand for labor will shift to the left. This effect is similar to that which increasing or decreasing the number of consumers in a market has on the demand for a good.

18.2 LEARNING OBJECTIVE   18.2 | Explain how people choose the quantity of labor to supply.

The Supply of Labor

Having discussed the demand for labor, we can now consider the supply of labor. Of the many trade-offs each of us faces in life, one of the most important is how to divide up the 24 hours in the day between labor and leisure. Every hour spent watching television, walking on the beach, or in other forms of leisure is one less hour spent working. Because in devoting an hour to leisure, we give up an hour's earnings from working, the *opportunity cost* of leisure is the wage. The higher the wage we could earn working, the higher the opportunity cost of leisure. Therefore, as the wage increases, we tend to take less leisure and work more. This relationship explains why the labor supply curve for most people is upward sloping, as Figure 18-2 shows.

Figure 18-2

The Labor Supply Curve

As the wage increases, the opportunity cost of leisure increases, causing individuals to supply a greater quantity of labor. Therefore, the labor supply curve is upward sloping.

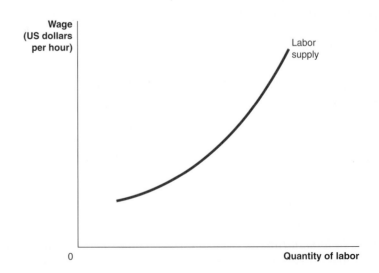

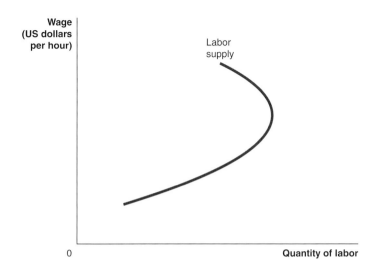

Figure 18-3

A Backward-Bending Labor Supply Curve

As the wage rises, a greater quantity of labor is usually supplied. As the wage climbs above a certain level, the individual is able to afford more leisure even though the opportunity cost of leisure is high. The result may be a smaller quantity of labor supplied.

Although we normally expect the labor supply curve for an individual to be upward sloping, it is possible that at very high wage levels, the supply curve of an individual might be *backward bending*, so that higher wages actually result in a *smaller* quantity of labor supplied, as shown in Figure 18-3. To understand why, recall the definitions of the *substitution effect* and the *income effect*, which is introduced in the previous chapters. The substitution effect of a price change refers to the fact that an increase in price makes a good more expensive *relative* to other goods. In the case of a wage change, the substitution effect refers to the fact that an increase in the wage raises the opportunity cost of leisure and causes a worker to devote *more* time to working and less time to leisure.

The income effect of a price change refers to the change in the quantity demanded of a good that results from changes in consumer purchasing power as a result of a price change. An increase in the wage will clearly increase a consumer's purchasing power for any given number of hours worked. For a normal good, the income effect leads to a larger quantity demanded. Because leisure is a normal good, the income effect of a wage increase will cause a worker to devote *less* time to working and more time to leisure. So, the substitution effect of a wage increase causes a worker to supply a larger quantity of labor, but the income effect causes a worker to supply a smaller quantity of labor. Whether a worker supplies more or less labor following a wage increase depends on whether the substitution effect is larger than the income effect. Figure 18-3 shows the typical case of the substitution effect being larger than the income effect at low levels of wages—so the worker supplies a larger quantity of labor as the wage rises—and the income effect being larger than the substitution effect at high levels of wages—so the worker supplies a smaller quantity of labor as the wage rises. For example, suppose a lawyer has become quite successful and can charge clients very high fees. Or suppose a musical band has become very popular and receives a large payment for every concert it performs. In these cases, there is a high opportunity cost for the lawyer to turn down another client to take a longer vacation or for the band to turn down another concert. But because their incomes are already very high, they may decide to give up additional income for more leisure. For the lawyer or the band, the income effect is larger than the substitution effect, and a higher wage causes them to supply *less* labor.

The Market Supply Curve of Labor

We can determine the market supply curve of labor in the same way we determine a market supply curve of a good. Earlier, we saw that the market supply curve of a good is determined by adding up the quantity of the good supplied by each firm at each price.

Similarly, the market supply curve of labor is determined by adding up the quantity of labor supplied by each worker at each wage, holding constant all other variables that might affect the willingness of workers to supply labor.

Factors That Shift the Market Supply Curve of Labor

In constructing the market supply curve of labor, we hold constant all other variables that would affect the willingness of workers to supply labor, except the wage. If any of these other variables change, the market supply curve will shift. The following are the three most important variables that cause the market supply curve of labor to shift:

- *Increases in population.* As the population grows because of natural increase and immigration, the supply curve of labor shifts to the right. The effects of immigration on labor supply are largest in the markets for unskilled workers. In some Arab countries in the Gulf, for example, the majority of taxi drivers and workers in hotels and restaurants are immigrants. Some supporters of reducing immigration argue that wages in these jobs have been depressed by the increased supply of labor from immigrants.

- *Changing demographics.* *Demographics* refers to the composition of the population. The more people who are between the ages of 16 and 65, the greater the quantity of labor supplied. According to the United Nations' *Population and Development Report* (2005), the rapid decline in infant mortality rates and the increase in life expectancy in the Arab world led to a change in the age structure of the population. In particular, the ratio of the economically active population (aged 15 to 64) has dramatically increased between 1980 and 2000. The biggest population increase occurred in the age group 25 to 64. This group increased from some 55.9 million in 1980 to 108.7 million in 2000, and is projected to reach 194 million in 2020. The percentage of this group in the total population increased from 32.9 percent in 1980 to 37.9 percent in 2000, and is projected to rise to 45 percent in 2020. Adding the age group 15 to 24, it is expected that by 2020 the economically active population will be more than 60 percent of the total population.

  Therefore, the Arab world's labor force is rapidly growing. So, the labor supply curve of the Arab world—as a block—is gradually shifting to the right, and will continue doing so in the 10 years ahead. In contrast, a low birth rate in Japan has resulted in an aging population. The number of working-age people in Japan actually began to decline during the 1990s, causing the labor supply curve to shift to the left.

  A related demographic issue is the changing role of women in the labor force. Despite an increase in the percentage of women in the labor force, it is still far below that of men in all Arab economies. According to a 2009 report by the Arab Labor Organization, the *labor force participation* of women increased to 26 percent in 2008. The increase in women's participation increases the supply of labor in the Arab world.

- *Changing alternatives.* The labor supply in any particular labor market depends, in part, on the opportunities available in other labor markets. For example, the construction bust in 2009 in the Gulf reduced the opportunities for civil engineers. Many workers left this market—causing the labor supply curve to shift to the left—and entered other markets, causing the labor supply curves to shift to the right in those markets. People who have lost jobs or who have low incomes may be eligible for unemployment insurance and other payments from the government in some countries. The more generous these payments are, the less pressure unemployed workers have to quickly find another job.

18.3 | Explain how equilibrium wages are determined in labor markets.

Equilibrium in the Labor Market

In Figure 18-4, we bring labor demand and labor supply together to determine equilibrium in the labor market. We can use demand and supply to analyze changes in the equilibrium wage and the level of employment for the entire labor market, or we can use it to analyze markets for different types of labor, such as football players or college professors.

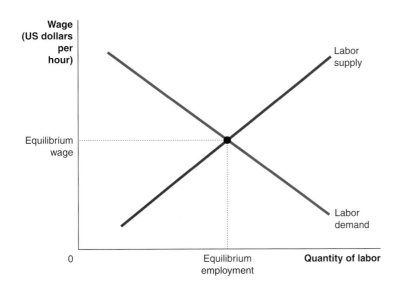

Figure 18-4

Equilibrium in the Labor Market

As in other markets, equilibrium in the labor market occurs where the demand curve for labor and the supply curve of labor intersect.

The Effect on Equilibrium Wages of a Shift in Labor Demand

In many labor markets, increases over time in labor productivity will cause the demand for labor to increase. As Figure 18-5 shows, if labor supply is unchanged, an increase in labor demand will increase both the equilibrium wage and the number of workers employed.

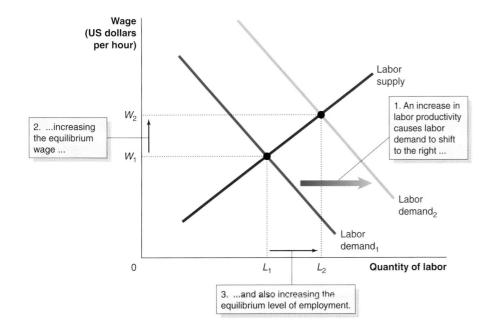

Figure 18-5

The Effect of an Increase in Labor Demand

Increases in labor demand will cause the equilibrium wage and the equilibrium level of employment to rise.
1. If the productivity of workers rises, the marginal revenue product increases, causing the labor demand curve to shift to the right.
2. The equilibrium wage rises from W_1 to W_2.
3. The equilibrium level of employment rises from L_1 to L_2.

Making the Connection | Will Your Future Income Depend on Which Courses You Take in College?

Most people realize the value of a college education. Why do college graduates earn more than others? The obvious answer would seem to be that a college education provides skills that increase productivity. Some economists, though, advocate an alternative explanation, known as the *signaling hypothesis*, first proposed by Nobel laureate A. Michael Spence of Stanford University in the United States. This hypothesis is based on the idea that job applicants will always have more information than will potential employers about how productive the applicants are likely to be. Although employers attempt through job interviews and background checks to distinguish 'good workers' from 'bad workers,' they are always looking for more information.

According to the signaling hypothesis, employers see a college education as a signal that workers possess certain desirable characteristics: self-discipline, the ability to meet deadlines, and the ability to make a sustained effort. Even if these characteristics are not related to the specifics of a particular job, employers value them because they usually lead to success in any activity. People generally believe that college graduates possess these characteristics, so employers often require a college degree for their best-paying jobs. In this view, the signal that a college education sends about a person's inherent characteristics—which the person presumably already possessed *before* entering college—is much more important than any skills the person may have learned in college. Or, as a college math professor of one of the authors put it (only half-jokingly), "The purpose of college is to show employers that you can succeed at something that's boring and hard."

Recently, though, several economic studies have provided evidence that the higher incomes of college graduates are due to their greater productivity rather than the signal that a college degree sends to employers. Orley Ashenfelter and Cecilia Rouse of Princeton University studied the relationship between schooling and income among 700 pairs of identical twins. Identical twins have identical genes, so differences in their inherent abilities should be relatively small. Therefore, if they have different numbers of years in school, differences in their earnings should be mainly due to the effect of schooling on their productivity. Ashenfelter and Rouse found that identical twins had returns of about 9 percent per additional year of schooling, enough to account for most of the gap in income between high school graduates and college graduates.

Sources: Orley Ashenfelter and Cecilia Rouse, "Income, Schooling, and Ability: Evidence from a New Sample of Identical Twins," *Quarterly Journal of Economics*, Vol. 113, No. 1 (February 1998), pp. 253–284.

YOUR TURN: Test your understanding by doing related problem 3.3 on page 612 at the end of this chapter.

Economists who studied the impact of education on earnings found that hard courses such as science and math significantly increase after-college earnings.

The Effect on Equilibrium Wages of a Shift in Labor Supply

What is the effect on the equilibrium wage of an increase in labor supply due to population growth? As Figure 18-6 shows, if labor demand is unchanged, an increase in labor supply will decrease the equilibrium wage but increase the number of workers employed.

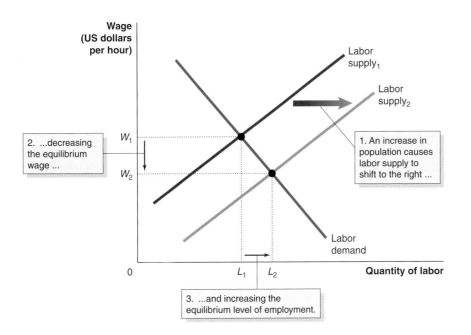

Figure 18-6

The Effect of an Increase in Labor Supply

Increases in labor supply will cause the equilibrium wage to fall but the equilibrium level of employment to rise.
1. As population increases, the labor supply curve shifts to the right.
2. The equilibrium wage falls from W_1 to W_2.
3. The equilibrium level of employment increases from L_1 to L_2.

Whether the wage rises in a market depends on whether demand increases faster than supply. For example, after the success of Walt Disney's animated film *The Lion King* in 1994, most movie studios in the U.S. increased production of animated films, increasing the demand for animators much faster than the supply of animators was increasing. The annual salary for a top animator rose from about US$125,000 in 1994 to US$550,000 in 1999. These high salaries led more people with artistic ability to choose to get training as film animators, causing the supply of animators to increase after 1999. Several of the animated films released between 1999 and 2001 failed to earn profits, which caused some companies to stop making these films, thereby decreasing the demand for animators. The decrease in demand for animators and the increase in supply caused the salaries of top animators to fall from US$550,000 in 1999 to US$225,000 in 2002.

Making the Connection | Restricting Immigration and the Supply of Labor in the Arab Gulf

What do you think happens when immigration increases labor supply in a particular market? The Nobel Prize-winning economist Paul A. Samuelson states in his most influential textbook, *Economics* (1948), that as immigrants increase the supply of a particular type of labor, the wage paid to that group (immigrants and non-immigrants alike) falls. This leads to the reasonable conclusion that immigration restrictions would tend "to keep wages high." The story then is two-sided. On the one hand, cheap, unlimited labor supply can be a catalyst for fast economic growth. Unrestricted immigration helps keep inflation low, boosts rents and housing values, and benefits the average local citizen. "Immigration provides overall economic gains to a country," wrote the economist Albert Saiz, in a 2003 article for the Federal Reserve Bank of Philadelphia. But on the downside, a surge of immigrants will increase the supply of such workers, driving down wages at the expense of local labor with similar skills. More importantly, as many see it today, immigrants can displace non-immigrants and make it harder for the latter to find jobs. This has become a whole area of research and debate in all parts of the world that receives immigrants.

(Continued)

The Arab world can be divided into two groups of countries: the group of labor exporting–capital importing countries, and the group of labor importing–capital exporting countries. Countries such as Egypt, Jordan, Tunisia, and Lebanon are net exporters of labor, while the oil-rich countries of the Gulf are net importers of labor. Not only do the latter receive millions of immigrant workers from the former every year, but they also tend to rely heavily on cheap imported labor from South Asia and the Indian subcontinent.

For more than three decades, expatriates have outnumbered nationals in most of the Gulf Cooperation Council (GCC) countries. Oman has the lowest percentage of non-nationals who have constituted almost one-quarter of the population in the past decade. On the other end of the scale lies the UAE, with almost three-quarters of its total population and two-thirds of the labor force being non-nationals. Moreover, non-nationals absorb 98 percent of the private sector jobs. In Saudi Arabia, the largest GCC country, foreigners constitute about one-third of the population, 70 percent of the total labor force, and 95 percent of the private sector labor force.

Foreign labor has helped in the rapid transformation of the infrastructure as well as institutional development in the Gulf, and immigrants were generally welcomed until a few years ago. The spectacular economic growth that many Gulf countries are experiencing today is undeniably due in part to their ability to import cheap, unlimited labor. Over a decade ago, Gulf countries started announcing new policies to help the nationalization of the labor force and the reduction in the expatriate population and workers.

In 2004, a UN survey of the GCC countries revealed that four out of the six countries considered that current immigration levels were too high and threatened their economies. Kuwait, Oman, Saudi Arabia, and the UAE announced new rules in order to tighten their foreign labor policies. Kuwait has perhaps the strictest policy to lower the permanent settlement of immigrants, and its policy for granting citizenship is highly restrictive. In addition, Kuwait also has a policy to lower the number of dependents of migrant workers. Bahrain and Qatar, on the other end, announced satisfaction over the level of foreign labor they currently have, with Bahrain announcing that no government intervention is expected in the near future. The full economic effects of nationalization policies and restricting expatriate labor are yet to be seen over the next two decades.

The construction industry is one of the many industries in the UAE that rely on immigrant workers.

Sources: N. Shah, "Restrictive Labor Immigration Policies in the Oil-Rich Gulf: Effectiveness and Implications for Sending Asian Countries," United Nations Expert Group Meeting on International Migration and Development in the Arab Region, UN/POP/EGM/2006/03, May, 2006; Nell Henderson "Effect of Immigration on Jobs: Wages Is Difficult for Economists to Nail Down," *Washington Post*, April 15, 2006; Paul A. Samuelson, *Economics: An Introductory Analysis*, McGraw-Hill, 1948

18.4 LEARNING OBJECTIVE

18.4 | Use demand and supply analysis to explain how compensating differentials, discrimination, and labor unions cause wages to differ.

Explaining Differences in Wages

A key conclusion of our discussion of the labor market is that the equilibrium wage equals the marginal revenue product of labor. The more productive workers are and the higher the price workers' output can be sold for, the higher the wages workers will receive. At the beginning of the chapter, we raised the question of why top football players are paid so much more than college professors. We are now ready to use demand and supply analysis to answer this question. Figure 18-7 shows the demand and supply curves for top football players and the demand and supply curves for college professors.

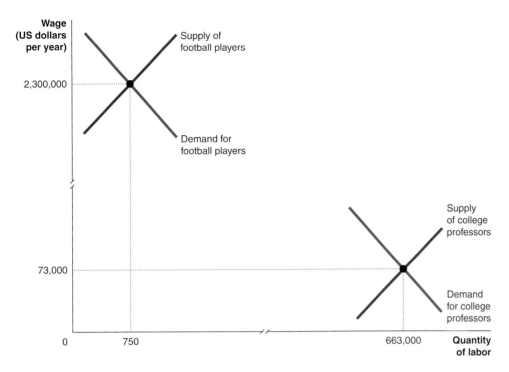

Figure 18-7

Football Players are Paid More than College Professors

The marginal revenue product of football players is very high, and the supply of people with the ability to play top-flight football is low. The result is that top-flight football players receive an average wage of US$2,300,000. The marginal revenue product of college professors is much lower, and the supply of people with the ability to be college professors is much higher. The result is that U.S. college professors receive an average wage of US$73,000, far below that of football players.

Consider first the marginal revenue product of football players, which is the additional revenue a team owner will receive from hiring one more player. Football players are hired to produce football games that are then sold to fans who pay admission to football stadiums and to radio and television stations that broadcast the games. Because a top football teams can sell each football game for a large amount, the marginal revenue product of football players is high. The supply of people with the ability to play top football is also very limited. As a result, the average annual salary of a top flight football player is about US$2,300,000.

The marginal revenue product of college professors is much lower than for football players. College professors are hired to produce college educations that are then sold to students and their parents. Although one year's college tuition is quite high at many colleges, hiring one more professor allows a college to admit at most a few more students. So, the marginal revenue product of a college professor is much lower than the marginal revenue product of a football player. There are also many more people who possess the skills to be a college professor than possess the skills to be a top football player. As a result, in a country like the U.S., it's 663,000 college professors are paid an average salary of about US$73,000.

This still leaves unanswered the question raised at the beginning of this chapter: Why is Real Madrid willing to pay Cristiano Ronaldo more than Manchester United were? Ronaldo's marginal product—which we can think of as the extra games a team will win by employing him—should be about the same in Real Madrid as it was in Manchester United. But his *marginal revenue product* will be higher in Real Madrid. The explanation is that, by having Ronaldo in its team, Real Madrid expects to sell more game tickets and to have more viewers for its games on television. Therefore, Real Madrid expects to be able to raise this difference in salary through higher game sales. That can explain why Real Madrid was willing to pay Ronaldo US$17 million per year when he had made 'only' US$8 million with the Manchester United.

Differences in marginal revenue products are the most important factor in explaining differences in wages, but they are not the whole story. To provide a more complete explanation for differences in wages, we must take into account three important aspects of labor markets: compensating differentials, discrimination, and labor unions. We begin with compensating differentials.

Why does Yusra earn more today relative to the typical actor than stars did in the 1940s?

Making the Connection | Technology and the Earnings of 'Superstars'

The gap between the 20 million Egyptian pounds Yusra is paid to star in a movie and the salary paid to an actor in a minor role is much greater than the gap between the salaries paid during the 1940s and 50s to stars such as Layla Murad and Sabah and the salaries paid to secondary players. In fact, in most areas of sports and entertainment, the highest-paid performers—the 'superstars'—now have much higher incomes relative to other members of their professions than was true a few decades ago.

The increase in the relative incomes of superstars is mainly due to technological advances. The spread of cable television has increased the number of potential viewers of movies, but many of those viewers will watch only if Yusra or Layla Elwi is the star. This increases the value of Yusra or Layla Elwi in a film and, therefore, increases their marginal revenue product and the salary they can earn.

With DVDs, Internet-streaming videos, and pay-per-view cable, the value to movie studios of producing a hit movie has risen greatly. Not surprisingly, movie studios have also increased their willingness to pay large salaries to stars like Yusra because they think these superstars will significantly raise the chances of a film being successful.

This process has been going on for a long time. For instance, before the invention of the motion picture, anyone who wanted to see a play had to attend the theatre and see a live performance. Limits on the number of people who could see the best actors and actresses perform created an opportunity for many more people to succeed in the acting profession, and the gap between the salaries earned by the best actors and the salaries earned by average actors was relatively small. Today, when a hit movie starring Yusra appears on DVD, millions of people will buy or rent it, and they will not be forced to spend money to see a lesser actress, as their great-great-grandparents might have been.

Compensating Differentials

Compensating differentials Higher wages that compensate workers for unpleasant aspects of a job.

Suppose Ahmad runs a video rental store and acquires a reputation for being a bad boss who yells at his workers and is generally unpleasant. Two blocks away, Ali also runs a video rental store, but Ali is always very polite to his workers. We would expect in these circumstances that Ahmed will have to pay a higher wage than Ali to attract and retain workers. Higher wages that compensate workers for unpleasant aspects of a job are called **compensating differentials**.

If working in a dynamite factory requires the same degree of training and education as working in a food processing factory but is much more dangerous, a larger number of workers will want to work making food than will want to work making dynamite. As a consequence, the wages of dynamite workers will be higher than the wages of food workers. We can think of the difference in wages as being the price of risk. As each worker decides on his or her willingness to assume risk and decides how much higher the wage must be to compensate for assuming more risk, wages will adjust so that dynamite factories will end up paying wages that are just high enough to compensate workers who choose to work there for the extra risk they assume. Only when workers in dynamite factories have been fully compensated with higher wages for the additional risk they assume will dynamite companies be able to attract enough workers.

One surprising implication of compensating differentials is that *laws protecting the health and safety of workers may not make workers better off*. To see this, suppose that dynamite factories pay wages of US$25 per hour, and food factories pay wages of US$20 per hour, with the US$5 difference in wages being a compensating differential for the greater risk of working in a dynamite factory. Suppose that the government passes a law regulating the manufacture of dynamite in order to improve safety in dynamite factories. As a result of this law, dynamite factories are no longer any more dangerous than food factories. Once this happens, the wages in dynamite factories will decline to US$20 per hour, the same as in food factories. Are workers in dynamite factories any better or worse off? Before the law was passed, their wages were US$25 per hour, but US$5 per hour was a compensating differential for the extra risk they were exposed to. Now their wages are only US$20 per hour, but the extra risk has been eliminated. The conclusion seems to be that dynamite workers are no better off as a result of the safety legislation.

This conclusion is only true, though, if the compensating differential actually does compensate workers fully for the additional risk. George Akerlof of the University of California, Berkeley, and William Dickens of the Brookings Institution have argued that the psychological principle known as *cognitive dissonance* might cause workers to underestimate the true risk of their jobs. According to this principle, people prefer to think of themselves as intelligent and rational and tend to reject evidence that seems to contradict this image. Because working in a very hazardous job may seem irrational, workers in such jobs may refuse to believe that the jobs really are hazardous. Akerlof and Dickens present evidence that workers in chemical plants producing benzene and workers in nuclear power plants underestimate the hazards of their jobs. If this is true, the wages of these workers will not be high enough to compensate them fully for the risk they have assumed. So, in this situation, safety legislation may make workers better off.

Discrimination

In many countries males, on average, earn more than females. One possible explanation for this is **economic discrimination**, which involves paying a person a lower wage, or excluding a person from an occupation, on the basis of an irrelevant characteristic such as race or gender.

Economic discrimination Paying a person a lower wage or excluding a person from an occupation on the basis of an irrelevant characteristic such as race or gender.

If employers discriminate by hiring only males for high-paying jobs or by paying males higher wages than females working the same jobs, males would have higher earnings. However, excluding females from certain jobs or paying one group more than another is illegal in some Arab countries. In Egypt, gender discrimination is not tolerated by the relatively new Egyptian labor law (no.12 of 2003). Article 88 states: "All employment regulations and policies should apply to female employees equalizing their status to that of their male counterparts without discrimination as long as their work conditions are [identical]." Nevertheless, it is possible that employers are ignoring the law and practicing economic discrimination.

Most economists believe that wage gaps, usually described as economic discrimination, can be explained by three main factors:

1 Differences in education

2 Differences in experience

3 Differing preferences for jobs

Differences in Education Some of the difference between the incomes of males and the incomes of females can be also explained by differences in education.

Differences in Experience Women are much more likely than men to leave their jobs for a period of time after having a child. Women with several children will sometimes have several interruptions in their careers. Some women leave the workforce for several years until their children are of school age. As a result, on average, women with children have less workforce experience than do men of the same age. Because workers with greater experience are, on average, more productive, the difference in levels of experience helps to explain some of the difference in earnings between men and women. One indication of this is that, on average, married women in the United States earn about 39 percent less than married men, but women who have never been married—and whose careers are less likely to have been interrupted—earn only about 10 percent less than men who have never been married.

Differing Preferences for Jobs Significant differences exist between the types of jobs held by women and men. Women are also likely to be overrepresented in low to average paying jobs, while men are overrepresented in higher paying jobs. While this pattern, if it exists, could be explained by women being excluded from some (high paying) occupations, it is also likely that this pattern reflects differences in job preferences between men and women. For example, because many women interrupt their careers—at least briefly—when their children are born, they are more likely to take jobs where work experience is less important. Women may also be more likely to take jobs, such as teaching, that allow them to be home in the afternoons when their children return from school. This is particularly true in the Arab world, where men—on average—earn higher income than women. This can be partly explained by the fact that working Arab women usually prefer less demanding, shorter-hours jobs. These jobs, on average, yield lower incomes.

The Gender Gap and the Labour Force in the Arab world Education contributes directly to the growth of national income by improving the productive capacities of the labor force. There have been a number of improvements in the Arab world towards education gender equality. Primary school enrollment is high or universal in most Arab countries and gender gaps in secondary school enrollment have already disappeared in several countries (see Figure 18-8). Women in the Arab world today are more likely to enroll in universities than they were in the past (see Figure 18-9); however these ratios are still low in many countries compared to other regions of the world.

Figure 18-8

Secondary School Enrollment Rate

The Arab world has almost closed the gender gap in secondary education.

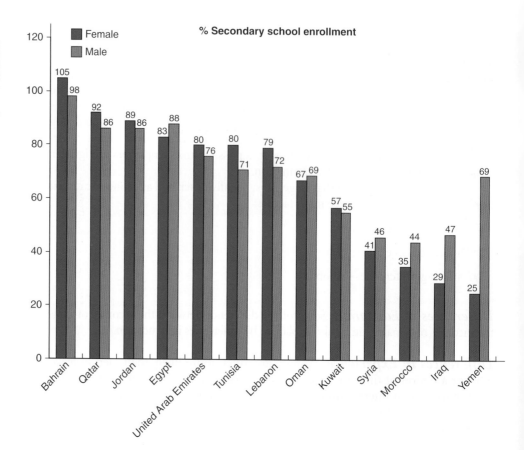

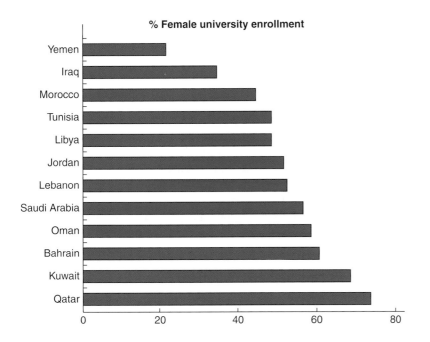

Figure 18-9

Percentage of Female University Enrollment

More women are enrolling in colleges and universities. This means more women are joining the labor force.

Literacy is the key to empowering women and to improving families' well-being. The Arab world has experienced a tremendous expansion in female education, outpacing other regions. However, that does not mean a complete success; challenges are still many. To date, Arab countries generally still have lower levels of women's literacy and labor force participation than other regions in the world with similar income levels. The region's economic structure and its conservative culture, in which traditional gender roles are strongly enforced, is largely responsible for such a gender gap.

As Figure 18-10 shows, some countries, such as Yemen, Morocco, Egypt, and Algeria are still struggling with high illiteracy rates in general. Other Arab countries, such as Jordan, Bahrain, and Lebanon were more successful in eradicating most of the illiteracy. Figure 18-11 depicts the gender gap in illiteracy and ranks countries according to the ratio of female to male illiteracy rates. At odds with the startling progress Jordan and Lebanon have made in fighting illiteracy and closing the gender

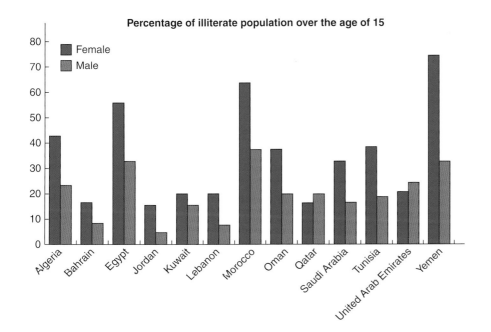

Figure 18-10

Illiteracy Rates Among Population Aged 15 or Above

High illiteracy rates among adults is still a problem in many Arab countries.

Figure 18-11

Ratio of Female to Male Illiteracy

Some Arab countries have more illiterate males than females, but in many others most of the remaining illiteracy is among women.

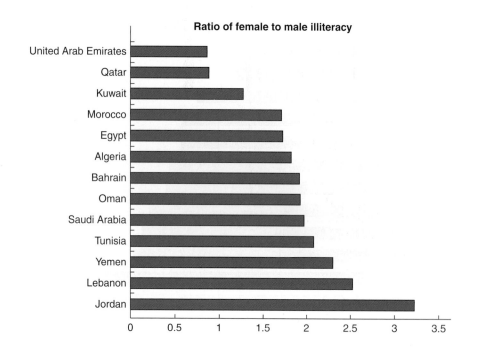

Ratio of female to male illiteracy

gap in secondary school education (Figure 18-8), we find that the two countries are ranked at the top for gender literacy inequality. In Jordan for example, despite the fact that illiteracy is only 16 percent among women aged 15 and above, the lowest in the Arab world, for each illiterate male there are three illiterate females. Similarly, this ratio is 2.5 for Lebanon. This means that most of the remaining illiteracy in society is among women. At the other end of the spectrum, Kuwait has almost closed the gender illiteracy gap with a ratio slightly higher than one. Qatar and the UAE, amazingly, have closed the gap with a ratio less than one; the two countries have more male illiterates than females.

Men in the Arab world are more likely to have direct access to waged employment and control over wealth, while women are largely economically dependent upon male family members. The region's oil-based economy reinforces the region's gender roles. The use of capital-intensive technologies that require few workers, along with relatively high wages for men, have depressed women's participation in the labor force. In the Gulf states, women's employment options have been limited to a small number of occupations and professions, perceived to be socially acceptable, while leaving many jobs to be filled by imported female laborers. In addition, the current high unemployment rates among men in most Arab countries make it harder for women to compete in the male-dominated job markets; hence women's unemployment rates are higher than those of men in the region. In Saudi Arabia, where Saudi women account for only 7 percent of the labor force, the unemployment rate for women is usually more than double that for men.

Despite a steady increase in women's participation in the labor force in many Arab countries in the past few decades, this figure is still low. On average, only 20 percent of women aged 15 and older in MENA countries are in the labor force; the lowest level of any world region. As can be seen from Figure 18-12, the highest levels of female labor force participation in the Arab world are found in Lebanon, Morocco, and Yemen, where women constitute more than 25 percent of the labor force; but this is still lower than rates found in developed and developing countries alike. In France and the U.S., for example, women make up 45 and 60 percent of the labor force, respectively. In Indonesia, the home to the world's largest Muslim population, women make up 38 percent of the labor force. Except for Kuwait where the participation of women is approaching 25 percent of the labor force, the lowest rates of

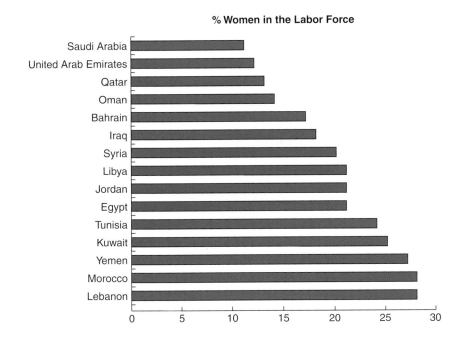

% Women in the Labor Force

Figure 18-12

Women's Participation in the Labor Force in Selected Arab Countries

Although more Arab women are joining the labor force, the female participation rate is still far below any other region in the world.

labor force participation are seen among national women of the countries of the Gulf Cooperation Council.

Women who live in countries with a large agricultural sector, such as Egypt, Syria, and Yemen, tend to work mainly in that sector. Most of the Arab women who work outside the agricultural sector are college-educated professionals employed mainly in government. A smaller share of women work in factories, and many lack the educational qualifications of factory workers in countries such as China.

However, the situation in the region is slowly changing. Women activists, who generally come from the educated segments of society, are challenging the status quo; demanding equality in the family and society; and calling for women's economic, political, and social empowerment. In addition, countries are dealing with economic changes, such as the rising cost of living, that require women to become more active outside the home.

Solved Problem | 18-4

Is 'Comparable Worth' Legislation the Answer to Closing the Gap between Men's and Women's Pay?

As we have seen, either because of discrimination or differing preferences, certain jobs are filled primarily by men, and other jobs are filled primarily by women. On average, the 'men's jobs' have higher wages than the 'women's jobs.' Some observers have argued that many 'men's jobs' are more highly paid than 'women's jobs,' despite the jobs being comparable in terms of the education and skills required and the working conditions involved. These observers have argued that the earnings gap between men and women could be closed at least partially if the government required employers to pay the same wages for jobs that have *comparable worth*. Many economists are skeptical of these proposals because they believe allowing markets to determine wages results in a more efficient outcome.

Suppose that electricians are currently being paid a market equilibrium wage of US$700 per week, and dental technicians are being paid a market equilibrium wage of

US$400 per week. Comparable-worth legislation is passed, and a study finds that an electrician and a dental technician have comparable jobs, so employers will now be required to pay workers in both jobs US$550 per week. Analyze the effects of this requirement on the market for electricians and on the market for dental technicians. Be sure to use demand and supply graphs.

SOLVING THE PROBLEM:

Step 1: **Review the chapter material.** This problem is about economic discrimination, so you may want to review the section "Discrimination," which begins on page 595.

Step 2: **Draw the graphs.** We saw in Chapter 4 that when the government sets the price in a market, the result is a surplus or a shortage, depending on whether the government-mandated price is above or below the competitive market equilibrium. A wage of US$550 per week is below the market wage for electricians and above the market wage for dental technicians. Therefore, we expect the requirement to result in a shortage of electricians and a surplus of dental technicians.

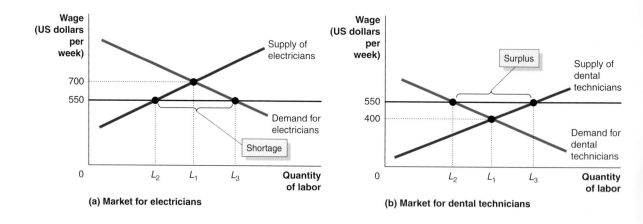

(a) Market for electricians   (b) Market for dental technicians

In panel (a), without comparable-worth legislation, the equilibrium wage for electricians is US$700, and the equilibrium quantity of electricians hired is L_1. Setting the wage for electricians below equilibrium at US$550 reduces the quantity of labor supplied in this occupation from L_1 to L_2 but increases the quantity of labor demanded by employers from L_1 to L_3. The result is a shortage of electricians equal to $L_3 - L_2$, as shown by the bracket in the graph.

In panel (b), without comparable-worth legislation, the equilibrium wage for dental technicians is US$400, and the equilibrium quantity of dental technicians hired is L_1. Setting the wage for dental technicians above equilibrium at US$550 increases the quantity of labor supplied in this occupation from L_1 to L_3 but reduces the quantity of labor demanded by employers from L_1 to L_2. The result is a surplus of dental technicians equal to $L_3 - L_2$, as shown by the bracket in the graph.

EXTRA CREDIT: Most economists are skeptical of government attempts to set wages and prices, as comparable-worth legislation would require. Supporters of comparable-worth legislation, by contrast, see differences between men's and women's wages as being mainly due to discrimination and are looking to government legislation as a solution.

YOUR TURN: For more practice, do related problems 4.7 and 4.8 on page 613 at the end of this chapter.

The Difficulty of Measuring Discrimination When two people are paid different wages, discrimination may be the explanation. But differences in productivity or preferences may also be an explanation. Labor economists have attempted to measure what part of differences in wages between men and women is due to discrimination and what part is due to other factors. Unfortunately, it is difficult to measure precisely differences in productivity or in worker preferences. As a result, we can't know exactly the extent of economic discrimination in the Arab world today. Most economists do believe, however, that most of the differences in wages between different groups are due to factors other than discrimination.

Does It Pay to Discriminate? Many economists argue that economic discrimination is no longer a major factor in labor markets in many countries. One reason is that *employers who discriminate pay an economic penalty.* To see why this is true, let's consider a simplified example. Suppose that men and women are equally qualified to be airline pilots and that, initially, airlines do not discriminate. In Figure 18-13, we divide the airlines into two groups: "A" airlines and "B" airlines. If neither group of airlines discriminates, we would expect them to pay an equal wage of US$1,100 per week to both men and women pilots. Now suppose that "A" airlines decide to discriminate and to fire all their women pilots. This action will reduce the supply of pilots to these airlines and, as shown in panel (a), that will force up the wage from US$1,100 to US$1,300. At the same time, as women fired from the jobs with "A" airlines apply for jobs with "B" airlines, the supply of pilots to "B" airlines will increase, and the equilibrium wage will fall from US$1,100 to US$900. All the women pilots will end up being employed at the non-discriminating airlines and be paid a lower wage than the men who are employed by the discriminating airlines.

But this situation cannot persist for two reasons. First, male pilots employed by "B" airlines will also receive the lower wage. This lower wage gives them an incentive to quit their jobs at "B" airlines and apply at "A" airlines, which will shift the labor supply curve for "B" airlines to the left and the labor supply curve for "A" airlines to the right. Second, "A" airlines are paying US$1,300 per week to hire pilots who are no more productive than the pilots being paid US$900 per week by "B" airlines. As a result, "B" airlines will have lower costs and will be able to charge lower prices. Eventually, "A" airlines will lose their customers to "B" airlines and be driven out of business. The market will have imposed

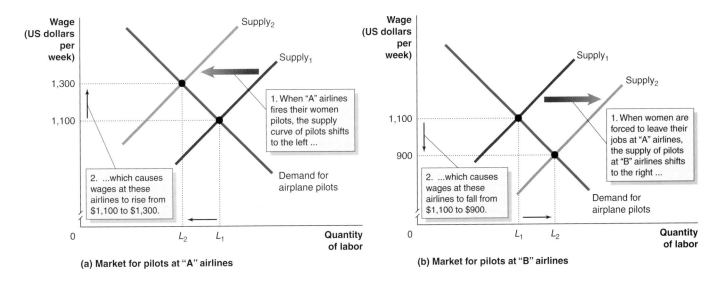

(a) Market for pilots at "A" airlines

(b) Market for pilots at "B" airlines

Figure 18-13 | Discrimination and Wages

In this hypothetical example, we assume that initially neither "A" airlines nor "B" airlines discriminate. As a result, men and women pilots receive the same wage of US$1,100 per week at both groups of airlines. We then assume that "A" airlines discriminates by firing all their women pilots. Panel (a) shows that this reduces the supply of pilots to "A" airlines and raises the wage paid by these airlines from

US$1,100 to US$1,300. Panel (b) shows that this increases the supply of pilots to "B" airlines and lowers the wage paid by these airlines from US$1,100 to US$900. All the women pilots will end up being employed at the nondiscriminating airlines and will be paid a lower wage than the men who are employed by the discriminating airlines.

an economic penalty on the discriminating airlines. So, discrimination will not persist, and the wages of men and women pilots will become equal.

Can we conclude from this analysis that competition in markets will eliminate all economic discrimination? Unfortunately, this optimistic conclusion is not completely accurate. Non-discriminating competitors will not drive the discriminating firms out of business. Why not? One factor is *negative feedback loops*. Our analysis in Figure 18-13 assumed that men and women pilots were equally qualified. However, if discrimination makes it difficult for women to find employment in a particular occupation, her incentive to be trained to enter that occupation is reduced.

Consider the legal profession as an example. Few decades ago in the Arab world, women were not appointed as judges or persecutors, and could not even work as independent defense lawyers. In fact, at the time of writing, women in many Arab countries such as Egypt, for example, are still struggling for the right to be appointed as court judges. It has always remained a 'solely' male profession and continues to be. Facing such bleak job prospects, it's not surprising that relatively few women entered law school. As a result, a law firm that did not discriminate would have been unable to act like the non-discriminating airlines in our example by hiring women lawyers at a lower salary and using this cost advantage to drive discriminating law firms out of business. In this situation, an unfortunate feedback loop was in place: Few women prepared to become lawyers because many law firms discriminated against women, and non-discriminating law firms were unable to drive discriminating law firms out of business because there were too few women lawyers available. Another example can be found in the medical profession. In the Arab world it is very hard to recall one known female surgeon in any country. The reason is that it is a predominantly male profession. Reputable hospitals would be very reluctant to hire a female surgeon. As a consequence, very few Arab females chose to specialize in surgery when they enter medical school.

Most economists agree that the market imposes an economic penalty on firms that discriminate, but it may take the market a very long time to eliminate discrimination entirely.

Labor Unions

Labor union An organization of employees that has the legal right to bargain with employers about wages and working conditions.

Workers' wages can differ depending on whether the workers are members of labor unions. **Labor unions** are organizations of employees that have the legal right to bargain with employers about wages and working conditions. If a union is unable to reach an agreement with a company, it has the legal right to call a *strike*, which means its members refuse to work until a satisfactory agreement has been reached.

Workers in unions usually receive higher wages than workers who are not in unions. Do union members earn more than nonunion members because they are in unions? The answer might seem to be "yes," but many union workers are in industries, such as automobile manufacturing, in which their marginal revenue products are high, so their wages would be high even if they were not unionized. Economists who have attempted to estimate statistically the impact of unionization on wages have concluded that being in a union increases a worker's wages about 10 percent, holding constant other factors, such as the industry the worker is in. A related question is whether unions raise the total amount of wages received by all workers, whether unionized or not. Because the share of national income received by workers has remained roughly constant over many years, most economists do not believe that unions have raised the total amount of wages received by workers.

18.5 LEARNING OBJECTIVE

18.5 | Discuss the role personnel economics can play in helping firms deal with human resources issues.

Personnel Economics

Traditionally, labor economists have focused on issues such as the effects of labor unions on wages or the determinants of changes in average wages over time. They have spent less time analyzing *human resources issues*, which address how firms hire, train, and promote workers and set their wages and benefits. In recent years, some labor economists, including Edward Lazear of Stanford University and William Neilson of Texas A&M University, in the United States, have begun exploring the application of economic analysis to human resources issues. This new focus has become known as **personnel economics**.

Personnel economics analyzes the link between differences among jobs and differences in the way workers are paid. Jobs have different skill requirements, require more or less interaction with other workers, have to be performed in more or less unpleasant environments, and so on. Firms need to design compensation policies that take into account these differences. Personnel economics also analyzes policies related to other human resources issues, such as promotions, training, and pensions. In this brief overview, we look only at compensation policies.

Personnel economics The application of economic analysis to human resources issues.

Should Workers' Pay Depend on How Much They Work or on How Much They Produce?

One issue personnel economics addresses is when workers should receive *straight-time pay*—a certain wage per hour or salary per week or month—and when they should receive *commission* or *piece-rate pay*—a wage based on how much output they produce.

Suppose, for example, that Aminah owns a car dealership and is trying to decide whether to pay her salespeople a salary of US$800 per week or a commission of US$200 on each car they sell. Figure 18-14 compares the compensation a salesperson would receive under the two systems, according to the number of cars the salesperson sells.

With a straight salary, the salesperson receives US$800 per week, no matter how many cars she sells. This outcome is shown by the horizontal line in Figure 18-14. If she receives a commission of US$200 per car, her compensation will increase with every car she sells. This outcome is shown by the upward-sloping line. A salesperson who sells fewer than 4 cars per week would earn more by receiving a straight salary of US$800 per week. A salesperson who sells more than 4 cars per week would be better off receiving the US$200-per-car commission. We can identify two advantages Aminah would receive from paying her salespeople commissions rather than salaries: she would attract and retain the most productive employees, and she would provide an incentive to her employees to sell more cars.

Suppose that other car dealerships were all paying salaries of US$800 per week. If Aminah pays her employees on commission, any of her employees who are unable to sell at least 4 cars per week can improve their pay by going to work for one of her competitors. By the same token, any salespeople at Aminah's competitors who can sell more than 4 cars per week can raise their pay by quitting and coming to work for Anne. Over time, Anne will find her least productive employees leaving, while she is able to hire new employees who are more productive.

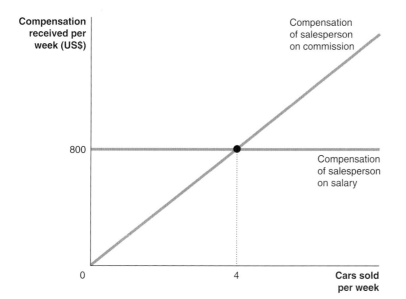

Figure 18-14

Paying Car Salespeople by Salary or by Commission

This figure compares the compensation a car salesperson receives if she is on a straight salary of US$800 per week or if she receives a commission of US$200 for each car she sells. With a straight salary, she receives US$800 per week, no matter how many cars she sells. This outcome is shown by the horizontal line in the figure. If she receives a commission of US$200 per car, her compensation will increase with every car she sells. This outcome is shown by the upward-sloping line. If she sells fewer than 4 cars per week, she would be better off with the US$800 salary. If she sells more than 4 cars per week, she would be better off with the US$200-per-car commission.

Paying a commission also increases the incentive Aminah's salespeople have to sell more cars. If Aminah paid a salary, her employees would receive the same amount no matter how few cars they sold. An employee on salary might decide on a particularly hot or cold day that it was less trouble to stay inside the building than to go out on the car lot to greet potential customers. An employee on commission would know that the additional effort expended on selling more cars would be rewarded with additional compensation.

Other Considerations in Setting Compensation Systems

The discussion so far indicates that companies will find it more profitable to use a commission or piece-rate system of compensation rather than a salary system. In fact, many firms continue to pay their workers salaries, which means they are paying their workers on the basis of how long they work rather than on the basis of how much they produce. Firms may choose a salary system for several good reasons:

- **Difficulty in measuring output.** Often it is difficult to attribute output to any particular worker. For example, projects carried out by an engineering firm may involve teams of workers whose individual contributions are difficult to distinguish. On assembly lines, such as those used in the automobile industry, the amount produced by each worker is determined by the speed of the line, which is set by managers rather than by workers. Managers at many firms perform such a wide variety of tasks that measuring their output would be costly, if it could be done at all.

- **Concerns about quality.** If workers are paid on the basis of the number of units produced, they may become less concerned about quality. An office assistant who is paid on the basis of the quantity of letters typed may become careless about how many typos the letters contain. In some cases, there are ways around this problem; for example, the assistant may be required to correct the mistakes on his or her own time without pay.

- **Worker dislike of risk.** Piece-rate or commission systems of compensation increase the risk to workers because sometimes output declines for reasons not connected to the worker's effort. For example, in the summer, in the Arab Gulf, many residents leave on vacation to escape the extremely hot weather, so few customers show up at Aminah's auto dealership. Through no fault of their own, her salespeople have great difficulty selling any cars. If the salespeople are paid a salary, their income would not be affected, but if they are on commission, their incomes would drop to low levels. The flip side of this is that by paying salaries, Aminah assumes a greater risk. During the summer, her payroll expenses will remain high even though her sales are low. With a commission system of compensation, her payroll expenses will decline along with her sales. But owners of firms are typically better able to bear risk than are workers. As a result, some firms may find that workers who would earn more under a commission system will prefer to receive a salary to reduce their risk. In these situations, paying a lower salary may reduce the firm's payroll expenses compared with what they would have been under a commission or piece-rate system.

Personnel economics is a relatively new field, but it holds great potential for helping firms deal more efficiently with human relations issues.

18.6 LEARNING OBJECTIVE

18.6 | Show how equilibrium prices are determined in the markets for capital and natural resources.

The Markets for Capital and Natural Resources

The approach we have used to analyze the market for labor can also be used to analyze the markets for other factors of production. We have seen that the demand for labor is determined by the marginal revenue product of labor because the value to a firm from hiring another worker equals the increase in the firm's revenue from selling the additional output it can produce by hiring the worker. The demand for capital and natural resources is determined in a similar way.

The Market for Capital

Physical capital includes machines, equipment, and buildings. Firms sometimes buy capital, but we will focus on situations in which firms rent capital. A chocolate manufacturer renting a warehouse and an airline leasing a plane are examples of firms renting capital. Like the demand for labor, the demand for capital is a derived demand. When a firm is considering increasing its capital by, for example, using another machine, the value it receives equals the increase in the firm's revenue from selling the additional output it can produce by using the machine. The *marginal revenue product of capital* is the change in the firm's revenue as a result of employing one more unit of capital, such as a machine. We have seen that the marginal revenue product of labor curve is the demand curve for labor. Similarly, the marginal revenue product of capital curve is also the demand curve for capital.

Firms producing capital goods face increasing marginal costs, so the supply curve of capital goods is upward sloping, as are the supply curves for other goods and services. Figure 18-15 shows equilibrium in the market for capital. In equilibrium, suppliers of capital receive a rental price equal to the marginal revenue product of capital, just as suppliers of labor receive a wage equal to the marginal revenue product of labor.

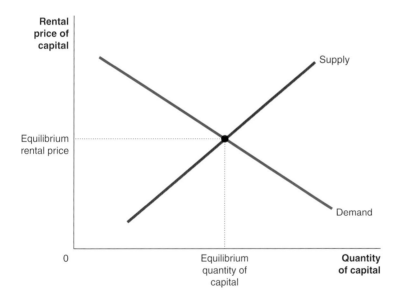

Figure 18-15

Equilibrium in the Market for Capital

The rental price of capital is determined by equilibrium in the market for capital. In equilibrium, the rental price of capital is equal to the marginal revenue product of capital.

The Market for Natural Resources

The market for natural resources can be analyzed in the same way as the markets for labor and capital. When a firm is considering employing more natural resources, the value it receives equals the increase in the firm's revenue from selling the additional output it can produce by buying the natural resources. So, the demand for natural resources is also a derived demand. The *marginal revenue product of natural resources* is the change in the firm's revenue as a result of employing one more unit of natural resources, such as a barrel of oil. The marginal revenue product of natural resources curve is also the demand curve for natural resources.

Although the total quantity of most natural resources is ultimately fixed in many cases, the quantity supplied still responds to the price. For example, although the total quantity of oil deposits in the world is fixed, an increase in the price of oil will result in an increase in the quantity of oil supplied during a particular period. The result, as

Economic rent (or pure rent) The price of a factor of production that is in fixed supply.

shown in panel (a) of Figure 18-16, is an upward-sloping supply curve. In some cases, however, the quantity of a natural resource that will be supplied is fixed and will not change as the price changes. The land available at a busy intersection is fixed, for example. In panel (b) of Figure 18-16, we illustrate this situation with a supply curve that is a vertical line, or perfectly inelastic. The price received by a factor of production that is in fixed supply is called an **economic rent (or pure rent)** because, in this case, the price of the factor is determined only by demand. For example, if a new highway diverts much of the traffic from a previously busy intersection, the demand for the land will decline and the price of the land will fall, but the quantity of the land will not change.

Monopsony

Monopsony The sole buyer of a factor of production.

Earlier we analyzed the case of *monopoly*, where a firm is the sole *seller* of a good or service. What happens if a firm is the sole *buyer* of a factor of production? This case, which is known as **monopsony**, is comparatively rare. An example is a plantation or mine in an isolated town that is the sole employer of labor in that location. In such case, not only would the firm own the mine or plantation, but it would also own the stores and other businesses in the town. Workers would have the choice of working for the sole employer in the town or moving to another town.

We know that a firm with a monopoly in an output market takes advantage of its market power to reduce the quantity supplied to force up the market price and increase its profits. A firm that has a monopsony in a factor market would employ a similar strategy: it would restrict the quantity of the factor demanded to force down the price of the factor and increase profits. A firm with a monopsony in a labor market will hire fewer workers and pay lower wages than would be the case in a competitive market. Because fewer workers are hired than would be true in a competitive market, monopsony results in a deadweight loss. Monopoly and monopsony have similar effects on the economy: in both cases a firm's market power results in a lower equilibrium quantity, a deadweight loss, and a reduction in economic efficiency compared with a competitive market. In some cases, monopsony in labor markets is offset by worker membership in a labor union.

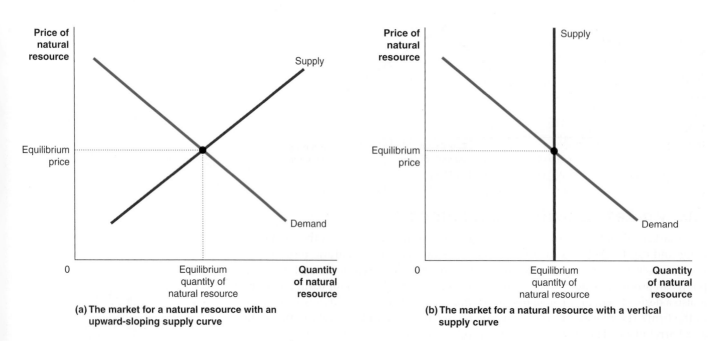

(a) The market for a natural resource with an upward-sloping supply curve

(b) The market for a natural resource with a vertical supply curve

Figure 18-16 | Equilibrium in the Market for Natural Resources

In panel (a), the supply curve of a natural resource is upward sloping. The price of the natural resource is determined by the interaction of demand and supply. In panel (b), the supply curve of the natural resource is a vertical line, indicating that the quantity supplied does not respond to changes in price. In this case, the price of the natural resource is determined only by demand. The price of a factor of production with a vertical supply curve is called an *economic rent* or a *pure rent*.

The Marginal Productivity Theory of Income Distribution

We have seen that in equilibrium, each factor of production receives a price equal to its marginal revenue product. We can use this fact to explain the distribution of income. Marginal revenue product represents the value of a factor's marginal contribution to producing goods and services. Therefore, individuals will receive income equal to the marginal contributions to production from the factors of production they own, including their labor. The more factors of production an individual owns and the more productive those factors are, the higher the individual's income will be. This approach to explaining the distribution of income is called the **marginal productivity theory of income distribution**. The marginal productivity theory of income distribution was developed by John Bates Clark, who taught at Columbia University in the U.S. in the late nineteenth and early twentieth centuries.

Marginal productivity theory of income distribution The theory that the distribution of income is determined by the marginal productivity of the factors of production that individuals own.

Economics in YOUR Life!

» Continued from page 581

At the beginning of the chapter, we asked you to imagine that you work at a local sandwich shop and that you plan to ask your manager for a raise. One way to show the manager your worth is to demonstrate how many dollars your work earns for the sandwich shop: your marginal revenue product. You could certainly suggest that as you have become better at your job and have gained new skills that you are a more productive employee, but more importantly, that your productivity results in increased revenue to the sandwich shop. By showing how your employment contributes to higher revenue and profit for the shop, you may be able to convince your manager to raise your pay.

Conclusion

In this chapter, we used the demand and supply model from Chapter 3 to explain why wages differ among workers. The demand for workers depends on their productivity and on the price that firms receive for the output the workers produce. The supply of workers to an occupation depends on the wages and working conditions offered by employers and on the skills required. The demand and supply for labor can also help us analyze such issues as economic discrimination and the impact of labor unions.

Read *An Inside Look* on the next page to see how flexible employment terms may increase labor market and business efficiency in the Arab countries of the Gulf.

Would Flexible Employment Enhance Labor Market Efficiency and Increase Labor Force Participation in the GCC countries?

AMEINFO.COM, SEPTEMBER 28, 2010

Making Case for Flexible Employment in GCC

Although Gulf Cooperation Council (GCC) countries' labor laws offer significant flexibility to employers, those regulations typically ignore part-time or temporary work arrangements, rendering such work contracts difficult, expensive, or impractical. This gap inhibits the region's economic competitiveness in three critical areas: labor participation, employment rate, and overall business agility. By adopting new laws and administrative policies promoting flexible work arrangements, the GCC countries could partially address these issues while strengthening their economic resilience to future downturns.

Benefit 1: Increasing labor participation

(a) "In the GCC, where the labor force participation rate stands at around 50 percent—well below the 70 percent average in OECD [Organization of Economic Cooperation and Development] countries—four main demographic segments could benefit from flexible employment arrangement: stay-at-home nationals, spouses of expats, students, and retired nationals," said Chucrallah Haddad, partner with Booz & Company.

GCC female workforce participation is among the lowest in the world. "Even compared to the overall participation rate in the region, which dips below global norms at 55 percent, the rate of participation among women is especially notable: out of roughly 8 to 9 million GCC female nationals of working age, no more than a third hold a regular professional position. The participation rates of women nationals in Saudi Arabia, the UAE, and Qatar stand at around 12 percent, 28 percent, and 35 percent, respectively. Cultural issues, such as the social stigma attached to women working in certain professions, may explain part of the gender gap. But some of these women would enter the workforce—especially in the private sector where schedules are typically more demanding than in public administrations—if they could limit their work hours during the day or tailor their work week to their duties outside the workplace," said Haddad.

Some countries in the GCC, such as the UAE and Qatar, have a substantial number of inactive expatriates. These inactive expatriates are usually sponsored by their spouses, and are technically forbidden from salaried activities unless they undergo a transfer of their sponsorship to a full-time employer. This could prove in certain cases lengthy or cumbersome and certainly does not account for part-time employment options. Fortunately, "In certain countries in the region, it is becoming easier for these inactive expatriates to enter the labor market. In 2008, Qatar allowed spouses of expatriates to work without transferring sponsors if they pay an annual fee. This could significantly reduce the need for additional foreign labor if 'in-country'

inactive expatriates can easily fill certain much-needed part-time or flexible activities," said Moncef Klouche, principal with Booz & Company.

Benefit 2: Reducing structural unemployment

(b) Beyond providing incentives for various segments of the inactive population to join the workforce, flexible employment could in some cases create the conditions that contribute to reducing part of a country's structural unemployment.

Traditional labor regulations—such as working conditions (e.g., mandatory rest days, standard hours), mandatory social program contributions (e.g., retirement or unemployment contributions), or lay-off protection programs (e.g., dismissal rules, severance packages)—are necessary to protect employees' rights, but they do increase the cost of employment. With the costs of employment higher, businesses are inclined to focus recruitment and hiring on experienced and tested workers, thereby marginalizing certain demographic groups, especially young and elderly workers.

"Young people's share of unemployment among nationals in the region is disproportionally high: For example, in 2008, 46 percent of the unemployed in Saudi Arabia consisted of youth, while they constituted only 12 percent of the overall workforce. In Qatar and the UAE, 62 percent and 40 percent respectively of the unemployed consisted of youth. Given the approaching 'youth bulge' in the populations of GCC countries and the reduction in the size of public administration (the default source of employment for many job entrants in the past), the challenge of finding work for young adults will need to lead public-policy agendas," said Klouche.

Flexible employment in OECD countries has proven to be extremely beneficial to companies and the economy. "Denmark has encouraged young adults and employers to engage in mutually beneficial part-time internships—or "school-to-work" programs—prior to and after vocational studies. As a result, it has the lowest youth unemployment rate in its region (6 percent, against an OECD average of 13 percent in 2008); 55 percent of Danish youth are employed part-time, compared to an OECD average of 28 percent," commented Haddad.

Benefit 3: Improving business agility

(c) Flexible employment also helps businesses remain agile by providing the tools for them to react seamlessly to economic cycles. The option to hire people for specific periods of time means companies can adapt labor forces to the business cycle, hire a temporary workforce during peak periods, and adjust easily when workers are no longer needed. In fact, part-time work arrangements appear to be significantly correlated to business competitiveness, as measured by the World Economic Forum Global Competitiveness Index.

"Industries subject to seasonal demand, such as retail or hospitality, have a great need for flexible employment to calibrate their staffing levels throughout the year. In some Western countries, retailers realize up to 50 percent of their yearly revenue during the last quarter of the year. To adequately respond to this surge, employers hire workers for the quarter only. Managing through such seasonality, or similar peaks in labor demand, with a full-time workforce would not be possible for a competitive seasonal business. In addition, even if demand is held constant, labor force availability can sometimes fluctuate due to maternity leaves and extended sick leave or vacations," added Klouche.

Source: "Making Case for Flexible Employment in GCC," AMEinfo.com, September 28, 2010: www.ameinfo.com/243314-more2.html.

Key Points in the Article

This article argues that developing a framework for flexible employment in GCC countries will substantially improve the efficiency of labor markets. It is expected to spur greater participation of workers from previously underrepresented groups, contribute to a reduction in unemployment and increase overall business agility. The benefit of these reforms will be felt by those demographic groups—especially national and expatriate women, young adults, and seniors—now overlooked by potential employers. For companies, especially those subject to cyclical and seasonal changes in demand, a more flexible labor market would contribute significantly to enhancing their competitiveness.

Analyzing the News

(a) GCC female workforce participation is less than one-third of the labor force; among the lowest in the world. But some of the national women excluded from the labour force will be encouraged to enter the workforce if they can have flexible schedules or the option of working part-time. Many inactive expatriates' spouses could also enter the labour force, reducing the need to import more foreign labour.

(b) Flexible employment could in some cases create the conditions that contribute to reducing part of a country's structural unemployment. Flexible employment can reduce the cost of employment, and hence increase the demand for labour. This will help reduce unemployment, especially among nationals.

(c) Industries subject to seasonal demand can adjust better to the business cycle by hiring labour during peak periods and reducing labour during low-sales periods. So, flexible employment terms can enhance a company's competitiveness.

Thinking Critically

1. On-the-job-training is an asset to both workers and employers. How can this affect employer's preferences towards flexible employment options? Do you think flexible options would have a sizable impact on the labour market, as the article claims?

2. Assume that an increase in flexible employment did not affect the average wage rate in the economy, what do you think must happen so that structural unemployment declines?

Flexible employment in the GCC could create conditions that reduce structural unemployment and strengthen the economy.

Key Terms

Compensating differentials, p. 594	Economic rent (or pure rent), p. 606	Labor union, p. 602	Marginal revenue product of labor (*MRP*), p. 583
Derived demand, p. 582	Factors of production, p. 582	Marginal product of labor, p. 582	
Economic discrimination, p. 595	Human capital, p. 585	Marginal productivity theory of income distribution, p. 607	Monopsony, p. 606
			Personnel economics, p. 603

Summary

18.1 LEARNING OBJECTIVE

Explain how firms choose the profit-maximizing quantity of labor to employ, **pages 582–586.**

The Demand for Labor

The demand for labor is a **derived demand** because it depends on the demand consumers have for goods and services. The additional output produced by a firm as a result of hiring another worker is called the **marginal product of labor**. The amount by which the firm's revenue will increase as a result of hiring one more worker is called the **marginal revenue product of labor** (*MRP*). A firm's marginal revenue product of labor curve is its demand curve for labor. Firms maximize profit by hiring workers up to the point where the wage is equal to the marginal revenue product of labor. The market demand curve for labor is determined by adding up the quantity of labor demanded by each firm at each wage, holding constant all other variables that might affect the willingness of firms to hire workers. The most important variables that shift the labor demand curve are changes in human capital, technology, the price of the product, the quantity of other inputs, and the number of firms in the market. **Human capital** is the accumulated training and skills that workers possess.

18.2 LEARNING OBJECTIVE

Explain how people choose the quantity of labor to supply, **pages 586–589.**

The Supply of Labor

As the wage increases, the opportunity cost of leisure increases, causing individuals to supply a greater quantity of labor. Normally, the labor supply curve is upward sloping, but it is possible that at very high wage levels, the supply curve might be backward bending. This outcome occurs when someone with a high income is willing to accept a somewhat lower income in exchange for more leisure. The market labor supply curve is determined by adding up the quantity of labor supplied by each worker at each wage, holding constant all other variables that might affect the willingness of workers to supply labor. The most important variables that shift the labor supply curve are increases in population, changing demographics, and changing alternatives.

18.3 LEARNING OBJECTIVE

Explain how equilibrium wages are determined in labor markets, **pages 589–592.**

Equilibrium in the Labor Market

The intersection between labor supply and labor demand determines the equilibrium wage and the equilibrium level of employment. If labor supply is unchanged, an increase in labor demand will increase both the equilibrium wage and the number of workers employed. If labor demand is unchanged, an increase in labor supply will lower the equilibrium wage and increase the number of workers employed.

18.4 LEARNING OBJECTIVE

Use demand and supply analysis to explain how compensating differentials, discrimination, and labor unions cause wages to differ, **pages 592–602.**

Explaining Differences in Wages

The equilibrium wage is determined by the intersection of the labor demand and labor supply curves. Some differences in wages are explained by **compensating differentials**, which are higher wages that compensate workers for unpleasant aspects of a job. Wages can also differ because of **economic discrimination**, which involves paying a person a lower wage or excluding a person from an occupation on the basis of irrelevant characteristics, such as race or gender. **Labor unions** are organizations of employees that have the legal right to bargain with employers about wages and working conditions. Being in a union increases a worker's wages about 10 percent, holding constant other factors, such as the industry in question.

Personnel Economics

Personnel economics is the application of economic analysis to human resources issues. One insight of personnel economics is that the productivity of workers often can be increased if firms move from straight-time pay to commission or piece-rate pay.

18.5 LEARNING OBJECTIVE

Discuss the role personnel economics can play in helping firms deal with human resources issues, **pages 602–604.**

The Markets for Capital and Natural Resources

The approach used to analyze the market for labor can also be used to analyze the markets for other factors of production. In equilibrium, the price of capital is equal to the marginal revenue product of capital, and the price of natural resources is equal to the marginal revenue product of natural resources. The price received by a factor that is in fixed supply is called an *economic rent*, or pure rent. A **monopsony** is the sole buyer of a factor of production. According to the **marginal productivity theory of income distribution**, the distribution of income is determined by the marginal productivity of the factors of production individuals own.

18.6 LEARNING OBJECTIVE

Show how equilibrium prices are determined in the markets for capital and natural resources, **pages 604–607.**

Review, Problems and Applications

18.1 LEARNING OBJECTIVE Explain how firms choose the profit-maximizing quantity of labor to employ, **pages 582–586.**

Review Questions

1.1 What is the difference between the marginal product of labor and the marginal revenue product of labor?

1.2 Why is the demand curve for labor downward sloping?

1.3 What are the five most important variables that cause the market demand curve for labor to shift?

Problems and Applications

1.4 Salem owns an apple orchard. He employs 87 apple pickers and pays them each US$8 per hour to pick apples, which he sells for US$1.60 per box. If Salem is maximizing profits, what is the marginal revenue product of the last worker he hired? What is that worker's marginal product?

1.5 **(Related to *Solved Problem 18-1* on page 584)** Fill in the blanks in the following table for Televisions:

NUMBER OF WORKERS (L)	OUTPUT OF TELEVISIONS PER WEEK (Q)	MARGINAL PRODUCT OF LABOR (TELEVISION SETS PER WEEK) (MP)	PRODUCT PRICE (P) IN US$	MARGINAL REVENUE PRODUCT LABOR (US$ PER WEEK) (W)	WAGE OF (DOLLARS PER WEEK) (W) IN US$	ADDITIONAL PROFIT FROM HIRING ONE MORE WORKER (US$ PER WEEK)
0	0	—	300	—	1,800	—
1	8	—	300	—	1,800	—
2	15	—	300	—	1,800	—
3	21	—	300	—	1,800	—
4	26	—	300	—	1,800	—
5	30	—	300	—	1,800	—
6	33	—	300	—	1,800	—

a. From the information in the table, can you determine whether this firm is a price taker or a price maker? Briefly explain.

b. Use the information in the table to draw a graph like Figure 18-1 on page 583 that shows the demand for labor by this firm. Be sure to indicate the profit-maximizing quantity of labor on your graph.

1.6 State whether each of the following events will result in a movement along the market demand curve for labor in electronics factories in Japan or whether it will cause the market demand curve for labor to shift. If the demand curve shifts, indicate whether it will shift to the left or to the right and draw a graph to illustrate the shift.

a. The wage rate declines.

b. The price of televisions declines.

c. Several firms exit the television market in Japan.

d. Japanese high schools introduce new vocational courses in assembling electronic products.

1.7 Under what circumstances would a firm's demand curve for labor be a horizontal line?

18.2 LEARNING OBJECTIVE   Explain how people choose the quantity of labor to supply, **pages 586–589.**

Review Questions

2.1 How can we measure the opportunity cost of leisure? Why is the supply curve of labor usually upward sloping?

2.2 What are the three most important variables that cause the market supply curve of labor to shift?

Problems and Applications

2.3 Ahmed had been earning US$65 per hour and working 45 hours per week. Then Ahmed's wage rose to US$75 per hour, and as a result, he now works 40 hours per week. What can we conclude from this information about the income effect and the substitution effect of a wage change for Ahmed?

2.4 Most labor economists believe that many adult males are on the vertical section of their labor supply curves. Explain when and why someone's supply of labor curve would be vertical, using the concepts of income and substitution effects.

Source: Robert Whaples, "Is There Consensus among American Labor Economists: Survey Results on Forty Propositions," *Journal of Labor Research*, Vol. 17, No. 4, Fall 1996.

2.5 Suppose that a large oil field is discovered in Saudi Arabia. By imposing a tax on the oil, the government is able to eliminate the state income tax on wages. What is likely to be the effect on the labor supply curve in Saudi Arabia?

2.6 State whether each of the following events will result in a movement along the market supply curve of agricultural labor in Jordan or whether it will cause the market supply curve of labor to shift. If the supply curve shifts, indicate whether it will shift to the left or to the right and draw a graph to illustrate the shift.
  a. The agricultural wage rate declines.
  b. Wages outside of agriculture increase.
  c. The law is changed to allow for unlimited immigration into Jordan.

18.3 LEARNING OBJECTIVE   Explain how equilibrium wages are determined in labor markets, **pages 589–592.**

Review Questions

3.1 If the labor demand curve shifts to the left and the labor supply curve remains unchanged, what will happen to the equilibrium wage and the equilibrium level of employment? Illustrate your answer with a graph.

3.2 If the labor supply curve shifts to the left and the labor demand curve remains unchanged, what will happen to the equilibrium wage and the equilibrium level of employment? Illustrate your answer with a graph.

Problems and Applications

3.3 **(Related to the *Making the Connection* on page 590)** Over time, the gap between the wages of workers with a college degree and the wages of workers without a college degree has been increasing. Shouldn't this gap have increased the incentive for workers to earn a college degree, thereby increasing the supply of college-educated workers, and reducing the size of the gap?

3.4 Suppose the Arab Gulf states had not allowed any immigration between 1960 and 1990. Which groups would have benefited from prohibiting immigration and which groups would have lost?

3.5 Labor supply in the Gulf has grown by millions in the past 30 years. How could the price of labor *not* fall? If there is an increase in labor supply, does the equilibrium wage have to fall?

18.4 LEARNING OBJECTIVE   Use demand and supply analysis to explain how compensating differentials, discrimination, and labor unions cause wages to differ, **pages 592–602.**

Review Questions

4.1 What is a compensating differential? Give an example.

4.2 Define economic discrimination. Is the fact that one group in the population has higher earnings than other groups evidence of economic discrimination? Briefly explain.

Problems and Applications

4.3 Do you agree or disagree with the argument that the free-market mechanism works well in labor markets by rewarding some people or professions more than others?

4.4 **(Related to the *Chapter Opener* on page 580)** A student remarks, "I don't think the idea of marginal revenue product really helps explain differences in wages. After all, a ticket to a soccer game costs much less than college tuition, yet football players are paid much more than college professors." Do you agree with the student's reasoning?

4.5 Provide an economic explanation of why football teams pay the teams' managers and general managers less than they pay most football players.

4.6 Tennis stars Venus Williams and Serena Williams do not play for teams. They enter tennis tournaments as individuals. Is the concept of marginal revenue product as important in explaining their earnings as it is in explaining the earnings of top-flight football players? Briefly explain.

4.7 (Related to *Solved Problem 18-4* on page 599) Use the following graphs to answer the questions.

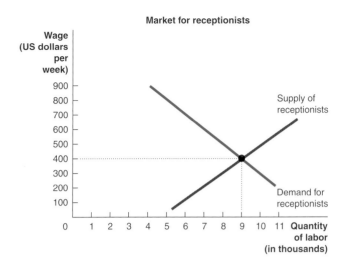

a. What is the equilibrium quantity of sanitary engineers hired, and what is the equilibrium wage?

b. What is the equilibrium quantity of receptionists hired, and what is the equilibrium wage?

c. Briefly discuss why sanitary engineers might earn a higher weekly wage than receptionists.

d. Suppose that legislation is passed and the government requires that sanitary engineers and receptionists must be paid the same wage of US$500 per week. Now how many sanitary engineers will be hired and how many receptionists will be hired?

4.8 (Related to *Solved Problem 18-4* on page 599) In most universities, economics professors receive larger salaries than English professors. Suppose that the government requires that from now on, all universities must pay economics professors the same salaries as English professors. Use demand and supply graphs to analyze the effect of this requirement.

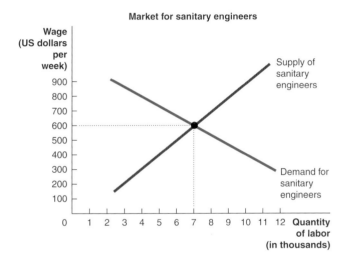

18.5 LEARNING OBJECTIVE   Discuss the role personnel economics can play in helping firms deal with human resources issues, **pages 602–604.**

Review Questions

5.1 What is personnel economics?

5.2 If piece-rate or commission systems of compensating workers have important advantages for firms, why don't more firms use them?

Problems and Applications

5.3 According to a recent economic study, the number of jobs in which firms used bonuses, commission, or piece rates to tie workers' pay to their performance increased from an estimated 30 percent of all jobs in the 1970s to 40 percent in the 1990s. Why would systems that tie workers pay to how much they produce have become increasingly popular with firms? The same study found that these pay systems were more common in higher-paid jobs than in lower-paid jobs. What explains this result?

Source: Thomas Lemieux, W. Bentley MacLeod, and Daniel Parent, "Performance Pay and Wage Inequality," NBER Working Paper No. 13128, May 2007.

5.4 Many companies that pay workers an hourly wage require some minimum level of acceptable output. Suppose a company that has been using this system decides to switch to a piece-rate system under which workers are compensated on the basis of how much output they produce but under which they are also free to choose how much to produce. Is it likely that workers under a piece-rate system will end up choosing to produce less than the minimum output required under the hourly wage system? Briefly explain.

5.5 In most jobs, the harder you work, the more you earn. Some workers would rather work harder and earn more; others would rather work less hard, even though as a result they earn less. Suppose, though, that all workers at a company fall into the "work harder and earn more" group. Suppose, also, that the workers all have the same abilities. In these circumstances, would output per worker be the same under an hourly wage compensation system as under a piece-rate system? Briefly explain.

5.6 For years, the Goodyear Tire & Rubber Company compensated its sales force by paying a salesperson a salary plus a bonus based on the number of tires he or she sold. In early 2002, Goodyear made two changes to this policy: (1) The basis for the bonus was changed from the *quantity* of tires sold to the *revenue* from the tires sold, and (2) salespeople were required to get approval from corporate headquarters before offering to sell tires to customers at reduced prices. Explain why these changes were likely to increase Goodyear's profits.

Source: Timothy Aeppel, "Amid Weak Inflation, Firms Turn Creative to Boost Prices," *Wall Street Journal*, September 18, 2002.

18.6 LEARNING OBJECTIVE   Show how equilibrium prices are determined in the markets for capital and natural resources, **pages 604–607.**

Review Questions

6.1 In equilibrium, what determines the price of capital? What determines the price of natural resources? What is the marginal productivity theory of income distribution?

6.2 What is an economic rent? What is a monopsony?

Problems and Applications

6.3 Mustafa operates a pin factory. Suppose Mustafa faces the situation shown in the following table and the cost of renting a machine is US$550 per week.

NUMBER OF MACHINES	OUTPUT OF PINS (BOXES PER WEEK)	MARGINAL PRODUCT OF CAPITAL	PRODUCT PRICE (US$ PER BOX)	TOTAL REVENUE	MARGINAL REVENUE PRODUCT OF CAPITAL	RENTAL COST PER MACHINE IN US$	ADDITIONAL PROFIT FROM RENTING ONE ADDITIONAL MACHINE
0	0	—	100	—		550	
1	12		100			550	
2	21		100			550	
3	28		100			550	
4	34		100			550	
5	39		100			550	
6	43		100			550	

a. Fill in the blanks in the table and determine the profit-maximizing number of machines for Mustafa to rent. Briefly explain why renting this number of machines is profit maximizing.

b. Draw Mustafa's demand curve for capital.

6.4 Many people have predicted, using a model like the one in panel (b) of Figure 18-2 on page 586, that the price of natural resources should rise consistently over time in comparison with the prices of other goods because the demand curve for natural resources is continually shifting to the right while the supply curve must be shifting to the left as natural resources are used up. However, the relative prices of most natural resources have not been increasing. Draw a graph that shows the demand and supply for natural resources that can explain why prices haven't risen even though demand has.

6.5 In 1879, economist Henry George published *Progress and Poverty*, which became one of the best-selling books of the nineteenth century. In this book, George argued that all existing taxes should be replaced with a single tax on land. In Chapter 4, we discussed the concept of tax incidence, or the actual division of the burden of a tax between buyers and sellers in a market. If land is taxed, how will the burden of the tax be divided between the sellers of land and the buyers of land? Illustrate your answer with a graph of the market for land.

6.6 The total amount of oil in the earth is not increasing. Does this mean that in the market for oil, the supply curve is perfectly inelastic? Briefly explain.

6.7 In a competitive labor market, imposing a minimum wage should reduce the equilibrium level of employment. Will this also be true if the labor market is a monopsony? Briefly explain.

Chapter 19

Output and Expenditure in the Short Run

The Fluctuating Demand in the Arab World: The Effects of the Recent Global Financial Crisis

In the past decade, many Arab countries took important steps to integrate their economies into the global economy. Emerging Arab markets such as Egypt, Jordan, and Tunisia became significant net recipients of foreign direct investment, and they witnessed large inflows of capital during the boom of 2004–2007. The Arab Gulf countries, on the other hand, positioned themselves as significant investors, especially in developed countries. With growing large sovereign wealth funds amid the big surge in oil prices in 2004, the United Arab Emirates, Saudi Arabia, Qatar, and Kuwait accumulated huge portfolios of financial investments and foreign assets. The greater openness and links to the global economy increased Arab countries' exposure to global downturns.

The reversal of the cycle started with the beginnings of the financial crisis at the end of 2008. The collapse of many real estate markets in the United States and Europe, the increasing unemployment, and the drying up of funds in the credit markets led to slower, and in many cases, negative growth of output in the developed world in the West. The global widespread recession led to a decline in demand for almost all goods and services, including crude oil. All parts of the world were affected by that drop in aggregate demand of developed countries, especially oil-exporters. Oil prices dropped sharply from a peak of US$147 per barrel in August 2008 to a low price of US$30 by the end of the same year. Facing this collapse in oil prices, OPEC countries cut production to prevent prices from falling further. The combined effect of a drop in prices and production sharply reduced the export receipts of most Arab Gulf countries. In addition, the direct effect of the global crisis, coupled with weak oil prices, was a sharp decline in capital inflows to buy real estate in the Arab world and the Middle East. Developers such as DAMAC, Emaar, and Nakheel, known for their prestigious and luxurious projects, suffered a larger drop in foreign demand.

Because the governments' fiscal revenues depend on the oil sector, Arab oil-exporting countries suffered a sharp fall in their main revenues. However, the governments in the Gulf continued spending, using the surplus they accumulated during the boom of 2004–2007 when oil prices were high. In fact, government spending was increased to compensate for the fall in private consumption and investment expenditure. Governments' demand for goods and services was high to prevent a sharp fall of aggregate demand.

The global recession also reduced the number of foreign tourists to the Middle East. Many MENA countries, especially Egypt, Morocco, Tunisia, Jordan, and Lebanon, rely heavily on tourism as an important source for job creation and foreign exchange revenue. Egypt, for example, reported a net decline in tourism income by 9.5 percent during the first half of 2009. In addition, in 2007, workers' remittances (i.e. income transfers while working abroad) in Jordan, Morocco, Egypt, and Tunisia accounted for 22.7 percent, 9 percent, 6 percent, and 5 percent of their GDP, respectively. In 2008, Arab countries enjoyed a positive growth of remittance incomes before being adversely impacted by the global crisis in 2009.

AN INSIDE LOOK on page 6 discusses the challenges that the Jordanian economy faced as a result of a drop in workers' remittances that was expected to cause the countries' aggregate demand to shrink.

Sources: Nader Habibi, "The Impact of the Global Economic Crisis on Arab Countries: A Year-End Assessment," *Middle East Brief No 40*, December, 2009, the Crown Center for Middle East Studies, Brandeis University, US.

Economics in YOUR Life!

Consumer Confidence Falls—is Your Job at Risk?

Suppose that you work part time assembling desktop computers for a large computer company. One morning, you read in the local newspaper that consumer confidence in the economy has fallen and, consequently, many households expect their future income to be dramatically less than their current income. Should you be concerned about losing your job? What factors should you consider in deciding how likely your company is to lay you off? As you read the chapter, see if you can answer these questions. You can check your answers against those we provide at the end of the chapter. **>> Continued on page 647**

Aggregate expenditure (*AE*) The total amount of spending in the economy: the sum of consumption, planned investment, government purchases, and net exports.

In the short run, as we saw in Chapter 17, the economy experiences a business cycle around the long-run upward trend in real GDP. In this chapter, we begin exploring the causes of the business cycle by examining the effect of changes in total spending on real GDP.

During some years, total spending in the economy, or **aggregate expenditure (*AE*)**, increases as much as does the production of goods and services. If this happens, most firms will sell about what they expected to sell, and they probably will not increase or decrease production or the number of workers hired. During other years, total spending in the economy increases more than the production of goods and services. In these years, firms will increase production and hire more workers. But at other times, such as in 2009, total spending does not increase as much as total production. As a result, firms cut back on production and lay off workers, and the economy moves into a recession. In this chapter, we will explore why changes in total spending play such an important role in the economy.

19.1 LEARNING OBJECTIVE

19.1 | Understand how macroeconomic equilibrium is determined in the aggregate expenditure model.

The Aggregate Expenditure Model

The business cycle involves the interaction of many economic variables. To understand the relationships among some of the most important of these variables, we begin our study of the business cycle in this chapter with a simple model called the *aggregate expenditure model*. Recall from Chapter 15 that GDP is the value of all the final goods and services produced in an economy during a particular year. Real GDP corrects nominal GDP for the effects of inflation. The **aggregate expenditure model** focuses on the short-run relationship between total spending and real GDP. An important assumption of the model is that the price level is constant. In Chapter 20, we will develop a more complete model of the business cycle that relaxes the assumption of constant prices.

Aggregate expenditure model A macroeconomic model that focuses on the relationship between total spending and real GDP, assuming that the price level is constant.

The key idea of the aggregate expenditure model is that *in any particular year, the level of GDP is determined mainly by the level of aggregate expenditure*. To understand the relationship between aggregate expenditure and real GDP, we need to look more closely at the components of aggregate expenditure.

Aggregate Expenditure

Economists first began to study the relationship between changes in aggregate expenditure and changes in GDP during the Great Depression of the 1930s. The United States, the United Kingdom, and other industrial countries suffered declines in real GDP of 25 percent or more during the early 1930s. In 1936, the English economist John Maynard Keynes published a book, *The General Theory of Employment, Interest, and Money*, that systematically analyzed the relationship between changes in aggregate expenditure and changes in GDP. Keynes identified four categories of aggregate expenditure that together equal GDP (these are the same four categories we discussed in Chapter 15):

- Consumption (*C*). This is spending by households on goods and services, such as automobiles and haircuts.

- Planned Investment (*I*). This is planned spending by firms on capital goods, such as factories, office buildings, and machine tools, and by households on new homes.

- Government Purchases (*G*). This is spending by local, state, and federal governments on goods and services, such as aircraft carriers, bridges, and the salaries of public sector employees.

So, we can write:

Aggregate expenditure = Consumption + Planned investment + Government purchases + Net exports

or:

$$AE = C + I + G + NX$$

Governments around the world gather statistics on aggregate expenditure on the basis of these four categories. Economists and business analysts usually explain changes in GDP in terms of changes in these four categories of spending.

The Difference between Planned Investment and Actual Investment

Before considering further the relationship between aggregate expenditure and GDP, we need to consider an important distinction: notice that it is *planned* investment spending, rather than actual investment spending, that is a component of aggregate expenditure. You might wonder how the amount that businesses plan to spend on investment can be different from the amount they actually spend. We can begin resolving this puzzle by remembering that goods that have been produced but have not yet been sold are referred to as **inventories**. Changes in inventories are included as part of investment spending along with spending on machinery, equipment, office buildings, and factories. We assume that the amount businesses plan to spend on machinery and office buildings is equal to the amount they actually spend, but the amount businesses plan to spend on inventories may be different from the amount they actually spend.

Inventories Goods that have been produced but not yet sold.

For example, Amazon may have in stock 0.5 million copies of a new book about Ibn Siena (Avicenna), expecting to sell them all. If Amazon does sell all 0.5 million copies, its inventories will be unchanged, but if it sells only 0.2 million, it will have an unplanned increase in inventories by the remaining 0.3 million copies. In other words, changes in inventories depend on sales of goods, which firms cannot always forecast with perfect accuracy.

For the economy as a whole, we can say that actual investment spending will be greater than planned investment spending when there is an unplanned increase in inventories. Actual investment spending will be less than planned investment spending when there is an unplanned decrease in inventories. *Therefore, actual investment will equal planned investment only when there is no unplanned change in inventories.* In this chapter, we will use *I* to represent planned investment. We will also assume that the government data on investment spending represents planned investment spending. This is a simplification, however, because the government collects data on actual investment spending, which equals planned investment spending only when unplanned changes in inventories are zero.

Macroeconomic Equilibrium

Macroeconomic equilibrium is similar to microeconomic equilibrium. In microeconomics, equilibrium in the apple market occurs at the point at which the demand for apples equals the supply of apples. When we have equilibrium in the apple market, the quantity of apples produced and sold will not change unless the demand for apples or the supply of apples changes. For the economy as a whole, macroeconomic equilibrium occurs where total spending, or aggregate expenditure, equals total production, or GDP:

Aggregate expenditure = GDP

As we saw in earlier chapters, over the long run, real GDP grows and the standard of living rises. In this chapter, we are interested in understanding why GDP fluctuates in the short run. To simplify the analysis of macroeconomic equilibrium, we assume that the economy is not growing. In the next chapter, we discuss the more realistic case of macroeconomic equilibrium in a growing economy. If we assume that the economy is not growing, then equilibrium GDP will not change unless aggregate expenditure changes.

Adjustments to Macroeconomic Equilibrium

The apple market isn't always in equilibrium because sometimes the quantity of apples demanded is greater than the quantity supplied, and sometimes the quantity supplied is greater than the quantity demanded. The same outcome holds for the economy as a whole. Sometimes the economy is in macroeconomic equilibrium, and sometimes it isn't. When aggregate expenditure is greater than GDP, the total amount of spending in the economy is greater than the total amount of production. With spending being greater than production, many businesses will sell more goods and services than they had expected. For example, the manager of one of Egypt's Carrefour stores might like to keep 50 refrigerators in stock to give customers the opportunity to see a variety of different sizes and models. If sales are unexpectedly high, the store may end up with only 20 refrigerators. In that case, the store will have an unplanned decrease in inventories: its inventory of refrigerators declines by 30.

How will the store manager react when more refrigerators are sold than expected? The manager is likely to order more refrigerators. If other stores selling refrigerators in Egypt are experiencing similar sales increases and are also increasing their orders, then refrigerator manufacturers such as Kiriazi, Zanussi, and Universal will significantly increase their production. These manufacturers may also increase the number of workers they hire. If the increase in sales is affecting not just refrigerators but also other appliances, automobiles, furniture, computers, and other goods and services, then GDP and total employment will begin to increase. In summary, *when aggregate expenditure is greater than GDP, inventories will decline, and GDP and total employment will increase.*

Now suppose that aggregate expenditure is less than GDP. With spending being less than production, many businesses will sell fewer goods and services than they had expected, so their inventories will increase. For example, the manager of the Carrefour store who wants 50 refrigerators in stock may find that because of slow sales, the store has 75 refrigerators, so the store manager will cut back on orders for new refrigerators. If other stores also cut back on their orders, Kiriazi, Zanussi, and Universal will reduce production and lay off workers.

If the decrease in sales is affecting not just refrigerators but also many different goods and services, GDP and total employment will begin to decrease. These events happened at many firms during the recent recession of 2009. In summary, *when aggregate expenditure is less than GDP, inventories will increase, and GDP and total employment will decrease.*

Only when aggregate expenditure equals GDP will firms sell what they expected to sell. In that case, their inventories will be unchanged, and they will not have an incentive to increase or decrease production. The economy will be in macroeconomic equilibrium. Table 19-1 summarizes the relationship between aggregate expenditure and GDP.

Increases and decreases in aggregate expenditure cause the year-to-year changes in GDP. Economists devote considerable time and energy to forecasting what will happen to each component of aggregate expenditure. If economists forecast that aggregate expenditure will decline in the future, that is equivalent to forecasting that GDP will decline and that the economy will enter a recession. Individuals and firms closely watch these forecasts because changes in GDP can have dramatic consequences. When GDP is increasing, so are wages, profits, and job opportunities. Declining GDP can be bad news for workers, firms, and job seekers.

When economists forecast that aggregate expenditure is likely to decline and that the economy is headed for a recession, the federal government may implement *macroeconomic*

TABLE 19-1

The Relationship between Aggregate Expenditure and GDP

IF ...	THEN ...	AND ...
Aggregate expenditure is *equal* to GDP	inventories are *unchanged*	the economy is in *macroeconomic equilibrium*.
Aggregate expenditure is *less* than GDP	inventories *rise*	GDP and employment *decrease*.
Aggregate expenditure is *greater* than GDP	inventories *fall*	GDP and employment *increase*.

policies in an attempt to head off the fall in expenditure and keep the economy from falling into recession. We discuss these macroeconomic polices in Chapters 22 and 23.

19.2 | Discuss the determinants of the four components of aggregate expenditure and define the marginal propensity to consume and the marginal propensity to save.

Determining the Level of Aggregate Expenditure in the Economy

To better understand how macroeconomic equilibrium is determined in the aggregate expenditure model, we look more closely at the components of aggregate expenditure for three selected Arab countries: Egypt, Jordan, and Saudi Arabia (KSA). Table 19-2 lists the four components of aggregate expenditure for the year 2007. For comparability, each component is measured in *real* terms, meaning that it is corrected for inflation by being measured in billions of year 2000 U.S. dollars. Consumption is clearly the largest component of aggregate expenditure in all three countries. The table shows that investment is more than double the size of government in Egypt, but in Jordan and Saudi, investment and government purchases are roughly similar in size. Net exports are negative in all three countries because they imported more goods and services than they exported. Next, we consider the variables that determine each of the four components of aggregate expenditure.

Consumption

Figure 19-1 shows movements in Kuwait's real consumption for the years 1970 to 2008. Notice that consumption follows an upward trend. Only during periods of recession does the growth in consumption slow or decline. For example, during the period 1981 to 1987 the sharp drop in oil prices and two consecutive recessions in the U.S. resulted in the slowing down of Kuwait's economy, which velied mainly on oil exports. Another interesting observation is the higher volatility of consumption when the economy is dependent on oil; consumption becomes more vulnerable to negative oil price shocks. Note the fluctuations of consumption between 1981 and 1986. Also, note the effect of the Iraqi invasion of Kuwait in 1990. Real consumption notably fell amid the liberation of Kuwait and did not start to recover until the beginning of the new century, responding to the booming oil sector. Indeed, the war with Iraq put Kuwait on a lower consumption path than it would have enjoyed without the war.

The following are the five most important variables that determine the level of consumption:

- Current disposable income
- Household wealth
- Expected future income
- The price level
- The interest rate

We can discuss how changes in each of these variables affect consumption.

TABLE 19-2

Components of Real Aggregate Expenditure, 2007

EXPENDITURE CATEGORY	REAL EXPENDITURE (BILLIONS OF CONSTANT 2000 US$)		
	Egypt	**Jordan**	**KSA**
Consumption	100,28	10.63	98,11
Investment	29,97	3.21	72,43
Government	13,40	2.86	77,45
Net Exports	–9,52	–3,22	–6,91

Source: WDI 2010, World Bank.

Figure 19-1

Kuwait's Real Consumption, 1970–2008

Consumption follows an upward trend, interrupted only infrequently by recessions.
Based on data from: Country National Accounts, United Nations, 2009.

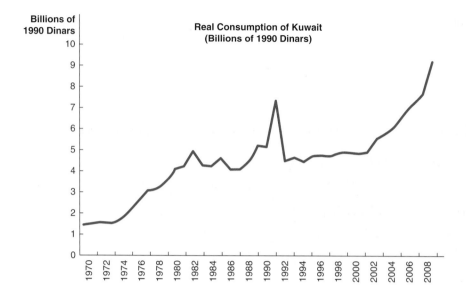

Current Disposable Income The most important determinant of consumption is the current disposable income of households. Recall from Chapter 15 that disposable income is the income remaining to households after they have paid personal income tax and received government *transfer payments*, such as social security payments. For most households, the higher their disposable income, the more they spend; and the lower their income, the less they spend. Macroeconomic consumption is the total of all the consumption by households. So, we would expect consumption to increase when the current disposable income of households increases, and to decrease when the current disposable income of households decreases. As we discussed in Chapter 15, total income expands during most years. Only during a recession, which happens infrequently, does total income decline. Then, if there is a general upward trend in consumption (as shown in Figure 19-1, after the year 2000), then disposable income must have followed a similar upward trend.

Household Wealth Consumption also depends on the wealth of households. A household's *wealth* is the value of its *assets* minus the value of its *liabilities*. An asset is anything of value owned by a person or a firm, and a liability is anything owed by a person or a firm. A household's assets include its home, stock and bond holdings, and bank accounts. A household's liabilities include any loans that it owes. A household with US$10 million in wealth is likely to spend more than a household with US$10,000 in wealth, even if both households have the same disposable income. Therefore, when the wealth of households increases, consumption should increase, and when the wealth of households decreases, consumption should decrease. Shares of stock are an important category of household wealth. When stock prices increase, household wealth will increase, and so should consumption. For example, a family whose stock holdings increase in value from US$50,000 to US$100,000 may be willing to spend a larger fraction of its income because it is less concerned with adding to its savings. A decline in stock prices should lead to a decline in consumption. Economists who have studied the determinants of consumption have concluded that permanent increases in wealth have a larger impact than temporary increases. A recent estimate of the effect of changes in wealth on consumption spending indicates that, for every permanent one US dollar increase in household wealth, consumption spending will increase by between four and five cents per year.

Expected Future Income Consumption also depends on expected future income. Most people prefer to keep their consumption fairly stable from year to year, even if their income fluctuates significantly. Real-estate brokers, for example, earn most of their income from commissions (fixed percentages of the sale price) on houses they sell. Real-estate brokers might have very high incomes some years and much lower incomes in other years. Most brokers keep their consumption steady and do not increase it during good years and then drastically cut back during slower years. If we looked just at a broker's current income, we might have difficulty estimating the broker's current consumption. Instead, we need to take into account the broker's expected future income. We can conclude that current income explains current consumption well *but only when current income is not unusually high or unusually low compared with expected future income.*

The Price Level Recall from Chapter 16 that the *price level* measures the average prices of goods and services in the economy. Consumption is affected by changes in the price level. It is tempting to think that an increase in prices will reduce consumption by making goods and services less affordable. In fact, the effect of an increase in the price of *one* product on the quantity demanded of that product is different from the effect of an increase in the price level on *total* spending by households on goods and services. Changes in the price level affect consumption mainly through their effect on household wealth. An increase in the price level will result in a decrease in the *real* value of household wealth. For example, if you have US$2,000 in a checking account, the higher the price level, the fewer goods and services you can buy with your money. If the price level falls, the real value of your US$2,000 would increase. Therefore, as the price level rises, the real value of your wealth declines, and so will your consumption, at least a little. Conversely, if the price level falls—which happens very rarely—your consumption will increase.

The Interest Rate Finally, consumption also depends on the interest rate. When the interest rate is high, the reward to saving is increased, and households are likely to save more and spend less. In Chapter 16 we distinguished between the *nominal interest rate* and the *real interest rate*. The nominal interest rate is the stated interest rate on a loan or a financial investment such as a bond. The real interest rate corrects the nominal interest rate for the impact of inflation and is equal to the nominal interest rate minus the inflation rate. Because households are concerned with the payments they will make or receive after the effects of inflation are taken into account, consumption spending depends on the real interest rate.

We saw in Chapter 15 that consumption spending is divided into three categories: spending on *services*, such as medical care, education, and haircuts; spending on *nondurable goods*, such as food and clothing; and spending on *durable goods*, such as automobiles and furniture. Spending on durable goods is most likely to be affected by changes in the interest rate because a high real interest rate increases the cost of spending financed by borrowing. The monthly payment on a four-year car loan will be higher if the real interest rate on the loan is 4 percent than if the real interest rate is 2 percent.

The Consumption Function There is a very close relationship between consumption and disposable income. Because changes in consumption depend on changes in disposable income, we can say that *consumption is a function of disposable income.*

The slope of the consumption function is equal to the change in consumption divided by the change in disposable income and is referred to as the **marginal propensity to consume (MPC)**. Using the Greek letter delta, Δ, to represent "change in," C to represent consumption spending, and YD to represent disposable income, we can write the expression for the *MPC* as follows:

$$MPC = \frac{\text{Change in consumption}}{\text{Change in disposable income}} = \frac{\Delta C}{\Delta YD}$$

For example, if between 2009 and 2010, consumption spending increased by US$30 billion, while disposable income increased by US$33 billion. The marginal propensity to consume was, therefore:

$$MPC = \frac{\Delta C}{\Delta YD} = \frac{30\,Billion}{33\,Billion} - 0.90$$

The value for the *MPC* tells us that households in 2010 spent 90 percent of the increase in their household income.

Consumption function The relationship between consumption spending and disposable income.

Marginal propensity to consume (MPC) The slope of the consumption function: The amount by which consumption spending changes when disposable income changes.

We can also use the *MPC* to determine how much consumption will change as income changes. To see this relationship, we rewrite the expression for the *MPC*:

$$MPC = \frac{\text{Change in consumption}}{\text{Change in disposable income}}$$

or:

$$\text{Change in consumption} = \text{Change in disposable income} \times MPC$$

For example, with an *MPC* of 0.90, a US$10 billion increase in disposable income will increase consumption by US$10 billion × 0.90, or US$9 billion.

The Relationship between Consumption and National Income

We have seen that consumption spending by households depends on disposable income. We now shift our focus slightly to the similar relationship that exists between consumption spending and GDP. We make this shift because we are interested in using the aggregate expenditure model to explain changes in real GDP rather than changes in disposable income. The first step in examining the relationship between consumption and GDP is noting that for most countries the differences between GDP and national income are usually small and can be ignored without affecting our analysis. In fact, in this and the following chapters, we will use the terms *GDP* and *national income* interchangeably. Also recall that disposable income is equal to national income plus government transfer payments minus taxes. Taxes minus government transfer payments are referred to as *net taxes*. So, we can write the following:

$$\text{Disposable income} = \text{National income} - \text{Net taxes}$$

We can rearrange the equation like this:

$$\text{National income} = \text{GDP} = \text{Disposable income} + \text{Net taxes}$$

The table in Figure 19-2 shows hypothetical values for national income (or GDP), net taxes, disposable income, and consumption spending. Notice that national income and disposable income differ by a constant amount, which is equal to net taxes of US$1,000 billion. In reality, net taxes are not a constant amount because they are affected by changes in income. As income rises, net taxes rise because some taxes, such as the personal income tax, increase and some government transfer payments, such as government payments to unemployed workers, fall. Nothing important is affected in our analysis, however, by our simplifying assumption that net taxes are constant. The graph in Figure 19-2 shows a line representing the relationship between consumption and national income. We defined the marginal propensity to consume (*MPC*) as the change in consumption divided by the change in disposable income, which is the slope of the consumption function. In fact, notice that if we calculate the slope of the line in Figure 19-2 between points *A* and *B*, we get a result that will not change whether we use the values for national income or the values for disposable income. Using the values for national income:

$$\frac{\Delta C}{\Delta Y} = \frac{\text{US\$5,250 billion} - \text{US\$3,750 billion}}{\text{US\$7,000 billion} - \text{US\$5,000 billion}} = 0.75$$

Using the corresponding values for disposable income from the table:

$$\frac{\Delta C}{\Delta YD} = \frac{\text{US\$5,250 billion} - \text{US\$3,750 billion}}{\text{US\$6,000 billion} - \text{US\$4,000 billion}} = 0.75$$

National income or GDP (billions of US$)	Net taxes (billions of US$)	Disposable income (billions of US$)	Consumption (billions of US$)	Change in national income (billions of US$)	Change in disposable income (billions of US$)
1,000	1,000	0	750	—	—
3,000	1,000	2,000	2,250	2,000	2,000
5,000	1,000	4,000	3,750	2,000	2,000
7,000	1,000	6,000	5,250	2,000	2,000
9,000	1,000	8,000	6,750	2,000	2,000
11,000	1,000	10,000	8,250	2,000	2,000
13,000	1,000	12,000	9,750	2,000	2,000

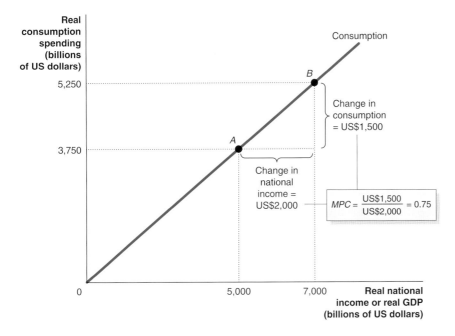

Figure 19-2

The Relationship between Consumption and National Income

Because national income differs from disposable income only by net taxes—which, for simplicity, we assume are constant—we can graph the consumption function using national income rather than disposable income. We can also calculate the *MPC*, which is the slope of the consumption function, using either the change in national income or the change in disposable income and always get the same value. The slope of the consumption function between point *A* and point *B* is equal to the change in consumption—US$1,500 billion—divided by the change in national income—US$2,000 billion—or 0.75.

It should not be surprising that we get the same result in either case. National income and disposable income differ by a constant amount, so changes in the two numbers always give us the same value, as is shown by the last two columns of the table in Figure 19-2. Therefore, we can graph the consumption function using national income rather than using disposable income. We can also calculate the *MPC* using either the change in national income or the change in disposable income and always get the same value.

Income, Consumption, and Saving

To complete our discussion of consumption, we can look briefly at the relationships among income, consumption, and saving. Households either spend their income, save it, or use it to pay taxes. For the economy as a whole, we can write the following:

$$\text{National income} = \text{Consumption} + \text{Saving} + \text{Taxes}$$

When national income increases, there must be some combination of an increase in consumption, an increase in saving, and an increase in taxes:

$$\text{Change in national income} = \text{Change in consumption} + \text{Change in saving} + \text{Change in taxes}$$

Using symbols, where Y represents national income (and GDP), C represents consumption, S represents saving, and T represents taxes, we can write the following:

$$Y = C + S + T$$

and,

$$\Delta Y = \Delta C + \Delta S + \Delta T$$

To simplify, we can assume that taxes are always a constant amount, in which case $\Delta T = 0$, so the following is also true:

$$\Delta Y = \Delta C + \Delta S$$

Marginal propensity to save (MPS) The change in saving divided by the change in disposable income.

We have already seen that the marginal propensity to consume equals the change in consumption divided by the change in income. We can define the **marginal propensity to save (MPS)** as the amount by which saving increases when disposable income increases and measure the MPS as the change in saving divided by the change in disposable income. In calculating the MPS, as in calculating the MPC, we can safely ignore the difference between national income and disposable income.

If we divide the last equation on the previous page by the change in income, ΔY, we get an equation that shows the relationship between the marginal propensity to consume and the marginal propensity to save:

$$\frac{\Delta Y}{\Delta Y} = \frac{\Delta C}{\Delta Y} + \frac{\Delta S}{\Delta Y}$$

or,

$$1 = MPC + MPS$$

This last equation tells us that when taxes are constant, the marginal propensity to consume plus the marginal propensity to save must always equal 1. They must add up to 1 because part of any increase in income is consumed, and whatever remains must be saved.

Solved Problem | 19-2

Calculating the Marginal Propensity to Consume and the Marginal Propensity to Save

Fill in the blanks in the following table. For simplicity, assume that taxes are zero. Show that the MPC plus the MPS equals 1.

NATIONAL INCOME AND REAL GDP (Y) IN US$	CONSUMPTION (C) IN US$	SAVING (S)	MARGINAL PROPENSITY TO CONSUME (MPC)	MARGINAL PROPENSITY TO SAVE (MPS)
9,000	8,000		—	—
10,000	8,600			
11,000	9,200			
12,000	9,800			
13,000	10,400			

SOLVING THE PROBLEM:

Step 1: **Review the chapter material.** This problem is about the relationship among income, consumption, and saving, so you may want to review the section "Income, Consumption, and Saving," which begins on page 625.

Step 2: **Fill in the table.** We know that $Y = C + S + T$. With taxes equal to zero, this equation becomes $Y = C + S$. We can use this equation to fill in the "Saving" column. We can use the expressions for the MPC and the MPS to fill in the other two columns:

$$MPC = \frac{\Delta C}{\Delta Y}$$

$$MPS = \frac{\Delta S}{\Delta Y}$$

For example, to calculate the value of the *MPC* in the second row, we have:

$$MPC = \frac{\Delta C}{\Delta Y} = \frac{US\$8,600 - US\$8,000}{US\$10,000 - US\$9,000} = \frac{US\$600}{US\$1,000} = 0.6$$

To calculate the value of the *MPS* in the second row, we have:

$$MPS = \frac{\Delta S}{\Delta Y} = \frac{US\$1,400 - US\$1,000}{US\$10,000 - US\$9,000} = \frac{US\$400}{US\$1,000} = 0.4$$

NATIONAL INCOME AND REAL GDP (Y) IN US$	CONSUMPTION (C) IN US$	SAVING (S) IN US$	MARGINAL PROPENSITY TO CONSUME (MPC)	MARGINAL PROPENSITY TO SAVE (MPS)
9,000	8,000	1,000	—	—
10,000	8,600	1,400	0.6	0.4
11,000	9,200	1,800	0.6	0.4
12,000	9,800	2,200	0.6	0.4
13,000	10,400	2,600	0.6	0.4

Step 3: **Show that the *MPC* plus the *MPS* equals 1.** At every level of national income, the *MPC* is 0.6 and the *MPS* is 0.4. Therefore, the *MPC* plus the *MPS* is always equal to 1.

YOUR TURN: For more practice, do related problem 2.9 on page 652 at the end of this chapter.

>> **End Solved Problem 19-2**

Planned Investment

Figure 19-3 shows movements in real investment spending in Egypt, as one example, for the years 1970–2008. Notice that investment does not follow a smooth, upward trend. Despite a very steady growth in the 1970s, investment declined significantly in the 1980s. Slower global trade as a result of the recessions in the West, mainly in the U.S., and the drying up of lending to the highly indebted developed world as a result of the international debt crisis had an adverse impact on capital inflows to Egypt: the cost of borrowing

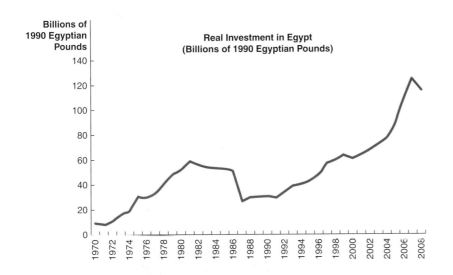

Billions of 1990 Egyptian Pounds

Real Investment in Egypt
(Billions of 1990 Egyptian Pounds)

Figure 19-3

Real Investment Spending In Egypt, 1970–2008

Investment is subject to more changes than is consumption. Investment declined significantly in the 1980s but started recovering during the 1990s.

Based on data from: Country National Accounts, United Nations, 2009.

increased and the trade balance worsened. This was later accentuated by the collapse of oil prices in 1986, which had a severe effect on Egypt's oil receipts and the remittances of Egyptian laborers working abroad. By the mid 1980s, the government not only was facing severe fiscal difficulties, but also very high external debt, and was struggling to restructure its debt with international debtors. As a consequence, both private and public investment fell sharply. The following decade witnessed a steady recovery as a result of following macroeconomic structural adjustment reforms, which included many incentives for foreign as well as domestic private investment. Since 2005, Egypt became one of the most attractive emerging markets in the Middle East region, attracting large direct foreign investment.

The four most important variables that determine the level of investment are:

- Expectations of future profitability
- The interest rate
- Taxes
- Cash flow

Expectations of Future Profitability
Investment goods, such as factories, office buildings, and machinery and equipment, are long lived. A firm is unlikely to build a new factory unless it is optimistic that the demand for its product will remain strong for a period of at least several years. When the economy moves into a recession, many firms postpone buying investment goods even if the demand for their own product is strong because they are afraid that the recession may become worse. The reverse may be true during an expansion. In the 2000s, many firms in the Middle East increased their investment spending, expecting that capital goods that embodied new information and telecommunication technologies would prove very profitable. The key point is this: *The optimism or pessimism of firms is an important determinant of investment spending.*

The Interest Rate
A significant fraction of business investment is financed by borrowing. This borrowing takes the form of issuing corporate bonds or borrowing from banks. Households also borrow to finance most of their spending on new homes. The higher the interest rate, the more expensive it becomes for firms and households to borrow. Because households and firms are interested in the cost of borrowing after taking into account the effects of inflation, investment spending depends on the real interest rate. Therefore, holding the other factors that affect investment spending constant, there is an inverse relationship between the real interest rate and investment spending: *A higher real interest rate results in less investment spending, and a lower real interest rate results in more investment spending.*

Taxes
Taxes also affect the level of investment spending. Firms focus on the profits that remain after they have paid taxes. The federal government imposes a *corporate income tax* on the profits corporations earn, including profits from the new buildings, equipment, and other investment goods they purchase. A reduction in the corporate income tax increases the after-tax profitability of investment spending. An increase in the corporate income tax decreases the after-tax profitability of investment spending. *Investment tax incentives* also increase investment spending. An investment tax incentive provides firms with a tax reduction when they spend on new investment goods. For example, Lebanon enacted an investment tax incentive for new investments by which the company gets a 75-percent tax-liability reduction. To qualify, the investment should be located in designated industrial zones and lead to an increase in production capacity and employment. Similarly, in Egypt, the profits of new manufacturing establishments in industrial zones are free of corporate tax for the first 10 years.

Cash Flow
Most firms do not borrow to finance spending on new factories, machinery, and equipment. Instead, they use their own funds. **Cash flow** is the difference between the cash revenues received by a firm and the cash spending by the firm. Noncash receipts or noncash spending would not be included in cash flow. For example, tax laws allow firms to count as a cost an amount for depreciation to replace worn out or obsolete machinery and equipment even if new machinery and equipment have not actually been purchased.

Cash flow The difference between the cash revenues received by a firm and the cash spending by the firm.

Because this is noncash spending, it would not be included when calculating cash flow. The largest contributor to cash flow is profit. The more profitable a firm is, the greater its cash flow and the greater its ability to finance investment. During periods of recession, many firms experience reduced profits, which in turn reduces their ability to finance spending on new factories or machinery and equipment.

Making the Connection | **The Construction Boom in the Gulf (2005–2008) Induces Steel Production Capacity Growth**

Started around 2005 and extended to the third quarter of 2008, a soaring demand for construction characterized growth in the Middle East during the first decade of the new century. After 2004, many Arab economies were booming as a result of the large surge in oil prices. Both oil countries and other emerging markets in the region, such as Egypt, Jordan, Lebanon, and Tunisia, were experiencing large capital inflows, especially into the real estate and the energy sectors. The fast growing economies, especially the Gulf Cooperation Council (GCC) countries, drove up infrastructure development and construction spending. The six countries, Bahrain, Kuwait, Oman, Qatar, Saudi Arabia, and the United Arab Emirates, have experienced an unprecedented growth in the spending on construction and real estate. As a result, there was a large increase in steel imports to fill out the growing gap between a limited local supply and a fast expanding demand.

In the UAE, for example, steel imports grew by almost 30 percent between 2004 and 2006. According to the Gulf Organization for Industrial Consulting (GOIC), the combined GCC demand for steel grew by more than 30 percent between 2005 and 2007, and steel import dependency has grown phenomenally over the past 10 years. Steel supply shortages were identified as a growing problem across the GCC.

The optimistic growth expectations, the flow of capital, and a growing building momentum had led investors to quickly take the opportunity to finance capacity expansions and new steel plants in the GCC area. The availability of energy at low cost gave this area a significant additional advantage in the expansion of its steel industry. Cheap natural gas and electricity make it potentially one of the world's most competitive regions. According to SteelConsult International, the costs of production are some US$80 per ton lower than in the USA. By the end of 2007, there had been a large amount of new capacity that was about to be added to the steel production capacity in the region. According to a report from Metal Bulletin Research (MBR), in its December 2006 issue, steel capacity expansion will be dominated by Egypt, Saudi Arabia, and UAE. The largest and most ambitious of the new steel projects is a complex of factories in Saudi Arabia that is expected to produce 500,000 tons of railway tracks and three million tons of iron annually.

The only perceived obstacles to economic steelmaking then were the lack of indigenous iron ore and the region's heavy reliance on immigrant workers. In addition, newly constructed steel plants could be vulnerable to imports of cheaper steel from low-cost producers such as China and India. No one really contemplated the risk of a turning business cycle or expected that a deep world recession was just a few months away. The 2008 financial crisis resulted in a halt to most construction development projects and a collapse in real-estate value. The direct consequence was a strong reversal of the cycle and a double-digit contraction in the construction sector, which sent thousands of construction workers home from the Gulf region. However, it is too soon yet to evaluate the effects of the 2009 downturn on the new iron industry investments in the region.

The construction boom in the GCC between 2004 and 2008 led to a huge expansion in steel production capacity in these countries.

Source: "Boom Time for Gulf," *Gulf Daily News*, May 21 2008, www.gulf-daily-news.com; James Renwick, "Gulf States' Steel Boom Drives Capacity Growth," *Steel Business Briefing Issue 36–26*, April, 2007, www.steelbb.com; Khalil Hanware, "Construction Boom Sparks Steel Demand in ME," *Arab News*, July 19, 2007, www.arabnews.com.

Figure 19-4

Saudi Arabia Real Government Purchases, 1970–2008

Government spending increased sharply after the first oil price shock in 1974, and kept growing but at a slower pace in the 1980s. At the beginning of the 1990s, concerns about the budget deficit caused real government purchases to fall for the following four years, beginning in 1991, before it started steadily rising in 1996.

Based on data from: Country National Accounts, United Nations, 2009.

Government Purchases

Total government purchases include all spending by federal, local, and state governments for goods and services. Recall that government purchases do not include transfer payments, such as Social Security payments or pensions paid by the federal or local governments because the government does not receive a good or service in return.

Figure 19-4 shows levels of Saudi Arabia's real government purchases during the years 1970–2008. Government spending increased sharply after the first oil price shock in 1974. This large increase in government consumption level was hard to cut when oil prices declined (and hence government revenues) during the 1980s. By the beginning of the 1990s, Saudi Arabia had accumulated a huge budget deficit that reached 26 percent of its GDP, surpassing by far all other GCC countries. Facing its largest deficit ever and increasing military spending requirements amid the first Gulf War, the government had to take strong measures to reduce its consumption. Figure 19-4 depicts the decline in the government's real consumption between 1991 and 1995. In 1996, government consumption started rebounding again with the exception of 1997/1998, when it declined as a result of the Asian financial crisis and the further drop in oil prices.

Net Exports

Net exports equal exports minus imports. We can calculate net exports by taking the value of spending by foreign firms and households on goods and services produced in a country and *subtracting* the value of spending by domestic firms and households on goods and services produced in other countries. Figure 19-5 illustrates movements in Jordan's real net exports during the years 1970–2008. From the figure we see that Jordan had a negative trade balance for all years. This means that the value of exports (adjusted for inflation) is not sufficient to cover the imports needs of Jordan. However, this (negative) difference improved in the 1990s and beginning of 2000s, but has worsened again in more recent years.

The following are the three most important variables that determine the level of net exports in any country:

- A country's domestic price level relative to the price levels in other countries
- The growth rate of GDP in the domestic economy relative to the growth rates of GDP in other countries
- The exchange rate between a country's currency and other currencies

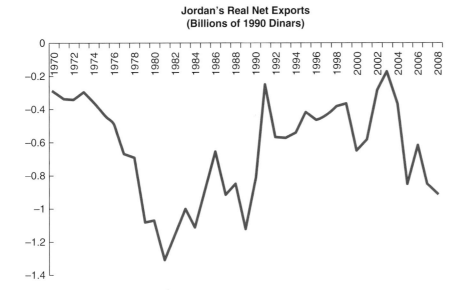

Jordan's Real Net Exports
(Billions of 1990 Dinars)

Figure 19-5

Jordan's Real Net Exports, 1970–2008

Net exports were negative in all years between 1970 and 2008.
Based on data from: Country National Accounts, United Nations, 2009

The Domestic Price Level in a country Relative to the Price Levels in Other Countries In the example of Jordan, if inflation in Jordan is lower than inflation in other countries, prices of Jordanian products increase more slowly than the prices of products of other countries. This difference in price levels increases the demand for Jordanian products relative to the demand for foreign products. So, Jordan's exports increase and Jordan's imports decrease, which increases net exports. The reverse happens during periods when the inflation rate in Jordan is higher than the inflation rates in other countries: Jordan's exports decrease and Jordan's imports increase, which decreases net exports.

The Growth Rate of GDP in a country Relative to the Growth Rates of GDP in Other Countries As GDP increases in Jordan, the incomes of households rise, leading them to increase their purchases of goods and services. Some of the additional goods and services purchased with rising incomes are produced in Jordan, but some are imported. When incomes rise faster in Jordan than in other countries, Jordanian consumers' purchases of foreign goods and services will increase faster than foreign consumers' purchases of Jordanian goods and services. As a result, net exports will fall. When incomes in Jordan rise more slowly than incomes in other countries, net exports will rise.

The Exchange Rate between a Country's Currency and Other Currencies As the value of the Jordanian dinar rises, the foreign currency price of Jordanian products sold in other countries rises, and the dinar price of foreign products sold in Jordan falls. For example, suppose that the exchange rate between the U.S. dollar and the Jordanian dinar (JD) is US$1.42 = JD1. At this exchange rate, someone in Jordan could buy US$1.42 for JD1, or Americans could buy JD1 for US$1.42. Leaving aside transportation costs, at this exchange rate, a Jordanian product that sells for JD1 in Jordan will sell for US$1.42 in the United Sates, and a U.S. product that sells for US$1.42 in the U.S. will sell for JD1 in Jordan. If the exchange rate changes to US$2 = JD1, then the value of the dinar will have risen because it takes more dollars to buy JD1. At the new exchange rate, Jordan's product that still sells for JD1 in Jordan will now sell for US$2 in the US, reducing the quantity demanded by American consumers. The U.S. product that still sells for US$1.42 in the U.S. will now sell for only JD0.70 in Jordan, increasing the quantity demanded by Jordanian consumers. An increase in the value of the dinar will reduce exports and increase imports, so net exports will fall. A decrease in the value of the dinar will increase exports and reduce imports, so net exports will rise.

19.3 | Use a 45°-line diagram to illustrate macroeconomic equilibrium.

Graphing Macroeconomic Equilibrium

Having examined the components of aggregate expenditure, we can now look more closely at macroeconomic equilibrium. We saw earlier in the chapter that macroeconomic equilibrium occurs when GDP is equal to aggregate expenditure. We can use a graph called the *45°-line diagram* to illustrate macroeconomic equilibrium. (The 45°-line diagram is also sometimes referred to as the *Keynesian cross* because it is based on the analysis of John Maynard Keynes.) To become familiar with this diagram, consider Figure 19-6, which is a 45°-line diagram that shows the relationship between the quantity of Pepsi sold (on the vertical axis) and the quantity of Pepsi produced (on the horizontal axis).

The line on the diagram forms an angle of 45° with the horizontal axis. The line represents all the points that are equal distances from both axes. So, points such as *A* and *B*, where the number of bottles of Pepsi produced equals the number of bottles sold, are on the 45° line. Points such as *C*, where the quantity sold is greater than the quantity produced, lie above the line. Points such as *D*, where the quantity sold is less than the quantity produced, lie below the line.

Figure 19-7 is very similar to Figure 19-6, except now we are measuring real national income or real GDP (*Y*) on the horizontal axis and planned real aggregate expenditure (*AE*) on the vertical axis. Because macroeconomic equilibrium occurs where planned aggregate expenditure equals GDP, *we know that all points of macroeconomic equilibrium must lie along the 45° line.* For all points above the 45° line, planned aggregate expenditure will be greater than GDP. For all points below the 45° line, planned aggregate expenditure will be less than GDP.

The 45° line shows many potential points of macroeconomic equilibrium. During any particular year, only one of these points will represent the actual level of equilibrium real GDP, given the actual level of planned real expenditure. To determine this point, we need to draw a line on the graph showing the *aggregate expenditure function*. The aggregate expenditure function shows us the amount of planned aggregate expenditure that will occur at every level of national income or GDP.

Figure 19-6

An Example of a 45°-Line Diagram

The 45° line shows all the points that are equal distances from both axes. Points such as *A* and *B*, at which the quantity produced equals the quantity sold, are on the 45° line. Points such as *C*, at which the quantity sold is greater than the quantity produced, lie above the line. Points such as *D*, at which the quantity sold is less than the quantity produced, lie below the line.

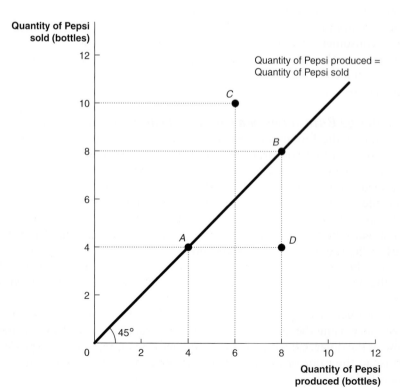

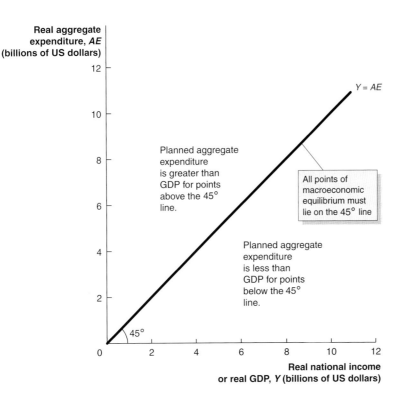

Real aggregate expenditure, *AE* (billions of US dollars)

Planned aggregate expenditure is greater than GDP for points above the 45° line.

All points of macroeconomic equilibrium must lie on the 45° line.

Planned aggregate expenditure is less than GDP for points below the 45° line.

Y = AE

45°

Real national income or real GDP, *Y* (billions of US dollars)

Figure 19-7

The Relationship between Planned Aggregate Expenditure and GDP on a 45°- Line Diagram

Every point of macroeconomic equilibrium is on the 45° line, where planned aggregate expenditure equals GDP. At points above the line, planned aggregate expenditure is greater than GDP. At points below the line, planned aggregate expenditure is less than GDP.

Changes in GDP have a much greater impact on consumption than on planned investment, government purchases, or net exports. We assume for simplicity that the variables that determine planned investment, government purchases, and net exports all remain constant, as do the variables other than GDP that affect consumption. For example, we assume that a firm's level of planned investment at the beginning of the year will not change during the year, even if the level of GDP changes.

Figure 19-8 on the next page shows the aggregate expenditure function on the 45°-line diagram. The lowest upward-sloping line, *C*, represents the consumption function. The quantities of planned investment, government purchases, and net exports are constant because we assumed that the variables they depend on are constant. So, the level of planned aggregate expenditure at any level of GDP is the amount of consumption spending at that level of GDP plus the sum of the constant amounts of planned investment, government purchases, and net exports. In Figure 19-8, we add each component of spending successively to the consumption function line to arrive at the line representing planned aggregate expenditure (*AE*). The *C* + *I* line is higher than the *C* line by the constant amount of planned investment; the *C* + *I* + *G* line is higher than the *C* + *I* line by the constant amount of government purchases; and the *C* + *I* + *G* + *NX* line is higher than the *C* + *I* + *G* line by the constant amount of *NX*. (Notice that in many years, *NX* is negative, which causes the *C* + *I* + *G* + *NX* line to be *below* the *C* + *I* + *G* line.) The *C* + *I* + *G* + *NX* line shows all four components of expenditure and is the aggregate expenditure (*AE*) function. At the point where the *AE* line crosses the 45° line, planned aggregate expenditure is equal to GDP, and the economy is in macroeconomic equilibrium.

Figure 19-9 on p. 635 makes the relationship between planned aggregate expenditure and GDP clearer by showing only the 45° line and the *AE* line. The figure shows that the *AE* line intersects the 45° line at a hypothetical level of real GDP of US$10 billion. Therefore, US$10 billion represents the equilibrium level of real GDP. To see why this is true, consider the situation if real GDP were only US$8 billion. By moving vertically from US$8 billion on the horizontal axis up to the *AE* line, we see that planned aggregate expenditure will be greater than US$8 billion at this level of real GDP. Whenever total spending is greater than total production, firms' inventories will

Figure 19-8

Macroeconomic Equilibrium on the 45°-Line Diagram

Macroeconomic equilibrium occurs where the aggregate expenditure line (*AE*) crosses the 45° line. The lowest upward-sloping line, *C*, represents the consumption function. The quantities of planned investment, government purchases, and net exports are constant because we assumed that the variables they depend on are constant. So, the total of planned aggregate expenditure at any level of GDP is just the amount of consumption at that level of GDP plus the sum of the constant amounts of planned investment, government purchases, and net exports. We successively add each component of spending to the consumption function line to arrive at the line representing aggregate expenditure.

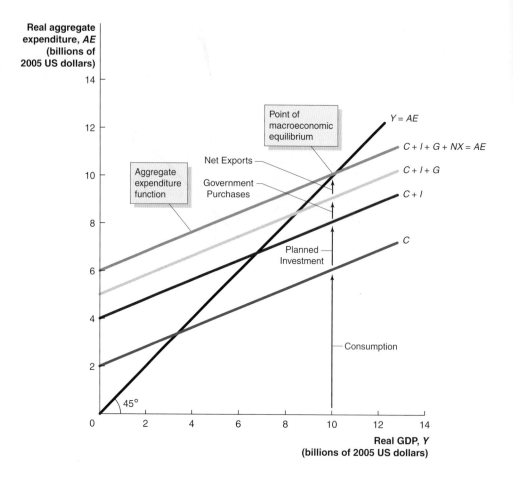

fall. The fall in inventories is equal to the vertical distance between the *AE* line, which shows the level of total spending, and the 45° line, which shows the US$8 billion of total production. Unplanned declines in inventories lead firms to increase their production. As real GDP increases from US$8 billion, so will total income and, therefore, consumption. The economy will move up the *AE* line as consumption increases. The gap between total spending and total production will fall, but as long as the *AE* line is above the 45° line, inventories will continue to decline, and firms will continue to expand production. When real GDP rises to US$10 billion, inventories stop falling, and the economy will be in macroeconomic equilibrium.

As Figure 19-9 shows, if GDP initially is US$12 billion, planned aggregate expenditure will be less than GDP, and firms will experience an unplanned increase in inventories. Rising inventories lead firms to decrease production. As GDP falls from US$12 billion, so will consumption, which causes the economy to move down the *AE* line. The gap between planned aggregate expenditure and GDP will fall, but as long as the *AE* line is below the 45° line, inventories will continue to rise, and firms will continue to cut production. When GDP falls to US$10 billion, inventories will stop rising, and the economy will be in macroeconomic equilibrium.

Showing a Recession on the 45°-Line Diagram

Notice that *macroeconomic equilibrium can occur at any point on the 45° line*. Ideally, we would like equilibrium to occur at *potential real GDP*. At potential real GDP, firms will be operating at their normal level of capacity, and the economy will be at the *natural rate of unemployment*. As we saw in Chapter 16, at the natural rate of unemployment, the economy will be at *full employment*: everyone in the labor force who wants a job will have one, except the structurally and frictionally unemployed. However, for equilibrium to occur at the level of potential real GDP, planned aggregate expenditure must be high enough.

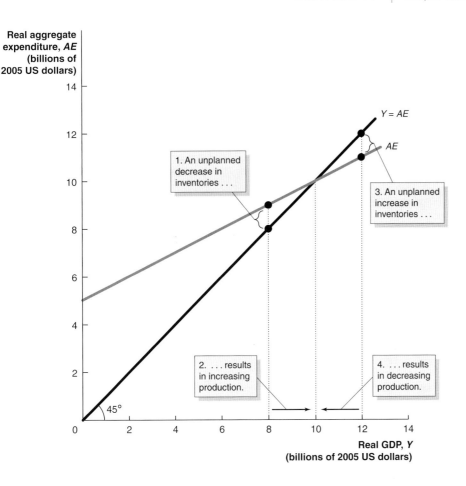

Figure 19-9

Macroeconomic Equilibrium

Macroeconomic equilibrium occurs where the *AE* line crosses the 45° line. In this case, that occurs at GDP of US$10 billion. If GDP is less than US$10 billion, the corresponding point on the *AE* line is above the 45° line, planned aggregate expenditure is greater than total production, firms will experience an unplanned decrease in inventories, and GDP will increase. If GDP is greater than US$10 billion, the corresponding point on the *AE* line is below the 45° line, planned aggregate expenditure is less than total production, firms will experience an unplanned increase in inventories, and GDP will decrease.

As Figure 19-10 on the next page shows, if there is insufficient total spending, equilibrium will occur at a lower level of real GDP. Many firms will be operating below their normal capacity, and the unemployment rate will be above the natural rate of unemployment.

Suppose that the level of potential real GDP is US$10 billion. As Figure 19-10 shows, when GDP is US$10 billion, planned aggregate expenditure is below US$10 billion, perhaps because business firms have become pessimistic about their future profitability and have reduced their investment spending. The shortfall in planned aggregate expenditure that leads to the recession can be measured as the vertical distance between the *AE* line and the 45° line at the level of potential real GDP. The shortfall in planned aggregate expenditure is exactly equal to the unplanned increase in inventories that would occur if the economy were initially at a level of GDP of US$10 billion. The unplanned increase in inventories measures the amount by which current planned aggregate expenditure is too low for the current level of production to be the equilibrium level. Or, put another way, if any of the four components of aggregate expenditure increased by this amount, the *AE* line would shift upward and intersect the 45° line at GDP of US$10 billion, and the economy would be in macroeconomic equilibrium at full employment.

Figure 19-10 shows that macroeconomic equilibrium will occur when real GDP is US$9.8 billion. Because this is 2 percent below the potential level of real GDP of US$10 billion, many firms will be operating below their normal capacity, and the unemployment rate will be well above the natural rate of unemployment. The economy will remain at this level of real GDP until there is an increase in one or more of the components of aggregate expenditure.

The Important Role of Inventories

Whenever planned aggregate expenditure is less than real GDP, some firms will experience an unplanned increase in inventories. If firms do not cut back their production

Figure 19-10

Showing a Recession on the 45°-Line Diagram

When the aggregate expenditure line intersects the 45° line at a level of GDP below potential real GDP, the economy is in recession. The figure shows that potential real GDP is US$10 billion, but because planned aggregate expenditure is too low, the equilibrium level of GDP is only US$9.8 billion, where the *AE* line intersects the 45° line. As a result, some firms will be operating below their normal capacity, and unemployment will be above the natural rate of unemployment. We can measure the shortfall in planned aggregate expenditure as the vertical distance between the *AE* line and the 45° line at the level of potential real GDP.

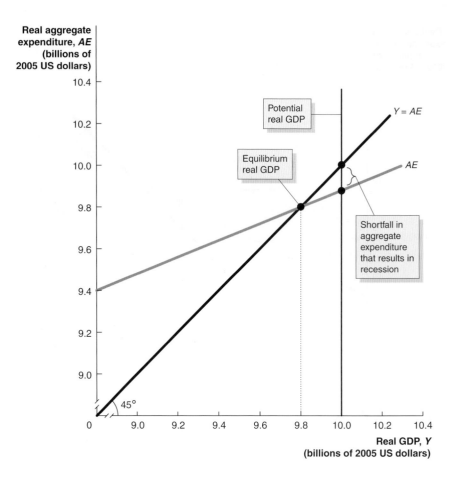

promptly when spending declines, they will accumulate inventories. If firms accumulate excess inventories, then even if spending quickly returns to its normal levels, firms will have to sell these excess inventories before they can return to producing at normal levels. The possibility that firms will accumulate excess inventories explains why a brief decline in spending can result in a fairly long recession. In the early twentieth century, the inability of many firms to control their inventories contributed to the length and severity of recessions. By the 1980s and 1990s, many firms used improved systems of inventory control, which helped make recessions shorter and less severe.

Making the Connection | **Business Attempts to Control Inventories, Then...and Now**

A failure to control inventories can cause a firm to suffer losses or even drive it into bankruptcy. For example, early in the twentieth century, excessive accumulation of inventories was a serious problem for the automobile industry. In his memoirs, Alfred Sloan, president of General Motors during the 1920s, described checking on inventory by travelling around the country by train and literally counting the number of unsold cars on dealers' lots. Not too surprisingly, this weak method of inventory control caused General Motors to suffer severe financial losses in 1920 and again in 1924. Eventually, automobile firms improved their inventory control methods, although not before a number of firms, including United States Motors, the predecessor of Chrysler Corporation, were driven into bankruptcy.

Modern computer firms, such as Dell and Hewlett-Packard, can also suffer significant losses if they accumulate large inventories of computer components because the prices of the components they buy from their suppliers can decline significantly, even from one week to the next. A firm that has large inventories of components may find that its costs of assembling computers are significantly greater than the costs of competitors who hold smaller inventories.

Dell Computer has pioneered in reducing costs by controlling inventories. Dell does not begin to assemble a new computer until it receives an order from a customer by telephone or over the Internet. As a result, Dell holds no inventories of finished computers. Dell still must hold some inventories of computer components, most of which are purchased from outside suppliers. Dell developed a system of *supply chain management* by which it quickly communicates orders to its suppliers and closely monitors their ability to fill its orders promptly. By the mid-1990s, Dell's suppliers could provide Dell with computer components in only two or three days. Dissatisfied with even this strong performance, in 1999, Dell set up an Internet site for suppliers to monitor Dell's need for components minute by minute and to track the components as they move through Dell's computer assembly process. As a

Dell Computer uses supply chain management to keep its inventory low.

result, the amount of time suppliers take to provide Dell with components has dropped to only six hours. When Dell assembles a computer, suppliers will have manufactured many of the components only a few hours earlier. The inventory control techniques that allow Dell to be a low-cost seller of computers also help the firm to respond quickly to sales declines without a significant build up of inventories.

A Numerical Example of Macroeconomic Equilibrium

In forecasting real GDP, economists rely on quantitative models of the economy. We can increase our understanding of the causes of changes in real GDP by considering a simple numerical example of macroeconomic equilibrium. Although simplified, this example captures some of the key features contained in the quantitative models used by economic forecasters. Table 19-3 shows several hypothetical combinations of real GDP and planned aggregate expenditure. The first column lists real GDP. The next four columns list levels of the four components of planned aggregate expenditure that occur at the corresponding level of real GDP. We assume that planned investment, government purchases, and net exports do not change as GDP changes. Because consumption depends on GDP, it increases as GDP increases.

TABLE 19-3 | Macroeconomic Equilibrium

REAL GDP (*Y*) IN US$	CONSUMPTION (*C*) IN US$	PLANNED INVESTMENT (*I*) IN US$	GOVERNMENT PURCHASES (*G*) IN US$	NET EXPORTS (*NX*) IN US$	PLANNED AGGREGATE EXPENDITURE (*AE*) IN US$	UNPLANNED CHANGE IN INVENTORIES IN US$	REAL GDP WILL...
8,000	6,200	1,500	1,500	−500	8,700	−700	increase
9,000	6,850	1,500	1,500	−500	9,350	−350	increase
10,000	7,500	1,500	1,500	−500	10,000	0	be in equilibrium
11,000	8,150	1,500	1,500	−500	10,650	+350	decrease
12,000	8,800	1,500	1,500	−500	11,300	+700	decrease

In the first row, GDP of US$8,000 billion results in consumption of US$6,200 billion. Adding consumption, planned investment, government purchases, and net exports across the row gives planned aggregate expenditure of US$8,700 billion, which is shown in the sixth column. Because planned aggregate expenditure is greater than GDP, inventories will fall by US$700 billion. This unplanned decline in inventories will lead firms to increase production, and GDP will increase. GDP will continue to increase until it reaches US$10,000 billion. At that level of GDP, planned aggregate expenditure is also US$10,000 billion, unplanned changes in inventories are zero, and the economy is in macroeconomic equilibrium.

In the last row of Table 19-3, GDP of US$12,000 billion results in consumption of US$8,800 billion and planned aggregate expenditure of US$11,300 billion. Because planned aggregate expenditure is less than GDP, inventories will increase by US$700 billion. This unplanned increase in inventories will lead firms to decrease production, and GDP will decrease. GDP will continue to decrease until it reaches US$10,000 billion, unplanned changes in inventories are zero, and the economy is in macroeconomic equilibrium.

Only when real GDP equals US$10,000 billion will the economy be in macroeconomic equilibrium. At other levels of real GDP, planned aggregate expenditure will be higher or lower than GDP, and the economy will be expanding or contracting.

Solved Problem | 19-3

Determining Macroeconomic Equilibrium

Fill in the blanks in the following table and determine the equilibrium level of real GDP.

REAL GDP (Y) IN US$	CONSUMPTION (C) IN US$	PLANNED INVESTMENT (I) IN US$	GOVERNMENT PURCHASES (G) IN US$	NET EXPORTS (NX) IN US$	PLANNED AGGREGATE EXPENDITURE (AE) IN US$	UNPLANNED CHANGE IN INVENTORIES IN US$
8,000	6,200	1,675	1,675	−500		
9,000	6,850	1,675	1,675	−500		
10,000	7,500	1,675	1,675	−500		
11,000	8,150	1,675	1,675	−500		
12,000	8,800	1,675	1,675	−500		

Note: The values are in billions of 2000 U.S. dollars.

SOLVING THE PROBLEM:

Step 1: Review the chapter material. This problem is about determining macroeconomic equilibrium, so you may want to review the section "A Numerical Example of Macroeconomic Equilibrium," which begins on page 637.

Step 2: Fill in the missing values in the table. We can calculate the missing values in the last two columns by using two equations:

$$\text{Planned aggregate expenditure } (AE) = \text{Consumption } (C) +$$
$$\text{Planned investment } (I) + \text{Government } (G) + \text{Net exports } (NX)$$

and:

$$\text{Unplanned change in inventories} = \text{Real GDP } (Y) -$$
$$\text{Planned aggregate expenditure } (AE)$$

For example, to fill in the first row, we have $AE =$ US$6,200 billion + US$1,675 billion + US$1,675 billion + (−US$500 billion) = US$9,050 billion; and Unplanned change in inventories = US$8,000 billion − US$9,050 billion = −US$1,050 billion.

REAL GDP (Y) IN US$	CONSUMPTION (C) IN US$	PLANNED INVESTMENT (I) IN US$	GOVERNMENT PURCHASES (G) IN US$	NET EXPORTS (NX) IN US$	PLANNED AGGREGATE EXPENDITURE (AE) IN US$	UNPLANNED CHANGE IN INVENTORIES IN US$
8,000	6,200	1,675	1,675	–500	9,050	–1,050
9,000	6,850	1,675	1,675	–500	9,700	–700
10,000	7,500	1,675	1,675	–500	10,350	–350
11,000	8,150	1,675	1,675	–500	11,000	0
12,000	8,800	1,675	1,675	–500	11,650	350

Step 3: **Determine the equilibrium level of real GDP.** Once you fill in the table, you should see that equilibrium real GDP must be US$11,000 billion because only at that level is real GDP equal to planned aggregate expenditure.

YOUR TURN: For more practice, do related problem 3.12 on page 653 at the end of this chapter.

>> End Solved Problem 19-3

19.4 | Define the multiplier effect and use it to calculate changes in equilibrium GDP.

19.4 LEARNING OBJECTIVE

The Multiplier Effect

To this point, we have seen that aggregate expenditure determines real GDP in the short run and how the economy adjusts if it is not in equilibrium. We have also seen that whenever aggregate expenditure changes, there will be a new level of equilibrium real GDP. In this section, we will look more closely at the effects of a change in aggregate expenditure on equilibrium real GDP. We begin the discussion with Figure 19-11, which illustrates the effects of an increase in planned investment spending. We assume that the economy starts in equilibrium at point A, at which real GDP is US$9.6 billion. Firms then become more optimistic about their future profitability and increase spending on factories, machinery, and equipment by US$100 million. This increase in investment spending shifts the AE line up by US$100 million, from the dark tan line (AE_1) to the light tan line (AE_2). The new equilibrium occurs at point B, at which real GDP is US$10.0 billion, which equals potential real GDP.

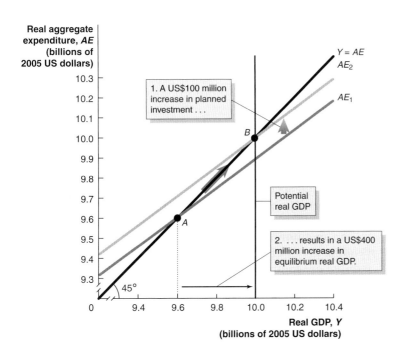

Figure 19-11

The Multiplier Effect

The economy begins at point A, at which equilibrium real GDP is US$9.6 billion. A US$100 million increase in planned investment shifts up aggregate expenditure from AE_1 to AE_2. The new equilibrium is at point B, where real GDP is US$10.0 billion, which is potential real GDP. Because of the multiplier effect, a US$100 million increase in investment results in a US$400 million increase in equilibrium real GDP.

Autonomous expenditure An expenditure that does not depend on the level of GDP.

Multiplier The increase in equilibrium real GDP divided by the increase in autonomous expenditure.

Multiplier effect The process by which an increase in autonomous expenditure leads to a larger increase in real GDP.

Notice that the initial US$10 million increase in planned investment spending results in a US$400 million increase in equilibrium real GDP. The increase in planned investment spending has had a *multiplied effect* on equilibrium real GDP. It is not only investment spending that will have this multiplied effect; any increase in **autonomous expenditure** will shift up the aggregate expenditure function and lead to a multiplied increase in equilibrium GDP. **Autonomous expenditure** does not depend on the level of GDP. In the aggregate expenditure model we have been using, planned investment spending, government spending, and net exports are all autonomous expenditures. Consumption actually has both an autonomous component, which does not depend on the level of GDP, and a non-autonomous—or *induced*—component that does depend on the level of GDP. For example, if households decide to spend more of their incomes—and save less—at every level of income, there will be an autonomous increase in consumption spending, and the aggregate expenditure function will shift up. If, however, real GDP increases and households increase their consumption spending, as indicated by the consumption function, the economy will move up the aggregate expenditure function, and the increase in consumption spending will be non-autonomous.

The ratio of the increase in equilibrium real GDP to the increase in autonomous expenditure is called the **multiplier**. The series of induced increases in consumption spending that results from an initial increase in autonomous expenditure is called the **multiplier effect**. The multiplier effect happens because an initial increase in autonomous expenditure will set off a series of increases in real GDP.

In Figure 19-11, we look more closely at the multiplier effect. Suppose the whole US$100 million increase in investment spending shown in the figure consists of firms buying additional factories and office buildings. Initially, this additional spending will cause the construction of factories and office buildings to increase by US$100 million, so GDP will also increase by US$100 million. Remember that increases in production result in equal increases in national income. So, this increase in real GDP of US$100 million is also an increase in national income of US$100 million. In this example, the income is received as wages and salaries by the employees of the construction firms, as profits by the owners of the firms, and so on. After receiving this additional income, these workers, managers, and owners will increase their consumption of cars, televisions, DVD players, and many other products. If the marginal propensity to consume (*MPC*) is 0.75, we know this increase in consumption spending will be US$75 million. This additional US$75 million in spending will cause the firms making the cars, televisions, and other products to increase production by US$75 million, so GDP will rise by US$75 million. This increase in GDP means national income has also increased by another US$75 million. This increased income will be received by the owners and employees of the firms producing the cars, televisions, and other products. These workers, managers, and owners in turn will increase their consumption spending, and the process of increasing production, income, and consumption will continue.

Eventually, the total increase in consumption will be US$300 million (we will soon show how we know this is true). This US$300 million increase in consumption combined with the initial US$100 million increase in investment spending will result in a total change in equilibrium GDP of US$400 million. Table 19-4 summarizes how changes in GDP and spending caused by the initial US$100 million increase in investment will result in equilibrium GDP rising by US$400 million. We can think of the multiplier effect occurring in rounds of spending. In round 1, there is an increase of US$100 million in autonomous expenditure—the US$100 million in planned investment spending in our example—which causes GDP to rise by US$100 million. In round 2, induced expenditure rises by US$75 million (which equals the US$100 million increase in real GDP in round 1 multiplied by the *MPC*). The US$75 million in induced expenditure in round 2 causes a US$75 million increase in real GDP, which leads to a US$56 million increase in induced expenditure in round 3, and so on. The final column sums up the total increases in expenditure, which equal the total increase in GDP. In each round, the additional induced expenditure becomes

TABLE 19-4

The Multiplier Effect in Action

	ADDITIONAL AUTONOMOUS EXPENDITURE (INVESTMENT) IN US$	ADDITIONAL INDUCED EXPENDITURE (CONSUMPTION) IN US$	TOTAL ADDITIONAL EXPENDITURE = TOTAL ADDITIONAL GDP IN US$
ROUND 1	100 million	0	100 million
ROUND 2	0	75 million	175 million
ROUND 3	0	56 million	231 million
ROUND 4	0	42 million	273 million
ROUND 5	0	32 million	305 million
⋮	⋮	⋮	⋮
ROUND 10	0	8 million	377 million
⋮		⋮	⋮
ROUND 15	0	2 million	395 million
⋮		⋮	⋮
ROUND 19	0	1 million	398 million
⋮	⋮	⋮	⋮
n	0	0	400 million

smaller because the *MPC* is less than 1. By round 10, additional induced expenditure is only US$8 million, and the total increase in GDP from the beginning of the process is US$377 million. By round 19, the process is almost complete: additional induced expenditure is only about US$1 million, and the total increase in GDP is US$398 million. Eventually, the process will be finished, although we cannot say precisely how many spending rounds it will take, so we simply label the last round "n" rather than give it a specific number.

We can calculate the value of the multiplier in our example by dividing the increase in equilibrium real GDP by the increase in autonomous expenditure:

$$\frac{\Delta Y}{\Delta I} = \frac{\text{Change in Real GDP}}{\text{Change in Investment Spending}} = \frac{\text{US\$400 million}}{\text{US\$100 million}} = 4$$

With a multiplier of 4, each increase in autonomous expenditure of US$1 will result in an increase in equilibrium GDP of US$4.

Making the Connection

The Multiplier in Reverse: The Great Depression of the 1930s

An increase in autonomous expenditure causes an increase in equilibrium real GDP, but the reverse is also true: a decrease in autonomous expenditure causes a decrease in real GDP. Many in the United States and around the world became aware of this fact in the 1930s when reductions in autonomous expenditure, first in the U.S. then in other parts of the world, were magnified by the multiplier into the largest decline in the U.S. and the world's real GDP.

In August 1929, the U.S. economy reached a business cycle peak, and a downturn in production began. In October, the stock market crashed, destroying billions of dollars of wealth and increasing pessimism among households and firms.

(Continued)

The multiplier effect contributed to the very high levels of unemployment in the U.S. during the Great Depression.

The crisis spread all around the world and international trade dropped to less than half its value. All countries experienced a large surge in unemployment and both consumption spending and planned investment spending declined. A series of banking crises that began in fall 1930, in the U.S. and then spread to all industrialized countries, limited the ability of households and firms to finance consumption and investment. As aggregate expenditure declined, many firms experienced declining sales and began to lay off more workers. Falling levels of production and income induced further declines in consumption spending, which led to further cutbacks in production and employment, leading to further declines in income, and so on, in a downward spiral.

We can use a 45°-line diagram to illustrate the multiplier effect in the U.S. working in reverse during these years. The U.S. economy was at potential real GDP in 1929 before the declines in aggregate expenditure began. Declining consumption, planned investment, and net exports shifted the aggregate expenditure function down from AE_{1929} to AE_{1933}, reducing equilibrium real GDP from US$865 billion in 1929 to US$636 billion in 1933. The depth and length of this economic downturn led to its being labeled the Great Depression.

The severity of the Depression meant bankruptcy for thousands of firms. Even firms that survived experienced sharp declines in sales. By 1933, production at U.S. Steel had declined by 90 percent, and production at General Motors had declined by more than 75 percent. High rates of unemployment forced many families into poverty and a daily struggle for survival. Recovery from the business cycle trough in 1933 was slow. Real GDP did not regain its 1929 level until 1936, and a growing labor force meant that the unemployment rate did not fall below 10 percent until the United States entered World War II in 1941.

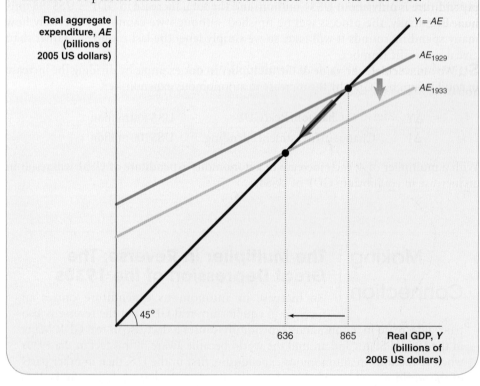

A Formula for the Multiplier

Table 19-4 shows that during the multiplier process, each round of increases in consumption is smaller than in the previous round, so eventually, the increases will come to an end, and we will have a new macroeconomic equilibrium. But how do we know that when we add all the increases in GDP, the total will be US$400 million? We can show this is true by first writing out the total change in equilibrium GDP:

Total change in GDP $=$ US$100 million $+$ $MPC \times$ US$100 million $+$ $MPC^2 \times$ US$100 million $+$ $MPC^3 \times$ US$100 million $+$ $MPC^4 \times$ US$100 million $+ \ldots$

where the ellipsis (...) indicates that the expression contains an infinite number of similar terms.

If we factor out the US$100 million from each expression, we have:

Total Change in GDP $=$ US$100 million $\times$ $(1 + MPC + MPC^2 + MPC^3 + MPC^4 + \ldots)$

Mathematicians have shown that an expression like the one in the parenthesis sums to:

$$\frac{1}{1 - MPC}$$

In this case, the MPC is equal to 0.75. So, we can now calculate that the change in equilibrium GDP $=$ US$1 million $\times [1/(1 - 0.75)]$ = US$100 million $\times 4$ = US$400 million. We have also derived a general formula for the multiplier:

$$\text{Multiplier} = \frac{\text{Change in equilibrium real GDP}}{\text{Change in autonomous expenditure}} = \frac{1}{1 - MPC}$$

In this case, the multiplier is $1/(1 - 0.75)$ or 4, which means that for each additional US$1 of autonomous spending, equilibrium GDP will increase by US$4. A US$100 million increase in planned investment spending results in a US$400 million increase in equilibrium GDP. Notice that the value of the multiplier depends on the value of the MPC. In particular, the larger is the value of the MPC, the larger the value of the multiplier. For example, if the MPC were 0.9 instead of 0.75, the value of the multiplier would increase from 4 to $1/(1 - 0.9) = 10$.

Summarizing the Multiplier Effect

You should note four key points about the multiplier effect:

1 The multiplier effect occurs both when autonomous expenditure increases and when it decreases. For example, with an MPC of 0.75, a *decrease* in planned investment of US$100 million will lead to a *decrease* in equilibrium income of US$400 million.

2 The multiplier effect makes the economy more sensitive to changes in autonomous expenditure than it would otherwise be. When firms decided to cut back their spending on construction following the financial crisis of 2008, the decision did not only affect real estate and infrastructure developers such as Nakheel or Emaar. Because the initial decline in investment spending set off a series of declines in production, income, and spending, firms such as automobile dealerships and furniture stores, which are not directly related to the construction sector, also experienced sales declines.

3 The larger is the MPC, the larger the value of the multiplier. With an MPC of 0.75, the multiplier is 4, but with an MPC of 0.50, the multiplier is only 2. This inverse relationship between the value of the MPC and the value of the multiplier holds true because the larger the MPC, the more additional consumption takes place after each rise in income during the multiplier process.

4 The formula for the multiplier, $1/(1 - MPC)$, is oversimplified because it ignores some real-world complications, such as the effect that an increasing GDP can have on imports, inflation, and interest rates. These effects combine to cause the simple formula to overstate the true value of the multiplier. In the following chapters, we will start to take into account these real-world complications.

Solved Problem | 19-4

Using the Multiplier Formula

Use the information in the table to answer the following questions.

REAL GDP (Y) IN US$	CONSUMPTION (C) IN US$	PLANNED INVESTMENT (I) IN US$	GOVERNMENT PURCHASES (G) IN US$	NET EXPORTS (NX) IN US$
8,000	6,900	1,000	1,000	−500
9,000	7,700	1,000	1,000	−500
10,000	8,500	1,000	1,000	−500
11,000	9,300	1,000	1,000	−500
12,000	10,100	1,000	1,000	−500

Note: The values are in billions of 2000 U.S. dollars.

a. What is the equilibrium level of real GDP?

b. What is the *MPC*?

c. Suppose government purchases increase by US$200 billion. What will be the new equilibrium level of real GDP? Use the multiplier formula to determine your answer.

SOLVING THE PROBLEM:

Step 1: **Review the chapter material.** This problem is about the multiplier process, so you may want to review the section "The Multiplier Effect," which begins on page 639.

Step 2: **Determine equilibrium real GDP.** Just as in Solved Problem 19-2 on page 626, we can find macroeconomic equilibrium by calculating the level of planned aggregate expenditure for each level of real GDP.

REAL GDP (Y) IN US$	CONSUMPTION (C) IN US$	PLANNED INVESTMENT (I) IN US$	GOVERNMENT PURCHASES (G) IN US$	NET EXPORTS (NX) IN US$	PLANNED AGGREGATE EXPENDITURE (AE) IN US$
8,000	6,900	1,000	1,000	−500	8,400
9,000	7,700	1,000	1,000	−500	9,200
10,000	8,500	1,000	1,000	−500	10,000
11,000	9,300	1,000	1,000	−500	10,800
12,000	10,100	1,000	1,000	−500	11,600

We can see that macroeconomic equilibrium will occur when real GDP equals US$10,000 billion.

Step 3: **Calculate *MPC*.**

$$MPC = \frac{\Delta C}{\Delta Y}$$

In this case,

$$MPC = \frac{\text{US\$800 billion}}{\text{US\$1,000 billion}} = 0.8$$

Step 4: **Use the multiplier formula to calculate the new equilibrium level of real GDP.** We could find the new level of equilibrium real GDP by constructing a new table with government purchases increased from US$1,000 to US$1,200. But the multiplier allows us to calculate the answer directly. In this case:

$$\text{Multiplier} = \frac{1}{1 - MPC} = \frac{1}{1 - 0.8} = 5$$

So:

Change in equilibrium real GDP = Change in autonomous expenditure × 5

Or:

Change in equilibrium real GDP = US$200 billion × 5 = US$1,000 billion

Therefore:

The new level of equilibrium GDP = US$10,000 billion +
US$1,000 billion = US$11,000 billion

YOUR TURN: For more practice, do related problem 4.3 on page 653 at the end of this chapter.

>> End Solved Problem 19-4

19.5 LEARNING OBJECTIVE

19.5 | Understand the relationship between the aggregate demand curve and aggregate expenditure.

The Aggregate Demand Curve

When demand for a product increases, firms usually respond by increasing production, but they are also likely to increase prices. Similarly, when demand falls, production falls, but often, prices also fall. We would expect, then, that an increase or a decrease in aggregate expenditure would affect not just real GDP but also the *price level*. So far, we haven't taken into account the effect of changes in the price level on the components of aggregate expenditure. In fact, as we will see, increases in the price level cause aggregate expenditure to fall, and decreases in the price level cause aggregate expenditure to rise. There are three main reasons for this inverse relationship between changes in the price level and changes in aggregate expenditure. We discussed the first two reasons earlier in this chapter when considering the factors that determine consumption and net exports:

- A rising price level decreases consumption by decreasing the real value of household wealth; a falling price level has the reverse effect.

- If the domestic price level in a country rises relative to the price levels in other countries, the country's exports will become relatively more expensive, and foreign imports will become relatively less expensive, causing net exports to fall. A falling domestic price level has the reverse effect.

- When prices rise, firms and households need more money to finance buying and selling. If the central bank does not increase the money supply, the result will be an increase in the interest rate. We will analyze in more detail why this happens in the following chapters. As we discussed earlier in this chapter, at a higher interest rate, investment spending falls as firms borrow less money to build new factories or to install new machinery and equipment, and households borrow less money to buy new houses. A falling price level has the reverse effect. Other things equal, interest rates will fall and investment spending will rise.

We can now incorporate the effect of a change in the price level into the basic aggregate expenditure model in which equilibrium real GDP is determined by the intersection of the aggregate expenditure (*AE*) line and the 45° line. Remember that we measure the price level as an index number with a value of 100 in the base year. If the price level rises from, say, 100 to 103, consumption, planned investment, and net exports will all fall, causing the *AE* line to shift down on the 45°-line diagram. The *AE* line shifts down because with higher prices, less spending will occur in the economy at every level of GDP. Panel (a) of Figure 19-12 shows that the downward shift of the *AE* line results in a lower level of equilibrium real GDP.

If the price level falls from, say, 100 to 97, then investment, consumption, and net exports would all rise. As panel (b) of Figure 19-12 shows, the *AE* line would shift up, which would cause equilibrium real GDP to increase.

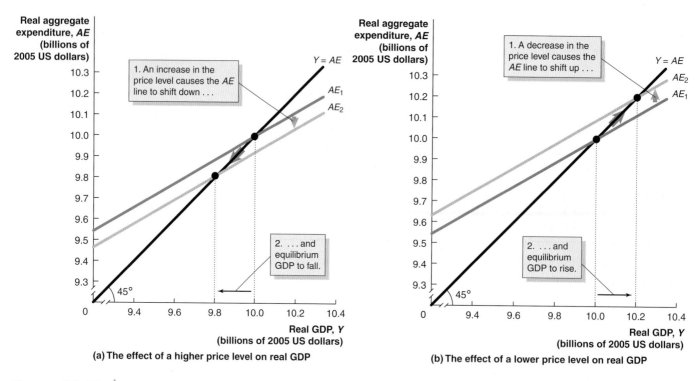

Figure 19-12 | The Effect of a Change in the Price Level on Real GDP

In panel (a), an increase in the price level results in declining consumption, planned investment, and net exports and causes the aggregate expenditure line to shift down from AE_1 to AE_2. As a result, equilibrium real GDP declines from US$10.0 billion to US$9.8 billion. In panel (b), a decrease in the price level results in rising consumption, planned investment, and net exports and causes the aggregate expenditure line to shift up from AE_1 to AE_2. As a result, equilibrium real GDP increases from US$10.0 billion to US$10.2 billion.

Aggregate demand curve A curve that shows the relationship between the price level and the level of planned aggregate expenditure in the economy, holding constant all other factors that affect aggregate expenditure.

Figure 19-13 summarizes the effect of changes in the price level on real GDP. The table shows the combinations of price level and real GDP from Figure 19-12. The figure plots the numbers from the table. In the figure, the price level is measured on the vertical axis, and real GDP is measured on the horizontal axis. The relationship shown in Figure 19-13 between the price level and the level of planned aggregate expenditure is known as the **aggregate demand curve**, or *AD* curve.

Figure 19-13

The Aggregate Demand Curve

The aggregate demand curve, labeled *AD*, shows the relationship between the price level and the level of planned aggregate expenditure in the economy. When the price level is 97, real GDP is US$10.2 billion. An increase in the price level to 100 causes consumption, investment, and net exports to fall, which reduces real GDP to US$10.0 billion.

Price level	Equilibrium real GDP
97	US$10.2 billion
100	US$10.0 billion
103	US$9.8 billion

Economics in YOUR Life!

>> Continued from page 617

At the beginning of this chapter, we asked you to suppose that you work part-time assembling desktop computers for a large computer company. You have learned that consumer confidence in the economy has fallen and that many households expect their future income to be dramatically less than their current income. Should you be concerned about losing your job? We have seen in this chapter that if consumers expect their future incomes to decline, they will cut their consumption spending, and consumption spending is about 70 percent of aggregate expenditure. So, there is some chance that consumption spending will fall, which would reduce aggregate expenditures and GDP. If the economy does move into a recession, spending on computers by households and firms may slow down, which could reduce your firm's sales and possibly cost you a job. Before you panic, though, keep in mind that surveys of consumer confidence do not have a good track record in predicting recessions, so you may not have to move back in with your parents after all.

Conclusion

In this chapter, we learned a key macroeconomic idea: in the short run, the level of GDP is determined mainly by the level of aggregate expenditure. When economists forecast changes in GDP, they do so by forecasting changes in the four components of aggregate expenditure. We constructed an aggregate demand curve by taking into account the effect on aggregate expenditure of changes in the price level.

But our story is incomplete. In the next chapter, we will analyze the *aggregate supply curve*. Then, we will use the aggregate demand curve and the aggregate supply curve to show how equilibrium real GDP *and* the equilibrium price level are simultaneously determined.

We also need to discuss the role the financial system and government policy play in determining real GDP and the price level in the short run. We will cover these important topics in the next three chapters. Before moving on, read *An Inside Look* on the next page, which discusses economists and businessmen's expectations of the impact of the 2008 financial crisis on the Jordanian economy's GDP and labor market.

Jordan Expected Thousands of Workers Home from the Gulf: Is it Good News for the Jordanian Economy?

GLOBAL POST, MARCH 14, 2009

Can Jordan Dodge the Downturn Bullet?

AMMAN—As other nations come to terms with mass layoffs, shattered fortunes, and home foreclosures, in Jordan the sense of impending economic catastrophe is … absent. Certainly, construction, tourism, and other industries are feeling the sting of the meltdown, but many economists here see it as more of an opportunity than a threat. As recession overtakes the Gulf countries, nations like Jordan are well situated to use the situation to restructure their economies and win back laborers who have long been lured by higher wages in the Gulf and overseas. Experts, however, warn that without fast action and government assistance, the chance may pass Jordan by. "The effect of the overall global recession on Jordan should be positive, not negative," says Yusuf Mansur, CEO of EnConsult, an economic consulting firm in Amman.

More than 20 percent of Jordan's gross domestic product comes from remittances sent home by citizens outside the country. The Arabian Gulf alone is home to nearly 10 percent of Jordan's population. The behavior of migrant workers in a downturn is hard to predict. As layoffs begin throughout the Gulf, some estimates have up to 25 percent of the Gulf workforce returning to their homes by the end of 2009. But many may also migrate to Gulf countries less affected by the downturn, or if there is a quick recovery they may return to the Gulf after only a short time in their home countries.

"It's not easy to say precisely what's going to happen," says Ahmed Oran, head of the economics department at the University of Jordan. "The magnitude of the international crisis is not known yet and it has not ended."

Despite its limited effect on Jordan thus far, the crisis is starting to send ripples through select segments of the economy here. Last year, Tony El-Khal established a real estate development branch of his UAE-based firm in Jordan. He had planned to begin building twin towers in Amman, but put the project on hold until his company could assess the economic situation going forward. While El-Khal didn't lay anyone off, he cancelled plans to hire new employees for the project.

He is, however, optimistic that, if not this year, the situation will begin to improve shortly thereafter. "We were hoping that the first half would be bad, and the second half would be the correction, but it seems no, the second half of this year will be not so good as well," he says. While businessmen like El-Khal remain optimistic, those on the receiving end of hiring freezes face a much bleaker predicament.

Wajdi El-Asir runs a small electrical engineering firm that contracts out to large construction projects. Just a year ago he had trouble keeping up with the amount of work available. Now, he's had to lay off two of his 15 employees and is struggling to find even a small project to keep others on the payroll. "No one is starting new projects right now, because they don't know what will happen," he says.

Though an influx of jobless workers may seem menacing, Yusuf Mansur (CEO of EnConsult) said,

those returning are likely to bring considerable savings they accrued in the Gulf. When Jordanian workers returned from Kuwait after the first Gulf War, for example, the economy grew by more than 16 percent. But that boom period was short-lived, as the returnees spent their money and then struggled to find work.

"In the immediate future these countries are going to be in a firefighting mode, with much of the labor returning," says Krishna Kumar, a senior economist who specializes in economic growth and development at the RAND Corporation. However, Kumar says that instead of seeing this as a burden, countries like Jordan could potentially use it as an opportunity to restructure the economic landscape. He states "This kind of a crisis gives political cover for a lot of reform-minded policy makers in these labor exporting countries to say, 'We've benefited from exporting labor; that was one step in the development. Now here is a perfect opportunity for us to move to the higher end of development and start making goods ourselves."

To date, though, Jordan has yet to take any major actions to facilitate such opportunities. Despite a healthy foreign reserve that grew by 12.7 percent in 2008, Jordanian officials have largely adhered to prudent financial policies and maintained high interest rates—in December the weighted average interest rate on loans and advances was 9.48 percent, according to the Central Bank of Jordan.

Source: Tom Peter, "Can Jordan Dodge the Downturn Bullet?," *Global Post*, March 14, 2009, www.Globalpost.com.

Key Points in the Article

This article discusses how economists and businessmen perceived the expected impact of the financial crisis on the Jordanian economy's national income and labor market. Some experts and business-men were pessimistic and others were opti-mistic. On the negative side, Jordan receives almost one fourth of its income from work-ers' remittances while working abroad, especially in the Gulf, which is home to 10 percent of the Jordanian population. Others see this as an opportunity for the Jordanian economy to seize. The returning population can be a boost to the economy during a bad downturn, and an engine of growth.

Analyzing the News

ⓐ In the wake of the global crisis, the lay-offs in the Gulf threatened to send many Jordanian workers home. This is an impending bombshell for an economy that derives more than 20 percent of its GDP from the remittances (income transfers) of workers abroad.

ⓑ The immediate impact of the crisis was a slowdown in new hiring, and freezing new projects, as businessmen tried to assess the final impact of the crisis. The most affected sector was construction and real estate development, and related services. This can be seen from the figure, which shows the drop from point C to point A. Aggregate demand fell to AE_1, and GDP fell as well at point E_1.

ⓒ Despite a limited and struggling job market, the return of Jordanian labor can be thought of as an opportunity to be seized. It could work as a stimulus

to aggregate demand in the economy at a time when income from net exports is shrinking. These workers are expected to spend their saved incomes inside the country, creating a new wave of demand and an increase in aggregate expenditure needed to reduce the impact of the global recession on the growth prospects of the Jordanian economy. We see this in the fig-ure, which that shows that the return of the labor force would raise the level of GDP to E_2 because of an increase in aggregate demand to AE_2. The gap of aggregate demand declines to BC.

Thinking Critically

1. As you read in this article, any crisis can be thought of as an impending catastro-phe or as an opportunity to seize. Which side would you support? What facts do you base your argument on?

2. What do you think happened to the Jordanian economy in 2009 and 2010? How well do you think they handled the crisis?

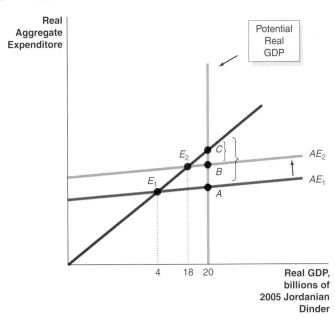

The global financial crisis and the economic downturn put many construction projects on hold in Jordan, as well as in other Arab countries.

Key Terms

Summary

19.1 LEARNING OBJECTIVE

Understand how macroeconomic equilibrium is determined in the aggregate expenditure model, **pages 618–621.**

The Aggregate Expenditure Model

Aggregate expenditure (*AE*) is the total amount of spending in the economy. The **aggregate expenditure model** focuses on the relationship between total spending and real GDP in the short run, assuming that the price level is constant. In any particular year, the level of GDP is determined by the level of total spending, or aggregate expenditure, in the economy. The four components of aggregate expenditure are consumption (*C*), planned investment (*I*), government purchases (*G*), and net exports (*NX*). When aggregate expenditure is greater than GDP, there is an unplanned decrease in **inventories**, which are goods that have been produced but not yet sold, and GDP and total employment will increase. When aggregate expenditure is less than GDP, there is an unplanned increase in inventories, and GDP and total employment will decline. When aggregate expenditure is equal to GDP, firms will sell what they expected to sell, production and employment will be unchanged, and the economy will be in macroeconomic equilibrium.

19.2 LEARNING OBJECTIVE

Discuss the determinants of the four components of aggregate expenditure and define the marginal propensity to consume and the marginal propensity to save, **pages 621–631.**

Determining the Level of Aggregate Expenditure in the Economy

The five determinants of consumption are current disposable income, household wealth, expected future income, the price level, and the interest rate. The consumption function is the relationship between consumption and disposable income. The marginal propensity to consume (*MPC*) is the change in consumption divided by the change in disposable income. The marginal propensity to save (*MPS*) is the change in saving divided by the change in disposable income. The determinants of planned investment are expectations of future profitability, the real interest rate, taxes, and cash flow, which is the difference between the cash revenues received by a firm and the cash spending by the firm. Government purchases include spending by the government on goods and services. Government purchases do not include *transfer payments*, such as Social Security payments by the government. The three determinants of net exports are the domestic price level relative to the price levels in other countries, the domestic growth rate of GDP relative to the growth rates of GDP in other countries, and the exchange rate between the local currency and other currencies.

19.3 LEARNING OBJECTIVE

Use a 45°-line diagram to illustrate macroeconomic equilibrium, **pages 632–639.**

Graphing Macroeconomic Equilibrium

The 45°-line diagram shows all the points where aggregate expenditure equals real GDP. On the 45°-line diagram, macroeconomic equilibrium occurs where the line representing the aggregate expenditure function crosses the 45° line. The economy is in recession when the aggregate expenditure line intersects the 45° line at a level of GDP that is below potential GDP. Numerically, macroeconomic equilibrium occurs when:

$$\text{Consumption} + \text{Planned investimet} +$$
$$\text{Government purchases} + \text{Net exports} = \text{GDP}$$

The Multiplier Effect

Autonomous expenditure is expenditure that does not depend on the level of GDP. An autonomous change is a change in expenditure not caused by a change in income. An *induced change* is a change in aggregate expenditure caused by a change in income. An autonomous change in expenditure will cause rounds of induced changes in expenditure. Therefore, an autonomous change in expenditure will have a *multiplier effect* on equilibrium GDP. The **multiplier effect** is the process by which an increase in autonomous expenditure leads to a larger increase in real GDP. The **multiplier** is the ratio of the change in equilibrium GDP to the change in autonomous expenditure. The formula for the multiplier is:

$$\frac{1}{1 - MPC}$$

19.4 LEARNING OBJECTIVE

Define the multiplier effect and use it to calculate changes in equilibrium GDP, **pages 639–645.**

The Aggregate Demand Curve

Increases in the price level cause a reduction in consumption, investment, and net exports. This causes the aggregate expenditure function to shift down on the 45°-line diagram, leading to a lower equilibrium real GDP. A decrease in the price level leads to a higher equilibrium real GDP. The **aggregate demand curve** shows the relationship between the price level and the level of aggregate expenditure, holding constant all factors that affect aggregate expenditure other than the price level.

19.5 LEARNING OBJECTIVE

Understand the relationship between the aggregate demand curve and aggregate expenditure, **pages 645–647.**

Review, Problems and Applications

myeconlab Visit www.pearsoned.co.uk/awe/hubbard to complete these exercises online and get instant feedback.
Get Ahead of the Curve

19.1 LEARNING OBJECTIVE Understand how macroeconomic equilibrium is determined in the aggregate expenditure model, **pages 618–621.**

Review Questions

1.1 What is the main reason for changes in GDP in the short run?

1.2 What are inventories? What usually happens to inventories at the beginning of a recession? At the beginning of an expansion?

Problems and Applications

1.3 Into which category of UAE aggregate expenditures would each of the following transactions fall?
   a. The Mohsen family buys a new car.
   b. United Arab Emirates University buys 12 new university busses.
   c. The Hamdan family buys a new house.
   d. A consumer in the UAE orders a computer online from Dell (in the U.S.).
   e. Zayed University in the UAE purchases 250 new computers from Dell (in the U.S.).

1.4 Suppose Apple plans to produce 16.2 million iPods this year. It expects to sell 16.1 million and add 100,000 to the inventories in its stores.

   a. Suppose that at the end of the year, Apple has sold 15.9 million iPods. What was Apple's planned investment spending? What was Apple's actual investment spending?
   b. Now suppose that at the end of the year, Apple has sold 16.3 million iPods. What was Apple's planned investment spending? What was Apple's actual investment spending?

1.5 In the second quarter of 2005, business inventories declined by US$10 billion. What does this information tell us about the relationship between aggregate expenditure and GDP during the second quarter of 2005?

1.6 Suppose you read that business inventories increased dramatically last month. What does this tell you about the state of the economy? Would your answer be affected by whether the increase in inventories was taking place at the end of a recession or the end of an expansion? Briefly explain.

Review Questions

2.1 What are the four categories of aggregate expenditure? Give an example of each.

2.2 What are the five main determinants of consumption spending? Which of these is the most important?

Problems and Applications

2.3 Suppose a major furniture manufacturer is forecasting demand for its products during the next year. How will the forecast be affected by each of the following?
a. A decrease in consumer spending in the economy
b. An increase in real interest rates
c. An increase in the exchange rate value of the domestic currency
d. A decrease in planned investment spending in the economy

2.4 Many people have difficulty borrowing as much money as they would like, even if they are confident that their incomes in the future will be high enough to pay it back easily. For example, many students in medical school will earn high incomes after they graduate and become physicians. If they could, they would probably borrow now in order to live more comfortably while in medical school and pay the loans back out of their higher future income. Unfortunately, banks are usually reluctant to make loans to people who currently have low incomes, even if there is a good chance their incomes will be much higher in the future. If people could always borrow as much as they would like, would you expect consumption to become more or less sensitive to current income? Why?

2.5 An economics student raises the following objection: "The textbook said that a higher interest rate lowers investment, but this doesn't make sense. I know that if I can get a higher interest rate, I am certainly going to invest more in my savings account." Do you agree with this reasoning?

2.6 Unemployed workers receive unemployment insurance payments from the government. Does the existence of unemployment insurance make it likely that consumption will fluctuate more or fluctuate less over the business cycle than it would in the absence of unemployment insurance? Briefly explain.

2.7 Explain whether you agree or disagree with the following argument: "Transfer payments should be counted as part of government purchases when we calculate aggregate expenditure. After all, spending is spending. Why does it matter whether the spending is for an aircraft carrier or for a social security payment to a retired person?"

2.8 Suppose we drop the assumption that net exports do not depend on real GDP. Draw a graph with the value of net exports on the vertical axis and the value of real GDP on the horizontal axis. Now, add a line representing the relationship between net exports and real GDP. Briefly explain why you drew the graph the way you did.

2.9 (Related to *Solved Problem 19-2* on page 626) Fill in the blanks in the table in the next column. Assume for simplicity that taxes are zero.

NATIONAL INCOME AND REAL GDP (Y) IN US$	CONSUMPTION (C) IN US$	SAVING (S) IN US$	MARGINAL PROPENSITY TO CONSUME (MPC)	MARGINAL PROPENSITY TO SAVE (MPS)
9,000	8,000		—	—
10,000	8,750			
11,000	9,500			
12,000	10,250			
13,000	11,000			

Review Questions

3.1 Use a 45°-line diagram to illustrate macroeconomic equilibrium. Make sure your diagram shows the aggregate expenditure function and the level of equilibrium real GDP and that your axes are properly labeled.

3.2 What is the macroeconomic consequence if firms accumulate large amounts of unplanned inventory at the beginning of a recession?

3.3 What is the difference between aggregate expenditure and consumption spending?

Problems and Applications

3.4 At point A in the following graph, is planned aggregate expenditure greater than, equal to, or less than GDP? What about at point B? At point C? For points A and C, indicate the vertical distance that measures the unintended change in inventories.

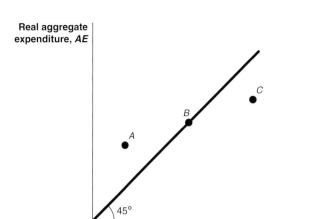

3.5 Is it possible for the economy to be in macroeconomic equilibrium at a level of real GDP that is greater than the potential level of real GDP? Illustrate using a 45°-line diagram.

3.6 The impact of inventory increases on the business cycle depends upon whether they are planned or unplanned. Do you agree with this statement? Briefly explain.

3.7 What is an "inventory drawdown"? What component of aggregate expenditure would be affected by an inventory drawdown? Why would this add to GDP growth?

3.8 In each of the following situations, indicate what happens to the firm's inventories and whether the firm will be likely to increase or decrease its production in the future.

   a. Universal expected to sell 120,000 microwaves during the current month but actually sold 100,000.

   b. Toyota Egypt expected to sell 80,000 Corollas during the current month but actually sold 90,000.

3.9 When the UAE's exports increase in one month more than the increase in imports, explain why this could mean a boost for the economy.

3.10 Briefly explain whether you agree with the following argument: "The equilibrium level of GDP is determined by the level of aggregate expenditure. Therefore, GDP will decline only if households decide to spend less on goods and services."

3.11 Explain how business spending on machinery, equipment, and other investments can "lift an economy" or "sink" it? Use a 45°-line diagram to illustrate your answer.

3.12 (Related to *Solved Problem 19-3* on page 638) Fill in the missing values in the following table. Assume that the value of the *MPC* does not change as real GDP changes.

REAL GDP (Y) IN US$	CONSUMPTION (C) IN US$	PLANNED INVESTMENT (I) IN US$	GOVERNMENT PURCHASES (G) IN US$	NET EXPORTS (NX) IN US$	PLANNED AGGREGATE EXPENDITURE (AE) IN US$	UNPLANNED CHANGE IN INVENTORIES
9,000	7,600	1,200	1,200	−400		
10,000	8,400	1,200	1,200	−400		
11,000		1,200	1,200	−400		
12,000		1,200	1,200	−400		
13,000		1,200	1,200	−400		

   a. What is the value of the *MPC*?
   b. What is the value of equilibrium real GDP?

19.4 LEARNING OBJECTIVE   Define the multiplier effect and use it to calculate changes in equilibrium GDP,

pages 639–645.

Review Questions

4.1 What is the multiplier effect? Use a 45°-line diagram to illustrate the multiplier effect of a decrease in government purchases.

4.2 What is the formula for the multiplier? Explain why this formula is considered to be too simple.

Problems and Applications

4.3 (Related to *Solved Problem 19-4* on page 644) Use the information in the following table to answer the following questions.

REAL GDP (Y) IN US$	CONSUMPTION (C) IN US$	PLANNED INVESTMENT (I) IN US$	GOVERNMENT PURCHASES (G) IN US$	NET EXPORTS (NX) IN US$
8,000	7,300	1,000	1,000	−500
9,000	7,900	1,000	1,000	−500
10,000	8,500	1,000	1,000	−500
11,000	9,100	1,000	1,000	−500
12,000	9,700	1,000	1,000	−500

a. What is the equilibrium level of real GDP?

b. What is the *MPC*?

c. Suppose net exports increase by US$400 billion. What will be the new equilibrium level of real GDP? Use the multiplier formula to determine your answer.

4.4 The direct contribution of net exports to China's income growth is not more than two percentage points. But if we include the multiplier effects, the total growth impact of net exports is certainly higher. What does "the multiplier effects" mean? What does "total growth impact" mean? Why would the multiplier effect increase the impact of exports on economic growth in China?

4.5 Explain whether you agree or disagree with the following statement:

> Many economists claim that the recession of 2001 was caused by a decline in investment. This can't be true. If there had just been a decline in investment, the only firms hurt would have been construction firms, computer firms, and other firms selling investment goods. In fact, many firms experienced falling sales during that recession, including automobile firms and furniture firms.

4.6 Suppose a booming economy in Europe causes net exports to rise by US$75 billion in Saudi Arabia. If the *MPC* is 0.8, what will be the change in equilibrium GDP?

4.7 Would a larger multiplier lead to longer and more severe recessions or shorter and less severe recessions? Briefly explain.

4.8 Use the following graph to answer the questions.

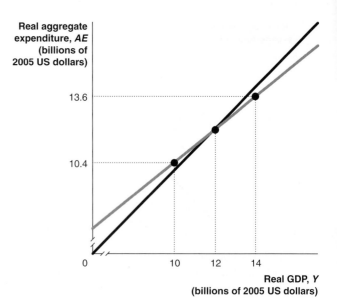

a. What is the value of equilibrium real GDP?

b. What is the value of the *MPC*?

c. What is the value of the multiplier?

d. What is the value of unplanned changes in inventories when real GDP has each of the following values?

- US$10 billion

- US$12 billion

- US$14 billion

4.9 When a business expands the number of buildings and employees at its headquarters, the newly created jobs will lead to a multiplier effect. How would this multiplier effect work?

Review Questions

5.1 Briefly explain the difference between aggregate expenditure and aggregate demand.

5.2 Briefly explain which components of aggregate expenditure are affected by a change in the price level.

Problems and Applications

5.3 Briefly explain why the aggregate expenditure line is upward sloping, while the aggregate demand curve is downward sloping.

5.4 Briefly explain whether you agree with the following statement: "The reason that the aggregate demand curve slopes downward is that when the price level is higher, people cannot afford to buy as many goods and services."

5.5 Suppose that exports become more sensitive to changes in the domestic price level in Qatar. That is, when the price level in Qatar rises, exports decline by more than they previously used to. Will this change make the aggregate demand curve steeper or less steep? Briefly explain.

Appendix

The Algebra of Macroeconomic Equilibrium

Apply the algebra of macroeconomic equilibrium.

In this chapter, we relied primarily on graphs and tables to illustrate the aggregate expenditure model of short-run real GDP. Graphs help us understand economic change *qualitatively*. When we write down an economic model using equations, we make it easier to make *quantitative estimates*. When economists forecast future movements in GDP, they often rely on *econometric models*. An econometric model is an economic model written in the form of equations, where each equation has been statistically estimated, using methods similar to the methods used in estimating demand curves that we briefly described in Chapter 3. We can use equations to represent the aggregate expenditure model described in this chapter.

The following equations are based on the example shown in Table 19-3 on page 637. Y stands for real GDP, and the numbers (with the exception of the *MPC*) represent billions of US dollars.

1	$C = 1,000 + 0.65\ Y$	Consumption function
2	$I = 1,500$	Planned investment function
3	$G = 1,500$	Government spending function
4	$NX = -500$	Net export function
5	$Y = C + I + G + NX$	Equilibrium condition

The first equation is the consumption function. The *MPC* is 0.65, and 1,000 is autonomous consumption, which is the level of consumption that does not depend on income. If we think of the consumption function as a line on the 45°-line diagram, 1,000 would be the intercept, and 0.65 would be the slope. The "functions" for the other three components of planned aggregate expenditure are very simple because we have assumed that these components are not affected by GDP and, therefore, are constant. Economists who use this type of model to forecast GDP would, of course, use more realistic investment, government, and net export functions. The *parameters* of the functions—such as the value of autonomous consumption and the value of the *MPC* in the consumption function—would be estimated statistically using data on the values of each variable over a period of years.

In this model, equilibrium GDP occurs where GDP is equal to planned aggregate expenditure. Equation 5—the equilibrium condition—shows us how to calculate equilibrium in the model: To calculate equilibrium, we substitute equations 1 through 4 into equation 5. This gives us the following:

$$Y = 1,000 + 0.65Y + 1,500 + 1,500 - 500$$

We need to solve this expression for Y to find equilibrium GDP. The first step is to subtract $0.65Y$ from both sides of the equation:

$$Y - 0.65Y = 1{,}000 + 1{,}500 + 1{,}500 - 500$$

Then, we solve for Y:

$$0.35Y = 3{,}500$$

Or:

$$Y = \frac{3{,}500}{0.35} = 10{,}000$$

To make this result more general, we can replace particular values with general values represented by letters:

1 $C = \bar{C} + MPC(Y)$ Consumption function

2 $I = \bar{I}$ Planned investment function

3 $G = \bar{G}$ Government spending function

4 $NX = \overline{NX}$ Net export function

5 $Y = C + I + G + NX$ Equilibrium condition

The letters with bars over them represent fixed, or autonomous, values. So, represents autonomous consumption, which had a value of 1,000 in our original example. Now, solving for equilibrium, we get:

$$Y = \bar{C} + MPC(Y) + \bar{I} + \bar{G} + \overline{NX}$$

or:

$$Y - MPC(Y) = \bar{C} + \bar{I} + \bar{G} + \overline{NX}$$

or:

$$Y(1 - MPC) = \bar{C} + \bar{I} + \bar{G} + \overline{NX}$$

or:

$$Y = \frac{\bar{C} + \bar{I} + \overline{GX} + \overline{NX}}{1 - MPC}$$

Remember that $1/(1-MPC)$ is the multiplier, and all four variables in the numerator of the equation represent autonomous expenditure. Therefore an alternative expression for equilibrium GDP is:

$$\text{Equilibrium GDP} = \text{Autonomous expenditure} \times \text{Multiplier}$$

Problems and Applications

LEARNING OBJECTIVE   Apply the algebra of macroeconomic equilibrium, **pages 655–656.**

19A.1 Write a general expression for the aggregate expenditure function. If you think of the aggregate expenditure function as a line on the 45°-line diagram, what would be the intercept and what would be the slope, using the general values represented by letters?

19A.2 Find equilibrium GDP using the following macroeconomic model (the numbers, with the exception of the MPC, represent billions of dollars).

a. $C = 1{,}500 + 0.75\ Y$ Consumption function
b. $I = 1{,}250$ Planned investment function

c. $G = 1,250$ Government spending function

d. $NX = -500$ Net export function

e. $Y = C + I + G + NX$ Equilibrium condition

19A.3 For the macroeconomic model in problem 19A.2, write the aggregate expenditure function. For GDP of US$16,000, what is the value of aggregate expenditure, and what is the value of the unintended change in inventories? For GDP of US$12,000, what is the value of aggregate expenditure, and what is the value of the unintended change in inventories?

19A.4 Suppose that autonomous consumption is US$500, government purchases are US$1,000, planned investment spending is US$1,250, net exports is US$–250, and the *MPC* is 0.8. What is equilibrium GDP?

>> **End Appendix Learning Objective**

Aggregate Demand and Aggregate Supply Analysis

The Fortunes of Aramex Follow the Business Cycle

The global economic environment plays a crucial role in the development of the air freight industry, which has witnessed a huge boom in recent years in the Middle East. The air freight market has grown at an average rate of about 15 percent per year since 1995, and the Middle East accounted for 5.7 percent of the world's air cargo traffic in tonnage.

The air freight and logistics business revenues follow closely seasonal demand and global and national business cycle patterns. At times when the world experiences faster growth and trade is booming, the air freight and logistics industry witnesses greater revenues and faster growth, and vice versa. In the Middle East, in addition, oil and petrochemical-related industries drive much of the region's economy. Increases in oil prices boosts local governments' revenues and spending, resulting in a larger flow of air freight

Like many successful businesses, Aramex began with a single bright idea by a Jordanian entrepreneur. In 1982, Fadi Ghandour founded Aramex, with headquarters in Amman, as an express wholesaler in the Middle East to

North American express delivery companies such as FedEX. The company rapidly grew and evolved into a global brand recognized for its customized services and innovative multi-product solutions. Today, Aramex employs more than 8,100 people in over 310 locations around the globe, and has a strong alliance network worldwide. Aramex offers many services such as international and domestic express delivery, freight forwarding, logistics and warehousing, records and information-management solutions, e-business solutions, and online shopping services.

Despite Aramex's great success over the past 30 years, the business cycle has always affected the company. For example, in the first two quarters of 2009 revenues dropped by 10 percent and 8 percent, respectively, as compared with the same quarters in 2008. This decrease in revenues was driven by the significant slowdown in global freight forwarding activity, which led to a drop of 22 percent in the network's freight revenues. When asked about the impact of the world recession on the company's performance in 2009, Fadi Ghandour, Aramex's founder and CEO, answered: "While the global economic slowdown continued to affect our revenue growth in this period, we maintained focus on operational cost efficiency and customization capabilities to better adapt to customers'

changing business needs…. This has enabled us to further improve our gross profit margins, control costs, and report an excellent net income growth." Indeed, Aramex reported positive overall profit growth of 25 percent in the first half of 2009 over profits reported in the first 6 months of 2008.

To understand why Aramex and other firms are affected by the business cycle, we need to explore the effects that recessions and expansions have on production, employment, and prices. As you will read in this chapter, although no two business cycles are identical, economists use the aggregate demand and aggregate supply model to explain their general features. In later chapters, we use aggregate demand and aggregate supply to understand how the government can employ fiscal policy and monetary policy to reduce the severity of business cycles.

AN INSIDE LOOK on **page 684** discusses how FedEx Middle East, one of Aramex's strong competitors, weathered the decline in the region's aggregate demand during the latest world recession.

Sources: "Middle Eastern Promise," *Mail & Express Review*, November 2009; "Aramex Profits Rise 30% as Firm Maintains Tough Cost Controls," *Gulf News*, July 29, 2009; Aramex 2008 report, The National Investor TNI, www.tni.ae; www.aramex.com.

Economics in YOUR Life!

Is an Employer Likely to Cut Your Pay During a Recession?

Suppose that you have worked as a barista for a local coffeehouse for two years. From on-the-job training and experience, you have enhanced your coffee-making skills and mastered the perfect latte. Suddenly, the economy moves into a recession, and sales at the coffeehouse decline. Is the owner of the coffeehouse likely to cut the prices of lattes and other drinks? Suppose the owner asks to meet with you to discuss your wages for next year. Is the owner likely to cut your pay? As you read the chapter, see if you can answer these questions. You can check your answers against those we provide at the end of the chapter. >> **Continued on page 683**

W e saw earlier that an Arab economy such as the Jordanian economy has experienced a long-run upward trend in real gross domestic product (GDP) between 1990 and 2008. In the short run, however, real GDP fluctuates around this long-run upward trend because of the business cycle. Fluctuations in GDP lead to fluctuations in employment. These fluctuations in real GDP and employment are the most visible and dramatic part of the business cycle. During recessions, for example, we are more likely to see factories close, small businesses declare bankruptcy, and workers lose their jobs. During expansions, we are more likely to see new businesses open and new jobs created. In addition to these changes in output and employment, the business cycle causes changes in wages and prices. Some firms react to a decline in sales by cutting back on production, but they may also cut the prices they charge and the wages they pay. Even more firms respond to a recession by raising prices and workers' wages by less than they would have otherwise.

In this chapter, we expand our story of the business cycle by developing the aggregate demand and aggregate supply model. This model will help us analyze the effects of recessions and expansions on production, employment, and prices.

20.1 LEARNING OBJECTIVE

20.1 | Identify the determinants of aggregate demand and distinguish between a movement along the aggregate demand curve and a shift of the curve.

Aggregate Demand

Aggregate demand and aggregate supply model A model that explains short-run fluctuations in real GDP and the price level.

Aggregate demand curve A curve that shows the relationship between the price level and the quantity of real GDP demanded by households, firms, and the government.

Short-run aggregate supply curve A curve that shows the relationship in the short run between the price level and the quantity of real GDP supplied by firms.

To understand what happens during the business cycle, we need an explanation of why real GDP, the unemployment rate, and the inflation rate fluctuate. We have already seen that fluctuations in the unemployment rate are caused mainly by fluctuations in real GDP. In this chapter, we use the **aggregate demand and aggregate supply model** to explain fluctuations in real GDP and the price level. As Figure 20-1 shows, real GDP and the price level in this model are determined in the short run by the intersection of the *aggregate demand curve* and the *aggregate supply curve*. Fluctuations in real GDP and the price level are caused by shifts in the aggregate demand curve or in the aggregate supply curve.

The **aggregate demand curve**, labeled *AD*, shows the relationship between the price level and the quantity of real GDP demanded by households, firms, and

Figure 20-1

Aggregate Demand and Aggregate Supply

In the short run, real GDP and the price level are determined by the intersection of the aggregate demand curve and the short-run aggregate supply curve. In the figure, real GDP is measured on the horizontal axis, and the price level is measured on the vertical axis by the GDP deflator. In this example, the equilibrium real GDP is US$10.0 billion, and the equilibrium price level is 100.

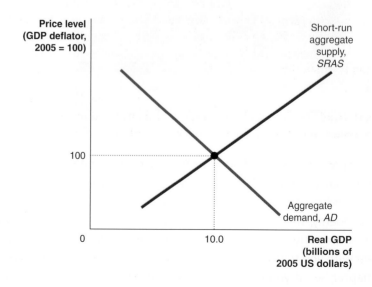

the government. The **short-run aggregate supply curve**, labeled *SRAS*, shows the relationship in the short run between the price level and the quantity of real GDP supplied by firms. The aggregate demand and short-run aggregate supply curves in Figure 20-1 look similar to the individual market demand and supply curves we studied in Chapter 3. However, because these curves apply to the whole economy, rather than to just a single market, the aggregate demand and aggregate supply model is very different from the model of demand and supply in individual markets. Because we are dealing with the economy as a whole, we need *macroeconomic* explanations of why the aggregate demand curve is downward sloping, why the short-run aggregate supply curve is upward sloping, and why the curves shift. We begin by explaining why the aggregate demand curve is downward sloping.

Why Is the Aggregate Demand Curve Downward Sloping?

We saw before that GDP has four components: consumption (C), investment (I), government purchases (G), and net exports (NX). If we let Y stand for GDP, we can write the following:

$$Y = C + I + G + NX$$

The aggregate demand curve is downward sloping because a fall in the price level increases the quantity of real GDP demanded. To understand why this is true, we need to look at how changes in the price level affect each of the components of aggregate demand. We begin with the assumption that government purchases are determined by the policy decisions of lawmakers and are not affected by changes in the price level. We can then consider the effect of changes in the price level on each of the other three components: consumption, investment, and net exports.

The Wealth Effect: How a Change in the Price Level Affects Consumption

Current income is the most important variable determining the consumption of households. As income rises, consumption will rise, and as income falls, consumption will fall. But consumption also depends on household wealth. A household's wealth is the difference between the value of its assets and the value of its debts. Consider two households, both with incomes of US$80,000 per year. The first household has wealth of US$5 million, whereas the second household has wealth of US$50,000. The first household is likely to spend more of its income than the second household. So, as total household wealth rises, consumption will rise. Some household wealth is held in cash or other *nominal assets* that lose value as the price level rises and gain value as the price level falls. For instance, if you have US$10,000 in cash, a 10 percent increase in the price level will reduce the purchasing power of that cash by 10 percent. When the price level rises, the *real value* of household wealth declines, and so will consumption. When the price level falls, the real value of household wealth rises, and so will consumption. This impact of the price level on consumption is called the *wealth effect*.

The Interest-Rate Effect: How a Change in the Price Level Affects

Investment When prices rise, households and firms need more money to finance buying and selling. Therefore, when the price level rises, households and firms will try to increase the amount of money they hold by withdrawing funds from banks, borrowing from banks, or selling financial assets, such as bonds. These actions tend to drive up the interest rate charged on bank loans and the interest rate on bonds. (In Chapter 22 we will analyze in more detail the relationship between money and interest rates.) A higher interest rate raises the cost of borrowing for firms and households. As a result, firms will borrow less to build new factories or to install new machinery and equipment, and households will borrow less to buy new houses. To a smaller extent, households will also borrow less to finance spending on automobiles, furniture, and other durable goods. Consumption will therefore be reduced. A lower price level will have the reverse effect, leading to an increase in investment and—to a lesser extent—consumption. This impact of the price level on investment is known as the *interest-rate effect*.

The International-Trade Effect: How a Change in the Price Level Affects Net Exports

Net exports equal: spending by foreign households and firms on goods and services domestically produced, minus spending by national households and firms on goods and services produced in other countries. If the domestic price level rises relative to the price levels in other countries, the country's exports will become relatively more expensive, and foreign imports will become relatively less expensive. Some consumers in foreign countries will shift from buying imported products to buying their own products, and some of our country's consumers will also shift from buying domestically made products to buying imported products. The country's exports will fall, and its imports will rise, causing net exports to fall. A lower domestic price level has the reverse effect, causing net exports to rise. This impact of the price level on net exports is known as the *international-trade effect*.

Shifts of the Aggregate Demand Curve versus Movements Along It

An important point to remember is that the aggregate demand curve tells us the relationship between the price level and the quantity of real GDP demanded, *holding everything else constant*. If the price level changes but other variables that affect the willingness of households, firms, and the government to spend are unchanged, the economy will move up or down a stationary aggregate demand curve. If any variable changes other than the price level, the aggregate demand curve will shift. For example, if government purchases increase and the price level remains unchanged, the aggregate demand curve will shift to the right at every price level. Or, if firms become pessimistic about the future profitability of investment and cut back spending on factories and machinery, the aggregate demand curve will shift to the left.

The Variables That Shift the Aggregate Demand Curve

The variables that cause the aggregate demand curve to shift fall into three categories:

- Changes in government policies
- Changes in the expectations of households and firms
- Changes in foreign variables

Monetary policy The actions the central bank takes to manage the money supply and interest rates to pursue macroeconomic policy objectives.

Fiscal policy Changes in taxes and purchases that are intended to achieve macroeconomic policy objectives, such as high employment, price stability, and high rates of economic growth.

Changes in Government Policies As we will discuss in Chapters 22 and 23, governments use monetary policy and fiscal policy to shift the aggregate demand curve. **Monetary policy** involves the actions the nation's central bank takes to manage the money supply and interest rates to pursue macroeconomic policy objectives. When the central bank takes actions to reduce interest rates, it lowers the cost to firms and households of borrowing. Lower borrowing costs increase consumption and investment spending, which shifts the aggregate demand curve to the right. Higher interest rates shift the aggregate demand curve to the left. **Fiscal policy** involves changes in taxes and purchases that are intended to achieve macroeconomic policy objectives, such as high employment, price stability, and high rates of economic growth. Because government purchases are one component of aggregate demand, an increase in government purchases shifts the aggregate demand curve to the right, and a decrease in government purchases shifts the aggregate demand curve to the left. An increase in personal income taxes reduces the amount of spendable income available to households. Higher personal income taxes reduce consumption spending and shift the aggregate demand curve to the left. Lower personal income taxes shift the aggregate demand curve to the right. Increases in business taxes reduce the profitability of investment spending and shift the aggregate demand curve to the left. Decreases in business taxes shift the aggregate demand curve to the right.

Changes in the Expectations of Households and Firms If households become more optimistic about their future incomes, they are likely to increase their current consumption. This increased consumption will shift the aggregate demand curve to the right. If households become more pessimistic about their future incomes, the aggregate demand curve will shift to the left. Similarly, if firms become more optimistic about the future profitability of investment spending, the aggregate demand curve will shift to the right. If firms become more pessimistic, the aggregate demand curve will shift to the left.

Changes in Foreign Variables If firms and households in other countries buy fewer of the goods a country produces or if local firms and households buy more foreign goods, net exports will fall, and the aggregate demand curve will shift to the left. As we saw in Chapter 15, when real GDP increases, so does the income available for consumers to spend. If our country's real GDP increases faster than real GDP in other countries, our imports will increase faster than our exports and net exports will fall. Net exports will also fall if the *exchange rate* between the local currency and foreign currencies rises because the price (in terms of foreign currency) of domestic products that are sold in other countries will rise, and the local price of foreign products sold in the local markets will fall. For example, in the UAE, if the current exchange rate for Arab Emirates dirhams (AED) is 1AED = US$1, then a 300AED hand-crafted item exported from Dubai to the U.S. will cost US$300 in the U.S., and a US$300 iPod imported from the U.S. to Dubai will cost 300AED in Dubai. But if the exchange rises to 1AED = US$1.50, then the hand-crafted item's price will rise to US$450 in the U.S., causing its sales to decline, and the price of the iPod in the UAE will fall to 200AED per iPod, causing its sales to increase. Exports to the U.S. will fall, and imports from the U.S. will rise, and the UAE aggregate demand curve will shift to the left.

An increase in net exports at every price level will shift the aggregate demand curve to the right. Net exports will increase if real GDP grows more slowly than in other countries or if the value of the local currency (AE dirhams in the previous example) falls against other currencies. A change in net exports that results from a change in the domestic price level will *not* cause the aggregate demand curve to shift.

Making the Connection | **In a Global Economy, How Can You Tell the Imports from the Domestic Goods?**

Some Arab groups appeal to the patriotism of the Arab consumers by urging them to boycott goods made in the West, and buy instead products made in the Arab world. They argue that Arabs should really buy Arab brands and abandon all Western labels and brands. Sometimes it is easy

(Continued)

Is the famous Egyptian Kushari dish as Egyptian as we think?

to tell imports from domestic goods. At the end of the day, what could be more American than imports of cloth or food from famous American chains such as Gap, McDonalds, KFC, Pizza Hut, and Starbucks? And what could obviously be more Egyptian than a Kushari dish or a falafel sandwich from a local food store, and a soft cotton T-shirt made by a local brand? After all, the headquarters of Gap, McDonalds, KFC, Pizza Hut, and Starbucks are all in the U.S.

But things are not so simple in the modern global economy. While the Kushari dish or falafel sandwich are obviously made in Egypt, the Big Mac, the Cheesy Bites pizza, and the Zinger dinner box are not made in the U.S. The Gap T-shirt as well; it may not be imported from the U.S. What is more, local firms may purchase the ingredients of their 'Kushari' products from anywhere in the world. For example, Egypt heavily depends on wheat imports. By contrast, a GAP T-shirt could be made of 100 percent Egyptian cotton and made by an Egyptian maker for GAP stores worldwide. So, what looks to be imported from firms located in other countries may turn out to be 100 percent locally made. So, an Arab consumer who buys a Big Mac meal in Egypt, or an Egyptian cotton GAP T-shirt, could actually be contributing more to increasing Egyptian aggregate demand than a consumer purchasing a Kushari dish.

YOUR TURN: Test your understanding by doing related problem 1.7 on page 687 at the end of this chapter.

Solved Problem | 20-1

Movements along the Aggregate Demand Curve versus Shifts of the Aggregate Demand Curve

Suppose the current price level is 120, and the current level of real GDP is US$12.2 billion. Illustrate each of the following situations on a graph.

a. The price level rises to 125, while all other variables remain constant.

b. Firms become pessimistic and reduce their investment. Assume that the price level remains constant.

SOLVING THE PROBLEM:

Step 1: **Review the chapter material.** This problem is about understanding the difference between movements along an aggregate demand curve and shifts of an aggregate demand curve, so you may want to review the section "Shifts of the Aggregate Demand Curve versus Movements Along It," which begins on page 662.

Step 2: **To answer question (a), draw a graph that shows a movement along the aggregate demand curve.** Because there will be a movement along the aggregate demand curve but no shift of the aggregate demand curve, your graph should look like this:

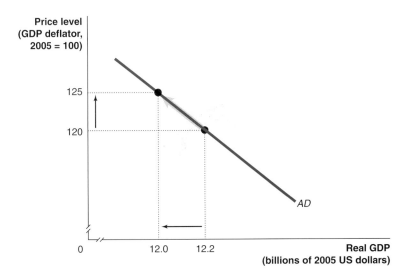

We don't have enough information to be certain what the new level of real GDP will be. We only know that it will be less than the initial level of US$12.2 billion; the graph shows the value as US$12.0 billion.

Step 3: **To answer question (b), draw a graph that shows a shift of the aggregate demand curve.** We know that the aggregate demand curve will shift to the left, but we don't have enough information to know how far to the left it will shift. Let's assume that the shift is US$300 million (or US$0.3 billion). In that case, your graph should look like this:

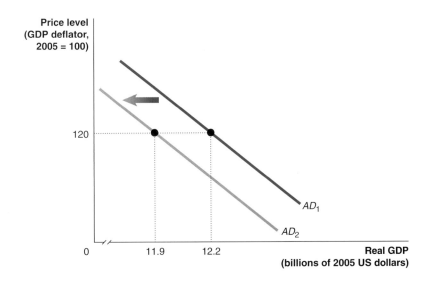

The graph shows a parallel shift in the aggregate demand curve so that at every price level, the quantity of real GDP demanded declines by US$300 million. For example, at a price level of 120, the quantity of real GDP demanded declines from US$12.2 billion to US$11.9 billion.

YOUR TURN: For more practice, do related problem 1.5 on page 687 at the end of this chapter.

>> **End Solved Problem 20-1**

Table 20-1 summarizes the most important variables that cause the aggregate demand curve to shift. It is important to notice that the table shows the shift in the aggregate demand curve that results from an increase in each of the variables. A *decrease* in these variables would cause the aggregate demand curve to shift in the opposite direction.

TABLE 20-1

Variables that Shift the Aggregate Demand Curve

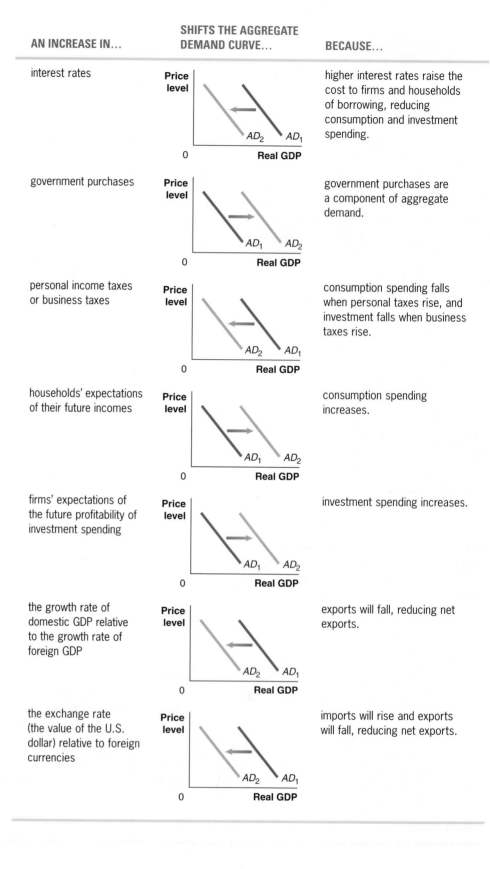

AN INCREASE IN...	SHIFTS THE AGGREGATE DEMAND CURVE...	BECAUSE...
interest rates		higher interest rates raise the cost to firms and households of borrowing, reducing consumption and investment spending.
government purchases		government purchases are a component of aggregate demand.
personal income taxes or business taxes		consumption spending falls when personal taxes rise, and investment falls when business taxes rise.
households' expectations of their future incomes		consumption spending increases.
firms' expectations of the future profitability of investment spending		investment spending increases.
the growth rate of domestic GDP relative to the growth rate of foreign GDP		exports will fall, reducing net exports.
the exchange rate (the value of the U.S. dollar) relative to foreign currencies		imports will rise and exports will fall, reducing net exports.

20.2 | Identify the determinants of aggregate supply and distinguish between a movement along the short-run aggregate supply curve and a shift of the curve.

Aggregate Supply

We just discussed the aggregate demand curve, which is one component of the aggregate demand and aggregate supply model. Now we turn to aggregate supply, which shows the effect of changes in the price level on the quantity of goods and services that firms are willing and able to supply. Because the effect of changes in the price level on aggregate supply is very different in the short run than in the long run, we use two aggregate supply curves: one for the short run and one for the long run. We start by considering the *long-run aggregate supply curve*.

The Long-Run Aggregate Supply Curve

We saw that in the long run, the level of real GDP is determined by the number of workers, the *capital stock*—including factories, office buildings, and machinery and equipment—and the available technology. Because changes in the price level do not affect the number of workers, the capital stock, or technology, *in the long run, changes in the price level do not affect the level of real GDP*. Remember that the level of real GDP in the long run is called *potential GDP* or *full-employment GDP*. At potential GDP, firms will operate at their normal level of capacity, and everyone who wants a job will have one, except the structurally and frictionally unemployed. There is no reason for this normal level of capacity to change just because the price level has changed. The **long-run aggregate supply curve** is a curve, labeled *LRAS*, that shows the relationship in the long run between the price level and the quantity of real GDP supplied. As Figure 20-2 shows, the price level was 120 in 2009, and potential real GDP was US$11.7 billion. If the price level had been 110, or if it had been 130, long-run aggregate supply would still have been a constant US$11.7 billion. Therefore, the *LRAS* curve is a vertical line.

Figure 20-2 also shows that the long-run aggregate supply curve shifts to the right every year. This shift occurs because potential real GDP increases each year, as the number of workers in the economy increases, the economy accumulates more machinery and equipment, and technological change occurs. As Figure 20-2 shows, potential real GDP increased from US$11.7 billion in 2009 to US$12.0 billion in 2010 and to US$12.3 billion in 2011.

Long-run aggregate supply curve
A curve that shows the relationship in the long run between the price level and the quantity of real GDP supplied.

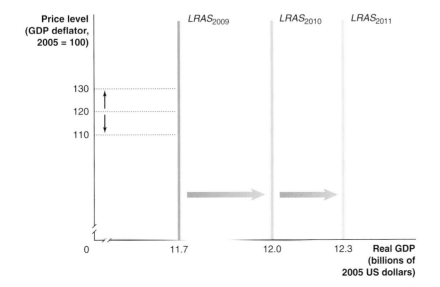

Figure 20-2

The Long-Run Aggregate Supply Curve

Changes in the price level do not affect the level of aggregate supply in the long run. Therefore, the long-run aggregate supply curve, labeled *LRAS*, is a vertical line at the potential level of real GDP. For instance, the price level was 120 in 2009, and potential real GDP was US$11.7 billion. If the price level had been 110, or if it had been 130, long-run aggregate supply would still have been a constant US$11.7 billion. Each year, the long-run aggregate supply curve shifts to the right as the number of workers in the economy increases, more machinery and equipment are accumulated, and technological change occurs.

The Short-Run Aggregate Supply Curve

Although the *LRAS* curve is vertical, the short-run aggregate supply curve, or *SRAS curve*, is upward sloping. The *SRAS* curve is upward sloping because, over the short run, as the price level increases, the quantity of goods and services firms are willing to supply will increase. The main reason firms behave this way is that, *as prices of final goods and services rise, prices of inputs—such as the wages of workers or the price of natural resources—rise more slowly.* Profits rise when the prices of the goods and services firms sell rise more rapidly than the prices they pay for inputs. Therefore, a higher price level leads to higher profits and increases the willingness of firms to supply more goods and services. A secondary reason the *SRAS* curve slopes upward is that, as the price level rises or falls, some firms are slow to adjust their prices. A firm that is slow to raise its prices when the price level is increasing may find its sales increasing and, therefore, will increase production. A firm that is slow to reduce its prices when the price level is decreasing may find its sales falling and, therefore, will decrease production.

Why do some firms adjust prices more slowly than others, and why might the wages of workers and the prices of other inputs change more slowly than the prices of final goods and services? Most economists believe the explanation is that *some firms and workers fail to predict accurately changes in the price level.* If firms and workers could predict the future price level exactly, the short-run aggregate supply curve would be the same as the long-run aggregate supply curve.

But how does the failure of workers and firms to predict the price level accurately result in an upward-sloping *SRAS* curve? Economists are not in complete agreement on this point, but we can briefly discuss the three most common explanations:

1 Contracts make some wages and prices 'sticky.'

2 Firms are often slow to adjust wages.

3 Menu costs make some prices sticky.

Contracts Make Some Wages and Prices 'Sticky' Prices or wages are said to be 'sticky' when they do not respond quickly to changes in demand or supply. Contracts can make wages or prices sticky. For example, suppose Orascom Telecom negotiates a three-year contract with the United Workers unions of Egypt at a time when demand for its Mobinil telecom services is increasing slowly. Suppose that after the contract is signed, the demand for mobile phone subscriptions starts to increase rapidly, and prices of new lines rise. Mobinil will find that providing more services will be profitable because it can increase call-minute prices, while the wages it pays its workers are fixed by contract. Or Qatar Airways could have signed a multiyear contract to buy jet fuel, which is used in its plans, at a time when the demand for oil was stagnant. If demand for air traveling and its air tickets prices begin to rise rapidly, increasing flights will be profitable because oil prices will remain fixed by contract. In both of these cases, rising prices lead to higher output. If these examples are representative of enough firms in the economy, a rising price level should lead to a greater quantity of goods and services supplied. In other words, the short-run aggregate supply curve will be upward sloping.

Notice, though, that if the workers at Orascom or the managers of the oil companies had accurately predicted what would happen to prices, this prediction would have been reflected in the contracts, and Orascom and Qatar airways would not have earned greater profits when prices rose. In that case, rising prices would not have led to higher output.

Firms Are Often Slow to Adjust Wages We just noted that the wages of many union workers remain fixed by contract for several years. Many nonunion workers also have their wages or salaries adjusted only once a year. For instance, suppose you accept a job at a management consulting firm in June at a salary of US$45,000 per year. The firm probably will not adjust your salary until the following June, even if the prices it can charge for its services later in the year are higher or lower than the firm had expected them to be when you were first hired. If firms are slow to adjust wages, a rise in the price level will increase the profitability of hiring more workers and producing more output. A fall in the price level will decrease the profitability of hiring more workers and producing more output. Once again, we have an explanation for why the short-run aggregate supply curve slopes upward.

It is worth noting that firms are often slower to *cut* wages than to increase them. Cutting wages can have a negative effect on the morale and productivity of workers and can also cause some of a firm's best workers to quit and look for jobs elsewhere.

Menu Costs Make Some Prices Sticky Firms base their prices today partly on what they expect future prices to be. For instance, a restaurant has to decide ahead of time the prices it will charge for meals before printing menus. Many firms print catalogs that list the prices of their products. If demand for their products is higher or lower than the firms had expected, they may want to charge prices that are different from the ones printed in their menus or catalogs. Changing prices would be costly, however, because it would involve printing new menus or catalogs. The costs to firms of changing prices are called **menu costs**. To see why menu costs can lead to an upward-sloping short-run aggregate supply curve, consider the effect of an unexpected increase in the price level. In this case, firms will want to increase the prices they charge. Some firms, however, may not be willing to increase prices because of menu costs. Because of their relatively low prices, these firms will find their sales increasing, which will cause them to increase output. Once again, we have an explanation for a higher price level leading to a larger quantity of goods and services supplied.

Menu costs The costs to firms of changing prices.

Shifts of the Short-Run Aggregate Supply Curve versus Movements Along It

It is important to remember the difference between a shift in a curve and a movement along a curve. The short-run aggregate supply curve tells us the short-run relationship between the price level and the quantity of goods and services firms are willing to supply, *holding constant all other variables that affect the willingness of firms to supply goods and services.* If the price level changes but other variables are unchanged, the economy will move up or down a stationary aggregate supply curve. If any variable other than the price level changes, the aggregate supply curve will shift.

Variables That Shift the Short-Run Aggregate Supply Curve

We now briefly discuss the five most important variables that cause the short-run aggregate supply curve to shift.

Increases in the Labor Force and in the Capital Stock A firm will supply more output at every price if it has more workers and more physical capital. The same is true of the economy as a whole. So, as the labor force and the capital stock grow, firms will supply more output at every price level, and the short-run aggregate supply curve will shift to the right. In Japan, the population is aging, and the labor force is decreasing. Holding other variables constant, this decrease in the labor force causes the short-run aggregate supply curve in Japan to shift to the left. On the contrary, the youth population in Saudi Arabia is growing, increasing the labor force. This would cause the short-run aggregate supply curve in Saudi Arabia to shift to the right.

Technological Change As technological change takes place, the productivity of workers and machinery increases, which means firms can produce more goods and services with the same amount of labor and machinery. This improvement reduces the firms' costs of production and, therefore, allows them to produce more output at every price level. As a result, the short-run aggregate supply curve shifts to the right.

Expected Changes in the Future Price Level If workers and firms believe that the price level is going to increase by 3 percent during the next year, they will try to adjust their wages and prices accordingly. For instance, if a labor union believes there will be 3 percent inflation next year, it knows that wages must rise 3 percent to preserve the purchasing power

Figure 20-3

How Expectations of the Future Price Level Affect the Short-Run Aggregate Supply

The *SRAS* curve shifts to reflect worker and firm expectations of future prices.

1. If workers and firms expect that the price level will rise by 3 percent, from 100 to 103, they will adjust their wages and prices by that amount.

2. Holding constant all other variables that affect aggregate supply, the short-run aggregate supply curve will shift to the left. If workers and firms expect that the price level will be lower in the future, the short-run aggregate supply curve will shift to the right.

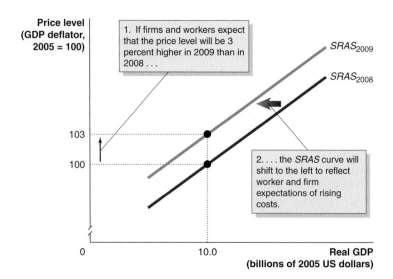

of those wages. Similar adjustments by other workers and firms will result in costs increasing throughout the economy by 3 percent. The result, shown in Figure 20-3, is that the short-run aggregate supply curve will shift to the left, so that any level of real GDP is now associated with a price level that is 3 percent higher. In general, *if workers and firms expect the price level to increase by a certain percentage, the* SRAS *curve will shift by an equivalent amount,* holding constant all other variables that affect the *SRAS* curve.

Adjustments of Workers and Firms to Errors in Past Expectations about the Price Level Workers and firms sometimes make wrong predictions about the price level. As time passes, they will attempt to compensate for these errors. Suppose, for example, that the United Workers Union of Egypt signs a contract with Mobinil that contains only small wage increases because the company and the union expect only small increases in the price level. If increases in the price level turn out to be unexpectedly large, the union will take this into account when negotiating the next contract. The higher wages Mobinil's workers receive under the new contract will increase Mobinil's costs and result in Mobinil needing to receive higher prices to produce the same level of output. If workers and firms across the economy are adjusting to the price level's being higher than expected, the *SRAS* curve will shift to the left. If they are adjusting to the price level being lower than expected, the *SRAS* curve will shift to the right.

Unexpected Changes in the Price of an Important Natural Resource An unexpected increase or decrease in the price of an important natural resource can cause firms' costs to be different from what they had expected. Oil prices can be particularly volatile. Some firms use oil in the production process. Other firms use products, such as plastics, that are made from oil. If oil prices rise unexpectedly, the costs of production will rise for these firms. Some utilities also burn oil to generate electricity, so electricity prices will rise. Rising oil prices lead to rising gasoline prices, which raise transportation costs for many firms. Because firms face rising costs, they will only supply the same level of output at higher prices, and the short-run aggregate supply curve will shift to the left. An unexpected event that causes the short-run aggregate supply curve to shift is known as a **supply shock**. Supply shocks are often caused by an unexpected increase or decrease in the price of an important natural resource.

Supply shock An unexpected event that causes the short-run aggregate supply curve to shift.

If an economy has experienced inflation every year of the past thirty years, for example, workers and firms always expect next year's price level to be higher than this year's price level. Holding everything else constant, expectations of a higher price level will cause the *SRAS* curve to shift to the left. But meanwhile the economy may experience an increase in the labor force and the capital stock expand and changes in technology occur, which cause the *SRAS* curve to shift to the right. Whether in any particular year the *SRAS*

TABLE 20-2

Variables that Shift the Short-Run Aggregate Supply Curve

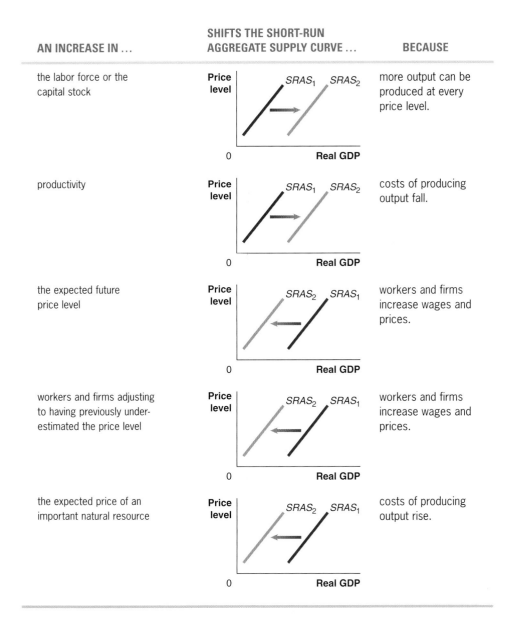

AN INCREASE IN ...	SHIFTS THE SHORT-RUN AGGREGATE SUPPLY CURVE ...	BECAUSE
the labor force or the capital stock		more output can be produced at every price level.
productivity		costs of producing output fall.
the expected future price level		workers and firms increase wages and prices.
workers and firms adjusting to having previously under-estimated the price level		workers and firms increase wages and prices.
the expected price of an important natural resource		costs of producing output rise.

curve shifts to the left or to the right depends on which of these variables has the largest impact during that year.

Table 20-2 summarizes the most important variables that cause the *SRAS* curve to shift. It is important to notice that the table shows the shift in the *SRAS* curve that results from an *increase* in each of the variables. A *decrease* in these variables would cause the *SRAS* curve to shift in the opposite direction.

20.3 LEARNING OBJECTIVE

20.3 | Use the aggregate demand and aggregate supply model to illustrate the difference between short-run and long-run macroeconomic equilibrium.

Macroeconomic Equilibrium in the Long Run and the Short Run

Now that we have discussed the components of the aggregate demand and aggregate supply model, we can use it to analyze changes in real GDP and the price level. In Figure 20-4, we bring the aggregate demand curve, the short-run aggregate supply curve, and the long-run

Figure 20-4

In long-run macroeconomic equilibrium, the *AD* and *SRAS* curves intersect at a point on the *LRAS* curve. In this case, equilibrium occurs at real GDP of US$10.0 billion and a price level of 100.

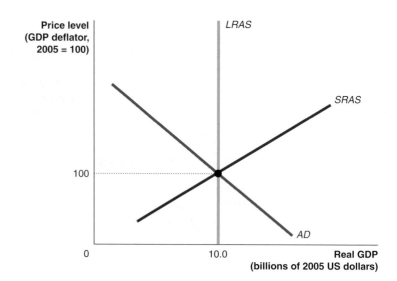

aggregate supply curve together in one graph, to show the *long-run macroeconomic equilibrium* for the economy. In the figure, equilibrium occurs at real GDP of US$10.0 billion and a price level of 100. Notice that in long-run equilibrium, the short-run aggregate supply curve and the aggregate demand curve intersect at a point on the long-run aggregate supply curve. Because equilibrium occurs at a point along the long-run aggregate supply curve, we know the economy is at potential real GDP: firms will be operating at their normal level of capacity, and everyone who wants a job will have one, except the structurally and frictionally unemployed. We know, however, that the economy is often not in long-run macroeconomic equilibrium. In the following section, we discuss the economic forces that can push the economy away from long-run equilibrium.

Recessions, Expansions, and Supply Shocks

Because the full analysis of the aggregate demand and aggregate supply model can be complicated, we begin with a simplified case, using two assumptions:

1 The economy has not been experiencing any inflation. The price level is currently 100, and workers and firms expect it to remain at 100 in the future.

2 The economy is not experiencing any long-run growth. Potential real GDP is US$10.0 billion and will remain at that level in the future.

In this section, we examine the short-run and long-run effects of recessions, expansions, and supply shocks.

Recession

The short-run effect of a decline in aggregate demand. For example, the recent outbreak of protests in early 2011 in some Arab countries, aimed at toppling their governments, has caused firms in other countries in the region such as KSA and the UAE to become pessimistic about the future profitability of new spending on factories and equipment. The decline in investment as a result will shift the aggregate demand curve of affected countries to the left, from AD_1 to AD_2, as shown in Figure 20-5. The economy moves from point A to a new *short-run macroeconomic equilibrium*, where the AD_2 curve intersects the SRAS curve at point B. In the new short-run equilibrium, real GDP has declined from US$10.0 billion to US$9.8 billion and is below its potential level. This lower level of GDP will result in declining profitability for many firms and layoffs for some workers: The economy will be in recession.

Adjustment back to potential GDP in the long run. We know that the recession will eventually end because there are forces at work that push the economy back to

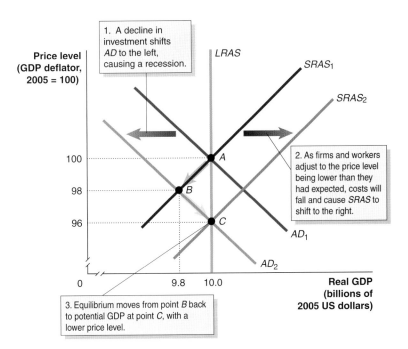

1. A decline in investment shifts *AD* to the left, causing a recession.

2. As firms and workers adjust to the price level being lower than they had expected, costs will fall and cause *SRAS* to shift to the right.

3. Equilibrium moves from point *B* back to potential GDP at point *C*, with a lower price level.

Figure 20-5

The Short-Run and Long-Run Effects of a Decrease in Aggregate Demand

In the short run, a decrease in aggregate demand causes a recession. In the long run, it causes only a decrease in the price level.

potential GDP in the long run. Figure 20-5 also shows how the economy moves from recession back to potential GDP. The shift from AD_1 to AD_2 initially leads to a short-run equilibrium with the price level having fallen from 100 to 98 (point *B*). Workers and firms will begin to adjust to the price level being lower than they had expected it to be. Workers will be willing to accept lower wages—because each dollar of wages is able to buy more goods and services—and firms will be willing to accept lower prices. In addition, the unemployment resulting from the recession will make workers more willing to accept lower wages, and the decline in demand will make firms more willing to accept lower prices. As a result, the *SRAS* curve will shift to the right, from $SRAS_1$ to $SRAS_2$. At this point, the economy will be back in long-run equilibrium (point *C*). The shift from $SRAS_1$ to $SRAS_2$ will not happen instantly. It may take the economy several years to return to potential GDP. The important conclusion is that a decline in aggregate demand causes a recession in the short run, but in the long run, it causes only a decline in the price level.

Economists refer to the process of adjustment back to potential GDP just described as an *automatic mechanism* because it occurs without any actions by the government. An alternative to waiting for the automatic mechanism to end the recession is for the government to use monetary and fiscal policy to shift the *AD* curve to the right and restore potential GDP more quickly. We will discuss monetary and fiscal policy in Chapters 22 and 23. Economists debate whether it is better to wait for the automatic mechanism to end recessions or whether it is better to use monetary and fiscal policy.

Expansion

The short-run effect of an increase in aggregate demand. Suppose that instead of becoming pessimistic, many firms become optimistic about the future profitability of new investment, as happened during the information technology and telecommunications booms of the late 1990s. The resulting increase in investment will shift the *AD* curve to the right, as shown in Figure 20-6. Equilibrium moves from point *A* to point *B*. Real GDP rises from US$10.0 billion to US$10.3 billion, and the price level rises from 100 to 103. The economy will be above potential real GDP: firms are operating beyond their normal level of capacity, and some workers are employed who ordinarily would be structurally or frictionally unemployed or who would not be in the labor force.

Figure 20-6

The Short-Run and Long-Run Effects of an Increase in Aggregate Demand

In the short run, an increase in aggregate demand causes an increase in real GDP. In the long run, it causes only an increase in the price level.

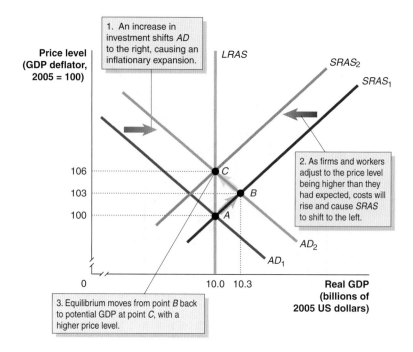

1. An increase in investment shifts *AD* to the right, causing an inflationary expansion.

2. As firms and workers adjust to the price level being higher than they had expected, costs will rise and cause *SRAS* to shift to the left.

3. Equilibrium moves from point *B* back to potential GDP at point *C*, with a higher price level.

Adjustment back to potential GDP in the long run. Just as an automatic mechanism brings the economy back to potential GDP from a recession, an automatic mechanism brings the economy back from a short-run equilibrium beyond potential GDP. Figure 20-6 illustrates this mechanism. The shift from AD_1 to AD_2 initially leads to a short-run equilibrium, with the price level rising from 100 to 103 (point *B*). Workers and firms will begin to adjust to the price level being higher than they had expected. Workers will push for higher wages—because each dollar of wages is able to buy fewer goods and services—and firms will charge higher prices. In addition, the low levels of unemployment resulting from the expansion will make it easier for workers to negotiate for higher wages, and the increase in demand will make it easier for firms to receive higher prices. As a result, the *SRAS* curve will shift to the left, from $SRAS_1$ to $SRAS_2$. At this point, the economy will be back in long-run equilibrium. Once again, the shift from $SRAS_1$ to $SRAS_2$ will not happen instantly. The process of returning to potential GDP may stretch out for more than a year.

Supply Shock

The short-run effect of a supply shock. Suppose oil prices increase substantially. This supply shock will increase many firms' costs and cause the *SRAS* curve to shift to the left, as shown in panel (a) of Figure 20-7. Notice that the price level is higher in the new short-run equilibrium (102 rather than 100), but real GDP is lower (US$9.7 billion rather than US$10 billion). This unpleasant combination of inflation and recession is called **stagflation**.

Stagflation A combination of inflation and recession, usually resulting from a supply shock.

Adjustment back to potential GDP in the long run. The recession caused by a supply shock increases unemployment and reduces output. This eventually results in workers being willing to accept lower wages and firms being willing to accept lower prices. In panel (b) of Figure 20-7, the short-run aggregate supply curve shifts from $SRAS_2$ to $SRAS_1$, moving the economy from point *B* back to point *A*. Potential GDP is regained at the original price level. It may take several years for this process to be completed. An alternative would be to use monetary and fiscal policy to shift the aggregate demand to the right. Using policy in this way would bring the economy back to potential GDP more quickly but would result in a permanently higher price level.

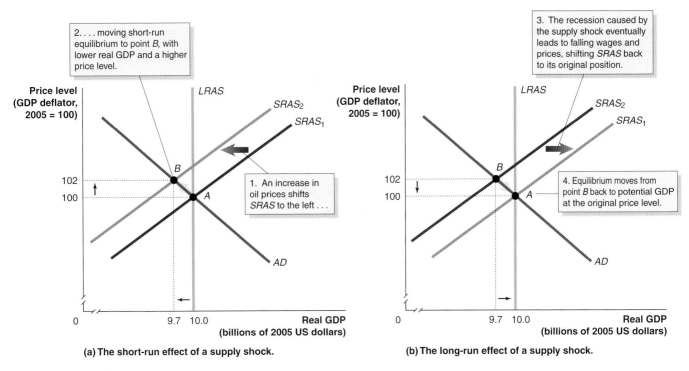

Figure 20-7 | The Short-Run and Long-Run Effects of a Supply Shock

Panel (a) shows that a supply shock, such as a large increase in oil prices, will cause a recession and a higher price level in the short run. The recession caused by the supply shock increases unemployment and reduces output. In panel (b), rising unemployment and falling output result in workers being willing to accept lower wages and firms being willing to accept lower prices. The short-run aggregate supply curve shifts from $SRAS_2$ to $SRAS_1$. Equilibrium moves from point B back to potential GDP and the original price level at point A.

20.4 | Use the dynamic aggregate demand and aggregate supply model to analyze macroeconomic conditions.

20.4 LEARNING OBJECTIVE

A Dynamic Aggregate Demand and Aggregate Supply Model

The basic aggregate demand and aggregate supply model used so far in this chapter gives us important insights into how short-run macroeconomic equilibrium is determined. Unfortunately, the model also gives us some misleading results. For instance, it incorrectly predicts that a recession caused by the aggregate demand curve shifting to the left will cause the price level to fall, which has not happened for an entire year since the 1930s. The difficulty with the basic model arises from the following two assumptions we made: (1) that the economy does not experience continuing inflation and (2) that the economy does not experience long-run growth. We can develop a more useful aggregate demand and aggregate supply model by dropping these assumptions. The result will be a model that takes into account that the economy is not *static*, with an unchanging level of potential real GDP and no continuing inflation, but *dynamic*, with potential real GDP that grows over time and inflation that continues every year. We can create a *dynamic aggregate demand and aggregate supply model* by making three changes to the basic model.

These changes recognize the following important macroeconomic facts:

- Potential real GDP increases continually, shifting the long-run aggregate supply curve to the right.

- During most years, the aggregate demand curve will be shifting to the right.

- Except during periods when workers and firms expect high rates of inflation, the short-run aggregate supply curve will be shifting to the right.

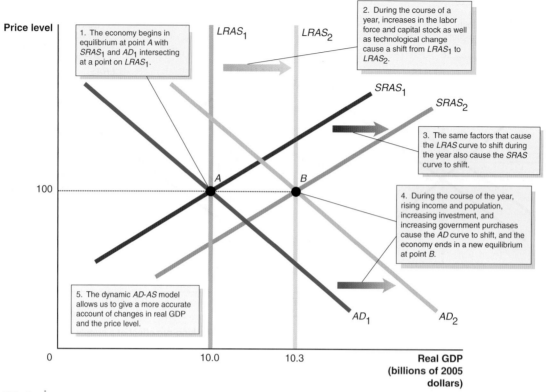

Figure 20-8 | A Dynamic Aggregate Demand and Aggregate Supply Model

We start with the basic aggregate demand and aggregate supply model. In the dynamic model, increases in the labor force and capital stock as well as technological change cause long-run aggregate supply to shift over the course of a year, from LRAS1 to LRAS2. Typically, these same factors cause short-run aggregate supply to shift from SRAS1 to SRAS2. Aggregate demand will shift from AD1 to AD2 if, as is usually the case, spending by consumers, firms, and the government increases during the year.

Figure 20-8 incorporates these three changes to the basic aggregate demand and aggregate supply model. We start with $SRAS_1$ and AD_1 intersecting at point A at a price level of 100 and real GDP of US$10.0 billion. Because this intersection occurs at a point on $LRAS_1$, we know the economy is in long-run equilibrium. The long-run aggregate supply curve shifts to the right from $LRAS_1$ to $LRAS_2$. This shift occurs because during the year potential real GDP increases as the labor force and the capital stock increase and technological progress occurs. The short-run aggregate supply curve shifts from $SRAS_1$ to $SRAS_2$. This shift occurs because the same variables that cause the long-run aggregate supply to shift to the right will also increase the quantity of goods and services that firms are willing to supply in the short run. Finally, the aggregate demand curve shifts to the right from AD_1 to AD_2. The aggregate demand curve shifts for several reasons: as population grows and incomes rise, consumption will increase over time. As the economy grows, firms will expand capacity, and new firms will be formed, increasing investment. An expanding population and an expanding economy require increased government services, such as more police officers and teachers, so government purchases will increase.

The new equilibrium in Figure 20-8 occurs at point B, where AD_2 intersects $SRAS_2$ on $LRAS_2$. In the new equilibrium, the price level remains at 100, while real GDP increases to US$10.3 billion. Notice that there has been no inflation because the price level is unchanged at 100. There was no inflation because aggregate demand and aggregate supply shifted to the right by exactly as much as long-run aggregate supply. We would not expect this to be the typical situation for two reasons: First, the $SRAS$ curve is also affected by workers' and firms' expectations of future changes in the price level and by supply shocks. These variables can partially, or completely, offset the normal tendency of the $SRAS$ curve to shift to the right over the course of a year. Second, we know that sometimes consumers,

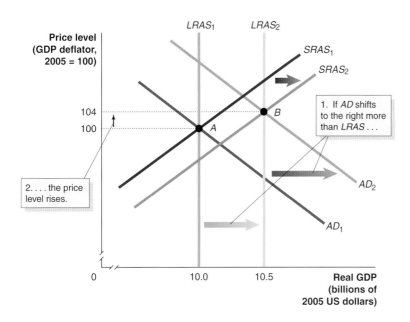

Figure 20-9

Using Dynamic Aggregate Demand and Aggregate Supply to Understand Inflation

The most common cause of inflation is total spending increasing faster than total production.

1. The economy begins at point *A*, with real GDP of US$10.0 billion and a price level of 100. An increase in full-employment real GDP from US$10.0 billion to US$10.5 billion causes long-run aggregate supply to shift from $LRAS_1$ to $LRAS_2$. Aggregate demand shifts from AD_1 to AD_2.
2. Because *AD* shifts to the right by more than the *LRAS* curve, the price level in the new equilibrium rises from 100 to 104.

firms, and the government may cut back expenditures. This reduced spending will result in the aggregate demand curve shifting to the right less than it normally would or, possibly, shifting to the left. In fact, as we will see shortly, *changes in the price level and in real GDP in the short run are determined by the shifts in the* SRAS *and* AD *curves.*

What Is the Usual Cause of Inflation?

The dynamic aggregate demand and aggregate supply model provides a more accurate explanation than the basic model of the source of most inflation. If total spending in the economy grows faster than total production, prices rise. Figure 20-9 illustrates this point by showing that if the *AD* curve shifts to the right by more than the *LRAS* curve, inflation results because equilibrium occurs at a higher price level, point *B*. In the new equilibrium, point *B*, the *SRAS* curve has shifted to the right by less than the *LRAS* curve because the anticipated increase in prices offsets some of the technological change and increases in the labor force and capital stock that occur during the year. Although inflation is generally the result of total spending growing faster than total production, a shift to the left of the short-run aggregate supply curve can also cause an increase in the price level, as we saw earlier in the discussion of supply shocks.

As we saw in Figure 20-8, if aggregate demand increases by the same amount as short-run and long-run aggregate supply, the price level will not change. In this case, the economy experiences economic growth without inflation.

The Slow Recovery from the Recession of 2009

We can use the dynamic aggregate demand and aggregate supply model to analyze the slow recovery from the recession of 2007–2010. The recession began in December 2007, as the long economic expansion after the year 2001 ended. The recession was caused by the financial crises that started in the U.S. and expanded to the whole world by the end of 2008. The crises resulted in a decline in global aggregate demand and also in the Arab world. The decline in the world demand for oil led to a large drop in its prices. This in turn reinforced the recessionary trends in the Arab world economies, which are dependent on oil to various degrees.

Some Arab countries, such as the GCC countries, Libya, and Algeria, directly depend on oil receipts as a major source of income. Other Arab countries, such as Egypt, Lebanon, Morocco, Jordan, Sudan, and Tunisia, rely to a great extent on workers' remittances from the Gulf and the rest of the oil countries. The price of a barrel of oil had been below US$30 in 2004 but was above US$140 in mid-2008. Petrol prices in the U.S. rose

Figure 20-10

Using Dynamic Aggregate Demand and Aggregate Supply to Understand the Recovery from the 2009 Recession

Between 2009 and 2010, *AD* shifted to the right but not by nearly enough to offset the shift to the right of *LRAS*, which represented the increase in potential real GDP from US$10.0 billion to US$10.3 billion. Although real GDP increased from US$9.9 billion in 2009 to US$10.1 billion in 2010, this was still far below the potential real GDP, shown by *LRAS*$_{2010}$. As a result, the unemployment rate rose from 4.7 percent in 2009 to 5.8 percent in 2010. Because the increase in aggregate demand was small, the price level increased only from 102.4 in 2009 to 104.2 in 2010, so the inflation rate for 2010 was only 1.8 percent.

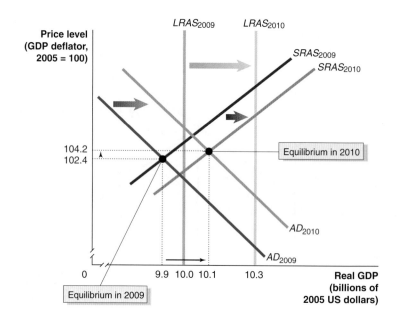

from US$1.50 per gallon in early 2004 to more than US$4.00 per gallon in mid-2008. As worldwide demand for oil decreased, oil prices fell to about US$40 per barrel in early 2009. Therefore, the decline in oil receipts and the worldwide slowing of trade resulted in a slowdown in almost all Arab countries, to differing extents. The more a country is integrated with the global economy, the more its economy will be impacted by the global business cycle. For example, an economy such as that of Dubai was hard hit by the crisis compared with other economies, such as Saudi Arabia or Egypt, that are less integrated with the global financial markets.

Few economists were surprised that the strong expansion of the 2000s eventually ended in recession. Although forecasting the exact date of a recession is very difficult, it was inevitable that the expansion would end, just as all previous expansions had. The recession effectively ended in 2010. Figure 20-10 illustrates the changes in an economy from 2009 to 2010 and shows that the economy remained well below potential GDP during 2010.

In Figure 20-10, the *AD* curve shifts to the right much less than does the *LRAS* curve. As a result, the price level increases only from 102.4 in 2009 to 104.2 in 2010, for a very low inflation rate of 1.8 percent. Real GDP increases only from US$9.9 billion to US$10.1 billion, which is below the potential level of US$10.3 billion, shown by *LRAS*$_{2010}$. Not surprisingly, the unemployment rate actually rose from 4.7 percent in 2001 to 5.8 percent in 2010.

The increase in aggregate demand during 2010 was weak because the factors that had caused the recession continued to be at work. Many firms still did not feel the need to increase investment spending. Uncertainty remained high as the Arab economies faced the consequences of the riots in Tunisia and Egypt demanding fairer income distribution and a democratic transition. However, the rebound and the increase in growth rates are expected to increase by 2012.

Making	**Saudi's Slow Economic Recovery**
the	
Connection	

Making the Connection

Saudi's Slow Economic Recovery

Following a stagnant and a difficult year in 2009, Saudi Arabia's economic recovery in 2010 and 2011 seems to follow a gradual but steady path of an accelerating growth performance. Inflation is expected to remain at manageable but historically high levels. Optimism started to spread with the expansion of the private sector and bank credit. Despite many key elements supporting the recovery of the Kingdom, economic growth forecasts for 2010 slightly dropped to 3.9 percent, based on the view that improvements in business activity, as we show in this chapter, will be gradual and cautious.

While most major world economies fell into recession, the Saudi economy witnessed a real growth of 0.15 percent in 2009. However, nominal GDP contracted by around 21 percent as a result of the decline in Saudi's oil exports. Meanwhile oil sector output contracted by only 6.4 percent; less than the 9.1 percent expected contraction. This was a direct effect of Saudi Aramco's expansion of investments in the oil sector. It helped in preventing a large drop in the oil sector.

Amid the global crisis in 2009, the private sector was reluctant to invest, and aggregate domestic demand declined, contributing to a slowdown in nonoil private sector performance. The private sector expanded 2.5 percent. down sharply from 4.7 percent in 2008. International and local credit dried up, which prompted many businesses to call off or cancel projects as they opted to hoard cash.

In 2010 the picture was more optimistic, witnessing an improvement in the private sector's performance. The sector grew at about 3 percent. With oil prices standing at around US$80 a barrel and key global economies beginning to return to growth, Saudi Arabia is likely to benefit from the improvement in global economic conditions. Real growth for the Saudi economy is expected to be 4.8 percent in 2011.

As the state continues to take the lead in the economic recovery, government sector estimates indicate that the government grew by about 4.1 percent in 2010, accelerating slightly from its 4 percent last year. In the 2010 budget, this expansionary fiscal policy was reflected in the 13.7 percent rise in projected state expenditure to a record level of SR540 billion (US$ 144 billion)—the largest budget in Saudi history—which is devised to stimulate the private sector to invest and urge banks to jumpstart lending, following a slow 2009.

After a record high inflation rate of 9.9 percent in 2008, inflationary pressures subsided in 2009 due to the slower domestic demand, lower oil (exports) prices, a decline in food prices, and a decline in domestic rents. The Saudi annual rate of inflation reached 4.3 percent in 2010, compared with 5.1 percent in 2009.

Source: John Sfakianakis, "Saudi Economic Growth Likely to Accelerate to 3.9% in 2010," *Arab News*, January 2010.

During a recession, businesses suffer from slower demand and less consumer spending. As a result, investment shrinks.

Figure 20-11 shows the results of the more rapid hypothetical increase in aggregate demand during 2012. In 2011, real GDP is forecasted to be 3.7 percent below its potential level, while the unemployment rate is around 6.0 percent. The figure shows that the large predicted shift in aggregate demand during 2012 would lead to an increase in real GDP from US$10.3 billion to US$10.8 billion. This level is still below potential real GDP of US$11.0 billion, but the gap had narrowed to 1.8 percent. As a result, the unemployment rate fell from 6.0 percent to 5.2 percent. The rapid increase in aggregate demand causes a rise in the inflation rate.

As a result of booming emerging markets in the Middle East and North Africa due to the huge surge in oil prices between 2004 and 2007, the construction industry was also booming, in particular in the Arab Gulf. Some of the rapid rise in prices for new and existing homes at that time was due to a speculative 'bubble.' A bubble occurs when people become less concerned with the underlying value of an asset—either a physical asset, such as a house, or a financial asset, such as a stock—and focus instead on expectations of the price of the asset increasing. In some areas of the Arab world—Dubai and Qatar, for example—many houses were being purchased by investors, who intended to resell them for higher prices than they paid for them and did not intend to live in them. The bubble was reinforced by the rising oil prices, and the availability of finance at reasonable costs.

Figure 20-11

Using Dynamic Aggregate Demand and Aggregate Supply to Understand the More Rapid Recovery of 2011–2012

The figure shows that the large shift in aggregate demand during 2012 led to an increase in real GDP from US$10.3 billion to US$10.8 billion. This was still below the potential real GDP of US$11.0 billion, but the gap had narrowed to 1.8 percent. As a result, the unemployment rate fell from 6.0 percent to 5.2 percent. The rapid increase in aggregate demand caused a rise in the inflation rate. The price level increased from 106.3 in 2011 to 109.1 in 2012, for an inflation rate of 2.6 percent.

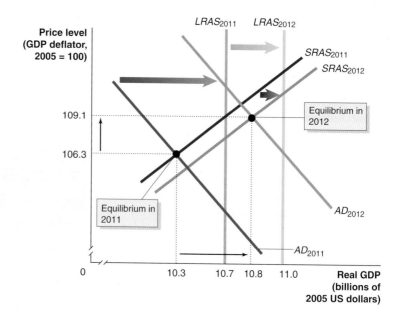

Speculative bubbles eventually come to an end, and this housing bubble began to deflate around the end of 2008 as a result of the mortgage crises in the U.S. that extended to Europe and the rest of the world, triggering a worldwide financial crisis. Many economies in 2009 felt the effects of hard times in the housing and real-estate market. When the world economies began to fall into recession during 2009, most central banks had taken action to lower interest rates. But the lower interest rates on mortgage loans were combined with less credit, and a sharp drop in consumer confidence in many countries.

In addition, emerging countries in the Middle East witnessed a drop in foreign capital inflows, which further led to a lower demand for houses, and a large drop (to various degrees) in their values. One of the most hard-hit markets was the Dubai real-estate market, which lost almost 40 percent of its value during the crisis and recession of 2009. This decline in new home sales, combined with a very large supply of new houses, helped deepen the severity of the 2009 recession in Arab markets. The real-estate markets showed a weak recovery in 2010, however, and are expected to pick up by 2012.

Solved Problem | 20-4

Showing the Effect of Oil Shock of 1974–1975 on the Economies of the West, Using a Dynamic Aggregate Demand and Aggregate Supply Graph

The 1974–1975 recession in the West, especially the U.S., clearly illustrates how a supply shock affects the economy. Following the Arab–Israeli War of 1973, the Organization of Petroleum Exporting Countries (OPEC) increased the price of a barrel of oil from less than US$3 to more than US$10. Use this information and the statistics in the following table to draw a dynamic aggregate demand and aggregate supply graph showing macroeconomic equilibrium for 1974 and 1975 for a country in the West, such as the U.S. Assume that

the aggregate demand curve did not shift between 1974 and 1975. Provide a brief explanation of your graph.

	ACTUAL REAL GDP IN US$	POTENTIAL REAL GDP IN US$	PRICE LEVEL
1974	4.32 billion	4.35 billion	34.7
1975	4.31 billion	4.50 billion	38.0

Source: U.S. Bureau of Economic Analysis.

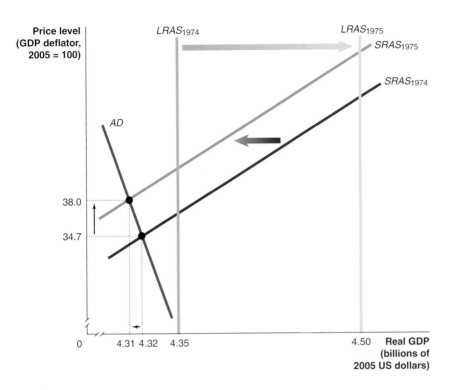

SOLVING THE PROBLEM:

Step 1: **Review the chapter material.** This problem is about using the dynamic aggregate demand and aggregate supply model, so you may want to review the section "A Dynamic Aggregate Demand and Aggregate Supply Model," which begins on page 675.

Step 2: **Use the information in the table to draw the graph.** You need to draw five curves: *SRAS* and *LRAS* for both 1974 and 1975 and *AD*, which is the same for both years. You know that the two *LRAS* curves will be vertical lines at the values given for potential GDP in the table. Because of the large supply shock, you know that the *SRAS* curve shifted to the left. You are instructed to assume that the *AD* curve did not shift. Your graph should look like this:

Step 3: **Explain your graph.** $LRAS_{1974}$ and $LRAS_{1975}$ are at the levels of potential real GDP for each year. Macroeconomic equilibrium for 1974 occurs where the *AD* curve intersects the $SRAS_{1974}$ curve, with real GDP of US$4.32 billion and a price level of 34.7. Macroeconomic equilibrium for 1975 occurs where the *AD* curve intersects the $SRAS_{1975}$ curve, with real GDP of US$4.31 billion and a price level of 38.0.

EXTRA CREDIT: As a result of the supply shock, the economy moved from an equilibrium output just below potential GDP in 1974 (the recession actually began right at the end of 1973) to an equilibrium well below potential GDP in 1975. With real GDP in 1975 about 4.2 percent below its potential level, the unemployment rate soared from 5.6 percent in 1974 to 8.5 percent in 1975.

YOUR TURN: For more practice, do related problems 4.4 and 4.5 on page 689 at the end of this chapter.

>> End Solved Problem 20-4

Making the Connection

Can FedEx and the U.S. Economy Withstand High Oil Prices?

FedEx burns a lot of gasoline and jet fuel to power its 70,000 trucks and 672 aircraft worldwide. An increase in oil prices causes FedEx to raise the prices it charges its customers, which reduces the quantity of packages those customers ship. If rising oil prices affect enough firms, the short-run aggregate supply curve will shift to the left, potentially pushing the economy into recession. This outcome occurred when oil prices rose from US$3 per barrel to US$10 per barrel in the early 1970s, pushing the U.S. economy into recession during 1974 and 1975. During those years, real GDP declined, and the unemployment rate rose to 9 percent.

FedEx's trucks and jets have become more fuel efficient.

The effects on the economy of earlier 'oil shocks' led some economists during the mid-2000s to predict that the United States would experience a recession as oil prices rose from about US$34 per barrel in 2004 to over US$140 per barrel in mid-2008. The increase in the price of oil appeared to be caused by increased demand in rapidly growing economies, particularly India and China, and by the difficulty in developing new supplies of oil in the short run. Surprisingly, at least through mid-2008, real GDP continued to grow despite soaring oil prices. Had the economy become less vulnerable to high oil prices? Some economists argued that, in fact, this was the case. Because of earlier increases in the price of oil, by the mid-2000s, many firms had switched to less oil-dependent production processes. For example, FedEx and other firms used more fuel efficient jets and trucks. As a result, the U.S. economy was consuming almost 60 percent less oil per dollar of GDP than it had in the mid-1970s. Today, oil price increases do not shift the short-run aggregate supply curve as far to the left as similar increases did 30 years ago.

In addition, the oil price increases of the mid-2000s occurred gradually, which gave individuals and firms time to adjust. Earlier increases in the price of oil had occurred more abruptly—usually as a result of conflict in the Middle East, where at the time more than half of world oil production took place. Finally, the oil price increases of the mid-2000s took place at a time when the U.S. economy was growing, so it was easier to absorb the adverse effects of higher oil prices. Economist Keith Sill of the Central Bank of Philadelphia in the U.S. state of pennsylvania has estimated that a 10 percent increase in oil prices will result in a temporary reduction in the annual growth of real GDP in the U.S. of about 0.5 percent. So, higher oil prices reduced the increases in real GDP during the mid-2000s but at least through mid-2008 had not yet tipped the economy into recession.

Sources: Justin Lahart and Connor Dougherty, "US Retools Economy, Curbing Thirst for Oil," *Wall Street Journal*, August 12, 2008, p. A1; and Keith Sill, "The Macroeconomics of Oil Shocks," *Business Review*, First Quarter 2007, pp. 21–31.

YOUR TURN: Test your understanding by doing related problem 4.9 on page 690 at the end of this chapter.

Economics in YOUR Life!

>> **Continued from page 659**

At the beginning of this chapter, we asked you to consider whether during a recession your employer is likely to reduce your pay and cut the prices of the products he or she sells. In this chapter, the dynamic aggregate demand and aggregate supply model showed that even during a recession, the price level rarely falls. A typical firm is therefore unlikely to cut its prices during a recession. So, the owner of the coffeehouse you work in will probably not cut the price of lattes unless sales have declined drastically. We also saw that most firms are more reluctant to cut wages than to increase them because wage cuts can have a negative effect on worker morale and productivity. Given that you are a highly skilled barista, your employer is particularly unlikely to cut your wages for fear that you might quit and work for a competitor.

Conclusion

Chapter 3 demonstrated the power of the microeconomic model of demand and supply in explaining how the prices and quantities of individual products are determined. This chapter showed that we need a different model to explain the behavior of the whole economy. We saw that the macroeconomic model of aggregate demand and aggregate supply explains fluctuations in real GDP and the price level.

One of the great disagreements among economists and political leaders is whether the governments should intervene to try to reduce fluctuations in real GDP and keep the unemployment and inflation rates low. We explore this important issue in Chapters 22 and 23, but first, in Chapter 21, we consider the role money plays in the economy.

Read *An Inside Look* on the next page to learn how FedEx in the Middle East met the recent global recession challenges.

How FedEx Middle East Weathered the Recent Global Recession

ARABIANSUPPLYCHAIN.COM, MARCH 16, 2009

Express Strategy

Hamdi Osman, FedEx's senior vice president for the Middle East, explains why the courier giant's regional developments will not be impacted by the global recession.

(a) Far flung destinations, bad weather and technical problems do not deter delivery company FedEx Express from transporting goods. And while beating global recession may be more challenging than posting birthday presents to Fiji, the organization is intent on rising to the challenge. By listening to customers' needs and economizing in certain areas, Hamdi Osman, FedEx Express' senior vice president for the Middle East, Indian Subcontinent and Africa, believes the company can easily sustain itself.

"One thing we're looking at is launching an economy service," he explains. "It will provide customers with an option where they can choose to have their package in three or four days rather than next day delivery, and I really think this will be the way of the future." Moreover, the company believes delivering packages via road transport whenever possible will save costs. "We may be expanding our road services rather than carrying the bulk of products by airfreight," says Osman.

FedEx is not the only company to be affected by the financial crisis. With transportation industry figures dropping rapidly, all sectors of the business are now feeling the pinch and need to take action. However, Osman maintains that the cargo industry, rather than the express business, is taking the brunt. "Cargo has definitely been the most affected.

"FedEx has been a good model for other companies year over year as we are so dedicated to the needs of customers."

(b) Ultimately, management believes it is this commitment that will ensure the company's survival. "Smaller companies, medium sized companies and even big companies have tough times and the only reason why they have problems or have to shut down is because somewhere or somehow they did not pay attention to or listen to what the customer wanted and this is something FedEx does very well."

(c) Established in the Middle East in 1989, Dubai has quickly become the central hub for FedEx in the region. "In the transportation business you have all these hot-spots when you consider the links in the chain and the Middle East is one of them. The region is as important as the US, as important as Europe or Asia. Out of this office alone we cover 82 countries," says Osman. The GCC in particular is at the forefront for industry in the area. "Oil has played a major role and also there has been a construction boom and a lot of the talent come here. The GCC all together is becoming a heavyweight."

…At present, FedEx uses a large fleet of freighter aircraft to provide round-the-clock air links between the GCC countries, Indian subcontinent and the Dubai regional facility.

…According to FedEx Middle East's management, the organization has experienced phenomenal growth in the past four years.

And despite this year's slowdown, business is still better than elsewhere in the world. "If you look at China, a country which we heavily rely on, the GDP (gross domestic product) growth has gone from 10% to 6.8% but it is still growing. Yes it is bad because it is dropping, but it is still growing at 6.8%," explains Osman. Meanwhile, closer to home, India has reduced its GDP growth expectations from 8% to 6%. "It may have dropped but there is still growth and I think this will push us to invest more into the future and expand our services, enhancing them and giving the customers more delivery options."

Source: Elizabeth Cernik, "Express Strategy," Arabiansupplychain.com, March 16, 2009, ITP Business Publishing Ltd.

Key Points in the Article

This article discusses how FedEx in the Middle East met the challenges of the global recession. Like all logistics businesses in the region, a decline in the World trade negatively affects the cargo industry, in particular, but not much the express delivery services. In addition, since oil is a major driver in the Middle East, a decline in oil prices slows down even further economic activity in this region. FedEx's strategy has been two-fold. First, they focused on consumer needs, providing more delivery options and economy services at times the consumer might be striving hard to cut expenses. One option is to offer a new option to consumers to deliver their packages in three to four days, alongside the regular express delivery services. The second aspect of their strategy to work around the recession was to cut all possible costs, in order to improve profitability despite a drop in demand.

Analyzing the News

(a) Recessions are challenging but FedEx's senior vice president for the Middle East, Indian Subcontinent and Africa believes the company has strong grounds for being up to the task. He laid out the "express strategy" of FedEx to weather the downturn in the region. The strategy is based on offering more economy options to customers, and cutting operational costs.

(b) All sectors of the industry are affected by the crisis, especially cargo shipments. It is time for all operators to take action. What helps one company to survive while others sink is the extent to which a company is paying attention to its customers' needs and adapting to it, in particular in tough times.

(c) The Middle East and the GCC is increasingly becoming of greater importance to the company's business. This is due to the greater potential of growth in the region with its rising oil prices

and growing businesses. In addition, the region managed to cope with the crisis better than the West. China and India, very important for FedEx business in the East, maintained relatively high growth rates as compared with other parts of the World, despite a clear slide in their growth rates figures.

Thinking Critically

1. How can cutting costs be one way to combat the effects of a recession in this situation? Briefly explain.

2. Freight-transportation companies such as FedEx provide domestic shipping services in many countries. How, if at all, might this geographic diversification alter how FedEx's earnings would otherwise respond to a slowing global and regional economy?

FedEx's strategy to weather the economic downturn is based on cost cutting and launching economy services to offer cheaper options to their customers.

Key Terms

Aggregate demand and aggregate supply model, p. 660

Aggregate demand curve, p. 660

Fiscal policy, p. 662

Long-run aggregate supply curve, p. 667

Menu costs, p. 669

Monetary policy, p. 662

Short-run aggregate supply curve, p. 660

Stagflation, p. 674

Supply shock, p. 670

Summary

Aggregate Demand

The **aggregate demand and aggregate supply model** enables us to explain short-run fluctuations in real GDP and price level. The **aggregate demand curve** shows the relationship between the price level and the level of planned aggregate expenditures by households, firms, and the government. The **short-run aggregate supply curve** shows the relationship in the short run between the price level and the quantity of real GDP supplied by firms. The **long-run aggregate supply curve** shows the relationship in the long run between the price level and the quantity of real GDP supplied. The four components of aggregate demand are consumption (C), investment (I), government purchases (G), and net exports (NX). The aggregate demand curve is downward sloping because a decline in the price level causes consumption, investment, and net exports to increase. If the price level changes but all else remains constant, the economy will move up or down a stationary aggregate demand curve. If any variable other than the price level changes, the aggregate demand curve will shift. The variables that cause the aggregate demand curve to shift are divided into three categories: changes in government policies, changes in the expectations of households and firms, and changes in foreign variables. For example, **monetary policy** involves the actions the central bank takes to manage the money supply and interest rates to pursue macroeconomic policy objectives. When the Central bank takes actions to change interest rates, consumption and investment spending will change, shifting the aggregate demand curve. **Fiscal policy** involves changes in federal taxes and purchases that are intended to achieve macroeconomic policy objectives. Changes in taxes and purchases shift the aggregate demand curve.

Aggregate Supply

The **long-run aggregate supply curve** is a vertical line because in the long run, real GDP is always at its potential level and is unaffected by the price level. The short-run aggregate supply curve slopes upward because workers and firms fail to predict accurately the future price level. The three main explanations of why this failure results in an upward-sloping aggregate supply curve are that (1) contracts make wages and prices 'sticky,' (2) businesses often adjust wages slowly, and (3) menu costs make some prices sticky. **Menu costs** are the costs to firms of changing prices on menus or catalogs. If the price level changes but all else remains constant, the economy will move up or down a stationary aggregate supply curve. If any variable other than the price level changes, the aggregate supply curve will shift. The aggregate supply curve shifts as a result of increases in the labor force and capital stock, technological change, expected increases or decreases in the future price level, adjustments of workers and firms to errors in past expectations about the price level, and unexpected increases or decreases in the price of an important raw material. A **supply shock** is an unexpected event that causes the short-run aggregate supply curve to shift.

Macroeconomic Equilibrium in the Long Run and the Short Run

In long-run macroeconomic equilibrium, the aggregate demand and short-run aggregate supply curves intersect at a point *on* the long-run aggregate supply curve. In short-run macroeconomic equilibrium, the aggregate demand and short-run aggregate supply curves often intersect at a point *off* the long-run aggregate supply curve. An automatic mechanism drives the economy to long-run equilibrium. If short-run equilibrium occurs at a point below potential real GDP, wages and prices will fall, and the short-run aggregate supply curve will shift to the right until potential GDP is restored. If short-run equilibrium occurs at a point beyond potential real GDP, wages and prices will rise, and the short-run aggregate supply curve will shift to the left until potential GDP is restored. Real GDP can be temporarily above or below its potential level, either because of shifts in the aggregate demand curve or because supply shocks lead to shifts in the aggregate supply curve. **Stagflation** is a combination of inflation and recession, usually resulting from a supply shock.

20.3 LEARNING OBJECTIVE

Use the aggregate demand and aggregate supply model to illustrate the difference between short-run and long-run macroeconomic equilibrium, **pages 671–675.**

A Dynamic Aggregate Demand and Aggregate Supply Model

To make the aggregate demand and aggregate supply model more realistic, we need to make it *dynamic* by incorporating three facts that were left out of the basic model: (1) Potential real GDP increases continually, shifting the long-run aggregate supply curve to the right; (2) during most years, aggregate demand will be shifting to the right; and (3) except during periods when workers and firms expect high rates of inflation, the aggregate supply curve will be shifting to the right. The dynamic aggregate demand and aggregate supply model allows us to analyze macroeconomic conditions, including the recovery from the 2009 recession.

20.4 LEARNING OBJECTIVE

Use the dynamic aggregate demand and aggregate supply model to analyze macroeconomic conditions, **pages 675–683.**

Review, Problems and Applications

 Visit www.pearsoned.co.uk/awe/hubbard to complete these exercises online and get instant feedback.

Get Ahead of the Curve

20.1 LEARNING OBJECTIVE Identify the determinants of aggregate demand and distinguish between a movement along the aggregate demand curve and a shift of the curve, **pages 660–666.**

Review Questions

1.1 Explain the three reasons the aggregate demand curve slopes downward.

1.2 What are the differences between the *AD* curve and the demand curve for an individual product, such as apples?

1.3 What are the variables that cause the *AD* curve to shift? For each variable, identify whether an increase in that variable will cause the *AD* curve to shift to the right or to the left.

Problems and Applications

1.4 Explain how each of the following events would affect the aggregate demand curve.
   a. An increase in the price level
   b. An increase in government purchases
   c. Higher income taxes
   d. Higher interest rate
   e. Faster income growth in other countries

1.5 (Related to *Solved Problem 20-1* on page 664) Explain whether each of the following will cause a shift of the *AD* curve or a movement along the *AD* curve.
   a. Firms become more optimistic and increase their spending on machinery and equipment.
   b. The government increases taxes in an attempt to reduce a budget deficit.
   c. The economy experiences 4 percent inflation.

1.6 A sharp decline in stock prices could have very significant effects on both businesses and consumers. Explain what are the expected consequences of this for the economy.

1.7 (Related to the *Making the Connection* on page 663) Suppose that a consumer in Qatar buys a Ford Mustang for a price of US$30,000. Do U.S. exports increase by US$30,000? Briefly explain.

Review Questions

2.1 Explain why the long-run aggregate supply curve is vertical.

2.2 What variables cause the long-run aggregate supply curve to shift? For each variable, identify whether an increase in that variable will cause the long-run aggregate supply curve to shift to the right or to the left.

2.3 Why does the short-run aggregate supply curve slope upward?

2.4 What variables cause the short-run aggregate supply curve to shift? For each variable, identify whether an increase in that variable will cause the short-run aggregate supply curve to shift to the right or to the left.

Problems and Applications

2.5 Explain how each of the following events would affect the long-run aggregate supply curve.
   a. A higher price level
   b. An increase in the labor force
   c. An increase in the quantity of capital goods
   d. Technological change

2.6 Explain how each of the following events would affect the short-run aggregate supply curve.
   a. An increase in the price level
   b. An increase in what the price level is expected to be in the future
   c. A price level that is currently higher than expected
   d. An unexpected increase in the price of an important raw material
   e. An increase in the labor force

2.7 Suppose that workers and firms could always predict next year's price level with perfect accuracy. Briefly explain whether in these circumstances the *SRAS* curve still slopes upward.

2.8 Workers and firms often enter into contracts that fix prices or wages, sometimes for years at a time. If the price level turns out to be higher or lower than was expected when the contract was signed, one party to the contract will lose out. Briefly explain why, despite knowing this, workers and firms still sign long-term contracts.

2.9 What are menu costs? How has the widespread use of computers and the Internet affected menu costs? If menu costs were eliminated, would the short-run aggregate supply curve be a vertical line? Briefly explain.

Review Questions

3.1 What is the relationship among the *AD*, *SRAS*, and *LRAS* curves when the economy is in macroeconomic equilibrium?

3.2 What is a supply shock? Why might a supply shock lead to stagflation?

3.3 Why are the long-run effects of an increase in aggregate demand on price and output different from the short-run effects?

Problems and Applications

3.4 Draw a basic aggregate demand and aggregate supply graph (with *LRAS* constant) that shows the economy in long-run equilibrium.
   a. Now assume that there is an increase in aggregate demand. Show the resulting short-run equilibrium on your graph. Explain how the economy adjusts back to long-run equilibrium.
   b. Now assume that there is an unexpected increase in the price of an important raw material. Show the resulting short-run equilibrium on your graph. Explain how the economy adjusts back to long-run equilibrium.

3.5 Many economists believe that some wages and prices are 'sticky downward,' meaning that these wages and prices increase quickly when demand is increasing

but decrease slowly, if at all, when demand is decreasing. Discuss the consequences of this for the automatic mechanism that brings the economy back to potential GDP after an increase in aggregate demand. Would your answer change if aggregate demand decreased rather than increased? Explain.

3.6 Consider the information in the following table:

YEAR	ACTUAL REAL GDP IN US$	POTENTIAL REAL GDP IN US$	UNEMPLOYMENT RATE
1969	3.77 trillion	3.67 trillion	3.5%
1970	3.77 trillion	3.80 trillion	4.9%

Sources: U.S. Department of Commerce; and Bureau of Economic Analysis.

   a. In 1969, actual real GDP was greater than potential real GDP. Explain how this is possible.
   b. Even though real GDP in 1970 was the same as real GDP in 1969, the unemployment rate increased substantially from 1969 to 1970. Why did this increase in unemployment occur?
   c. Was the inflation rate in 1970 likely to have been higher or lower than the inflation rate in 1969? Does your answer depend on whether the recession was caused by a change in a component of aggregate demand or by a supply shock?

3.7 Use the following graph to answer the questions.

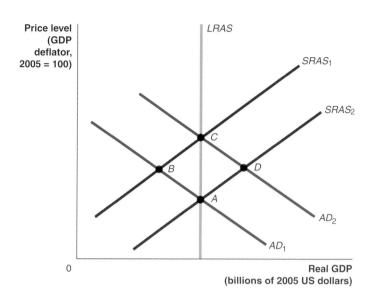

a. Which of the points *A*, *B*, *C*, or *D* can represent a long-run equilibrium?

b. Suppose that initially the economy is at point *A*. If aggregate demand increases from AD_1 to AD_2, which point represents the economy's short-run equilibrium? Which point represents the eventual long-run equilibrium? Briefly explain how the economy adjusts from the short-run equilibrium to the long-run equilibrium.

20.4 LEARNING OBJECTIVE — Use the dynamic aggregate demand and aggregate supply model to analyze macroeconomic conditions, **pages 675–683.**

Review Questions

4.1 What are the key differences between the basic aggregate demand and aggregate supply model and the dynamic aggregate demand and aggregate supply model?

4.2 In the dynamic aggregate demand and aggregate supply model, what is the result of aggregate demand increasing faster than potential real GDP? What is the result of aggregate demand increasing slower than potential real GDP?

Problems and Applications

4.3 Draw a dynamic aggregate demand and aggregate supply graph showing the economy moving from potential GDP in 2012 to potential GDP in 2013, with no inflation. Your graph should contain the *AD*, *SRAS*, and *LRAS* curves for both 2012 and 2013, and should indicate the short-run macroeconomic equilibrium for each year and the directions in which the curves have shifted. Identify what must happen to have growth during 2013 without inflation.

4.4 **(Related to *Solved Problem 20-4* on page 680)** Consider the information in the following table for the first two years of the Great Depression (the values for real GDP are in 2000 U.S. dollars).

YEAR	ACTUAL REAL GDP IN US$	POTENTIAL REAL GDP IN US$	PRICE LEVEL
1929	865.2 billion	865.2 billion	12.0
1930	790.7 billion	895.7 billion	11.5

Sources: U.S. Department of Commerce; and Bureau of Economic Analysis.

a. The table shows that something happened during 1929–1930 that has not happened during the recessions of the past 50 years. What is it?

b. Draw a dynamic aggregate demand and aggregate supply graph to illustrate what happened during these years. Your graph should contain the *AD*, *SRAS*, and *LRAS* curves for both 1929 and 1930 and should indicate the short-run macroeconomic equilibrium for each year and the directions in which the curves have shifted.

4.5 **(Related to *Solved Problem 20-4* on page 680)** Look again at Solved Problem 20-4 on the supply shock of 1974–1975. In the table, the price level for 1974 is given as 34.7, and the price level for 1975 is given as 38.0. The values for the price level are well below 100. Does this indicate that inflation must have been low during these years? Briefly explain.

4.6 In the graph, suppose that the economy moves from point *A* in year 1 to point *B* in year 2. Using the graph, briefly explain your answers to each of the questions.

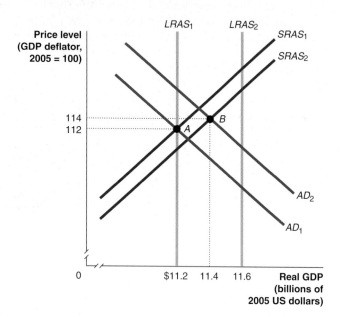

a. What is the growth rate in potential real GDP from year 1 to year 2?

b. Is the unemployment rate in year 2 higher or lower than in year 1?

c. What is the inflation rate in year 2?

d. What is the growth rate of real GDP in year 2?

4.7 The worldwide recession of 2009 resulted from a cutback in business spending when the real-estate market bubble in the U.S. burst and exported the financial crisis to other parts of the world through the global financial system.

a. What does "business spending" mean?

b. What does the "real-estate market bubble" mean?

c. Why would the bursting of this bubble affect business spending?

4.8 (Related to the *Chapter Opener* on page 658) Briefly compare how sensitive Aramex's sales are to changes in the business cycle with how sensitive the following firms' sales are to changes in the business cycle: Toyota, Starbucks, Emaar, Adair (home builders), and Paramount Pictures (movies). In other words, do Aramex's sales fluctuate more or less than the sales of each of these other firms as the economy moves from recession to expansion and back to recession?

4.9 (Related to the *Making the Connection* on page 682) Suppose the price of a barrel of oil increases from US$100 to US$130. Use a basic aggregate demand and aggregate supply graph to show the short-run and long-run effects on an oil-importing economy.

Appendix

Macroeconomic Schools of Thought

Understand Macroeconomic Schools of Thought

Macroeconomics as a separate field of economics began with the publication in 1936 of John Maynard Keynes's book *The General Theory of Employment, Interest, and Money*. Keynes, an economist at the University of Cambridge in England, was attempting to explain the devastating Great Depression of the 1930s. As we discussed in Chapter 19, real GDP in the United States declined by more than 25 percent between 1929 and 1933 and did not return to its potential level until the United States entered World War II in 1941. The unemployment rate soared to 25 percent by 1933 and did not return to its 1929 level until 1942. Keynes developed a version of the aggregate demand and aggregate supply model to explain these facts. The widespread acceptance during the 1930s and 1940s of Keynes's model became known as the **Keynesian revolution**.

In fact, the aggregate demand and aggregate supply model remains the most widely accepted approach to analyzing macroeconomic issues. Because the model has been modified significantly from Keynes's day, many economists who use the model today refer to themselves as *new Keynesians*. The new Keynesians emphasize the importance of the stickiness of wages and prices in explaining fluctuations in real GDP. A significant number of economists, however, dispute whether the aggregate demand and aggregate supply model, as we have discussed in this chapter, is the best way to analyze macroeconomic issues. These alternative *schools of thought* use models that differ significantly from the standard aggregate demand and aggregate supply model. We can briefly consider each of the three major alternative models:

1 The monetarist model

2 The new classical model

3 The real business cycle model

Keynesian revolution The name given to the widespread acceptance during the 1930s and 1940s of John Maynard Keynes's macroeconomic model.

The Monetarist Model

The monetarist model—also known as the neo-Quantity Theory of Money model—was developed beginning in the 1940s by Milton Friedman, an economist at the University of Chicago in the United States who was awarded the Nobel Prize in Economics in 1976. Friedman argued that the Keynesian approach overstates the amount of macroeconomic instability in the economy. In particular, he argued that the economy will ordinarily be at potential real GDP. In the book *A Monetary History of the United States: 1867–1960*, written with Anna Jacobson Schwartz, Friedman argued that most fluctuations in real output were caused by fluctuations in the money supply rather than by fluctuations in consumption spending or investment spending. Friedman and Schwartz argued that the severity of the Great Depression was caused by the U.S. Federal Reserve's allowing the quantity of money in the economy to fall by more than 25 percent between 1929 and 1933.

In the United States, the Federal Reserve is responsible for managing the quantity of money. As we will discuss further in Chapter 22, the Federal Reserve has typically

Monetary growth rule A plan for increasing the quantity of money at a fixed rate that does not respond to changes in economic conditions.

Monetarism The macroeconomic theories of Milton Friedman and his followers; particularly the idea that the quantity of money should be increased at a constant rate.

focused more on controlling interest rates than on controlling the money supply. Friedman has argued that the Federal Reserve should change its practices and adopt a **monetary growth rule**, which is a plan for increasing the quantity of money at a fixed rate. Friedman believed that adopting a monetary growth rule would reduce fluctuations in real GDP, employment, and inflation.

Friedman's ideas, which are referred to as **monetarism**, attracted significant support during the 1970s and early 1980s, when the economy experienced high rates of unemployment and inflation. The support for monetarism declined during the late 1980s and 1990s, when the unemployment and inflation rates were relatively low. In Chapter 21, we will discuss the *quantity theory of money*, which underlies the monetarist model.

The New Classical Model

The new classical model was developed in the mid-1970s by a group of economists including Nobel laureate Robert Lucas of the University of Chicago, Thomas Sargent of New York University, and Robert Barro of Harvard University in the United States. Some of the views held by the new classical macroeconomists are similar to those held by economists before the Great Depression. Keynes referred to the economists before the Great Depression as "classical economists." Like the classical economists, the new classical macroeconomists believe that the economy normally will be at potential real GDP. They also believe that wages and prices adjust quickly to changes in demand and supply. Put another way, they believe the stickiness in wages and prices emphasized by the new Keynesians is unimportant.

New classical macroeconomics The macroeconomic theories of Robert Lucas and others, particularly the idea that workers and firms have rational expectations.

Lucas argued that workers and firms have *rational expectations*, meaning that they form their expectations of the future values of economic variables, such as the inflation rate, by making use of all available information, including information on variables—such as changes in the quantity of money—that might affect aggregate demand. If the actual inflation rate is lower than the expected inflation rate, the actual real wage will be higher than the expected real wage. These higher real wages will lead to a recession because they will cause firms to hire fewer workers and cut back on production. As workers and firms adjust their expectations to the lower inflation rate, the real wage will decline, and employment and production will expand, bringing the economy out of recession. The ideas of Lucas and his followers are referred to as the **new classical macroeconomics**. Supporters of the new classical model agree with supporters of the monetarist model that the Federal Reserve should adopt a monetary growth rule. They argue that a monetary growth rule will make it easier for workers and firms to accurately forecast the price level, thereby reducing fluctuations in real GDP.

The Real Business Cycle Model

Real business cycle model A macroeconomic model that focuses on real, rather than monetary, causes of the business cycle.

Beginning in the 1980s, some economists, including Nobel laureates Finn Kydland of Carnegie Mellon University and Edward Prescott of Arizona State University in the U.S., argued that Lucas was correct in assuming that workers and firms formed their expectations rationally and that wages and prices adjust quickly to supply and demand but wrong about the source of fluctuations in real GDP. They argued that fluctuations in real GDP are caused by temporary shocks to productivity. These shocks can be negative, such as a decline in the availability of oil or other raw materials, or positive, such as technological change that makes it possible to produce more output with the same quantity of inputs.

According to this school of thought, shifts in the aggregate demand curve have no impact on real GDP because the short-run aggregate supply curve is vertical. Other schools of thought all believe that the short-run aggregate supply curve is upward sloping and that only the *long-run* aggregate supply curve is vertical. Fluctuations in real GDP occur when a negative productivity shock causes the short-run aggregate supply curve to shift to the left—reducing real GDP—or a positive productivity shock causes the short-run aggregate supply curve to shift to the right—increasing real GDP. Because this model focuses on 'real' factors—productivity shocks—rather than changes in the quantity of money to explain fluctuations in real GDP, it is known as the **real business cycle model**.

Making the Connection

Karl Marx: Capitalism's Severest Critic

The schools of macroeconomic thought we have discussed in this appendix are considered part of mainstream economic theory because of their acceptance of the market system as the best means of raising living standards in the long run. One quite influential critic of mainstream economic theory was Karl Marx. Marx was born in Trier, Germany, in 1818. After graduating from the University of Berlin in 1841, he began a career as a political journalist and agitator. His political activities caused him to be expelled first from Germany and then from France and Belgium. In 1849, he moved to London, where he spent the remainder of his life.

In 1867, he published the first volume of his greatest work, *Das Kapital*. Marx read closely the most prominent mainstream economists, including Adam Smith, David Ricardo, and John Stuart Mill. But Marx believed that he understood how market systems would evolve in the long run much better than those earlier authors. Marx argued that the market system would eventually be replaced by a Communist economy in which the workers would control production. He believed in the *labor theory of value*, which attributed all of the value of a good or service to the labor that was embodied in it. According to Marx, the owners of businesses—capitalists—did not earn profits by contributing anything of value to the production of goods or services. Instead, capitalists earned profits because their "monopoly of the means of production"—their ownership of factories and machinery—allowed them to exploit workers by paying them wages that were much less than the value of workers' contribution to production.

Marx argued that wages of workers would be driven to levels that allowed only bare survival. He also argued that small firms would eventually be driven out of business by larger firms, forcing owners of small firms into the working class. Control of production would ultimately be concentrated in the hands of a few firms. These few remaining firms would have difficulty selling the goods they produced to the impoverished masses. A final economic crisis would lead the working classes to rise up, seize control of the economy, and establish Communism. Marx died in 1883 without providing a detailed explanation of how the Communist economy would operate.

Marx had relatively little influence on mainstream thinking in the United States, but several political parties in Europe were guided by his ideas. In 1917, the Bolshevik party seized control of Russia and established the Soviet Union, the first Communist state. Although the Soviet Union was a vicious dictatorship under Vladimir Lenin and his successor, Joseph Stalin, its prestige rose when it avoided the macroeconomic difficulties that plagued the market economies during the 1930s. By the late 1940s, Communist parties had also come to power in China and the countries of Eastern Europe. Poor economic performance contributed to the eventual collapse of the Soviet Union and its replacement by a market system, although one in which government intervention is still widespread. The Communist Party remains in power in China, but the economy is evolving toward a market system. Today, only North Korea and Cuba have economies that claim to be based on the ideas of Karl Marx.

Karl Marx predicted that a final economic crisis would lead to the collapse of the market system.

Key Terms

>> End Appendix Learning Objective

Most people in modern economies are highly specialized. They do only one thing—work as a nurse, an accountant, or an engineer—and use the money they earn to buy everything else they need. As we discussed in Chapter 2, people become much more productive by specializing because they can pursue their *comparative advantage*. The high income levels in modern economies are based on the specialization that money makes possible. We can now answer the question, "Why do we need money?" *By making exchange easier, money allows for specialization and higher productivity.*

The Functions of Money

Anything used as money—whether a deerskin, a cowrie seashell, cigarettes, a dollar bill, or a dinar—should fulfill the following four functions:

- Medium of exchange
- Unit of account
- Store of value
- Standard of deferred payment

Medium of Exchange Money serves as a medium of exchange when sellers are willing to accept it in exchange for goods or services. When the local supermarket accepts your US$5 bill in exchange for bread and milk, the US$5 bill is serving as a medium of exchange. To go back to our earlier example, with a medium of exchange, the farmer with the extra goat does not have to want wheat, and the farmer with the extra wheat does not have to want a goat. Both can exchange their products for money and use the money to buy what they want. An economy is more efficient when a single good is recognized as a medium of exchange.

Unit of Account In a barter system, each good has many prices. A cow may be worth 15 sheep, or 20 bushels of wheat. Using a good as a medium of exchange results in another benefit: it reduces the need to quote many different prices in trade. Instead of having to quote the price of a single good in terms of many other goods, each good has a single price quoted in terms of the medium of exchange. This function of money gives buyers and sellers a *unit of account*, a way of measuring value in the economy in terms of money. In every economy there is a currency used as money; each good has a price in terms of that currency. For example, in Lebanon the lira is the unit of account, while the dinar is Kuwait's unit of account, and so on.

Store of Value Money allows value to be stored easily: if you do not use all your accumulated money to buy goods and services today, you can hold the rest to use in the future. In fact, a fisherman and a farmer would be better off holding money rather than inventories of their perishable goods. The acceptability of money in future transactions depends on its not losing value over time. Money is not the only store of value. Any asset—stocks, Treasury bonds, real-estate, or Renoir paintings, for example—represents a store of value. Indeed, financial assets offer an important benefit relative to holding money because they generally pay a higher rate of interest or offer the prospect of gains in value. Other assets also have advantages relative to money because they provide services. A house, for example, offers you a place to sleep.

Why, then, would you bother to hold any money? The answer has to do with *liquidity*, or the ease with which a given asset can be converted into the medium of exchange. When money is the medium of exchange, it is the most liquid asset. You incur costs when you exchange other assets for money. When you sell bonds or shares of stock to buy a car, for example, you pay a commission to your broker. If you have to sell your house on short notice to finance an unexpected major medical expense, you pay a commission to a real-estate agent and probably have to accept a lower price to exchange the house for money quickly. To avoid such costs, people are willing to hold some of their wealth in the form of money, even though other assets offer a greater return as a store of value.

Standard of Deferred Payment Money is useful because it can serve as a standard of deferred payment in borrowing and lending. Money can facilitate exchange at a *given point in time* by providing a medium of exchange and unit of account. It can facilitate exchange *over time* by providing a store of value and a standard of deferred payment. For example, a furniture maker may be willing to sell you a chair today in exchange for money in the future.

How important is it that money be a reliable store of value and standard of deferred payment? People care about how much food, clothing, and other goods and services their money will buy. The value of money depends on its purchasing power, which refers to its ability to buy goods and services. Inflation causes a decline in purchasing power because rising prices cause a given amount of money to purchase fewer goods and services. With deflation, the value of money increases because prices are falling.

You have probably heard relatives or friends exclaim, "A dollar doesn't buy what it used to!" They really mean that the purchasing power of a dollar has fallen, that a given amount of money will buy a smaller quantity of the same goods and services than it once did.

What Can Serve as Money?

Having a medium of exchange helps to make transactions easier, allowing the economy to work more smoothly. The next logical question is this: What can serve as money? That is, which assets should be used as the medium of exchange? We saw earlier that an asset must, at a minimum, be generally accepted as payment to serve as money. In practical terms, however, it must be even more.

Five criteria make a good suitable to use as a medium of exchange:

1 The good must be *acceptable* to (that is, usable by) most people.

2 It should be of *standardized quality* so that any two units are identical.

3 It should be *durable* so that value is not lost by spoilage.

4 It should be *valuable* relative to its weight so that amounts large enough to be useful in trade can be easily transported.

5 The medium of exchange should be *divisible* because different goods are valued differently.

Dollar bills, Kuwaiti dinars, UAE dirhams, and other currencies meet all these criteria. What determines the acceptability of the Kuwaiti dinar as a medium of exchange? Basically, it is through self-fulfilling expectations: you value something as money only if you believe that others will accept it from you as payment. Kuwaitis' willingness to use the Kuwaiti dinar as money makes the dinar an acceptable medium of exchange. This property of acceptability is not unique to money. Your personal computer has the same keyboard organization of letters as other computer keyboards because manufacturers agreed on a standard layout. You learned to speak Arabic because it is probably the language that most people around you speak.

Commodity Money Commodity money meets the criteria for a medium of exchange. Gold, for example, was a common form of money in the nineteenth century because it was a medium of exchange, a unit of account, a store of value, and a standard of deferred payment. But commodity money has a significant problem: its value depends on its purity. Therefore, someone who wanted to cheat could mix impure metals with a precious metal. Unless traders trusted each other completely, they needed to check the weight and purity of the metal at each trade. In the Middle Ages, respected merchants, who were the predecessors of modern bankers, solved this problem by assaying metals and stamping them with a mark certifying weight and purity and earned a commission in the process. Unstamped (uncertified) commodity money was acceptable only at a discount. Another problem with using gold as money was that the money supply was difficult to control because it depended partly on unpredictable discoveries of new gold fields.

Fiat Money It can be inefficient for an economy to rely on only gold or other precious metals for its money supply. What if you had to transport bars of gold to settle your transactions? Not only would doing so be difficult and costly, but you would also run the risk of being robbed. To get around this problem, private institutions or governments began to store gold and issue paper certificates that could be redeemed for gold. In modern economies, paper currency is generally issued by a **central bank**, which is an agency of the government that regulates the money supply. Today, no government in the world issues paper currency that can be redeemed for gold. Paper currency has no value unless it is used as money and is therefore not a commodity money. Instead, paper currency is a **fiat money**, which has no value except as money. If paper currency has no value except as money, why do consumers and firms use it?

    If you look at the top of Egypt's one pound bill, you will see that it is actually a *Central Bank Note*, issued by the Central Bank of Egypt. Because Egyptian pounds are fiat money, the Central Bank is not required to give you gold or silver for your pound. Central bank currency is *legal tender* in all Arab countries, which means the government requires that it be accepted in payment of debts and requires that cash or checks denominated in the country's currency be used in payment of taxes. Despite being legal tender, without everyone's acceptance, a country's currency would not be a good medium of exchange and could not serve as money. In practice, you, along with everyone else, agree to accept central bank currency as money. The key to this acceptance is that *households and firms have confidence that if they accept banknotes in exchange for goods and services, the banknotes will not lose much value during the time they hold them*. Without this confidence, a currency would not serve as a medium of exchange.

    For example, when riots started in Egypt, in January of 2011, demanding President Mubarak to step down, the Central Bank of Egypt feared that people would lose confidence in the Egyptian pound. This loss of confidence would arise from fears of the pound losing its value in a short period of time. If this had happened, Egypt would have faced a currency crisis in which people would rush to exchange their pounds for U.S. dollars or euros when the banks next opened their doors. In fact, this did not happen, despite the currency losing some of its value. The loss of value was not severe enough to accelerate the public's mistrust in the currency.

Central Bank An agency of the government that regulates the money supply.

Fiat money Money, such as paper currency, that is authorized by a central bank or governmental body and that does not have to be exchanged by the central bank for gold or some other commodity money.

An Egyptian Pound bill is fiat money.

Making the Connection | Money without a Government? The Strange Case of the Iraqi Dinar

    The value of the Iraqi dinar was rising against the U.S. dollar. This result may not seem surprising. We saw in Chapter 20 that the exchange rate, or the value of one currency in exchange for another currency, fluctuates— but this was May 2003. The Iraqi government of Saddam Hussein had collapsed the month before, following the invasion by U.S. and British forces. No new Iraqi government had been formed yet, but people continued to use Iraqi paper currency with pictures of Saddam for buying and selling.

(Continued)

U.S. officials in Iraq had expected that as soon as the war was over and Saddam had been forced from power, the currency with his picture on it would lose all its value. This result had seemed inevitable once the United States had begun paying Iraqi officials in U.S. dollars. However, many Iraqis continued to use the dinar because they were familiar with that currency. As one Iraqi put it, "People trust the dinar more than the dollar. It's Iraqi." In fact, for some weeks after the invasion, increasing demand for the dinar caused its value to rise against the dollar. In early April, when U.S. troops first entered Baghdad, it took about 4,000 dinar to buy 1 U.S. dollar. Six weeks later, in mid-May, it took only 1,500 dinar.

Eventually, a new Iraqi government was formed, and the government ordered that dinars with Saddam's picture be replaced by a new dinar. The new dinar was printed in factories around the world, and 27 Boeing 747s filled with paper dinars were flown to Baghdad. By January 2004, 2 billion paper dinars in varying denominations had been distributed to banks throughout Iraq, and the old Saddam dinars disappeared from circulation. That dinars issued by Saddam's government actually increased in value for a period after his government had collapsed illustrates an important fact about money: *anything can be used as money as long as people are willing to accept it in exchange for goods and services*, even paper currency issued by a government that no longer exists.

Many Iraqis continued to use currency with Saddam's picture on it, even after he was forced from power.

Sources: Edmund L. Andrews, "His Face Still Gives Fits as Saddam Dinar Soars," *New York Times*, May 18, 2003; Yaroslav Trofimov, "Saddam Hussein Is Scarce, but Not the Saddam Dinar," *Wall Street Journal*, April 24, 2003; and "A Tricky Operation," *The Economist*, June 24, 2004.

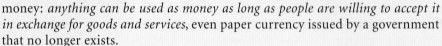

21.2 LEARNING OBJECTIVE

21.2 | Discuss the definitions of the money supply used today.

How Is Money Measured in the Arab World Today?

The definition of money as a medium of exchange depends on beliefs about whether others will use the medium in trade now and in the future. This definition offers guidance for measuring money in an economy. Interpreted literally, this definition says that money should include only those assets that obviously function as a medium of exchange: currency, checking account deposits, and traveler's checks. These assets can easily be used to buy goods and services and thus act as a medium of exchange.

This strict interpretation is too narrow, however, as a measure of the money supply in the real world. Many other assets can be used as a medium of exchange, but they are not as liquid as a checking account deposit or cash. For example, you can convert your savings account at a bank to cash. Likewise, if you have an account at a brokerage firm, you can write checks against the value of the stocks and bonds the firm holds for you. Although these assets have restrictions on their use and there may be costs to converting them into cash, they can be considered part of the medium of exchange.

The job of defining the money supply has become more difficult during the past two decades as innovation in financial markets and institutions has created new substitutes

Kuwait December 2010: M1 [Million dinar]

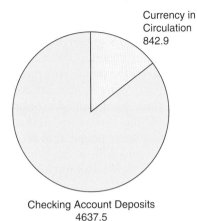

Currency in
Circulation
842.9

Checking Account Deposits
4637.5

(a) M1 = 5480.4 million dinar.

Kuwait December 2010: M2 [Million dinar]

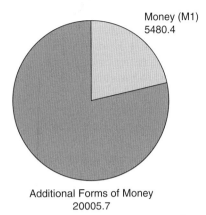

Money (M1)
5480.4

Additional Forms of Money
20005.7

(b) M2 = 25486.1 million dinar. It includes small-time
deposits and savings deposits.

Figure 21-1

Measuring the Money Supply in Kuwait in 2010

The Central Bank uses two different measures of the money supply: M1 and M2. M2 includes all the assets in M1, as well as additional assets. Source: Central Bank of Kuwait, monthly reports, December 2010.

for the traditional measures of the medium of exchange. During the 1980s, central banks changed their definitions of money in response to financial innovation. Despite differences in the level of development and maturity of financial markets, it is important to note that central banks around the world use similar measures of money supply, as we see next.

M1: The Narrowest Definition of the Money Supply

Figure 21-1 illustrates the definitions of the money supply in Kuwait, as an example. The narrowest definition of the money supply is called **M1**. It includes:

1 *Currency*, which is all the paper money and coins that are in circulation, where "in circulation" means not held by banks or the government

2 The value of all checking account deposits at banks

3 The value of traveler's checks (this last category is so small that we will ignore it in our discussion of the money supply).

As we see from panel (a) of Figure 21-1, according to the Central Bank of Kuwait's figures, although currency in circulation has a relatively large value (842.9 million dinar), checking account deposits are used much more often than currency to make payments. Checking deposits amount to 4637.5 million dinar or almost 85 percent of M1.

M1 The narrowest definition of the money supply: The sum of currency in circulation, checking account deposits in banks, and holdings of traveller's checks.

Making the Connection

Do We Still Need the Fils, Piaster, or Penny?

We have seen that fiat money has no value except as money. Governments actually make a profit from issuing fiat money because fiat money is usually produced using paper or low-value metals that cost far less than the face value of the money. For example, it only costs about four cents to manufacture a US$20 bill. The government's profit from issuing fiat money—which is equal to the difference between the face value of the money and its production cost—is called *seigniorage*.

With small-denomination coins—such as a fils or piaster or a penny—there is always the possibility that the coins will cost more to produce than their face

(*Continued*)

value. This was true in the early 1980s when the rising price of copper meant that governments were spending more than a fils, piaster, or a penny to produce each of these coins. That led some governments, such as the U.S. government, to switch from making pennies from copper to making them from zinc. Unfortunately, by 2007, the rising price of zinc meant that once again, the penny cost more than one cent to produce, let alone coins made of copper. Many economists began to ask whether the penny, fils, or piaster should simply be abolished. Not only do they cost more to produce than they are worth, but inflation has eroded their purchasing power to such an extent that some people find the fils or piaster to be a nuisance. Seeing a Bahraini 5-fils or Egyptian piaster coin on the sidewalk, many people will walk on by, not bothering to pick it up. In fact, most, if not all, Arab countries, including Egypt, Bahrain, the UAE, and Kuwait among others, have eliminated their lowest-denomination coins.

Some economists, though, have argued that eliminating the fils or piaster would subject consumers to a 'rounding tax.' For example, a good that had been priced at EGP 2.99 will cost EGP 3.00 if the Egyptian piaster is eliminated. As in most Arab countries, it seems very likely that the penny in the U.S. will also vanish from the U.S. money supply, as did the fils and the piaster.

Sources: Robert Whaples, "Why Keeping the Penny No Longer Makes Sense," *USA Today*, July 12, 2006; and Austan Goolsbee, "Now That a Penny Isn't Worth Much, It's Time to Make It Worth 5 Cents," *New York Times*, Feb. 1, 2007

These coins are circulating in Bahrain today. One fils is 1/1000 Bahraini dinar

M2: A Broader Definition of Money

Before the 1980s, firms and some households in the Arab world held checking account deposits primarily to buy goods and services. Most transactions, however, were done in terms of currency. M1 was, therefore, very close to the function of money as a medium of exchange. Almost all currency, checking account deposits, and traveler's checks were held with the intention of buying and selling, not to store value. People could store value and receive interest by placing funds in savings accounts in banks or by buying other financial assets, such as stocks and bonds. Nowadays, we may see banks paying interest on certain types of checking accounts and sometimes for a specific class of customers. This change reduced the difference between checking accounts and savings accounts, although people are still not allowed to write checks against their savings account balances.

M2 A broader definition of the money supply: M1 plus savings account balances, small-denomination time deposits, balances in money market deposit accounts in banks, and noninstitutional money market fund shares.

M2 includes everything that is in M1, plus savings account deposits, small-denomination time deposits, such as certificates of deposit (CDs), balances in money market deposit accounts in banks. Small-denomination time deposits are similar to savings accounts, but the deposits are for a fixed period of time—usually from six months to several years—and withdrawals before that time are subject to a penalty. Mutual fund companies sell shares to investors and use the funds raised to buy financial assets such as stocks and bonds. Some of these mutual funds are called *money market mutual funds* because they invest in very short-term bonds, such as Treasury bills (a very short-term government bond). The balances in these funds are included in M2. Central banks publish statistics on M1 and M2 on a weekly or monthly basis. In the discussion that follows, we will use the M1 definition of the money supply because it corresponds most closely to money as a medium of exchange.

There are two key points about the money supply to keep in mind:

1 The money supply consists of *both* currency and checking account deposits.

2 Because balances in checking account deposits are included in the money supply, banks play an important role in the process by which the money supply increases and decreases. We will discuss this second point further in the next section.

Solved Problem | 21-2

The Definitions of M1 and M2

Suppose you decide to withdraw US$2,000 from your checking account and use the money to buy a bank certificate of deposit (CD). Briefly explain how this will affect M1 and M2.

SOLVING THE PROBLEM:

Step 1: **Review the chapter material.** This problem is about the definitions of the money supply, so you may want to review the section "How Is Money Measured in the World Today?", which begins on page 702.

Step 2: **Use the definitions of M1 and M2 to answer the problem.** Funds in checking accounts are included in both M1 and M2. Funds in certificates of deposit are included in only M2. It is tempting to answer this problem by saying that shifting US$2,000 from a checking account to a certificate of deposit reduces M1 by US$2,000 and increases M2 by US$2,000, but the US$2,000 in your checking account was already counted in M2. So, the correct answer is that your action reduces M1 by US$2,000 but leaves M2 unchanged.

YOUR TURN: For more practice, do related problems 2.4 and 2.5 on page 724 at the end of this chapter.

>> End Solved Problem 21-2

What about Credit Cards and Debit Cards?

Many people buy goods and services with credit cards, yet credit cards are *not* included in definitions of the money supply. The reason is that when you buy something with a credit card, you are in effect taking out a loan from the bank that issued the credit card. Only when you pay your credit card bill at the end of the month—often with a check or an electronic transfer from your checking account—is the transaction complete. In contrast, with a debit card, the funds to make the purchase are taken directly from your checking account. In either case, the cards themselves do not represent money.

Making *the* **Connection** | **Is Money the Same as Income or Wealth?**

Prince Al-Waleed bin Talal is a member of the Saudi Royal Family. He is the nephew of the Saudi Arabian King Abdullah and a well-known entrepreneur and international investor. According to *Forbes* magazine, Prince Al-Waleed bin Talal's estimated net wealth is US$19.4 billion, making him the 19th richest person in the world on their list, published in March 2010. He also has a very large income, but how much money does he have?

A person's *wealth* is equal to the value of his or her assets minus the value of any debts they have. A person's *income* is equal to his or her earnings during the year. Al-Waleed bin Talal's earnings are very large. But his *money* is just equal to what he has in currency and in checking accounts. Only a small proportion of Al-Waleed's US$19 billion in wealth is likely to be in currency or checking accounts. Most of his wealth is invested in real estate, stocks, and bonds and other financial assets that are not included in the definition of money.

(Continued)

Prince Al-Waleed bin Talal has a very large income, but how much money does he have?

In everyday conversation, we often describe someone who is wealthy or who has a high income as "having a lot of money." But when economists use the word money, they are usually referring to currency plus checking account deposits. It is important to keep a focus on the differences between wealth, income, and money.

Just as money and income are not the same for every person, they are not the same for the whole economy. There is no reason why national income in a country should be equal to the country's money supply, nor will an increase in a country's money supply necessarily increase the country's national income.

Sources: "World's Billionaires," *Forbes*, March 10, 2010, www.forbes.com.

21.3 LEARNING OBJECTIVE

21.3 | Explain how banks create money.

How Do Banks Create Money?

We have seen that the most important component of the money supply is checking accounts in banks. To understand the role money plays in the economy, we need to look more closely at how banks operate. Banks are profit-making private businesses, just like bookstores and supermarkets. Some banks are quite small, with just a few branches, and they do business in a limited area. Others are among the largest corporations in the Arab world, with hundreds of branches spread across many countries. The key role that banks play in the economy is to accept deposits and make loans. By doing this, they create checking account deposits.

Bank Balance Sheets

To understand how banks create money, we need to briefly examine a typical bank balance sheet. On a balance sheet, a firm's assets are listed on the left and its liabilities and stockholders' equity are listed on the right. Assets are the value of anything owned by the firm, liabilities are the value of anything the firm owes, and stockholders' equity is the difference between the total value of assets and the total value of liabilities. Stockholders' equity represents the value of the firm if it had to be closed, all its assets were sold, and all its liabilities were paid off. A corporation's stockholders' equity is also referred to as its *net worth*.

The key assets on a bank's balance sheet are its *reserves*, loans, and holdings of securities, such as Treasury bills. **Reserves** are deposits that a bank has retained, rather than loaned out or invested by, for instance, buying Treasury bills. Banks keep reserves either physically within the bank, as *vault cash*, or on deposit with the central bank. Banks are required by law to keep as reserves a certain percentage of their checking account deposits above a threshold level. For simplicity, we will assume that banks are required to keep 10 percent of all reserves. These reserves are called **required reserves**. The minimum fraction of deposits that banks are required to keep as reserves is called the **required reserve ratio**. We can abbreviate the required reserve ratio as *RR*. Any reserves that banks hold over and above the legal requirement are called **excess reserves**. Loans are usually the largest asset in most banks' balance sheets, and the largest liability is their deposits.

Banks make *consumer loans* to households and *commercial loans* to businesses. A loan is an asset to a bank because it represents a promise by the person taking out the loan to make certain specified payments to the bank. A bank's reserves and its holdings of securities are also assets because they are things of value owned by the bank.

Deposits include checking accounts, savings accounts, and certificates of deposit. Deposits are liabilities to banks because they are owed to the households or firms that have deposited the funds. If you deposit US$100 in your checking account, the bank owes you the US$100, and you can ask for it back at any time.

Reserves Deposits that a bank keeps as cash in its vault or on deposit with the Central Bank.

Required reserves Reserves that a bank is legally required to hold, based on its checking account deposits.

Required reserve ratio (RR) The minimum fraction of deposits banks are required by law to keep as reserves.

Excess reserves Reserves that banks hold over and above the legal requirement.

Using T-Accounts to Show How a Bank Can Create Money

It is easier to show how banks create money by using a T-account that shows only how a transaction *changes* a bank's balance sheet. For example, suppose you deposit US$1,000 in currency into your account at National Commercial Bank (NCB). This transaction raises the total deposits of the NCB by US$1,000 and also raises its reserves by US$1,000. We can show this on the following T-account:

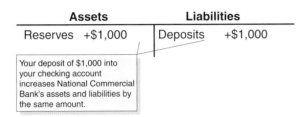

Remember that because the total value of all the entries on the right side of a balance sheet must always be equal to the total value of all the entries on the left side of a balance sheet, any transaction that increases (or decreases) one side of the balance sheet must also increase (or decrease) the other side of the balance sheet. In this case, the T-account shows that we increased both sides of the balance sheet by US$1,000.

Initially, this transaction does not increase the money supply. The currency component of the money supply declines by US$1,000 because the US$1,000 you deposited is no longer in circulation and, therefore, is not counted in the money supply. But the decrease in currency is offset by a US$1,000 increase in the checking account deposit component of the money supply.

This initial change is not the end of the story, however. Banks are required to keep 10 percent of deposits as reserves. Because banks do not earn interest on reserves, they have an incentive to loan out or buy securities with the other 90 percent. In this case, the bank can keep US$100 as required reserves and loan out the other US$900, which represents excess reserves. Suppose the NCB loans out the US$900 to someone to buy a very inexpensive used car. The bank could give the US$900 to the borrower in currency, but usually banks make loans by increasing the borrower's checking account. We can show this with another T-account:

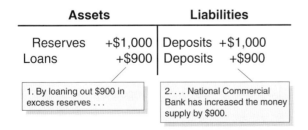

A key point to recognize is that *by making this US$900 loan, NCB has increased the money supply by US$900.* The initial US$1,000 in currency you deposited into your checking account has been turned into US$1,900 in checking account deposits—a net increase in the money supply of US$900.

But the story does not end here. The person who took out the US$900 loan did so to buy a used car. To keep things simple, let's suppose he buys the car for exactly US$900 and pays by writing a check on his account at the NCB. The owner of the used car will now deposit the check in her bank. Let's assume that the seller of the car has her account at a branch of Arab Bank. Once she deposits the check, Arab Bank will send it to NCB to *clear* the check and collect the US$900. We can show the result using T-accounts:

National Commercial Bank

Assets		Liabilities
Reserves	+$100	Deposits +$1,000
Loans	+$900	

1. When the $900 check that was deposited in an Arab Bank account arrives to be cleared, the increase in National Commercial Bank's reserves (shown in the previous T-account) falls by $900 to $100 . . .

2. . . . and the increase in National Commercial Bank deposits falls by $900 to $1,000.

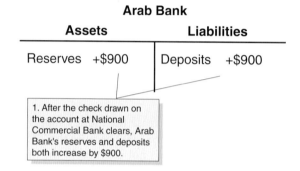

Arab Bank

Assets		Liabilities
Reserves +$900		Deposits +$900

1. After the check drawn on the account at National Commercial Bank clears, Arab Bank's reserves and deposits both increase by $900.

Once the car buyer's check has cleared, NCB has lost US$900 in deposits—the amount loaned to the car buyer—and US$900 in reserves—the amount it had to pay Arab Bank. The latter has an increase in checking account deposits of US$900—the deposit of the car seller—and an increase in reserves of US$900—the amount it received from NCB.

Arab Bank has 100 percent reserves against this new US$900 deposit, when it only needs 10 percent reserves. The bank has an incentive to keep US$90 as reserves and to loan out the other US$810, which are excess reserves. If Arab Bank does this, we can show the change in its balance sheet using another T-account:

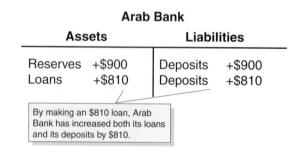

Arab Bank

Assets		Liabilities	
Reserves	+$900	Deposits	+$900
Loans	+$810	Deposits	+$810

By making an $810 loan, Arab Bank has increased both its loans and its deposits by $810.

In loaning out the US$810 in excess reserves, Arab Bank creates a new checking account deposit of US$810. The initial deposit of US$1,000 in currency into NCB has now resulted in the creation of US$1,000 + US$900 + US$810 = US$2,710 in checking account deposits. The money supply has increased by US$2,710 − US$1,000 = US$1,710.

The process is still not finished. The person who borrows the US$810 will spend it by writing a check against his account. Whoever receives the US$810 will deposit it in her bank, which could be a branch of NCB or Arab Bank, or a branch of some other bank. That Third Bank will send the check to Arab Bank and will receive US$810 in new reserves. That Third Bank will have an incentive to loan out 90 percent of these reserves—keeping 10 percent to meet the legal requirement—and the process will go on. At each stage, the additional loans being made and the additional deposits being created are shrinking by 10 percent, as each bank has to withhold that amount as required reserves. We can use a table to show the total increase in checking account deposits set off by your initial deposit of US$1,000. The dots in the table represent additional rounds in the money creation process:

BANK	INCREASE IN CHECKING ACCOUNT DEPOSITS IN US$	
NCB	1,000	
Arab Bank	+ 900	(= 0.9 – 1,000)
Third Bank	+ 810	(= 0.9 – 900)
Fourth Bank	+ 729	(= 0.9 – 810)
•	+ •	
•	+ •	
•	+ •	
Total change in checking account deposits	= 10,000	

The Simple Deposit Multiplier

Your initial deposit of US$1,000 increased the reserves of the banking system by US$1,000 and led to a total increase in checking account deposits of US$10,000. The ratio of the amount of deposits created by banks to the amount of new reserves is called the **simple deposit multiplier**. In this case, the simple deposit multiplier is equal to US$10,000/US$1,000 = 10. Why 10? How do we know that your initial US$1,000 deposit ultimately leads to a total increase in deposits of US$10,000?

There are two ways to answer this question. First, each bank in the process is keeping reserves equal to 10 percent of its deposits. For the banking system as a whole, the total increase in reserves is US$1,000—the amount of your original currency deposit. Therefore, the system as a whole will end up with US$10,000 in deposits, because US$1,000 is 10 percent of US$10,000.

A second way to answer the question is by deriving an expression for the simple deposit multiplier. The total increase in deposits equals:

$$\$1,000 + [0.9 \times \$1,000] + [(0.9 \times 0.9) \times \$1,000] + [(0.9 \times 0.9 \times 0.9) \times \$1,000] + \ldots$$

Or:

$$\$1,000 + [0.9 \times \$1,000] + [0.9^2 \times \$1,000] + [0.9^3 \times \$1,000] + \ldots$$

Or:

$$\$1,000 \times (1 + 0.9 + 0.9^2 + 0.9^3 + \ldots)$$

The rules of algebra tell us that an expression like the one in the parentheses sums to:

$$\frac{1}{1 - 09}$$

Simplifying further, we have:

$$\frac{1}{0.10} = 10$$

So:

$$\text{Total increase in deposits} = \$1,000 \times 10 = \$10,000$$

Simple deposit multiplier The ratio of the amount of deposits created by banks to the amount of new reserves.

Note that 10 is equal to 1 divided by the required reserve ratio, *RR*, which in this case is 10 percent, or 0.10. This gives us another way of expressing the simple deposit multiplier:

$$\text{Simple deposit multiplier} = \frac{1}{RR}$$

This formula makes it clear that the higher the required reserve ratio, the smaller the simple deposit multiplier. With a required reserve ratio of 10 percent, the simple deposit multiplier is 10. If the required reserve ratio were 20 percent, the simple deposit multiplier would fall to 1/0.20, or 5. We can use this formula to calculate the total increase in checking account deposits from an increase in bank reserves due to, for instance, currency being deposited in a bank:

$$\text{Change in checking account deposits} = \text{Change in bank reserves} \times \frac{1}{RR}$$

For example, if US$100,000 in currency is deposited in a bank and the required reserve ratio is 10 percent, then:

$$\text{Change in checking account deposits} = \$100,000 \times \frac{1}{0.10} = \$100,000 \times 10 = \$1,000,000$$

Solved Problem | 21-3

Showing How Banks Create Money

Suppose you deposit US$5,000 in currency into your checking account at a branch of Arab Bank, which we will assume has no excess reserves at the time you make your deposit. Also assume that the required reserve ratio is 0.10.

a. Use a T-account to show the initial effect of this transaction on Arab Bank's balance sheet.

b. Suppose that Arab Bank makes the maximum loan it can from the funds you deposited. Use a T-account to show the initial effect on Arab Bank's balance sheet from granting the loan. Also include in this T-account the transaction from question (a).

c. Now suppose that whoever took out the loan in question (b) writes a check for this amount and that the person receiving the check deposits it in NCB. Show the effect of these transactions on the balance sheets of Arab Bank and NCB *after the check has been cleared.* On the T-account for Arab Bank, include the transactions from questions (a) and (b).

d. What is the maximum increase in checking account deposits that can result from your US$5,000 deposit? What is the maximum increase in the money supply? Explain.

SOLVING THE PROBLEM:

Step 1: **Review the chapter material.** This problem is about how banks create checking account deposits, so you may want to review the section "Using T-Accounts to Show How a Bank Can Create Money," which begins on page 707.

Step 2: **Answer question (a) by using a T-account to show the impact of the deposit.** Keeping in mind that T-accounts show only the changes in a balance sheet that result from the relevant transaction and that assets are on the left side of the account and liabilities are on the right side, we have:

ARAB BANK			
ASSETS IN US$		**LIABILITIES IN US$**	
Reserves	+5,000	Deposits	+5,000

Because the bank now has your US$5,000 in currency in its vault, its reserves (and, therefore, its assets) have risen by US$5,000. But this transaction also increases your checking account balance by US$5,000. Because the bank owes you this money, the bank's liabilities have also risen by US$5,000.

Step 3: **Answer question (b) by using a T-account to show the impact of the loan.** The problem tells you to assume that Arab Bank currently has no excess reserves and that the required reserve ratio is 10 percent. This requirement means that if the bank's checking account deposits go up by US$5,000, the bank must keep US$500 as reserves and can loan out the remaining US$4,500. Remembering that new loans usually take the form of setting up, or increasing, a checking account for the borrower, we have:

ARAB BANK

ASSETS IN US$		LIABILITIES IN US$	
Reserves	+5,000	Deposits	+5,000
Loans	+4,500	Deposits	+4,500

The first line of the T-account shows the transaction from question (a). The second line shows that Arab Bank has loaned out US$4,500 by increasing the checking account of the borrower by US$4,500. The loan is an asset to Arab Bank because it represents a promise by the borrower to make certain payments spelled out in the loan agreement.

Step 4: **Answer question (c) by using T-accounts for Arab Bank and NCB to show the impact of the check clearing.** We now show the effect of the borrower having spent the US$4,500 he received as a loan from Arab Bank. The person who received the US$4,500 check deposits it in her account at NCB. We need two T-accounts to show this:

ARAB BANK

ASSETS IN US$		LIABILITIES IN US$	
Reserves	+500	Deposits	+5,000
Loans	+4,500		

NCB

Assets		Liabilities	
Reserves	+4,000	Deposits	+4,000

Look first at the T-account for Arab Bank. Once NCB sends the check written by the borrower to Arab Bank, Arab Bank loses US$4,500 in reserves and NCB gains US$4,500 in reserves. The US$4,500 is also deducted from the account of the borrower. Arab Bank is now satisfied with the result. It received a US$5,000 deposit in currency from you. When that money was sitting in the bank vault, it wasn't earning any interest for Arab Bank. Now US$4,500 of the US$5,000 has been loaned out and is earning interest. These interest payments allow Arab Bank to cover its costs and earn a profit, which it has to do to remain in business.

NCB now has an increase in deposits of US$4,500, resulting from the check deposited by the contractor, and an increase in reserves of US$4,500. NCB is in the same situation as Arab Bank was in question (a): It has excess reserves as a result of this transaction and a strong incentive to lend them out in order to earn some interest.

Step 5: **Answer question (d) by using the simple deposit multiplier formula to calculate the maximum increase in checking account deposits and the**

maximum increase in the money supply. The simple deposit multiplier expression is (remember that RR is the required reserve ratio):

$$\text{Change in checking account deposits} = \text{Change in bank reserves} \times \frac{1}{RR}$$

In this case, bank reserves rose by US$5,000 as a result of your initial deposit, and the required reserve ratio is 0.10, so:

$$\text{Change in checking account deposits} = \$5,000 \times \frac{1}{0.10}$$

$$= \$5,000 \times 10 = \$50,000$$

Because checking account deposits are part of the money supply, it is tempting to say that the money supply has also increased by US$50,000. Remember, though, that your US$5,000 in currency was counted as part of the money supply while you had it, but it is not included when it is sitting in a bank vault. Therefore:

$$\text{Change in the money supply} = \text{Increase in checking account deposits} -$$
$$\text{Decline in currency in circulation} = \$50,000 - \$5,000 = \$45,000$$

>> **End Solved Problem 21-3**

YOUR TURN: For more practice, do related problem 3.7 on page 724 at the end of the chapter.

The Simple Deposit Multiplier versus the Real-World Deposit Multiplier

The story we have told about the way an increase in reserves in the banking system leads to the creation of new deposits and, therefore, an increase in the money supply has been simplified in two ways. First, we assumed that banks do not keep any excess reserves. That is, we assumed that when you deposited US$1,000 in currency into your checking account at NCB, the bank loaned out US$900, keeping only the US$100 in required reserves. In fact, banks often keep at least some excess reserves to guard against the possibility that many depositors may simultaneously make withdrawals from their accounts. The more excess reserves banks keep, the smaller the deposit multiplier. Imagine an extreme case where the bank keeps your entire US$1,000 as reserves. If the bank does not loan out any of your deposit, the process described earlier of loans leading to the creation of new deposits, leading to the making of additional loans, and so on will not take place. The US$1,000 increase in reserves will lead to a total increase of US$1,000 in deposits, and the deposit multiplier will be only 1, not 10.

Second, we assumed that the whole amount of every check is deposited in a bank; no one takes any of it out as currency. In reality, households and firms keep roughly constant the amount of currency they hold relative to the value of their checking account balances. So, we would expect to see people increasing the amount of currency they hold as the balances in their checking accounts rise. Once again, think of the extreme case. Suppose that when NCB Bank makes the initial US$900 loan to the borrower who wants to buy a used car, the seller of the car cashes the check instead of depositing it. In that case, Arab Bank does not receive any new reserves and does not make any new loans. Once again, the US$1,000 increase in your checking account at the NCB is the only increase in deposits, and the deposit multiplier is 1.

The effect of these two factors is to reduce the real-world deposit multiplier to about 2.5. That means that a US$1 increase in the reserves of the banking system results in about a US$2.50 increase in deposits.

Although the story of the deposit multiplier can be complicated, the key point to bear in mind is that the most important part of the money supply is the checking account balance component. When banks make loans, they increase checking account balances, and the money supply expands. Banks make new loans whenever they gain reserves. The whole process can also work in reverse. If banks lose reserves, they reduce their outstanding loans and deposits, and the money supply contracts.

We can summarize these important conclusions:

1 Whenever banks gain reserves, they make new loans, and the money supply expands.

2 Whenever banks lose reserves, they reduce their loans, and the money supply contracts.

21.4 | Discuss the three policy tools the Central Bank uses to manage the money supply.

The Central Bank

Many people are surprised to learn that banks do not keep in their vaults all the funds that are deposited into checking accounts. Nearly all countries, has a *fractional reserve banking system*. In a **fractional reserve banking system**, banks keep less than 100 percent of deposits as reserves. When people deposit money in a bank, the bank loans most of the money to someone else. What happens, though, if depositors want their money back? This would seem to be a problem because banks have loaned out most of the money and can't get it back easily.

In practice, though, withdrawals are usually not a problem for banks. On a typical day, about as much money is deposited as is withdrawn. If a small amount more is withdrawn than deposited, banks can cover the difference from their excess reserves or by borrowing from other banks. Sometimes depositors lose confidence in a bank when they question the value of the bank's underlying assets, particularly its loans. Often, the reason for a loss of confidence is bad news, whether true or false. When many depositors simultaneously decide to withdraw their money from a bank, there is a **bank run**. If many banks experience runs at the same time, the result is a **bank panic**. It is possible for one bank to handle a run by borrowing from other banks, but if many banks simultaneously experience runs, the banking system may be in trouble.

A *central bank* can help stop a bank panic by acting as a *lender of last resort*. In acting like a lender of last resort, a central bank makes loans to banks that cannot borrow funds elsewhere. The bank can use these loans to pay off depositors. When the panic ends and the depositors put their money back in their accounts, the bank can repay the loan to the central bank. Bank panics lead to severe disruptions in business activity because neither households nor firms can gain access to their accounts. Not surprisingly, each bank panic in history in the late nineteenth and early twentieth centuries was accompanied by a recession. Perhaps during the latest world recession, which started around the end of 2007 with a widespread global financial crisis, there was an imminent threat that the largest bank panic in history could happen. Most developed and developing countries' central banks alike had to intervene and to coordinate in order to defend their banking systems. The crisis took its toll on the UAE banking system when news spread that Dubai World, a public investment company, was seeking the deferral of its huge debt bill. Depositors were worried that defaults by Dubai World could undermine much of the banking system. The UAE federal government and its central bank announced that they would back up all bank deposits, preventing a potential bank panic in the region.

Fractional reserve banking system A banking system in which banks keep less than 100 percent of deposits as reserves.

Bank run A situation in which many depositors simultaneously decide to withdraw money from a bank.

Bank panic A situation in which many banks experience runs at the same time.

How the Central Bank Manages the Money Supply

Today the most important activity for the central banks around the world is managing the money supply. As we will discuss in more detail in Chapter 22, managing the money supply is part of **monetary policy**, which the central bank undertakes to pursue economic objectives.

To manage the money supply, central banks usually have three tools, which are called *monetary policy tools*:

1 Open market operations

2 Discount policy

3 Reserve requirements

Monetary policy The actions the Central Bank takes to manage the money supply and interest rates to pursue macroeconomic policy objectives.

Remember that the most important component of the money supply is checking account deposits. Not surprisingly, all three of the central bank's policy tools are aimed at affecting the reserves of banks as a means of changing the volume of checking account deposits.

Open Market Operations

Open market operations The buying and selling of Treasury securities by the Central Bank in order to control the money supply.

Many Arab countries, such as Egypt, Jordan, the UAE, Qatar, and Kuwait conduct open market operations to control money supply. **Open market operations** consist of the buying and selling of Treasury securities. The Treasury borrows money by selling bills, notes, and bonds to the public. Remember that the *maturity* of a financial asset is the period of time until the purchaser receives payment of the face value or principal. To increase the money supply, the central bank directs the *trading desk*, to *buy* Treasury securities (known in some Arab countries as certificates of deposit, or CDs). These are most frequently short-term bills. When the sellers of the Treasury securities deposit the funds in their banks, the reserves of the banks rise. This increase in reserves starts the process of increasing loans and checking account deposits, which increases the money supply. To decrease the money supply, the central bank directs the trading desk to *sell* Treasury securities. When the buyers of the Treasury securities pay with checks, the reserves of their banks fall. This decrease in reserves starts a contraction of loans and checking account deposits that reduces the money supply.

There are three reasons the central bank conducts monetary policy principally through open market operations. First, because the central bank initiates open market operations, it completely controls their volume. Second, the central bank can make both large and small open market operations. Third, the central bank can implement its open market operations quickly, with no administrative delay or required changes in regulations. Many other central banks, including the European Central Bank and the Bank of Japan, also use open market operations to conduct monetary policy.

The central bank is responsible for putting the paper currency into circulation. Recall that if you look at the top of the Egyptian pound, you see the words "Central Bank Note." When the central bank takes actions to increase the money supply, the public sometimes say that it is "printing more money." The main way the central bank increases the money supply, however, is not by printing more money but by buying Treasury securities. Similarly, to reduce the money supply, the central bank does not set fire to stacks of paper currency. Instead, it sells Treasury securities. We will spend more time discussing how and why the central bank manages the money supply in the next chapter, when we discuss monetary policy.

Discount Policy

Discount loans Loans the Central Bank makes to banks.

Discount rate The interest rate the Central Bank charges on discount loans.

The loans the central bank makes to banks are called **discount loans**, and the interest rate it charges on the loans is called the **discount rate**. When a bank receives a loan from the central bank, its reserves increase by the amount of the loan. By lowering the discount rate, the central bank can encourage banks to take additional loans and thereby increase their reserves. With more reserves, banks will make more loans to households and firms, which will increase checking account deposits and the money supply. Raising the discount rate will have the reverse effect.

Reserve Requirements

When the central bank reduces the required reserve ratio, it converts required reserves into excess reserves. For example, suppose a bank has US$100 million in checking account deposits and the required reserve ratio is 10 percent. The bank will be required to hold US$10 million as reserves. If the central bank reduces the required reserve ratio to 8 percent, the bank will need to hold only US$8 million as reserves. The central bank has converted US$2 million worth of reserves from required to excess. This US$2 million is now available for the bank to lend out. If the central bank *raises* the required reserve ratio from 10 percent to 12 percent, it would have the reverse effect.

The central bank changes reserve requirements much more rarely than it conducts open market operations or changes the discount rate. Because changes in reserve requirements require significant alterations in banks' holdings of loans and securities, frequent changes would be disruptive. Also, because reserves earn no interest, the use of reserve requirements to manage the money supply effectively places a tax on banks' deposit-taking and lending activities, which can be costly for the economy.

Putting It All Together: Decisions of the Nonbank Public, Banks, and the Central Bank

Using its three tools—open market operations, the discount rate, and reserve requirements—the central bank has substantial influence over the money supply, but that influence is not absolute. Two other actors—the nonbank public and banks—also influence the money supply.

The nonbank public—households and firms—must decide how much money to hold as deposits in banks. The larger the money holdings in deposits, the greater the reserves of banks and the more money the banking system can create. The smaller the money holdings in deposits, the lower the reserves of banks and the less money the banking system can create. In addition, the central bank can influence, but does not control, the amount bankers decide to lend. Banks create money only if they lend their reserves. If bankers retain excess reserves, they make a smaller volume of loans and create less money. At the end of this chapter you can read an article in *An Inside Look at Policy* that shows how the Central Bank of Kuwait tried to stimulate credit growth and bank lending at the beginning of 2010 by lowering the discount rate twice. Despite this action, bank lending did not respond much and banks continued strict credit policy that limited credit expansion.

The roles of the nonbank public and banks in the money supply process do not mean that the central bank lacks meaningful control of the money supply. The central bank's staff monitors information on banks' reserves and deposits every week, and the central bank can respond quickly to shifts in behavior by depositors or banks. The central bank can therefore steer the money supply close to the level it desires.

21.5 LEARNING OBJECTIVE

21.5 | Explain the quantity theory of money and use it to explain how high rates of inflation occur.

The Quantity Theory of Money

People have been aware of the connection between increases in the money supply and inflation for centuries. In the sixteenth century, the Spanish conquered Mexico and Peru and shipped large quantities of gold and silver back to Spain. The gold and silver were minted into coins and spent across Europe to further the political ambitions of the Spanish kings. Prices in Europe rose steadily during these years, and many observers discussed the relationship between this inflation and the flow of gold and silver into Europe from the Americas.

Connecting Money and Prices: The Quantity Equation

In the early twentieth century, Irving Fisher, an economist at Yale University in the U.S., formalized the connection between money and prices using the *quantity equation*:

$$M \times V = P \times Y$$

The equation states that the money supply (M) multiplied by the *velocity of money* (V) equals the price level (P) multiplied by real output (Y). Fisher defined the **velocity of money**, often referred to simply as 'velocity,' as the average number of times each dollar of the money supply is used to purchase goods and services included in GDP. Rewriting the original equation by dividing both sides by M, we have the equation for velocity:

Velocity of money The average number of times each dollar in the money supply is used to purchase goods and services included in GDP.

$$V = \frac{P \times Y}{M}$$

We can use M1 to measure the money supply, the GDP price deflator to measure the price level, and real GDP to measure real output. Suppose these were:

$$V = \frac{1.197 \times \$11.567 \text{ billon}}{\$1,368 \text{ billion}} = 10.1$$

Quantity theory of money A theory of the connection between money and prices that assumes that the velocity of money is constant.

This result tells us that, on average during a particular year, each dollar of M1 was spent about 10 times on goods or services included in GDP.

Irving Fisher turned the quantity equation into the **quantity theory of money** by asserting that velocity was constant. He argued that the average number of times a dollar is spent depends on how often people get paid, how often they do their grocery shopping, how often businesses mail bills, and other factors that do not change very often. Because this assertion may be true or false, the quantity theory of money is, in fact, a theory.

The Quantity Theory Explanation of Inflation

The quantity equation gives us a way of showing the relationship between changes in the money supply and changes in the price level, or inflation. To see this relationship more clearly, we can use a handy mathematical rule that states that an equation where variables are multiplied together is equal to an equation where the *growth rates* of these variables are *added* together. So, we can transform the quantity equation from:

$$M \times V = P \times Y$$

to:

Growth rate of the money supply + Growth rate of velocity =
Growth rate of the price level (or inflation rate) + Growth rate of real output

This way of writing the quantity equation is more useful for investigating the effect of changes in the money supply on the inflation rate. Remember that the growth rate for any variable is just the percentage change in the variable from one year to the next. The growth rate of the price level is just the inflation rate, so we can rewrite the quantity equation to help us understand the factors that determine inflation:

Inflation rate = Growth rate of the money supply +
Growth rate of velocity − Growth rate of real output

If Irving Fisher was correct that velocity is constant, then the growth rate of velocity will be zero. That is, if velocity is, say, always 10.1, then its percentage change from one year to the next will always be zero. This assumption allows us to rewrite the equation one last time:

Inflation rate = Growth rate of the money supply − Growth rate of real output

This equation leads to the following predictions:

1 If the money supply grows at a faster rate than real GDP, there will be inflation.

2 If the money supply grows at a slower rate than real GDP, there will be deflation. (Recall that *deflation* is a decline in the price level.)

3 If the money supply grows at the same rate as real GDP, the price level will be stable, and there will be neither inflation nor deflation.

It turns out that Irving Fisher was wrong in asserting that the velocity of money is constant. From year to year, there can be significant fluctuations in velocity. As a result, the predictions of the quantity theory of money do not hold every year, but most economists agree that the quantity theory provides a useful insight into the long-run relationship between the money supply and inflation: *In the long run, inflation results from the money supply growing at a faster rate than real GDP.*

High Rates of Inflation

Why do governments allow high rates of inflation? The quantity theory can help us to understand the reasons for high rates of inflation, such as that experienced in Argentina during the 1980s. Very high rates of inflation—in excess of hundreds or thousands of percentage points per year—are known as *hyperinflation*. Hyperinflation is caused by central banks increasing the money supply at a rate far in excess of the growth rate of real GDP. A high rate of inflation causes money to lose its value so rapidly that households and firms avoid holding it. If the inflation becomes severe enough, people stop using paper currency, so it no longer serves the important functions of money discussed earlier in this chapter. Economies suffering from high inflation usually also suffer from very slow growth, if not severe recession.

Given the dire consequences that follow from high inflation, why do governments allow it by expanding the money supply so rapidly? The main reason is that governments often want to spend more than they are able to raise through taxes. Developed countries, such as the United States, can usually bridge gaps between spending and taxes by borrowing through selling bonds to the public. Developing countries often have difficulty selling bonds because the public is skeptical of their ability to pay back the money. If they are unable to sell bonds to the public, governments in developing countries will force their central banks to purchase them. As we discussed previously, when a central bank buys bonds, the money supply will increase.

High Inflation in Argentina

The link between rapid money growth and high inflation was evident in the experience of Argentina during the 1980s. Panel (a) of Figure 21-2 shows rates of growth of the money supply and the inflation rate in Argentina in the years from 1981 to 1991. Both the average annual growth rate of the money supply and the average annual inflation rate from 1981 to 1990 were greater than 750 percent. With prices rising so quickly, Argentine currency could not fulfill the normal functions of money. Not surprisingly, the Argentine economy struggled during these years, with real GDP in 1990 ending up 6 percent lower than it had been in 1981.

This weak economic performance was particularly frustrating to many people in Argentina because early in the twentieth century, the country had had one of the highest standards of living in the world. In 1910, only the United States and Great Britain had higher levels of real GDP per capita than Argentina. In U.S.-made films of the 1920s and 1930s, the rich foreigner was often from Argentina.

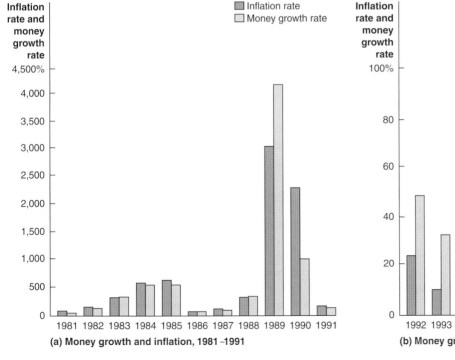

Figure 21-2 | Money Growth and Inflation in Argentina

Panel (a) shows rates of growth of the money supply and the inflation rate in Argentina in the years from 1981 to 1991. Both the average growth rate of the money supply and the average annual inflation rate from 1981 to 1990 were greater than 750 percent. In 1991, the Argentine government enacted a new policy that fixed the exchange rate of the peso versus the U.S. dollar at one to one. As panel (b) shows, the new policy greatly reduced increases in the money supply and the inflation rate. (Notice that the scale of panel (b) is different form the scale in panel (a), which partly disguises the fall in money growth and inflation.) Source: International Monetary Fund.

It was clear to policymakers in Argentina that the only way to bring inflation under control was to limit increases in the money supply. In 1991, the Argentine government enacted a new policy that fixed the exchange rate of the peso versus the U.S. dollar at one to one. In addition, the Argentine central bank was allowed to issue pesos only in exchange for dollars. As panel (b) in Figure 21-2 shows, the new policy greatly reduced increases in the money supply and the inflation rate. (Notice that the scale of panel (b) is different from the scale of panel (a), which partly disguises the fall in money growth and inflation.) Economic growth also revived, with real GDP increasing at an average annual rate of almost 6 percent from 1991 to 1998. Unfortunately, though, Argentina had not come to grips with several underlying economic problems, perhaps the most important of which was the continuing gap between government expenditures and tax receipts.

By 2000, many observers expected that the Argentine government would not be able to maintain the one-to-one exchange rate between the peso and the U.S. dollar. As Argentine firms and households, along with foreign investors, began exchanging pesos for dollars, the Argentine money supply declined. The money supply declined by 9 percent in 2000 and by an additional 20 percent in 2001. Argentina experienced falling prices, or deflation, during both years, along with falling real GDP. Finally, in January 2002, the Argentine government abandoned its commitment to the one-to-one exchange rate between the peso and the dollar, and the money supply increased rapidly. During 2002, the money supply increased by nearly 80 percent, and deflation was transformed to an inflation rate of 25 percent. Although the inflation rate declined over the next few years, Argentina continues to struggle to keep its money supply from growing at rates likely to result in high inflation.

Making the Connection	**The German Hyperinflation of the Early 1920s**

When Germany lost World War I, a revolution broke out that overthrew Kaiser Wilhelm II and installed a new government known as the Weimar Republic. In the peace treaty of 1919, the Allies—the United States, Great Britain, France, and Italy—imposed payments called *reparations* on the new German government. The reparations were meant as compensation to the Allies for the damage Germany had caused during the war. It was very difficult for the German government to use tax revenue to cover both its normal spending and the reparations.

The German government decided to pay for the difference between its spending and its tax revenues by selling bonds to the central bank, the Reichsbank. After a few years, the German government fell far behind in its reparations payment. In January 1923, the French government sent troops into the German industrial area known as the Ruhr to try to collect the payments directly. German workers in the Ruhr went on strike, and the German government decided to support them by paying their salaries. Raising the funds to do so was financed by an inflationary monetary policy—the German government sold bonds to the Reichsbank, thereby increasing the money supply.

The inflationary increase in the money supply was very large: the total number of marks—the German currency—in circulation rose from 115 million in January 1922 to 1.3 billion in January 1923 and then to 497 billion *billion,* or 497,000,000,000,000,000,000, in December 1923. Just as the quantity theory predicts, the result was an extremely high rate of inflation that has never been heard of in modern history. The German price index that stood at 100 in 1914 and 1,440 in January 1922 had risen to 126,160,000,000,000 in December 1923. The German mark became worthless. The German government ended the hyperinflation by (1) negotiating a new agreement with the Allies that reduced its reparations payments,

During the hyperinflation of the 1920s, people in Germany used paper currency to light their stoves.

(2) reducing other government expenditures and raising taxes to balance its budget, and (3) replacing the existing mark with a new mark. Each new mark was worth 1 *trillion* old marks. The German central bank was also limited to issuing a total of 3.2 billion new marks.

These steps were enough to bring the hyperinflation to an end—but not before the savings of anyone holding the old marks had been wiped out. Most middle-income Germans were extremely resentful of this outcome. Many historians believe that the hyperinflation helped pave the way for Hitler and the Nazis to seize power 10 years later.

Source: Thomas Sargent, "The End of Four Big Hyperinflations," in *Rational Expectations and Inflation*, New York: Harper and Row, 1986.

YOUR TURN: Test your understanding by doing related problem 5.6 on page 726 at the end of this chapter.

Economics in YOUR Life!

>> Continued from page 697

At the beginning of the chapter, we asked you to consider whether you would like to live in an economy in which the purchasing power of money rose every year. The first thing to consider when thinking about the advantages and disadvantages of this situation is that the only way for the purchasing power of money to increase is for the price level to fall; in other words, *deflation* must occur. Most people alive today in the Arab world have experienced only rising price levels—and declining purchasing power of money. Would replacing rising prices with falling prices necessarily be a good thing? It might be tempting to say yes, because if you have a job, then your salary will buy more goods and services each year. But, in fact, just as a rising price level results in most wages and salaries rising each year, a falling price level is likely to mean falling wages and salaries each year. So, it is likely that, on average, people would not see the purchasing power of their incomes increase, even if the purchasing power of any currency they hold would increase. There can also be a significant downside to deflation, particularly if the transition from inflation to deflation happens suddenly. In previous chapters, we defined the real interest rate as being equal to the nominal interest rate minus the inflation rate. If an economy experiences deflation, then the real interest rate will be greater than the nominal interest rate. A rising real interest rate can be bad news for anyone who has borrowed, including homeowners who may have substantial mortgage loans. So, you are probably better off living in an economy experiencing mild inflation rather than one experiencing deflation.

Conclusion

Money plays a key role in the functioning of an economy by facilitating trade in goods and services and by making specialization possible. Without specialization, no advanced economy can prosper. Households and firms, banks, and the central bank are participants in the process of creating the money supply. In Chapter 22, we will explore how the central bank uses monetary policy to promote its economic objectives.

An Inside Look at Policy on the next page discusses how Kuwait's Central Bank is trying to control the money supply by encouraging bank lending and conducting open market operations.

Lowering the Discount Rate Failed to Encourage Bank Lending in Kuwait

ARAB TIMES, MAY 2, 2011

Kuwait Money Supply Surges to KD25.6b in Feb [2010]

(a) [In February 2010] private sector deposits denominated in Kuwaiti Dinar compromised the majority of private sector deposits as it accounted for 77.4% or KWD22.16 billion, whereas private sector deposits in foreign currencies constituted 9.4% or KWD2.68 billion....

In comparison to February 2009, private sector deposits have grown [by] 6.7% or around KWD1.56 billion fuelled by the KWD1 billion increase in Time deposits over the same period. The volatile performance of the local and regional stock markets shifted investors' preference to low-risk return assets rather than risky financial instruments, which in turn have led to a flow back of money into the banking system ... strengthening the deposit base of local banks....

For the Full Year 2009, government deposits grew by 12.71% or KWD449 million, down from an increase of KWD1.31 billion during Q4-08 ... the government intervention maintained confidence in local banks and improved their liquidity. The growth in government deposits witnessed during the year 2009 came on the back of the government agencies attempts to boost the economy and improve the tight liquidity conditions that prevailed in the local financial system, amid the critical financial

circumstances, through available monetary tools and fund injections into the banking system to compensate for the withdrawal of funds by foreign depositors and to enhance the liquidity in the market.

However, these actions failed to stimulate credit growth over 2009 (credit grew at 6% during 2009) as local banks remained reluctant in extending additional credit to the various economic sectors, namely financial, trade, and manufacturing, triggered by the slump in the local stock market and the depreciation in the value of financial assets...

(b) Credit facilities extended by local banks to residents witnessed a moderate increase of KWD37.6 million compared to Jan-10 to record at the end of the month around KWD25.15 billion.... The marginal growth rate in credit facilities during the first two months of this year (around KWD40 million) is mainly due to the liquidity squeeze in the market, tight credit conditions, rise of default risk by highly indebted local firms along with the deterioration in the prices of financial assets which together pushed banks to implement a conservative and strict lending policies in extending additional facilities particularly with the lack of viable investment opportunities in the real economic sectors and the slowdown in the property market accompanied by the high fluctuations in stock prices and instability in the Kuwait Stock Exchange....

Loans to Real Estate sector, the second major component of credit facilities, dropped by around

KWD52.1 million, to reach KWD6.57 billion, accounting for around 26% of banks' loan portfolio. Kuwaiti banks' exposure to the real estate & construction sector is believed to be one of the highest levels in the Gulf region, representing around 33% of local banks' loan portfolio....

(c) **Interest Rates:** No further cut in CBK discount rate was seen following the 50 basis point slash during February 2010 to 2.5%. The CBK continuous efforts to strengthen the foundations of growth in the domestic economy in the face of the challenges of the global financial and economic crisis, helps establishing an appropriate atmosphere to reinforce growth in non-oil sectors in the national economy by reducing the cost of credit and thus enhance the stimulus effect of the CBK monetary policy in the current stage.

During the month of March, the CBK continued its policy of helping banks, [which] have excess liquidity, to find short-term investment opportunities.... As a result, the CBK announced the issuance of 3 tranches of one-year Treasury Bonds during the month for a total value of KWD400 million with all carrying a coupon of 1.25% p.a. Treasury Bonds issued by the CBK, which exceeded KWD 2 billion since Jan-09, have been formulated to absorb excess liquidity with local banks and to create investment opportunities for risk-averse banks that are still reluctant to extend additional credit to local corporates.

Source: "Kuwait money supply surges to KD256b in Feb," *Arabian Times*, May 2, 2011.

Key Points in the Article

This article discusses how bank lending and credit in Kuwait in the first quarter of 2010 did not significantly expand, despite the central bank and government actions to expand bank lending. Despite a large increase in private time deposits, which led to soaring bank liquidity, bank lending growth remained very slow in 2010. Banks were still reluctant to lend because of the high risk of default in the private sector and the depreciation in financial assets. The devaluation of real estate also damaged banks' collaterals, causing banks to reduce lending. The Central Bank of Kuwait, to encourage bank lending, reduced the discount rate twice at the beginning of 2010. Meanwhile, to offer banks some investment opportunities in low-risk assets, the Central Bank sold short-term Treasury bills. So, on the one hand, reducing the discount rate reduces the cost of credit and helps expand credit, thus increasing the money supply; on the other hand, selling Treasury bills to the public absorbs the excess liquidity at banks, reducing the money supply.

Analyzing the News

(a) Private deposits (local and foreign) increased dramatically, especially time deposits. This was a direct result of the high risks associated with the local and regional financial markets amid the global financial crisis. Investors preferred holding low-return, low-risk liquid assets, such as time deposits. Government deposits, on the other hand, shrank in 2010, after largely expanding in 2009 to pump new liquidity in the financial system.

(b) The soaring liquidity of the banking system in 2010 did not translate much into an increase in credit as was expected as liquidity conditions eased. The main reason for this remained the high risk of default by private corporations. Banks remained reluctant to lend and applied a strict credit policy. Bank credit witnessed very small growth. One element that contributed to this situation was the decline in the real estate market, which led to deterioration in the value of collaterals.

(c) The Central Bank took two steps that appear contradictory. One was to reduce the discount rate to encourage more bank lending and reduce the cost of credit. If successful, this action would increase the money supply. The second measure was to conduct open market operations, selling Treasury bills to absorb the excess liquidity of commercial banks, which lead to a reduction in money supply.

Thinking Critically

1. Do you believe the Central Bank of Kuwait had a clear strategy of increasing money supply through expanding credit? Was conducting open market operations helpful to achieve this goal?

2. The article mentions that private deposits increased to an all-time high figure at the same time that the money supply also increased. Is it correct to say that the increase in quasi money (checking and savings deposits) contributed directly to the increase in money supply? Explain why?

Despite a surge in Kuwait's private deposits and a soaring bank liquidity, bank lending growth remained very slow in 2010.

Key Terms

Summary

21.1 LEARNING OBJECTIVE

Define money and discuss its four functions, **pages 698–702.**

What Is Money and Why Do We Need It?

A *barter economy* is an economy that does not use money and in which people trade goods and services directly for other goods and services. Barter trade occurs only if there is a *double coincidence of wants*, where both parties to the trade want what the other one has. Because barter is inefficient, there is strong incentive to use **money**, which is any **asset** that people are generally willing to accept in exchange for goods or services or in payment of debts. An *asset* is anything of value owned by a person or a firm. A *commodity money* is a good used as money that also has value independent of its use as money. Money has four functions: it is a medium of exchange, a unit of account, a store of value, and a standard of deferred payment. The *gold standard* was a monetary system under which the government produced gold coins and paper currency that were convertible into gold. The gold standard collapsed in the early 1930s. Today, no government in the world issues paper currency that can be redeemed for gold. Instead, paper currency is **fiat money**, which has no value except as money.

21.2 LEARNING OBJECTIVE

Discuss the definitions of the money supply used today, **pages 702–706.**

How Is Money Measured Today?

The narrowest definition of the money supply today is **M1**, which includes currency, checking account balances, and traveler's checks. A broader definition of the money supply is **M2**, which includes everything that is in M1, plus savings accounts, small-denomination time deposits (such as certificates of deposit [CDs]), money market deposit accounts in banks, and noninstitutional money market fund shares.

21.3 LEARNING OBJECTIVE

Explain how banks create money, **pages 706–713.**

How Do Banks Create Money?

On a bank's balance sheet, *reserves* and loans are assets, and deposits are liabilities. **Reserves** are deposits that the bank has retained rather than loaned out or invested. **Required reserves** are reserves that banks are legally required to hold. The fraction of deposits that banks are required to keep as reserves is called the **required reserve ratio**. Any reserves banks hold over and above the legal requirement are called **excess reserves**. When a bank accepts a deposit, it keeps only a fraction of the funds as reserves and loans out the remainder. In making a loan, a bank increases the checking account balance of the borrower. When the borrower uses a check to buy something with the funds the bank has loaned, the seller deposits the check in his bank. The seller's bank keeps part of the deposit as reserves and loans out the remainder. This process continues until no banks have excess reserves. In this way, the process of banks making new loans increases the volume of checking account balances and the money supply. This money creation process can be illustrated with T-accounts, which are stripped-down versions of balance sheets that show only how a transaction changes a bank's balance sheet. The **simple deposit multiplier** is the ratio of the amount of deposits created by banks to the amount of new reserves. An expression for the simple deposit multiplier is $1/RR$.

The Central Bank

In a **fractional reserve banking system** banks keep less than 100 percent of deposits as reserves. In a **bank run**, many depositors decide simultaneously to withdraw money from a bank. In a **bank panic**, many banks experience runs at the same time. The **central bank's** main role is to carry out *monetary policy*. **Monetary policy** refers to the actions the central bank takes to manage the money supply and interest rates to pursue macroeconomic policy objectives. The three monetary policy tools are open market operations, discount policy, and reserve requirements. **Open market operations** are the buying and selling of Treasury securities by the central bank. The loans the central bank makes to banks are called **discount loans**, and the interest rate central bank charges on discount loans is the **discount rate**.

21.4 LEARNING OBJECTIVE

Discuss the three policy tools the Central Bank uses to manage the money supply, **pages 713–715.**

The Quantity Theory of Money

The *quantity equation* relates the money supply to the price level: $M \times V = P \times Y$, where M is the money supply, V is the *velocity of money*, P is the price level, and Y is real output. The **velocity of money** is the average number of times each dollar in the money supply is spent during the year. Economist Irving Fisher developed the **quantity theory of money**, which assumes that the velocity of money is constant. If the quantity theory of money is correct, the inflation rate should equal the rate of growth of the money supply minus the rate of growth of real output. Although the quantity theory of money is not literally correct because the velocity of money is not constant, it is true that in the long run, inflation results from the money supply growing faster than real GDP. When governments attempt to raise revenue by selling large quantities of bonds to the central bank, the money supply will increase rapidly, resulting in a high rate of inflation.

21.5 LEARNING OBJECTIVE

Explain the quantity theory of money and use it to explain how high rates of inflation occur, **pages 715–720.**

Review, Problems and Applications

 Visit www.pearsoned.co.uk/awe/hubbard to complete these exercises online and get instant feedback.

21.1 LEARNING OBJECTIVE   Define money and discuss its four functions, **pages 698–702.**

Review Questions

1.1 What is the difference between commodity money and fiat money?

1.2 What are the four functions of money? Can something be considered money if it does not fulfill all four functions?

Problems and Applications

1.3 Consider a singer in ancient times, who performed in a concert for one-third of the receipts. This turned out to be a cow, 20 turkeys, 50 chickens, and 5,000 kilos of bananas, lemons, and oranges. She of course could not consume the receipts by herself and also had to feed the cow and poultry. Do the goods the singer received as payment fulfill the four functions of money described in the chapter? Briefly explain.

1.4 In the late 1940s, the Communists under Mao Zedong were defeating the government of China in a civil war. The paper currency issued by the Chinese government was losing much of its value, and most businesses refused to accept it. At the same time, there was a paper shortage in Japan. During these years, Japan was still under military occupation by the United States, following its defeat in World War II. Some of the U.S. troops in Japan realized that they could use dollars to buy up vast amounts of paper currency in China, ship it to Japan to be recycled into paper, and make a substantial profit. Under these circumstances, was the Chinese paper currency a commodity money or a fiat money? Briefly explain.

1.5 In the 1970s, Pol Pot, the dictator of Cambodia, proclaimed that he intended to cancel money in his country because money represents the decadence of the West (Western Europe and the United States). Historically, did money only exist in the West? What effect would the elimination of money have on the economy?

1.6 According to a news story, during 2007, businesses in the city of Magdeburg, Germany, were printing their own currency called the Urstromtaler. The lawyer who started the currency was quoted as saying, "All the businesses have signed contracts, and it's official. We have our own banknotes and we have an issuing office in the city centre." The new currency is issued at a rate of one for one against the euro: anyone bringing euros to the issuing office in the city will receive the same number of Urstomtalers in exchange. Although issuing this local currency is apparently technically illegal, the German government has taken no action. Unlike euros, the local currency no longer

has value after a certain date, which means consumers have an incentive to spend it quickly. Does this local German currency fulfill the four functions of money described in the chapter? Briefly explain.

Source: Tristana Moore, "Germans Take Pride in Local Money," BBC News, February 6, 2007.

21.2 LEARNING OBJECTIVE Discuss the definitions of the money supply used today, **pages 702–706**.

Review Questions

2.1 What is the main difference between the M1 and M2 definitions of the money supply?

2.2 Why does the central bank use two definitions of the money supply rather than one?

Problems and Applications

2.3 Briefly explain whether each of the following is counted in M1.
  a. The coins in your pocket
  b. The funds in your checking account
  c. The funds in your savings account
  d. The traveler's check that you have left over from a trip
  e. Your Citibank Platinum MasterCard

2.4 (Related to *Solved Problem 21-2* on page 705) Suppose you have US$2,000 in currency in a shoebox in your closet. One day, you decide to deposit the money in a checking account. Briefly explain how this will affect M1 and M2.

2.5 (Related to *Solved Problem 21-2* on page 705) Suppose you decide to withdraw US$100 in currency from your checking account. What is the effect on M1? Ignore any actions the bank may take as a result of your having withdrawn the US$100.

2.6 Briefly explain whether you agree or disagree with the following statement: "I recently read that more than half of the money issued by the government is actually held by people in foreign countries. If that's true, then the country is less than half as wealthy as government statistics indicate."

21.3 LEARNING OBJECTIVE Explain how banks create money, **pages 706–713**.

Review Questions

3.1 What are the largest asset and the largest liability of a typical bank?

3.2 Suppose you decide to withdraw US$100 in cash from your checking account. Draw a T-account showing the effect of this transaction on your bank's balance sheet.

3.3 Give the formula for the simple deposit multiplier. If the required reserve ratio is 20 percent, what is the maximum increase in checking account deposits that will result from an increase in bank reserves of US$20,000?

Problems and Applications

3.4 Deposits are the fuel to any bank, through which they can make loans and mortgages, and can extend credit. Briefly explain what this means.

3.5 "Most of the money supply is created by banks making loans." Briefly explain whether you agree or disagree with this statement.

3.6 Would a series of bank runs in a country decrease the total quantity M1? Wouldn't a bank run simply move funds in a checking account to currency in circulation? How could that movement of funds decrease the quantity of money?

3.7 (Related to *Solved Problem 21-3* on page 710) Suppose you deposit US$2,000 in currency into your checking account at a branch of Bank Misr, which we will assume has no excess reserves at the time you make your deposit. Also assume that the required reserve ratio is 0.20.

  a. Use a T-account to show the initial impact of this transaction on Bank Misr's balance sheet.

  b. Suppose that Bank Misr makes the maximum loan it can from the funds you deposited. Using a T-account, show the initial impact of granting the loan on Bank Misr's balance sheet. Also include on this T-account the transaction from (a).

  c. Now suppose that whoever took out the loan in (b) writes a check for this amount and that the person receiving the check deposits it in a branch of Citibank. Show the effect of these transactions on the balance sheets of Bank Misr and Citibank *after the check has been cleared*. (On the T-account for Bank Misr, include the transactions from [a] and [b].)

  d. What is the maximum increase in checking account deposits that can result from your US$2,000 deposit? What is the maximum increase in the money supply? Explain.

3.8 Consider the following simplified balance sheet for a bank.

ASSETS IN US$		LIABILITIES IN US$	
Reserves	10,000	Deposits	70,000
Loans	66,000	Stockholders' equity	6,000

   a. If the required reserve ratio is 10 percent, how much in excess reserves does the bank hold?

   b. What is the maximum amount by which the bank can expand its loans?

   c. If the bank makes the loans in (b), show the *immediate* impact on the bank's balance sheet.

3.9 Briefly explain whether you agree or disagree with the following statement: "Assets are things of value that people own. Liabilities are debts. Therefore, a bank will always consider a checking account deposit to be an asset and a car loan to be a liability."

3.10 "Banks don't really create money, do they?" How would you answer this question?

21.4 LEARNING OBJECTIVE   Discuss the three policy tools the Central Bank uses to manage the money supply, **pages 713–715.**

Review Questions

4.1 Today, what is the most important role of the central bank in any economy?

4.2 What are the policy tools the central bank uses to control the money supply? Which tool is the most important?

Problems and Applications

4.3 Why do most depositors seem to be unworried that banks loan out most of the deposits they receive?

4.4 Suppose that you are a bank manager, and the central bank raises the required reserve ratio from 10 percent to 12 percent. What actions would you need to take? How would your actions and those of other bank managers end up affecting the money supply?

4.5 Reserve requirements have been referred to as a 'tax on bank profits.' Briefly explain whether you agree.

How would your answer change if the central bank began paying interest on banks' reserve accounts?

4.6 Suppose that the central bank makes a US$10 million discount loan to the National Commercial Bank (NCB) by increasing NCB's account at the Central Bank.

   a. Use a T-account to show the impact of this transaction on NCB's balance sheet. Remember that the funds a bank has on deposit at the central bank count as part of its reserves.

   b. Assume that before receiving the discount loan, NCB has no excess reserves. What is the maximum amount of this US$10 million that NCB can lend out?

   c. What is the maximum total increase in the money supply that can result from the central bank's discount loan? Assume that the required reserve ratio is 10 percent.

21.5 LEARNING OBJECTIVE   Explain the quantity theory of money and use it to explain how high rates of inflation occur, **pages 715–720.**

Review Questions

5.1 What is the quantity theory of money? How does the quantity theory explain why inflation occurs?

5.2 What is hyperinflation? Why do governments sometimes allow it to occur?

Problems and Applications

5.3 If the money supply is growing at a rate of 6 percent per year, real GDP is growing at a rate of 3 percent per year, and velocity is constant, what will the inflation rate be? If velocity is increasing 1 percent per year instead of remaining constant, what will the inflation rate be?

5.4 Suppose that during one period, the velocity of money is constant and during another period, it undergoes large fluctuations. During which period will the

quantity theory of money be more useful in explaining changes in the inflation rate? Briefly explain.

5.5 The following is from an article in the *Wall Street Journal*: "[Japan's] money supply is surging. If that doesn't curtail Japan's debilitating price deflation, a lot of economics textbooks may need to be rewritten."

   a. What is "price deflation"?

   b. If rapid increases in the money supply don't stop deflation, why will economics textbooks need to be rewritten?

   c. (This is a more difficult question.) Why might price deflation in Japan be "debilitating"? (*Hint*: What reaction might consumers have to price deflation?)

Source: Peter Landers, "Japan Shows Vague Signs of Recovery," *Wall Street Journal*, March 5, 2002.

5.6 (Related to *Making the Connection* on page 718) During the German hyperinflation of the 1920s, many households and firms in Germany were hurt economically. Did you think any groups in Germany benefited from the hyperinflation? Briefly explain.

5.7 In the summer of 2006, the African country of Zimbabwe decided to change its currency. The government announced that at the end of the day on August 21, 2006, the old dollar would no longer be legal tender. It would be replaced with new currency, with each new dollar worth 1,000 times what the old dollar was worth. According to a newspaper article "Under the changeover rules, individuals were permitted to exchange a limit of 100 million old Zimbabwe dollars (US$40) for new currency in a single transaction each week since Aug. 1." Predict what happened to prices in Zimbabwe in terms of the old dollar as the August 21 deadline approached. What would the government of Zimbabwe hope to gain from swapping a new currency for an old currency?

Source: "Zimbabwe Swaps Currency Amid Runaway Inflation," *Wall Street Journal*, August 21, 2006.

5.8 An article in *The Economist* on Zimbabwe, described conditions in summer 2007: "inflation is hovering around 4,500%, and eight Zimbabweans in ten do not have formal jobs." Is there a connection between the very high inflation rate and the high rate of unemployment? Briefly explain.

Source: "Rumblings Within," *The Economist*, June 21, 2007.

Chapter 22

Monetary Policy

Monetary Policy, Drake and Scull, and the Housing Market in Dubai

Negative real interest rates were a major reason behind the Dubai property boom between 2005 and 2007. But, what are negative real interest rates? This is a situation where local inflation is higher than the return on bank deposits and the interest rate banks charge on loans (the cost of borrowing). So, it is not a wise decision to keep your money in the bank. In fact, borrowing and investing the money in real assets, such as houses, is a smart decision. The UAE's Central Bank ties UAE interest rate to the U.S. rate set by the American Federal Reserves because the dirham is fixed against the U.S. dollar. Therefore, mortgage finance (house loans) during these years ranged from 6.75 percent to 7.5 percent. Inflation, on the other hand, was running at the 20 percent level, causing an almost 13 percent negative interest rate (the difference between the UAE interest rate and the inflation rate). This heated the boom in the housing and construction sectors, till it peaked in 2008.

The global downturn after the outbreak of the worldwide financial crisis in 2008 was tough, and many economies around the world started suffering from a recession. During a typical recession, sales of new homes decline sharply as unemployment increases and incomes fall. Home builders are usually among the businesses hit hardest during recessions. One of the few firms that escaped dramatic swings in sales between 2009 and 2010 was the Dubai-based real-estate contractor Drake and Scull International (DSI). DSI owes this to its geographically diverse operations not only in the UAE, but also in all other GCC states, and India, Thailand, Nigeria, and China. DSI was among the few companies that hired when others laid off workers, and its shares were among the few securities that outperformed the DFM (Dubai Financial Market) General Index during the second half of 2009. DSI maintained this performance in 2010. By November, its shares were still traded at a 9.2 percent gain compared with last year; 1 percent higher than the gain in the average DFM index and more than 3 percent higher than the gain in Emaar's shares, for the same period. Despite this relatively better response to the recession, the crisis finally had its toll on DSI's profits. During the third quarter of 2010, DSI's net profit fell significantly by 45 percent.

In 2010, the UAE central bank decided to cut interest rates to encourage lending and rescue the housing market. Commercial banks, in turn, lowered their mortgage interest rate for new customers. For example, HSBC reduced the mortgage rate from 8.5 percent to 6.75 percent, making mortgage finance more affordable. As we will see in this chapter, in addition to being concerned about recessions, the central bank tries to keep the inflation rate at a low level. During 2006 and 2007, the inflation rate was above the level the central bank considers acceptable. Lowering interest rates might worsen inflation if it leads to a large increase in spending by households and firms. But fears of a deeper recession were enough to have the central bank reducing interest rates. In 2009, the UAE Central Bank, following the U.S. Federal Reserves, was forced to turn to new policies as it tried to keep the economy out of recession while inflation was at its lowest levels in years.

AN INSIDE LOOK AT POLICY on **page 754** discusses how the drop in Dubai houses prices helped keeping inflation low throughout 2010.

Sources: "DSI Weathers the Crisis in the Middle East Construction Sector," www.ameinfo.com, December 8, 2010; "Negative Real Interest Rates Sustain Dubai Property Boom," www.ameinfo.com, June 5, 2006; "HSBC Lowers UAE Mortgage Rate to 6.75 pct," March 10, 2010, www.arabianbusiness.com.

LEARNING Objectives

After studying this chapter, you should be able to:

22.1 Define **monetary policy** and describe the central bank's **monetary policy goals**, page 730.

22.2 Describe the central bank's monetary policy targets and explain how **expansionary** and **contractionary monetary policies** affect the **interest rate**, page 732.

22.3 Use aggregate demand and aggregate supply graphs to show the **effects** of **monetary policy** on **real GDP** and the **price level**, page 738.

22.4 Discuss the central bank's setting of **monetary policy targets**, page 748.

Economics in YOUR Life!

Should You Buy a House During a Recession?

If you are like most college students, buying a house is one of the farthest things from your mind. But suppose you think forward a few years to when you might be married and maybe even have children. Leaving years of renting apartments behind, you are considering buying a house. But, suppose that according to an article in the *Gulf News*, a majority of economists are predicting that a recession is likely to begin soon. What should you do? Would this be a good time or a bad time to buy a house? As you read the chapter, see if you can answer these questions. You can check your answers against those we provide at the end of the chapter. >> Continued on page 752

I n the previous chapter, we saw that banks play an important role in creating the money supply. We also saw that the central bank manages the money supply to achieve its policy goals. As we will see in this chapter, the central bank has four policy goals: (1) price stability, (2) high employment, (3) economic growth, and (4) stability of financial markets and institutions. In this chapter, we will explore how the central bank decides which *monetary policy* actions to take to achieve its goals.

Monetary policy The actions the Central Bank takes to manage the money supply and interest rates to pursue its macroeconomic policy objectives.

22.1 | Define monetary policy and describe the central bank's monetary policy goals.

What Is Monetary Policy?

Monetary policy refers to the actions central banks take to manage the money supply and interest rates to pursue its macroeconomic policy objectives.

The Goals of Monetary Policy

Central banks usually have four *monetary policy goals* that are intended to promote a well-functioning economy:

1 Price stability

2 High employment

3 Economic growth

4 Stability of financial markets and institutions.

We briefly consider each of these goals.

Price Stability As we have seen in previous chapters, rising prices erode the value of money as a medium of exchange and a store of value. Especially after inflation rose dramatically and unexpectedly during the 1970s, policymakers in most industrial countries have price stability as a policy goal. Figure 22-1 shows inflation rates in three selected Arab countries. Jordan and Egypt are non-oil countries and Kuwait is an oil country. Kuwait had the lowest average inflation rate of about 4 percent during the period 1979–2008, while Egypt, on the other hand, had the highest rates. Between 1975 and 1995 Egypt suffered from two-digit rates of inflation, which approached 25 percent in 1986. After 1995, inflation declined and was contained below 5 percent, till it started rising again in 2004. Jordan had relatively high rates of inflation in the 1970s, but started steadily declining from 1979, to hit almost zero in 1985, and fall below zero in 1986. Inflation hiked during the first Gulf War. As in the case of Egypt, after 1995, inflation was contained below 5 percent, till it started rising in 2006. Jordan seems to closely follow inflation trends in Kuwait. One explanation is that almost 20 percent of the Jordanian population works in GCC countries and sends its income home. In other words, inflation in Jordan is 'imported' from the Gulf. When inflation is low over the long run, the central bank will have the flexibility it needs to lessen the impact of recessions. And many economists agree.

High Employment High employment, or a low rate of unemployment, is another monetary policy goal. Unemployed workers and underused factories and office buildings reduce GDP below its potential level. Unemployment causes financial distress and decreases self-esteem for workers who lack jobs. The goal of high employment extends beyond the central bank to other branches of the government.

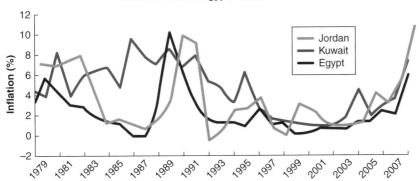

Inflation rates in Egypt, Jordan and Kuwait

Figure 22-1

Inflation Rates in Three Selected Arab Countries

This figure shows inflation rates in three selected Arab countries. Kuwait has the lowest average inflation rate, while Egypt has the highest. In Jordan, it seems that inflation follows the same trend of the Arab Gulf countries. Source: World Development Indicators, World Bank, 2010.

Economic Growth We discussed in earlier chapters the importance of economic growth to raising living standards. Policymakers aim to encourage *stable* economic growth because stable growth allows households and firms to plan accurately and encourages the long-run investment that is needed to sustain growth. Policy can spur economic growth by providing incentives for saving to ensure a large pool of investment funds, as well as by providing direct incentives for business investment. Policies to increase saving and investment may be better carried out by the parliament and the president than by the central bank, however. For example, parliament and the president can change the tax laws to increase the return to saving and investing. In fact, some economists question whether the central bank can play a role in promoting economic growth beyond attempting to meet its goals of price stability and high employment. These economists note that high employment typically occurs only when real GDP is near potential GDP and growing at a sustained rate. So, in attaining its goal of high employment, the central bank will also have promoted economic growth. Similarly, most economists believe that economic growth is generally slow during periods of high inflation. So, in achieving price stability, the central bank will also be promoting economic growth.

Stability of Financial Markets and Institutions When financial markets and institutions are not efficient in matching savers and borrowers, resources are lost. Firms with the potential to produce goods and services valued by consumers cannot obtain the financing they need to design, develop, and market those products. Savers waste resources looking for satisfactory investments. The central bank promotes the stability of financial markets and institutions so that an efficient flow of funds from savers to borrowers will occur. For example, during the turmoil in the market for subprime mortgages in 2007 and 2008 in the U.S., the Federal Reserve decided to expand its role as a lender of last resort.

The crisis in the mortgage market during 2007 and 2008 was similar to the banking crises that led the U.S. Congress to create the Federal Reserve System in 1913. A key difference is that while earlier banking crises affected commercial banks, investment banks were heavily involved in the events of 2007–2008. Investment banks can be subject to *liquidity problems* because they often borrow short term—sometimes as short as overnight—and invest the funds in longer term investments. Commercial banks borrow from households and firms in the form of checking and saving deposits, while investment banks borrow primarily from other financial firms, such as other investment banks, mutual funds, or hedge funds, which are similar to mutual funds but typically engage in more complex—and risky—investment strategies. Just as commercial banks can experience a crisis if depositors begin to withdraw funds, investment banks can experience a crisis if other financial firms stop offering them short-term loans.

In the next section, we will look at how the central bank attempts to attain its monetary policy goals. Although the central bank has multiple monetary policy goals, during most periods, the most important goals of monetary policy are price stability and high employment.

22.2 | Describe the central bank's monetary policy targets and explain how expansionary and contractionary monetary policies affect the interest rate.

The Money Market and the Central Bank's Choice of Monetary Policy Targets

The central bank's objective in undertaking monetary policy is to use its policy tools to achieve its monetary policy goals. Recall from Chapter 21 that the central bank's policy tools are open market operations, discount policy, and reserve requirements. At times, the central bank encounters conflicts between its policy goals. For example, as we will discuss later in this chapter, the central bank can raise interest rates to reduce the inflation rate. But, as we saw earlier, higher interest rates typically reduce household and firm spending, which may result in slower growth and higher unemployment. So, a policy that is intended to achieve one monetary policy goal, such as lower inflation, may have an adverse effect on another policy goal, such as high employment.

Monetary Policy Targets

The central bank tries to keep both the unemployment and inflation rates low, but it can't affect either of these economic variables directly. The central bank cannot tell firms how many people to employ or what prices to charge for their products. Instead, the central bank uses variables, called *monetary policy targets*, that it can affect directly and that, in turn, affect variables, such as real GDP, employment, and the price level, that are closely related to the central bank's policy goals. The two main monetary policy targets are the money supply and the interest rate. As we will see, the central bank typically uses the interest rate as its policy target.

The Demand for Money

The central bank's two monetary policy targets are related in an important way. To see this relationship, we first need to examine the demand and supply for money. Figure 22-2 shows the demand curve for money. The interest rate is on the vertical axis, and the quantity of money is on the horizontal axis. Here we are using the M1 definition of money, which equals currency in circulation plus checking account deposits. Notice that the demand curve for money is downward sloping.

To understand why the demand curve for money is downward sloping, consider that households and firms have a choice between holding money and holding other financial assets, such as Treasury bills. Money has one particularly desirable characteristic: you can use it to buy goods, services, or financial assets. Money also has one undesirable characteristic: it earns either no interest or a very low rate of interest. The currency in your wallet earns no interest, and the money in your checking account earns either no interest or very little interest. Alternatives to money, such as Treasury bills, pay interest but have to be sold if you want to use the funds to buy something. When interest rates rise on financial assets such as Treasury bills, the amount of interest that households and firms lose by holding money increases. When interest rates fall, the amount of interest households and firms lose by holding money decreases. Remember that *opportunity cost*

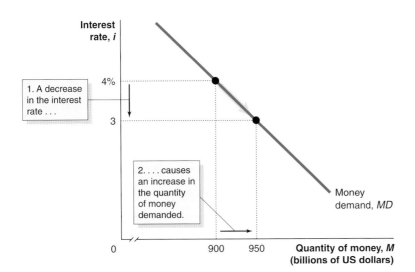

Figure 22-2

The Demand for Money

The money demand curve slopes downward because lower interest rates cause households and firms to switch from financial assets like Treasury bills to money. All other things being equal, a fall in the interest rate from 4 percent to 3 percent will increase the quantity of money demanded from US$900 billion to US$950 billion. An increase in the interest rate will decrease the quantity of money demanded.

is what you have to forgo to engage in an activity. The interest rate is the opportunity cost of holding money.

We now have an explanation for why the demand curve for money slopes downward: when interest rates on Treasury bills and other financial assets are low, the opportunity cost of holding money is low, so the quantity of money demanded by households and firms will be high; when interest rates are high, the opportunity cost of holding money will be high, so the quantity of money demanded will be low. In Figure 22-2, a decrease in interest rates from 4 percent to 3 percent causes the quantity of money demanded by households and firms to rise from US$900 billion to US$950 billion.

Shifts in the Money Demand Curve

We saw in Chapter 3 that the demand curve for a good is drawn holding constant all variables, other than the price, that affect the willingness of consumers to buy the good. Changes in variables other than the price cause the demand curve to shift. Similarly, the demand curve for money is drawn holding constant all variables, other than the interest rate, that affect the willingness of households and firms to hold money. Changes in variables other than the interest rate cause the demand curve to shift. The two most important variables that cause the money demand curve to shift are real GDP and the price level.

An increase in real GDP means that the amount of buying and selling of goods and services will increase. This additional buying and selling increases the demand for money as a medium of exchange, so the quantity of money households and firms want to hold increases at each interest rate, shifting the money demand curve to the right. A decrease in real GDP decreases the quantity of money demanded at each interest rate, shifting the money demand curve to the left. A higher price level increases the quantity of money required for a given amount of buying and selling. Eighty years ago, for example, when the price level was much lower and someone could purchase a new car for US$500 and a salary of US$30 per week put you in the middle class, the quantity of money demanded by households and firms was much lower than today, even adjusting for the effect of the lower real GDP and smaller population of those years. An increase in the price level increases the quantity of money demanded at each interest rate, shifting the money demand curve to the right. A decrease in the price level decreases the quantity of money demanded at each interest rate, shifting the money demand curve to the left. Figure 22-3 illustrates shifts in the money demand curve.

Figure 22-3

Shifts in the Money Demand Curve

Changes in real GDP or the price level cause the money demand curve to shift. An increase in real GDP or an increase in the price level will cause the money demand curve to shift from MD_1 to MD_2. A decrease in real GDP or a decrease in the price level will cause the money demand curve to shift from MD_1 to MD_3.

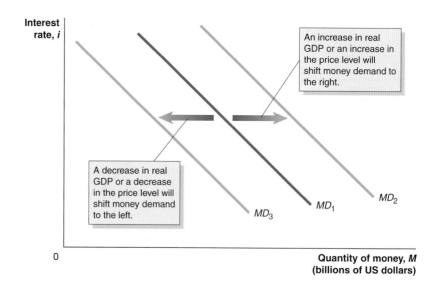

How the Central Bank Manages the Money Supply: A Quick Review

Having discussed money demand, we now turn to money supply. In the previous chapter, we saw how the central bank manages the money supply. If the central bank decides to increase the money supply, it purchases Treasury securities. The sellers of these Treasury securities deposit the funds they receive from the central bank in banks, which increases the banks' reserves. Banks loan out most of these reserves, which creates new checking account deposits and expands the money supply. If the central bank decides to decrease the money supply, it sells Treasury securities, which decreases banks' reserves and contracts the money supply.

Equilibrium in the Money Market

In Figure 22-4, we include both the money demand and money supply curves. We can use this figure to see how the central bank affects both the money supply and the interest rate. For simplicity, we assume that the central bank is able to completely fix the money supply (although, in fact, the behavior of the public and banks can also affect the money supply). Therefore, the money supply curve is a vertical line, and changes in the interest

Figure 22-4

The Impact on the Interest Rate When the Central Bank Increases the Money Supply

When the central bank increases the money supply, households and firms will initially hold more money than they want, relative to other financial assets. Households and firms buy Treasury bills and other financial assets with the money they don't want to hold. This increase in demand drives up the prices of these assets and drives down their interest rates. Eventually, interest rates will fall enough that households and firms will be willing to hold the additional money the central bank has created. In the figure, an increase in the money supply from US$900 billion to US$950 billion causes the money supply curve to shift to the right, from MS_1 to MS_2, and causes the equilibrium interest rate to fall from 4 percent to 3 percent.

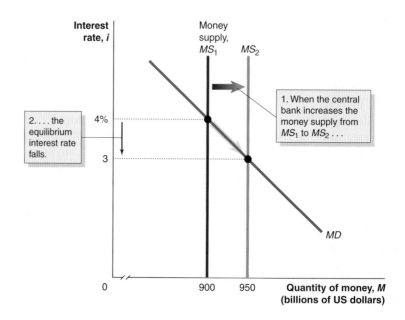

rate have no effect on the quantity of money supplied. Just as with other markets, equilibrium in the *money market* occurs where the money demand curve crosses the money supply curve. If the central bank increases the money supply, the money supply curve will shift to the right, and the equilibrium interest rate will fall. In Figure 22-4, when the central bank increases the money supply from US$900 billion to US$950 billion, the money supply curve shifts from MS_1 to MS_2, and the equilibrium interest rate falls from 4 percent to 3 percent.

In the money market, the adjustment from one equilibrium to another equilibrium is a little different from the adjustment in the market for a good. In Figure 22-4, the money market is initially in equilibrium with an interest rate of 4 percent and a money supply of US$900 billion. When the central bank increases the money supply by US$50 billion, households and firms have more money than they want to hold at an interest rate of 4 percent. What do households and firms do with the extra US$50 billion? They are most likely to use the money to buy short-term financial assets, such as Treasury bills. Short-term financial assets have maturities—the date when the last payment by the seller is made—of one year or less. By buying short-term assets, households and firms drive up their prices and drive down their interest rates.

To see why an increasing demand for Treasury bills will lower their interest rate, recall that *the prices of financial assets and their interest rates move in opposite directions.* Suppose you buy a Treasury bill today for US$962 that matures in one year, at which time the Treasury will pay you US$1,000. The government sells Treasury bills at a price below their face value of US$1,000. The difference between the price of the bill and its US$1,000 face value represents the return to investors for lending their money to the Treasury. In this case, you will earn US$38 in interest on your investment of US$962. The interest rate on the Treasury bill is:

$$\left(\frac{\$38}{\$962} \right) \times 100 = 4\%$$

Now suppose that many households and firms increase their demand for Treasury bills. This increase in demand will have the same effect on Treasury bills that an increase in the demand for apples has on apples: the price will rise. Suppose the price of Treasury bills rises from US$962 to US$971. Now if you buy a Treasury bill, you will receive only US$29 in interest on your investment of US$971. The interest rate on the Treasury bill is now:

$$\left(\frac{\$29}{\$971} \right) \times 100 = 3\%$$

Therefore, as the price of a Treasury bill increases, the interest rate on the Treasury bill falls.

As the interest rate on Treasury bills and other financial assets falls, the opportunity cost of holding money also falls. Households and firms move down the money demand curve. Eventually the interest rate will have fallen enough that households and firms are willing to hold the additional US$50 billion worth of money the central bank has created, and the money market will be back in equilibrium. To summarize: *When the central bank increases the money supply, the short-term interest rate must fall until it reaches a level at which households and firms are willing to hold the additional money.*

Figure 22-5 shows what happens when the central bank decreases the money supply. The money market is initially in equilibrium, at an interest rate of 4 percent and a money supply of US$900 billion. If the central bank decreases the money supply to US$850 billion, households and firms will be holding less money than they would like—relative to other financial assets—at an interest rate of 4 percent. To increase their money holdings, they will sell Treasury bills and other financial assets. The increased supply of Treasury bills for sale will decrease their prices and increase their interest rates. Rising short-term interest rates increase the opportunity cost of holding money, causing households and firms to move up the money demand curve. Equilibrium is finally restored at an interest rate of 5 percent.

Figure 22-5

The Impact on Interest Rates when the Central Bank Decreases the Money Supply

When the central bank decreases the money supply, households and firms will initially hold less money than they want, relative to other financial assets. Households and firms will sell Treasury bills and other financial assets, reducing their prices and increasing their interest rates. Eventually, interest rates will rise to the point at which households and firms will be willing to hold the smaller amount of money that results from the central bank's actions. In the figure, a reduction in money supply from US$900 billion to US$850 billion causes the money supply curve to shift to the left, from MS_1 to MS_2, and causes the equilibrium interest rate to rise from 4 percent to 5 percent.

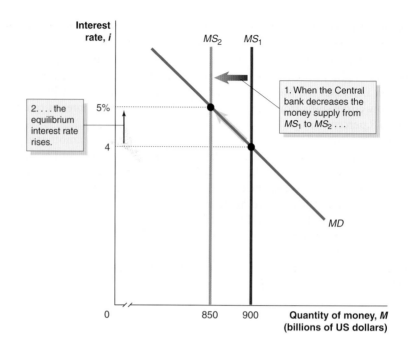

Solved Problem | 22-2

The Relationship between Treasury Bill Prices and Their Interest Rates

---

What is the price of a Treasury bill that pays US$1,000 in one year, if its interest rate is 4 percent? What is the price of the Treasury bill if its interest rate is 5 percent?

SOLVING THE PROBLEM:

Step 1: **Review the chapter material.** This problem is about the relationship between Treasury bill prices and interest rates, so you may want to review the section "Equilibrium in the Money Market," which begins on page 734.

Step 2: **Use the formula for calculating interest rates to determine the Treasury bill price when the interest rate is 4 percent.** In this situation, the interest rate will be equal to the percentage increase from the initial purchase price of the bill to the US$1,000 buyers will receive in one year. We can set up the problem like this, where P is the purchase price of the Treasury bill:

$$\left(\frac{\$1,000 - P}{P} \right) \times 100 = 4$$

Dividing both sides by 100 and multiplying both sides by P, we get:

$$\$1,000 - P = 0.04P$$

or:

$$\$1,000 = 1.04P$$

or:

$$\frac{\$1,000}{1.04} = P$$

or, rounding to the nearest dollar:

$$P = \$962$$

Step 3: **Use the formula for calculating interest rates to determine the Treasury bill price when the interest rate is 5 percent.** We can apply the same formula to find the price when the interest rate is 5 percent:

$$\left(\frac{\$1,000 - P}{P}\right) \times 100 = 5$$

Once again, dividing both sides by 100 and multiplying both sides by P, we get:

$$\$1,000 - P = 0.05P$$

or:

$$\$1,000 = 1.05P$$

or:

$$\frac{\$1,000}{1.05} = P$$

or:

$$P = \$952$$

EXTRA CREDIT: The interest rate on a Treasury bill or other financial asset is also called its *yield*. It's important to remember that prices of financial assets and their yields move in opposite directions.

YOUR TURN: For more practice, do related problem 2.6 on page 758 at the end of this chapter.

>> End Solved Problem 22-2

A Tale of Two Interest Rates

In Chapter 17, we discussed the loanable funds model of the interest rate. In that model, the equilibrium interest rate was determined by the demand and supply for loanable funds. Why do we need two models of the interest rate? The answer is that the loanable funds model is concerned with the *long-term real rate of interest*, and the money-market model is concerned with the *short-term nominal rate of interest*. The long-term real rate of interest is the interest rate that is most relevant when savers consider purchasing a long-term financial investment such as a corporate bond. It is also the rate of interest that is most relevant to firms that are borrowing to finance long-term investment projects such as new factories or office buildings, or to households that are taking out mortgage loans to buy new homes.

When conducting monetary policy, however, the short-term nominal interest rate is the most relevant interest rate because it is the interest rate most affected by increases and decreases in the money supply. Often—but not always—there is a close connection between movements in the short-term nominal interest rate and movements in the long-term real interest rate. So, when the central bank takes actions to increase the short-term nominal interest, usually the long-term real interest rate also increases. In other words, as we will discuss in the next section, when the interest rate on Treasury bills rises, the real interest rate on mortgage loans usually also rises, although sometimes only after a delay.

Choosing a Monetary Policy Target

As we have seen, the central bank uses monetary policy targets to affect economic variables such as real GDP or the price level, which are closely related to the central bank's policy goals. The central bank chooses the money supply or the interest rate as its monetary policy target. As Figure 22-5 shows, the central bank is capable of affecting both. Since the early 1980s many financial innovations were introduced in developed nations, including paying interest on checking accounts and the introduction of money market mutual funds. This has made M1 less relevant as a measure of the medium of exchange. These developments led central banks to rely for a time on M2, a broader measure of the money supply that had a more stable historical relationship to economic growth. But over time most central banks increased its reliance on interest rate targets.

There are many different interest rates in the economy. For purposes of monetary policy, the central bank targeted the interest rate known as the *Central Bank's funds rate*. In the next section, we discuss the Central Bank's funds rate before examining how targeting the interest rate can help the central bank achieve its monetary policy goals.

The Importance of the Central Bank's Funds Rate

Central Bank's funds rate The interest rate banks charge each other for overnight loans.

Recall from Chapter 21 that every bank must keep some percentage, say 10 percent, of its checking account deposits above a certain threshold as reserves, either as currency held in the bank or as deposits with the central bank. Banks receive no interest on their reserves, so they have an incentive to invest reserves above the 10-percent minimum. Banks that need additional reserves can borrow in the *Central Bank's funds market* from banks that have reserves available. The **Central Bank's funds rate** is the interest rate banks charge on loans in the Central Bank's funds market. The loans in the Central Bank's funds market are usually very short term, often just overnight.

Despite the name, the Central Bank's funds rate is not set administratively by the central bank. Instead, the rate is determined by the supply of reserves relative to the demand for them. Because the central bank can increase and decrease the supply of bank reserves through open market operations, it can set a target for the Central Bank's funds rate and come very close to hitting it. The central bank usually announces a target for the Central Bank's funds rate every period.

The Central Bank's funds rate is not directly relevant for households and firms. No households or firms, except banks, can borrow or lend in the Central Bank's funds market. However, changes in the Central Bank's funds rate usually result in changes in interest rates on other short-term financial assets, such as Treasury bills, and changes in interest rates on long-term financial assets, such as corporate bonds and mortgages. The effect of a change in the Central Bank's funds rate on long-term interest rates is usually smaller than it is on short-term interest rates, and the effect may occur only after a lag in time. Although a majority of economists support the central bank's choice of the interest rate as its monetary policy target, some economists believe the central bank should concentrate on the money supply instead. We will discuss the views of these economists later in this chapter.

22.3 LEARNING OBJECTIVE

22.3 | Use aggregate demand and aggregate supply graphs to show the effects of monetary policy on real GDP and the price level.

Monetary Policy and Economic Activity

Remember that the central bank uses the Central Bank's funds rate as a monetary policy target because it has good control of the Central Bank's funds rate through open market operations and because it believes that changes in the Central Bank's funds rate will ultimately affect economic variables that are related to its monetary policy goals. Here it is important to consider again the distinction between the nominal interest rate and the real interest rate. Recall that we calculate the real interest rate by subtracting the inflation rate from the nominal interest rate. Ultimately, the ability of the central bank to use monetary policy to affect economic variables such as real GDP depends on its ability to affect real interest rates, such as the real interest rates on mortgages and corporate bonds. Because the Central Bank's funds rate is a short-term nominal interest rate, the central bank sometimes has difficulty affecting long-term real interest rates. Nevertheless, for purposes of the following discussion, we will assume that the central bank is able to use open market operations to affect long-term real interest rates.

How Interest Rates Affect Aggregate Demand

Changes in interest rates affect *aggregate demand*, which is the total level of spending in the economy. Recall from Chapter 20 that aggregate demand has four components: consumption, investment, government purchases, and net exports. Changes in interest rates will not affect government purchases, but they will affect the other three components of aggregate demand in the following ways:

- *Consumption.* Many households finance purchases of consumer durables, such as automobiles and furniture, by borrowing. Lower interest rates lead to increased spending on durables because they lower the total cost of these goods to consumers by lowering the interest payments on loans. Higher interest rates raise the cost of consumer durables, and households will buy fewer of them. Lower interest rates also reduce the return to saving, leading households to save less and spend more. Higher interest rates increase the return to saving, leading households to save more and spend less.

- *Investment.* Firms finance most of their spending on machinery, equipment, and factories out of their profits or by borrowing. Firms borrow either from the financial markets by issuing corporate bonds or from banks. Higher interest rates on corporate bonds or on bank loans make it more expensive for firms to borrow, so they will undertake fewer investment projects. Lower interest rates make it less expensive for firms to borrow, so they will undertake more investment projects. Lower interest rates can also increase investment through their impact on stock prices. As interest rates decline, stocks become a more attractive investment relative to bonds. The increase in demand for stocks raises their price. An increase in stock prices sends a signal to firms that the future profitability of investment projects has increased. By issuing additional shares of stocks, firms can acquire the funds they need to buy new factories and equipment, thereby increasing investment.

   Finally, spending by households on new homes is also part of investment. When interest rates on mortgage loans rise, the cost of buying new homes rises, and fewer new homes will be purchased. When interest rates on mortgage loans fall, more new homes will be purchased.

- *Net exports.* Recall that net exports are equal to spending by foreign households and firms on goods and services produced in the economy minus spending by domestic households and firms on goods and services produced in other countries. The value of net exports depends partly on the exchange rate between the dollar and foreign currencies. When the value of the dollar rises, households and firms in other countries will pay more for goods and services produced in your country, but a country's households and firms will pay less for goods and services produced in other countries. As a result, the economy will export less and import more, so net exports fall. When the value of the local currency falls (in terms of dollars), net exports will rise. If interest rates in the economy rise relative to interest rates in other countries, investing locally in financial assets will become more desirable, causing foreign investors to increase their demand for domestic currency (by selling their dollars), which will increase the value of the local currency. As the value of the local currency (in terms of dollars) increases, net exports will fall. If interest rates in the economy decline relative to interest rates in other countries, the value of the domestic currency (in terms of dollars) will fall, and net exports will rise.

The Effects of Monetary Policy on Real GDP and the Price Level: An Initial Look

In Chapter 20, we developed the *aggregate demand and aggregate supply model* to explain fluctuations in real GDP and the price level. In the basic version of the model, we assume that there is no economic growth, so the long-run aggregate supply curve does not shift. In panel (a) of Figure 22-6, we assume that the economy is in short-run equilibrium at point A, where the aggregate demand curve (AD_1) intersects the short-run aggre-

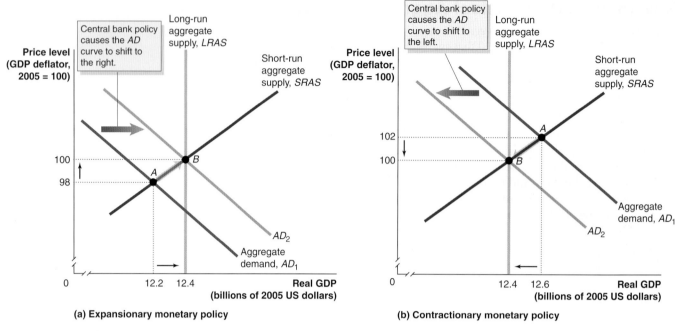

Figure 22-6 | Monetary Policy

In panel (a), the economy begins in recession at point *A*, with real GDP of US$12.2billion and a price level of 98. An expansionary monetary policy causes aggregate demand to shift to the right, from *AD*₁ to *AD*₂, increasing real GDP from US$12.2 billion to US$ 12.4 billion and the price level from 98 to 100 (point *B*). With real GDP back at its potential level, the central bank can meet its goal of high employment. In panel (b), the economy begins at point *A*, with real GDP at US$12.6

billion and the price level at 102. Because real GDP is greater than potential GDP, the economy experiences rising wages and prices. A contractionary monetary policy causes aggregate demand to shift to the left, from *AD*₁ to *AD*₂, decreasing real GDP from US$12.6 billion to US$12.4 billion and the price level from 102 to 100 (point *B*). With real GDP back at its potential level, the central bank can meet its goal of price stability.

Expansionary monetary policy The Central Bank's increasing the money supply and decreasing interest rates to increase real GDP.

Contractionary monetary policy The Central Bank's adjusting the money supply to increase interest rates to reduce inflation.

gate supply curve (*SRAS*). Real GDP is below potential real GDP, as shown by the *LRAS* curve, so the economy is in recession, with some firms operating below normal capacity and some workers having been laid off. To reach its goal of high employment, the central bank needs to carry out an **expansionary monetary policy** by increasing the money supply and decreasing interest rates. Lower interest rates cause an increase in consumption, investment, and net exports, which shifts the aggregate demand curve to the right, from *AD*₁ to *AD*₂. Real GDP increases from US$12.2 billion to potential GDP of US$12.4 billion, and the price level rises from 98 to 100 (point *B*). The policy successfully returns real GDP to its potential level. Rising production leads to increasing employment, allowing the central bank to achieve its goal of high employment.

In panel (b) of Figure 22-6, the economy is in short-run equilibrium at point *A*, with real GDP of US$12.6 billion, which is above potential real GDP of US$12.4 billion. With some firms producing beyond their normal capacity and the unemployment rate very low, wages and prices are increasing. To reach its goal of price stability, the central bank needs to carry out a **contractionary monetary policy** by decreasing the money supply and increasing rates. Higher interest rates cause a decrease in consumption, investment, and net exports, which shifts the aggregate demand curve from *AD*₁ to *AD*₂. Real GDP decreases from US$12.6 billion to US$12.4 billion, and the price level falls from 102 to 100 (point *B*). Why would the central bank want to intentionally cause real GDP to decline? Because in the long run, real GDP cannot continue to remain above potential GDP. Attempting to keep real GDP above potential GDP would result in rising inflation. As aggregate demand declines and real GDP returns to its potential level, upward pressure on wages and prices will be reduced, allowing the central bank to achieve its goal of price stability.

We can conclude that the central bank can use monetary policy to affect the price level and, in the short run, the level of real GDP, allowing it to attain its two most important policy goals: high employment and price stability.

The Effects of Monetary Policy on Real GDP and the Price Level: A More Complete Account

The overview of monetary policy we just finished contains a key idea: the central bank can use monetary policy to affect aggregate demand, thereby changing the price level and the level of real GDP. The account is simplified, however, because it ignores two important facts about the economy: (1) the economy experiences continuing inflation, with the price level rising every year, and (2) the economy experiences long-run growth, with the LRAS curve shifting to the right every year. In Chapter 20, we developed a *dynamic aggregate demand and aggregate supply model* that took these two facts into account. In this section, we use the dynamic model to gain a more complete understanding of monetary policy. Let's briefly review the dynamic model: Recall from Chapter 20 that over time, the labor force and capital stock will increase. Technological change will also occur. The result will be an increase in potential real GDP, which we show by the long-run aggregate supply curve shifting to the right. These factors will also result in firms supplying more goods and services at any given price level in the short run, which we show by the short-run aggregate supply curve shifting to the right. During most years, the aggregate demand curve will also shift to the right, indicating that aggregate expenditure will be higher at every price level. There are several reasons aggregate expenditure usually increases: as population grows and incomes rise, consumption will increase over time. Also, as the economy grows, firms expand capacity, and new firms are established, increasing investment spending. Finally, an expanding population and an expanding economy require increased government services, such as more police officers and teachers, so government purchases will expand.

During certain periods, however, AD does not increase enough during the year to keep the economy at potential GDP. This slow growth in aggregate demand may be due to households and firms becoming pessimistic about the future state of the economy, leading them to cut back their spending on consumer durables, houses, and factories. Other possibilities exist, as well: the government might decide to balance the budget by cutting back its purchases, or recessions in other countries might cause a decline in a country's exports. In Figure 22-7 on the next page, in the first year, the economy is in equilibrium, at potential real GDP of US$12.0 billion and a price level of 100 (point A). In the second year, LRAS increases to US$12.4 billion, but AD increases only to $AD_{2(\text{without policy})}$, which is not enough to keep the economy in macroeconomic equilibrium at potential GDP. If the central bank does not intervene, the short-run equilibrium will occur at US$12.3 billion (point B). The US$100 million gap between this level of real GDP and potential real GDP at $LRAS_2$ means that some firms are operating at less than their normal capacity. Incomes and profits will fall, firms will begin to lay off workers, and the unemployment rate will rise.

The economists at the central bank closely monitor the economy and continually update forecasts of future levels of real GDP and prices. When these economists anticipate that aggregate demand is not growing fast enough to allow the economy to remain at full employment, they decide whether circumstances require a change in monetary policy. For example, suppose that the central bank meets and considers a forecast from the staff indicating that during the following year a gap of US$100 million will open between equilibrium real GDP and potential real GDP. In other words, the situation shown in Figure 22-7 will occur. The central bank may then decide to carry out an expansionary monetary policy to lower interest rates to stimulate aggregate demand. The figure shows the results of a successful attempt to do this: AD has shifted to the right, and equilibrium occurs at potential GDP (point C). The central bank will have successfully headed off the falling incomes and rising unemployment that otherwise would have occurred.

Notice that in Figure 22-7, the expansionary monetary policy caused the inflation rate to be higher than it would have been. Without the expansionary policy, the price level would have risen from 100 to 102, so the inflation rate for the year would have been 2 percent. By shifting the aggregate demand curve, the expansionary policy caused the price level to increase from 102 to 103, raising the inflation rate from 2 percent to 3 percent.

Figure 22-7

An Expansionary Monetary Policy

The economy begins in equilibrium at point A, with real GDP of US$12.0 billion and a price level of 100. Without monetary policy, aggregate demand will shift from AD_1 to $AD_{2(without\ policy)}$, which is not enough to keep the economy at full employment because long-run aggregate supply has shifted from $LRAS_1$ to $LRAS_2$. The economy will be in short-run equilibrium at point B, with real GDP of US$12.3 billion and a price level of 102. By lowering interest rates, the central bank increases investment, consumption, and net exports sufficiently to shift aggregate demand to $AD_{2(with\ policy)}$. The economy will be in equilibrium at point C, with real GDP of US$12.4 billion, which is its full employment level, and a price level of 103. The price level is higher than it would have been if the central bank had not acted to increase spending in the economy.

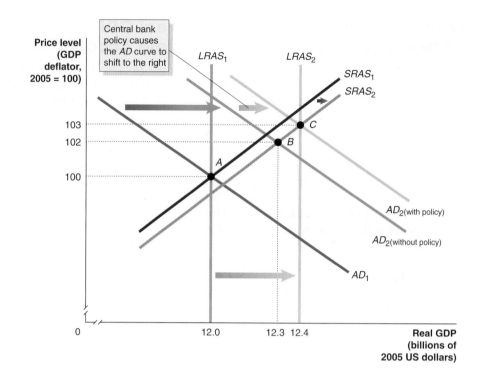

Can the Central Bank Eliminate Recessions?

Figure 22-7 shows an expansionary monetary policy that performs so well that no recession actually takes place. The central bank manages to shift the AD curve to keep the economy continually at potential GDP. In fact, however, this ideal is very difficult for the central bank to achieve. Keeping recessions shorter and milder than they would otherwise be is usually the best the central bank can do. In fact, the central bank has no realistic hope of 'fine-tuning' the economy to eliminate the business cycle and achieve absolute price stability.

Using Monetary Policy to Fight Inflation

In addition to using monetary policy to reduce the severity of recessions, the central bank can also use a contractionary monetary policy to keep aggregate demand from expanding so rapidly that the inflation rate begins to increase. Figure 22-8 shows a hypothetical situation during 2005 and 2006 where the central bank faces this possibility. Suppose that the economy was at equilibrium beyond potential GDP, although the inflation rate for the entire year was only about 1.5 percent. Months later, the central bank announces its worries that aggregate demand was increasing so rapidly, exceeding the growth in potential supply, that the inflation rate would begin to accelerate. The central bank decides to assess available information on the possible need for monetary policy adjustment to contain inflationary pressures.

At its next meeting, the central bank decides to take action by raising the target for the Central Bank's funds rate. The decision is intended to help aligning the growth of aggregate demand with the expansion of aggregate supply in an effort to combat inflationary pressures in the economy. Figure 22-8 shows that without the central bank's actions to increase interest rates, aggregate demand would have shifted farther to the right, and equilibrium would have occurred at a level of real GDP that was even further beyond the potential level. The price level would have risen to 102.0. Because the central bank kept aggregate demand from increasing as much as it otherwise would have, equilibrium occurred closer to potential real GDP, and the price level rose to only 100.0. Notice the central bank was unable to fine-tune the economy: real GDP was still above its potential level.

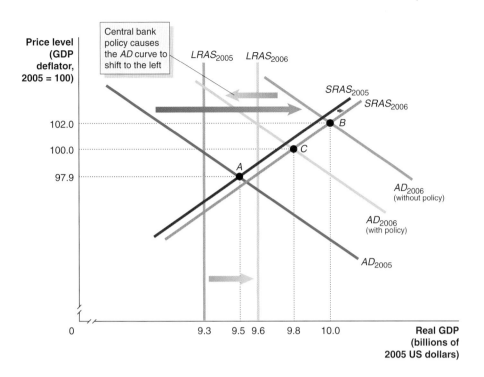

Figure 22-8

A Contractionary Monetary Policy in 2006

The economy began 2005 in equilibrium at point A, with real GDP of US$9.5 billion and a price level of 97.9. From 2005 to 2006, potential real GDP increased from US$9.3 billion to US$9.6 billion, as long-run aggregate supply increased from $LRAS_{2005}$ to $LRAS_{2006}$. The central bank raised interest rates because it believed aggregate demand was increasing too rapidly. Without the increase in interest rates, aggregate demand would have shifted from AD_{2005} to $AD_{2006\ (without\ policy)}$, and the new short-run equilibrium would have occurred at point B. Real GDP would have been US$10.0 billion—US$200 billion higher than it actually was—and the price level would have been 102.0. The increase in interest rates resulted in aggregate demand increasing only to $AD_{2006\ (with\ policy)}$. Equilibrium occurred at point C, with real GDP of US$9.8 billion and the price level rising only to 100.0

Solved Problem | 22-3

The Effects of Monetary Policy

The hypothetical information in the following table shows what the values for real GDP and the price level will be in 2015 if the central bank does *not* use monetary policy.

YEAR	POTENTIAL REAL GDP IN US$	REAL GDP IN US$	PRICE LEVEL IN US$
2014	13.3 billion	13.3 billion	140
2015	13.7 billion	13.6 billion	142

a. If the central bank wants to keep real GDP at its potential level in 2015, should it use an expansionary policy or a contractionary policy? Should the trading desk buy Treasury bills or sell them?

b. Suppose the central bank's policy is successful in keeping real GDP at its potential level in 2015. State whether each of the following will be higher or lower than if the central bank had taken no action:

i. Real GDP

ii. Potential real GDP

iii. The inflation rate

iv. The unemployment rate

c. Draw an aggregate demand and aggregate supply graph to illustrate your answer. Be sure that your graph contains *LRAS* curves for 2014 and 2015; *SRAS* curves for 2014 and 2015; *AD* curve for 2014 and 2015, with and without monetary policy action; and equilibrium real GDP and the price level in 2015, with and without policy.

SOLVING THE PROBLEM:

Step 1: **Review the chapter material.** This problem is about the effects of monetary policy on real GDP and the price level, so you may want to review the section "The Effects of Monetary Policy on Real GDP and the Price Level: A More Complete Account," which begins on page 741.

Step 2: **Answer question (a) by explaining how the central bank can keep real GDP at its potential level.** The information in the table tells us that without monetary policy, the economy will be below potential real GDP in 2015. To keep real GDP at its potential level, the central bank must undertake an expansionary policy. To implement an expansionary policy, the trading desk needs to buy Treasury bills. Buying Treasury bills will increase reserves in the banking system. Banks will increase their loans, which will increase the money supply and lower the interest rate.

Step 3: **Answer question (b) by explaining the effect of the central bank's policy.** If the central bank's policy is successful, real GDP in 2015 will increase from the level given in the table of US$13.3 billion to its potential level of US$13.7 billion. Potential real GDP is not affected by monetary policy, so its value will not change. Because the level of real GDP will be higher, the unemployment rate will be lower than it would have been without policy. The expansionary monetary policy shifts the *AD* curve to the right, so short-run equilibrium will move up the short-run aggregate supply curve (*SRAS*), and the price level will be higher.

Step 4: **Answer question (c) by drawing the graph.** Your graph should look similar to Figure 22-7.

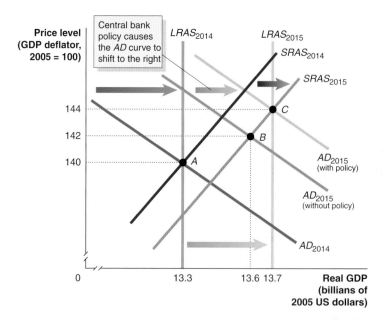

The economy starts in equilibrium in 2014 at point *A*, with the *AD* and *SRAS* curves intersecting along the *LRAS* curve. Real GDP is at its potential level of US$13.3 billion, and the price level is 140. Without monetary policy, the *AD* curve shifts to $AD_{2015(\text{without policy})}$, and the economy is in short-run equilibrium at point *B*. Because potential real GDP has increased from US$13.3 billion to US$13.7 billion, short-run equilibrium real GDP of US$13.6 billion is below the potential level. The price level has increased from 140 to 142. With policy, the *AD* curve shifts to $AD_{2015(\text{with policy})}$, and the economy is in equilibrium at point *C*. Real GDP is at its potential level of US$13.7 billion. We don't have enough information to be sure of the new equilibrium price level. We do know that it will be higher than 142. The graph shows the price level rising to 144. Therefore, without policy, the inflation rate in 2015 would have been about 1.4 percent. With policy, it will be about 2.9 percent.

EXTRA CREDIT: It's important to bear in mind that in reality, the central bank is unable to use monetary policy to keep real GDP exactly at its potential level, as this problem suggests. In a later section, we will discuss some of the difficulties the central bank encounters in conducting monetary policy.

YOUR TURN: For more practice, do related problems 3.10 and 3.11 on pages 758 and 759 at the end of this chapter.

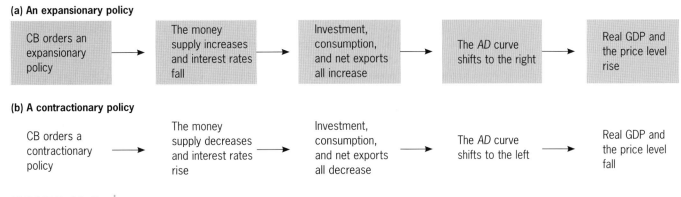

(a) An expansionary policy

CB orders an expansionary policy → The money supply increases and interest rates fall → Investment, consumption, and net exports all increase → The *AD* curve shifts to the right → Real GDP and the price level rise

(b) A contractionary policy

CB orders a contractionary policy → The money supply decreases and interest rates rise → Investment, consumption, and net exports all decrease → The *AD* curve shifts to the left → Real GDP and the price level fall

FIGURE 22-9 | Expansionary and Contractionary Monetary Policies

A Summary of How Monetary Policy Works

Figure 22-9 compares the steps involved in expansionary and contractionary monetary policies. We need to add a very important qualification to this summary. At every point, we should add the phrase "relative to what would have happened without the policy." Figure 22-9 is isolating the impact of monetary policy, *holding constant all other factors affecting the variables involved*. In other words, we are invoking the *ceteris paribus condition*, discussed in Chapter 3. This point is important because, for example, a contractionary monetary policy does not cause the price level to fall. As Figure 22-8 on page 743 shows, a contractionary monetary policy causes the price level *to rise by less than it would have without the policy*. One final note on terminology: an expansionary monetary policy is sometimes referred to as a *loose* or an *easy* policy. A contractionary monetary policy is sometimes referred to as a *tight* policy.

Making the Connection

Why Does *Khaleej Times* Care about Monetary Policy?

You have probably seen newspaper headlines similar to these:

"Appreciating Central Bank's move"
"UAE Central Bank issues new system for bank loans"
"Central Bank tightens lending rules"

Newspapers report stock traders' predictions of possible central bank actions and whether those actions will cause stock prices to increase or decrease. Some stock markets analysts are known as *Central Bank watchers* because they study the central bank and attempt to forecast future changes in the target for the Central Bank's funds rate. Why do changes in the Central Bank's funds rate affect the stock market? There are two main explanations. In thinking about both explanations, remember that changes in the Central Bank's funds rate usually cause changes in other interest rates.

The first reason that stock prices react to the central bank raising or lowering interest rates is because changes in interest rates affect the economy. As we have seen, lower interest rates usually result in increases in real GDP. Fundamentally, the value of a share of stock depends on the profitability of the firm that issued the stock. When real GDP is increasing, the profitability of many firms is also increasing. Stock prices tend to rise when investors expect that the central bank will be lowering interest rates to stimulate the economy. When investors expect that the central bank will be raising interest rates to slow down an economy at risk of rising inflation, stock prices tend to fall.

The stock market reacts when the Central Bank raises or lowers interest rates.

(Continued)

The second reason that stock prices react to changes in interest rates is that changes in interest rates make it more or less attractive for people to invest in stock rather than in other financial assets. Investors look for the highest return possible on their investments, holding constant the risk level of the investments. If the interest rates on Treasury bills, bank certificates of deposit, and corporate bonds are all low, an investment in stocks will be more attractive. When interest rates are high, an investment in stocks will be less attractive.

Can the Central Bank Get the Timing Right?

The central bank's ability to quickly recognize the need for a change in monetary policy is a key to its success. If the central bank is late in recognizing that a recession has begun or that the inflation rate is increasing, it may not be able to implement a new policy soon enough to do much good. In fact, if the central bank implements a policy too late, it may actually destabilize the economy. To see how this can happen, consider Figure 22-10. The straight line represents the long-run growth trend in real GDP. On average, real GDP grows about 3.5 percent per year. The actual path of real GDP differs from the underlying trend because of the business cycle, which is shown by the curving line. As we saw in Chapter 17, the actual business cycle is more irregular than the stylized cycle shown here.

Suppose that a recession begins in August 2014. Because it takes months for economic statistics to be gathered by a government's statistical department, and the central bank itself, there is often a *lag*, or delay, before the central bank recognizes that a recession has begun. Then it takes time for the central bank's economists to analyze the data. Finally, say in June 2015, the central bank concludes that the economy is in recession and begins an expansionary monetary policy. As it turns out, June 2015 is actually the trough of the recession, meaning that the recession has already ended, and an expansion has begun. In these circumstances, the central bank's expansionary policy is not needed to end the recession. The increase in aggregate demand caused by the central bank's lowering interest rates is likely to push the economy beyond potential real GDP and cause a significant acceleration in inflation. Real GDP ends up following the path indicated by the curving blue line. The central bank has inadvertently engaged in a *procyclical policy*, which increases the severity of the business cycle, as opposed to a *countercyclical policy*, which is

Figure 22-10

The Effect of a Poorly Timed Monetary Policy on the Economy

The upward-sloping straight line represents the long-run growth trend in real GDP. The red curving line represents the path real GDP takes because of the business cycle. If the central bank implements a change in monetary policy too late, real GDP will follow the blue curving line. The central bank's expansionary monetary policy results in too great an increase in aggregate demand during the next expansion, which causes an increase in the inflation rate.

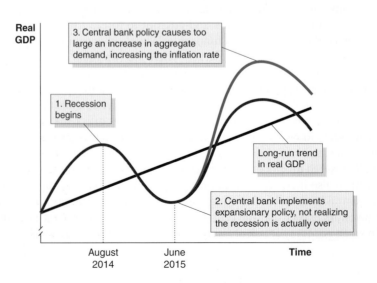

meant to reduce the severity of the business cycle, and which is what the central bank intends to use.

It is not unusual for employment or manufacturing production to decline for a month or two in the middle of an expansion. Distinguishing these minor ups and downs from the beginning of a recession is difficult.

Making the Connection

With Monetary Policy, It's the Interest Rates—Not the Money—That Counts

It is tempting to think of monetary policy working like this: if the central bank wants more spending in the economy, it increases the money supply, and people spend more because they now have more money. If the central bank wants less spending in the economy, it decreases the money supply, and people spend less because they now have less money. In fact, that is *not* how monetary policy works. Remember the important difference between money and income: the central bank increases the money supply by buying Treasury bills. The sellers of the Treasury bills have just exchanged one asset— Treasury bills—for another asset—a check from the central bank; the sellers have *not* increased their income. Even though the money supply is now larger, no one's income has increased, so no one's spending should be affected.

It is only when this increase in the money supply results in lower interest rates that spending is affected. When interest rates are lower, households are more likely to buy new homes and automobiles, and businesses are more likely to buy new factories and computers. Lower interest rates also lead to a lower value of local currency, which lowers the prices of exports and raises the prices of imports, thereby increasing net exports. It isn't the increase in the money supply that has brought about this additional spending, *it's the lower interest rates*. To understand how monetary policy works, and to interpret news reports about the central bank's actions, remember that it is the change in interest rates, not the change in the money supply, that is most important.

The Central Bank increases the stock of money or the money supply, which leads to a decline in interest rates, which encourages more spending.

22.4 | Discuss the central bank's setting of monetary policy targets.

22.4 LEARNING OBJECTIVE

A Closer Look at the Central Bank's Setting of Monetary Policy Targets

We have seen that in carrying out monetary policy, the central bank changes its target for the Central Bank's funds rate depending on the state of the economy. Is using the Central Bank's funds rate as a target the best way to conduct monetary policy? If the central bank targets the Central Bank's funds rate, how should it decide what the target level should be? In this section, we consider some important issues concerning the central bank's targeting policy.

Should the Central Bank Target the Money Supply?

Some economists have argued that rather than use an interest rate as its monetary policy target, the central bank should use the money supply. Many of the economists who make this argument belong to a school of thought known as *monetarism*. The leader of the monetarist school was Nobel laureate Milton Friedman, who was critical of the central bank's ability to correctly time changes in monetary policy.

Friedman and his followers favored replacing *monetary policy* with a *monetary growth rule*. Ordinarily, we expect monetary policy to respond to changing economic conditions: when the economy is in recession, the central bank reduces interest rates, and when inflation is increasing, the central bank raises interest rates. A monetary growth rule, in contrast, is a plan for increasing the money supply at a constant rate that does not change in response to economic conditions. Friedman and his followers proposed a monetary growth rule of increasing the money supply every year at a rate equal to the long-run growth rate of real GDP, which varies from one country to another. If the central bank adopted this monetary growth rule, it would stick to it through changing economic conditions.

But what happens under a monetary growth rule if the economy moves into recession? Shouldn't the central bank abandon the rule to drive down interest rates? Friedman argued that the central bank should stick to the rule even during recessions because, he believed, active monetary policy destabilizes the economy, increasing the number of recessions and their severity. By keeping the money supply growing at a constant rate, Friedman argued, the central bank would greatly increase economic stability.

Why Doesn't the Central Bank Target Both the Money Supply and the Interest Rate?

Most economists believe that an interest rate is the best monetary policy target, but, as we have just seen, other economists believe the central bank should target the money supply. Why doesn't the central bank satisfy both groups by targeting both the money supply and an interest rate? The simple answer to this question is that the central bank can't target both at the same time. To see why, look at Figure 22-11, which shows the money market.

Remember that the central bank controls the money supply, but it does not control money demand. Money demand is determined by decisions of households and firms as they weigh the trade-off between the convenience of money and its low interest rate compared with other financial assets. Suppose the central bank is targeting the interest rate and decides, given conditions in the economy, that the interest rate should be 5 percent. Or, suppose the central bank is targeting the money supply and decides that the money

Figure 22-11

The Central Bank Can't Target Both the Money Supply and the Interest Rate

The central bank is forced to choose between using either an interest rate or the money supply as its monetary policy target. In this figure, the central bank can set a target of a money supply of US$900 billion or a target of an interest rate of 5 percent, but it can't have both because only combinations of the interest rate and the money supply that represent equilibrium in the money market are possible.

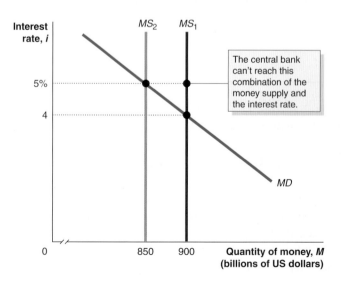

supply should be US$900 billion. Figure 22-10 shows that the central bank can bring about an interest rate of 5 percent, or a money supply of US$900 billion, but it can't bring about both. The point representing an interest rate of 5 percent and a money supply of US$900 billion is not on the money demand curve, so it can't represent an equilibrium in the money market. Only combinations of the interest rate and the money supply that represent equilibrium in the money market are possible. The central bank has to choose between targeting an interest rate and targeting the money supply.

The central bank is forced to choose between using either an interest rate or the money supply as its monetary policy target. In this figure, the central bank can set a target of a money supply of US$900 billion or a target of an interest rate of 5 percent, but it can't have both because only combinations of the interest rate and the money supply that represent equilibrium in the money market are possible.

The Taylor Rule

How does the central bank choose a target for the central bank's funds rate? The discussions at the meetings of the central bank can be complex, and they take into account many economic variables. John Taylor of Stanford University in the U.S. has analyzed the factors involved in central bank decision making and developed the **Taylor rule** to explain Central Bank's funds rate targeting. The Taylor rule begins with an estimate of the value of the equilibrium real Central Bank's funds rate, which is the Central Bank's funds rate—adjusted for inflation—that would be consistent with real GDP being equal to potential real GDP in the long run. According to the Taylor rule, the central bank should set the target for the Central Bank's funds rate so that it is equal to the sum of the inflation rate, the equilibrium real Central Bank's funds rate, and two additional terms. The first of these additional terms is the *inflation gap*—the difference between current inflation and a target rate; the second is the *output gap*—the percentage difference between real GDP and potential real GDP. The inflation gap and output gap are each given 'weights' that reflect their influence on the Central Bank's funds target rate. With weights of 1/2 for both gaps, we have the following Taylor rule:

Taylor rule A rule developed by John Taylor that links the Central Bank's target for the Central Bank's funds rate to economic variables.

Central Bank's funds target rate = Current inflation rate +
Real equilibrium Central Bank's funds rate + (1/2) × Inflation gap + (1/2) × Output gap

The Taylor rule includes expressions for the inflation gap and the output gap because the central bank is concerned about both inflation and fluctuations in real GDP. Taylor demonstrated that if the equilibrium real Central Bank's funds rate is 2 percent and the target rate of inflation is 2 percent, the preceding expression does a good job of explaining changes in the central bank's target for the Central Bank's funds rate. Consider an example in which the current inflation rate is 1 percent, and real GDP is 1 percent below potential real GDP. In that case, the inflation gap is 1 percent − 2 percent = −1 percent, and the output gap is also −1 percent. Inserting these values in the Taylor rule, we can calculate the predicted value for the Central Bank's funds target rate:

Central Bank's funds target rate = 1% + 2% + ((1/2 × −1%)) + ((1/2) × −1%) = 2%

Although the Taylor rule does not account for changes in the target inflation rate or the equilibrium interest rate, many economists view the rule as a convenient way to analyze the Central Bank's funds target.

Should the Central Bank Target Inflation?

Over the past decade, many economists and central bankers, including the current U.S. Federal Reserve's chairman, Ben Bernanke, have proposed using *inflation targeting* as a framework for carrying out monetary policy. With **inflation targeting**, the central bank commits to conducting policy to achieve a publicly announced inflation target of, for example, 2 percent. Inflation targeting need not impose an inflexible rule on the central bank. The central bank would still be free, for example, to take action in case

Inflation targeting Conducting monetary policy so as to commit the Central Bank to achieving a publicly announced level of inflation.

of a severe recession. Nevertheless, monetary policy goals and operations would focus on inflation and inflation forecasts. Inflation targeting has been adopted by the Central Banks of New Zealand (1989), Canada (1991), the United Kingdom (1992), Finland (1993), Sweden (1993), and Spain (1994), and by the European Central Bank. Inflation targeting has also been used in some newly industrializing countries, such as Chile, South Korea, Mexico, and South Africa, as well as in some transition economies in Eastern Europe, such as the Czech Republic, Hungary, and Poland. In the Arab world, inflation targeting has not been implemented yet, since it requires the independence of central banks from the government. This basic condition is not yet fulfilled in any Arab country since central banks, despite having some independence in some cases such as Egypt, are still very tied to government financing decisions and governments' control. Experience with inflation targeting has varied, but typically, the move to inflation targeting has been accompanied by lower inflation (sometimes at the cost of temporarily higher unemployment).

Should the central bank adopt an inflation target? Arguments in favor of inflation targeting focus on four points. First, as we have already discussed, in the long run, real GDP returns to its potential level, and potential real GDP is not affected by monetary policy. Therefore, in the long run, the central bank can have an impact on inflation but not on real GDP. Having an explicit inflation target would draw the public's attention to this fact. Second, by announcing an inflation target, the central bank would make it easier for households and firms to form accurate expectations of future inflation, improving their planning and the efficiency of the economy. Finally, an inflation target would promote accountability for the central bank by providing a yardstick against which its performance could be measured.

Inflation targeting also has opponents, who typically raise three points. First, having a numerical target for inflation reduces the flexibility of monetary policy to address other policy goals. Second, inflation targeting assumes that the central bank can accurately forecast future inflation rates, which is not always the case. Finally, holding the central bank accountable only for an inflation goal may make it less likely that the central bank will achieve other important policy goals.

In the wake of the recession in 2007–2009, in 2010, for example, we saw low inflation and a beginning of some economic expansion. In recent years, the central bank has acted to head off the threat of future inflation before it can become established. Even without a formal inflation target, the central bank has been successful at building public support for the idea that low inflation is important to the efficient performance of the economy. The central bank's strategy is not without risk, however. The central bank's prestige during the past two decades has been dependent on public trust in the effectiveness of central bank leadership in containing inflation while maintaining economic growth. But the central bank's leadership changes over time, which highlights what may be a need for more formal procedures to reassure both the public and elected officials about the continuity of policy.

Making the Connection | How Does the Central Bank Measure Inflation?

When the central bank puts increased emphasis on the goal of price stability, it has therefore to consider carefully the best way to measure the inflation rate. As we saw in Chapter 16, the consumer price index (CPI) is the most widely used measure of inflation. But we also saw that the CPI suffers from biases that cause it to overstate the true underlying rate of inflation. An alternative measure of changes in consumer prices can be constructed from the data gathered to calculate GDP. We saw in Chapter 15 that the GDP deflator is a broad measure of the price level that includes the price of every good or service that is in GDP. Changes in the GDP deflator are not a good measure of inflation experienced by the typical consumer, worker, or firm, however, because the deflator include prices of goods, such as industrial equipment, that are not widely purchased. In Arab oil-producing countries, the GDP deflator would be a misleading measure for inflation since it will mostly reflect the changes in oil prices; the major export of these countries. On the other hand, the GDP deflator does not reflect the prices of imports since it is a measure of the prices of domestically produced goods and services. In Arab oil-producing countries most consumption goods are imported from abroad, and hence their prices do not affect the GDP deflator. Therefore, the latter is a poor measure for the cost of living of a typical consumer in Arab oil-exporters. The following graph shows movements in the CPI and GDP deflator in the UAE from 1980 to 2007. You can see that both measures were clearly rising over years. However, the CPI, which reflects the prices of imported consumption goods, is relatively more stable than the GDP deflator, which reflects movements in the prices of oil.

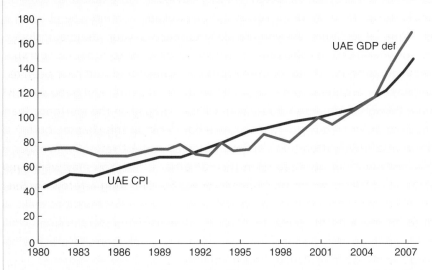

Despite the fact that the CPI is still the most used measure of inflation, in some developed countries, such as the U.S., Central Banks started relying on a concept called the *personal consumption expenditures price index* (PCE). The PCE is a measure of the price level that is similar to the GDP deflator, except it includes only the prices of goods from the consumption category of GDP.

There are at least three advantages that the PCE has over the CPI:

1. The PCE is a so-called chain-type price index, as opposed to the market-basket approach used in constructing the CPI. As we saw earlier, because consumers shift the mix of products they buy each year, the market-basket approach makes the CPI overstate actual inflation. A chain-type price index allows the mix of products to change each year.

2. The PCE includes the prices of more goods and services than the CPI, so it is a broader measure of inflation.

3. Past values of the PCE can be recalculated as better ways of computing price indexes are developed and as new data become available. This allows the central bank to better track historical trends in the inflation rate.

In 2004, the U.S. Federal Reserve announced that it would begin to rely on a subcategory of the PCE: the so-called core PCE, which excludes food and energy

(Continued)

prices. Prices of food and energy tend to fluctuate up and down for reasons that may not be related to the causes of general inflation and that cannot easily be controlled by monetary policy. Oil prices, in particular, have moved dramatically up and down in recent years. Therefore, a price index that includes food and energy prices may not give a clear view of underlying trends in inflation.

YOUR TURN: Test your understanding by doing related problem 4.6 on page 759 at the end of this chapter.

Economics in YOUR Life!

>> **Continued from page 729**

At the beginning of this chapter, we asked whether buying a house during a recession is a good idea. Clearly, there are many considerations to keep in mind when buying a house, which is the largest purchase you are likely to make in your lifetime. Included among these considerations are the price of the house relative to other comparable houses in the neighborhood, whether house prices in the neighborhood have been rising or falling, and the location of the house relative to stores, work, and good schools. Also important, though, is the interest rate you will have to pay on the mortgage loan you would need in order to buy the house. As we have seen in this chapter, during a recession, the central bank often takes actions to lower interest rates. So, mortgage rates are typically lower during a recession than at other times. You may well want to take advantage of these low interest rates to buy a house during a recession. But, recessions are also times of rising unemployment, and you would not want to make a commitment to borrow a lot of money for 15 or more years if you were in significant danger of losing your job. We can conclude, then, that if your job seems secure, buying a house during a recession may actually be a good idea.

Conclusion

Monetary policy is one way governments pursue goals for inflation, employment, and financial stability. The central bank can strongly affect the economy through conducting monetary policy. In the next chapter, we discuss how *fiscal policy*—changes in government spending and taxes—affect the economy.

Read *An Inside Look at Policy* on the next page to see how the slowing down of the housing market in Dubai has affected the rate of inflation in the United Arab Emirates.

Dubai Housing Market Slowdown Affects the Rate of Inflation in the UAE

AMEINFO.COM, JANUARY 27, 2011

Drop in Dubai House Prices Causes Inflation to Fall Dramatically

In the first half of 2008, at the height of an unprecedented construction- and real estate-led economic boom, inflation in the UAE reached a record 13%. According to US investment bank Merrill Lynch, inflation had become a "major problem" for the Gulf state— a conclusion no doubt echoed by the millions of UAE residents facing soaring housing costs and suffering from the dirham's peg to a weak dollar, as well as negative real interest rates.

Merrill estimated the UAE's GDP growth would hit around 7.2% for the full year, underpinned by an oil price which averaged around US$115 a barrel in the first half of the year, and had hit a record high of US$147.27 in July. What's more, 2008 was by no means an unusual year—GDP growth in the UAE had averaged close to 10% over the previous five years.

Fast-forward to early 2011 and those who are still left in the UAE in the wake of the credit crisis and Dubai's tumble from grace, are at least paying less for the privilege. According to government figures, inflation in the UAE eased to 0.9% in 2010, its lowest annual level since the first Gulf War rocked the region in 1990, and down from 1.6% in 2009, the height of the financial crisis.

The real estate sector slump has seen rents drop sharply and excess supply all but flatten property sales. According to the UAE Central Bank, banks in the country provisioned more than US$11.2bn for non-performing loans by end-November 2010, severely denting their lending appetites in the process. And the debt woes of Dubai state-owned firms have added to the uncertain climate: Dubai World has struck a US$25bn debt restructuring deal with creditors, but a heavy debt repayment schedule means the state has significant obligations falling in 2011, when cash flows are expected to remain weak.

"Rents represent almost half of the CPI in the UAE," says Philippe Dauba-Pantanacce, senior economist for the MENA region at Standard Chartered. "As a result, the collapse in the real estate prices in the UAE has mechanically put a substantial downward pressure on the headline inflation figure."

The real estate slump has hit Dubai particularly hard. Once famed for reshaping its coastline to build ambitious mega-projects such as the Palm islands and World archipelagos, the Emirate is now littered with oversupply. According to property consultant Jones Lang LaSalle, around 36,000 new units came onto the Dubai market in 2010, while 25,000 new units are scheduled to come onto the market in 2011.

Inflation in the Emirate slowed to 0.6% in 2010, from 4% in 2009, according to figures from the Dubai Statistics Center. Ongoing weakness in the property sector has accounted for much of this drop: despite significant increases in water and electricity costs in 2010, housing and utilities costs slumped 1.3% in the year, after a 2.4% rise the previous year.

"Housing is obviously a significant component of living costs, but Dubai has seen a significant adjustment in pricing, and that's been of great benefit to tenants," says Craig Plumb, Jones Lang LaSalle's Head of Research for the MENA region.

"Rental prices have fallen consistently, about 50 to 60% from the beginning of 2009, and now there's no question that the market is oversupplied.

The Economist Intelligence Unit forecasts that total inflation across the entire UAE will average 2% between 2011 and 2015, owing largely to an ongoing decline in housing costs. But for once, it is likely the decline in costs will be felt more acutely in UAE capital Abu Dhabi, than its troubled desert neighbor.

"There is more good news ahead for tenants, but you have to talk about Dubai and Abu Dhabi separately, as they are very different markets," says Plumb at Jones Lang LaSalle. "Dubai has always seen the majority of the decline in pricing, but while we will see further falls, it won't be as steep. Abu Dhabi will probably be the opposite: we have seen some falls but the pace of decline is likely to increase in 2011."

At Standard Chartered, however, Dauba-Pantanacce predicts that inflation will rise to an average of 3% in 2011. The disinflationary impact of the real estate sector should be much more moderate this year compared to last year, he warns…

Key Points in the Article

This article discusses how the Dubai real estate sector was hit hard by the financial crisis of 2008. As the housing market became oversupplied in 2009 and 2010, real estate prices declined, driving down the rental value as well. After many years of suffering from high inflation rates that were considered a great concern between 2005 and 2008, Dubai residents now are at least paying less to live in the city. The inflation rate dropped to less than 1 percent in 2010 after hovering at around 13 percent in 2008. The disinflationary impact of the slump in the real estate sector was significant because rents constitute almost half of the CPI basket of goods and services.

Analyzing the News

(a) In 2010, the UAE witnessed its lowest rate of inflation since 1990. The squeeze in credit due to bad loans and the position of weaker banks reduced house purchases; meanwhile, the housing supply increased in 2009 and 2010 to exceed demand. This led to a large decline in rents in the city. As you can see in the figure, before the recession the housing market was at equilibrium at point a. With the downturn and loss of jobs and the credit squeeze, the demand for new houses shifted to D2, pushing housing prices down to P_b at the equilibrium point b. When the market added more unites in the subsequent year, shifting supply to the right, a new equilibrium occurs at point c and prices are further pushed down to P_c.

(b) Housing and rents constitute about 50 percent of the CPI basket, and therefore the inflation rate declined to a historic low rate of less than 1 percent. The sharp decline in rents by about 40 percent to 50 percent and the declining housing costs contributed to much of this sharp reduction in prices.

(c) The average inflation rate is expected to be low, on average, for the whole UAE. However, real estate experts see that the dynamics and developments in the housing market in the next five years are expected to significantly differ between Dubai and the capital, Abu Dhabi. While Dubai saw most of the correction in house values and is about to stabilize, Abu Dhabi is starting an episode of a declining housing market. Experts expect a strong decline in real estate value in Abu Dhabi in 2011.

Thinking Critically About Policy

1. The Central Bank reduced the interest rate in 2010 in order to encourage lending and to revive the housing market. What do you expect happens to inflation and the price level?

2. Oil prices started rising again to exceed US$100 per barrel in February of 2011 due to the uprisings in the Middle East. If oil prices continued rising, how would this affect housing prices in the oil-producing countries? Carefully, explain.

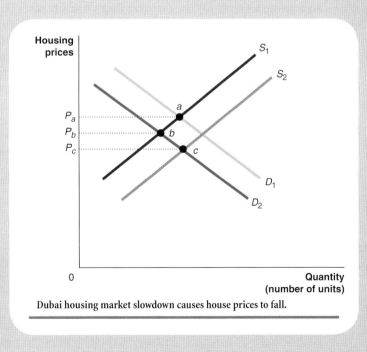

Dubai housing market slowdown causes house prices to fall.

Key Terms

Summary

What Is Monetary Policy?

Monetary policy is the actions the central bank takes to manage the money supply and interest rates to pursue its macroeconomic policy objectives. The central bank has set four *monetary policy goals* that are intended to promote a well-functioning economy: price stability, high employment, economic growth, and stability of financial markets and institutions.

The Money Market and the Central Bank's Choice of Monetary Policy Targets

The central bank's *monetary policy targets* are economic variables that it can affect directly and that in turn affect variables such as real GDP and the price level that are closely related to the central bank's policy goals. The two main monetary policy targets are the money supply and the interest rate. The central bank has most often chosen to use the interest rate as its monetary policy target. The central bank announces a target for the **Central Bank's funds rate**. The Central Bank's funds rate is the interest rate banks charge each other for overnight loans. To fight a recession, the central bank conducts an *expansionary policy* by increasing the money supply. The increase in the money supply lowers the interest rate. To reduce the inflation rate, the central bank conducts a *contractionary monetary policy* by adjusting the money supply to increase the interest rate. In a graphical analysis of the money market, an *expansionary monetary policy* shifts the money supply curve to the right, causing a movement down the money demand curve and a new equilibrium at a lower interest rate. A contractionary policy shifts the money supply curve to the left, causing a movement up the money demand curve and a new equilibrium at a higher interest rate.

Monetary Policy and Economic Activity

An **expansionary monetary policy** lowers interest rates to increase consumption, investment, and net exports. This increased spending causes the aggregate demand curve (*AD*) to shift out more than it otherwise would, raising the level of real GDP and the price level. An expansionary monetary policy can help the central bank achieve its goal of high employment. A **contractionary monetary policy** raises interest rates to decrease consumption, investment, and net exports. This decreased spending causes the aggregate demand curve to shift out less than it otherwise would, reducing both the level of real GDP and the inflation rate below what they would be in the absence of policy. A contractionary monetary policy can help the central bank achieve its goal of price stability.

A Closer Look at the Central Bank's Setting of Monetary Policy Targets

20.4 LEARNING OBJECTIVE

Discuss the central bank's setting of monetary policy targets, **pages 748–753.**

Some economists have argued that the central bank should use the money supply, rather than an interest rate, as its monetary target. Milton Friedman and other monetarists argued that the central bank should adopt a monetary growth rule of increasing the money supply every year at a fixed rate. John Taylor has analyzed the factors involved in central bank decision making and developed the *Taylor rule* for Central Bank's funds rate targeting. The *Taylor rule* links the central bank's target for the Central Bank's funds rate to economic variables. Over the past decade, many economists and central bankers have expressed significant interest in using **inflation targeting**, under which monetary policy is conducted to commit the central bank to achieving a publicly announced inflation target. A number of foreign central banks have adopted inflation targeting.

Review, Problems and Applications

22.1 LEARNING OBJECTIVE Define monetary policy and describe the central bank's monetary policy goals, **pages 730–732.**

Review Questions

1.1 What is the central bank's main responsibility?

1.2 What are the central bank's four monetary policy goals?

Problems and Applications

1.3 Why is price stability one of the central bank's monetary policy goals? What problems can high inflation rates cause for the economy?

1.4 It can be argued that the central bank's objectives of price stability and low long-term interest rates are essentially the same. Briefly explain the reasoning behind this argument.

1.5 Gulf countries stock prices registered a rapid rise in 2007 and then fell rapidly amid the financial crisis in 2008. Housing prices in many parts of the UAE and Qatar also rose rapidly between 2005 and 2007 and then declined in 2009. Some economists have argued that rapid increases and decreases in the prices of assets such as shares of stock or houses can damage the economy. Currently, stabilizing asset prices is not one of the central bank's policy goals. In what ways would a goal of stabilizing asset prices be different from the four goals listed on page 730? Do you believe that stabilizing asset prices should be added to the list of the central bank's policy goals? Briefly explain.

22.2 LEARNING OBJECTIVE Describe the central bank's monetary policy targets and explain how expansionary and contractionary monetary policies affect the interest rate, **pages 732–738.**

Review Questions

2.1 What is a monetary policy target? Why does the central bank use policy targets?

2.2 Draw a demand and supply graph showing equilibrium in the money market. Suppose the central bank wants to lower the equilibrium interest rate. Show on the graph how the central bank would accomplish this objective.

2.3 Explain the effect an open market purchase has on the equilibrium interest rate.

2.4 What is the Central Bank's funds rate? What role does it play in monetary policy?

Problems and Applications

2.5 A 'basis point' is one one-hundredth of a percentage point. If an interest rate increases by 50 basis points, it has gone up by one-half of a percentage point. 'Monetary aggregates' are measures of the money supply, such as M1 and M2. Arab Gulf countries lowered interest rates in December of 2008 after the U.S. Federal Reserve slashed its target level for the overnight Central Bank funds rate by 475 basis points, to 1.75 percent. Also during the year, money supply increased in both the U.S. and the Arab states.

a. If the target for the U.S. rate was reduced by 475 basis points, to 1.75 percent, what was its original level?

b. Is there a connection between the Central Bank funds rate falling and the money supply increasing? Briefly explain.

2.6 **(Related to *Solved Problem 22-2* on page 736)** Suppose the interest rate is 2 percent on a Treasury bill that will pay its owner US$1,000 when it matures in one year.

a. What is the price of the Treasury bill?

b. Suppose that the central bank engages in open market sales resulting in the interest rate on one-year Treasury bills rising to 3 percent. What will the price of these bills be now?

2.7 In this chapter, we depict the money supply curve as a vertical line. Is there any reason to believe the money supply curve might actually be upward sloping? (*Hint:* Think about the role of banks in the process of creating the money supply.) Draw a money demand and money supply graph with an upward-sloping money supply curve. Suppose that households and firms decide they want to hold more money at every interest rate. Show the result on your graph. What is the impact on the size of M1? How does this differ from the impact if the money supply curve were a vertical line?

2.8 If the central bank purchases US$100 million worth of Treasury bills from the public, predict what will happen to the money supply. Explain your reasoning.

22.3 LEARNING OBJECTIVE   Use aggregate demand and aggregate supply graphs to show the effects of monetary policy on real GDP and the price level, **pages 738–747.**

Review Questions

3.1 How does an increase in interest rates affect aggregate demand? Briefly discuss how each component of aggregate demand is affected.

3.2 If the central bank believes the economy is about to fall into recession, what actions should it take? If the central bank believes the inflation rate is about to increase, what actions should it take?

Problems and Applications

3.3 Companies usually invest when the central bank sets interest rates low. Explain the connection between the monetary policy pursued by the central bank and the companies' investment behavior.

3.4 How can central bank policies explain the strength of a housing market during a recession?

3.5 In 2010, some economists were worried that the U.S. and the global economy might make only a slow recovery from the 2008/2009 recession. Given the uncertainty about consumer demand and the overall health of an economy, the main force that could hinder the recovery is firms' expectations that the rates of return on new investments are too low. Explain how such perception would make monetary policy less effective in ending a recession.

3.6 According to an article in the *New York Times*, an official at the Bank of Japan had the following explanation of why monetary policy was not pulling the country out of recession: "Despite recent major increases in the money supply, he said, the money stays in banks." Explain what the official meant by the phrase "the money stays in banks." Where does the money go if an expansionary monetary policy is successful?

Source: James Brooke, "Critics Say Koizumi's Economic Medicine Is a Weak Tea," *New York Times*, February 27, 2002.

3.7 What is the term for a falling price level? Why would a country's central bank be reluctant to raise its target for short-term interest rates if the price level is falling? And why would the central bank consider a falling price level to be undesirable?

3.8 If the central bank is wary of inflation, why might it be reluctant to lower the target for the Central Bank funds rate?

3.9 If a country's central bank targets the inflation rate, why would it be increasing interest rates?

3.10 **(Related to *Solved Problem 22-3* on page 743)** Use the following graph to answer the questions.

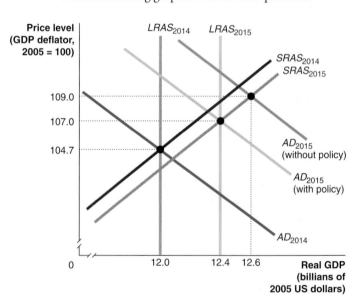

a. If the central bank does not take any policy action, what will be the level of real GDP and the price level in 2015?

b. If the central bank wants to keep real GDP at its potential level in 2015, should it use an expansionary policy or a contractionary policy? Should the trading desk be buying Treasury bills or selling them?

c. If the central bank takes no policy action, what will be the inflation rate in 2015? If the central bank uses monetary policy to keep real GDP at its full-employment level, what will be the inflation rate in 2015?

3.11 (Related to *Solved Problem 22-3* on page 743) The hypothetical information in the following table shows what the situation will be in 2015 if the central bank does *not* use monetary policy:

YEAR	POTENTIAL REAL GDP IN US$	REAL GDP IN US$	PRICE LEVEL IN US$
2014	12.8 billion	12.8 billion	140
2015	13.3 billion	13.4 billion	147

a. If the central bank wants to keep real GDP at its potential level in 2015, should it use an expansionary policy or a contractionary policy? Should the trading desk be buying T-bills or selling them?

b. If the central bank's policy is successful in keeping real GDP at its potential level in 2015, state whether each of the following will be higher, lower, or the same as it would have been if the central bank had taken no action:
   i. Real GDP
   ii. Potential real GDP
   iii. The inflation rate
   iv. The unemployment rate

3.12 Briefly explain whether you agree or disagree with the following statement: "The Central Bank has an easy job. Say it wants to increase real GDP by US$200 billion. All it has to do is increase the money supply by that amount."

3.13 Why would some lending banks be willing to grant mortgages to borrowers who are believed to have high credit risk? Why might many borrowers be particularly willing to take on mortgage debt, even if their credit was not very good? What risks to the economy might this type of lending involve?

3.14 Why would stock prices increase if investors believed that the central bank will not be raising interest rates and may even be cutting them?

22.4 LEARNING OBJECTIVE Discuss the central bank's setting of monetary policy targets, **pages 748–753.**

Review Questions

4.1 What is a monetary rule, as opposed to a monetary policy? What monetary rule would Milton Friedman have liked central banks to follow?

4.2 Central banks sometimes use the Central Bank's funds rate as its monetary policy target. Why don't they target the money supply at the same time?

Problems and Applications

4.3 Suppose that the equilibrium real Central Bank's funds rate is 2 percent, and the target rate of inflation is 2 percent. Use the following information and the Taylor rule to calculate the Central Bank's funds rate target:

Current inflation rate = 4 percent
Potential real GDP = US$14.0 billion
Real GDP = US$14.14 billion

4.4 Why is keeping interest rates unusually low an indication that a country's central bank is more concerned about economic growth than inflation?

4.5 This chapter states, "Experience with inflation targeting has varied, but typically, the move to inflation targeting has been accompanied by lower inflation (sometimes at the cost of temporarily higher unemployment)." Why might a move to inflation targeting temporarily increase the unemployment rate?

4.6 (Related to the *Making the Connection* on page 750) If the core PCE is a better measure of the inflation rate than is the CPI, why is the CPI more widely used? In particular, can you think of reasons why central banks use the CPI when deciding how much to increase social security payments to retired workers to keep the purchasing power of the payments from declining?

Chapter 23

Fiscal Policy

Arab Governments to the Rescue

High unemployment rates, economic instability, fewer investment opportunities, and low economic growth rates are typical economic problems facing the Arab countries. How have Arabs reacted to these problems? In general, there are two players in any economy that can play a role in mitigating these problems: the government and the private market. Since private markets in Arab countries are generally weak and unstable, policymakers in Arab governments always find themselves responsible for tackling these economic problems, mainly through the formation of several government expenditure programs and also by adjusting tax laws, i.e. through the use of *fiscal policy* tools.

The 2008 economic crisis could be taken as a good example of how important government intervention is. The crisis resulted in a reduction in both domestic and foreign investment, economic recession (higher unemployment rate), and thus, slower economic growth rates. This was because of the reduction in oil prices (for Arab oil-based economies), or the reduction in capital inflows, exports, and citizens'

remittances (for Arab non-oil-based economies). Although there are disparities between Arab countries, many Arab governments have adopted quite similar policies to lessen the adverse effects of the crisis. The oil-based economies, in GCC countries in particular, have designed comprehensive rescue packages and have devoted considerable resources to support economic activities. For example, the Saudi Arabian government has increased public spending to maintain all current and planned projects in construction, petrochemicals, oil and gas, and water with an estimated fund of US$600 billion. A significant portion of government expenditure in Saudi Arabia has been also directed toward subsidizing the price of basic

goods, increasing public wages, and enhancing education and health services. On the other hand, the government of Morocco (a non-oil-based economy), has adopted economic policy measures (a fiscal stimulus package) to maintain growth rates by increasing public investment by US$16.7 billion, subsidizing citizen purchasing power with a US$5 billion fund, introducing tax cuts to small- and medium-size enterprises, and spending around US$12.8 billion on the education and health sectors. Finally, Egypt, Jordan, Lebanon, and Syria are in a more difficult position after the crisis due to their limited financial resources and prolonged budget deficits. While Lebanon and Syria show almost no signs of increasing public expenditure, Egypt and Jordan reacted to the 2008 economic crisis by applying fiscal stimulus packages. The Egyptian government has approved a fiscal stimulus of around 3 billion dollars. The government also has charged the Social Development Fund to focus more on labor-intensive and small-scale income generating projects for young people. In addition, the Egyptian government exempted certain industries

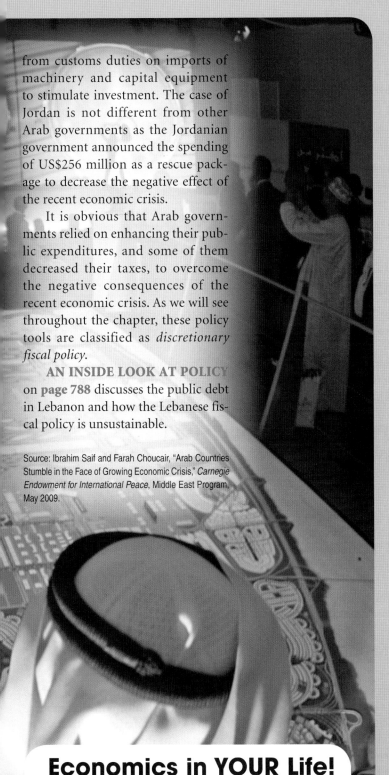

from customs duties on imports of machinery and capital equipment to stimulate investment. The case of Jordan is not different from other Arab governments as the Jordanian government announced the spending of US$256 million as a rescue package to decrease the negative effect of the recent economic crisis.

It is obvious that Arab governments relied on enhancing their public expenditures, and some of them decreased their taxes, to overcome the negative consequences of the recent economic crisis. As we will see throughout the chapter, these policy tools are classified as *discretionary fiscal policy*.

AN INSIDE LOOK AT POLICY on **page 788** discusses the public debt in Lebanon and how the Lebanese fiscal policy is unsustainable.

Source: Ibrahim Saif and Farah Choucair, "Arab Countries Stumble in the Face of Growing Economic Crisis," *Carnegie Endowment for International Peace*, Middle East Program, May 2009.

LEARNING Objectives

After studying this chapter, you should be able to:

23.1 Define **fiscal policy**, page 762.

23.2 Explain how **fiscal policy** affects **aggregate demand** and how the government can use fiscal policy to stabilize the economy, page 764.

23.3 Explain how **government purchases** and **tax multipliers** work, page 768.

23.4 Discuss the **difficulties** that can arise in **implementing fiscal policy**, page 773.

23.5 Define **budget deficit** and **government debt** and explain how the budget can serve as an **automatic stabilizer**, page 777.

23.6 Discuss the effects of **fiscal policy** in the **long run**, page 782.

APPENDIX Apply the **multiplier formula**, page 795.

Economics in YOUR Life!

What Would You Do with US$500?

Suppose that the government announces that it will immediately provide you, and everyone else in the economy, with a US$500 tax cut. In addition, you expect that in future years, your taxes will also be US$500 less than they would otherwise have been. How will you respond to this increase in your disposable income? What effect will this tax cut likely have on equilibrium real GDP in the short run? As you read the chapter, see if you can answer these questions. You can check your answers against those we provide at the end of the chapter. >> **Continued on page 787**

I n Chapter 22, we discussed how the central bank uses monetary policy to pursue macroeconomic policy goals, including price stability and high employment. In this chapter, we will explore how the government uses *fiscal policy*, which involves changes in taxes and government purchases, to achieve similar policy goals. As we have seen, in the short run, the price level and the levels of real GDP and total employment in the economy depend on aggregate demand and short-run aggregate supply. The government can affect the levels of both aggregate demand and aggregate supply through fiscal policy. We will explore how parliament decides which fiscal policy actions to take to achieve their goals. We will also discuss the disagreements among economists and policymakers over the effectiveness of fiscal policy.

23.1 | Define fiscal policy.

Fiscal Policy

As we saw in Chapter 22, central banks closely monitor the economy, and Open Market Committees meet several times per year to decide whether to change monetary policy. Less frequently, parliament also makes changes in taxes and government purchases to achieve macroeconomic policy objectives, such as high employment, price stability, and high rates of economic growth. Changes in taxes and spending that are intended to achieve macroeconomic policy objectives are called **fiscal policy**.

Fiscal policy Changes in taxes and government purchases that are intended to achieve macroeconomic policy objectives, such as high employment, price stability, and high rates of economic growth.

What Fiscal Policy Is and What It Isn't

Economists restrict the term *fiscal policy* to refer only to the actions of the central government. So for countries with a federal system of government, such as the U.S., Canada, and India, state and local governments sometimes change their taxing and spending policies to aid their local economies, but these are not fiscal policy actions because they are not intended to affect the national economy. The central government makes many decisions about taxes and spending, but not all of these decisions are fiscal policy actions because they are not intended to achieve macroeconomic policy goals. For example, a decision to cut the taxes of people who buy hybrid cars is an environmental policy action, not a fiscal policy action. Similarly, the defense and internal security spending increases in the Arab world are part of defense and internal security policy, not fiscal policy.

Automatic Stabilizers versus Discretionary Fiscal Policy

There is an important distinction between *automatic stabilizers* and *discretionary fiscal policy*. Some types of government spending and taxes, which automatically increase and decrease along with the business cycle, are referred to as **automatic stabilizers**. The word *automatic* in this case refers to the fact that changes in these types of spending and taxes happen without actions by the government. For example, when the economy is expanding and employment is increasing, government spending on unemployment insurance payments to workers who have lost their jobs will automatically decrease. During a recession, as employment declines, this type of spending will automatically increase. Similarly, when the economy is expanding and incomes are rising, the amount the government collects in taxes will increase as people pay additional taxes on their higher incomes. When the economy is in recession, the amount the government collects in taxes will fall.

Automatic stabilizers Government spending and taxes that automatically increase or decrease along with the business cycle.

With discretionary fiscal policy, the government is taking actions to change spending or taxes. The personal income tax cut applied by the Egyptian government in 2005 (where the maximum income tax rate for individuals is now 20 percent instead of 40 percent) is an example of a discretionary fiscal policy action.

Figure 23-1

Government Purchases as a Percentage of GDP in the Arab World, 1975–2009

There is a downward trend in the Arab governments' purchases to GDP ratio starting in the early 1990s because of the ongoing tendency in many Arab countries to diversify their economies and give more weight to the private market to contribute to GDP.
Source: World Development Indicators, World Bank.

An Overview of Government Spending and Revenue in the Arab World

To provide a context for understanding fiscal policy, it is important to understand the big picture of government revenue and spending.

Economists often measure government spending relative to GDP. Remember that there is a difference between government *purchases* and government *expenditures*. When the government purchases an aircraft carrier or hires a nurse at a public hospital, it receives a good (aircraft carrier) or service (nursing) in return. Government expenditures include purchases plus all other government spending. Figure 23-1 shows government *purchases* as a percentage of GDP in the Arab world during the period 1975–2009. The figure shows a downward trend in the Arab governments' purchases to GDP ratio starting in the early 1990s. This could be because of the ongoing tendency in many Arab countries to diversify their economies and give more weight to the private market to contribute to GDP.

Since Arab countries are not similar in their economic structure, it is better to take a closer look at government purchases to GDP ratio in both Arab oil-based and Arab non-oil-based economies. Figure 23-2 shows government *purchases* as a percentage of GDP in four selected Arab countries: Egypt and Jordan (non-oil-based economies) and

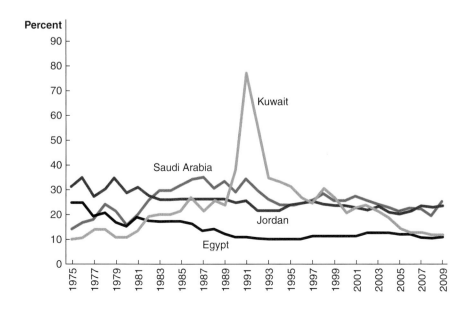

Figure 23-2

Government Purchases as a Percentage of GDP in Selected Arab Countries, 1975–2009

The ups and downs in the percentage of government purchases to GDP in Jordan and Egypt are smoother than those in Saudi Arabia and Kuwait because of the fluctuations in the international oil prices, which significantly affect both the value of GDP and government expenditure programs in oil-based economies.
Source: World Development Indicators.

Figure 23-3

Non-oil-based economies depend on income
taxes, sales taxes, and oil revenues to fund
government expenses, while oil-based economies get most of their revenues from oil. In
addition, the fluctuations in the percentage of
government revenue to GDP in oil-based economies are larger than those in non-oil-based
economies due to the variation in international oil prices.
Source: Arab Statistics, the United Nations
Development Programme on Governance
in the Arab Region (UNDP-POGAR),
www. arabstats.org.

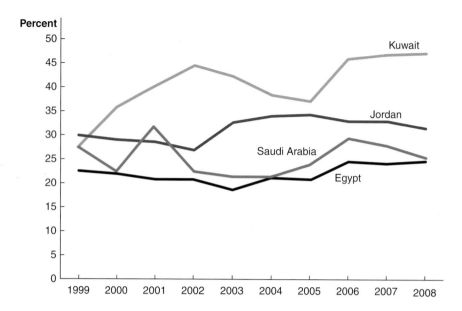

Saudi Arabia and Kuwait (oil-based economies) during the period 1975–2009. Note
that the ups and downs in the percentage of government purchases to GDP in Jordan
and Egypt are smoother than those in Saudi Arabia and Kuwait. This is because of the
fluctuations in the international oil prices, which significantly affect both the value
of GDP and government expenditure programs in oil-based economies. The sharp
increase in the percentage of government purchases to GDP in Kuwait in 1991 is due to
the first Gulf War.

In addition to purchases, there are two other categories of government expenditures: *interest on the national debt* and *transfer payments*. Interest on the national debt
represents payments to holders of the bonds the government has issued to borrow
money. One of the largest categories of government expenditures is transfer payments.
Examples of these transfer payments include several programs, such as: social security,
unemployment insurance, medical care, and government assistance to the poor.

Figure 23-3 shows the percentage of government revenue to GDP in the same countries mentioned above during the period 1999–2008. While non-oil-based economies
depend on income taxes, sales taxes, customs duties, and sometimes oil revenues to fund
government expenses, oil-based economies get most of their revenues from one source:
oil revenue. For example, the government revenue from oil is greater than 80 percent of
total government revenue in Saudi Arabia and more than 90 percent of total government
revenue in Kuwait. Again, the fluctuations in the percentage of government revenue to
GDP in oil-based economies are larger than those in non-oil-based economies due to the
variation in the international oil prices.

23.2 LEARNING OBJECTIVE

23.2 | Explain how fiscal policy affects aggregate demand and how
the government can use fiscal policy to stabilize the economy.

The Effects of Fiscal Policy on Real GDP and the Price Level

Governments use stabilization policy to offset the effects of the business cycle on the
economy. We saw in Chapter 22 that the central bank carries out monetary policy
through changes in the money supply and interest rates. Parliament, the president, or
the king carries out fiscal policy through changes in government purchases and taxes.
Because changes in government purchases and taxes lead to changes in aggregate
demand, they can affect the level of real GDP, employment, and the price level. When
the economy is in a recession, *increases* in government purchases or *decreases* in taxes

will increase aggregate demand. As we saw in Chapter 20 the inflation rate may increase when real GDP is beyond potential GDP. Decreasing government purchases or raising taxes can slow the growth of aggregate demand and reduce the inflation rate.

Expansionary and Contractionary Fiscal Policy: An Initial Look

Expansionary fiscal policy involves increasing government purchases or decreasing taxes. An increase in government purchases will increase aggregate demand directly because government expenditures are a component of aggregate demand. A cut in taxes has an indirect effect on aggregate demand. Remember from Chapter 15 that the income households have available to spend after they have paid their taxes is called *disposable income*. Cutting the individual income tax will increase household disposable income and consumption spending. Cutting taxes on business income can increase aggregate demand by increasing business investment.

Figure 23-4 shows the results of an expansionary fiscal policy using the basic version of the aggregate demand and aggregate supply model. In this model, there is no economic growth, so the long-run aggregate supply curve does not shift. Notice that this figure is very similar to Figure 22-6 on page 740, which showed the effects of an expansionary monetary policy. The goal of both expansionary monetary policy and expansionary fiscal policy is to increase aggregate demand relative to what it would have been without the policy.

In panel (a) of Figure 23-4, we assume that the economy is in short-run equilibrium at point *A*, where the aggregate demand curve (*AD*₁) intersects the short-run aggregate supply curve (*SRAS*). Real GDP is below potential real GDP, so the economy is in recession, with some firms operating below normal capacity and some workers having been laid off. To bring real GDP back to potential GDP, the government asks parliament to approve increasing government purchases or cut taxes, which will shift the aggregate

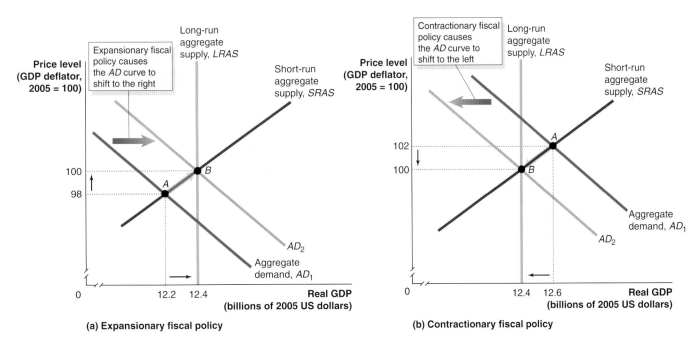

(a) Expansionary fiscal policy

(b) Contractionary fiscal policy

Figure 23-4 | Fiscal Policy

In panel (a), the economy begins in recession at point *A*, with real GDP of US$12.2 billion and a price level of 98. An expansionary fiscal policy will cause aggregate demand to shift to the right, from *AD*₁ to *AD*₂, increasing real GDP from US$12.2 billion to US$12.4 billion and the price level from 98 to 100 (point *B*). In panel (b), the economy begins at point *A*, with real GDP at US$12.6 and the price level at 102. Because real GDP is greater than potential GDP, the economy will experience rising wages and prices. A contractionary fiscal policy will cause aggregate demand to shift to the left, from *AD*₁ to *AD*₂, decreasing real GDP from US$12.6 billion to US$12.4 billion and the price level from 102 to 100 (point *B*).

demand curve to the right, from AD_1 to AD_2. Real GDP increases from US$12.2 billion to potential GDP of US$12.4 billion, and the price level rises from 98 to 100 (point B). The policy has successfully returned real GDP to its potential level. Rising production will lead to increasing employment, reducing the unemployment rate.

Contractionary fiscal policy involves decreasing government purchases or increasing taxes. Policymakers use contractionary fiscal policy to reduce increases in aggregate demand that seem likely to lead to inflation. In panel (b) of Figure 23-4, the economy is in short-run equilibrium at point A, with real GDP of US$12.6 billion, which is above potential real GDP of US$12.4 billion. With some firms producing beyond their normal capacity and the unemployment rate very low, wages and prices will be increasing. To bring real GDP back to potential GDP, the government asks parliament to approve decreasing government purchases or increase taxes, which will shift the aggregate demand curve from AD_1 to AD_2. Real GDP falls from US$12.6 billion to US$12.4 billion, and the price level falls from 102 to 100 (point B).

We can conclude that governments can attempt to stabilize the economy by using fiscal policy to affect the price level and the level of real GDP.

Using Fiscal Policy to Influence Aggregate Demand: A More Complete Account

In this section, we use the *dynamic model of aggregate demand and aggregate supply* to gain a more complete understanding of fiscal policy. To briefly review the dynamic model, recall that over time, potential real GDP increases, which we show by the long-run aggregate supply curve shifting to the right. The factors that cause the *LRAS* curve to shift also cause firms to supply more goods and services at any given price level in the short run, which we show by the short-run aggregate supply curve shifting to the right. Finally, during most years, the aggregate demand curve will also shift to the right, indicating that aggregate expenditure will be higher at every price level.

Figure 23-5 shows the results of an expansionary fiscal policy using the dynamic aggregate demand and aggregate supply model. Notice that this figure is very similar to Figure 22-7 on page 742, which showed the effects of an expansionary monetary policy. The goal of both expansionary monetary policy and expansionary fiscal policy is to increase aggregate demand relative to what it would have been without the policy.

In the hypothetical situation shown in Figure 23-5, the economy begins in equilibrium at potential real GDP of US$12.0 billion and a price level of 100 (point A). In the second year, *LRAS* increases to US$12.4 billion, but *AD* increases only to $AD_{2(\text{with policy})}$, which is not enough to keep the economy in macroeconomic equilibrium at potential

Figure 23-5

An Expansionary Fiscal Policy

The economy begins in equilibrium at point A, at potential real GDP of US$12.0 billion and a price level of 100. Without an expansionary policy, aggregate demand will shift from AD_1 to $AD_{2(\text{without policy})}$, which is not enough to keep the economy at potential GDP because long-run aggregate supply has shifted from $LRAS_1$ to $LRAS_2$. The economy will be in short-run equilibrium at point B, with real GDP of US$12.3 billion and a price level of 102. Increasing government purchases or cutting taxes will shift aggregate demand to $AD_{2(\text{with policy})}$. The economy will be in equilibrium at point C, with real GDP of US$12.4 billion, which is its potential level, and a price level of 103. The price level is higher than it would have been if expansionary fiscal policy had not been used.

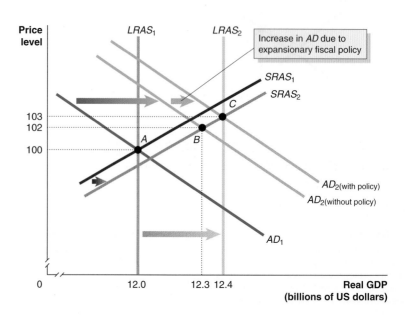

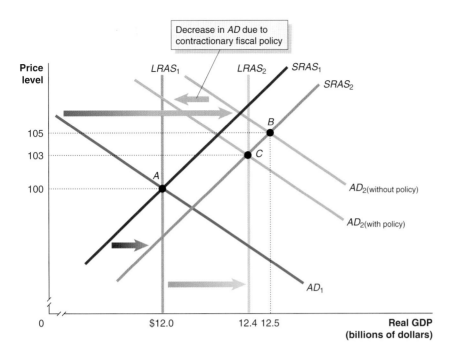

Figure 23-6

A Contractionary Fiscal Policy

The economy begins in equilibrium at point A, with real GDP of US$12.0 billion and a price level of 100. Without a contractionary policy, aggregate demand will shift from $AD_{2(without\ policy)}$, which results in a short-run equilibrium beyond potential GDP at point B, with real GDP of US$12.5 billion and a price level of 105. Decreasing government purchases or increasing taxes can shift aggregate demand to $AD_{2(with\ policy)}$. The economy will be in equilibrium at point C, with real GDP of US$12.4 billion, which is its potential level, and a price level of 103. The inflation rate will be 3 percent as opposed to the 5 percent it would have been without the contractionary fiscal policy.

GDP. Let's assume that the central bank does not react to the situation with an expansionary monetary policy. In that case, without an expansionary fiscal policy of spending increases or tax reductions, the short-run equilibrium will occur at US$12.3 billion (point B). The US$100 billion gap between this level of real GDP and the potential level means that some firms are operating at less than their full capacity. Incomes and profits will be falling, firms will begin to lay off workers, and the unemployment rate will rise.

Increasing government purchases or cutting taxes can shift aggregate demand to $AD_{2(with\ policy)}$. The economy will be in equilibrium at point C, with real GDP of US$12.4 billion, which is its potential level, and a price level of 103. The price level is higher than it would have been if expansionary fiscal policy had not been used.

Contractionary fiscal policy involves decreasing government purchases or increasing taxes. Policymakers use contractionary fiscal policy to reduce increases in aggregate demand that seem likely to lead to inflation. In Figure 23-6, the economy again begins at potential real GDP of US$12.0 billion and a price level of 100 (point A). Once again, *LRAS* increases to US$12.4 billion in the second year. In this scenario, the shift in aggregate demand to $AD_{2(without\ policy)}$ results in a short-run macroeconomic equilibrium beyond potential GDP (point B). If we assume, once again, that the central bank does not respond to the situation with a contractionary monetary policy, the economy will experience a rising inflation rate. Decreasing government purchases or increasing taxes can keep real GDP from moving beyond its potential level. The result, shown in Figure 23-6, is that in the new equilibrium at point C, the inflation rate is 3 percent rather than 5 percent.

A Summary of How Fiscal Policy Affects Aggregate Demand

Table 23-1 summarizes how fiscal policy affects aggregate demand. Just as we did with monetary policy, we must add a very important qualification to this summary of fiscal policy: the table isolates the impact of fiscal policy *by holding constant monetary policy and all other factors affecting the variables involved.* In other words, we are again invoking the *ceteris paribus* condition we discussed in Chapter 3. This point is important because, for example, a contractionary fiscal policy does not cause the price level to fall. A contractionary fiscal policy causes the price level *to rise by less than it would have without the policy*, which is the situation shown in Figure 23-6.

TABLE 23-1

Countercyclical Fiscal Policy

PROBLEM	TYPE OF POLICY	ACTIONS BY THE GOVERNMENT	RESULT
Recession	Expansionary	Increase government spending or cut taxes	Real GDP and the price level rise.
Rising inflation	Contractionary	Decrease government spending or raise taxes	Real GDP and the price level fall.

23.3 LEARNING OBJECTIVE

23.3 | Explain how the government purchases and tax multipliers work.

Government Purchases and Tax Multipliers

Suppose that during a recession, the government decides to use discretionary fiscal policy to increase aggregate demand by spending US$100 billion more on construct-ing subway systems in several cities. How much will equilibrium real GDP increase as a result of this increase in government purchases? We know that the answer is greater than US$100 billion because we know the initial increase in aggregate demand will lead to additional increases in income and spending. To build the subways, the government hires private construction firms. These firms will hire more workers to carry out the new construction projects. Newly hired workers will increase their spending on cars, furniture, appliances, and other products. Sellers of these products will increase their production and hire more workers, and so on. At each step, real GDP and income will rise, thereby increasing consumption spending and aggregate demand.

Economists refer to the initial increase in government purchases as *autonomous* because it does not depend on the level of real GDP. The increases in consumption spending that result from the initial autonomous increase in government purchases are *induced* because they are caused by the initial increase in autonomous spending. Economists refer to the series of induced increases in consumption spending that result from an initial increase in autonomous expenditures as the **multiplier effect**.

Figure 23-7 illustrates how an increase in government purchases affects the aggre-gate demand curve. The initial increase in government purchases causes the aggregate demand to shift to the right because total spending in the economy is now higher at

Multiplier effect The series of induced increases in consumption spending that results from an initial increase in autonomous expenditures.

Figure 23-7

The Multiplier Effect and Aggregate Demand

An initial increase in government purchases of US$100 billion causes the aggregate demand curve to shift to the right from AD_1 to the dot-ted AD curve and represents the impact of the initial increase of US$100 billion in govern-ment purchases. Because this initial increase raises incomes and leads to further increases in consumption spending, the aggregate demand curve will ultimately shift further to the right, to AD_2.

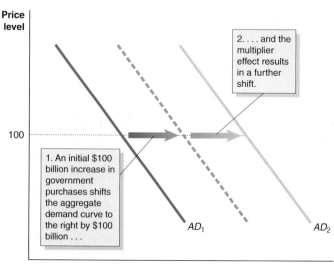

2. . . . and the multiplier effect results in a further shift.

1. An initial $100 billion increase in government purchases shifts the aggregate demand curve to the right by $100 billion . . .

AD_1 AD_2

Period	Additional spending this period	Cumulative increase in spending and real GDP
1	$100 billion in government purchases	$100 billion
2	$50 billion in consumption spending	$150 billion
3	$25 billion in consumption spending	$175 billion
4	$12.5 billion in consumption spending	$187.5 billion
5	$6.25 billion in consumption spending	$193.75 billion
6	$3.125 billion in consumption spending	$196.875 billion
⋮	⋮	⋮
n	0	$200 billion

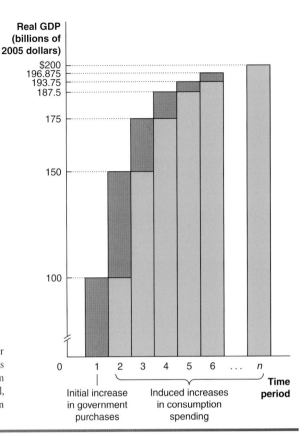

Figure 23-8 | The Multiplier Effect of an Increase in Government Purchases

Following an initial increase in government purchases, spending and real GDP increase over a number of periods due to the multiplier effect. The new spending and increased real GDP in each period is shown in green, and the level of spending from the previous period is shown in orange, so the sum of the orange and green areas represents the cumulative increase in spending and real GDP. In total, equilibrium real GDP will increase by US$200 billion as a result of an initial increase of US$100 billion in government purchases.

every price level. The shift to the right from AD_1 to the dotted AD curve represents the impact of the initial increase of US$100 billion in government purchases. Because this initial increase in government purchases raises incomes and leads to further increases in consumption spending, the aggregate demand curve will ultimately shift from AD_1 all the way to AD_2.

To understand the multiplier effect, let's start with a simplified analysis in which we assume that the price level is constant. In other words, initially we will ignore the effect of an upward-sloping *SRAS*. Figure 23-8 shows how spending and real GDP increase over a number of periods, beginning with the initial increase in government purchases in the first period, holding the price level constant. The initial spending in the first period raises real GDP and total income in the economy by US$100 billion. How much additional consumption spending will result from US$100 billion in additional income? We know that in addition to increasing their consumption spending on domestically produced goods, households will save some of the increase in income, use some to pay income taxes, and use some to purchase imported goods, which will have no direct effect on spending and production in the economy. In Figure 23-8, we assume that in the second period, households increase their consumption spending by one-half of the increase in income from the first period—or by US$50 billion. This spending in the second period will, in turn, increase real GDP and income by an additional US$50 billion. In the third period, consumption spending will increase by US$25 billion, or one-half of the US$50 billion increase in income from the second period.

The multiplier effect will continue through a number of periods, with the additional consumption spending in each period being half of the income increase from the previous period. Eventually, the process will be complete, although we cannot say precisely how many periods it will take, so we simply label the final period n rather than give it a specific number. In the graph in Figure 23-8, the new spending and increased real GDP in each period is shown in green, and the level of spending from the previous period is shown in orange, so the sum of the orange and green areas represents the cumulative increase in spending and real GDP.

How large will the total increase in equilibrium real GDP be as a result of the initial increase of US$100 billion in government purchases? The ratio of the change in equilibrium real GDP to the initial change in government purchases is known as the *government purchases multiplier*:

$$\text{Goverment purchases multiplier} = \frac{\text{Change in equilibrium real GDP}}{\text{Change in government purchases}}$$

Economists have estimated that the government purchases multiplier has a value of about 2. Therefore, an increase in government purchases of US$100 billion should increase equilibrium real GDP by 2 × US$100 billion = US$200 billion. We show this in Figure 23-8 by having the cumulative increase in real GDP equal US$200 billion.

Tax cuts also have a multiplier effect. Cutting taxes increases the disposable income of households. When household disposable income rises, so will consumption spending. These increases in consumption spending will set off further increases in real GDP and income, just as increases in government purchases do. Suppose we consider a change in taxes of a specific amount—say, a tax cut of US$100 billion—with the tax *rate* remaining unchanged. The expression for this tax multiplier is:

$$\text{Tax multiplier} = \frac{\text{Change in equilibrium real GDP}}{\text{Change in taxes}}$$

The tax multiplier is a negative number because changes in taxes and changes in real GDP move in opposite directions: an increase in taxes reduces disposable income, consumption, and real GDP, and a decrease in taxes raises disposable income, consumption, and real GDP. For example, if the tax multiplier is –1.6, a US$100 billion *cut* in taxes will increase real GDP by –1.6 × –US$100 billion = US$160 billion. We would expect the tax multiplier to be smaller in absolute value than the government purchases multiplier. To see why, think about the difference between a US$100 billion increase in government purchases and a US$100 billion decrease in taxes. The whole of the US$100 billion in government purchases results in an increase in aggregate demand. But households will save rather than spend some portion of a US$100 billion decrease in taxes, and spend some portion on imported goods. The fraction of the tax cut that households save or spend on imports will not increase aggregate demand. Therefore, the first period of the multiplier process will see a smaller increase in aggregate demand than occurs when there is an increase in government purchases, and the total increase in equilibrium real GDP will be smaller.

Fiscal Policy in Action: The Egyptian Tax Cut of 2005

As we have seen, the government can use tax cuts to increase aggregate demand to avoid a recession or to shorten the length or severity of a recession that is already underway. In July 2005, Egypt sharply lowered tax rates on personal income. The personal tax rate schedule was cut from a progressive tax schedule that ranged from a minimum rate of 20 percent to a maximum rate of 40 percent, to a new schedule that ranged from 10 percent to 20 percent. In general, cutting taxes would increase aggregate demand by increasing household disposable income, which would in turn increase consumption spending.

How effective is the tax cut in increasing consumption spending? Economic analysis can give us some answers to this question. Many economists believe that consumers base their spending on their *permanent income*, rather than just on their *current income*. A consumer's permanent income reflects the consumer's expected future income. By basing spending on permanent income, a consumer can smooth out consumption over a period of years, rather than having to adjust spending to every blip in current income. For example, a real-estate agent may have income that is quite high during some years when the real-estate market is booming and much lower in other years when the real-estate market is declining. The agent will find it less disruptive to keep her consumption roughly constant by basing it on her average income over a number of years, rather than to increase and decrease her consumption as her current income fluctuates. Similarly, a newly graduated doctor may have very low current income, but a high expected future income. The doctor may borrow against this high expected future income, rather than having to consume at a very low level in the present. Some people, however, have difficulty borrowing against their future income because banks or other lenders may not be convinced that a borrower's future income really will be significantly higher than his or her current income. Consumers who have difficulty smoothing out their consumption spending on the basis of their permanent income are said to be *liquidity constrained*. The spending of consumers who are liquidity constrained is more likely to depend on their current income than is the spending of consumers who are better able to borrow against their future income. If the tax cut is a one-time (temporary) procedure, it leads to an increase in consumers' current income, but not their permanent income. A similar effect was expected to happen when the King of Bahrain ordered a one-time BD1,000 cash payment (US$2,600) to be paid to Bahraini families in February 2011. Only a permanent decrease in taxes increases consumers' permanent income. Therefore, the 2005 permanent tax cut in Egypt was likely to increase consumption spending more than a temporary tax cut would, and is likely to have its greatest effect on the spending of consumers who are not liquidity constrained since it increases future permanent income. On the other hand, the temporary cash payment to Bahraini families is expected to increase consumption spending less than a permanent cash payment would, and is likely to have its greatest effect on the spending of consumers who are liquidity constrained.

The Effect of Changes in Tax Rates

A change in tax *rates* has a more complicated effect on equilibrium real GDP than does a tax cut of a fixed amount. To begin with, the value of the tax rate affects the size of the multiplier effect. The higher the tax rate, the smaller the multiplier effect. To see why, think about the size of the additional spending increases that take place in each period following an increase in government purchases. The higher the tax rate, the smaller the amount of any increase in income that households have available to spend, which reduces the size of the multiplier effect. So, a cut in tax rates affects equilibrium real GDP through two channels: (1) a cut in tax rates increases the disposable income of households, which leads them to increase their consumption spending, and (2) a cut in tax rates increases the size of the multiplier effect.

Taking into Account the Effects of Aggregate Supply

To this point, as we discussed the multiplier effect, we assumed that the price level was constant. We know, though, that because the *SRAS* curve is upward sloping, when the *AD* curve shifts to the right, the price level will rise. As a result of the rise in the price level, equilibrium real GDP will not increase by the full amount the multiplier effect indicates. Figure 23-9 illustrates how an upward-sloping *SRAS* curve affects the size of the multiplier. To keep the graph relatively simple, assume that the *SRAS* and *LRAS* curves do not shift. The economy starts at point *A*, with real GDP below its potential level. An increase in government purchases shifts the aggregate demand curve from AD_1 to the dotted *AD* curve. Just as in Figure 23-7, the multiplier effect causes a further shift in aggregate demand to AD_2. If the price level remained constant, real GDP would increase from US$11.0 billion at point *A* to US$12.2 billion at point *B*. However, because the *SRAS* curve is upward sloping, the price level rises from 100 to 103, reducing the total quantity of goods and services demanded in the economy. The new equilibrium occurs at point *C*, with real GDP having risen to US$12.0 billion, or by US$200 billion less than if the price level had remained unchanged. We can conclude that the actual change in real GDP resulting from an increase in government purchases or a cut in taxes will be less than indicated by the simple multiplier effect with a constant price level.

Figure 23-9

The Multiplier Effect and Aggregate Supply

The economy is initially at point *A*. An increase in government purchases causes the aggregate demand to shift to the right, from AD_1 to the dotted *AD* curve. The multiplier effect results in the aggregate demand curve shifting further to the right, to AD_2 (point *B*). Because of the upward-sloping supply curve, the shift in aggregate demand results in a higher price level. In the new equilibrium at point *C*, both real GDP and the price level have increased. The increase in real GDP is less than indicated by the multiplier effect with a constant price level.

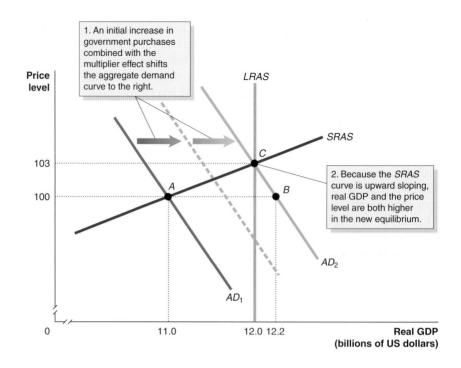

The Multipliers Work in Both Directions

Increases in government purchases and cuts in taxes have a positive multiplier effect on equilibrium real GDP. Decreases in government purchases and increases in taxes also have a multiplier effect on equilibrium real GDP, only in this case, the effect is negative. For example, an increase in taxes will reduce household disposable income and consumption spending. As households buy fewer cars, furniture, refrigerators, and other products, the firms that sell these products will cut back on production and begin laying off workers. Falling incomes will lead to further reductions in consumption spending. A reduction in government spending on defense would set off a similar process of decreases in real GDP and income. The cutback would be felt first by defense contractors selling directly to the government, but then it would spread to other firms.

We look more closely at the government purchases multiplier and the tax multiplier in the appendix to this chapter.

Solved Problem | 23-3

Fiscal Policy Multipliers

Briefly explain whether you agree or disagree with the following statement: "Real GDP is currently US$12.2 billion, and potential real GDP is US$12.4 billion. If the government would increase its purchases by US$200 million or cut taxes by US$200 million, the economy could be brought to equilibrium at potential GDP."

SOLVING THE PROBLEM:

Step 1: **Review the chapter material.** This problem is about the multiplier process, so you may want to review the section "The Government Purchases and Tax Multipliers," which begins on page 768.

Step 2: **Explain how the necessary increase in purchases or cut in taxes is less than US$200 million because of the multiplier effect.** The statement is incorrect because it neglects the multiplier effect. Because of the multiplier effect, an increase in government purchases or a decrease in taxes of less than US$200 million is necessary to increase equilibrium real GDP by US$200 million. For instance, assume that the government purchases multiplier is 2 and the tax multiplier is –1.6. We can then calculate the necessary increase in government purchases as follows:

$$\text{Government purchases multiplier} = \frac{\text{Change in equilibrium real GDP}}{\text{Change in government purchases}}$$

$$2 = \frac{\$200 \text{ million}}{\text{Change in government purchases}}$$

$$\text{Change in government purchases} = \frac{\$200 \text{ million}}{2} = \$100 \text{ million}$$

And the necessary change in taxes:

$$\text{Tax multiplier} = \frac{\text{Change in equilibrium real GDP}}{\text{Change in taxes}}$$

$$-1.6 = \frac{\$200 \text{ million}}{\text{Change in taxes}}$$

$$\text{Change in taxes} = \frac{\$200 \text{ million}}{-1.6} = -\$125 \text{ million}$$

YOUR TURN: For more practice, do related problem 3.5 on page 792 at the end of this chapter.

>> **End Solved Problem 23-3**

23.4 | Discuss the difficulties that can arise in implementing fiscal policy.

The Limits of Using Fiscal Policy to Stabilize the Economy

Poorly timed fiscal policy, like poorly timed monetary policy, can do more harm than good. As we discussed in Chapter 22, it takes time for policymakers to collect statistics and identify changes in the economy. If the government decides to increase spending or cut taxes to fight a recession that is about to end, the effect may be to increase the inflation rate. Similarly, cutting spending or raising taxes to slow down an economy that has actually already moved into recession can make the recession longer and deeper.

Getting the timing right can be more difficult with fiscal policy than with monetary policy for two main reasons. Control over monetary policy is concentrated in the hands of the Open Market Committee in the central bank, which can change monetary policy at any of its meetings. By contrast, the president (or the king) and a majority of the members of parliament have to agree on changes in fiscal policy. The delays caused by the legislative process can be very long, especially in democratic countries. For example, in 1962, U.S. President John F. Kennedy concluded that the U.S. economy was operating below potential GDP and proposed a tax cut to stimulate aggregate demand. Congress eventually agreed to the tax cut—but not until 1964.

Once a change in fiscal policy has been approved, it takes time to implement the policy. Suppose that parliament agrees to increase aggregate demand by spending US$30 billion more on constructing subway systems in several cities. It will probably take at least several months to prepare detailed plans for the construction. The government will then ask for bids from private construction companies. Once the winning bidders have been selected, they will usually need several months to begin the project.

Only then will significant amounts of spending actually take place. This delay may push the spending beyond the end of the recession that the spending was intended to fight. Recently, the 2008 financial crisis pushed both developed and developing countries to move quickly and apply expansionary fiscal policies that were approved by their parliaments in a timely manner. In many countries, governments use fiscal policies relatively infrequently to stabilize the economy because they are well aware of the timing problem. Central banks play a larger role in stabilizing the economy because they can quickly change monetary policy in response to changing economic conditions.

Does Government Spending Reduce Private Spending?

In addition to the timing problem, using increases in government purchases to increase aggregate demand presents another potential problem. We have been assuming that when the government increases its purchases by US$30 billion, the multiplier effect will cause the increase in aggregate demand to be greater than US$30 billion. However, the size of the multiplier effect may be limited if the increase in government purchases causes one of the nongovernment, or private, components of aggregate expenditures—consumption, investment, or net exports—to fall. A decline in private expenditures as a result of an increase in government purchases is called **crowding out**.

> **Crowding out** A decline in private expenditures as a result of an increase in government purchases.

Crowding Out in the Short Run

First, consider the case of a temporary increase in government purchases. Suppose the government decides to fight a recession by spending US$30 billion more this year on subway construction. When the US$30 billion has been spent, the program will end, and government spending will drop back to its previous level. As the spending takes place, income and real GDP will increase. These increases in income and real GDP will cause households and firms to increase their demand for currency and checking account balances to accommodate the increased buying and selling. Figure 23-10 shows the result, using the money market graph introduced in Chapter 22.

At higher levels of real GDP and income, households and firms demand more money at every level of the interest rate. When the demand for money increases, the equilibrium interest rate will rise. Higher interest rates will result in a decline in each component of private expenditures. Consumption spending and investment spending will decline because households will borrow less to buy cars, furniture, and appliances, and firms will borrow less to buy factories, computers, and machine tools. In addition,

Figure 23-10

An Expansionary Fiscal Policy Increases Interest Rates

If the federal government increases spending, the demand for money will increase from Money demand₁ to Money demand₂ as real GDP and income rise. With the supply of money constant, at US$950 billion, the result is an increase in the equilibrium interest rate from 3 percent to 5 percent, which crowds out some consumption, investment, and net exports.

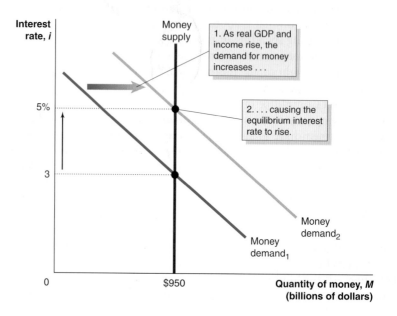

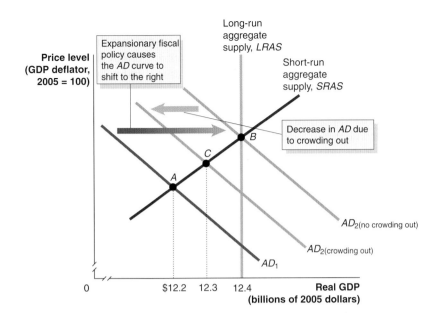

Figure 23-11

The Effect of Crowding Out in the Short Run

The economy begins in a recession with real GDP of US$12.2 billion (point *A*). In the absence of crowding out, an increase in government purchases would shift aggregate demand to $AD_{2(\text{no crowding out})}$ and bring the economy to equilibrium at potential real GDP of US$12.4 billion (point *B*). But the higher interest rate resulting from the increased government purchases reduces consumption, investment, and net exports, causing aggregate demand to shift to $AD_{2(\text{crowding out})}$. The result is a new short-run equilibrium at point *C*, with real GDP of US$12.3 billion, which is US$100 billion short of potential real GDP.

net exports will also decline because higher interest rates in the home country will attract foreign investors. This will cause an appreciation in the home country's currency and thus, a reduction in net exports. For example, an increase in the interest rate on the Kuwaiti dinar will make foreign investors more willing to exchange the currencies of their countries for Kuwaiti dinars to invest in Kuwaiti financial assets. This increased demand for Kuwaiti dinars will cause an increase in the exchange rate between the dinar and other currencies. When the dinar increases in value, the prices of products made in Kuwait in foreign countries rise—causing a reduction in Kuwait's exports—and the prices of foreign products in Kuwait fall—causing an increase in Kuwait's imports. Falling exports and rising imports mean that net exports are falling.

The greater the sensitivity of consumption, investment, and net exports to changes in interest rates, the more crowding out will occur. In a deep recession, many firms may be so pessimistic about the future and have so much excess capacity that investment spending falls to very low levels and is unlikely to fall much further, even if interest rates rise. In this case, crowding out is unlikely to be a problem. If the economy is close to potential GDP, however, and firms are optimistic about the future, then an increase in interest rates may result in a significant decline in investment spending.

Figure 23-11 shows that crowding out may reduce the effectiveness of an expansionary fiscal policy. The economy begins in short-run equilibrium at point *A*, with real GDP at US$12.2 billion. Real GDP is below potential GDP, so the economy is in recession. Suppose that the government decided to increase government purchases to bring the economy back to potential GDP. In the absence of crowding out, the increase in government purchases would shift aggregate demand to $AD_{2(\text{no crowding out})}$ and bring the economy to equilibrium at real GDP of US$12.4 billion, which is the potential level of GDP (point *B*). But the higher interest rate resulting from the increased government purchases reduces consumption, investment, and net exports, causing aggregate demand to shift back to $AD_{2(\text{crowding out})}$. The result is a new short-run equilibrium at point *C*, with real GDP of US$12.3 billion, which is US$100 billion short of potential GDP.

Crowding Out in the Long Run

Most economists agree that in the short run, an increase in government spending results in partial, but not complete, crowding out. What is the long-run effect of a *permanent* increase in government spending? In this case, most economists agree that the result is complete crowding out. In the long run, the decline in investment, consumption, and net exports exactly offsets the increase in government purchases, and aggregate demand remains unchanged. To understand crowding out in the long run, recall from Chapter 20 that *in the long run, the economy returns to potential GDP.* Suppose that the economy is currently at potential GDP and that government purchases are 35 percent of GDP. In that case, private expenditures—the sum of consumption, investment, and net exports—will make up the other 65 percent of GDP. If government purchases are increased permanently to 37 percent of GDP, in the long run, private expenditures must fall to 63 percent of GDP. There has been complete crowding out: private expenditures have fallen by the same amount that government purchases have increased. If government spending is taking a larger share of GDP, then private spending must take a smaller share.

An expansionary fiscal policy does not have to cause complete crowding out in the short run. If the economy is below potential real GDP, it is possible for both government purchases and private expenditures to increase. But in the long run, any permanent increase in government purchases must come at the expense of private expenditures. Keep in mind, however, that it may take several—possibly many—years to arrive at this long-run outcome.

Making the Connection | Is Losing Your Job Good for Your Health?

Recessions cause lost output and cyclical unemployment, which reduce welfare. It makes sense, then, that monetary and fiscal policies that shorten recessions would increase welfare. Someone experiencing cyclical unemployment will clearly experience declining income. Will the unemployed also suffer from declining health? For many years, most economists believed that they would. If this belief were correct, effective macroeconomic policies would improve welfare by both raising the incomes and improving the health of people who might otherwise be cyclically unemployed.

Recently, however, Christopher Ruhm, an economist at the University of North Carolina in the United State, has found substantial evidence that during recessions, the unemployed may on average experience improving health. Ruhm analyzed data gathered by the federal Centers for Disease Control. He found that during recessions, people tend to smoke less, drink less alcohol, eat a healthier diet, lose weight, and exercise more. As a result, death rates and sickness rates decline during business cycle recessions and increase during business cycle expansions. Why do recessions apparently have a positive impact on health? The reasons are not completely clear, but Ruhm offers several possibilities. The unemployed may have more time available to exercise, prepare healthy meals, and visit the doctor. Temporary joblessness also may reduce the workplace stress that some people attempt to relieve by smoking and drinking alcohol. In addition, during a recession, traffic congestion and air pollution decline, which may reduce deaths from coronary heart disease. In fact, Ruhm estimates that during business cycle expansions, a one percent decline in the unemployment rate is associated with an additional 3,900 deaths from heart disease.

Ruhm has found that health problems, such as cancer, that tend to develop over many years, are not affected by the business cycle. In addition, unlike physical health, mental health apparently does decline during recessions and improve during expansions. It is important to understand that Ruhm's research is analyzing the effects on health of temporary fluctuations in output and employment during the business cycle. Over the long-run, economic research has shown that rising incomes result in better health.

Recent research shows that, surprisingly, the health of people who are temporarily unemployed may improve.

The results of the new research on health and the business cycle do not mean that the government should abandon using monetary and fiscal policy to stabilize the economy. Although the physical health of the unemployed may, on average, increase during recessions, their incomes and their mental health may decline. No one doubts that losing your job can be a heavy blow, as the rising suicide rate during recessions shows. So, most economists would still agree that a successful policy that reduced the severity of the business cycle would improve average well-being in the economy.

Sources: Christopher J. Ruhm, "A Healthy Economy Can Break Your Heart," *Demography*, 44(4) Nov. 2007; Christopher J. Ruhm, "Healthy Living in Hard Times," *Journal of Health Economics*, Vol. 24, No. 2, March 2005, pp. 341–363; and Christopher J. Ruhm, "Are Recessions Good for Your Health?" *Quarterly Journal of Economics*, Vol. 115, No. 2, May 2000, pp. 617–650.

YOUR TURN: Test your understanding by doing related problem 4.6 on page 793 at the end of this chapter.

23.5 | Define budget deficit and government debt and explain how the budget can serve as an automatic stabilizer.

Deficits, Surpluses, and Government Debt

The government's budget shows the relationship between its expenditure and its tax revenue. If the government's expenditure is greater than its revenue, a **budget deficit** results. If the government's expenditure is less than its tax revenue, a **budget surplus** results. As with many other macroeconomic variables, it is useful to consider the size of the surplus or deficit relative to the size of the overall economy. Figure 23-12 shows the budget deficit/surplus as a percentage of GDP in selected Arab countries: Lebanon, Egypt, Saudi Arabia, and Kuwait. Again, the fluctuations are more obvious in oil-based economies as the budget balance is severely affected by changes in oil prices. The budget deficit in Kuwait and Saudi Arabia in the early 2000s turned into a considerable surplus, starting in 2002 and 2005, respectively, due to the gradual increase in the international oil prices. The largest budget surplus in the two countries was achieved in 2006 and 2008, when oil prices reached a record of US$145 per barrel in July 2008. On the contrary, Arab non-oil-based economies suffer from a prolonged deficit. The political instability in Lebanon is an important reason for the budget deficit since it affects investment activities and, thus, tax revenues sharply. Lebanon depends on customs duties, income taxes, and value added taxes to raise the government's revenue. Figure 23-12 shows an increase in the Lebanese budget deficit in 2006 and 2007 due to the 2006 war in Lebanon. Egypt is in slightly better shape in terms of budget deficit compared with Lebanon as its budget deficit to GDP ranges from 2 percent to 7 percent during the past 10 years compared with a range of 7 percent to 18 percent in Lebanon in the same period. The government revenue structure in Egypt is close to that of Lebanon since the Egyptian government depends mainly on taxes on goods and services (sales taxes), income taxes, and customs duties to raise most of its revenue. The revenue from publicly owned enterprises, such as the Suez Canal and oil revenues, also accounts for a significant part of the Egyptian government's revenue (around 28 percent of the total revenue in 2010). This partially explains the increase in budget deficit in Egypt during the fiscal year 2008/2009 and 2009/2010. The recent international economic crisis

Budget deficit The situation in which the government's expenditure is greater than its tax revenue.

Budget surplus The situation in which the government's expenditure is less than its tax revenue.

Figure 23-12

The budget deficit in Kuwait and Saudi Arabia (oil-based economies) in the early 2000s turned into a considerable surplus, starting in 2002 and 2005, respectively, due to the gradual increase in international oil prices. On the contrary, Egypt and Lebanon (non-oil-based) economies suffer from a prolonged deficit.

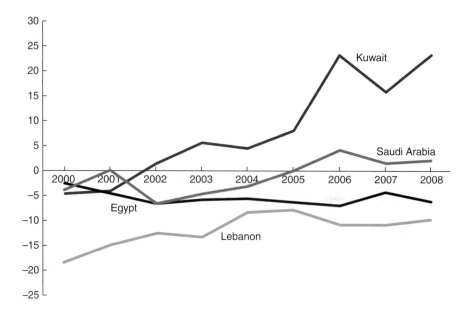

resulted in slower international trade and, thus, a reduction in Suez Canal revenue. The Suez Canal Authority announced in 2010 that Suez Canal revenue decreased by 7.2 percent in 2008/2009 and by 20 percent in 2009/2010 due to the global recession.

How the Budget Can Serve as an Automatic Stabilizer

The budget deficit sometimes increases during recessions because of discretionary fiscal policy actions. Discretionary increases in spending or cuts in taxes to increase aggregate demand during a recession will increase the budget deficit. For example, the decision to cut taxes in Egypt in 2005 reduced the government's revenues, holding constant other factors that affect the budget. As we saw earlier, because of the poorly timed fiscal policy, many countries take no significant fiscal policy actions during recessionary periods. In fact, most of the increase in the budget deficit during a recession takes place without the government taking any action because of the effects of the *automatic stabilizers* we briefly mentioned earlier in this chapter.

Deficits occur automatically during recessions for two reasons: first, during a recession, wages and profits fall, causing government tax revenues to fall; second, the government automatically increases its spending on transfer payments when the economy moves into recession. The government's contribution to the unemployment insurance program will increase as unemployment rises. Spending will also increase on programs to aid poor people, such as the social aid from the Bahraini Social Development Ministry, and the food stamp and Medicaid programs in the U.S. These spending increases take place without the government taking any action. Existing laws already specify who is eligible for unemployment insurance and these other programs. As the number of eligible persons increases during a recession, so does government spending on these programs.

Because budget deficits automatically increase during recessions and decrease during expansions, economists often look at the *cyclically adjusted budget deficit or surplus*, which can provide a more accurate measure of the effects on the economy of the government's spending and tax policies than the actual budget deficit or surplus. The **cyclically adjusted budget deficit or surplus** measures what the deficit or surplus would be if the economy were at potential GDP. An expansionary fiscal policy should result in a cyclically adjusted budget deficit, and a contractionary fiscal policy should result in a cyclically adjusted budget surplus.

Cyclically adjusted budget deficit or surplus The deficit or surplus in the government's budget if the economy were at potential GDP.

Automatic budget surpluses and deficits can help to stabilize the economy. When the economy moves into a recession, wages and profits fall, which reduces the taxes that households and firms owe the government. In effect, households and firms have received an automatic tax cut, which keeps their spending higher than it otherwise would have been. In a recession, workers who have been laid off receive unemployment insurance payments, and households whose incomes have dropped below a certain level become eligible for social aid and other government transfer programs. As a result of receiving this extra income, these households will spend more than they otherwise would have spent. This extra spending helps reduce the length and severity of the recession. Many economists argue that lack of an unemployment insurance system and other government transfer programs contributed to the severity of the Great Depression. During the Great Depression, workers who lost their jobs saw their wage incomes drop to zero and had to rely on their savings, what they could borrow, or what they received from private charities. As a result, many cut back drastically on their spending, which made the downturn worse.

When GDP increases above its potential level, households and firms have to pay more taxes to the government, and the government makes fewer transfer payments. Higher taxes and lower transfer payments cause total spending to rise by less than it otherwise would have, which helps reduce the chance that the economy will experience higher inflation.

Making the Connection | Did Fiscal Policy Fail during the Great Depression?

Modern macroeconomics began during the 1930s with publication of *The General Theory of Employment, Interest, and Money* by John Maynard Keynes. One conclusion many economists drew from Keynes's book was that an expansionary fiscal policy would be necessary to pull the United States out of the Great Depression. When Franklin D. Roosevelt became president in 1933, federal government expenditures increased, and there was a federal budget deficit each remaining year of the decade, except for 1937. The U.S. economy recovered very slowly, however, and did not reach potential real GDP again until the U.S. entered World War II in 1941.

Some economists and policymakers at the time argued that because the economy recovered slowly despite increases in government spending, fiscal policy had been ineffective. In separate studies, economists E. Cary Brown of MIT and Larry Peppers of Washington and Lee University in the United States argued that, in fact, fiscal policy had not been expansionary during the 1930s. The following table provides the data supporting the arguments of Brown and Peppers (all variables in the table are nominal rather than real). The second column shows federal government expenditures increasing from 1933 to 1936, falling in 1937, and then increasing in 1938 and 1939. The third column shows a similar pattern, with the federal budget being in deficit each year after 1933, with the exception of 1937. The fourth column, though, shows that in each year after 1933, the federal government ran a cyclically adjusted budget *surplus*. Because the level of income was so low and the unemployment rate was so high during these years, tax collections were far below what they would have been if the economy had been at potential GDP. As the fifth column shows, in 1933 and again in the years 1937 to 1939, the cyclically adjusted surpluses were quite large relative to GDP.

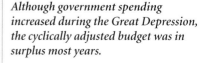

Although government spending increased during the Great Depression, the cyclically adjusted budget was in surplus most years.

(Continued)

YEAR	FEDERAL GOVERNMENT EXPENDITURES (BILLIONS OF U.S. DOLLARS)	ACTUAL FEDERAL BUDGET DEFICIT OR SURPLUS (BILLIONS OF U.S. DOLLARS)	CYCLICALLY ADJUSTED BUDGET DEFICIT OR SURPLUS (BILLIONS OF U.S. DOLLARS)	CYCLICALLY ADJUSTED BUDGET DEFICIT OR SURPLUS (AS A PERCENTAGE OF GDP)
1929	2.6	1.0	1.24	1.20
1930	2.7	0.2	0.81	0.89
1931	4.0	−2.1	−0.41	−0.54
1932	3.0	−1.3	0.50	0.85
1933	3.4	−0.9	1.06	1.88
1934	5.5	−2.2	0.09	0.14
1935	5.6	−1.9	0.54	0.74
1936	7.8	−3.2	0.47	0.56
1937	6.4	0.2	2.55	2.77
1938	7.3	−1.3	2.47	2.87
1939	8.4	−2.1	2.00	2.17

Although President Roosevelt did propose many new government spending programs, he had also promised during the 1932 presidential election campaign to balance the federal budget. He achieved a balanced budget only in 1937, but his reluctance to allow the actual budget deficit to grow too large helps explain why the cyclically adjusted budget remained in surplus. Many economists today would agree with E. Cary Brown's conclusion: "Fiscal policy, then, seems to have been an unsuccessful recovery device in the 'thirties—not because it did not work, but because it was not tried."

Sources: E. Cary Brown, "Fiscal Policy in the 'Thirties: A Reappraisal," *American Economic Review,* Vol. 46, No. 5, December 1956, pp. 857–879; Larry Peppers, "Full Employment Surplus Analysis and Structural Changes," *Explorations in Economic History,* Vol. 10, Winter 1973, pp. 197–210; and Bureau of Economic Analysis.

Solved Problem | 23-5

The Effect of Economic Fluctuations on the Budget Deficit

The Lebanese government's budget deficit was US$2.7 billion in 2001 and US$2.4 billion in 2002. A student comments, "The government must have acted during 2002 to raise taxes or cut spending or both." Do you agree? Briefly explain.

SOLVING THE PROBLEM:

Step 1: **Review the chapter material.** This problem is about the budget as an automatic stabilizer, so you may want to review the section "How the Budget Can Serve as an Automatic Stabilizer," which begins on page 778.

Step 2: **Explain how changes in the budget deficit can occur without the government acting.** If the government takes action to raise taxes or cut spending, the budget deficit will decline. But the deficit will also decline automatically when GDP increases, even if the government takes no action. When GDP increases, rising household incomes and firm profits result in higher tax revenues. Increasing GDP also usually means falling unemployment, which reduces government spending on transfer payments. So, you should disagree with the comment. A falling deficit does not mean that the government *must* have acted to raise taxes or cut spending.

EXTRA CREDIT: Although you don't have to know it to answer the question, real GDP in Lebanon did increase from US$11.9 billion in 2001 to US$12.3 billion in 2002.

YOUR TURN: For more practice, do related problem 5.5 on page 793 at the end of this chapter.

>> End Solved Problem 23-5

Should the Budget Always Be Balanced?

Although many economists believe that it is a good idea for the government to have a balanced budget when the economy is at potential GDP, few economists believe that the government should attempt to balance its budget every year. To see why economists take this view, consider what the government would have to do to keep the budget balanced during a recession, when the budget automatically moves into deficit. To bring the budget back into balance, the government would have to raise taxes or cut spending, but these actions would reduce aggregate demand, thereby making the recession worse. Similarly, when GDP increases above its potential level, the budget automatically moves into surplus. To eliminate this surplus, the government would have to cut taxes or increase government spending. But these actions would increase aggregate demand, thereby increasing GDP further beyond potential GDP and raising the risk of higher inflation. To balance the budget every year, the government might have to take actions that would destabilize the economy.

Some economists argue that the government should normally run a deficit, even at potential GDP. When the budget is in deficit, the Ministry of Finance (Treasury) sells bonds to investors to raise the funds necessary to pay the government's bills. Borrowing to pay the bills is a bad policy for a household, firm, or government when the bills are for current expenses, but it is not a bad policy if the bills are for long-lived capital goods. For instance, businesses often borrow the funds to buy machinery, equipment, and factories by selling 30-year corporate bonds. Because these capital goods generate profits for the businesses over many years, it makes sense to pay for them over a period of years as well. By similar reasoning, when the government contributes to the building of a new highway, bridge, or subway, it may want to borrow funds by selling Treasury bonds. The alternative is to pay for these long-lived capital goods out of the tax revenues received in the year the goods were purchased. But that means that the taxpayers in that year have to bear the whole burden of paying for the projects, even though taxpayers for many years in the future will be enjoying the benefits.

The Government Debt

Every time the government runs a budget deficit, the Treasury must borrow funds from investors by selling Treasury securities. For simplicity, we will refer to all Treasury securities as 'bonds.' When the government runs a budget surplus, the Treasury pays off some existing bonds. Figure 23-12 on page 778 shows that the Egyptian government budget is in deficit in all years of the first decade of this century. As a result, the total number of Treasury bonds has grown over the years. The total value of a country's Treasury bonds outstanding is referred to as the *government debt* or, sometimes, as the *national debt*. Each year the budget is in deficit, the government debt grows. Each year the budget is in surplus, the debt shrinks.

It makes more sense if we study the government debt concept in one of the non-oil-based Arab economies (since, over the years, many Arab oil-based economies realize a surplus in their budgets by more than the years of deficit). Figure 23-13 shows the net public domestic debt in Egypt as a percentage of GDP over the past 10 years. The ratio of debt to GDP increased in 2005 and 2006 due to the increase in the budget deficit in those years, as we mentioned earlier. The sharp reduction in the government debt to GDP in 2007 and 2008 is mainly because of the strong economic growth rates achieved in those years. The Egyptian real GDP grew by 7.1 and 7.2 percent in 2007 and 2008, respectively, before it declined to 4.7 in 2009 due to the global financial crisis.

Figure 23-13

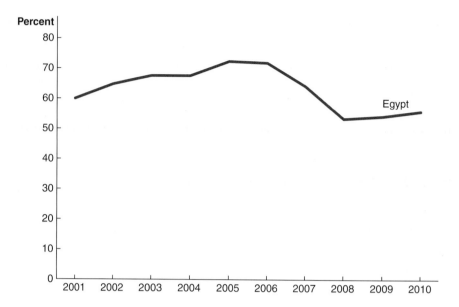

Net Public Domestic Debt as Percent of GDP in Egypt, 2001–2010

The ratio of government debt to GDP increased in 2005 and 2006 due to the increase in the budget deficit. The sharp reduction in the government debt to GDP in 2007 and 2008 is because of the strong economic growth rates achieved in those years as the Egyptian real GDP grew by 7.1 and 7.2 percent in 2007 and 2008, respectively.

Source: Egyptian Ministry of Finance, www.mof.gov.eg.

Is Government Debt a Problem?

Debt can be a problem for a government for the same reasons that debt can be a problem for a household or a business. If a family has difficulty making the monthly car loan payment, it will have to cut back spending on other things. If the family is unable to make the payments, it will have to *default* on the loan and will probably lose their house. The government is in no danger of defaulting on its debt. Ultimately, the government can raise the funds it needs through taxes to make the interest payments on the debt. If the debt becomes very large relative to the economy, however, the government may have to raise taxes to high levels or cut back on other types of spending to make the interest payments on the debt. For example, interest payments in Egypt are expected to reach about 22.2 percent of total government expenditure in the fiscal year 2010/2011 compared with 19.8 percent in the fiscal year 2009/2010. This level of interest payments is fairly high and might need serious procedures from the Egyptian government to cut public expenditure that is not related to social issues, i.e. not related to social security, education, and health care, as these are more politically acceptable procedures compared with raising taxes.

In the long run, a debt that increases in size relative to GDP can pose a problem. As we discussed previously, crowding out of investment spending may occur if an increasing debt drives up interest rates. Lower investment spending means a lower capital stock in the long run and a reduced capacity of the economy to produce goods and services. This effect is somewhat offset if some of the government debt was incurred to finance improvements in *infrastructure*, such as bridges, highways, and ports; to finance education; or to finance research and development. Improvements in infrastructure, a better-educated labor force, and additional research and development can add to the productive capacity of the economy.

23.6 LEARNING OBJECTIVE   23.6 | Discuss the effects of fiscal policy in the long run.

The Effects of Fiscal Policy in the Long Run

Some fiscal policy actions are intended to meet short-run goals of stabilizing the economy. Other fiscal policy actions are intended to have long-run effects by expanding the productive capacity of the economy and increasing the rate of economic growth. Because these policy actions primarily affect aggregate supply rather than aggregate demand, they are sometimes referred to as *supply-side economics*. Most fiscal policy actions that attempt to increase aggregate supply do so by changing taxes to increase the incentives to work, save, invest, and start a business.

The Long-Run Effects of Tax Policy

The difference between the pre-tax and post-tax return to an economic activity is known as the **tax wedge**. The tax wedge applies to the *marginal tax rate*, which is the fraction of each additional dollar of income that must be paid in taxes. For example, the Egyptian personal income tax has several tax brackets, which are the income ranges within which a tax rate applies. In 2010, the tax rate is zero percent on the first EGP5,000 earned during a year. The tax rate rises for higher income brackets, until it reaches 20 percent on income earned above EGP40,000. Suppose you are paid a wage of EGP20 per hour. If your marginal income tax rate is 20 percent, then your after-tax wage is EGP16, and the tax wedge is EGP4. When discussing the model of demand and supply in Chapter 3, we saw that increasing the price of a good or service increases the quantity supplied. So, we would expect that reducing the tax wedge by cutting the marginal tax rate on income would result in a larger quantity of labor supplied because the after-tax wage would be higher. Similarly, we saw in Chapter 16 that a reduction in income tax would increase the after-tax return on saving, causing an increase in the supply of loanable funds, a lower equilibrium interest rate, and an increase in investment spending. In general, economists believe that the smaller the tax wedge for any economic activity—such as working, saving, investing, or starting a business—the more that economic activity will occur.

We can look briefly at the effects on aggregate supply of cutting each of the following taxes:

Tax wedge The difference between the pre-tax and post-tax return to an economic activity.

- *Individual income tax.* As we have seen, reducing the marginal tax rates on individual income will reduce the tax wedge faced by workers, thereby increasing the quantity of labor supplied. Many small businesses are *sole proprietorships*, whose profits are taxed at the individual income tax rates. Therefore, cutting the individual income tax rates also raises the return to entrepreneurship, encouraging the opening of new businesses. Most households are also taxed on their returns from saving at the individual income tax rates. Reducing marginal income tax rates, therefore, also increases the return to saving.

- *Corporate income tax.* Many governments tax the profits earned by corporations under the corporate income tax. For example, manufacturing corporations in Egypt face a marginal corporate tax rate of 20 percent. Cutting the marginal corporate income tax rate would encourage investment spending by increasing the return corporations receive from new investments in equipment, factories, and office buildings. Because innovations are often embodied in new investment goods, cutting the corporate income tax can potentially increase the pace of technological change.

- *Taxes on dividends and capital gains.* Corporations distribute some of their profits to shareholders in the form of payments known as *dividends*. Shareholders also may benefit from higher corporate profits by receiving *capital gains*. A capital gain is the change in the price of an asset, such as a share of stock. Rising profits usually result in rising stock prices and capital gains to shareholders. Some countries ask individuals to pay taxes on both dividends and capital gains (although the tax on capital gains can be postponed if the stock is not sold). As a result, the same earnings are, in effect, taxed twice: once when corporations pay the corporate income tax on their profits and a second time when the profits are received by individual investors in the form of dividends or capital gains. Economists debate the costs and benefits of a separate tax on corporate profits. With the corporate income tax remaining in place, one way to reduce the 'double taxation' problem is to reduce the taxes on dividends and capital gains. Lowering the tax rates on dividends and capital gains increases the supply of loanable funds from household to firms, increasing saving and investment and lowering the equilibrium real interest rate.

Tax Simplification

In addition to the potential gains from cutting individual taxes, there are also gains from tax simplification. For example, the complexity of the tax code in the U.S. has created a whole industry of tax preparation services, such as H&R Block (a tax preparation company). The U.S. tax code is extremely complex and is almost 3,000 pages long. The Internal Revenue Service (the U.S. tax administration) estimates that taxpayers spend more than 6.4 billion hours each year filling out their tax forms, or about 45 hours per tax return. Households and firms have to deal with more than 480 tax forms to file their federal taxes. It is not surprising that there are more H&R Block offices around the country than Starbucks coffeehouses. Even Albert Einstein supposedly remarked, "The hardest thing in the world to understand is the income tax." It is not surprising that millions of Americans have given up filling out their own income tax forms, or have to rely on software such as Intuit's TurboTax or H&R Block's TaxCut.

If the tax code were greatly simplified, the economic resources currently used by the tax preparation industry would be available to produce other goods and services. In addition to wasting resources, the complexity of the tax code may also distort the decisions made by households and firms. For example, the tax rate on dividends has clearly affected whether corporations pay dividends. When the U.S. Congress passed a reduction in the tax on dividends in 2003, many firms—including Microsoft—began paying a dividend for the first time. A simplified tax code would increase economic efficiency by reducing the number of decisions households and firms make solely to reduce their tax payments.

Making the Connection | **Should Arab Non-Oil-Based Economies Adopt the 'Flat Tax'?**

In thinking about fundamental tax reform, some economists and policymakers have advocated simplifying the individual income tax by adopting a 'flat tax.' A flat tax would replace the current individual income tax system in many Arab countries, with its many tax brackets, exemptions, and deductions, with a new system containing few, or perhaps no, deductions and exemptions and a single tax rate.

In 1994, Estonia became the first country to adopt a flat tax when it began imposing a single tax rate of 26 percent on individual income. As the table shows, a number of other countries in Eastern Europe have followed Estonia's lead. Although all these countries have a flat tax rate on income, they vary in the amount of annual income they allow to be exempt from the tax and on which income is taxable. For example, Estonia does not tax corporate profits directly, although it does tax dividends paid by corporations to shareholders.

Governments in Eastern Europe are attracted by the simplicity of the flat tax. It is easy for taxpayers to understand and easy for the government to administer.

COUNTRY	FLAT TAX RATE	YEAR FLAT TAX WAS INTRODUCED
Estonia	26 percent	1994
Lithuania	33	1994
Latvia	25	1995
Russia	13	2001
Serbia	14	2003
Ukraine	13	2004
Slovakia	19	2004
Georgia	12	2005
Romania	16	2005

The result has been greater compliance with the tax code. A study of the effects of Russia's moving to a flat tax found that, before tax reform, Russians whose incomes had placed them in the two highest tax brackets had on average been reporting only 52 percent of their income to the government. In 2001, with the new, single 13 percent tax bracket in place, these high-income groups, on average, reported 68 percent of their income to the government.

In the United States and Western Europe, proponents of the flat tax have focused on the reduction in paperwork and compliance cost and the potential increases in labor supply, saving, and investment that would result from a lower marginal tax rate. Opponents of the flat tax believe it has two key weaknesses. First, they point out that many of the provisions that make the current tax code so complex were enacted for good reasons. For example, in some countries, taxpayers are allowed to deduct from their taxable income the interest they pay on mortgage loans. For many people, this provision of the tax code reduces the after-tax cost of owning a home, thereby aiding the government's goal of increasing home ownership. Similarly, the limited deduction for educational expenses increases the ability of many people to further their or their children's educations. The tax credit of up to US$3,000 applied in the U.S. in 2008 for the purchase of hybrid cars that combine an electric motor with a gasoline-powered engine was intended to further the goal of reducing air pollution and oil consumption. These and other deductions would be eliminated under most flat tax proposals, thereby reducing the ability of the government to pursue some policy goals. Second, opponents of the flat tax believe that it would make the distribution of income more unequal by reducing the marginal tax rate on high-income taxpayers. Because high-income taxpayers now can sometimes use the complexity of the tax code to shelter some of their income from taxes, it is unclear whether the amount of taxes paid by high-income people actually would decrease under a flat tax.

This issue of income distribution after applying the flat tax is of great concern to policymakers in the countries of the Arab world when thinking of replacing the progressive tax with a flat tax. People in many Arab countries feel that the national income is distributed fairly and that the gap between the rich and poor is getting larger and larger. Applying a flat tax means that both the rich and the working poor pay the same percentage of their income in tax. This equal sacrifice by both the rich and the poor is not acceptable socially and politically. Thus, some voices now are calling for not only keeping the progressive income tax, but also increasing the maximum tax rate, regardless of its negative impact on investment and, thus, economic growth. This reminds us of the famous tradeoff in economics: equity versus efficiency. So it is unlikely that a flat personal income tax will be applied in the Arab non-oil-based countries, where the disparity between the rich and poor is large.

Sources: "The Case for Flat Taxes," *The Economist*, April 14, 2005; and Juan Carlos Conesa and Dirk Krueger, "On the Optimal Progressivity of the Income Tax Code," *Journal of Monetary Economics*, Vol. 53, No. 7, October 2006, pp. 1425–1450.

YOUR TURN: Test your understanding by doing related problem 6.7 on page 794 at the end of this chapter.

The Economic Effect of Tax Reform

We can analyze the economic effects of tax reduction and simplification by using the aggregate demand and aggregate supply model. Figure 23-14 shows that without tax changes, the long-run aggregate supply curve will shift from $LRAS_1$ to $LRAS_2$. This shift represents the increases in the labor force and the capital stock and the technological change that would occur even without tax reduction and simplification. As we know from our discussion of the AD–AS model in Chapter 20, during any year, the aggregate demand and short-run aggregate supply curves will also shift. To focus on the impact

Figure 23-14

The economy's initial equilibrium is at point
A. With no tax change, long-run aggregate
supply shifts to the right, from $LRAS_1$ to
$LRAS_2$. Equilibrium moves to point B, with
the price level falling from P_1 to P_2 and real
GDP increasing from Y_1 to Y_2. With tax reductions and simplifications, long-run aggregate
supply shifts further to the right, to $LRAS_3$,
and equilibrium moves to point C, with the
price level falling to P_3 and real GDP increasing to Y_3.

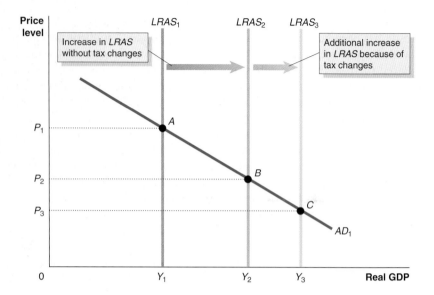

of tax changes on aggregate supply, we will ignore the short-run aggregate supply curve,
and we will assume that the aggregate demand remains unchanged, at AD_1. In this case,
equilibrium moves from point A to point B, with real GDP increasing from Y_1 to Y_2 and
the price level decreasing from P_1 to P_2.

If tax reduction and simplification are effective, the economy will experience increases
in labor supply, saving, investment, and the formation of new firms. Economic efficiency
will also be improved. Together these factors will result in an increase in the quantity of
real GDP supplied at every price level. We show the effects of the tax changes in Figure
23-14 by a shift in the long-run aggregate supply curve to $LRAS_3$. With aggregate demand
remaining unchanged, the equilibrium in the economy moves from point A to point C
(rather than to point B, which is the equilibrium without tax changes), with real GDP
increasing from Y_1 to Y_3 and the price level decreasing from P_1 to P_3. An important point
to notice is that compared with the equilibrium without tax changes (point B), the equilibrium with tax changes (point C) occurs at a lower price level and a higher level of real
GDP. We can conclude that the tax changes have benefited the economy by increasing
output and employment while at the same time reducing the price level.

Clearly, our analysis is unrealistic because we have ignored the changes in aggregate
demand and short-run aggregate supply that will actually occur. How would a more realistic analysis differ from the simplified one in Figure 23-14? The change in real GDP would
be the same because in the long run, real GDP is equal to its potential level, which is represented by the long-run aggregate supply curve. The results for the price level would be different, however, because we would expect both aggregate demand and short-run aggregate
supply to shift to the right. The likeliest case is that the price level would end up higher in
the new equilibrium than in the original equilibrium. However, because the position of the
long-run aggregate supply curve is further to the right as a result of the tax changes, the
increase in the price level will be smaller; that is, the price level at point C is likely to be lower
than at point B, even if it is higher than at point A, although—as we will discuss in the next
section—not all economists would agree. We can conclude that a successful policy of tax
reductions and simplifications will benefit the economy by increasing output and employment and, at the same time, may result in smaller increases in the price level.

How Large Are Supply-Side Effects?

Most economists would agree that there are supply-side effects to reducing taxes: decreasing
marginal income tax rates will increase the quantity of labor supplied, cutting the corporate
income tax will increase investment spending, and so on. The magnitude of the effects is subject to considerable debate, however. For example, some economists argue that the increase
in the quantity of labor supplied following a tax cut will be limited because many people
work a number of hours set by their employers and lack the opportunity to work additional

hours. Similarly, some economists believe that tax changes have only a small effect on saving and investment. In this view, saving and investment are affected much more by changes in income or changes in expectations of the future profitability of new investment due to technological change or improving macroeconomic conditions than they are by tax changes.

Economists who are skeptical of the magnitude of supply-side effects believe that tax cuts have their greatest impact on aggregate demand rather than on aggregate supply. In their view, focusing on the impact of tax cuts on aggregate demand, while ignoring any impact on aggregate supply, yields accurate forecasts of future movements in real GDP and the price level, which indicates that the supply-side effects must be small. If tax changes have only small effects on aggregate supply, it is unlikely that they will reduce the size of price increases, as they did in the analysis in Figure 23-14.

Ultimately, the size of the supply-side effects of tax policy can be resolved only through careful study of the effects of differences in tax rates on labor supply and saving and investment decisions. Some recent studies have arrived at conflicting conclusions, however. For example, a study by Nobel laureate Edward Prescott of Arizona State University in the U.S. concludes that the differences between the United States and Europe with respect to the average number of hours worked per week and the average number of weeks worked per year are due to differences in taxes. The lower marginal tax rates in the United States compared with Europe increase the return to working for U.S. workers and result in a larger quantity of labor supplied. But another U.S. study by Alberto Alesina and Edward Glaeser of Harvard University and Bruce Sacerdote of Dartmouth College argues that the more restrictive labor market regulations in Europe explain the shorter work weeks and longer vacations of European workers and that differences in taxes have only a small effect.

As in other areas of economics, over time, differences among economists in their estimates of the supply-side effects of tax changes may narrow as additional studies are undertaken.

Economics in YOUR Life!

>> Continued from page 761

At the beginning of the chapter we posed the question: How will you respond to a US$500 tax cut? and What effect will this tax cut likely have on equilibrium real GDP in the short run? This chapter has shown that tax cuts increase disposable income, and, when there is a permanent increase in disposable income, consumption spending increases. So, you will likely respond to a permanent US$500 increase in your disposable income by increasing your spending. In addition, this chapter has also shown that tax cuts such as this one have a multiplier effect on the economy. That is, an increase in consumption spending sets off further increases in real GDP and income. So, if the economy is not already at potential GDP, this tax cut will likely increase equilibrium real GDP in the short run.

Conclusion

In this chapter, we have seen how the government uses changes in government purchases and taxes to achieve its economic policy goals. We have seen that economists debate the effectiveness of discretionary fiscal policy actions intended to stabilize the economy. The government shares responsibility for economic policy with the central bank. In Chapter 24, we will discuss further some of the challenges that the central bank encounters as it carries out monetary policy. In Chapter 25, we will look more closely at the international economy, including how monetary and fiscal policy are affected by the linkages between economies.

Read *An Inside Look at Policy* on the next page for a discussion on the sustainability of fiscal policy in Lebanon and how large the public debt is.

How Severe is the Lebanese Public Debt?

THE DAILY STAR, OCTOBER 9, 2009

EU Commission: Fiscal Policy in Lebanon "Unsustainable":

Despite some positive indicators in terms of economic growth and resilience to the global financial crisis, Lebanon's economy faces grave challenges in its efforts to reduce the national debt and reform its financial institutions, the European Commission to Lebanon said on Thursday.

Economic and social reforms were the topic of discussion as commission representatives met with Lebanese political authorities and public representatives during the third round of opening hearings on the European Neighborhood Policy (ENP) action plan. "As the ENP assessment has said, the fiscal situation [in Lebanon] is unsustainable," said Dr Toufic Gaspard, an economist, noting that anything unsustainable must, by definition, reform or stop.

Lebanon's financial difficulties, and in particular its inability to balance its spending against its debt, stem from mismanagement of government spending, he said. Lebanon's debt is estimated to be around 160 percent of its GDP, the third highest in the world after Zimbabwe and Japan.

"When you look at total government expenditures between 1993 and 2009, you see a total of US$116 billion collected," said Saba. "Of that amount, US$43 billion was spent on paying the interest on the debt—not even on the principle.

"Interest and wages combined accounted for two-thirds of government spending. Add Electricite du Liban to that and you have eaten up three-fourths of the government spending." The money that the government pours into Electricite du Liban is unmonitored, he said, noting that the last budget report submitted by the company to the government appeared in 2005. As for the wages of public-sector employees, he said that compensation in the public sector amounted to a system of "political patronage." Public-sector employees, on average, make significantly more than those in the private sector, he said.

Dr Marwen Soueid, an adviser to the prime minister, cautioned critics not to condemn Lebanon's political stewards without taking into consideration the significant progress the nation has made in expanding the economy and attracting international investment.

He also congratulated the Lebanese economy, and the Lebanese public, for their resilience and ongoing faith in the country, which, as he said, has allowed it to maintain a strong growth rate during the worst financial crisis in living memory.

However, as the ENP progress report points out, Lebanon has not been untouched by the world economic crisis. Remittances from expatriates working abroad—a major contributor to GDP—have slackened, the report notes, contributing to an overall slowdown in GDP growth from 6 percent in 2008 to 3 percent in 2009.

Another factor pressuring the Lebanese public is the rising cost of imports, and in particular food, which has recently led to tensions and some public demonstrations. The cost of living continues to rise at a higher pace than wage inflation, and unemployment remains a critical problem, with only 42 percent of the public entered into the labor force, as opposed to 51 percent in Tunisia and 61 percent in Europe.

Most of the economic reforms recommended in the ENP 2008 action plan have not been undertaken, due in large part to recent political difficulties and the absence of an established parliament.

Speakers noted that, while major resolutions have been passed in line with the ENP's recommendations, in many cases those resolutions have yet to be implemented on the ground.

Source: Nathanael Massey, "EU Commission: Fiscal policy in Lebanon 'Unsustainable': Economy faces grave challenges in efforts to reduce debt," *The Daily Star*, published in *Zawya*, October 9, 2009.

Key Points in the Article

This article discusses the fiscal policy in Lebanon and how it is unsustainable because of the large national debt. The European Commission to Lebanon announced that the Lebanese economy faces great challenges in its efforts to reduce the national debt, which had reached around 160 percent of the GDP. There is a misallocation of the Lebanese public expenditure since around two-thirds of the expenditure is allocated to interest payments on the national debt and wages. In addition, the 2008 global financial crisis affected the Lebanese economy through its negative impact on Lebanese remittances. The European Neighborhood Policy progress report pointed out that the reduction in remittances from Lebanese expatriates working abroad contributed to an overall slowdown in GDP growth from 6 percent in 2008 to 3 percent in 2009.

Analyzing the News

A sustainable fiscal policy simply means controlling the budget deficit and public debt, and keeping them within specific limits as a percentage of GDP, in order to achieve the desired levels of economic stability and economic growth. For example, the Maastricht Treaty (a treaty signed in 1991 by members of the European Union (EU) to work toward a monetary union) requires EU member countries to keep budget deficits below 3 percent of GDP, and public debt below 60 percent of GDP, in order for the EU economies to be

stable. In addition, the empirical study on sovereign default, i.e. the inability of a government to repay its debt because the government's debt obligations exceed its capacity to pay, conducted by the International Monetary Fund (IMF), shows that the median public debt to GDP ratio among countries that defaulted on their public debt during the 1980s and 1990s is about 50 percent. Now comparing between the thresholds set by the EU members and the IMF empirical study to the Lebanese debt to GDP ratio of 160 percent, we can explain why the European Commission to Lebanon claims that the fiscal policy in Lebanon is "unsustainable." This considerably high debt to GDP ratio threatens both the economic growth and economic stability in Lebanon in the future. If the Lebanese government decides to raise taxes to repay its debts, private investment will be affected negatively and, thus, a slower economic growth rate will be expected, which will create recessionary pressures on the economy. An efficient allocation and management of government expenditure is required to decrease the debt to GDP ratio.

A key factor in assuring the sustainability and efficiency of the fiscal policy is political stability and the existence of a strong parliament. As we learned throughout the chapter, the government cannot implement fiscal policies (discretionary or automatic stabilizers) without the approval of parliament. Unfortunately, some external and internal factors in Lebanon create periods of political instability more

often than other countries in the region. This makes the process of discussing and monitoring the execution of the proposed fiscal policies by the government very difficult. This could lead to a sharp increase in government expenditure and, thus, the budget deficit and public debt. On the other hand, although the 2008 global financial crisis affected the Lebanese economy negatively, mainly through its negative impact on remittances by Lebanese expatriates, the good news is that it resulted in a reduction in the debt service to GDP ratio in 2010. As indicated by Dr Youssef Khalil, Senior Director of the Financial Operations Department at Banque du Liban, Beirut, the reason behind this reduction in the debt service to GDP ratio is that the crisis led to a reduction in the interest rate.

Source: "International and Arab Perspectives on the Recent Economic Crisis," Jordan, June 21, 2010.

Thinking Critically About Policy

1. Suppose that parliament passes increased spending for an expansionary fiscal policy. All else being equal, is the policy's effect on aggregate demand relatively larger or smaller if an increase in taxes is also in effect? Briefly explain your reasoning.

2. Suppose that the Saudi government announces that it will not renew the 15-percent cost-of-living allowances in 2015. How is this announcement likely to affect aggregate demand today?

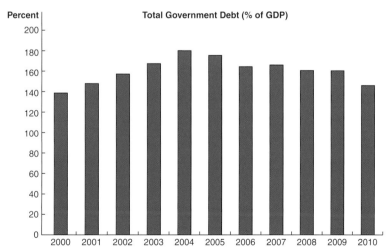

The fiscal policy in Lebanon is considered unsustainable because of the large national debt as a percentage of GDP.

The Central Bank of Lebanon, www.bdl.gov.lb/edata/elements.asp?Table=t531-1, and World Development Indicators, www.worldbank.org.

Key Terms

Automatic stabilizers,
   p. 762

Budget deficit, p. 777

Budget surplus, p. 777

Crowding out, p. 774

Cyclically adjusted budget
   deficit or surplus, p. 778

Fiscal policy, p. 762

Multiplier effect, p. 768

Tax wedge, p. 783

Summary

23.1 LEARNING OBJECTIVE

Define fiscal policy, **pages 762–764.**

Fiscal Policy

Fiscal policy involves changes in government taxes and purchases that are intended to achieve macroeconomic policy objectives. **Automatic stabilizers** are government spending and taxes that automatically increase or decrease along with the business cycle. The main categories of government spending are: government purchases, transfer payments, and interest payments. The ups and downs in the percentage of government purchases to GDP in Arab non-oil-based economies are smoother than those in Arab oil-based economies. This is because of the fluctuations in the international oil prices, which significantly affect both the value of GDP and government expenditure programs in oil-based economies. While non-oil-based economies depend on income taxes, sales taxes, customs duties, and sometimes oil revenues to fund government expenses, oil-based economies get most of their revenues from oil.

23.2 LEARNING OBJECTIVE

Explain how fiscal policy affects aggregate demand and how the government can use fiscal policy to stabilize the economy, **pages 764–768.**

The Effects of Fiscal Policy on Real GDP and the Price Level

To fight recessions, the government can propose to increase government purchases or cut taxes. After getting approval from parliament, this expansionary policy causes the aggregate demand curve to shift out more than it otherwise would, raising the level of real GDP and the price level. To fight rising inflation, the government can decrease government purchases or raise taxes. This contractionary policy causes the aggregate demand curve to shift out less than it otherwise would, reducing the increase in real GDP and the price level.

23.3 LEARNING OBJECTIVE

Explain how government purchases and tax multipliers work, **pages 768–773.**

Government Purchases and Tax Multipliers

Because of the **multiplier effect**, an increase in government purchases or a cut in taxes will have a multiplied effect on equilibrium real GDP. The *government purchases multiplier* is equal to the change in equilibrium real GDP divided by the change in government purchases. The *tax multiplier* is equal to the change in equilibrium real GDP divided by the change in taxes. Increases in government purchases and cuts in taxes have a positive multiplier effect on equilibrium real GDP. Decreases in government purchases and increases in taxes have a negative multiplier effect on equilibrium real GDP.

23.4 LEARNING OBJECTIVE

Discuss the difficulties that can arise in implementing fiscal policy, **page 773–777.**

The Limits of Using Fiscal Policy to Stabilize the Economy

Poorly timed fiscal policy can do more harm than good. Getting the timing right with fiscal policy can be difficult because obtaining approval from parliament for a new fiscal policy can be a very long process and because it can take months for an increase in authorized spending to actually take place. Because an increase in government purchases may lead to a higher interest rate, it may result in a decline in consumption, investment, and net exports. A decline in private expenditures as a result of an increase in government purchases is called **crowding out**. Crowding out may cause an expansionary fiscal policy to fail to meet its goal of keeping the economy at potential GDP.

Deficits, Surpluses, and Government Debt

A **budget deficit** occurs when the government's expenditures are greater than its tax revenues. A **budget surplus** occurs when the government's expenditures are less than its tax revenues. The budget deficit automatically increases during recessions and decreases during expansions. The automatic movements in the budget help to stabilize the economy by cushioning the fall in spending during recessions and restraining the increase in spending during expansions. The **cyclically adjusted budget deficit or surplus** is the deficit or surplus in the government's budget if the economy were at potential GDP. The government debt is the value of outstanding bonds issued by the government Treasury. The national debt is a problem if interest payments on it require taxes to be raised substantially or require other government expenditures to be cut.

23.5 LEARNING OBJECTIVE

Define budget deficit and government debt and explain how the budget can serve as an automatic stabilizer, **pages 777–782.**

The Effects of Fiscal Policy in the Long Run

Some fiscal policy actions are intended to have long-run effects by expanding the productive capacity of the economy and increasing the rate of economic growth. Because these policy actions primarily affect aggregate supply rather than aggregate demand, they are sometimes referred to as *supply-side economics*. The difference between the pre-tax and post-tax return to an economic activity is known as the **tax wedge**. Economists believe that the smaller the tax wedge for any economic activity—such as working, saving, investing, or starting a business—the more of that economic activity will occur. Economists debate the size of the supply-side effects of tax changes.

23.6 LEARNING OBJECTIVE

Discuss the effects of fiscal policy in the long run, **pages 782–787.**

Review, Problems and Applications

 Visit www.pearsoned.co.uk/awe/hubbard to complete these exercises online and get instant feedback.

Get Ahead of the Curve

23.1 LEARNING OBJECTIVE   Define fiscal policy, **pages 762–764.**

Review Questions

1.1 What is fiscal policy? Who is responsible for fiscal policy?
1.2 What is the difference between fiscal policy and monetary policy?
1.3 What is the difference between purchases and expenditures? Are government purchases in Saudi Arabia and Kuwait higher today as a percentage of GDP than they were in early 1990? Why?

Problems and Applications

1.4 What does it mean if government expenditure is increasing more rapidly than government purchases?
1.5 After the Egyptian and Tunisian revolutions in early 2011, which type of government expenditure is likely to increase the most, in the future, in these two countries? Briefly explain.

23.2 LEARNING OBJECTIVE   Explain how fiscal policy affects aggregate demand and how the government can use fiscal policy to stabilize the economy, **pages 764–768.**

Review Questions

2.1 What is an expansionary fiscal policy? What is a contractionary fiscal policy?
2.2 If the government decides an expansionary fiscal policy is necessary, what changes should they make in government spending or taxes? What changes should they make if they decide a contractionary fiscal policy is necessary?

Problems and Applications

2.3 Briefly explain whether you agree or disagree with the following statements: "An expansionary fiscal policy involves an increase in government purchases or an increase in taxes. A contractionary fiscal policy involves a decrease in government purchases or a decrease in taxes."
2.4 Identify each of the following as (i) part of an expansionary fiscal policy, (ii) part of a contractionary fiscal policy, or (iii) not part of fiscal policy.
    a. The corporate income tax rate is increased.
    b. Defense spending is increased.
    c. Families are allowed to deduct all their expenses for daycare from their income taxes.
    d. The individual income tax rate is decreased.

e. The government builds a new highway in an attempt to expand employment in the state.

2.5 Briefly explain whether you agree with the following remark: "Real GDP is US$250 billion below its full-employment level. With a multiplier of 2, if the government increases government purchases by US$125 billion or the central bank increases the money supply by US$125 billion, real GDP can be brought back to its full-employment level."

2.6 Use the graph to answer the following questions.

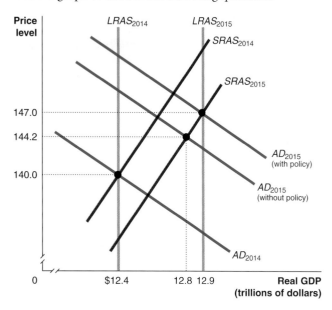

a. If the government does not take any policy actions, what will be the values of real GDP and the price level in 2015?

b. If the government purchases multiplier is 2, how much will government purchases have to be increased to bring real GDP to its potential level in 2015? (Assume that the multiplier value takes into account the impact of a rising price level on the multiplier effect.)

c. If the tax multiplier is −1.6, how much will taxes have to be cut to bring real GDP to its potential level in 2015? (Again, assume that the multiplier value takes into account the impact of a rising price level.)

d. If the government takes no policy actions, what will be the inflation rate in 2015? If the government uses fiscal policy to keep real GDP at its potential level, what will be the inflation rate in 2015?

Review Questions

3.1 Why does a US$1 increase in government purchases lead to more than a US$1 increase in income and spending?

3.2 Define the government purchases multiplier and the tax multiplier.

Problems and Applications

3.3 In *The General Theory of Employment, Interest, and Money*, John Maynard Keynes wrote this:

> If the Treasury were to fill old bottles with banknotes, bury them at suitable depths in disused coal mines which are then filled up to the surface with town rubbish, and leave it to private enterprise…to dig the notes up again…there need be no more unemployment and, with the help of the repercussions, the real income of the community…would probably become a good deal greater than it is.

Which important macroeconomic effect is Keynes discussing here? What does he mean by "repercussions"? Why does he appear unconcerned if government spending is wasteful?

3.4 Suppose that real GDP is currently US$13.1 trillion, potential real GDP is US$13.5 trillion, the government purchases multiplier is 2, and the tax multiplier is −1.6.

a. Holding other factors constant, by how much will government purchases need to be increased to bring the economy to equilibrium at potential GDP?

b. Holding other factors constant, by how much will taxes have to be cut to bring the economy to equilibrium at potential GDP?

c. Construct an example of a *combination* of increased government spending and tax cuts that will bring the economy to equilibrium at potential GDP.

3.5 (Related to *Solved Problem 23-3* on page 772) Briefly explain whether you agree or disagree with the following statement: "Real GDP is currently US$12.7 trillion, and potential real GDP is US$12.4 trillion. If the government would decrease government purchases by US$200 billion or increase taxes by US$200 billion, the economy could be brought to equilibrium at potential GDP."

3.6 If the short-run aggregate supply curve (*SRAS*) were a horizontal line, what would be the impact on the size of the government purchases and tax multipliers?

Review Questions

4.1 Which can be changed more quickly: monetary policy or fiscal policy? Briefly explain.

4.2 What is meant by crowding out? Explain the difference between crowding out in the short run and in the long run.

Problems and Applications

4.3 In a column published in the *Wall Street Journal* on July 19, 2001, David Wessel wrote, "Most economic forecasters don't foresee recession this year or next." In fact, a recession had already begun in March 2001. Does this tell us anything about the difficulty of U.S. Congress and the president implementing a fiscal policy that stabilizes rather than destabilizes the economy?

Source: David Wessel, "Economic Forecasting in Three Steps," *Wall Street Journal*, July 19, 2001, p. A1.

4.4 Figure 23-10 on page 774 shows the equilibrium interest rate rising as the demand for money increases.

Describe what must be happening in the market for government Treasury bills.

4.5 Some economists argue that because increases in government spending crowd out private spending, increased government spending will reduce the long-run growth rate of real GDP.

a. Is this most likely to happen if the private spending being crowded out is consumption spending, investment spending, or net exports? Briefly explain.

b. In terms of its effect on the long-run growth rate of real GDP, would it matter if the additional government spending involves (i) increased spending on highways and bridges or (ii) increased spending on the national parks? Briefly explain.

4.6 (Related to the *Making the Connection* on page 776) Why might the effects on health of a temporary increase or decrease in income be different than the effects of a permanent increase or decrease?

Review Problems

5.1 In what ways does the budget serve as an automatic stabilizer for the economy?

5.2 What is the cyclically adjusted budget deficit or surplus? Suppose that the economy is currently at potential GDP and the budget is balanced. If the economy moves into recession, what will happen to the budget?

5.3 Why do few economists argue that it would be a good idea to balance the budget every year?

5.4 What is the difference between the budget deficit and government debt?

Problems and Applications

5.5 (Related to *Solved Problem 23-5* on page 780) Suppose that the government's budget deficit was US$22.4 billion in 2009 and US$26.2 billion in 2010. What does this information tell us about fiscal policy actions that this government took during these years?

5.6 The following is from an article in the *Wall Street Journal*: "The Treasury Department said it expected to borrow a net US$1 billion during the April-to-June quarter—not repay a net US$89 billion, as it said it would earlier this year." Why does the Treasury Department borrow? When the Treasury "repays," who is it repaying? Why would the Treasury say it was going to repay debt and then end up borrowing?

Source: Rebecca Christie and Deborah Lagomarsino, "US Debt Is Set to Rise in Quarter as Tax Receipts Come Up Short," *Wall Street Journal*, April 30, 2002.

5.7 A government calculates its budget on a fiscal year that begins each year on October 1 and ends on the following September 30. Suppose that at the beginning of the 1997 fiscal year, the Budget Office (Committee) in parliament forecasts that the budget deficit would be $127.7 billion. The actual budget deficit for fiscal 1997 was only $21.9 billion. Expenditures were $30.3 billion less than the Budget Office had forecast, and revenue was $75.5 billion more than the Budget Office had forecast.

a. Is it likely that the economy grew faster or slower during fiscal 1997 than the CBO had expected? Explain your reasoning.

b. Suppose that the government and the president were committed to balancing the budget each year. Does what happened during 1997 provide any insight into difficulties they might run into in trying to balance the budget every year?

5.8 Nobel laureate Paul Samuelson, an economist at MIT, argued that "it was harmful to let a large budget surplus develop in the weak 1959–60 revival and thereby help to choke off that recovery." Why would a large budget surplus "choke off" a recovery from economic recession? What could the government have done to have kept a large budget surplus from developing?

Source: Paul A. Samuelson, "Economic Policy for 1962," *American Economic Review*, Vol. 44, No. 1 (February 1962), p. 6.

5.9 In testifying before Congress in 2003, then U.S. Federal Reserve Chairman Alan Greenspan observed,

"There is no question that if you run substantial and excessive deficits over time you are draining savings from the private sector." What did Greenspan mean by "draining savings from the private sector"? How might this be bad for the economy?

Source: Martin Crutsinger, "Greenspan Warns of Rising Deficits," Associated Press, July 17, 2003.

5.10 Budget forecasts depend on so many variables. What variables would a forecast of future budget deficits depend on? What is it about these variables that makes future budget deficits difficult to predict?

5.11 According to an article in the *Wall Street Journal* "US tax revenue for fiscal 2006,...is expected to be 5 percent—or US$115 billion—higher, than the administration projected in February. Largely as a result, the budget deficit is expected to be US$296 billion this year, instead of US$423 billion." Why would higher than expected tax revenues cause the budget deficit to be smaller than expected? What might make tax revenues be higher than expected? (*Hint:* For one possibility, note the title of the article given in the source line below.)

Source: Greg Ip and Deborah Solomon, "As Bigger Piece of Economic Pie Shifts to Wealthiest, US Deficit Heads Downward," *Wall Street Journal*, July 17, 2006, p. A2.

5.12 During 2003, China ran large government budget deficits to stimulate its economy. The *Wall Street Journal* quoted an official in China's ministry of finance as saying, "The proactive fiscal policy has brought some negative effects because it has squeezed out the private investor." What did the official mean by a "proactive fiscal policy"? Why would such a policy "squeeze out" the private investor? Does that mean the policy should not have been used?

Source: Karby Leggett and Kathy Chen, "China's Rising Debt Raises Questions about the Future," *Wall Street Journal*, January 20, 2003.

5.13 A political columnist wrote the following:

Today...the main purpose [of government's issuing bonds] is to let craven politicians launch projects they know the public, at the moment, would rather not fully finance. The tab for these projects will not come due, probably, until after the politicians have long since departed for greener (excuse the expression) pastures.

Do you agree with this commentator's explanation for why some government spending is financed through tax receipts and other government spending is financed through borrowing, by issuing bonds? Briefly explain.

Source: Paul Carpenter, "The Bond Issue Won't Be Repaid by Park Tolls," *(Allentown, PA) Morning Call*, May 26, 2002, p. B1.

23.6 LEARNING OBJECTIVE   Discuss the effects of fiscal policy in the long run, **pages 782–787.**

Review Questions

6.1 What is meant by supply-side economics?

6.2 What is the 'tax wedge'?

Problems and Applications

6.3 It would seem that both households and businesses would benefit if the income tax were simpler and tax forms were easier to fill out. Why then have the tax laws become increasingly complicated?

6.4 Suppose a political candidate hired you to develop two arguments in favor of a flat tax. What two arguments would you advance? Alternatively, if you were hired to develop two arguments against the flat tax, what two arguments would you advance?

6.5 Suppose that an increase in marginal tax rates on individual income affects both aggregate demand and aggregate supply. Briefly describe the effect of the tax increase on equilibrium real GDP and the equilibrium price level. Will the changes in equilibrium real GDP and the price level be larger or smaller than they would be if the tax increase affected only aggregate demand? Briefly explain.

6.6 An editorial in the *Wall Street Journal* in early 2007 observed: "The other news you won't often hear concerns the soaring tax revenues in the wake of the 2003 supply-side tax cuts. Tax collections have risen by US$757 billion, among the largest revenue gushers in history." What is a "supply-side" tax cut? How would a supply-side tax cut lead to higher tax revenues? Would a supply-side tax cut always result in higher tax revenues?

Source: "Fiscal Revelation," *Wall Street Journal*, February 6, 2007.

6.7 **(Related to the *Making the Connection* on page 784)** As the Czech Republic considered converting to a flat tax, an editorial in the *Wall Street Journal* noted, "If the [Czech] Prime Minister manages to push his plans through a divided parliament in June, it would bring to 14 the number of single-rate tax systems in the world, all but four of them in Eastern Europe. (Hong Kong, Iceland, Mongolia and Kyrgyzstan are the exceptions.)" Why would the countries of Eastern Europe and the other small countries mentioned be more likely to adopt a flat tax than the United States, Canada, Japan, or the countries of Western Europe?

Source: "Flat Czechs," *Wall Street Journal*, April 13, 2007.

Appendix

A Closer Look at the Multiplier

In this chapter, we saw that changes in government purchases and changes in taxes have a multiplied effect on equilibrium real GDP. In this appendix, we will build a simple economic model of the multiplier effect. When economists forecast the effect of a change in spending or taxes, they often rely on *econometric models*. As we saw in the appendix to Chapter 19, an econometric model is an economic model written in the form of equations, where each equation has been statistically estimated, using methods similar to those used in estimating demand curves, as briefly described in Chapter 3. In this appendix, we will start with a model similar to the one we used in the appendix to Chapter 19.

An Expression for Equilibrium Real GDP

We can write a set of equations that includes the key macroeconomic relationships we have studied in this and previous chapters. It is important to note that in this model, we will be assuming that the price level is constant. We know that this is unrealistic because an upward-sloping *SRAS* curve means that when the aggregate demand curve shifts, the price level will change. Nevertheless, our model will be approximately correct when changes in the price level are small. It also serves as an introduction to more complicated models that take into account changes in the price level. For simplicity, we also start out by assuming that taxes, T, do not depend on the level of real GDP, Y. We also assume that there are no government transfer payments to households. Finally, we assume that we have a closed economy, with no imports or exports. The numbers (with the exception of the *MPC*) represent billions of dollars:

(1) $C = 1{,}000 + 0.75(Y - T)$ Consumption function

(2) $I = 1{,}500$ Planned investment function

(3) $G = 1{,}500$ Government purchases function

(4) $T = 1{,}000$ Tax function

(5) $Y = C + I + G$ Equilibrium condition

The first equation is the consumption function. The marginal propensity to consume, or *MPC*, is 0.75, and 1,000 is the level of autonomous consumption, which is the level of consumption that does not depend on income. We assume that consumption depends on disposable income, which is $Y - T$. The functions for planned investment spending, government spending, and taxes are very simple because we have assumed that these variables are not affected by GDP and, therefore, are constant. Economists who use this type of model to forecast GDP would, of course, use more realistic planned investment, government purchases, and tax functions.

Equation (5)—the equilibrium condition—states that equilibrium GDP equals the sum of consumption spending, planned investment spending, and government purchases. To calculate a value for equilibrium real GDP, we need to substitute equations (1) through (4) into equation (5). This substitution gives us the following:

$$Y = 1,000 + 0.75(Y - 1,000) + 1,500 + 1,500$$
$$= 1,000 + 0.75Y - 750 + 1,500 + 1,500$$

We need to solve this equation for Y to find equilibrium GDP. The first step is to subtract $0.75Y$ from both sides of the equation:

$$Y - 0.75Y = 1,000 - 750 + 1,500 + 1,500$$

Then, we solve for Y:

$$0.25Y = 3,250$$

or:

$$Y = \frac{3,250}{0.25} = 13,000$$

To make this result more general, we can replace particular values with general values represented by letters:

(1) $C = \bar{C} + MPC(Y-T)$	Consumption function
(2) $I = \bar{I}$	Planned Investment function
(3) $G = \bar{G}$	Government purchases function
(4) $T = \bar{T}$	Tax function
(5) $Y = C + I + G$	Equilibrium condition

The letters with 'bars' represent fixed, or *autonomous*, values that do not depend on the values of other variables. So, represents autonomous consumption, which had a value of 1,000 in our original example. Now, solving for equilibrium, we get:

$$Y = \bar{C} + MPC(Y - \bar{T}) + \bar{I} + \bar{G}$$

or:

$$Y - MPC(Y) = \bar{C} - (MPC \times \bar{T}) + \bar{I} + \bar{G}$$

or:

$$Y(1 - MPC) = \bar{C} - (MPC \times \bar{T}) + \bar{I} + \bar{G}$$

or:

$$Y = \frac{\bar{C} - (MPC \times \bar{T}) + \bar{I} + \bar{G}}{1 - MPC}$$

A Formula for the Government Purchases Multiplier

To find a formula for the government purchases multiplier, we need to rewrite the last equation for changes in each variable rather than levels. Letting – stand for the change in a variable, we have:

$$\Delta Y = \frac{\Delta\bar{C} - (MPC \times \Delta\bar{T}) + \Delta\bar{I} + \Delta\bar{G}}{1 - MPC}$$

If we hold constant changes in autonomous consumption spending, planned investment spending, and taxes, we can find a formula for the government purchases multiplier, which is the ratio of the change in equilibrium real GDP to the change in government purchases:

$$\Delta Y = \frac{\Delta G}{1 - MPC}$$

or:

$$\text{Government purchases multiplier} = \frac{\Delta Y}{\Delta G} = \frac{1}{1 - MPC}$$

For an *MPC* of 0.75, the government purchases multiplier will be:

$$\frac{1}{1 - 0.72} = 4$$

A government purchases multiplier of 4 means that an increase in government spending of US$10 billion will increase equilibrium real GDP by 4 × US$10 billion = US$40 billion.

A Formula for the Tax Multiplier

We can also find a formula for the tax multiplier. We start again with this equation:

$$\Delta Y = \frac{\Delta \overline{C} - (MPC \times \Delta \overline{T}) + \Delta \overline{I} + \Delta \overline{G}}{1 - MPC}$$

Now we hold constant the values of autonomous consumption spending, planned investment spending, and government purchases, but we allow the value of taxes to change:

$$\Delta Y = \frac{-MPC \times \Delta T}{1 - MPC}$$

or:

$$\text{The tax multiplier} = \frac{\Delta Y}{\Delta T} = \frac{-MPC}{1 - MPC}$$

For an *MPC* of 0.75, the tax multiplier will be:

$$\frac{-0.75}{1 - 0.75} = -3$$

The tax multiplier is a negative number because an increase in taxes causes a decrease in equilibrium real GDP, and a decrease in taxes causes an increase in equilibrium real GDP. A tax multiplier of –3 means that a decrease in taxes of US$10 billion will increase equilibrium real GDP by –3 × –US$10 billion = US$30 billion. In this chapter, we discussed the economic reasons for the tax multiplier being smaller than the government spending multiplier.

The 'Balanced Budget' Multiplier

What will be the effect of equal increases (or decreases) in government purchases and taxes on equilibrium real GDP? At first, it might appear that the tax increase would exactly offset the government purchases increase, leaving real GDP unchanged. But we have just seen that the government purchases multiplier is larger (in absolute value) than the tax multiplier. We can use our formulas for the government purchases multiplier and the tax multiplier to calculate the net effect of increasing government purchases by US$10 billion at the same time that taxes are increased by US$10 billion:

Increase in real GDP from the increase in government purchases =

$$\$10 \text{ billion} \times \frac{1}{1 - MPC}$$

Decrease in real DGP from the increase in taxes = $\$10$ billion $\times \dfrac{-MPC}{1 - MPC}$

So, the combined effect equals:

$$\$10 \text{ billion} \times \left[\left(\frac{1}{1 - MPC} \right) + \left(\frac{-MPC}{1 - MPC} \right) \right]$$

or:

$$\$10 \text{ billion} \times \left(\frac{1 - MPC}{1 - MPC} \right) = \$10 \text{ billion}$$

The balanced budget multiplier is, therefore, equal to $(1 - MPC)/(1 - MPC)$, or 1. Equal dollar increases and decreases in government purchases and in taxes lead to the same dollar increase in real GDP in the short run.

The Effects of Changes in Tax Rates on the Multiplier

We now consider the effect of a change in the tax *rate*, as opposed to a change in a fixed amount of taxes. Changing the tax rate actually changes the value of the multiplier. To see this, suppose the tax rate is 20 percent, or 0.2. In that case, an increase in household income of US$10 billion will increase *disposable income* by only US$8 billion [or US$10 billion $\times (1 - 0.2)$]. In general, an increase in income can be multiplied by $(1 - t)$ to find the increase in disposable income, where t is the tax rate. So, we can rewrite the consumption function as:

$$C = \bar{C} + MPC(1 - t)Y$$

We can use this expression for the consumption function to find an expression for the government purchases multiplier using the same method we used previously:

$$\text{Government purchases multiplier} = \frac{\Delta Y}{\Delta G} = \frac{1}{1 - MPC(1 - t)}$$

We can see the effect of changing the tax rate on the size of the multiplier by trying some values. First, assume that $MPC = 0.75$ and $t = 0.2$. Then:

$$\text{Government purchases multiplier} = \frac{\Delta Y}{\Delta G} = \frac{1}{1 - 0.75(1 - 0.2)}$$

$$= \frac{1}{1 - 0.6} = 2.5$$

This value is smaller than the multiplier of 4 that we calculated by assuming that there was only a fixed amount of taxes (which is the same as assuming that the marginal tax *rate* was zero). This multiplier is smaller because spending in each period is now reduced by the amount of taxes households must pay on any additional income they earn. We can calculate the multiplier for an *MPC* of 0.75 and a lower tax rate of 0.1:

$$\text{Government purchases multiplier} = \frac{\Delta Y}{\Delta G} = \frac{1}{1 - 0.75(1 - 0.1)}$$

$$= \frac{1}{1 - 0.675} = 3.1$$

Cutting the tax rate from 20 percent to 10 percent increased the value of the multiplier from 2.5 to 3.1.

The Multiplier in an Open Economy

Up to now, we have assumed that the economy is closed, with no imports or exports. We can consider the case of an open economy by including net exports in our analysis. Recall that net exports equal exports minus imports. Exports are determined primarily by factors—such as the exchange value of the dollar and the levels of real GDP in other countries—that we do not include in our model. So, we will assume that exports are fixed, or autonomous:

$$\text{Exports} = \overline{Exports}$$

Imports will increase as real GDP increases because households will spend some portion of an increase in income on imports. We can define the *marginal propensity to import* (*MPI*) as the fraction of an increase in income that is spent on imports. So, our expression for imports is:

$$\text{Imports} = MPI \times Y$$

We can substitute our expressions for exports and imports into the expression we derived earlier for equilibrium real GDP:

$$Y = \overline{C} + MPC(1 - t)Y + \overline{I} + \overline{G} + [\overline{Imports} - (MPI \times Y)]$$

where the expression $\overline{Imports} - (MPI \times Y)$, represents net exports. We can now find an expression for the government purchases multiplier by using the same method as we did previously:

$$\text{Government purchases multiplier} = \frac{\Delta Y}{\Delta G} = \frac{1}{1 - [MPC(1 - t) - MPI]}$$

We can see the effect of changing the value of the marginal propensity to import on the size of the multiplier by trying some values of key variables. First, assume *MPC* = 0.75, *t* = 0.2, and *MPI* = 0.1. Then:

$$\text{Government purchases multiplier} = \frac{\Delta Y}{\Delta G} = \frac{1}{1 - (0.75)(1 - 0.2) - 0.1)}$$

$$= \frac{1}{1 - 0.5} = 2$$

This value is smaller than the multiplier of 2.5 that we calculated by assuming that there were no exports or imports (which is the same as assuming that the marginal propensity to import was zero). This multiplier is smaller because spending in each period is now reduced by the amount of imports households buy with any additional income they earn. We can calculate the multiplier with *MPC* = 0.75, *t* = 0.20, and a higher *MPI* of 0.2:

$$\text{Government purchases multiplier} = \frac{\Delta Y}{\Delta G} = \frac{1}{1 - (0.75(1 - 0.2) - 0.2)}$$

$$= \frac{1}{1 - 0.4} = 1.7$$

Increasing the marginal propensity to import from 0.1 to 0.2 decreases the value of the multiplier from 2 to 1.7. We can conclude that countries with a higher marginal propensity to import will have smaller multipliers than countries with a lower marginal propensity to import.

It is always important to bear in mind that the multiplier is a short-run effect which assumes that the economy is below the level of potential real GDP. In the long run, the economy is at potential real GDP, so an increase in government purchases causes a decline in the nongovernment components of real GDP, but it leaves the level of real GDP unchanged.

The analysis in this appendix is simplified compared to what would be carried out by an economist forecasting the effects of changes in government purchases or changes in taxes on equilibrium real GDP in the short run. In particular, our assumption that the price level is constant is unrealistic. However, looking more closely at the determinants of the multiplier has helped us see more clearly some important macroeconomic relationships.

Problem and Applications

 Visit www.pearsoned.co.uk/awe/hubbard to complete these exercises online and get instant feedback.

Get Ahead of the Curve

23A.1 Assuming a fixed amount of taxes and a closed economy, calculate the value of the government purchases multiplier, the tax multiplier, and the balanced budget multiplier if the marginal propensity to consume equals 0.6.

23A.2 Calculate the value of the government purchases multiplier if the marginal propensity to consume equals 0.8, the tax rate equals 0.25, and the marginal propensity to import equals 0.2.

23A.3 Show on a graph the change in the aggregate demand curve resulting from an increase in government purchases if the government purchases multiplier equals 2. Now, on the same graph, show the change in the aggregate demand curve resulting from an increase in government purchases if the government purchases multiplier equals 4.

23A.4 Using your understanding of the multiplier process, explain why an increase in the tax rate would decrease the size of the government purchases multiplier. Similarly, explain why a decrease in the marginal propensity to import would increase the size of the government purchases multiplier.

>> **End Appendix Learning Objective**

Inflation, Unemployment, and Central Bank Policy

How Do Central Banks React to Economic Downturns?

How do economic downturns affect monetary policy, and how does monetary policy affect economic downturns? The following examples of central banks' actions answer these questions.

In 2008, the global financial crisis started to have a negative impact on economic activities in general, and investment in particular, in the Arab world. Central banks in the Arab countries responded to the low investment and lending rates by applying expansionary (easy) monetary policies. For example, the Governor of the Central Bank of Kuwait (CBK), Sheikh Salem Al-Sabah, announced in an interview with Emirates 24/7 Business that "since the fourth quarter of 2008, the Central Bank had adopted a policy of expanding its supervisory policy to enhance the banks' role in meeting the financing needs of Kuwait's economic sectors by sharply cutting rates, injecting liquidity into the banking sector, and revising (deposit) ratios to allow banks to increase their financing activities in the country."

In the same trend, the latest Economic Review of the Central Bank of Egypt (CBE) shows the Central Bank's reaction toward the global financial crisis as follows: "The Monetary Policy Committee (MPC) took a number of decisions responsive to changes in inflation and its own assessment of inflationary pressures (six MPC meetings were held during July/March 2009/2010). Accordingly, the MPC decided in the two meetings dated July 30 and September 17, 2009 to cut down the CBE's key interest rates (the overnight deposit and lending rates), with a cumulative drop of 0.75 percent to 8.25 percent and 9.75 percent, respectively, at the end of Sept. 2009. The discount rate was also cut by 0.50 percent to 8.5 percent per annum."

In simple words, it is clear that both central banks decided to lower the target for the overnight interest rate to fight the negative effects of the global financial crisis on both firms and households.

We saw in Chapter 3, when introducing the model of demand and supply, that the ability of firms to produce is determined partly by microeconomic factors input cost and technology. The previous expansionary monetary policy implemented by the Central Banks of Kuwait and Egypt indicates that macroeconomic factors, such as monetary policy in this case study, also play a role. By lowering the overnight lending rate (and the discount rate), the cost of borrowing between banks (and from the Central Bank) decreases, which increases banks' ability to make new loans. Thus, the new loans will be offered to firms (investors) at a lower market interest rate, which will encourage firms to borrow more and expand their investment since the cost of capital is now less than before. At the aggregate level, when many firms enlarge their investment, the aggregate demand shifts rightward and pushes the aggregate output closer to the potential GDP and, thus, the economy goes into recovery.

AN INSIDE LOOK AT POLICY on **page 824** discusses the Central Bank of Jordan's monetary policy during the 2009 recession and the 2010 inflation.

Sources: "Kuwaiti Central Bank Defends Monetary Policy," emirates247.com, August 3, 2010; and the Central Bank of Egypt, *Economic Review*, Vol. 50, No. 3, 2009/2010.

LEARNING Objectives

After studying this chapter, you should be able to:

24.1 Describe the **Phillips curve** and the nature of the **short-run trade-off** between **unemployment** and **inflation**, page 804.

24.2 Explain the relationship between the **short-run** and **long-run Phillips curves**, page 809.

24.3 Discuss how **expectations** of the **inflation rate** affect monetary policy, page 814.

24.4 Use a Phillips curve graph to show how the **central bank** can permanently **lower** the **inflation rate**, page 817.

Economics in YOUR Life!

How Big of a Raise Should You Ask For?

Suppose that you meet with your boss to discuss your raise for next year. One factor in deciding how big an increase to request is your expectation of what the inflation rate will be. If the central bank pledges to keep the unemployment rate at 3 percent in the long run, what effect will this pledge have on the size of the raise you request? As you read this chapter, see if you can answer this question. You can check your answer against the one we provide at the end of the chapter.

>> Continued on page 822

A
s we saw in Chapter 22, two of the central bank's monetary policy goals are price stability and high employment. These goals can sometimes be in conflict, however. An important consideration for the central bank is that in the short run, there can be a trade-off between unemployment and inflation: lower unemployment rates can result in higher inflation rates. In the long run, however, this trade-off disappears, and the unemployment rate is independent of the inflation rate. In this chapter, we will explore the relationship between inflation and unemployment in both the short run and the long run, and we will discuss what this relationship means for monetary policy.

24.1 LEARNING OBJECTIVE

24.1 | Describe the Phillips curve and the nature of the short-run trade-off between unemployment and inflation.

The Discovery of the Short-Run Trade-off between Unemployment and Inflation

Unemployment and inflation are the two great macroeconomic problems the central bank must deal with in the short run. As we saw in Chapter 20, when aggregate demand increases, unemployment usually falls and inflation rises. When aggregate demand decreases, unemployment usually rises and inflation falls. As a result, there is a *short-run trade-off* between unemployment and inflation: higher unemployment is usually accompanied by lower inflation, and lower unemployment is usually accompanied by higher inflation. As we will see later in this chapter, this trade-off exists in the short run—a period that may be as long as several years—but disappears in the long run.

Although today the short-run trade-off between unemployment and inflation plays a role in the central bank's monetary policy decisions, this trade-off was not widely recognized until the late 1950s. In 1957, New Zealand economist A. W. Phillips plotted data on the unemployment rate and the inflation rate in Great Britain and drew a curve showing their average relationship. Since that time, a graph showing the short-run relationship between the unemployment rate and the inflation rate has been called a **Phillips curve**. (Phillips actually measured inflation by the percentage change in wages rather than by the percentage change in prices. Because wages and prices usually move together, this difference is not important to our discussion.) Figure 24-1 shows a graph similar to the one Phillips prepared. Each point on the Phillips curve represents a possible combination of the unemployment rate and the inflation rate that might be observed in a given

Phillips curve A curve showing the short-run relationship between the unemployment rate and the inflation rate.

Figure 24-1

The Phillips Curve

A. W. Phillips was the first economist to show that there is usually an inverse relationship between unemployment and inflation. Here we can see this relationship at work: in the year represented by point *A*, the inflation rate is 4 percent and the unemployment rate is 5 percent. In the year represented by point *B*, the inflation rate is 2 percent and the unemployment rate is 6 percent.

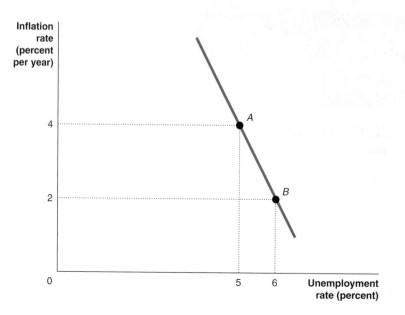

year. Point *A* represents a year in which the inflation rate is 4 percent and the unemployment rate is 5 percent, and point *B* represents a different year in which the inflation rate is 2 percent and the unemployment rate is 6 percent. Phillips documented that there is usually an *inverse relationship* between unemployment and inflation. During years when the unemployment rate is low, the inflation rate tends to be high, and during years when the unemployment rate is high, the inflation rate tends to be low.

Explaining the Phillips Curve with Aggregate Demand and Aggregate Supply Curves

The inverse relationship between unemployment and inflation that Phillips discovered is consistent with the aggregate demand and aggregate supply analysis we developed in Chapter 20. Figure 24-2 shows the factors that cause this inverse relationship.

Panel (a) shows the aggregate demand and aggregate supply *(AD–AS)* model from Chapter 20, and panel (b) shows the Phillips curve. For simplicity, in panel (a), we are using the basic *AD–AS* model, which assumes that the long-run aggregate supply curve and the short-run aggregate supply curve do not shift. Assume that a hypothetical economy in 2011 is at point *A*, with real GDP of US$14.0 billion and a price level of 100. If there is weak growth in aggregate demand, in 2012, the economy moves to point *B*, with real GDP of US$14.3 billion and a price level of 102. The inflation rate is 2 percent and the unemployment rate is 6 percent, which corresponds to point *B* on the Phillips curve in panel (b). If there is strong growth in aggregated demand, in 2012, the economy moves to point *C*, with real GDP of US$14.5 billion and a price level of 104. Strong aggregate demand growth results in a higher inflation of 4 percent but a lower unemployment rate of 5 percent. This combination of higher inflation and lower unemployment is shown as point *C* on the Phillips curve in panel (b).

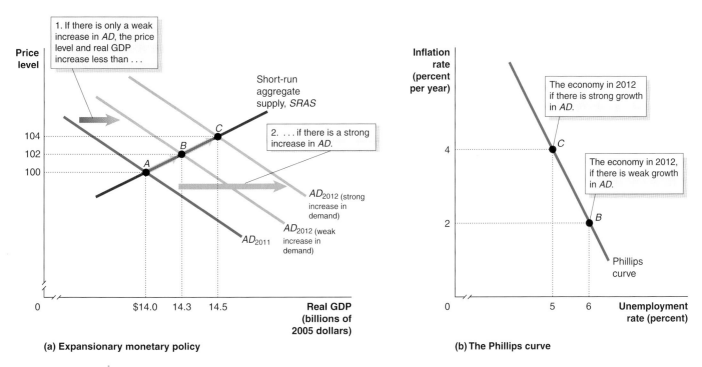

Figure 24-2 | Using Aggregate Demand and Aggregate Supply to Explain the Phillips Curve

In panel (a), the economy in 2011 is at point *A*, with real GDP of US$14.0 billion and a price level of 100. If there is weak growth in aggregate demand, in 2012, the economy moves to point *B*, with real GDP of US$14.3 billion and a price level of 102. The inflation rate is 2 percent and the unemployment rate is 6 percent, which corresponds to point *B* on the Phillips curve in panel (b). If there is strong growth in aggregated demand, in 2012, the economy moves to point *C*, with real GDP of US$14.5 billion and a price level of 104. Strong aggregate demand growth results in a higher inflation rate of 4 percent but a lower unemployment rate of 5 percent. This combination of higher inflation and lower unemployment is shown as point *C* on the Phillips curve in panel (b).

To summarize, the *AD–AS* model indicates that slow growth in aggregate demand leads to both higher unemployment and lower inflation. This relationship explains why there is a short-run trade-off between unemployment and inflation, as shown by the downward-sloping Phillips curve. The *AD–AS* model and the Phillips curve are different ways of illustrating the same macroeconomic events. The Phillips curve has an advantage over the *AD–AS* model, however, when we want to analyze explicitly *changes* in the inflation and unemployment rates.

Is the Phillips Curve a Policy Menu?

Structural relationship A relationship that depends on the basic behavior of consumers and firms and remains unchanged over long periods.

During the 1960s, some economists argued that the Phillips curve represented a **structural relationship** in the economy. A structural relationship depends on the basic behavior of consumers and firms and remains unchanged over long periods. Structural relationships are useful in formulating economic policy because policymakers can anticipate that these relationships are constant—that is, the relationships will not change as a result of changes in policy.

If the Phillips curve were a structural relationship, it would present policymakers with a reliable menu of combinations of unemployment and inflation. Potentially, policymakers could use expansionary monetary and fiscal policies to choose a point on the curve that had lower unemployment and higher inflation. They could also use contractionary monetary and fiscal policies to choose a point that had lower inflation and higher unemployment. Because many economists and policymakers in the 1960s viewed the Phillips curve as a structural relationship, they believed it represented a *permanent trade-off between unemployment and inflation*. As long as policymakers were willing to accept a permanently higher inflation rate, they would be able to keep the unemployment rate permanently lower. Similarly, a permanently lower inflation rate could be attained at the cost of a permanently higher unemployment rate. As we discuss in the next section, however, economists came to realize that the Phillips curve did *not*, in fact, represent a permanent trade-off between unemployment and inflation.

Is the Short-Run Phillips Curve Stable?

During the 1960s, the basic Phillips curve relationship seemed to hold because a stable trade-off appeared to exist between unemployment and inflation. In the early 1960s, the inflation rate was low, and the unemployment rate was high. In the late 1960s, the unemployment rate had declined, and the inflation rate had increased. Then in 1968, in his presidential address to the American Economic Association, Milton Friedman of the University of Chicago argued that the Phillips curve did *not* represent a *permanent* trade-off between unemployment and inflation. At almost the same time, Edmund Phelps of Columbia University in the U.S. published an academic paper making a similar argument. Friedman and Phelps noted that economists had come to agree that the long-run aggregate supply curve was vertical (a point we discussed in Chapter 20). If this observation were true, the Phillips curve could not be downward sloping in the long run. A critical inconsistency existed between a vertical long-run aggregate supply curve and a long-run Phillips curve that is downward sloping. Friedman and Phelps argued, in essence, that there is no trade-off between unemployment and inflation in the long run.

The Long-Run Phillips Curve

Natural rate of unemployment The unemployment rate that exists when the economy is at potential GDP.

To understand the argument that there is no permanent trade-off between unemployment and inflation, first recall that the level of real GDP in the long run is also referred to as *potential real GDP*. At potential real GDP, firms will operate at their normal level of capacity, and everyone who wants a job will have one, except the structurally and frictionally unemployed. Friedman defined the **natural rate of unemployment** as the unemployment rate that exists when the economy is at potential GDP. The actual unemployment rate will fluctuate in the short run but will always come back to the natural rate in the long run. In the same way, the actual level of real GDP will fluctuate in the short run but will always come back to its potential level in the long run.

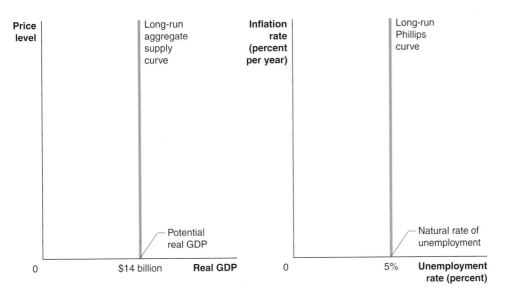

Figure 24-3

A Vertical Long-Run Aggregate Supply Curve Means a Vertical Long-Run Phillips Curve

Milton Friedman and Edmund Phelps argued that there is no trade-off between unemployment and inflation in the long run. If real GDP automatically returns to its potential level in the long run, the unemployment rate must return to the natural rate of unemployment in the long run. In this figure, we assume that potential real GDP is US$14 billion and the natural rate of unemployment is 5 percent.

In the long run, a higher or lower price level has no effect on real GDP because real GDP is always at its potential level in the long run. In the same way, in the long run, a higher or lower inflation rate will have no effect on the unemployment rate because the unemployment rate is always equal to the natural rate in the long run. Figure 24-3 illustrates Friedman's conclusion that the long-run aggregate supply curve is a vertical line at the potential real GDP, and *the long-run Phillips curve is a vertical line at the natural rate of unemployment.*

The Role of Expectations of Future Inflation

If the long-run Phillips curve is a vertical line, *no trade-off exists between unemployment and inflation in the long run.* This conclusion seemed to contradict the experience of the 1950s and 1960s, which showed a stable trade-off between unemployment and inflation. Friedman argued that the statistics from those years actually showed only a short-run trade-off between inflation and unemployment.

The short-run trade-off existed—but only because workers and firms sometimes expected the inflation rate to be either higher or lower than it turned out to be. Differences between the expected inflation rate and the actual inflation rate could lead the unemployment rate to rise above or dip below the natural rate. To see why, consider a simple case of Saudi Aramco, the largest oil company in the world, negotiating a wage contract with Zamil CoolCare, the service and maintenance business of Zamil Air Conditioners, to maintain and service thousands of room air conditioners. Assume that both Aramco and Zamil CoolCare are interested in the real wage, which is the nominal wage, corrected for inflation. Suppose, for example, that Aramco and Zamil CoolCare agree on a wage of US$31.50 per hour to be paid during 2015. Both Aramco and Zamil CoolCare expect that the price level will increase from 100 in 2014 to 105 in 2015, so the inflation rate will be 5 percent. We can calculate the real wage Aramco expects to pay and Zamil CoolCare workers expect to receive as follows:

$$\text{Real wage} = \frac{\text{Nominal wage}}{\text{Price level}} \times 100 = \frac{\$31.50}{105} \times 100 = \$30$$

But suppose that the actual inflation rate turns out to be higher or lower than the expected inflation rate of 5 percent. Table 24-1 shows the effect on the actual real wage. If the price level rises only to 102 during 2015, the inflation rate will be 2 percent, and the actual real wage will be US$30.88, which is higher than Aramco and Zamil CoolCare had expected. With a higher real wage, Aramco will hire fewer workers than it had planned to at the expected real wage of US$30. If the inflation rate is 8 percent, the actual real wage

TABLE 24-1

The Impact of Unexpected Price
Level Changes on the Real Wage

NOMINAL WAGE IN US$	EXPECTED REAL WAGE IN US$	ACTUAL REAL WAGE IN US$	
	Expected P_{2012} = 105 Expected inflation = 5%	Actual P_{2015} = 102 Actual inflation = 2%	Actual P_{2015} = 108 Actual inflation = 8%
31.50	$\frac{31.50}{105} \times 100 = 30$	$\frac{31.50}{102} \times 100 = 30.88$	$\frac{31.50}{108} \times 100 = 29.17$

will be US$29.17, and Aramco will hire more workers than it had planned. If Aramco and Zamil CoolCare expected a higher or lower inflation rate than actually occurred, other firms and workers probably made the same mistake.

If actual inflation is higher than expected inflation, actual real wages in the economy will be lower than expected real wages, and many firms will hire more workers than they had planned to hire. Therefore, the unemployment rate will fall. If actual inflation is lower than expected inflation, actual real wages will be higher than expected; many firms will hire fewer workers than they had planned to hire, and the unemployment rate will rise. Table 24-2 summarizes this argument.

Friedman and Phelps concluded that an increase in the inflation rate increases employment (and decreases unemployment) only if the increase in the inflation rate is unexpected. Friedman argued that in 1968, the unemployment rate in the U.S. was 3.6 percent rather than 5 percent only because the inflation rate of 4 percent was above the 1 percent to 2 percent inflation that workers and firms had expected: "There is always a temporary trade-off between inflation and unemployment; there is no permanent trade-off. The temporary trade-off comes not from inflation per se, but from unanticipated inflation."

TABLE 24-2

The Basis for the Short-Run
Phillips Curve

IF...	THEN...	AND...
actual inflation is greater than expected inflation,	the actual real wage is less than the expected real wage,	the unemployment rate falls.
actual inflation is less than expected inflation,	the actual real wage is greater than the expected real wage,	the unemployment rate rises.

Making the Connection | Do Workers Understand Inflation?

A higher inflation rate can lead to lower unemployment if *both* workers and firms mistakenly expect the inflation rate to be lower than it turns out to be. But this same result might be due to firms forecasting inflation more accurately than workers do or to firms understanding better the effects of inflation. Some large firms employ economists to help them gather and analyze information that is useful in forecasting inflation. Many firms also have human resources or employee compensation departments that gather data on wages paid at competing firms and analyze trends in compensation. Workers generally rely on much less systematic information about wages and prices. Workers also often fail to realize a fact we discussed in Chapter 16: *expected inflation increases the value of total production and the value of total income by the same amount.* Therefore, although not all wages will rise as prices rise, inflation will increase the average wage in the economy at the same time that it increases the average price.

Robert Shiller, an economist at Yale University the United States, conducted a survey on inflation and discovered that, although most economists believe an increase in inflation will lead quickly to an increase in wages, a majority of the general public thinks otherwise. In one question, Shiller asked how "the effect of general inflation on wages or salary relates to your own experience and your own job." The most popular response was: "The price increase will create extra profits for my employer, who can now sell output for more; there will be no effect on my pay. My employer will see no reason to raise my pay."

Shiller also asked the following question:

> Imagine that next year the inflation rate unexpectedly doubles. How long would it probably take, in these times, before your income is increased enough so that you can afford the same things as you do today? In other words, how long will it be before a full inflation correction in your income has taken place?

Eighty-one percent of the public answered either that it would take several years for the purchasing power of their income to be restored or that it would never be restored.

If workers fail to understand that rising inflation leads over time to comparable increases in wages, then when inflation increases, in the short run, firms can increase wages by less than inflation without needing to worry about workers quitting or their morale falling. Once again, we have a higher inflation rate, leading in the short run to lower real wages and lower unemployment. In other words, we have an explanation for a downward-sloping short-run Phillips curve.

Source: Robert J. Shiller, "Why Do People Dislike Inflation?" in *Reducing Inflation: Motivation and Strategy*, Christina D. Romer and David H. Romer, eds., Chicago: University of Chicago Press, 1997.

YOUR TURN: Test your understanding by doing related problems 1.12 and 1.13 on page 828 at the end of this chapter.

Will his wage increases keep up with inflation?

24.2 LEARNING OBJECTIVE

The Short-Run and Long-Run Phillips Curves

If there is both a short-run Phillips curve and a long-run Phillips curve, how are the two curves related? We can begin answering this question with the help of Figure 24-4, which represents macroeconomic conditions in the United States during the 1960s. In the late 1960s, workers and firms were still expecting the inflation rate to be about 1.5 percent, as it had been from 1960 to 1965. Expansionary monetary and fiscal policies, however, had moved the short-run equilibrium up the short-run Phillips curve to an inflation rate of 4.5 percent and an unemployment rate of 3.5 percent. This very low unemployment rate was possible only because the real wage rate was unexpectedly low.

Once workers and firms began to expect that the inflation rate would continue to be about 4.5 percent, they changed their behavior. Firms knew that only nominal wage increases of more than 4.5 percent would increase real wages. Workers realized that unless they received a nominal wage increase of at least 4.5 percent, their real wage would be falling. Higher expected inflation rates had an impact throughout the economy. For example, as we saw in Chapter 21, when banks make loans, they are interested in the *real interest rate* on the loan. The real interest rate is the nominal interest rate

Figure 24-4

The Short-Run Phillips Curve of the 1960s and the Long-Run Phillips Curve

In the late 1960s, U.S. workers and firms were expecting the 1.5 percent inflation rates of the recent past to continue. However, expansionary monetary and fiscal policies moved the short-run equilibrium up the short-run Phillips curve to an inflation rate of 4.5 percent and an unemployment rate of 3.5 percent.

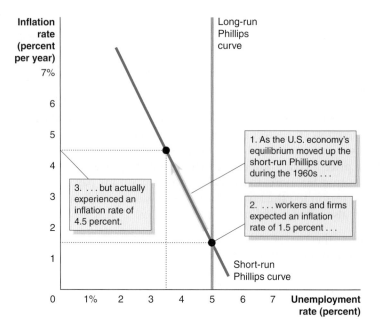

minus the expected inflation rate. If banks need to receive a real interest rate of 3 percent on home mortgage loans and expect the inflation rate to be 1.5 percent, they will charge a nominal interest rate of 4.5 percent. If banks revise their expectations of the inflation rate to 4.5 percent, they will increase the nominal interest rate they charge on mortgage loans to 7.5 percent.

Shifts in the Short-Run Phillips Curve

The new, higher expected inflation rate can become *embedded* in the economy, meaning that workers, firms, consumers, and the government all take the inflation rate into account when making decisions. The short-run trade-off between unemployment and inflation now takes place from this higher, less favorable level, as shown in Figure 24-5.

Figure 24-5

Expectations and the Short-Run Phillips Curve

By the end of the 1960s, workers and firms had revised their expectations of inflation from 1.5 percent to 4.5 percent. As a result, the short-run Phillips curve shifted up, which made the short-run trade-off between unemployment and inflation worse.

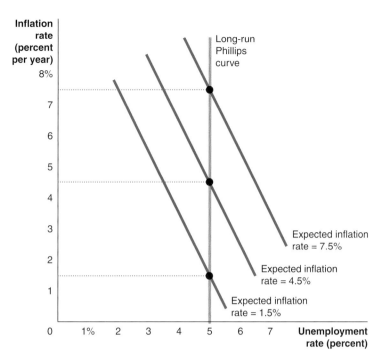

Figure 24-6

A Short-Run Phillips Curve for Every Expected Inflation Rate

There is a different short-run Phillips curve for every expected inflation rate. Each short-run Phillips curve intersects the long-run Phillips curve at the expected inflation rate.

As long as workers and firms expected the inflation rate to be 1.5 percent, the short-run trade-off between unemployment and inflation was the more favorable one shown by the lower Phillips curve. Along this Phillips curve, an inflation rate of 4.5 percent was enough to drive down the unemployment rate to 3.5 percent. Once workers and firms adjusted their expectations to an inflation rate of 4.5 percent, the short-run trade-off deteriorated to the one shown by the higher Phillips curve. At this higher expected inflation rate, the real wage rose, causing some workers to lose their jobs, and the economy's equilibrium returned to the natural rate of unemployment of 5 percent, but now with an inflation rate of 4.5 percent rather than 1.5 percent. On the higher short-run Phillips curve, an inflation rate of 7.5 percent would be necessary to reduce the unemployment rate to 3.5 percent. An inflation rate of 7.5 percent would keep the unemployment rate at 3.5 percent only until workers and firms revised their expectations of inflation up to 7.5 percent. In the long run, the economy's equilibrium would return to the 5 percent natural rate of unemployment.

As Figure 24-6 shows, there is a short-run Phillips curve for every level of expected inflation. Each short-run Phillips curve intersects the long-run Phillips curve at the expected inflation rate.

How Does a Vertical Long-Run Phillips Curve Affect Monetary Policy?

By the 1970s, most economists accepted the argument that the long-run Phillips curve is vertical. In other words, economists realized that the common view of the 1960s had been wrong: it was *not* possible to buy a permanently lower unemployment rate at the cost of a permanently higher inflation rate. The moral of the vertical long-run Phillips curve is that *in the long run, there is no trade-off between unemployment and inflation*. In the long run, the unemployment rate always returns to the natural rate, no matter what the inflation rate is.

Figure 24-7 shows that the inflation rate is stable only when the unemployment rate is equal to the natural rate. If the central bank were to attempt to use expansionary monetary policy to push the economy to a point such as *A*, where the unemployment rate is below the natural rate, the result would be increasing inflation as the economy moved up the short-run Phillips curve. If the economy remained below the natural rate long enough, the short-run Phillips curve would shift up as workers and firms adjusted to the

Figure 24-7

The Inflation Rate and the Natural Rate of Unemployment in the Long Run

The inflation rate is stable only if the unemployment rate equals the natural rate of unemployment (point *C*). If the unemployment rate is below the natural rate (point *A*), the inflation rate increases, and, eventually, the short-run Phillips curve shifts up. If the unemployment rate is above the natural rate (point *B*), the inflation rate decreases, and, eventually, the short-run Phillips curve shifts down.

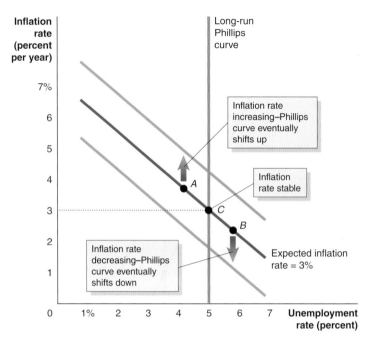

new, higher inflation rate. During the 1960s and 1970s, the short-run Phillips curve did shift up, presenting the economy with a more unfavorable short-run trade-off between unemployment and inflation.

If the central bank used contractionary policy to push the economy to a point such as *B*, where the unemployment rate is above the natural rate, the inflation rate would decrease. If the economy remained above the natural rate long enough, the short-run Phillips curve would shift down as workers and firms adjusted to the new, lower inflation rate. Only at a point such as *C*, where the unemployment rate is equal to the natural rate, will the inflation rate be stable. As a result, the natural rate of unemployment is sometimes called the **nonaccelerating inflation rate of unemployment (NAIRU)**. We can conclude this: *In the long run, the central bank can affect the inflation rate but not the unemployment rate.*

Nonaccelerating inflation rate of unemployment (NAIRU) The unemployment rate at which the inflation rate has no tendency to increase or decrease.

Making the Connection | **Does the Natural Rate of Unemployment Ever Change?**

Life would be easier for the central bank if it knew exactly what the natural rate of unemployment was and if that rate never changed. Unfortunately for the central bank, the natural rate does change over time. Remember that at the natural rate of unemployment, only frictional and structural unemployment remain. Frictional or structural unemployment can change—thereby changing the natural rate—for several reasons:

- *Demographic changes.* Younger and less skilled workers have higher unemployment rates, on average, than do older and more skilled workers. We saw in Chapter 16 that unskilled Arab youth, between the ages of 15 and 24, and women account for a large portion of those who are unemployed in the Arab world. Most of those unemployed youth and women are classified as structurally unemployed. As a result, the natural rate of unemployment in the Arab world is expected to be higher than that in other countries with a less unskilled labor force.

- *Labor market institutions.* As we discussed in Chapter 16, labor market institutions, such as the unemployment insurance system, unions, and legal barriers to firing workers, can increase the economy's unemployment rate. For example, because many European countries have generous unemployment insurance systems, strong unions, and restrictive policies on firing workers, the natural rate of unemployment in most European countries has been well above the rate in the United States. In addition, since most of the Arab countries suffer from a high structural unemployment rate, as discussed in Chapter 16, the natural rate of unemployment in the Arab world is usually higher than that of the United States.

- *Past high rates of unemployment.* Evidence indicates that if high unemployment persists for a period of years, the natural rate of unemployment may increase. When workers have been unemployed for longer than a year or two, their skills deteriorate, they may lose confidence that they can find and hold a job, and they may become dependent on government payments to survive. Robert Gordon, an economist at Northwestern University, has argued that in the late 1930s, so many U.S. workers had been out of work for so long that the natural rate of unemployment may have risen to more than 15 percent. He has pointed out that even though the unemployment rate in the United States was 17 percent in 1939, the inflation rate did not change. Similarly, many economists have argued that the high unemployment rates experienced by European countries during the 1970s increased their natural rates of unemployment.

What makes the natural rate of unemployment increase or decrease?

YOUR TURN: Test your understanding by doing related problem 2.4 on page 829 at the end of this chapter.

Solved Problem | 24-2

Changing Views of the Phillips Curve

Writing in a publication for the U.S. Federal Reserve Bank (the Fed—the central bank of the United States), Bennett McCallum, an economist at Carnegie Mellon University, argues that during the 1970s, the Fed was "acting under the influence of 1960s academic ideas that posited the existence of a long-run and exploitable Phillips-type tradeoff between inflation and unemployment rates." What does he mean by a "long-run and exploitable Phillips-type tradeoff"? How would the Fed have attempted to exploit this long-run tradeoff? What would be the consequences for the inflation rate?

SOLVING THE PROBLEM:

Step 1: **Review the chapter material.** This problem is about the relationship between the short-run and long-run Phillips curves, so you may want to review the section "The Short-Run and Long-Run Phillips Curves," which begins on page 809.

Step 2: **Explain what a "long-run exploitable Phillips-type tradeoff" means.** A "long-run exploitable Phillips-type tradeoff" means a Phillips curve that in the long run is downward sloping rather than vertical. An "exploitable" trade-off is one that the Fed could take advantage of to *permanently* reduce unemployment at the expense of higher inflation or to permanently reduce inflation at the expense of higher unemployment.

Step 3:   **Explain how the inflation rate will accelerate if the Fed tries to exploit a long-run trade-off between unemployment and inflation.** As we have seen, during the 1960s, the Fed conducted expansionary monetary policies to move up what it thought was a stationary short-run Phillips curve. By the late 1960s, these policies resulted in very low unemployment rates. In the long run, there is no stable trade-off between unemployment and inflation. Attempting to permanently keep the unemployment rate at very low levels leads to a rising inflation rate, which is what happened in the late 1960s and early 1970s.

Source: Bennett T. McCallum, "Recent Developments in Monetary Policy Analysis: The Roles of Theory and Evidence," Federal Reserve Bank of Richmond, *Economic Quarterly*, Winter 2002, p. 73.

>> **End Solved Problem 24-2**

YOUR TURN: For more practice, do related problem 2.5 on page 829 at the end of this chapter.

24.3 LEARNING OBJECTIVE

24.3 | Discuss how expectations of the inflation rate affect monetary policy.

Expectations of the Inflation Rate and Monetary Policy

How long can the economy remain at a point that is on the short-run Phillips curve, but not on the long-run Phillips curve? It depends on how quickly workers and firms adjust their expectations of future inflation to changes in current inflation. In general, there are three possibilities on how workers and firms adjust their expectations of inflation. This adjustment of expectations depends on how high the inflation rate is. The three possibilities are:

- *Low inflation.* When the inflation rate is low, workers and firms tend to ignore it. For example, if the inflation rate is low, a restaurant may not want to pay for printing new menus that would show slightly higher prices.

- *Moderate but stable inflation.* This inflation rate is high enough that workers and firms cannot ignore it without seeing their real wages and profits decline. Workers and firms believe that it is also likely that the next year's inflation rate would be very close to the current year's inflation rate. In this case, people are said to have adaptive expectations of inflation if they assume that future rates of inflation will follow the pattern of rates of inflation in the recent past.

- *High and unstable inflation.* Industrial countries suffered from high inflation rates (above 5 percent) during the first and second oil shocks (1973 and 1980) when oil prices increased sharply. Not only were inflation rates high during these years, they were also unstable. For example, the inflation rate in the U.S. economy rose from 6 percent in 1973 to 11 percent in 1974, before falling below 6 percent in 1976 and rising again to 13.5 percent in 1980. In the mid-1970s, Nobel laureate Robert Lucas of the University of Chicago and Thomas Sargent of New York University in the U.S. argued that the gains to forecasting inflation accurately had dramatically increased. Workers and firms that failed to correctly anticipate the fluctuations in inflation during these years could experience substantial declines in real wages and profits. Therefore, Lucas and Sargent argued, people should use all available information when forming their expectations of future inflation. Expectations formed by using all available information about an economic variable are called **rational expectations**.

Rational expectations Expectations formed by using all available information about an economic variable.

The Effect of Rational Expectations on Monetary Policy

Lucas and Sargent pointed out an important consequence of rational expectations: an expansionary monetary policy would not work. In other words, there might not be a trade-off between unemployment and inflation, even in the short run. By the mid-1970s, most economists had accepted the idea that an expansionary monetary policy could cause the actual inflation rate to be higher than the expected inflation rate. This gap between actual and expected inflation would cause the actual real wage to fall below the expected real wage, and the unemployment rate would be pushed below the natural rate. The economy's short-run equilibrium would move up the short-run Phillips curve.

Lucas and Sargent argued that this explanation of the Phillips curve assumed that workers and firms either ignored inflation or used adaptive expectations in making their forecasts of inflation. If workers and firms have rational expectations, they will use all available information, *including knowledge of the effects of central bank policy*. If workers and firms know that an expansionary monetary policy will raise the inflation rate, they should use this information in their forecasts of inflation. If they do, an expansionary monetary policy will not cause the actual inflation rate to be above the expected inflation rate. Instead, the actual inflation rate will equal the expected inflation rate, the actual real wage will equal the expected real wage, and the unemployment rate will not fall below the natural rate.

Figure 24-8 illustrates this argument. Suppose the economy begins at point *A*, where the short-run Phillips curve intersects the long-run Phillips curve. The actual and expected inflation rates are both equal to 1.5 percent, and the unemployment rate equals the natural rate of 5 percent. Then suppose the central bank engages in an expansionary monetary policy. If workers ignore inflation or if they form their expectations adaptively, the expansionary monetary policy will cause the actual inflation rate to be higher than the expected inflation rate, and the short-run equilibrium will move from point *A* on the short-run Phillips curve to point *B*. The inflation rate will rise to 4.5 percent, and the unemployment rate will fall to 3.5 percent. The decline in unemployment will be only temporary, however. Eventually, workers and firms will adjust to the fact that the actual inflation rate is 4.5 percent, not the 1.5 percent they had expected. The short-run Phillips curve will shift up, and the unemployment rate will return to 5 percent at point *C*.

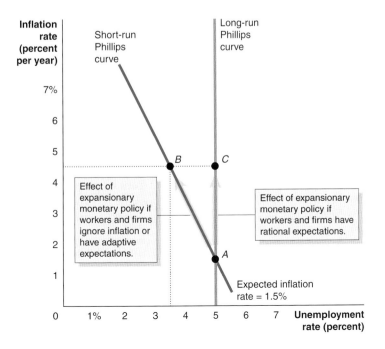

Figure 24-8

Rational Expectations and the Phillips Curve

If workers and firms ignore inflation, or if they have adaptive expectations, an expansionary monetary policy will cause the short-run equilibrium to move from point *A* on the short-run Phillips curve to point *B*; inflation will rise, and unemployment will fall. If workers and firms have rational expectations, an expansionary monetary policy will cause the short-run equilibrium to move up the long-run Phillips curve from point *A* to point *C*. Inflation will still rise, but there will be no change in unemployment.

Lucas and Sargent argued that if workers and firms have rational expectations, they will realize that the central bank's expansionary policy will result in an inflation rate of 4.5 percent. Therefore, as soon as the new policy is announced, workers and firms should adjust their expectations of inflation from 1.5 percent to 4.5 percent. There will be no temporary decrease in the real wage, leading to a temporary increase in employment and real GDP. Instead, the short-run equilibrium will move immediately from point *A* to point *C* on the long-run Phillips curve. The unemployment rate will never drop below 5 percent, and the *short-run* Phillips curve will be vertical.

Is the Short-Run Phillips Curve Really Vertical?

The claim by Lucas and Sargent that the short-run Phillips curve was vertical and that an expansionary monetary policy could not reduce the unemployment rate below the natural rate surprised many economists. An obvious objection to the argument of Lucas and Sargent was that the record of the 1950s and 1960s seemed to show that there was a short-run trade-off between unemployment and inflation and that, therefore, the short-run Phillips curve was downward sloping and not vertical. Lucas and Sargent argued that the apparent short-run trade-off was actually the result of *unexpected* changes in monetary policy. During those years, the U.S. Federal Reserve Bank did not announce changes in policy, so workers, firms, and financial markets had to *guess* when the Fed had begun using a new policy. In that case, an expansionary monetary policy might cause the unemployment rate to fall because workers and firms would be taken by surprise, and their expectations of inflation would be too low. Lucas and Sargent argued that a policy that was announced ahead of time would not cause a change in unemployment.

Many economists have remained skeptical of the argument that the short-run Phillips curve is vertical. The two main objections raised are that (1) workers and firms actually may not have rational expectations, and (2) the rapid adjustment of wages and prices needed for the short-run Phillips curve to be vertical will not actually take place. Many economists doubt that people are able to use information on the Fed's monetary policy to make a reliable forecast of the inflation rate. If workers and firms do not know what impact an expansionary monetary policy will have on the inflation rate, the actual real wage may still end up being lower than the expected real wage. Also, firms may have contracts with their workers and suppliers that keep wages and prices from adjusting quickly. If wages and prices adjust slowly, then even if workers and firms have rational expectations, an expansionary monetary policy may still be able to reduce the unemployment rate in the short run.

Real Business Cycle Models

During the 1980s, some economists, including Nobel laureates Finn Kydland of Carnegie Mellon University and Edward Prescott of Arizona State University in the U.S., argued that Robert Lucas was correct in assuming that workers and firms formed their expectations rationally and that wages and prices adjust quickly, but that he was wrong in assuming that fluctuations in real GDP are caused by unexpected changes in the money supply. Instead, they argued that fluctuations in 'real' factors, particularly *technology shocks*, explained deviations of real GDP from its potential level. Technology shocks are changes to the economy that make it possible to produce either more output—a positive shock—or less output—a negative shock—with the same number of workers, machines, and other inputs. Real GDP will be above its previous potential level following a positive technology shock and below its previous potential level following a negative technology shock. Because these models focus on real factors—rather than on changes in the money supply—to explain fluctuations in real GDP, they are known as **real business cycle models**.

The approach of Lucas and Sargent and the real business cycle models are sometimes grouped together under the label *the new classical macroeconomics* because these

Real business cycle models Models that focus on real rather than monetary explanations of fluctuations in real GDP.

approaches share the assumptions that people have rational expectations and that wages and prices adjust rapidly. Some of the assumptions of the new classical macroeconomics are similar to those held by economists before the Great Depression of the 1930s. John Maynard Keynes, in his 1936 book *The General Theory of Employment, Interest, and Money*, referred to these earlier economists as "classical economists." Like the classical economists, the new classical macroeconomists believe that the economy will normally be at its potential level.

Economists who find the assumptions of rational expectations and rapid adjustment of wages and prices appealing are likely to accept the real business cycle model approach. Other economists are skeptical of these models because the models explain recessions as being caused by negative technology shocks. Negative technology shocks are uncommon and, apart from the oil price increases of the 1970s, real business cycle theorists have had difficulty identifying shocks that would have been large enough to cause recessions. Some economists have begun to develop real business cycle models that allow for the possibility that changes in the money supply may affect the level of real GDP. If real business cycle models continue to develop along these lines, they may eventually converge with the approaches used by the U.S. Federal Reserve.

24.4 LEARNING OBJECTIVE

24.4 | Use a Phillips curve graph to show how the central bank can permanently lower the inflation rate.

The Effect of a Supply Shock on the Phillips Curve in the Industrial Countries: the Case of Oil Shocks

The increases in oil prices in 1974 resulting from actions by the Organization of Petroleum Exporting Countries (OPEC) caused the short-run aggregate supply curve to shift to the left (a negative supply shock in the industrial countries). This shift is shown in panel (a) of Figure 24-9 on the next page. (For simplicity, in this panel, we use the basic rather than dynamic *AD–AS* model.) The result was a higher price level and a lower level of real GDP. On a Phillips curve graph—panel (b) of Figure 24-9—we can shift the short-run Phillips curve up to show that the inflation rate and unemployment rate both increased.

As the Phillips curve shifted up, the economy moved from an unemployment rate of about 5 percent and an inflation rate of about 5.5 percent in 1973 to an unemployment rate of 8.5 percent and an inflation rate of about 9.5 percent in 1975. This combination of rising unemployment and rising inflation placed the central banks in industrial countries in a difficult position. Let us take the U.S. Federal Reserve Bank as an example: if the Fed used an expansionary monetary policy to fight the high unemployment rate, the *AD* curve would shift to the right, and the economy's equilibrium would move up the short-run Phillips curve. Real GDP would increase, and the unemployment rate would fall—but at the cost of higher inflation. If the Fed used a contractionary monetary policy to fight the high inflation rate, the *AD* curve would shift to the left, and the economy's equilibrium would move down the short-run Phillips curve. As a result, real GDP would fall, and the inflation rate would be reduced—but at the cost of higher unemployment. In the end, the Fed chose to fight high unemployment with an expansionary monetary policy, even though that decision worsened the inflation rate.

Contractionary Monetary Policy and Disinflation

By the late 1970s, the Federal Reserve had gone through a two-decade period of continually increasing the rate of growth of the money supply. In August 1979, along with most other economists, Paul Volcker (the chairman of the Fed) was convinced that high

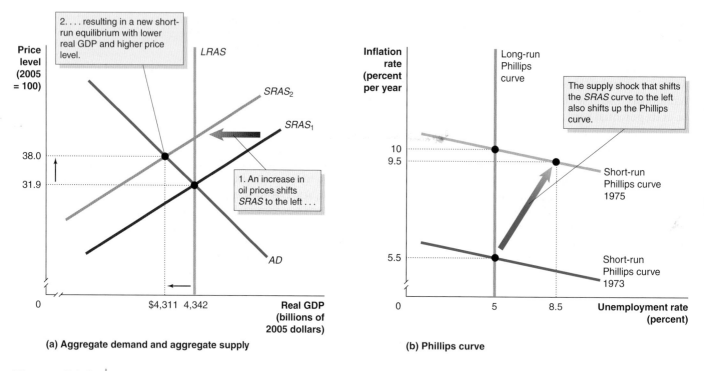

Figure 24-9 | A Supply Shock Shifts the *SRAS* and the Short-Run Phillips Curve

When OPEC increased the price of a barrel of oil from less than US$3 to more than US$10, in panel (a), the *SRAS* curve shifted to the left. Between 1973 and 1975, real GDP declined from US$4,342 billion to US$4,311 billion, and the price level rose from 31.9 to 38.0. Panel (b) shows that the supply shock shifted up the Phillips curve. In

1973, the U.S. economy had an inflation rate of about 5.5 percent and an unemployment rate of about 5 percent. By 1975, the inflation rate had risen to about 9.5 percent and the unemployment rate to about 8.5 percent.

inflation rates were inflicting significant damage on the economy and should be reduced. To reduce inflation, Volcker decided to reduce the annual growth rate of the money supply. This contractionary monetary policy raised interest rates, causing a decline in aggregate demand. Figure 24-10 uses the Phillips curve model to analyze the movements in unemployment and inflation from 1979 to 1989.

Figure 24-10

The Fed Tames Inflation, 1979–1989

The Fed, under Chairman Paul Volcker, began fighting inflation in 1979 by reducing the growth of the money supply, thereby raising interest rates. By 1982, the unemployment rate had risen to 10 percent, and the inflation rate had fallen to 6 percent. As workers and firms lowered their expectations of future inflation, the short-run Phillips curve shifted down, improving the short-run trade-off between unemployment and inflation. This adjustment in expectations allowed the Fed to switch to an expansionary monetary policy, which by 1987 brought the economy back to the natural rate of unemployment, with an inflation rate of about 4 percent. The orange line shows the actual combinations of unemployment and inflation for each year from 1979 to 1989. Note that during these years, the natural rate of unemployment was estimated to be about 6 percent.

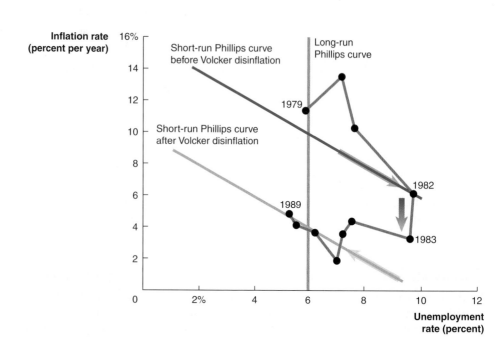

The Fed's contractionary monetary policy shifted the economy's short-run equilibrium down the short-run Phillips curve, lowering the inflation rate from 11 percent in 1979 to 6 percent in 1982—but at a cost of raising the unemployment rate from 6 percent to 10 percent. As workers and firms lowered their expectations of future inflation, the short-run Phillips curve shifted down, improving the short-run trade-off between unemployment and inflation. This adjustment in expectations allowed the Fed to switch to an expansionary monetary policy. By 1987, the economy was back to the natural rate of unemployment, which during these years was about 6 percent. The orange line in Figure 24-10 shows the actual combinations of unemployment and inflation for each year from 1979 to 1989.

Under Volcker's leadership, the Fed had reduced the inflation rate from more than 10 percent to less than 5 percent. The inflation rate has generally remained below 5 percent ever since. A significant reduction in the inflation rate is called **disinflation**. In fact, this episode is often referred to as the "Volcker disinflation." The disinflation had come at a very high price, however. From September 1982 through June 1983, the unemployment rate was above 10 percent. This period is the only one since the end of the Great Depression of the 1930s when unemployment has been above 10 percent in the United States.

Disinflation A significant reduction in the inflation rate.

Some economists argue that the Volcker disinflation provided evidence against the view that workers and firms have rational expectations. Volcker's announcement in October 1979 that he planned to use a contractionary monetary policy to bring down the inflation rate was widely publicized. If workers and firms had had rational expectations, we might have expected them to have quickly reduced their expectations of future inflation. The economy should have moved smoothly down the long-run Phillips curve. As we have seen, however, the economy moved down the existing short-run Phillips curve, and only after several years of high unemployment did the Phillips curve shift down. Apparently, workers and firms had adaptive expectations—only changing their expectations of future inflation after the current inflation rate had fallen.

Robert Lucas and Thomas Sargent argue, however, that a less painful disinflation would have occurred if workers and firms had *believed* Volcker's announcement that he was fighting inflation. The problem was that previous Fed chairmen had made similar promises throughout the 1970s, but inflation had continued to get worse. By 1979, the credibility of the Fed was at a low point. Some support for Lucas's and Sargent's argument comes from surveys of business economists at the time, which showed that they also reduced their forecasts of future inflation only slowly, even though they were well aware of Volcker's announcement of a new policy.

Solved Problem | 24-4

Using Monetary Policy to Lower the Inflation Rate

Consider the following hypothetical situation: the economy is currently at the natural rate of unemployment of 5 percent. The actual inflation rate is 6 percent and, because it has remained at 6 percent for several years, this is also the rate that workers and firms expect to see in the future. The central bank decides to reduce the inflation rate permanently to 2 percent. How can the central bank use monetary policy to achieve this objective? Be sure to use a Phillips curve graph in your answer.

SOLVING THE PROBLEM:

Step 1: **Review the chapter material.** This problem is about using a Phillips curve graph to show how the central bank can fight inflation, so you may want to review the section "Contractionary Monetary Policy and Disinflation," which begins on page 817.

Step 2:   Explain how the central bank can use monetary policy to reduce the inflation rate. To reduce the inflation rate significantly, the central bank will have to raise the target for the overnight lending rate. Higher interest rates will reduce aggregate demand, raise unemployment, and move the economy's equilibrium down the short-run Phillips curve.

Step 3:   Illustrate your argument with a Phillips curve graph. How much the unemployment rate would have to rise to drive down the inflation rate from 6 percent to 2 percent depends on the steepness of the short-run Phillips curve. Here we have assumed that the unemployment rate would have to rise from 5 percent to 7 percent.

Step 4:   Show on your graph the reduction in the inflation rate from 6 percent to 2 percent. For the decline in the inflation rate to be permanent, the expected inflation rate has to decline from 6 percent to 2 percent. We can show this on our graph:

Once the short-run Phillips curve has shifted down, the central bank can push the economy back to the natural rate of unemployment with an expansionary monetary policy. This policy is similar to the one carried out by the U.S. Federal Reserve Bank after Paul Volcker became chairman in 1979. The downside to these policies of disinflation is that they lead to significant increases in unemployment.

EXTRA CREDIT: A follower of the new classical macroeconomics approach would have a more optimistic view of the consequences of using monetary policy to lower the inflation rate from 6 percent to 2 percent. According to this approach, the central bank's policy announcement should cause people to immediately revise downward their expectations of future inflation from 6 percent to 2 percent. The economy's short-run equilibrium would move directly down the long-run Phillips curve from an inflation rate of 6 percent to an inflation rate of 2 percent, while keeping the unemployment rate constant at 5 percent. For the reasons discussed in this chapter, many economists are skeptical that disinflation can be brought about that painlessly.

YOUR TURN: For more practice, do related problems 4.6 and 4.7 on page 830 at the end of this chapter.

>> **End Solved Problem 24-4**

Monetary Policy Credibility

There is a continuing debate over policies to increase central banks' credibility. Some economists and policymakers believe that central banks are more credible if they adopt and follow rules. A *rules strategy* for monetary policy involves the central bank's following specific and publicly announced guidelines for policy. This strategy requires that when the central bank chooses a rule, it follows the rule, whatever the state of the economy. For example, the central bank might commit to increasing the money supply 5 percent each year, regardless of whether the economy enters a recession or suffers a financial crisis. (Note that support among economists for a monetary growth rule of this type has declined over the past 25 years.) The rule the central bank adopts should apply to variables that the central bank can control. For example, a rule stating that the central bank was committed to maintaining the growth rate of real GDP at 4 percent per year would not be useful because the central bank has no direct control over GDP.

Economists and policymakers who oppose the rules strategy support a *discretion strategy* for monetary policy. With a discretion strategy, the central bank should adjust monetary policy as it sees fit to achieve its policy goals, such as price stability and high employment. This approach differs from the rules strategy in that it allows the central bank to adjust its policy based on changes in the economy.

Many economists believe a middle course between a rules strategy and a discretion strategy is desirable. In this view, the central bank should be free to make adjustments in policy as long as the adjustments are stated as part of the rules. The *Taylor rule*, which we discussed in Chapter 22, is an example of a modified rule of this type. According to the Taylor rule, the central bank should set the target for the overnight lending rate according to an equation that includes the inflation rate, the equilibrium real overnight rate, the 'inflation gap,' and the 'output gap.' Even a modified rule isn't foolproof. Rules are credible because they reduce central bank flexibility, thereby giving firms, workers, and investors more confidence that the central bank will actually do what it says it will do. But the same lack of flexibility that can make a rule credible can also limit the central bank's ability to respond during a financial crisis, such as a stock market crash.

Most economists believe the best way to achieve commitment to rules is to remove political pressures on the central bank. When the central bank is free of political pressures, the public is more likely to believe the central bank's announcements.

A Failure of Credibility at the Bank of Japan

Is it possible for the inflation rate to be too *low*? The answer is yes, particularly if inflation becomes deflation. Since the early 1990s, the Japanese economy has been plagued by slow growth and significant periods of *deflation*—or a falling price level. Deflation can contribute to slow growth by raising real interest rates, increasing the real value of debts, and causing consumers to postpone purchases in the hope of experiencing even lower prices in the future. The Bank of Japan attempted to end deflation and spur economic growth by using expansionary monetary policy to drive down interest rates and stop deflation.

By 1999, the Bank of Japan had reduced the target interest rate on overnight bank loans—the equivalent of the U.S. federal funds rate—to zero. Because Japan was experiencing deflation, however, the *real* interest rate on these loans was greater than zero. The real interest rate on mortgages and long-term bonds also remained too high to stimulate the increase in investment spending needed to bring the Japanese economy back to potential GDP. Why was the Bank of Japan unable to end deflation and reduce real interest rates? Some economists argue that the key problem was that the Bank of Japan's policies lacked credibility. Because firms, workers, and participants in financial markets doubted the Bank of Japan's willingness to continue an expansionary monetary policy long enough to end the deflation, the price level continued to fall, and real interest rates remained high. In fact, this view was reinforced when the Bank of Japan raised the target interest rate on overnight bank loans in August 2000, even though deflation continued. The lack of credibility also may have stemmed in part from the unwillingness of the Bank of Japan to state an explicit target for inflation. An explicit inflation rate target of, say, 2 percent may have caused firms, workers, and investors to raise their expectations of inflation, which could have brought the deflation to an end. Some officials at the Bank of Japan also appeared reluctant to pursue too aggressive an expansionary policy for fear of reigniting the inflation in stock prices and real estate prices that Japan had experienced in the 1980s.

Although deflation was not the only reason economic growth in Japan was so weak, failing to end deflation made other problems, such as reform of the banking system, harder to manage. The Bank of Japan's failure of credibility helps to explain its weak performance compared with the performance of the Federal Reserve during the same period.

Economics in YOUR Life!

>> Continued from page 803

At the beginning of the chapter, we posed this question: If the central bank pledges to keep the economy's long-run unemployment rate below 3 percent, what effect will this pledge have on the size of the raise you request? To answer this question, recall that the long-run, or natural, rate of unemployment is determined by the economy's long-run aggregate supply curve, not monetary policy, and is probably about 5 percent. The central bank's attempt to keep the economy's long-run unemployment rate below its natural level will cause the inflation rate to increase and eventually raise the public's expectations of future inflation and, by doing so, will keep inflation relatively high. Therefore, you should ask your boss for a relatively large wage increase in order to preserve the future purchasing power of your wage.

Conclusion

The workings of the contemporary economy are complex. The attempts by central banks to keep their economies near the natural rate of unemployment with a low rate of inflation have not always been successful. Economists continue to debate the best way for central banks to proceed.

An Inside Look at Policy on the next page discusses how the Central Bank of Jordan responded to the 2009 recession and the 2010 inflation.

The Monetary Policy of the Central Bank of Jordan

THE JORDAN TIMES, **JANUARY 24, 2011**

Inflation in 2010

The cost of living index as calculated by the Department of Statistics indicates that the average index for 2010 was 5 percent higher, year-on-year. It is only natural that this figure will be widely used to indicate inflation rate in 2010.

This percentage does not show what actually happened during 2010. It shows the change that took place vis-à-vis the previous year. The 5 percent figure would have been different had the cost of living index in 2009 been different. In fact, inflation in 2009 was negative.

The right method to define the inflation pattern in 2010 is to measure the rise in prices that took place between January 1, 2010, and December 31, 2010. This is a very easy and practical measure.

(a) The cost of living index at the end of 2009 was 121.3 (2006=100). It rose to reach 128.7 in December, thus the rise during 2010 in particular is 6.11 percent not 5 percent.

This percentage is high by all standards. If we take into account the rise in fuel and foodstuff prices, especially of the domestic agricultural products, the inflation rate in this year 2011 can reach 7 percent, even though the International Monetary Fund's experts predicted inflation in 2011

to be around 5.5 percent. The IMF experts are of the opinion that the inflation rate will rise further in 2011.

This overall picture is worth dwelling upon a little bit to see if it warrants a change in the monetary policy. The Central Bank of Jordan is still applying the policies required by the economic recession and the negative inflation. One wonders if it is time to shift the Central Bank's stance from easy to tight money.

The interest rate on the dinar is currently higher than the interest rate commanded by the dollar, yet it is at a record low. In fact, real interest on the dinar during 2010 was negative, as the inflation rate was higher than the interest rate.

(b) The answer to this policy question depends to a certain extent on the way the inflation rate is analyzed. If inflation is due mainly to petroleum prices determined by the world market or by the high prices of agricultural products, determined by seasonal factors, then there is no dynamic inflation that needs to be tackled.

The core inflation is lower than the above-mentioned rate. In general, inflation in Jordan, as high as it may be, is not the result of an overheated economy that needs to be cooled down. If anything, many commentators still call on the government to

stimulate the economy and encourage investments.

Most likely, the Central Bank will not act at this stage. It will watch the situation develop. It will not take a measure that may hurt the economic growth until there is a compelling reason to do so.

Despite the above logic, the government, under the pressure of the psychological effect of the Tunis factor, may give inflation priority over growth and take measures to reduce the cost of living or prevent it from rising at the expense of higher deficit and more debt.

Source: Fahed Fanek, "Inflation 2010," *The Jordan Times*, February 4, 2011.

Key Points in the Article

This article discusses the Central Bank of Jordan's monetary policy during the 2008–2009 economic recession and whether the Central Bank should alter its expansionary monetary policy in 2011. The method of measuring inflation in Jordan and the government concerns about economic growth determine the Central Bank's monetary policy in 2011. In addition, the political instability in the Middle East that started in late 2010 might have a strong impact on the direction of the monetary policy implemented by the Central Bank of Jordan.

Analyzing the News

(a) As we discussed in the opening of this chapter, the 2008 global financial crisis affected many Arab economies negatively, including the Jordanian economy. In terms of the *AD–AS* framework, low investment activities in Jordan in 2009 resulted in economic recession and pushed the aggregate demand backward. The only blessing of economic recession is that it led to a significant reduction in the Jordanian inflation rate—*disinflation*. According to the World Bank Indicators, the inflation rate in Jordan decreased from 14.9 in 2008 to –0.67 in 2009. The Central Bank of Jordan responded to this economic recession and the negative inflation by applying an easy (expansionary) monetary policy, via reducing the interest rate, in order to stimulate economic growth. The situation was reversed in 2010 when the inflation rate jumped from a negative value to the announced 5 percent (or the calculated 6.11 percent). This increase in inflation during 2010 was high enough to exceed the market interest rate. This resulted in a negative real interest rate. As we discussed in Chapter 16, a negative real interest rate encourages firms to borrow and engage in debt contracts, on the one hand, since the cost of borrowing is low, but on the other hand, discourages depositors from saving, since the return on savings is low in real terms.

(b) As the inflation rate went up in 2010, economists may have thought that the Central Bank of Jordan should raise the interest rate (a tight monetary policy) in order to mitigate the inflationary pressure. In fact, the Jordanian Central Bank did not alter its policy and kept the interest rate low. There are two explanations to the Central Bank's decision to keep its expansionary monetary policy. First, it seems that the estimated economic growth rate of 3.4 percent in 2010, according to the International Monetary Fund estimates, was less than the one targeted by the Jordanian government, especially as the economic growth rate reached 6.6 percent in 2007 (right before the global financial crisis). Thus, the Central Bank of Jordan continued its easy monetary policy to keep pushing the aggregate demand rightward and achieve higher economic growth rate. Second, as mentioned in the article, the Central Bank might be relying on the core inflation rate as a measure of the overall price change. The core inflation rate excludes items (goods) with high price fluctuations, such as food and energy products, and, thus, its measure of inflation is lower than the one that depends on the percentage change in the consumer price index, which reflects all consumer goods and services. The recent high international price of food makes the core inflation rate considerably lower than the regular inflation rate. Finally, with regard to the recent political instability in many Arab countries, the Central Bank of Jordan might give up its easy monetary policy that favors economic growth, and apply a tight monetary policy in order to control inflation and keep the cost of living for Jordanians within a reasonable level.

Thinking Critically About Policy

1. According to the current expansionary monetary policy applied by the Central Bank of Jordan and the high inflation rate, real interest rate is estimated to be negative. How will this negative real interest rate affect households' decisions? (*Hint*: think about households' decision regarding consumption, saving, and their preferred asset holdings.) How will these decisions affect the aggregate demand?

2. Suppose that, because of the high international food prices and political instability in the Middle East, both workers and firms in Jordan revised their expectations regarding inflation in 2011 to be 7 percent. How would this expectation adjustment affect the short-run Phillips curve? (*Hint*: draw the short-run Phillips curve in 2010 when the inflation rate was estimated to be 3.4 percent, and then think how the revised expectations of inflation would affect the short-run Phillips curve in 2011.)

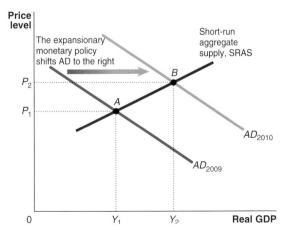

(a) The Central Bank's expansionary monetary policy shifts aggregate demand (*AD*) to the right and results in a higher real GDF and price level.

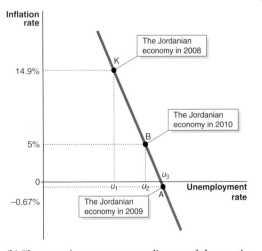

(b) The expansionary monetary policy turned the negative inflation rate of 2009 into positive in 2010.

Key Terms

Summary

24.1 LEARNING OBJECTIVE

Describe the Phillips curve and
the nature of the short-run trade-
off between unemployment and
inflation, **pages 804–809.**

The Discovery of the Short-Run Trade-off between Unemployment and Inflation

The **Phillips curve** illustrates the short-run trade-off between the unemployment rate and the inflation rate. The inverse relationship between unemployment and inflation shown by the Phillips curve is consistent with the aggregate demand and aggregate supply analysis developed in Chapter 19. The *AD–AS* model indicates that slow growth in aggregate demand leads to both higher unemployment and lower inflation, and rapid growth in aggregate demand leads to both lower unemployment and higher inflation. This relationship explains why there is a short-run trade-off between unemployment and inflation. Many economists initially believed that the Phillips curve was a **structural relationship** that depended on the basic behavior of consumers and firms and that remained unchanged over time. If the Phillips curve were a stable relationship, it would present policymakers with a menu of combinations of unemployment and inflation from which they could choose. Nobel laureate Milton Friedman argued that there is a **natural rate of unemployment**, which is the unemployment rate that exists when the economy is at potential GDP and to which the economy always returns. As a result, there is no trade-off between unemployment and inflation in the long run, and the long-run Phillips curve is a vertical line at the natural rate of unemployment.

24.2 LEARNING OBJECTIVE

Explain the relationship between
the short-run and long-run Phillips
curves, **pages 809–814.**

The Short-Run and Long-Run Phillips Curves

There is a short-run trade-off between unemployment and inflation only if the actual inflation rate differs from the inflation rate that workers and firms had expected. There is a different short-run Phillips curve for every expected inflation rate. Each short-run Phillips curve intersects the long-run Phillips curve at the expected inflation rate. With a vertical long-run Phillips curve, it is not possible to buy a permanently lower unemployment rate at the cost of a permanently higher inflation rate. If the central bank attempts to keep the economy below the natural rate of unemployment, the inflation rate will increase. Eventually, the expected inflation rate will also increase, which causes the short-run Phillips curve to shift up and pushes the economy back to the natural rate of unemployment. The reverse happens if the central bank attempts to keep the economy above the natural rate of unemployment. In the long run, the central bank can affect the inflation rate but not the unemployment rate.

24.3 LEARNING OBJECTIVE

Discuss how expectations of the
inflation rate affect monetary
policy, **pages 814–817.**

Expectations of the Inflation Rate and Monetary Policy

When the inflation rate is moderate and stable, workers and firms tend to have *adaptive expectations*. That is, they form their expectations under the assumption that future inflation rates will follow the pattern of inflation rates in the recent past. During the high and unstable inflation rates of the mid- to late-1970s, Robert Lucas and Thomas Sargent argued that workers and firms would have *rational expectations*. **Rational expectations** are formed by using all the available information about an economic variable, including the effect of the policy being used by the U.S. Federal Reserve Bank. Lucas and Sargent argued that if people have rational expectations, expansionary monetary policy will not work. If workers and firms know that an expansionary monetary policy is going to raise the inflation rate, the actual inflation rate will be the same as the expected inflation rate. Therefore, the unemployment rate won't fall. Many economists remain skeptical of Lucas and Sargent's argument in its strictest form. **Real business cycle models** focus on 'real' factors—technology shocks—rather than changes in the money supply to explain fluctuations in real GDP.

The Effect of a Supply Shock on the Phillips Curve in the industrial Countries: the Case of Oil Shocks

The increases in oil prices in 1974, resulting from actions by the Organization of Petroleum Exporting Countries (OPEC), caused the short-run aggregate supply curve to shift to the left. The result was a higher price level and a lower level of real GDP. This resulted in an upward shift in the Phillips curve graph, which means that the inflation rate and unemployment rate both increased. This combination of rising unemployment and rising inflation placed the central banks in industrial countries in a difficult position. For example, the U.S. Federal Reserve Bank initially used a contractionary monetary policy to reduce inflation. A significant reduction in the inflation rate is called **disinflation**. This contractionary monetary policy pushed the economy down the short-run Phillips curve. As workers and firms lowered their expectations of future inflation, the short-run Phillips curve shifted down, improving the short-run trade-off between unemployment and inflation. This change in expectations allowed the Fed to switch to an expansionary monetary policy to bring the economy back to the natural rate of unemployment. Some economists and policymakers believe that a central bank's credibility is increased if it follows a *rules strategy* for monetary policy, which involves the central bank's following specific and publicly announced guidelines for policy. Other economists and policymakers support a *discretion strategy* for monetary policy, under which the central bank adjusts monetary policy as it sees fit to achieve its policy goals, such as price stability and high employment.

24.4 LEARNING OBJECTIVE

Use a Phillips curve graph to show how the central bank can permanently lower the inflation rate, **pages 817–823.**

Review, Problems and Applications

myeconlab Visit www.pearsoned.co.uk/awe/hubbard to complete these exercises online and get instant feedback.
Get Ahead of the Curve

24.1 LEARNING OBJECTIVE Describe the Phillips curve and the nature of the short-run trade-off between unemployment and inflation, **pages 804–809.**

Review Questions

1.1 What is the Phillips curve? Draw a graph of a short-run Phillips curve.

1.2 What actions should the central bank take if it wants to move from a point on the short-run Phillips curve representing high unemployment and low inflation to a point representing lower unemployment and higher inflation?

1.3 Why did economists during the early 1960s think of the Phillips curve as a "policy menu"? Were they correct to think of it in this way? Briefly explain.

1.4 Why did Milton Friedman argue that the Phillips curve did not represent a permanent trade-off between unemployment and inflation? In your answer, be sure to explain what Friedman meant by the "natural rate of unemployment."

Problems and Applications

1.5 In fall 2003, the economy had not yet returned to the natural rate of unemployment following the end of the recession of 2001 in the U.S. An article in the *Wall Street Journal* noted the following:

> Perhaps the best cure for [unemployed workers'] woes would be a return to the unusually strong economy of the late 1990s, when unemployment fell so low that employers couldn't be picky. President Bush and Federal Reserve Chairman Alan Greenspan are working on that, [using] tax cuts and interest-rate cuts.

   a. Which of these two actions (tax cuts and interest-rate cuts) is fiscal policy and which is monetary policy?

   b. Briefly explain how tax cuts and interest-rate cuts reduce unemployment.

Source: David Wessel, "Clues to the Cure for Unemployment Begin to Emerge," *Wall Street Journal*, October 13, 2003.

1.6 Use the graphs provided to answer the following questions.

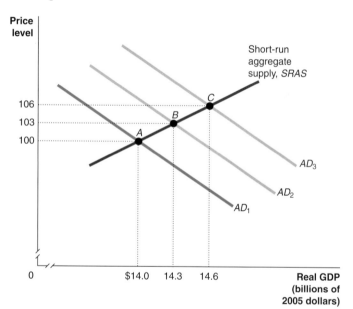

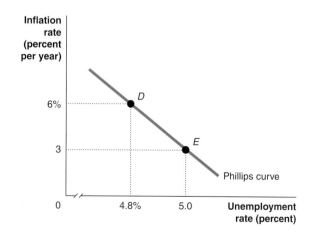

   a. Briefly explain which point on the Phillips curve graph represents the same economic situation as point *B* on the aggregate demand and aggregate supply graph.

   b. Briefly explain which point on the Phillips curve graph represents the same economic situation as point *C* on the aggregate demand and aggregate supply graph.

1.7 Given that the Phillips curve is derived from the aggregate demand and aggregate supply model, why use the Phillips curve analysis? What benefits does the Phillips curve analysis offer compared to the *AD–AS* model?

1.8 Briefly explain whether you agree or disagree with the following statement: "Any economic relationship that changes as economic policy changes is not a structural relationship."

1.9 In macroeconomics courses in the 1960s and early 1970s, some professors taught that some countries were willing to have higher unemployment in order to achieve lower inflation while some other countries were willing to have higher inflation in order to achieve lower unemployment. Why might such views of the trade-off between inflation and unemployment have existed in the 1960s? Why are such views rare today?

1.10 General Juan Perón, the former dictator of Argentina, once said of the labor market in his country, "Prices have gone up the elevator, and wages have had to use the stairs." In this situation, what was happening to real wages in Argentina? Was unemployment likely to have been relatively high or relatively low?

Source: Robert J. Shiller, "Why Do People Dislike Inflation?" in Christina D. Romer and David H. Romer, eds., *Reducing Inflation: Motivation and Strategy*, Chicago: University of Chicago Press, 1997.

1.11 This chapter argues that if the price level increases, over time, the average wage should increase by the same amount. Why is this true?

1.12 **(Related to the *Making the Connection* on page 808)** Robert Shiller asked a sample of the general public and a sample of economists the following question: "Do you agree that preventing high inflation is an important national priority, as important as preventing drug abuse or preventing deterioration in the quality of our schools?" Fifty-two percent of the general public, but only 18 percent of economists, fully agreed. Why does the general public believe inflation is a bigger problem than economists do?

1.13 **(Related to the *Making the Connection* on page 808)** When Shiller asked a sample of the general public what they thought caused inflation, the most frequent answer he received was "greed." Do you agree that greed causes inflation? Briefly explain.

1.14 Use the following information to draw a graph showing the short-run and long-run Phillips curves:

Natural rate of unemployment = 5 percent
Current rate of unemployment = 4 percent
Expected inflation rate = 4 percent
Current inflation rate = 6 percent

   Be sure your graph shows the point where the short-run and long-run Phillips curves intersect.

Review Questions

2.1 What is the relationship between the short-run Phillips curve and the long-run Phillips curve?

2.2 Why is it inconsistent to believe that the long-run aggregate supply curve is vertical and the long-run Phillips curve is downward sloping?

Problems and Applications

2.3 In 1968, Herbert Stein, who would later serve on President Nixon's Council of Economic Advisers, wrote, "Some who would opt for avoiding inflation would say that in the long run such a policy would cost little, if any, additional unemployment." Was Stein correct? Did most economists in 1968 agree with him? Briefly explain.

Source: Herbert Stein, *The Fiscal Revolution in America*, Chicago: University of Chicago Press, 1969, p. 382.

2.4 **(Related to the *Making the Connection* on page 812)** An article in *The Economist* magazine discussing the natural rate of unemployment, makes the observation: "'Natural' does not mean optimal." Do you agree that the natural rate of unemployment is not the optimal rate of unemployment? In your answer, be sure to explain what you mean by *optimal*.

Source: "A Natural Choice," *The Economist*, October 12, 2006.

2.5 **(Related to *Solved Problem 24-2* on page 813)** In a speech in September 1975, then Fed Chairman Arthur Burns said the following:

> There is no longer a meaningful trade-off between unemployment and inflation. In the current environment, a rapidly rising level of consumer prices will not lead to the creation of new jobs.... Highly expansionary monetary and fiscal policies might, for a short time, provide some additional thrust to economic activity. But inflation would inevitably accelerate—a development that would create even more difficult economic problems than we have encountered over the past year.

How do Burns's views in this speech compare with the views at the Fed in the late 1960s? Why do you think he specifically says "in the current environment" there is no trade-off between unemployment and inflation?

Source: Arthur F. Burns, "The Real Issues of Inflation and Unemployment," in Federal Reserve Bank of New York, *Federal Reserve Readings on Inflation*, February 1979.

Review Questions

3.1 Why do workers, firms, banks, and investors in financial markets care about the future rate of inflation? How do they form their expectations of future inflation? Do current conditions in the economy have any bearing on how they form their expectations?

3.2 What does it mean to say that workers and firms have rational expectations?

3.3 Why did Robert Lucas and Thomas Sargent argue that the Phillips curve might be vertical in the short run? What difference would it make for monetary policy if they were right?

Problems and Applications

3.4 During a time when the inflation rate is increasing each year for a number of years, are adaptive expectations or rational expectations likely to give the more accurate forecasts? Briefly explain.

3.5 An article in *The Economist* notes: "A government's inability to demonstrate sincerity in achieving low inflation can...lead consumers to make high inflation a self-fulfilling prophecy." What does "a government's inability to demonstrate sincerity in achieving low inflation" mean in terms of the central bank policy?

If consumers have rational expectations, why will this policy failure make high inflation a self-fulfilling prophecy?

Source: "Cycles and Commitment," *The Economist*, October 10, 2004.

3.6 Would a monetary policy intended to bring about disinflation cause a greater increase in unemployment if workers and firms have adaptive expectations or if they have rational expectations? Briefly explain.

3.7 If both the short-run and long-run Phillips curves are vertical, what will be the effect on the inflation rate and the unemployment rate of an expansionary monetary policy? Use a Phillips curve graph to illustrate your answer.

3.8 An article in the *Wall Street Journal* contained the following about the views of William Poole, the president of the Federal Reserve Bank of St. Louis in the U.S.:

> Mr Poole said both inflation expectations and the output gap—the spare room the economy has between what it's producing and what it could potentially produce—go into the inflation process. But "inflation expectations...trump the gap. If inflation expectations were to rise, that development by itself would tend to drag

the inflation rate up…and it might take a very long time before the (output gap) would be able to offset what's going on with inflation expectations."

a. Explain using the short-run and long-run Phillips curves what Poole meant in saying that both inflation expectations and the output gap affect the current inflation rate.

b. In terms of Phillips curve analysis, what are the implications of Poole's claim that "it might take a very long time before the (output gap) would be able to offset what's going on with inflation expectations"?

c. Why might inflation expectations be slow to respond to the output gap?

Source: Greg Ip, "Fed Policy Maker Warns of Rising Inflation," *Wall Street Journal*, June 6, 2006.

24.4 LEARNING OBJECTIVE | Use a Phillips curve graph to show how the central bank can permanently lower the inflation rate, **pages 817–823.**

Review Questions

4.1 Explain the difference between the rules strategy and discretion strategy for monetary policy.

4.2 Describe how the first oil shock in 1973 resulted in shifting the short-run Phillips curve in the industrial countries.

Problems and Applications

4.3 Economists always expect that disinflation will be accompanied by a fall in interest rates. What is disinflation and why should it lead to a fall in interest rates?

4.4 Marvin Goodfriend, an economist at Carnegie Mellon University, argues that one of the advances in macroeconomic thinking since 1979 is "the proven power of monetary policy to reduce and stabilize inflation and inflation expectations at a low rate." How has monetary policy proven its power to reduce inflation and inflation expectations?

Source: Marvin Goodfriend, "The Monetary Policy Debate Since October 1979: Lessons for Theory and Practice," Federal Reserve Bank of St. Louis *Review*, March/April 2005, Vol. 87, No. 2, Part 2, pp. 243– 262.

4.5 Suppose the current inflation rate and the expected inflation rate are both 4 percent. The current unemployment rate and the natural rate of unemployment are both 5 percent. Use a Phillips curve graph to show the effect on the economy of a severe supply shock. If the central bank keeps monetary policy unchanged, what will hapen eventually to the unemployment rate? Show this on your Phillips curve graph.

4.6 (Related to *Solved Problem 24-4* on page 819) Suppose the inflation rate has been 15 percent for the past four years. The unemployment rate is currently at the natural rate of unemployment of 5 percent. The central bank decides that it wants to permanently reduce the inflation rate to 5 percent.

How can the central bank use monetary policy to achieve this objective? Be sure to use a Phillips curve graph in your answer.

4.7 (Related to *Solved Problem 24-4* on page 819) Suppose that some economists in your country argue that the natural rate of unemployment is 4 percent but the chairman of the central bank is convinced that the natural rate is actually about 6 percent. Suppose also that the current unemployment rate is around 6 percent too. If the chairman of the central bank had accepted the view that the natural rate of unemployment is 4 percent, how might the monetary policy applied by him change?

4.8 According to an article in the *Wall Street Journal*, "J.P. Morgan Chase economist Michael Feroli finds that in the past two decades it has taken a far larger drop in the jobless rate to boost inflation by one percentage point than it did in the previous 25 years." If this economist is correct, has the short-run Phillips curve become steeper during the past 25 years or less steep? If true, would this fact have any implications for monetary policy? Briefly explain.

Source: Greg Ip, "Fed Sees Inflation Rise as Fleeting," *Wall Street Journal*, August 4, 2006, p. A2.

4.9 Robert Lucas was recently quoted as saying: "In practice, it is much more painful to put a modern economy through a deflation than the monetary theory we have would lead us to expect. I take this to mean that we have 'price stickiness.'" What does Lucas mean by "the monetary theory we have"? What events may have led him to conclude that it is more painful to reduce the inflation rate than theory would predict? Why does he conclude the U.S. economy apparently has "price stickiness"?

Source: Paul A. Samuelson and William A. Barnett, eds., *Inside the Economist's Mind: Conversations with Eminent Economists*, Malden, MA: Blackwell Publishing, 2007, p. 63.

Chapter 25

Macroeconomics in an Open Economy

Chinese Products Threaten Local Industries in Both Developed and Developing Countries

Mohamed Ahmed Dawood Investment Company is an Egyptian company specializing in electric motors. NewPage is a U.S. paper manufacturer specializing in the glossy paper used in catalogs and magazines. In recent years, these two firms have been facing strong competition from Chinese firms.

Chinese exports of glossy paper to the United States in 2006 were 10 times higher than they were in 2002. Chinese firms have the advantage of paying their workers the equivalent of about US$2.10 per hour, while U.S. firms pay their workers at least 10 times as much. In addition, NewPage claimed, Chinese firms have received subsidies from the Chinese government in the form of special tax breaks and low-cost loans.

Under existing international trade agreements, governments are not allowed to subsidize firms that export to other countries, and NewPage filed a complaint with the U.S. Department of Commerce. According to Mark Suwyn, CEO of NewPage, "We've had to shut down machines and lay off people because [Chinese firms] are dumping product way below their costs."

In March 2007, the Department of Commerce announced that, in response to NewPage's complaint, it was imposing tariffs of 10 percent to 20 percent on imports of glossy paper from China. Although U.S. paper manufacturers such as NewPage applauded the tariffs, U.S. publishing firms that use glossy paper complained that their costs would rise and that U.S. consumers would face rising prices for magazines and other publications.

In the case of the electric motors in Egypt, in July 2009, the Mohamed Ahmed Dawood Investment Company filed a complaint to the Anti-Dumping Agency of Egypt claiming that low-priced Chinese electric motors were being dumped in abundance on the Egyptian market, and that this dumping action was harming Egyptian companies that produce similar products to those imported from China. The investigation found the complaint to be accurate and that domestic companies were being affected negatively by the dumping of the Chinese products.

By June 2010, the committee designated to carry out the investigation had decided to enforce a recommendation to apply anti-dumping duties on imported Chinese electric motors. The Egyptian Ministry of Trade and Industry then decided to implement anti-dumping duties that range from 80 percent to 85 percent of the value of the Chinese electric motors depending on the horse-power.

Of course, Chinese firms are exporting much more than just paper to the United States and electric motors to Egypt. For example, in 2010, total Chinese exports to the U.S. were US$364.9 billion, while Chinese imports from the U.S. were only US$91.8 billion. The trade balance between China and Egypt is also in favor of China. Chinese exports to Egypt in 2007 were US$4.4 billion, while Chinese imports from Egypt were around US$240 million. The Chinese government has found that high levels of exports have led to political problems not only with the U.S., but also with Japan and the countries of the European Union. As we will see in this chapter, any country that has a high level of net exports must also have a high level of *net foreign investment*. When the foreign investment takes the form of buying foreign stocks and bonds, relatively little political friction usually results. But when the foreign investment takes the form of purchasing foreign firms, it can result in political difficulties. For example, in 2005, Chinese firms attempted to buy the U.S. oil company Unocal Corporation and the U.S. appliance-maker Maytag. Ultimately, neither purchase was successful, and CNOOC, the Chinese oil company that failed to buy Unocal, blamed

the political environment in the U.S. and "the unprecedented political opposition."

AN INSIDE LOOK on page 856 discusses why most global investors aren't worried about America's current account deficit.

Sources: James Hanah, "U.S. Paper Mills See Glimmer of Hope," *Charlotte Observer*, June 8, 2007; Gregg Hitt, "U.S. Sets New China Duties," *Wall Street Journal*, March 31, 2007, p. A3; Matt Pottinger, Russell Gold, Michael M. Phillips, and Kate Linebaugh, "CNOOC Drops Offer for Unocal, Exposing U.S.–Chinese Tensions," *Wall Street Journal*, August 3, 2005, p. A1; and "Egypt Places Anti-Dumping Duties on Chinese Electric Motors", *Zawya*, June 2, 2010.

LEARNING Objectives

After studying this chapter, you should be able to:

25.1 Explain how the **balance of payments** is calculated, page 834.

25.2 Explain how **exchange rates** are determined and how changes in exchange rates affect the **prices** of **imports** and **exports**, page 839.

25.3 Explain the **saving and investment equation**, page 847.

25.4 Explain the effect of a **government budget deficit** on **investment** in an **open economy**, page 850.

25.5 Discuss the difference between the effectiveness of **monetary and fiscal policy** in an **open economy** and in a **closed economy**, page 852.

Economics in YOUR Life!

Foreign Investors and Your Car Loan

Suppose that you are shopping for a new car, which you plan to finance with a loan from a local bank. One morning, as you head out the door to visit another automobile dealership, you hear the following newsflash on the radio: "many foreign investors are intending to sell their large holdings of your government's Treasury bonds." What likely effect will the foreign investors' decision to sell their Treasury bonds, issued by your government, have on the interest rate that you pay on your car loan? As you read this chapter, see if you can answer this question. You can check your answer against the one we provide at the end of the chapter. >> Continued on page 854

I n Chapter 14, we looked at the basics of international trade. In this chapter, we look more closely at the linkages among countries at the macroeconomic level. Countries are linked by trade in goods and services and by flows of financial investment. We will see how policymakers in all countries take these linkages into account when conducting monetary and fiscal policy.

25.1 LEARNING OBJECTIVE

25.1 | Explain how the balance of payments is calculated.

The Balance of Payments: Linking the Arab World to the International Economy

Today, consumers, firms, and investors routinely interact with consumers, firms, and investors in other economies. A consumer in Bahrain may use a computer produced in the China, listen to music on a CD player made in Japan, and wear a sweater made in Jordan. A firm in Kuwait may sell its products in dozens of countries around the world. An investor in London may sell a U.S. Treasury bill to an investor in Doha City. Nearly all economies are **open economies** and have extensive interactions in trade or finance with other countries. Open economies interact by trading goods and services and by making investments in each other's economies. A **closed economy** has no interactions in trade or finance with other countries. No economy today is completely closed. A few countries, such as North Korea, have very limited economic interactions with other countries.

The best way to understand the interactions between one economy and other economies is through the *balance of payments*. The **balance of payments** is a record of a country's trade with other countries in goods, services, and assets. The Ministry of Trade is usually responsible for collecting data on the balance of payments. Tables 25-1-A and 25-1-B show the balance of payments of two Arab counties: an oil-based economy (Kuwait) and a non-oil-based economy (Egypt) in 2007. Notice that the table contains three accounts: the *current account*, the *financial account*, and the *capital account*.

Open economy An economy that has interactions in trade or finance with other countries.

Closed economy An economy that has no interactions in trade or finance with other countries.

Balance of payments The record of a country's trade with other countries in goods, services, and assets.

TABLE 25-1-A

The Balance of Payments of Kuwait, 2007 (billions of US dollars)

ITEM	2007
CURRENT ACCOUNT	
1. Goods (balance of trade)	43,056
Goods Exports (FOB)	63,681
Goods Imports (FOB)	−20,625
2. Services (transportation, travel, insurance, …, etc.)	−3,447
Receipts (Credit)	9,636
Payments (Debit)	−13,083
3. Net Investment Income	12,937
Receipts (Credit)	15,688
Payments (Debit)	−2,751
Balance on Goods, Services and Income	52,546
4. Net Current Transfers	−5,076
Receipts (Credit)	127
General government	127
Other sectors of which:	…
Workers' remittances	…
Payments (Debit)	−5,203
General government	−574
Other sectors of which:	−4,630
Workers' remittances	−3,824
Current Account Balance	**47,471**

ITEM	2007
CAPITAL AND FINANCIAL ACCOUNT	
1. Capital Account (balance)	**1,573**
Capital transfers (Credit)	1,596
Capital transfers (Debit)	−23
2. Financial Account (balance)	**−40,503**
Direct investment	−13,563
Abroad	−13,682
In reporting economy	119
Portfolio Investment	−32,900
−Portfolio Investment Assets	−33,575
Equity securities	…
Debt securities	−33,575
−Portfolio Investment Liabilities	675
Equity securities	…
Debt securities	675
Other investment	9,178
−Other Investment Assets	−10,915
Loans	−1,089
Currency & Deposits	−5,069
Trade Credits	−2,639
Other assets	−2,118
−Other Investment Liabilities	20,093
Loans	5,747
Currency & Deposits	10,832
Trade Credits	…
Reserve and Related Items	**−3,218**
Capital and Financial Account Balance	**−38,930**
3. Net Errors and Omissions (Statistical discrepancy)	−8,541
Balance of Payments	**0**

Source: Arab Monetary Fund, www.amf.org.ae/bop.

TABLE 25-1-A

The Balance of Payments of Kuwait, 2007 (billions of US dollars) (*Continued*)

ITEM	2007
CURRENT ACCOUNT	
1. Goods (balance of trade)	−14,899.7
Goods Exports (FOB)	24,454.6
Goods Imports (FOB)	−39,354.3
2. Services (transportation, travel, insurance, …, etc.)	5,601
Receipts (Credit)	19,943.4
Payments (Debit)	−14,342.4
3. Net Investment Income	1,388.2
Receipts (Credit)	3,309
Payments (Debit)	−1,920.8
Balance on Goods, Services and Income	**−7,910.5**
4. Net Current Transfers	8,322.1
Receipts (Credit)	8,561.8
General government	823.8
Other sectors of which:	7,738
Workers' remittances	7,655.8
Payments (Debit)	−239.7
General government	−59.8
Other sectors of which:	−179.9
Workers' remittances	−179.6
Current Account Balance	**411.6**
	(Continued)

TABLE 25-1-B

The Balance of Payments of Egypt, 2007 (billions of US dollars)

TABLE 25-1-C

The Balance of Payments of Egypt, 2007 (billions of US dollars)

ITEM	2007
CAPITAL AND FINANCIAL ACCOUNT	
1. Capital Account	**1.9**
Capital transfers (Credit)	5.3
Capital transfers (Debit)	−3.4
2. Financial Accounts	**−664.1**
Direct investment	10,913.3
Abroad	−664.8
In reporting economy	11,578.1
Portfolio Investment	−3,573.9
–Portfolio Investment Assets	−846.4
Equity securities	−846.4
Debt securities	…
–Portfolio Investment Liabilities	−2,727.5
Equity securities	−3,198.9
Debt securities	471.4
Other investment	−4,316.6
–Other Investment Assets	−5,498.1
Loans	…
Currency & Deposits	−4,585.2
Trade Credits	…
Other assets	−912.9
–Other Investment Liabilities	1,181.5
Loans	−1,791.6
Currency & Deposits	929.6
Trade Credits	2,027.8
Reserve and Related Items	**−3,686.9**
Capital and Financial Account Balance	**−662.2**
3. Net Errors and Omissions	250.6
Balance of Payments	**0**

Source: Arab Monetary Fund, www.amf.org.ae/bop.

The Current Account

The **current account** records *current*, or short-term, flows of funds into and out of a country. The current account includes imports and exports of goods and services (*net exports*), income received by residents of Kuwait/Egypt from investments in other countries, income paid on investments in Kuwait/Egypt owned by residents of other countries (*net investment income*), and the difference between transfers made to residents of other countries and transfers received by Kuwait/Egypt residents from other countries (*net transfers*). If you make a donation to a charity caring for orphans in Somalia, it would be included in net transfers. Any payments received by Kuwait/Egypt residents are positive numbers in the current account, and any payments made by Kuwait/Egypt residents are negative numbers in the current account.

The Balance of Trade Part of the current account is the **balance of trade**, which is the difference between the value of the goods a country exports and the value of the goods a country imports. The balance of trade is the largest item in the current account and is often a topic politicians and the media discuss. If a country exports more than it imports, it has a *trade surplus*. If it exports less than it imports, it has a *trade deficit*. For example, in 2007, Kuwait had a trade surplus of US$43 billion, while Egypt had a trade deficit of around US$15 billion. Examples in developed economies are: the United States had a trade deficit of US$816 billion, Japan had a trade surplus of US$105 billion, and China had a trade surplus of US$316 billion.

Current account The part of the balance of payments that records a country's net exports, net investment income, and net transfers.

Balance of trade The difference between the value of the goods a country exports and the value of the goods a country imports.

Net Exports Equals the Sum of the Balance of Trade and the Balance of Services In previous chapters, we saw that *net exports* is a component of aggregate expenditures. Net exports is not explicitly shown in Tables 25-1-A and 25-1-B, but we can calculate it by adding together the balance of trade and the balance of services. The *balance of services* is the difference between the value of the services a country exports and the value of the services a country imports. Notice that, technically, net exports is *not* equal to the current account balance because the current account balance also includes net investment income and net current transfers. But these other two items are relatively small, so it is often a convenient simplification to think of net exports as equal to the current account balance, as we will see later in this chapter.

The Financial Account

The **financial account** records purchases of assets a country has made abroad and foreign purchases of assets in the country. The financial account records long-term flows of funds into and out of a country. There is a *capital outflow* from Kuwait/Egypt when an investor in Kuwait/Egypt buys a bond issued by a foreign company or government or when a Kuwaiti/Egyptian firm builds a factory in another country. There is a *capital inflow* into Kuwait/Egypt when a foreign investor buys a bond issued by a Kuwaiti/Egyptian firm or by the government or when a foreign firm builds a factory in Kuwait/Egypt. Notice that we are using the word *capital* here to apply not just to physical assets, such as factories, but also to financial assets, such as shares of stock. When firms build or buy facilities in foreign countries, they are engaging in *foreign direct investment*. When investors buy stock or bonds issued in another country, they are engaging in *foreign portfolio investment*.

Another way of thinking of the balance on the financial account is as a measure of *net capital flows*, or the difference between capital inflows and capital outflows. (Here we are omitting a few transactions included in the capital account, as discussed in the next section.) A closely related concept to net capital flows is **net foreign investment**, which is equal to capital outflows minus capital inflows. Net capital flows and net foreign investment are always equal but have opposite signs: when net capital flows are positive, net foreign investment is negative, and when net capital flows are negative, net foreign investment is positive. Net foreign investment is also equal to net foreign direct investment plus net foreign portfolio investment. Later in this chapter, we will use the relationship between the balance on the financial account and net foreign investment to understand an important aspect of the international economic system.

Financial account The part of the balance of payments that records purchases of assets a country has made abroad and foreign purchases of assets in the country.

Net foreign investment The difference between capital outflows from a country and capital inflows, also equal to net foreign direct investment plus net foreign portfolio investment.

The Capital Account

A third, less important, part of the balance of payments is called the *capital account*. The **capital account** records relatively minor transactions, such as migrants' transfers—which consist of goods and financial assets people take with them when they leave or enter a country—and sales and purchases of nonproduced, nonfinancial assets. A nonproduced, nonfinancial asset is a copyright, patent, trademark, or right to natural resources. The definitions of the financial account and the capital account are often misunderstood because the capital account prior to 1999 recorded all the transactions included now in both the financial account and the capital account. In other words, capital account transactions went from being a very important part of the balance of payments to being a relatively unimportant part. Because the balance on what is now called the capital account is so small, for simplicity we will ignore it in the remainder of this chapter.

Capital account The part of the balance of payments that records relatively minor transactions, such as migrants' transfers, and sales and purchases of nonproduced, nonfinancial assets.

Why Is the Balance of Payments Always Zero?

The sum of the current account balance, the financial account balance, and the capital account balance equals the balance of payments. Tables 25-1-A and 25-1-B show that the balance of payments for Kuwait, and also Egypt, in 2007 was zero. It's not just by chance that this balance was zero; *the balance of payments is always zero.* Notice that the current account balance of Kuwait in 2007 was US$47.471 billion. This value is not quite equal (with opposite sign) to the balance on the capital and financial account, which was US$–38,930 billion. To make the balance on the current account equal the balance on the capital and financial account, the balance of payments includes an entry called the *statistical discrepancy*. (In this example we are adding the balance on the capital account to the balance on financial account. So if we ignored the balance on the capital account, we would say that the statistical discrepancy takes on a value equal to the difference between the current account balance and the balance on the financial account only.)

Why does the Ministry of Trade include the statistical discrepancy entry to force the balance of payments to equal zero? The Ministry knows that the sum of the current account balance and the financial account balance must equal zero. If the sum does not equal zero, some imports or exports of goods and services or some capital inflows or capital outflows were not measured accurately.

To understand why the balance of payments must equal zero every year, consider the following: in 2007, the state of Kuwait spent US$47.471 billion less on goods, services, and other items in the current account than it paid. What happened to that US$47.471 billion? We know that every dollar of that US$47.471 billion was used by Kuwaiti individuals or firms in investments abroad or was added to the Kuwaiti holdings of dollars. We know this because logically there is nowhere else for the dollars to go: if the dollars weren't spent on foreign goods and services—and we know they weren't because in that case they would have shown up in the current account—they must have been spent on investments in foreign countries or not spent at all. Again, dollars that aren't spent are added to the Kuwaiti holdings of dollars. Changes in the Kuwaiti holdings of dollars are known as *official reserve transactions*. Kuwaiti investments abroad or additions to Kuwaiti holdings of dollars both show up as negative entries in the Kuwaiti financial account. Therefore, a current account surplus must be exactly offset by a financial account deficit, leaving the balance of payments equal to zero. The same scenario applies to Egypt, China, and Japan, in 2007, since they also realize a surplus in their current accounts. Similarly, a country that runs a current account deficit, such as the U.S., must run a financial account surplus of exactly the same size. If a country's current account surplus is not exactly equal to its financial account deficit, or if a country's current account deficit is not exactly equal to its financial account surplus, some transactions must not have been accounted for. The statistical discrepancy is included in the balance of payments to compensate for these uncounted transactions.

Solved Problem | **25-1**

Understanding the Arithmetic of Open Economies

Test your understanding of the relationship between the current account and the financial account by evaluating the following assertion by a political commentator: "The industrial countries are committing economic suicide. Every year, they invest more and more in developing countries. Every year, more U.S., Japanese, and European manufacturing firms move their factories to developing countries. With extensive new factories and low wages, developing countries now export far more to the industrial countries than they import."

SOLVING THE PROBLEM:

Step 1: **Review the chapter material.** This problem is about the relationship between the current account and the capital account, so you may want to review the section "Why Is the Balance of Payments Always Zero?" which begins on page 837.

Step 2: **Explain the errors in the commentator's argument.** The argument sounds plausible. It would be easy to find similar statements to this one in recent books and articles by well-known political commentators. But the argument contains an important error: the commentator has failed to understand the relationship between the current account and the financial account. The commentator asserts that developing countries are receiving large capital inflows from industrial countries. In other words, developing countries are running financial account surpluses. The commentator also asserts that developing countries are exporting more than they are importing. In other words, they are running current account surpluses. As we have seen in this section, it is impossible to run a current account surplus *and* a financial account surplus simultaneously. A country that runs a current account surplus *must* run a financial account deficit and vice versa.

EXTRA CREDIT: Most emerging economies that have received large inflows of foreign investment during the past decade, such as South Korea, Thailand, and Malaysia, have run current account deficits: they import more goods and services than they export. Emerging economies, such as Singapore, that run current account surpluses also run financial account deficits: they invest more abroad than other countries invest in them.

The point here is not obvious, otherwise it wouldn't confuse so many intelligent politicians, journalists, and political commentators. Unless you understand the relationship between the current account and the financial account, you won't be able to understand a key aspect of the international economy.

YOUR TURN: For more practice, do related problems 1.6, 1.7, and 1.8 on page 860 at the end of this chapter.

>> **End Solved Problem 25-1**

25.2 | Explain how exchange rates are determined and how changes in exchange rates affect the prices of imports and exports.

The Foreign Exchange Market and Exchange Rates

A firm that operates entirely within Kuwait will price its products in Kuwaiti dinars and will use dinars to pay local suppliers, workers, interest to bondholders, and dividends to shareholders. A multinational corporation, in contrast, may sell its product in many different countries and receive payment in many different currencies. Its suppliers and workers may also be spread around the world and may have to be paid in local currencies. Corporations may also use the international financial system to borrow in a foreign currency. During the 1990s, for example, many large firms located in East Asian countries, such as Thailand and South Korea, received dollar loans from foreign banks. When firms make extensive use of foreign currencies, they must deal with fluctuations in the exchange rate.

The **nominal exchange rate** is the value of one country's currency in terms of another country's currency. Economists also calculate the *real exchange rate*, which corrects the nominal exchange rate for changes in prices of goods and services. We discuss the real exchange rate later in this chapter. The nominal exchange rate determines how many units of a foreign currency you can purchase with your local currency. For example, the exchange rate between the U.S. dollar and the Japanese yen (¥) can be expressed as ¥100 = US$1. (This exchange rate can also be expressed as how many U.S. dollars are required to buy 1 Japanese yen: US$0.01 = ¥1.) Similarly, the exchange rate between the U.S. dollar and the Saudi riyal is expressed as SR3.75=US$1, or in terms of how many U.S. dollars you can buy with one Saudi riyal: US$0.266= SR1 (it is simply the reciprocal of how many Saudi riyals you can buy with one U.S. dollar). The market for foreign exchange is very active. Every day, the equivalent of more than US$1 trillion worth of currency is traded in the foreign exchange market. The exchange rates that result from this trading are reported each day in the business or financial sections of most newspapers.

Nominal exchange rate The value of one country's currency in terms of another country's currency.

Banks and other financial institutions around the world employ currency traders, who are linked together by computer. Rather than exchange large amounts of paper currency, they buy and sell deposits in banks. A bank buying or selling dollars will actually be buying or selling dollar bank deposits. Dollar bank deposits exist not just in banks in the United States but also in banks around the world. Suppose that the Credit Lyonnais bank in France wishes to sell U.S. dollars and buy Japanese yen. It may exchange U.S. dollar deposits that it owns for Japanese yen deposits owned by the Deutsche Bank in Germany. Businesses and individuals usually obtain foreign currency from banks in their own country.

Making the Connection | Exchange Rates in the Financial Pages

The business pages of most newspapers list the exchange rates between the dollar and other important currencies. The exchange rates in the following table are for July 2, 2008. The euro is the common currency used by 15 European countries, including France, Germany, and Italy.

EXCHANGE RATE BETWEEN THE DOLLAR AND THE INDICATED CURRENCY

CURRENCY	UNITS OF FOREIGN CURRENCY PER U.S. DOLLAR	U.S. DOLLARS PER UNIT OF FOREIGN CURRENCY
Canadian dollar	1.014	0.987
Japanese yen	106.000	0.009
Mexican peso	10.390	0.096
British pound	0.502	1.992
Euro	0.630	1.587

As you might have noticed in the previous section, when we discussed the nominal exchange rate between the U.S. dollar and the Japanese yen, on the one hand, and between the U.S. dollar and the Saudi Riyal, on the other, the expression for the exchange rate stated as units of foreign currency per U.S. dollar is the *reciprocal* of the exchange rate stated as U.S. dollars per unit of foreign currency. So, the exchange rate between the U.S. dollar and the British pound can be stated as either 0.502 British pounds per U.S. dollar or 1/0.502 = 1.992 U.S. dollars per British pound.

Banks are the most active participants in the market for foreign exchange. Typically, banks buy currency for slightly less than the amount for which they sell it. This spread between the buying and selling prices allows banks to cover their expenses from currency trading and to make a profit. Therefore, when most businesses and individuals buy foreign currency from a bank, they receive fewer units of foreign currency per dollar than would be indicated by the exchange rate printed in the newspaper.

Source: *Wall Street Journal*, July 2, 2008.

YOUR TURN: Test your understanding by doing related problem 2.5 on page 860 at the end of this chapter.

The financial pages of most newspapers provide information on exchange rates.

The market exchange rate is determined by the interaction of demand and supply, just as other prices are. Let's consider the demand for U.S. dollars in exchange for Japanese yen. There are three sources of foreign currency demand for the U.S. dollar:

1 Foreign firms and households who want to buy goods and services produced in the United States.

2 Foreign firms and households who want to invest in the United States either through foreign direct investment—buying or building factories or other facilities in the United States—or through foreign portfolio investment—buying stocks and bonds issued in the United States.

3 Currency traders who believe that the value of the dollar in the future will be greater than its value today.

Equilibrium in the Market for Foreign Exchange

Figure 25-1 shows the demand and supply of U.S. dollars for Japanese yen. Notice that as we move up the vertical axis in Figure 25-1, the value of the dollar increases relative to the value of the yen. When the exchange rate is ¥150 = US$1, the dollar is worth 1.5 times as much relative to the yen as when the exchange rate is ¥100 = US$1. Consider, first, the demand curve for dollars in exchange for yen. The demand curve has the normal downward slope. When the value of the dollar is high, the quantity of dollars demanded will be low. A Japanese investor will be more likely to buy a US$1,000 bond issued by the U.S. Treasury when the exchange rate is ¥100 = US$1 and the investor pays only ¥100,000 to buy US$1,000 than when the exchange rate is ¥150 = US$1 and the investor must pay ¥150,000. Similarly, a Japanese firm is more likely to buy US$150 million worth of microchips from Intel Corporation when the exchange rate is ¥100 = US$1 and the microchips can be purchased for ¥15 billion than when the exchange rate is ¥150 = US$1 and the microchips cost ¥22.5 billion.

Consider, now, the supply curve of dollars in exchange for yen. The supply curve has the normal upward slope. When the value of the dollar is high, the quantity of dollars supplied in exchange for yen will be high. A U.S. investor will be more likely to buy a ¥200,000 bond issued by the Japanese government when the exchange rate is ¥200 = US$1 and he needs to pay only US$1,000 to buy ¥200,000 than when the exchange rate is ¥100 = US$1 and he must pay US$2,000. The owner of a U.S. electronics store is more likely to buy ¥20 million worth of television sets from the Sony Corporation when the exchange rate is ¥200 = US$1 and she only needs to pay US$100,000 to purchase the televisions than when the exchange rate is ¥100 = US$1 and she must pay US$200,000.

As in any other market, equilibrium occurs in the foreign exchange market where the quantity supplied equals the quantity demanded. In Figure 25-1, ¥120 = US$1 is the equilibrium exchange rate. At exchange rates above ¥120 = US$1, there will be a surplus of dollars and downward pressure on the exchange rate. The surplus and the downward pressure will not be eliminated until the exchange rate falls to ¥120 = US$1. If the

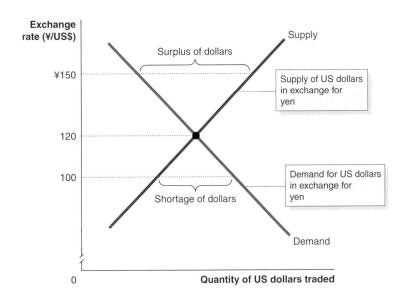

Figure 25-1

Equilibrium in the Foreign Exchange Market

When the exchange rate is ¥150 to the U.S. dollar, it is above its equilibrium level, and there will be a surplus of dollars. When the exchange rate is ¥100 to the dollar, it is below its equilibrium level, and there will be a shortage of dollars. At an exchange rate of ¥120 to the dollar, the foreign exchange market is in equilibrium.

Based on data from the Federal Reserve Bank of St Louis.

Currency appreciation An increase in the market value of one currency relative to another currency.

Currency depreciation A decrease in the market value of one currency relative to another currency.

exchange rate is below ¥120 = US$1, there will be a shortage of dollars and upward pressure on the exchange rate. The shortage and the upward pressure will not be eliminated until the exchange rate rises to ¥120 = US$1. Surpluses and shortages in the foreign exchange market are eliminated very quickly because the volume of trading in major currencies such as the dollar and the yen is very large, and currency traders are linked together by computer.

Currency appreciation occurs when the market value of a country's currency increases relative to the value of another country's currency. **Currency depreciation** occurs when the market value of a country's currency decreases relative to the value of another country's currency.

How Do Shifts in Demand and Supply Affect the Exchange Rate?

Shifts in the demand and supply curves cause the equilibrium exchange rate to change. Three main factors cause the demand and supply curves in the foreign exchange market to shift:

1 Changes in the demand for domestically produced goods and services and changes in the demand for foreign-produced goods and services

2 Changes in the desire to invest in the country and changes in the desire to invest in foreign countries

3 Changes in the expectations of currency traders about the likely future value of the local currency and the likely future value of foreign currencies.

Speculators Currency traders who buy and sell foreign exchange in an attempt to profit from changes in exchange rates.

Shifts in the Demand for Foreign Exchange Consider how the three factors listed above will affect the demand for U.S. dollars in exchange for Japanese yen. During an economic expansion in Japan, the incomes of Japanese households will rise, and the demand by Japanese consumers and firms for U.S. goods will increase. At any given exchange rate, the demand for U.S. dollars will increase, and the demand curve will shift to the right. Similarly, if interest rates in the United States rise, the desirability of investing in U.S. financial assets will increase, and the demand curve for dollars will also shift to the right. Some buyers and sellers in the foreign exchange market are *speculators*. **Speculators** buy and sell foreign exchange in an attempt to profit from changes in exchange rates. If a speculator becomes convinced that the value of the dollar is going to rise relative to the value of the yen, the speculator will sell yen and buy dollars. If the current exchange rate is ¥120 = US$1, and the speculator is convinced that it will soon rise to ¥140 = US$1, the speculator could sell ¥600,000,000 and receive US$5,000,000 (= ¥600,000,000/¥120) in return. If the speculator is correct and the value of the dollar rises against the yen to ¥140 = US$1, the speculator will be able to exchange US$5,000,000 for ¥700,000,000 (= US$5,000,000 × ¥140), leaving a profit of ¥100,000,000.

To summarize, the demand curve for dollars shifts to the right when incomes in Japan rise, when interest rates in the United States rise, or when speculators decide that the value of the dollar will rise relative to the value of the yen.

During a recession in Japan, Japanese incomes will fall, reducing the demand for U.S.-produced goods and services and shifting the demand curve for dollars to the left. Similarly, if interest rates in the United States fall, the desirability of investing in U.S. financial assets will decrease, and the demand curve for dollars will shift to the left. Finally, if speculators become convinced that the future value of the dollar will be lower than its current value, the demand for dollars will fall, and the demand curve will shift to the left.

Shifts in the Supply of Foreign Exchange The factors that affect the supply curve for dollars are similar to those that affect the demand curve for dollars. An economic expansion in the United States increases the incomes of Americans and increases their demand for goods and services, including goods and services made in Japan. As U.S. consumers and

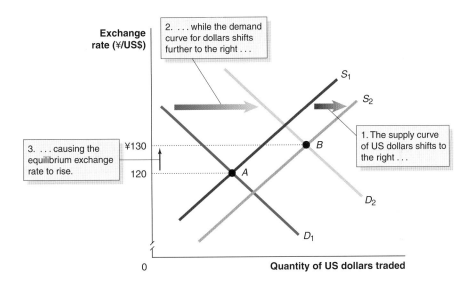

Figure 25-2

Shifts in the Demand and Supply Curve Resulting in a Higher Exchange Rate

Holding other factors constant, an increase in the supply of dollars will decrease the equilibrium exchange rate. An increase in the demand for dollars will increase the equilibrium exchange rate. In the case shown in this figure, the demand curve and the supply curve have both shifted to the right. Because the demand curve has shifted to the right by more than the supply curve, the equilibrium exchange rate has increased from ¥120 to US$1 at point A to ¥130 to US$1 at point B.

firms increase their spending on Japanese products, they must supply dollars in exchange for yen, which causes the supply curve for dollars to shift to the right. Similarly, an increase in interest rates in Japan will make financial investments in Japan more attractive to U.S. investors. These higher Japanese interest rates will cause the supply of dollars to shift to the right, as U.S. investors exchange dollars for yen. Finally, if speculators become convinced that the future value of the yen will be higher relative to the dollar than it is today, the supply curve of dollars will shift to the right as traders attempt to exchange dollars for yen.

A recession in the United States will decrease the demand for Japanese products and cause the supply curve for dollars to shift to the left. Similarly, a decrease in interest rates in Japan will make financial investments in Japan less attractive and cause the supply curve of dollars to shift to the left. If traders become convinced that the future value of the yen will be lower relative to the dollar, the supply curve will also shift to the left.

Adjustment to a New Equilibrium The factors that affect the demand and supply for currencies are constantly changing. Whether the exchange rate increases or decreases depends on the direction and size of the shifts in the demand curve and supply curve. For example, as Figure 25-2 shows, if the demand curve for dollars in exchange for Japanese yen shifts to the right by more than the supply curve does, the equilibrium exchange rate will increase.

Making the Connection | **What Explains the Fall and Rise and Fall of the U.S. Dollar?**

An American vacationing in Paris during the spring of 2002 could have bought a meal for 50 and paid the equivalent of US$44 for it. In the summer of 2008, that same 50 meal would have cost the equivalent of US$79. A few months later, in early 2009, it would have cost only US$64, before rising again to US$70 in the summer. Clearly, during these years the value of the dollar in exchange for the euro was going through substantial fluctuations. And it wasn't just against the euro that the dollar was losing value, then regaining some of it, and then losing it again. The graph below shows fluctuations for the period from 1990 to mid-2009 in an index of the value of the dollar against an average of other major currencies, such as the euro, the British pound, the Canadian dollar, and the Japanese yen.

(Continued)

The graph indicates that although the dollar gained value against other currencies for a brief period during late 2008 and early 2009, overall it has lost value since 2002. What explains the decline in the value of the dollar? We have just seen that an increase in the demand by foreign investors for U.S. financial assets can increase the value of the dollar, and a decrease in the demand for U.S. financial assets can decrease the value of the dollar. The increase in the value of the dollar in the late 1990s, as shown in the graph, was driven by strong demand from foreign investors for U.S. stocks and bonds, particularly U.S. Treasury securities. This increase in demand was not primarily due to higher U.S. interest rates, but to problems in the international financial system. Many investors saw U.S. financial assets as a safe haven in times of financial problems because the chance that the U.S. Treasury would default on its bonds was believed to be very small.

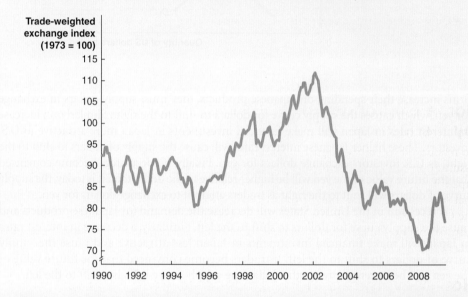

Based on data from the Federal Reserve Bank of St Louis.

Conditions began to change in 2002, however, for a couple of reasons. First, as we saw in Chapter 22, the U.S. Federal Reserve began aggressively cutting the target for the federal funds rate to deal with the recession of 2001 and the initially slow recovery that followed. By May 2003, the target for the federal funds rate was at a historically low level of 1 percent. Low U.S. interest rates mean that investors are likely to buy foreign assets rather than U.S. assets, which depresses the demand for dollars and lowers the exchange value of the dollar. Although the Fed did begin raising the target for the federal funds rate in 2004, it resumed cutting the target in the fall of 2007. Low U.S. interest rates have played a role in the declining value of the dollar. Second, many investors and some central banks became convinced that the value of the dollar was too high in 2002 and that it was likely to decline in the future. As we will see later in this chapter, the United States has run large current account deficits during the early 2000s. Many investors believed that the substantial increase in the supply of dollars in exchange for foreign currencies that resulted from these current account deficits would ultimately result in a significant decline in the value of the dollar. Once investors become convinced that the value of a country's currency will decline, they become reluctant to hold that country's financial assets. For example, Japanese purchases of U.S. financial assets declined from US$59 billion in 2006 to only £6 billion in 2008. European purchases, for all countries other than the United Kingdom, dropped from US$128 billion in 2006 to US$8 billion in 2008. A decreased willingness by foreign investors to buy U.S. financial assets decreases the demand for dollars and lowers the exchange value of the dollar.

What explains the increase in the value of the dollar in late 2008 and early 2009? The increase in the value of the dollar during this period caused problems for companies, as their foreign currency earnings could be exchanged for fewer dollars. The increase in the value of the dollar was largely the result of the deepening of the financial crisis in the fall of 2008. Just as during the financial crisis of the late 1990s, many investors saw U.S. Treasury securities as a safe haven and demanded dollars in order to invest in them. By the summer of 2009, the easing in the financial crisis resulted in the dollar resuming its decline.

The fall in the value of the dollar over the long run has been bad news for U.S. tourists traveling abroad and for anyone in the United States buying foreign goods and services. It has been good news, however, for U.S. firms exporting goods and services to other countries.

YOUR TURN: Test your understanding by doing related problem 2.13 on page 861 at the end of this chapter.

Some Exchange Rates Are Not Determined by the Market

To this point, we have assumed that exchange rates are determined in the market. This assumption is a good one for many currencies, including the U.S. dollar, the euro, the Japanese yen, and the British pound. Some currencies, however, have *fixed exchange rates* that do not change over long periods. For example, for more than 10 years, the value of the Chinese yuan was fixed against the U.S. dollar at a rate of 8.28 yuan to the dollar. Also, as mentioned earlier, the value of Saudi riyals against the U.S. dollars is fixed at a rate of 3.75 riyals to the dollar.

How Movements in the Exchange Rate Affect Exports and Imports

When the market value of the dollar increases, the foreign currency price of U.S. exports rises, and the dollar price of foreign imports falls. For example, suppose that initially the market exchange rate between the U.S. dollar and the euro is US\$1 = €1. In that case, an Apple iPod Nano that has a price of US\$200 in the United States will have a price of €200 in France. Now suppose the market exchange rate between the U.S. dollar and the euro changes to US\$1.20 = €1. Because it now takes more dollars to buy a euro, the dollar has *depreciated* against the euro, and the euro has *appreciated* against the dollar.

The depreciation of the dollar has decreased the euro price of the iPod from €200 to US\$200/(1.20 dollars/euro) = €167. As a result, we would expect more iPods to be sold in France since it is now cheaper than before when evaluated at euros. On the other hand, French products will be more expensive when imported in the U.S. since more dollars are needed now to get the same amount of euros as before (when the exchange rate was US\$1=€1). For example, a pack of French cookies priced at €10 used to have a price of US\$10 when imported in the U.S., but after the depreciation of the dollar against the euro, the same pack now costs US\$12. To generalize, we can conclude that a depreciation in the domestic currency will increase exports and decrease imports, thereby increasing net exports. As we saw in previous chapters, net exports is a component of aggregate demand. If the economy is currently below potential GDP, then, holding all other factors constant, a depreciation in the domestic currency should increase net exports, aggregate demand, and real GDP. An appreciation in the domestic currency should have the opposite effect: exports should fall, and imports should rise, which will reduce net exports, aggregate demand, and real GDP.

Solved Problem | 25-2

The Effect of Changing Exchange Rates on the Prices of Imports and Exports

Suppose that in March 2011, the average price of goods imported into Saudi Arabia from Egypt fell by 10 percent. Is it likely that the value of the Saudi riyal appreciated or depreciated versus the Egyptian pound during this period?

Is it likely that the average price in Egyptian pounds of goods exported from Saudi Arabia to Egypt during March 2011 rose or fell?

SOLVING THE PROBLEM:

Step 1: **Review the chapter material.** This problem is about changes in the value of a currency, so you may want to review the section "How Movements in the Exchange Rate Affect Exports and Imports," which appears on page 845.

Step 2: **Explain whether the value of the Saudi riyal appreciated or depreciated against the Egyptian pound.** We know that if the Saudi riyal appreciates against the Egyptian pound, it will take more Egyptian pounds to purchase one Saudi riyal, and, equivalently, fewer Saudi riyals will be required to purchase one Egyptian pound. An Egyptian consumer or business will need to pay more Egyptian pounds to buy products imported from Saudi Arabia: a good or service that had been selling for 100 Egyptian pounds will now sell for more than 100 Egyptian pounds. A Saudi consumer or business will have to pay fewer Saudi riyals to buy products imported from Egypt: a good or service that had been selling for 100 Saudi riyals will now sell for fewer than 100 Saudi riyals. We can conclude that if the price of goods imported into Saudi Arabia from Egypt fell, the value of the Saudi riyal must have appreciated versus the Egyptian pound.

Step 3: **Explain what happened to the average price in Egyptian pounds of goods exported from Saudi Arabia to Egypt.** If the Saudi riyal appreciated relative to the Egyptian pound, the average price in Egyptian pounds of goods exported from Saudi Arabia to Egypt will have risen.

>> **End Solved Problem 25-2**

YOUR TURN: For more practice, do related problem 2.9 on page 861 at the end of this chapter.

The Real Exchange Rate

Real exchange rate The price of domestic goods in terms of foreign goods.

We have seen that an important factor in determining the level of a country's exports to and imports from another country is the relative prices of each country's goods. The relative prices of two countries' goods are determined by two factors: the relative price levels in the two countries and the nominal exchange rate between the two countries' currencies. Economists combine these two factors in the *real exchange rate*. The **real exchange rate** is the price of domestic goods in terms of foreign goods. Recall that the price level is a measure of the average prices of goods and services in an economy. We can calculate the real exchange rate between two currencies as:

$$\text{Real exchange rate} = \text{Nominal exchange rate} \times \left(\frac{\text{Domestic price level}}{\text{Foreign price level}} \right)$$

Notice that changes in the real exchange rate reflect both changes in the nominal exchange rate and changes in the relative price levels. For example, suppose that, for simplicity, the exchange rate between the U.S. dollar and the Bahraini dinar is US$1 = BD1, the price level in the United States is 100, and the price level in Bahrain is also 100. Then the real exchange rate between the US dollar and the Bahraini dinar is:

$$\text{Real exchange rate} = 1 \text{ dinar/dollar} \times (100/100) = 1.00$$

Now suppose that the nominal exchange rate increases to 1.1 dinars per dollar, while the price level in the United States rises to 105 and the price level in Bahrain remains 100. In this case, the real exchange rate will be:

$$\text{Real Exchange rate} = 1.1 \text{ dinar/dollar} \times (105/100) = 1.15$$

The increase in the real exchange rate from 1.00 to 1.15 tells us that the prices of U.S. goods and services are now 15 percent higher than they were relative to Bahraini goods and services.

Real exchange rates are reported as index numbers, with one year chosen as the base year. As with the consumer price index, the main value of the real exchange rate is in tracking changes over time—in this case, changes in the relative prices of domestic goods in terms of foreign goods.

25.3 | Explain the saving and investment equation.

Net Exports Equal Net Foreign Investment

If your spending is greater than your income, what can you do? You can sell some assets—maybe some of your shares of stock in Etisalat Company—or you can borrow money. A firm can be in the same situation: if a firm's costs are greater than its revenues, it has to make up the difference by selling assets or by borrowing. A country is in the same situation when it imports more than it exports. The country must finance the difference by selling assets—such as land, office buildings, or factories—or by borrowing.

In other words, for any country, a current account deficit must be exactly offset by a financial account surplus. When a country sells more assets to foreigners than it buys from foreigners, or when it borrows more from foreigners than it lends to foreigners—as it must if it is running a current account deficit—the country experiences a net capital inflow and a financial account surplus. Remember that net exports is roughly equal to the current account balance. Remember also that the financial account balance is roughly equal to net capital flows, which are in turn equal to net foreign investment but with the opposite sign. To review these two points, look again at Tables 25-1-A and 25-1-B on page 834, which show that the current account balance is determined mainly by the balance of trade and the balance of services, and the financial account is equal to net capital flows. Also, remember the definition of net foreign investment.

When imports are greater than exports, net exports are negative, and there will be a net capital inflow as people in your country sell assets and borrow to pay for the surplus of imports over exports. Therefore, net capital flows will be equal to net exports (but with the opposite sign), and net foreign investment will also be equal to net exports (and with the same sign). Because Kuwait realizes positive net exports, it must be a net lender to foreign countries and the net foreign investment of Kuwait will be positive. On the contrary, because net exports are usually negative for the United States, in most years, the United States must be a net borrower from abroad, and U.S. net foreign investment will be negative.

We can summarize this discussion with the following equations:

$$\text{Current account balance} + \text{Financial account balance} = 0$$

or:

$$\text{Current account balance} = -\text{Financial account balance}$$

or:

$$\text{Net exports} = \text{Net foreign investment}$$

This equation tells us, once again, that countries such as the United States that import more than they export must borrow more from abroad than they lend abroad: if net exports are negative, net foreign investment will also be negative by the same amount. Countries such as Kuwait, Qatar, Japan, and China that export more than they import must lend abroad more than they borrow from abroad: if net exports are positive, net foreign investment will also be positive by the same amount.

Domestic Saving, Domestic Investment, and Net Foreign Investment

As we saw in Chapter 17, the total saving in any economy is equal to saving by the private sector plus saving by the government sector, which we called *public saving*. When the government runs a budget surplus by spending less than it receives in taxes, it is saving. When the government runs a budget deficit, public saving is negative. Negative saving is also known as *dissaving*. We can write the following expression for the level of saving in the economy:

$$\text{National saving} = \text{Private saving} + \text{Public saving}$$

or:

$$S = S_{\text{private}} + S_{\text{public}}$$

Private saving is equal to what households have left of their income after spending on consumption goods and paying taxes (for simplicity, we assume that transfer payments are zero):

$$\text{Private saving} = \text{National income} - \text{Consumption} - \text{Taxes}$$

or:

$$S_{\text{private}} = Y - C - T$$

Public saving is equal to the difference between government spending and taxes:

$$\text{Government saving} = \text{Taxes} - \text{Government spending}$$

or:

$$S_{\text{public}} = T - G$$

Finally, remember the basic macroeconomic equation for GDP or national income:

$$Y = C + I + G + NX$$

Saving and investment equation An equation that shows that national saving is equal to domestic investment plus net foreign investment.

We can use this last equation, our definitions of private and public saving, and the fact that net exports equal net foreign investment to arrive at an important relationship, known as the **saving and investment equation**:

$$\text{National saving} = \text{Domestic investment} + \text{Net foreign investment}$$

or:

$$S = I + NFI$$

This equation is an *identity* because it must always be true, given the definitions we have used.

The saving and investment equation tells us that a country's saving will be invested either domestically or overseas. If you save US$1,000 and use the funds to buy a bond issued by General Motors, GM may use the US$1,000 to renovate a factory in the United States (*I*) or to build a factory in Egypt (*NFI*) as a joint venture with an Egyptian firm.

Solved Problem | 25-3

Arriving at the Saving and Investment Equation

Use the definitions of private and public saving, the equation for GDP or national income, and the fact that net exports must equal net foreign investment to arrive at the saving and investment equation.

SOLVING THE PROBLEM:

Step 1: **Review the chapter material.** This problem is about the saving and investment equation, so you may want to review the section "Domestic Saving, Domestic Investment, and Net Foreign Investment," which begins on page 848.

Step 2: **Derive an expression for national saving (S) in terms of national income (Y), consumption (C), and government purchases (G).** We can bring together the four equations we need to use:

1. $S_{private} = Y - C - T$
2. $S_{public} = T - G$
3. $Y = C + I + G + NX$
4. $NX = NFI$

Because national saving (S) appears in the saving and investment equation, we need to find an equation for it in terms of the other variables. Adding equation 1. plus equation 2. yields national saving:

$$S = S_{private} + S_{public} = (Y - C - T) + (T - G) = Y - C - G$$

Step 3: **Use the result from Step 2 to derive an expression for national saving in terms of investment (I) and net exports (NX).** Because GDP (Y) does not appear in the saving and investment equation, we need to substitute the expression for it given in equation 3:

$$S = (C + I + G + NX) - C - G$$

and simplify:

$$S = I + NX$$

Step 4: **Use the results of Steps 2 and 3 to derive the saving and investment equation.** Finally, substitute net foreign investment for net exports:

$$S = I + NFI$$

YOUR TURN: For more practice, do related problem 3.8 on page 862 at the end of this chapter.

>> End Solved Problem 25-3

A country such as the United States that has negative net foreign investment must be saving less than it is investing domestically. To see this, rewrite the saving and investment equation by moving domestic investment to the left side:

$$S - I = NFI$$

If net foreign investment is negative—as it is for the United States nearly every year—domestic investment (I) must be greater than national saving (S).

The level of saving in Japan has been well above domestic investment. The result has been high levels of Japanese net foreign investment. For example, Japanese automobile companies Toyota, Honda, and Nissan have all constructed factories in the United States. Sony purchased the Columbia Pictures film studio. Japanese investors are also estimated to hold more than US$200 billion worth of U.S. Treasury bonds. Japan has made many similar investments in countries around the world, which has sometimes caused resentment in these countries. There were some protests in the United States in the 1980s, for example, when Japanese investors purchased the Pebble Beach golf course in California and the Rockefeller Center complex in New York City.

Japan needs a high level of net exports to help offset a low level of domestic investment. When exports of a product begin to decline and imports begin to increase, governments are often tempted to impose tariffs or quotas to reduce imports. (See Chapter 14 to review tariffs and quotas and their negative effects on the economy.) In fact, many Japanese firms have been urging the Japanese government to impose trade restrictions on exports from China.

25.4 | Explain the effect of a government budget deficit on investment in an open economy.

The Effect of a Government Budget Deficit on Investment

The link we have just developed among saving, investment, and net foreign investment can help us understand some of the effects of changes in a government's budget deficit. When the government runs a budget deficit, national saving will decline unless private saving increases by the amount of the budget deficit, which is unlikely. As the saving and investment equation $(S = I + NFI)$ shows, the result of a decline in national saving must be a decline in either domestic investment or net foreign investment. Why, though, does an increase in the government budget deficit cause a fall in domestic investment or net foreign investment?

To understand the answer to this question, remember that if the government runs a budget deficit, the Ministry of Finance (Treasury) must raise an amount equal to the deficit by selling bonds. To attract investors, the Treasury may have to raise the interest rates on its bonds. As interest rates on Treasury bonds rise, other interest rates, including those on corporate bonds and bank loans, will also rise. Higher interest rates will discourage some firms from borrowing funds to build new factories or to buy new equipment or computers. Higher interest rates on financial assets in the United States will attract foreign investors. Investors in Kuwait, Saudi Arabia, Canada, Japan, or China will have to buy U.S. dollars to be able to purchase bonds in the United States. This greater demand for dollars will increase their value relative to foreign currencies. As the value of the dollar rises, exports from the United States will fall, and imports to the United States will rise. Net exports and, therefore, net foreign investment will fall.

When a government budget deficit leads to a decline in net exports, the result is sometimes referred to as the *twin deficits*, which refers to the possibility that a government budget deficit will also lead to a current account deficit. The twin deficits idea first became widely discussed in the United States during the early 1980s when the federal government ran a large budget deficit that resulted in high interest rates, a high exchange value of the dollar, and a large current account deficit.

Figure 25-3 shows that in the early 1980s, the United States had large federal budget deficits and large current account deficits. The figure also shows, however, that the twin deficits idea does not match the experience of the United States after 1990. The large federal budget deficits of the early 1990s occurred at a time of relatively small current account deficits, and the budget surpluses of the late 1990s occurred at a time of then-record current account deficits. Both the current account deficit and the federal budget deficit increased in the early 2000s, but the federal budget deficit declined in the mid-2000s much more than did the current account deficit. In 2008, the federal budget deficit soared, more than doubling as a percentage of GDP, while the current account deficit declined.

The experience of other countries also shows only mixed support for the twin deficits idea. Germany ran large budget deficits and large current account deficits during the early 1990s, but both Canada and Italy ran large budget deficits during the 1980s without running current account deficits. The saving and investment equation shows that an increase in the government budget deficit will not lead to an increase in the current account deficit, provided that either private saving increases or domestic investment declines. According to the twin deficits idea, when the federal government ran budget

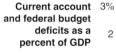

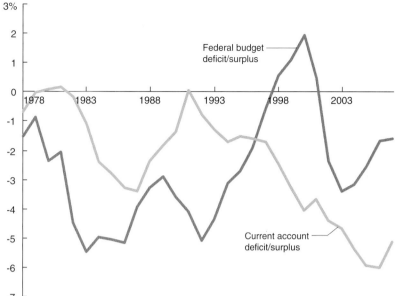

Figure 25-3

The Twin Deficits, 1978–2008

During the early 1980s, large federal budget deficits occurred at the same time as large current account deficits, but twin deficits did not occur in the 1990s.
Source: U.S. Bureau of Economic Analysis.

surpluses in the late 1990s, the current account should also have been in surplus, or at least the current account deficit should have been small. In fact, the increase in national saving due to the budget surpluses was more than offset by a sharp decline in private saving, and the United States ran very large current account deficits.

Making the Connection

Why Is the United States Called the "World's Largest Debtor"?

The following graph shows the current account balance as a percentage of GDP for the United States for the period 1950–2008. The United States has had a current account deficit every year since 1982, with the exception of 1991. Between 1950 and 1975, the United States ran a current account deficit in only five years. Many economists believe that the current account deficits of the 1980s were closely related to the federal budget deficits of those years. High interest rates attracted foreign investors to U.S. bonds, which raised the exchange rate between the dollar and foreign currencies. The high exchange rate reduced U.S. exports and increased imports, leading to current account deficits.

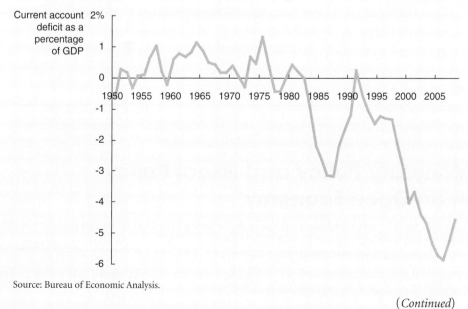

Source: Bureau of Economic Analysis.

(Continued)

Large current account deficits have resulted in foreign investors purchasing large amounts of U.S. assets.

As the federal budget deficit narrowed in the mid-1990s and disappeared in the late 1990s, the foreign exchange value of the dollar remained high—and large current account deficits continued—because foreign investors persisted in investing in the United States despite low interest rates. In the late 1990s, a number of countries around the world, such as South Korea, Indonesia, Brazil, and Russia, suffered severe economic problems. In a process known as a *flight to quality*, many investors sold their investments in those countries and bought investments in the United States. In addition, the strong performance of the U.S. stock market through the spring of 2000 attracted many investors. Finally, the sharp decline in private saving in the United States that began during the late 1990s also contributed to the U.S. current account deficit. The fall in the value of the dollar during 2007 and 2008 helped reduce the size of the current account deficit, although the deficit still remained substantial.

Do persistent current account deficits represent a problem for the United States? Current account deficits result in U.S. net foreign investment being negative. Each year, foreign investors accumulate many more U.S. assets than U.S. investors accumulate foreign assets. At the end of 2008, foreign investors owned about US$3.5 trillion more of U.S. assets—such as stocks, bonds, and factories—than U.S. investors owned of foreign assets, which is why the United States is sometimes called "the world's largest debtor." But the continued willingness of foreign investors to buy U.S. stocks and bonds and foreign companies to build factories in the United States can be seen as a vote of confidence in the strength of the U.S. economy and the buying power of U.S. consumers. When private saving rates declined in the United States to historically low levels, only the continued flow of funds from foreign investors has made it possible for the United States to maintain the high levels of domestic investment required for economic growth. In 2009, private saving rates increased, but public saving turned sharply negative as the federal budget deficit soared. Domestic investment in the United States remains reliant on funds from foreign investment.

YOUR TURN: Test your understanding by doing related problem 4.6 on page 863 at the end of this chapter.

25.5 | Discuss the difference between the effectiveness of monetary and fiscal policy in an open economy and in a closed economy.

Monetary Policy and Fiscal Policy in an Open Economy

Now that we have explored some of the links between economies, we can look at the difference between how monetary and fiscal policy work in an open economy as opposed to a closed economy. Economists refer to the ways in which monetary and fiscal policy affect the domestic economy as *policy channels*. An open economy has more policy channels than does a closed economy.

Monetary Policy in an Open Economy

When the central bank engages in an expansionary monetary policy, it buys Treasury securities to lower interest rates and stimulate aggregate demand. In a closed economy, the main effect of lower interest rates is on domestic investment spending and purchases of consumer durables. In an open economy, lower interest rates will also affect the exchange rate between the dollar and foreign currencies. For example, lower interest rates in Egypt will cause some Egyptian investors in and abroad to switch from investing in Egyptian financial assets to investing in foreign financial assets. This switch will lower the demand for the Egyptian pound relative to foreign currencies and cause its value to decline. A lower exchange rate will decrease the price of Egyptian products in foreign markets and increase the price of foreign products in Egypt. As a result, net exports will increase. This additional policy channel will increase the ability of an expansionary monetary policy to affect aggregate demand.

When the central bank wants to reduce the rate of economic growth to reduce inflation, it engages in contractionary monetary policy. The central bank sells Treasury securities to increase interest rates and reduce aggregate demand. In a closed economy, the main effect is once again on domestic investment spending and purchases of consumer durables. In an open economy, higher interest rates will lead to a higher foreign exchange value of the domestic currency (the Egyptian pound in our example). The prices of Egyptian products in foreign markets will increase, and the prices of foreign products in the Egypt will fall. As a result, net exports will fall. The contractionary policy will have a larger impact on aggregate demand, and therefore it will be more effective in slowing down the growth in economic activity. To summarize: *Monetary policy has a greater impact on aggregate demand in an open economy than in a closed economy.*

Fiscal Policy in an Open Economy

To engage in an expansionary fiscal policy, the government increases its purchases or cuts taxes. Increases in government purchases directly increase aggregate demand. Tax cuts increase aggregate demand by increasing household disposable income and business income, which results in increased consumption spending and investment spending. An expansionary fiscal policy may result in higher interest rates. In a closed economy, the main effect of higher interest rates is to reduce domestic investment spending and purchases of consumer durables. In an open economy, higher interest rates will also lead to an increase in the foreign exchange value of the domestic currency and a decrease in net exports. Therefore, in an open economy, an expansionary fiscal policy may be less effective because the *crowding out effect* may be larger. In a closed economy, only consumption and investment are crowded out by an expansionary fiscal policy. In an open economy, net exports may also be crowded out.

The government can fight inflation by using a contractionary fiscal policy to slow the rate of economic growth. A contractionary fiscal policy cuts government purchases or raises taxes to reduce household disposable income and consumption spending. It also reduces the budget deficit (or increases the budget surplus), which may lower interest rates. Lower interest rates will increase domestic investment and purchases of consumer durables, thereby offsetting some of the reduction in government spending and increases in taxes. In an open economy, lower interest rates will also reduce the foreign exchange value of the domestic currency and increase net exports. Therefore, in an open economy, a contractionary fiscal policy will have a smaller impact on aggregate demand and therefore will be less effective in slowing down an economy. In summary: *Fiscal policy has a smaller impact on aggregate demand in an open economy than in a closed economy.*

Economics in YOUR Life!

>> Continued from page 833

At the beginning of the chapter, we posed this question: What likely effect will foreign investors' decision to sell their treasury bonds, issued by your government, have on the interest rate that you pay on your car loan? To sell its holdings of treasury bonds, foreign investors may have to offer them at a lower price. When the prices of bonds fall, the interest rates on them rise. As the interest rates on your government's Treasury bonds increase, the interest rates on corporate bonds and bank loans, including car loans, may also increase. So, the decision of the foreign investors has the potential to increase the interest rate you pay on your car loan. In practice, the interest rate on your car loan is likely to be affected only if foreign investors sell a very large number of bonds and if domestic investors consider it likely that more foreign investors may soon do the same thing. The basic point is important, however: economies are interdependent, and interest rates in a specific country are not determined entirely by the actions of people in that specific country.

Conclusion

At one time, some policymakers—and economics textbooks—ignored the linkages between the domestic economy and other economies (the rest of the world). In the modern world, these linkages have become increasingly important, and economists and policymakers must take them into account when analyzing the economy.

Read *An Inside Look* on the next page for a discussion of how the U.S. current account deficit affects global investors.

Can the U.S. Current Account Deficit Be Sustained?

THE ECONOMIST, **MARCH 15, 2007**

Sustaining the Unsustainable

Sour subprime mortgages, sluggish retail sales, the spectre of a broader retreat in credit and consumer spending. These are the American shadows that spooked investors across the globe this week, once again sending share prices tumbling from Manhattan to Mumbai.

For years, the longest shadow of all was cast by America's imposing current-account deficit. But in these fretful times, no one seems to be fretting much about the country's heavy reliance on foreign funding. New figures released on March 14th showed that Americans spent some US$857 billion more than they produced in 2006, the equivalent of 6.5% of GDP, and a new record ....

China's government, one of America's best creditors, has announced it is seeking a better return on a chunk of its foreign-exchange reserves. It will create a new investment agency, which looks sure to diversify some of the central bank's assets out of the American Treasury bonds that now dominate its portfolio ....

None of this had much effect on the dollar. Measured on a trade-weighted basis, it has fallen by a mere 0.04% since the recent financial turbulence began on February 27th. And as investors yawn at America's deficit, so too do policymakers. A year ago, finance ministers and central bankers from the G7 group of big, rich countries promised to take "vigorous action" to resolve the imbalances between the world's savers (particularly China, Japan and the oil exporters) and borrowers (especially America). The IMF was hoping to reinvent itself as the overseer of this grand macroeconomic bargain. A year later the venture has fizzled ....

What explains this nonchalance? By some measures, the world is already rebalancing. The dollar after all has fallen by 16% from its 2002 peak in real terms. Compared with the previous quarter, America's current-account deficit shrank in the last three months of 2006 and was below US$200 billion for the first time in more than a year .... That decline owes a lot to lower oil prices. But even excluding oil, America's trade balance seems to be stabilizing as exports boom and imports slow .... A few years ago most economists argued that the spectacle of poor countries bankrolling America's deficits was the perverse and unsustainable consequence of American profligacy. Economic theory suggested that capital should flow from rich countries to poor ones, and that America could not increase its foreign borrowing forever. Empirical studies showed that deficits of more than 5% of GDP caused trouble.

Since then, economists have vied with each other to overturn this orthodoxy. Indeed, rejecting the conventional wisdom is now itself entirely conventional, as Jeffrey Frankel, an economist at Harvard University, has pointed out ....

In 2005 Ben Bernanke, now chairman of the Federal Reserve, pointed out that global interest rates were oddly low, suggesting a glut of saving abroad, not a shortfall of saving at home, was responsible for the flow of capital to America.

More recent papers have picked up similar threads, arguing that imbalances might prove to be both more persistent and less perverse than once thought. A study last summer by three economists at the IMF, for instance, showed that poor countries which export capital have grown faster than those which rely on importing it from abroad.

One reason may be the feebleness of their financial markets. That is a thesis explored by Ricardo Caballero and Emmanuel Farhi of the Massachusetts Institute of Technology, as well as Pierre-Olivier Gourinchas of the University of California, Berkeley. They point out that emerging economies have been frantically accumulating real assets, such as assembly lines and office towers, but their generation of financial assets has not kept pace. Thanks to weak property rights, fear of expropriation, and poor bankruptcy procedures, many newly rich countries are unable to create enough trustworthy claims on their future incomes. Lacking vehicles for saving at home, the thrifty buy assets abroad instead. In China, Mr Caballero argues, this is done indirectly through the state, which buys foreign securities, such as Treasuries, then issues bonds of its own, which are held by Chinese banks, companies, and households.

Because emerging economies' supply of financial instruments is so unreliable, people may hoard more of them as a precautionary measure. Firms and households fear they will not be able to borrow to tide themselves over bad times, therefore they choose to save for a rainy day instead. Because they cannot transfer purchasing power from the future to the present, they must store it from the past ....

Source: "Sustaining the Unsustainable," *Economist*, © The Economist Newspaper Limited, London (15 March 2007).

Key Points in the Article

This article discusses the U.S. balance of payments and, in particular, the country's large current account deficit. The U.S. current account deficit in 2006 was US$857 billion, or 6.5 percent of U.S. GDP. The article explains why economists have long argued that large current account deficits are unsustainable and why some economists believe that the U.S. current account deficit may prove to be the exception to this rule.

Analyzing the News

(a) Most macroeconomists contend that large deficits in a country's current account—the part of the balance of payments that records a country's net exports, net investment income, and net transfers—are unsustainable. This is because a country's current account deficit is matched by foreigners' (net) purchases of the country's real and financial assets. Hence, current account deficits can last

only as long as foreigners are willing to hold the deficit country's currency, which typically decreases in value as its supply in the world market increases. For example, the U.S. current account deficit in 2006 was US$857 billion, or 6.5 percent of U.S. GDP.

(b) As the U.S. current account deficit increases, so does the supply of U.S. dollars in the foreign exchange market. And, as you read in this chapter, an increase in the supply of dollars decreases the foreign exchange value of the dollar. Nonetheless, despite the growing U.S. current account deficit and, the resulting increase in the supply of U.S. dollars, the foreign exchange value of the U.S. dollar has not fallen as much as most economists and policymakers had expected. This pattern is shown in the figure below, where the trade-weighted exchange value of the U.S. dollar remained relatively stable through 2005 and 2006, during which time the U.S. current account deficit continued to increase. (The trade-weighted exchange rate shows the value of the U.S. dollar against an average of other countries' currencies, with the average determined by how much trade the United States does with each country.) This apparent resilience of the U.S. dollar has—for better or worse—eased the concerns of policymakers.

(c) Economists have developed several theories that explain why the U.S. dollar remains so resilient and, consequently, the United States continues to run a current account deficit. One explanation focuses on the fact that many investors in developing countries are unable to buy stocks and bonds issued by domestic firms because relatively weak property rights and court systems have made it difficult for financial markets to function in these countries So, investors in developing countries who wish to buy stocks and bonds have chosen to invest abroad, particularly in the United States. This explains, in part, foreigners' willingness to hold U.S. dollars, despite the enormous current account deficit of the United States.

Thinking Critically

1. Suppose the foreign exchange value of the U.S. dollar fell to an extent that reflected the country's large current account deficit. What segment of the U.S. economy would, all else being equal, benefit from such an adjustment? Why?

2. As you read in this article, the United States has a larger trade deficit with China than with any other country. How would China's economy be affected by a significant decline in the value of the U.S. dollar? Briefly explain your reasoning.

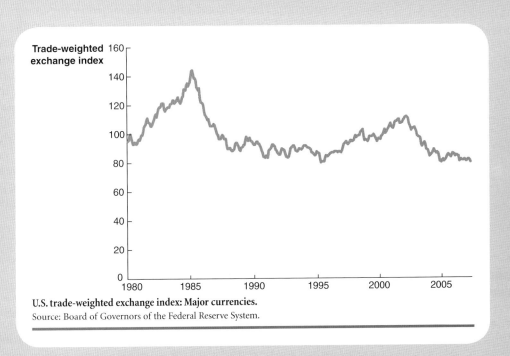

U.S. trade-weighted exchange index: Major currencies.
Source: Board of Governors of the Federal Reserve System.

Key Terms

Summary

25.1 LEARNING OBJECTIVE

Explain how the balance of payments is calculated, **pages 834–839.**

The Balance of Payments: Linking the Arab World to the International Economy

Nearly all economies are **open economies** that trade with and invest in other economies. A **closed economy** has no transactions in trade or finance with other economies. The **balance of payments** is the record of a country's trade with other countries in goods, services, and assets. The **current account** records a country's net exports, net investment income, and net transfers. The **financial account** shows investments a country has made abroad and foreign investments received by the country. The **balance of trade** is the difference between the value of the goods a country exports and the value of the goods a country imports. **Net foreign investment** is the difference between capital outflows from a country and capital inflows. The **capital account** is a part of the balance of payments that records relatively minor transactions. Apart from measurement errors, the sum of the current account and the financial account must equal zero. Therefore, the balance of payments must also equal zero.

25.2 LEARNING OBJECTIVE

Explain how exchange rates are determined and how changes in exchange rates affect the prices of imports and exports, **pages 839–847.**

The Foreign Exchange Market and Exchange Rates

The **nominal exchange rate** is the value of one country's currency in terms of another country's currency. The exchange rate is determined in the foreign exchange market by the demand and supply of a country's currency. Changes in the exchange rate are caused by shifts in demand or supply. The three main sets of factors that cause the supply and demand curves in the foreign exchange market to shift are: changes in the demand for domestically produced goods and services and change in the demand for foreign-produced goods and services; changes in the desire to invest inside the country and changes in the desire to invest in foreign countries; and changes in the expectations of currency traders—particularly **speculators**—concerning the likely future values of the domestic currency and the likely future values of foreign currencies. **Currency appreciation** occurs when a currency's market value increases relative to another currency. **Currency depreciation** occurs when a currency's market value decreases relative to another currency. The **real exchange rate** is the price of domestic goods in terms of foreign goods. The real exchange rate is calculated by multiplying the nominal exchange rate by the ratio of the domestic price level to the foreign price level.

25.3 LEARNING OBJECTIVE

Explain the saving and investment equation, **pages 847–850.**

Net Exports Equal Net Foreign Investment

A current account deficit must be exactly offset by a financial account surplus. The financial account is equal to net capital flows, which is equal to net foreign investment but with the opposite sign. Because the current account balance is roughly equal to net exports, we can conclude that net exports will equal net foreign investment. National saving is equal to private saving plus government saving. Private saving is equal to national income minus consumption and minus taxes. Government saving is the difference between taxes and government spending. As we saw in previous chapters, GDP (or national income) is equal to the sum of investment, consumption, government spending, and net exports. We can use this fact, our definitions of private and government saving, and the fact that net exports equal net foreign investment, to arrive at an important relationship known as the **saving and investment equation**: $S = I + NFI$.

The Effect of a Government Budget Deficit on Investment

When the government runs a budget deficit, national saving will decline unless private saving increases by the full amount of the budget deficit, which is unlikely. As the saving and investment equation ($S = I + NFI$) shows, the result of a decline in national saving must be a decline in either domestic investment or net foreign investment.

25.4 LEARNING OBJECTIVE

Explain the effect of a government budget deficit on investment in an open economy, **pages 850–852.**

Monetary Policy and Fiscal Policy in an Open Economy

When the central bank engages in an expansionary monetary policy, it buys government bonds to lower interest rates and increase aggregate demand. In a closed economy, the main effect of lower interest rates is on domestic investment spending and purchases of consumer durables. In an open economy, lower interest rates will also cause an increase in net exports. When the central bank wants to slow the rate of economic growth to reduce inflation, it engages in a contractionary monetary policy. With a contractionary policy, the central bank sells government bonds to increase interest rates and reduce aggregate demand. In a closed economy, the main effect is once again on domestic investment and purchases of consumer durables. In an open economy, higher interest rates will also reduce net exports. We can conclude that monetary policy has a greater impact on aggregate demand in an open economy than in a closed economy. To engage in an expansionary fiscal policy, the government increases government spending or cuts taxes. An expansionary fiscal policy can lead to higher interest rates. In a closed economy, the main effect of higher interest rates is on domestic investment spending and spending on consumer durables. In an open economy, higher interest rates will also reduce net exports. A contractionary fiscal policy will reduce the budget deficit and may lower interest rates. In a closed economy, lower interest rates increase domestic investment and spending on consumer durables. In an open economy, lower interest rates also increase net exports. We can conclude that fiscal policy has a smaller impact on aggregate demand in an open economy than in a closed economy.

25.5 LEARNING OBJECTIVE

Discuss the difference between the effectiveness of monetary and fiscal policy in an open economy and in a closed economy, **pages 852–853.**

Review, Problems and Applications

myeconlab Visit www.pearsoned.co.uk/awe/hubbard to complete these exercises online and get instant feedback.
Get Ahead of the Curve

25.1 LEARNING OBJECTIVE   Explain how the balance of payments is calculated, **pages 834–839.**

Review Questions

1.1 What is the relationship among the current account, the financial account, and the balance of payments?

1.2 What is the difference between net exports and the current account balance?

1.3 Explain why you agree or disagree with the following statement: "Kuwait has run a balance of payments surplus every year for quite long time."

Problems and Applications

1.4 In 2007, suppose that Sudan had a current account deficit of US$31 billion. Did Sudan experience a net capital outflow or a net capital inflow during 2007? Briefly explain.

1.5 Use the information in the table on the next page to prepare a balance of payments account, like the one shown in Tables 25-1-A and 25-1-B on pages 834–835. Assume that the balance on the capital account is zero.

Increase in foreign holdings of assets in Lebanon	$1,181
Exports of goods	856
Imports of services	−256
Statistical discrepancy	?
Net transfers	−60
Exports of services	325
Income received on investments	392
Imports of goods	−1,108
Increase in Lebanon's holdings of assets in foreign countries	−1,040
Income payments on investments	−315

1.6 (Related to *Solved Problem 25-1* on page 838) Is it possible for a country to run a trade deficit and a financial account deficit simultaneously? Briefly explain.

1.7 (Related to *Solved Problem 25-1* on page 838) Suppose we know that a country has been receiving large inflows of foreign investment. What can we say about its current account balance?

1.8 (Related to *Solved Problem 25-1* on page 838) The United States ran a current account surplus every year during the 1960s. What must have been true about the U.S. financial account balance during those years?

1.9 The only year since 1982 that the United States has run a current account surplus was 1991. In that year, Japan made a large payment to the United States to help pay for the Gulf War. Explain the connection between these two facts. (*Hint:* Where would Japan's payment to the United States appear in the balance of payments?)

1.10 According to this chapter, the Egypt balance of trade was in deficit in 2007 while the Egyptian current account was in surplus. How does this happen?

1.11 According to an article in *BusinessWeek*, "The U.S. is depending on an ever-rising influx of foreign funds to pay for all the imported automobiles, TVs, and clothing that U.S. consumers crave." Convert this sentence into a statement about changes in the U.S. current account and the U.S. financial account.

Source: Rich Miller and David Fairlamb, "The Greenback's Setback: Cause for Concern?" *BusinessWeek*, May 20, 2002, p. 44.

25.2 LEARNING OBJECTIVE   Explain how exchange rates are determined and how changes in exchange rates affect the prices of imports and exports, **pages 839–847.**

Review Questions

2.1 If the exchange rate between the Japanese yen and the U.S. dollar expressed in terms of yen per dollar is ¥110 = US$1, what is the exchange rate when expressed in terms of dollars per yen?

2.2 Suppose that the current exchange rate between the US dollar and the euro is 1.1 euros per US dollar. If the exchange rate changes to 1.2 euros per US dollar, has the euro appreciated or depreciated against the US dollar?

2.3 What are the three main sets of factors that cause the supply and demand curves in the foreign exchange market to shift?

Problems and Applications

2.4 If we know the exchange rate between Country A's currency and Country B's currency and we know the exchange rate between Country B's currency and Country C's currency, then we can compute the exchange rate between Country A's currency and Country C's currency.

    a. Suppose the exchange rate between the Japanese yen and the U.S. dollar is currently ¥120 = US$1 and the exchange rate between the British pound and the U.S. dollar is £0.60 = US$1. What is the exchange rate between the yen and the pound?

    b. Suppose the exchange rate between the yen and dollar changes to ¥130 = US$1 and the exchange rate between the pound and dollar changes to £0.50 = US$1. Has the dollar appreciated or depreciated against the yen? Has the dollar appreciated or depreciated against the pound? Has the yen appreciated or depreciated against the pound?

2.5 (Related to the *Making the Connection* on page 840) Beginning January 1, 2002, 12 of the 15 member countries of the European Union eliminated their own individual currencies and began using a new common currency, the euro. For a three-year period from January 1, 1999, through December 31, 2001, these 12 countries priced goods and services in terms of both their own currencies and the euro. During this period, the value of their currencies was fixed against each other and against the euro. So during this time, the U.S. dollar had an exchange rate against each of these currencies and against the euro. The information in the following table shows the fixed exchange rates of four European currencies against the euro and their exchange rates against the U.S. dollar on March 2, 2001. Use the information on the next page to calculate the exchange rate between the US dollar and the euro (in euros per US dollar) on March 2, 2001.

CURRENCY	UNITS PER EURO (FIXED)	UNITS PER U.S. DOLLAR (AS OF MARCH 2, 2001)
German mark	1.9558	2.0938
French franc	6.5596	7.0223
Italian lira	1,936.2700	2,072.8700
Portuguese escudo	200.4820	214.6300

2.6 Graph the demand and supply of U.S. dollars for euros and label each axis. Show graphically and explain the effect of an increase in interest rates in Europe by the European Central Bank (ECB) on the demand and supply of dollars and the resulting change in the exchange rate of euros for U.S. dollars.

2.7 Graph the demand and supply of Egyptian pounds for euros and label each axis. Show graphically and explain the effect of an increase in the Egyptian government budget deficit that increases interest rates in Egypt on the demand and supply of Egyptian pounds and the resulting change in the exchange rate of euros for Egyptian pounds. Why might the change in the exchange rate lead to a current account deficit?

2.8 Use the graph to answer the following questions.

a. Briefly explain whether the dollar appreciated or depreciated against the yen.

b. Which of the following events could have caused the shift in demand shown in the graph?
  i. Interest rates in the United States have declined.
  ii. Income rises in Japan.
  iii. Speculators begin to believe the value of the dollar will be higher in the future.

2.9 **(Related to *Solved Problem 25-2* on page 846)** When a country's currency appreciates, is this generally good news or bad news for the country's consumers? Is it generally good news or bad news for the country's businesses? Explain your reasoning.

2.10 The following appeared in an article in the *Wall Street Journal*: "...Japanese exporters got a lift from the sagging yen."

a. What does the reporter mean by a "sagging yen"?

b. Why would the yen's sagging help Japanese exporters?

Source: Tim Annett, "Housing Still Hurting," *Wall Street Journal*, February 22, 2007.

2.11 **(Related to the *Chapter Opener* on page 832)** Some Egyptian and U.S. firms, such as Mohamed Ahmed Dawood Investment Company and the paper manufacturer NewPage, argued that the Chinese government was keeping the value of the yuan artificially low against the Egyptian pound and the dollar, which gave Chinese exporters an advantage when selling their products in Egypt and the United States. Why would a low value of the yuan in exchange for the Egyptian pound and the U.S. dollar help Chinese firms exporting to Egypt and the United States?

2.12 Phil Treadway is president and owner of Erie Molded Plastics, Inc., which is located in Erie, Pennsylvania, and makes electrical connectors and plastic bottle caps. Treadway was quoted as follows in the *New York Times*: "Our customers have a market without borders, and we know that. We can compete against China's low labor costs.... But we cannot compete with them if they have a 20 percent to 40 percent currency advantage." What does Treadway mean by a "currency advantage"? How would a currency advantage make it hard for his firm to compete with Chinese firms?

Source: Elizabeth Becker and Edmund L. Andrews, "Currency of China Is Emerging as Tough Business Issue in U.S.," *New York Times*, August 26, 2003.

2.13 **(Related to the *Making the Connection* on page 843)** An article in the *Wall Street Journal* contained the following observations on the foreign exchange market:

> Many eyes in currency markets Friday were on Mexico, where the dollar fell below 10 pesos for the first time since October 2002.... The peso's rise to its strongest level in nearly six years has been largely attributed to the widening of yield spreads—U.S. interest rates have been kept low to counter economic weakness, and the Bank of Mexico has raised rates to keep inflation expectations in check.

> Over in Australia, however, the U.S. dollar came out on the winning end Friday. Australia's dollar fell to a 2 1/2-month low of US$0.9298 Friday as investors began betting that Australia's central bank may reduce its relatively high lending rates before the end of the year.

Why would interest rates in Mexico being higher than interest rates in the United States cause the value of the peso to be high relative to the U.S. dollar? Why would the expectation that Australia's central bank will reduce its lending rates cause the value of the Australian dollar to fall relative to the value of the U.S. dollar?

Source: Dan Molinski, "Jobs Data Lift Dollar Against Euro," *Wall Street Journal*, August 1, 2008.

Review Questions

3.1 Explain the relationship between net exports and net foreign investment.

3.2 What is the saving and investment equation? If national saving declines, what will happen to domestic investment and net foreign investment?

3.3 If a country saves more than it invests domestically, what must be true of its net foreign investment?

Problems and Applications

3.4 Writing in the *Wall Street Journal*, David Wessel makes the following observation:

> Trend one: The U.S. has been buying more than US$1 billion a day more from the rest of the world than it has been selling…. Trend two: Foreigners have been investing more than US$1 billion a day of their savings in U.S. stocks, bonds, office towers, factories, and companies.

Is it coincidence that both of his "trends" involve US$1 billion per day? Briefly explain.

Source: David Wessel, "Pain from the Dollar's Decline Will Mostly Be Felt Overseas," *Wall Street Journal*, June 13, 2002.

3.5 In 2006, domestic investment in Japan was 24.1 percent of GDP, and Japanese net foreign investment was 3.9 percent of GDP. What percentage of GDP was Japanese national saving?

3.6 In 2006, France's net foreign investment was negative. Which was larger in France in 2006: national saving or domestic investment? Briefly explain.

3.7 Briefly explain whether you agree with the following statement: "Because in 2006 national saving was a smaller percentage of GDP in the United States than in the United Kingdom, domestic investment must also have been a smaller percentage of GDP in the United States than in the United Kingdom."

3.8 **(Related to *Solved Problem 25-3* on page 849)** Look again at Solved Problem 25-3, in which we derived the saving and investment equation $S = I + NX$. In deriving this equation, we assumed that national income was equal to Y. But Y only includes income *earned* by households. In the modern U.S.

economy, households receive substantial transfer payments—such as social security payments and unemployment insurance payments—from the government. Suppose that we define national income to be equal to $Y + TR$, where TR equals government transfer payments, and we also define government spending to be equal to $G + TR$. Show that after making these adjustments, we end up with the same saving and investment equation.

3.9 Use the saving and investment equation to explain why the United States experienced large current account deficits in the late 1990s.

3.10 Former Congressman and presidential candidate Richard Gephardt once proposed that tariffs be imposed on imports from countries with which the United States has a trade deficit. If this proposal were enacted and if it were to succeed in reducing the U.S. current account deficit to zero, what would be the likely effect on domestic investment spending within the United States? Assume that no other federal government economic policy is changed. (*Hint:* Use the saving and investment equation to answer this question.)

3.11 **(Related to the *Chapter Opener* on page 832)** Suppose that the Egyptian government decides to raise tariffs on Chinese exports of electric motors even higher. Discuss the impact on the following:
  a. The Egyptian electric motors manufacturers
  b. Chinese electric motors manufacturers
  c. Egyptian consumers
  d. Egyptian net exports
  e. Egyptian net foreign investment

3.12 According to an article in *BusinessWeek*, "In the past year, foreign purchases of stocks and bonds are down 24%, and foreign direct investment is off 63%…. And a key victim is the dollar, down 12% vs. the euro and 10% vs. the yen." From the U.S. point of view, do the changes mentioned in the first sentence represent an increase or a decrease in net foreign investment? Why would this change in net foreign investment cause the exchange value of the dollar to decline?

Source: James C. Cooper and Kathleen Madigan, "The Twin Deficits Are Back—And as Dangerous as Ever," *BusinessWeek*, July 8, 2002, pp. 29–30.

Review Questions

4.1 What happens to national saving when the government runs a budget surplus? What is the twin deficits idea? Briefly explain.

4.2 Why were the early and mid-1980s particularly difficult times for U.S. exporters?

Problems and Applications

4.3 Writing in the April 1997 issue of *International Economic Trends*, published by the Federal Reserve Bank of St Louis, economist Michael Pakko observed the following:

The current account...reached a deficit of US$165 billion in 1996, second only to the deficit of US$167 billion in 1987.... The evidence suggests that strong investment demand underlies the current economic expansion. Since the recession of 1990–91, real fixed investment spending has been growing at a rate of 6.9 percent...compared to 2.6 percent growth of GDP.... Only time will tell what the payoff to these investments will be, but they do give some reason to interpret the U.S. current account deficit with less apprehension.

Why should the fact that investment spending in the United States has been strong reduce apprehension about the size of the current account deficit? What does the current account deficit have to do with investment spending?

4.4 Lee Morgan, chairman of Caterpillar, was quoted in 1985 as saying this of his company's difficulties in exporting: "We believe that there should be a 25% to 30% improvement in the exchange rate with the Japanese yen, because U.S. manufacturers are finding themselves disadvantaged by that amount." When Morgan talked about an "improvement" in the exchange rate between the US dollar and the yen, did he want the US dollar to exchange for more yen or for fewer yen? Why was the exchange value of the US dollar particularly high during the mid-1980s?

4.5 The text states, "The budget surpluses of the late 1990s occurred at a time of then-record current account deficits." Holding everything else constant, what would the likely impact have been on domestic investment in the United States if the current account had been balanced instead of being in deficit?

4.6 **(Related to the *Making the Connection* on page 851)** Why might "the continued willingness of foreign investors to buy U.S. stocks and bonds and foreign companies to build factories in the United States" result in the United States running a current account deficit?

25.5 LEARNING OBJECTIVE   Discuss the difference between the effectiveness of monetary and fiscal policy in an open economy and in a closed economy, **pages 852–853.**

Review Questions

5.1 Why does monetary policy have a greater effect on aggregate demand in an open economy than in a closed economy?

5.2 Why does fiscal policy have a smaller impact in an open economy than in a closed economy?

Problems and Applications

5.3 What is meant by a 'policy channel'? Why would an open economy have more policy channels than a closed economy?

5.4 Suppose that the central bank policy leads to higher interest rates in Jordan.

a. How will this policy affect real GDP in the short run if Jordan is a closed economy?

b. How will this policy affect real GDP in the short run if Jordan is an open economy?

c. How will your answer to part b change if interest rates also rise in the countries that are the major trading partners of Jordan?

5.5 Suppose the government increases spending without also increasing taxes. In the short run, how will this action affect real GDP and the price level in a closed economy? How will the effects of this action differ in an open economy?

Additional References

Chapter 1

2008 Country Reports on Human Rights Practices, US Department of State.

Samir Salama, "GCC must tackle unemployment," *Guly News*, February 2, 2010.

Chapter 2

For more information see, M.A. Cook, ed. *Studies in the Economic History of the Middle East*, 1970. Also, Afaf Loutfi El Sayed, Reviewed Work: "Egyptian Guilds in Modern Times" by Gabriel Baer, *Middle Eastern Studies*, Vol. 2, No. 3 (Apr., 1966), pp. 272–6.

Chapter 5

Quintin Smith, "Microsoft Vista Price Cuts Extends to Gulf Nations," arabianbusiness.com, March 3, 2008.

Chapter 11

Amira Salah-Ahmed, "Mona Yassine: Chairperson, Egyptian Competition Authority," May 2006, *Business Today Egypt*, http://www.businesstodayegypt.com/article .aspx?ArticleID =6725; A, F, Ghoneim, "Competition Law and Competition Policy: What Does Egypt Really Need?" ERF Working Paper 0239, 2006; M. El-Far, "Enforcement Policy of the Egyptian Competition Law," Competition Law International, April 2010, electronic copy available at: http://ssrn.com/abstract=1580056.

Chapter 14

European Institute for Research on Mediterranean and Euro-Arab Cooperation: www.medea.be/index.html?page=2&lang= en&doc=286.

League of Arab States: Greater Arab Free Trade Agreement, The Institute for Domestic and International Affairs, Inc. (IDIA), United Nations 2007.

Paul Rivlin, (2009), *Arab Economies in the Twenty-First Century*, Cambridge: Cambridge University Press.

Table 4.1, 2007 International Trade Statistics Yearbook, *United Nations,* p. 134.

The American Chamber of Commerce in Egypt, www.amcham .org.eg; and the Egyptian Ministry of Trade and industry, www.qizegypt.gov.eg

The Arab World Competitiveness Report 2007: www.weforum .org/en/initiatives/gcp/Arab percent20World percent20 Competitiveness percent20Report/index.htm

The Great Arab Free Trade Area: An Explanatory Guide, The General Assembly of the Arab League (in Arabic), 2007.

World Trade Organization, International Trade Statistics 2007 at www.wto.org

Chapter 18

Information on p. 599 sourced from: The Arab Human Development Report 2005: *Towards the Rise of Women in the Arab World*, New York: United Nations Development Programme, Regional Bureau for Arab States, 2006; F. Roudi-Fahimi, and V. Moghadam, *Empowering Women, Developing Society: Female Education in the Middle East and North Africa*, MENA Policy Brief, Population Reference Bureau (PRP), 2003.

Glossary

Absolute advantage | الميزة المطلقة
The ability of an individual, a firm, or a country to produce more of a good or service than competitors, using the same amount of resources.

Accounting profit | الربح المحاسبي
A firm's net income measured by revenue minus operating expenses and taxes paid.

Aggregate demand and aggregate supply model | نموذج الطلب الإجمالي و العرض الإجمالي
A model that explains short-run fluctuations in real GDP and the price level.

Aggregate demand curve | منحنى الطلب الإجمالي
A curve that shows the relationship between the price level and the quantity of real GDP demanded by households, firms, and the government.

Aggregate expenditure (AE) | منحنى الإنفاق الإجمالي
The total amount of spending in the economy: the sum of consumption, planned investment, government purchases, and net exports.

Aggregate expenditure model | نموذج الإنفاق الإجمالي
A macroeconomic model that focuses on the relationship between total spending and real GDP, assuming that the price level is constant.

Allocative efficiency | الكفاءة التخصيصيه
A state of the economy in which production is in accordance with consumer preferences; in particular, every good or service is produced up to the point where the last unit provides a marginal benefit to society equal to the marginal cost of producing it.

Antitrust laws | قوانين مقاومة الإحتكار
Laws aimed at eliminating collusion and promoting competition among firms.

Autarky | الاكتفاء الذاتي
A situation in which a country does not trade with other countries.

Automatic stabilizers | مثبتات تلقائية للاقتصاد
Government spending and taxes that automatically increase or decrease along with the business cycle.

Autonomous expenditure | النفقات التلقائية
An expenditure that does not depend on the level of GDP.

Average fixed cost | متوسط التكلفة الثابتة
Fixed cost divided by the quantity of output produced.

Average product of labor | متوسط إنتاج العمال
The total output produced by a firm divided by the quantity of workers.

Average revenue (AR) | الايراد المتوسط
Total revenue divided by the quantity of the product sold.

Average total cost | متوسط إجمالي التكاليف
Total cost divided by the quantity of output produced.

Average variable cost | معدل التكلفة المتغيرة
Variable cost divided by the quantity of output produced.

Balance of payments | ميزان المدفوعات
The record of a country's trade with other countries in goods, services, and assets.

Balance of trade | الميزان التجاري
The difference between the value of the goods a country exports and the value of the goods a country imports.

Bank panic | ذعر بنكي
A situation in which many banks experience runs at the same time.

Bank run | سحب غير اعتيادي للودائع
A situation in which many depositors simultaneously decide to withdraw money from a bank.

Barrier to entry | حاجز تجاري، عائق تجاري
Anything that keeps new firms from entering an industry in which firms are earning economic profits.

Behavioral economics | الاقتصاد السلوكي
The study of situations in which people make choices that do not appear to be economically rational.

Black market | سوق سوداء، سوق موازية
A market in which buying and selling take place at prices that violate government price regulations.

Brand management | إدارة العلامه التجاريه
The actions of a firm intended to maintain the differentiation of a product over time.

Budget constraint | قيد الموازنة
The limited amount of income available to consumers to spend on goods and services

Budget deficit | عجز الموازنة
The situation in which the government's expenditures are greater than its tax revenue.

Budget surplus | فائض الموازنة
The situation in which the government's expenditures are less than its tax revenue.

Business cycle | دورة الأعمال التجارية
Alternating periods of economic expansion and economic recession.

Business strategy | استراتيجية إدارة الأعمال
Actions taken by a firm to achieve a goal, such as maximizing profits

Capital | رأس المال
Manufactured goods that are used to produce other goods and services.

Capital account | حساب رأس المال
The part of the balance of payments that records relatively minor transactions, such as migrants' transfers, and sales and purchases of nonproduced, nonfinancial assets.

Cartel | اتفاق احتكاري، اتحاد احتكاري للمنتجين
A group of firms that collude by agreeing to restrict output to increase prices and profits

Cash flow | تدفق نقدي
The difference between the cash revenues received by a firm and the cash spending by the firm.

Central Bank | البنك المركزي
An agency of the government that regulates the money supply.

Central Bank's funds rate | سعر فائدة البنك المركزي
The interest rate banks charge each other for overnight loans

Centrally planned economy | الإقتصاد المخطط مركزيا
An economy in which the government decides how economic resources will be allocated

Ceteris paribus ("all else equal"): | بقاء العوامل الأخرى على حالها
The requirement that when analyzing the relationship between two variables—such as price and quantity demanded—other variables must be held constant

Circular-flow diagram | مخطط التدفق الدائري
A model that illustrates how participants in markets are linked

Closed economy | اقتصاد مغلق
An economy that has no interactions in trade or finance with other countries.

Coase theorem | نظرية كوز
The argument of economist Ronald Coase that if transactions costs are low, private bargaining will result in an efficient solution to the problem of externalities.

Collusion | تحالف احتكاري
An agreement among firms to charge the same price or otherwise not to compete

Command and control approach | نهج الضبط والتحكم
An approach that involves the government imposing quantitative limits on the amount of pollution firms are allowed to emit or requiring firms to install specific pollution control devices.

Commodity money | النقود السلعية
A good used as money that also has value independent of its use as money.

Common resource | المورد المشترك
A good that is rival but not excludable.

Comparative advantage | الميزة النسبية
The ability of an individual, a firm, or a country to produce a good or service at a lower opportunity cost than competitors.

Comparative advantage | الميزة النسبية
The ability of an individual, a firm, or a country to produce a good or service at a lower opportunity cost than competitors

Compensating differentials | تعويض الفوارق
Higher wages that compensate workers for unpleasant aspects of a job.

Competitive market equilibrium | توازن السوق التنافسي
A market equilibrium with many buyers and many sellers

Complements | سلع متكاملة
Goods and services that are used together

Constant returns to scale | عوائد ثابتة بالنسبة للحجم
The situation when a firm's long-run average costs remain unchanged as it increases output

Consumer price index (CPI) | مؤشر أسعار المستهلكين
An average of the prices of the goods and services purchased by the typical urban family of four.

Consumer surplus | فائض المستهلك
The difference between the highest price a consumer is willing to pay and the price the consumer actually pays

Consumption | استهلاك
Spending by households on goods and services, not including spending on new houses.

Consumption function | دالة الاستهلاك
The relationship between consumption spending and disposable income.

Contractionary monetary policy | سياسة مالية إنكماشية
The Federal Reserve's adjusting the money supply to increase interest rates to reduce inflation.

Cooperative equilibrium | التوازن التعاوني
An equilibrium in a game in which players cooperate to increase their mutual payoff

Copyright | حقوق النشر
A government-granted exclusive right to produce and sell a creation

Cross-price elasticity of demand | المرونة السعرية التقاطعية للطلب
The percentage change in quantity demanded of one good divided by the percentage change in the price of another good

Crowding out | التزاحم الطارد
A decline in private expenditures as a result of an increase in government purchases.

Currency appreciation | ارتفاع سعر العملة
An increase in the market value of one currency relative to another currency.

Currency depreciation | انخفاض قيمة العملة
A decrease in the market value of one currency relative to another currency.

Current account | الحساب الجاري
The part of the balance of payments that records a country's net exports, net investment income, and net transfers.

Cyclical unemployment | بطالة دورية
Unemployment caused by a business cycle recession

Cyclically adjusted budget deficit or surplus | عجز أو فائض الميزانية المعدل دورياً
The deficit or surplus in the federal government's budget if the economy were at potential GDP.

Deadweight loss | الخسارة الساكنة (غير المعوضه)
The reduction in economic surplus resulting from a market not being in competitive equilibrium

Deflation | الانكماش
A decline in the price level.

Demand curve | منحنى الطلب
A curve that shows the relationship between the price of a product and the quantity of the product demanded

Demand schedule | جدول الطلب
A table showing the relationship between the price of a product and the quantity of the product demanded

Demographics | التغيُّرات السُكانية
The characteristics of a population with respect to age, race, and gender

Derived demand | طلب مشتق
The demand for a factor of production that is derived from the demand for the good the factor produces.

Discount loans | القروض المخفضة / المخصومة
Loans the Federal Reserve makes to banks.

Discount rate | سعر الخصم
The interest rate the Federal Reserve charges on discount loans.

Discouraged workers | العمال المثبطين
People who are available for work but have not looked for a job during the previous four weeks because they believe no jobs are available for them.

Diseconomies of scale |
ارتفاع سعر التكلفة عند زيادة الإنتاج / تبذيرات زيادة الحجم
The situation when a firm's long-run average costs rise as the firm increases output

Disinflation | إنقاص حدة التضخم
A significant reduction in the inflation rate.

Dominant strategy | الاستراتيجية السائدة
A strategy that is the best for a firm, no matter what strategies other firms use

Dumping | الإغراق
Selling a product for a price below its cost of production.

Economic discrimination | التمييز الاقتصادي
Paying a person a lower wage or excluding a person from an occupation on the basis of an irrelevant characteristic such as race or gender.

Economic efficiency | الكفاءة الاقتصادية
A market outcome in which the marginal benefit to consumers of the last unit produced is equal to its marginal cost of production and in which the sum of consumer surplus and producer surplus is at a maximum

Economic growth | النمو الاقتصادي
The ability of an economy to produce increasing quantities of goods and services.

Economic growth | النمو الاقتصادي
The ability of an economy to produce increasing quantities of goods and services

Economic loss | خسارة اقتصادية
The situation in which a firm's total revenue is less than its total cost, including all implicit costs

Economic model | نموذج اقتصادي
A simplified version of reality used to analyze real-world economic situations

Economic profit | ربح اقتصادي
A firm's revenues minus all its costs, implicit and explicit

Economic rent (or pure rent) | الريع الاقتصادي
The price of a factor of production that is in fixed supply.

Economic surplus | فائض اقتصادي
The sum of consumer surplus and producer surplus

Economic variable | متغير اقتصادي
Something measurable that can have different values, such as the wages of software programmers

Economics | علم الاقتصاد
The study of the choices people make to attain their goals, given their scarce resources

Economies of scale | وفورات زيادة الحجم
The situation when a firm's long-run average costs fall as it increases output

Efficiency wage | أجر الكفاءة
A higher-than market wage that a firm pays to increase worker productivity.

Elastic demand | الطلب المرن
Demand is elastic when the percentage change in quantity demanded is *greater* than the percentage change in price, so the price elasticity is *greater* than 1 in absolute value

Elasticity | المرونة
A measure of how much one economic variable responds to changes in another economic variable

Endowment effect | تأثير الاقتناء
The tendency of people to be unwilling to sell a good they already own even if they are offered a price that is greater than the price they would be willing to pay to buy the good if they didn't already own it

Entrepreneur | رجل الأعمال
Someone who operates a business, bringing together the factors of production—labor, capital, and natural resources—to produce goods and services

Equity | المساواة
The fair distribution of economic benefits

Excess reserves | إحتياطات فائضة
Reserves that banks hold over and above the legal requirement.

Excludability | الإقصاء
The situation in which anyone who does not pay for a good cannot consume it.

Expansion | توسع
The period of a business cycle during which total production and total employment are increasing.

Expansionary monetary policy | سياسة نقدية توسعية
The Federal Reserve's increasing the money supply and decreasing interest rates to increase real GDP.

Explicit cost | تكلفة صريحة
A cost that involves spending money

Exports | الصادرات
Goods and services produced domestically but sold to other countries.

External economies | وفورات خارجية
Reductions in a firm's costs that result from an increase in the size of an industry.

Externality | اثر خارجي
A benefit or cost that affects someone who is not directly involved in the production or consumption of a good or service.

Factor markets | أسواق عناصر الإنتاج
Markets for the factors of production, such as labor, capital, natural resources, and entrepreneurial ability

Factors of production | عناصر الإنتاج
Labor, capital, natural resources, and other inputs used to produce goods and services

Federal Open Market Committee (FOMC) |
لجنة السوق المفتوحة الاتحادية
The Federal Reserve committee responsible for open market operations and managing the money supply in the United States.

Fiat money | عملة مصدرة بلا غطاء
Money, such as paper currency, that is authorized by a central bank or governmental body and that does not have to be exchanged by the central bank for gold or some other commodity money.

Final good or service | سلع نهائية
A good or service purchased by a final user.

Financial account | الحساب المالي
The part of the balance of payments that records purchases of assets a country has made abroad and foreign purchases of assets in the country.

Financial intermediaries | الوسطاء الماليين
Firms, such as banks, mutual funds, pension funds, and insurance companies, that borrow funds from savers and lend them to borrowers.

Financial markets | الأسواق المالية
Markets where financial securities, such as stocks and bonds, are bought and sold.

Financial system | النظام المالي
The system of financial markets and financial intermediaries through which firms acquire funds from households.

Fiscal policy | السياسة المالية
Changes in federal taxes and purchases that are intended to achieve macroeconomic policy objectives, such as high employment, price stability, and high rates of economic growth.

Fixed costs | التكاليف الثابتة
Costs that remain constant as output changes

Fractional reserve banking system | نظام الاحتياطي النسبي المصرفي
A banking system in which banks keep less than 100 percent of deposits as reserves.

Free market | السوق الحر
A market with few government restrictions on how a good or service can be produced or sold or on how a factor of production can be employed

Free riding | استغلال مجاني
Benefiting from a good without paying for it.

Free trade | التجارة الحرة
Trade between countries that is without government restrictions.

Frictional unemployment | البطالة الاحتكاكية
Short-term unemployment that arises from the process of matching workers with jobs.

Game theory | نظرية الألعاب
The study of how people make decisions in situations in which achieving their goals depends on their interactions with others; in economics, the study of the decisions of firms in industries where the profits of each firm depend on its interactions with other firms

GDP deflator | مكمش الناتج المحلي الإجمالي
A measure of the price level, calculated by dividing nominal GDP by real GDP and multiplying by 100.

Globalization | العولمة
The process of countries becoming more open to foreign trade and investment.

Government purchases | المشتريات الحكومية
Spending by federal, state, and local governments on goods and services.

Gross domestic product (GDP) | الناتج المحلي الإجمالي
The market value of all final goods and services produced in a country during a period of time, typically one year.

Horizontal merger | اندماج أفقي
A merger between firms in the same industry

Human capital | رأس المال البشري
The accumulated knowledge and skills that workers acquire from education and training or from their life experiences.

Implicit cost | التكلفة الضمنية
A nonmonetary opportunity cost

Imports | الواردات
Goods and services bought domestically but produced in other countries.

Income effect | أثر الدخل
The change in the quantity demanded of a good that results from the effect of a change in the good's price on consumers' purchasing power holding all other factors constant

Income elasticity of demand | مرونة الطلب الدخلية
A measure of the responsiveness of quantity demanded to changes in income, measured by the percentage change in quantity demanded divided by the percentage change in income

Inelastic demand | الطلب غير المرن
Demand is inelastic when the percentage change in quantity demanded is *less* than the percentage change in price, so the price elasticity is *less* than 1 in absolute value

Inferior good | سلع رديئة
A good for which the demand increases as income falls and decreases as income rises

Inflation rate | معدل التضخم
The percentage increase in the price level from one year to the next.

Inflation targeting | استهداف التضخم
Conducting monetary policy so as to commit the central bank to achieving a publicly announced level of inflation.

Intermediate good or service | سلع وسيطة
A good or service that is an input into another good or service, such as a tire on a truck.

Inventories | مخزون السلع
Goods that have been produced but not yet sold.

Investment | استثمار
Spending by firms on new factories, office buildings, machinery, and additions to inventories, and spending by households on new houses.

Labor force | القوى العاملة
The sum of employed and unemployed workers in the economy.

Labor force participation rate | نسبة المشاركة في القوى العاملة
The percentage of the working-age population in the labor force.

Labor productivity | إنتاجية القوى العاملة
The quantity of goods and services that can be produced by one worker or by one hour of work.

Labor union | نقابة العمال
An organization of employees that has the legal right to bargain with employers about wages and working conditions.

Law of demand | قانون الطلب
The rule that, holding everything else constant, when the price of a product falls, the quantity demanded of the product will increase, and when the price of a product rises, the quantity demanded of the product will decrease

Law of diminishing marginal utility | قانون تناقص المنفعة الحدية
The principle that consumers experience diminishing additional satisfaction as they consume more of a good or service during a given period of time

Law of diminishing returns | قانون الغلة المتناقصة / قانون المردود المتناقص
The principle that, at some point, adding more of a variable input, such as labor, to the same amount of a fixed input, such as capital, will cause the marginal product of the variable input to decline

Law of supply | قانون العرض
The rule that, holding everything else constant, increases in price cause increases in the quantity supplied, and decreases in price cause decreases in the quantity supplied

Long run | المدى الطويل
The period of time in which a firm can vary all its inputs, adopt new technology, and increase or decrease the size of its physical plant

Long-run aggregate supply curve | منحنى العرض الإجمالي
A curve that shows the relationship in the long run between the price level and the quantity of real GDP supplied.

Long-run average cost curve | منحنى متوسط التكاليف طويل الأجل
A curve showing the lowest cost at which a firm is able to produce a given quantity of output in the long run, when no inputs are fixed

Long-run competitive equilibrium | التوازن التنافسي طويل المدى
The situation in which the entry and exit of firms has resulted in the typical firm breaking even

Long-run economic growth | النمو الاقتصادي على المدى الطويل
The process by which rising productivity increases the average standard of living.

Long-run supply curve | منحنى العرض طويل المدى
A curve that shows the relationship in the long run between market price and the quantity supplied

M1 | مفهوم العرض النقدي المبسّط (الضيق)
The narrowest definition of the money supply: The sum of currency in circulation, checking account deposits in banks, and holdings of traveler's checks.

M2 | مفهوم العرض النقدي الموسّع
A broader definition of the money supply: M1 plus savings account balances, small-denomination time deposits, balances in money market deposit accounts in banks, and non institutional money market fund shares.

Macroeconomics | الاقتصاد الكلي
The study of the economy as a whole, including topics such as inflation, unemployment, and economic growth.

Marginal analysis | التحليل الهامشي
Analysis that involves comparing marginal benefits and marginal costs

Marginal benefit | المنفعة الإضافية
The additional benefit to a consumer from consuming one more unit of a good or service

Marginal cost | التكلفة الحدية/الهامشية
The additional cost to a firm of producing one more unit of a good or service
   The change in a firm's total cost from producing one more unit of a good or service

Marginal product of labor | الناتج الحدى للعمالة
The additional output a firm produces as a result of hiring one more worker.

Marginal productivity theory of income distribution | نظرية الإنتاجية الحدية وتوزيع الدخل
The theory that the distribution of income is determined by the marginal productivity of the factors of production that individuals own.

Marginal propensity to consume (MPC) | الميل الحدى للإستهلاك
The slope of the consumption function: The amount by which consumption spending changes when disposable income changes.

Marginal propensity to save (MPS) | الميل الحدى للإدخار
The change in saving divided by the change in disposable income.

Marginal revenue (MR) | عائد هامشي/ إيراد حدي
Change in total revenue from selling one more unit of a product

Marginal revenue product of labor (MRP) | الإيراد الحدى للعمالة
The change in a firm's revenue as a result of hiring one more worker.

Marginal utility | المنفعة الحدية
The change in total utility a person receives from consuming one additional unit of a good or service

Market | السوق
A group of buyers and sellers of a good or service and the institution or arrangement by which they come together to trade

Market demand | طلب السوق
The demand by all the consumers of a given good or service

Market economy | إقتصاد السوق
An economy in which the decisions of households and firms interacting in markets allocate economic resources

Market equilibrium | توازن السوق
A situation in which quantity demanded equals quantity supplied

Market failure | فشل السوق
A situation in which the market fails to produce the efficient level of output.

Market for loanable funds | سوق الأموال المتاحة للإقراض
The interaction of borrowers and lenders that determines the market interest rate and the quantity of loanable funds exchanged.

Market power | القوة السوقية (الإحتكارية)
The ability of a firm to charge a price greater than marginal cost

Marketing | التسويق
All the activities necessary for a firm to sell a product to a consumer

Menu costs | تكاليف تغيير القائمة (الأسعار)
The costs to firms of changing prices.

Microeconomics | اقتصاد جزئي
The study of how households and firms make choices, how they interact in markets, and how the government attempts to influence their choices

Microeconomics | الاقتصاد الجزئي
The study of how households and firms make choices, how they interact in markets, and how the government attempts to influence their choices.

Minimum efficient scale | الحجم الأدنى لتحقيق الفاعلية
The level of output at which all economies of scale are exhausted

Mixed economy | اقتصاد مختلط
An economy in which most economic decisions result from the interaction of buyers and sellers in markets but in which the government plays a significant role in the allocation of resources

Monetary policy | السياسة النقدية
The actions the Federal Reserve takes to manage the money supply and interest rates to pursue macroeconomic policy objectives.

Money | النقود
Assets that people are generally willing to accept in exchange for goods and services or for payment of debts.

Monopolistic competition | المنافسة الاحتكارية
A market structure in which barriers to entry are low and many firms compete by selling similar, but not identical, products

Monopoly | الاحتكار
A firm that is the only seller of a good or service that does not have a close substitute

Monopsony | احتكار الشراء
The sole buyer of a factor of production.

Multiplier | المضاعف
The increase in equilibrium real GDP divided by the increase in autonomous expenditure.

Multiplier effect | أثر المضاعف
The series of induced increases in consumption spending that results from an initial increase in autonomous expenditure.

Nash equilibrium | توازن ناش
A situation in which each firm chooses the best strategy, given the strategies chosen by other firms

Natural monopoly | الاحتكار الطبيعي
A situation in which economies of scale are so large that one firm can supply the entire market at a lower average total cost than can two or more firms

Natural rate of unemployment | نسبة البطالة الطبيعية
The normal rate of unemployment, consisting of frictional unemployment plus structural unemployment.

Net exports | صافي الصادرات
Exports minus imports.

Net foreign investment | صافي الاستثمار الأجنبي
The difference between capital outflows from a country and capital inflows, also equal to net foreign direct investment plus net foreign portfolio investment.

Network externalities | الأثار الخارجية للشبكات
The situation where the usefulness of a product increases with the number of consumers who use it

Network externality | تأثير الشبكة الخارجية
The situation where the usefulness of a product increases with the number of consumers who use it

Nominal GDP | الناتج المحلى الإجمالي الاسمي
The value of final goods and services evaluated at current-year prices.

Nominal exchange rate | سعر الصرف الاسمي
The value of one country's currency in terms of another country's currency.

Nominal interest rate | سعر الفائدة الاسمي
The stated interest rate on a loan.

Nonaccelerating inflation rate of unemployment (NAIRU) | معدل البطالة الذي لايؤدى الى تسارع التضخم
The unemployment rate at which the inflation rate has no tendency to increase or decrease.

Noncooperative equilibrium | التوازن اللاتعاوني
An equilibrium in a game in which players do not cooperate but pursue their own self-interest

Normal good | سلعة عادية
A good for which the demand increases as income rises and decreases as income falls

Normative analysis | التحليل المعياري
Analysis concerned with what ought to be

Oligopoly | احتكار القلة
A market structure in which a small number of interdependent firms compete

Open economy | الاقتصاد المفتوح
An economy that has interactions in trade or finance with other countries.

Open market operations | معاملات السوق المفتوحة
The buying and selling of Treasury securities by the Federal Reserve in order to control the money supply.

Opportunity cost | البديلة تكلفة الفرصة
The highest-valued alternative that must be given up to engage in an activity.

Patent | براءة اختراع
The exclusive right to a product for a period of 20 years from the date the product is invented

Payoff matrix | مصفوفة المكافأت
A table that shows the payoffs that each firm earns from every combination of strategies by the firms

Perfectly competitive market | سوق المنافسة الكاملة
A market that meets the conditions of (1) many buyers and sellers, (2) all firms selling identical products, and (3) no barriers to new firms entering the market

Perfectly elastic demand | طلب تام المرونة
The case where the quantity demanded is infinitely responsive to price, and the price elasticity of demand equals infinity

Perfectly inelastic demand | طلب غير تام المرونة
The case where the quantity demanded is completely unresponsive to price, and the price elasticity of demand equals zero

Personnel economics | اقتصاديات الأفراد
The application of economic analysis to human resources issues.

Phillips curve | منحنى فيليبس
A curve showing the short-run relationship between the unemployment rate and the inflation rate.

Pigovian taxes and subsidies | الضرائب والإعانات الحكومية التصحيحية
Government taxes and subsidies intended to bring about an efficient level of output in the presence of externalities.

Positive analysis | التحليل الإيجابي (واقعى)
Analysis concerned with what is

Potential GDP | الناتج المحلي الإجمالي المحتمل
The level of GDP attained when all firms are producing at capacity.

Price ceiling | السقف السعري
A legally determined maximum price that sellers may charge

Price discrimination | التمييز السعًري
Charging different prices to different customers for the same product when the price differences are not due to differences in cost

Price elasticity of demand | المرونة السعرية للطلب
The responsiveness of the quantity demanded to a change in price, measured by dividing the percentage change in the quantity demanded of a product by the percentage change in the product's price

Price elasticity of supply | المرونة السعرية للعرض
The responsiveness of the quantity supplied to a change in price, measured by dividing the percentage change in the quantity supplied of a product by the percentage change in the product's price

Price floor | الأرضية السعرية (الحد الأدنى للسعر)
A legally determined minimum price that sellers may receive

Price leadership | ريادة تحديد السعر
A form of implicit collusion where one firm in an oligopoly announces a price change, which is matched by the other firms in the industry

Price level | مستوى السعر
A measure of the average prices of goods and services in the economy.

Price taker | متلقّي للسعر
A buyer or seller that is unable to affect the market price

Prisoners' dilemma | معضلة المساجين
A game in which pursuing dominant strategies results in noncooperation that leaves everyone worse off

Private benefit | المنفعة الخاصة
The benefit received by the consumer of a good or service.

Private cost | التكلفة الخاصة
The cost borne by the producer of a good or service.

Private good | السلعة الخاصة
A good that is both rival and excludable.

Producer price index (PPI) | مؤشّر أسعار الإنتاج
An average of the prices received by producers of goods and services at all stages of the production process.

Producer surplus | فائض المنتج
The difference between the lowest price a firm would be willing to accept and the price it actually receives

Product markets | أسواق السلع
Markets for goods—such as computers—and services—such as medical treatment

Production function | دالة الإنتاج
The relationship between the inputs employed by a firm and the maximum output it can produce with those inputs

Production possibilities frontier (*PPF*) | منحنى إمكانيات الإنتاج
A curve showing the maximum attainable combinations of two products that may be produced with available resources and current technology

Profit | الربح
Total revenue minus total cost

Property rights | حقوق الملكية
The rights individuals or firms have to the exclusive use of their property including the right to buy or sell it

Protectionism | الحماية
The use of trade barriers to shield domestic firms from foreign competition.

Public franchise | امتياز حكومي
A designation by the government that a firm is the only legal provider of a good or service

Public good | سلعة عامة
A good that is both non rivalrous and non excludable.

Quantity demanded | الكمية المطلوبة
The amount of a good or service that a consumer is willing and able to purchase at a given price

Quantity supplied | كمية العرض
The amount of a good or service that a firm is willing and able to supply at a given price

Quantity theory of money | النظرية الكمية للنقود
A theory of the connection between money and prices that assumes that the velocity of money is constant.

Quota | الحصة
A numeric limit imposed by a government on the quantity of a good that can be imported into the country.

Rational expectations | التوقعات الرشيدة
Expectations formed by using all available information about an economic variable.

Real business cycle models | نماذج دورة الأعمال الحقيقية
A macroeconomic model that focuses on real, rather than monetary, causes of the business cycle.

Real exchange rate | سعر الصرف الحقيقى
The price of domestic goods in terms of foreign goods.

Real GDP | الناتج المحلي الإجمالي الحقيقي
The value of final goods and services evaluated at base-year prices.

Real interest rate | معدل الفائدة الحقيقى
The nominal interest rate minus the inflation rate.

Recession | ركود
The period of a business cycle during which total production and total employment are decreasing.

Required reserve ratio | نسبة الاحتياطي الإلزامي
The minimum fraction of deposits banks are required by law to keep as reserves.

Required reserves | الاحتياطيات الإلزامية
Reserves that a bank is legally required to hold, based on its checking account deposits.

Reserves | الاحتياطيات
Deposits that a bank keeps as cash in its vault or on deposit with the Federal Reserve.

Rivalry | منافسة
The situation that occurs when one person's consuming a unit of a good means no one else can consume it.

Saving and investment equation | معادلة التوفير والاستثمار
An equation that shows that national saving is equal to domestic investment plus net foreign investment.

Scarcity | الندرة
The situation in which unlimited wants exceed the limited resources available to fulfill those wants

Short run | المدى القصير
The period of time during which at least one of a firm's inputs is fixed

Shortage | عجز ، نقص
A situation in which the quantity demanded is greater than the quantity supplied

Short-run aggregate supply curve | منحنى العرض الكلي على المدى القصير
A curve that shows the relationship in the short run between the price level and the quantity of real GDP supplied by firms.

Shutdown point | نقطة الإغلاق/ حد الإغلاق
The minimum point on a firm's average variable cost curve; if the price falls below this point, the firm shuts down production in the short run

Simple deposit multiplier | مضاعف الوديعة البسيط
The ratio of the amount of deposits created by banks to the amount of new reserves.

Social benefit | منفعة اجتماعية
The total benefit from consuming a good or service, including both the private benefit and any external benefit.

Social cost | تكلفة اجتماعية
The total cost of producing a good or service, including both the private cost and any external cost.

Stagflation | الركود التضخمي
A combination of inflation and recession, usually resulting from a supply shock.

Structural relationship | العلاقة الهيكلية
A relationship that depends on the basic behavior of consumers and firms and remains unchanged over long periods.

Structural unemployment | البطالة الهيكلية
Unemployment arising from a persistent mismatch between the skills and characteristics of workers and the requirements of jobs.

Substitutes | بدائل
Goods and services that can be used for the same purpose

Substitution effect | أثر الإحلال
The change in the quantity demanded of a good that results from a change in price, making the good more or less expensive relative to other goods that are substitutes. The change in the quantity demanded of a good that results from a change in price making the good more or less expensive relative to other goods, holding constant the effect of the price change on consumer purchasing power

Sunk cost | التكلفة المفقودة (الغارقة)
A cost that has already been paid and cannot be recovered

Supply curve | منحنى العرض
A curve that shows the relationship between the price of a product and the quantity of the product supplied

Supply schedule | جدول العرض
A table that shows the relationship between the price of a product and the quantity of the product supplied

Supply shock | صدمة العرض
An unexpected event that causes the short-run aggregate supply curve to shift.

Surplus | فائض
A situation in which the quantity supplied is greater than the quantity demanded

Tariff | التعرفة الجمركية
A tax imposed by a government on imports.

Tax incidence | العبء النهائي للضريبة
The actual division of the burden of a tax between buyers and sellers in a market

Tax wedge | فرق الضريبة
The difference between the pretax and posttax return to an economic activity.

Taylor rule | قانون تايلور
A rule developed by John Taylor that links the Fed's target for the federal funds rate to economic variables.

Technological change | التغير التكنولوجي
A positive or negative change in the ability of a firm to produce a given level of output with a given quantity of inputs. A change in

the ability of a firm to produce a given level of output with a given quantity of inputs

Technology | تكنولوجيا / تقنية
The processes a firm uses to turn inputs into outputs of goods and services

Terms of trade | معدلات التبادل التجاري
The ratio at which a country can trade its exports for imports from other countries.

Total cost | إجمالي التكلفة / تكلفة كلية
The cost of all the inputs a firm uses in production

Total revenue | الإيراد الكلى
The total amount of funds received by a seller of a good or service, calculated by multiplying price per unit by the number of units sold

Trade | التجارة
The act of buying or selling

Trade-off | المبادلة (المقايضة)
The idea that because of scarcity, producing more of one good or service means producing less of another good or service

Tragedy of the commons | مأساة الموارد ذات الإستهلاك المشترك (الشائع)
The tendency for a common resource to be overused.

Transactions costs | تكلفة المعاملات
The costs in time and other resources that parties incur in the process of agreeing to and carrying out an exchange of goods or services.

Transactions costs | تكلفة المعاملات
The costs in time and other resources that parties incur in the process of agreeing to and carrying out an exchange of goods or services

Transfer payments | المدفوعات التحويلية
Payments by the government to individuals for which the government does not receive a new good or service in return.

Two-part tariff | تعرفة ذات جزئين / تعرفة مزدوجة
A situation in which consumers pay one price (or tariff) for the right to buy as much of a related good as they want at a second price

Underground economy | اقتصاد سري
Buying and selling of goods and services that is concealed from the government to avoid taxes or regulations or because the goods and services are illegal.

Unemployment rate | نسبة البطالة
The percentage of the labor force that is unemployed.

Unit-elastic demand | الطلب أحادي المرونة
Demand is unit-elastic when the percentage change in quantity demanded is *equal to* the percentage change in price, so the price elasticity is equal to 1 in absolute value

Utility | المنفعة
The enjoyment or satisfaction people receive from consuming goods and services

Variable costs | التكاليف المتغيرة
Costs that change as output changes

Velocity of money | سرعة دوران النقود
The average number of times each dollar in the money supply is used to purchase goods and services included in GDP.

Vertical merger ا الاندماج الرأسي
A merger between firms at different stages of production of a good

Voluntary exchange ا تبادل طوعي
The situation that occurs in markets when both the buyer and seller of a product are made better off by the transaction

Voluntary export restraint (VER) ا القيد الطوعي على الصادرات
An agreement negotiated between two countries that places a numeric limit on the quantity of a good that can be imported by one country from the other country.

World Trade Organization (WTO) ا منظمة التجارة العالمية
An international organization that oversees international trade agreements.

Index

Key Terms and their Page numbers are in **boldface.**

Credits

Figures

Figures 1A-1, 1A-6, 14.1 from International Bank for Reconstruction and Development/ The World Bank: World Development Indicators, 2009, reproduced with permission; Figure 1A-2 from United Nations Development Programme (UNDP), *Human Development Report, 2009,* published 2009, Palgrave, reproduced with permission of Palgrave Macmillan; Figure 9.7 adapted from *The Economics of Strategy*, 4 ed., Wiley, Inc. (David Besanko, David Dranove, Mark Shanley, and Scott Schaefer, 2007) Fig. 11.3, Copyright (c) 2007 John Wiley & Sons, Inc. Reproduced with permission of John Wiley & Sons, Inc.; Figure on page 346 from Telegeography, GlobalComms Database, 1 March 2005, reproduced with permission; Figure 10.4 from International Monetary Fund, *International Financial Statistics*, 2010, reproduced with permission; Figure 10.8 from *Competitive Strategy: Techniques for Analyzing Industries and Competitors,* The Free Press (Porter, Michael E. 1998) Reprinted with the permission of The Free Press, a Division of Simon & Schuster, Inc., Copyright © 1980, 1998 by The Free Press. All rights reserved; Figures on page 474, page 475, page 506, page 507, 15.4, 15.5, 15.6, 22.1 from International Bank for Reconstruction and Development/The World Bank: *World Development Indicators* (WDI), 2010, reproduced with permission; Figures 14.2 and 14.4 from WTO, *International Trade Statistics (ITS)*, 2009, reproduced with permission; Figures on page 502 from International Bank for Reconstruction and Development/The World Bank: *World Governance Indicators (Control of Corruption)*, 2010, reproduced with permission;

Figures 15.2, 15.3 from International Monetary Fund, *World Economic Outlook*, 2010, reproduced with permission; Figure on page 543 from Labour Office, International Labour Organization, "Global Employment Trends for Youth," August 2010, Copyright © International Labour Organization, 2010, reproduced with permission; Figure 16.1 from Index Mundi, **www.indexmundi.com**., Based on data from the *CIA World Factbook*, reproduced with permission; Figures on page 554, page 573, 17.1, 17.7, 17.8, 17.9, 23.1, 23.2 from International Bank for Reconstruction and Development/The World Bank: World Development Indicators, 2011, **http://databank.worldbank .org/ddp/home.do?Step=12&id= 4&CNO=2**, reproduced with permission; Figure 17.3 from International Bank for Reconstruction and Development/The World Bank: Saudi Arabian Ministry of Finance Statistics, World Development Indicators, 2011, **http://databank.worldbank.org/ ddp/home.do?Step=12&id= 4&CNO=2**, reproduced with permission; Figure 21.2 from International Monetary Fund, reproduced with permission.

Tables

Table on page 71 from A Modeling Framework for Category Assortment Planning, *Manufacturing & Service Operations Management*, vol. 3, no. 3, pp. 191–210 (Juin-Kuan Chong, Teck-Hua Ho, and Christopher S. Tang 2002), Adapted with permission. Copyright 2002, the Institute for Operations Research and the Management Sciences, 7240 Parkway Drive, Suite 300, Hanover, Maryland 21076.; Table on page 147 from The

Price Elasticity of Demand for Breakfast Cereal, *Timothy F. Bresnahan and Robert J. Gordon, eds., The Economics of New Goods* (Hausman, Jerry A. 1997), Chicago: University of Chicago Press, 1997. Used with permission of The University of Chicago Press.; Table on page 155 from Understanding Crude Oil Prices, *The Energy Journal*, vol. 30, no. 2, pp. 179-206 (Hamilton, James D.), This table is copyrighted and reprinted by permission from the International Association for Energy Economics. The table first appeared in The Energy Journal; Table on page 169 from Determinants of Store-Level Price Elasticity, *Journal of Marketing Research*, Vol. 32, February, pp. 17–29 (Hoch, Stephen J., Kim, Byung-do, Montgomery, Alan L. and Rossi, Peter E. 1995), Reprinted with permission from the publisher, American Marketing Association; Table on page 224 from *Handbook for Academic Authors*, 4 ed., Cambridge University Press (Luey, Beth 2002) p. 244; Table on page 376 from Monopoly: The Case of Egyptian Steel, *Journal of Business Case Studies*, vol. 2, no. 3, p. 87 (Selim, Tarek H. 2006), Journal of Business Case Studies by Clute Institute for Academic Research. Copyright 2006 Reproduced with permission of THE CLUTE INSTITUTE in the format Textbook via Copyright Clearance Center; Table on page 456 from International Bank for Reconstruction and Development / The World Bank: World Bank Economic Developments and Prospects Report: "Regional Integration for Global Competitiveness", 2008, reproduced with permission; Table on page 516 from United Nations Development Programme, *Human Development Report, 2007/2008*, published 2007, Palgrave, reproduced with permission of Palgrave Macmillan; Table 16.1 from Jad

Chaaban, "Job Creation in The Arab Economies: Navigating Through Difficult Waters", *Arab Human Development Report*, Research Paper Series, 2010. United Nations Development Programme (UNDP), Regional Bureau for Arab States, reproduced with permission.

Text

Article on pages 87–88 from Menareport.com, February 28, 2010, © 2000–2011 Al Bawaba (**www.albawaba.com**), reproduced with permission; Article on page 124 from UAE Landlords Find Ways to Beat the Rent Control, *Gulf News*, 31/05/2008 (Al Serkal, Mariam M., El Shammaa, Dina, and Ali, Fuad, Staff Reporters), reproduced with permission from Gulf News, Dubai; Article on page 198 from Nokia Cooperates with Popular Singer Mohamed Hamaki to Promote 'Comes With Music', **www.ameinfo.com**, April 14, 2010, Copyright (c) AME Info FZ LLC. Middle East business news website **www.AMEinfo.com** has been providing information on the region for over 16 years in the form of daily news updates, analysis, press releases and special reports in both English and Arabic; Article on page 242 from Flat-Panel TVs, Long Touted, Finally Are Becoming the Norm, *Wall Street Journal*, 15/04/2006, p. A1 (Ramstad, Evan), Reprinted by permission, Copyright © 2006 Dow Jones & Company, Inc. All Rights Reserved Worldwide. License number 2744221405368; Article on page 320 from Criselda E. Diala, "Coffee Culture Thrives in Middle East," **http://www.english .alrroya.com**, June 29, 2010, reproduced with permission; Article on page 348 from LuLu Continues Oman Expansion, *Gulf News*, 22/06/2010 (Lowe, Aya), reproduced with permission from Gulf News, Dubai; Article on page 380 from BuddeCom telecommunications research and consultancy company, "Kuwait–Telecoms, Mobile, Broadband and Forecasts," 2011 report, **www.budde.com.au**, reproduced with permission; Extract on page 478 from World Trade Organization, **www.wto.org/english/news_e/spmm_e/spmm65_e.htm**, reproduced with permission; Article on page 482 from First GCC Trade Accord Signed with Singapore Gulf News, 15/12/2008 (Staff Report), reproduced with permission from Gulf News, Dubai; Article on page 512 adapted from Regional Economic Outlook, "Middle East, North Africa Weathering Global Crisis," IMF Survey online, **www.imf.org**, May 10, 2009, reproduced with permission; Article on page 572 from Peter Feuilherade, "Arab Economic Growth Predicted to Rebound After 2009 Drop," suite101.com, November 10, 2010, Peter Feuilherade, a former BBC World Service journalist, is a UK-based Middle East writer and analyst; Article on page 608 from Making Case for Flexible Employment in GCC, AMEIinfo.com, September 28, 2010:. **http://www.ameinfo.com/243314-more2.html**, Copyright (c) AME Info FZ LLC. Middle East

business news website **www.AMEinfo.com** has been providing information on the region for over 16 years in the form of daily news updates, analysis, press releases and special reports in both English and Arabic.; Article on page 648 from Tom Peter, "Can Jordan dodge the downturn bullet?", Global Post, 14 March 2009, **www.Globalpost.com**, © 2009 GlobalPost; Article on pages 678-679 from Saudi Economic growth likely to accelerate to 3.9% in 2010, Arab News, January 2010 (Sfakianakis, John), With permission from Arab News; Article on page 754 from "Drop in Dubai House Prices Causes Inflation Tto Fall Dramatically," **www.ameinfo.com**, January 27, 2011, Copyright (c) AME Info FZ LLC. Middle East business news website **www.AMEinfo.com** has been providing information on the region for over 16 years in the form of daily news updates, analysis, press releases and special reports in both English and Arabic.; Article on page 760 from Ibrahim Saif and Farah Choucair, "Arab Countries Stumble in the Face of Growing Economic Crisis," (Washington, D.C., Carnegie Endowment for International Peace, Middle East Program, May 2009), Carnegie Endowment.

org , Reprinted by permission of the publisher; Article on page 856 from Sustaining the Unsustainable, Economist, © The Economist Newspaper Limited, London (15 March 2007)

The Financial Times

Article on page 18 from Gulf Companies Learn the Price of Globalization, *The Financial Times*, 15/04/2009 (Cooper, Tristan), reproduced with permission from the author. *In some instances we have been unable to trace the owners of copyright material, and we would appreciate any information that would enable us to do so.*

Photos

The publisher would like to thank the following for their kind permission to reproduce their photographs:

(Key: b-bottom; c-centre; l-left; r-right; t-top)

Alamy Images: 14cl, 66-67c, 82br, 93tl, 121tr, 138-139c, 147cr, 165tl, 187br, 191br, 196tl, 243tl, 310tl, 317tr, 328-329c, 339tr, 349c, 362cl, 388-389c, 397tr, 421br, 452-453c, 483tl, 495t, 495c, 590tl, 609tl, 616-617c, 664tl, 696-697c, 701cr, 721b, 728-729c, 747cr, 802-803c, 813tr, 832-833c, 857tl, Art Directors & TRIP; **Arabian Eye:** 495r; **Author's own work:** 42l; **Corbis:** 2-3c, 36-37c, 53br, 55br, 59tl, 100-101c, 125tl, 199tl, 356-357c, 381tl, 441tr, 513tl, 518-519c, 580-581c, 592tl, 629cr, 642tl, 702tl, 705br, 718tl, 745br, 755tl, 760-761c; **Getty Images:** 19b, 51l, 76tl, 88tl, 152l, 174-175c, 220-221c, 224bl, 230l, 239br, 264-265c, 300-301c, 321tl, 527cr, 594l, 679tr, 776bl, 809tr, 840cl; **Glow Images:** 115br, 361tr, 434cl, 460tl, 550-551c, 685b, 693tr, 785cr; **Masterfile UK Ltd:** 51r; **Pearson Education Ltd:** 51t; **Photolibrary.com:** 51b, 495b; **Press Association Images:** 682tl, 779br, 852tl; **Reuters:** 359tr, 637tr, 649b; **Shutterstock.com:** 416-417c, 420l, 445tl

Cover images: *Front:* **Corbis:** c

All other images © Pearson Education

Every effort has been made to trace the copyright holders and we apologise in advance for any unintentional omissions. We would be pleased to insert the appropriate acknowledgement in any subsequent edition of this publication.